HANDBOOK OF BEHAVIORAL NEUROSCIENCE

VOLUME 17

HANDBOOK OF ANXIETY AND FEAR

Other volumes in HANDBOOK OF BEHAVIORAL NEUROSCIENCE
(*formerly* Techniques in the Behavioral and Neural Sciences)

HANDBOOK OF BEHAVIORAL NEUROSCIENCE

Series Editor

J.P. HUSTON
Düsseldorf

VOLUME 17

HANDBOOK OF ANXIETY AND FEAR

Edited by

ROBERT J. BLANCHARD

Department of Psychology, University of Hawaii at Manoa, Honolulu, HI, USA

D. CAROLINE BLANCHARD

*Pacific Biosciences Research Institute, and Department of Genetics and Molecular Biology, John A. Burns
School of Medicine, University of Hawaii at Manoa, Honolulu, HI, USA*

GUY GRIEBEL

Sanofi-Aventis, Psychopharmacology Department, Bagneux, France

DAVID NUTT

Psychopharmacology Unit, University of Bristol, Bristol, UK

ELSEVIER

AMSTERDAM – BOSTON – HEIDELBERG – LONDON – NEW YORK – OXFORD
PARIS – SAN DIEGO – SAN FRANCISCO – SINGAPORE – SYDNEY – TOKYO
Academic Press is an imprint of Elsevier

ACADEMIC
PRESS

Academic Press is an imprint of Elsevier
Radarweg 29, PO Box 211, 1000 AE Amsterdam, The Netherlands
Linacre House, Jordan Hill, Oxford OX2 8DP, UK

First edition 2008

Notice
No responsibility is assumed by the publisher for any injury and/or damage to persons
or property as a matter of products liability, negligence or otherwise, or from any use
or operation of any methods, products, instructions or ideas contained in the material
herein. Because of rapid advances in the medical sciences, in particular, independent
verification of diagnoses and drug dosages should be made

Library of Congress Cataloging-in-Publication Data
A catalog record for this book is available from the Library of Congress

British Library Cataloguing in Publication Data
A catalogue record for this book is available from the British Library

ISBN: 978-0-444-53065-3 (this volume)
ISSN: 1569-7339 (Series) (formerly 0921-0709)

For information on all Academic Press publications
visit our website at books.elsevier.com

Printed and bound in The Netherlands

08 09 10 11 12   10 9 8 7 6 5 4 3 2 1

Working together to grow
libraries in developing countries

www.elsevier.com | www.bookaid.org | www.sabre.org

ELSEVIER   BOOK AID
            International   Sabre Foundation

List of Contributors

James L. Abelson (455), Department of Psychiatry, University of Michigan, Rachel Upjohn Building, 4250 Plymouth Road Ann Arbor, MI 48109-5765, USA

David S. Baldwin (395), Clinical Neuroscience Division, School of Medicine, University of Southampton, University Department of Mental Health, RSH Hospital, Brintons Terrace, Southampton SO14 OYG, UK

Catherine Belzung (325), EA3248 Psychobiologie des Emotions, Université François Rabelais, UFR Sciences et Techniques, Parc Grandmont, 37200 Tours, France

D. Caroline Blanchard (3, 63, 81, 141), Department of Genetics and Molecular Biology, John A. Burns School of Medicine; and Pacific Biosciences Research Center, University of Hawaii at Manoa, 1993 East West Road, Honolulu, HI 96822, USA

Robert J. Blanchard (3, 63, 81), Department of Psychology, University of Hawaii at Manoa, Gartley Hall 2430 Campus Road, Honolulu, HI 96822, USA

Marco Bortolato (303), Department of Cardiovascular and Neurological Sciences, Policlinico Universitario, University of Cagliari, S.S. 554 km 4.500, 09042 Monserrato (CA), Italy

Christopher K. Cain (103), Center for Neural Science, New York University, 4 Washington Place, Room 809, New York, NY 10003, USA

Newton S. Canteras (125, 141), Departamento de Anatomia, Instituto de Ciências Biomédicas, Universidade de São Paulo, Av. Lineu Prestes, 2415 CEP 05508-900, São Paulo, SP, Brazil

Antonio Pádua Carobrez (241), Department of Pharmaoclogy, CCB, Universidade Federal de Santa Catarina, Campus Universitário-Trindade, Florianópolis, SC 88040-900, Brazil

John F. Cryan (269), School of Pharmacy, Department of Pharmacology and Therapeutics, Alimentary Pharmabiotic Centre, Cavanagh Pharmacy Building, University College Cork, Cork, Ireland

Simon J.C. Davies (365), Academic Unit of Psychiatry, University of Bristol, Cotham House, Cotham Hill, Bristol BS6 6JL, UK

Michael Davis (49), Department of Psychiatry and Behavioral Sciences, Center for Behavioral Neuroscience, Emory University, 4th Floor, WMB, 1639 Pierce Drive, Atlanta, GA 30322, USA

Kumlesh K. Dev (269), Department of Anatomy, Biosciences Institute, University College Cork, Cork, Ireland

Gabriel Esquivel (413), Experimental and Clinical Psychiatry Section, Department of Psychiatry and Neuropsychology, Faculty of Health, Medicine and Life Sciences, Maastricht University, Vijverdalseweg 1, k.2.039, Gebouw Concorde, 6226 NB Maastricht, The Netherlands

Michael S. Fanselow (29), Psychology and the Brain Research Institute, University of California, 1285 Franz Hall, Los Angeles, CA 90095, USA

Berta Garcia de Miguel (365), Psychopharmacology Unit, University of Bristol, Dorothy Hodgkin Building, Whitson Street, Bristol BS1 3NY, UK

Matthew Garner (395), Clinical Neuroscience Division, School of Medicine, University of Southampton, Southampton SO14 OYG, UK

Frederico Guilherme Graeff (241), Department of Neurology, Psychiatry and Medical Psychology, Hospital das Clínicas da Faculdade de Medicina de Ribeirão Preto, Universidade de São Paulo, Avenida Bandeirantes 3900, Ribeirão Preto, SP 14090-900, Brazil

Guy Griebel (3, 325), Sanofi-Aventis, Psychopharmacology Department, 31 Avenue Paul Vaillant-Couturier, 92220 Bagneux, France

Eric Griez (413), Experimental and Clinical Psychiatry Section, Department of Psychiatry and Neuropsychology, Faculty of Health, Medicine and Life Sciences, Maastricht University, Vijverdalseweg 1, k.2.039, Gebouw Concorde, 6226 NB Maastricht, The Netherlands

Francisco Silveira Guimarães (241), Department of Pharmacology, Faculdade de Medicina de Ribeirão Preta, Universidade de São Paulo, Avenida Bandeirantes 3900, Ribeirão Preto, SP 14090-900, Brazil

John M. Hettema (475), Virginia Institute for Psychiatric and Behavioral Genetics, Department of Psychiatry, Virginia Commonwealth University, 800 East Leigh Street, Room 1-116, Richmond, VA 23219, USA

Andrew Holmes (355), Section on Behavioral Science and Genetics, Laboratory for Integrative Neuroscience, National Institute on Alcohol Abuse and Alcoholism, 5625 Fishers Lane Room 2N09, Rockville, MD 20852-9411, USA

Joseph E. LeDoux (103), Center for Neural Science, New York University, 4 Washington Place, Room 809, New York, NY 10003, USA

Samuel Leman (325), EA3248 Psychobiologie des Emotions, Université François Rabelais, UFR Sciences et Techniques, Parc Grandmont, 37200 Tours, France

Israel Liberzon (455), Department of Psychiatry, University of Michigan, Rachel Upjohn Building, 4250 Plymouth Road, Ann Arbor, MI 48109-5765, USA

Yoav Litvin (81), Department of Psychology, University of Hawaii at Manoa, 2430 Campus Road, Gartley Hall 110, Honolulu, HI 96822, USA

Andrea L. Malizia (437), Academic Unit of Psychiatry and Psychopharmacology Unit, University of Bristol, Cotham House, Cotham Hill, Bristol BS6 6JL, UK

Eduard Maron (475), Department of Psychiatry, University of Tartu, Tartu, Estonia; and Research Department of Mental Health, The North Estonian Regional Hospital, Psychiatry Clinic, Tallinn, Estonia

Karyn M. Myers (49), Department of Psychiatry and Behavioral Sciences, Center for Behavioral Neuroscience, Emory University, 954 Gatewood Road NE, Atlanta, GA 30329, USA

Neil McNaughton (11), Department of Psychology, University of Otago, P.O. Box 56, Dunedin, New Zealand

David Nutt (3, 365, 437), Psychopharmacology Unit, University of Bristol, Dorothy Hodgkin Building, Whitson Street, Bristol BS1 3NY, UK

Nathan S. Pentkowski (81), Department of Psychology, University of Hawaii at Manoa, 2430 Campus Road, Gartley Hall 110, Honolulu, HI 96822, USA

Daniele Piomelli (303), Department of Pharmacology and Center for Drug Discovery, 3101 Gillespie Neuroscience Facility, University of California, Irvine, CA 92697-4625, USA

Roger L. Pobbe (81), Pacific Biosciences Research Center, 1993 East-West Road, Honolulu, HI 96822, USA

Ravikumar Ponnusamy (29), Psychology and the Brain Research Institute, University of California, 1285 Franz Hall, Los Angeles, CA 90095, USA

James K. Rowlett (223), Harvard Medical School, New England Primate Research Center, Box 9102, One Pine Hill Drive, Southborough, MA 01772-9102, USA

Koen Schruers (413), Experimental and Clinical Psychiatry Section, Department of Psychiatry and Neuropsychology, Faculty of Health, Medicine and Life Sciences, Maastricht University, Vijverdalseweg 1, k.2.039, Gebouw Concorde, 6226 NB Maastricht, The Netherlands

Jakov Shlik (475), Department of Psychiatry, University of Ottawa, Royal Ottawa Health Care Group, 1145 Carling Avenue, Ottawa, Ont. K1Z7K4, Canada

Thomas Steckler (157), Department of Psychiatry, Research and Early Development Europe, Johnson & Johnson Pharmaceutical Research and Development, Turnhoutseweg 30, 2340 Beerse, Belgium

Elizabeth A. Young (455), Molecular and Behavioral Neurosciences Institute, 205 Zina Pitcher Place, Ann Arbor, MI 48109-5720, USA

Hélio Zangrossi Jr. (11), Department of Pharmacology, School of Medicine of Ribeirão Preto, University of São Paulo, Av. Bandeirantes 3900, 14049-900, Ribeirão Preto-SP, Brazil

Preface

Fear and anxiety constitute crucial emotional behaviors, manifest to some degree in virtually all chordates and magnificently represented in human behavior and history. Because of their importance, they have been intensively investigated from a number of scientific perspectives. The commonalities and consistencies of their cross species representation, while by no means total, also suggest a foundation for their analysis that is not available for more evanescent, subtle, or idiosyncratic emotions. This volume provides examples of the variety and intensity of scientific attention to fear and anxiety. We hope that it also indicates good progress toward understanding the mechanisms and functions of these emotions and the behavior patterns with which they are associated.

R.J. Blanchard
D.C. Blanchard
G. Griebel
D. Nutt
(*The Editors*)

Acknowledgments

Sarah Mae Arbo and Amy Vasconcellos at the University of Hawaii helped in organizing and managing editorial details. At Elsevier, Maureen Twaig and Johannes Menzel served as efficient sounding boards and timekeepers. Joe Huston, as Series Editor for the Elsevier "*Handbook of Behavioral Neuroscience*" series, initiated the project. The editors thank all of these people for their competent, gracious, and kind efforts.

Contents

Section 1. Introduction

Section 2. Animal Models of Anxiety, Fear and Defense

Section 3. Neural Systems for Anxiety, Fear, and Defense

Section 4.   The Pharmacology of Anxiety, Fear, and Defense

Section 5.   Handbook of Fear and Anxiety: Clinical and Experimental Considerations

Introduction

Introduction to the handbook on fear and anxiety

Robert J. Blanchard[1],*, D. Caroline Blanchard[2],*, Guy Griebel[3] and David Nutt[4]

[1]*Department of Psychology, University of Hawaii at Manoa, Honolulu, HI, USA*
[2]*Department of Genetics and Molecular Biology, John A. Burns School of Medicine; and Pacific
Biosciences Research Center, University of Hawaii at Manoa, Honolulu, HI, USA*
[3]*Sanofi-Aventis, Psychopharmacology Department, Bagneux, France*
[4]*Psychopharmacology Unit, University of Bristol, Bristol, UK*

Any volume that seeks to analyze two concepts – here fear and anxiety – needs to start by differentiating them. This volume will bring up this distinction in a number of contexts, and it will become clear that different authors may have somewhat different conceptions of what the distinction may be (e.g., chapter by McNaughton and Zangrossi). For current purposes, and because the editors have a robust position on this topic, we will start with this distinction: fear is the motivation associated with a number of behaviors that normally occur on exposure to clearly threatening stimuli. Anxiety is the motivation associated with behaviors that occur to potential, signaled, or ambiguous threat. Both anxiety and fear are often measured through the intensity or persistence of the behaviors with which they are associated, and may further be assessed by their ability to be conditioned to stimuli associated with these threats. These characterizations make it clear that fear and anxiety may intergrade or overlap, just as the stimuli that elicit them represent extremes of continua of clarity and immediacy of threat, such that a particular threat might appear at various points along these continua.

From an ethological perspective, both fear and anxiety are highly adaptive responses. Both are persistent and intense under appropriate conditions, in all vertebrate species in which they have been examined. However, the behaviors associated with fear and anxiety are time- and labor intensive; they may have to be, in order to be successful in meeting the array of dangers that every living organism faces. Failures of intensity or persistence are some of, but certainly not all, the ways that fear and anxiety systems may be insufficient. The simple fact that each of us is alive to read these words indicates that every one of our direct ancestors, human or prehuman, displayed fear and anxiety patterns that were at least adequate to keep them alive through successful reproduction. It is not a negligible legacy.

The problem with all such intense and persistent reactions is that they take effort and time. The evolutionary history of all species has included a world of threatening events. Left unchecked, the motivations and behavioral expression of fear and anxiety might easily consume a disproportionate portion of the energy and time budgets of individual animals, to the detriment of other crucial behaviors like obtaining food, sex, reproduction, and self-care. The major mechanisms limiting fear and anxiety, such as habituation and extinction, and behaviors facilitating these limitation processes, for example, risk assessment, are

*Corresponding authors. E-mail: blanchar@hawaii.edu

R.J. Blanchard, D.C. Blanchard, G. Griebel and D. Nutt (Eds.)
Handbook of Anxiety and Fear, Vol. 17
ISBN 978-0-444-53065-3

DOI: 10.1016/S1569-7339(07)00001-X

described in several chapters in this volume (Fanselow and Ponnusamy; Myers and Davis; Blanchard et al.). The Myers and Davis chapter, in particular, highlights some of the potential therapeutic values of promoting factors that limit the duration of conditioned fear or anxiety reactions.

Fear and anxiety are both complex reactions. The range of ways in which they can be maladaptive reflects this complexity. In addition to being too intense or too persistent, they may be elicited by incorrect stimuli, that is, those that are not genuinely threatening. In turn, the perceived threat qualities of a given stimulus may depend on many factors, including innate or preprogrammed tendencies, specific learning by direct experience or by observation of the experiences of others, nonspecific stressors past or present, etc. This multiplicity of factors contributing to the threatening qualities of stimuli that elicit fear and anxiety has led to parallel variation in the stimuli used as models of anxiety (see chapters by Fanselow and Ponnusamy for conditioned, and by Litvin et al. for unconditioned models of anxiety).

The behavioral expression of these emotions is another area where fear, anxiety, and, in particular, anxiety disorders, show great variability. A foundation for this, in terms of normal mammalian response to threat, is outlined in the chapter by Blanchard and Blanchard, potentially providing a counterpart to the later chapter by Nutt, describing, in part, behavioral aspects of current classifications of anxiety disorders. Other focal behaviors commonly used in animal models relevant to fear or anxiety are described in Myers and Davis, as well as in Cain and LeDoux: both chapters additionally provide information on neural systems and neurotransmitters involved in these behaviors and their conditioning. Canteras outlines brain systems that are activated in response to a particularly high intensity, unconditioned, threat stimulus, a predator; and Canteras and Blanchard compare the brain systems engaged in particular unconditioned and conditioned paradigms, as well as trends in use of these paradigms.

The use of animal models is described in greater detail in the third section of the text, which deals with the pharmacology of fear and anxiety. It would perhaps be more precise to say the pharmacology of anxiety, as the goal of discovering new mechanisms in the pharmacological treatment of anxiety disorders is a major driving force behind research in this area. These chapters are organized in terms of major neurotransmitter systems, including peptide receptor ligands (Steckler); $GABA_A$/benzodiazepine receptor ligands (Rowlett); 5-HT interacting drugs (Guimarães et al.); glutamatergic compounds (J. Cryan and K. Dev); and the endocannabinoid system (D. Piomelli and M. Bortolato). Andrew Holmes provides an overview of the pharmacology of anxiolysis, and Catherine Belzung et al. provide a meta-analysis of rodent studies of targeted mutations of neurotransmission genes related to anxiety.

The clinical section of the book was designed to clarify and focus on the key issues that often complicate and confuse individuals researching translational approaches to fear and anxiety disorders. The chapter by Young et al. offers a powerful fusion of animal and human research approaches to the neuroendocrinology and related brain mechanisms of fear and anxiety. The chapter on diagnostics (Nutt et al.) provides an approach to the issues of diagnostic specificities and overlaps, to give a clear and succinct overview of this complex field that animal model researchers will find of benefit in understanding their current models and developing new ones. The drug treatment chapter (Baldwin and Garner) presents an overview of the current clinical treatments of anxiety disorders, based on recent high-level consensus meetings.

The chapter on imaging by Malizia and Nutt looks at the achievements of this approach in anxiety and fear, and the ways in which current and future developments may – or may not – help in drug discovery and possibly in future animal research. Similarly, the section on challenge tests (Esquivel et al.) offers a current state of the art in this complex arena that has only little been translated to the human drug discovery field despite its clear potential; it also presents a real challenge – or opportunity – to those working in the animal study field as a way of improving translational models. Finally the genetics section (Maron et al.) will provide a useful framework for those working on both human disorders and those exploring related issues in rodents, especially transgenics and trait loci approaches.

As these brief descriptions of the chapters indicate, the scope of the phenomena encompassed by the concepts of fear and anxiety is very wide, reaching from an analysis of animal behavior through neural systems and pharmacology to human psychopathologies. Many readers of this volume, perhaps the majority, are likely to be interested primarily because of the latter, which brings up the question of how firm is the relationship between these anxiety psychopathologies, and the procedures designed to model them, using animal subjects. It is a question that also speaks directly to the value of both neural system and pharmacological research that is based largely on such models, but aimed at intervention and treatment of the human disorders. Some trends in the use of these models are presented in the Canteras and Blanchard chapter.

Our basic goal for this handbook was simply to present this multiplicity of facets to fear and anxiety, describing particular aspects of relevant animal models and their physiological mechanisms, as well as research and analysis on anxiety psychopathologies. This material speaks to great progress on both "pure science" and "applied" fronts during the past couple of decades.

Nonetheless, it is tempting to try to go one step further, to attempt to integrate this material in such a way as to point out a systematic future direction to research on anxiety. A useful corrective for such dramatic effort is that the editors are by no means in total agreement about a core premise for much of this work, that there is a substantial relationship between at least some, or some components of, animal models of anxiety and clinical anxiety. On this topic, our views range

from "animal models say little about human anxiety disorders" to "animal models tell more about the biology of the systems than do current classifications of human anxiety disorders." However, what we can and do agree on is the importance of understanding fear and anxiety, and we expect that some of the disagreements as well as the convergences may clarify views of where refinements are needed or may be particularly useful, in research approaches to fear and anxiety. The perceived strength of this relationship has clear implications for the relevance of neural systems based on such models, as well as the adequacy of preclinical research to identify new treatment mechanisms, with regard to anxiety disorders.

The problem driving the need for this relationship can be illustrated by examination of a very recent phenomenon in research: the increasing development and use of a concept of the endophenotype, as applied to psychiatric conditions. Endophenotypes are very broadly defined as components along the pathway between genotype and disease state (Gottesman and Gould, 2003) or as "heritable, quantitative traits hypothesized to more closely represent genetic risk for complex polygenic mental disorders than overt symptoms and behaviors" (Fineberg et al., 2007). What they represent are strategies for deconstruction and simplification of the elements that may be associated with psychiatric diagnostic categories, by focusing on a coherent, usually heritable, biological process that may be involved in a disorder. Ideally, identification and characterization of such an endophenotype (e.g., reduced predictive pursuit response in schizophrenics and their unaffected first-degree relatives; Hong et al., 2007) may enable tracking backward, to the genome and to experiential and epigenetic factors that modulate the endophenotype; and forward to endophenotype-related aspects of behavior that comprise components of the psychopathological condition.

This is clearly a complex and difficult business, and moreover one that is likely to be relatively fruitless in many cases. There is no guarantee that a particular endophenotype selected for analysis will eventually prove to have an integral relationship to the disorder of interest. As Keck and Strohle (2005) acknowledge: "…identification of reliable endophenotypes is currently one of the major rate-limiting steps in psychiatric genetic studies." Nonetheless, the endophenotype approach appears to represent a valuable new strategy in research on biological contributions to psychiatric disorders, precisely because contemporary diagnoses and classification of these disorders currently pay so little attention to their biological underpinnings (Gottesman and Gould, 2003).

The concept of animal modeling as it applies to anxiety has at least two major sources: first, a desire to understand basic emotional processes. This has been a consistent thread throughout most of the history of psychology, and it has resulted in research that typically had no specific conceptual connection to psychopathology. Second, a more recent trend has been development of models specifically to evaluate the effects of pharmacological and other potential treatments for anxiety disorders in general, or for particular categories of anxiety disorder. What both of these have in common is the use of subject species that are a great deal more amenable to both genetic and physiological/pharmacological interventions and analyses than are people. The result, as various chapters in this handbook illustrate, is that a good deal is known about the neural and biochemical systems involved in animal models of anxiety, along with a much more recent but rapidly expanding knowledge base on genetic factors relevant to some of these models.

The point is that this information is available, and that it is currently informing and being informed by findings from new technologies that provide some information on brain processes without possible damage to human subjects. In particular, imaging studies have tended to verify the basic "emotional brain" findings based on animal models, while adding some additional sites that appear to be more important in humans than in nonhuman mammals (Malizia and Nutt). However, as yet imaging studies are far from capable of determining which structures or systems are integral to a process, as opposed to merely active during that process. Human genetic analyses of anxiety are also capable of providing important information, but the likely combination of polygenic regulation (Lesch, 2001) with a strong influence of both experiential and epigenetic factors (e.g., Korte, 2001; Barr et al., 2004; Diorio and Meaney, 2007) in anxiety suggests that an adequate analysis of the role of genetics would require disproportionate effort and expense in investigations using only human populations. Indeed, even for a condition such as autism spectrum disorder (ASD), which has much higher twin concordance rates than do anxiety disorders, the genetics component has proved resistant to analysis: Although many individual genes have been evaluated for association with ASD, replication of positive results has been rare (Gupta and State, 2007).

Such considerations suggest that the study of anxiety, although largely fueled by the desire to understand and ameliorate human anxiety-linked psychopathologies, will continue to rely heavily on animal models. This being the case, the optimal strategy would appear to be to improve both the animal models, and the clarity of our conceptions of human anxiety. Building bridges requires an adequate foundation on both sides of the river. We hope this volume contributes to this effort.

References

Barr, C.S., Newman, T.K., Shannon, C., Parker, C., Dvoskin, R.L., Becker, M.L., Schwandt, M., Champoux, M., Lesch, K.P., Goldman, D., Suomi, S.J. and Higley, J.D. (2004) Rearing condition and rh5-HTTLPR interact to influence limbic-hypothalamic-pituitary-adrenal axis response to stress in infant macaques. Biol. Psychiatry, 55: 733–738.

Diorio, J. and Meaney, M.J. (2007) Maternal programming of defensive responses through sustained effects on gene expression. J. Psychiatry Neurosci., 32: 275–284.

Fineberg, N.A., Saxena, S., Zohar, J. and Craig, K.J. (2007) Obsessive-compulsive disorder: boundary issues. CNS Spectr., 12: 359–364. 367–375.

Gottesman, I.I. and Gould, T.D. (2003) The endophenotype concept in psychiatry: etymology and strategic intentions. Am. J. Psychiatry, 160: 636–645.

Gupta, A.R. and State, M.W. (2007) Recent advances in the genetics of autism. Biol. Psychiatry, 61: 429–437.

Hong, L.E., Turano, K.A., O'Neill, H., Hao, L., Wonodi, I., McMahon, R.P., Elliott, A. and Thaker, G.K. (2007) Refining the predictive pursuit endophenotype in schizophrenia. *Biol. Psychiatry* (In press).

Keck, M.E. and Strohle, A. (2005) Challenge studies in anxiety disorders. Handb. Exp. Pharmacol., 169: 449–468.

Korte, S.M. (2001) Corticosteroids in relation to fear, anxiety and psychopathology. Neurosci. Biobehav. Rev., 25: 117–142.

Lesch, K.P. (2001) Molecular foundation of anxiety disorders. J. Neural Transm., 108: 717–746.

Animal Models of Anxiety, Fear and Defense

CHAPTER 2.1

Theoretical approaches to the modeling of anxiety in animals

Neil McNaughton[1,*] and Hélio Zangrossi Jr.[2]

[1]*Department of Psychology, University of Otago, Dunedin, New Zealand*
[2]*Department of Pharmacology, School of Medicine of Ribeirão Preto, University of São Paulo, Ribeirão Preto-SP, Brazil*

Abstract: Theory influences what we mean by the word "anxiety", what we require of any animal model, and what specific theoretical constructs are embedded in any specific animal model of anxiety. We argue that, in the ideal case, the animal models we use should be embedded in a large-scale theory that integrates all of the theoretical levels of each animal model. We argue that face validity of a model should be ignored and that true predictive validity reduces ultimately to construct validity. So all models should aim to have construct validity based on strong theory. Theoretical analysis shows that anxiety should be distinguished from fear; that different anxiety disorders should be distinguished from each other; and that the components of any single apparent type of anxiety can have distinct neural control. Theory can show how a model is unsatisfactory, but it can also show that it is not the model but rather our translation from the clinical situation that is faulty. To model the many flavors of clinical disorder and variations in drug effectiveness, we must use theory to link multiple animal models, neural analysis and pharmacological analysis. The goal is to provide us with truly predictive tests that can be used for drug discovery as well as drug development. Most importantly, theory is required if we are to correctly match a particular measure from a particular model with the clinical entity we desire to model.

Keywords: anxiety; fear; defense; pharmacology; theory; model; anxiolytic; panicolytic

I. Introduction

Theory can impact on the assessment of animal models of anxiety at several levels. What we mean by the word "anxiety" is itself a theoretical issue that needs to be settled, at least in a preliminary fashion, before we can define what is to be modeled. What is required of an animal model depends on one's theoretical perspective on such models. Finally, specific theoretical constructs are embedded in any specific animal model of anxiety – either during its construction or, post hoc, when a new theory has to account for the properties of

an older model. We will discuss these three levels in turn and argue that, in the ideal case, the animal models we use should be embedded in a large-scale theory that integrates all of the theoretical levels of each animal model.

II. The nature of anxiety

It is tempting to take the meaning of the word "anxiety" as approximately given and then proceed to uncover the neural or behavioral basis of this entity. But not only are we then assuming rather than demonstrating an answer to the question "What is anxiety?", we are assuming an answer to the fundamental question posed by William James over 120 years ago, "What is an

*Corresponding author. E-mail: nmcn@psy.otago.ac.nz

R.J. Blanchard, D.C. Blanchard, G. Griebel and D. Nutt (Eds.)
Handbook of Anxiety and Fear, Vol. 17
ISBN 978-0-444-53065-3

11

DOI: 10.1016/S1569-7339(07)00002-1

emotion?'' (James, 1884). The problem is that, despite our everyday use of ''an emotion'' to talk about some entity we think is inside us, there may be no strictly matching scientific concept. ''An emotion'' may not be a single entity within an organism. Where this is true, we may need multiple animal models, each one assessing its own independent aspect of ''the emotion''. Or, we may need to choose a model in which multiple different measures capture each of the different aspects.

II.A. What is emotion?

We have argued elsewhere (McNaughton, 1989), that the key feature of whatever are variously called emotions (by lay, academic or clinical persons) is that they are products of evolution (Darwin, 1965). Certainly, phylogenetic continuity is an implicit assumption made by all who use ''animal models''. The superficial form of an emotion is shaped by development and includes species-specific details. But its underlying structure is conserved not only between individuals but, in terms of things like the action patterns of muscles, across species (Ekman et al., 1980; Ekman, 1982; Redican, 1982; Ekman and Friesen, 1986). In some respects this is not contentious. But we would go further and suggest that it is the recurrence of a particular class of evolutionary requirement – of a specific adaptive pressure – that not only shapes the parts of an emotion (as labeled by us) but also allows the parts to been seen as combined into a nominal whole.

The problem is that evolution does not work in the logical, tidy, way that a human engineer would like. It is the result of a continuous interaction between available mutations and local adaptive advantages. Critically, there are many cases where a number of specific neural mechanisms have each evolved to provide a particular ''rule of thumb'' (Krebs et al., 1983) that provides a local simple answer to part of a more complex global problem. It is the agglomeration of a sufficient number of such independent reactions that then provides the illusory appearance of a single, higher-order, class

of response to that adaptive requirement across many situations.

An example of this is provided by ''separation anxiety''. This is easily and regularly identified both by the means of producing it (removal of the primary caregiver, usually the mother) and by the characteristic pattern of responses that then ensues in children and in the young of other mammals such as rats, dogs and primates. In rats, as in humans, separation anxiety is manifest in both behavioral and autonomic responses. These appear together when the mother is removed and disappear together when she is returned.

The behavioral and autonomic components of this ''emotion'' give the appearance of joint outputs of a single, unified central state. Certainly, one could argue that, if either output were missing, the result would not be separation anxiety. However, it has been shown that, in rats, the behavioral reactions can be eliminated by the presence of a non-lactating foster mother, whereas the autonomic reactions can be eliminated by regular feeding with milk – but not, in either case, vice versa (Hofer, 1972). Thus, the two effector aspects of the ''one emotion'' can be doubly dissociated in the laboratory.

''Separation anxiety'' remains a nameable set of entities that are coherent under normal ecological circumstances and our analysis does not require any change in the everyday use of the term. The combined occurrence of the behavioral and autonomic components of the emotion is guaranteed by the fact that, under normal ecological circumstances, removing the mother necessarily removes, simultaneously, the separate stimuli (milk and mothering) that drive the separate autonomic and behavioral reactions. But, for scientific purposes, we must view the term as grounded in a particular class of evolutionarily recurring situation (loss of parents) which gives rise to a consistent set of adaptive requirements and so a consistent effector pattern (behavioral and autonomic) that constitutes a fairly consistent central state. However, ''separation anxiety'' does not refer to, or in any way imply, a single internal control mechanism governing the two sorts of pattern and guaranteeing their co-occurrence (Fig. 1).

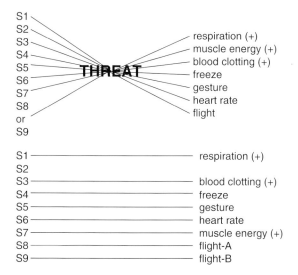

Fig. 1. The extremes of the possible neural relations which could have evolved to control responses to threat. The top half of the figure shows the functional relations linking stimuli (S1–S9) to responses where the stimuli are either regular predictors of threat (S1–S7) or where different stimuli are predictive of threat at different times (S8, S9). It can also be viewed as a representation of the simplest view of emotional states, namely that all stimuli activate a single neural representation of threat and this in turn activates the separate response systems. The bottom half of the figure shows, in its most extreme form, the opposite type of neural organization suggested by Hofer's experiments (see text). Here, each response system is under its own private stimulus control. Some stimuli (S2) may have not acquired control over any response system and some stimuli (S8, S9) may have acquired control over a particular response (flight) but only under some circumstances (A, B). Redrawn from McNaughton (1989).

II.B. What is anxiety?

Having concluded that we may need to invoke more than one measure or model to encompass "anxiety", we now need to distinguish models of anxiety from models of other emotions. In the past, anxiety has often been conflated with fear and panic:

> anxiety may be focused on an object, situation, or activity, which is avoided (phobia), or may be unfocused (free-floating anxiety). It may be experienced in discrete periods of sudden onset

and be accompanied by physical symptoms (panic attacks). When anxiety is focused on physical signs or symptoms and causes preoccupation with the fear or belief of having a disease, it is termed hypochondriasis. (American Psychiatric Association, 1987, p. 392)

This conflation continues in current clinical classifications – DSM, for example, continues to include phobias, panic and generalized anxiety within a single class of "anxiety disorders" (American Psychiatric Association, 1994). However, while extreme anxiety can result in panic as a symptom (Marks, 1988) panic in its purest sense can occur in the absence of anxiety (Holt, 1990; Carter et al., 1994; Shear and Maser, 1994) and elimination of anxiety can reduce arousal-related panic while leaving primary panic attacks intact (Franklin, 1990). Critically, some drugs, at doses that alleviate generalized anxiety and social anxiety, do not alleviate panic or specific phobia, whereas other drugs do (Table 1). This suggests a neural and functional separation between phobia and panic on the one hand and anxiety on the other. So, how are we to distinguish such entities?

If, as we have argued, a historically recurring adaptive requirement[1] in phylogeny is what links the parts of an emotion, it follows that we can define an emotion by

> analysis of its possible functional significance. ... Important and pervasive human action tendencies, particularly those which occur across a wide range of cultures and specific learning situations, are very likely to have their origin in the functionally significant behavior patterns of non-human animals. ... This approach, working through the characteristic behavior patterns seen in response to important ecological demands (e.g. feeding, reproduction, defense) when animals are given the rather wide range of behavioral choices typical of most natural habitats, is called ethoexperimental analysis. It involves a view that the functional significance of behavior attributed to anxiety (or other emotions) needs to be taken into

---

[1] This can be loosely translated as "purpose" but without any implication of a purposer. Strictly, it should be referred to as teleonomy (Pittendrigh, 1958).

Table 1. Relative effectiveness of drugs in treating different aspects of defensive disorders

	"Antianxiety"			"Antidepressant"			
	BDZ_1	BUS	BDZ_2	IMI	CMI	MAOI	SSRI
Specific phobia	0	?	?	0	?	(–)	(–)
Generalized anxiety	–	–	–	–	–	?	–
Social anxiety	–	(–)	(–)	0	(–)	–	–
Unipolar depression	0	–	–	–	–	–	–
Atypical depression	0	?	?	(–)	?	–	?
Panic attacks	0	0	–	–	—	–	–
Obsessions/compulsions	0	(–)	0	(–)	—	(–)	—

BDZ_1, early benzodiazepines, e.g., chlordiazepoxide and diazepam administered at typical antianxiety doses. Other sedative antianxiety drugs (barbiturates, meprobamate) have similar effects. BDZ_2, later high-potency benzodiazepines, e.g., alprazolam. The antipanic effect is achieved at higher doses and this has also been reported with equivalent high doses for BDZ_1 (Noyes et al., 1996). BUS, buspirone and related $5HT1_A$ agonists; CMI, clomipramine; IMI, imipramine and related tricyclic antidepressants, but excluding clomipramine; MAOI, monoamine oxidase inhibitors, e.g., phenelzine; SSRI, selective serotonin reuptake inhibitors, e.g., fluoxetine, citalopram.

Different patterns of response in the table can be attributed to the variation in receptor occupancy or interaction by particular drugs in different parts of the brain. No drug or drug class produces a specific limited effect (despite the omission of side effects from the table) but the variation in relative effectiveness across the different aspects of disorders of fear and anxiety argues for distinct neural control of each effect.

Source: Stein et al. (1992), Westenberg (1999), Gray and McNaughton (2000), McNaughton (2002), Rickels and Rynn (2002), Stein et al. (2004), Stevens and Pollack (2005).

Symbols: 0, no effect; –, reduction; —, extensive reduction; +, increase; (–), small or discrepant effects.

account; and that this functional significance reflects the dynamics of that behavior in interaction with the ecological systems in which the species has evolved, implying that these dynamics … can be determined far more efficiently when the behavior is studied under conditions typical of life for the particular species.

(Blanchard and Blanchard, 1990a,b, p. 125)

Such detailed ethoexperimental analysis suggests a categorical separation of fear from anxiety in the defensive responses elicited by a predator (Blanchard and Blanchard, 1988, 1989, 1990a,b). The immediate presence of a predator elicits a distinctive set of behaviors that are identifiable with a state of fear. These behaviors, defined purely ethologically, turn out to be sensitive to anti-panic, but not anti-anxiety drugs (Blanchard et al., 1997). The potential presence of a predator (i.e., its recent disappearance from view, or the presence only of its odor) produces a quite different set of behaviors (especially "risk assessment") that are identifiable with a state of anxiety. These behaviors, again defined purely ethologically, turn out to be sensitive to anxiolytic drugs. This analysis of fear predicts, for example, the well-demonstrated insensitivity to anxiolytic

drugs of active avoidance in a wide variety of species and of phobia in humans (Sartory et al., 1990) and the sensitivity of passive avoidance to anxiolytic drugs (Gray, 1977). The critical factor distinguishing fear and anxiety (Gray and McNaughton, 2000) appears to be what can be called "defensive direction" (McNaughton and Corr, 2004). Fear operates to allow an animal to leave a dangerous situation (active avoidance); anxiety operates to allow an animal to enter a dangerous situation (e.g., cautious "risk assessment", approach behavior) or withhold entrance (passive avoidance).

In constructing "animal models of anxiety", then, we need to distinguish anxiety from fear. We should also note that different drugs (Table 1) could have different relative potencies in relation to, for example, generalized anxiety as compared to social anxiety. So, even within the category of anxiety (or fear) we may need different models to best approximate different sub-types. It should be noted, also, that the theoretical approach taken to the concept of anxiety in this section has been highly general. Our choice of animal models will also be shaped by specific theories of anxiety and fear but we will deal with this issue later when discussing specific models.

II.C. What is pathological anxiety?

There is a final issue that we need to consider when choosing an animal model of anxiety: what we understand to be the nature of an anxiety disorder. Anxiety can present as a symptom of some physical, non-neural pathology. In such cases we would seek an animal model of the physical pathology (expecting anxiety to be a symptom) but we would not seek an animal model of anxiety in any general sense. Anxiety disorders, in general, as classified by systems such as DSM, involve unwanted reactions that are either extreme or occur to inappropriate eliciting stimuli but which are otherwise indistinguishable from normal behavior. Thus, when the "reaction is beyond that expected for the child's developmental level", separation anxiety becomes separation anxiety disorder (American Psychiatric Association, 1994).

In practice, the more recently developed animal models of anxiety generate anxiety with ecologically relevant stimuli; and the resultant changes in behavior are (as noted above) sensitive to drugs that treat the symptoms of human clinical anxiety. This suggests that "anxiety disorder" will often simply represent an extreme tail of the normal distribution of population sensitivity to anxiety-provoking stimuli. However, as we develop deeper, neurally based, theories of defensive disorders it is likely that in some cases there may be genuine neural pathology underlying the symptoms. This seems likely with some cases of panic and obsession (notably those that lack any concurrent symptoms of anxiety); and, where this is true, we may want to develop pathology-specific models.

We have treated fear and anxiety, here, as specific distinct emotional states that can occur in both an adaptive and a pathological form. This matches the loose forms of common usage (where neither word entails pathology) and to some extent what is said within DSM. However, it should be noted that there are those who use the term anxiety to mean "pathological fear" (with "fear" being by definition adaptive) and, contrariwise, those who use the term fear to mean "extreme anxiety" (with the implication that this is often

pathological). We think that a major advantage of the usage we have adopted, based on both animal experimental data and ethoexperimental analysis, is that it provides a clear basis for a consistent terminology that roughly encompasses the various different prior usages – and resolves the inconsistencies between them. Critically, clinical categories (such as social anxiety) that involve approach-avoidance conflict are sensitive to anxiolytic drugs such as diazepam and buspirone; but those (such as simple phobia) that involve pure avoidance are not sensitive to these drugs.

III. The nature of an animal model

The nature of an animal model, and the division of models into subtypes, has been approached from a wide range of perspectives (Joel, 2006; van der Staay, 2006). We think it preferable to use the word "model" rather loosely and to not attempt to characterize types and subtypes of model. Pragmatically, an animal model is something you use instead of a direct test on humans. The animal model may be a restricted, simplified, measure or set of measures and so "model" aspects of the test animal's neural or behavioral repertoire as well as aspects of the human condition. But the model could also involve a complex situation that can simultaneously produce many aspects of a particular human condition. In this case we are likely to have chosen to use an animal for economical, ethical or pragmatic reasons rather than for simplicity.

III.A. Validating animal models

The key issue in relation to an animal model is whether it delivers measures that can stand in for ones that we would have taken in a direct human test. This is an issue usually referred to as "validity" and we will consider types of validity and their relation to each other below. It is important to bear in mind, given our discussion of the parts of an emotion and of distinctions between types of defensive emotion that a model may be a valid measure of some aspect of anxiety but be an invalid measure of some other aspect.

So, in determining the fitness for our current purpose of a particular model, it is as important to be as clear about the aspect of anxiety that we wish to assess as it is to know the validity of the model in relation to the aspect that it nominally measures.

> While different authors may disagree on terminology and classification, there seems to be a wide agreement that it is impossible to develop an animal model that mimics a psychiatric syndrome in its entirety, and that therefore the criteria that an animal model must satisfy to establish its validity depend on the purpose of the model (Matthysse, 1986; McKinney, 1988; Willner, 1991; Geyer and Markou, 1995). In the context of neurobiological research, in which the aim of animal models is to promote our understanding of the modeled condition by elucidating its neurobiological mechanisms (Geyer and Markou, 1995), it is widely agreed that a common physiological basis of the model and the modeled condition contributes greatly to the model's validity, although authors disagree on whether this contributes to the model's face, predictive, and/or construct validity (Yadin et al., 1991; Rapoport et al., 1992; Altemus et al., 1996; Nurnberg et al., 1997; Sagvolden, 2000; Bourin et al., 2001; Geyer et al., 2001; Szechtman et al., 2001). It should be noted that a critical component in the demonstration of a common physiological basis is the demonstration of a similar response to treatment, because the latter suggests similarity in the neurotransmitter systems involved. This makes pharmacological isomorphism an important factor in assessing the validity of an animal model, and indeed, the validation process of most animal models of psychopathology involves testing the effects of relevant pharmacological treatments.
>
> Joel (2006)

As indicated by Joel, the type of validation required for animal models of disorder is not clear; (Willner, 1984, 1985, 1991; Joel, 2006; van der Staay, 2006). We will argue that a higher-order theoretical validity (linked to the neurobiological isomorphism focused on by Joel) is to be preferred. To see why, we will consider the most common forms of validity invoked in relation to animal models: face validity, predictive validity and construct validity. We think these are all best evaluated in the context of the evolutionary perspective on anxiety described above.

III.B. Face, predictive and construct validity

"Face validity" normally refers to a superficial resemblance of the measures taken to the equivalent human measures. In practice, such similarity provides no guarantee that changes in a measure will predict changes in the equivalent human measure and so "face validity", although still used as a descriptive term, is not generally seen as conferring validity on an animal model in any real sense (Joel, 2006; van der Staay, 2006). This issue is neatly exemplified by the facial expressions of monkeys. The monkey expression most similar, in a photograph, to a wide human smile uses quite different muscles from a smile and is a display of aggression. By contrast, the "play face" uses the same muscles as a human smile, and is displayed in similar emotional contexts, and despite its superficial difference is a true homolog (Redican, 1982). We will argue below that, with anxiety and fear, homology is an important ingredient for validity. That is, as argued in the quotation from the Blanchards above, it is the matching of functional significance of behaviors across species that is important not the matching of the detailed behaviors themselves.

"Predictive validity" is, at first blush, the only validity required of a model: the proven capacity to predict, from the model, future findings in the modeled case. Certainly, where prediction truly fails, a model must be invalid. However, a model that, for example, detects classical anti-anxiety drugs such as benzodiazepines and predicts their clinical effects may simply involve a $GABA_A$ receptor, have no physiological relationship to the generation of anxiety, and so fail to detect the effects of novel anti-anxiety drugs that act via the $5HT1_A$ system. The latter do not interact with GABA, and so have quite different effects on euphoria, muscle relaxation and addiction, while having the same capacity to alleviate anxiety. True predictive validity, then, should have a guarantee that the model should detect quite novel classes of drug in the future and not simply have been shown to detect many members of older classes of drug in the past. In this stronger form, predictive validity is, essentially, construct validity.

"Construct validity" is conferred on animal models "if their procedures are theoretically sound. The construct validity is not established by determining the relation between a test and an accepted criterion but is instead based on the establishment of relationships, which are in turn based on the definition of a trait. Implicitly, a construct is defined by a network of associations" (van der Staay, 2006). The key point here is that the model embodies a construct that, in turn, is part of a theory. A properly developed theory summarizes, integrates and encapsulates a vast database and it is the capturing of the essence of this database that validates the construct and, subject to the validity and generality of the theory, provides it with the strong form of predictive validity that we desire.

When anxiety is viewed from an evolutionary point of view, it is important to note that, whatever the surface behaviors that fulfill a function, the neural and hormonal systems controlling behavior will contain components that are conserved. Indeed, since substantial alteration in an existing defensive system is likely to be catastrophic in evolutionary terms, we can expect the core aspects of defensive systems to be particularly well conserved. The properties of the homologous systems in other animals are likely, therefore, to be highly similar to those in humans. Comparative, and particularly neural, theories of anxiety and fear should thus provide a particularly strong theoretical base for the derivation of animal models of specific aspects of human anxiety.

There are two unique aspects of construct validity that flow on from its theoretical derivation and do not follow from face or simple predictive validity. First, is that novel models can be generated directly from a theory. A model that has only current predictive validity, with no obvious construct validity, can only have been discovered by accident. By contrast, a theory provides a range of constructs from which a suitable model can be extracted by design. Second, is that apparent failure of predictive validity will not automatically invalidate a model but can lead

instead to a deeper understanding of the human condition being modeled.

III.C. Deriving a model from a theory

To derive a model from a theory, one first needs a substantial theory. Probably one of the most substantial and well-developed theories of the neural basis of anxiety is that of Jeffrey Gray. This arose, over 30 years ago, in the hypothesis that anti-anxiety drugs change hippocampal function (Gray, 1970) and that this structure is an important part of a "behavioral inhibition system" (Gray, 1976). Further development of the theory, based only on analysis of classical (GABA-acting) anxiolytic drugs resulted in a full theory of the "Neuropsychology of Anxiety" (Gray, 1982). This has recently been modified and elaborated (Gray and McNaughton, 2000; McNaughton and Corr, 2004).

Given Gray's theory, the demonstration that an anxiolytic drug can reduce the frequency of hippocampal theta rhythm (McNaughton and Sedgwick, 1978) provided a potential model of anti-anxiety drug action with high construct validity; although there was no obvious way to assess face validity and, initially, no data on predictive validity. To date this model has shown predictive validity with ethanol (Coop et al., 1990); benzodiazepines (McNaughton et al., 1986); the $5HT1_A$ agonist, buspirone (Coop and McNaughton, 1991); the tricyclic antidepressant, imipramine (Zhu and McNaughton, 1991) and the specific serotonin reuptake inhibitor, fluoxetine (Munn and McNaughton, unpublished data). Of particular interest, it shows a similarly linear dose–response curve with $5HT1_A$ anxiolytics as with $GABA_A$ anxiolytics. By contrast, many behavioral models show only weak effects, and inverted-U dose–response curves, with $5HT1_A$ drugs.

We would argue that the demonstrated robustness of this model derives from its tight construct validity – it assesses a core construct of the theory. Indeed, from the theoretical point of view, its apparent robustness is greater than expected as there are aspects of anxiolytic action, within the most recent versions of the theory (Gray and

McNaughton, 2000) that should be mediated by other systems and so not be detectable in this model (see section on neuropsychology, below).

III.D. Does failure of prediction automatically invalidates a model?

Genuine failure of prediction will, of course, invalidate any model. However, where construct validity is high, we may want to ask how far an apparent failure reflects a failure of the model, as such, or a failure of our understanding of the situation being modeled.

As noted above, a number of behavioral models that detect classical (GABA$_A$) anxiolytic drugs show weak responses and inverted U-shaped dose–response curves with novel (5HT) anxiolytics. Fixed-interval responding is an interesting example of this (Panickar and McNaughton, 1991). It is a prime test of behavioral inhibition and so reflects a key construct in Gray's theory of the behavioral inhibition system, mentioned above. Further, anxiolytic drugs have been shown to affect fixed interval responding through the control of theta rhythm (Woodnorth and McNaughton, 2002), changes in which (as we saw above) appear to have strong predictive validity.

The failure of buspirone to affect fixed interval responding, except at very low doses, turns out not to be entirely general. First, if buspirone and a benzodiazepine are each given repeatedly for some time before training starts, rather than being tested with acute injections, they turn out to have the same effect on fixed-interval responding, with the chronic benzodiazepine having a relatively smaller effect than usual and buspirone having a larger one (Zhu and McNaughton, 1995). This matches the clinical situation where the two types of drug only have equivalent effects after longer-term administration. Second, buspirone releases, and benzodiazepines block the release of, stress hormones and, if these effects are blocked, again the acute effects of the two on fixed-interval responding become similar as a result of a decrease in the benzodiazepine's and an increase in buspirone's effects (McNaughton et al., 1996). Thus, close inspection of the fixed-interval model's apparent

failure shows that: (1) where the human treatment matches the treatment applied to the model then the model does not fail; and, (2) the differences in effects of the major classes of anxiolytic, both in the model and in the clinic, can be attributed to their additional, opposite, effects on the pituitary–adrenal axis interacting with the fundamental anxiolytic effect.

III.E. Conclusions

In discussing the nature of emotion in general, and anxiety in particular, we concluded that we must use multiple models (or at least measures) to capture the different aspects of "a single emotion" and to be able to assess different defensive emotions (e.g., fear and anxiety) and different subtypes of those emotions (e.g., generalized anxiety and social anxiety). This imposes one type of requirement on the validity of a model: the chosen model must map to the specific aspect of the specific subtype of anxiety (or fear) in which we are interested.

In discussing types of validity, we rejected face validity as being appropriate and concluded that in its strongest form predictive validity reduces to construct validity. We also argued that construct validity needs to be based on a strong, general theory and that, where this is the case, carefully chosen models can detect quite novel classes of compound and on occasion inform us about unexpected aspects of the modeled condition.

Both the nature of anxiety and the nature of animal models, then, require us to base our models (and our choice of a particular model for a particular purpose) on well-developed neuropsychological theory. In the remainder of this chapter we will look at particular models and their relation to particular theories to gain a more detailed picture of the interactions between the two.

IV. The nature of a specific test: the elevated plus-maze

We have provided a council of perfection: models, if they are to correctly perform their modeling function, should be derived from neuropsychological theory. However, this first requires an adequate neuropsychological theory. Such theories must be derived from behavioral, neural and pharmacological experiments. These experiments often use paradigms that are either intended to be, or in practice are used as, models. In such cases, even with models that are only partially successful, we need to analyze them, post hoc, in terms of available (especially competing) theories.

As an example of such analysis we will look at the theoretical concepts behind, and alternative interpretations of results in the most popular animal model of anxiety of the last two decades: the elevated plus-maze. Briefly, this test, originally developed by Handley and Mithani (1984), consists of two opposed arms enclosed by walls and united, in perpendicular, to two open arms of equal dimensions, which are devoid of lateral walls. The whole apparatus is elevated above the floor. It has been shown that rats and mice, when freely exploring the maze, have a clear preference for the enclosed arms when compared to the open arms.

There are a number of reasons for the popularity of the elevated plus-maze. It is fast, requires no food deprivation or delivery of shock, and uses very simple apparatus. The matching disadvantage is that, without extensive analysis, it is not clear what the reinforcers are – whether, for example, any particular behavior is driven by positive (approach arm A) or negative (avoid arm B) drives. With operant tests these things are explicit and controlled – but at considerable expense. So, we will provide a theoretical analysis of the elevated plus-maze both in terms of experiments testing variations on its basic parameters and by linking these findings to the results of other operant and ethologically oriented tests.

IV.A. Theoretical analysis of the elevated plus-maze

The elevated plus-maze test was based on previous work by Montgomery (1955) that intended to analyze the factors underlying animals' exploratory behavior in novel situations. Using Y-shaped mazes comprising different numbers of enclosed and open alleys, he showed that rats prefer to explore the closed arms. He attributed the exploration of both types of arm to the positive value of novelty. However, novelty also has negative aspects that can lead to avoidance behavior. Both the open and the closed arms evoke both positive and negative aspects of novelty. Montgomery stated that open arms evoke a greater strength of fear drive than enclosed arms. Hence, the animals tended to avoid the open arms and to explore the closed arms. However, he did not make clear the source of this greater fear and his context implies that it could have been negative aspects of novelty.

When the elevated plus-maze was developed as a model of anxiety, it was based on the fundamental conclusions of Montgomery's studies. It presented rats with a simple choice of exploring open or protected closed alleys. The opposition of two arms of the same type meant that a genuine choice could be made. If there were only one open and one closed arm, the animal might stay in a closed arm simply through inertia – that is, a lack of exploratory drive. But, in the plus-maze, leaving a closed arm (as a result of a reduction in its novelty) presents the rat with a choice (initially) of two open and one closed arm, all of equal novelty. Choice of the other closed arm then indicates either a preference for closed arms or an avoidance of open arms.

There are two issues that need to be settled, here, in assessing the nature of the plus-maze in terms of possible influences of anxiety. The first is whether the behavior is approach to the closed arm (which would result from a positive exploratory drive and so be unlikely to result from anxiety which is, especially in the clinic, perceived as negative). The second issue is, assuming that the measured behavior is the result of avoidance, whether the test can be seen as one driven simply by avoidance, or by a conflict between approach and avoidance.

Treit and co-workers (1993) examined the extent to which stimuli in the open arms of the elevated plus-maze motivate avoidance behavior. They showed that open arm avoidance did not habituate across trials. It was also not reduced in animals that received three previous confinement sessions to the open arms (flooding exposures). Neither negative nor positive aspects of novelty could, then, account for the pattern of behavior. The level of open arm avoidance was, also, similar in animals tested in plus-mazes elevated to different heights, leading to the conclusion that height is not an anxiogenic stimulus in this test. In contrast, they reported that rats explored an open arm with a raised Plexiglas edge more than an open arm with a standard flat edge. This suggests that fear of open spaces is the main aversive stimulus in the elevated plus-maze. This has been related to the fact that rats in open spaces are more exposed to predation. They show thigmotaxis – a preference, in a range of apparatus and situations, to stay near vertical surfaces and avoid the center of open spaces.

We have, then, good reason to see the plus-maze test (however elevated) as pitting two different motivations against each other. The positive (albeit mixed) motivation driving exploration of all the arms is novelty. The negative motivation specifically associated with the open as opposed to closed arms, is the avoidance of open spaces. We will deal later with the issue of whether the conflict between the motivations is critical or whether the positive one simply provides a baseline against which the effects of the negative can be assessed.

IV.B. Pharmacological analysis of the elevated plus-maze

Handley and Mithani (1984) used the ratio of the number of entries into open arms relative to closed as a potential measure of anxiety and challenged this with putative or clinically effective anxiolytic and anxiogenic compounds. They observed that non-sedative doses of anxiolytic drugs such as diazepam and amylobarbitone increased exploration of the open arms, without significantly changing exploration of the enclosed arms. Anxiogenic drugs such as picrotoxin and ACTH caused the opposite effect. Since these first observations, the anxiolytic-like effect of benzodiazepines and barbiturates in the elevate plus-maze has been extensively replicated. This highly reliable pharmacological isomorphism coupled with its simplicity, economy and lack of either lengthy training procedures or the use of food/water deprivation or electric shock made the elevated plus-maze enormously popular.

However, confidence in the elevated plus-maze test was undermined when buspirone was introduced in the clinic for the treatment of generalized anxiety disorder. Unlike GABA-related anxiolytics such as the benzodiazepines and barbiturates, buspirone is a $5HT_{1A}$ receptor agonist. It was found that the elevated plus-maze did not consistently demonstrate an anxiolytic effect of this new class of anxiolytics. This was also true regarding the anxiolytic effects of other 5HT-modulating drugs such as imipramine and fluoxetine (Griebel, 1995).

To understand this failure of the test's predictive validity, we need to return to the issue of whether the key element of the plus-maze as a model is simple avoidance or approach-avoidance conflict. This is theoretically important as conflict is a pervasive concept associated with anxiety. It emerged from the psychoanalytic idea that human anxiety results from inner conflict. While there is considerable scientific doubt about many psychoanalytic premises, the association between approach-avoidance conflicts and anxiety is much more a superficial description of situations and behavior than specific to psychoanalytic theory. The idea of conflict in one form or another, then, remains a cornerstone for many current theories (Blanchard and Blanchard, 1990a,b; Blanchard et al., 1991; Gray and McNaughton, 2000; Graeff, 2002).

One could simply argue that, since anxiolytic drugs affect passive but not active avoidance in many learning-based tests, the effect of the drugs in the plus-maze must also be on conflict and not on simple avoidance. However, we do not have to rely on such inference. A variant of the elevated plus-maze, the elevated T-maze, was developed to separate out the different elements embedded in the plus-maze (Viana et al., 1994; Zangrossi and Graeff, 1997; Graeff et al., 1998; Jardim et al., 1999; Sanson and Carobrez, 1999). This model was designed to separate different motivational components by shutting the entrance of one of the enclosed arms of the plus-maze and presenting the animal with specific trials rather than allowing free behavior. To assess inhibitory avoidance, the rat is placed at the end of the remaining enclosed arm and the latency to exit this arm with the four paws is recorded in three successive trials made at 30-s intervals. Learning can be indicated by an increase in withdrawal latency across trials. To assess active escape, the rat is placed, 30 s after the completion of avoidance training, at the end of one of the open arms and the withdrawal latency from this arm is similarly recorded.

As would be expected from previous data in operant experiments, benzodiazepine anxiolytics such as diazepam and midazolam, but also 5HT-related drugs such as buspirone, ipsapirone and ritanserin impair inhibitory avoidance in the T maze while leaving one-way escape unchanged (Graeff and Zangrossi, 2002). This selective effect in favour of defensive approach correlates with the clinical effectiveness of these drugs on generalized anxiety, as opposed to their lack of efficacy (at least at anxiolytic doses) on panic disorder. Similarly, one-way escape is impaired by chronic (but not acute) administration of the tricyclic antidepressants such as imipramine (Teixeira et al., 2000) and clomipramine as well as by the selective 5HT reuptake blocker fluoxetine (Poltronieri et al., 2003) – all drugs that are used to treat panic disorder.

We have shown that the plus-maze is a mixed test, in the sense that the rat can display multiple different strategies of defense while exploring any specific part of the maze. This has been recognized for some time and can explain the inconsistent effects of 5HT-acting drugs (Handley et al., 1993). As indicated by results in the elevated T-maze, at least two of them can be clearly named: avoidance of open arms when the rat is in an enclosed arm, and escape from an open arm toward an enclosed arm. Since it has been shown that 5HT pathways may influence these defense strategies in different, even opposite ways (for a review see Graeff, 2002, and Chapter 4.3 in this book) the effect of 5HT-acting drugs in the plus-maze would vary as a function of the predominance of one or the other of these defense reactions.

IV.C. Ethological analysis of the elevated plus-maze

In parallel to the introduction of buspirone in the clinic, there was a worldwide acceptance of the separation of "anxiety" disorders into distinct diagnostic categories, a trend that was initiated by the DSM III classification of psychiatric disorders (American Psychiatric Association, 1980). (Note that DSM conflates what we would see as distinct anxiety and fear disorders.) Later studies showed that buspirone was effective in treating generalized anxiety disorder and depression but not panic, post-traumatic stress disorder or obsessive compulsive disorder.

This led to a different way of dealing with the failure of predictive validity of the elevated plus-maze. The idea was that the successful detection of a drug effect could depend on the types of defensive behaviors actually measured in this test. On this view, as we have already argued on the basis of both the earlier work and Treit's results, the plus-maze does in fact contain the critical elements required of an animal model of anxiety. But, in contrast to Montgomery's focus on choice behavior (and so, as we have seen, a contaminated measure of behavioral inhibition), we can focus on the kind of elicited behaviors, such as risk assessment, that are fundamental to the ethological approach advocated by the Blanchards.

Application of this ethological approach showed that the incorporation of defensive acts and postures toward risk assessment in the scoring of the plus-maze notably improved the test's capability for detecting the effects on anxiety of 5HT-modulating drugs (Griebel et al., 1997). Again we see that careful theoretical analysis of the content of a test can account for, and lead to ways to deal with, apparent failures of the test as a model. In this case by using measures of elicited behavior instead of measures of behavioral inhibition to assess anxiety.

V. Other animal models of anxiety

Let us now apply the principles we have elucidated in the elevated plus-maze to other animal models of anxiety. These turn out to involve, as we might expect, both behavioral inhibition and anxiety-specific elicited behavior.

The elevated plus-maze was popular because it was seen as having many advantages over pre-existing animal models of anxiety. These were mostly based on approach-avoidance conflict. Before the plus-maze era, two main classes of animal model were commonly used: those using response-contingent shock and those using non-contingent shock. For example, "conditioned suppression" is the inhibition of ongoing behavior elicited by conditioned stimuli that predict *unavoidable* electric shock. "Conditioned punishment" involves the suppression of rewarded responding by concurrent *response-contingent* electric shock. These tests all require food or water deprivation and administration of shock. (The fixed-interval test, discussed earlier, can be viewed as a form of punishment schedule where, in the early part of the interval, frustration rather than shock acts as the punisher.) The earlier tests also required very extensive pre-training. While their expense was considerable, it can be argued that these tests allow a clear identification of the key anxiolytic-sensitive parameter (behavioral inhibition) and also contain (in their un-shocked baseline periods) controls for non-specific effects on motivation, perception, motor control, etc. By contrast, it has taken considerable analysis – and development of a second-generation test, the elevated T-maze – for us to identify the factors governing behavior in the elevated plus-maze.

Drug results are theoretically clearest with conditioned suppression. Animals are trained to respond for reward and then periods of signaled non-contingent punishment are superimposed – the shock can therefore never be avoided and anxiety is always present. Anxiolytic drugs selectively release the inhibition of responding by shock. Similar results are obtained with the Geller–Seifter punishment schedule (Geller and Seifter, 1960), in which shock is contingent. However, it should be noted that, with well-learned punishment (unlike conditioned suppression), the animal comes to avoid the shock or, when it occurs, can predict its occurrence with complete accuracy. At this point, genuine anxiolytic effects are lost and are replaced by state-dependent changes (McNaughton, 1985).

A simpler, and so cheaper, punishment test – the Vogel conflict test – was later developed that involved administration of shock on an unlearned licking baseline (Vogel et al., 1971). We can thus see a progression from tests where approach and avoidance are tightly controlled, and approach-avoidance conflict is clear; through tests that combine innate and learned components; to tests, such as the elevated plus-maze, where the sources of approach and avoidance were initially unknown – and where, as we have seen, their control is problematic. These are all tests of approach-avoidance conflict, with anxiolytics reducing behavioral inhibition. We would argue that, at present, the elevated T-maze provides the best compromise between control of approach and avoidance and the cost of administering the test.

A range of other "innate"/"ethological" tests have been developed since the advent of the plus-maze (for descriptions see Chapter 2.5 by Litvin et al.). The key parameters in the social interaction test, the light–dark exploration test, and the shock-probe burying test include clear measures of behavioral inhibition – and so require no further psychological analysis here (but see the neural analysis below). However, it should be noted that the Blanchard's analysis of anxiety-related behavior (Blanchard et al., 1990, 1991) focuses equally on specific anxiety-elicited behaviors and on behavioral inhibition.

The shock-probe burying test, as the name implies, has as its major measure the extent to which a rat will bury the shock probe. This is an elicited behavior that, consistent with our analysis of fear versus anxiety, will only occur when the animal approaches the source of threat. Shock-probe burying is sensitive to anxiolytic drugs. It also shows how such elicited responses are shaped by the context of the threat (burying the scent or memory of a cat is not a functional defensive option; nor is risk assessment of the environment around a shock probe). It also shows that approach to threat is critical in determining anxiolytic sensitivity, as opposed to whether threat is actual or potential, since the shock probe is a clear and definite threat – but still one that it can make sense to approach.

Ultrasonic vocalization is less easy to categorize. It occurs in rat pups experiencing separation anxiety (which we have already discussed above) and in adult rats subject to inescapable footshock. It is clear that in neither case is this part of a simple threat avoidance repertoire. But, on the other hand, it is far from clear, particularly in the adult case, that the response is elicited in the context of threat approach (the basis for risk-assessment behaviors or shock-probe burying). In the case of the rat pups it could be argued that they are in a safe place and, for sustenance, need to leave it and so approach threat. In that context vocalization is a means of solving the problem (by bringing their sustenance back to them) and so an appropriate part of a threat-approach repertoire. But not only is this speculative; it does not clearly apply to the adult case.

VI. Models of anxiety and their control by the brain

We have already argued from the clinical profile of drugs used to treat disorders of fear and anxiety (Table 1) that specific models and measures need to be chosen carefully to ensure that the model captures the desired type or component of anxiety. The need for this, at the neural level, is demonstrated by Menard and Treit (1999) and by more detailed consideration of the neuropsychological theory of anxiety we discussed earlier (see Section III.C; Figure 2).

Menard and Treit (1999) review the effects of different anxiolytic drugs; across a wide range of animal models (e.g., open field, elevated + maze, fear potentiated startle, etc.); and injected into different sites in the brain. Their key findings are:

1. Anxiolytic drugs can produce changes in unlearned tests of anxiety when injected into any part of the defensive approach hierarchy illustrated in Fig. 2.
2. Within different parts of the same general neural area (such as the amygdala), the same drug can dissociate measures from two different

models (such as the elevated plus maze and the shock probe burying test).
3. Within a single part of a structure, a drug can dissociate two measures within a single test (such as burying and probe avoidance within the shock probe burying test).
4. An anxiolytic effect of a $GABA_A$ drug does not guarantee an effect of a $5HT_{1A}$ drug within the same structure despite the fact that systemic injection is effective in both cases.
5. Effects on multiple structures can combine to produce the systemic profile of the drug within a single test ($GABA_A$ drugs affect shock probe avoidance but not probe burying in the amygdala and vice versa in the septum).

We must view the effects of anxiolytic drugs, then, as having potentially variable profiles of action across a range of measures derived from a range of tests. Depending on variables such as defensive direction (fear vs. anxiety) and defensive distance (which translates to neural level within the hierarchies of Fig. 2) individual drugs will have different effects on different measures of "anxiety". Different drugs (including members of the same class with only slightly different structures such as imipramine and clomipramine) will have different quantitative profiles across ranges of measures depending on the precise location within the distributed defense system of the receptors to which they bind with greatest affinity.

VII. Conclusions

We have shown that anxiety should be distinguished from fear; that, less categorically, different anxiety disorders and different fear disorders should be distinguished from each other; and that the components of an apparently unitary type of anxiety can be neurally distinct. Theoretical analysis of animal models is, therefore, required if we are to match a particular measure from a particular model with the clinical entity we desire to model.

We have also shown that face validity of a model is meaningless and we have argued that true predictive validity reduces to construct validity.

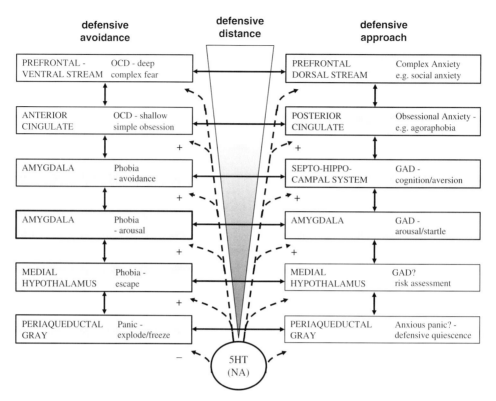

Fig. 2. The two-dimensional defense system (Gray and McNaughton, 2000; McNaughton and Corr, 2004). On either side are defensive avoidance and defensive approaches, respectively – a categorical dimension. Each is divided, down the page, into a number of hierarchical levels (Deakin and Graeff, 1991; Graeff, 1994). These are ordered from high to low (top to bottom) both with respect to neural level (and cytoarchitectonic complexity) and to functional level. Each level is associated with specific classes of behavior and so symptom and syndrome. Syndromes are associated with hyper-reactivity of a structure and symptoms with high activity. Given the interconnections within the system (and effects of, e.g., conditioning) symptoms will not be a good guide to syndromes. At short defensive distances the avoidance system is more likely to be activated, whereas at longer defensive distances the approach system is more likely to be activated (shading of boxes). Systemic drugs can target via serotonin (5HT), noradrenaline (NA) and the GABA$_A$–benzodiazepine-receptor complex – a range of anatomical sites. Different drugs have different profiles of action (Table 1) due to variation in receptor types among structures. Injection of different drugs into different structures fractionates both animal models and measures within a model (see Engin and Treit, 1999).

That is, the models we choose to use should be based on strong theory and should have been tested for their detailed conformation to theoretical constructs.

We believe we have shown that when theory is given such primacy it will not only allow us to determine ways in which particular models are unsatisfactory. In many cases a strong theory will demonstrate that a model is actually valid and that it is our picture of the clinical situation being modeled that requires adjustment. This brings us full circle to the point that theory is required

as much to decide what our model should be modeling as which model we wish to use.

Animal models have, in the past, often been constructed ad hoc. However, we would argue that theory, particularly neurally based theory, has now advanced to the point where proper theoretical analysis should be the first step in considering any new model or in assessing the predictive validity of an existing model. Critically, neural theory may allow us to develop tests (such as the reticular activation of hippocampal theta described earlier) that can detect specific actions of drugs in the absence of the confounding side effects that often make behavioral models difficult to use. Conversely, behavioral models have the advantage of capturing *all* the neural circuitry on which drugs might act, without the need to first determine the specific sites of action.

As we attempt to model the many flavors of defensive disorder demonstrated by variation of drug effectiveness (Table 1), we must use theory to link multiple animal models, neural analysis and pharmacological analysis. This will provide us with a means of developing batteries of test with clear predictive (i.e., construct) validity that can be used for drug discovery of genuinely new classes of drug as well as development of improved variants of already known classes.

References

American Psychiatric Association (1980) DSM-III: diagnostic and statistical manual of mental disorders, 3rd edn.

American Psychiatric Association (1987) DSM-III: diagnostic and statistical manual of mental disorders, 3rd edn - Revised.

American Psychiatric Association (1994) DSM-IV: diagnostic and statistical manual of mental disorders, 4th edn.

Blanchard, D.C. and Blanchard, R.J. (1988) Ethoexperimental approaches to the biology of emotion. Ann. Rev. Psychol., 39: 43–68.

Blanchard, D.C., Blanchard, R.J. and Rodgers, R.J. (1991) Risk assessment and animal models of anxiety. In: Olovier, B. Mos, J. and Slangen, J.L. (Eds.), Animal Models in Psychopharmacology. Birkhauser Verlag, Basel, pp. 117–134.

Blanchard, D.C., Blanchard, R.J., Tom, P. and Rodgers, R.J. (1990) Diazepam changes risk assessment in an anxiety/defense test battery. Psychopharmacology (Berlin), 101: 511–518.

Blanchard, R.J. and Blanchard, D.C. (1989) Antipredator defensive behaviors in a visible burrow system. J. Comp. Psychol., 103: 70–82.

Blanchard, R.J. and Blanchard, D.C. (1990a) An ethoexperimental analysis of defense, fear and anxiety. In: McNaughton, N. and Andrews, G. (Eds.), Anxiety. Otago University Press, Dunedin, pp. 124–133.

Blanchard, R.J. and Blanchard, D.C. (1990b) Antipredator defense as models of animal fear and anxiety. In: Brain, P.F. Parmigiani, S. Blanchard, R.J. and Mainardi, D. (Eds.), Fear and Defense. Church Harwood Academic Publishers, Chur, pp. 89–108.

Blanchard, R.J., Griebel, G., Henrie, J.A. and Blanchard, D.C. (1997) Differentiation of anxiolytic and panicolytic drugs by effects on rat and mouse defense test batteries. Neurosci. Biobehav. Rev., 21: 783–789.

Carter, C., Maddock, R., Zoglio, M., Lutrin, C., Jella, S. and Amsterdam, E. (1994) Panic disorder and chest pain: a study of cardiac stress scintigraphy patients. Am. J. Cardiol., 74: 296–298.

Coop, C.F. and McNaughton, N. (1991) Buspirone affects hippocampal rhythmical slow activity through serotonin$_{1A}$ rather than dopamine D_2 receptors. Neuroscience, 40: 169–174.

Coop, C.F., McNaughton, N., Warnock, K. and Laverty, R. (1990) Effects of ethanol and Ro 15-4513 in an electrophysiological model of anxiolytic action. Neuroscience, 35: 669–674.

Darwin, C. (1965) The Expression of the Emotions in Man and Animals. University of Chicago Press, Chicago, IL.

Deakin, J.F.W. and Graeff, F.G. (1991) 5-HT and mechanisms of defense. J. Psychopharmacol., 5: 305–315.

Ekman, P. (1982) Emotion in the Human Face. Cambridge University Press, Cambridge.

Ekman, P. and Friesen, W.V. (1986) A new pan-cultural facial expression of emotion. Motiv. Emot., 10: 159–168.

Ekman, P., Friesen, W.V. and Ancoli, S. (1980) Facial signs of emotional experience. J. Pers. Soc. Psychol., 39: 1125–1134.

Franklin, J.A. (1990) Behavioral treatment for panic disorder. In: McNaughton, N. and Andrews, G. (Eds.), Anxiety. University of Otago, Dunedin, pp. 84–91.

Geller, I. and Seifter, J. (1960) The effects of meprobamate, barbiturates, D-amphetamine and promazine on experimentally induced conflict in the rat. Psychopharmacologia, 1: 482–492.

Graeff, F.G. (1994) Neuroanatomy and neurotransmitter regulation of defensive behaviors and related emotions in mammals. Braz. J. Med. Biol. Res., 27: 811–829.

Graeff, F.G. (2002) On serotonin and experimental anxiety. Psychopharmacology, 163: 467–476.

Graeff, F.G., Netto, C.F. and Zangrossi Jr., H. (1998) The elevated T-maze as an experimental model of anxiety. Neurosci. Biobehav. Rev., 23: 237–246.

Graeff, F.G. and Zangrossi Jr., H. (2002) Animal models of anxiety disorders. In: D'Haenen, H. den Boer, J.A. Westenberg, H. and Willner, P. (Eds.), Textbook of Biological Psychiatry. Wiley, London, pp. 879–893.

Gray, J.A. (1970) The psychophysiological basis of introversion–extraversion. Behav. Res. Ther., 8: 249–266.

Gray, J.A. (1976) The behavioral inhibition system: a possible substrate for anxiety. In: Feldman, M.P. and

Broadhurst, A.M. (Eds.), Theoretical and Experimental Bases of Behavior Modification. Wiley, London, pp. 3–41.

Gray, J.A. (1977) Drug effects on fear and frustration: possible limbic site of action of minor tranquilizers. In: Iversen, L.L. Iversen, S.D. and Snyder, S.H. (Eds.), Handbook of Psychopharmacology. Vol. 8. Drugs, Neurotransmitters and Behavior. Plenum Press, New York, pp. 433–529.

Gray, J.A. (1982) The Neuropsychology of Anxiety: An Enquiry in to the Functions of the Septo-Hippocampal System. Oxford University Press, Oxford.

Gray, J.A. and McNaughton, N. (2000) The Neuropsychology of Anxiety: An Enquiry into the Functions of the Septo-Hippocampal System. Oxford University Press, Oxford.

Griebel, G. (1995) 5-Hydroxytryptamine-interacting drugs in animal models of anxiety disorders: more than 30 years of research. Pharmacol. Ther., 65: 319–395.

Griebel, G., Rodgers, R.J., Perrault, G. and Sanger, D.J. (1997) Risk assessment behavior: evaluation of utility in the study of 5-HT-related drugs in the rat elevated plus-maze test. Pharmacol. Biochem. Behav., 57: 817–827.

Handley, S.L. and Mithani, S. (1984) Effects of alpha-adrenoceptor agonists in a maze-exploration model of "fear"-motivated behavior. Naunyn Schmiedebergs Arch. Pharmacol., 327: 1–5.

Handley, S.L., McBlane, J.W., Critchley, M.A.E. and Njung'e, K. (1993) Multiple serotonin mechanisms in animal models of anxiety: environmental, emotional and cognitive factors. Behav. Brain Res., 58: 203–210.

Hofer, M.A. (1972) Physiological and behavioral processes in early maternal deprivation. In: Porter, R., Knight, J. (Eds.), Physiology, Emotion and Psychosomatic Illness. CIBA Symposium No. 8 (new series). Elsevier, pp. 175–186.

Holt, P. (1990) Panic disorder: some historical trends. In: McNaughton, N. and Andrews, G. (Eds.), Anxiety. University of Otago Press, Dunedin, pp. 54–65.

James, W. (1884) What is an emotion? Mind, 9: 188–205.

Jardim, M.C., Nogueira, R.L., Graeff, F.G. and Nunes-de-Souza, R.L. (1999) Evaluation of the elevated T-maze as an animal model of anxiety in the mouse. Brain Res. Bull., 48: 407–411.

Joel, D. (2006) Current animal models of obsessive compulsive disorder: a critical review. Prog. Neuropsychopharmacol. Biol. Psychiatry, 30: 374–388.

Krebs, J.R., Stephens, D.W. and Sutherland, W.J. (1983) Perspectives in optimal foraging. In: Clark, G.A. and Brush, A.H. (Eds.), Perspectives in Ornithology. Cambridge University Press, Cambridge, pp. 165–221.

Marks, I.M. (1988) The syndromes of anxious avoidance: classification of phobic and obsessive-compulsive phenomena. In: Noyes, Jr., R. Roth, M. and Burrows, G.D. (Eds.), Handbook of Anxiety, Vol. 2: Classification, Etiological Factors and Associated Disturbances. Elsevier Science Publishers B.V., Amsterdam, pp. 109–146.

Montgomery, K.C. (1955) The relationship between fear induced by novel stimulation and exploratory behavior. J. Comp. Physiol. Psychol., 48: 254–260.

McNaughton, N. (1985) Chlordiazepoxide and successive discrimination: different effects on acquisition and performance. Pharmacol. Biochem. Behav., 23: 487–494.

McNaughton, N. (1989) Biology and Emotion. Cambridge University Press, Cambridge.

McNaughton, N. (2002) Aminergic transmitter systems. In: D'haenen, H. Den Boer, J.A. Westenberg, H. and Willner, P. (Eds.), Textbook of Biological Psychiatry. Wiley, pp. 895–914.

McNaughton, N. and Corr, P.J. (2004) A two-dimensional neuropsychology of defense: fear/anxiety and defensive distance. Neurosci. Biobehav. Rev., 28: 285–305.

McNaughton, N., Panickar, K.S. and Logan, B. (1996) The pituitary-adrenal axis and the different behavioral effects of buspirone and chlordiazepoxide. Pharmacol. Biochem. Behav., 54: 51–56.

McNaughton, N., Richardson, J. and Gore, C. (1986) Reticular elicitation of hippocampal slow waves: common effects of some anxiolytic drugs. Neuroscience, 19: 899–903.

McNaughton, N. and Sedgwick, E.M. (1978) Reticular stimulation and hippocampal theta rhythm in rats: effects of drugs. Neuroscience, 2: 629–632.

Menard, J. and Treit, D. (1999) Effects of centrally administered anxiolytic compounds in animal models of anxiety. Neurosci. Biobehav. Rev., 23: 591–613.

Noyes Jr., R., Burrows, G.D., Reich, J.H., Judd, F.K., Garvey, M.J., Norman, T.R., Cook, B.L. and Marriott, P. (1996) Diazepam versus alprazolam for the treatment of panic disorder. J. Clin. Psychiatry, 57: 349–355.

Panickar, K.S. and McNaughton, N. (1991) Effects of buspirone on fixed interval responding in rats. J. Psychopharmacol., 5: 410–417.

Pittendrigh, C.S. (1958) Adaptation, natural selection and behavior. In: Roes, A. and Simpson, G.G. (Eds.), Behavior and Evolution. Yale University Press, New Haven.

Poltronieri, S.C., Zangrossi Jr., H. and de Barros Viana, M. (2003) Antipanic-like effect of serotonin reuptake inhibitors in the elevated T-maze. Behav. Brain Res., 147: 185–192.

Redican, W.K. (1982) An evolutionary perspective on human facial displays. In: Ekman, P. (Ed.), Emotion in the Human Face. Cambridge University Press, Cambridge.

Rickels, K. and Rynn, M. (2002) Pharmacotherapy of generalized anxiety disorder. J. Clin. Psychiatry, 63: 9–16.

Sanson, L.T. and Carobrez, A.P. (1999) Long-lasting inhibitory avoidance acquisition in rats submitted to the elevated T-maze model of anxiety. Behav. Brain Res., 101: 59–64.

Sartory, G., MacDonald, R. and Gray, J.A. (1990) Effects of diazepam on approach, self-reported fear and psychophysiological responses in snake phobics. Behav. Res. Ther., 28: 273–282.

Shear, M.K. and Maser, J.D. (1994) Standardized assessment for panic disorder research: a conference report. Arch. Gen. Psychiatry, 51: 346–354.

Stein, D.J., Hollander, E., Mullen, L.S., DeCaria, C.M. and Liebowitz, M.R. (1992) Comparison of clomipramine, alprazolam and placebo in the treatment of obsessive-compulsive disorder. Hum. Psychopharmacol., 7: 389–395.

Stein, D.J., Vythilingum, B. and Seedat, S. (2004) Pharmacotherapy of phobias. In: Maj, M. (Ed.), Evidence and Experience in Psychiatry. Vol. 7. Phobias. Wiley.

Stevens, J.C. and Pollack, M.H. (2005) Benzodiazepines in clinical practice: consideration of their long-term use and alternative agents. J. Clin. Psychiatry, 66: 21–27.

Teixeira, R.C., Zangrossi Jr., H. and Graeff, F.G. (2000) Behavioral effects of acute and chronic imipramine in the elevated T-maze model of anxiety. Pharmacol. Biochem. Behav., 65: 571–576.

Treit, D., Menard, J. and Royan, C. (1993) Anxiogenic stimuli in the elevated plus-maze. Pharmacol. Biochem. Behav., 44: 463–469.

van der Staay, F.J. (2006) Animal models of behavioral dysfunctions: basic concepts and classifications, and an evaluation strategy. Brain Res. Rev., 52: 131–159.

Viana, M.B., Tomaz, C. and Graeff, F.G. (1994) The elevated T-maze: a new animal model of anxiety and memory. Pharmacol. Biochem. Behav., 49: 549–554.

Vogel, J.R., Beer, B. and Clody, D.E. (1971) A simple and reliable conflict procedure for testing antianxiety agents. Psychopharmacology (Berlin), 21: 1–7.

Westenberg, H.G.M. (1999) Facing the challenge of social anxiety disorder. Eur. Neuropsychopharmacol., 9: S93–S99.

Willner, P. (1984) The validity of animal models of depression. Psychopharmacology, 83: 1–16.

Willner, P. (1985) Animal models of depression: theory and applications. In: Willner, P. (Ed.), Depression: A Psychobiological Synthesis. Wiley, London, pp. 119–143.

Willner, P. (1991) Behavioral models in psychopharmacology. In: Willner, P. (Ed.), Behavioral Models in Psychopharmacology: Theoretical, Industrial and Clinical Perspectives. Cambridge University Press, Cambridge, pp. 3–18.

Woodnorth, M.A. and McNaughton, N. (2002) Similar effects of medial supramammillary or systemic injections of chlordiazepoxide on both theta frequency and fixed-interval responding. Cogn. Affect. Behav. Neurosci., 2: 76–83.

Zangrossi Jr., H. and Graeff, F.G. (1997) Behavioral validation of the elevated T-maze, a new animal model of anxiety. Brain Res. Bull., 44: 1–5.

Zhu, X.O. and McNaughton, N. (1991) Effects of long-term administration of imipramine on reticular-elicited hippocampal rhythmical slow activity. Psychopharmacology, 105: 433–438.

Zhu, X.O. and McNaughton, N. (1995) Similar effects of buspirone and chlordiazepoxide on a fixed interval schedule with long-term, low-dose administration. J. Psychopharmacol., 9: 326–330.

CHAPTER 2.2

The use of conditioning tasks to model fear and anxiety

Michael S. Fanselow* and Ravikumar Ponnusamy

Psychology and the Brain Research Institute, University of California, Los Angeles, CA, USA

Abstract: Pavlovian fear conditioning is a process that normally plays an adaptive role in generating defensive behaviors in threatening situations. Since this learning process is powerful, rapid and lasts indefinitely, it renders neutral stimuli reminiscent of a threatening situation capable of generating inappropriate fear reactions in non-threatening situations. Here we describe some of the normal functions of Pavlovian fear conditioning and then review how it was used as a model to generate several breakthroughs in our understanding of learning processes and mechanisms. Pavlovian conditioning is not only a model of fear acquisition but also a model of the loss of fear called extinction. We review the processes responsible for extinction, emphasizing recovery of fear following extinction. We describe the long history of translating fear acquisition and extinction to humans and the clinic. We end with a discussion of the use of fear conditioning to understand individual differences in anxiety disorders and post-traumatic stress disorder (PTSD).

Keywords: fear; anxiety; PTSD; model; conditioning; extinction; translation

Fear and anxiety have two, seemingly irreconcilable, sides. The clinician sees them as devastating symptoms of psychopathology that render normal adaptive behavior impossible. The biologist sees them as remarkable and necessary adaptations sculpted by powerful evolutionary forces. For all animals throughout time attack by predators or rival conspecifics bring the potential for life ending peril and an immediate end to future reproductive success. Under such harsh conditions natural selection led to powerful processes and mechanisms capable of taking complete and immediate control over behavior. What makes such a state so critical when activated under actual threat also makes it so destructive to adaptive functioning when inappropriately activated. Anxiety disorders may then be seen as the inappropriate activation

of natural defensive behavioral systems (Rau and Fanselow, 2007).

If the inappropriate activation of defensive systems (fear and anxiety) is so devastating, why are they not better constrained? Why do non-threatening (i.e., neutral) situations sometimes provoke such distress? One key reason is found in the way animals evolved to activate defensive systems. Threatening situations provoke an instantaneous form of learning, a unique type of Pavlovian conditioning, that immediately bestows even the neutral features of the situation the ability to provoke full blown fear reactions. This learning is so rapid that it even contributes to the immediate fear reactions that occur in response to the first time a particular threat is encountered. But the learning lasts a lifetime and can forever engender similar reactions in non-threatening situations. This Pavlovian fear conditioning has received extensive laboratory analyses that tells us

*Corresponding author. E-mail: mfanselow@gmail.com

R.J. Blanchard, D.C. Blanchard, G. Griebel and D. Nutt (Eds.)
Handbook of Anxiety and Fear, Vol. 17
ISBN 978-0-444-53065-3

29

DOI: 10.1016/S1569-7339(07)00003-3

what conditions are likely to lead to inappropriate fear and perhaps more importantly, how to treat this condition. The goal of this chapter is to review these features of Pavlovian fear conditioning and relate them to anxiety disorders. But first we will describe an example of how this learning contributes to even the very initial reaction to threat.

I. A deceptively simple experiment

We start with a laboratory rat that has spent its life safe, fed and happy in a home cage. At the start of this simple experiment, we place it in a novel observation chamber and after 3 min give it a brief (2.0 s) but aversive electric footshock. Prior to the shock the rat freely explores the chamber, walking about, sniffing corners and rearing up on walls. This behavior comes to an abrupt end with the shock. During the shock the rat vigorously runs, jumps, hops and vocalizes. These behaviors, termed the activity burst, persist for a brief period after shock after which point they are replaced by freezing (Fanselow, 1982). Freezing is a complete immobility, where even the whiskers stop moving. The only movements that can be detected are small respiration-related movements of the flanks caused by breathing.

These behaviors are the exactly the sort of behaviors seen in response to predators in natural environments. The activity burst is associated with predatory contact and serves, at least momentarily, to separate prey from predator. The freezing response reduces the likelihood of attack for two reasons. First, if the predator has not yet spotted the prey, it is more difficult to detect when motionless. However, as anyone who has played with a housecat knows, even when the prey is detected it is less likely to be attacked if it keeps still (Fanselow and Lester, 1988).

One is tempted to give such a simple experiment a simple explanation: The explanation is based on the assumption that because defense is so important, prey must be hardwired to innately recognize their predators and such innate recognition must trigger hardwired defenses (Hirsch and Bolles, 1980). In the experiment described above, shock is simply treated like an innately recognized predator, perhaps because the rat evolved no other way to deal with such a strange stimulus (Bolles, 1970). According to this explanation, shock innately, or unconditionally, provoked the freezing response. There is no need to posit complex processes, such as learning to explain such a rapidly provoked and automatic response. As it turns out, this simple analysis is simply wrong. Learning, specifically Pavlovian fear conditioning, is a necessary and sufficient explanation of the behavior in this experiment. To appreciate this analysis, one has to appreciate three currently accepted aspects of Pavlovian conditioning that differ from standard textbook treatments (Rescorla, 1988). First, some forms of Pavlovian conditioning evidence robust learning with just a single trial (Garcia et al., 1955). Second, the conditional stimulus (CS; Pavlov used a bell) does not have to be a separate discrete stimulus. The CS can be the static or contextual features of the situation where the unconditional stimulus (US; Pavlov's meat) occurred. Third, unlike Pavlov's typical example, the conditional response (CR) to the CS need not be anything like the unconditional response (UR) to the US. Applied to our experiment, a single shock US was able to condition a CR of freezing to the context even though the UR to shock was not freezing but an activity burst. Fig. 1 shows a schematic comparison of Pavlov's experiment and the fear experiment. Note that in both cases the shock US starts after presentation of the CS. Pavlov called this relationship between the CS and US "delay" conditioning and noted that it is the most potent arrangement of stimuli for the acquisition of a CR.

In the lower panel of Fig. 1, if the test after one pairing begins with the shock termination, we have procedurally duplicated the simple experiment. This occurs because the CS in this case is the context and the context is not only "on" before the shock, it is continuously "on" both during and after the shock. This is schematized in the top portion of Fig. 2. As the figure shows, this analysis perfectly predicts both the behaviors and their temporal distribution as was observed in our example experiment. However, it provides a very different interpretation than the simple one first provided. In this analysis freezing is never an

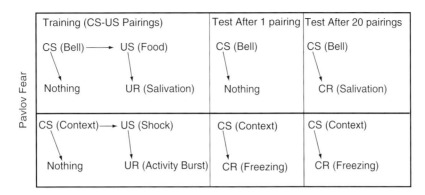

Fig. 1. Illustration of the basic Pavlovian conditioning paradigm showing training and testing. The upper portion shows the proverbial conditional salivation procedure and the bottom fear conditioning. Notice that unlike salivation fear shows learning after one trial and the CR is different than the UR.

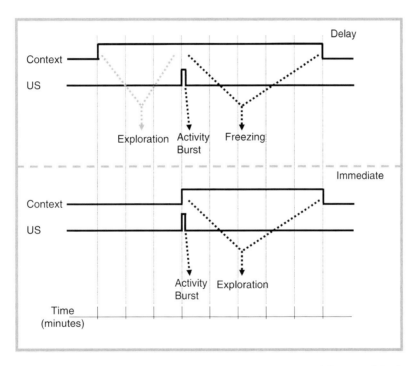

Fig. 2. This figure schematizes the "simple experiment" (see text) as a contextual fear conditioning experiment in the upper portion. Upon shock the rat stops exploring and shows an unconditional activity burst. This is followed by a conditional freezing response to the context as a CS. The bottom portion shows the immediate shock procedure, where eliminating exposure to the context before shock eliminates the freezing response.

innate, unlearned or unconditional response to the shock. Rather, freezing is portrayed as entirely a learned or conditional response to the context that has been paired with shock. Note that, like Bolles (1970) and others, we assume that the freezing response itself is a hardwired motor program that was shaped by evolution. What is learned, and learned instantaneously, is the relationship between the contextual CS and shock. The expression of the hardwired freezing response depends on learning of this relationship. Such a pattern combines the benefits of having an immediately available adaptive behavior with the flexibility to use it effectively even though the situation was not genetically encoded as dangerous.

While this may not seem to be the most parsimonious interpretation of freezing following a single shock there is now a volume of literature indicating that is the correct interpretation (Fanselow, 1980; Fanselow and Lester, 1988; Landeira-Fernandez et al., 2006). The most powerful test is to prevent the animal from processing the context prior to shock. This is accomplished by giving the rat the shock immediately upon placement in the chamber as illustrated in the lower portion of Fig. 2. When this is done freezing is completely abolished (Blanchard et al., 1976; Fanselow, 1986a, 1990; Landeira-Fernandez et al., 2006). There appears to be no component of the freezing response that is unconditionally (innately) provoked by the shock. While this "immediate shock deficit" has been most extensively evaluated with freezing, it has been extended to several measures of fear including defecation (Fanselow, 1986a), fear potentiated startle (Kiernan et al., 1995), passive avoidance (Kiernan et al., 1995) and fear-induced analgesia (Fanselow et al., 1994). Additionally, several of the neuronal changes observed during fear conditioning, do not occur with immediate context–shock pairings (Rosen et al., 1998; Pham et al., 2005). Another line of evidence indicating that the freezing following shock is a CR comes from studies that change the context after shock. This manipulation essentially removes the CS and it reduces freezing in a manner that is proportional to the degree of context change; sufficiently large context changes eliminate freezing (Bolles and Collier, 1976; Fanselow, 1980, 1981). Blanchard and Blanchard (1969) obtained similar results measuring crouching rather than freezing.

These findings are critically important to understanding why conditioning tasks provide an extremely appropriate model of fear and anxiety. During a single highly threatening or traumatic experience an important part of the behavior in the situation will be conditional behavior regardless of prior experience. Additionally, a single threatening experience has the ability to condition fear to many inherently non-threatening features of the experience. Experiencing those features at another time will bring back reactions much like those in the originally threatening situation – remember both are CRs. Furthermore, at least in the rat, these fears can last unabated for a lifetime (Gale et al., 2004). Fear conditioning is not simply a laboratory model. It normally plays a role in the adaptive behavioral reactions to a threat and it plays a role when these reactions occur in non-threatening environments, that is, in anxiety disorders. It is also a phenomenon that can be directly and objectively studied in the laboratory. That brings the hope that advances in the laboratory will translate to the clinic. Therefore, we will now turn to the laboratory analysis of Pavlovian fear conditioning.

II. A brief history of Pavlovian fear conditioning

In one of the earliest demonstrations of Pavlovian conditioning in the United States, Watson and Rayner (1920) used a human infant to show that anxiety was a Pavlovian phenomenon. Baby Albert reacted with fear of a rat and other visually similar stimuli after the rat was paired with a very loud noise. Thus from the outset, Pavlovian fear conditioning was known to apply to humans. Later, Estes and Skinner (1941) adapted this procedure to rats showing that a tone that was paired with electric footshock acquired the ability to suppress on-going behavior. Rats were first trained to lever press for food. Initially, the tone produced no changes in the food-reinforced response but after the tone was paired with shock, lever pressing during the tone stopped. Indeed, the suppression to the tone was often greater than that produced by the shock itself. Note that in Pavlovian conditioned suppression the lever-press response itself had no effect on the tone or shock, the frightened rat simply stopped lever pressing for food. Later, Estes (1944) modified this task so that bar pressing was explicitly punished. This punishment tasks was a precursor to other procedures such as the Vogel test (Vogel et al., 1971) that punish otherwise positively reinforced responses. Such conflict tasks are highly sensitive to anxiolytic drugs such as the benzodiazepines.

Annau and Kamin (1961) described a quantitative measure of conditioned suppression that was highly sensitive to parametric manipulations that should be related to the strength of conditioning and the amount of fear (e.g., shock intensity and number of trials). The measure, called a suppression ratio, was the ratio of responding during a test presentation of the CS to the overall amount of responding both before and during the CS. With this measure in hand, Pavlovian fear conditioning became one of the major models of learned behavior and spurred a rapid advancement in our knowledge of general learning processes. For example, the conditioned suppression procedure provided the first demonstrations of blocking (Kamin, 1968) and the importance of CS–US contingency over contiguity (Rescorla, 1968). Both of these findings indicated that conditioning was determined not only by CS–US pairings but also what happened outside of the CS–US pairing. For example, when CS–US pairings are held constant, unsignaled US presentations degrade conditioning to the CS (Rescorla, 1968). These findings led to a sea change in the rules of Pavlovian conditioning, framing it as a basic information integration and selection process where stimuli compete for associative strength between the CS and US (e.g., Rescorla and Wagner, 1972).

While models such as the Rescorla–Wagner model describe how acquisition of a CR should be influenced by changes in conditioning procedures, they do not say anything about how the brain achieves these operations. Insight into neural mechanisms supporting the competitive learning envisioned by Rescorla and Wagner (1972) awaited integration of findings on descending control of pain systems (Liebeskind and Paul, 1977) with these ideas about competitive learning in Pavlovian conditioning (Bolles and Fanselow, 1980). During fear conditioning a potent analgesic response occurs (Chance et al., 1977; Fanselow and Bolles, 1979). Bolles and Fanselow (1980)

recognized that this fear-induced analgesia could modify the reinforcing impact of the shock US because the perceived nociceptiveness of shock depended not only the physical intensity of shock but also the level of activation of descending analgesic systems. They combined this idea with the notion that competitive learning models such as that of Rescorla and Wagner (1972) could be thought of as describing a process where "error in the expectation (of the nociceptive properties of shock) is fed back so as to reduce future errors (Bolles and Fanselow, 1980, p. 293)". Thus in Pavlovian fear conditioning, error correction driven learning occurs because the CS engages an analgesic CR that reduces the impact of the shock, making already predicted shock a less effective reinforcer (Fanselow, 1979). As fear is acquired, the analgesic CR increases, in essence providing negative feedback on the ability for an aversive shock to support conditioning (Bolles and Fanselow, 1980; Fanselow, 1986b, 1998). The findings that fear conditioning loses its error correction and competitive features when opioid antagonists are given during training provided compelling support for this model (Fanselow and Bolles, 1979; Fanselow et al., 1991; Young and Fanselow, 1992; McNally and Cole, 2006). This negative feedback model anticipated other circuit-based models of error correction driven learning (Kim et al., 1998; Schultz and Dickinson, 2000).

III. Behavioral measures of conditional fear

III.A. Freezing as a measure of conditional fear

Conditioned suppression is an indirect measure of fear; it is an assay of what a frightened animal is not doing. Motivated by Robert Bolles' species-specific defense reaction theory (Bolles, 1970), which said that fear limits an animal's behavioral repertoire to its natural defensive behaviors, several of Bolles' students began to use freezing as an assay of fear conditioning (Fanselow and Bolles, 1979; Sigmundi et al., 1980). Like conditioned suppression, freezing is highly sensitive to parametric manipulations that are expected to affect the level of learning and the level of fear. It increases with both the number of trials and with the intensity of shock (Fanselow, 1979, 1980; Young and Fanselow, 1992). As with most learning preparations, increasing the spacing between training trials also increases the amount of conditional freezing (Fanselow and Tighe, 1988). This parametric dependence of freezing, which is illustrated in Fig. 3, establishes the internal validity of the model as an index of learning and emotional processes. It also means that researchers can tailor the sensitivity of the preparation to the demands of the experimental question being addressed.

There are several advantages to freezing as a measure of fear. As reviewed at the start of this chapter, in conditioning situations one can be confident that freezing is fully a CR to shock-associated stimuli. It can be used in unconstrained, freely moving animals. Unlike suppression, it does not require the potentially confounding influences of food or water deprivation and positive reinforcement. It does not require the delivery of any extraneous probe stimuli as does fear-potentiated startle. Partly for these reasons, since the late

1970s freezing has remerged as one the most common measures of conditional fear. A large increase in the use of freezing was spurred by the discovery that it can be used to assess both hippocampus-dependent and hippocampus-independent memory (Kim and Fanselow, 1992) and that besides rats it is a highly reliable response in mice (Abeliovich et al., 1993; Bourtchouladze et al., 1994).

III.B. Fear-potentiated startle as a measure of fear conditioning

Fear-potentiated startle refers to the increase or potentiation of the acoustic startle reflex during fear states elicited by the anticipation of an aversive stimulus (e.g., a shock). This effect was first described in animals using aversive conditioning procedures by Brown et al. (1951), and has been investigated extensively by Davis and his collaborators (Davis, 1998). This potentiation of the acoustic startle reflex is but one example of a more general facilitation of reflexive behaviors (Lam et al., 1996).

In a typical fear-potentiated startle experiment, the amplitude of the startle reflex elicited by a loud noise is measured either in the presence or in the absence of a CS previously paired with an aversive US. Under these conditions, the amplitude of the startle reflex is greater in the presence of the CS than in the absence of the CS. The same effect has been found in humans (Spence and Norris, 1950; Hamm et al., 1993; Grillon and Davis, 1997).

One significant advantage of potentiated startle as a measure of fear is that it can assess the level of fear at a precise moment in time. This is not possible for diffuse responses such as freezing. However, it should be noted that fear-potentiated startle requires administration of potent extraneous test stimuli (i.e., the startle stimulus) that may affect behavior directly or indirectly. For example, the startle stimulus itself is capable of supporting fear conditioning (Leaton and Cranney, 1990), so the test itself is anxiety producing.

Reliable FPS requires more training than the typical context or cue fear-conditioning techniques using freezing as a measure. Fear-potentiated

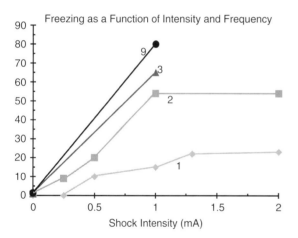

Fig. 3. Illustration of parametric dependency of fear conditioning using freezing. Each curve looks at female long-Evans that received context conditioning with different number of trials. The data points are all independent groups trained at various shock intensities and show the percentage of an 8 min test period spent freezing. Shock duration was 0.75 s. The data are based on Fanselow and Bolles (1979b) and Fanselow and Tighe (1988).

startle has been demonstrated with as few as five CS-shock trials but the inclusion of a large number of CS–startle stimulus pairings during testing makes the actual amount of training unclear (Campeau et al., 1990). Because the test for fear-potentiated startle requires many CS–startle stimulus pairings it does not offer a clear separation of learning from performance. Robust one-trial fear learning with freezing as a measure allows specification of the exact instant a fear memory was formed (Fanselow, 1990). Thus, each procedure (fear-potentiated startle and freezing) has its advantages and disadvantages.

III.C. Conditional fear-induced analgesia

As mentioned earlier, a conditional fear CS produces an analgesia that reduces responses to pain. This conditional fear-induced analgesia produces a loss of simple spinal reflexes to pain such as the tail-flick to radiant heat (Chance et al., 1979) as well as more highly integrated pain responses assessed by the hot plate (Ross and Randich, 1985) and formalin (Fanselow and Baackes, 1982) tests. The suppression of the tail-flick reflex is particularly interesting in comparison to the fact that most other simple reflexes are enhanced by fear (see section on fear-potentiated startle above). Bolles and Fanselow (1980) suggested that one function of this analgesia is to prevent pain-related responses from interfering with fear-related defensive behavior.

Another property of painful stimuli is the ability to support fear conditioning and this response to pain is also reduced by conditional-fear-induced analgesia (Fanselow, 1979). In this way, the acquisition of analgesia provides a negative feedback regulation of the acquisition of fear. One result of this negative feedback is that it makes the level of fear proportional to the level of threat (Young and Fanselow, 1992). As reviewed above, this negative feedback also provides a mechanism that allows the brain to perform Rescorla–Wagner type calculations (Fanselow, 1998).

The formalin test, which does not require any physical constraint, allows freezing and analgesia to be assessed simultaneously. Studies that have assessed the development of both responses indicate that conditional-fear-induced analgesia appears to be acquired in parallel to freezing. However, unlike freezing, analgesia depends on functional endogenous opioid receptors (Fanselow and Baackes, 1982; Fanselow, 1984). Different opioid receptors appear to contribute to different components of the analgesia. For example, conditional-fear-induced analgesia assessed by the formalin test depends on both mu- and delta-type opioid receptors (Calcagnetti et al., 1988, 1989; Fanselow et al., 1989), while the regulation of conditional fear depends exclusively on mu-opioid receptors (Fanselow et al., 1991).

Like potentiated startle, conditional analgesia requires administration of a potent (i.e., painful) extraneous stimulus. Thus, it has been examined more for its theoretical significance than as a routine method for the assessment of fear.

IV. Other unconditional stimuli

While the vast majority of fear conditioning research has used shock as an US, the finding is certainly not limited to shock. It is not possible to cover all the USs that have been used to support fear conditioning; here we will describe some of the more interesting. Remember that Watson and Rayner (1920) "Little Albert" experiment used a loud noise to condition fear and this basic effect has been replicated both in humans (Bechara et al., 1995) and rats (Leaton and Cranney, 1990). Like shock, inhalation of carbon dioxide causes panic reactions in humans and rats; it also functions as a US that supports fear conditioning (Mongeluzi et al., 1996). A sudden air blast is an effective US for fear conditioning in children (Grillon et al., 1999).

In the initial section of the review we developed how fear conditioning is a normal component of natural defensive behaviors. Thus, it should not be surprising that attack by a predator (cat) produces behavioral and neural changes consistent with fear conditioning in rats (Adamec et al., 2001). Predator odors alone are also effective reinforcers for fear conditioning and engage similar circuitry to shock-paired stimuli (Takahashi et al., 2007).

Even non-lethal predators can serve as USs for fear conditioning. Kavaliers et al. (1999) demonstrated that mice, which have been exposed to biting flies, react with fear responses to the presence of non-biting flies.

Lithium chloride causes a pronounced nausea. However, a context paired with LiCl treatment produces freezing and analgesia as a conditional response (McNally et al., 1999) much the way a context paired with shock does. This is another good example of how the UR (nausea) is quite different from the CR (freezing and analgesia). It also resembles how stimuli that predict the "avian flue" cause a panic reaction that is quite different from the flue itself.

There are also very effective social USs. Mineka et al. (1980) observed that while wild caught rhesus monkeys responded fearfully to real and toy snakes, lab-reared rhesus, at least on their initial exposure did not. These researchers went on to show that the fear was actually acquired and the US was observation of a fear reaction on the part of other monkeys (Mineka et al., 1984). Perhaps the most intriguing version of such observational learning is that mice that observe others having a fear reaction to biting flies acquire a fear of flies themselves. Given the degree of observational learning in mice and monkeys, it seems likely that observational US are effective reinforcers in humans as well.

V. Key developments in the neuroanatomy of fear conditioning

V.A. Amygdala afferents

Perhaps the first indication of the amygdala's involvement in fear conditioning was that of Fuster and Uyeda (1971). Using monkeys they found that after light–shock pairings a light evoked activity in the amygdala. Subsequently, Blanchard and Blanchard (1972) found that large electrolytic lesions of the amygdaloid region dramatically reduced freezing to a context that was paired with shock. Kapp et al. (1979) made lesions restricted to the central nucleus of the amygdala of rabbits and found that these lesions

blocked the normal heart rate deceleration to conditional fear stimuli. They also found that this same region had direct projections to the brainstem regions that control heart rate (Schwaber et al., 1980). Hitchcock and Davis (1986) report that central nucleus lesions produced a selective loss of conditional fear measured with potentiated startle, launched an explosion of research on the amygdala's involvement in learned fear that is extensively reviewed in Cain and LeDoux's chapter in this volume.

While the amygdala may be a neural hub for fear conditioning, it needs to receive information about the environment and then contact appropriate regions to generate fear CRs. Swanson and Petrovich (1998) provide an excellent anatomical review of the sensory inputs to the amygdala. For fear conditioning to simple sounds, inputs from the thalamus and auditory cortex are capable of supporting conditioning (Romanski and LeDoux, 1992), with the auditory cortex normally playing the dominant role (Boatman and Kim, 2006). However, fear conditioning to complex auditory signals and simple visual stimuli is supported by projections from perirhinal cortex to amygdala (Rosen et al., 1992; Lindquist et al., 2004). Contextual fear conditioning is supported by the hippocampus (Kim and Fanselow, 1992; Kim et al., 1993) through direct projections through the ventral angular bundle (Maren and Fanselow, 1995) and indirect projections through perirhinal, entorhinal and parahippocampal cortex (Maren and Fanselow, 1997; Burwell et al., 2004). Thus as the CS increases in complexity, from a pure tone to complex unimodal (auditory) stimuli to polymodal (contextual) stimuli, there is a progressive recruitment of brain regions that encode increasingly processed information (see the upper portion of Fig. 4).

V.B. Amygdala efferents

The integration and flow of information through the amygdala is detailed by Cain and Ledoux's chapter (see their Fig. 2A). The amygdala makes contact with the structures that support fear conditioning via the central nucleus and bed nuclei

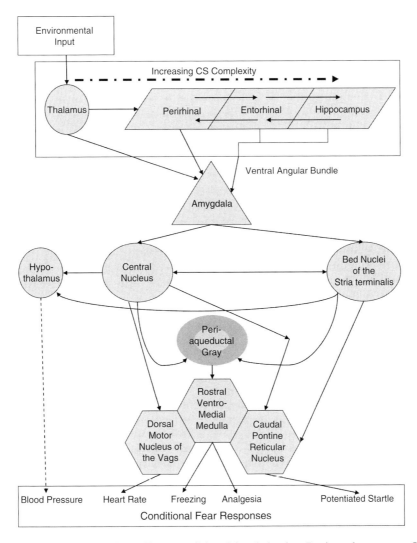

Fig. 4. The primary circuit that normally mediates conditional fear behavior. Regions that process CS input are at the top of the figure. Regions that generate specific responses are at the bottom of the figure.

of the stria terminalis (Rosen et al., 1991; Petrovich and Swanson, 1997; Dong et al., 2001a,b). Freezing and analgesic CRs depend on projections to the ventral and dorsal horns of the spinal cord, respectively, with relays in ventral periaqueductal gray and rostral ventral medulla (LeDoux et al., 1988; Fanselow, 1991; Kim et al., 1993; Helmstetter and Tershner, 1994; Morgan and Fields, 1994; Foo and Helmstetter, 1999). Based on tract tracing data, it was initially suggested that potentiation of acoustic startle by fear was mediated by a monosynpatic projection

from the central nucleus to the brainstem startle reflex circuit (Rosen et al., 1991). However, subsequent elctrophysiological collision studies suggest that a disynaptic circuit with a relay in the midbrain plays a large role in this response (Yeomans and Pollard, 1993). The lower portion of Fig. 4 illustrates these efferent projections from the amygdala.

The "fear circuit" described in Fig. 4 is the circuit that normally mediates conditional fear. Research from several laboratories examining very different components of the circuit have found that post-training lesions cause greater impairment than pre-training lesions (Maren et al., 1997; Maren, 1999; Anglada-Figueroa and Quirk, 2005; Boatman and Kim, 2006; Wiltgen et al., 2006). Ponnusamy et al. (2007) proposed a model to account for this general pattern. They suggest that when the normal fear circuit is compromised, fear can be acquired using alternate pathways. These alternate circuits are usually less efficient, for example, they learn at slower rates. However, the alternate pathway does not acquire fear when the primary pathway functions normally.

V.C. Neural basis of fear conditioning in humans

V.C.1. Neuropsychological studies

While the field of fear conditioning may have begun with a study of a human subject (Watson and Rayner, 1920), clearly most of the scientific advancements owe to the extensive research from the rodent laboratory. However, several findings from non-human animal research have more recently been substantiated and extended in humans, using neuropsychological and neuroimaging methodologies. Research across species concur that the neural correlates of fear conditioning include involvement of the amygdala during all stages of fear learning. Human research participants subjected to conditioning procedures, for example, show increased skin conductance responses to a fear CS. Patients with unilateral (LaBar et al., 1995) and bilateral lesions of the amygdala (Bechara et al., 1995), however, fail to exhibit these increases in skin conductance to the fear CS even though the loud noise US provokes the response. Despite the finding that participants with selective amygdala lesions fail to show emotional CRs, they still have explicit knowledge of the contingency between CS and US (Bechara et al., 1995). Thus, emotional learning and explicit knowledge are separable memory systems.

The dissociation between explicit knowledge and emotional memory can go the other way as well. A skin conductance CR occurs even when a brief CS is masked to prevent conscious awareness (Esteves et al., 1994). Furthermore, fear conditioning also occurs in amnesic patients, who have hippocampal damage but intact amygdala, even though they are unable to explicitly report that the CS was associated with an US (Fried et al., 1997). Thus, there is a double dissociation in that hippocampal damage eliminates explicit memory for the conditioning situation but leaves emotional memory intact, while amygdala damage eliminates emotional memory but spares explicit memory.

V.C.2. Imaging studies

This neuropsychological work is supported by functional magnetic resonance imaging methodology. Buchel et al. (1998) measured regional blood flow on trials that predicted the occurrence (CS+) or absence (CS−) of the US. They found bilateral amygdala activation in response to processing of the CS+, which was higher early on during learning and subsequently decreased. At the same time, LaBar et al. (1998) used neutral stimuli (i.e., colored squares) paired (CS+) or unpaired (CS−) with mild shocks, in a procedure that closely resembled traditional animal studies. They found activation of the amygdala when comparing CS+ versus CS− acquisition trials. In addition, such activation correlated with the strength of the fear CR. In both of these neuroimaging studies, the observed response in the amygdala was temporally graded, consistent with physiological recordings in the rat amygdala (Quirk et al., 1997). A series of elegant studies from Helmstetter's laboratory found that activation of structures and circuits in the human brain have a close and direct parallel to those isolated in the rat brain (Knight et al., 1999; Cheng et al., 2006). Importantly, human amygdala activity predicts trials when humans will show autonomic indices of fear (Cheng et al., 2003); activity in the amygdala increases only when the CS both predicts shock and causes increases skin conductance (Cheng et al., 2006).

VI. Pavlovian extinction

While Pavlovian acquisition corresponds to the increase in conditional responding when the US is presented in a manner dependent on the CS,

Pavlovian extinction corresponds to the loss of conditional responding when the CS is presented without the US. Like acquisition, extinction is not simply a laboratory model. Rather it is a robust real-world phenomenon that is conveniently reproduced in the laboratory. Indeed, Pavlovian principles have had a remarkable application to the treatment of anxiety disorders. Cognitive-behavioral therapies (CBT) based on Pavlovian extinction were one of the first and remain the most effective treatment for anxiety disorders (Wolpe, 1969; Wolpe and Plaud, 1997). In CBT, the feared stimulus is presented or visualized in a situation where the patient is protected from harm. In the typical rodent laboratory experiment, a CS previously associated with a footshock US is presented alone.

VI.A. Recovery from extinction

Pavlov was the first to suggest that the loss of conditional responding during extinction is not a weakening of the original CS–US association (Pavlov, 1927). Rather, Pavlov believed that extinction training engendered acquisition of a second learning process, one capable of inhibiting expression of the CR. This interpretation was motivated by his finding that after extinction, distracting the dog or merely waiting for a sufficient period of time restored responding to the CS. Pavlov suggested that inhibition was more fragile than excitation and was disrupted by the distractor (disinhibition) or waiting period (spontaneous recovery). When the more fragile inhibition was gone, only the more robust excitation remained.

Pavlovian fear conditioning has been very useful in extending the general pattern of recovered conditional responding after extinction that Pavlov observed with a salivation CR. Presenting a shock US by itself after extinction leads to recovery of fear responding to an extinguished CS. Rescorla and Heth (1975) named this phenomenon reinstatement. Bouton and colleagues have described an extensive series of experiments showing that after extinction of a tone previously paired with shock, conditional responding reco-

vers if testing is done in a different environment. Unlike reinstatement, this type of recovery does not depend on delivery of the US (Bouton and King, 1983) and was therefore labeled renewal to differentiate it from reinstatement. Thus, reinstatement and renewal join disinhibition and spontaneous recovery on the list of post-extinction recovery phenomenon.

Much of the advancements in our theoretical understanding of extinction come from the study of renewal. It is now clear that the essential feature for renewal is a change in stimulus conditions between extinction and test. Renewal occurs if testing is in the original fear conditioning environment or a completely novel environment as long as there was a change between extinction and testing (Bouton and Bolles, 1979). Importantly, if fear conditioning and extinction are in the same environment, fear is still renewed if testing is done in a second environment (Bouton and Ricker, 1994). A very important finding is that renewal occurs if drug treatment conditions change between extinction and testing (Bouton et al., 1990). This suggests that if care is not taken to equate drug treatment during extinction and testing, an agent thought to impair extinction might act by supporting renewal rather than an influence on the mechanisms of extinction.

VI.B. What causes extinction and recovery?

These recovery phenomena have generated much debate over the nature of extinction. It now appears likely that extinction is an example of a more general type of learning called occasion setting (Ross and Holland, 1982; Swartzentruber and Bouton, 1986; Rescorla, 1997). Occasion setting occurs when a CS is inconsistently reinforced. Animals will readily use an additional cue (modulator) to resolve the inconsistency. A positive occasion setter provides information that the target CS will be reinforced; a negative occasion setter tells the subject that the target CS will not be reinforced. By definition, an extinguished CS has had periods of reinforcement and non-reinforcement so its meaning with respect to the US is inconsistent (Bouton, 1994). Basically, stimuli that are present during extinction, but not acquisition, will come to assert negative occasion-setting control over the CS. If those occasion-setting stimuli are present the CR will be inhibited, if they are not the CR will occur (Brooks and Bouton, 1994; Rescorla, 1997).

As described above, recovery of the extinguished response is a robust finding that occurs with several manipulations. Insight into why this is such a pronounced effect can be gleaned from studies of the transfer of occasion setting (Holland, 1992). Transfer of occasion setting is highly limited. The key is that in order for a CS to be susceptible to modulation by an occasion setter it must be trained in an occasion-setting relationship. That CS is susceptible to modulation by other occasion setters only if the occasion setter (modulator) was involved in the same type of occasion-setting relationship. An inconsistently reinforced CS that was trained in a positive occasion-setting relationship will be modulated only by positive and not negative occasion setters. If the CS was trained in a negative occasion-setting relationship, only negative occasion setters can modulate the response to that CS. Normally, during acquisition there is no inconsistency; the CS is reliably reinforced. Inconsistency is first introduced with extinction. If inconsistency is what drives occasion-setting learning, then occasion-setting learning will first occur during extinction, making extinction a negative occasion-setting phenomenon. Essentially, during extinction the subject learns that the CS is "inhibitable" and that inhibition only occurs when stimuli trained as negative occasion setters are also present (Bouton and Nelson, 1994). Any stimulus change that removes the negative occasion setter will lead to recovery of fear responding. Strong support for this view comes from a study by Bouton and Nelson (1994). They first trained a stimulus as an inhibitor and then reinforced it. In this example it is the CS–US pairings that introduce inconsistency and should come under occasion-setting control. They found under this arrangement that it is the excitatory conditioning that is lost when there is a switch in the environment and it is the inhibitory learning that "recovers".

VI.C. *Translating extinction to the clinic*

In addition to providing critical insight into the processes responsible for extinction, recovery phenomena are directly relevant to the success of exposure therapy. Obviously, the return of fear after therapy is an undesirable outcome. There are clearly renewal effects with human phobia following exposure therapy. Studies to date have evaluated effects of environmental shifts on renewal in individuals who are highly fearful of spiders and undergo exposure therapy with graduated presentations of a live spider. Loss of fear is assessed immediately post-treatment, and retesting occurs 1–2 weeks later. Fear typically is measured via self-report, behavioral avoidance and heart rate during a behavioral approach test to a live spider. In general, renewal effects have been observed when participants are retested 1–2 weeks later in an environment that differs from the treatment environment (Mineka et al., 1999; Rodriguez et al., 1999). The effects became stronger as the environments are made more distinct (Mystkowski et al., 2002).

VII. Individual differences in anxiety disorders

VII.A. *Human studies*

In human there are marked individual differences to the susceptibility to anxiety disorders. For example, only a fraction of the people who experience trauma go on to develop post-traumatic stress disorder (PTSD; Breslau et al., 1991; Kessler et al., 1995). Additionally, all major subtypes of anxiety disorders aggregate in families (Merikangas et al., 1998). The investigation of offspring of parents with these conditions is, therefore, a powerful strategy to identify premorbid risk and protective factors, as well as early signs of expression of these disorders. The finding of increased baseline startle reactivity in individuals with PTSD and panic disorder raises the possibility that a proclivity to react fearfully to situations that are only mildly challenging to others is a risk marker for subsequent development of anxiety disorders. Grillon et al. (1998)

examined fear-potentiated startle to threat in children of parents with an anxiety disorder. Because shocks may be more difficult to use with children than with adults, they developed a procedure in which a strong puff of air (air blast) delivered to the neck was substituted for the shock. Anticipation of such an air blast produced a robust startle potentiation in children (Grillon et al., 1999) and was associated with increased activity in the amygdala based on fMRI studies in adults (Pine et al., 2001). These findings pointed to gender-specific abnormal startle reactivity in the high-risk group. High-risk girls were overly sensitive to contextual threat but exhibited normal fear-potentiated startle to explicit threat, and boys showed the inverse pattern (normal contextual fear and increased fear potentiation to threat). These results suggest that vulnerability to anxiety disorders may involve a gender-specific differential sensitivity of fear pathways.

VII.B. Genetically modified mice as a model of individual differences in anxiety disorders

VII.B.1. GABA$_A$-receptor variations as a potential mechanism for individual differences

Animal studies using fear conditioning are beginning to provide insight into potential genetic mechanisms that predispose individuals to anxiety disorders. Of particular relevance are studies using mice that have been genetically engineered to have alterations in GABA$_A$-receptor function (Anagnostaras et al., 1999). GABA is the major inhibitory transmitter in the brain and pharmacological agents that target GABA$_A$-receptor function have been used by humans for eons to attenuate anxiety (e.g., alcohol and benzodiazepines). GABA$_A$ receptors are pentamers made of five subunits (Barnard et al., 1998). There are a large number of subunits and the resulting combinatorial possibilities result in a great heterogeneity both in the anatomical distribution of specific combinations and the function of the particular subunit combinations. All GABA$_A$ receptors have two alpha and two beta subunits. Most often the fifth subunit is a $\gamma 2$ subunit and it is these GABA$_A$ receptors that are sensitive to

modulation by benzodiazepines. Mice that have one allele of the $\gamma 2$ gene deleted (i.e., those heterozygous for a knockout of the gene encoding $\gamma 2$) show a profile of heightened anxiety (Crestani et al., 1999). In particular, these mice have an abnormally strong fear response to CSs that have a weak relationship with the US. In this genetic variant, CS–US arrangements that do not normally support fear conditioning result in pronounced conditional fear.

In some GABA$_A$ receptors a delta subunit replaces the $\gamma 2$. While these δ containing GABA$_A$ receptors are insensitive to benzodiazepines, they are highly sensitive to alcohol and neurosteroids (Mihalek et al., 1999; Wallner et al., 2006). Female mice with a genetic deletion of the δ subunit show increased fear to hippocampus-dependent trace conditioning, where the CS and US are separated by 20 s, even though standard delay fear conditioning is normal (Wiltgen et al., 2005). Interestingly, δ subunit expression varies over the ovarian cycle (Maguire and Mody, 2007). Thus, δ containing GABA$_A$ receptors may play a role in both gender and cycle differences in fear. Combining Pavlovian fear conditioning with genetically engineered mice holds tremendous promise for uncovering the specific genetic patterns that predispose individuals to anxiety disorders.

VIII. Post-traumatic stress disorder

Fear conditioning is most clearly analogous to simple phobias. However, animal models using fear conditioning may prove helpful in analyzing other aspects of anxiety disorders. About 20% of humans exposed to traumatic events go on to develop PTSD. The symptoms of PTSD include re-experiencing the trauma, passively avoiding reminders of the trauma, numbing of affect and heightened general arousal. It is unlikely that simple fear conditioning alone provides an adequate model of all of the complexities of PTSD. One important aspect of PTSD is that even asymptomatic patients (e.g., those that have undergone CBT) may become symptomatic again following exposure to a new stressor. Additionally, PTSD patients show exaggerated reactions to a mild stressor. As pointed out earlier, fear conditioning is tightly regulated to the level of threat and by definition is under immediate control of threatening stimuli in the environment. Furthermore, as described above fear conditioning is reversed by extinction, but PTSD is quite resistant to exposure therapy, the clinical analogue of extinction (Rothbaum and Davis, 2003). These aspects of PTSD are not completely consistent with simple fear conditioning.

Recently, we developed an animal model that retains the analytical power of Pavlovian fear conditioning but also appears to capture some of the symptoms of PTSD. We found that pre-exposure to a severe stressor (15 shocks) enhances conditional fear responding to a single context–shock pairing (Rau et al., 2005). The data from this series of experiments suggest that the traumatic event causes a change in the state of functioning of the animal. Rather than expressing a normal fear reaction to a mild shock, these rats show exaggerated responses to a mild stressor (a single shock). Also, we found that the exaggerated fear conditioning is not eliminated by extinction of the original trauma context. That is, while the rats no longer show fear following extinction of the place where they received the 15 shocks, they still show the exaggerated fear response to a subsequent shock. This enhanced fear learning to the single shock depends on experience with prior trauma, if the single shock is given before the trauma, but tested after trauma, the rats show a normal fear reaction to the single shock context. Thus, prior trauma seems to permanently sensitize the fear conditioning circuit; extensive aversive experience enhances susceptibility to subsequent fear conditioning. PTSD is comorbid with phobias (Zayfert et al., 2005). The stress-induced sensitization of the fear-learning circuit may provide a mechanism for this comorbidity. If trauma sensitizes fear learning, then new phobias are likely to develop.

In this experimental procedure, the 15-shock stressor causes a sensitization in conditional fear responding to a less intense but qualitatively similar stressor (the single shock). In this way the model can be used to study at least one symptom of PTSD, the increased reactivity to things or events that resemble the traumatic stressor (American Psychiatric Association, 2000). In this way, the 1-shock session can be viewed as a less severe "reminder" of the 15-shock session. Additionally, the finding that a single shock causes an exaggerated response, even after the rats had undergone exposure therapy, is consistent with the re-emergence of PTSD symptoms after a reminder of the original trauma.

The Rau et al. (2005) experiments used the same stimulus to induce stress and to condition fear. However, work in other laboratories suggests that different stressors can enhance aversive Pavlovian conditioning. Rats exposed to inescapable tail-shocks show an impaired ability to escape footshocks, a phenomenon called learned helplessness (Overmier and Seligman, 1967). In addition, these rats show enhanced freezing when re-exposed to the box in which they previously received footshock (Maier, 1990). Shors and colleagues have shown that a session of inescapable tailshock or swim stress enhances the acquisition of the conditional eyeblink response (Shors et al., 1992; Shors and Servatius, 1997; Shors, 2001). Additionally, a 2 h session of restraint stress enhances fear produced by three context–shock pairings (Cordero et al., 2003). Our results are consistent with these findings, but extend the overall pattern to a situation that uses the same qualitative stressor for both the trauma and conditioning; exposure to several shocks enhances conditional fear responding to one.

These experiments suggest that the traumatic event, the 15 shocks, causes a change in the state of functioning of the animal. This change is not dependent on the memory of the traumatic event, but may depend instead on a psychobiological change induced by the stressor (Rau et al., 2005). One possible mechanism responsible for the state change may be kindling of neural pathways involved in fear and anxiety. Traditionally, kindling describes a phenomenon in which repeated subthreshold electrical stimulation eventually leads to a full-blown seizure (Goddard et al., 1969). A similar biological mechanism has been proposed to contribute to the development of PTSD (Adamec, 1997; Post et al., 1997; Hageman et al., 2001). In PTSD, a traumatic event activates the stress response. Upon re-experiencing events similar to the trauma or less intense stressors, the stress response reactivates. Eventually this repeated activation leads to a dysregulated response that has a lower threshold of activation (Rosen and Schulkin, 1998). This then facilitates sensitized reactions to neutral stimuli that are perceived as threatening. Repeated traumatizations or re-experiencing aspects of a traumatic event may kindle regions of the fear circuit susceptible to traditional electrically induced kindling (e.g., amygdala) leading to the dramatic reactions seen in PTSD patients. Animal studies have shown that kindling can have anxiogenic effects in behavioral tests such as the elevated plus-maze and open-field (Nieminen et al., 1992; Helfer et al., 1996; Adamec and Shallow, 2000) and can increase fear-potentiated startle (Rosen et al., 1996).

IX. Conclusion

Fear conditioning research testifies to the strength and power of the use of animal models for anxiety disorders. In many ways fear conditioning was originally developed in humans (Watson and Rayner, 1920) and then translated to animals (Estes and Skinner, 1941). As an animal model it has allowed major progress in our understanding of defensive behavior in particular (Bolles, 1970; Fanselow and Lester, 1988) and learning and memory in general (Kamin, 1968; Rescorla, 1968). It has provided an exceptionally tractable model for analyzing the physiology of learning and memory that has proven to be directly applicable to the human brain. Treatments based on this animal model of been tremendously successful at treating anxiety in humans. And the animal research has pushed further refinements in cognitive behavior therapy (Bouton et al., 2001; Mystkowski et al., 2002; Mineka and Zinbarg, 2006). This past success, suggests that fear conditioning will advance our understanding of other anxiety disorders such as PTSD and the genetic factors that lead to vulnerability to anxiety disorders.

Acknowledgment

Preparation of this chapter was supported by NIMH R01 MH62122 and NINDS P01NS35985.

References

Abeliovich, A., Paylor, R., Chen, C., Kim, J.J., Wehner, J.M. and Tonegawa, S. (1993) PKC gamma mutant mice exhibit mild deficits in spatial and contextual learning. Cell, 75: 1263–1271.

Adamec, R. (1997) Transmitter systems involved in neural plasticity underlying increased anxiety and defense – implications for understanding anxiety following traumatic stress. Neurosci. Biobehav. Rev., 21: 755–765.

Adamec, R. and Shallow, T. (2000) Effects of baseline anxiety on response to kindling of the right medial amygdala. Physiol. Behav., 70: 67–80.

Adamec, R.E., Blundell, J. and Collins, A. (2001) Neural plasticity and stress induced changes in defense in the rat. Neurosci. Biobehav. Rev., 25: 721–744.

American Psychiatric Association. (2000) Diagnostic and Statistical Manual of Mental Disorders, IV ed. American Psychiatric Association, Washington, DC.

Anagnostaras, S.G., Craske, M.G. and Fanselow, M.S. (1999) Anxiety: at the intersection of genes and experience. Nat. Neurosci., 2: 780–782.

Anglada-Figueroa, D. and Quirk, G.J. (2005) Lesions of the basal amygdala block expression of conditioned fear but not extinction. J. Neurosci., 25: 9680–9685.

Annau, Z. and Kamin, L.J. (1961) The conditioned emotional response as a function of intensity of the US. J. Comp. Physiol. Psychol., 54: 428–432.

Barnard, E.A., Skolnick, P., Olsen, R.W., Mohler, H., Sieghart, W., Biggio, G., Braestrup, C., Bateson, A.N. and Langer, S.Z. (1998) International union of pharmacology. XV. Subtypes of gamma-aminobutyric acidA receptors: classification on the basis of subunit structure and receptor function. Pharmacol. Rev., 50: 291–313.

Bechara, A., Tranel, D., Damasio, H., Adolphs, R., Rockland, C. and Damasio, A.R. (1995) Double dissociation of conditioning and declarative knowledge relative to the amygdala and hippocampus in humans. Science, 269: 1115–1118.

Blanchard, D.C. and Blanchard, R.J. (1972) Innate and conditioned reactions to threat in rats with amygdaloid lesions. J. Comp. Physiol. Psychol., 81: 281–290.

Blanchard, R.J. and Blanchard, D.C. (1969) Crouching as an index of fear. J. Comp. Physiol. Psychol., 67: 370–375.

Blanchard, R.J., Fukunaga, K.K. and Blanchard, D.C. (1976) Environmental control of defensive reactions to footshock. Bull. Psychon. Soc., 8: 129–130.

Boatman, J.A. and Kim, J.J. (2006) A thalamo-cortico-amygdala pathway mediates auditory fear conditioning in the intact brain. Eur. J. Neurosci., 24: 894–900.

Bolles, R.C. (1970) Species-specific defense reactions and avoidance learning. Psychol. Rev., 77: 32–48.

Bolles, R.C. and Collier, A.C. (1976) The effect of predictive cues on freezing in rats. Anim. Learn. Behav., 4: 6–8.

Bolles, R.C. and Fanselow, M.S. (1980) A perceptual-defensive-recuperative model of fear and pain. Behav. Brain Sci., 3: 291–323.

Bourtchouladze, R., Patterson, S., Kelly, M., Kreibich, A., Kandel, E. and Abel, T. (1994) Chronically increased Gs signaling disrupts associative and spatial learning. Learn. Mem., 13: 745–752.

Bouton, M.E. (1994) Conditioning, remembering, and forgetting. J. Exp. Psychol. Anim. Behav. Process., 20: 219–231.

Bouton, M.E. and Bolles, R.C. (1979) Role of conditioned contextual stimuli in reinstatement of extinguished fear. J. Exp. Psychol. Anim. Behav. Process., 5: 368–378.

Bouton, M.E., Kenney, F.A. and Rosengard, C. (1990) State-dependent fear extinction with two benzodiazepine tranquilizers. Behav. Neurosci., 104: 44–55.

Bouton, M.E. and King, D.A. (1983) Contextual control of the extinction of conditioned fear: tests for the associative value of the context. J. Exp. Psychol. Anim. Behav. Process., 9: 248–265.

Bouton, M.E., Mineka, S. and Barlow, D.H. (2001) A modern learning theory perspective on the etiology of panic disorder. Psychol. Rev., 108: 4–32.

Bouton, M.E. and Nelson, J.B. (1994) Context-specificity of target versus feature inhibition in a feature-negative discrimination. J. Exp. Psychol. Anim. Behav. Process., 20: 51–65.

Bouton, M.E. and Ricker, S.T. (1994) Renewal of extinguished responding in a second context. Anim. Learn. Behav., 22: 317–324.

Breslau, N., Davis, G.C., Andreski, P. and Peterson, E. (1991) Traumatic events and posttraumatic stress disorder in an urban population of young adults. Arch. Gen. Psychiatry, 48: 216–222.

Brooks, D.C. and Bouton, M.E. (1994) A retrieval cue for extinction attenuates response recovery (renewal) caused by a return to the conditioning context. J. Exp. Psychol. Anim. Behav. Process., 20: 366–379.

Brown, J.S., Kalish, H.I. and Farber, I.E. (1951) Conditioned fear as revealed by magnitude of startle response to an auditory stimulus. J. Exp. Psychol., 41: 317–328.

Buchel, C., Morris, J., Dolan, R.J. and Friston, K.J. (1998) Brain systems mediating aversive conditioning: an event-related fMRI study. Neuron, 20: 947–957.

Burwell, R.D., Bucci, D.J., Sanborn, M.R. and Jutras, M.J. (2004) Perirhinal and postrhinal contributions to remote memory for context. J. Neurosci., 24: 11023–11028.

Calcagnetti, D.J., Fanselow, M.S., Helmstetter, F.J. and Bowen, W.D. (1989) [D-Ala2,Leu5,Cys6]enkephalin: short-term agonist effects and long-term antagonism at delta opioid receptors. Peptides, 10: 319–326.

Calcagnetti, D.J., Helmstetter, F.J. and Fanselow, M.S. (1988) Analgesia produced by centrally administered DAGO, DPDPE and U50488H in the formalin test. Eur. J. Pharmacol., 153: 117–122.

Campeau, S., Liang, K.C. and Davis, M. (1990) Long-term retention of fear-potentiated startle following a short training session. Anim. Learn. Behav., 18: 462–468.

Chance, W.T., White, A.C., Krynock, G.M. and Rosecrans, J.A. (1977) Autoanalgesia: behaviorally activated antinociception. Eur. J. Pharmacol., 44: 283–284.

Chance, W.T., White, A.C., Krynock, G.M. and Rosecrans, J.A. (1979) Autoanalgesia: acquisition, blockade and relationship to opiate binding. Eur. J. Pharmacol., 58: 461–468.

Cheng, D.T., Knight, D.C., Smith, C.N. and Helmstetter, F.J. (2006) Human amygdala activity during the expression of fear responses. Behav. Neurosci., 120: 1187–1195.

Cheng, D.T., Knight, D.C., Smith, C.N., Stein, E.A. and Helmstetter, F.J. (2003) Functional MRI of human amygdala activity during Pavlovian fear conditioning: stimulus processing versus response expression. Behav. Neurosci., 117: 3–10.

Cordero, M.I., Venero, C., Kruyt, N.D. and Sandi, C. (2003) Prior exposure to a single stress session facilitates subsequent contextual fear conditioning in rats. Evidence for a role of corticosterone. Horm. Behav., 44: 338–345.

Crestani, F., Lorez, M., Baer, K., Essrich, C., Benke, D., Laurent, J.P., Belzung, C., Fritschy, J.M., Luscher, B. and Mohler, H. (1999) Decreased GABAA-receptor clustering results in enhanced anxiety and a bias for threat cues. Nat. Neurosci., 2: 833–839.

Davis, M. (1998) Anatomic and physiologic substrates of emotion in an animal model. J. Clin. Neurophysiol., 15: 378–387.

Dong, H.W., Petrovich, G.D. and Swanson, L.W. (2001a) Topography of projections from amygdala to bed nuclei of the stria terminalis. Brain Res. Rev., 38: 192–246.

Dong, H.W., Petrovich, G.D., Watts, A.G. and Swanson, L.W. (2001b) Basic organization of projections from the oval and fusiform nuclei of the bed nuclei of the stria terminalis in adult rat brain. J. Comp. Neurol., 436: 430–455.

Estes, W.K. (1944) An experimental study of punishment. Psychol. Monog., 57: 40.

Estes, W.K. and Skinner, B.F. (1941) Some quantitative properties of anxiety. J. Exp. Psychol., 29: 390–400.

Esteves, F., Parra, C., Dimberg, U. and Ohman, A. (1994) Nonconscious associative learning: Pavlovian conditioning of skin conductance responses to masked fear-relevant facial stimuli. Psychophysiology, 31: 375–385.

Fanselow, M.S. (1979) Naloxone attenuates rat's preference for signaled shock. Phys. Psychol., 7: 70–74.

Fanselow, M.S. (1980) Conditioned and unconditional components of post-shock freezing. Pavlov. J. Biol. Sci., 15: 177–182.

Fanselow, M.S. (1981) Naloxone and Pavlovian fear conditioning. Learn. Motiv., 12: 398–419.

Fanselow, M.S. (1982) The post-shock activity burst. Anim. Learn. Behav., 10: 448–454.

Fanselow, M.S. (1984) Shock-induced analgesia on the formalin test: effects of shock severity, naloxone, hypophysectomy, and associative variables. Behav. Neurosci., 98: 79–95.

Fanselow, M.S. (1986a) Associative vs topographical accounts of the immediate shock-freezing deficit in rats: Implications for the response selection rules governing species-specific defensive reactions. Learn. Motiv., 17: 16–39.

Fanselow, M.S. (1986b) Conditioned fear-induced opiate analgesia: a competing motivational state theory of stress analgesia. Ann. N.Y. Acad. Sci., 467: 40–54.

Fanselow, M.S. (1990) Factors governing one-trial contextual conditioning. Anim. Learn. Behav., 18: 264–270.

Fanselow, M.S. (1991) The midbrain periaqueductal gray as a coordinator of action in response to fear and anxiety. In: Depaulis, A. and Bandler, R. (Eds.), The Midbrain Periaqueductal Gray Matter: Functional, Anatomical and Immunohistochemical Organization. Plenum Publishing Corporation, New York, pp. 151–173.

Fanselow, M.S. (1998) Pavlovian conditioning, negative feedback, and blocking: mechanisms that regulate association formation. Neuron, 20: 625–627.

Fanselow, M.S. and Baackes, M.P. (1982) Conditioned fear-induced opiate analgesia on the formalin test: evidence for two aversive motivational systems. Learn. Motiv., 13: 200–221.

Fanselow, M.S. and Bolles, R.C. (1979) Naloxone and shock-elicited freezing in the rat. J. Comp. Physiol. Psychol., 93: 736–744.

Fanselow, M.S., Calcagnetti, D.J. and Helmstetter, F.J. (1989) Role of mu and kappa opioid receptors in conditional fear-induced analgesia: the antagonistic actions of nor-binaltorphimine and the cyclic somatostatin octapeptide, Cys2Tyr3Orn5Pen7-amide. J. Pharmacol. Exp. Ther., 250: 825–830.

Fanselow, M.S., Kim, J.J., Young, S.L., Calcagnetti, D.J., DeCola, J.P., Helmstetter, F.J. and Landeira-Fernandez, J. (1991) Differential effects of selective opioid peptide antagonists on the acquisition of Pavlovian fear conditioning. Peptides, 12: 1033–1037.

Fanselow, M.S., Landeira-Fernandez, J., DeCola, J.P. and Kim, J.J. (1994) The immediate-shock deficit and postshock analgesia: implications for the relationship between the analgesic CR and UR. Anim. Learn. Behav., 22: 72–76.

Fanselow, M.S. and Lester, L.S. (1988) A functional behavioristic approach to aversively motivated behavior: predatory imminence as a determinant of the topography of defensive behavior. In: Bolles, R.C. and Beecher, M.D. (Eds.), Evolution and Learning. Lawrence Erlbaum Associates, Inc., Hillsdale, NJ, England, pp. 185–212.

Fanselow, M.S. and Tighe, T.J. (1988) Contextual conditioning with massed versus distributed unconditional stimuli in the absence of explicit conditional stimuli. J. Exp. Psychol. Anim. Behav. Process., 14: 187–199.

Foo, H. and Helmstetter, F.J. (1999) Hypoalgesia elicited by a conditioned stimulus is blocked by a mu, but not a delta or a kappa, opioid antagonist injected into the rostral ventromedial medulla. Pain, 83: 427–431.

Fried, I., MacDonald, K.A. and Wilson, C.L. (1997) Single neuron activity in human hippocampus and amygdala during recognition of faces and objects. Neuron, 18: 753–765.

Fuster, J.M. and Uyeda, A.A. (1971) Reactivity of limbic neurons of the monkey to appetitive and aversive signals. Electroencephalogr. Clin. Neurophysiol., 30: 281–293.

Gale, G.D., Anagnostaras, S.G., Godsil, B.P., Mitchell, S., Nozawa, T., Sage, J.R., Wiltgen, B. and Fanselow, M.S. (2004) Role of the basolateral amygdala in the storage of fear memories across the adult lifetime of rats. J. Neurosci., 24: 3810–3815.

Garcia, J., Kimeldorf, D.J. and Koelling, R.A. (1955) Conditioned aversion to saccharin resulting from exposure to gamma radiation. Science, 122: 157–158.

Goddard, G.V., McIntyre, D.C. and Leech, C.K. (1969) A permanent change in brain function resulting from daily electrical stimulation. Exp. Neurol., 25: 295–330.

Grillon, C. and Davis, M. (1997) Fear-potentiated startle conditioning in humans: explicit and contextual cue conditioning following paired versus unpaired training. Psychophysiology, 34: 451–458.

Grillon, C., Dierker, L. and Merikangas, K.R. (1998) Fear-potentiated startle in adolescent offspring of parents with anxiety disorders. Biol. Psychiatry, 44: 990–997.

Grillon, C., Merikangas, K.R., Dierker, L., Snidman, N., Arriaga, R.I., Kagan, J., Donzella, B., Dikel, T. and Nelson, C. (1999) Startle potentiation by threat of aversive stimuli and darkness in adolescents: a multi-site study. Int. J. Psychophysiol., 32: 63–73.

Hageman, I., Andersen, H.S. and Jorgensen, M.B. (2001) Post-traumatic stress disorder: a review of psychobiology and pharmacotherapy. Acta Psychiatr. Scand., 104: 411–422.

Hamm, A.O., Greenwald, M.K., Bradley, M.M. and Lang, P.J. (1993) Emotional learning, hedonic change, and the startle probe. J. Abnorm. Psychol., 102: 453–465.

Helfer, V., Deransart, C., Marescaux, C. and Depaulis, A. (1996) Amygdala kindling in the rat: anxiogenic-like consequences. Neuroscience, 73: 971–978.

Helmstetter, F.J. and Tershner, S.A. (1994) Lesions of the periaqueductal gray and rostral ventromedial medulla disrupt antinociceptive but not cardiovascular aversive conditional responses. J. Neurosci., 14: 7099–7108.

Hirsch, S.M. and Bolles, R.C. (1980) On the ability of prey to recognize predators. Zeitschrift für Tierpsychologie, 54: 71–84.

Hitchcock, J. and Davis, M. (1986) Lesions of the amygdala, but not of the cerebellum or red nucleus, block conditioned fear as measured with the potentiated startle paradigm. Behav. Neurosci., 100: 11–22.

Holland, P.C. (1992) Occasion setting in Pavlovian conditioning. In: Medin, D. (Ed.), The Psychology of Learning and Motivation. Academic Press, San Diego, CA, pp. 69–125.

Kamin, L.J. (1968) Attention-like processes in classical conditioning. In: Jones, M.R. (Ed.), In Miami Symposium on Predictability, Behavior and Aversive Stimulation. Miami University Press, Miami, pp. 9–31.

Kapp, B.S., Frysinger, R.C., Gallagher, M. and Haselton, J.R. (1979) Amygdala central nucleus lesions: effect on heart rate conditioning in the rabbit. Physiol. Behav., 23: 1109–1117.

Kavaliers, M., Colwell, D.D., Choleris, E. and Ossenkopp, K.P. (1999) Learning to cope with biting flies: rapid NMDA-mediated acquisition of conditioned analgesia. Behav. Neurosci., 113: 126–135.

Kessler, R.C., Sonnega, A., Bromet, E., Hughes, M. and Nelson, C.B. (1995) Posttraumatic stress disorder in the National Comorbidity Survey. Arch. Gen. Psychiatry, 52: 1048–1060.

Kiernan, M.J., Westbrook, R.F. and Cranney, J. (1995) Immediate shock, passive avoidance, and potentiated startle: implications for the unconditioned response to shock. Anim. Learn. Behav., 23: 22–30.

Kim, J.J. and Fanselow, M.S. (1992) Modality-specific retrograde amnesia of fear. Science, 256: 675–677.

Kim, J.J., Krupa, D.J. and Thompson, R.F. (1998) Inhibitory cerebello-olivary projections and blocking effect in classical conditioning. Science, 279: 570–573.

Kim, J.J., Rison, R.A. and Fanselow, M.S. (1993) Effects of amygdala, hippocampus, and periaqueductal gray lesions on short- and long-term contextual fear. Behav. Neurosci., 107: 1093–1098.

Knight, D.C., Smith, C.N., Stein, E.A. and Helmstetter, F.J. (1999) Functional MRI of human Pavlovian fear conditioning: patterns of activation as a function of learning. Neuroreport, 10: 3665–3670.

LaBar, K.S., Gatenby, J.C., Gore, J.C., LeDoux, J.E. and Phelps, E.A. (1998) Human amygdala activation during conditioned fear acquisition and extinction: a mixed-trial fMRI study. Neuron, 20: 937–945.

LaBar, K.S., LeDoux, J.E., Spencer, D.D. and Phelps, E.A. (1995) Impaired fear conditioning following unilateral temporal lobectomy in humans. J. Neurosci., 15: 6846–6855.

Lam, Y.W., Wong, A., Canli, T. and Brown, T.H. (1996) Conditioned enhancement of the early component of the rat eyeblink reflex. Neurobiol. Learn. Mem., 66: 212–220.

Landeira-Fernandez, J., DeCola, J.P., Kim, J.J. and Fanselow, M.S. (2006) Immediate shock deficit in fear conditioning: effects of shock manipulations. Behav. Neurosci., 120: 873–879.

Leaton, R.N. and Cranney, J. (1990) Potentiation of the acoustic startle response by a conditioned stimulus paired with acoustic startle stimulus in rats. J. Exp. Psychol. Anim. Behav. Process., 16: 279–287.

LeDoux, J.E., Iwata, J., Cicchetti, P. and Reis, D.J. (1988) Different projections of the central amygdaloid nucleus mediate autonomic and behavioral correlates of conditioned fear. J. Neurosci., 8: 2517–2529.

Liebeskind, J.C. and Paul, L.A. (1977) Psychological and physiological mechanisms of pain. Annu. Rev. Psychol., 28: 41–60.

Lindquist, D.H., Jarrard, L.E. and Brown, T.H. (2004) Perirhinal cortex supports delay fear conditioning to rat ultrasonic social signals. J. Neurosci., 24: 3610–3617.

Maguire, J. and Mody, I. (2007) Neurosteroid synthesis-mediated regulation of GABA(A) receptors: relevance to the ovarian cycle and stress. J. Neurosci., 27: 2155–2162.

Maier, S.F. (1990) Role of fear in mediating shuttle escape learning deficit produced by inescapable shock. J. Exp. Psychol. Anim. Behav. Process., 16: 137–149.

Maren, S. (1999) Neurotoxic basolateral amygdala lesions impair learning and memory but not the performance of conditional fear in rats. J. Neurosci., 19: 8696–8703.

Maren, S., Aharonov, G. and Fanselow, M.S. (1997) Neurotoxic lesions of the dorsal hippocampus and Pavlovian fear conditioning in rats. Behav. Brain Res., 88: 261–274.

Maren, S. and Fanselow, M.S. (1995) Synaptic plasticity in the basolateral amygdala induced by hippocampal formation stimulation in vivo. J. Neurosci., 15: 7548–7564.

Maren, S. and Fanselow, M.S. (1997) Electrolytic lesions of the fimbria/fornix, dorsal hippocampus, or entorhinal cortex produce anterograde deficits in contextual fear conditioning in rats. Neurobiol. Learn. Mem., 67: 142–149.

McNally, G.P. and Cole, S. (2006) Opioid receptors in the midbrain periaqueductal gray regulate prediction errors during Pavlovian fear conditioning. Behav. Neurosci., 120: 313–323.

McNally, G.P.G., Marika, C., Low, L.F. and West-brook, R.F. (1999) Effects of contextual cues previously paired with footshock or illness on behavior and pain sensitivity in the rat. Anim. Learn. Behav., 27: 416–425.

Merikangas, K.R., Dierker, L.C. and Szatmari, P. (1998) Psychopathology among offspring of parents with substance abuse and/or anxiety disorders: a high-risk study. J. Child Psychol. Psychiatry, 39: 711–720.

Mihalek, R.M., Banerjee, P.K., Korpi, E.R., Quinlan, J.J., Firestone, L.L., Mi, Z.P., Lagenaur, C., Tretter, V., Sieghart, W., Anagnostaras, S.G., Sage, J.R., Fanselow, M.S., Guidotti, A., Spigelman, I., Li, Z., DeLorey, T.M., Olsen, R.W. and Homanics, G.E. (1999) Attenuated sensitivity to neuroactive steroids in gamma-aminobutyrate type A receptor delta subunit knockout mice. Proc. Natl. Acad. Sci. USA, 96: 12905–12910.

Mineka, S., Davidson, M., Cook, M. and Keir, R. (1984) Observational conditioning of snake fear in rhesus monkeys. J. Abnorm. Psychol., 93: 355–372.

Mincka, S., Keir, R. and Price, V. (1980) Fear of snakes in wild- and laboratory-reared rhesus monkeys (*Macaca mulatta*). Anim. Learn. Behav., 8: 653–663.

Mineka, S., Mystkowski, J.L., Hladek, D. and Rodriguez, B.I. (1999) The effects of changing contexts on return of fear following exposure therapy for spider fear. J. Consult. Clin. Psychol., 67: 599–604.

Mineka, S. and Zinbarg, R. (2006) A contemporary learning theory perspective on the etiology of anxiety disorders: it's not what you thought it was. Am. Psychol., 61: 10–26.

Mongeluzi, D.L., Rosellini, R.A., Caldarone, B.J., Stock, H.S. and Abrahamsen, G.C. (1996) Pavlovian aversive context conditioning using carbon dioxide as the unconditional stimulus. J. Exp. Psychol. Anim. Behav. Process., 22: 244–257.

Morgan, M.M. and Fields, H.L. (1994) Pronounced changes in the activity of nociceptive modulatory neurons in the rostral ventromedial medulla in response to prolonged thermal noxious stimuli. J. Neurophysiol., 72: 1161–1170.

Mystkowski, J.L., Craske, M.G. and Echiverri, A.M. (2002) Treatment context and return of fear in spider phobia. Behav. Ther., 33: 399–416.

Nieminen, S.A., Sirvio, J., Teittinen, K., Pitkanen, A., Airaksinen, M.M. and Riekkinen, P. (1992) Amygdala kindling increased fear-response, but did not impair spatial memory in rats. Physiol. Behav., 51: 845–849.

Overmier, J.B. and Seligman, M.E. (1967) Effects of inescapable shock upon subsequent escape and avoidance responding. J. Comp. Physiol. Psychol., 63: 28–33.

Pavlov, I.P. (1927) Conditioned Reflexes. Oxford University Press, London.

Petrovich, G.D. and Swanson, L.W. (1997) Projections from the lateral part of the central amygdalar nucleus to the postulated fear conditioning circuit. Brain Res., 763: 247–254.

Pham, K., McEwen, B.S., Ledoux, J.E. and Nader, K. (2005) Fear learning transiently impairs hippocampal cell proliferation. Neuroscience, 130: 17–24.

Pine, D.S., Fyer, A., Grun, J., Phelps, E.A., Szeszko, P.R., Koda, V., Li, W., Ardekani, B., Maguire, E.A., Burgess, N. and Bilder, R.M. (2001) Methods for developmental studies of fear conditioning circuitry. Biol. Psychiatry, 50: 225–228.

Ponnusamy, R., Poulos, A.M. and Fanselow, M.S. (2007) Amygdala-dependent and amygdala-independent pathways for contextual fear conditioning, 147(4): 919–927.

Post, R.M., Weiss, S.R., Smith, M., Li, H. and McCann, U. (1997) Kindling versus quenching. Implications for the evolution and treatment of posttraumatic stress disorder. Ann. N. Y. Acad. Sci., 821: 285–295.

Quirk, G.J., Armony, J.L. and LeDoux, J.E. (1997) Fear conditioning enhances different temporal components of tone-evoked spike trains in auditory cortex and lateral amygdala. Neuron, 19: 613–624.

Rau, V., DeCola, J.P. and Fanselow, M.S. (2005) Stress-induced enhancement of fear learning: an animal model of posttraumatic stress disorder. Neurosci. Biobehav. Rev., 29: 1207–1223.

Rau, V. and Fanselow, M.S. (2007) Neurobiological and Neuroethological Perspectives on Fear and Anxiety. Cambridge University Press, New York, NY.

Rescorla, R.A. (1968) Probability of shock in the presence and absence of CS in fear conditioning. J. Comp. Physiol. Psychol., 66: 1–5.

Rescorla, R.A. (1988) Behavioral studies of Pavlovian conditioning. Annu. Rev. Neurosci., 11: 329–352.

Rescorla, R.A. (1997) Spontaneous recovery after Pavlovian conditioning with multiple outcomes. Anim. Learn. Behav., 25: 99–107.

Rodriguez, B.I., Craske, M.G., Mineka, S. and Hladek, D. (1999) Context-specificity of relapse: effects of therapist and environmental context on return of fear. Behav. Res. Ther., 37: 845–862.

Rescorla, R.A. and Heth, C.D. (1975) Reinstatement of fear to an extinguished conditioned stimulus. J. Exp. Psychol. Anim. Behav. Process., 1: 88–96.

Rescorla, R.A. and Wagner, A.R. (1972) A theory of Pavlovian conditioning: variations in the effectiveness of reinforcement and nonreinforcement. In: Black, A.H. and Prokasy, W.F. (Eds.), Classical

Conditioning II: Current Theory and Research. Appleton-Century-Crofts, New York, pp. 64–69.

Romanski, L.M. and LeDoux, J.E. (1992) Equipotentiality of thalamo-amygdala and thalamo-cortico-amygdala circuits in auditory fear conditioning. J. Neurosci., 12: 4501–4509.

Rosen, J.B., Fanselow, M.S., Young, S.L., Sitcoske, M. and Maren, S. (1998) Immediate-early gene expression in the amygdala following footshock stress and contextual fear conditioning. Brain Res., 796: 132–142.

Rosen, J.B., Hamerman, E., Sitcoske, M., Glowa, J.R. and Schulkin, J. (1996) Hyperexcitability: exaggerated fear-potentiated startle produced by partial amygdala kindling. Behav. Neurosci., 110: 43–50.

Rosen, J.B., Hitchcock, J.M., Miserendino, M.J., Falls, W.A., Campeau, S. and Davis, M. (1992) Lesions of the perirhinal cortex but not of the frontal, medial prefrontal, visual, or insular cortex block fear-potentiated startle using a visual conditioned stimulus. J. Neurosci., 12: 4624–4633.

Rosen, J.B., Hitchcock, J.M., Sananes, C.B., Miserendino, M.J. and Davis, M. (1991) A direct projection from the central nucleus of the amygdala to the acoustic startle pathway: anterograde and retrograde tracing studies. Behav. Neurosci., 105: 817–825.

Rosen, J.B. and Schulkin, J. (1998) From normal fear to pathological anxiety. Psychol. Rev., 105: 325–350.

Ross, R.T. and Holland, P. (1982) Serial positive patterning: implications for occasion setting. Bull. Psychon. Soc., 19: 159–162.

Ross, R.T. and Randich, A. (1985) Associative aspects of conditioned analgesia evoked by a discrete CS. Anim. Learn. Behav., 13: 419–431.

Rothbaum, B.O. and Davis, M. (2003) Applying learning principles to the treatment of post-trauma reactions. Ann. N. Y. Acad. Sci., 1008: 112–121.

Schultz, W. and Dickinson, A. (2000) Neuronal coding of prediction errors. Annu. Rev. Neurosci., 23: 473–500.

Schwaber, J.S., Kapp, B.S. and Higgins, G. (1980) The origin and extent of direct amygdala projections to the region of the dorsal motor nucleus of the vagus and the nucleus of the solitary tract. Neurosci. Lett., 20: 15–20.

Shors, T.J. (2001) Acute stress rapidly and persistently enhances memory formation in the male rat. Neurobiol. Learn. Mem., 75: 10–29.

Shors, T.J. and Servatius, R.J. (1997) The contribution of stressor intensity, duration, and context to the stress-induced facilitation of associative learning. Neurobiol. Learn. Mem., 68: 92–96.

Shors, T.J., Weiss, C. and Thompson, R.F. (1992) Stress-induced facilitation of classical conditioning. Science, 257: 537–539.

Sigmundi, R.A., Bouton, M.E. and Bolles, R.C. (1980) Conditioned freezing in the rat as a function of shock intensity and CS modality. Bull. Psychon. Soc., 15: 254–256.

Spence, K.W. and Norris, E.B. (1950) Eyelid conditioning as a function of the inter-trial interval. J. Exp. Psychol., 40: 716–720.

Swanson, L.W. and Petrovich, G.D. (1998) What is the amygdala? Trends Neurosci., 21: 323–331.

Swartzentruber, D. and Bouton, M.E. (1986) Contextual control of negative transfer produced by prior CS–US pairings. Learn. Motiv., 17: 366–385.

Takahashi, L.K., Hubbard, D.T., Lee, I., Dar, Y. and Sipes, S.M. (2007) Predator odor-induced conditioned fear involves the basolateral and medial amygdala. Behav. Neurosci., 121: 100–110.

Vogel, J.R., Beer, B. and Clody, D.E. (1971) A simple and reliable conflict procedure for testing anti-anxiety agents. Psychopharmacologia, 21: 1–7.

Wallner, M., Hanchar, H.J. and Olsen, R.W. (2006) Low-dose alcohol actions on alpha4beta3delta $GABA_A$ receptors are reversed by the behavioral alcohol antagonist Ro15-4513. Proc. Natl. Acad. Sci. USA, 103: 8540–8545.

Watson, J.B. and Rayner, R. (1920) Conditioned emotional reactions. J. Exp. Psychol., 3: 1–14.

Wiltgen, B.J., Sanders, M.J., Anagnostaras, S.G., Sage, J.R. and Fanselow, M.S. (2006) Context fear learning in the absence of the hippocampus. J. Neurosci., 26: 5484–5491.

Wiltgen, B.J., Sanders, M.J., Ferguson, C., Homanics, G.E. and Fanselow, M.S. (2005) Trace fear conditioning is enhanced in mice lacking the delta subunit of the $GABA_A$ receptor. Learn. Mem., 12: 327–333.

Wolpe, J. (1969) The practice of behavior therapy, 1st ed. Pergamon Press, New York.

Wolpe, J. and Plaud, J.J. (1997) Pavlov's contributions to behavior therapy. The obvious and not so obvious. Am. Psychol., 52: 966–972.

Yeomans, J.S. and Pollard, B.A. (1993) Amygdala efferents mediating electrically evoked startle-like responses and fear potentiation of acoustic startle. Behav. Neurosci., 107: 596–610.

Young, S.L. and Fanselow, M.S. (1992) Associative regulation of Pavlovian fear conditioning: unconditional stimulus intensity, incentive shifts, and latent inhibition. J. Exp. Psychol. Anim. Behav. Process., 18: 400–413.

Zayfert, C., DeViva, J.C. and Hofmann, S.G. (2005) Comorbid PTSD and social phobia in a treatment-seeking population: an exploratory study. J. Nerv. Ment. Dis., 193: 93–101.

CHAPTER 2.3

Extinction of fear: from animal studies to clinical interventions

Karyn M. Myers[1,3,]* and Michael Davis[1,2,3]

[1]Department of Psychiatry and Behavioral Sciences, Center for Behavioral Neuroscience, Emory University, Atlanta, GA, USA
[2]Department of Psychology, Emory University, Atlanta, GA, USA
[3]Yerkes National Primate Research Center, Emory University, Atlanta, GA, USA

Abstract: Excessive fear and anxiety are hallmarks of a variety of disabling anxiety disorders that affect millions of people throughout the world. Hence, a greater understanding of the brain mechanisms involved in the inhibition of fear and anxiety is attracting increasing interest in the research community. In the laboratory, fear inhibition most often is studied through a procedure in which an organism previously trained to fear a cue is exposed to it in the absence of any aversive event. This procedure results in a decline in conditioned fear responses that is attributed to a process called fear extinction. In this chapter, we describe recent research on extinction of conditioned fear, focusing on observations in the laboratory that promise to inform clinical interventions for fear and anxiety disorders in humans. In particular, we will focus on research indicating that fear extinction in rodents and exposure therapy in humans are facilitated by a compound called D-cycloserine. We also will describe recent research suggesting that different mechanisms of extinction operate at different intervals between fear acquisition and extinction training.

Keywords: fear; extinction; memory; learning; Pavlovian conditioning; exposure therapy; D-cycloserine; amygdala

I. Introduction

In recent years a great deal has been learned about the behavioral characteristics and neural mechanisms of fear acquisition, as described in earlier chapters of this volume as well as in several excellent reviews (e.g., Davis, 2000; Rodrigues et al., 2004). Much of this progress may be attributed to the use of Pavlovian fear conditioning as a model system. In this paradigm, an initially innocuous stimulus (the to-be conditioned stimulus – CS; e.g., a light, tone, or distinctive place) is paired with an innately aversive unconditioned stimulus (US; e.g., a footshock) and the subject

(typically a rat or mouse) comes to exhibit a conditioned fear response (CR) to the CS. In rodents, fear is defined operationally as a cessation of all bodily movements except those required for respiration (freezing), an increase in the amplitude of an acoustically elicited startle response (potentiated startle), an increase in blood pressure, changes in respiration, emission of ultrasonic distress calls, avoidance of the place where shock occurred, or any of a number of other measures, in the presence of the CS.

Much less is known about the mechanisms of fear inhibition although this question is attracting increasing interest because of its clinical importance. Using the same Pavlovian fear conditioning paradigm described above, inhibition of fear typically is studied through a procedure in which,

*Corresponding author. E-mail: kmmyers@emory.edu

R.J. Blanchard, D.C. Blanchard, G. Griebel and D. Nutt (Eds.)
Handbook of Anxiety and Fear, Vol. 17
ISBN 978-0-444-53065-3

49

DOI: 10.1016/S1569-7339(07)00004-5

after fear conditioning, the organism is exposed to the fear-eliciting CS in the absence of the aversive US. This procedure results in a decline in conditioned fear responses that is attributed to a process called fear extinction. As we will see, extinction is a deceptively complex phenomenon, and one that has resisted simple explanation since its initial characterization by Pavlov (1927).

This chapter will explore recent research on extinction of conditioned fear, focusing on observations in the laboratory that promise to inform clinical interventions for fear and anxiety disorders in humans. We will begin by describing basic behavioral features and some theoretical accounts of extinction. We then will discuss research indicating that extinction in rodents is facilitated by a compound called D-cycloserine, and describe the rapid translation of this finding into a tangible clinical advance. Finally, we will consider the possibility that the mechanism of extinction may differ depending on the interval between fear acquisition and extinction training, and speculate on the potential clinical implications of this finding.

Before beginning we should note that the term "extinction" commonly is used in more than one sense, to refer to (1) the experimental procedure used to produce a decrement in the fear response; (2) the decremental effect of this procedure upon the fear response, which can be measured both at the time of the experimental procedure and at a later time; or (3) the hypothesized associative or cellular process responsible for that effect. In this chapter we will define the experimental procedure as *extinction training*, the decrement in the fear response measured during extinction training as *within-session extinction*, and the decrement measured at some interval after extinction training as *extinction retention*. The term *extinction* will be reserved for the theoretical process underlying the loss of the fear response.

II. Behavioral features of extinction

Extinction is a remarkably complex phenomenon that has attracted the attention of behavioral psychologists for over a century. As a full discussion of the literature would take us far afield, we will highlight only the most relevant observations here. For a more comprehensive account, interested readers are referred to several fine reviews prepared by leaders in this field (Mackintosh, 1974; Rescorla, 2001; Bouton, 2004; Delamater, 2004).

II.A. Extinction is not the same as forgetting

Although it is difficult to be sure that forgetting does not occur to some extent in extinction, numerous studies show that extinction cannot fully be explained by forgetting because it requires exposure to the CS in the absence of the US as opposed to the simple passage of time. This is especially true with fear extinction because fear memories can last months or even years with little forgetting (Gale et al., 2004).

II.B. Extinction is cue specific

Although Pavlov (1927) reported that extinction of one CS generalizes to other CSs trained with the same US, subsequent investigations have indicated that extinction is cue specific. Several studies have defined generalization gradients of extinction following training of cues falling along a spectrum, such as series of increasing auditory frequencies, and extinction of a single value of the continuum (Bass and Hull, 1934; Hovland, 1949; Dubin and Levis, 1974). The gradient of extinction is remarkably similar to that of acquisition, but inverted, with the lowest levels of responding occurring to the extinguished cue and increasingly greater responding occurring to cues falling farther away along the continuum. Other reports have shown that generalization of extinction is negligible across cues drawn from different sensory modalities, or drawn from a single modality but differing substantially in their physical characteristics (Kasprow et al., 1984; Richards and Sargent, 1984; Vervliet et al., 2004, 2005).

II.C. Extinction generally is not permanent

The decrement in conditioned fear responses during and shortly after extinction training generally is not permanent, as there are several instances in which extinguished fear responses are observed to reappear. The most thoroughly studied of these are reinstatement, renewal, and spontaneous recovery.

II.C.1. Reinstatement

Reinstatement refers to a reappearance of extinguished fear responses following exposure to unsignaled presentations of the US after the completion of extinction training (Fig. 1A). Reinstatement was first observed by Rescorla and Heth (1975), who determined that the effect was specific to extinguished CSs (i.e., it did not extend to neutral CSs) and persisted at least 24 h after unsignaled shock presentations, suggesting that the reappearance of fear responses was not due to sensitization. Subsequent work established that unsignaled US presentations must occur within the context in which animals ultimately are tested if recovery is to be observed, and that extinction (nonreinforced exposure) to that context between unsignaled US presentations and test attenuates fear recovery (Bouton and Bolles, 1979b; Bouton and King, 1983). Thus, reinstatement seems to depend on context conditioning and is likely to involve summation of two fear-inducing tendencies, each behaviorally subthreshold when considered independently, but suprathreshold when combined (cf. Reberg, 1972; Hendry, 1982): weak conditioning to context and residual conditioned fear to the extinguished CS. Other context-dependent mechanisms may contribute as well (Westbrook et al., 2002).

II.C.2. Renewal

Renewal refers to a reappearance of extinguished CRs when animals are tested in a context different from the one in which extinction training took place (Fig. 1B). For example, when animals first are trained to fear a light CS in context A, then receive extinction training to the light in context B, and finally are tested for fear to the light in either context A or context B, different outcomes are obtained: animals tested in context B (the same context where extinction training took place) exhibit little fear to the light, whereas animals

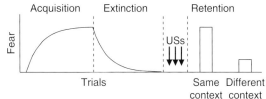

A. Reinstatement

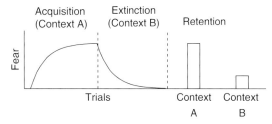

B. Renewal

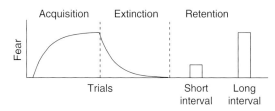

C. Spontaneous recovery

Fig. 1. Extinguished fear responses recover under a variety of circumstances. (A) *Reinstatement* occurs when unsignaled presentations of the US are interposed between the completion of extinction training and a subsequent retention test. Reinstatement is observed only if the USs are presented in the context in which the retention test will occur, indicating that the effect is context specific. (B) Extinction itself is context specific, as indicated by *renewal*. For example, if animals are fear conditioned in context A and extinguished in context B, they will exhibit extinction (i.e., little to no fear) if subsequently tested in context B, but they will show little evidence of extinction (i.e., renewed fear) if tested in context A. (C) *Spontaneous recovery* of extinguished fear responses occurs with the passage of time following extinction in the absence of any further training. The magnitude of recovery increases with the length of the extinction-to-test interval. From Myers and Davis (2007), with permission of Nature Publishing Group.

tested in context A exhibit robust fear to the light (Bouton and Bolles, 1979a; Bouton and King, 1983). A similar post-extinction return of fear is observed when animals are tested in a third, novel context C following acquisition in context A and extinction in context B (Bouton and Bolles, 1979a; Harris et al., 2000). The renewal effect is not due to simple context conditioning (Bouton and King, 1983; Bouton and Swartzentruber, 1986), but rather appears to reflect an occasion-setting or modulatory role of context in gating performance to the CS (Bouton, 1993). Thus, rather than learning that "now the cue is no longer paired with the shock," the animal learns that "now, in this place, the cue is no longer paired with the shock." There is some debate as to whether renewal may be mitigated by overtraining of extinction (Rauhut et al., 2001; Denniston et al., 2003) or extinction in multiple contexts (Gunther et al., 1998; Chelonis et al., 1999; Bouton et al., 2006; Neumann et al., 2006).

II.C.3. Spontaneous recovery

Spontaneous recovery refers to a reappearance of extinguished CRs with the passage of time following extinction training in the absence of any further explicit training (Fig. 1C). Generally the degree of CR recovery is directly related to the length of the retention interval, such that more robust CRs are observed at longer delays (Robbins, 1990; Quirk, 2002). It has been suggested that spontaneous recovery may be accounted for in terms of handling cues acting as a signal of the impending delivery of the US (Skinner, 1950), although findings suggesting that spontaneous recovery is observed even when test trials are inserted into the middle of a session seem inconsistent with that idea (Thomas and Sherman, 1986; Robbins, 1990). That is, even when handling cues are temporally remote and unlikely to signal US delivery, response recovery occurs upon reintroduction of the CS.

III. Theoretical accounts of extinction

Contemporary theories of extinction have been influenced heavily by observations of reinstatement, renewal, and spontaneous recovery. Thus, although the simplest account of extinction attributes the disappearance of responding to an erasure of previous learning about the significance of the CS (e.g., Rescorla and Wagner, 1972;

Wagner and Rescorla, 1972), an erasure mechanism is considered by most investigators to be untenable because it does not easily account for recovery phenomena.

A popular alternative is one in which original learning emerges from extinction relatively intact, but is counteracted by a second learning process that accrues over the course of extinction training. In the context of associative theory, this second learning process is referred to as "inhibitory" learning, as opposed to the original "excitatory" learning that occurred during CS–US pairings. These two types of learning work at cross-purposes in terms of their tendency to stimulate or oppose, respectively, fear output (e.g., Konorski, 1948; Wagner, 1981; Bouton, 1993). Stated in different terms, the CS emerges from extinction training with two meanings: following acquisition, the CS signals that the US is coming, and following extinction, the CS signals that the US will be withheld (Bouton, 1993).

In order to account for recovery of fear following extinction, many of these sorts of "new learning" accounts propose that the inhibitory learning that accrues in extinction is not always expressed, either because it is particularly "fragile" or subject to disruption (Pavlov, 1927) or because it is gated by context, where "context" is defined broadly to include temporal and interoceptive cues, as well as spatial ones (Bouton, 1993). That is, following extinction, the meaning of the CS is disambiguated by contextual cues, such that extinction-appropriate behavior (no fear) is expressed within the temporal and spatial context of extinction training, whereas acquisition-appropriate behavior (fear) is expressed at other times and in other places.

IV. Facilitation of extinction by D-cycloserine

Extinction has attracted the attention not only of psychologists but also of neuroscientists as well, and in recent years great strides have been made in dissecting the neural mechanisms of the development, expression, and consolidation of extinction memory (for a review see Myers and Davis, 2007). Among the most thoroughly investigated aspects of the neurobiology of fear extinction is the involvement of glutamate, the major excitatory neurotransmitter in the mammalian brain, acting at glutamate receptors of the N-methyl-D-aspartate (NMDA) subtype (henceforth referred to as "NMDA receptors").

IV.A. Extinction of conditioned fear in rodents

Several studies have shown that high-frequency stimulation of amygdala afferents in vitro (Chapman et al., 1990; Clugnet and LeDoux, 1990; Huang and Kandel, 1998) or exposure to tone–shock pairings in behaving animals (McKernan and Shinnick-Gallagher, 1997; Rogan et al., 1997) results in long-term potentiation (LTP) of neuro-transmission at amygdala synapses. Both amygdalar LTP and the acquisition of conditioned fear are blocked by application of NMDA receptor antagonists prior to LTP induction (Watanabe et al., 1995; Lee et al., 2002) or behavioral training (Miserendino et al., 1990).

Fear extinction also depends on NMDA receptors within the basolateral amygdala. Falls et al. (1992) reported that intra-amygdala infusions of the NMDA receptor antagonist D,L-2-amino-5-phosphonovaleric acid (AP5) prior to extinction training dose-dependently blocked extinction of fear-potentiated startle. Additional experiments indicated that this impairment could not be attributed to an effect on NMDA receptors outside the amygdala, to damage or destruction of the amygdala, or to an impairment of sensory transmission during extinction training. A similar blockade of extinction of contextual fear conditioning, inhibitory avoidance, and eyeblink conditioning also has been reported with both systemic and localized administration of AP5 and other NMDA receptor antagonists (Kehoe et al., 1996; Lee and Kim, 1998; Szapiro et al., 2003), and additional studies have confirmed that these effects cannot be explained by state dependency (Cox and Westbrook, 1994; Baker and Azorlosa, 1996). Blockade of NMDA receptors immediately after extinction training also impairs extinction under some circumstances, suggesting that NMDA-receptor-mediated transmission may

be important for the consolidation of extinction memory (Santini et al., 2001; Szapiro et al., 2003; Bevilaqua et al., 2006).

In light of these findings, the question arose as to whether it would be possible to improve extinction by enhancing the functioning of the NMDA receptor. D-cycloserine (DCS) is a partial agonist that binds to the NMDA receptor complex in such a way that the functioning of the receptor is facilitated. In a series of experiments conducted very similarly to those of Falls et al. (1992), Walker et al. (2002) administered DCS either systemically or directly into the basolateral amygdala prior to extinction training and then tested retention of extinction the next day without administering any more of the drug. DCS dose-dependently enhanced extinction of fear-potentiated startle in rats exposed to lights in the absence of shock but not in rats that did not receive extinction training (Fig. 2). This indicated that the drug's facilitatory effect was specific to extinction and did not result from a general dampening of fear expression. Consistent with these findings, DCS administered either systemically or directly into the amygdala also facilitates extinction of conditioned freezing (Ledgerwood et al., 2003; Bertotto et al., 2006; Lee et al., 2006) and conditioned suppression of bar pressing (Woods and Bouton, 2006). Interestingly, DCS still works when given up to about 3 h after extinction training, suggesting that it acts upon extinction memory consolidation (Ledgerwood et al., 2003).

The mechanism by which DCS facilitates extinction is controversial. Among the possibilities that have been considered are that (1) DCS enhances inhibitory learning that normally occurs in extinction; (2) DCS fundamentally alters the mechanism of extinction, such that it causes erasure of fear memory; and (3) DCS modulates learning about the experimental context. However, none of these mechanisms is able to account for all of the available data. Potentially supporting the erasure hypothesis, for example, is an observation that DCS reduces the ability of unsignaled US presentations to disrupt extinction through reinstatement (Ledgerwood et al., 2004). However, DCS-facilitated extinction exhibits normal renewal following a shift to a different context

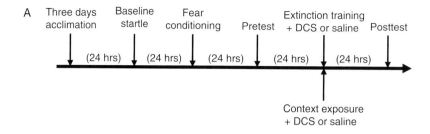

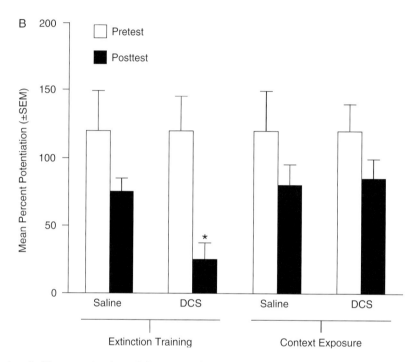

Fig. 2. D-cycloserine facilitates extinction of fear-potentiated startle in rats. Shown is mean percent potentiation of startle in the presence of the light CS, relative to startle in the absence of the light. (A) At 24 h intervals, rats were exposed to light-footshock pairings; a pretest of fear-potentiated startle to the light; 30 non-reinforced light exposures (extinction training) or the context without light presentations (context exposure); and a post-test. Saline or DCS (15 mg/kg, i.p.) was administered 30 min prior to extinction training or context exposure. (B) Fear-potentiated startle was significantly lower in rats that received DCS plus extinction training compared with rats that received saline plus extinction training. Fear-potentiated startle was not affected by DCS in rats that did not receive extinction training. *$p < 0.05$ versus saline plus extinction training. Adapted from Walker et al. (2002), with permission of the Society for Neuroscience.

after extinction training (Woods and Bouton, 2006), indicating that fear memory at least partially endures. Woods and Bouton (2006) suggested that DCS might facilitate the development of conditioned inhibition to the context during extinction training – that is, the context in which DCS-facilitated extinction training occurs might become a safety signal, or a predictor of the absence of shock. This type of mechanism could account for both the lack of reinstatement and normal renewal observed following DCS-facilitated extinction, since reinstatement depends critically on the development of context-US associations, whereas renewal reflects a more modulatory type of contextual learning that proceeds independently of explicit contextual learning (Bouton and

Swartzentruber, 1986). This account also predicts generalization of DCS-facilitated extinction to comparably fear conditioned but non-extinguished cues (Ledgerwood et al., 2005), but runs into difficulty in explaining the observation that context fear reacquisition is not retarded following DCS-facilitated extinction (Ledgerwood et al., 2005).

Further complicating matters are two studies examining the neural mechanisms of DCS effect. Yang and Lu (2005) reported modest increases in both phosphorylated mitogen-activated protein kinase (pMAPK) and phosphorylated Akt (pAkt) within the basolateral amygdala following exposure to a behaviorally subthreshold extinction training protocol, and significantly larger increases in pMAPK and pAkt following exposure to the same protocol after administration of D-cycloserine. This suggests that DCS potentiates activation within pathways normally engaged in extinction. Consistent with this, extinction in the presence or absence of DCS is blocked by administration of inhibitors of MAPK (Lu et al., 2001; Yang and Lu, 2005) or PI3 kinase (which is upstream of Akt) (Chen et al., 2005; Yang and Lu, 2005). On the other hand, Mao et al. (2006) found that DCS causes a reversal of an acquisition-induced increase in the expression of the GluR1 subunit of the alpha-amino-3-hydroxy-5-methyl-4-isoxazolepropionic acid (AMPA) glutamate receptor within the basolateral amygdala, and facilitates the induction of synaptic depotentiation (defined as a physiological reversal of long-term potentiation) in amygdala slices (Mao et al., 2006), suggesting that DCS causes erasure of fear memory.

IV.B. Exposure therapy to treat pathological fear in humans

Fear- and anxiety-related disorders such as phobias and post-traumatic stress disorder (PTSD) seem to be disorders of fear regulation in which inhibition of fear is absent or insufficient in situations that are patently safe (Rothbaum and Davis, 2003). In this regard, the study of the mechanisms of fear inhibition and identification of behavioral or pharmacological interventions to facilitate inhibitory learning in rodent models can inform clinical interventions for these sorts of disorders in clinical populations. Procedurally, extinction is very similar to several types of exposure-based psychotherapeutic treatments and thus has a great deal of face validity. Exposure therapy, for example, involves exposure to the feared object or situation in the absence of any danger, coupled with reassurance and soothing from the therapist to reduce anxiety.

In light of these considerations, it is not surprising that significant progress has been made in bringing insights gained in the laboratory to bear on clinical practice. A case in point is the facilitation of exposure therapy for anxiety disorders by D-cycloserine. Because DCS has been FDA-approved for some time as an antibiotic treatment for tuberculosis at high doses, clinical studies examining the utility of this compound in humans were fairly easily and quickly set up. Although the antibiotic effects have nothing to do with DCS's ability to facilitate extinction, its widespread use with minimal side effects when given acutely allowed it to be used as an adjunct to psychotherapy right away.

The first of the DCS clinical studies was conducted by members of our laboratory in collaboration with Barbara Rothbaum, Kerry Ressler, and colleagues, and examined the ability of DCS to enhance exposure therapy for acrophobia, or fear of heights, using the most optimally controlled form of psychotherapy available: virtual reality exposure (VRE) therapy (Ressler et al., 2004). In VRE a person is exposed to a 3D computer-generated virtual reality image of their feared object or situation. This is ideal for clinical research because exposure and testing is identical between patients, is well-controlled by the therapist, and occurs within the spatial and temporal confines of the limited therapy environment (Rothbaum et al., 1995). VRE has proved to be successful for the treatment of specific phobias as well as PTSD (Rothbaum et al., 1995, 2000, 2001).

In the DCS study the virtual reality situation involved a glass elevator ascending to progressively higher floors of a virtual hotel. Previous work had shown improvements on all acrophobia outcome measures for treated as compared to untreated groups after seven weekly therapy sessions using this scenario (Rothbaum et al., 1995). Volunteer participants who met DSM-IV criteria for acrophobia were assigned randomly to groups receiving placebo or one of two doses of DCS (50 or 500 mg) in conjunction with VRE. Participants underwent a suboptimal amount of exposure therapy for acrophobia (two VRE sessions) (Rothbaum et al., 1995) and were instructed to take a single dose of study medication 2–4 h before each session (sessions were separated by 1–2 weeks; mean 12.9 days). Post-treatment assessments were performed 1–2 weeks after therapy.

Similar to the rats in the preclinical work, participants receiving either dose of DCS exhibited significantly more improvement than did participants receiving placebo, with no statistical difference between the two doses. DCS-treated patients exhibited less fear and fewer skin conductance fluctuations at the 1-week follow-up in the VRE. Overall acrophobia symptoms were significantly lower at the 3-month follow-up, and self-reports of exposure to heights in the "real world" increased, suggesting decreased avoidance. Finally, self-ratings of improvement were significantly higher in the DCS-treated subjects (Fig. 3).

Recently it has been reported that social anxiety disorder (SAD) with public-speaking anxiety also responds to exposure therapy and that its treatment is facilitated by DCS (Hofmann et al., 2006). In this study participants were assigned randomly to groups receiving placebo or DCS prior to each of four individual or group therapy sessions in which participants were asked to engage in increasingly challenging public-speaking episodes (speaking in front of other group participants, an audience composed of research confederates, and a video camera). At the conclusion of therapy and at a 1-month follow-up, participants receiving DCS showed significantly larger improvements relative to participants receiving placebo, as measured by clinician-administered and self-report instruments. This extends the usefulness of DCS as a therapeutic agent to a disorder (SAD) that is more prevalent and arguably more debilitating than acrophobia.

There has been one report of a failure to obtain a facilitation of exposure therapy with D-cycloserine and another report of a failure to facilitate experimental extinction in a laboratory situation in humans. Guastella et al. (2006a) randomly assigned undergraduates attaining high, but generally sub-clinical, scores on spider phobia indices to groups receiving DCS or placebo, and performed a single session of exposure therapy involving a graded sequence of approach toward and contact with a large (8 cm) Australian spider. Two separate experiments, both double-blind, were performed in which participants received one of two doses of DCS (50 or 500 mg, as in Ressler et al., 2004) or placebo prior to exposure therapy and were given optimal or sub-optimal exposure (i.e., exposure that produced marked or minimal improvement, respectively, in the placebo group). Multiple measures were taken including heart rate, subjective units of discomfort, and approach proximity during exposure and at two post-exposure assessments occurring immediately (on the same day) or 3.5 weeks after exposure therapy. In no case was there an enhancement of therapeutic efficacy by DCS. There were several procedural differences between this study and those of Ressler et al. (2004) and Hofmann et al. (2006) that may have contributed to the failure to replicate the findings of those earlier studies, although the use of a non-clinical population and/or possible floor effects may be the most significant factors. Additional work is required to determine if the therapeutic efficacy of DCS is observable only in severely impaired clinical populations, as Guastella et al. (2006a) suggest. Perhaps consistent with this general idea, a relatively low dose of DCS recently was found to be effective at facilitating extinction in rats that were undergoing alcohol withdrawal as compared to controls (Bertotto et al., 2006).

V. Emerging evidence for multiple mechanisms of extinction

While it is generally accepted that extinction is, under most circumstances, a new learning process as opposed to an erasure of fear memory, recent work in our laboratory and others has raised the possibility that extinction may not be a unitary phenomenon. For example, we (Myers et al., 2006)

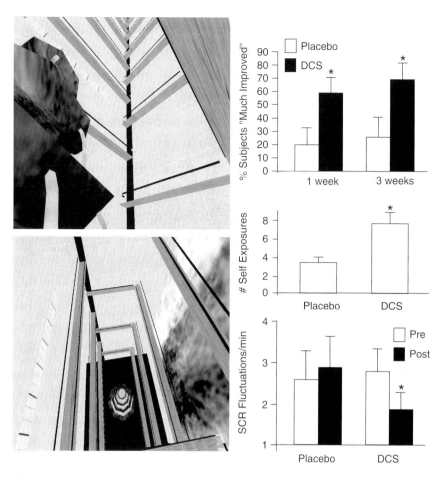

Fig. 3. D-cycloserine facilitates exposure therapy for acrophobics using a computer-generated virtual reality glass elevator. Participants were administered a tablet containing either 50 or 500 mg DCS, or were given a placebo, prior to each of two sessions in the virtual reality environment (left panels). Following treatment, those participants receiving DCS reported both more improvement and increased numbers of self-exposures to heights, and exhibited fewer spontaneous skin conductance response (SCR) fluctuations per minute during an assessment in the virtual environment than did participants receiving placebo (right panels). $*p < 0.05$ versus placebo. Adapted from Ressler et al. (2004), with permission of the American Medical Association.

have suggested that extinction may be mediated by either unlearning or new learning, depending on the time after fear conditioning when extinction training is initiated. In this study, different groups of rats were fear conditioned and then given extinction training either 10 min, or 1, 24, or 72 h after acquisition and their susceptibility to recovery of fear through reinstatement (following exposure to unsignaled foot shocks), renewal (following a shift of context), and spontaneous recovery (after an interval of 3 weeks had elapsed) was evaluated. Animals extinguished at 72 h

exhibited robust recovery in all cases, whereas animals extinguished at 10 min exhibited no recovery in any of them (Fig. 4). Animals extinguished at intermediate intervals exhibited intermediate recovery. In many cases extinction at the shortest time point was less complete than that at the longest time point (cf. Cain et al., 2005; Cammarota et al., 2005; Maren, 2005), but this did not seem to explain the lack of recovery in the 10-min group. That is, even in an experiment in which animals extinguished at 10 min demonstrably were not at a measurement ceiling, they were

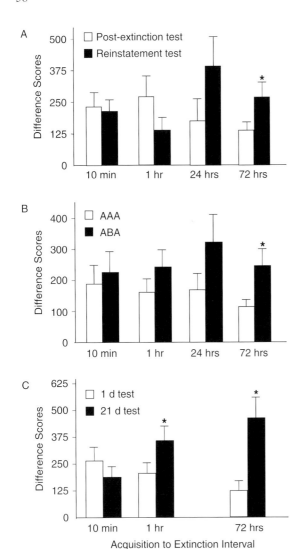

Fig. 4. Extinction of fear-potentiated startle is susceptible to recovery only if the interval between acquisition
and extinction training is sufficiently long. Shown are
mean difference scores (startle amplitude in the presence
of the light CS minus startle amplitude in the absence of
the light). In three experiments, rats were exposed to 15
light-footshock pairings (acquisition) followed 10 min
and 1, 24, or 72 h later by 90 lights in the absence of
shock (extinction training). They then were tested for
recovery of fear through reinstatement, renewal, and
spontaneous recovery. (A) In the reinstatement experiment, rats were given a post-extinction test of fear-
potentiated startle, then were exposed to five unsignaled
footshock presentations and retested for reinstatement.
Only rats in the 72 h group exhibited significant
reinstatement. (B) In the renewal experiment, half of
the rats of each group were extinguished in the same

resistant to reinstatement. Because recovery effects
have served as the impetus for new learning
accounts of extinction, the lack of recovery in the
short interval group would seem to be explained
most parsimoniously in terms of erasure of
conditioned fear and/or prevention of consolidation of the fear memory.

Evidence is emerging for a neurobiological
difference between short- and long-interval extinction as well. Cain et al. (2005) reported that
immediate extinction is not affected by the L-type
voltage-gated calcium channel (L-VGCC) inhibitor
nifedipine, whereas delayed extinction is impaired.
Mao et al. (2006) found that fear extinction
initiated 1 h after fear acquisition reversed a fear
conditioning-induced increase in the expression of
the GluR1 subunit of the AMPA receptor within
the amygdala, whereas this reversal did not occur
when extinction was initiated 24 h after acquisition.
(Intriguingly, as we have seen, 24 h extinction in the
presence of D-cycloserine did reverse the increase in
GluR1 expression, suggesting that DCS-facilitated
long-interval extinction may be similar mechanistically to short-interval extinction.)

The apparent difference in the mechanisms of
short- and long-interval extinction may be under-
standable in the context of consolidation theory,
which holds that memories, once acquired,
undergo a time-dependent process by which they
are converted from a short-term, labile state into a
long-term, permanent state (McGaugh, 2000).
When extinction training is initiated 10 min after
acquisition, fear memory has only just begun to

context in which acquisition and test occurred (AAA),
and the other half was extinguished in a different context
(ABA). Rats were tested for fear-potentiated startle 24 h
after extinction training. Only rats in the 72 h group
exhibited significant renewal. (C) In the spontaneous
recovery experiment, half of the rats of each group were
tested for fear-potentiated startle 1 day after extinction
training, and the other half was tested 21 days after
extinction training. The 24 h extinction interval group
was omitted in this experiment. Rats in the 72 and 1 h
groups, but not in the 10 min group, exhibited significant
spontaneous recovery. $^*p < 0.05$ recovery versus the
appropriate comparison condition. Adapted from
Myers et al. (2006), with permission of Cold Spring
Harbor Laboratory Press.

consolidate, whereas when extinction training is initiated 72 h after acquisition, consolidation probably is complete or close to it. This difference in the consolidation state of fear memory at the two time points may offer a different substrate for extinction to act upon, and thus may be a critical factor in determining the mechanism of extinction (Cain et al., 2005; Sotres-Bayon et al., 2006). A similar idea has been discussed in the literature on memory reconsolidation, where similar time-dependent mechanistic changes have been reported by some investigators (Dudai and Eisenberg, 2004; Kemenes et al., 2006).

Clinically, the finding that short-interval extinction is resistant to recovery effects might imply that intervention shortly following trauma will be more effective in reducing fear and counteracting the development of disorders such as PTSD than is delayed intervention. Of course, this implication rests on the assumption that humans exhibit a similar sensitivity to extinction training interval as do rats, and it is not yet clear whether this is true. Some response measures, such as conditioned skin conductance and cognitive awareness of experimental contingencies, exhibit reinstatement and renewal even when extinction training occurs immediately upon the termination of acquisition (LaBar and Phelps, 2005; Milad et al., 2005), whereas fear-potentiated startle in humans, as in rats, exhibits spontaneous recovery only when acquisition and extinction training are temporally separated (Norrholm et al., in preparation). Additional research is needed to make sense of these discrepancies, which could relate to differences among response measures in terms of the degree to which they tap into arousal and explicit versus implicit memory processes, among other factors. Generally speaking, however, the implication is that intervention soon after trauma may be useful in suppressing pathological fear responses, assuming the intervention is structured in such a way as to produce significant extinction over the course of the session (as contrasted with relatively brief, unstructured sorts of early interventions, such as debriefing, that have not proved to be effective) (Rose and Bisson, 1998), and, perhaps, assuming the level of fear exhibited at the outset of the session is not too great (cf. Maren and Chang, 2006).

VI. Conclusion

The experimental analysis of fear extinction has been, and continues to be, a success story. Because of the availability of intensively studied fear acquisition paradigms for which the underlying neural circuitry is well understood, the literature on fear extinction has expanded at an incredible rate. Moreover, because of the validity of extinction as a model system for therapeutic interventions for fear- and anxiety-related disorders, the "bench to bedside" translation of this basic research has occurred very rapidly. Ongoing efforts will almost certainly provide further insights into the conduct of clinical interventions, affording this literature a great deal of practical utility in addition to its obvious merits from a basic science perspective. In fact, some have said that the use of cognitive enhancers to facilitate exposure-based psychotherapy could represent a paradigm shift in psychiatry. Thus, instead of treating the symptoms of anxiety pharmacologically, this strategy attempts to improve the extinction learning that occurs during cognitive behavioral therapy.

Acknowledgments

This work was supported by Kirchstein National Research Service Award Individual Fellowship 1 F32MH77420 (K.M.M.); National Institute of Mental Health grants MH47840, MH57250, and MH59906 (M.D.); the Science and Technology Center (The Center for Behavioral Neuroscience of the National Science Foundation under Agreement No. IBN-9876754); and the Yerkes Base Grant.

Dr. Davis has submitted a patent for the use of D-cycloserine for the specific enhancement of learning during psychotherapy and is entitled to royalties from Therapade in the event this invention is commercialized. The terms of these arrangements have been reviewed and approved by Emory University in accordance with its conflict of interest policies.

References

Baker, J.D. and Azorlosa, J.L. (1996) The NMDA antagonist MK-801 blocks the extinction of Pavlovian fear conditioning. Behav. Neurosci., 110: 618–620.

Bass, M.J. and Hull, C.L. (1934) The irradiation of a tactile conditional reflex in man. J. Comp. Psychol., 17: 47–65.

Bertotto, M.E., Bustos, S.G., Molina, V.A. and Martijena, I.D. (2006) Influence of ethanol withdrawal on fear memory: effect of D-cycloserine. Neuroscience, 142: 979–990.

Bevilaqua, L.R., Bonini, J.S., Rossato, J.I., Izquierdo, L.A., Cammarota, M. and Izquierdo, I. (2006) The entorhinal cortex plays a role in extinction. Neurobiol. Learn. Mem., 85: 192–197.

Bouton, M.E. (1993) Context, time, and memory retrieval in the interference paradigms of Pavlovian learning. Psychol. Bull., 114: 80–99.

Bouton, M.E. (2004) Context and behavioral processes in extinction. Learn. Mem., 11: 485–494.

Bouton, M.E. and Bolles, R.C. (1979a) Contextual control of the extinction of conditioned fear. Learn. Motiv., 10: 455–466.

Bouton, M.E. and Bolles, R.C. (1979b) Role of conditioned contextual stimuli in reinstatement of extinguished fear. J. Exp. Psychol. Anim. Behav. Process., 5: 368–378.

Bouton, M.E., Garcia-Gutierrez, A., Zilski, J. and Moody, E.W. (2006) Extinction in multiple contexts does not necessarily make extinction less vulnerable to relapse. Behav. Res. Ther., 44: 983–994.

Bouton, M.E. and King, D.A. (1983) Contextual control of conditioned fear: tests for the associative value of the context. J. Exp. Psychol. Anim. Behav. Process., 9: 248–256.

Bouton, M.E. and Swartzentruber, D. (1986) Analysis of the associative and occasion-setting properties of contexts participating in a Pavlovian discrimination. J. Exp. Psychol. Anim. Behav. Process., 12: 333–350.

Cain, C.K., Godsil, B.P., Jami, S. and Barad, M. (2005) The L-type calcium channel. blocker nifedipine impairs extinction, but not reduced contingency effects, in mice. Learn. Mem., 12: 277–284.

Cammarota, M., Bevilaqua, L.R.M., Rossato, J.I., Ramirez, M., Medina, J.H. and Izquierdo, I. (2005) Relationship between short- and long-term memory and short- and long-term extinction. Neurobiol. Learn. Mem., 84: 25–32.

Chapman, P.F., Kairiss, E.W., Keenan, C.L. and Brown, T.H. (1990) Long-term synaptic potentiation in the amygdala. Synapse, 6: 271–278.

Chelonis, J.J., Calton, J.L., Hart, J.A. and Schachtman, T.R. (1999) Attenuation of the renewal effect by extinction in multiple contexts. Learn. Motiv., 30: 1–14.

Chen, X., Garelick, M.G., Wang, H., Lil, V., Athos, J. and Storm, D.R. (2005) PI3 kinase signaling is required for retrieval and extinction of contextual memory. Nat. Neurosci., 8: 925–931.

Clugnet, M.C. and LeDoux, J.E. (1990) Synaptic plasticity in fear conditioning circuits: induction of LTP in the lateral nucleus of the amygdala by stimulation of the medial geniculate body. J. Neurosci., 10: 2818–2824.

Cox, J. and Westbrook, R.F. (1994) The NMDA receptor antagonist MK-801 blocks acquisition and extinction of conditioned hypoalgesia responses in the rat. Q. J. Exp. Psychol. B, 47: 187–210.

Davis, M. (2000) The role of the amygdala in conditioned and unconditioned fear and anxietyIn: Aggleton, J.P. (Ed.), The Amygdala, Oxford University Press, Oxford, UK, Vol. 2, pp. 213–287.

Delamater, A.R. (2004) Experimental extinction in Pavlovian conditioning: behavioural and neuroscience perspectives. Q. J. Exp. Psychol. B, 57: 97–132.

Denniston, J.C., Chang, R.C. and Miller, R.R. (2003) Massive extinction treatment attenuates the renewal effect. Learn. Motiv., 34: 68–86.

Dubin, W.J. and Levis, D.J. (1974) Generalization of extinction gradients: a systematic analysis. J. Exp. Psychol., 100: 403–412.

Dudai, Y. and Eisenberg, M. (2004) Rites of passage of the engram: reconsolidation and the lingering consolidation hypothesis. Neuron, 44: 93–100.

Falls, W.A., Miserendino, M.J. and Davis, M. (1992) Extinction of fear-potentiated startle: blockade by infusion of an NMDA antagonist into the amygdala. J. Neurosci., 12: 854–863.

Gale, G.D., Anagnostaras, S.G., Godsil, B.P., Mitchell, S., Nozawa, T., Sage, J.R., Wiltgen, B. and Fanselow, M.S. (2004) Role of the basolateral amygdala in the storage of fear memories across the adult lifetime of rats. J. Neurosci., 24: 3810–3815.

Guastella, A.J., Dadds, M.R., Lovibond, P.F., Mitchell, P. and Richardson, R. (2006a) A randomized controlled trial of the effect of D-cycloserine on exposure therapy for spider fear. J. Psychiatr. Res., 41: 466–471.

Gunther, L.M., Denniston, J.C. and Miller, R.R. (1998) Conducting exposure treatment in multiple contexts can prevent relapse. Behav. Res. Ther., 36: 75–91.

Harris, J.A., Jones, M.L., Bailey, G.K. and Westbrook, R.F. (2000) Contextual control over conditioned responding in an extinction paradigm. J. Exp. Psychol. Anim. Behav. Process., 26: 174–185.

Hendry, J.S. (1982) Summation of undetected excitation following extinction of the CER. Anim. Learn. Behav., 10: 476–482.

Hofmann, S.G., Meuret, A.E., Smits, J.A., Simon, N.M., Pollack, M.H., Eisenmenger, K., Shiekh, M. and Otto, M.W. (2006) Augmentation of exposure therapy with D-cycloserine for social anxiety disorder. Arch. Gen. Psychiatry, 63: 298–304.

Hovland, C.I. (1949) Comments on Littman's conditioned generalization of the galvanic skin reaction to tones. J. Exp. Psychol., 39: 892–896.

Huang, Y.Y. and Kandel, E.R. (1998) Postsynaptic induction and PKA-dependent expression of LTP in the lateral amygdala. Neuron, 21: 169–178.

Kasprow, W.J., Schachtman, T.R., Cacheiro, H. and Miller, R.R. (1984) Extinction does not depend on degradation of event memories. Bull. Psychon. Soc., 22: 95–98.

Kehoe, E.J., Macrae, M. and Hutchinson, C.L. (1996) MK-801 protects conditioned response from extinction in the rabbit nictitating membrane preparation. Psychobiology, 24: 127–135.

Kemenes, G., Kemenes, I., Michel, M., Papp, A. and Muller, U. (2006) Phase-dependent molecular requirements for memory reconsolidation: differential roles for protein synthesis and protein kinase A activity. J. Neurosci., 26: 6298–6302.

Konorski, J. (1948) Conditioned reflexes and neuronal organization. Cambridge University Press, London.

LaBar, K.S. and Phelps, E.A. (2005) Reinstatement of conditioned fear in humans is context dependent and impaired in amnesia. Behav. Neurosci., 119: 677–686.

Ledgerwood, L., Richardson, R. and Cranney, J. (2003) D-cycloserine facilitates extinction of conditioned fear as assessed by freezing in rats. Behav. Neurosci., 117: 341–349.

Ledgerwood, L., Richardson, R. and Cranney, J. (2004) D-cycloserine and the facilitation of extinction of conditioned fear: consequences for reinstatement. Behav. Neurosci., 118: 505–513.

Ledgerwood, L., Richardson, R. and Cranney, J. (2005) D-cycloserine facilitates extinction of learned fear: effects on reacquisition and generalized extinction. Biol. Psychiatry, 57: 841–847.

Lee, J.L., Milton, A.L. and Everitt, B.J. (2006) Reconsolidation and extinction of conditioned fear: inhibition and potentiation. J. Neurosci., 26: 10051–10056.

Lee, H. and Kim, J.J. (1998) Amygdalar NMDA receptors are critical for new fear learning in previously fear-conditioned rats. J. Neurosci., 18: 8444–8454.

Lee, O., Lee, C.J. and Choi, S. (2002) Induction mechanisms for L-LTP at thalamic input synapses to the lateral amygdala: requirement of mGluR5 activation. Neuroreport, 13: 685–691.

Lu, K.T., Walker, D.L. and Davis, M. (2001) Mitogen-activated protein kinase cascade in the basolateral nucleus of amygdala is involved in extinction of fear-potentiated startle. J. Neurosci., 21: RC162.

Mackintosh, N.J. (1974) The psychology of animal learning. Academic Press, New York.

Mao, S.C., Hsiao, Y.H. and Gean, P.W. (2006) Extinction training in conjunction with a partial

agonist of the glycine site on the NMDA receptor erases memory trace. J. Neurosci., 26: 8892–8899.

Maren, S. (2005) Building and burying fear memories in the brain. Neuroscientist, 11: 89–99.

Maren, S. and Chang, C.H. (2006) Recent fear is resistant to extinction. Proc. Natl. Acad. Sci. USA, 103: 18020–18025.

McGaugh, J.L. (2000) Memory – a century of consolidation. Science, 287: 248–251.

McKernan, M.G. and Shinnick-Gallagher, P. (1997) Fear conditioning induces a lasting potentiation of synaptic currents in vitro. Nature, 390: 607–611.

Milad, M.R., Orr, S.P., Pitman, R.K. and Rauch, S.L. (2005) Context modulation of memory for fear extinction in humans. Psychophysiology, 42: 456–464.

Miserendino, M.J., Sananes, C.B., Melia, K.R. and Davis, M. (1990) Blocking of acquisition but not expression of conditioned fear-potentiated startle by NMDA antagonists in the amygdala. Nature, 345: 716–718.

Myers, K.M. and Davis, M. (2007) Mechanisms of fear extinction. Mol. Psychiatry, 12: 120–150.

Myers, K.M., Ressler, K.J. and Davis, M. (2006) Different mechanisms of fear extinction dependent on length of time since fear acquisition. Learn. Mem., 13: 216–223.

Neumann, D.L., Lipp, O.V. and Cory, S.E. (2006) Conducting extinction in multiple contexts does not necessarily attenuate the renewal of shock expectancy in a fear-conditioning procedure with humans. Behav. Res. Ther., 45: 385–394.

Pavlov, I.P. (1927) Conditioned Reflexes. Dover Publications, Inc., New York, NY.

Quirk, G.J. (2002) Memory for extinction of conditioned fear is long-lasting and persists following spontaneous recovery. Learn. Mem., 9: 402–407.

Rauhut, A.S., Thomas, B.L. and Ayres, J.J. (2001) Treatments that weaken Pavlovian conditioned fear and thwart its renewal in rats: implications for treating human phobias. J. Exp. Psychol. Anim. Behav. Process., 27: 99–114.

Reberg, D. (1972) Compound tests for excitation in early acquisition and after prolonged extinction of conditioned suppression. Learn. Motiv., 3: 246–248.

Rescorla, R.A. (2001) Experimental extinction. In: Mowrer, R.R. and Klein, S. (Eds.), Handbook of Contemporary Learning Theories. Erlbaum, Mahwah, NJ, pp. 119–154.

Rescorla, R.A. and Heth, C.D. (1975) Reinstatement of fear to an extinguished conditioned stimulus. J. Exp. Psychol. Anim. Behav. Process., 1: 88–96.

Rescorla, R.A. and Wagner, A.R. (1972) A theory of Pavlovian conditioning: variations in the effectiveness of reinforcement and nonreinforcement. In: Prokasy, W.F. and Black, A.H. (Eds.), Classical Conditioning II: Current Research and Theory. Appleton-Century-Crofts, New York.

Ressler, K.J., Rothbaum, B.O., Tannenbaum, L., Anderson, P., Graap, K., Zimand, E., Hodges, L. and Davis, M. (2004) Cognitive enhancers as adjuncts to psychotherapy: use of D-cycloserine in phobic individuals to facilitate extinction of fear. Arch. Gen. Psychiatry, 61: 1136–1144.

Richards, R.W. and Sargent, D.M. (1984) The order of presentation of conditioned stimuli during extinction. Anim. Learn. Behav., 11: 229–236.

Robbins, S.J. (1990) Mechanisms underlying spontaneous recovery in autoshaping. J. Exp. Psychol. Anim. Behav. Process., 16: 235–249.

Rodrigues, S.M., Schafe, G.E. and LeDoux, J.E. (2004) Molecular mechanisms underlying emotional learning and memory in the lateral amygdala. Neuron, 44: 75–91.

Rogan, M.T., Staubli, U.V. and LeDoux, J.E. (1997) Fear conditioning induces associative long-term potentiation in the amygdala. Nature, 390: 604–607.

Rose, S. and Bisson, J. (1998) Brief early psychological interventions following trauma: a systematic review of the literature. J. Trauma. Stress., 11: 697–710.

Rothbaum, B.O. and Davis, M. (2003) Applying learning principles to the treatment of post-trauma reactions. Ann. N.Y. Acad. Sci., 1008: 112–121.

Rothbaum, B.O., Hodges, L., Smith, S., Lee, J.H. and Price, L. (2000) A controlled study of virtual reality exposure therapy for the fear of flying. J. Consult. Clin. Psychol., 68: 1020–1026.

Rothbaum, B.O., Hodges, L.F., Kooper, R., Opdyke, D., Williford, J.S. and North, M. (1995) Effectiveness of computer-generated (virtual reality) graded exposure in the treatment of acrophobia. Am. J. Psychiatry, 152: 626–628.

Rothbaum, B.O., Hodges, L.F., Ready, D., Graap, K. and Alarcon, R.D. (2001) Virtual reality exposure therapy for Vietnam veterans with posttraumatic stress disorder. J. Clin. Psychiatry, 62: 617–622.

Santini, E., Muller, R.U. and Quirk, G.J. (2001) Consolidation of extinction learning involves transfer from NMDA-independent to NMDA-dependent memory. J. Neurosci., 21: 9009–9017.

Skinner, B.F. (1950) Are theories of learning necessary? Psychol. Rev., 57: 193–216.

Sotres-Bayon, F., Cain, C.K. and LeDoux, J.E. (2006) Brain mechanisms of fear extinction: historical perspectives on the contribution of prefrontal cortex. Biol. Psychiatry, 60: 329–336.

Szapiro, G., Vianna, M.R., McGaugh, J.L., Medina, J.H. and Izquierdo, I. (2003) The role of NMDA glutamate receptors, PKA, MAPK, and CAMKII in the hippocampus in extinction of conditioned fear. Hippocampus, 13: 53–58.

Thomas, D.R. and Sherman, L. (1986) An assessment of the role of handling cues in 'spontaneous recovery' after extinction. J. Exp. Anal. Behav., 46: 305–314.

Vervliet, B., Vansteenwegen, D., Baeyens, F., Hermans, D. and Eelen, P. (2005) Return of fear in a human differential conditioning paradigm caused by a stimulus change after extinction. Behav. Res. Ther., 43: 357–371.

Vervliet, B., Vansteenwegen, D. and Eelen, P. (2004) Generalization of extinguished skin conductance responding in human fear conditioning. Learn. Mem., 11: 555–558.

Wagner, A.R. (1981) SOP: a model of automatic memory processing in animal behavior. In: Miller, R.R. and Spear, N.E. (Eds.), Information Processing in Animals: Memory Mechanisms. Lawrence Erlbaum Associates, Hillsdale, NJ, pp. 5–47.

Wagner, A.R. and Rescorla, R.A. (1972) Inhibition in Pavlovian conditioning: application of a theory. In: Boakes, R.A. and Halliday, M.S. (Eds.), Inhibition and Learning. Academic Press, London, pp. 301–336.

Walker, D.L., Ressler, K.J., Lu, K.T. and Davis, M. (2002) Facilitation of conditioned fear extinction by systemic administration or intra-amygdala infusions of D-cycloserine as assessed with fear-potentiated startle in rats. J. Neurosci., 22: 2343–2351.

Watanabe, Y., Ikegaya, Y., Saito, H. and Abe, K. (1995) Roles of $GABA_A$, NMDA and muscarinic receptors in induction of long-term potentiation in the medial and lateral amygdala in vitro. Neurosci. Res., 21: 317–322.

Westbrook, R.F., Iordanova, M., McNally, G., Richardson, R. and Harris, J.A. (2002) Reinstatement of fear to an extinguished conditioned stimulus: two roles for context. J. Exp. Psychol. Anim. Behav. Process., 28: 97–110.

Woods, A.M. and Bouton, M.E. (2006) D-cycloserine facilitates extinction but does not eliminate renewal of the conditioned emotional response. Behav. Neurosci., 120: 1159–1162.

Yang, Y.L. and Lu, K.T. (2005) Facilitation of conditioned fear extinction by D-cycloserine is mediated by mitogen-activated protein kinase and phosphatidylinositol 3-kinase cascades and requires de novo protein synthesis in basolateral nucleus of amygdala. Neuroscience, 134: 247–260.

CHAPTER 2.4

Defensive behaviors, fear, and anxiety

D. Caroline Blanchard[1] and Robert J. Blanchard[2,*]

[1]*Department of Genetics and Molecular Biology, John A. Burns School of Medicine; and Pacific Biosciences Research Center, University of Hawaii at Manoa, Honolulu, HI, USA*
[2]*Department of Psychology, University of Hawaii at Manoa, Honolulu, HI, USA*

Abstract: Defensive behaviors are a set of responses to threat stimuli and situations that have evolved on the basis of their adaptiveness in reducing harm to the threatened organism. These behaviors are highly conserved across mammals and rapidly conditioned to stimuli and situations associated with threat. Because the effectiveness of particular defenses may depend on features of the threat stimulus and the situation in which it is encountered, the presence of these "enabling" features strongly modulates the strength of specific responses, resulting in highly consistent patterns of defensive behavior under controlled conditions; and additionally suggesting a basic differentiation between fear-related defenses and anxiety-related defenses. Use of such controlled conditions indicates that particular defenses may be differentially sensitive to drugs effective against generalized anxiety disorder, and panic. Recent scenario studies suggest that normal humans show patterns of defense that are relatively similar to those of laboratory rodents, supporting the possibility that evolved/unconditioned defensive behaviors may be involved in some of the behavioral variability found in anxiety disorders.

Keywords: defense; defensive behaviors; threat stimuli; threat ambiguity; fear–anxiety distinction; flight; freezing; defensive threat and attack; risk assessment; human defensive behaviors; antipredator defensive behaviors; antipredator defense; enabling or expediting stimuli

I. Fear and anxiety

The word "fear", in a context indicating emotional responsivity to danger, first appeared in (middle) English in the thirteenth century. "Anxiety" has almost as ancient a lineage in the English language, appearing in the sixteenth century (Online Etymology Dictionary, 2007). Although definitions of anxiety frequently refer to fear, they contain the additional nuance of involving apprehension with regard to uncertain events. This view that, while both fear and anxiety are emotional responses to aversive events, anxiety is the response to potential, rather than clear and present threat, has been taken

up by a surprisingly diverse range of influential psychiatrists and psychologists, including both Freud (1930) and Skinner (Estes and Skinner, 1941).

A second component of the conceptualized division between fear and anxiety relates to the behaviors with which they are associated. The view that fear may be linked to and expressed in a pattern involving several different behaviors is a very old one. In an early report containing anecdotes of variable credibility, Thompson (1851) nonetheless offers this interesting analysis of flight- and terror-based immobility in animals: "Fear .... (has) the greatest influence on the lives of animals, as aids and excitements for their preservation; (it) impels them to shun a threatened danger by flight which terror disqualifies them from attempting…". In considerable contrast, anxiety has typically been

*Corresponding author. E-mail: blanchar@hawaii.edu

R.J. Blanchard, D.C. Blanchard, G. Griebel and D. Nutt (Eds.)
Handbook of Anxiety and Fear, Vol. 17
ISBN 978-0-444-53065-3

DOI: 10.1016/S1569-7339(07)00005-7

conceptualized in terms of subjective feelings such as apprehension or dread, associated with worry in which the individual's thoughts are focused on some (often poorly specified) potential or future bad outcome or event.

A final component of the fear/anxiety distinction, brought to the fore in modern psychiatry, is that fear is generally regarded as adaptive, while anxiety is generally regarded as maladaptive. There are no "Fear Disorders" in DSM-IV, while the categories of "Anxiety Disorders" expands with every new edition. This is despite the fact that phobias are, in terms of the ordinary distinction between the two, much closer to fear than to anxiety. The apparent underlying assumption, although perhaps nothing more than a matter of convenience, is that when what might otherwise be classified as fear is maladaptive, it falls under the rubric of anxiety.

This nomenclature, while doubtless based on a history in which the terms were initially used without precise definitions or even clear distinctions, reflects that anxiety tends to be applied when the source of threat is uncertain, ambiguous, or unrealistic; and the associated emotional response is subjectively unpleasant, pervasive (i.e., not linked to the actual presence of the threat), and typically involves a prominent cogitating or thought element focusing on the perceived threat. While both fear and anxiety may involve autonomic arousal, fear is the response to a realistic, often imminent, threat and it involves relatively discrete responses such as flight or avoidance.

These analyses initially represented ordinary usages, later encapsulated in dictionaries and more recently, and indirectly, conceptualized in terms of a number of categories of psychopathologies. What, however, is their biological reality? Are fear and anxiety different behavior patterns? What specific behaviors do they encompass? How can such behaviors be used to investigate the biology of these emotions, with the ultimate goal of understanding and treating relevant pathologies? The behaviors, neural systems, and pharmacology of fear/anxiety, with these concepts often not differentiated in terms of animal models, have been examined in a number of conditioning paradigms, with interesting and important results (see chapters by Fanselow and Ponnusamy; Myers and Davis,

and Cain and LeDoux, in this volume). More recently, a complementary, ethological, approach to the analysis of fear and anxiety has sought to analyze the defensive behaviors of several mammalian species in response to natural but non-painful threats such as (non-contacting) confrontation with a predator.

II. Defensive behaviors: what, when, where, and why?

II.A. What?

Defensive behaviors are a group of responses or response patterns elicited by threat. For animals of the vast majority of species these threat-responsive behaviors do not rely on specific experience, but instead are based on evolution. They are adaptive responses to threat stimuli and situations that are common in the evolutionary histories of the species that exhibit them, and they evolve through the differential survival/reproductive success that they afford to individuals that display them appropriately. As there is considerable, indeed overwhelming, consistency in the types of stimuli or factors that provide a direct threat to the bodily well-being of animals of different species, it is not surprising that a corresponding consistency is seen in the behaviors that are elicited in response to these threats.

There is no reason to believe that the full spectrum of defensive behaviors has been described. However, flight, avoidance, freezing, defensive threat, defensive attack, and risk assessment have been characterized in a variety of species (e.g., Blanchard, 1997), as have some other behaviors, for example, burying of novel, aversive, or potentially dangerous objects (Treit et al., 1981) that may be functionally related to one or more of the above-named defense patterns. Behaviors that warn potentially related conspecifics of danger, such as alarm cries, might also be considered under this category, with the proviso that they would be expected to occur more frequently in species in which related conspecifics typically live in close proximity (Litvin et al., 2006). Ceasing to do something that may direct the attention of an animate threat toward the defensive animal, for example, when rat pups cease separation/distress vocalizations in the presence of an adult male (Takahashi, 1992a,b), is also a common element of defense across many species and situations. Other defense-related behaviors, sometimes relatively species-specific (e.g., stotting) may been seen in wild animals in response to threat in natural situations (Caro, 1994). The functions of some of these are not clear, as the conditions of observation in free-living animals typically do not permit a very precise analysis of the relationship between features of the threat stimulus and situation, and these particular behaviors; or of the outcomes of these behaviors in terms of success or failure.

Although the category of defense remains somewhat open-ended, it is clear that the typical forms of defense are common to most if not all mammalian species (Hediger, 1968; Edmunds, 1974). While the term "species-specific" is commonly used as a modifier for "defensive behavior" it is simply incorrect. Even such rare actions as rolling up into a ball to present attackers with armor or spines are seen in more than a single species, while virtually all vertebrates and many invertebrates show some form of flight, avoidance, or hiding, while most also show freezing, defensive threat, and defensive attack.

II.B. When?

A crucial element in the analysis of defense is that particular defenses need to be effective against the type of threat that is actually being experienced. It is true that some threat situations, such as actually being caught by a predator that is much larger than oneself, are unlikely to have happy outcomes regardless of the prey's behavior. Even here, however, some defenses (e.g., defensive attack) may provide a sliver of advantage over others or over offering no defense at all, and may evolve on that basis. In fact, when the immediate alternative is death, even tiny advantages should produce rapid "selection" of the more adaptive behavior. This advantage, specifically in response to a particular threat, would be expected to result in a relatively unique connection between that type of threat/ situation and the specific defense, manifest as a high

probability of that response in that situation. As will be described, defensive behaviors are highly stimulus-bound with regard to both threat type, and situation, in most of the studies in which they have been investigated (e.g., Blanchard, 1997). This suggests that, rather than relying on a single category of "threat stimulus" analysis of defensive behavior will gain in depth and specificity by consideration of different types of threat, and particular features of the threat stimulus that impact the success or failure of defensive responses made to that stimulus.

II.B.1. Types of threat stimuli

Animals emit defensive behavior when they are confronted by some type of threatening stimulus. Predators, attack by conspecifics, and dangerous features of the environment represent three classes of threat stimuli that are found in almost any natural environment (Endler, 1986). The range and complexity of stimuli to be found within each of these categories, and the relative mix of stimuli between the various categories, may vary for different species and in different locales, but it is probably safe to say that all of these classes of threat are relevant to the overwhelming majority of animal species living now or in the past.

Predators obviously vary across species. For small herbivorous mammals such as rodents, the class of predators includes amphibians (e.g., the giant African frog); reptiles (many snakes and large lizards); birds (most raptors); and mammals (most felids, canids, many viverids, and a few primates). For large reptiles and mammals (considering only terrestrial animals), most of these potential predators drop out, leaving only a few carnivorous mammals and perhaps a reptile or two, as serious predatory threats. Some prey species differentiate common predators on the basis of their approach modes, with terrestrial, aerial, and even subterranean predators eliciting different types of cries from prey, that in turn produce different and appropriate defensive responses in the conspecific recipients of these cries.

Conspecific threats are obviously different for each species. This, paradoxically, leads to some similarities in defense across species, in that there is typically a substantial match in the capabilities of the attacker and those of the defender. Moreover, the defender has had ample (evolutionary) time and occasion to develop particular defenses against such attack, as has the conspecific attacker to develop more effective counters to these defenses. It is this immediately responsive relationship of defense to attack, and of attack to defense, in conspecific fighting that results in its "dance-like" aspect (Blanchard et al., 1975). Dangerous environmental features include some, such as spreading fire, flood, and earth movements that pose a danger to many if not all animals in the vicinity. Some combination of avoidance and flight may be successful against such moving but inanimate threats, whereas defensive threat/attack and freezing are not only useless, but often counterproductive. Non-moving hazards such as high places may also generally require avoidance. The point is that in order to be successful in reducing the probability of damage, defensive responses must be finely attuned to the particular characteristics of the threat source.

While these three classes of threat stimuli cover most cases, other threats may also emerge as important. For example, a body of literature is developing on fighting between predators of different species, over prey (Durant, 1998, 2000). These fights involve both aggression and defense, as may conspecific attack situations, but the defense elements are as clear and functional as those occurring to other types of threat.

II.B.2. Differentiations among threat stimuli

If the features of a threat stimulus are important in determining defensive behavior, threatened animals must be able to recognize different types of threat stimuli, in order to respond appropriately to them. In the case of predator stimuli, there is an established literature indicating that this is true. The well-known studies of Cheney and Seyfarth (see Seyfarth and Cheney, 2003 for review) indicate that a number of birds and mammals have distinct alarm cries or calls to different predator species: As one of many possible examples, vervet and diana monkeys have different alarm calls for leopards, eagles, and snakes, and these calls elicit different defensive behaviors from conspecifics, as appropriate to the capabilities of each such type of predator. In each case,

the call is not specific to the species by which it is labeled; "eagle" cries are made to other raptors as well, but seldom to non-raptors. The cry appears to be relatively specific to dangers that can approach by flying, a factor that would be expected to have a strong influence on the differential effectiveness of the defenses available to these monkeys. These findings are useful, both as direct indications that these two monkey species can differentiate among various types of predators, and, in indicating that these differentiations do result in varied and appropriate defenses. Suricates (meerkats) also have different cries for different types of predators, and in addition, can acoustically signal the urgency of danger, as indexed by the distance between the threat stimulus and the caller (Manser, 2001). This "urgency" factor for an alarm vocalization may contribute to an important motivational or emotional response parameter that results in lesser or greater strength of responding by the recipient.

II.B.3. Defensive distance

Defensive distance, the distance between prey and predator, also strongly impacts the type of defense offered, with closer predators eliciting more rapid flight when flight is possible and stronger freezing when it is not. Defensive threat, then defensive attack, appear as defensive distance decreases and contact with the predator becomes imminent (Blanchard, 1997). All of these behaviors are oriented with reference to the predator, and sometimes also with reference to a way out or place of comparative safety: In one elegant study, Ellard and Goodale (1988) found that when the silhouette of a predator was displayed overhead, gerbils that had established a place preference during a 15-min exploratory period in the test situation showed a flight path that maximized the distance to the threat stimulus, minus the distance to the preferred area. More generally, flight is away from the threat; and freezing and defensive threat and attack are oriented toward the threat, when a specific threat stimulus is available. Thus, in almost all cases, defense must be appropriately oriented with regard to the threat source. This is not a minor matter. Disoriented defensive behaviors are often not particularly useful or adaptive;

no more than a mother bird attempting to feed the wrong end of her chick.

II.B.4. Threat ambiguity

One particularly influential characteristic of the threat stimulus may cut across these categories of threat stimuli and situations. All of the threats yet described are discrete stimuli or events. But many threats are not discrete, at least not until it is too late for any specific antipredator defenses to have a good chance of success. Stealth is often an important component of the predatory pattern, effective in enabling the predator to reach striking distance to the prey without being detected. Conversely, from the perspective of the prey animal, early detection of danger is extremely useful, and any behavior that enables a prey animal to determine the presence or potential presence of danger is adaptive.

In field studies such prey behaviors are grouped under the concept of "vigilance". This involves inhibition of normal activities such as eating, grooming, or care of young, in favor of a pattern of scanning the environment, focused listening, or sniffing, for signs of danger. The behaviors of other animals may be observed for indications that the latter have detected danger. These activities, generally involving multiple senses but often focusing on the particular sense that is best developed in the species under observation, are functional in enabling the vigilant animal to assess risk levels. In laboratory studies, they are typically labeled "risk assessment" behaviors. While "risk assessment" is roughly synonymous with "vigilance", in laboratory studies most of which involve rodents, it is typically measured by the subject's assumption of a stretched posture oriented to threat, or by stretched approach to the threat source (Blanchard and Blanchard, 1989; Pinel et al., 1989).

This pattern is particularly common when the subject encounters ambiguous or non-specific stimuli potentially associated with threat. Such stimuli include novel or unexpected places, objects, sounds, smells, etc. These often induce initial but fairly brief flight/freezing/avoidance, typically followed by approach, investigation, sniffing, or other information-gathering activities, with relatively rapid habituation of these behaviors if no actual danger is found. This is in contrast to actual predator stimuli, to which much less habituation is seen (Blanchard et al., 1998; Dielenberg and McGregor, 1999). As an information-gathering mode in situations where caution may be adaptive, risk assessment is also a component of approach involving appetitive motivations such as sex or predation, especially when the acquiescence and retaliatory capabilities of the approached animal are unclear.

II.C. Where? Enabling or expediting stimuli

An additional component in the analysis of the relationship between threat stimuli and particular defensive behaviors involves particular features of the situation in which threat occurs. If evolution is responsible for the development of defensive behaviors, the mechanism of this evolution is that animals showing adaptive defenses, i.e., defenses that are appropriate to the situation, have been more likely to survive and reproduce than those that did not. For an optimal outcome, these behaviors should represent the most effective defense possible, given the specific features of the situation in which the threat is encountered. Such features enable particular responses to be effective, and their presence or absence can determine which defense is most effective in a given situation. Thus, flight as rapid locomotion away from a threat, is physically possible in any fairly large enclosure, but it is not effective against an equally fleet predator or conspecific attacker unless there is a way for the subject to actually escape the enclosure; when no way out is available, flight is a very dangerous response, in terms of the number of wounds suffered. Indeed, in typical enclosed test situations both predators and conspecific attackers may show enhanced or more effective attack when the subject flees, and less when it displays one of several non-locomotory defenses, such as freezing and defensive threat/attack. The switch from flight to freezing when an escape route is blocked can be clearly demonstrated in rats (Blanchard, 1997). Other enabling stimuli include the presence of a concealing or protecting area, crucial for hiding or sheltering to be effective, and the presence of

Table 1. Defensive behaviors as a function of the discreteness or ambiguity of threat, defensive distance, and presence of particular enabling stimuli

	Defensive behaviors		
Source of threat (and distance)	Enabling stimuli	Behavior	Typical outcome
Discrete	"Way out" available	Flight	Escapes
Discrete	No means of escape	Freezing	Reduces attack
Discrete	Conspecifics nearby	Alarm cry	Warns conspecifics
Discrete	Hiding place available	Hiding	No detection/access
Discrete (close in)		Defensive threat	Threatens attacker
Discrete (contacting)		Defensive attack	Hurts attacker
Discrete (contacting)		Startle	Startles attacker
Uncertain (potential)		Risk assessment	Localize, identify threat
Uncertain (potential)	Substrate	Defensive burying	Elicit animate movement

conspecifics, necessary for alarm cries to fulfill the function of alerting relatives to the presence of danger. Re the latter, conspecific presence has indeed been shown to facilitate rat ultrasonic alarm calls after encountering a cat (Blanchard et al., 1991).

These enabling features determine the functionality of a response, not whether it is physically possible. Animals can make alarm cries when no conspecifics are present, or run fruitlessly about when no escape or hidey-hole is available. Features of the threat stimulus itself are similar: It is possible for an animal to make a full threat display and emit the actual actions involved in attack when the threat is at such a distance that neither action, and particularly the latter, is effective. The fact that they do not do so but instead show extremely consistent differences as a function of defensive distance, or ambiguity of threat, attests to the strong relationship between threat and/or situational features, on the one hand, and the effectiveness of particular defenses, on the other. Some of these relationships are outlined in the summary Table 1.

II.D. Why?

The last column of Table 1 provides some information on typical adaptive outcomes, i.e., outcomes when successful, of each of these behaviors in the threat/situational circumstances in which they are most likely to occur. These "outcome" indications stem from a number of sources, including personal observations in laboratory and field studies, findings from published studies, and to some degree, speculation. A few examples of relevant published findings are:

(1) In an (endless) oval runway that contains a central wall, mice fleeing from a predator almost invariably run around the wall, "escaping" visual contact with the predator. They typically pause in this location (hiding?) until the pursuing predator rounds the same corner to confront them again (Blanchard et al., 2003a).

(2) For rats in predator confrontation situations, freezing is the dominant response when a way out is precluded by lack of an exit, or by punishment of flight (Blanchard and Blanchard, 1971; Blanchard et al., 1981).

(3) The relative mix of freezing and flight is different for species living in different habitats (Edut and Eilam, 2003). However, freezing and flight are controlled by features of the threat stimulus and situation, with freezing most effective when the prey subject has not yet been spotted by a predator (Eilam, 2005). Flight is influenced by both the distance to a predator and the predator's approach speed (Cooper, 2006).

(4) Alarm cries, actual or recorded, elicit defensive behaviors in listening conspecifics, consonant with a view that they serve to warn the latter. Insofar as these hearers are relatives, this provides a benefit to the genes of the

vocalizing animal (Brudzynski and Chiu, 1995; Seyfarth and Cheney, 2003; Litvin et al., 2006).

(5) Defensive threat and attack reduce predation by signaling an intention to attack (threat) or by actually hurting the attacker. Prey that attempt to retaliate by defensive threat and attack may truncate predatory attacks (Cowlishaw, 1994).

(6) Risk assessment enables the subject to learn about the characteristics of a threat stimulus, or to determine that there is no threat, enabling a return to non-defensive behavior (Pinel et al., 1989). Risk assessment occurs, on a long-term basis, to potential threat stimuli, whereas flight and freezing dominate when an actual predator is encountered (Blanchard et al., 1989). In field situations this situation can be more finely tuned: A lion tends to elicit only intermittent risk assessment (vigilance) by prey when its behavior suggests it is not in hunting or attacking mode. When the lion is hunting, more vigorous risk assessment and specific behaviors such as flight are elicited in prey (Schaller, 1976).

(7) Defensive burying may reduce the risk of accidental contact with noxious stimuli. However, a risk assessment view of burying is promoted by findings that after burying potentially dangerous stimuli, rats may dig them up again and continue by touching and manipulating them (Blanchard, unpublished observations). When a shock probe is the threat stimulus rats frequently bury it. However, their orientation/investigation behaviors following shock suggest that rats continue to risk assess stimuli after being hurt (Pinel et al., 1989).

Interpretations of functions are a tricky business. The study of defense in animals is in its infancy, and it is by no means impossible that additional, or even different, mechanisms by which these defenses are effective wait to be discovered. Particular behaviors may sometimes confer multiple adaptive advantages. However, the close ties of particular defenses to specific combinations of threat and situational stimuli strongly suggest differential efficacy in these situations. The fact that this pattern of modulation occurs consistently in animals that have had no experience of a predator and almost none of life outside a cage strongly suggests the existence of neural and neurochemical mechanisms that promote these complex but unconditioned stimulus (US) – modulatory relationships in a number of mammalian species.

III. Relationships to learning

III.A. Learning of defensive behaviors

In keeping with the robust and varied influences of both genetic and experiential factors in successful defense, there is a very complex relationship between defensive behaviors and learning. One aspect of this is the degree to which the actual actions involved in a particular defensive behavior may be considered to have been acquired through experience, perhaps through some form of differential reinforcement, or by observation of another performing the same actions. Of late, this has been a somewhat under-investigated aspect of defense, probably reflecting consistent findings that both rats and mice show a clearly differentiated range of defensive behaviors on first, non-painful, exposure to a predator or predator stimuli (e.g., Blanchard and Blanchard, 1972; Griebel et al., 1995a,b), and that such defenses appear very early in development (Takahashi, 1992a,b; Hubbard et al., 2004). The latter findings, of cessation in separation-induced ultrasonic vocalizations of rat pups to an adult male rat at 12 days of age and avoidance of the same, adult male, stimulus, and freezing to it, by 14 days of age (Takahashi, 1992a,b, 1994); and avoidance of a cat odor stimulus by 18 days of age; (Hubbard et al., 2004) also argue against a view that the specific behaviors comprising defense are learned in early interactions of sibling rat or mouse pups. Play fighting among rat pups does not begin until about 16 days postnatal (Pellis and Pellis, 1997), precluding defenses learned in this context from serving as the source of responses that are seen earlier.

Both sets of findings strongly suggest that in these particular animals the development of defensive behaviors is minimally dependent on reward or punishment contingencies during experience of pain or danger, or observation of others in such situations. This is in agreement with earlier findings on punishment contingencies. For example, entry latencies, 2 h later, for rats shocked immediately on entering a chamber, were not different than for animals receiving equivalent shock after being placed in the chamber; both were much higher than for non-shocked controls (Blanchard and Blanchard, 1968a). This was interpreted as indicating that behavior/shock associations may have a less important or immediate effect than stimulus/shock associations, with reference to the development of such passive avoidance behaviors. Moreover, the form of a defensive behavior in a particular context is hard to alter: Cain and LeDoux (this volume) discuss findings indicating that many more experiences (trials) with differential reinforcement are required to produce substantial changes in the type of defensive behavior seen in response to the presentation of a conditioned stimulus (CS), again suggesting that specific defenses have a substantial preprogrammed aspect that is difficult to alter.

As with many other complex response patterns, the degree to which the form and patterning of defensive responses are truly independent of learning based on response contingencies or observation learning, is very likely different from one species to another, with a general increase in such dependency for more highly encephalized mammals. However, there is considerable physiological evidence for the continuation of some primitive physiological defense systems in humans (Liddell et al., 2005), as well as behavioral evidence for basic "mammalian" patterns of defense in this species. The latter will be described in a later section of this chapter.

IV. Danger learning: conditioning to painful unconditioned stimuli (US)

Defensive behaviors do, however, show robust and rapid conditioning to stimuli, particularly situational stimuli, when pain is used as the US. Many studies of this phenomenon have focused on defensive immobility behaviors, variously labeled "crouching" or "freezing". Early studies indicated that long-lasting immobility in the shock situation occurs after a single footshock, but that postshock crouching is much higher when the shocks are delivered in a relatively unfamiliar environment: When the environment is very familiar (24 h habituation) postshock crouching is minimal (Blanchard et al., 1968b), indicating a possible latent inhibition (Lubow, 1989) effect. Both of these findings suggested that immobility is conditioned to the shock situation, an inference confirmed (Blanchard and Blanchard, 1969) by findings that a single, brief, 1.3 mA shock produced significant immobile crouching in the shock situation, whereas an identically shocked group shifted to another situation was not different from non-shocked controls. Replacement of this shocked and shifted group to the original box elicited robust immobility. An additional study in the same report indicated that this immobile response increased as a function of intensity of the single shock.

Blanchard et al. (1970) provided the first indication that there may be a particular connection between defensive immobility and situational as opposed to discrete cue stimuli. They reported that footshock produces one trial conditioning of avoidance when a highly discriminable object is used as the shock stimulus (seven out of eight experimental subjects touched the object only once, although they were free to do so). However, when this highly discriminable box served as the shock object, there was little immobility in the shock situation. In contrast, when a poorly discriminable box was used, such that the entire situation served as the CS, an equal number of shocks produced very high levels of immobility. Thus these studies, while further supporting a view of rapid – one-trial – conditioning of defensive behaviors to stimuli associated with shock, also indicated that the primary defensive behavior emitted to a CS depends on the type of stimulus; here, a discriminable object versus situational CS. These findings, based on single shocks, additionally indicate that differential reinforcement cannot account for the difference between avoidance of the discriminable object and freezing into the contextual CS.

V. Unconditioned and conditioned responses to non-painful stimuli (predators or predator odors)

The first detailed experimental report of freezing immobility to a predator was that of Curti (1935), who exposed rats to a cat. As contact between the two animals was allowed, it is not clear that this freezing reflected responsivity to a non-painful stimulus or, indeed, if such freezing might have developed during the encounter, perhaps on the basis of reduced attack when the rat was immobile rather than moving. However, studies involving a non-contacting cat (Blanchard and Blanchard, 1971) make it clear that pain is not necessary for either freezing, or active avoidance, to occur in rats that have not previously encountered a cat: Rats encountering a cat in a circular runway showed avoidance, albeit with reduced activity in the intertrial intervals. When the situation was a closed chamber with a single way out, over an electrified grid, they crossed the grid until high levels of shock were given, and showed freezing when failing to cross. This immobile freezing shows robust one-trial contextual conditioning to a cat US after a single experience (Blanchard et al., 1975), a finding that again attests to the adaptive value of learning about places where danger has been experienced. Rats with amygdala lesions showed strongly reduced avoidance and freezing, both to the cat and to a shock prod or situational stimulus associated with shock. This pattern, of freezing and discriminated avoidance, was enhanced by movement of the cat, and was also robustly elicited by another non-contacting predator, a dog (Blanchard et al., 1975). More recently, an additional prey–predator dyad, mice and rats, respectively, have been used in a number of studies of defensive behaviors, in the Mouse Defense Test Battery (Griebel et al., 1995a,b,c; Blanchard et al., 2001 for review).

VI. Learning of defense to partial predator stimuli

Even within the same species, predators represent a range of imminence of threat. Active lions, as noted, elicit a strong vigilance reaction in prey, whereas resting lions do not (Schaller, 1976, p. 234). Similarly, active cats elicit greater defensiveness than quiet ones, but even quiet predators are capable of eliciting some freezing and avoidance (Blanchard et al., 1975). Partial predator stimuli such as cat fur/skin odor tend to elicit more risk assessment, but may also produce strong specific defenses such as freezing and avoidance (Blanchard et al., 1990; McGregor et al., 2002). The risk assessment component is particularly associated with learning about potential threat stimuli (Pinel et al., 1989), and McGregor et al., 2002 have suggested that the ability of a partial predator stimulus to elicit risk-assessment behavior is a factor in the ability of that stimulus to support one-trial conditioning.

If contextual danger learning, such as that which occurs when a predator or other strong threat is encountered, is evolutionarily adaptive because it results in defensiveness in situations where danger is likely, it is predictable that partial predator stimuli should also be capable of serving as a US in the rapid (one-trial) conditioning that occurs with an actual predator, or shock, as the US. Such conditioning, using cat fur/skin odor was first demonstrated by McGregor and Dielenberg (1999) and Dielenberg and McGregor (1999), and has since proved to be a highly replicable phenomenon. While initial demonstrations of this ability of cat fur/skin odor to support both cue and context conditioning involved longer, albeit single, trials (20 min), subsequent work has indicated that a single, 10-min experience of cat fur/skin odor, but not cat feces or urine, will produce contextual conditioning of defensiveness (Blanchard et al., 2003b). Consistent findings that cat feces, as well as substances such as trimethylthiazoline (TMT) – a synthetic chemical derived from fox anal gland extracts, produce some defensive behaviors during presentation but do not support one-trial conditioning (e.g., Wallace and Rosen, 2000; McGregor et al., 2002; Blanchard et al., 2003b) has been interpreted in terms of the reduced ability of such odorants, compared to fur/skin odor, to predict the actual presence of a predator (Blanchard et al., 2001).

VII. Effects of stress and stress ameliorating conditions on defense

In terms of the relationship between defensive behavior and anxiety, it is important that experience with unconditioned threat stimuli that elicit defense may also enhance anxiety-like behaviors in other contexts and without the presence of threat-conditioned stimuli. Adamec and Shallow (1993) found that exposure to a cat produces anxiety-like responses in the rat that are manifest up to 21 days later, in an elevated plus maze. Perhaps more surprising, partial predator stimuli such as cat fur/ skin odor stimuli, in addition to supporting one-trial contextual and cue conditioning (Blanchard et al., 2001) also enhance defensiveness in other situations (Zangrossi and File, 1992a,b; Adamec et al., 1998), suggesting that longer-term changes in defensiveness may be a common accompaniment of exposure to predators or partial predator stimuli.

This facilitation of anxiety-like behavior by stressful experience may be a complex process. Adamec et al. (1998) evaluated anxiety-linked behaviors in the hole board and elevated plus maze tests, for rats previously placed in a room with a cat, or in the same room but with the cat having been just removed, leaving residual odors. The cat odor exposed rats showed enhanced frequency and duration of risk assessment in the plus maze, compared to (no-odor) controls, but the cat exposed rats showed reduced risk assessment compared to the same controls. Notably, much the same pattern of changes occurs during the initial exposure to the threat stimulus; reduced risk assessment during cat exposure, but enhanced risk assessment during cat odor exposure. This reinforces the view that risk assessment is particularly associated with partial or ambiguous predator stimuli, even in terms of the residual effects of such stimuli.

VIII. Defense and learning: relationship to anxiety

These findings, along with many recent developments in the study of fear conditioning (see chapters by Fanselow and Ponnusamy, Myers and Davis, and Caine and LeDoux, this volume), suggest that defensive behaviors to both painful and non-painful but threatening stimuli are easily acquired and difficult to extinguish. Such results make defensive behaviors particularly interesting candidates for involvement in many phenomena

related to anxiety and fear. First, defensive behaviors, at least in rats and mice, involve highly structured response patterns that are not based on specific experience. Second, these behaviors are nonetheless capable of becoming strongly conditioned to either situational or cue stimuli with a single pairing or trial. Moreover, US that elicit strong defensive emotions can support this rapid conditioning without pain; such US may be predictive cues for danger, in the absence of the actual danger stimulus itself. It is obvious that these features could promote rapid observation learning, in addition to avoidance of stimuli based on pain: In people, and other primates, it is clear that the conditioning of defensive behaviors to previously neutral stimuli does not require any direct experience, but can be mediated through observation (Mineka et al., 1984; Davey et al., 2003). Moreover, in people parallels between the features of the CS and the US can facilitate this process, for example, use of predatory animal stimuli can differentially facilitate acquisition of defensiveness to a pain-relevant US (Davey et al., 2003). Finally, single exposures to threat stimuli such as predators may also result in long-term enhancements of emotionality, manifest as increases in general "anxiety" measures such as the EPM.

IX. Responses to anxiolytic and panicolytic drugs

A traditional mode of validating animal models of anxiety involves determining their responsivity to drugs that are known to reduce or exacerbate anxiety in clinical populations (Willner, 1991). While this pharmacological validation approach has significant limitations, it remains the most commonly used type of validation for potential models of conditions that are known to show a relatively consistent and robust response to drugs. One particularly intriguing feature of the dozen or so conditions currently classified as anxiety disorders (American Psychiatric Association, 2000) is that they do not all respond consistently to the same classes of drugs (Baldwin et al., 2005). In this context it is interesting to note that defensive behaviors also show differential responsivity to drugs that are effective against generalized anxiety disorder (GAD), compared to those that reduce panic attacks. Specifically, anti-GAD drugs show a more consistent reduction in two defensive behaviors: risk assessment and defensive threat/attack, than to flight/avoidance; whereas drugs that are effective against panic disorder consistently reduce, and propanic drugs consistently enhance, flight (Blanchard et al., 2001, 2003a). This outcome is also intriguing because of situational or response parallels between these particular defensive behaviors and the clinical disorders with which they share a consistent drug response. Risk assessment – investigation of potentially but not clearly dangerous stimuli – may have a parallel in the "vigilance and scanning" component of GAD (APA, 2000) and in the excessive cognitive "rumination" and "worry" that are seen as frequent accompaniments of both GAD and depression, particularly in women (Robichaud et al., 2003). While defensive threat and attack are less clearly paralleled in the concept of GAD, this disorder is noted as associated with "irritability" as well as "muscle tension"; both potentially contributing to a heightened defensive threat/attack response to minimal provocation.

In contrast, analyses of the motivations and core response tendencies involved in panic attacks have focused on flight. This formulation (Deakin and Graeff, 1991) was largely based on clinical data, and spurred attempts to determine if antipanic drugs do selectively impact flight. This adds a behavioral parallel (sometimes called "face validity" or "phenomenological validity") to consistent findings that antipanic drugs and drug schedules increase flight; propanic drugs and drug schedules decrease flight; and drugs without effect on flight also have no effect on panic (Griebel et al., 1995a; Blanchard et al., 2001). While face validity based on parallels in behavior alone may be a poor index of the value of an animal model (see McNaughton and Zangrossi, this volume) when combined with parallels in other crucial aspects of a phenomenon such as eliciting situations and drug response, as here, it adds to a view that analysis of particular defensive behaviors may provide a useful and appropriate method for unraveling the neurobiological systems involved in different anxiety disorders (see Canteras and Blanchard, this volume).

X. Human defensive behaviors

Behavioral studies of defense outline the relationships between flight, freezing, hiding, defensive threat/attack, and risk assessment of rats and mice, and particular features of the eliciting (threat) stimulus and the situation in which it is encountered. They further indicate that some of these behaviors show considerable specificity of response to drugs effective against GAD or panic. While no systematic attempt has yet been made to determine whether the defensive behaviors described in rodents are characteristic of all mammalian species, laboratory and especially field studies make it clear that many of them are at least part of the defensive repertory of most other mammals (e.g., Edmunds, 1974). However, if defense behaviors are to serve as major models for investigating and understanding the biology of emotional response to aversive stimuli, it is essential to evaluate whether these systems show strong parallels in human responsivity to threat. In generalizing from rodent defenses to human anxiety disorders, two major areas of concern need to be considered. First, rodents are different from people. Second, the defensive behaviors that have been characterized are those that are found in relatively normal animals, to threat stimuli (typically predators) that are influential in the evolution of the subject species; whereas anxiety disorders are characteristic of people who have been diagnosed with psychopathologies and in most cases the threat stimuli and situations by which they are elicited are not normative for people. The obvious solution is to examine normal human defensive behaviors, in the same contexts, i.e., of eliciting and enabling stimuli, that modulate the defenses of rodents.

For obvious practical and ethical reasons experimental studies of attack by predators or even conspecifics on people are very difficult to do. However, human subjects are sufficiently obliging as to tell you what they think they would do, or what they have done, under a variety of circumstances. While such self-reports may be faulty due to poor recall, lack of interest or understanding, or deliberate lying on the part of the subjects, these problems can to some degree be assessed through various analyses of the data. Blanchard et al (2001) devised 12 brief threat scenarios, each involving a present or potential threatening conspecific in a situation chosen to reflect clear and often polarized values of the situational/enabling stimulus characteristics previously shown to modulate defense patterns in rodents. These threat/situational characteristics – magnitude of threat, escapability of the situation, ambiguity of the threat stimulus, distance between the threat and the subject, presence of a hiding place – were also evaluated by raters who were not involved in the study and did not know its purpose. The decision to use conspecific rather than predator attack represented an attempt to reduce the "ridiculousness" factor that can be a problem with scenarios, and to expand the number of situations where attack might reasonably be expected.

Each scenario was read by 160 male and female undergraduate students, who then chose, from a list of 10 possible responses, the first defensive response they would show to that situation. This list included six responses characteristic of rodents, and four that were more "human", for example, "beg", or "negotiate". Subjects were also allowed to write in choices that were not on the list. Across all scenarios, over 92% of responses were from the list of 10 provided, and about 75% of all responses were from the group of 6 "rodent-like" behaviors. For the 24 gender/scenario combinations, 23 first choices were from this group. Male and female responses to the various scenarios were highly correlated, except for "yell, scream, or call for help" which was frequent for females but rare for males, who tended to choose "attack" to the same scenarios. When the "scream" and "attack" categories were combined, the correlation of male and female responses was high and positive (+0.96) across scenarios. This finding also provides considerable assurance that subjects were paying attention to the scenarios and not answering randomly or with intent to deceive.

The following correlations between situational/stimulus characteristics and first defense selected were statistically significant.

Hypothesis	Relevant findings
Supported by statistically significant correlations	
Ambiguous threat stimuli increase risk assessment	$r = +0.86$ (women), $+0.89$ (men)
Ambiguous threat stimuli decrease flight	$r = -0.63$ (women), (NS for men)
A place of concealment/protection increases hiding	$r = +0.63$ (women), $+0.59$ (men)
A place of concealment/protection decreases defensive attack	$r = -0.71$ (women), -0.77 (men)
Distant threat stimuli reduce defensive attack	$r = -0.64$ (women), -0.59 (men)
Distant threat stimuli reduce freezing	$r = -0.71$ (women), -0.63 (men)
Inescapable situations increase defensive threat	$r = +0.74$ (women), (NS for men)
Inescapable situations increase defensive attack	$r = +0.65$ (women), $+0.76$ (men)

Some additional relationships hypothesized on the basis of animal findings (e.g., inescapable situations enhance freezing; ambiguous stimuli reduce defensive attack) received limited support, with combined male–female correlations of 0.4 or greater. The only significant correlation that was not predicted from the animal literature was between threat distance and hiding, with more distant threat stimuli eliciting a greater tendency to hide.

Additional studies using these scenarios, in Brazil and Wales, provide information on the degree to which these choices persist over different cultures. One of these studies, conducted in Swansea, Wales, replicated the findings of Blanchard et al., 2001 with reference to preference for defenses among the six "rodent-like" behaviors (about 90%); sex differences related to "scream" versus "attack"; and correlations for a number of the specific hypotheses relating to the relationship between threat stimuli and situations and particular behaviors. The correlations given were generally very similar indeed to those of the earlier study, for example, correlations of $+0.89$ (men) and $+0.85$ (women) versus the $+0.89$ and $+0.86$ for men and women, respectively of the Blanchard et al., 2001 study, for the relationship between risk assessment and threat ambiguity. However, "hide" was rarely selected in the Welsh sample, and the positive relationship between availability of a place of protection/concealment in the Hawaii study was not significant in the Welsh study. Intriguingly, one hypothesis from the animal literature that was not supported in either study was that flight is enhanced by availability of a way out of the situation: correlations were <0.15 in either study. This could perhaps reflect a difference between an attacking predator, as in the rodent studies, and attack by a human conspecific, for which other defenses might be regarded as more useful. Perkins and Corr (2006) further analyzed the direction (avoiding or approaching the threat) and intensity of threat as indexed by patterns of particular defenses, for each subject, finding highly significant correlations of up to 0.76 between this measure, over all scenarios, and a variety of psychometric measures of personality, such as trait anxiety, assessed by the Spielberger State-Trait Anxiety Inventory (Spielberger et al., 1983).

The Brazilian study is currently being analyzed. However, the first choices for each gender/scenario are available (Frederico Graeff, personal communication). Of the 24 first choices of defense for men or women with regard to each scenario, 22 were from the "rodent-like" list (compare with 23 of 24 for Blanchard et al., 2001). Including ties, there was agreement between the two studies on 17 of these first choices. Where disagreement occurred, Brazilian subjects favored risk assessment, or "apologize" whereas the Hawaiian subjects favored a variety of active behaviors. While these may relate to general cultural differences between the two sites, it is also possible that it more reflects a socioeconomic difference, in that the Blanchard

et al. (2001) subjects were students at a blue-collar community college, while the Brazilian subjects were students at one of the most selective Brazilian Universities (University of Sao Paulo). One clearly cultural difference did emerge, however. Brazilians, like the Welsh subjects in Perkins and Corr (2006) showed almost no defensiveness in response to a scenario about being tailgated in an automobile; a potential commentary on driving customs in the three sites involved.

In summary, the data from all of these studies were strongly and consistently consonant with a view that people utilize many of the same defensive behaviors as do rodents, and that major features of threat stimuli and situations that are determinative of defensive responses for rodents have parallels in human behavior. While at least one cultural difference was obtained in how threatening respondents regarded a particular situation (being tailgated), the degree to which particular findings were replicated in studies from two very different cultures suggest an overwhelming similarity in patterns of defense to these relatively commonly encountered types of situations.

These findings do not address a number of important issues, such as the role of weapons in defense. No weapons were described as readily available in the scenarios. If they had been, it seems very likely that use of them would have substantially enhanced the "attack" choice, although it is difficult to say if this would have altered the overall pattern of responding. The question of individual learning is similarly not addressed. Obviously each of the participants in all of these studies had a great deal of direct or indirect (e.g., media) experience with conspecific attack, in striking contrast to laboratory rodents' lack of experience with predators. It might well be argued that the choices made by human subjects reflect the chances of each such behavior being successful in that specific situation, based on what they have learned or experienced about responding to attack. This view, while likely true, does not detract from the hypothesized relationships between characteristics of threat stimuli and situations, and the most appropriate defensive response to them. Instead, it emphasizes a point made by B.F. Skinner many years ago, that behaviors "selected" by evolution on the basis of success are typically the same behaviors that are learned individually, again on the basis of success, in a particular type of situation (Skinner, 1984). Here, we are suggesting that evolution and individual learning under normal circumstances both tend to promote tendencies toward the same patterns of behavior. In laboratory rodents it is possible to assert with some certainty that the patterns are largely independent of individual experience, whereas in people both etiological factors are likely represented, along with neurobiological systems by which their motivations and action patterns are expressed.

XI. Defensive behavior, fear, and anxiety

Defensive behaviors constitute a range of responses to threat. While they are typically unconditioned in less encephalized mammals such as rodents, relatively little is known of the degree to which they reflect unconditioned and conditioned tendencies in more highly encephalized mammals. Laboratory rodent studies indicate that particular defensive behaviors are tightly controlled by specific features of the threat stimulus and the situation in which it is encountered. These analyses apply to human defensive responses as well, and agreements between studies of these phenomena make it clear that the patterns of relationships between threat/situational characteristics and the types of defensive behaviors emitted are consistent and robust across different cultures.

Etymological analyses of the terms "fear" and "anxiety" suggest that, while both describe reactions to threat or danger, they are different in terms of their eliciting stimuli; the behaviors they encompass; and the degree to which they are regarded as normal and adaptive. Specifically, anxiety is a response to an ambiguous or poorly defined danger, and its behavioral manifestations tend to be more pervasive than are those of fear; involving extended worry or rumination, often without a definitive outcome.

The parallels between behaviors of rodents, or people, to ambiguous vs unambiguous or discrete threat stimuli, in combination with these brief excursions into the etymology of the terms suggest that the common differentiation between fear and anxiety in what has been termed the "ordinary psychological language" has a substantial basis in biology. Ambiguous threat stimuli do elicit different defensive responses than do clear/discrete threat stimuli. Moreover, these risk-assessment responses have a strong parallel in one of the core features of human anxiety, i.e., worry and rumination, in which the anxious individual attempts, by focusing cognitive efforts toward understanding a poorly conceptualized difficulty, to attain a solution to it. However, the existence of a biological basis for the differentiation of fear and anxiety is at variance with the view that fear is more normal and adaptive than is anxiety. A case can be made for the view that when threat is ambiguous, risk assessment is the best possible defense, enabling identification and localization of the threat source, if one is actually present; or facilitating a return to non-defensive behavior if it is not (Blanchard et al., 1990).

Why, then, is human anxiety so often regarded as maladaptive, or even pathological? An adequate answer to that very interesting question might involve components that range from pure convenience in labeling, through recognition that the situations to which anxiety is an appropriate response are, in general, more difficult to understand and deal with than are the relatively simple threats that elicit fear. There are a number of points where a defensive behavior might earn the label "maladaptive" or "abnormal". These include elicitation by a non-threatening or insufficiently intense threat stimulus/situation; hyperexpression of general defensiveness or overemphasis on specific defenses; abnormal persistence of any or all aspects of defensiveness to threat stimuli, for example, failure to show habituation when a stimulus/situation is resolved; an inappropriate match to the eliciting threat or threat situation (e.g., risk assessment to a clearly present and threatening stimulus; flight or defensive attack to an ambiguous threat stimulus, etc.); or poor execution of a defense such that it becomes ineffective. We suggest that these aspects of maladaptiveness are embedded in many, if not most, of the currently recognized anxiety disorders, and that an analysis in terms of defensiveness will prove useful in understanding of both the normal and abnormal manifestations of fear and anxiety in people.

References

Adamec, R., Kent, P., Anisman, H., Shallow, T. and Merali, Z. (1998) Neural plasticity, neuropeptides and anxiety in animals – implications for understanding and treating affective disorder following traumatic stress in humans. Neurosci. Biobehav. Rev., 23: 301–318.

Adamec, R.E. and Shallow, T. (1993) Lasting effects on rodent anxiety of a single exposure to a cat. Physiol. Behav., 54: 101–109.

American Psychiatric Association. (2000) DSM-IV-TR: Diagnostic and Statistical Manual of Mental Disorders. American Psychiatric Publishing, Washington DC, USA.

Baldwin, D.S., Anderson, I.M., Nutt, D.J., Bandelow, B., Bond, A., Davidson, J.R., den Boer, J.A., Fineberg, N.A., Knapp, M., Scott, J. and Wittchen, H.U. (2005) Evidence-based guidelines for the pharmacological treatment of anxiety disorders: recommendations from the British Association for Psychopharmacology. J. Psychopharmacol., 19: 567–596.

Blanchard, D.C. (1997) Stimulus and environmental control of defensive behaviors. In: Bouton, M. and Fanselow, M. (Eds.), The Functional Behaviorism of Robert C. Bolles: Learning, Motivation and Cognition. American Psychological Association, Washington, DC, pp. 283–305.

Blanchard, D.C. and Blanchard, R.J. (1972) Innate and conditioned reactions to threat in rats with amygdaloid lesions. J. Comp. Physiol. Psychol., 81: 281–290.

Blanchard, D.C., Griebel, G. and Blanchard, R.J. (2003a) The Mouse Defense Test Battery: pharmacological and behavioral assays for anxiety and panic. Eur. J. Pharmacol., 463: 97–116.

Blanchard, D.C., Lee, E.M.C., Williams, G. and Blanchard, R.J. (1981) Taming of Rattus norvegicus by lesions of the mesencephalic central gray. Physiol. Psychol., 9: 157–163.

Blanchard, D.C., Markham, C., Yang, M., Hubbard, D., Madarang, E. and Blanchard, R.J. (2003b) Failure to produce conditioning with low-doseTMT, or, cat feces, as unconditioned stimuli. Behav. Neurosci., 117: 360–368.

Blanchard, R.J. and Blanchard, D.C. (1968a) Passive avoidance; a variety of fear conditioning? Psychon. Sci., 13: 17–18.

Blanchard, R.J. and Blanchard, D.C. (1969) Crouching as an index of fear. J. Comp. Physiol. Psychol., 67: 370–375.

Blanchard, R.J. and Blanchard, D.C. (1971) Defensive reactions in the albino rat. Learn. Motiv., 21: 351–362.

Blanchard, R.J. and Blanchard, D.C. (1989) Antipredator defensive behaviors in a visible burrow system. J. Comparat. Psychol., 103: 70–82.

Blanchard, R.J., Blanchard, D.C., Agullana, R. and Weiss, S.M. (1991) Twenty-two kHz alarm cries to presentation of a predator, by laboratory rats living in visible burrow systems. Physiol. Behav., 50: 967–972.

Blanchard, R.J., Blanchard, D.C. and Fial, R.A. (1970) Hippocampal lesions in rats and their effect on activity, avoidance, and aggression. J. Comp. Physiol. Psychol., 71: 92–101.

Blanchard, R.J., Blanchard, D.C. and Hori, K. (1989) Ethoexperimental approaches to the study of defensive behavior. In: Blanchard, R.J., Brain, P.F., Blanchard, D.C. and Parmigiani, S. (Eds.), Ethoexperimental Approaches to the Study of Behavior. Kluwer Academic Publishers, Dordrecht, pp. 114–136.

Blanchard, R.J., Blanchard, D.C., Weiss, S.M. and Meyer, S. (1990) The effects of ethanol and diazepam on reactions to predatory odors. Pharmacol. Biochem. Behav., 35: 775–780.

Blanchard, R.J., Dielman, T.E. and Blanchard, D.C. (1968b) Post-shock crouching; familiarity with the shock situation. Psychon. Sci., 10: 371–373.

Blanchard, R.J., Mast, M. and Blanchard, D.C. (1975) Stimulus control of defensive reactions in the albino rat. J. Comp. Physiol. Psychol., 88: 81–88.

Blanchard, R.J., Nikulina, J.N., Sakai, R.R., McKittrick, C., McEwen, B.S. and Blanchard, D.C. (1998) Behavioral and endocrine change following chronic predatory stress. Physiol. Behav., 63: 561–569.

Blanchard, R.J., Yang, M., Li, C.I., Gervacio, A. and Blanchard, D.C. (2001) Cue and context conditioning of defensive behaviors to cat odor stimuli. Neurosci. Biobehav. Rev., 25: 587–595.

Brudzynski, S.M. and Chiu, E.M. (1995) Behavioral response of laboratory rats to playback of 22kHz ultrasonic calls. Physiol. Behav., 57: 1039–1044.

Caro, T.M. (1994) Ungulate antipredator behaviour: preliminary and comparative data from African bovids. Behaviour, 128: 189–228.

Cooper, W.E. Jr. (2006) Dynamic risk assessment: prey rapidly adjust flight initiation distance to changes in predator approach speed. Ethology, 112: 858–864.

Cowlishaw, G. (1994) Vulnerability to predation in baboon populations. Behaviour, 131: 293–304.

Curti, M.W. (1935) Native responses of white rats in the presence of cats. Psychol. Monogr., 46: 76–98.

Davey, G.C., Cavanagh, K. and Lamb, A. (2003) Differential aversive outcome expectancies for high- and low-predation fear-relevant animals. J. Behav. Ther. Exp. Psychiatry, 34: 117–128.

Deakin, J.F. and Graeff, F.G. (1991) 5-HT and mechanisms of defence. J. Psychopharmacol., 5: 305–315.

Dielenberg, R.A. and McGregor, I.S. (1999) Habituation of the hiding response to cat odor in rats (*Rattus norvegicus*). J. Comp. Psychol., 113: 376–387.

Durant, S.M. (1998) Competition refuges and coexistence: an example from Serengeti carnivores. J. Anim. Ecol., 67: 370–386.

Durant, S.M. (2000) Predator avoidance, breeding experience and reproductive success in endangered cheetahs, *Acinonyx jubatus*. Anim. Behav., 60: 121–130.

Edmunds, M. (1974) Defence in Animals: A Survey of Anti-Predator Defences. Longman, Harlow.

Edut, S. and Eilam, D. (2003) Rodents in open space adjust their behavioral response to the different risk levels during barn-owl attack. BMC Ecol., 3: 10.

Eilam, D. (2005) Die hard: a blend of freezing and fleeing as a dynamic defense – implications for the control of defensive behavior. Neurosci. Biobehav. Rev., 29: 1181–1191.

Ellard, C.G. and Goodale, M.A. (1988) A functional analysis of collicular output pathways: a dissociation of deficits following lesions of the dorsal tegmental decussation and the ipsilateral efferent bundle in the Mongolian gerbil. Exp. Brain Res., 71: 307–319.

Endler, J.A. (1986) Natural Selection in the Wild. Princeton University Press, New Jersey.

Estes, W.K. and Skinner, B.F. (1941) Some quantitative properties of anxiety. J. Exper. Psychol., 29: 390–400.

Freud, S. (1930) Inhibitions, Symptoms and Anxiety. London, Hogarth Press.

Griebel, G., Blanchard, D.C., Agnes, R. and Blanchard, R.J. (1995a) Differential modulation of antipredator defensive behavior in Swiss-Webster mice following acute and chronic treatment with imipramine and fluoxetine. Psychopharmacology, 120: 57–66.

Griebel, G., Blanchard, D.C., Jung, A. and Blanchard, R.J. (1995b) A model of "antipredator" defense in Swiss-Webster mice: effects of benzodiazepine receptor ligands with different intrinsic activities. Behav. Pharmacol., 6: 732–745.

Griebel, G., Blanchard, D.C., Jung, A., Masuda, C.K. and Blanchard, R.J. (1995c) Further evidence that the Mouse Defense Test Battery is useful for screening anxiolytic and panicolytic drugs: effects of acute and chronic treatment with alprazolam. Neuropharmacology, 34: 1625–1633.

Hediger, H. (1968) The Psychology of Animals in Zoos and Circuses. Dover, New York.

Hubbard, D.T., Blanchard, D.C., Yang, M., Markham, C.M., Gervacio, A., Chun, I.L. and Blanchard, R.J. (2004). Development of defensive behavior and conditioning to cat odor in the rat. Physiol. Behav., 80: 525–530.

Liddell, B.J., Brown, K.J., Kemp, A.H., Barton, M.J., Das, P., Peduto, A., Gordon, E. and Williams, L.M. (2005) A direct brainstem-amygdala-cortical 'alarm' system for subliminal signals of fear. Neuroimage, 24: 235–243.

Litvin, Y., Blanchard, D.C. and Blanchard, R.J. (2006). Rat 22kHz ultrasonic vocalizations as alarm cries. *Behav. Brain. Res.*, [E-pub ahead of print]

Lubow, R.E. (1989) Latent Inhibition and Conditioned Attention Theory. Cambridge University Press, Cambridge.

Manser, M.B. (2001) The acoustic structure of suricates' alarm calls varies with predator type and the level of response urgency. Proc. Biol. Sci., 268: 2315–2324.

McGregor, I.S. and Dielenberg, R.A. (1999) Differential anxiolytic efficacy of a benzodiazepine on first versus second exposure to a predatory odor in rats. Psychopharmacology (Berlin), 147: 174–181.

McGregor, I.S., Schrama, L., Ambermoon, P. and Dielenberg, R.A. (2002) Not all 'predator odours' are equal: cat odour but not 2,4,5 trimethylthiazoline (TMT; fox odour) elicits specific defensive behaviours in rats. Behav. Brain Res., 129: 1–16.

Mineka, S., Davidson, M., Cook, M. and Keir, R. (1984) Observational conditioning of snake fear in rhesus monkeys. J. Abnorm. Psychol., 93: 355–372.

Online Etymology Dictionary (2007) <http://www.etymonline.com/>

Pellis, S.M. and Pellis, V.C. (1997) The prejuvenile onset of play fighting in laboratory rats (*Rattus norvegicus*). Dev. Psychobiol., 31: 193–205.

Perkins, A.M. and Corr, P.J. (2006) Reactions to threat and personality: psychometric differentiation of intensity and direction dimensions of human defensive behaviour. Behav. Brain Res., 169: 21–28.

Pinel, J.P.J., Mana, M.J. and Ward, J.A. (1989) Stretched-approach sequences directed at a localized shock source by *Rattus norvegicus*. J. Comp. Psychol., 103: 140–148.

Robichaud, M., Dugas, M.J. and Conway, M. (2003) Gender differences in worry and associated cognitive-behavioral variables. J. Anxiety Disord., 17: 501–516.

Schaller, G.B. (1976) The Serengeti Lion: A Study of Predator-Prey Relations. University of Chicago Press, Chicago.

Seyfarth, R.M. and Cheney, D.L. (2003) Signalers and receivers in animal communication. Annu. Rev. Psychol., 54: 145–173.

Skinner, B.F. (1984) The evolution of behavior. J. Exp. Anal. Behav., 41: 217–221.

Spielberger, C.D., Gorsuch, R.L., Lushene, R., Vagg, P.R. and Jacobs, G.A. (1983) Manual for the state-trait anxiety inventory: STAI (form Y). Consulting Psychological Press, Palo Alto, CA.

Takahashi, L.K. (1992a) Developmental expression of defensive responses during exposure to conspecific adults in preweanling rats (*Rattus norvegicus*). J. Comp. Psychol., 106: 69–77.

Takahashi, L.K. (1992b) Ontogeny of behavioral inhibition induced by unfamiliar adult male conspecifics in preweanling rats. Physiol. Behav., 52: 493–498.

Takahashi, L.K. (1994) Stimulus control of behavioral inhibition in the preweanling rat. Physiol. Behav., 55: 717–721.

Thompson, E.P. (1851) The Passions of Animals. Chapman and Hall, London, pp. 116.

Treit, D., Pinel, J.P. and Fibiger, H.C. (1981) Conditioned defensive burying: a new paradigm for the study of anxiolytic agents. Pharmacol. Biochem. Behav., 15: 619–626.

Wallace, K.J. and Rosen, J.B. (2000) Predator odor as an unconditioned fear stimulus in rats: elicitation of freezing by trimethylthiazoline, a component of fox feces. Behav. Neurosci., 114: 912–922.

Willner, P. (1991) Animal models as simulations of depression. Trends Pharmacol. Sci., 12: 131–136.

Zangrossi, H. Jr. and File, S.E. (1992a) Behavioral consequences in animal tests of anxiety and exploration of exposure to cat odor. Brain Res. Bull., 29: 381–388.

Zangrossi, H. Jr. and File, S.E. (1992b) Chlordiazepoxide reduces the generalised anxiety, but not the direct responses, of rats exposed to cat odor. Pharmacol. Biochem. Behav., 43: 1195–1200.

Unconditioned models of fear and anxiety

Yoav Litvin[1,*], Nathan S. Pentkowski[1], Roger L. Pobbe[3], D. Caroline Blanchard[2,3]
and Robert J. Blanchard[1]

[1]Department of Psychology, University of Hawaii at Manoa, Honolulu, HI, USA
[2]John A. Burns School of Medicine, Department of Genetics and Molecular Biology, Honolulu, HI, USA
[3]Pacific Biosciences Research Center, Honolulu, HI, USA

Abstract: Preclinical animal models are utilized in the study of unconditioned states related to fear and anxiety. They are used to screen novel pharmaceuticals, study behavioral phenomena, and understand underlying etiology. In this chapter, we will present a brief overview of the most prevalently used models, discuss their various applications, and state their main behavioral indices. We will conclude by discussing the importance of factors associated with the environment and the chosen experimental subjects to appropriately model preclinical states associated with fear and anxiety.

Keywords: fear; anxiety; unconditioned; animal models; defense; high throughput

I. Introduction

Animal models are experimental devices developed for the study of behavioral and physiological phenomena with a view to analysis of these phenomena in other species than the one actually used (McKinney, 1984). In particular, animal models are aimed at mimicking different aspects of human diseases or disorders. They may reduce time and cost requirements of research; expand the range of experimental techniques available, and are especially useful when ethical considerations make parallel human research procedures difficult or impossible. Although animal research includes work with primates, fish, felines, canines, and other species, the common laboratory rat (*Rattus norvegicus*) has been the favored research subject for over a century (Iwaniuk, 2005). However, recent burgeoning interest in, and resulting work with, genetic techniques, genetically modified animals and gene therapy has created

a growing need for relevant behavioral models for the mammalian species of choice involved in such research, namely mice (Crawley and Paylor, 1997).

In this chapter, we will focus on the standard indices of fear and anxiety as measured in a sample of common unconditioned laboratory models. We will present a sample of paradigms, which utilize a variety of threat stimuli along a continuum of intensity; starting at one end with relatively weak stimuli such as exposure to novel, elevated, or brightly lit spaces and closing with paradigms which utilize relatively strong stimuli such as direct predator exposure. The paradigms presented are not exhaustive, and are only a sample of paradigms based on the categorical division of Table 1. They have been chosen largely on the basis of how commonly they are used, and some material will also be presented on trends in use patterns. This analysis also suggests a division between tests that have been conceived and designed as models of anxiety, and those that originated for other, or more general purposes, but have come to be regarded as anxiety models.

*Corresponding author. E-mail: litvin@hawaii.edu

R.J. Blanchard, D.C. Blanchard, G. Griebel and D. Nutt (Eds.)
Handbook of Anxiety and Fear, Vol. 17
ISBN 978-0-444-53065-3

DOI: 10.1016/S1569-7339(07)00006-9

Table 1. Unconditioned models of anxiety

1. Novelty/exploration
   a. Open field
   b. Free exploration
   c. Elevated plus-maze
   d. Elevated T-maze
   e. Zero maze
   f. Light/dark box
   g. Staircase test
2. Social tests
   a. Separation-induced ultrasonic vocalizations
   b. Social competition
   c. Social interaction
3. Antipredator tests
   a. Mouse defense test battery
   b. Cat exposure
   c. Cat odor
   d. Rat exposure test
   e. Anxiety/defense test battery
   f. Fear/defense test battery
4. Others
   a. Hyponeophagia
   b. Pain-induced ultrasonic vocalizations
   c. Startle response

II. Models

II.A. Open field

The open field is an extremely popular model for the study of behavior in general, and fear and anxiety in particular (Belzung, 1999). Its use has been extended to calves, pigs, lambs, rabbits, pullets, primates, bush babies, honeybees, and lobsters (Prut and Belzung, 2003).

Hall (1934) first described the open field as a test for assessment of "emotionality". The open field apparatus consists of a brightly illuminated circular arena containing palatable mash, the floor of which is marked into sectors by concentric circles. In essence, the procedure involves individually placing rats in the brightly lit center of a novel arena from which escape is prevented by a high surrounding wall. In his classic studies, Hall tested rats that were food deprived and later determined that "emotional" rats ate less, defecated more, and preferred the outer perimeter of the apparatus rather than its center. Later, others modified various aspects of the open field, differentially manipulating lighting, and the shape of the test apparatus.

When initially placed in the open field, animals begin investigating the context. Test animals spontaneously prefer the periphery of the open field to activity in central parts of the apparatus and display risk assessment behaviors toward the center area. This high level of peripheral activity is often accompanied by thigmotaxis (wall-hugging) behavior, a reaction in which the animal remains close to vertical surfaces (Wilson et al., 1976; Treit and Fundytus, 1989). Emotionality in the open field is also evaluated by indices of sympathetic activation, i.e., defecation and urination (Hall, 1934) and by latency to consume palatable mash (positioned in the center of the field), a measure reflecting the conflict aspect of anxiety.

In the 1950s and 1960s there was considerable debate around the issue of the motivation behind exploratory behavior in a novel open field (Montgomery, 1954; Welker, 1959; Fowler, 1965). Many authors suggested that exploratory behaviors resemble an animal's approach–avoidance conflict. The open field paradigm tests forced exploration; animals are placed directly into a novel environment and are forced to explore their surroundings. In contrast to forced exploration whereby animals are "flown" into the apparatus, animals in free exploration situations are given the choice of entering a novel arena from a familiar home base (e.g. see Griebel et al., 1993; Kopp et al., 1997). Animals usually orient themselves toward the novel area and frequently exhibit risk assessment behavior, an established index of anxiety (Blanchard and Blanchard, 1971b, 1989). Blanchard et al. (1974) compared animals previously housed in a home base with animals "flown" into it, and demonstrated that fear, rather than exploration, is the driving incentive behind behaviors witnessed in the open field.

The popularity of the open field has also produced several problems with its usage. Over the years the open field has become a convenient procedure to measure not only anxiety-like behaviors, but also sedation or locomotor (ambulatory) activity. The utility of such use of the open field has been recently questioned by some very interesting reviews and commentaries (Prut and Belzung, 2003; Rodgers, 2007). As demonstrated by Blanchard et al. (1974) and recently emphasized by Prut and Belzung, researchers that make use of the open field to measure locomotor activity are not (as is often claimed) measuring activity or exploration per se but rather behavior in a stressful situation. Rodgers (2007) points out that multiple sources of "background" stress, which may include environmental conditions or prior treatments, such as handling, surgery, and drug injections, intensely affect the performance of animals exposed to the open field. In addition, studies of the open field show less standardization than most anxiety models, in terms of apparatus and test procedures (for a review see Choleris et al., 2001; Stanford, 2007).

Despite these problems, pharmacological results obtained with the administration of clinically effective anxiolytics, including benzodiazepine (BZ) receptor full agonists (e.g., diazepam) and serotonin (5-HT)$_{1A}$ receptor agonists (e.g., buspirone) tend to show a consistent increase in the percentage of entries in the central part of the open field (Prut and Belzung, 2003). However, open field measures are not sensitive to compounds that are now recommended as a first line treatment for most clinical anxiety disorders, such as alprazolam and chronic SSRIs (Griebel, 1996; Belzung, 2001), indicating that this test cannot claim true predictive validity as a model relevant to most clinical anxiety disorders (see Griebel, this volume).

II.B. Elevated plus-maze

The elevated plus-maze (EPM) has become the most widely used animal model in contemporary preclinical research on anxiety. The EPM affords a good example of a model based on the study of unconditioned responses to less intense threatening situations.

The EPM is based on a conflict between the tendency of rodents to explore a novel environment and the aversive properties of the open arms (Pellow et al., 1985). Its origin derived from the observation that when faced with a choice between alleys enclosed within walls versus unprotected open ones, rodents prefer to stay in the protected areas (Montgomery, 1955). It was initially argued that the reluctance of animals to explore the open arms of the EPM was due either to rodent aversion to open spaces or to the maze height (Lister, 1990). Nevertheless, other studies showed that height alone is not a sufficiently intense anxiogenic stimulus, suggesting that rodent aversion to open spaces could be related to thigmotaxis (Treit et al., 1993). Furthermore, as enclosed spaces afford good protection from potential predators this model might be viewed as a predation model, but of lesser stimulus intensity than is direct predator confrontation (Dawson and Tricklebank, 1995).

The primary indices of anxiety in the EPM include spatiotemporal as well as behavioral measures. The classic spatiotemporal measures are open arm entries, and duration, both expressed as a percentage of entries or time, respectively, on the open and closed arms combined. These measures disregard entries/time in the central square, as central square time can vary between groups. However, it has been suggested that time spent on the central square may be related to decision-making and/or risk assessment (Rodgers et al., 1996). A modification of the EPM in the form of a "zero maze" is meant to circumvent the ambiguity in interpretation of time spent on the central platform of the EPM (Shepherd et al., 1994).

Ethological approaches to the EPM have evaluated defensive behaviors, especially those associated with risk assessment; for example, stretch-attend posture and head dipping (Rodgers et al., 1997; Carobrez and Bertoglio, 2005). These measures of defense have improved the analysis of the effects observed in this paradigm (Griebel et al., 1997; Wall and Messier, 2001; Roy and Chapillon, 2004), yet unfortunately they are not widely implemented (Carobrez and Bertoglio, 2005).

Handley and Mithani (1984) carried out the first study reporting drug effects in the EPM. Using a simple X- or plus-shaped maze configuration, with two open and enclosed arms, these authors showed that anxiolytic drugs (e.g., diazepam) reduced open arm avoidance, while anxiogenic compounds (e.g., picrotoxin) enhanced it. This seminal work was quickly followed by comprehensive validations of the test for use with both rats (Pellow et al., 1985) and mice (Lister, 1987), and recent research has suggested its potential utility for other species including guinea pigs (Rex and Fink, 1998), hamsters (Prendergast and Nelson, 2005), gerbils (Varty et al., 2002), and wild voles (Hendrie et al., 1997).

It is well established that the plus-maze is highly sensitive to the influence of BZ/GABA- and glutamate-related manipulations (Rodgers, 1997; Carobrez et al., 2001). However, effects obtained with other anxiety-modulating compounds (e.g., the 5-HT$_{1A}$ receptor partial agonist buspirone) have been very much more variable (Handley and McBlane, 1993; Borsini et al., 2002). The reasons for this variability have been extensively analyzed. For instance, Handley et al. (1993) suggested the EPM is sensitive to multiple effects of drugs interacting with the 5-HT system. Differing EPM methodologies between laboratories, while less than for the open field, may also be involved in inconsistent findings (Rodgers, 1997; Salome et al., 2002).

Interestingly, rats previously exposed to the EPM (a single 5 min exposure) often show complete avoidance of the open arms when retested. These effects are not reversed by anxiolytics; i.e., these animals no longer exhibit increases in open-arm exploration when reexposed to the test (File, 1993; File and Zangrossi, 1993). It has been suggested that brain areas involved in anxiety-linked memory systems may modulate this loss of anxiolysis on the second trial. For instance, reversible deactivation of the basolateral nucleus of the amygdala with lidocaine immediately after the first trial restores the anxiolytic-like effect of BZs on the second (File et al., 1998). A similar pattern of results was observed after the deactivation of either the dorsomedial hypothalamus (File et al., 1999) or the dorsolateral periaqueductal gray (Bertoglio et al., 2005).

II.C. Elevated T-maze

As noted, pharmacological results obtained with several 5-HT related drugs assayed in the EPM

have produced inconsistent results (Griebel, 1995). Handley (1995) has argued that such inconsistencies may be explained by the fact that the plus-maze is a mixed test, in the sense that rodents display different defense strategies while exploring the maze. Two such strategies are: avoidance of open arms when the animal is in a closed arm, and escape from an open arm into the enclosed arm. The elevated T-Maze consists of three elevated arms – one enclosed and two open. To assess inhibitory avoidance, a subject is placed at the end of the enclosed arm and the latency to exit this arm is recorded in three consecutive trials. Inhibitory avoidance learning is indicated by the increase in withdrawal latency across trials. Thirty seconds after the completion of avoidance training, the second behavioral task (one-way escape) is measured. For this, the animal is placed at the end of one of the open arms of the maze and the withdrawal latency from this arm is similarly registered in three consecutive trials.

Since these defense strategies are influenced in opposite ways by serotonin (5-HT) (Deakin and Graeff, 1991), the effect of compounds that act on this neurotransmitter system should vary depending on the predominance of one or the other – avoidance or escape – of such defense reactions. The ETM was designed to separate these defensive behaviors (Graeff et al., 1993; Viana et al., 1994). The underlying premise for this model is that generalized anxiety and panic-related defensive responses are differentially regulated by serotonin (5-HT) released from fibers in the dorsal raphe nucleus (DRN), a midbrain structure that innervates neural substrates particularly involved in anxiety (e.g., amygdala, frontal cortex, dorsal periaqueductal gray (dPAG), among others) (Lowry et al., 2005). According to these authors, activation of the DRN results in facilitation of the defense strategies that are mainly integrated at the levels of the amygdala, such as avoidance and risk assessment behaviors. At the same time, more intense defensive reactions such as fight or flight behaviors, which are mainly organized in the dPAG are inhibited by 5-HT (for recent reviews see Graeff, 2002, 2004).

Zangrossi and Graeff (1997) have conducted several experiments in order to behaviorally validate the ETM. Their results showed that rats trained on an ETM with three enclosed arms did not show the increase in withdrawal latency along three consecutive trials that is often observed in the standard ETM procedure. Therefore, open arm experience seems to be critical for inhibitory avoidance learning. Moreover, over five trials in an open arm, animals left at increasingly higher speeds. Both findings are consonant with a view that the open arms are aversive, and that repeated placement in the closed or open arm elicits avoidance, or escape, respectively.

For pharmacological validation, it has been shown that systemic and acute administration of anxiolytic compounds (e.g., diazepam, buspirone, and ritanserin) impairs avoidance acquisition (shortening withdrawal latency of the enclosed arm) while leaving one-way escape unchanged (Graeff et al., 1998). This selective effect on avoidance is in accordance with the clinical effectiveness of these drugs on generalized anxiety disorder, as opposed to their inefficacy with regard to panic disorder (Nutt, 1991). Moreover, chronic administration of 5-HT reuptake inhibitors such as imipramine, fluoxetine, and chlorimipramine inhibits escape in this test (Teixeira et al., 2000; Poltronieri et al., 2003), again in agreement with the clinical effectiveness of these drugs on panic disorder (Johnson et al., 1995). These results suggest that both behavioral tasks assessed in the ETM model two different anxiety disorders, generalized anxiety and panic disorders.

II.D. Light/dark box

The light/dark box is based on rodents' innate aversion to two mild stressors; bright light and a novel environment (Crawley and Goodwin, 1980). The primary indices of anxiety in this test are spatiotemporal; i.e., the time spent in the bright side and the number of transitions made by animals between the two compartments. Anxiolytics have been shown to significantly increase the number of transits between compartments (Crawley, 1981).

Many authors have made procedural modifications from the original two-compartment paradigm (for a recent review see Bourin and Hascoet, 2003). These modifications include the introduction of a connecting tunnel between the two compartments (Belzung et al., 1987, 1994), changes in the dimensions or spatial disposition of the compartments (Shimada et al., 1995), and analyses of additional behavioral indices of anxiety and locomotor activity (Chaouloff et al., 1997; Hascoet and Bourin, 1998).

Although at first glance these modifications may seem slight, they may profoundly influence the way animals respond to the situation. For instance, increasing the light intensity of the bright side may reduce the expression of risk assessment behaviors made by the animals in the transition area between the two compartments. Although this alteration may not necessarily lead to changes in the total amount of time spent in both compartments, it may interfere with the expression of an important set of generalized anxiety disorder-related behaviors (Graeff and Zangrossi, 2002).

Despite the above caveats, pharmacological results with classic anti-anxiety compounds are remarkably consistent, using either the original protocol or modified versions of the test. Thus, reported results show that acute injection of BZs (e.g., diazepam, chlordiazepoxide, and alprazolam) or buspirone-like drugs induce anxiolytic effects in both mice and rats (Shimada et al., 1995; Griebel et al., 1996c; Hascoet and Bourin, 1998).

II.E. Social interaction

The social interaction paradigm was developed on the basis that anxiety levels selectively modulate social behavior in rats. The time spent in social interaction (sniffing, following, and grooming the partner, boxing and wrestling) provides an inverse measure of anxiety. Recently, infrared beams have been utilized to provide an automated measure of locomotor activity (e.g. see Tucci et al., 2003).

This task has been shown to successfully model both extremes of anxiety-related profiles, and was pharmacologically validated as such using classic anxiolytic and anxiogenic substances. In addition, social interaction involves a variety of neurotransmitters and neuropeptides including 5-HT CCK, substance P, neuropeptide Y, cortico-tropin-releasing factor (CRF), and corticotropins (for review see File and Seth, 2003).

Environmental factors modulate social behaviors in this paradigm. Familiarity with the test arena significantly reduces levels of anxiety, i.e., by increasing interaction, with male rats more strongly effected than females (Johnston and File, 1991). Second, aversive cues, such as bright lights, loud noise, or exposure to cat odor or fresh rat blood increase anxiety, i.e., reduce interaction (Zangrossi and File, 1992a; File, 1994). Interestingly, cat odor effects are reversed by treatment with chlordiazepoxide (Zangrossi and File, 1992b). Lastly, early-life trauma in the form of maternal separation for 8 h every other day between postnatal days 2–10, significantly decreased interaction levels in adult male rats, an effect reversed by application of an antagonist DMD696 (Maciag et al., 2002).

Swiss albino mice showed similar sensitivity to light changes, although manipulations of the test arena were not as reliable (de Angelis and File, 1979). In addition, mice did not show the clear anxiolytic and anxiogenic profiles of rats (Lister and Hilakivi, 1988; Hilakivi et al., 1989).

In addition to common usage in rats and mice, the social interaction paradigm has also been utilized in Gerbils (Salome et al., 2006; Cheeta et al., 2001; File et al., 2001). These studies show that diazepam, nicotine, 8-hydroxy-2-di-*n*-(propylami-no)tetralin (8-OH-DPAT) and a substance P receptor antagonist all produced increased social interaction (i.e., anxiolytic), while an acute dose of fluoxetine decreased time spent in social interaction (i.e., anxiogenic).

II.F. Separation-induced ultrasonic vocalizations

Infant rats emit ultrasonic vocalizations (USV) as a response to isolation from the dam and conspecifics (Bell et al., 1974; Shair, 2007), and when exposed to thermal or olfactory challenges (Allin and Banks, 1971; Oswalt and Meier, 1975; Conely and Bell, 1978; Hofer and Shair, 1980). Rat pups reduce the emission of USV when exposed to familiar maternal odors (Oswalt and Meier, 1975), or to threatening odors, such as those of an adult male conspecific (Takahashi, 1992). The classical interpretation posits that infant USV serve to restore tactile, olfactory, and thermal conditions associated with the nest by eliciting maternal retrieval and are thus pertinent during the early postnatal period in which pups cannot fend for their basic physiological needs.

Separation-induced USV have been regarded as an index of separation anxiety and are used to study the pharmacological basis of associated disorders. Interestingly, several studies show that both BZ anxiolytics and 5-HT associated compounds effectively reduce USV (Insel et al., 1986; Winslow and Insel, 1991; Zimmerberg et al., 1994; Miczek et al., 1995; Podhorna and Brown, 2000). Furthermore, studies have shown that morphine (Kehoe and Blass, 1986) and ethanol (Barron et al., 2000) both reduce USV, while naltrexone, an opioid antagonist, potentiates them (Kehoe and Blass, 1986).

III. Ethological approaches: predator confrontation

A number of recent fear and anxiety models are based on an ethological approach that involves a detailed description of defensive behaviors in response to predatory stimuli. In these models, fear and anxiety-like behaviors are often differentiated on the basis of either the eliciting stimuli or on the resulting behavioral output, or on a combination of both. Whereas ambiguous stimuli such as predator odor elicit risk assessment behaviors (e.g., stretch attend, stretch approach, olfactory investigation) and are associated with a state of anxiety, discrete, present threats elicit flight, avoidance, defensive threat, and attack and are associated with a state of fear. Features of the test situation further modify defensive behaviors: escapability potentiates flight while its lack thereof, freezing. The defensive distance between predator and prey shifts defensive coping strategies from avoidance to escape, with short distances and contact culminating in defensive threat and attack postures (for review see D.C. Blanchard, this volume).

A major factor contributing to the heightened interest in investigating the neurobiology of defensive behaviors is their potential relevance to certain human psychiatric disorders. Pharmacological studies have demonstrated predictive validity for these behaviors, as drugs effective against human psychiatric disorders tend to produce reliable changes in defense (Blanchard et al., 2001a). As such, drugs effective in treating certain forms of human anxiety (i.e., generalized anxiety disorder) selectively affect risk assessment and defensive threat/attack, while panicolytic drugs appear to selectively alter flight responses (Blanchard et al., 2003a).

These behavior descriptions reflect observations of prey–predator behaviors in seminatural visible burrow systems (VBS) and other situations where rats or mice are confronted by predators or predator-related stimuli. Because of the presence of a colony of rats containing both males and females in a VBS, and the time-course of observations (up to 24 h after predator presentation), the VBS itself is seldom used to evaluate drugs, but a number of shorter tests based on analyses of defensive behaviors of a single rat, and utilizing a predator or predator stimuli as threat sources, are used in preclinical research on anxiety.

Here, we will present only a brief overview of behaviors from the rat and mouse VBS (see Blanchard et al., this volume for a more extensive analysis) but the specific tests incorporating these behaviors as measures of anxiety will be described.

III.A. Visible burrow system

III.A.1. Rats

The VBS is a paradigm, which elicits a full range of defensive behaviors toward a predator threat (a cat). When a cat is presented to the surface of the VBS, rats initially display flight to a side chamber, general avoidance of the surface, and freezing (Blanchard and Blanchard, 1989; Blanchard et al., 2001a). After this initial period of immobility, a pattern of risk assessment emerges accompanied by 22 kHz ultrasonic alarm cries (Blanchard et al., 1991b; Litvin et al., 2007a). After the potential for risk is assessed, and no further signs of the

predator are detected (assuming the predator has been removed), the rats return to a nondefensive state; this process occurs over hours, with the initial period of immobility lasting up to 30 min. In the control procedure a toy cat stimulus is presented, resulting in brief flight to the burrow system, and short-lived 22 kHz ultrasonic alarm cries, after which rats quickly reenter the open area and resume their regular activities. A second cat exposure the following day induces responses virtually identical to the first, indicating that no habituation has occurred in the defenses elicited by predator presentation. Acute presentation of cat odor in a VBS produces initial flight to, and freezing in the side chambers (avoidance), followed by risk assessment behaviors including stretch attends, stretch/flat back approaches to, and head outs of the tunnel, and minimal contact with the discrete odor source (cloth covered block) (Blanchard et al., 1989).

Classic anxiolytics such as the BZs diazepam and chlordiazepoxide (Blanchard et al., 1990a), alcohol (Blanchard et al., 1990b), the 5-HT$_{1a}$ agonists 8-OH-DPAT and Gepirone (Blanchard et al., 1992a), and the tricyclic antidepressant imipramine (Blanchard et al., 1992a) all lower general levels of defensiveness in the VBS, functioning to decrease avoidance (time spent in the burrows) while increasing risk assessment, resulting in a faster return to a nondefensive state (Blanchard et al., 1997). In addition, a modification of this model has been used to study the effects of chronic social stress on behavior, the endocrine system, and associated neural mechanisms (Blanchard et al., 1995a).

III.A.2. Mice

A full range of mouse anti-predator behaviors has been assessed in a mouse sized VBS (Blanchard et al., 1995b). Mice typically display flight, avoidance, and cessation of nondefensive activities such as foraging and mating. Mice exposed to a cat on the surface area of the VBS show rapid flight to the burrows and a marked reduction in nondefensive behaviors for 14 h or more, a very similar pattern of behaviors to that displayed by rats in a similar situation (Blanchard and

Blanchard, 1989). In contrast to rats, mice display initial high levels of risk assessment (frequent approach-withdrawals to the surface), and do not display 22 kHz ultrasonic alarm cries, behaviors that may be inversely related (Blanchard et al., 1995b). Aside from these relatively minor differences in defensive responsiveness, mice and rats show a very similar defensive repertoire when confronted with a predator threat, and are thus highly comparable.

III.B. Predator exposure

In an attempt to analyze behaviors related to the state of fear, defensive reactions to an inescapable and discrete stimulus, a cat, were evaluated (Blanchard and Blanchard, 1971a). The specific behaviors elicited in response to direct cat exposure depend on the exposure context, particularly the ability to flee and hide (Blanchard et al., 1976). In an inescapable test situation, rats exposed to a predator exhibit cessation of ongoing activity (freeze) and show hypertension for almost the entire exposure duration (Markham et al., 2004; Pentkowski et al., 2006). When animals are reexposed to the context alone 24 h later, they show freezing, similar to the response shown when rats are reexposed to a context in which they received shock (Blanchard and Blanchard, 1969).

Situations involving potential threats (predatory odors or contexts in which predators are briefly presented then removed) tend to elicit defensive behaviors amendable to anxiolytics, while direct predator encounters appear to be more closely tied to a state of fear as anxiolytics during these unavoidable/direct predator encounters are generally ineffective (Blanchard et al., 1993). Pharmacological studies have demonstrated predictive validity for this notion, as drugs effective against certain forms of human anxiety (i.e., generalized anxiety disorder) selectively affect risk assessment behaviors during exposure to cues or contexts associated with predators (Blanchard et al., 2003a). Diazepam fails to reliably alter levels of risk assessment or freezing, but again increases measures of risk assessment immediately following predator removal (Blanchard et al., 1990a). In contrast to standard anxiolytic compounds, anti-panic agents such as the tricyclic anti-depressant imipramine reduce avoidance during and following direct predator exposure (Blanchard et al., 1993).

III.C. Cat odor exposure

The use of predator odors as models of anxiety is based on the natural defensive proclivity of rodents to locate not only predators, but also predatory cues, including aspects of their size, shape, movement, and/or chemical odor (Apfelbach et al., 2005). From an evolutionary perspective, the avoidance of predatory cues is quite adaptive in that it decreases the chances of coming into contact with an actual predator. In laboratory settings, their use thus affords researchers an ethologically valid model for investigating the neuroanatomical and pharmacological mechanisms of reactions toward ambiguous threat stimuli related to fear and anxiety.

Testing using this procedure is relatively simple and utilizes spontaneous behavior thus requiring no training. Context, or context plus cue learning, as well as extinction processes can also be tested subsequent to cat odor exposure (Blanchard et al., 2001b), allowing for the investigation of conditioned anxiety-like behaviors. The behaviors occurring in response to predator odors are extensive and depend on several factors including the exposure context (semi-natural or controlled/laboratory), the type of predator odor (TMT: 2,5-dihydro-2,4,5-trimethylthiazoline-a component of fox feces, or cat and ferret fur/skin odors), and the duration and intensity of the odor presentation.

Rats exposed to a cat odor block enclosed in a long narrow runway apparatus without a hiding place (hide box, burrow, side chamber, etc.) exhibit flight, freezing, and high levels of risk assessment (Blanchard et al., 2001b). While exposure to TMT produces similar patterns of freezing and avoidance, risk assessment behaviors generally only occur during exposure to cat fur/skin odors (Takahashi et al., 2005). A further consideration regarding risk assessment is that these behaviors also require a discrete point source to locate and investigate, and thus testing environments that present the odor by covering the apparatus with a cat worn cloth elicit high levels of freezing and avoidance, but not risk assessment (Takahashi, unpublished observations). These results suggest that when presented using this method, nonspecific odor saturation of the environment may occur, limiting the subjects' defensive repertoire to avoidance and freezing.

The intensity of predatory odors as a variable in altering defensive behaviors has recently been investigated using cat and ferret fur skin odor, as well as TMT. Wallace and Rosen (2000) demonstrated that increasing the doses of TMT produced higher levels of freezing, although these effects occurred in small test chambers resulting in an unavoidable, saturated stimulus; TMT has never produced freezing in large, or habituated to environments (Blanchard et al., 2003b). In contrast, Takahashi et al. (2005) have recently shown that increasing the concentration of cat odor by varying the size of cat odor-saturated cloths produces a dose-dependent (size of the cloth) reduction in contact with the odor source and increase in freezing. Furthermore, rats exposed to a large cat odor collar (compared to controls and smaller collars) exhibited increased fear-like responses (avoidance and freezing) over a 7-day habituation period, as well as increased avoidance during extinction trials. Despite some questions regarding TMT, these results collectively indicate that exposure to predator odors do not trigger unconditioned reflexive responses similar in magnitude across varying odor intensities; rather, predator odors exert stimulus control over the magnitude of the defensive behaviors expressed (Takahashi et al., 2005).

High levels of risk assessment produced in this paradigm correspond with increased vigilance seen in various anxiety disorders, both of which are amendable to standard anxiolytic treatments, thus establishing predictive pharmacological validity. For example, irrespective of environmental context, anxiolytic compounds such as alcohol, the BZs diazepam (Blanchard et al., 1990c), and midazolam (McGregor et al., 2004), the tricyclic antidepressant imipramine (Blanchard et al., 1993), and the 5-HT$_{1a}$ agonist 8-OH-DPAT

(Blanchard et al., 1992a) all decrease levels of risk assessment and avoidance during cat odor exposure. Conditioning to cat odor responds to standard anxiolytics (Blanchard et al., 1990a, b).

III.D. Mouse defense test battery

The mouse defense test battery (MDTB) enables well-controlled elicitation of a range of unconditioned behavioral responses to a predator threat (Blanchard et al., 2003a) (for review of methods see Blanchard et al., 2005). These behaviors span over much of the typical defensive response, and include: flight, avoidance, freezing, risk assessment, defensive threat, and attack.

The MDTB was constructed with the purpose of evaluating responses to stimuli varying in intensity; ranging from a light stressor such as novelty (pretest), to an intense stressor, i.e., forced contact with a potential predator (a hand-held anesthetized laboratory rat), thus increasing levels of anxiety/fear over the subsets of the test. Behaviors in the MDTB are tightly constrained by the circular shape of the apparatus, which does not enable escape or any form of concealment from a threat, and by temporal restrictions, which may selectively modulate time dependent risk assessment and other defensive behaviors.

The pharmacological validity of the MDTB has been shown with respect to a number of BZ anxiolytics (alprazolam and clonazepam), chronic treatments with various antidepressants, specifically effecting flight behavior (imipramine, fluoxetine, moclobemide, and phenelzine) (Griebel et al., 1996b, 1998, Blanchard et al., 1997) (for review of pharmacology see Griebel, this volume). It is noteworthy to mention that flight behavior induced by predator presentation is goal-oriented, not an abrupt release in forward locomotion (Blanchard et al., 1998). In a factor-analytic study, Griebel et al. (1996a) addressed the questions whether the different subtests of the MDTB signify different measures of the same state, or whether they measure distinct states of defensiveness, fear, or anxiety. Results showed that the behaviors may be divided into five factors: anxiety-related behaviors modulated by BZ, those modulated by 5-HT related neurotransmission, non-risk assessment "affective" defense, defenses to specific threat stimuli (or "terminal defenses"), and behaviors related to escape from an area in which threat has been encountered. These results confirm that the MDTB provides an appropriate model for evaluating several conditions, which may be related to human anxiety and panic disorders.

III.E. Rat exposure test

In the rat exposure test (RET) a mouse subject is presented with a discrete predator threat (an awake, amphetamine injected rat), which is located in a compartment behind a mesh screen (Yang et al., 2004). The mouse can either stay in close proximity to the rat in an adjacent chamber (the "surface"), or pass via a tunnel to a smaller hide box (or "home chamber") (for review of methods see Blanchard et al., 2005). Bedding material is provided in all chambers of the RET, and mice can seal off the tunnel from within the home chamber, leaving a crack from which they can display risk assessment toward the rat compartment. Prior to testing in the RET, subjects are habituated to the context for 3 days (10-min per day without the rat threat) in order to minimize novelty-associated anxiety. Thus, reactivity on the test day can be attributed solely to the presence of the predator.

Central administration of anxiogenic compounds prior to testing in the RET produces enhanced avoidance (Farrokhi, 2006), while BZ administration produces an anxiolytic profile (Tovote et al., 2006). In addition, findings from our lab show enhanced burying in the RET with intra-dPAG administration of anxiogenic compounds such as ovine CRF (oCRF) (Carvalho-Netto et al., 2007) or cortagine, a novel CRF receptor type 1 agonist (Litvin et al., 2007b). These effects are consonant with findings that show burying as a reaction toward a threat (a shock probe) (for review see De Boer and Koolhaas, 2003).

Although an extensive pharmacological validation (e.g., BZ, 5-HT-related compounds) similar to that conducted on the MDTB, is vital for the continuing use and potential applicability of the results derived from the RET, these behavioral findings render this model of considerable interest for the study of fear and anxiety states in animals.

Although some similarities between the MDTB and RET paradigms are present, they model fundamentally different situations. These models differentially manipulate temporal, spatial and learned factors in order to selectively adjust both the presented threat intensity, and the prepotency of individual defensive behaviors. Enhanced threat together with strict temporal and spatial restrictions provide less controllability for the mouse in the MDTB context, a factor which has been known to render situations more stressful (for review see Maier and Watkins, 2005).

IV. Conclusions

IV.A. High-throughput modeling

Pharmaceutical and genetic research has largely dictated the development of novel unconditioned models for research on fear and anxiety (for trends, see Canteras and Blanchard, this volume). A particularly influential development in such research is an emphasis on "high throughput": favoring tests and measures that can be run, evaluated, and analyzed quickly and with a minimum of costs that are incurred by the involvement of trained personnel. This emphasis reflects increasing numbers of new drugs that must be evaluated with a variety of different models during the preclinical testing phase. High throughput is also important in accommodating an even more recent upsurge in the demand for quick, inexpensive, and highly standardized (thus potentially comparable) tests of anxiety for genetic analyses. In line with these emphases, the use of tasks requiring extensive pretraining of subjects has diminished in favor of those that can be accomplished in a single, brief, period using naïve animals for which no other background manipulations are required; preferably in an automated apparatus for which the output can be channeled directly into a computer. This requirement clearly favors the use of unconditioned, as opposed to conditioned tests, because it eliminates the need for (time and labor intensive) conditioning prior to the actual test of anxiety-like behavior.

In particular, this trend has promoted the use of the EPM and its daughter, the elevated zero maze, as well as the open field and, to a lesser degree, the light/dark box (see Canteras and Blanchard, this volume for details of changes over time in the use of these models). The EPM is approaching a level of regard as the "gold standard" for analysis of anxiolytic or anxiogenic action that formerly was reserved for conditioned conflict models. Conditioned models, in contrast, have declined substantially in comparison to the overall trend for tests of anxiety. This relative decrease in usage of tests requiring extensive pretraining of subjects fits well with a view of increased emphasis on high throughput for tests.

However, the desire for high-throughput tests may inadvertently oversimplify the interpretation of the obtained results, resulting in false negatives. For example, although the EPM is considered an ethological model of anxiety (Rodgers et al., 1997), and the addition of corresponding measures (e.g., risk assessment) has been shown to improve its sensitivity toward anxioselective compounds (Cruz et al., 1994; Rodgers and Johnson, 1995; Weiss et al., 1998), a minority of studies have incorporated such an analysis (Carobrez and Bertoglio, 2005), most likely due to the financial and temporal advantages of automated procedures and scoring methods. Furthermore, usage of the EPM must consider factors associated with stressful pretest conditions (e.g., excessive movement) and particular testing conditions (e.g., strong lighting), both of which have been shown to enhance the affect of anxiolytics (for a review of variability in the EPM see Hogg, 1996).

Defensive responses, largely produced in response to predators, provide an additional approach to the analysis of unconditioned anxiety measures; favoring a different set of tasks than the EPM, open field, or light/dark test. Models based on defense, such as the MDTB, are less attractive from the perspective of high throughput as they may require training of personnel and typically involve videotaping and later analysis of

behaviors. However, some researchers (e.g., McGregor and Dielenberg, 1999) have successfully automated test situations to accommodate differential measurement of these behaviors.

IV.B. Other uses of unconditioned models

In addition to modeling fear and anxiety, associated unconditioned paradigms are utilized for a variety of other purposes. Under the premise whereby unconditioned models serve as stressors, many have studied their effects on mechanisms of learning and memory by testing animals exposed to an anxiety paradigm in learning-based tasks, such as the Morris water maze (e.g., Diamond et al., 2006) or on behavior in a subsequent test of emotionality. For example, direct cat exposure has been shown to produce lasting effects on performance in the EPM in rats (Adamec and Shallow, 1993) and mice (Adamec et al., 2004). In addition, direct exposure of adult (Cohen and Zohar, 2004) and juvenile (Cohen et al., 2007) rats to cat litter has been shown to affect EPM performance. The latter study adds to a plethora of evidence linking early-life stress with the development and persistence of anxiety-related disorders (Ford and Kidd, 1998; Heim and Nemeroff, 2001).

The open field, originally designed as a model of "emotionality" (Hall, 1934), has frequently been used to model locomotor activity. This is intuitively appealing and can be automated for even higher throughput. While fear, anxiety, and locomotion do interact (Rodgers et al., 1997), most uses of the open field separate center (emotionality linked) from peripheral (locomotion linked) line crossings.

IV.C. Subjects

Successful modeling entails careful consideration of the test subjects to be utilized with regard to particular attributes such as strain and sex. Results show that the various models differentially interact with these parameters.

IV.C.1. Strain

Griebel et al. (2000) compared the sensitivity to diazepam of nine mouse strains in two models of anxiety, the EPM and light/dark task. Results showed clear differences between the strains, indicating that some strains are better suited for investigating the effects of GABA/BZ receptor ligands. Moreover, due to an unequal distribution of sensitivity to the light/dark test and EPM, the authors concluded that these tasks entail differential behaviors.

It is especially important to evaluate the different behavioral profiles of mice used in the making of genetic knockouts. In a study which compared the behavioral profiles of three commonly used background strains (C57BL/6JOlaHsd, 129/SvEv, and 129S2/SvHsd) in the EPM and light/dark exploration test, results indicated enhanced anxiety in the 129 strains, and reduced activity of all three inbred strains when compared to an outbred (Swiss-Webster) control (Rodgers et al., 2002).

When two inbred (BALB/c and C57BL/6) and two outbred (CD-1 and Swiss-Webster) strains of mice were compared in an ethological model of anxiety, the RET, results indicated enhanced defense in inbred strains, with C57BL/6 mice showing enhanced avoidance, risk assessment and freezing (Yang et al., 2004).

IV.C.2. Sex

Defensive behaviors have evolved on the basis that in response to particular types of threat stimuli and in particular situations, each such behavior has proved to be optimally adaptive in terms of enhancing the overall fitness of the individual (Blanchard et al., 2007). Because the fitness of females may largely reflect the survival of their offspring, the optimal defensive behaviors for males and females may differ: The mechanisms underlying these gender differences are poorly understood, yet there is speculation that these may be related to the substantial and consistent differences in vulnerability to particular psychiatric disorders for men and women. These include higher prevalence of females with panic disorder, generalized anxiety disorder, and phobias (DSM-IV, 1994). These findings suggest a difference between male and female reactivity toward stressful or threatening situations, with females showing enhanced defensiveness, or enhancements in the type of defensiveness emphasized in these disorders.

Results from preclinical models support this notion; in the anxiety/defense test battery (A/DTB), a model in which animals are presented with ambiguous predator stimuli (i.e., cat odor), females show enhanced avoidance and crouching, with a general reduction in nondefensive behaviors (Blanchard et al., 1991a). These results are in contrast to studies utilizing the fear defense test battery (F/DTB), in which direct cat presentation failed to produce gender differences. However, females did show differences in the sonographic characteristics (i.e., frequency and duration) of circa 22-kHz USV in response to cat presentation (Blanchard et al., 1992b). These alarm vocalizations are a valid index of anxiety, and equivalents in a variety of species have been detailed (Litvin et al., 2007a).

A number of studies implicate the estrous cycle in modulating defensive mechanisms, with this effect attributed to the fluctuations of the ovarian sex hormones estrogen and progesterone (Zimmerberg and Farley, 1993; Mora et al., 1996). Female rats in the proestrus stage spend more time in the open arms of an EPM when compared to those during the diestrus stage. Interestingly, application of estradiol to diestrus females abolishes this difference, implicating estradiol in the modulation of this response (Marcondes et al., 2001). The brain 5-HT system is more highly expressed in females (Carlsson and Carlsson, 1988) and is influenced by the estrous cycle (Biegon et al., 1980), as well as by the administration of estradiol (Biegon and McEwen, 1982).

Sexual experience has also been shown to affect levels of anxiety, with experienced rats showing significantly less anxiety-like behavior in the open field and EPM when compared to inexperienced male rats (Edinger and Frye, 2007). Levels of testosterone show an inverse relation in these groups, with experienced rats showing higher levels than inexperienced rats.

IV.C.3. Laboratorization

The long history of work with laboratory animals, especially rodents and nonhuman primates, raises the question of the effect of laboratorization on defensive behaviors. In both rats and mice, many generations of human handling have created an artificial rift between common laboratory strains and their counterparts in the wild (Huck and Price, 1975; Price, 1984; Blanchard et al., 1986; Blanchard, 1997; Blanchard et al., 1998; Blanchard and Blanchard, 2005). Specifically, wild rats show enhanced defensive behaviors when compared to laboratory rats, with an emphasis on elevations in escape and confrontational defensive postures (Blanchard et al., 1986; Blanchard, 1997). On the other hand, laboratory rats favor freezing as a response toward threat.

Wild mice (*mus musculus*) tested in an EPM show a preference for the open arms, a behavior conventionally attributed to lower levels of anxiety (Holmes et al., 2000). In comparison, male laboratory Swiss-Webster mice exhibit reduced exploratory activities and increased duration in the closed arms of the EPM. When reexposed to the EPM, wild mice show further increases in exploration of the open arms, while Swiss-Webster mice maintain and even enhance their preference for the enclosed parts of the EPM. When a more ethological approach is applied, it reveals a profile of high reactivity and escape motivation for wild mice, characterized by attempted and actual jumps from the apparatus, spontaneous freezing, and exploration of the upper ledges of the closed arms (Holmes et al., 2000). However, Augustsson and Meyerson (2004) reported that when wild mice are tested in an EPM and open field, they show lower activity and higher avoidance of the open areas when compared to the BALB/c or C57BL/6 laboratory strains, a finding opposite to that of Holmes et al.

Laboratory Swiss-Webster mice tested in a MDTB show the full range of defensive behaviors, albeit exhibiting lower levels of both flight and freezing when compared to their wild counterparts, but show high levels of other defensive behaviors such as risk assessment, defensive threat, and defensive attack (Blanchard et al., 1998). Different strains of wild mice have recently been shown to have differential reactivity in the MDTB, illustrating the effects of their natural habitats and associated predatory threats on defensivity (Litvin, Eilam, Blanchard, and Blanchard, unpublished observations).

References

Adamec, R., Walling, S. and Burton, P. (2004) Long-lasting, selective, anxiogenic effects of feline predator stress in mice. Physiol. Behav., 83: 401–410.

Adamec, R.E. and Shallow, T. (1993) Lasting effects on rodent anxiety of a single exposure to a cat. Physiol. Behav., 54: 101–109.

Allin, J.T. and Banks, E.M. (1971) Effects of temperature on ultrasound production by infant albino rats. Dev. Psychobiol., 4: 149–156.

American Psychiatric Association (1994) (DSM-IV) Diagnostic and statistical manual of mental disorders, 4th edition. American Psychiatric Press Inc., Washington, DC.

Apfelbach, R., Blanchard, C.D., Blanchard, R.J., Hayes, R.A. and McGregor, I.S. (2005) The effects of predator odors in mammalian prey species: a review of field and laboratory studies. Neurosci. Biobehav. Rev., 29: 1123–1144.

Augustsson, H. and Meyerson, B.J. (2004) Exploration and risk assessment: a comparative study of male house mice (*Mus musculus musculus*) and two laboratory strains. Physiol. Behav., 81: 685–698.

Barron, S., Segar, T.M., Yahr, J.S., Baseheart, B.J. and Willford, J.A. (2000) The effects of neonatal ethanol and/or cocaine exposure on isolation-induced ultrasonic vocalizations. Pharmacol. Biochem. Behav., 67: 1–9.

Bell, R.W., Nitschke, W., Bell, N.J. and Zachman, T.A. (1974) Early experience, ultrasonic vocalizations, and maternal responsiveness in rats. Dev. Psychobiol., 7: 235–242.

Belzung, C. (1999) Measuring exploratory behavior. In: Crusio, W.E. and Gerlai, R.T. (Eds.), Handbook of Molecular Techniques for Brain and Behavior Research (Techniques in the Behavioral and Neural Sciences). Elsevier, Amsterdam.

Belzung, C. (2001) Rodent models of anxiety-like behaviors: are they predictive for compounds acting via non-benzodiazepine mechanisms? Curr. Opin. Invest. Drugs, 2: 1108–1111.

Belzung, C., Misslin, R., Vogel, E., Dodd, R.H. and Chapouthier, G. (1987) Anxiogenic effects of methyl-beta-carboline-3-carboxylate in a light/dark choice situation. Pharmacol. Biochem. Behav., 28: 29–33.

Belzung, C., Pineau, N., Beuzen, A. and Misslin, R. (1994) PD135158, a CCK-B antagonist, reduces "state," but not "trait" anxiety in mice. Pharmacol. Biochem. Behav., 49: 433–436.

Bertoglio, L.J., Anzini, C., Lino-de-Oliveira, C. and Carobrez, A.P. (2005) Enhanced dorsolateral periaqueductal gray activity counteracts the anxiolytic response to midazolam on the elevated plus-maze Trial 2 in rats. Behav. Brain Res., 162: 99–107.

Biegon, A., Bercovitz, H. and Samuel, D. (1980) Serotonin receptor concentration during the estrous cycle of the rat. Brain Res., 187: 221–225.

Biegon, A. and McEwen, B.S. (1982) Modulation by estradiol of serotonin receptors in brain. J. Neurosci., 2: 199–205.

Blanchard, D.C. (1997) Stimulus, environmental and pharmacological control of defensive behaviors. In: Bouton, M. and Fanselow, M.S. (Eds.), Learning, Motivation and Cognition. The Functional Behaviorism of Robert C. Bolles. American Psychological Association, Washington, DC.

Blanchard, D.C. and Blanchard, R.J. (2005) Antipredator defense. In: Whishaw, I.Q. and Kolb, B. (Eds.), The Behavior of the Laboratory Rat. Oxford University Press, New York.

Blanchard, D.C., Blanchard, R.J. and Griebel, G. (2005) Current protocols in neuroscience. In: Crawley, J.N., Gerfen, C.R., Rogawski, M.A., Sibley, D.R., Skolnick, P. and Wray, S. (Eds.), Behavioral Neuroscience. Wiley, New York.

Blanchard, D.C., Blanchard, R.J., Tom, P. and Rodgers, R.J. (1990a) Diazepam changes risk assessment in an anxiety/defense test battery. Psychopharmacology (Berlin), 101: 511–518.

Blanchard, D.C., Griebel, G. and Blanchard, R.J. (2001a) Mouse defensive behaviors: pharmacological and behavioral assays for anxiety and panic. Neurosci. Biobehav. Rev., 25: 205–218.

Blanchard, D.C., Griebel, G. and Blanchard, R.J. (2003a) The mouse defense test battery: pharmacological and behavioral assays for anxiety and panic. Eur. J. Pharmacol., 463: 97–116.

Blanchard, D.C., Markham, C., Yang, M., Hubbard, D., Madarang, E. and Blanchard, R.J. (2003b) Failure to produce conditioning with low-dose trimethylthiazoline or cat feces as unconditioned stimuli. Behav. Neurosci., 117: 360–368.

Blanchard, D.C., Shepherd, J.K., De Padua Carobrez, A. and Blanchard, R.J. (1991a) Sex effects in defensive behavior: baseline differences and drug interactions. Neurosci. Biobehav. Rev., 15: 461–468.

Blanchard, D.C., Shepherd, J.K., Rodgers, R.J. and Blanchard, R.J. (1992a) Evidence for differential effects of 8-OH-DPAT on male and female rats in the anxiety/defense test battery. Psychopharmacology (Berlin), 106: 531–539.

Blanchard, D.C., Spencer, R.L., Weiss, S.M., Blanchard, R.J., McEwen, B. and Sakai, R.R. (1995a) Visible burrow system as a model of chronic social stress: behavioral and neuroendocrine correlates. Psychoneuroendocrinology, 20: 117–134.

Blanchard, D.C., Yang, M., Hebert, M. and Blanchard, R.J. (2007) Defensive behaviors. In: Fink, G. (Ed.), Encyclopedia of Stress. 2nd edn. Academic Press, Oxford.

Blanchard, R.J., Agullana, R., McGee, L., Weiss, S. and Blanchard, D.C. (1992b) Sex differences in the incidence and sonographic characteristics of antipredator ultrasonic cries in the laboratory rat (Rattus norvegicus). J. Comp. Psychol., 106: 270–277.

Blanchard, R.J. and Blanchard, D.C. (1969) Crouching as an index of fear. J. Comp. Physiol. Psychol., 67: 370–375.

Blanchard, R.J. and Blanchard, D.C. (1971a) Defensive reactions in the albino rat. Learn. Motiv., 21: 351–362.

Blanchard, R.J. and Blanchard, D.C. (1971b) Defensive reactions in the albino rat. Learn. Motiv., 2: 351–362.

Blanchard, R.J. and Blanchard, D.C. (1989) Antipredator defensive behaviors in a visible burrow system. J. Comp. Psychol., 103: 70–82.

Blanchard, R.J., Blanchard, D.C., Agullana, R. and Weiss, S.M. (1991b) Twenty-two kHz alarm cries to presentation of a predator, by laboratory rats living in visible burrow systems. Physiol. Behav., 50: 967–972.

Blanchard, R.J., Blanchard, D.C. and Hori, K. (1989) An ethoexperimental approach to the study of defense. In: Blanchard, R.J. Brain, P.F. Blanchard, D.C. and Parmigiani, S. (Eds.), Ethoexperimental Approaches to the Study of Behavior. Kluver Academic, Boston.

Blanchard, R.J., Blanchard, D.C. and Weiss, S.M. (1990b) Ethanol effects in an anxiety/defense test battery. Alcohol, 7: 375–381.

Blanchard, R.J., Blanchard, D.C., Weiss, S.M. and Meyer, S. (1990c) The effects of ethanol and diazepam on reactions to predatory odors. Pharmacol. Biochem. Behav., 35: 775–780.

Blanchard, R.J., Flannelly, K.J. and Blanchard, D.C. (1986) Defensive behavior of laboratory and wild Rattus norvegicus. J. Comp. Psychol., 100: 101–107.

Blanchard, R.J., Fukunaga, K.K. and Blanchard, D.C. (1976) Environmental control of defensive reactions to a cat. Bull. Psychon. Soc., 8: 179–181.

Blanchard, R.J., Griebel, G., Henrie, J.A. and Blanchard, D.C. (1997) Differentiation of anxiolytic and panicolytic drugs by effects on rat and mouse defense test batteries. Neurosci. Biobehav. Rev., 21: 783–789.

Blanchard, R.J., Hebert, M.A., Ferrari, P.F., Palanza, P., Figueira, R., Blanchard, D.C. and Parmigiani, S. (1998) Defensive behaviors in wild and laboratory (Swiss) mice: the mouse defense test battery. Physiol. Behav., 65: 201–209.

Blanchard, R.J., Kelley, M.J. and Blanchard, D.C. (1974) Defensive reactions and exploratory behavior in rats. J. Comp. Physiol. Psychol., 87: 1129–1133.

Blanchard, R.J., Parmigiani, S., Bjornson, C., Masuda, C., Weiss, S.M. and Blanchard, D.C. (1995b) Antipredator behavior of Swiss-Webster mice in a visible burrow system. Aggress. Behav., 21: 123–136.

Blanchard, R.J., Shepherd, J.K., Rodgers, R.J., Magee, L. and Blanchard, D.C. (1993) Attenuation of antipredator defensive behavior in rats following chronic treatment with imipramine. Psychopharmacology (Berlin), 110: 245–253.

Blanchard, R.J., Yang, M., Li, C.I., Gervacio, A. and Blanchard, D.C. (2001b) Cue and context conditioning of defensive behaviors to cat odor stimuli. Neurosci. Biobehav. Rev., 25: 587–595.

Borsini, F., Podhorna, J. and Marazziti, D. (2002) Do animal models of anxiety predict anxiolytic-like effects of antidepressants? Psychopharmacology (Berlin), 163: 121–141.

Bourin, M. and Hascoet, M. (2003) The mouse light/dark box test. Eur. J. Pharmacol., 463: 55–65.

Carlsson, M. and Carlsson, A. (1988) A regional study of sex differences in rat brain serotonin. Prog. Neuropsychopharmacol. Biol. Psychiatry, 12: 53–61.

Carobrez, A.P. and Bertoglio, L.J. (2005) Ethological and temporal analyses of anxiety-like behavior: the elevated plus-maze model 20 years on. Neurosci. Biobehav. Rev., 29: 1193–1205.

Carobrez, A.P., Teixeira, K.V. and Graeff, F.G. (2001) Modulation of defensive behavior by periaqueductal gray NMDA/glycine-B receptor. Neurosci. Biobehav. Rev., 25: 697–709.

Carvalho-Netto, E.F., Litvin, Y., Nunes-De-Souza, R.L., Blanchard, D.C. and Blanchard, R.J. (2007) Effects of Intra-PAG infusion of ovine CRF (oCRF) on defensive behaviors in Swiss-Webster Mice. Behav. Brain Res., 176: 222 229.

Chaouloff, F., Durand, M. and Mormede, P. (1997) Anxiety- and activity-related effects of diazepam and chlordiazepoxide in the rat light/dark and dark/light tests. Behav. Brain Res., 85: 27–35.

Cheeta, S., Tucci, S., Sandhu, J., Williams, A.R., Rupniak, N.M. and File, S.E. (2001) Anxiolytic actions of the substance P (NK1) receptor antagonist L-760735 and the 5-HT1A agonist 8-OH-DPAT in the social interaction test in gerbils. Brain Res., 915: 170–175.

Choleris, E., Thomas, A.W., Kavaliers, M. and Prato, F.S. (2001) A detailed ethological analysis of the mouse open field test: effects of diazepam, chlordiazepoxide and an extremely low frequency pulsed magnetic field. Neurosci. Biobehav. Rev., 25: 235–260.

Cohen, H., Kaplan, Z., Matar, M.A., Loewenthal, U., Zohar, J. and Richter-Levin, G. (2007) Long-lasting behavioral effects of juvenile trauma in an animal model of PTSD associated with a failure of the autonomic nervous system to recover. Eur. Neuropsychopharmacol., 17: 464–477.

Cohen, H. and Zohar, J. (2004) An animal model of posttraumatic stress disorder: the use of cut-off behavioral criteria. Ann. N.Y. Acad. Sci., 1032: 167–178.

Conely, L. and Bell, R.W. (1978) Neonatal ultrasounds elicited by odor cues. Dev. Psychobiol., 11: 193–197.

Crawley, J. (1981) Neuropharmacological specificity of a simple animal model for the behavioral actions of the benzodiazepines. Pharmacol. Biochem. Behav., 15: 695–699.

Crawley, J. and Goodwin, F.K. (1980) Preliminary report of a simple animal behavior model for the anxiolytic effects of benzodiazepines. Pharmacol. Biochem. Behav., 13: 167–170.

Crawley, J.N. and Paylor, R. (1997) A proposed test battery and constellations of specific behavioral paradigms to investigate the behavioral phenotypes of transgenic and knockout mice. Horm. Behav., 31: 197–211.

Cruz, A.P., Frei, F. and Graeff, F.G. (1994) Ethopharmacological analysis of rat behavior on the elevated plus-maze. Pharmacol. Biochem. Behav., 49: 171–176.

Dawson, G.R. and Tricklebank, M.D. (1995) Use of the elevated plus-maze in the search for novel anxiolytic agents. Trends Pharmacol. Sci., 16: 33–36.

Deakin, J.F.W. and Graeff, F.G. (1991) 5-HT and mechanisms of defence. J. Psychopharmacol., 5: 305–315.

de Angelis, L. and File, S.E. (1979) Acute and chronic effects of three benzodiazepines in the social interaction anxiety test in mice. Psychopharmacology (Berlin), 64: 127–129.

De Boer, S.F. and Koolhaas, J.M. (2003) Defensive burying in rodents: ethology, neurobiology and psychopharmacology. Eur. J. Pharmacol., 463: 145–161.

Diamond, D.M., Campbell, A.M., Park, C.R., Woodson, J.C., Conrad, C.D., Bachstetter, A.D. and Mervis, R.F. (2006) Influence of predator stress on the consolidation versus retrieval of long-term spatial memory and hippocampal spinogenesis. Hippocampus, 16: 571–576.

Edinger, K.L. and Frye, C.A. (2007) Sexual experience of male rats influences anxiety-like behavior and androgen levels. Physiol. Behav., 2(3): 443–453.

Farrokhi, C. (2006) Comparative effects of the CRF agonist, ovine CRF, and CRF antagonist, astressin, on homecage behavior patterns and defense in the mouse. *Psychology*. Honolulu, University of Hawaii at Manoa.

File, S.E. (1993) The interplay of learning and anxiety in the elevated plus-maze. Behav. Brain Res., 58: 199–202.

File, S.E. (1994) Chronic exposure to noise modifies the anxiogenic response, but not the hypoactivity, detected on withdrawal from chronic ethanol treatment. Psychopharmacology (Berlin), 116: 369–372.

File, S.E., Cheeta, S. and Akanezi, C. (2001) Diazepam and nicotine increase social interaction in gerbils: a test for anxiolytic action. Brain Res., 888: 311–313.

File, S.E., Gonzalez, L.E. and Gallant, R. (1998) Role of the basolateral nucleus of the amygdala in the formation of a phobia. Neuropsychopharmacology, 19: 397–405.

File, S.E., Gonzalez, L.E. and Gallant, R. (1999) Role of the dorsomedial hypothalamus in mediating the response to benzodiazepines on trial 2 in the elevated plus-maze test of anxiety. Neuropsychopharmacology, 21: 312–320.

File, S.E. and Seth, P. (2003) A review of 25 years of the social interaction test. Eur. J. Pharmacol., 463: 35–53.

File, S.E. and Zangrossi, H. Jr. (1993) "One-trial tolerance" to the anxiolytic actions of benzodiazepines in the elevated plus-maze, or the development of a phobic state? Psychopharmacology (Berlin), 110: 240–244.

Ford, J.D. and Kidd, P. (1998) Early childhood trauma and disorders of extreme stress as predictors of treatment outcome with chronic posttraumatic stress disorder. J. Trauma Stress, 11: 743–761.

Fowler, H. (1965) Curiosity and exploratory behavior. Macmillan, New York.

Graeff, F.G. (2002) On serotonin and experimental anxiety. Psychopharmacology (Berlin), 163: 467–476.

Graeff, F.G. (2004) Serotonin, the periaqueductal gray and panic. Neurosci. Biobehav. Rev., 28: 239–259.

Graeff, F.G., Netto, C.F. and Zangrossi, H. Jr. (1998) The elevated T-maze as an experimental model of anxiety. Neurosci. Biobehav. Rev., 23: 237–246.

Graeff, F.G., Viana, M.B. and Tomaz, C. (1993) The elevated T maze, a new experimental model of anxiety and memory: effect of diazepam. Braz. J. Med. Biol. Res., 26: 67–70.

Graeff, F.G. and Zangrossi, H. (2002) Animal models of anxiety disorders. In: D'Haenen, H. den Boer, J.A. and Willner, P. (Eds.), Biological Psychiatry. Wiley, Chichester.

Griebel, G. (1995) 5-Hydroxytryptamine-interacting drugs in animal models of anxiety disorders: more than 30 years of research. Pharmacol. Ther., 65: 319–395.

Griebel, G. (1996) Variability in the effects of 5-HT-related compounds in experimental models of anxiety: evidence for multiple mechanisms of 5-HT in anxiety or never ending story? Pol. J. Pharmacol., 48: 129–136.

Griebel, G., Belzung, C., Misslin, R. and Vogel, E. (1993) The free-exploratory paradigm: an effective method for measuring neophobic behaviour in mice and testing potential neophobia-reducing drugs. Behav. Pharmacol., 4: 637–644.

Griebel, G., Belzung, C., Perrault, G. and Sanger, D.J. (2000) Differences in anxiety-related behaviours and in sensitivity to diazepam in inbred and outbred strains of mice. Psychopharmacology (Berlin), 148: 164–170.

Griebel, G., Blanchard, D.C. and Blanchard, R.J. (1996a) Evidence that the behaviors in the mouse defense test battery relate to different emotional states: a factor analytic study. Physiol. Behav., 60: 1255–1260.

Griebel, G., Blanchard, D.C. and Blanchard, R.J. (1996b) Predator-elicited flight responses in Swiss-Webster mice: an experimental model of panic attacks. Prog. Neuropsychopharmacol. Biol. Psychiatry, 20: 185–205.

Griebel, G., Curet, O., Perrault, G. and Sanger, D.J. (1998) Behavioral effects of phenelzine in an experimental model for screening anxiolytic and anti-panic drugs: correlation with changes in monoamine-oxidase activity and monoamine levels. Neuropharmacology, 37: 927–935.

Griebel, G., Rodgers, R.J., Perrault, G. and Sanger, D.J. (1997) Risk assessment behaviour: evaluation of utility in the study of 5-HT-related drugs in the rat elevated plus-maze test. Pharmacol. Biochem. Behav., 57: 817–827.

Griebel, G., Sanger, D.J. and Perrault, G. (1996c) Further evidence for differences between non-selective and BZ-1 (omega 1) selective, benzodiazepine receptor ligands in murine models of "state" and "trait" anxiety. Neuropharmacology, 35: 1081–1091.

Hall, C.S. (1934) Emotional behavior in the rat: I, Defecation and urination as measures of individual differences in emotionality. J. Comp. Psychol., 18: 385–403.

Handley, S.L. (1995) 5-Hydroxytryptamine pathways in anxiety and its treatment. Pharmacol. Ther., 66: 103–148.

Handley, S.L. and McBlane, J.W. (1993) 5HT drugs in animal models of anxiety. Psychopharmacology (Berlin), 112: 13–20.

Handley, S.L., McBlane, J.W., Critchley, M.A.E. and Njung'e, K. (1993) Multiple serotonin mechanisms in animal models of anxiety: environmental, emotional and cognitive factors. Behav. Brain Res., 58: 203–210.

Handley, S.L. and Mithani, S. (1984) Effects of alpha-adrenoceptor agonists and antagonists in a maze-exploration model of 'fear'-motivated behaviour. Naunyn Schmiedebergs Arch. Pharmacol., 327: 1–5.

Hascoet, M. and Bourin, M. (1998) A new approach to the light/dark test procedure in mice. Pharmacol. Biochem. Behav., 60: 645–653.

Heim, C. and Nemeroff, C.B. (2001) The role of childhood trauma in the neurobiology of mood and anxiety disorders: preclinical and clinical studies. Biol. Psychiatry, 49: 1023–1039.

Hendrie, C.A., Eilam, D. and Weiss, S.M. (1997) Effects of diazepam and buspirone on the behaviour of wild voles (Microtus socialis) in two models of anxiety. Pharmacol. Biochem. Behav., 58: 573–576.

Hilakivi, L.A., Durcan, M.J. and Lister, R.G. (1989) Effects of caffeine on social behavior, exploration and locomotor activity: interactions with ethanol. Life Sci., 44: 543–553.

Hofer, M.A. and Shair, H. (1980) Sensory processes in the control of isolation-induced ultrasonic vocalization by 2-week-old rats. J. Comp. Physiol. Psychol., 94: 271–279.

Hogg, S. (1996) A review of the validity and variability of the elevated plus-maze as an animal model of anxiety. Pharmacol. Biochem. Behav., 54: 21–30.

Holmes, A., Parmigiani, S., Ferrari, P.F., Palanza, P. and Rodgers, R.J. (2000) Behavioral profile of wild mice in the elevated plus-maze test for anxiety. Physiol. Behav., 71: 509–516.

Huck, U.W. and Price, E.O. (1975) Differential effects of environmental enrichment on the open-field behavior of wild and domestic Norway rats. J. Comp. Physiol. Psychol., 89: 892–898.

Insel, T.R., Hill, J.L. and Mayor, R.B. (1986) Rat pup ultrasonic isolation calls: possible mediation by the benzodiazepine receptor complex. Pharmacol. Biochem. Behav., 24: 1263–1267.

Iwaniuk, A.N. (2005) Evolution. In: Whishaw, I.Q. and Kolb, B. (Eds.), The Behavior of the Laboratory Rat. Oxford University Press, Oxford.

Johnson, M.R., Lydiard, R.B. and Ballenger, J.C. (1995) Panic disorder. Pathophysiology and drug treatment. Drugs, 49: 328–344.

Johnston, A.L. and File, S.E. (1991) Sex differences in animal tests of anxiety. Physiol. Behav., 49: 245–250.

Kehoe, P. and Blass, E.M. (1986) Opioid-mediation of separation distress in 10-day-old rats: reversal of stress with maternal stimuli. Dev. Psychobiol., 19: 385–398.

Kopp, C., Misslin, R., Vogel, E., Rettori, M.C., Delagrange, P. and Guardiola-Lemaître, B. (1997) Effects of day-length variations on emotional responses toward unfamiliarity in Swiss mice. Behav. Proc., 41: 151–157.

Lister, R.G. (1987) The use of a plus-maze to measure anxiety in the mouse. Psychopharmacology (Berlin), 92: 180–185.

Lister, R.G. (1990) Ethologically-based animal models of anxiety disorders. Pharmacol. Ther., 46: 321–340.

Lister, R.G. and Hilakivi, L.A. (1988) The effects of novelty, isolation, light and ethanol on the social behavior of mice. Psychopharmacology (Berlin), 96: 181–187.

Litvin, Y., Blanchard, D.C. and Blanchard, R.J. (2007a) Rat 22 kHz ultrasonic vocalizations as alarm cries. Behav. Brain Res., 182: 166–172.

Litvin, Y., Pentkowski, N.S., Blanchard, D.C. and Blanchard, R.J. (2007b) CRF type 1 receptors in the dorsal periaqueductal gray modulate anxiety-induced defensive behaviors. Horm. Behav., 52: 244–251.

Lowry, C.A., Johnson, P.L., Hay-Schmidt, A., Mikkelsen, J. and Shekhar, A. (2005) Modulation of anxiety circuits by serotonergic systems. Stress, 8: 233–246.

Maciag, C.M., Dent, G., Gilligan, P., He, L., Dowling, K., Ko, T., Levine, S. and Smith, M.A. (2002) Effects of a non-peptide CRF antagonist (DMP696) on the behavioral and endocrine sequelae of maternal separation. Neuropsychopharmacology, 26: 574–582.

Maier, S.F. and Watkins, L.R. (2005) Stressor controllability and learned helplessness: the roles of the dorsal raphe nucleus, serotonin, and corticotropin-releasing factor. Neurosci. Biobehav. Rev., 29: 829–841.

Marcondes, F.K., Miguel, K.J., Melo, L.L. and Spadari-Bratfisch, R.C. (2001) Estrous cycle influences the response of female rats in the elevated plus-maze test. Physiol. Behav., 74: 435–440.

Markham, C.M., Blanchard, D.C., Canteras, N.S., Cuyno, C.D. and Blanchard, R.J. (2004) Modulation of predatory odor processing following lesions to the dorsal premammillary nucleus. Neurosci. Lett., 372: 22–26.

McGregor, I.S. and Dielenberg, R.A. (1999) Differential anxiolytic efficacy of a benzodiazepine on first versus second exposure to a predatory odor in rats. Psychopharmacology (Berlin), 147: 174–181.

McGregor, I.S., Hargreaves, G.A., Apfelbach, R. and Hunt, G.E. (2004) Neural correlates of cat odor-induced anxiety in rats: region-specific effects of the benzodiazepine midazolam. J. Neurosci., 24: 4134–4144.

McKinney, W.T. (1984) Animal models of depression: an overview. Psychiatry Dev., 2: 77–96.

Miczek, K.A., Weerts, E.M., Vivian, J.A. and Barros, H.M. (1995) Aggression, anxiety and vocalizations in animals: GABAA and 5-HT anxiolytics. Psychopharmacology (Berlin), 121: 38–56.

Montgomery, K.C. (1954) The role of the exploratory drive in learning. J. Comp. Physiol. Psychol., 47: 60–64.

Montgomery, K.C. (1955) The relation between fear induced by novelty stimulation and exploratory behavior. J. Comp. Physiol. Psychol., 48: 254–260.

Mora, S., Dussaubat, N. and Diaz-Veliz, G. (1996) Effects of the estrous cycle and ovarian hormones on behavioral indices of anxiety in female rats. Psychoneuroendocrinology, 21: 609–620.

Nutt, D.J. (1991) Anxiety and its therapy: today and tomorrow. In: Briley, M. and File, S.E. (Eds.), New Concepts in Anxiety. MacMillan Press, London.

Oswalt, G.L. and Meier, G.W. (1975) Olfactory, thermal, and tactual influences on infantile ultrasonic vocalization in rats. Dev. Psychobiol., 8: 129–135.

Pellow, S., Chopin, P., File, S.E. and Briley, M. (1985) Validation of open: closed arm entries in an elevated plus-maze as a measure of anxiety in the rat. J. Neurosci. Methods, 14: 149–167.

Pentkowski, N.S., Blanchard, D.C., Lever, C., Litvin, Y. and Blanchard, R.J. (2006) Effects of lesions to the dorsal and ventral hippocampus on defensive behaviors in rats. Eur. J. Neurosci., 23: 2185–2196.

Podhorna, J. and Brown, R.E. (2000) Flibanserin has anxiolytic effects without locomotor side effects in the infant rat ultrasonic vocalization model of anxiety. Br. J. Pharmacol., 130: 739–746.

Poltronieri, S.C., Zangrossi, H. Jr. and de Barros Viana, M. (2003) Antipanic-like effect of serotonin reuptake inhibitors in the elevated T-maze. Behav. Brain Res., 147: 185–192.

Prendergast, B.J. and Nelson, R.J. (2005) Affective responses to changes in day length in Siberian hamsters (*Phodopus sungorus*). Psychoneuroendocrinology, 30: 438–452.

Price, E.O. (1984) Behavioral aspects of animal domestication. Q. Rev. Biol., 59: 1–32.

Prut, L. and Belzung, C. (2003) The open field as a paradigm to measure the effects of drugs on anxiety-like behaviors: a review. Eur. J. Pharmacol., 463: 3–33.

Rex, A. and Fink, H. (1998) Effects of cholecystokinin-receptor agonists on cortical 5-HT release in guinea pigs on the X-maze. Peptides, 19: 519–526.

Rodgers, R.J. (1997) Animal models of 'anxiety': where next? Behav. Pharmacol., 8: 477–496. discussion 497–504.

Rodgers, R.J. (2007) More haste, considerably less speed. J. Psychopharmacol., 21: 141–143.

Rodgers, R.J., Boullier, E., Chatzimichalaki, P., Cooper, G.D. and Shorten, A. (2002) Contrasting phenotypes of C57BL/6JOlaHsd, 129S2/SvHsd and 129/SvEv mice in two exploration-based tests of anxiety-related behaviour. Physiol. Behav., 77: 301–310.

Rodgers, R.J., Dalvi, A. and Holmes, A. (1997) Animal models of anxiety: an ethological perspective. Braz. J. Med. Biol. Res., 30: 289–304.

Rodgers, R.J. and Johnson, N.J. (1995) Factor analysis of spatiotemporal and ethological measures in the murine elevated plus-maze test of anxiety. Pharmacol. Biochem. Behav., 52: 297–303.

Rodgers, R.J., Johnson, N.J., Cole, J.C., Dewar, C.V., Kidd, G.R. and Kimpson, P.H. (1996) Plus-maze retest profile in mice: importance of initial stages of trail 1 and response to post-trail cholinergic receptor blockade. Pharmacol. Biochem. Behav., 54: 41–50.

Roy, V. and Chapillon, P. (2004) Further evidences that risk assessment and object exploration behaviours are useful to evaluate emotional reactivity in rodents. Behav. Brain Res., 154: 439–448.

Salome, N., Stemmelin, J., Cohen, C. and Griebel, G. (2006) Selective blockade of NK2 or NK3 receptors produces anxiolytic- and antidepressant-like effects in gerbils. Pharmacol. Biochem. Behav., 83: 533–539.

Salome, N., Viltart, O., Darnaudery, M., Salchner, P., Singewald, N., Landgraf, R., Sequeira, H. and Wigger, A. (2002) Reliability of high and low anxiety-related behaviour: influence of laboratory environment and multifactorial analysis. Behav. Brain Res., 136: 227–237.

Shair, H.N. (2007) Acquisition and expression of a socially mediated separation response. Behav. Brain Res., 182: 180–192.

Shepherd, J.K., Grewal, S.S., Fletcher, A., Bill, D.J. and Dourish, C.T. (1994) Behavioural and pharmacological characterisation of the elevated "zero-maze" as an animal model of anxiety. Psychopharmacology (Berlin), 116: 56–64.

Shimada, T., Matsumoto, K., Osanai, M., Matsuda, H., Terasawa, K. and Watanabe, H. (1995) The modified light/dark transition test in mice: evaluation of classic and putative anxiolytic and anxiogenic drugs. Gen. Pharmacol., 26: 205–210.

Stanford, S.C. (2007) The open field test: reinventing the wheel. J. Psychopharmacol., 21: 134–135.

Takahashi, L.K. (1992) Ontogeny of behavioral inhibition induced by unfamiliar adult male conspecifics in preweanling rats. Physiol. Behav., 52: 493–498.

Takahashi, L.K., Nakashima, B.R., Hong, H. and Watanabe, K. (2005) The smell of danger: a behavioral and neural analysis of predator odor-induced fear. Neurosci. Biobehav. Rev., 29: 1157–1167.

Teixeira, R.C., Zangrossi, H. and Graeff, F.G. (2000) Behavioral effects of acute and chronic imipramine in the elevated T-maze model of anxiety. Pharmacol. Biochem. Behav., 65: 571–576.

Tovote, P., Farrokhi, C.B., Todorovic, C., Blanchard, R.J. and Blanchard, D.C. (2006). The rat exposure test: a semi-natural model for anxiety-like behavior in the mouse. *Society for Neuroscience*. Atlanta, USA.

Treit, D., Menard, J. and Royan, C. (1993) Anxiogenic stimuli in the elevated plus-maze. Pharmacol. Biochem. Behav., 44: 463–469.

Treit, D. and Fundytus, M. (1989) Thigmotaxis as a test for anxiolytic activity in rats. Pharmacol. Biochem. Behav., 31: 959–962.

Tucci, S., Cheeta, S., Seth, P. and File, S.E. (2003) Corticotropin releasing factor antagonist, alpha-helical CRF(9-41), reverses nicotine-induced conditioned, but not unconditioned, anxiety. Psychopharmacology (Berlin), 167: 251–256.

Varty, G.B., Morgan, C.A., Cohen-Williams, M.E., Coffin, V.L. and Carey, G.J. (2002) The gerbil elevated plus-maze I: behavioral characterization and pharmacological validation. Neuropsychopharmacology, 27: 357–370.

Viana, M.B., Tomaz, C. and Graeff, F.G. (1994) The elevated T-maze: a new animal model of anxiety and memory. Pharmacol. Biochem. Behav., 49: 549–554.

Wall, P.M. and Messier, C. (2001) Methodological and conceptual issues in the use of the elevated plus-maze as a psychological measurement instrument of animal anxiety-like behavior. Neurosci. Biobehav. Rev., 25: 275–286.

Wallace, K.J. and Rosen, J.B. (2000) Predator odor as an unconditioned fear stimulus in rats: elicitation of freezing by trimethylthiazoline, a component of fox feces. Behav. Neurosci., 114: 912–922.

Weiss, S.M., Wadsworth, G., Fletcher, A. and Dourish, C.T. (1998) Utility of ethological analysis to overcome locomotor confounds in elevated maze models of anxiety. Neurosci. Biobehav. Rev., 23: 265–271.

Welker, W.I. (1959) Escape, exploratory, and food-seeking responses of rats in a novel situation. J. Comp. Physiol. Psychol., 52: 106–111.

Wilson, R.C., Vacek, T., Lanier, D.L. and Dewsbury, D.A. (1976) Open-field behavior in muroid rodents. Behav. Biol., 17: 495–506.

Winslow, J.T. and Insel, T.R. (1991) Infant rat separation is a sensitive test for novel anxiolytics. Prog. Neuropsychopharmacol. Biol. Psychiatry, 15: 745–757.

Yang, M., Augustsson, H., Markham, C.M., Hubbard, D.T., Webster, D., Wall, P.M., Blanchard, R.J. and Blanchard, D.C. (2004) The rat exposure test: a model of mouse defensive behaviors. Physiol. Behav., 81: 465–473.

Zangrossi, H. Jr. and File, S.E. (1992a) Behavioral consequences in animal tests of anxiety and exploration of exposure to cat odor. Brain Res. Bull., 29: 381–388.

Zangrossi, H. Jr. and File, S.E. (1992b) Chlordiazepoxide reduces the generalised anxiety, but not the direct responses, of rats exposed to cat odor. Pharmacol. Biochem. Behav., 43: 1195–1200.

Zangrossi, H. Jr. and Graeff, F.G. (1997) Behavioral validation of the elevated T-maze, a new animal model of anxiety. Brain Res. Bull., 44: 1–5.

Zimmerberg, B., Brunelli, S.A. and Hofer, M.A. (1994) Reduction of rat pup ultrasonic vocalizations by the neuroactive steroid allopregnanolone. Pharmacol. Biochem. Behav., 47: 735–738.

Zimmerberg, B. and Farley, M.J. (1993) Sex differences in anxiety behavior in rats: role of gonadal hormones. Physiol. Behav., 54: 1119–1124.

Neural Systems for Anxiety, Fear, and Defense

CHAPTER 3.1

Brain mechanisms of Pavlovian and instrumental aversive conditioning

Christopher K. Cain* and Joseph E. LeDoux

Center for Neural Science, New York University, New York, NY, USA

Abstract: Fear learning can be broadly divided into two categories: the acquisition of fear reactions, modeled by Pavlovian conditioning, and the acquisition of fear actions, modeled by instrumental avoidance/escape conditioning. Brain research on Pavlovian conditioning has been especially successful at delineating the cellular and molecular mechanisms of fear-reaction learning. Instrumental conditioning research is beginning to shed light on fear-action learning at the brain systems level. In the present chapter we review recent advances in both fields and suggest that the Escape from Fear (EFF) paradigm is an excellent model for studying how these two types of learning interact to subserve fear behavior. The mechanisms of such learning may be related to passive versus active coping strategies in humans suffering from pathological fear and understanding these mechanisms may have important treatment implications.

Keywords: Pavlovian; instrumental; conditioning; avoidance; amygdala; coping

I. Introduction

The predatory defense, or fear, system has been a particularly useful model system for exploring questions about brain mechanisms of emotional processing. Stimuli associated with predators or other dangers elicit defensive responses that function to keep the organism safe. Each species has certain stimuli that are innately wired to activate the fear system. Other stimuli, when associated with innate stimuli, acquire the capacity to activate the system. By examining how the brain processes information about innate and/or learned fear stimuli, and how it generates specific defensive responses on the basis of this processing, the defense circuitry is being mapped. In this sense, emotion can be thought of as the process by which the brain computes the value of a stimulus for the purpose of responding adaptively.

Activation of the fear system leads to the automatic elicitation of emotional reactions (i.e. freezing behavior, autonomic nervous system activity, hormonal release). It also mobilizes brain and body resources and prepares the organism to perform active responses that cope with the danger (i.e. flight). The former is usually referred to as fear, and the latter as escape or avoidance. Fear-elicited reactions prevent escalation of the threat and fear-motivated actions function to remove the organism from the threat. Note that fear responses (reactions/actions) are adaptive in the sense that they protect individual organisms from life-threatening circumstances and improve the evolutionary fitness of a species. However, in the context of human pathology, fear responses can be maladaptive if they are activated by innocuous stimuli or are activated in a recurring, excessive, or prolonged way that goes beyond the requirements of the situation.

The present chapter reviews recent advances in our understanding of brain mechanisms mediating fear learning. We focus on animal research using

*Corresponding author. E-mail: cc110@nyu.edu

R.J. Blanchard, D.C. Blanchard, G. Griebel and D. Nutt (Eds.)
Handbook of Anxiety and Fear, Vol. 17
ISBN 978-0-444-53065-3

103

DOI: 10.1016/S1569-7339(07)00007-0

two basic learning protocols to study fear reactions and fear actions: Pavlovian conditioning and instrumental escape/avoidance conditioning. Pavlovian conditioning research has been especially successful at delineating the anatomical, cellular, and molecular substrates of fear learning. Research on avoidance conditioning, a more complex form of learning, is beginning to shed light on how fear-conditioning systems interact with motor learning systems to subserve fear-motivated action learning. We conclude by proposing a hypothetical brain "motive circuit" to use as a framework for future investigations of Pavlovian–instrumental interactions in the aversive context.

II. Pavlovian fear conditioning

Pavlovian fear conditioning involves the generation of defensive reactions to a stimulus that predicts an aversive consequence. In a typical fear-conditioning experiment, rodents are presented with an emotionally neutral conditioned stimulus (CS), often a tone, that is paired in time with an aversive footshock unconditioned stimulus (US). Prior to the pairing, the subjects exhibit weak defensive responses to the tone. After pairing, tone presentations elicit a cassette of defensive responses including freezing (Blanchard and Blanchard, 1969; Fanselow and Bolles, 1979), autonomic reactions (Schneiderman et al., 1974; Fitzgerald and Brackbill, 1976; LeDoux et al., 1980; Smith et al., 1980), neuroendocrine responses (Mason et al., 1961; Korte et al., 1992a, b), as well as potentiation of somatic reflexes such as startle (Davis, 1986) and eyeblink (Weisz and McInerney, 1990) (Fig. 1). Collectively these CS-elicited learned responses are referred to as conditioned fear responses (Miller, 1951; Brown and Wagner, 1964; McAllister and McAllister, 1971). Fear responses elicited by the CS after pairing with the US indicate that associative learning took place

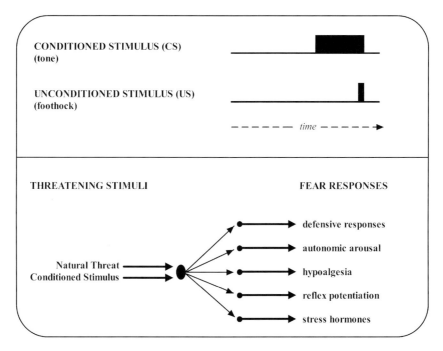

Fig. 1. Pavlovian fear conditioning involves temporal pairings of an emotionally neutral conditioned stimulus (CS), such as a tone, with an aversive unconditioned stimulus (US), such as a footshock (*top*). Prior to conditioning, the CS does not elicit fear responses. After conditioning, CS presentations elicit a number of fear reactions (*bottom*). Figure recreated with permission from *Annual Reviews of Neuroscience* (LeDoux, 2000).

during conditioning, provided that similar responses fail to occur when the CS and US are unpaired during conditioning (Rescorla, 1967). Conditioned fear responses can be generated with a single CS–US pairing (Anagnostaras et al., 2000) and can last for the lifetime of the animal (Gale et al., 2004). Fear conditioning also establishes the CS as secondary incentive that can motivate avoidance behaviors (discussed below).

II.A. Circuitry

The amygdala, an almond-shaped cluster of nuclei in the temporal lobe, is critical for the learning, storage, and expression of fear conditioning (Fanselow and LeDoux, 1999; LeDoux, 2000; Maren and Quirk, 2004; Pare et al., 2004). The amygdala is composed of a dozen or so nuclei (Pitkänen et al., 1997). Of these, three have been the focus of much of the research on fear conditioning: the lateral nucleus (LA), central nucleus (CE), and the basal nucleus (B) (Fig. 2a).

Neurons in the LA receive auditory (CS) and somatosensory (US) inputs from thalamic and cortical processing regions (LeDoux, 1990; Turner and Herkenham, 1991; Amaral et al., 1992; Mascagni et al., 1993; Romanski et al., 1993; McDonald, 1998). Tone signals arrive in the LA as early as 12 ms following stimulus onset and the

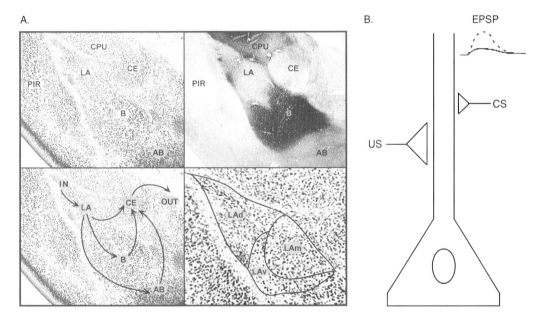

Fig. 2. A. At least 12 nuclei comprise the mammalian amygdala. Particularly important for fear conditioning are the lateral nucleus (LA), the basal nucleus (B), and the central nucleus (CE). Top panels show coronal slices taken from rat brain (*Left*: Nissl stain, *Right*: Acetylcholinesterase stain) including LA, B, and CE. The basic amygdala circuit mediating auditory fear conditioning is shown in the *Lower Left* panel. Sensory inputs enter through the LA, and LA connects to CE both directly and indirectly by way of B. CE is the major output nucleus mediating expression of conditioned responses. *Bottom Right*: higher magnification image of the LA demonstrating that amygdala nuclei can also be divided into functional subregions called subnuclei. Abbreviations: Pir = piriform cortex, AB = accessory basal nucleus, CPU = caudate putamen, LAd = dorsal subdivision of the LA, LAm = medial subdivision of the LA, LAv = ventral subdivision of the LA. B. Schematic illustrating the basic cellular hypothesis of fear conditioning. Prior to conditioning, CS afferents synapse on dendrites of LA principle cells resulting in small EPSPs, which are incapable of driving LA neurons and downstream regions important for fear expression. When CS and US inputs are correlated in time, as during a CS–US pairing, synaptic plasticity occurs so that subsequent CS presentations elicit larger EPSPs that are capable of driving LA principle cells and downstream regions important for fear expression. Figures reprinted with permission from *Annual Reviews of Neuroscience* (LeDoux, 2000) and *Learning and Memory* (Blair et al., 2001).

same neurons receive shock inputs (Clugnet et al., 1990; Bordi and LeDoux, 1992; Bordi et al., 1993; Romanski et al., 1993; Bordi and LeDoux, 1994a, b). LA neurons in turn connect with CE both directly and indirectly via projections to B (Pitkänen et al., 1997; Pare and Smith, 1998).

The LA appears to be critical for the acquisition and retention of fear conditioning. Both electrolytic and excitotoxic lesions of the LA prevent acquisition and expression of fear conditioning (LeDoux, 1990; Campeau and Davis, 1995; Amorapanth et al., 2000; Gale et al., 2004). Temporary inactivation of the LA with muscimol prevents CS-elicited freezing when given before training or testing, but not if given immediately after training (Muller et al., 1997; Wilensky et al., 1999). Further, pharmacological manipulations of LA function using local infusions support a role for LA in acquisition and storage of the fear-conditioning trace. For instance, infusions of NMDA receptor blockers before conditioning, but not after, impair both short- and long-term fear memory (Miserendino et al., 1990; Campeau et al., 1992; Maren et al., 1996; Rodrigues et al., 2001). Agents that block gene transcription and translation in LA specifically block long-term memory for conditioning (Bourtchouladze et al., 1994; Bailey et al., 1999; Schafe and LeDoux, 2000; Kida et al., 2002; Maren et al., 2003). A particularly striking demonstration that the LA is required for the long-term storage of fear-conditioning plasticity comes from recent work in the Fanselow laboratory (Gale et al., 2004). They found that excitotoxic lesions of the LA conducted 16 months after fear conditioning, nearly the entire adult lifetime of the rat, severely disrupted subsequent conditioned freezing.

Substantial evidence suggests that CE, via projections to the hypothalamus and brainstem (LeDoux et al., 1988; Bellgowan and Helmstetter, 1996; Davis, 1998; De Oca et al., 1998), is important for the expression of fear conditioning (Hitchcock and Davis, 1986; Kapp et al., 1992; Amorapanth et al., 1999; Goosens and Maren, 2001; but see: Killcross et al., 1997a; Koo et al., 2004). Initial studies suggested that CE was not important for acquisition of fear conditioning because agents that impaired acquisition when

delivered to LA failed to impair acquisition when delivered to CE (e.g. Fanselow and Kim, 1994). Very recent data, however, questions the notion that CE is merely a passive relay of conditioning plasticity arriving from LA (Wilensky et al., 2006). Inactivation of CE prior to fear conditioning impairs short- and long-term memory, and CE infusion of anisomycin, a protein synthesis inhibitor, disrupts long-term memory. Thus CE appears to also participate in the learning and storage of fear conditioning. It is important to note, however, that CE processes alone appear incapable of supporting learning/memory for fear conditioning since LA-specific manipulations result in severe impairments of fear conditioning. It is also unclear at present whether fear-conditioning plasticity in CE depends on LA processes or is mediated by direct CS and US inputs (LeDoux et al., 1987; Bernard and Besson, 1990; Turner and Herkenham, 1991; Jasmin et al., 1997; McDonald, 1998), independent of LA (see: Cardinal et al., 2002; Balleine and Killcross, 2006).

The role of the basal nucleus (B) in fear conditioning is somewhat controversial at present. Pre-training lesions of B have no effect on learning or expression (Amorapanth et al., 2000; Goosens and Maren, 2001; Nader et al., 2001; Sotres-Bayon et al., 2004) but a recent study indicates that post-training lesions impair expression of learning (Anglada-Figueroa and Quirk, 2005). This suggests that B is not required for learning or expression of fear conditioning, but may participate in one or both of these processes when the brain is intact. Thus, the null findings with pre-training lesions of B may result from functional compensation by other brain regions.

Taken together, anatomic, lesion, and pharmacological studies suggest that LA is critical for the learning and storage of Pavlovian fear conditioning, CE participates in learning, storage and expression and B participates, at least, in fear expression. Notably, LA and CE manipulations that impair fear conditioning do not alter tone or shock sensitivity, the ability to freeze, or even non-associative learning processes such as shock-induced sensitization (Fanselow and LeDoux, 1999; Wilensky et al., 2006). Thus, LA and CE appear to be selectively involved in associative learning about emotionally significant stimuli.

II.B. Synaptic plasticity

Short latency ($<15\,ms$) auditory-evoked unit responses of LA neurons are enhanced following behavioral fear conditioning (Quirk et al., 1995; Collins and Pare, 2000; Repa et al., 2001). These changes are believed to reflect synaptic plasticity induced by the associative pairing of the tone and shock. To examine this, Rogan et al. (1997) assessed auditory CS-evoked field responses in the LA, and CS-evoked fear behavior in freely behaving rats before, during and after fear conditioning. They found an increase in slope and amplitude of this response during fear condition- ing that paralleled fear behavior and persisted. Importantly, unpaired CS and US presentations produced no enhancement of this response or fear of the CS. These and other studies also highlight the thalamus→LA synapse as an important mediator of fear conditioning. The earliest CS-evoked LA responses occur less than $15\,ms$ after tone onset, are modified by fear conditioning and are likely driven by direct connections from the thalamus (Quirk et al., 1995; Rogan and LeDoux, 1995; Quirk et al., 1997; Rogan et al., 1997). Consistent with this notion, LA excitatory post-synaptic potentials evoked by stimulation of thalamic afferents are selectively enhanced in brain slices taken from fear-conditioned rats (McKernan and Shinnick-Gallagher, 1997).

Fear conditioning also results in synaptic plasticity in structures afferent to the LA (e.g. thalamus, cortex; Weinberger, 1995; Quirk et al., 1997). However, these are unlikely to be essential for fear learning at the level of behavior for three reasons: (1) inactivation of the LA prevents fear learning and memory indicating that these struc- tures alone cannot support learning (Muller et al., 1997; Wilensky et al., 1999), (2) plasticity in these afferent structures appears to depend on LA function (Armony et al., 1998; Maren, 2001a), and (3) conditioning-related plasticity in the LA often emerges before changes in afferent regions (Quirk et al., 1997; Repa, 2002). Together these

findings suggest that fear conditioning changes the way a CS is processed in an emotional circuit involving LA, and this plasticity allows the CS to control expression of defensive responses after the aversive experience.

The demonstrated importance of the LA to learning and memory for fear conditioning, coupled with discoveries of synaptic plasticity in LA, led to a cellular hypothesis of fear conditioning (Blair et al., 2001) (Fig. 2b). Briefly, prior to auditory fear conditioning, tone presentations result in weak depolarization of LA neurons and little to no activation of downstream brain areas mediating expression of defensive responses. However, when tone and shock stimuli are paired in time, neurons are strongly depolarized resulting in initiation of an LTP-like process that strengthens the synapses between auditory afferents and LA neurons. Following fear conditioning, tone presentations result in strong depolarization of LA neurons and activation of downstream brain areas mediating expression of defensive responses.

II.C. Molecular mechanisms of fear conditioning in LA

With mounting anatomical, physiological, and behavioral evidence implicating the LA in fear conditioning, many researchers have focused their efforts on deciphering the molecular signaling cascades important for learning/memory in this region. The majority of studies employ genetic and pharmacological manipulations coupled with fear conditioning to determine the function of specific molecules. Manipulations carefully timed with respect to training and testing allow researchers to distinguish between involvement in learning, short-term memory, and long-term memory pro- cesses (Rodrigues et al., 2004). Related studies have also probed the molecular mechanisms of LTP, usually using *in vitro* brain slice preparations while stimulating sensory afferents and recording in the LA. However, we will omit coverage of *in vitro* LTP as this topic has been covered in detail elsewhere (Sigurdsson et al., 2007) and the results are generally in agreement with *in vivo* manipula- tions. A detailed review of the large body of molecular work related to fear conditioning is beyond the scope of this chapter (for reviews see: Maren, 2001a; Rodrigues et al., 2004), however we will highlight the contributions of a few key molecular players to illustrate how long-lasting changes in plasticity between sensory afferent and principle neurons in the LA are achieved.

There appear to be several important molecular stages to fear-conditioning related plasticity in the LA (Fig. 3). First, receptors and ion channels at the synapse translate presynaptic activity into postsynaptic activation of intracellular signaling cascades. NMDA receptors, L-type voltage-gated calcium channels and metabotropic glutamate receptors are crucial for this process. When activated they couple presynaptic neural activity (glutamate release from sensory afferents) to postsynaptic kinase cascades by elevating

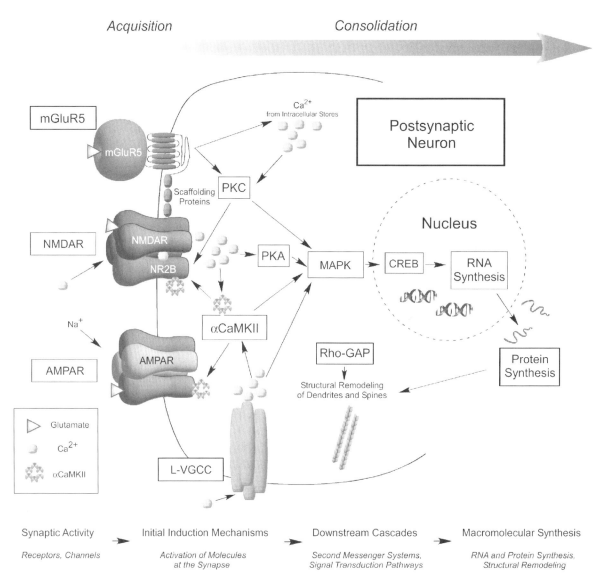

Fig. 3. Lateral amygdala intracellular signaling pathways related to learning and memory for Pavlovian fear conditioning. Reprinted with permission from *Neuron* (Rodrigues et al., 2004).

intracellular calcium. αCaMKII is particularly important for short-term memory/plasticity and may covalently modify existing synaptic proteins, like the AMPA receptor, to facilitate glutamatergic transmission. PKA and MAPK are important for long-term memory/plasticity. When they are activated they translocate to the nucleus to simulate CREB-mediated transcription. Long-term changes in synaptic transmission are ultimately achieved by transcription of the appropriate genes, translation of new proteins, and incorporation of these new proteins at the synapse. For instance, a very recent study demonstrates that the production and synaptic insertion of new AMPA receptors is critical for long-term fear-conditioning memory (Rumpel et al., 2005). In addition to facilitating the function of existing synapses, transcription and translation may also be necessary for the formation of new synapses between sensory afferents and LA neurons. Together, molecular work in the fear-conditioning pathway demonstrates that synaptic receptors/channels, intracellular kinases and nuclear machinery respond to CS–US pairings in a coordinated fashion to change CS processing in the LA.

III. Aversive instrumental conditioning

For many decades following Pavlov's work, conditional fear (Mowrer and Lamoreaux, 1946; Miller, 1948; Solomon and Wynne, 1954; Bolles, 1969) and its neural basis (Weiskrantz, 1956; Goddard, 1969; Sarter and Markowitsch, 1985; Gabriel et al., 1986) were commonly studied with avoidance protocols. We focus here on signaled active avoidance, although there are many procedural variations on this theme, such as passive/inhibitory avoidance (Blanchard and Blanchard, 1970, 1992; McGaugh, 2002), Sidman avoidance (Sidman, 1953) and conditioned taste aversion (Guitton and Dudai, 2004). In a typical active avoidance experiment, rats are presented with tone-shock pairings on one side of a two-compartment chamber. Movement to the opposite side terminates the tone and prevents the shock presentation. These avoidance responses serve as

the dependent measure of fear learning and animals exhibit responses more frequently and with shorter latencies as training progresses.

Avoidance proved to be a difficult paradigm for the analysis and explanation of learning mechanisms. First, learning occurs on trials where the animal successfully avoids shock, and it was difficult to explain how absence of a US could reinforce a response. Second, researchers realized that avoidance was actually a complex learning process where animals first learned that the tone predicted shock, and then learned to escape the tone and prevent shock delivery.

Two-factor theory quickly arose hypothesizing that avoidance conditioning involves both classical fear conditioning and instrumental response conditioning (Mowrer, 1947; Miller, 1948). In the 60 years since the emergence of two-factor theory, researchers have heatedly debated the contents (i.e. S–S, S–R, or R–S), conditions (Pavlovian operations, Instrumental operations or both), and mechanisms (drives, perceptions, memory etc…) of avoidance conditioning. However, one idea was proposed early and remains a viable possibility today: Escape from fear (EFF) (Mowrer, 1947; Miller, 1948; Levis, 1989; McAllister and McAllister, 1991).

III.A. Escape from fear

EFF learning was proposed to explain how classical conditioning and instrumental conditioning could interact to mediate active avoidance. The basic idea is that classical conditioning first establishes fear of the CS. Then on later trials, active responding is reinforced by fear reduction associated with CS-termination. Another way to say this is that the response is instrumental in leading to the reinforcement: fear reduction. Formally, this sort of learning is called conditioned negative reinforcement of a stimulus-response association. Importantly, expression of EFF learning is also believed to be motivated by fear. As training progresses, escape responding is motivated by fear of the CS and reinforced by CS-termination. Thus, EFF learning may be a useful paradigm for studying how fear processing can lead to the reinforcement and motivation of active instrumental responses. A major benefit of adopting this strategy is that the neural mechanisms of classical fear conditioning have largely been worked out (see above) giving us a firm foundation to examine aversive motivation and instrumental learning.

Unlike typical avoidance conditioning, EFF learning involves first subjecting animals to CS–US pairings with no escape contingency to establish fear of the CS. Then in a later session, usually in a different chamber, the CS is presented alone and escape responses result in CS termination. Note that no shock is ever delivered in the EFF training session so learning is attributable to fear-reduction and performance is attributable to fear motivation.

Despite the promise and simplicity of EFF, it has itself been the subject of considerable controversy over the years (Herrnstein, 1969; Bolles, 1970; Seligman and Johnston, 1973; Levis, 1989; McAllister and McAllister, 1991). The main reason is that some researchers have had trouble reliably reproducing EFF learning (independent of avoidance conditioning) in the laboratory. Many have reported successful EFF learning but failures to obtain EFF learning are also common and may be underreported (see Cain and LeDoux, 2007 for complete list of references).

We recently conducted an extensive behavioral examination of EFF in order to address reasons for the controversy and to suggest procedural improvements to optimize learning (Cain and LeDoux, 2007). The procedure for the critical experiment is as follows: On day 1, Paired-EFF and Paired-Yoked rats received five Pavlovian conditioning trials in context A (5 kHz, 60 s tone CS paired with a 0.7 mA × 1 s footshock US, no escape contingency). Unpaired-EFF rats received the same stimuli in an explicitly unpaired fashion. On day 2 all rats were presented with 25 CSs in context B during the EFF training session. Paired-EFF and Unpaired-EFF rats could terminate the CS presentation by standing up on their hind legs (behavioral rearing). Paired-Yoked rats received the same number and temporal pattern of CS presentations as their master rat, but could not terminate the CS by rearing. Finally, on day 3 all

rats were returned to context B and presented with a continuous 10 min CS that could not be turned off by rearing (extinction test for EFF memory). Note that the experimental group (Paired-EFF) feared the CS and could later escape it by rearing. The yoked group controlled for the instrumental escape contingency whereas the unpaired group controlled for CS-fear. If the instrumental contingency and CS-fear are required for EFF learning then the Paired-EFF group should rear more during EFF training and testing. Behavioral freezing was also assessed during EFF training and testing to evaluate the relationship between passive fear reactions and active responding associated with EFF learning.

We found that EFF training led to a two-fold increase in CS-evoked rearing relative to yoked control animals (Fig. 4A and B). This learning was long-lasting (24 h) and response-specific (no increase in other non-reinforced behaviors; data not shown). Interestingly, successful EFF learning also resulted in a transition from passive freezing reactions to active escaping; rats that learned the EFF response showed no spontaneous recovery of freezing following the extinguishing CS presentations used for EFF training (Fig. 4D). Importantly, expression of EFF learning was also motivated by fear of the CS; animals that went through EFF training did not rear differently than yoked controls until the CS was presented. Finally, CS-fear was necessary for EFF learning as Paired-EFF rats also reared considerably more than Unpaired-EFF rats who could terminate the CS but were not afraid of it. Thus, our data lead us to conclude that instrumental escape responses can be reinforced by CS-termination and be motivated by fear.

It is very likely that EFF learning contributes to signaled active avoidance conditioning especially since failures to respond result in US delivery in active avoidance, thus maintaining high levels of fear to the CS. EFF and active avoidance rely on Pavlovian fear conditioning to establish the CS as a secondary incentive, important for reinforcement (fear reduction) and motivation of responding. Thus, we can now build on our extensive knowledge of the fear-conditioning circuitry to begin understanding more complex learning phenomena

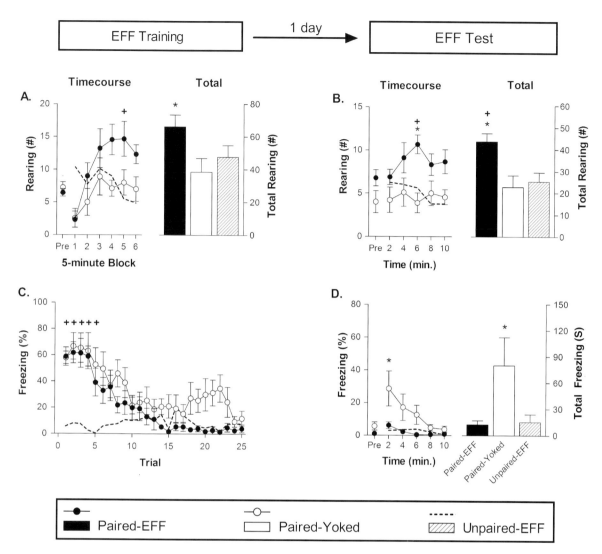

Fig. 4. Escape from fear (EFF) learning represents instrumental learning that is motivated by fear and reinforced by fear reduction. One day after Pavlovian tone–shock pairings, rats were presented with 25 tone-alone presentations in a novel context (EFF training, *left*). For Paired-EFF rats, rearing during a tone presentation led to its immediate termination (response-reinforcement pairing). Paired-Yoked rats received identical tone presentations independent of their behavior. One day after EFF training, rats were presented with a single, continuous 10 min tone presentation to assess long-term EFF memory (EFF test, *right*). Rearing and freezing were assessed during both phases. Paired-EFF rats showed a two-fold increase in the EFF escape response (rearing) during the training and testing sessions compared to Paired-Yoked rats (A & B, note change in scales between training and testing). Unpaired-EFF rats had no fear of the CS and did not acquire the EFF response (enhanced rearing). Successful acquisition of this active escape response was also associated with less passive freezing to the tone (C & D). Further analysis demonstrated that EFF learning was response-specific and performance was motivated by fear (no difference in rearing in the absence of the CS; data not shown). Figure adapted with permission from *Journal of Experimental Psychology: Animal Behavior Processes* (Cain and LeDoux, 2007).

like EFF and avoidance conditioning (LeDoux, 2002).

Research on EFF learning has been sporadic over the last half century and only one study to date has investigated brain mechanisms of EFF learning. Amorapanth et al. (2000) created selective electrolytic lesions of amygdaloid subnuclei to investigate their potential involvement in EFF learning. Lesions of the LA, CE, or B were made prior to fear conditioning and EFF training and both conditioned freezing and escape responding were measured. In this case, chamber crossing served as the escape response. The results were clear (Fig. 5). LA lesions disrupted both conditioned freezing and EFF learning. CE lesions disrupted freezing but not escape responding. And B lesions disrupted escape responding but not conditioned freezing. Thus, consistent with the model proposed above, LA damage prevented the acquisition of CS-elicited fear, which is necessary for both fear reactions (freezing) and fear actions (escaping). The double dissociation between CE and B on freezing and EFF suggest that CE mediates fear reactions and B participates in the motivation/reinforcement of fear actions like instrumental escape learning.

Ongoing experiments in our laboratory are investigating the downstream brain regions potentially responsible for receiving information from B and translating it into instrumental escape responding. One possibility is the nucleus accumbens (NAcc) which contributes to appetitive motivated action learning (Koob, 1996; Ikemoto and Panksepp, 1999; Salamone et al., 2003; Cardinal and Everitt, 2004; Kelley, 2004), including action learning about conditioned reinforcers (Robbins et al., 1990; Kelley and Delfs, 1991; de Borchgrave et al., 2002). Anatomically, NAcc shares direct connections with B (Robbins et al., 1989; Everitt and Robbins, 1992) and is situated at the "neural crossroads of emotion and movement" (Graybiel, 1976; Mogenson et al., 1980) making it a particularly attractive candidate region.

III.B. Signaled Active Avoidance

Investigations into the brain mechanisms of signaled active avoidance peaked midway through the last century and then tapered off (Goddard, 1964; Sarter and Markowitsch, 1985). This may be partly due to the emergence of Pavlovian

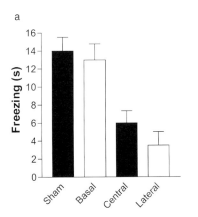
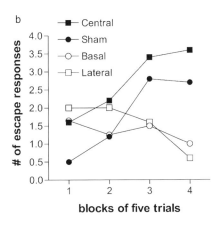

Fig. 5. EFF learning depends on the lateral and basal, but not central, amygdala. Prior to behavioral training rats received bilateral electrolytic lesions of LA, CE, or B. Rats were first subjected to Pavlovian fear conditioning and then EFF training using chamber crossing as the escape response. LA and CE lesions disrupted performance of a passive fear reaction to the CS (A, freezing). LA and B lesions disrupted performance of an active EFF response (B, chamber crossing). These data suggest that LA is necessary for establishing the CS as a conditioned incentive. This information is then relayed to CE to initiate passive Pavlovian reactions and to B for active escape responding. Reproduced with permission from *Nature Neuroscience* (Amorapanth et al., 2000).

conditioning as an ideal model for relating behavioral learning to brain activity and partly to the theoretical controversies regarding instrumental conditioning (Masterson and Crawford, 1982). Many of these studies focused on the amygdala as a region potentially critical for active avoidance. The techniques most commonly employed to investigate amydalar involvement in avoidance were lesions, local drug infusions, and sub-seizure electrical stimulation (Sarter and Markowitsch, 1985). However, it is important to note that many, if not most, of these studies were conducted before researchers appreciated the importance of investigating the function of amygdala subnuclei separately, and thus the results are mixed and bit difficult to interpret. Also, the majority of studies involved pre-learning manipulations that can potentially affect acquisition, consolidation, and storage functions.

The most common finding from early studies was that impairing amygdala function disrupts the acquisition and recall of active avoidance. For instance, pre-training lesions that included the entire amygdala (King, 1958; Thatcher and Kimble, 1966; Bush et al., 1973; Molino, 1975; Schultz and Izquierdo, 1979; Eclancher and Karli, 1980), or the basolateral complex (Coover et al., 1973) resulted in slower rates of within-session acquisition that persisted across days. However, a number of studies employing complete or partial amygdala lesions resulted in no impairment of avoidance (McNew and Thompson, 1966; Kleiner et al., 1967; Campenot, 1969; Molino, 1975; Thompson, 1981), or even facilitated avoidance conditioning (Hearst and Pribram, 1964; Grossman et al., 1975; Kemble and Davis, 1981).

More recent investigations also implicate the amygdala in signaled active avoidance learning. Pre-training lesions restricted to the LA and B impaired acquisition and retention of two-way active avoidance without affecting general activity levels. LA/B infusions of an NMDAr blocker also impaired two-way active avoidance learning in rats (Savonenko et al., 2003). Immunoctyochemical studies also suggest that the LA is important for signaled active avoidance; phosphorylation of extracellular signal-related kinase was most

prominent in the LA following training (Radwanska et al., 2002).

Work from the laboratory of Michael Gabriel has been especially successful at dissecting brain mechanisms of signaled active avoidance at the systems level in rabbits. In their preparation, rabbits are trained to discriminate between a CS+ and CS− in an avoidance paradigm that requires the animals to perform a step response on a rotating wheel apparatus to avoid shock delivery during CS+ presentations (Gabriel et al., 2003). Using an elegant combination of lesion, pharmacology, and multi-site single unit recording techniques, this group has implicated the amygdala (LA, B, and CE), cingulate cortex (anterior and posterior), thalamus (medial geniculate and anterior nuclei), and auditory cortex in the acquisition and storage of signaled active avoidance. The amygdala appears to be particularly important in this task and is required for behavioral learning and the development of training-induced neuronal activity changes in all of the other regions (Gabriel et al., 2003). These authors also demonstrate that discriminative changes in neuronal firing in the LA develop with the initial active avoidance training session (Duvel et al., 2001), consistent with previous reports in Pavlovian conditioning (Collins and Pare, 2000; Maren, 2000; Quirk et al., 1995; Quirk et al., 1997; Repa et al., 2001). The work from this laboratory emphasizes the interactivity of multiple brain regions in coordinating the learning and performance of complex active avoidance.

Recent work in our own laboratory has focused on dissecting the contributions of specific amygdala subnuclei to signaled active avoidance learning (Choi and LeDoux, 2003). Rats were trained in a two-way active avoidance paradigm where the animal was required to perform a shuttle response to the opposite chamber side in order to avoid shock delivery at the end of a tone CS presentation. Post-training lesions of LA or B severely impaired learning and retention of this task. CE lesions had no effect on learning or retention in animals that showed high levels of initial avoidance conditioning. Interestingly, CE lesions rescued the ability to learn active avoidance in poor learning rats. Unoperated rats that failed to acquire the active avoidance response with three training sessions ($<20\%$ avoidance) were subsequently given sham or CE lesions. After recovery from surgery, poor learners in the sham group remained unable to acquire active avoidance with five additional training sessions. CE-lesioned rats, on the other hand, were now able to acquire the response reaching an asymptote of 70% successful avoidance by the fifth post-lesion session. These data are consistent with the notion that LA is important for the acquisition of CS–US associations important for both Pavlovian fear reactions and instrumental fear action learning. B may be important for using this conditioned incentive information to guide goal-directed action learning and CE for mediating Pavlovian reactions. Given that the primary rodent fear reaction to a conditioned CS is freezing, it seems likely that some reciprocal inhibitory mechanism between B and CE outputs exists that determines the likelihood of reaction versus action responding, although it is currently unknown how this might occur. The present findings may also help explain apparent inconsistencies present in early studies of signaled avoidance brain mechanisms, where some manipulations impaired avoidance and others facilitated avoidance. These contradictory effects may be due to the degree the manipulations affected LA/B versus CE.

Another interesting study supports the notion that LA and B are involved in aversive instrumental learning about a conditioned reinforcer, although this study employed conditioned punishment rather than signaled avoidance (Killcross et al., 1997a). Rats pretrained to lever press for food were given lesions that included both LA and B or sham lesions. They were then trained to press either of two levers for food. Pressing one lever resulted in presentation of a tone associated with footshock (CS+) where pressing the other lever resulted in presentation of different neutral tone (CS−). In this way the researchers could simultaneously assess Pavlovian conditioning (suppression of responding on the CS− lever when the CS+ was presented) and instrumental conditioning (reduced likelihood of pressing the CS+ lever). They found that LA/B lesions impaired conditioned punishment relative to sham controls; rats with the lesions continued to press the CS+ lever

for food. However, they also found that animals with LA/B lesions had no impairment in Pavlovian fear conditioning as measured by conditioned suppression. This latter finding is at odds with many previous reports and may be explained by compensation related to overtraining of the CS–US association (for more on this debate see: Nader and LeDoux, 1997; Killcross et al., 1997b; Maren, 2001b; Lee et al., 2005). Interestingly, they also found that CE lesions impaired conditioned suppression but not conditioned punishment consistent with the notion that CE mediates Pavlovian fear reactions but not acquisition of aversive instrumental learning with a conditioned cue.

IV. Using EFF to investigate an aversive "motive circuit"

A brain processing account of motivation/learning must first include an explanation of how emotional stimuli are established and then how they lead to the invigoration and direction of behavior toward positive goals and away from aversive ones. The brain state evoked by emotional stimuli has been called a "motive state" (Morgan, 1943, 1957; Bindra, 1969; Gallistel, 1980) and studies in the aversive and appetitive fields suggest that the amygdala and NAcc are important mediators of this state (Kalivas and Nakamura, 1999). In the following paragraphs we will outline a hypothetical motive circuit responsible for EFF learning. The model relies heavily on appetitive research demonstrating that the amygdala is important for incentive learning and the NAcc is important for using incentive information to invigorate and guide active behaviors. In the appetitive context, invigoration is evidenced by the ability of a Pavlovian CS to facilitate active behaviors like eating (i.e. cue-potentiated feeding; (Holland and Petrovich, 2005) and food-seeking [i.e. Pavlovian–instrumental transfer; (Corbit and Balleine, 2005)]. The direction of behavior is represented by approach conditioning where a CS paired with food, for instance, results in movement towards the CS (Parkinson et al., 2002). It has been suggested that avoidance/escape behavior may be a form of approach, approach to *safety* (Weisman and

Litner, 1972; Ikemoto and Panksepp, 1999), and thus may rely on similar brain regions and mechanisms. The goal-object in EFF learning is fear. Invigoration is evidenced by the demonstration that EFF responses are only expressed in the presence of the fear-eliciting CS. The EFF response is directed away from fear (towards safety) since it is instrumental in terminating the fear-eliciting CS.

Before describing the motive circuit as it relates to EFF, a brief discussion of dopamine transmission is warranted. Dopamine, especially NAcc dopamine, has been intensely studied for decades as it relates to reward-related processes (Salamone et al., 2005). Although NAcc dopamine was initially believed to mediate the primary motivational value of rewards like food and sex, this notion has been called into question. Mounting evidence suggests that NAcc dopamine is important for generating anticipatory/preparatory responses in the presence of a secondary incentive (e.g. CS paired with food), but not for consummatory responses. Thus, manipulations of NAcc dopamine affect how hard a rat will work for food (Aberman et al., 1998), but they do not generally affect how much food the rat will eat once it is obtained (Berridge and Robinson, 1998; Everitt and Robbins, 1999; Everitt et al., 1999; Ikemoto and Panksepp, 1999). Simple NAcc infusion of dopamine, or drugs that mimic dopamine, result in the invigoration of active exploratory behaviors such that the animals appear to be searching for something (Ikemoto and Panksepp, 1999). This may apply to aversive motivation as well, and in this context, it is important to note that fear-eliciting CS presentations cause dopamine (from ventral tegmental neurons) to be released in the NAcc core (Wilkinson et al., 1998; Levita et al., 2002; Pezze and Feldon, 2004). The amygdaloid CE nucleus, important for learning/expression of fear conditioning and approach conditioning, projects to the ventral tegmental area (VTA) and may stimulate dopamine release in the NAcc (Cardinal et al., 2002).

Fig. 6 shows a hypothetical motive circuit as it relates to EFF. Recall that in EFF, rats first learn to fear the tone through Pavlovian pairings with an aversive footshock. Then, in a separate session, tone presentations are terminated when the rat makes the appropriate escape response (e.g. rearing or chamber crossing). Early in the session, rats primarily freeze to the tone. But eventually they exhibit the escape response and the tone terminates (Fig. 4). Fear-reduction associated with tone-termination is believed to reinforce the instrumental response, and tone-evoked fear is believed to motivate escape responding on subsequent trials.

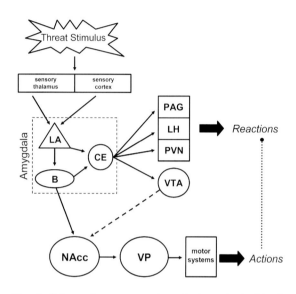

Fig. 6. Schematic representation of a hypothetical brain motive circuit mediating EFF learning. After fear conditioning, threatening stimuli, processed in the sensory thalamus and cortex, drive activity in the LA and CE leading to passive fear reactions (like freezing), and also activate arousal centers like the VTA. Incentive information flows also from LA to B which projects to the nucleus accumbens (NAcc). The NAcc processing of incentive information invigorates and guides active behavior via projections to the ventral pallidum (VP) and downstream motor systems, with the aid of dopamine arriving from VTA (dashed line). Note that early portions of this model are derived from work on amygdala-dependent fear conditioning and EFF learning (Amorapanth et al., 2000) while downstream portions of the model are borrowed from work in appetitive conditioning (e.g. Ikemoto and Panksepp, 1999; Kalivas and Nakamura, 1999; Cardinal et al., 2002). Once EFF is well-learned, there is a hypothetical inhibition of passive fear actions (dotted line). Additional abbreviations: PAG = periaqueductal gray, LH = lateral hypothalamus, PVN = paraventricular nucleus, LA = lateral amygdala, B = basal amygdala, CE = central amygdala.

In EFF, tone processing begins in the auditory system (thalamus, cortex) and is relayed to the LA. As a consequence of LTP generated by Pavlovian conditioning, activity in sensory afferents can now drive firing in LA neurons. This activity is then relayed to both the CE and B. CE outputs trigger expression of species-typical defensive responses (e.g. freezing) subserved by brainstem and hypothalamic regions. CE outputs also activate brainstem "arousal" centers like dopaminergic neurons in the VTA. Conditioned incentive information is relayed from B to the NAcc core region where this signal may be "gain amplified" (Floresco et al., 1998; Everitt et al., 1999; Parkinson et al., 1999; Floresco et al., 2001a, b) by dopamine arriving from the VTA. This NAcc signal may access motor control regions in the cortex and brainstem via projections to the ventral pallidum (VP). Thus, dopamine in the NAcc, triggered by the tone presentation, may invigorate behavior.

Rodents and humans initially respond to a CS warning of danger with suppression of active behavior, which may be regarded as a "passive" default response to moderate/high levels of threat. The performance of active responses, like rearing or shuttle behavior, is necessary to establish an escape response to the CS. According to predatory imminence theory (Fanselow and Lester, 1988), active responses occur when the threat level is extremely high (i.e. flight) or when the threat level is more moderate or low. We propose that EFF may be learned at both ends of this spectrum, as long as an active response is performed and there is fear of the CS for reinforcement (fear reduction). Our EFF demonstration (Fig. 4) takes advantage of fear extinction to reduce freezing and allow for response–CS_{off} pairings. In the present model, CS processing during EFF learning flows from the LA to B and then out to the striatum and ultimately motor response regions to mediate active response learning. Inhibition of passive responding (Fig. 6, dotted line) presumably occurs somewhere in this circuit although the mechanism is unknown.

The manner in which behavior is reinforced and subsequently directed is presently unclear, although the incentive signal arriving from B

seems critical. Some studies suggest that striatal processing of incentive stimuli facilitates the acquisition of instrumental stimulus–response (i.e. tone–escape) associations in the cortex, perhaps motor cortex or the anterior cingulate (Wise et al, 1996; White, 1997; LeDoux, 2002; Cardinal et al, 2003). If true, this model may explain how fear-eliciting tone presentations can first elicit passive freezing and later lead to the acquisition of an active escape response. We should point out, however, that well-learned instrumental habits may no longer rely on incentive processing by the amygdala and NAcc (Solomon and Wynne, 1954; Linden, 1969; Ikemoto and Panksepp, 1999; Poremba and Gabriel, 1999).

Although clearly very speculative, the present model draws on systems-level appetitive findings to build on the solid foundation of aversive incentive learning (fear-conditioning) providing strong hypotheses about a motive circuit for EFF learning. These hypotheses are directly testable using currently available techniques. The model will surely be refined in the coming years as more experimental evidence comes to light. Other brain regions that may be part of the motive circuit include the prefrontal cortex (for motivated decision making and working memory), the hippocampus (for working memory and contextualizing motivated behavior) and the mediodorsal thalamus (for the coordination of information between limbic and motor circuits) (Kalivas et al., 1999; Cardinal et al., 2002; LeDoux, 2002).

V. Summary/conclusions

Research on brain mechanisms of aversive conditioning in the past two decades has greatly increased our understanding of how an emotion-evoking stimulus is established and maintained in the brain. Pavlovian fear-conditioning research has been especially successful at delineating the cellular and molecular mechanisms of fear-reaction learning in a defensive brain system that involves the amygdala. The LA plays prominent role in establishing an aversive CS, important for fear reactions and also for motivating and reinforcing subsequent fear actions, like escape and avoidance responding. Although research on brain mechanisms of avoidance has been less intense in recent years, work in several laboratories also suggests that the amygdala plays an important early role in CS processing. Avoidance and appetitive instrumental research have made great strides in describing active responding at the systems level, particularly in demonstrating the importance of amygdala–striatum interactions in action learning with conditioned stimuli. We propose that EFF may be ideal for advancing research on how Pavlovian learning interacts with instrumental learning to generate learned fear actions.

Understanding such brain mechanisms may have important implications for the treatment of pathological anxiety in humans. Many forms of human anxiety involve the triggering of fear responses by environmental stimuli associated with trauma, similar to fear expression following Pavlovian conditioning in experimental animals. Humans also undergo fear conditioning and respond to trauma-associated stimuli with many of the same passive reactions (e.g. freezing, hormonal responses, etc). This is widely accepted by therapists and behavioral therapy of fear/anxiety disorders almost universally employs some degree of safe exposure to fear-eliciting cues aimed at extinguishing passive fear reactions (Wolpe, 1969; Craske, 1999). However, fear extinction in animals and humans is an imperfect treatment mainly because passive fear reactions return under a variety of circumstances including the simple passage of time (spontaneous recovery; Rescorla, 2004). Recently it has been suggested that more permanent recovery from pathological anxiety may be achieved by learning functionally adaptive actions when confronted with fear-eliciting stimuli (Keay and Bandler, 2001; LeDoux and Gorman, 2001; LeDoux, 2002; van der Kolk, 2006). Indeed, this is supported by our own recent data in rats indicating that EFF learning prevents spontaneous recovery of freezing (Cain and LeDoux, 2007; Fig. 4). Thus, action learning dependent on fear-eliciting conditional stimuli (EFF) may represent an important animal model for understanding human coping in the face of threat. Although it is important to point out that identical mechanisms may also mediate the generation of maladaptive

active responses. Indeed, avoidance behavior is a hallmark of human anxiety disorders and an important component of behavior therapy involves replacing maladaptive avoidance responses with adaptive coping strategies. It may even be the case that exaggerated Pavlovian fear reactions hinder the establishment of beneficial active coping strategies much like excessive freezing in rats hinders the acquisition of EFF learning. Thus, research on brain mechanisms of EFF may advance our understanding of Pavlovian–instrumental interactions with the promise of improving treatment for human anxiety.

Abbreviations

αCaMKII	alpha calcium-calmodulin dependent kinase type II
AMPA	alpha-amino-3-hydroxy-5-methyl-4-isoxazolepropionic acid
B	basal amygdala
CE	central amygdala
CR	conditioned response
CREB	cAMP response element-binding protein
CS	conditioned stimulus
EFF	escape from fear
LA	lateral amygdala
LH	lateral hypothalamus
MAPK	mitogen-activated protein kinase
NAcc	nucleus accumbens
NMDA	N-methyl-D-aspartic acid
NMDAr	N-methyl-D-aspartic acid type glutamate receptor
PAG	periaqueductal gray
PKA	protein kinase A
PVN	paraventricular nucleus
R-S	response–stimulus association
S-S	stimulus–stimulus association
S-R	stimulus–response association
US	unconditioned stimulus
VTA	ventral tegmental area

References

Aberman, J.E., Ward, S.J. and Salamone, J.D. (1998) Effects of dopamine antagonists and accumbens dopamine depletions on time-constrained progressive-ratio performance. Pharmacol. Biochem. Behav., 61: 341–348.

Amaral, D.G., Price, J.L., Pitkänen, A. and Carmichael, S.T. (1992) Anatomical organization of the primate amygdaloid complex. In: Aggleton, J.P. (Ed.), The Amygdala: Neurobiological Aspects of Emotion, Memory, and Mental Dysfunction. Wiley-Liss, Inc., New York, NY, pp. 1–66.

Amorapanth, P., Nader, K. and LeDoux, J.E. (1999) Lesions of periaqueductal gray dissociate-conditioned freezing from conditioned suppression behavior in rats. Learn. Mem., 6: 491–499.

Amorapanth, P., LeDoux, J.E. and Nader, K. (2000) Different lateral amygdala outputs mediate reactions and actions elicited by a fear-arousing stimulus. Nat. Neurosci., 3: 74–79.

Anagnostaras, S.G., Josselyn, S.A., Frankland, P.W. and Silva, A.J. (2000) Computer-assisted behavioral assessment of Pavlovian fear conditioning in mice. Learn. Mem., 7: 58–72.

Anglada-Figueroa, D. and Quirk, G.J. (2005) Lesions of the basal amygdala block expression of conditioned fear but not extinction. J. Neurosci., 25: 9680–9685.

Armony, J.L., Quirk, G.J. and LeDoux, J.E. (1998) Differential effects of amygdala lesions on early and late plastic components of auditory cortex spike trains during fear conditioning. J. Neurosci., 18: 2592–2601.

Bailey, D.J., Kim, J.J., Sun, W., Thompson, R.F. and Helmstetter, F.J. (1999) Acquisition of fear conditioning in rats requires the synthesis of mRNA in the amygdala. Behav. Neurosci., 113: 276–282.

Balleine, B.W. and Killcross, S. (2006) Parallel incentive processing: an integrated view of amygdala function. Trends Neurosci., 29: 272–279.

Bellgowan, P.S.F. and Helmstetter, F.J. (1996) Neural systems for the expression of hypoalgesia during nonassociative fear. Behav. Neurosci., 110: 727–736.

Bernard, J.F. and Besson, J.M. (1990) The spino(trigemino)pontoamygdaloid pathway: electrophysiological evidence for an involvement in pain processes. J. Neurophys., 63: 473–489.

Berridge, K.C. and Robinson, T.E. (1998) What is the role of dopamine in reward: hedonic impact, reward learning, or incentive salience? Brain Res. Rev., 28: 309–369.

Bindra, D. (1969) The interrelated mechanisms of reinforcement and motivation, and the nature of their influence on response. In: Arnold, W.J. and Levine, D. (Eds.), Nebraska Symposium on Motivation. Lincoln University of Nebraska, Lincoln, NE, pp. 1–33.

Blair, H.T., Schafe, G.E., Bauer, E.P., Rodrigues, S.M. and LeDoux, J.E. (2001) Synaptic plasticity in the lateral amygdala: a cellular hypothesis of fear conditioning. Learn. Mem., 8: 229–242.

Blanchard, R.J. and Blanchard, D.C. (1969) Passive and active reactions to fear-eliciting stimuli. J. Comp. Physiol. Psychol., 68: 129–135.

Blanchard, R.J. and Blanchard, D.C. (1970) Dual mechanisms in passive avoidance: I. Psychonomic Sci., 19: 1–2.

Blanchard, R.J. and Blanchard, D.C. (1992) Dual mechanisms in passive avoidance: II. Psychonomic Sci., 19: 3–4.

Bolles, R.C. (1969) Avoidance and escape learning: simultaneous acquisition of different responses. J. Comp. Physiol. Psychol., 68: 355–358.

Bolles, R.C. (1970) Species-specific defense reactions and avoidance learning. Psychol. Rev., 77: 32–48.

Bordi, F. and LeDoux, J. (1992) Sensory tuning beyond the sensory system: an initial analysis of auditory response properties of neurons in the lateral amygdaloid nucleus and overlying areas of the striatum. J. Neurosci., 12: 2493–2503.

Bordi, F. and LeDoux, J.E. (1994a) Response properties of single units in areas of rat auditory thalamus that project to the amygdala. II. Cells receiving convergent auditory and somatosensory inputs and cells antidromically activated by amygdala stimulation. Exp. Brain. Res., 98: 275–286.

Bordi, F. and LeDoux, J.E. (1994b) Response properties of single units in areas of rat auditory thalamus that project to the amygdala. I. Acoustic discharge patterns and frequency receptive fields. Exp. Brain Res., 98: 261–274.

Bordi, F., LeDoux, J., Clugnet, M.C. and Pavlides, C. (1993) Single-unit activity in the lateral nucleus of the amygdala and overlying areas of the striatum in freely behaving rats: rates, discharge patterns, and responses to acoustic stimuli. Behav. Neurosci., 107: 757–769.

Bourtchouladze, R., Frenguelli, B., Blendy, J., Cioffi, D., Schutz, G. and Silva, A.J. (1994) Deficient long-term memory in mice with a targeted mutation of the cAMP-responsive element-binding protein. Cell, 79: 59–68.

Brown, R.T. and Wagner, A.R. (1964) Resistance to punishment and extinction following training with shock or nonreinforcement. J. Exp. Psychol., 68: 503–507.

Bush, D.F., Lovely, R.H. and Pagano, R.P. (1973) Injection of ACTH induces recovery from shuttle-box avoidance deficits in rats with amygdaloid lesions. J. Comp. Physiol. Psychol., 83: 163–172.

Cain, C.K. and LeDoux, J.E. (2007). Escape from fear: a detailed behavioral analysis of two atypical responses reinforced by CS-termination. J. Exp. Psych.: Anim. Behav. Proc., 33(4): 451–463.

Campeau, S. and Davis, M. (1995) Involvement of the central nucleus and basolateral complex of the amygdala in fear conditioning measured with fear-potentiated startle in rats trained concurrently with auditory and visual conditioned stimuli. J. Neurosci., 15: 2301–2311.

Campeau, S., Miserendino, M.J. and Davis, M. (1992) Intra-amygdala infusion of the *N*-methyl-D-aspartate receptor antagonist AP5 blocks acquisition but not expression of fear-potentiated startle to an auditory conditioned stimulus. Behav. Neurosci., 106: 569–574.

Campenot, R.B. (1969) Effect of amygdaloid lesions upon active avoidance acquisition and anticipatory responding in rats. J. Comp. Physiol. Psych., 69: 492–497.

Cardinal, R.N. and Everitt, B.J. (2004) Neural and psychological mechanisms underlying appetitive learning: links to drug addiction. Curr. Opin. Neurobiol., 14: 156–162.

Cardinal, R.N., Parkinson, J.A., Marbini, H.D., Toner, A.J., Bussey, T.J., Robbins, T.W. and Everitt, B.J. (2003) Role of the anterior cingulate cortex in the control over behavior by Pavlovian conditioned stimuli in rats. Behav. Neurosci., 17: 566–587.

Cardinal, R.N., Parkinson, J.N., Hall, J. and Everitt, B.J. (2002) Emotion and motivation: the role of the amygdala, ventral striatum, and prefrontal cortex. Neurosci. Biobehav. Rev., 26: 321–352.

Choi, J.S. and LeDoux, J.E. (2003) Lesions of the lateral/basal but not the central nucleus of the amygdala impair post-training performance of fear-induced 2-way active avoidance signaled by a conditioned stimulus. *Soc. Neurosci. Abst.*, Program No. 623.5.

Clugnet, M.C., LeDoux, J.E. and Morrison, S.F. (1990) Unit responses evoked in the amygdala and striatum by electrical stimulation of the medial geniculate body. J. Neurosci., 10: 1055–1061.

Collins, D.R. and Pare, D. (2000) Differential fear conditioning induces reciprocal changes in the sensory responses of lateral amygdala neurons to the CS(+) and CS(−). Learn. Mem., 7: 97–103.

Coover, G., Ursin, H. and Levine, S. (1973) Corticosterone and avoidance in rats with basolateral amygdaloid lesions. J. Comp. Physiol. Psych., 85: 111–122.

Corbit, L.H. and Balleine, B.W. (2005) Double dissociation of basolateral and central amygdala lesions on the general and outcome-specific forms of Pavlovian-instrumental transfer. J. Neurosci., 25: 962–970.

Craske, M.G. (1999) Anxiety Disorders: Psychological Approaches to Theory and Treatment. Westview Press, Boulder, CO.

Davis, M. (1986) Pharmacological and anatomical analysis of fear conditioning using the fear-potentiated startle paradigm. Behav. Neurosci., 100: 814–824.

Davis, M. (1998) Anatomic and physiologic substrates of emotion in an animal model. J. Clin. Neurophysiol., 15: 378–387.

de Borchgrave, R., Rawlins, J.N., Dickinson, A. and Balleine, B.W. (2002) Effects of cytotoxic nucleus accumbens lesions on instrumental conditioning in rats. Exp. Brain Res., 144: 50–68.

De Oca, B.M., DeCola, J.P., Maren, S. and Fanselow, M.S. (1998) Distinct regions of the periaqueductal gray are involved in the acquisition and expression of defensive responses. J. Neurosci., 18: 3426–3432.

Duvel, A.D., Smith, D.M., Talk, A. and Gabriel, M. (2001) Medial geniculate, amygdalar and cingulate cortical training-induced neuronal activity during discriminative avoidance learning in rabbits with auditory cortical lesions. J. Neurosci., 21: 3271–3281.

Eclancher, F. and Karli, P. (1980) Effects of infant and adult amygdaloid lesions upon acquisition of two-way avoidance by the adult rat: influence of rearing conditions. Physiol. Behav., 24: 887–893.

Everitt, B. and Robbins, T. (1999) Motivation and reward. In: Zigmond, M.J. Bloom, F.E. Landis, S.C. Roberts, J.L. and Squire, L.R. (Eds.), Fundamental Neuroscience. Academic Press, San Diego, CA.

Everitt, B.J., Parkinson, J.A., Olmstead, M.C., Arroyo, M., Robledo, P. and Robbins, T.W. (1999) Associative processes in addiction and reward. The role of amygdala–ventral striatal subsystems. In: McGintry, J. (Ed.), Advancing from the Ventral Striatum to the Extended Amygdala. New York Academy of Sciences, New York, NY, pp. 412–438.

Everitt, B.J. and Robbins, T.W. (1992) Amygdala–ventral striatal interactions and reward-related processes. In: Aggleton, J.P. (Ed.), The Amygdala: Neurobiological Aspects of Emotion, Memory, and Mental Dysfunction. Wiley-Liss, Inc., New York, NY, pp. 401–429.

Fanselow, M.S. and Bolles, R.C. (1979) Naloxone and shock-elicited freezing in the rat. J. Comp. Physiol. Psychol., 93: 736–744.

Fanselow, M.S. and Lester, L.S. (1988) A functional behavioristic approach to aversively motivated behavior: predatory imminence as a determinant of the topography of defensive behavior. In: Bolles, R.C. and Beecher, M.D. (Eds.), Evolution and Learning. Erlbaum, Hillsdale, NJ, pp. 185–211.

Fanselow, M.S. and Kim, J.J. (1994) Acquisition of contextual Pavlovian fear conditioning is blocked by application of an NMDA receptor antagonist D,L-2-amino-5-phosphonovaleric acid to the basolateral amygdala. Behav. Neurosci., 108: 210–212.

Fanselow, M.S. and LeDoux, J.E. (1999) Why we think plasticity underlying Pavlovian fear conditioning occurs in the basolateral amygdala. Neuron, 23: 229–232.

Fitzgerald, H.E. and Brackbill, Y. (1976) Classical conditioning in infancy: development and constraints. Psychol. Bull., 83: 353–376.

Floresco, S.B., Blaha, C.D., Yang, C.R. and Phillips, A.G. (2001a) Dopamine D1 and NMDA receptors mediate potentiation of basolateral amygdala-evoked firing of nucleus accumbens neurons. J. Neurosci., 21: 6370–6376.

Floresco, S.B., Blaha, C.D., Yang, C.R. and Phillips, A.G. (2001b) Modulation of hippocampal and amygdalar-evoked activity of nucleus accumbens neurons by dopamine: cellular mechanisms of input selection. J. Neurosci., 21: 2851–2860.

Floresco, S.B., Yang, C.R., Phillips, A.G. and Blaha, C.D. (1998) Basolateral amygdala stimulation evokes glutamate receptor-dependent dopamine efflux in the nucleus accumbens of the anaesthetized rat. Eur. J. Neurosci., 10: 1241–1251.

Gabriel, M., Burhans, L. and Kashef, A. (2003) Consideration of a unified model of amygdalar associative functions. Ann. NY Acad. Sci., 985: 206–217.

Gabriel, M., Sparenborg, S. and Stolar, N. (1986) The neurobiology of memory. In: LeDoux, J.E. and Hirst, W. (Eds.), Mind and Brain: Dialogues in Cognitive Neuroscience. Cambridge University Press, New York, NY, pp. 215–254.

Gale, G.D., Anagnostaras, S.G., Godsil, B.P., Mitchell, S., Nozawa, T., Sage, J.R., Wiltgen, B. and Fanselow, M.S. (2004) Role of the basolateral amygdala in the storage of fear memories across the adult lifetime of rats. J. Neurosci., 24: 3810–3815.

Gallistel, R. (1980) The organization of action: A new synthesis. Erlbaum, Hillsdale, NJ.

Goddard, G. (1964) Functions of the amygdala. Psychol. Rev., 62: 89–109.

Goddard, G.V. (1969) Analysis of avoidance conditioning following cholinergic stimulation of amygdala in rats. J. Comp. Physiol. Psychol., 68: 1–18.

Goosens, K.A. and Maren, S. (2001) Contextual and auditory fear conditioning are mediated by the lateral, basal, and central amygdaloid nuclei in rats. Learn. Mem., 8: 148–155.

Graybiel, A. (1976) Input–output anatomy of the basal ganglia. In: Toronto, Canada: *Lecture at the Society for Neuroscience*.

Grossman, S.P., Grossman, L. and Walsh, L. (1975) Functional organization of the rat amygdala with respect to avoidance behavior. J. Comp. Physiol. Psych., 88: 829–850.

Guitton, M.J. and Dudai, Y. (2004) Anxiety-like state associates with taste to produce conditioned taste aversion. Biol. Psychiatry, 56: 901–904.

Hearst, E. and Pribram, K.H. (1964) Facilitation of avoidance behavior by unavoidable shocks in normal and amydalectomized monkeys. J. Comp. Physiol. Psych.,, 39–42.

Herrnstein, R.J. (1969) Method and theory in the study of avoidance. Psychol. Rev., 76: 49–69.

Hitchcock, J. and Davis, M. (1986) Lesions of the amygdala but not of the cerebellum or red nucleus block conditioned fear as measured with the potentiated startle paradigm. Behav. Neurosci., 100: 11–22.

Holland, P.C. and Petrovich, G.D. (2005) A neural systems analysis of the potentiation of feeding by conditioned stimuli. Physiol. Behav., 86: 747–761.

Ikemoto, S. and Panksepp, J. (1999) The role of nucleus accumbens dopamine in motivated behavior: a unifying interpretation with special reference to reward-seeking. Brain Res. Rev., 31: 6–41.

Jasmin, L., Burkey, A.R., Card, J.P. and Basbaum, A.I. (1997) Transneuronal labeling of a nociceptive pathway, the spino-(trigemino-)parabrachio-amygdaloid, in the rat. J. Neurosci., 17: 3751–3765.

Kalivas, P.W., Churchill, L. and Romanides, A. (1999) Involvement of the pallidal–thalamocortical circuit in adaptive behavior. Ann. NY Acad. Sci., 877: 64–70.

Kalivas, P.W. and Nakamura, M. (1999) Neural systems for behavioral activation and reward. Curr. Opin. Neurobiol., 9: 223–227.

Kapp, B.S., Whalen, P.J., Supple, W.F. and Pascoe, J.P. (1992) Amygdaloid contributions to conditioned arousal and sensory information processing. In: Aggleton, J.P. (Ed.), The Amygdala: Neurobiological Aspects of Emotion, Memory, and Mental Dysfunction. Wiley-Liss, New York, NY, pp. 229–254.

Keay, K.A. and Bandler, R. (2001) Parallel circuits mediating distinct emotional coping reactions to different types of stress. Neurosci. Biobehav. Rev., 25: 669–678.

Kelley, A.E. (2004) Ventral striatal control of appetitive motivation: role in ingestive behavior and reward-related learning. Neurosci. Biobehav. Rev., 27: 765–776.

Kelley, A.E. and Delfs, J.M. (1991) Dopamine and conditioned reinforcement. I. Differential effects of amphetamine microinjections into striatal subregions. Psychopharm. (Berl), 103: 187–196.

Kemble, E.D. and Davis, V.A. (1981) Effects of prior environmental enrichment and amygdaloid lesions on consumatory behavior, activity, predation, and shuttlebox avoidance in male and female rats. Physiol. Psychol., 9: 340–346.

Kida, S., Josselyn, S.A., de Ortiz, S.P., Kogan, J.H., Chevere, I., Masushige, S. and Silva, A.J. (2002) CREB required for the stability of new and reactivated fear memories. Nat. Neurosci., 5: 348–355.

Killcross, S., Robbins, T.W. and Everitt, B.J. (1997a) Different types of fear-conditioned behaviour mediated by separate nuclei within amygdala. Nature, 388: 377–380.

Killcross, S., Robbins, T.W. and Everitt, B.J. (1997b) Response from Killcross, Robbins and Everitt. Trends Cogn. Sci., 1: 244–246.

King, F.A. (1958) Effects of septal and amygdaloid lesions on emotional behavior and conditioned avoidance responses in the rat. J. Nerv. Ment. Dis., 126: 57–63.

Kleiner, F.B., Meyer, P.M. and Meyer, D.R. (1967) Effects of simultaneous septal and amygdaloid lesions upon emotionality and retention of a black–white discrimination. Brain Res., 5: 459–468.

Koob, G.F. (1996) Hedonic valence, dopamine and motivation. Mol. Psychiatry, 1: 186–189.

Koo, J.W., Han, J.S. and Kim, J.J. (2004) Selective neurotoxic lesions of basolateral and central nuclei of the amygdala produce differential effects on fear conditioning. J. Neurosci., 24: 7654–7662.

Korte, S.M., Bouws, G.A., Koolhaas, J.M. and Bohus, B. (1992a) Neuroendocrine and behavioral responses during conditioned active and passive behavior in the defensive burying/probe avoidance paradigm: effects of ipsapirone. Physiol. Behav., 52: 355–361.

Korte, S.M., Buwalda, B., Bouws, G.A., Koolhaas, J.M., Maes, F.W. and Bohus, B. (1992b) Conditioned neuroendocrine and cardiovascular stress responsiveness accompanying behavioral passivity and activity in aged and in young rats. Physiol. Behav., 51: 815–822.

LeDoux, J.E. (1990) Fear pathways in the brain: implications for theories of the emotional brain. In: Brain, P. Parmigiani, S. Maindardi, D. and Blanchard, R.J. (Eds.), Fear and Defense. Gordon and Breach, London.

LeDoux, J.E. (2000) Emotion circuits in the brain. Ann. Rev. Neurosci., 23: 155–184.

LeDoux, J.E. (2002) The lost world. In: Synaptic Self. Viking, New York, NY, pp. 235–259.

LeDoux, J.E. and Gorman, J.M. (2001) A call to action: overcoming anxiety through active coping. Am. J. Psychiatry, 158: 1953–1955.

LeDoux, J.E., Iwata, J., Cicchetti, P. and Reis, D.J. (1988) Different projections of the central amygdaloid nucleus mediate autonomic and behavioral correlates of conditioned fear. J. Neurosci., 8: 2517–2529.

LeDoux, J.E., Ruggiero, D.A., Forest, R., Stornetta, R. and Reis, D.J. (1987) Topographic organization of convergent projections to the thalamus from the inferior colliculus and spinal cord in the rat. J. Comp. Neurol., 264: 123–146.

LeDoux, J.E., Tucker, L.W., Del Bo, A., Harshfield, G., Green, L., Talman, W.T. and Reis, D.J. (1980) A hierarchical organization of blood pressure during natural behaviour in rat and the effects of central catecholamine neurons thereon. Clin. Sci. (Lond), 59(Suppl 6): 271–273.

Lee, J.L., Dickinson, A. and Everitt, B.J. (2005) Conditioned suppression and freezing as measures of aversive Pavlovian conditioning: effects of discrete amygdala lesions and overtraining. Behav. Brain. Res., 159: 221–233.

Levis, D.J. (1989) The case for a return to a two-factor theory of avoidance: the failure of non-fear interpretations. In: Klein, S.B. and Mowrer, R.R. (Eds.), Contemporary Learning Theories: Pavlovian Conditioning and the Status of Traditional Learning Theory. Lawrence Erlbaum Associate, Hillsdale, pp. 227–277.

Levita, L., Dalley, J.W. and Robbins, T.W. (2002) Nucleus accumbens dopamine and learned fear revisited: a review and some new findings. Behav. Brain Res., 137: 115–127.

Linden, D.R. (1969) Attenuation and reestablishment of the CER by discriminated avoidance conditioning in rats. J. Comp. Physiol. Psychol., 69: 573–578.

Maren, S. (2000) Auditory fear conditioning increases CS-elicited spike firing in lateral amygdala neurons even after extensive overtraining. Eur. J. Neurosci., 12: 4047–4054.

Maren, S. (2001a) Neurobiology of Pavlovian fear conditioning. Annu. Rev. Neurosci., 24: 897–931.

Maren, S. (2001b) Is there savings for Pavlovian fear conditioning after neurotoxic basolateral amygdala lesions in rats? Neurobiol. Learn. Mem., 76: 268–283.

Maren, S., Aharonov, G., Stote, D.L. and Fanselow, M.S. (1996) N-methyl-D-aspartate receptors in the basolateral amygdala are required for both acquisition and expression of conditional fear in rats. Behav. Neurosci., 110: 1365–1374.

Maren, S., Ferrario, C.R., Corcoran, K.A., Desmond, T.J. and Frey, K.A. (2003) Protein synthesis in the amygdala, but not the auditory thalamus, is required for consolidation of Pavlovian fear conditioning in rats. Eur. J. Neurosci., 18: 3080–3088.

Maren, S. and Quirk, G.J. (2004) Neuronal signalling of fear memory. Nat. Rev. Neurosci., 5: 844–852.

Mascagni, F., McDonald, A.J. and Coleman, J.R. (1993) Corticoamygdaloid and corticocortical projections of the rat temporal cortex: A Phaseolus vulgaris leucoagglutinin study. Neuroscience, 57: 697–715.

Mason, J.W., Mangan, G., Brady, J.V., Conrad, D. and Rioch, D.M. (1961) Concurrent plasma epinephrine, norepinephrine and 17-hydroxycorticosteroid levels during conditioned emotional disturbances in monkeys. Psychosom. Med., 23: 344–353.

Masterson, F.A. and Crawford, M. (1982) The defensive motivation system: A theory of avoidance behavior. Behav. Brain Sci., 5: 661–689.

McAllister, D.E. and McAllister, W.R. (1991) Fear theory and aversively motivated behavior: Some controversial issues. In: Denny, M.R. (Ed.), Fear, Avoidance, and Phobias: A Fundamental Analysis. Erlbaum, Hillsdale, NJ, pp. 135–163.

McAllister, W.R. and McAllister, D.E. (1971) Behavioral measurement of conditioned fear. In: Brush, F.R. (Ed.), Aversive Conditioning and Learning. Academic Press, New York, NY, pp. 105–179.

McDonald, A.J. (1998) Cortical pathways to the mammalian amygdala. Prog. Neurobiol., 55: 257–332.

McGaugh, J.L. (2002) Memory consolidation and the amygdala: a systems perspective. Trends Neurosci., 25: 456.

McKernan, M.G. and Shinnick-Gallagher, P. (1997) Fear conditioning induces a lasting potentiation of synaptic currents in vitro. Nature, 390: 607–611.

McNew, J.J. and Thompson, R. (1966) Role of the limbic system in active and passive avoidance conditioning in the rat. J. Comp. Physiol. Psychol., 61: 173–180.

Miller, N.E. (1948) Studies of fear as an acquirable drive: I. Fear as motivation and fear-reduction as reinforcement in the learning of new responses. J. Exp. Psychol., 38: 89–101.

Miller, N.E. (1951) Learnable drives and rewards. In: Stevens, S.S. (Ed.), Handbook of Experimental Psychology. Wiley, New York, NY, pp. 435–472.

Miserendino, M.J., Sananes, C.B., Melia, K.R. and Davis, M. (1990) Blocking of acquisition but not expression of conditioned fear-potentiated startle by NMDA antagonists in the amygdala. Nature, 345: 716–718.

Mogenson, G.J., Jones, D.L. and Yim, C.Y. (1980) From motivation to action: functional interface between the limbic system and the motor system. Prog. Neurobiol., 14: 69–97.

Molino, A. (1975) Sparing of function after infant lesions of selected limbic structures in the rat. J. Comp. Physiol. Psych., 89: 868–881.

Morgan, C.T. (1943) Physiological Psychology. McGraw Hill, New York, NY.

Morgan, C.T. (1957) Physiological mechanisms of motivation. Nebraska Symp. Motivation, 5: 1–43.

Mowrer, O.H. (1947) On the dual nature of learning: A reinterpretation of "conditioning" and "problem solving". Harvard Educational Review, 17: 102–148.

Mowrer, O.H. and Lamoreaux, R.R. (1946) Fear as an intervening variable in avoidance conditioning. J. Comp. Psychol., 39: 29–50.

Muller, J., Corodimas, K.P., Fridel, Z. and LeDoux, J.E. (1997) Functional inactivation of the lateral and basal nuclei of the amygdala by muscimol infusion prevents fear conditioning to an explicit conditioned stimulus and to contextual stimuli. Behav. Neurosci., 111: 683–691.

Nader, K. and LeDoux, J.E. (1997) Is it time in invoke multiple fear learning systems in the amygdala? Trends Cogn. Sci., 1: 241–244.

Nader, K., Majidishad, P., Amorapanth, P. and LeDoux, J.E. (2001) Damage to the lateral and central, but not other, amygdaloid nuclei prevents the acquisition of auditory fear conditioning. Learn. Mem., 8: 156–163.

Pare, D. and Smith, Y. (1998) Intrinsic circuitry of the amygdaloid complex: common principles of organization in rats and cats. Trends Neurosci., 21: 240–241.

Pare, D., Quirk, G.J. and Ledoux, J.E. (2004) New vistas on amygdala networks in conditioned fear. J. Neurophysiol., 92: 1–9.

Parkinson, J.A., Dalley, J.W., Cardinal, R.N., Bamford, A., Fehnert, B., Lachenal, G., Rudarakanchana, N., Halkerston, K.M., Robbins, T.W. and Everitt, B.J. (2002) Nucleus accumbens dopamine depletion impairs both acquisition and performance of appetitive Pavlovian approach behaviour: implications for mesoaccumbens dopamine function. Behav. Brain Res., 137: 149–163.

Parkinson, J.A., Olmstead, M.C., Burns, L.H., Robbins, T.W. and Everitt, B.J. (1999) Dissociation in effects of lesions of the nucleus accumbens core and shell on appetitive Pavlovian approach behavior and the potentiation of conditioned reinforcement and locomotor activity by D-amphetamine. J. Neurosci., 19: 2401–2411.

Pezze, M.A. and Feldon, J. (2004) Mesolimbic dopaminergic pathways in fear conditioning. Prog. Neurobiol., 74: 301–320.

Pitkänen, A., Savander, V. and LeDoux, J.E. (1997) Organization of intra-amygdaloid circuitries in the rat: an emerging framework for understanding functions of the amygdala. Trends Neurosci., 20: 517–523.

Poremba, A. and Gabriel, M. (1999) Amygdala neurons mediate acquisition but not maintenance of instrumental avoidance behavior in rabbits. J. Neurosci., 19: 9635–9641.

Quirk, G.J., Armony, J.L. and LeDoux, J.E. (1997) Fear conditioning enhances different temporal components of tone-evoked spike trains in auditory cortex and lateral amygdala. Neuron, 19: 613–624.

Quirk, G.J., Repa, C. and LeDoux, J.E. (1995) Fear conditioning enhances short-latency auditory responses of lateral amygdala neurons: parallel recordings in the freely behaving rat. Neuron, 15: 1029–1039.

Radwanska, K., Nikolaev, E., Knapska, E. and Kaczmarek, L. (2002) Differential response of two subdivisions of lateral amygdala to aversive conditioning as revealed by c-Fos and P-ERK mapping. Neuroreport, 13: 2241–2246.

Repa, J.C. (2002) The neural basis for emotional learning: Electrophysiological investigations of fear conditioning. In: Center for Neural Science. New York: New York University.

Repa, J.C., Muller, J., Apergis, J., Desrochers, T.M., Zhou, Y. and LeDoux, J.E. (2001) Two different lateral amygdala cell populations contribute to the initiation and storage of memory. Nat. Neurosci., 4: 724–731.

Rescorla, R.A. (1967) Pavlovian conditioning and its proper control procedures. Psychol. Rev., 74: 71–80.

Rescorla, R.A. (2004) Spontaneous recovery. Learn. Mem., 11: 501–509.

Robbins, T.W., Cador, M., Taylor, J.R. and Everitt, B.J. (1989) Limbic–striatal interactions in reward-related processes. Neurosci. Biobehav. Rev., 13: 155–162.

Robbins, T.W., Giardini, V., Jones, G.H., Reading, P. and Sahakian, B.J. (1990) Effects of dopamine depletion from the caudate-putamen and nucleus accumbens septi on the acquisition and performance of a conditional discrimination task. Behav. Brain Res., 38: 243–261.

Rodrigues, S.M., Schafe, G.E. and LeDoux, J.E. (2001) Intra-amygdala blockade of the NR2B subunit of the NMDA receptor disrupts the acquisition but not the expression of fear conditioning. J. Neurosci., 21: 6889–6896.

Rodrigues, S.M., Schafe, G.E. and LeDoux, J.E. (2004) Molecular mechanisms underlying emotional learning and memory in the lateral amygdala. Neuron, 44: 75–91.

Rogan, M.T. and LeDoux, J.E. (1995) LTP is accompanied by commensurate enhancement of auditory-evoked responses in a fear conditioning circuit. Neuron, 15: 127–136.

Rogan, M.T., Staubli, U.V. and LeDoux, J.E. (1997) Fear conditioning induces associative long-term potentiation in the amygdala. Nature, 390: 604–607.

Romanski, L.M., LeDoux, J.E., Clugnet, M.C. and Bordi, F. (1993) Somatosensory and auditory convergence in the lateral nucleus of the amygdala. Behav. Neurosci., 107: 444–450.

Rumpel, S., LeDoux, J., Zador, A. and Malinow, R. (2005) Postsynaptic receptor trafficking underlying a form of associative learning. Science, 308: 83–88.

Salamone, J.D., Correa, M., Mingote, S. and Weber, S.M. (2003) Nucleus accumbens dopamine and the regulation of effort in food-seeking behavior: implications for studies of natural motivation, psychiatry, and drug abuse. J. Pharmacol. Exp. Ther., 305: 1–8.

Salamone, J.D., Correa, M., Mingote, S.M. and Weber, S.M. (2005) Beyond the reward hypothesis: alternative functions of nucleus accumbens dopamine. Curr. Opin. Pharmacol., 5: 34–41.

Sarter, M.F. and Markowitsch, H.J. (1985) Involvement of the amygdala in learning and memory: a critical review, with emphasis on anatomical relations. Behav. Neurosci., 99: 342–380.

Savonenko, A., Werka, T., Nikolaev, E., Zielinski, K. and Kaczmarek, L. (2003) Complex effects of NMDA receptor antagonist APV in the basolateral amygdala on acquisition of two-way avoidance reaction and long-term fear memory. Learn. Mem., 10: 292–303.

Schafe, G.E. and LeDoux, J.E. (2000) Memory consolidation of auditory Pavlovian fear conditioning requires protein synthesis and protein kinase A in the amygdala. J. Neurosci., 20: RC96.

Schneiderman, N., Francis, J., Sampson, L.D. and Schwaber, J.S. (1974) CNS integration of learned cardiovascular behavior. In: DiCara, L.V. (Ed.), Limbic and Autonomic Nervous System Research. Plenum, New York, NY, pp. 277–309.

Schultz, R.A. and Izquierdo, I. (1979) Effect of brain lesions on rat shuttle behavior in four different tests. Physiol. Behav., 23: 97–105.

Seligman, M.E. and Johnston, J.C. (1973) A cognitive theory of avoidance learning. In: McGuigan, F.J. and Lumsden, D.B. (Eds.), Contemporary Approaches to Conditioning and Learning. V. H. Winston & Sons, Oxford, England.

Sidman, M. (1953) Avoidance conditioning with brief shock and no exteroceptive warning signal. Science, 118: 157–158.

Sigurdsson, T., Doyere, V., Cain, C.K. and LeDoux, J.E. (2007) Long-term potentiation in the amygdala: A cellular mechanism of fear learning and memory. Neuropharmacology, 52: 215–227.

Smith, O.A., Astley, C.A., Devito, J.L., Stein, J.M. and Walsh, R.E. (1980) Functional analysis of hypothalamic control of the cardiovascular responses accompanying emotional behavior. Federation Proc., 39: 2487–2494.

Solomon, R.L. and Wynne, L.C. (1954) Traumatic avoidance learning: The principles of anxiety conservation and partial irreversibility. Psychol. Rev., 61: 353.

Sotres-Bayon, F., Bush, D.E. and LeDoux, J.E. (2004) Emotional perseveration: an update on prefrontal-amygdala interactions in fear extinction. Learn. Mem., 11: 525–535.

Thatcher, R.W. and Kimble, D.P. (1966) Effect of amygdaloid lesions on retention of an avoidance response in overtrained and non-overtrained rats. Psychon. Sci., 6: 9–10.

Thompson, C.I. (1981) Learning in rhesus monkeys after amygdalectomy in infancy or adulthood. Behav. Brain Res., 2: 81–101.

Turner, B. and Herkenham, M. (1991) Thalamoamygdaloid projections in the rat: a test of the amygdala's role in sensory processing. J. Comp. Neurol., 313: 295–325.

van der Kolk, B.A. (2006) Clinical implications of neuroscience research in PTSD. Ann. NY Acad. Sci., 1071: 277–293.

Weinberger, N.M. (1995) Retuning the brain by fear conditioning. In: Gazzaniga, M.S. (Ed.), The Cognitive Neurosciences. The MIT Press, Cambridge, MA, pp. 1071–1090.

Weiskrantz, L. (1956) Behavioral changes associated with ablation of the amygdaloid complex in monkeys. J. Comp. Physiol. Psychol., 49: 381–391.

Weisman, R.G. and Litner, J.S. (1972) The role of Pavlovian events in avoidance training. In: Boakes, R.A. and Halliday, M.S. (Eds.), Inhibition and Learning. Academic Press, London, pp. 253–270.

Weisz, D.J. and McInerney, J. (1990) An associative process maintains reflex facilitation of the unconditioned nictitating membrane response during the early stages of training. Behav. Neurosci., 104: 21–27.

White, N.M. (1997) Mnemonic functions of the basal ganglia. Curr. Opin. Neurobiol., 7: 164–169.

Wilensky, A.E., Schafe, G.E., Kristensen, M.P. and LeDoux, J.E. (2006) Rethinking the fear circuit: the central nucleus of the amygdala is required for the acquisition, consolidation, and expression of Pavlovian fear conditioning. J. Neurosci., 26: 12387–12396.

Wilensky, A.E., Schafe, G.E. and LeDoux, J.E. (1999) Functional inactivation of the amygdala before but not after auditory fear conditioning prevents memory formation. J. Neurosci., 19: RC48.

Wilkinson, L.S., Humby, T., Killcross, A.S., Torres, E.M., Everitt, B.J. and Robbins, T.W. (1998) Dissociations in dopamine release in medial prefrontal cortex and ventral striatum during the acquisition and extinction of classical aversive conditioning in the rat. Eur. J. Neurosci., 10: 1019–1026.

Wise, S.P., Murray, E.A. and Gerfen, C.R. (1996) The frontal cortex–basal ganglia system in primates. Crit. Rev. Neurobiol., 10: 317–356.

Wolpe, J. (1969) The practice of behavior therapy. Pergamon, Oxford, England.

Neural systems activated in response to predators and partial predator stimuli

Newton S. Canteras*

Departamento de Anatomia, Instituto de Ciências Biomédicas, Universidade de São Paulo, São Paulo, SP, Brazil

Abstract: Interest in unconditioned anti-predator defenses has a long history and helps to portray a more complete view of the neural system mediating fear reactions under natural conditions. In this chapter, we review advances in understanding the neural basis of unconditioned and conditioned anti-predator defensive responses. A number of recent studies have identified a key medial hypothalamic circuit critically involved in the expression of anti-predator defensive responses – the medial hypothalamic zone (MHZ) defensive system. Current evidence suggests that the neural network putatively involved in organizing both unconditioned and conditioned anti-predator related defensive responses is centered around the MHZ defensive system. Thus, on one hand, this hypothalamic system is in a position to organize the neural processing related to predator cues, and on the other hand, it influences brain stem sites responsible for the expression of anti-predator defensive responses. We present here a comprehensive review of the anatomical and functional data available to indicate how this network is organized.

Keywords: defensive behavior; fear conditioning; hypothalamus; hippocampus; amygdala; dorsal premammillary nucleus; periaqueductal gray

I. Introduction

Studies on defensive behaviors in psychology have overwhelmingly employed aversive conditioning procedures, typically a shock stimulus paired with a discrete cue, or, more recently, a situation or context. Nonetheless, interest in unconditioned anti-predator defenses has a long history (see Curti, 1935; Small, 1899). Studies from the Blanchard laboratory have provided much of the background on defensive responses in rodents to cats and other predators, and to cat fur/skin odor (see Blanchard et al., 1989). These studies suggest a much wider array of unconditioned defensive behaviors than measured in aversive learning procedures and this view is strongly

supported by field studies of anti-predator defense. Of particular relevance, the study of defense and defensive conditioning mechanisms to nonpainful threat has been proved particularly helpful to understand the neural basis of fear and anxiety.

Rodent unconditioned defensive behaviors appear to consist of at least the following: flight, hiding, freezing, defensive threat, defensive attack, and risk assessment. These are species-typical (i.e., typically expressed by individuals of a given species under appropriate circumstances), but not species-specific, in the sense that they occur in the same form across a variety of mammalian species (Blanchard et al., 2001). The unconditioned defensive behaviors are elicited in wild or laboratory strains without prior relevant experience. In particular, cat exposure to rats produces in the latter intense freezing, avoidance (and hiding, if a place of concealment is available), and elements of risk

*Corresponding author. E-mail: newton@icb.usp.br

R.J. Blanchard, D.C. Blanchard, G. Griebel and D. Nutt (Eds.)
Handbook of Anxiety and Fear, Vol. 17
ISBN 978-0-444-53065-3

DOI: 10.1016/S1569-7339(07)00008-2

assessment, such as orientation to the predator (see Blanchard et al., 1989). When the cat is removed, intense long-term risk assessment, as well as freezing and avoidance, are seen in the area where the cat was encountered (Ribeiro-Barbosa et al., 2005). Responses to cat exposure are very resistant to habituation, and conditioning occurs to the context in which the cat was encountered.

Because of difficulties in maintaining cats or other predators in laboratory settings as an experimental technique, the use of predator odor has recently become more common than direct exposure to a cat. Cat fur/skin odor elicits some freezing and avoidance, typically less intensely than when a live cat is present, combined with higher levels of risk assessment than are seen to a live cat (Zangrossi and File, 1992; Dielenberg and McGregor, 1999; Blanchard et al., 2001; McGregor et al., 2002). These behaviors show rapid conditioning to the context in which the cat fur/skin odor was present (Blanchard et al., 2001; Dielenberg et al., 2001; McGregor et al., 2002). Notably, cat fur/skin odor produces a graded response, with small portions of cloth rubbed on a cat eliciting lower magnitude defensive behaviors than do larger portions (Takahashi et al., 2005). Efforts to define and quantify odor stimuli more precisely have led to the use of extracts of predator feces and anal gland secretions, such as trimethylthiazoline, as predator stimuli. Although these odorants may elicit some defensive response (e.g., McGregor et al., 2002; Staples and McGregor, 2006), in contrast to cat fur/skin odor, they do not serve as effective unconditioned stimuli for rapid context conditioning (Wallace and Rosen, 2000; Blanchard et al., 2001; Dielenberg et al., 2001; McGregor et al., 2002; Staples and McGregor, 2006).

In the present chapter, we will provide an overview of the neural systems underlying unconditioned and conditioned defensive responses to a cat, as well as cat fur/skin odor exposure.

II. The hypothalamus and its central role in the organization of anti-predator defensive responses

By the end of the nineteenth century, it was known that the expression of emotional behavior does not depend on the cerebral cortex. Goltz (1892) had demonstrated that fully integrated rage responses could be elicited after surgical removal of the cortex in dogs, acting as if a profoundly threatening situation had confronted them. Cannon and Britton (1925) termed the hyperexcitability of anger in decorticate animals "sham rage." Working in Cannon's laboratory, Bard (1928) localized the subcortical brain regions necessary for the expression of sham rage. In a series of 46 surgically lesioned cats, Bard demonstrated that the central emotional system underlying sham rage involved an area comprising the caudal half of the hypothalamus and the adjacent caudoventral thalamus. Considering the work of Karplus and Kreidl (1909), who had observed that electrical stimulation of the hypothalamus produces diffuse sympathetic excitation comparable to that seen in sham rage, Bard proposed the hypothalamus as a key site involved in emotional expression.

By the 1950s, the hypothalamic defense response of Hess and Brugger (1943) had replaced sham rage as the prototypical model of emotional behavior. These authors electrically stimulated various points throughout the diencephalon, and identified the perifornical region of the lateral hypothalamic area as a key site for eliciting integrated defensive responses. However, debate soon arose regarding the location of the hypothalamic defensive zone. While the studies of Hess and Brugger (1943) implicated the perifornical region, and Hilton and Zbrozyna (1963) also evoked defensive displays from perifornical and adjacent regions of the lateral hypothalamus, Wasman and Flynn (1962) found that defensive behavior was elicited primarily from medial sites in the hypothalamus. Indeed, a number of studies in the cat (Romaniuk, 1965), rat (Panksepp, 1971), opossum (Roberts et al., 1967), and monkey (Delgado, 1964) have emphasized the role of the medial hypothalamus, particularly the ventromedial nucleus, in defensive behavior.

Using the methods of $[^{14}C]$2-deoxyglucose (2-DG) and $[^3H]$leucine radioautography, along with the technique of electrical brain stimulation, Fuchs et al. (1985) suggested that the pathway mediating affective defense behavior from the ventromedial hypothalamus involves an initial synapse within the region of the anteromedial hypothalamus, and a second synapse in the midbrain central gray substance.

However, this view was challenged by Bandler (1982), who found that excitatory amino acid (glutamate) injection into the medial hypothalamus failed to elicit any defensive response, implying that electrical stimulation in the ventromedial hypothalamus activates fibers whose cell bodies are located elsewhere. This issue was clarified by Silveira and Graeff (1992). Using a subtoxic dose (60 pmol) of another excitatory amino acid (kainic acid) injected into the medial hypothalamus, they evoked a pattern of responses resembling the behavior of animals facing natural threats. Similar results have also been obtained following microinjection of drugs impairing GABAergic neurotransmission (Di Scala et al., 1984; Schmitt et al., 1985; Brandão et al., 1986; Milani and Graeff, 1987), indicating that the medial hypothalamus contains groups of neurons commanding defensive behavior, which are tonically inhibited by GABAergic neurotransmission.

The defense reaction induced by chemical stimulation of the medial hypothalamus is characterized by coordinated rapid bouts of locomotion interspersed with well-directed attempts to escape (Di Scala et al., 1984; Brandão et al., 1986; Milani and Graeff, 1987; Silveira and Graeff, 1992), which contrasts with the explosive behavioral reaction evoked from the periaqueductal gray (PAG), characterized by sudden running bouts and aimless vertical jumps (Di Scala et al., 1984; Bandler et al., 1985).

III. The medial hypothalamic defensive system

Although stimulation methods were useful for pointing out the medial zone of the hypothalamus as a key site for orchestrating defensive responses, they are inadequate to provide a clear delineation of the medial hypothalamic defensive circuits. The medial hypothalamic zone (MHZ) consists of a series of well-defined cell groups and is thought to play an important role in the initiation of specific motivated behaviors (Fig. 1). A comprehensive analysis of MHZ axonal projections was made by

Swanson and colleagues, who investigated the connections of each medial hypothalamic nucleus using the *Phaseolus vulgaris* leucoagglutinin (PHAL) technique (Simerly and Swanson, 1988; Canteras and Swanson, 1992; Canteras et al., 1992, 1994; Risold et al., 1994). Of particular relevance, these studies revealed two distinct circuits in the MHZ, where the anterior hypothalamic nucleus (AHN), the dorsomedial part of the ventromedial nucleus (VMHdm), and the dorsal premammillary nucleus (PMd) are particularly interconnected (Fig. 1B), and they are segregated from another medial zone circuit including the medial preoptic nucleus, the ventrolateral part of the ventromedial nucleus, the tuberal nucleus, and the ventral premammillary nucleus (Fig. 1C).

As we shall discuss below, the former hypothalamic circuit is involved in integrating innate antipredator defensive responses (Fig. 1B, medial hypothalamic defensive system), and the latter is part of the sexually dimorphic circuit mediating reproductive and social agonistic behaviors (Fig. 1C, medial hypothalamic reproductive system) (Kollack-Walker and Newman, 1995; Coolen et al., 1996; Canteras et al., 1997). Importantly, in contrast to these medial hypothalamic sites, the mammillary body does not seem to be involved in the initiation of specific motivated behaviors (Swanson, 1987), and is likely instead to mediate other neural functions, including spatial working memory (Sziklas and Petrides, 1998) and navigation (Stackman and Taube, 1998).

To delineate hypothalamic circuits underlying the integration of anti-predator defensive responses, we started by examining Fos immunoreactivity in rats during cat exposure (Canteras et al., 1997). Direct exposure to the predator induced marked freezing and flight responses, and upregulated Fos expression in the medial hypothalamus, which was largely restricted to the circuit formed by the AHN, VMHdm, and PMd (Canteras et al., 1997). The brain regions activated during cat odor exposure have also been explored using Fos immunohistochemistry, and the results indicate that cat odor is processed as a pheromone-like stimulus, activating the accessory olfactory pathways (Dielenberg et al., 2001; McGregor et al., 2004). The same hypothalamic circuit formed by

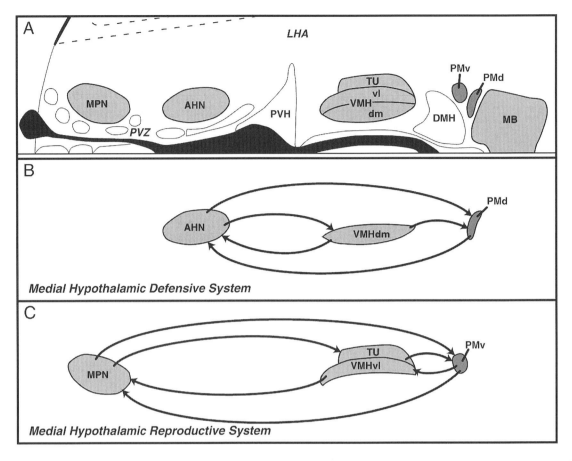

Fig. 1. (A) A schematic horizontal view of the rat brain to show the major subdivisions of the hypothalamus. The organization of major direct connections between the components of the medial hypothalamic defensive (B) and reproductive (C) systems. See text for details. Abbreviations – AHN: anterior hypothalamic nucleus; DMH: dorsomedial hypothalamic nucleus; LHA: lateral hypothalamic area; MB: mammillary body; MPN: medial preoptic nucleus; PMd: dorsal premammillary nucleus; PMv: ventral premammillary nucleus; PVH: paraventricular hypothalamic nucleus; PVZ: periventricular hypothalamic zone; TU: tuberal nucleus; VMH, vl, dm: ventromedial hypothalamic nucleus, ventrolateral part, dorsomedial part.

the AHN, VMHdm, and PMd also showed strong activation to cat odor (Dielenberg et al., 2001). Remarkably, the PMd was the hyptothalamic site presenting the most striking increase in Fos levels in response to both stimuli (Canteras et al., 1997; Dielenberg et al., 2001), and lesions centered in the PMd severely reduced the defensive response to both a live cat and to cat odor, while having a minimal effect on nonpredator threat stimuli, such as an elevated plus maze and postshock contextual cues (Canteras et al., 1997; Blanchard et al., 2003). Considering these anatomical and functional results together brought into focus a distinct medial hypothalamic circuit critical for the expression of anti-predator defensive behavior.

IV. Neural inputs to the medial hypothalamic defensive system

Understanding neural inputs integrated into the medial hypothalamic defensive system (MHZ defensive system) serves as a convenient springboard to reveal brain systems processing predator-related stimuli likely to influence anti-predator defensive responses. The MHZ defensive system receives inputs from widely distributed areas in the forebrain and, to a lesser extent, from the brainstem as well. The major telencephalic sources of inputs to the MHZ defensive system arise from the amygdala and bed nuclei of the stria terminalis (BST), as well as from the septohippocampal system. The MHZ defensive circuit is also modulated by particular regions of the lateral hypothalamic area and a few sites in the brainstem, as well.

IV.A. Amygdalar and BST inputs

The amygdalar region is known to be critically involved in the expression of innate fear responses during encounters with a predator (Blanchard and Blanchard, 1972a). As shown in Fig. 2, specific sites in the amygdala provide substantial inputs to the MHZ defensive system, particularly aimed at the VMHdm, which integrates amygdalar information arising from the posteroventral part of the medial amygdalar nucleus and from the posterior part of the basomedial nucleus (Canteras et al., 1995; Petrovich et al., 1996). The posteroventral part of the medial amygdalar nucleus provides a massive projection to the VMHdm and presents a very strong and selective activation following exposure to cat odor, suggesting that this particular region of the vomeronasal amygdala is involved in pheromone-like processing of predator odor (Canteras et al., 1995; Dielenberg et al., 2001; McGregor et al., 2004). In line with this view, rats with cytotoxic lesions in the medial nucleus, but not in the central nucleus, exhibited a significant reduction in unconditioned fear responses to cat odor (Li et al., 2004). On the other hand, the posterior part of the basomedial amygdalar nucleus receives massive inputs from the lateral amygdalar nucleus (Swanson and Petrovich, 1998). During exposure to a live predator, in addition to activation of the posteroventral part of the medial amygdalar nucleus, we have also observed a distinct increase in Fos levels both in the posterior basomedial amygdalar nucleus and caudal levels of the lateral amygdalar nucleus (Fig. 2C), which, according to Dielenberg et al. (2001), do not appear to

upregulate Fos expression in response to cat odor, suggesting that these two amygdalar sites respond to the totality of predator stimuli rather than the odor alone. The caudal lateral amygdalar nucleus, and to a lesser extent, the posterior basomedial nucleus receive inputs from visual and auditory association areas (i.e., Te1, Te2, and dorsal bank of the perirhinal cortex), likely to integrate predator-derived sensory clues, other than olfactory clues (McDonald, 1998; Shi and Cassell, 1999). The lateral amygdalar nucleus has been implicated as a site of plasticity and storage of emotional memory; damage to this area dramatically reduces cue and contextual conditioning to footshock (LeDoux et al., 1990; Campeau and Davis, 1995; Wallace and Rosen, 2001). At this point, it would be very interesting to define these cortico-amygdalar paths for predator detection and to know how they influence the expression of anti-predator responses.

Amygdalar inputs to the VMHdm, as well as to other components of the MHZ system (e.g., AHN and PMd), may also be relayed through the interfascicular nucleus of the BST (Dong and Swanson, 2004), which represents the BST region most responsive to predator exposure (Fig. 2, E.R. Ribeiro-Barbosa and N.S. Canteras, personal observations). It has been shown that the BST modulates defensive rage (Shaikh et al., 1986; Brutus et al., 1988) and unconditioned startle reflex (Walker and Davis, 1997); however, its specific roles in the context of anti-predator defensive responses remains to be investigated.

IV.B. Septohippocampal inputs

A number of studies have shown that the hippocampus helps to modulate anxiety-related behaviors (Gray and McNaughton, 2000; Bannerman et al., 2004) and innate defensive responses to various threat stimuli (Blanchard et al., 1970; Kim et al., 1971; Blanchard and Blanchard, 1972b; Blanchard et al., 1977; Canteras, 2002). According to Gray and McNaughton (2000), all anxiolytic drugs produce their effects by acting on the behavioral inhibition system, the most important neural component of which is the septo-hippocampal

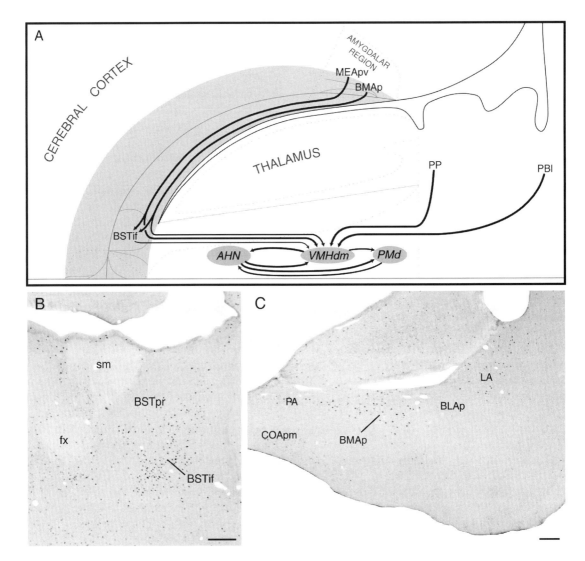

Fig. 2. (A) Main neural inputs to the dorsomedial part of the ventromedial nucleus (VMHdm). (B, C) Photomicrographs of transverse Fos-stained sections at the levels of interfascicular nucleus of the bed nuclei of the stria terminalis (B) and caudal amygdalar region (C) from an animal exposed to a cat. Abbreviations – AHN: anterior hypothalamic nucleus; BLAp: basolateral amygdalar nucleus, posterior part; BMAp: basomedial amygdalar nucleus, posterior part; BSTif: bed nuclei of the stria terminalis, interfascicular nucleus; BSTpr: bed nuclei of the stria terminalis, principal nucleus; COApm: cortical amygdalar nucleus, posterior part, medial zone; fx: fornix; LA: lateral amygdalar nucleus; MEApv: medial amygdalar nucleus, posteroventral part; PA: posterior amygdalar nucleus; PBl: parabrachial nucleus, lateral part; PMd: dorsal premammillary nucleus; PP: peripeduncular nucleus; sm: stria medullaris; VMHdm: ventromedial hypothalamic nucleus, dorsomedial part. Scale Bars = 200 μm.

system. The Blanchards have shown that complete electrolytic hippocampal lesions reduce unconditioned freezing to, and increase avoidance of, a live cat (Blanchard and Blanchard, 1972b). Tract-

tracing studies have shown that the septohippocampal system is in a position to influence the MHZ defensive system. As can be seen in Fig. 3A, the projection from the septal area to the MHZ

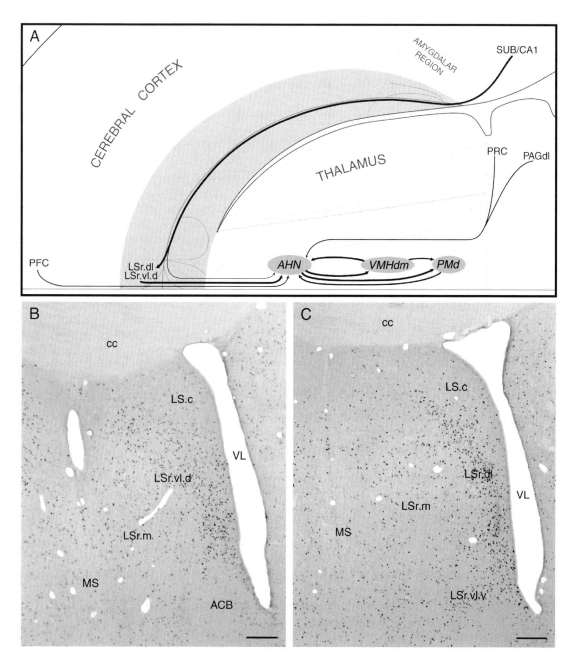

Fig. 3. (A) Main neural inputs to the anterior hypothalamic nucleus (AHN). (B, C) Photomicrographs of transverse Fos-stained sections at rostral (B) and caudal (C) levels of the rostral part of the lateral septal nucleus from an animal exposed to a cat. Abbreviations – ACB: nucleus accumbens; CA1: field CA1, Ammon's horn; cc: corpus callosum; LSc: lateral septal nucleus, caudal part; LSr.dl: lateral septal nucleus, rostral part, dorsolateral zone; LSr.m: lateral septal nucleus, rostral part, medial zone; LSr.vl.d: lateral septal nucleus, rostral part, ventrolateral zone, dorsal region; LSr.vl.v: lateral septal nucleus, rostral part, ventrolateral zone, ventral region; MS: medial septal nucleus; PAGdl: periaqueductal gray, dorsolateral part; PFC: prefrontal cortex; PMd: dorsal premammillary nucleus; PRC: precommissural nucleus; SUB: subiculum; VL: lateral ventricle; VMHdm: ventromedial hypothalamic nucleus, dorsomedial part. Scale Bars = 200 μm.

defensive system is mainly directed to the AHN and arises predominantly from the dorsal region of the ventrolateral zone of the rostral part of the lateral septal nucleus (LSr.vl.d), which also provides a sparser innervation to the PMd and capsular region of the VMHdm (Risold and Swanson, 1997). In addition, retrograde tracer findings from our laboratory indicated that the caudal part of the AHN receives a distinctive input from the dorsolateral zone of the rostral part of the lateral septal nucleus (LSr.dl). Notably, both the LSr.dl and LSr.vl.d seem to be involved in septal lesions most effective in producing the hyperdefensiveness state referred to as "septal rage" (Albert and Chew, 1980). According to previous observations from our laboratory, in the septal region, we noted that both of these districts were particularly mobilized in terms of Fos expression during cat exposure (Fig. 3B, C). These septal districts are known to receive inputs from intermediate regions of field CA1 and the subiculum (Risold and Swanson, 1997), which may also provide modest direct inputs to the AHN (Fig. 3A). Of particular relevance in the present context is the fact that intermediate regions of field CA1 and the subiculum integrate information from amygdalar regions likely to process sensory clues related to the predator, such as the lateral and posterior basomedial amygdalar nuclei (Petrovich et al., 2001). Recent findings from the Blanchards' laboratory indicate that ventral hippocampal lesions (including intermediate regions of field CA1 and subiculum), but not dorsal hippocampal lesions, significantly reduced unconditioned defensive behaviors during exposure to cat odor without producing any observable effects during cat exposure (Pentkowski et al., 2006). Furthermore, ventral hippocampal lesions significantly attenuated conditioned defensive behaviors during re-exposure to the context associated with either direct exposure to the cat or cat odor alone (Pentkowski et al., 2006).

IV.C. Lateral hypothalamic inputs

The MHZ defensive system is modulated by specific lateral hypothalamic districts, including the periformical region and the lateral hypothalamic retinoceptive field. All elements of the MHZ defensive system receive substantial inputs from a distinct periformical site located ventral to the fornix at caudal levels of the AHN (Goto et al., 2005). Several studies have associated this part of the periformical region with aggressive behavior, where electrical or chemical stimulation evoke either attack or escape responses, and it has been included within the hypothalamic "attack area" (Siegel et al., 1999). Roberts and Nagel (1996), combining electrical stimulation of this periformical region with ^{14}C-deoxyglucose auto-radiograph maps of metabolic activity, found increased metabolic activity in all elements of the MHZ defensive system particularly correlated with escape, but not with attack responses. In line with this view, a conspicuous activation of this periformical region occurs when rats present anti-predator defensive responses to direct cat exposure, but not to cat odor alone (Dielenberg et al., 2001; Canteras et al., 2001). This periformical region is known to share strong bidirectional connections with the dorsolateral zone of the rostral part of the lateral septal nucleus (LSrdl) (Risold and Swanson, 1997; Goto et al., 2005), which, as previously discussed, is likely to be involved in septal lesions that are most effective in producing "septal rage" (Albert and Chew, 1980). Moreover, this periformical district is positioned to integrate a complex set of input information from nociception system and brainstem networks involved in coordinating behavioral responses (see Goto et al., 2005). It has been suggested that this hypothalamic region is in a position to match current internal motivational status and external environmental conditions to appropriate behavioral responses (i.e., either escape or attack responses).

In the MHZ defensive system, the PMd also receives inputs from another lateral hypothalamic region located immediately dorsal to the supraoptic nucleus, heavily targeted by the lateral component of the retinohypothalamic tract (Comoli et al., 2000). According to Leak and Moore (1997), retinal ganglion cells projecting to this lateral hypothalamic region are likely to convey information about environmental light intensity. In the context of anti-predator defensive responses, it seems plausible to suggest that different behavioral strategies might be expressed depending on environmental luminescence. For example, instead of flight behaviors, freezing immobility seems to be particularly effective as a camouflage in darkness, where freezing greatly reduces prey visibility and noise generation. Moreover, it seems reasonable to believe that this path may, at least in part, mediate the well-documented anxiogenic profile induced by high levels of environmental luminescence (File and Hyde, 1978; File, 1980).

IV.D. Brainstem inputs

Only a few sites in the brainstem appear to provide direct inputs to the MHZ defensive system. Previous anatomical studies have shown that the AHN receives ascending projection from the precommissural nucleus and dorsolateral PAG (PAGdl) (Cameron et al., 1995a; Canteras and Goto, 1999a), which, as we shall discuss below, represent the main brainstem targets of the MHZ defensive system. As we shall consider, the PAGdl is activated in response to "psychological stressors," such as the presence of a natural predator, and it in turn triggers "active emotional coping responses," including increased somatomotor activity (e.g., freezing, fight, or flight), hyperreactivity, hypertension, tachycardia, and a nonopioid-mediated analgesia (for references, see Floyd et al., 2000). It is reasonable to suggest that this pathway from the PAGdl to the MHZ defensive system is likely to convey critical feedback information related to the outcome of anti-predator defensive responses. It has been suggested that the PAG is in a position to influence the motivational drive for a number of behavioral responses, and that these ascending projections to the hypothalamus should, perhaps, be thought of as underlying the long-lasting behavioral inhibition that follows predator exposure (Sukikara et al., 2006).

Previous anatomical and functional studies have shown that the VMHdm is heavily targeted by lateral parabrachial sites involved in transmitting noxious stimuli (Bester et al., 1997). The VMHdm also integrates inputs from the peripeduncular nucleus (Arnault and Roger, 1987). Considering the peripeduncular nucleus' role in underlying aggressive behavior (see Roberts and Nagel, 1996), this path to the MHZ defensive system is in a position to relay information regarding agonistic interactions.

V. Neural outputs from the medial hypothalamic defensive system

The precommissural nucleus and the PAG represent the main brainstem targets of the MHZ defensive system. As originally noted by Hunsperger (1956), the PAG is a key site to organize defensive responses, where lesions result in passive animals that rarely, if ever, show defensive behavior. The projection from the VMHdm and the PMd to the PAG is very dense and presents a clear topography (Canteras and Swanson, 1992; Canteras et al., 1994). Thus, at the level of the nucleus of Darkschewitsch, the dorsomedial part of the PAG receives a massive innervation from the VMHdm in addition to a significant, but sparser, projection from the PMd. At the level of the oculomotor and trochlear nuclei, this latter hypothalamic site provides a strikingly dense projection to the dorsolateral part of the PAG, which, in addition to the dorsomedial PAG, is also heavily targeted by fibers arising from the VMHdm. At caudal levels, axons from the VMHdm spread to innervate the dorsomedial, dorsolateral, lateral, and ventrolateral parts of the PAG, whereas those from the PMd continue to provide a relatively circumscribed projection to the dorsolateral PAG. Compared to other components of the MHZ defensive system, the AHN provides a much lighter projection to the PAG, particularly directed to the rostral dorsomedial and caudal ventrolateral parts of the PAG (Risold et al., 1994). Of special relevance, the pattern of projection from the MHZ defensive system to the PAG largely overlaps the pattern of PAG activation in animals exposed to a predator, where Fos expression was mostly seen in the rostral two-thirds of the PAG in the dorsomedial and dorsolateral regions, whereas in the caudal PAG, a less intense but more widespread activation was observed (Canteras and Goto, 1999b). A similar pattern of

PAG activation was also described after administration of drugs known to induce panic in humans (Singewald and Sharp, 2000), differing, however, from the one seen after physical stressors (e.g., cutaneous pain, footshock, restraint stress, swim stress, opiate withdrawal), which fail to evoke consistent Fos expression within the dorsolateral PAG (Keay and Bandler, 1993; Pezzone et al., 1993; Cullinan et al., 1995; Bellchambers et al., 1998; Li and Sawchenko, 1998). Taken together, this evidence strongly supports the idea that the dorsolateral PAG appears to play a critical role in the PAG for integrating forebrain limbic information related to "psychological stressors," such as the presence of a natural predator.

The PAG is known to play an important role in a number of anti-predator related responses, such as the modulation of nociceptive sensory transmission (Besson et al., 1991; Lovick, 1993; Bandler and Shipley, 1994), regulation of the cardiovascular system (Lovick, 1993; Bandler and Shipley, 1994), vocalization (Jürgens, 1994), and organization of motor patterns in response to live predators (Bandler and Shipley, 1994; Keay and Bundler, 2001). By and large, PAG-related responses have been regarded as rather stereotyped and are thought to depend on descending projections to the brainstem and spinal cord. Recent findings from our lab have challenged this view and suggested an additional rather integrative PAG function in influencing motivational drives for the expression of more complex behavioral responses, such as foraging and risk-assessment responses (Sukikara et al., 2006). According to this view, such responses could rely predominantly on PAG-ascending projections to certain hypothalamic and thalamic sites, and apparently to a considerably lesser extent on descending paths to the brainstem.

All elements of the MHZ defensive system provide a particularly dense projection to the precommissural nucleus, which, like PAG regions densely targeted by this system, also presents a dramatic increase in Fos immunoreactivity in animals exposed to a predator (Canteras and Goto, 1999b). Unfortunately, we are not aware of any reports on possible functional roles played by the precommissural nucleus. However, we have found

that this nucleus presents a connective pattern similar in many ways to the rostral part of the dorsolateral PAG (Cameron et al., 1995a,b; Canteras and Goto, 1999a), and therefore, it is likely to share with this latter region a number of integrative functions.

The elements of the MHZ defensive system also project to medial regions of the intermediate and deep layers of the superior colliculus (Canteras and Swanson, 1992; Canteras et al., 1994; Risold et al., 1994). Significantly, this region is particularly responsive to visual-threatening stimuli like suddenly expanding shadows in the upper visual field, and, via a projection to the rostral part of the PAGdl, is thought to exert a marked influence on the control of defensive responses (Redgrave and Dean, 1991).

Interestingly, the MHZ defensive system provides feedback loops to several telencephalic sites that we have just described as being involved in processing predator-related information, including the interfascicular nucleus of the BST, the lateral septal nucleus and the lateral amygdalar nucleus. Moreover, the MHZ defensive system also projects to a number of thalamic sites that are also likely to influence the anti-predator defensive responses.

In the dorsal thalamus, the nucleus reuniens and the ventral part of the anteromedial nucleus receive a dense innervation from the MHZ defensive system. The AHN contributes with a considerable projection to rostral parts of the nucleus reuniens, which also receive significant, but less dense, inputs from the VMHdm and PMd (Canteras and Swanson, 1992; Canteras et al., 1994; Risold et al., 1994). The nucleus reuniens represents the major source of thalamic projections to the hippocampal formation, and is thought to play a key role in modulating transmission through the hippocampal system (Herkenham, 1978; Wouterlood et al., 1990; Risold et al., 1997). In the present context, it is important to consider potential roles of this path in emotion-related learning and memory, which may be particularly relevant for influencing contextual responses to predator-related environmental cues.

The PMd provides a massive projection to the ventral anteromedial thalamic nucleus, which, in turn, projects to the lateral retrosplenial area thought to be involved in modulating eye and head movements associated with attentional mechanisms (Risold and Swanson, 1995).

In the ventral thalamus, all components of the MHZ defensive system provide a substantial projection to the rostral pole of the zona incerta (Canteras and Swanson, 1992; Canteras et al., 1994; Risold et al., 1994). Although a great deal remains to be learned about the connectivity and possible functional roles of this region of the zona incerta, hodologic evidence indicates that it is intimately related to the main brainstem targets of this hypothalamic system, for example, the precommissural nucleus and the dorsolateral PAG (Cameron et al., 1995a; Elias and Bittencourt, 1997; Canteras and Goto, 1999a).

VI. Overview of the circuits involved in processing anti-predator defensive responses

In Fig. 4, we provide a provisional delineation of the neural systems reviewed here as involved in organizing unconditioned predator-induced responses. During exposure to a live cat or to cat fur/skin odor, specific amygdalar systems are involved in detecting predator-related cues and in activating the MHZ defensive circuit. Concomitantly, the hippocampal formation is likely to be involved in some aspect of the association between these predator threats and the environment where the rat encounters this stimulus. The hippocampal–septal complex, in turn, also provides inputs to the MHZ defensive system. The MHZ defensive system may provide either direct or indirect (via certain thalamic nuclei) feedback loops (not shown in Fig. 4), which may influence both amygdalar and hippocampal processing. In conclusion, the MHZ defensive system – integrating amygdalar, hippocampal, and retinal inputs – is in a position to modulate the PAG (as well as other brainstem targets). The PAG, in turn, is likely to organize a number of unconditioned anti-predator defensive

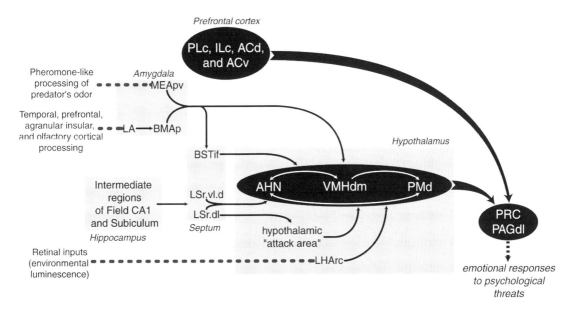

Fig. 4. Summary diagram showing the organization of major parallel prosencephalic pathways involved in the control of innate fear responses to psychological threats. Abbreviations – Acd: anterior cingulate area, dorsal part; Acv: anterior cingulate area, ventral part; AHN: anterior hypothalamic nucleus; BMAp: basomedial amygdalar nucleus, posterior part; BSTif: bed nuclei of the stria terminalis, interfascicular nucleus; Ilc: imfralimbic area, caudal part; LA: lateral amygdalar nucleus; LHArc: lateral hypothalamic area, retinoceptive region; LSr.dl: lateral septal nucleus, rostral part, dorsolateral zone; LSr.vl.d: lateral septal nucleus, rostral part, ventrolateral zone, dorsal region; MEApv: medial amygdalar nucleus, posteroventral part; PAGdl: periaqueductal gray, dorsolateral part; PLc: prelimbic area, caudal part; PMd: dorsal premammillary nucleus; PRC: precommissural nucleus; VMHdm: ventromedial hypothalamic nucleus, dorsomedial part.

responses, such as flight, hiding, freezing, defensive threat, defensive attack, and risk assessment.

VII. Neural systems involved in anti-predator contextual conditioning responses

Defensive behaviors in response to threatening cues and context have been well-documented, chiefly using unconditioned aversive stimuli, such as footshock. Interestingly, rats rapidly acquire contextual conditioned defensive responses to the environment where they had previously encountered a predator, or the odor of a predator (Ribeiro-Barbosa et al., 2005; Staples et al, 2005). Thus, long-term risk assessment, as well as freezing and avoidance, are seen in the area where a live cat or its skin/fur odor had been encountered.

Staples et al. (2005), examining the neural system responsible for contextual conditioned responses to cat odor, observed a robust activation of the PMd in response to cat-odor-associated context and suggested that there is an overlap between the neural systems associated with the expression of unconditioned and contextual-conditioned anti-predator defensive responses. In line with this view, we have found that rats exposed to a hostile environment, where a live cat had been previously encountered, present a partial activation of the MHZ defensive system, where increased Fos expression was found in the AHN and PMd (E.R. Ribeiro-Barbosa and N.S. Canteras, personal observation). As previously noted, the AHN integrates most of the septohippocampal inputs to the MHZ defensive system, and lesion studies have shown that damage to the ventral hippocampus significantly attenuated conditioned defensive behaviors following re-exposure to contexts associated with either a live cat or its odor (Pentkowski et al., 2006). Moreover, we have found that pharmacological PMd inactivation with muscimol drastically reduced conditioned defensive behaviors during exposure to the hostile environment, where a live cat had been previously encountered (A.F. Cezário and N.S. Canteras, personal observation).

In contrast to the AHN and PMd, the VMHdm and its allied amygdalar paths seem particularly involved in detecting the actual predator-related stimuli, either a live cat or its odor, but do not respond to predator-related contextual cues. Taken as a whole, the evidence suggests that the MHZ defensive system, in particular the AHN and the PMd, may be involved in integrating anti-predator contextual conditioning responses, as well.

Curiously, previous fear-conditioning studies using footshock do not identify the involvement of any element of the MHZ defensive system (Beck and Fibiger, 1995; Pezzone et al., 1992; Smith et al., 1992). Therefore, it is of particular interest to note the fact that conditioning, using a predator-related stimulus, seems to be mediated by a neural system that is distinct from the one known to underlie contextual fear acquired using footshock as an unconditioned stimulus.

As with unconditioned anti-predator defensive responses, the PAG seems to be a critical site for organizing the expression of contextual conditioned anti-predator responses. We have found that animals exposed to the environment where a live cat had been previously encountered present a pattern of PAG activation similar to the one seen in response to the actual predator, but considerably less intense. Thus, the PAGdl seems to be particularly responsive to both the actual predator and, to a lesser extent, to the predator-related context cues. A somewhat different finding has been reported by Staples et al. (2005), who found Fos upregulation in the ventrolateral part, but not in other parts of the PAG, in response to cat-odor related context. This view seems to be at odds with recent findings showing that NMDA glutamate receptor blockade with AP5 into the dorsal PAG significantly reduced defensive behaviors during cat odor conditioning (A.P. Carobrez, personal communication).

Although a great deal remains to be learned about the neural basis of anti-predator contextual conditioning responses, the evidence gathered so far clearly suggests that there is a large overlap of neural circuits mediating both unconditioned and conditioned anti-predator related defensive responses. Thus, in both situations a pathway using the ventral hippocampus, the AHN, the PMd, and the dorsolateral PAG seems to be particularly critical for the expression of fear responses.

References

Albert, D.J. and Chew, G.L. (1980) The septal forebrain and the inhibitory modulation of attack and defense in the rat. A review. Behav. Neural. Biol., 30: 357–388.

Arnault, P. and Roger, M. (1987) The connections of the peripeduncular area studied by retrograde and anterograde transport in the rat. J. Comp. Neurol., 258: 463–476.

Bandler, R. (1982) Induction of "rage" following microinjections of glutamate into midbrain but not hypothalamus of cats. Neurosci. Lett., 30: 183–188.

Bandler, R., Depaulis, A. and Vergnes, M. (1985) Identification of midbrain neurons mediating defensive behavior in the rat by microinjections of excitatory amino acids. Behav. Brain Res., 15: 107–119.

Bandler, R. and Shipley, M.T. (1994) Columnar organization of the midbrain periaqueductal gray: modules for emotional expression. Trends Neurosci., 17: 379–389.

Bannerman, D.M., Rawlins, J.N.P., McHugh, S.B., Deacon, R.M.J., Yee, B.K., Bast, T., Zhang, W.-N., Pothuizen, H.H.J. and Feldon, J. (2004) Regional dissociations within the hippocampus-memory and anxiety. Neurosci. Biobehav. Rev., 28: 273–283.

Bard, P. (1928) A diencephalic mechanism for the expression of rage with special reference to the sympathetic nervous system. Am. J. Physiol., 84: 490–515.

Beck, C.H.M. and Fibiger, H.C. (1995) Conditioned fear-induced changes in behavior and in the expression of the immediate early gene c-Fos: with and without diazepam treatment. J. Neurosci., 15: 709–720.

Bellchambers, C.E., Chieng, B., Keay, K.A. and Christie, M.J. (1998) Swim-stress but not opioid withdrawal increases expression of c-fos immunoreactivity in rat periaqueductal gray neurons which project to the rostral ventromedial medulla. Neuroscience, 83: 517–524.

Besson, J.M., Fardin, V. and Oliveras, J.L. (1991) Analgesia produced by stimulation of the periaqueductal gray matter: true antinoceptive effects versus stress effects. In: Depaulis, A. and Bandler, R. (Eds.), The Midbrain Periaqueductal Gray Matter: Functional, Anatomical, and Neurochemical Organization. Plenum, New York, pp. 121–138.

Bester, H., Besson, J.M. and Bernard, J.F. (1997) Organization of efferent projections from the parabrachial area to the hypothalamus: a *Phaseolus vulgaris* leucoagglutinin study in the rat. J. Comp. Neurol., 383: 245–281.

Blanchard, D.C. and Blanchard, R.J. (1972a) Innate and conditioned reactions to threat in rats with amygdaloid lesions. J. Comp. Psychol. Psychol., 81: 281–290.

Blanchard, D.C., Blanchard, R.J., Lee, E.M.C. and Fukunaga, K.K. (1977) Movement arrest and the hippocampus. Physiol. Psychol., 5: 331–335.

Blanchard, D.C., Li, C.I., Hubbard, D., Markham, C.M., Yang, M., Takahashi, L.K. and Blanchard, R.J. (2003) Dorsal premammillary nucleus differentially modulates defensive behaviors induced different threat stimuli in rats. Neurosci. Lett., 345: 145–148.

Blanchard, R.J. and Blanchard, D.C. (1972b) Effects of hippocampal lesions on the rat's reaction to a cat. J. Comp. Physiol. Psychol., 78: 77–82.

Blanchard, R.J., Blanchard, D.C. and Fial, R.A. (1970) Hippocampal lesions in rats and their effect on activity, avoidance, and aggression. J. Comp. Physiol. Psychol., 71: 92–102.

Blanchard, R.J., Blanchard, D.C. and Hori, K. (1989) An ethoexperimental approach to the study of defense. In: Blanchard, R.J. Brain, P.F. Blanchard, D.C. and Parmigiani, S. (Eds.), Ethoexperimental approaches to the study of behavior. Kluwer Academic Publishing, Dordrecht, pp. 114–136.

Blanchard, R.J., Yang, M., Li, C.I., Gervacio, A. and Blanchard, D.C. (2001) Cue and context conditioning of defensive behaviors to cat odor stimuli. Neurosci. Biobehav. Rev., 26: 587–595.

Brandão, M.L., Di Scala, G., Bouchet, M.J. and Schmitt, P. (1986) Escape behavior produced by blockade of glutamic acid decarboxylase (GAD) in mesencephalic central gray or medial hypothalamus. Pharmacol. Biochem. Behav., 24: 497–501.

Brutus, M., Zuabi, S. and Siegel, A. (1988) Effects of D-ala2-met5-enkephalinamide microinjections placed into the bed nucleus of the stria terminalis upon affective defense behavior in the cat. Brain Res., 473: 147–152.

Cameron, A.A., Khan, I.A., Westlund, K.N., Cliffer, K.D. and Willis, W.D. (1995a) The efferent projections of the periaqueductal gray in the rat: a *Phaseolus vulgaris* leucoagglutinin study: I. Ascending projections. J. Comp. Neurol., 351: 568–584.

Cameron, A.A., Khan, I.A., Westlund, K.N. and Willis, W.D. (1995b) The efferent projections of the periaqueductal gray in the rat: a *Phaseolus vulgaris* leucoagglutinin study: II. Descending projections. J. Comp. Neurol., 351: 585–601.

Campeau, S. and Davis, M. (1995) Involvement of the central and basolateral complex of the amygdala in fear conditioning measured with fear-potentiated startle in rats trained concurrently with auditory and visual conditioned stimuli. J. Neurosci., 15: 2301–2311.

Cannon, W.B. and Britton, S.W. (1925) Pseudo-affective medulliadrenal secretion. Am. J. Physiol., 72: 283–294.

Canteras, N.S., Chiavegatto, S., Ribeiro do Valle, L.E. and Swanson, L.W. (1997) Severe reduction of defensive behavior to a predator by discrete hypothalamic chemical lesions. Brain Res. Bull., 44: 297–305.

Canteras, N.S. and Goto, M. (1999a) Connections of the precommissural nucleus. J. Comp. Neurol., 408: 23–45.

138

Canteras, N.S. and Goto, M. (1999b) Fos-like immunoreactivity in the periaqueductal gray of rats exposed to a natural predator. Neuroreport, 10: 413–418.

Canteras, N.S., Simerly, R.B. and Swanson, L.W. (1992) Projections of the ventral premammillary nucleus. J. Comp. Neurol., 324: 195–212.

Canteras, N.S., Simerly, R.B. and Swanson, L.W. (1994) Organization of projections from the ventromedial nucleus of the hypothalamus: a *Phaseolus vulgaris* leucoagglutinin study in the rat. J. Comp. Neurol., 348: 41–79.

Canteras, N.S., Simerly, R.B. and Swanson, L.W. (1995) Organization of projections from the medial nucleus of the amygdala: a PHAL study in the rat. J. Comp. Neurol., 360: 213–245.

Canteras, N.S. and Swanson, L.W. (1992) The dorsal premammillary nucleus: an unusual component of the mammillary body. Proc. Natl. Acad. Sci. USA, 89: 10089–10093.

Canteras, N.S. (2002) The medial hypothalamic defensive system: hodological organization and functional implications. Pharmacol. Biochem. Behav., 71: 481–491.

Canteras, N.S., Ribeiro-Barbosa, E.R. and Comoli, E. (2001) Tracing from the dorsal premammillary nucleusprosencephalic systems involved in the organization of innate fear responses. Neurosci. Biobehav. Rev., 25: 661–668.

Comoli, E., Ribeiro-Barbosa, E.R. and Canteras, N.S. (2000) Afferent connections of the dorsal premammillary nucleus. J. Comp. Neurol., 423: 83–98.

Coolen, L.M., Peters, H.J.P.W. and Veening, J.G. (1996) Fos immunoreactivity in the rat brain following consummatory elements of sexual behavior: a sex comparison. Brain Res., 738: 67–82.

Cullinan, W.E., Herman, J.P., Battaglia, D.F., Akil, H. and Watson, S.J. (1995) Pattern and time course of immediate early gene expression in rat brain following acute stress. Neuroscience, 64: 477–505.

Curti, M.W. (1935) Native responses of white rats in the presence of cats. Psychol. Monogr., 46: 76–98.

Delgado, J.M.R. (1964) Free behavior and brain stimulation. Int. Rev. Neurobiol., 6: 349–449.

Di Scala, G., Schmitt, P. and Karli, P. (1984) Flight induced by infusion of bicuculline methiodide into periventricular structures. Brain Res., 309: 199–208.

Dielenberg, R.A., Hunt, G.E. and McGregor, I.S. (2001) "When a rat smells a cat": the distribution of c-fos expression in rat brain following exposure to a predator odor. Neuroscience, 104: 1085–1097.

Dielenberg, R.A. and McGregor, I.S. (1999) Habituation of the hiding response to cat odor in rats (*Rattus norvegicus*). J. Comp. Psychol., 113: 376–387.

Dong, H.W. and Swanson, L.W. (2004) Projections from bed nuclei of the stria terminalis, posterior division: implications for cerebral hemisphere regulation of defensive and reproductive behaviors. J. Comp. Neurol., 471: 396–433.

Elias, C.F. and Bittencourt, J.C. (1997) Study of origins of melanin-concentrating hormone and neuropeptide EI immunoreactive projections to the periaqueductal gray matter. Brain Res., 755: 255–271.

File, S.E. (1980) The use of social interaction as a method of detecting anxiolytic activity of chlordiazepoxide-like drugs. J. Neurosci. Methods, 2: 219–238.

File, S.E. and Hyde, J.R.G. (1978) Can social interaction be used to measure anxiety? Br. J. Pharmacol., 62: 19–24.

Floyd, N.S., Price, J.L., Ferry, A.T., Keay, K.A. and Bandler, R. (2000) Orbitomedial prefrontal cortical projections to distinct longitudinal columns of the periaqueductal gray in the rat. J. Comp. Neurol., 422: 556–578.

Fuchs, S.A.G., Edinger, H.M. and Siegel, A. (1985) The organization of the hypothalamic pathways mediating affective defensive behavior in the cat. Brain Res., 330: 77–92.

Goltz, F. (1892) Der Hund ohne Grosshirn. Pfluegers Arch. Gesamte Physiol. Menschen Tiere, 51: 570–614.

Goto, M., Canteras, N.S., Burns, G. and Swanson, L.W. (2005) Projections from the subfornical region of the lateral hypothalamic area. J. Comp. Neurol., 493: 412–438.

Gray, J.A. and McNaughton, N. (2000) The Neuropsychology of Anxiety. , 2nd edn. Oxford University Press, Oxford, pp. 424.

Herkenham, M. (1978) The connections of the nucleus reuniens thalami: evidence for a direct thalamo-hippocampal pathway in the rat. J. Comp. Neurol., 177: 589–610.

Hess, W.R. and Brugger, M. (1943) Das subkortikale Zentrum der affektiven Abwehrreaktion. Helv. Physiol. Pharmacol. Acta, 1: 33–52.

Hilton, S.M. and Zbrozyna, A.W. (1963) Amygdaloid region for defence reactions and its efferent pathway to the brain stem. J. Physiol. (Lond.), 165: 160–173.

Hunsperger, R.W. (1956) Affektreaktionen auf elektrische Reizung im Hirnstamm der Katze. Helv. Physiol. Pharmacol. Acta, 14: 70–92.

Jürgens, U. (1994) The role of the periaqueductal grey in vocal behavior. Behav. Brain. Res., 62: 107–117.

Karplus, J.P. and Kreidl, A. (1909) Gehirn und Sympathicus. I. Zwischenhirnbasis und Halssympathicus. Pfluegers Arch. Gesamte Physiol. Menschen Tiere, 129: 138–144.

Keay, K.A. and Bandler, R. (1993) Deep and superficial noxious stimulation increases Fos like immunoreactivity in different regions of the midbrain periaqueductalgray of the rat. Neurosci. Lett., 154: 143–158.

Keay, K.A. and Bundler, R. (2001) Parallel circuits mediating distinct emotional coping reactions to different types of stress. Neurosci. Biobehav. Rev., 25: 669–678.

Kim, C., Kim, C.C., Kim, J.K., Kim, S.M., Chang, H.K., Kim, J.Y. and Lee, I.G. (1971) Fear response and aggressive behavior of hippocampectomized house rats. Brain Res., 29: 237–251.

Kollack-Walker, S. and Newman, S.W. (1995) Mating and agonistic behavior produce different patterns of fos immunolabeling in the male Syrian hamster brain. Neuroscience, 66: 721–736.

Leak, R.K. and Moore, R.Y. (1997) Identification of retinal ganglion cells projecting to the lateral hypothalamic area of the rat. Brain Res., 770: 105–114.

LeDoux, J.E., Cicchetti, P., Xagoraris, A. and Rominski, L.M. (1990) The lateral amygdaloid nucleus: sensory interface of the amygdala in fear conditioning. J. Neurosci., 10: 1062–1069.

Li, C.I., Maglinao, T.L. and Takahashi, L.K. (2004) Medial amygdala modulation of predator odor-induced unconditioned fear in the rat. Behav. Neurosci., 118: 324–332.

Li, H.Y. and Sawchenko, P.E. (1998) Hypothalamic effector neurons and extended circuitries activated in "neurogenic" stress: a comparison of footshock effects exerted acutely, chronically, and in animals with controlled glucocorticoid levels. J. Comp. Neurol., 393: 244–266.

Lovick, T.A. (1993) Integrated activity of cardiovascular and pain regulatory systems: role in adaptive behavioral responses. Prog. Neurobiol., 40: 631–644.

McDonald, A.J. (1998) Cortical pathways to mammalian amygdale. Prog. Neurobiol., 55: 257–332.

McGregor, I.S., Hargreaves, G.A., Apfelbach, R. and Hunt, G.E. (2004) Neural correlates of cat odor-induced anxiety in rats: region-specific effects of the benzodiazepine midazolam. J. Neurosci., 24: 4134–4144.

McGregor, I.S., Schrama, L., Ambermoon, P. and Dielenberg, R.A. (2002) Not all "predartor odours" are equal: cat odour but not 2,4,5 trimethylthiazoline (TMT; fox odor) elicits specific defensive behaviours in rats. Behav. Brain Res., 129: 1–16.

Milani, H. and Graeff, F.G. (1987) GABA-benzodiazepine modulation of aversion in the medial hypothalamus of the rat. Pharmacol. Biochem. Behav., 28: 21–27.

Panksepp, J. (1971) Aggression elicited by electrical stimulation of the hypothalamus in albino rats. Physiol. Behav., 6: 321–329.

Pentkowski, N.S., Blanchard, D.C., Lever, C., Litvin, Y. and Blanchard, R.J. (2006) Effects of lesions to the dorsal and ventral hippocampus on defensive behaviors in rats. Eur. J. Neurosci., 23: 2185–2196.

Petrovich, G.D., Canteras, N.S. and Swanson, L.W. (2001) Combinatorial amygdalar inputs to hippocampal domains and hypothalamic behavior systems. Brain Res. Rev., 38: 247–289.

Petrovich, G.D., Risold, P.Y. and Swanson, L.W. (1996) Organization of the projections of the basomedial nucleus of the amygdala: a PHAL study in the rat. J. Comp. Neurol., 374: 387–420.

Pezzone, M.A., Lee, W.S., Hoffman, G.E. and Rabin, B.S. (1992) Induction of c-Fos immunoreactivity in the rat forebrain by conditioned and unconditioned aversive stimuli. Brain Res., 597: 41–50.

Redgrave, P. and Dean, P. (1991) Does the PAG learn about emergencies from the superior colliculus? In: Depaulis, A. and Bandler, R. (Eds.), The Midbrain Periaqueductal Gray Matter. Plenum, New York, pp. 199–209.

Ribeiro-Barbosa, E.R., Canteras, N.S., Cezario, A.F., Blanchard, R.J. and Blanchard, D.C. (2005) An alternative experimental procedure for studying predator-related defensive responses. Neurosci. Biobehav. Rev., 29: 1255–1263.

Risold, P.Y., Canteras, N.S. and Swanson, L.W. (1994) Organization of projections from the anterior hypothalamic nucleus: a *Phaseolus vulgaris* leucoagglutinin study in the rat. J. Comp. Neurol., 348: 1–40.

Risold, P.Y. and Swanson, L.W. (1995) Evidence for a hypothalamocortical circuit mediating pheromonal influences on eye and head movements. Proc. Natl. Acad. Sci. USA, 99: 3898–3902.

Risold, P.Y. and Swanson, L.W. (1997) Connections of the rat lateral septal complex. Brain Res. Rev., 24: 115–195.

Risold, P.Y., Thompson, R.H. and Swanson, L.W. (1997) The structural organization of connections between hypothalamus and cerebral cortex. Brain Res. Rev., 24: 197–254.

Roberts, W.W. and Nagel, J. (1996) First-order projections activated by stimulation of hypothalamic sites eliciting attack and flight in rats. Behav. Neurosci., 110: 509–527.

Roberts, W.W., Steinberg, M.L. and Means, L.W. (1967) Hypothalamic mechanisms for sexual, aggressive, and other motivational behaviors in the opossum, *Didelphis virginiana*. J. Comp. Physiol. Psychol., 64: 1–15.

Romaniuk, A. (1965) Representation of aggression and flight reactions in the hypothalamus of the cat. Acta Biol. Exp. Warsaw, 25: 177–186.

Schmitt, P., Di Scala, G., Brandão, M.L. and Karli, P. (1985) Behavioral effects of microinjections of SR 95103, a new GABA-A antagonist, into the medial hypothalamus or the mesencephalic central gray. Eur. J. Pharmacol., 117: 149–158.

Shaikh, M.B., Brutus, M., Siegel, A. and Siegel, H.E. (1986) Regulation of feline aggression by the bed nucleus of stria terminalis. Brain Res. Bull., 16: 179–182.

Shi, C.J. and Cassell, M.D. (1999) Perirhinal cortex projections to the amygdaloid complex and hippocampalformation in the rat. J. Comp. Neurol., 406: 299–328.

Siegel, A., Roeling, T.A.P., Gregg, T.R. and Kruk, M.R. (1999) Neuropharmacology of brain-stimulation-evoked aggression. Neurosci. Biobehav. Rev., 23: 359–389.

Silveira, M.C.L. and Graeff, F.G. (1992) Defense reaction elicited by microinjection of kainic acid into the medial hypothalamus of the rat: antagonism by GABAA receptor agonist. Behav. Neural. Biol., 57: 226–232.

Simerly, R.B. and Swanson, L.W. (1988) Projections of the medial preoptic nucleus: a *Phaseolus vulgaris* leucoagglutinin anterograde tract-tracing study in the rat. J. Comp. Neurol., 270: 209–242.

Singewald, N. and Sharp, T. (2000) Neuroanatomical targets of anxiogenic drugs in the hindbrain as revealed by Fos immunocytochemistry. Neuroscience, 98: 759–770.

Small, W.S. (1899) Notes on the psychic development of the young white rat. Am. J. Psychol., 11: 80–100.

Smith, M.A., Banerjee, S., Gold, P.W. and Glowa, J. (1992) Induction of c-fos mRNA in rat brain by conditioned and unconditioned stressors. Brain Res., 578: 135–141.

Stackman, R.W. and Taube, J.S. (1998) Firing properties of rat lateral mammillary single units: head direction, head pitch, and angular head velocity. J. Neurosci., 18: 9020–9037.

Staples, L.G., Hunt, G.E., Cornish, J.L. and McGregor, I.S. (2005) Neural activation during cat odor-induced conditioned fear and 'trial 2' fear in rats. Neurosci. Biobehav. Rev., 29: 1265–1277.

Staples, L.G. and McGregor, I.S. (2006) Defensive responses of Wistar and Sprague-Dawley rats to cat odour and TMT. Behav. Brain Res., 172: 351–354.

Sukikara, M.H., Mota-Ortiz, S.R., Baldo, M.V., Felicio, L.F. and Canteras, N.S. (2006) A role for the periaqueductal gray in switching adaptive behavioral responses. J. Neurosci., 26: 2583–2589.

Swanson, L.W. (1987) The hypothalamus. In: Hökfelt, T. Björklund, A. and Swanson, L.W. (Eds.), Handbook of Chemical Neuroanatomy. Integrated Systems. Elsevier, Amsterdam, Vol. 5, pp. 1–124.

Swanson, L.W. and Petrovich, G.D. (1998) What is the amygdala? Trends Neurosci., 21: 323–331.

Sziklas, V. and Petrides, M. (1998) Memory and the region of the mammillary bodies. Prog. Neurobiol., 54: 55–77.

Takahashi, L.K., Nakashima, B.R., Hong, H. and Watanabe, K. (2005) The smell of danger: a behavioral and neural analysis of predator odor-induced fear. Neurosci. Biobehav. Rev., 29: 1157–1167.

Walker, D.L. and Davis, M. (1997) Double dissociation between the involvement of the bed nucleus of the stria terminalis and the central nucleus of the amygdala in startle increases produced by conditioned versus unconditioned fear. J. Neurosci., 17: 9375–9383.

Wallace, K.J. and Rosen, J.B. (2000) Predator odor as an unconditioned fear stimulus in rats: elicitation of freezing by trimethylthiazoline, a component of fox feces. Behav. Neurosci., 114: 912–922.

Wallace, K.J. and Rosen, J.B. (2001) Neurotoxic lesions of the lateral nucleus of the amygdala decrease conditioned fear but not unconditioned fear of a predator odor: comparison with electrolytic lesions. J. Neurosci., 21: 3619–3627.

Wasman, M. and Flynn, J.P. (1962) Directed attack elicited from hypothalamus. Arch. Neurol., 6: 220–227.

Wouterlood, F.G., Saldana, E. and Witter, M.P. (1990) Projection from the nucleus reunions thalami to the hippocampal region: light and electron microscopic tracing study in the rat with the anterograde tracer *Phaseolus vulgaris* leucoagglutinin. J. Comp. Neurol., 296: 179–203.

Zangrossi Jr., H. and File, S.E. (1992) Behavioral consequenses in animal tests of anxiety and exploration of exposure to cat odor. Brain Res. Bull., 29: 381–388.

CHAPTER 3.3

A behavioral and neural systems comparison of unconditioned and conditioned defensive behavior

Newton S. Canteras[1] and D. Caroline Blanchard[2,3,*]

[1]*Departamento de Anatomia, Instituto de Ciências Biomédicas, Universidade de São Paulo, São Paulo, SP, Brazil*
[2]*Pacific Biosciences Research Center, University of Hawaii, Honolulu, HI, USA*
[3]*Genetics and Molecular Biology, John A. Burns School of Medicine, University of Hawaii, Honolulu, HI, USA*

Abstract: This chapter is an overview of some comparisons of unconditioned and conditioned models of anxiety, as well as a brief and general discussion of the topic of validity of animal models. The comparisons involve, first, an attempt to compare the neural systems underlying experimental models of anxiety that involve exposure to a predator or predator odor (anti-predator models) versus models based on conditioned responses to stimuli associated with painful stimuli such as footshock. Second, the chapter provides some quantitative data on changes in use patterns for unconditioned versus conditioned models over time, with a focus on those models that currently epitomize the evaluation of fear and anxiety in laboratory animals. Finally, the chapter provides an overview of some recent developments in views of the validity of animal models, asserting the value of such models in enabling research that may be too complex, expensive, or invasive for use with human subjects. It further notes the interdependence of analyses of animal model and clinical disorder, and suggests that advances in understanding either of these may be synergistic with reference to the other.

Keywords: unconditioned models of anxiety (use patterns over time); conditioned models of anxiety (use patterns over time); unconditioned models of anxiety (neural systems); conditioned models of anxiety (neural systems); validity; translational validity; endophenotypes

This brief chapter is designed to provide some integration of materials from chapters in the first two sections of this volume, on animal models, and neural systems for fear and anxiety. It will focus on three areas: First, comparison of the neural systems associated with unconditioned and conditioned fear/anxiety-relevant behaviors; second, descriptions of changes in usage patterns for unconditioned and conditioned models of anxiety during the last 20+ years; and last, some

consideration of classic and emerging approaches to the evaluation of validity of animal models.

I. Neural system analysis: comparison among models using Pavlovian fear conditioning or predator-related unconditioned and conditioned responses

Two main experimental approaches have been used to investigate the question of the brain systems underlying fear and anxiety; i.e., Pavlovian fear conditioning to a context or to a neutral stimulus, and exposure to a real predator or its

*Corresponding author. E-mail: blanchar@hawaii.edu

R.J. Blanchard, D.C. Blanchard, G. Griebel and D. Nutt (Eds.)
Handbook of Anxiety and Fear, Vol. 17
ISBN 978-0-444-53065-3

DOI: 10.1016/S1569-7339(07)00009-4

odor. Pavlovian conditioning is by far the more commonly used approach. The phenomenon of Pavlovian fear conditioning is highly reproducible; and, it generates clearly measurable responses. Moreover, the main responses measured in this context, freezing and startle, are both seen in the repertory of animals confronting unconditioned threats (see chapters by Fanselow and Ponnusamy; Caine and LeDoux; Myers and Davis; Blanchard et al., this volume), providing additional validation to both sets of models.

Studies on the neural basis of Pavlovian conditioned fear indicate the amygdala as a major player in learning, storage, and expression of fear conditioning. Among the amygdalar regions, three nuclei have been particularly focused on the fear conditioning research, namely, the lateral nucleus,

the central nucleus, and the basolateral nucleus (see chapter by Cain and LeDoux).

As shown in Fig. 1, associative learning between the conditioned and unconditioned stimuli is likely to occur in the lateral nucleus. In fact, both acquisition and retention of fear conditioning occur in the lateral nucleus, where electrolytic and excitotoxic lesions, as well as pharmacological blockade, prevent acquisition and expression of fear conditioning (Campeau and Davis, 1995; Muller et al., 1997; LeDoux, 2000; Gale et al., 2004). The lateral nucleus presents clear synapse plasticity during fear conditioning, and changes the way a conditioned stimulus is processed after the shock pairing (see chapter by Cain and LeDoux). The lateral nucleus, in turn, projects to the central nucleus both directly and indirectly via

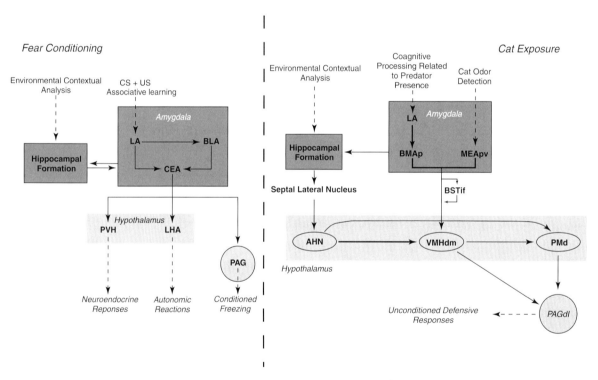

Fig. 1. Schematic representation comparing brain circuits mediating fear conditioning (on the left) and unconditioned fear during cat exposure (on the right). Abbreviations: AHN, anterior hypothalamic nucleus; BLA, basolateral amygdalar nucleus; BMAp, basomedial amygdalar nucleus, posterior part; BSTif, bed nuclei of the stria terminalis, interfascicular nucleus; CEA, central amygdalar nucleus; CS, conditioned stimulus; LA, lateral amygdalar nucleus; LHA, lateral hypothalamic area; MEApv, medial amygdalar nucleus, posteroventral part; PAGdl, periaqueductal gray, dorsolateral part; PMd, dorsal premammillary nucleus; PVH, paraventricular hypothalamic nucleus; US, unconditioned stimulus; VMHdm, ventromedial hypothalamic nucleus, dorsomedial part.

projections to the basolateral nucleus (Pitkänen et al., 1997; Pare and Smith, 1998).

The central nucleus, via projections to the hypothalamus and brainstem, is critical for the expression of fear conditioning. In fact, lesions of the central nucleus disrupt freezing, along with the autonomic reactions observed during fear conditioning (see chapter by Cain and LeDoux). More recent studies, however, have also suggested a role for the central nucleus in learning and storage of fear conditioning (see chapter by Cain and LeDoux). The role of the basolateral nucleus in fear conditioning is more controversial, and only post-training, but not pre-training, lesions appear to interfere with the expression of conditioned fear (see chapter by Cain and LeDoux).

This well-developed neural circuitry model for the processing of fear conditioning provides an excellent framework for comparison to the neural processing for innate fear responses, such as those that occur during exposure to a predator. Some differences are immediately apparent, as lesions of the central nucleus, a key region for the expression of fear conditioning, produce only marginal deficits, at best, on defensive responses to a predator (De Oca and Fanselow, 2004) or its odor (Li et al., 2004). Also, latent *Toxoplasma* infection resulting in entry into rodent brains of parasites that presumably affect the circuits involved in responding to predator threats, inducing loss of innate defensive responses toward cat odor, has recently been reported to have no effect on fear responses to a conditioned stimulus previously paired to a shock (Berdoy et al., 1995; Vyas et al., 2007). Taken together, the evidence suggests that, at least in rats, innate defensive behavior to a predator or its odor is likely to be processed by neural circuits somewhat different from those for fear conditioning.

Over the last years, a great deal has been learned about the neural system involved in processing innate defensive behaviors to a predator or its odor. Similarly to what has been discussed for fear conditioning, the amygdala also occupies a central role in integrating the sensory clues related to the predator. A recent finding is that predator odors may in fact be processed by prey species in the accessory olfactory bulb (AOB), rather than the main olfactory bulb (MOB) (McGregor et al., 2004). This suggests that cat odor is processed by rats more as a pheromone than a conventional odor, and the authors suggested that cat odor may be an example of a "kairomone" – a semiochemical released by one species that has a favorable adaptive effect on a different "receiving" species (Dicke and Grostal, 2001). The AOB projects principally to the medial amygdala, and rats exposed to cat odor also show substantial activation in this nucleus, particularly in its posteroventral part (Dielenberg et al., 2001; McGregor et al., 2004). In line with this view, rats with cytotoxic lesions in the medial nucleus, but not in the central nucleus, exhibited a significant reduction in unconditioned fear responses to cat odor (Li et al., 2004). During exposure to a live predator, in addition to activation of the posteroventral part of the medial amygdalar nucleus, we have also observed a distinct Fos increase in two other amygdalar sites, namely, the posterior basomedial amygdalar nucleus and caudal levels of the lateral amygdalar nucleus (see chapter by Canteras). Importantly, these amygdalar nuclei receive inputs from visual and auditory association areas, and are likely to integrate predator-derived sensory clues, other than olfactory ones (McDonald, 1998; Shi and Cassell, 1999). As shown in Fig. 1, the amygdalar sites related to predator detection project either directly or indirectly, via the transverse nucleus of the BST, to the ventromedial nucleus of the hypothalamus, where its dorsomedial part receives most of the direct projections from the amygdala and is particularly mobilized during exposure to a live predator or its odor. Therefore, the studies using rats exposed to a live cat or its fur odor suggest an amygdalar-BST-hypothalamic path to detect a live predator or its cues (see chapter by Canteras). However, these observations were limited to one prey species which have been exposed to a particular predator, and further studies are needed to evaluate how this predator-detector circuit works in other prey species, and how it responds to a wider variety of predators.

Curiously, previous studies examining the responses to shock-based fear conditioning and the unconditioned freezing to trimethylthiazoline (TMT) odor suggested that the BST, but not the amygdala, mediates unconditioned fear reactions (Walker and Davis, 1997; Wallace and Rosen, 2001; Fendt et al., 2003). In contrast to this view, however, more recent studies have shown that cytotoxic lesions or pharmacological inactivation of the medial amygdalar nucleus drastically reduce unconditioned fear responses to both TMT and cat odor (Li et al., 2004; Muller and Fendt, 2006). In fact, examining the role of the BST in several fear-related conditions using different fear conditioning paradigms, a number of studies have suggested that, in contrast to the amygdala, the BST may mediate slower-onset, longer-lasting fear responses evoked by long-duration conditioned or unconditioned stimuli (see Walker et al., 2003). Unfortunately, to our knowledge, so far there has been no study examining the BST roles in innate defensive behaviors to a predator or its cues.

As shown in Fig. 1, the hippocampal formation, in its turn, receives inputs from the amygdalar sites involved in detecting predator-related cues, and is likely to be involved in some aspect of the association between these predator threats and the environment where the rat encounters this stimulus (Petrovich et al., 2001). Hippocampal processing, via projections to the lateral septal nucleus, may influence the anterior hypothalamic nucleus, which also upregulates cfos expression during predator exposure. Both the anterior hypothamic nucleus and the dorsomedial part of the ventromedial nucleus project to the dorsal premammillary nucleus, which, by far, represents the most sensitive brain region responding to a predator or its clues, and where lesions have been most effective in reducing anti-predator defensive responses (see chapter by Canteras). In fact, the anterior hypothalamic nucleus, the dorsomedial part of the ventromedial hypothalamic nucleus, and the dorsal premammillary nucleus are particularly interconnected, forming a partially segregated circuit in the medial zone of the hypothalamus, the so-called medial hypothalamic defensive circuit (Canteras, 2002). Notably, the dorsal premamillary nucleus appears to work as an amplifier for the neural processing in the medial hypothalamic defensive circuit. This would explain why this region is so responsive to predator threats, and why lesions therein are able to reduce

defensive responses so drastically (Canteras et al., 1997; Blanchard et al., 2003, 2005; Markham et al., 2004). This amplifier region in the hypothalamus certainly favors a ceiling effect on the antipredator defensive responses, perhaps accounting for the poor results in reducing defensive responses to a live cat when lesions have been applied in just one specific telencephalic site that influences the hypothalamic defensive system, such as the medial amygdalar nucleus or the ventral hippocampus account (Blanchard et al., 2005; Pentkowski et al., 2006). In sharp contrast to that seen during exposure to a cat or its odor, lesions in the dorsal premammillary nucleus have no effect on behavioral responses to shock, or shock-based fear conditioning (Blanchard et al., 2003).

The hypothalamic systems are well known for integrating a number of behaviors critical for the survival of the individual or the species (Swanson, 1987), and it comes as no surprise that the hypothalamus, and not the amygdala (as previously suggested by fear conditioning studies), should occupy this central role in integrating antipredator defensive responses.

The periaqueductal gray (PAG) represents the main brainstem targets of the medial hypothalamic defensive system, and is critical for the expression of defensive responses. Of special relevance, the pattern of projection from the medial hypothalamic defensive system to the PAG largely overlaps the pattern of PAG activation in animals exposed to a predator or its odor, where Fos expression was mostly seen in the rostral two-thirds of the PAG in the dorsomedial and dorsolateral regions, whereas in the caudal PAG, a less intense, but more widespread activation, was observed (Canteras and Goto, 1999; Dielenberg et al., 2001). A similar pattern of PAG activation was also described after administration of drugs known to induce panic in humans (Singewald and Sharp, 2000). In fact, particularly, the dorsolateral PAG appears to play a critical role for integrating forebrain limbic information related to "psychological stressors," such as the presence of a natural predator (see chapter by Canteras). Fear-conditioning-induced freezing is also known to depend on the PAG. However, in contrast to what was found in animals exposed to a predator or its odor, the ventrolateral PAG, but not the dorsolateral PAG, is mostly mobilized during fear conditioning to a context previously associated with footshocks (Carrive et al., 1997).

Considering what we have learned about the neural systems underlying fear conditioning and the anti-predator defensive responses, an important conclusion to be drawn is that animals have indeed a more complex way of dealing with different kinds of threat stimuli, and certainly differentiate between an actual predator or its clues from other threats such as electrical shock or shock-paired stimulus. This fact may explain why fear conditioning using electrical shocks paired to a neutral stimulus fails to predict the neural systems underlying natural anti-predator fear responses.

However, in contrast to innate defensive responses to a predator, one can argue that fear conditioning involves learning, and perhaps should work for predicting the neural systems underlying learned fear to a predator or its clues. This does not seem to be the case either, and the evidence gathered so far clearly suggests that there is a large overlap of neural circuits mediating both unconditioned and conditioned anti-predator related defensive responses, and a pathway using the ventral hippocampus, the anterior hypothalamic nucleus, the dorsal premammillary nucleus, and the dorsolateral PAG seems to be involved in the expression of contextual conditioning fear responses to a predator or its odor (see chapter by Canteras).

The vast majority of studies investigating the neural basis of anti-predator defensive responses have examined the neural processing in rat brains when a cat is used as the potential predator. At this point, there is an important question to be addressed, whether or not there is a general neural circuit responsible for processing predatory threats. In this regard, we need to know whether the findings from this particular relationship rat versus cat could be generalized to other situations with different prey and predators, and whether we can bring into focus a general circuit serving all predatory threats.

If the assumption is valid that rats treat electrical shock or shock-paired stimulus as if they represented an actual predator, then one would expect that both fear conditioning and innate fear would share the same basic circuitry. However, this does not seem to be the case.

II. Comparisons of use of conditioned and unconditioned animal models of anxiety over time

An important point for comparison of conditioned and unconditioned models of anxiety involves their use patterns, and how these have changed over time. We attempted to evaluate this by examining the numbers of PubMed articles accessed by search terms reflecting major conditioned and unconditioned models. Details of the search terms used and rationales for them are presented in an appendix at the end of the chapter. These data were obtained in mid-2007, and the figures for 2005–2007 were accordingly corrected by doubling the count for the first 6 months of 2007 and adding it to the 2005–2006 count; a procedure that slightly underestimates the count for term combinations showing steadily increasing use in recent years.

Fig. 2 presents the result obtained by searching PubMed for the total number of articles detailing anxiety tests on animal models; articles on conditioned models (obtained by summing accessed articles for potentiated startle, fear conditioning, and conflict tests); and on unconditioned models (elevated plus maze – EPM, open field – OF, light/dark, and ethological models) in 3-year groups, from 1984 to 2007. This figure indicates that the absolute number of studies in each category increased dramatically during this 24-year period. However, in contrast to the "conditioned" test increase, about 15 times, the "unconditioned" tests increased nearly 60-fold. These findings indicate that the use of unconditioned tests of anxiety has increased disproportionately over the past two decades.

Fig. 3 presents articles accessed by reference to the three major conditioned tests: "conflict", fear conditioning, and startle. Whereas "conflict" tests appeared to have a modest peak around 1990–1995, declining thereafter to a level typical of the mid-1980s, both fear conditioning and

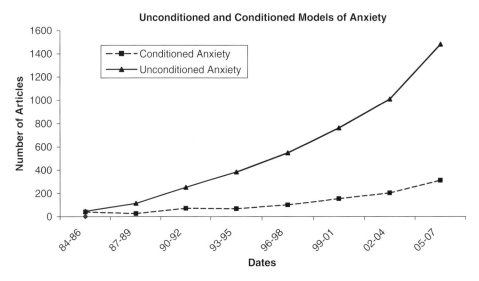

Fig. 2. Articles reporting use of unconditioned or conditioned animal models of anxiety, in 3-year blocks, between 1984 and 2007. Data for 2005–2007 includes extrapolations for the second half of 2007, based on January–June 2007 figures. See Appendix for details of PubMed search procedure.

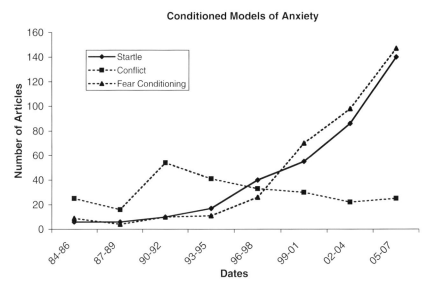

Fig. 3. Articles reporting use of three conditioned animal models of anxiety: startle, conflict, and fear conditioning in 3-year blocks, between 1984 and 2007. Data for 2005–2007 includes extrapolations for the second half of 2007, based on January–June 2007 figures. See Appendix for details of PubMed search procedure.

potentiated startle showed dramatic increase, during recent years. This was slightly more pronounced for fear conditioning, which showed a 16-fold increase from the 1996–1998 period to 2005–2007. As noted in the appendix, numbers for all of these specific tests were compared with or without the additional term "anxiety" and it is notable that "fear conditioning" without anxiety accessed nearly 1,200 articles, nearly seven times as many as were found with "anxiety" added. However, the distribution over time of "fear conditioning" without anxiety (not shown) was very similar to that with anxiety included, suggesting that the dramatic increase in recent years in studies of fear conditioning that also referenced anxiety simply reflects the increasing popularity of fear conditioning tests, not a time-based change in the relative tendency to make an anxiety interpretation of this test. For startle, the difference between results of searches with or without the term "anxiety" was much smaller (about 2 to 1), suggesting that fewer studies of this phenomenon failed to involve anxiety interpretations. Although "startle" is included in conditioned tests of anxiety, a few studies included under this rubric evaluated startle responses in the presence of unconditioned stimuli such as bright lights.

Fig. 4 presents four types of unconditioned models. Of these, the EPM is clearly the most often used unconditioned model of anxiety, with almost as many articles utilizing this test as all other models, conditioned as well as unconditioned, combined. It appears to be regarded as a relatively dedicated model of anxiety, in that there are very few "EPM" articles that do not contain "anxiety" in their search terms. In contrast, although there are many articles reporting use of the open field AND anxiety, nearly four times as many use the open field (OF) without an anxiety notation, strongly suggesting that the open field has been, and is, frequently used for purposes other than the evaluation of anxiety. However, in an anxiety context, it is increasingly combined with the EPM: Of 600+ articles pairing the EPM and OF, over 75% have been reported since 2000. Although less frequent, the light/dark test also appears to differentially occur in concert with the EPM and the OF. Such a three-test combination, all fitting very well with the requirements of "high throughput" (see chapter by Litvin et al., this volume) appears to additionally satisfy demands that drugs be evaluated with a variety of anxiety-related measures rather than a single measure alone.

Models involving defensive behaviors (defense OR defence OR defensive AND anxiety) do not quite fit with the above categories. First, while most defense-based tests for anxiety-like behaviors

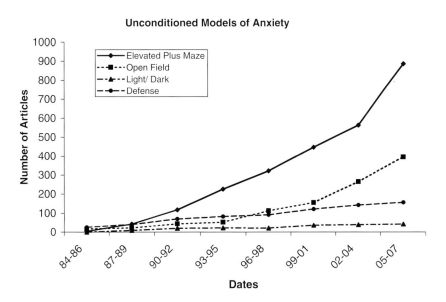

Fig. 4. Articles reporting use of four animal models of anxiety: elevated plus maze, open field, light/dark, and defense in 3-year blocks, between 1984 and 2007. Data for 2005–2007 includes extrapolations for the second half of 2007, based on January–June 2007 figures. See Appendix for details of PubMed search procedure.

do involve unconditioned behavior patterns, some studies of such behaviors do use conditioned stimuli such as situations in which a predator or predator stimuli have previously been encountered. Nonetheless they are here included under the unconditioned test rubric, as the vast majority use unconditioned threat stimuli to elicit these behaviors. A second circumstance of interest was the much wider array of defense-related tests that did not involve rats or mice: 2,052 accessed articles versus 836 when rats and mice were part of the search combination. While many of these are studies involving people, from a variety of non-experimental perspectives, this number also includes many studies of nonhuman species other than rats or mice, reflecting the clear cross-species focus of analyses of defensive behaviors as a set of evolved patterns of responsivity to threat. The increase over time for this category, like that of light/dark tests, is at an intermediate level, not showing the rapid escalation of use of either the EPM or OF tests.

In summary, there has been a clear trend, especially over the past decade, in use of unconditioned as compared to conditioned animal models of anxiety. Of the unconditioned models, the EPM is by far the most commonly used: It is frequently used in conjunction with the OF, and not infrequently with the light/dark box. There is a substantial difference among the various tests of anxiety in the degree to which the test is regarded as "dedicated" – reflecting specific relevance to anxiety. The EPM is a particularly dedicated test, seldom used to measure anything but anxiety, whereas tests such as the OF, fear conditioning, or defense have many additional uses.

III. Validity of animal models of fear and anxiety

Any treatment of the role of animal models in understanding fear and anxiety brings up the topic of validity. Here, we will only briefly discuss some general and current concepts for analysis of validity of animal models. These cannot be compared and contrasted for the general categories of unconditioned and conditioned models, due to differences in the models within each group, and

are only provided to point out some recent changes in strategies for approaching and improving the parallels between animal models and psychiatric conditions. The classic analysis of animal models of psychiatric disorders is that of Willner (1991a).

Willner's analysis largely deals with two separable aspects of the validity of such models; their use as screening devices in preclinical research (predictive validity) and their value in analysis and integration of phenomena to develop and clarify the concept of what is to be modeled (construct validity). Geyer and Markou (1995) further develop the view that validity has a variety of meanings, depending on the particular questions that are to be answered.

Anxiety encompasses a vast literature on the effects of drugs on individuals diagnosed with relevant disorders. This provides ample opportunity for analysis of predictive validity of models based on parallels in responsivity to drugs that are effective against, or, that elicit or potentiate the clinical condition. Specificity of the model can be further evaluated by its nonresponse to drugs that are known to have little clinical effect on this condition. There are some important practical difficulties with this approach, including cross-species differences in drug kinetics, appropriate dose levels, receptor subtypes, and the like. Moreover, when a model has been developed on the basis of response to a well-established clinical treatment, it may run into difficulties in predicting the effects of treatments with different mechanisms (e.g., BZP-based models respond poorly to 5HT1A agonists such as buspirone; Rodgers et al., 1997). Nonetheless, "predictive validity" is undoubtedly the most utilized method of evaluating the validity of models of anxiety. This form of evaluation is not often applied to models of "fear" for the simple reason that drug development is not aimed at fear, per se.

Obviously, an approach through predictive validity is difficult when there are no robustly effective drugs (or other clearly defined and easily quantified treatments) that reduce or promote the clinical condition, a situation that still applies to some anxiety disorders (e.g., OCD, PTSD). This factor shifts the validity emphasis toward phenomenological similarity, or "face validity". This is often interpreted very narrowly, as requiring that the behaviors of the animal are structurally similar to those characterizing the anxiety or depressive disorder. As Willner (1991b) notes, a focus on this interpretation does not give a favorable view of most animal models: Mouse killing is not a common activity for depressed patients. However, face validity – sometimes also called phenomenological validity (e.g., van der Staay, 2006) – has also been interpreted (e.g., McKinney and Bunney, 1969) as similarity with reference to etiology, symptomatology, and underlying processes and treatment, views that encompass a much broader interpretation of where the parallels between the animal model and the clinical condition might lie.

In general, a requirement of simple behavioral identity seems unlikely to be useful. Aside from simple reflex systems there are relatively few important behaviors for which rats and mice show exactly the same pattern of movements or action as do humans. Rodents usually locomote on 4 feet, humans on 2; they fight, copulate, give birth, rear young, etc., using actions that are frequently different than those of humans performing the same functions. For example, perhaps the most frequent single component of care of neonates by mouse or rat mothers is licking, with a particular emphasis on obligate licking of the perianal region to stimulate excretion of feces and urine. The context, the two parties to the interaction, and the consistently poor outcome when this behavior is prevented (the infant dies) all make it clear that maternal licking is a crucial component of maternal care and a legitimate part of any rat/mouse model of maternal behavior: clearly, there is no direct parallel in human maternal care. Yet these additional factors: eliciting situation and/or stimulus; interaction with conspecifics or other biologically important animals (e.g., predators or prey); and the outcome of the interaction; all contribute to the specification of the phenomenon and provide crucial clues to the function of the behaviors that are central to this situation.

It might be noted that consideration of these particular factors is not the same as attention to "construct validity" – often considered the ultimate criterion for validity of an animal model. Construct validity, in fact, is a rather elusive concept. It was initially applied (e.g., Cronbach and Meehl, 1955) in the context of analysis of human traits such as "intelligence" or "anxiety", through convergences of (usually pen and pencil) test-based measures. Its goal was the clarification of what the focal test, or the test nexus, measured, resulting in a sound theoretical construct; this route being taken in situations where there appeared to be little hope of establishing any direct evaluation of the criterion phenomenon which was typically an intervening variable construct. This is essentially a psychological, as opposed to biological, approach, albeit with some parallels in attempts to factor analyze (e.g., Wall and Messier, 2000; Ohl et al., 2001; Henderson et al., 2004; Francia et al., 2006) measures of various animal models of anxiety. In contrast, functional analyses of behavior are aimed at establishing specific points of relationship to the three specific factors noted above; determination of a "problem situation" (e.g., need for nourishment; response to danger; reproduction, care of young, etc.) by characterizing the relevant situation and/or the organismic conditions (e.g., hunger) to which the situation gives rise; relating this situation to particular behaviors; determination of the outcome when those behaviors occur, or, are blocked. Such an analysis is aimed at determining the validity of a functional relationship, not at clarifying or reifying a construct or intervening variable.

Neither construct validity nor an approach to validity through functional systems directly involves specification of underlying mechanisms. However, such specification remains a major goal of research on both the clinical level and for animal models. Acknowledgment of both the importance of underlying genetic and physiological mechanisms, and of the present state of uncertainly concerning them, appears to be a factor in the recent development and use of the concept of the endophenotype. Endophenotypes provide an additional strategy for investigation of potential linkages between genetic and biological mechanisms, on the one hand, and psychopathologies, on the other. They may offer substantial advantages such as an enhanced precision and quantification of the focal endophenotypic trait, in comparison to the more complex, less easily quantified, and potentially multifaceted or even heterogeneous symptom-cluster that may be involved in a particular psychopathology. This emphasis on quantitative and heritable traits can potentially fit very well with the methods and goals of functional analysis, and with the use of animal models. In particular, given the unknown but potentially large numbers of endophenotypes that may be identified for any psychopathology, functional analyses may prove to be useful in helping to select those that are most promising in terms of an actual relationship to the disorder. In addition, if the enhanced precision and quantitative power promised by the endophenotype concept can transfer to the new criteria that such endophenotypes may suggest for animal models, this should substantially strengthen an aspect of animal modeling that has long been acknowledged to be troublesome; the previously mentioned "face validity".

How might functional analyses be used to improve detection and identification of endophenotypes that will prove to be successful? One suggestion is to analyze what is normally functional, but now functions poorly, in a given disorder, and to seek out endophenotypes that are specifically related to these now dysfunctional elements. The additional step would be to examine animal models that tap these same functional systems, specifically seeking to identify traits that may represent the same type of dysfunction that is represented by the human endophenotype.

As noted, this would necessarily involve analysis of eliciting stimuli, behaviors, and the potentially adaptive or maladaptive consequences of those behaviors, rather than behavior alone, in order to understand how this system is functional in a particular "problem" context, on both the human and the animal model levels. Any endophenotype identified for the human disorder could then be evaluated in terms of its relationship to the well-characterized model, using laboratory animal species that are conducive to analyses and manipulations that are difficult in people.

Why would this tactic represent an improvement in the probability that such a model would facilitate the identification of useful endophenotypes? The underlying assumption is that functional systems have a relatively dedicated set of genetic and physiological mechanisms, in comparison to behaviors that have less functionality; and, that systems that remain consistently functional over evolutionary time tend to be relatively unchanged, providing some assurance of consistency across species. If these assumptions are true, functional systems should show a great deal more cross-species similarity than those that are not functional, enhancing both the value of the model, and its use as a testing medium for endophenotypes: Still a cumbersome approach, but one that may considerably enhance early identification of successful endophenotypes. Although this analysis may appear to run counter to the clear present trend toward high throughput models, it might be noted that the depth of analysis that goes into the creation of a model, and the time and effort required to evaluate an individual animal subject in that model, are not necessarily related.

These considerations also suggest that better animal models need to be developed in parallel with improved conceptualizations of psychiatric disorders. This is not a new idea.

Almost 30 years ago, Frank Beach (1978) suggested that there are

"... two cardinal rules that should govern not only the construction of animal models for human behaviour, but for all interspecific comparisons regardless of the behaviour and the species involved. The first rule is that meaningful comparisons are based not upon the formal characteristics of behaviour, but upon its causal mechanisms and functional outcomes.... The second rule is that the validity of interspecific generalization cannot exceed the reliability of intraspecific analysis. Significant comparison of a particular type of behaviour in two different species is impossible unless and until the behaviour has been adequately analyzed in each species by itself".

This factor is, to the authors of this chapter, a core component of the successful use of animal models to investigate phenomena of importance to human health and well-being. It suggests that the translational validity of a model, the ability of research with that model to provide information that is relevant to the understanding and treatment of a human disorder, is not only a function of the animal model itself, but of the match between the two. The creation of better, and more valid, models of anxiety will ultimately reflect improved knowledge of anxiety-like behaviors in species that are subjects for these models, and of the functional systems that anxiety disorders disrupt in people. Advances on each front may be expected to have synergistic effects with regard to understanding the systems involved. Conversely, confusion on either end drags down the entire system. This is a point that should be kept in mind by researchers on both sides of the gap.

Appendix: accessing articles using conditioned and unconditioned models of anxiety

Our survey was done in July 2007, on PubMed. It turned out to involve quite a bit of judgment, in terms of finding search terms that would provide a reasonably accurate view of these data. First, the total tabulation for "'animal models" AND anxiety' produced less than 500 articles, immediately indicating that this is an inadequate search term for such models, as needed to show an overall trend over time that could be contrasted to the changes seen for individual tests. At the other extreme, the combination "rat OR mouse AND anxiety" produced nearly 9,000 articles, far more than was indicated to be relevant by data summing the articles accessed by reference to several frequently used anxiety tests (see Fig. 2). Examination of a sample of these 9,000 articles suggested that many involved hypothalamic pituitary adrenal axis activity, or other physiological measures that did not involve behavioral tests of anxiety. The addition of "test" to the "rat OR mouse AND anxiety" search term, reflecting the common label of "test" for behavioral models, reduced the number to slightly more than 3,000 articles. This compared relatively well to figures obtained for the individual tests, being about 25% smaller than a sum based on individual tests. This likely reflects that several tests of anxiety may

occur in the same article, such that when tests are compiled separately their sum is higher than the total number of articles. In addition, names of particular tests (e.g., elevated plus maze) are sometimes used without the qualifier "test"; a view supported by examination of some of the abstracts involved. Despite this discrepancy, and because the focus here was on trends over time, and much less on absolute values, this last term (rat OR mouse AND anxiety AND test) was used to provide a picture of time-based changes in the overall use of animal models in the study of anxiety. Additionally, the use of only tests for rats and mice is defensible on the basis that inclusion of other species, such as hamsters, gerbils, and guinea pigs added relatively little to the totals obtained, for all categories except defense (see below).

An additional problem was that many animal tests of anxiety-like behavior do not present "unconditioned" or "conditioned" as search terms, forcing a reliance on names of specific tests that clearly fall into one or the other of these categories. Also, tests originally used for some other purpose have sometimes evolved into "animal models of anxiety" over time. To handle these problems, a first step in analysis of individual tests was incorporated that compared the number of PubMed articles containing the name of a specific test, such as "elevated plus maze" to the articles accessed by same term '...AND "anxiety"'. This process appeared to divide such tests into two groups. "Elevated plus maze", used alone, accessed about 2,450 articles. When the term ".... AND anxiety" was included, this was only slightly reduced, to about 2,000 articles. Scanning of abstracts for a few of the "elevated plus maze" alone (i.e., without "anxiety") articles suggested that there was no real difference in the goal or interpretation of these tests, compared to those used in articles that additionally cited "anxiety"; suggesting that the EPM is so clearly regarded as a test of anxiety that some portion of abstracts, about 20%, saw no need to state this relationship. In contrast, "open field" alone produced over 6,000 articles, whereas '"open field" AND anxiety' came up with only about 1,000. This difference indicated substantial additional uses and interpretations of the open field test, such that it was necessary to restrict the accessed articles to those with the search term "anxiety". This procedure was followed throughout. For tests that failed to show robust differences when tracked with or without the additional term "anxiety", all articles were included. Tests showing a striking difference, e.g., 50% or more, were tabulated with "anxiety" included. This likely does not inflate the figures for tests that are uniquely associated with anxiety, as these specific tests appear to be used as measures of anxiety even when this relationship was not explicitly stated.

For conditioned models of anxiety, the classic conflict tests were accessed by "'conflict test OR Geller–Seifter OR Vogel test" AND anxiety NOT social'; the last qualification was to exclude unconditioned tests of social interaction or social conflict. The other major categories of conditioned models were accessed by the terms "'rat OR mouse AND fear conditioning" AND anxiety'; or, the same sequence but with "fear-potentiated startle" substituted for "fear conditioning".

Among specific unconditioned models, only three were accessed: the elevated plus maze (EPM); the open field test (OF); and the light/dark test. Each of these was evaluated separately, due to data suggesting that this procedure might be informative. An additional category of "rat OR mouse AND defense OR defence OR defensive AND anxiety" was designed to capture such tests as the mouse defense test battery, the elevated T maze, predator and predator-odor elicited behaviors, and the like.

References

Beach, F.A. (1978) Animal models for human sexuality. Ciba Found. Symp., 62: 113–143.

Berdoy, M., Webster, J.P. and Macdonald, D.W. (1995) Parasite-altered behaviour: is the effect of *Toxoplasma gondii* on *Rattus norvegicus* specific?. Parasitology, 111: 403–409.

Blanchard, D.C., Canteras, N.S., Markham, C.M., Pentkowski, N.S. and Blanchard, R.J. (2005) Lesions of structures showing FOS expression to cat presentation: effects on responsivity to a cat, cat odor, and nonpredator threat. Neurosci. Biobehav. Rev., 29: 1243–1253.

Blanchard, D.C., Li, C.I., Hubbard, D., Markham, C.M., Yang, M., Takahashi, L.K. and Blanchard, R.J. (2003) Dorsal premammillary nucleus differentially modulates defensive behaviors induced by different threat stimuli in rats. Neurosci. Lett., 345: 145–148.

Campeau, S. and Davis, M. (1995) Involvement of the central nucleus and basolateral complex of the amygdala in fear conditioning measured with fear-potentiated startle in rats trained concurrently with auditory and visual conditioned stimuli. J. Neurosci., 15: 2301–2311.

Canteras, N.S. (2002) The medial hypothalamic defensive system: hodological organization and functional implications. Pharmacol. Biochem. Behav., 71: 481–491.

Canteras, N.S., Chiavegatto, S., Valle, L.E. and Swanson, L.W. (1997) Severe reduction of rat defensive behavior to a predator by discrete hypothalamic chemical lesions. Brain Res. Bull., 44: 297–305.

Canteras, N.S. and Goto, M. (1999) Fos-like immunoreactivity in the periaqueductal gray of rats exposed to a natural predator. Neuroreport, 10: 413–418.

Carrive, P., Leung, P., Harris, J. and Paxinos, G. (1997) Conditioned fear to context is associated with increased Fos expression in the caudal ventrolateral region of the midbrain periaqueductal gray. Neuroscience, 78: 165–177.

Cronbach, L.J. and Meehl, P.E. (1955) Construct validity in psychological tests. Psychol. Bull., 52: 281–302.

De Oca, B.M. and Fanselow, M.S. (2004) Amygdala and periaqueductal gray lesions pastially attenuate unconditional defensive responses in rats exposed to a cat. Integr. Physiol. Behav. Sci., 39: 318–333.

Dicke, M. and Grostal, P. (2001) Chemical detection of natural enemies by arthropods: an ecological perspective. Annu. Rev. Ecol. Syst., 32: 1–23.

Dielenberg, R.A., Hunt, G.E. and McGregor, I.S. (2001) "When a rat smells a cat": the distribution of c-fos expression in rat brain following exposure to a predator odor. Neuroscience, 104: 1085–1097.

Fendt, M., Endres, T. and Apfelbach, R. (2003) Temporary inactivation of the bed nucleus of the stria terminalis but not of the amygdala blocks freezing induced by trimethylthiazoline, a component of fox feces. J. Neurosci., 23: 23–28.

Fineberg, N.A., Saxena, S., Zohar, J. and Craig, K.J. (2007) Obsessive-compulsive disorder: boundary issuesCNS Spectr., 12: 359–364. 367–375.

Francia, N., Cirulli, F., Chiarotti, F., Antonelli, A., Aloe, L. and Alleva, E. (2006) Spatial memory deficits in middle-aged mice correlate with lower exploratory activity and a subordinate status: role of hippocampal neurotrophins. Eur. J. Neurosci., 23: 711–728.

Gale, G.D., Anagnostaras, S.G., Godsil, B.P., Mitchell, S., Nozawa, T., Sage, J.R., Wiltgen, B. and Fanselow, M.S. (2004) Role of the basolateral amygdala in the storage of fear memories across the adult lifetime of rats. J. Neurosci., 24: 3810–3815.

Geyer, M.A. and Markou, A. (1995) Animal models of psychiatric disorders. In: Bloom, F.E. and Kupfer, D.J. (Eds.), Psychopharmacology: the fourth generation of progress. Raven Press, New York.

Gottesman, I.I. and Gould, T.D. (2003) The endophenotype concept in psychiatry: etymology and strategic intentions. Am. J. Psychiatry, 160: 636–645.

Henderson, N.D., Turri, M.G., DeFries, J.C. and Flint, J. (2004) QTL analysis of multiple behavioral measures of anxiety in mice. Behav. Genet., 34: 267–293.

Hong, L.E., Turano, K.A., O'Neill, H., Hao, L., Wonodi, I., McMahon, R.P., Elliott, A. and Thaker, G.K. (2007) Refining the predictive pursuit endophenotype in schizophrenia. Biol. Psychiatry, (in press).

Keck, M.E. and Strohle, A. (2005) Challenge studies in anxiety disorders. Handb. Exp. Pharmacol., 169: 449–468.

LeDoux, J.E. (2000) Emotion circuits in the brain. Ann. Rev. Neurosci., 23: 155–184.

Li, C.I., Maglinao, T.L. and Takahashi, L.K. (2004) Medial amygdala modulation of predator odor-induced unconditioned fear in the rat. Behav. Neurosci., 118: 324–332.

Markham, C.M., Blanchard, D.C., Canteras, N.S., Cuyno, C.D. and Blanchard, R.J. (2004) Modulation of predatory odor processing following lesions to the dorsal premammillary nucleus. Neurosci. Lett., 372: 22–26.

McDonald, A.J. (1998) Cortical pathways to mammalian amygdale. Prog. Neurobiol., 55: 257–332.

McGregor, I.S., Hargreaves, G.A., Apfelbach, R. and Hunt, G.E. (2004) Neural correlates of cat odor-induced anxiety in rats: region-specific effects of the benzodiazepine midazolam. J. Neurosci., 24: 4134–4144.

McKinney Jr., W.T. and Bunney Jr., W.E. (1969) Animal model of depression. I. Review of evidence: implications for research. Arch. Gen. Psychiatry, 21: 240–248.

Muller, J., Corodimas, K.P., Fridel, Z. and LeDoux, J.E. (1997) Functional inactivation of the lateral and basal nuclei of the amygdala by muscimol infusion prevents fear conditioning to an explicit conditioned stimulus and to contextual stimuli. Behav. Neurosci., 111: 683–691.

Muller, M. and Fendt, M. (2006) Temporary inactivation of the medial and basolateral amygdala differentially affects TMT-induced fear behavior in rats. Behav. Brain Res., 167: 57–62.

Ohl, F., Toschi, N., Wigger, A., Henniger, M.S. and Landgraf, R. (2001) Dimensions of emotionality in a rat model of innate anxiety. Behav. Neurosci., 115: 429–436.

Pare, D. and Smith, Y. (1998) Intrinsic circuitry of the amygdaloid complex: common principles of organization in rats and cats. Trends Neurosci., 21: 240–241.

Pentkowski, N.S., Blanchard, D.C., Lever, C., Litvin, Y. and Blanchard, R.J. (2006) Effects of lesions to the dorsal and ventral hippocampus on defensive behaviors in rats. Eur. J. Neurosci., 23: 2185–2196.

Petrovich, G.D., Canteras, N.S. and Swanson, L.W. (2001) Combinatorial amygdalar inputs to hippocampal domains and hypothalamic behavior systems. Brain Res. Rev., 38: 247–289.

Pitkänen, A., Savander, V. and LeDoux, J.E. (1997) Organization of intra-amygdaloid circuitries in the rat: an emerging framework for understanding functions of the amygdala. Trends Neurosci., 20: 517–523.

Rodgers, R.J., Cao, B.J., Dalvi, A. and Holmes, A. (1997) Animal models of anxiety: an ethological perspective. Braz. J. Med. Biol. Res., 30: 289–304.

Shi, C.J. and Cassell, M.D. (1999) Perirhinal cortex projections to the amygdaloid complex and hippocampal formation in the rat. J. Comp. Neurol., 406: 299–328.

Singewald, N. and Sharp, T. (2000) Neuroanatomical targets of anxiogenic drugs in the hindbrain as revealed by Fos immunocytochemistry. Neuroscience, 98: 759–770.

Swanson, L.W. (1987) The hypothalamus. In: Hökfelt, T. Björklund, A. and Swanson, L.W. (Eds.), Handbook of Chemical Neuroanatomy. Integrated Systems Vol. 5, Elsevier, Amsterdam, pp. 1–124.

van der Staay, F.J. (2006) Animal models of behavioral dysfunctions: basic concepts and classifications, and an evaluation strategy. Brain Res. Rev., 52: 131–159.

Vyas, A., Kim, S.K., Giacomini, N., Boothroyd, J.C. and Sapolsky, R.M. (2007) Behavioral changes induced by Toxoplasma infection of rodents are highly specific to aversion of cat odors. Proc. Natl. Acad. Sci. USA, 104: 6442–6447.

Walker, D.L. and Davis, M. (1997) Double dissociation between the involvement of the bed nucleus of the stria terminalis and the central nucleus of the amygdala in light-enhanced versus fear-potentiated startle. J. Neurosci., 17: 9375–9383.

Walker, D.L., Toufexis, D.J. and Davis, M. (2003) Role of the bed nucleus of the stria terminalis versus the amygdale in fear, stress, and anxiety. Eur. J. Pharmacol., 463: 199–216.

Wall, P. and Messier, C. (2000) Ethological confirmatory factor analysis of anxiety-like behaviour in the murine elevated plus-maze. Behav. Brain Res., 114: 199–212.

Wallace, K.J. and Rosen, J.B. (2001) Neurotoxic lesions of the lateral nucleus of the amygdala decrease conditioned fear but not unconditioned fear of a predator odor: comparison with electrolytic lesions. J. Neurosci., 21: 3619–3627.

Willner, P. (1991a) Behavioral models in Psychopharmacology. Cambridge University Press, Cambridge.

Willner, P. (1991b) Animal models as simulations of depression. Trends Pharmacol. Sci., 12: 131–136.

The Pharmacology of Anxiety, Fear, and Defense

CHAPTER 4.1

Peptide receptor ligands to treat anxiety disorders

Thomas Steckler*

Department of Psychiatry, Research and Early Development Europe, Johnson & Johnson Pharmaceutical Research and Development, Beerse, Belgium

Abstract: Neuropeptides seem to play critical roles in the modulation of anxiety and in the pathophysiology of anxiety disorders. Specific, small-molecule, non-peptide receptor ligands targeting these peptide systems have been developed and are at various stages of the drug development process, such as antagonists acting at the corticotropin-releasing factor, cholecystokinin, neurokinin, neuropeptide Y, vasopressin, melanocortin, angiotensin, galanin, bombesin, or melanin-stimulating hormone receptors. Furthermore, oxytocin, δ-opiate, and orphanin FQ/nociceptin receptor agonists have been developed and shown to have anxiolytic-like properties in preclinical models. Some of these compounds are currently in clinical testing. This review provides an update of the preclinical and clinical status of the field. Although a number of obstacles need to be overcome in this area, it can be concluded that compounds acting at neuropeptide targets represents a highly promising approach for the development of the next generation drugs to treat anxiety disorders.

Keywords: anxiety; fear; neuropeptide; drug development; small molecule

I. Introduction

Anxiety disorders can be conceptualized as the pathological counterpart of normal fear. They are amongst the most common psychiatric disorders and represent major health problems in our society. Psychological symptoms can range from discrete episodes of intense fear, such as in panic disorder, marked and persistent anxiety in social situations, such as in social phobia, or fear of specific objects or situations, such as in specific phobias, to anxiety or worry not attributable to specific factors, lasting for prolonged periods of time, such as in generalized anxiety disorder. Often these psychological symptoms are accompanied by a range of autonomic (vegetative, cardiovascular,

gastrointestinal, and other) symptoms, as well as activation of the hypothalamic–pituitary–adrenal (HPA) axis, which is the main hormonal axis mediating the stress response.

Pharmacologically, anxiety disorders are frequently treated with benzodiazepines or antidepressants, especially selective serotonin re-uptake inhibitors (SSRIs). Although benzodiazepines have a fast onset of action, they suffer from abuse potential, can induce tolerance and withdrawal, sedation, psychomotor retardation, memory impairment, and rebound anxiety. Antidepressants such as SSRIs have a better safety and tolerability profile compared to benzodiazepines, but delayed onset of action and can induce other side effects, such as sexual dysfunction. Moreover, many patients do not respond to existing treatment or show only partial response. Thus, it would be desired to develop novel drugs to treat anxiety

*Corresponding author. E-mail: tsteckle@prdbe.jnj.com

R.J. Blanchard, D.C. Blanchard, G. Griebel and D. Nutt (Eds.)
Handbook of Anxiety and Fear, Vol. 17
ISBN 978-0-444-53065-3

157

DOI: 10.1016/S1569-7339(07)00010-0

disorders that combine fast onset of action with improved side-effect profile and efficacy.

In the search for novel therapeutic approaches to the clinically used benzodiazepines and anti-depressants, it has been suggested that drugs that target certain neuropeptide systems could represent promising alternatives. Neuropeptides are molecules made of short amino acid chains that function as neurotransmitters and/or neuromodulators. More than one hundred of them have been identified over the years, which can be classified according to their structure, function, or major sites of synthesis (Table 1). They differ from classical neurotransmitters, such as serotonin, dopamine, noradrenaline, acetylcholine, glutamate, or GABA, in their biosynthesis, storage, intracellular transport, release, and inactivation, but can also co-exist with classical neurotransmitters within the same neuron and can be co-transmitted (Valentino and Commons, 2005; Belzung et al., 2006). Similar to the classical neurotransmitters, the majority of neuropeptides binds to seven-transmembrane G-protein-coupled receptors (GPCRs), although some action through ion channel-associated receptors has been reported.

To better conceptualize the role of neuropeptides in the modulation of anxiety and the therapeutic value of drugs acting at these neuropeptide systems for the treatment of anxiety disorders, it is important to discuss some of the differences between neuropeptide and classical neurotransmitter systems. Amongst the most relevant difference between neuroeptides and classical neurotransmitters is the fact that neuropeptides need conditions of relatively high neuronal discharge to be released at quantities, which activate their receptors, while classical neurotransmitters are already released by low neuronal frequency bursts (Hokfelt et al., 2003). This in turn implies that selective blockade of the receptor by neuropeptide antagonists should be without consequences under resting conditions (unless the molecule has an intrinsic activity on its own), but should only have effects after activation of the targeted neuropeptidergic system, also at the behavioral level. Evidence supporting this view comes, for example, from studies investigating the effects of corticotropin-releasing factor (CRF)

receptor antagonists on anxiety-related behavior. The anxiolytic-like effects of CRF receptor antagonists in animal models of anxiety are more readily detected after activation of the CRF system by prior stress exposure (e.g., see Holmes et al., 2003a; Steckler, 2005; Steckler and Dautzenberg, 2006, for review). Such state-dependency of the behavioral effects of neuropeptides on anxiety-related behavior has also been reported, for example, for vasopressin (AVP) receptor antagonists (see Holmes et al., 2003a, for review),

Table 1. Classification of neuropeptides

Category	Major neuropeptides
Opioid neuropeptides	Methionin-enkephalin (Met-ENK) Leucin-enkephalin (Leu-ENK) β-endorphin (END) Dynorphin (DYN) Orphanin FQ/nociceptin (OFQ/N)
Gut-brain peptides	Substance P/neurokinin (SP/NK) Cholecystokinin (CCK) Galanin (GAL) Gastrin-releasing peptide (GRP) Neurotensin (NT) Neuropeptide Y (NPY) Somatostatin (SST) Vasoactive intestinal peptide (VIP) Pituitary adenylate cyclase activating polypeptide (PACAP) Glucagon (GLC) Glucagon-like peptide 1 (GLP-1) Calcitonin gene-related peptide (CGRP) Ghrelin Relaxin-3 (INSL-7)
Hypothalamic peptides	Corticotropin-releasing factor/hormone (CRF/CRH) Thyrotropin-releasing hormone (TRH) Hypocretin/orexin (HCRT/ORX) Melanin-concentrating hormone (MCH)
Pituitary peptides	Vasopressin/antidiuretic hormone (AVP/ADH) Oxytocin (OT) Thyroid-stimulating hormone (TSH) Corticoliberin/adrenocorticotropin (ACTH) Melanin-stimulating hormone (MSH)
Natriuretic peptides Other peptides	Atrial natriuretic peptide (ANP) Angiotensin II (ANG II) Neuromedin U (NMU) Neuropeptide AF (NPAF) Neuropeptide FF (NPFF) Neuropeptide S (NPS) Bradykinin

Source: Adapted from Belzung et al. (2006).

manipulation of the galanin (GAL) system (see Holmes et al., 2003a, for review), and cholecystokinin (CCK4) (Harro et al., 1993; Dauge and Lena, 1998). This in turn would suggest that peptide receptor antagonists should be particularly efficacious in patients under conditions activating these neuropeptide systems, as can be seen following stress exposure, or in patients with a disease-related overactivity of the targeted peptide system.

Second, the mode of transmission between neuropeptides and classical neurotransmitters can differ. Comparable to classical neurotransmitters, neuropeptides can be released into the synaptic cleft, thereby affecting pre- and postsynaptic receptors and contributing to synaptic transmission. In addition, it has been shown that neuropeptides can be released from other sites of the neuronal membrane, especially on dendrites, from where they can diffuse over several micrometers – a phenomenon called volume transmission (Fuxe and Agnati, 1991). This concept implies that the distribution of the peptide receptors may be more relevant for defining the consequences of neuropeptide system activation than the patterns of projections from peptidergic neurons (Landgraf, 2005).

Another important concept, applicable to both classical neurotransmitter and neuropeptide systems, is that of fast receptor desensitization and internalization from the cell surface into the cytoplasm after prolonged exposure to an agonist. For example, desensitization of pituitary CRF receptors has been demonstrated after CRF administration in rats (Wynn et al., 1988). In general, receptor desensitization and internalization, and hence the development of tolerance, must be considered in the development of peptide receptor agonists, but is of particular importance for the treatment of conditions requiring repeated or chronic treatment, as would be the case in many types of anxiety disorders.

In addition, a phenomenon called peptide conversion has been described. Following receptor stimulation and exerting their effects peptides are inactivated by enzymatic degradation, which can lead to fragments with additional, either agonistic or antagonistic, bioactivity. In case of antagonistic properties, these biodegraded products may counteract the action of the parent peptide. This phenomenon has been shown for a number of peptides, including the opioids, tachykinins (TKs), and angiotensin II (ANG II) (Nyberg and Hallberg, 2007) and may further complicate predictions of net effects of peptide receptor agonists and antagonists.

Further, peptides are generally poorly bioavailable after oral administration, metabolically instable, and hardly pass the blood–brain barrier. Therefore, considerable efforts have been undertaken to develop small molecule receptor ligands targeting peptide systems (but differing from peptide structures) for the treatment of CNS disorders, including anxiety disorders. Although notable exceptions seem to exist, for example, the opioid or the MCH systems, the development of such small molecule ligands for the majority of peptide systems constituted a major challenge when compared to the development of ligands acting at the receptors for the classical neurotransmitters. Nevertheless, a number of successful developments have been achieved, as will be discussed below.

Because of the poor brain penetration and bioavailability, many animal studies on the role of neuropeptides in the modulation of anxiety-related behavior report the effects of intracerebroventricular (ICV) or direct intracerebral infusions of the neuropeptide or neuropeptide fragments (which can have agonistic or antagonistic properties). Where available, small molecule peptide receptor agonists or antagonists can be used, which ideally should allow oral administration and can also be used in man. Alternative approaches reported in the animal literature are the generation of knockout mice, the use of antisense oligodeoxynucleotides or small interfering RNA (siRNA).

In healthy volunteers and patients, challenge studies, for example with the tetrapeptide CCK fragment CCK-4, have been reported. CCK-4 provocation can induce panic symptoms in volunteers and exacerbate symptoms in panic disorder patients (Van Megen et al., 1996; Bradwejn and Koszycki, 2001). Since CCK can also be used to induce anxiety-related behavior in animals (see below), CCK-4 challenge in human represents an interesting translational model to study the potential role of CCK in panic disorder. Another challenge test frequently used in human is the CRF stimulation test (Hermus et al., 1984). Here, CRF is administered intravenously and the hormonal response of the HPA axis (release of adrenocorticotropin (ACTH) and cortisol) is measured. Since the HPA axis will play a central role in this review, it seems useful to briefly discuss its different components: The HPA axis consists of the hypothalamic paraventricular nucleus (PVN), from where CRF and vasopressin (AVP) are released and transported to the adenohypophysis, leading to release of ACTH from pituitary corticotrophs. ACTH in turn triggers the release of glucocorticoids (corticosterone in many animal species, cortisol in some animal species, and human) from the adrenal cortex. CRF stimulation allows measurement of the function of the HPA axis, which has been reported to be deregulated in at least some types of anxiety disorders (see below).

II. Neuropeptide systems in anxiety patients

Since blockade of peptide receptors should be particularly efficacious under conditions of a hyperactive neuropeptide system, the development of peptide receptor antagonists targeting these systems showing overactivity in patients should be most promising. In the following section, clinical findings showing abnormalities in different neuropeptide systems in anxiety disorders will be summarized.

II.A. Opioid peptides

Investigating the role of endogenous opioid peptides in anxiety disorders, Eriksson et al. (1989) and Pitkanen et al. (1989) reported elevated levels of β-endorphin (END) in the cerebrospinal fluid (CSF) of panic disorder patients, but this was not confirmed by others (Lepola et al., 1989, 1990; Brady et al., 1991). Further, CSF dynorphin (DYN) levels were comparable between panic disorder patients and controls in the study by Brady et al. (1991).

II.B. Gut-brain peptides

II.B.1. Substance P
Within the family of the gut-brain family of peptides, several have been implicated in the

modulation of anxiety disorder. Plasma levels of the 11-amino acid peptide substance P (SP) were elevated in humans after a traumatic event (Weiss et al., 1996), under conditions of psychosocial anxiety (Fehder et al., 1997) and in subjects with high-state anxiety relative to subjects with low-state anxiety during anticipatory anxiety (Schedlowski et al., 1995). However, an inverse relationship was found between CSF SP levels and the personality trait of psychic anxiety in patients with chronic pain syndromes (Almay et al., 1988).

II.B.2. Cholecystokinin
A possible association with a CCK promoter polymorphism with panic disorder was reported by Wang et al. (1998), but such association was not confirmed in a subsequent study (Kennedy et al., 1999). However, Kennedy et al. (1999) found an association of panic disorder with a polymorphism in the CCK_2 receptor, but not with the CCK_1 receptor, gene. The CCK_2 receptor (also named CCK-B receptor – for brain) is the main CCK receptor expressed in the brain, while the CCK_1 receptor (also know as CCK-A receptor) is primarily peripherally expressed.

Significant inverse correlations were found between CCK levels and anxiety parameters in a group of depressed patients (Lofberg et al., 1998) and with the anger-hostility, anxiety, and interpersonal sensitivity subscales of the Symptom Check List 90 in bulimic patients (Lydiard et al., 1993). Likewise, patients suffering from panic disorder have been reported to have reduced CCK levels in CSF (Lydiard et al., 1992; Brambilla et al., 1993) but enhanced CCK_1 receptor function (Akiyoshi et al., 1996). At first sight, this would argue for a possible underactivity of the CCK system in anxiety disorders, rather than an overactive CCK system. However, these findings could also be interpreted as a compensatory effect secondary to overactivity of other parts of the central CCK system.

Indeed, an overactive CCK system has been suggested to play a role in the pathophysiology especially of panic disorders based on the findings that acute, intravenous injection of CCK-4 in healthy volunteers (de Montigny, 1989) and patients suffering from panic disorder (Bradwejn et al., 1990) can induce panic symptoms, with dose-dependent increases in anxiety, heart rate, HPA axis activation (plasma ACTH and cortisol), and physical symptoms of panic, also on repeated challenge (Bradwejn et al., 1992; Bradwejn, 1993; Van Megen et al., 1997a; Jarabek et al., 1999). Comparable results were reported in panic disorder patients after treatment with the CCK_2 receptor agonist pentagastrin, a synthetic analog of CCK-4 (Abelson and Nesse, 1994; Abelson et al., 1994; McCann et al., 1994–1995; Van Megen et al., 1994; Abelson and Liberzon, 1999; Bradwejn and Koszycki, 2001; Radu et al., 2003; Zedkova et al., 2003). Increased sensitivity to pentagastrin challenge was also seen in studies with patients suffering from social phobia (Van Vliet et al., 1997; McCann et al., 1997b) and generalized anxiety disorder (GAD) patients (Brawman-Mintzer et al., 1997), while CCK-4 failed to provoke flashbacks in PTSD patients (Kellner et al., 2000), suggesting that the effect is not specific to panic disorder but can also be seen in at least some other types of anxiety disorders.

Because of the reproducibility of the effect, CCK-4 challenge was suggested as a tool to study the effects of drug treatment on CCK-4-induced panic in panic disorder patients (Bradwejn et al., 1992; Bradwejn, 1993). True positive findings have been shown with the benzodiazepine alprazolam (Zwanzger et al., 2003) and the SSRIs citalopram (Shlik et al. 1997) and fluvoxamine (Van Megen et al., 1997a). An example for a true negative finding represents the $5\text{-}HT_3$ antagonist ondansetron in a study by McCann et al. (1997a). However, a reduction of CCK-4-induced panic symptoms by chronic ondansetron was reported by others (Depot et al., 1999).

The mechanism by which CCK-4 and pentagastrin exert their effects on anxiety symptoms is unclear as CCK-4 or pentagastrin do not cross the blood–brain barrier (Durieux et al., 1991). Three possible mechanisms have been discussed: (i) CCK-4 and pentagastrin may exert their effects either via peripheral activation of CCK receptors expressed at vagal nerve endings, leading to secondary effects mediated by vagal afferents (Crawley and Corwin, 1994; Rinaman et al., 1995), (ii) they may have direct effects at brain areas outside the blood–brain barrier, such as the nucleus of the tractus solitarius or the area postrema (Rinaman et al., 1995), and/or (iii) they may have indirect effects via vasodilatation of cerebral arteries, thereby increasing hypothalamic blood flow (Cano et al., 2003; Sanchez-Fernandez et al., 2003). Interestingly, there seems to be an uncoupling between anxiety symptoms and HPA axis response as CCK-4 can activate the HPA axis, but to comparable degree in panic disorder patients and controls (Abelson et al., 2007), suggesting that the psychological and neuroendocrine effects are mediated by different and independent mechanisms.

II.B.3. Galanin

The 29–30-amino acid polypeptide GAL has also received considerable attention for its possible involvement in the modulation of anxiety-related behavior in animals (see below). A distinction in the genetic GAL haplotype association was found between Finish alcoholics with high– and low–personality anxiety traits, but not between GAL haplotypes and anxiety disorders in a recent study by Belfer et al. (2006). No alterations of GAL levels in CSF have been reported in anxiety disorder patients up to now.

II.B.4. Neurotensin

Plasma levels of the tridecapeptide neurotensin (NT) were elevated in humans after a traumatic event (Weiss et al., 1996). However, further evidence linking alterations of the neurotensin system to anxiety disorders is lacking.

II.B.5. Neuropeptide Y

A negative study by Lindberg et al. (2006) failed to find an association between polymorphism in the neuropeptide Y (NPY) gene and panic disorder in a Danish population. Others, however, reported a risk locus for anxiety disorders, including phobias and panic disorder, in a region of the human chromosome 4 (Kaabi et al., 2006). This is of interest as this chromosomal region also contains the gene for one of the NPY receptors, the Y_1 receptor.

Furthermore, decreased levels of plasma NPY have been observed in PTSD patients (Rasmusson et al., 2000), although this was not confirmed by others (Morgan et al., 2003; Seedat et al., 2003; Yehuda et al., 2006). Rather, Yehuda et al. (2006) reported increased NPY levels in combat veterans with a history of PTSD relative to veterans without past PTSD, as well as in combat veterans without history of PTSD when compared to controls. It has been argued that this could reflect a role of NPY as a protective stress factor, possibly counteracting the anxiogenic effects of CRF (Sajdyk et al., 2004; see also below). An increase in plasma NPY levels was also seen in panic disorder patients (Boulenger et al., 1996). Interestingly, NPY acts as a co-transmitter in the sympathetic nervous system and may be released from cardiac sympathetic nerve endings during a panic attack (Esler et al., 2004). However, unaltered plasma levels of NPY were reported in panic, as well as in GAD and social phobia in another study (Stein et al., 1996). Thus, clinical studies investigating changes in the NPY system in anxiety disorders must be considered inconclusive at the moment.

II.B.6. Somatostatin and glucagon
Somatostatin (SST) levels have been reported to be unchanged in patients with GAD (Banki et al., 1992). Likewise, no changes were seen in plasma levels of glucagon in patients suffering from phobic anxiety (Nesse et al., 1985). Thus, clinical evidence for a role of this peptide system in anxiety disorders is lacking.

II.C. Hypothalamic peptides

II.C.1. Corticotropin-releasing factor
Possibly the strongest evidence for overactivity of a neuropeptide system in anxiety disorders comes from studies on one of the main hypothalamic peptide: CRF. There is good clinical evidence for an overactivity of the CRF system in anxiety disorders. In post-traumatic stress disorder (PTSD) patients, levels of the 41-amino acid polypeptide CRF in CSF are increased (Bremner et al., 1997; Arborelius et al., 1999; Baker et al., 1999; Kasckow et al., 2001; Newport et al., 2003).

Interestingly, despite this central overactivity of the CRF system in PTSD, ACTH release was blunted in this patient group in response to CRF challenge (Smith et al., 1989; Bremner et al., 2003, but see Rasmusson et al., 2001), which may reflect an increased negative feedback inhibition of the pituitary secondary to altered glucocorticoids receptor sensitivity or number (Yehuda et al., 1991).

Although CSF levels of CRF seem unaltered in GAD or panic disorder (Jolkkonen et al., 1993; Fossey et al., 1996), there is substantial evidence that ACTH response to CRF challenge is blunted in patients with panic disorder (Roy-Byrne et al., 1986a; Holsboer et al., 1987; Von Bardeleben and Holsboer, 1988; Rapaport et al., 1989; Curtis et al., 1997), suggesting again increased negative feedback inhibition. Moreover, an association has been found between the CRF gene and behavioral inhibition in children at risk for panic disorder (Smoller et al., 2005), providing further support for an important role of abnormalities of the CRF system in panic disorder.

II.C.2. Thyroid-releasing hormone
A blunted thyroid-stimulating hormone (TSH) response was seen following thyrotropin-releasing hormone (TRH) stimulation in patients suffering from PTSD (Reist et al., 1995). Likewise, a blunted TSH response to TRH has been observed in panic disorder patients following challenge of the hypothalamic–pituitary–thyroidal (HPT) axis (Roy-Byrne et al., 1986b), although others reported normal TSH response to TRH challenge in panic disorder patients (Stein and Uhde, 1988). Moreover, CSF TRH has been reported unchanged in patients with panic disorder or GAD (Fossey et al., 1993). However, more recently, a positive correlation between plasma TSH levels and severity of panic attacks was found in patients suffering from panic disorder (Kikuchi et al., 2005). TRH has also been reported to induce some somatic symptoms resembling a panic attack in healthy volunteers, for example, cardiorespiratory responses comparable to those induced by penta-gastrin, but its efficacy to induce feelings of anxiety was inferior to that of pentagastrin

(Zedkova et al., 2003). Thus, there is evidence supporting a role of the thyroid axis in anxiety disorders, although the findings are controversial.

II.D. Pituitary peptides

II.D.1. Vasopressin

Despite evidence supporting a role of the non-apeptide vasopressin (AVP), and especially its V_{1A} receptor, in the modulation of anxiety-related behavior from the preclinical animal literature (see below), there is a remarkable paucity of clinical data. A correlation between plasma AVP levels and anxiety symptoms was seen after an anxiety-provoking challenge of healthy volunteers with pentagastrin (Abelson et al., 2001). Moreover, higher levels of plasma AVP were seen in anxious-retarded depressed patients when compared to non-anxious-retarded depressed patients in a study by De Winter et al. (2003), but these patients all suffered from concurrent depressive disorder which could have confounded the findings. No difference in plasma AVP response to a sodium lactate challenge was apparent between untreated panic disorder patients (who experienced panic) and healthy controls or panic disorder patients chronically treated with alprazolam (who had minimal symptoms) (Carr et al., 1986), the latter of which would not support a major role of AVP in this type of anxiety disorder. Thus, on the human site the picture is still blurred.

II.D.2. Oxytocin

No changes in oxytocin (OT) have been reported in patients suffering from anxiety disorders. However, it has been recently shown that OT administration in humans had anxiolytic effects in the Trier Social Stress Test (Heinrichs et al., 2003) and led to an increase in trust (Kosfeld et al., 2005). Moreover, using functional magnetic resonance imaging, activation of the human amygdala was reduced following intranasal OT administration compared to placebo in response to fear-inducing visual stimuli, suggesting that OT plays a role in the modulation of anxiety in man (Kirsch et al., 2005).

II.E. The natriuretic peptide family

II.E.1. Atrial natriuretic peptide and angiotensin II

Plasma levels of atrial natriuretic peptide (ANP) have been reported to be low in patients with PTSD (Kellner et al., 2003). Furthermore, treatment with ANP was anxiolytic in patients with panic disorder (Strohle et al., 2001) and attenuated CCK-4-induced panic attacks in panic disorder patients (Wiedemann et al., 2001). However, it is unclear how peripherally administered ANP exerts its anxiolytic effects, as the peptide is not brain penetrant. Possible modes of action could be stimulation of natriuretic peptide receptors at the level of the circumventricular organ, and in particular the subfornical organ, in the brain, which lack the normal blood–brain barrier and regulate blood pressure and sympathetic tone (Saavedra and Pavel, 2005).

Angiotensin II has been considered the natural counterplayer to ANP. Although one study reported an association between the angiotensin converting enzyme (ACE) gene and panic disorder in male but not in female patients (Olsson et al., 2004), this was not confirmed in another study (Shimizu et al., 2004). No association was found between the angiotensinogen gene or the gene encoding for the angiotensin II type 1 (AT_1) receptor and panic disorder (Olsson et al., 2004).

To summarize (Table 2), convincing evidence for overactivity of neuropeptide systems in patients suffering from anxiety disorders is seen for CRF only, and primarily in PTSD patients. Although CCK-4 and pentagastrin challenges also suggest overactivity of the CCK system in anxiety disorders, studies investigating CSF levels are contradictory. This is important in view of the fact that CCK challenge might involve a peripheral rather than a central mechanism and hence does not necessarily allow conclusions about changes in the CCK system in the brain. There is also limited evidence that SP and AVP system overactivity may lead to anxiety disorder, but of note almost all studies in human failed to study anxiety patients, but either investigated healthy volunteers or patients suffering from anxiety in combination with other disorders. Only for ANP a direct therapeutic benefit could be shown in

Table 2. Neuropeptide changes in anxiety disorders

Anxiety disorder	Neuropeptide	Outcome	Reference
Panic disorder	β-endorphin (END)	↑ CSF levels	Eriksson et al. (1989) and Pitkanen et al. (1989)
		Ø CSF levels	Brady et al. (1991) and Lepola et al. (1989)
	Dynorphin (DYN)	Ø CSF levels	Brady et al. (1991)
	Cholecystokinin (CCK)	Linkage with promoter polymorphism	Wang et al. (1998)
		No linkage with promoter polymorphism	Kennedy et al. (1999)
		Linkage with CCK_2 polymorphism	Kennedy et al. (1999)
		No linkage with CCK_1 polymorphism	Kennedy et al. (1999)
		↓ CSF levels	Brambilla et al. (1993) and Lydiard et al. (1992)
		↑ CCK_2 function (T-cells)	Akiyoshi et al. (1996)
		↑ CCK-4/ pentagastrin sensitivity	Abelson and Nesse (1994), Abelson et al. (1994, 2007), Bradwejn (1993), Bradwejn et al. (1990, 1992), Depot et al. (1999), McCann et al. (1997a), Shlik et al. (1997), Van Megen et al. (1994, 1997a), and Zwanzger et al. (2003)
	Neuropeptide Y (NPY)	No linkage with NPY polymorphism	Lindberg et al. (2006)
		↑ Plasma levels	Boulenger et al. (1996)
		Ø Plasma levels	Stein et al. (1996)
	Corticotropin-releasing factor (CRF)	Ø CSF level	Jolkkonen et al. (1993)
		↓ CRF sensitivity	Curtis et al. (1997), Holsboer et al. (1987), Rapaport et al. (1989), Roy-Byrne et al. (1986a), and Von Bardeleben and Holsboer (1988
	Thyrotropin-releasing hormone (TRH)	Ø TRH CSF level	Fossey et al. (1993)
		↓ TRH sensitivity	Roy-Byrne et al. (1986b)
		Ø TRH sensitivity	Stein and Uhede (1988)
	Vasopressin (AVP)	Ø Plasma levels	Carr et al. (1986)
	Atrial natriuretic peptide (ANP)	Anxiolytic	Strohle et al. (2001) and Wiedemann et al. (2001)

Table 2 (*continued*)

Anxiety disorder	Neuropeptide	Outcome	Reference
	Angiotensin II	Linkage with ACE polymorphism	Olsson et al. (2004)
		No linkage with ACE polymorphism	Shimizu et al. (2004)
		No linkage with angiotensinogen polymorphism	Olsson et al. (2004)
		No linkage with AT_1 polymorphism	Olsson et al. (2004)
GAD	Cholecystokinin (CCK)	↑ Pentagastrin sensitivity	Brawman-Mintzer et al. (1997)
	Neuropeptide Y (NPY)	Ø Plasma levels	Stein et al. (1996)
	Somatostatin (SST)	Ø CSF levels	Banki et al. (1992)
	Corticotropin-releasing factor (CRF)	Ø CSF level	Fossey et al. (1996)
	Thyrotropin-releasing hormone (TRH)	Ø TRH CSF level	Fossey et al. (1993)
Social phobia	Cholecystokinin (CCK)	↑ Pentagastrin sensitivity	McCann et al. (1997b) and Van Vliet et al. (1997)
	Neuropeptide Y (NPY)	Ø Plasma levels	Stein et al. (1996)
	Glucagon	Ø Plasma levels	Nesse et al. (1985)
PTSD	Cholecystokinin (CCK)	Ø CCK-4 sensitivity	Kellner et al. (2000)
	Neuropeptide Y (NPY)	↓ Plasma levels	Rasmusson et al. (2000)
		Ø Plasma levels	Morgan et al. (2003) and Seedat et al. (2003)
		↑ Plasma levels with past Hx	Yehuda et al. (2006)
	Corticotropin-releasing factor (CRF)	↑ CSF level	Arborelius et al. (1999), Baker et al. (1999), Bremner et al. (1997), Kasckow et al. (2001), and Newport et al. (2003)
		↓ CRF sensitivity	Bremner et al. (2003) and Smith et al. (1989)
		↑ CRF sensitivity	Rasmusson et al. (2001)
	Thyrotropin-releasing hormone (TRH)	↓ TRH sensitivity	Reist et al. (1995)
	Atrial natriuretic peptide (ANP)	↓ Plasma levels	Kellner et al. (2003)

Ø, unchanged; ↑, increased; ↓, decreased; "sensitivity", refers to challenge studies; Hx, past history of disorder.

patients suffering from panic disorders. The limited evidence available from studies in man does not support a major role of END, SST, or TSH in the pathogenesis of anxiety disorders.

Although it is tempting to suggest a protective effect of the NPY system in the pathogenesis of anxiety disorders, further clinical studies are required to confirm this hypothesis. Moreover, studies of the NPY system in anxiety disorders focused on peripheral alterations in plasma. Since these changes may reflect sympathetic alterations but do not necessarily translate into NPY abnormalities in the human brain, caution must be taken when interpreting these results. Clearly, more studies are needed to clarify also the role of other peptide systems in the modulation of anxiety and anxiety disorders in man.

Despite these caveats, the current data suggest that drugs that normalize activity of the CRF, CCK, SP, and/or AVP systems could be clinically useful anxiolytics. Conversely, compounds that enhance the activity of the NPY system may also have anxiolytic properties. Of course, neuropeptide levels in the CSF always reflect the net concentration of the peptide diffusing from different brain areas and individual brain areas, known to play important roles in the mediation of anxiety, could differ substantially in their peptide levels. By just measuring neuropeptide concentrations in CSF one might miss increased neuropeptide levels in a circumscribed brain area due to limited sensitivity of this technology. Thus, the possibility that other peptide systems are also involved in human anxiety disorders should not be discarded solely based on negative findings in studies measuring changes in peptide concentrations in the CSF. Animal data may help to shed further light on the role of these systems in anxiety-related behavior, as discussed below.

III. Anxiety-related behavior and neuropeptides: preclinical evidence

Although the validity of animal studies to predict for effects in anxiety patients is not always clear, they represent another important source for information on the role of neuropeptides in the modulation of anxiety, because they allow for direct, acute, and chronic manipulation of peptide systems in the target organ, i.e., in brain. The focus of section review will be on targeted pharmacological and molecular manipulations.

III.A. Opioid peptides

III.A.1. Enkephalin
The endogenous pentapeptides met- and leu-enkephalin bind to μ- and δ-opioid receptors in the brain, with an approximately ten times higher affinity for the δ- than for the μ-opioid receptor (Lord et al., 1977). Knockout of the precursor peptide preproenkephalin induced anxiogenic-like responses in mice (Konig et al., 1996; Ragnauth et al., 2001). Conversely, anxiolytic-like effects were observed in mice following intraperitoneal (i.p.) administration of RB101, an inhibitor of zink-metallopeptidases (Nieto et al., 2005). Zink-metallopeptidases rapidly degrade enkephalins in the brain under physiological conditions, and hence blockade of these peptidases increases extracellular concentrations of enkephalins in the brain (Nieto et al., 2005). Taken together, this suggests that activation of μ- and/or δ-opiate receptors by enkephalin elicits anxiolytic properties. Along similar lines, it has been shown that central administration of the mixed μ/δ receptor agonist enkephalin analog D-Ala^2-Met^5-enkephalinamide (DALA) attenuated the anxiogenic-like effects of central CCK infusions in mice (Hebb and Zacharko, 2003). Interestingly, anxiolytic-like effects of RB101 were also seen in μ-opioid knockout mice (Nieto et al., 2005), suggesting that this effect is mediated by enkephalins acting at δ-opioid receptors. In further support of this notion, it has been reported that knockout of the δ- but not of the μ-opiate receptor leads to increases in anxiety-related behavior (Filliol et al., 2000). These preclinical data would suggest that δ-opiate receptor agonists have anxiolytic properties (Table 4).

III.A.2. Dynorphin
Dynorphin-A (DYNA) and dynorphin-B (DYNB), opiate peptides generated from the precursor pro-dynorphin, are endogenous ligands of the third opiate receptor, the κ-opiate receptor.

Different splice variants have been reported for these peptides with different sequence length. Of note, these peptides do not only activate κ-opiate receptors, but also block glutamatergic N-methyl-D-aspartate (NMDA) receptor channels, and affinity for the NMDA receptor increases with increasing peptide length (Chen and Huang, 1998). This is an important consideration as NMDA receptor blockade has anxiolytic-like properties on its own (e.g., Stephens et al., 1986; Kehne et al., 1991; Fraser et al., 1996; Gatch et al., 1999).

Central administration of DYNA or DYNB failed to alter anxiety-related behavior in mice (Kuzmin et al., 2006). Likewise, anxiety-related behavior was unchanged in knockout mice lacking the κ-opiate receptor (Filliol et al., 2000). In contrast, big dynorphin (BDYN), a pro-dynorphin-derived peptide consisting of DYNA and DYNB, induced anxiolytic-like behavior. This effect was blocked by the NMDA channel blocker MK 801, suggesting that the effect is NMDA receptor-mediated and not through κ-opiate receptors (Kuzmin et al., 2006). Others have reported that activation of the κ-opiate receptor by subcutaneous treatment with the peptidergic dynorphin analog E2078 induced anxiolytic-like effects in a conflict paradigm in mice (Tsuda et al., 1996), but the peptidergic nature of the analog likely will compromise brain penetration. It, therefore, remains questionable whether this effect is centrally mediated. Moreover, peripheral κ-opiate receptor activation has antinociceptive properties (Vanderah et al., 2004; Kumar et al., 2005), which could have confounded these data generated in a task using aversive, painful stimuli. However, as will be discussed below, there is increasing evidence suggesting that small molecule, non-peptidergic κ-opiate receptor agonists might indeed hold therapeutic potential.

III.A.3. Orphanin FQ/nociceptin
Anxiolytic-like effects have been reported following central administration of the 17-amino acid peptide orphanin FQ/nociceptin (OFQ/N) (Jenck et al., 1997; Griebel et al., 1999; Gavioli et al., 2002b; Kamei et al., 2004; Vitale et al., 2006; see Gavioli and Calo', 2006 for review), the endogenous ligand of the so-called opioid-receptor-like receptor (ORL$_1$), also referred to as NOP (nociceptin/orphanin FQ peptide receptor). The ORL$_1$ receptor does not bind any of the known opiates but shows 67–82% sequence identity with the other opiate receptors (Mollereau et al., 1994). In line with the idea that OFQ/N or agonists acting at the ORL$_1$ receptor could have anxiolytic-like properties, it has been shown that mice lacking OFQ/N display enhanced anxiety-related behavior (Koster et al., 1999; Ouagazzal et al., 2003). Fernandez et al. (2004), however, reported anxiogenic-like effects induced by OFQ/N, but more recent data suggest that these effects may be confounded by acute hypoactivity induced by the peptide (Vitale et al., 2006). Taken together, these findings would suggest that drugs acting as ORL$_1$ agonists could also have anxiolytic properties (Table 4).

III.B. Gut-brain peptides

III.B.1. Substance P
Within the group of the TKs, possibly most attention has been given to SP, while less is known about the role of neurokinin A (NKA) and neurokinin B (NKB). Two other TKs, hemokinin-1 and endokinin, are primarily peripherally expressed. The effects of the TKs are mediated through three G-protein coupled neurokinin receptors, called NK$_1$, NK$_2$, and NK$_3$. Although SP, NKA, and NKB are agonists at all three NK receptors, the receptors differ in affinity for the different TKs (rank order of potency: NK$_1$: SP ≥ NKA ≥ NKB; NK$_2$: NKA > NKB > SP; NK$_3$: NKB > NKA > SP; Pennefather et al., 2004). Central administration of SP induces anxiogenic-like effects in mice and rats (Unger et al., 1988; Krase et al., 1994; Teixeira et al., 1996, 2004; Kramer et al., 1998), an effect likely mediated by activation of the NK$_1$ receptor (Teixeira and De Lima, 2003). Likewise, local injection of SP into the periaqueductal gray, which receives major SP positive projections from the amygdala (Gray and Magnuson, 1992), elicits an anxiogenic-like effect (Aguiar and Brandao, 1996). Conversely, knockout or the Tac-1 gene, which encodes both SP and NKA, reduced anxiety-related behavior in

mice (Bilkei-Gorzo et al., 2002). Studies of NK_1 knockout mice gave somewhat inconsistent results, with some reporting decreased anxiety-related behavior of mice lacking the NK_1 receptor (Rupniak et al., 2000; Santarelli et al., 2001), while others showed anxiolytic-like effects of knockout of the NK_1 receptor in some (e.g., separation-induced vocalization) but not all (e.g., elevated plus-maze) paradigms (Kramer et al., 1998; Rupniak et al., 2001). One reason for this inconsistency may be related to the state-dependent effects reported for several neuropeptides, i.e., that anxiolytic-like effects are more readily detected under more stressful conditions (Holmes et al., 2003a). However, it should also be noted that the effects of manipulations of the SP system may vary depending on the exact brain areas involved as infusions of SP directly into the ventral pallidum of rats induced anxiolytic-like behavior, not anxiogenic effects, and these effects seem also NK_1 receptor mediated (Hasenohrl et al., 1998; Nikolaus et al., 1999).

III.B.2. Cholecystokinin

Corroborating the human literature, several animal experiments have shown that CCK plays an important role in anxiogenesis through the activation of the CCK_2 receptor (Harro et al., 1993). ICV administration of CCK-8 sulfate (CCK-8s, which is the most abundant form of CCK in the brain; Dockray, 1979; Rehfeld and Hansen, 1986) induced anxiety-related behavior in rats in the elevated plus maze and activated the HPA axis (Biro et al., 1993). Rat social interaction was reduced following ICV infusions of non-sulfated CCK-8 (To and Bagdy, 1999). Likewise, ICV administration of caerulein (a frog skin peptide with comparable activity at CCK receptors, but better stability than CCK-8; Deschodt-Lanckman et al., 1981; Fujimoto et al., 1985) was anxiogenic-like in rats (Singh et al., 1991). Similar effects were seen following ICV infusion of the CCK_2 receptor agonist pentagastrin (Singh et al., 1991), suggesting a CCK_2-mediated effect. Direct intraperiaqueductal gray (Zanoveli et al., 2004), intra-amygdala (Belcheva et al., 1994), or intra-hippocampal (Rezayat et al., 2005) infusions of

non-sulfated or sulfated CCK-8, also induced an increase in anxiety-related behavior in rats, suggesting that these brain areas mediate some of the effects of CCK on this type of behavior.

Conversely, ICV administration of antisense oligodeoxynucleotides directed against the CCK precursor protein (Cohen et al., 1998) or the CCK_2 receptor (Tsutsumi et al., 2001) reduced anxiety-related behavior in rats. Although an early study by Dauge et al. (2001) failed to reveal changes in anxiety-related behavior in CCK_2 receptor knockout mice, more recent data from Horinouchi et al. (2004) suggest anxiolytic-like effects as a result of CCK_2 receptor knockout. Anxiolytic-like effects have also been reported in female CCK_2 receptor knockout mice in the elevated plus maze (Raud et al., 2003) and in the light–dark box (Raud et al., 2005), another test of exploratory anxiety, but not in conditioned models of anxiety (fear conditioning; Raud et al., 2005; but see Miyasaka et al., 2002, reporting even increased anxiety-related behavior in CCK_2 knockout mice in the elevated plus maze). Part of these discrepancies may be due to a gender effect, possibly in interaction with stress history, as knockout of the CCK_2 receptor has been reported to reduce anxiety-related behavior in socially isolated female but not male mice exploring an elevated plus maze (Abramov et al., 2004). Overexpression of the CCK_2 receptor in the mouse forebrain, on the other hand, led to increased anxiety-related behavior (Chen et al., 2006).

Given the prominent effects of peripherally administered CCK-4 or pentagastrin in human, it is of course of interest to see whether similar effects can be obtained in animals. Indeed, i.p. administration of CCK-4 increased anxiety-related behavior in guinea pigs in an elevated plus maze (Rex et al., 1997) and in an exploration box in rats (Matto et al., 1997). An increase in one-way escape behaviors was also seen in rats following peripheral CCK-8s administration (Zanoveli et al., 2004). Likewise, subcutaneous injection of caerulein was anxiogenic-like in rats (Mannisto et al., 1994). Others, however, failed to find changes in anxiety-related behavior following intravenous administration of CCK-4 in the rat elevated plus maze test (Greisen et al., 2005). Moreover, Rupniak et al.

(1993) reported that pentagastrin failed to induce panic-like symptoms after intravenous infusions in rhesus monkeys. The reasons for these discrepant findings with CCK peptide fragments are unclear. But despite some inconsistencies, the majority of preclinical animal data would suggest that CCK_2 antagonism could be beneficial for the treatment of anxiety disorders (Table 4).

III.B.3. Galanin

GAL mediates its action via three receptor subtypes: GAL_1, GAL_2, and GAL_3, all of which are expressed in the brain, although distribution patterns differ (Branchek et al., 2000). GAL_1 and GAL_3 are coupled to inhibitory G-proteins, i.e., will have mainly inhibitory effects after activation, while GAL_2 is positively coupled to phospholipase C. Hence its activation by GAL will have stimulatory effects (Branchek et al., 2000).

GAL has been reported to produce anxiolytic-like effects in the rat lick suppression test after ICV administration (Bing et al., 1993). Direct infusions of GAL into the amygdala, on the other hand, increases anxiety-related behavior on punished responding in lick suppression (Moller et al., 1999). This may suggest site-specific effects of GAL. However, intra-amygdala GAL had no effect on exploratory anxiety in the elevated plus maze in rats (Moller et al., 1999) and central administration of GAL also failed to affect anxiety-related behavior in the elevated plus maze and in the light–dark box paradigm in mice, while it reduced murine contextual fear conditioning if administered prior to training (Karlsson et al., 2005). This may suggest that GAL is particularly effective under aversive or stressful conditions. In line with this suggestion, it has been shown that GAL injected directly into the central nucleus of the amygdale was anxiolytic-like in the elevated plus maze in rats after exposure to immobilization stress (Khoshbouei et al., 2002). Thus, explorative anxiety may not be under control of the GAL system, at least not under baseline conditions of low stress levels, but GAL may gain importance under conditions of increased stress levels. Along similar lines, no change in anxiety-related behavior was seen in GAL overexpressing mice under baseline conditions in an elevated plus maze, a light–dark box and an open field (Holmes et al., 2002; Kuteeva et al., 2005), but GAL overexpressors displayed less anxiety-related behavior in the light dark box than wild-type mice following treatment with the anxiogenic α_2-adrenoceptor antagonist yohimbine (Holmes et al., 2002).

GAL_1 knockout mice, on the other hand, displayed increased anxiety-related behavior in the elevated plus maze, while anxiety-related behavior in the light–dark box, emergence and open field tests were normal (Holmes et al., 2003b), suggesting that part of the anxiolytic-like effects of GAL could be mediated through GAL_1 activation. GAL_2 knockout mice failed to display any changes in anxiety-related behavior as measured by open field or light–dark box exploration, fear conditioning or stress-induced hyperthermia (Gottsch et al., 2005). From these findings, it may be concluded that GAL seems to play a role in the modulation of anxiety-related behavior, at least under stressful conditions, and this effect may in part be mediated by GAL_1 receptor activation (Tables 3 and 4). However, it would be premature to drive to firm conclusions of the exact GAL receptor subtypes being involved in anxiety simply based on the limited knockout data.

III.B.4. Bombesin-like peptides

Bombesin-like peptides comprise of peptides such as the 14-amino acid peptide bombesin, originally isolated from frog skin, the mammalian analog gastrin-releasing peptide (GRP), and neuromedin B (NMB). GRP binds with high affinity to the GRP receptor, also called bombesin receptor 2 (BB_2), while NMB binds with higher affinity to the NMB receptor, also called bombesin receptor 1 (BB_1; Moody and Merali, 2004). Other bombesin receptor subtypes are BRS-3 and BB_4, although the natural ligands for these receptors in the mammalian brain still need to be uncovered.

Data on bombesin-like peptides are relatively scarce, although bombesin has been clearly implicated in the modulation of anxiety-related behavior (Roesler et al., 2004). ICV administration of

Table 3. Neuropeptides and anxiety: weighted according to evidence

| Neuropeptide | Clinical | Behavior | Preclinical | | | |
			GABA	Neurochemistry 5-HT	Neurochemistry NA	HPA
Corticotropin-releasing factor (CRF)	+	A	↓BNST	↑H,Am,PfC↓LS	↑H,PfC	↑
Cholecystokinin (CCK)	+†	A		↑PfC		↑
Atrial natriuretic peptide	a†	a				↓
Oxytocin (OT)	a*	a				↓
Neuropeptide Y (NPY)	(+)	a	↑BNST		±PVN	↓
Angiotensin II (ANG II)	±†	A	↓H		↑PVN	↑
β-endorphin (END)	±†	a			↓H,Am	↑
Thyrotropin-releasing hormone (TRH)	(+)	Ø	↑H			
Substance P (SP)	O	A		↑H	↑PfC§	↓
Galanin (GAL)	O	a		↓H	↓H,↑PVN	↓
Orphanin FQ/nociceptin (OFQ/N)	O	a	↓Am		↓Am	↑
Vasopressin (AVP)	O	±			↑H	↑
ACTH	O	A				↑
Melanin-stimulating hormone (MSH)	O	A				↑
Melanin-concentrating hormone (MCH)	O	±				↑
Hypocretin/orexin (HCRT/ORX)	O	(±)		↑DR	↑H	↑
Urocortin 1 (UCN1)	O	(A)		↑H	↑H	
Urocortin 2 (UCN2)	O	(A)		↑H,Am	↑H	
Urocortin 3 (UCN3)	O	(a)		↑H	↑H	
Gastrin-releasing peptide (GRP)	O	(a)	↑H			
Pituitary adenylate cyclase activating polypeptide (PACAP)	O	(A)				↑
Glucagon-like peptide 1 (GLP-1)	O	(A)				↑
Calcitonin-gene related peptide (CGRP)	O	(A)				↑
Ghrelin	O	(A)				↑
Neuropeptide S (NPS)	O	(a)	↓PAG			
Somatostatin (SST)	O	(a)		↑H		
Neurotensin (NT)	O		↑H, PfC			↑
Dynorphin (DYN)	O					
Neuropeptide FF (NPFF)	O		↑PVN		↓H	
Neuromedin U (NMU)	O					↑
Neuropeptide W (NPW)	O					↑
Neuromedin B (NMB)	O					↑
Bradykinin	O					
Vasoactive intestinal peptide (VIP)	O					
Glucagon	O					
Relaxin-3 (INSL-7)	O					

Note: preclinical evidence cited is limited to studies where peptides were exogenously administered or using mouse mutants.

+, good evidence for involvement; ±, conflicting evidence; O, insufficient evidence; A, anxiogenic; a, anxiolytic; ↑, increased release; ↓, decreased release; ( ), limited evidence; *, in healthy volunteers only; †, in patients with panic disorder; §, effect of senktide; Am, amygdala; BNST, bed nucleus of the stria terminalis; DR, dorsal raphe; H, hippocampus; LS, lateral septum; PfC, prefrontal cortex; PVN, paraventricular hypothalamic nucleus. See text for references.

Table 4. Potential anxiolytic properties of neuropeptide GPCR manipulation, based on peptide infusions and knockout studies

Neuropeptide	GPCR	Anxiolytic efficacy
Antagonism		
Corticotropin-releasing factor (CRF)	CRF_1	−
Cholecystokinin (CCK)	CCK_2	−
Neuropeptide Y	Y_2	−
Substance P (SP)	NK_1	−
Vasopressin (AVP)	V_{1A}	−
ACTH/α-melanin-stimulating hormone (α-MSH)	MC_3/MC_4	−
Angiotensin II (ANG II)	AT_2	(−)
Pituitary adenylate cyclase activating polypeptide (PACAP)	PAC_1	(−)
Glucagon-like peptide 1 (GLP-1)	GLP-1R	(−)
Calcitonin-gene related peptide (CGRP)	CGRPR	(−)
Ghrelin	GHS_{1A}	(−)
Neuromedin B (NMB)	BB_1	−
C-type atrial natriuretic peptide (CNP)	NPR-B?	(−)
Agonism		
Atrial natriuretic peptide (ANP)	NPR-A?	(+)
Oxytocin (OT)	OTR	+
Neuropeptide Y (NPY)	Y_1	+
	Y_5	+
β-endorphin (END)	δ-opiate	+
Galanin (GAL)	GAL_1	+
Orphanin FQ/nociceptin (OFQ/N)	OFQ_1	+
Hypoctretin/orexin (HCRT/ORX)	OX_2	(+)
Gastrin-releasing peptide (GRP)	BB_2	(+)
Neuropeptide S (NPS)	GPR154/NPSR	(+)
Somatostatin (SST)	sst_2	+
Conflicting evidence		
Corticotropin-releasing factor (CRF)	CRF_2	±
Melanin-concentrating hormone (MCH)	MCH_1	±

+, agonism; −, antagonism; ±, conflicting evidence; ( ), limited evidence; ?, indirect evidence through limited reports on the effects of ANP and CNP. See text for references.

bombesin itself induced excessive grooming in rats (Crawley and Moody, 1997), which could be an indication for increased anxiety-related behavior. Likewise, direct injection of NMB into the serotonergic dorsal raphe nucleus induced anxiogenic-like behavior, as indicated by a decrease in social interaction in rats (Merali et al., 2006). NMB injections into the third ventricle, on the other hand, failed to affect anxiety-related behavior in rats tested on an elevated plus maze (Bedard et al., 2007).

GRP injected into the third ventricle (Bedard et al., 2007) or into the infralimbic cortex (Mountney et al., 2006) attenuated fear potentiated startle, and GRP infusions directly into the prelimbic cortex, infralimbic cortex, or central nucleus of the amygdala reduced freezing to contextual cues (Mountney et al., 2006), suggesting that GRP reduces learned fear. However, ICV injections of GRP in rats (Bedard et al, 2007) or knockout of the mammalian GRP/BB_2 receptor in mice (Yamada et al., 2002) failed to affect performance in the elevated plus maze or the light–dark box. The reason for these discrepant findings are unclear and could be related to compensatory processes or the fact that GRP is involved in learned but not innate fear responses.

NMB/BB$_1$ receptor knockout mice failed to differ from wild-type mice in conventional measures (time spent in open arms, etc.) in tests of exploratory anxiety, irrespective whether they had been exposed to a stressor or not prior to test (Yamada et al., 2000, 2002, 2003; Yamano et al., 2002). However, BB$_1$ receptor knockout mice showed a reduction in risk assessment both in the elevated plus maze and the light dark box (Yamada et al., 2002), suggesting a reduction in anxiety-related behavior if these measures were considered. Furthermore, Shumyatsky et al. (2002) found a decreased inhibition of principal neurons by the interneurons in the lateral nucleus of the amygdala, enhanced long-term potentiation (LTP), and greater and more persistent long-term fear memory in BB$_2$ receptor knockout mice. Since BB$_2$ receptors are expressed at these interneurons, it would suggest that GRP operates in a negative feedback regulating fear at amygdala level. Thus, there is emerging evidence for a role of these bombesin-like peptides in the modulation of anxiety, but data are still limited (Table 3). For completeness, it should also be mentioned that one study looked at the effects of knocking out BRS-3 (Yamada et al., 2002). These mice spent more time on the open arms of an elevated plus maze, suggesting an anxiolytic-like effect, while at the same time displaying an increased risk assessment, suggesting an anxiogenic-like effect.

III.B.5. Neuropeptide Y

The 36-amino acid member of the pancreatic polypeptide family, NPY, acts at five functional receptors in the brain, Y$_1$–Y$_5$, differing in expression patterns and density, and pre- and postsynaptic localization (Michel et al., 1998). ICV administration of NPY has been shown to elicit anxiolytic like effects in the open field (Sorensen et al., 2004), the elevated plus maze (Heilig et al., 1989; Britton et al., 2000; Sorensen et al., 2004), the light–dark box (Pich et al., 1993), lick suppression (Heilig et al., 1989), and in the Geller–Seifter conflict test (Heilig et al., 1992;

Britton et al., 1997, 2000; see Carvajal et al., 2006b, for overview). ICV administration of the closely related peptides peptide YY (PYY) or NPY(2–36) also elicited anxiolytic-like activity in the elevated plus maze and fear-potentiated startle (Broqua et al., 1995). Moreover, transgenic rats overexpressing prepro-NPY exhibited reduced anxiety-related behavior in two studies (Thorsell et al., 2000; Carvajal et al., 2004), providing further evidence for the anxiolytic-like properties of NPY (Table 3). Sites where NPY seems to exert its anxiolytic-like effects are the basolateral, but not the central, nucleus of the amygdala (Sajdyk et al., 1999b), and the lateral septum (Kask et al., 2001).

In an attempt to delineate the NPY receptor subtypes mediating these effects, a number of NPY analogs were tested, differing in their affinity for to different NPY receptor subtypes. Anxiolytic-like effects were also seen following ICV administration of the NPY analog [Leu^{31},Pro^{34}]NPY, a non-selective Y$_1$/Y$_4$/Y$_5$ agonist (Heilig et al., 1993; Broqua et al., 1995), of [D-His^{26}]NPY, which acts as a selective Y$_1$ agonist (Sorensen et al., 2004), of the Y$_5$ agonistic NPY analog [cPP (1–7),NPY19–23),Ala^{31},Aib^{32},Gln^{34}]hPP (Sorensen et al., 2004), but not of the Y$_2$ agonistic peptide C2-NPY (Broqua et al., 1995; Sorensen et al., 2004), suggests that these effects are primarily Y$_1$ and Y$_5$ receptor mediated (Table 4). Conversely, Y$_1$ antagonism increased anxiety-related behavior (Kask et al., 1997). Anxiolytic-like effects were also seen in social interaction following administration of the Y$_2$/Y$_5$ agonist NPY(3–36) directly into the basolateral amygdala (Sajdyk et al., 2002). If this were a Y$_5$-mediated effect, it would suggest that NPY acts at Y$_5$ receptors in the basolateral amygdala to elicit its anxiolytic-like properties. However, ICV injection of NPY(3–36) have also been reported to increase anxiety-related behavior (Heilig et al., 1989). Given that Y$_5$ receptor stimulation has been shown to be anxiolytic-like, this may suggest that it is the Y$_2$ receptor, which mediates anxiogenic-like properties of NPY. Indeed, infusions of the Y$_2$ agonistic peptide C2-NPY directly into the basolateral amygdala decreased social behavior (Sajdyk et al., 2002), suggesting that selective

Y_2 receptor activation may be anxiogenic-like. Since the Y_2 receptor is a presynaptic autoreceptor, anxiogenic-like properties of Y_2 stimulation could be explained by negative feedback and consequently reduced NPY release (Table 4).

Consistent with the studies mentioned above, an anxiogenic-like phenotype was seen in NPY knockout mice (Bannon et al., 2000). Y_1 antisense oligodeoxynucleotide injected ICV or directly into the central nucleus of the amygdala attenuated the anxiolytic-like effects of NPY (Wahlestedt et al., 1993; Heilig, 1995), while knockout mice lacking the Y_2 receptor showed an anxiolytic-like phenotype (Redrobe et al., 2003; Tschenett et al., 2003; Carvajal et al., 2006a). More recently, this picture was slightly blurred by findings that Y_1 knockout mice exhibited anxiogenic-like behavior in an elevated plus maze, although still an anxiogenic-like effect was seen in the light–dark box (Karl et al., 2006). However, it has been shown that Y_2 receptor expression is upregulated in Y_1 receptor knockout mice (Wittmann et al., 2005), which could explain part of these effects.

Taken together, there is substantial preclinical evidence suggesting that the Y_1 and the Y_5 receptors mediate the anxiolytic-like properties of NPY, while Y_2 receptor activation has anxiogenic-like properties, possibly secondary to negative feedback mechanisms and a reduction in NPY release.

III.B.6. Somatostatin

The actions of somatostatin (SST, also named somatotropin-release inhibiting factor, SRIF), which exists in two isoforms (a tetradecapeptide, SST-14, and an N-terminally extended form, SST-28) are mediated through five SST receptor subtypes (sst1–sst5; Hoyer et al., 1995).

The literature on the involvement of somatostatin in anxiety is relatively sparse: The SST receptor agonist peptide sandostatin blocked fear potentiation if injected into the pontine reticular nucleus of rats (Fendt et al., 1996), suggesting SST could have anxiolytic-like properties. Along similar lines, it has been suggested that SST dampens cell excitability in amygdaloid projection neurons and thereby reduces fear responsiveness (Meis et al., 2005). Conversely, knockout mice lacking the sst2 receptor exhibited increased anxiety-related behavior when tested in an elevated plus maze, as well as increased neophobia (Viollet et al., 2000), suggesting that at least part of the effects of SST on the modulation of anxiety-related behavior could be mediated through this receptor (Tables 3 and 4). However, more studies are required before firm conclusions on the role of SST in anxiety can be drawn.

III.B.7. Pituitary adenylate cyclase activating polypeptide

Pituitary adenylate cyclase activating polypeptide (PACAP) is a member of the vasoactive intestinal peptide (VIP)/secretin/glucagon peptide family, originally isolated from ovine hypothalamus, but expressed more widely throughout the brain. It exists in two splice variants, PACAP-27 and PACAP-38. PACAP binds to three GPCRs, called PAC_1, $VPAC_1$, and $VPAC_2$ (Arimura and Shioda, 1995; Arimura, 1998) Mice lacking PACAP have been reported to display less anxiety-related behavior (Hashimoto et al., 2001). Likewise, mice lacking the PAC_1 receptor exhibited less anxiety-related behavior (Otto et al., 2001), suggesting that PAC_1 antagonists could have therapeutic utility in the treatment of anxiety disorders.

No published evidence exists linking VIP or glucagon to the modulation of anxiety-related behavior in animals. In fact, one study reported that central administration of glucagon failed to affect anxiety-related behavior in rats (Morawska et al., 1998).

III.B.8. Glucagon-like peptide

There is limited evidence linking glucagon-like peptide (GLP-1) with anxiety-related behavior. GLP-1 positive neurons are located in the nucleus of the solitary tract (Han et al., 1986), from where projections originate to various brain areas involved in the modulation of anxiety, such as the amygdala (Goke et al., 1995). More recently, GLP-1 has been shown to exert anxiogenic-like effects following ICV administration (Moller et al., 2002) or infusions into the amygdala or the PVN (Kinzig et al., 2003).

III.B.9. Calcitonin gene-related peptide

Calcitonin gene-related peptide (CGRP), a 37-amino acid polypeptide, is a member of the calcitonin family of peptides (Rosenfeld et al., 1983) and widely distributed throughout the brain (Van Rossum et al., 1997). It has been suggested to play an important role in migraine and pain (e.g., Edvinsson, 2001). Injections of CGRP into the lateral ventricle (Poore and Helmstetter, 1996) or into the amygdala (Kocorowski and Helmstetter, 2001) produced fear-like behavior in a rat fear conditioning paradigm, even before any aversive stimuli were presented. Thus, limited evidence suggests CGRP to be involved in anxiety and fear responses.

III.B.10. Ghrelin

Ghrelin is a 28-amino acid, recently discovered gastrointestinal peptide with orexigenic properties. Low levels of ghrelin are also expressed in the brain (Dornonville de la Cour et al., 2001). The peptide is involved in the control of growth hormone secretion and is considered as the endogenous ligand of the growth hormone secretagogue receptor (GHS_{1A}) (Kojima et al., 1999; Tschop et al., 2000). In the brain, the GHS_{1A} receptor is most strongly expressed in the hypothalamic arcuate nucleus and the ventromedial hypothalamus, but is also found in other brain areas (Guan et al., 1997). ICV administration of ghrelin increased anxiety-related behavior in rats (Carlini et al., 2002) and mice (Asakawa et al., 2001). Anxiogenic-like effects were also seen following peripheral administration in mice (Asakawa et al., 2001). Likewise, infusions of ghrelin directly into the amygdala, the hippocampus or the dorsal raphe nucleus have been reported to induce anxiogenic-like effects in the rat elevated plus maze task (Carlini et al., 2004). Conversely, ICV administration of antisense DNA against ghrelin had anxiolytic-like effects in rats (Kanehisa et al., 2006). This would suggest that GHS_{1A} antagonists could have anxiolytic properties.

III.C. Hypothalamic peptides

III.C.1. Corticotropin-releasing factor

The CRF family of peptides comprises of the 41-amino acid peptide CRF and the more recently discovered endogenous peptide agonists urocortin 1, 2, and 3 (UCN1, UCN2, UCN3; Vaughan et al., 1995; Lewis et al., 2001; Reyes et al., 2001). These peptides differ in expression patterns and bind to two main CRF receptors in the brain, designated CRF_1 and CRF_2 (Dautzenberg and Hauger, 2002). CRF is considered to be the primary endogenous ligand for the CRF_1 receptor, while the UCNs are considered the primary endogenous ligands for the CRF_2 receptor, based on their respective affinities and projection patterns.

Numerous studies have shown anxiogenic-like effects of CRF, either after ICV administration (Spina et al., 1996, 2002; Moreau et al., 1997; Jones et al., 1998; Radulovic et al., 1999; Okuyama et al., 1999a; Britton et al., 2000; Dirks et al., 2002; Zorrilla et al., 2002; Kagamiishi et al., 2003; Matys et al., 2004; Pelleymounter et al., 2004; Meloni et al., 2006) or infusion into distinct brain areas, such as the amygdala (Sajdyk et al., 1999a; Daniels et al., 2004), the bed nucleus of the stria terminalis (Sahuque et al., 2006), the lateral septum (Kask et al., 2001), or the hippocampus (Radulovic et al., 1999). Mice overexpressing CRF also showed anxiogenic-like effects (Stenzel-Poore et al., 1994; Van Gaalen et al., 2002; but see Groenink et al., 2003, reporting reduced freezing of CRF overexpressing transgenic mice in fear conditioning). Despite this overwhelming evidence, there is still debate around the exact role of CRF in the modulation of anxiety-related behavior, and it has been suggested more recently that CRF might prepare the organism to cope with aversive situations, rather than to be a prime mediator of fear and anxiety per se (Merali et al., 2004).

The effects of the other CRF-related peptides are less clear. ICV administration of UCN1 had no effects on anxiety-related behavior (Spina et al., 1996), weaker effects than CRF (Jones et al., 1998; Radulovic et al., 1999), time-dependent effects (Spina et al., 2002), induced anxiogenic-like effects comparable to CRF (Moreau et al., 1997;

Radulovic et al., 1999), or was even more potent than CRF in inducing anxiety-related behavior (Sajdyk et al., 1999a), which seems to depend on task, time of testing after peptide administration, and/or brain area where the peptide was injected (see Steckler and Holsboer, 1999, for review). UCN2 also elicited anxiogenic-like effects after ICV in some (Pelleymounter et al., 2002, 2004; Risbrough et al., 2003) but not all (Henry et al., 2006) studies. However, the same group failing to find effects of UCN2 after ICV infusions reported anxiogenic-like effects following infusions of UCN2 directly into the lateral septum, and the strength of this effect depended on the stress level of the animal (Henry et al., 2006). ICV infusions of UCN3, on the other hand, were either without effects (Pelleymounter et al., 2004) or even elicited anxiolytic-like effects (Valdez et al., 2003; Venihaki et al., 2004). To complicate matters, delayed anxiolytic-like effects were also seen following central UCN2 infusions (Valdez et al., 2002).

Conceptually, equipotent effects of UCN1 and CRF on anxiety-related behavior could be expected after central administration. While the affinity of UCN1 for the CRF_2 receptor is higher than that of CRF, both UCN1 and CRF have comparable affinity for the CRF_1 receptor, (Dautzenberg and Hauger, 2002). Although the projection patterns of UCN1 and CRF neurons differ, it is unlikely that the effects of UCN1 after ICV or local injection do reflect physiological responses but rather mimic the effects of CRF. Indeed, direct infusions of UCN1 into the basolateral amygdala also elicited anxiety-related responses (Gehlert et al., 2005; Sajdyk et al., 2006; Spiga et al., 2006) and this effect is CRF_1 receptor mediated (Gehlert et al., 2005). However, results obtained with UCN2 (Pelleymounter et al., 2004; Henry et al., 2006) suggest that at least part of the effects of CRF-related peptides can be mediated via the CRF_2 receptor.

Increased anxiety-related behavior was also seen following ICV administration of the CRF fragment CRF(6–33), which does not bind to the CRF receptor subtypes but displaces CRF from its binding protein in the brain (Radulovic et al., 1999), although some earlier studies failed to find changes in anxiety-related behavior after

treatment with CRF(6–33) (Behan et al., 1995). Along similar lines, lack of CRF binding protein also led to increased anxiety-related behavior in knockout mice (Karolyi et al., 1999). Thus, increasing CRF activity either endogenously via displacement from its binding protein or by exogenous administration has clear anxiogenic-like effects (Table 3).

Further evidence for an import role of the CRF_1 receptor in the CRF-induced anxiogenic effects comes from Tezval et al. (2004), showing that ICV administration of the synthetic peptide cortagine, which preferentially acts as CRF_1 agonist, also induced anxiogenic-like effects in mice. Conversely, central administration of antisense deoxynucleotides directed against the CRF_1 receptor (Liebsch et al., 1995, 1999; Skutella et al., 1998; but see Heinrichs et al., 1997, for negative results), or conventional or conditional knockout of the CRF_1 receptor (Smith et al., 1998; Timpl et al., 1998; Contarino et al., 1999; Muller et al., 2003; Gammie and Stevenson, 2006) reduces anxiety-related behavior, indicating that the anxiogenic-like effects of CRF-related peptides are CRF_1 mediated (Table 4).

Central application of antisense oligodeoxynucleotides against the CRF_2 receptor failed to affect anxiety-related behavior (Heinrichs et al., 1997; Liebsch et al., 1999). However, more recent studies using CRF_2 antisense oligodeoxynucleotides showed anxiogenic effects following ICV administration (Isogawa et al., 2003). In CRF_2 knockout mice, the picture is less clear and anxiogenic-like effects in males and females (Bale et al., 2000), gender-specific anxiogenic-like effects (Kishimoto et al., 2000) or unaltered anxiety-related behavior, irrespective of gender (Coste et al., 2000), have been reported.

Taken together, these studies confirm a major role of CRF and CRF-related peptides in the modulation of anxiety-related behavior and further support the clinical findings. Clearly, preclinical data support the idea that the anxiogenic-like effects of CRF are CRF_1 receptor mediated. Although there is also evidence for a role of the CRF_2 receptor, findings are less clear, and both anxiolytic- and anxiogenic-like effects of CRF_2 receptor activation could be suggested from the data (Table 4).

III.C.2. Thyrotropin-releasing hormone

Systemic injections of prepro-thyrotropin-releasing hormone(178–199) (PP-TRH(178–199)) in postnatal 3-day-old rat pups has been reported to ameliorate separation-induced increases in anxiety related behavior, as indicated by an increase in exploration and a reduction in distress vocalizations (Stahl et al., 2002). This peptide fragment has been considered an "endogenous corticotropin-release inhibiting factor (CRIF)", inhibiting stress-induced ACTH secretion in vivo (Redei et al., 1998). However, ICV administration of TRH had no effects on anxiety-related behavior in rats exploring an elevated plus maze, but rather induced stereotyped behavior (Gargiulo and Donoso, 1996). Thus, evidence from the animal literature for a role of TRH on anxiety-related behavior is limited.

III.C.3. Hypocretin/orexin

The hypocretin/orexin system in the brain has been associated with the modulation of sleep and arousal (Jones and Muhlethaler, 2005). Two hypocretin/orexin peptides have been identified, named hypocretin-1 or orexin-A (HCRT-1/ORX-A), and hypocretin-2 or orexin-B (HCRT-2/ORX-B), acting via two receptor subtypes, HCRT-1 (also named OX_1) and HCRT-2 (also named OX_2) (Sakurai et al., 1998). Limited evidence for a role of orexin in the modulation of anxiety-related behavior has been presented: Suzuki et al. (2005) showed an increase in anxiety-related behavior in rats following ICV administration of ORX-A. Conversely, mice with specific lesions of the cells expressing the OX_2 receptor following administration of the neurotoxin OX_2-saporin into the lateral hypothalamus were less fearful (Easton et al., 2006). However, another recent study pointed toward possible anxiolytic-like properties of ORX-A and ORX-B as both peptides decreased startle (Singareddy et al., 2006) and more studies are needed to further address this system and its role in anxiety.

III.C.4. Melanin-concentrating hormone

Melanin-concentrating hormone (MCH) is a cyclic 19-amino acid, anabolic neuropeptide, exerting both central orexigenic effects and inducing a positive peripheral energy balance (Hervieu, 2003, 2006). MCH-positive neurons originate from the lateral hypothalamic area and project widely throughout the brain (Hervieu, 2003; Kennedy et al., 2003). The peptide binds to two receptors, named MCH_1 (also called orphan somatostatin-like receptor, SLC-1) and MCH_2. In the rodent brain, the MCH_2 receptor is not functional and central effects are mediated via the MCH_1 receptor (Boutin et al., 2002).

The MCH system received growing attention over the last years as a system playing an important role in the modulation of anxiety, not at least due to the seminal paper by Borowsky et al. (2002), showing that the small molecule, non-peptide MCH_1 antagonist SNAP-7941 had anxiolytic-like properties (see also below). However, the effects of central MCH administration are controversial (Table 3): No effects on anxiety-related behavior were seen in rats after MCH infusions into the third cerebral ventricle (Duncan et al., 2005). Anxiogenic-like effects have been reported following ICV injections of MCH (Smith et al., 2006) or infusions of MCH into the medial preoptic hypothalamic area (Gonzalez et al., 1996), while others did see anxiolytic-like effects following ICV (Monzon and De Barioglio, 1999; Monzon et al., 2001; Kela et al., 2003), intra-amygdala (Monzon et al., 2001), or intrahippocampal (Carlini et al., 2006) administration of MCH.

Given that only the MCH_1 receptor is functional the rodent brain, it can be expected that the effects of central MCH administration – be it anxiolytic- or anxiogenic-like – are MCH_1 mediated. Somewhat mixed reports have also been published with MCH_1 knockout mice, showing either anxiolytic-like behavior (Roy et al., 2006; Smith et al., 2006), or no change in anxiety-related behavior (Adamantidis et al., 2005). These data would not allow drawing a clear picture on the value of MCH_1 manipulations and their therapeutic potential to treat anxiety disorders (Table 4).

Another recently discovered gut-brain peptide that has been linked to the modulation of stress and that may hold potential in the regulation of anxiety is relaxin (INSL-7) (Sutton et al., 2004; Tanaka et al., 2005). However, no behavioral data have been published so far directly addressing this possibility.

III.D. Pituitary peptides

III.D.1. Vasopressin

Vasopressin (AVP) is another stress-related peptide and closely linked to the CRF family of peptides. AVP is secreted peripherally at the level of the posterior pituitary and median eminence and plays a pivotal role in the modulation of the HPA axis. As with CRF, AVP is also released centrally where it has neuromodulatory function. Two main receptors mediate the central effects of AVP, classified as V_{1a} and V_{1b} receptor subtypes (Lolait et al., 1995).

There is strong preclinical evidence indicating an important role of the AVP system in the modulation of anxiety-related behavior, especially on the relationship between anxiety states and physiologically released AVP (e.g., see Landgraf, 2006, for review), although the effects of central administration of AVP itself on anxiety-related behavior are contradictory: While ICV administration of AVP (Appenrodt and Schwarzberg, 2000) or infusion of AVP into the lateral septum (Appenrodt et al., 1998; Appenrodt and Schwarzberg, 2000), but also peripheral application of AVP (Appenrodt et al., 1998), have been reported to induce anxiolytic-like effects in rats, others failed to see any effect of AVP into the lateral septum (Liebsch et al., 1996), or reported anxiogenic-like effects following ICV treatment with AVP (Bhattacharya et al., 1998). Anxiogenic-like effects were also seen in conditioned freezing following peripheral administration AVP(4–9) (Stoehr et al., 1992).

Reports on the effects of selective V_{1A} receptor manipulations are more consistent: Mild increases in anxiety-related behavior were observed in mice overexpressing the V_{1A} receptor in the lateral septum (Bielsky et al., 2005a), and male prairie voles overexpressing the V_{1A} receptor in the ventral pallidum showed anxiogenic-like behavior in the elevated plus maze (Pitkow et al., 2001).

Conversely, downregulation of the V_{1A} receptor with antisense oligodeoxynucleotides had anxiolytic-like effects in rats (Landgraf et al., 1995). Along similar lines, male, but not female, mice lacking the V_{1A} receptor displayed reduced anxiety-related behavior (Bielsky et al., 2004, 2005b). The latter results may be due to sexual dimorphism, which has been reported in relation to the AVP system (Bielsky et al., 2005b). Taken together, it can be suggested that AVP affects anxiety-related behavior via activation of the V_{1A} receptor and that blockade of this receptor has anxiolytic properties (Tables 3 and 4). However, as will be seen below, pharmacological data also point to an important involvement of the V_{1B} receptor in the regulation of anxiety.

III.D.2. Oxytocin

Anxiolytic-like effects have been reported following ICV (Windle et al., 1997), central amygdala (Bale et al., 2001), and peripheral (Uvnas-Moberg et al., 1994; McCarthy et al, 1996), but not ventromedial hypothalamic (Bale et al., 2001), infusions of OT in rats. Similar reductions in anxiety-related behavior were seen in mice following central or peripheral treatment with OT (Ring et al., 2006). Furthermore, peripheral administration of an OT fragment reduced conditioned freezing in rats (Stoehr et al., 1992). Female OT knockout mice, on the other hand, exhibit an increase in anxiety-related behavior (Mantella et al., 2003; Amico et al., 2004), although no change (De Vries et al., 1997), or a reduction in anxiety-related behavior was reported by others phenotyping OT knockout mice (Winslow et al., 2000). Taken together, the data suggest that activation of the central OT receptor could be of benefit in the treatment of anxiety disorders.

III.D.3. The melanocortin peptide family

The melanocortins, α-, β-, and γ-melanin-stimulating hormone (α-, β-, and γ-MSH), as well as ACTH, derive via post-translational processing from the POMC pro-hormone. Five melanocortin receptors have been reported, MC_1–MC_5. Of those, mainly the MC_3 and MC_4 receptors, as well as the MC_5 receptor, are expressed in the brain. Both α-MSH and ACTH have comparably high affinity for the MC$_3$ and MC$_4$ receptors, while the affinity for the MC$_5$ receptor is higher for α-MSH than for ACTH. The MC$_2$ receptor is expressed in the adrenal cortex where it mediates the steroidogenic effects of ACTH (see Chaki and Okuyama, 2005, for review).

Both ACTH and α-MSH have been shown to exert anxiogenic-like effects in the rat punished drinking paradigm (Chaki et al., 2003b; Corda et al., 1990). Likewise, increased anxiety-related behavior was seen following ICV infusions of α-MSH (Rao et al., 2003; Kokare et al., 2006), injections of α-MSH into the medial preoptic hypothalamic area and the ventromedial hypothalamic nucleus (Gonzalez et al., 1996), or into the amygdala (Kokare et al., 2005). Furthermore, anxiogenic-like responses were seen in the social interaction test in rats receiving ACTH infusions into the lateral ventricles (File and Clarke, 1980). These data would suggest that blockade of MC$_3$ and/or MC$_4$ receptors would have anxiolytic-like properties.

III.E. The natriuretic peptide family

III.E.1. Atrial natriuretic peptide and angiotensin II

The natriuretic peptide family includes ANP, brain natriuretic peptide (BNP) and C-type atrial natriuretic peptide (CNP) (Saavedra and Pavel, 2005). Despite their names, both ANP and CNP, but not BNP, are expressed in the brain (Saavedra et al., 2000). The natriuretic peptides act via three GPCRs in the brain, NPR-A, NPR-B, and NPR-C (Saavedra et al., 2000).

ANP has an endogenous counterpart, the octapeptide angiotensin II (ANG II). ANG II can be considered a natural antagonist of ANP, as it counterregulates the effects of ANP, especially on cardiovascular function (Saavedra and Pavel, 2005). ANG II is also both peripherally and centrally expressed and acts via two receptors in the brain, designated as AT$_1$ and AT$_2$ (Tsutsumi and Saavedra, 1991; Saavedra and Pavel, 2005).

ICV infusions of ANP (Bhattacharya et al., 1996) as well as central administration of the ANP derivative atriopeptin II (ANP(103–125)) into the ventricles or into the amygdala, but also peripheral administration of atriopeptin II (Strohle et al., 1997), have anxiolytic-like effects in rats. Conversely, limited evidence suggests that ICV administration of CNP exerts anxiogenic-like effects (Montkowski et al., 1998; Jahn et al., 2001). One explanation for the dissociation between ANP and CNP could be their different receptor affinities. ANP has higher affinity for the NPR-A receptor than CNP, while CNP binds with higher affinity to the NPR-B receptor than ANP (Saavedra and Pavel, 2005).

As might be expected from the antagonistic role of ANG II on the ANP system, central administration of ANG II has anxiogenic-like properties in rats (Wright and Harding, 1992; Braszko et al., 2003). Moreover, direct injections of ANG II into the dorsomedial hypothalamus in "panic-prone" rats with chronic disruption of the GABA-mediated inhibition of the dorsomedial hypothalamus elicited panic-like behavior (Shekhar et al., 2006). Increased anxiety-related behavior was also seen in transgenic rats with elevated brain and plasma ANG II levels (Wilson et al., 1996b). From this, it may be expected that knockout of ANG II would lead to anxiolytic-like effects. However, mice deficient of ANG II due to lack of expression of angiotensinogen, the precursor of ANG II, did not differ from wild-type mice in anxiety-related behavior (Walther et al., 1999). However, transgenic rats expressing antisense RNA against angiotensinogen showed increases in anxiety-related behavior (Voigt et al., 2005), which cannot readily be explained with a direct effect on the ANG II system but may suggest compensatory effects. Okuyama et al. (1999b) have shown that AT$_2$ knockout mice display anxiolytic-like behavior (Okuyama et al., 1999b), suggesting that the effects of ANG II on anxiety-related behavior could at least in part be mediated via this receptor subtype. Moreover, it would suggest that blockade of the AT$_2$ receptor may have anxiolytic properties (Table 4), although – as will be seen below – there is also good pharmacological evidence linking the AT$_1$ receptor to anxiety.

III.F. Other peptides

III.F.1. Neuropeptide S

A relatively new player in the field of neuropeptides and anxiety is the 20-amino acid peptide neuropeptide S (NPS) (Xu et al., 2004). NPS is the endogenous ligand of an orphan GPCR, named GPR154 or NPSR. Neurons expressing NPS precursor mRNA are located in the brain stem between the locus coeruleus (LC) and Barrington's nucleus (Xu et al., 2004, 2007). The GPR154 receptor, amongst other sites, is expressed in the amygdaloid complex and the hypothalamic PVN (Xu et al., 2007), i.e., at sites linked to the mediation of anxiety- and stress-related behavior. Central administration of NPS has been shown to increase locomotor activity in mice, to promote arousal and interfere with sleep, and to produce anxiolytic-like effects in the open field, the light–dark box, the elevated plus maze and the marble burying test (Xu et al., 2004). Most neuropeptides promoting arousal will show anxiogenic-like effects. Thus, the findings with NPS are remarkable in that respect as the peptide is arousing and anxiolytic-like at the same time.

The limited findings open the possibility that GPR154 agonists might have anxiolytic potential (Table 4). However, so far only one study has been published on the effects of NPS on anxiety-related behavior and more experiments are needed to fully position this new peptide and its role in anxiety.

Other recently discovered neuropeptides are, for example, neuromedin U (NMU), neuropeptide FF (NPFF), neuropeptide AF (NPAF), and neuropeptide W (NPW). Although NMU (Brighton et al., 2004), NPFF, and NPAF (Liu et al., 2001) have been implicated in the regulation of anxiety, direct evidence is lacking. An interesting feature of peptides characterized by a Phe–Met–Arg–Phe–NH$_2$ sequence, the so-called FMRFamide peptides, such as NPFF and NPAF, is the fact that they do not only exert their action through GPCRs, but also ion channel-associated receptors. In mammals this is the so-called acid-sensing ion channel (ASIC) (Lingueglia et al., 2006). The ASIC channel in turn has been shown to play a role in the modulation of conditioning fear (Wemmie et al., 2003). But clearly more studies are needed before firm conclusions can be drawn.

Taken together, it becomes obvious that the preclinical literature links a wide variety of different neuropeptides to anxiety. Table 3 summarizes these findings, grouping the peptides into different categories according to the evidence provided to suggest therapeutic benefit. Since the most compelling evidence comes from human studies, those peptides showing alterations in anxiety disorders or having effects on anxiety in healthy volunteers score highest, followed by the strength of evidence from the animal literature. According to this scheme, TRH stands relatively high in the list, even though there is only inconsistent evidence from human studies and no animal data to support an important role in anxiety. Insufficient evidence to make a link to anxiety exists for a number of peptides. This can either be due to the fact that negative data have been reported or, more often that no data exist yet in the literature.

Table 4 summarizes those peptides that have been linked to anxiety and their binding sites, which could provide potential targets for the development of novel anxiolytic drugs. Because the development of agonists poses different challenges from the development of antagonistic drugs, peptide targets are grouped according to their presumed antagonistic or agonistic requirements to induce anxiolytic effects.

IV. Neurochemical evidence linking neuropeptides and the mechanism of action of clinically used anxiolytic drugs

Currently used anxiolytic drugs either increase GABAergic activity, such as the benzodiazepines, or serotonergic activity, such as the selective serotonin reuptake inhibitors (SSRIs). Another part in the puzzle to answer whether neuropeptides could play an important role as novel therapeutic targets for treatment of anxiety disorders is the evaluation of the effects of currently used clinical anxiolytic drugs on peptide systems.

IV.A. Effects of benzodiazepines on peptidergic systems

Possibly the strongest evidence for a modulatory function of anxiolytic drugs on peptidergic activity comes from the CRF field: Chronic benzodiazepine treatment has been reported to downregulate CRF receptor expression in the frontal cortex and hippocampus in rats, and similar tendencies have been reported in other brain areas, except for the pituitary, where a tendency for an increase was seen (Grigoriadis et al., 1989). Although CRF receptor subtypes were not specified in this study, the expression pattern suggests that it is a decrease of CRF_1 receptor binding that is seen following chronic benzodiazepine treatment, at least at the level of the frontal cortex. In addition, $GABA_A$ receptor subunits containing the benzodiazepine binding site are expressed on CRF-positive neurons in the PVN (Cullinan, 2000), benzodiazepines attenuate stress-induced CRF mRNA expression (Imaki and Vale, 1993) and CRF-like immunoreactivity in the PVN (Inglefield et al., 1993). A decrease in CRF mRNA expression was also seen in the LC following benzodiazepines (Owens and Nemeroff, 1993). A reduction of CRF mRNA expression has also been reported in the central nucleus of the amygdala following treatment with the benzodiazepine alprazolam (Stout et al., 2001). In line with these findings, it has been reported that the stress-induced increase in plasma ACTH is antagonized by benzodiazepines (Wilson et al., 1996a; Welt et al., 2006). Benzodiazepine withdrawal, on the other hand, has been shown to activate the HPA axis in animals (Skelton et al., 2004) and human (Wichniak et al., 2004), and to increase CRF mRNA expression in the cerebral cortex in rats (Skelton et al., 2004). This suggests that some of the anxiolytic effects of benzodiazepines could be mediated through downregulation of the CRF system.

A number of studies also investigated the effects of manipulations of the benzodiazepine receptor on the CCK system, although the picture is less clear than with CRF. The anxiogenic benzodiazepine receptor inverse agonist FG7142 induced CCK mRNA expression in the basolateral amygdala and hippocampus (Pratt and Brett, 1995). Likewise, withdrawal from diazepam led to an upregulation of CCK receptors in frontal cortex and hippocampus (Harro et al., 1990). However, chronic benzodiazepine treatment also seems to increase activity of the CCK system, as CCK-like immunoreactivity was upregulated in the cingulate cortex, periaqueductal gray, and ventral tegmental area of rats receiving continuous clonazepam infusions for 14 days (Brodin et al., 1994). Moreover, long-term diazepam treatment increased the number of CCK binding sites in the olfactory cortex (Harro et al., 1990). However, a reduction in neuronal responsiveness to CCK in the hippocampus has also been reported following chronic treatment with benzodiazepines (Bouthillier and De Montigny, 1988). Interestingly, CCK_2 receptor antagonism failed to substitute for diazepam in a drug discrimination procedure (Jackson et al., 1994), suggesting that the interoceptive state induced by the benzodiazepine cue differs from the effect of CCK_2 receptor blockade. Along similar lines, CCK-8 was unable to block the discriminative stimulus effect of chlordiazepoxide in rats (Fox et al., 2001).

Fewer studies have been published on the effects of benzodiazepines on other peptide systems in the brain. A role for benzodiazepines in the modulation of SST activity has also been suggested, as sub-chronic to chronic diazepam administration has been reported to reduce the number and function of sst receptors in the frontoparietal cortex and hippocampus of rats (Martinez and Arilla, 1993; Martinez-Ferrer et al., 2000). Preprotachykinin mRNA was also reduced in the striatum following chronic diazepam treatment (Lucas et al., 1997). Moreover, diazepam has been reported to reverse conditioned fear-induced alterations in NPY-like immunoreactivity in the amygdala, nucleus accumbens, hypothalamus, and frontal cortex in rats (Krysiak et al., 2000). Both acute (Llorens-Cortes et al., 1990) and chronic (Lucas et al., 1997) treatment with diazepam reduced the activity of the ENK in the striatum. Furthermore, long-term diazepam treatment has been shown to increase mRNA levels of DYN (Lucas et al., 1997), although others reported reduced DYN levels found in various brain regions following chronic midazolam treatment (Rattan and Tejwani, 1997).

More recently, an increase in AVP release was reported at the level of the PVN following treatment with the benzodiazepine temazepam (Welt et al., 2006). At that level, AVP has been suggested to facilitate normalization of an activated HPA axis (Wotjak et al., 2002). Table 5 summarizes the findings with benzodiazepines on the peptide systems mentioned above.

IV.B. Effects of selective serotonin re-uptake inhibitors (SSRIs) on peptidergic systems

The second large group of drugs used to treat anxiety disorders are the SSRIs. The activity of the HPA axis was also downregulated following chronic treatment with the SSRI citalopram (Jensen et al., 1999; Hesketh et al., 2005; Jongsma et al., 2005), comparable to what has been reported following chronic benzodiazepine treatment. Moreover, it has been reported that chronic treatment with citalopram upregulated AVP mRNA in the PVN (Hesketh et al., 2005), which again could be interpreted as an enhanced ability of the system to normalize an activated HPA axis (Wotjak et al., 2002). Interestingly, the SSRI paroxetine normalized an AVP hyperdrive in rats originally bred for the expression of high anxiety (HAB), while it had no significant effect on AVP mRNA expression in animals exhibiting low anxiety-related behavior (LAB) (Keck et al., 2003). This may imply that the effects of SSRIs differ, depending on whether the activity of the HPA axis has been acutely or chronically upregulated, the latter of which is the case in HAB rats and also seen in various psychopathological conditions. Contrary to benzodiazepines, however, it has been reported that acute SSRI administration activated the HPA axis (Jensen et al., 1999). Likewise, acute treatment with an SSRI prolonged the activation of the HPA axis induced by acute stress, presumably via upregulation of AVP in the PVN (Hesketh et al., 2005), in line with the fact that acute SSRI administration can lead to a transiently increased anxiety (Grillon et al., 2007). Acute citalopram

Table 5. Effects of benzodiazepines and SSRIs on peptide systems in the brain

Neuropeptide	Benzodiazepine effect	SSRI effect
CRF	↓	↓ (chronic)
CCK	±	
SST	(↓)	
NPY	(↓)	Ø (chronic)
ENK	(↓)	
DYN	(±)	
AVP	(↑)	(↑) (chronic)
OT		(↑) (acute)

Note: data may be region-specific and activity may differ according to area under investigation, as well as whether drugs were given acute or chronic. See text for further details.
Ø, unchanged; ↑, activation; ↓, inhibition; ±, conflicting evidence; ( ), limited evidence.

treatment, however, also increased OT mRNA in the PVN (Hesketh et al., 2005), which, if at all, could be associated with anxiolytic-like rather than anxiogenic-like effects (see above) – although it is currently unclear whether it is the PVN where OT mediates its anxiolytic-like effects (Table 5). No effects were seen in NPY activity following chronic citalopram treatment (Husum et al., 2000).

IV.C. Effects of peptides on GABA function

Conversely, the neuropeptides mentioned above may interact with the target systems of benzodiazepines and SSRIs, i.e., the GABAergic and serotonergic systems, or with the noradrenergic system, which has also been strongly implicated in anxiety-related processes.

Studies investigating the effects of neuropeptides on in vivo GABA release in brain areas relevant to anxiety, such as the amygdala, the bed nucleus of the stria terminalis, the prefrontal cortex, the hippocampus, the periaqueductal gray or the PVN, are sparse. However, it can be assumed that a number of peptides are co-released with GABA as GABA and neuropeptides are co-localized in these areas. Thus, co-localization with GABA has been described for CCK (Sloviter et al., 2001; Somogyi et al., 2004), NPY (Sloviter et al., 2001), SST (Esclapez and Houser, 1995; Sloviter et al., 2001), and VIP (Sloviter et al., 2001) in the hippocampus. GABAergic interneurons containing

SST have also been described in the prefrontal cortex (Jones et al., 1988; Kubota et al., 1994) and in the amygdala (McDonald and Mascagni, 2002). Frontal GABAergic interneurons also contain NPY (Jones et al., 1988; Kubota et al., 1994) and SP (Jones et al., 1988). Furthermore, amygdaloid GABAergic neurons co-express CRF (Day et al., 1999), CCK (McDonald and Pearson, 1989), ENK (Day et al., 1999), END (Oertel et al., 1983), NPY (McDonald and Pearson, 1989; Oberto et al., 2001), SST (McDonald and Pearson, 1989), NT (Day et al., 1999), and VIP (McDonald and Pearson, 1989).

A role of bombesin-like peptides may be suggested as GRP infused into the ventral hippocampus by reverse dialysis led to an increase in hippocampal GABA levels (Andrews et al., 2000). This finding would be in line with the anxiolytic-like effects reported for GRP (Table 3). Moreover, hippocampal, as well as prefrontal cortical, GABA release were activated by NT (Rakovska et al., 1998; Petrie et al., 2005). TRH has also been reported to increases GABA release in the hippocampus (Deng et al., 2006). However, the behavioral consequences of this effect for the modulation of anxiety remain unclear at this moment, given the limited evidence for a role of both NT and TRH in the modulation of this type of behavior.

A number of in vitro and ex vivo experiments also reported inhibitory effects of neuropeptides on the hippocampal GABAergic system: ANG II inhibited potassium-induced GABA release in hippocampal slices (Hadjiivanova and Georgiev, 1998), which would be in line with the anxiogenic-like properties of this peptide. Likewise, a reduction in GABA release, but this time at the level of the periaqueductal gray was reported for SST (Connor et al., 2004). The relevance of the latter finding for the modulation of anxiety-related behavior can be questioned, given the rather weak association of SST with anxiolytic-like effects. Even more confusing is the finding that OFQ/N decreased GABAergic transmission in slice preparations from the amygdala (Meis and Pape, 2001; Roberto and Siggins, 2006). It is possible that modulation of GABAergic interneurons at these sites may lead to inhibition of brain areas downstream the BNST, thereby leading to anxiolytic-like effects, but it is clear that the effect differs from that of the classical benazodiazepines. Along similar lines, it has been shown that GABAergic transmission in the bed nucleus of the stria terminalis is enhanced by CRF, while NPY inhibits it at this brain level (Kash and Winder, 2006), findings which are difficult to conceptualize with the anxiogenic- and anxiolytic-like effects of the two neuropeptides. Moreover, a modulatory role of GABAergic neurotransmission has been reported for NPFF. This peptide activates GABAergic neurons in the PVN, thereby inhibiting magnocellular neurosecretory cells that synthesize AVP and OT (Jhamandas et al., 2006), which subsequently could lead to altered stress-responsivity and anxiety-related behavior.

IV.D. Effects of peptides on serotonergic function

More evidence indicates important interactions between different neuropeptides and the serotonergic system. One peptide that has been strongly indicated in the modulation of serotonergic activity is CRF and it has been suggested that this interaction plays an important role in the mediation of anxiety-related behavior (Linthorst, 2005). A number of studies reported that ICV administration of CRF induces serotonin release in the hippocampus in rats (Linthorst et al., 2002; Kagamiishi et al., 2003; De Groote et al., 2005), although reductions of 5-HT release have been reported in the lateral septum after ICV or intradorsal raphe nucleus injections of CRF (Price and Lucki, 2001). It is interesting to note that acute stress also has differential effects on serotonin release in different brain areas and stressors such as swim stress also lead to a reduction of serotonin release in the lateral septum – effects likely mediated by distinct projections from the dorsal raphe nucleus to the forebrain (Waselus et al., 2006). Moreover, an immediate increase in serotonin release was seen in the central nucleus of the amygdala following infusion of CRF into the dorsal raphe, and this increase was positively correlated with the induction of freezing behavior in rats, opening the possibility that an increase in serotonin in the central nucleus of the amygdala may be necessary for the expression of fear behavior (Forster et al., 2006). This effect may be CRF_1 or CRF_2 receptor mediated as both are expressed within the dorsal raphe. The exact localization of the CRF_1 receptor remains unclear. However, the CRF_2 receptor is expressed at both serotonergic neurons and at GABAergic interneurons within this area (Day et al., 2004). Interestingly, cessation of freezing behavior correlated with a delayed and prolonged increase in serotonin release within the medial prefrontal cortex in the study of Forster et al. (2006). This opens the possibility that the increase in prefrontal serotonin levels may be necessary for the termination of this fear reaction (Forster et al., 2006). Thus, serotonin may play different roles in the mediation of this behavior, depending on the brain area under investigation.

ICV administrations of UCN1 (Linthorst et al., 2002; De Groote et al., 2005), UCN2, or UCN3 (De Groote et al., 2005) all induce 5-HT release in the hippocampus in rats. Similar effects were seen in the basolateral amygdala following infusion of UCN2 directly into the dorsal raphe nucleus (Amat et al., 2004). These findings indicate that it is not only the CRF_1 but also the CRF_2 receptor mediating the effects of CRF-related peptides on serotonin release. Likewise, AVP has been reported to augment serotonergic activity in the hippocampus (Auerbach and Lipton, 1982).

Rex and colleagues investigated the effects of CCK on serotonergic activity. Although CCK does not seem to have major effects under resting conditions on serotonin release in the lateral prefrontal cortex of guinea pigs, both CCK-4 and the CCK_2 agonist BOC-CCK-4 potentiated the rise in prefrontal serotonin in guinea pigs when exposed to an aversive situation (Rex et al., 1997; Rex and Fink, 1998). Likewise, activation of the serotonergic system has been reported for SP, SST, and ORX. Microinjections of the tachykinin SP directly into the dorsal raphe nucleus increased extracellular levels of serotonin in the ventral hippocampus in rats (Gradin et al., 1992). This effect has been suggested to be indirect, i.e., via NK_1 receptors expressed on GABAergic

interneurons within the dorsal raphe (Ma and Bleasdale, 2002). However, a recent study by Lacoste et al. (2006) showed that NK1 receptors are also expressed on serotonergic neurons in the rat. Thus, the effects induced by SP infusions directly into the dorsal raphe may depend on the exact type of neuron affected. Along these lines, it has been shown that most of the dorsal raphe neurons were inhibited by SP microinfusion, but that in some cases this was preceded by a brief activation, and pure excitation was also observed in a small population of neurons (Valentino et al., 2003).

Augmented serotonin release was also observed in cortical, hippocampal, and hypothalamic slice preparations from rat brain following superfusion with SST (Tanaka and Tsujimoto, 1981). Both ORX-A and ORX-B induce raphe serotonin release following infusions into the raphe nucleus (Tao et al., 2006; see Table 3). Conversely, hippocampal serotonin release was attenuated by ICV administration of GAL (Ogren et al., 1998; Kehr et al., 2002; Yoshitake et al., 2003a, b) or infusions of GAL directly into the dorsal raphe nucleus (Kehr et al., 2002; Table 3). GAL is co-expressed in serotonergic neurons in the dorsal raphe nucleus, where it causes hyperpolarization at high concentrations and prolongs monoamine-induced outward currents at low concentrations (Hokfelt et al., 1999).

Taken together, it appears that peptides with anxiogenic-like properties lead to an increase in serotonin in brain areas such as the hippocampus, prefrontal cortex and amygdala, while peptides with anxiolytic-like properties may lead to decreased serotonergic activity – this at least holds true for GAL at hippocampal level. It is, therefore, conceivable that part of the acute effects of neuropeptides on anxiety-related behavior may be mediated via the serotonergic system. This is in line with the anxiogenic-like effects sometimes reported following acute treatment with SSRIs (Bagdy et al., 2001). It would be interesting to better understand the effects of these peptides following chronic administration. However, no studies investigating the effects of chronic administration of neuropeptides on serotonin release are reported in the literature.

184

IV.E. Effects of peptides on noradrenergic function

Activation of the noradrenergic system has also been associated with stress responsivity, arousal (Berridge, 2005), and increased anxiety-related behavior (Brunello et al., 2003). Both CRF and UCN1 administration increased hippocampal noradrenaline (Page and Abercrombie, 1999; Palamarchouk et al., 2002; De Groote et al., 2005). Likewise, ICV CRF increased hypothalamic (Lavicky and Dunn, 1993) and prefrontal (Lavicky and Dunn, 1993; Finlay et al., 1997; Murphy et al., 2003) noradrenaline release in rats, especially under stressful conditions (Finlay et al., 1997). Furthermore, direct infusions of CRF into the LC have been reported to increase noradrenaline release in the parietal cortex of rats (Schulz and Lehnert, 1996). This effect may be CRF_1 receptor mediated as the CRF_1 receptor is expressed on noradrenergic LC neurons (Sauvage and Steckler, 2001). Activation of the CRF_2 receptor also affects the noradrenergic system, although the effects may be qualitatively and quantitatively different: De Groote et al. (2005) showed that UCN2 and UCN3 elevated the noradrenaline metabolite MHPG in the hippocampus, but did not alter noradrenaline itself. Moreover, the temporal pattern of these effects differed when compared to the effects of CRF and UCN1 (De Groote et al., 2005).

There are a number of other peptides with anxiogenic-like properties that interact with the noradrenergic system: ANG II administered ICV (Stadler et al., 1992) or microinjected into the subfornical organ (Tanaka et al., 2001) elicited noradrenaline release at the level of the hypothalamic PVN. Increased noradrenaline activity in turn leads to the release of AVP from the PVN (Veltmar et al., 1992). Thus, ANG II-induced activation of the noradrenergic projection to the PVN is one mechanism through which ANG II can stimulate the HPA axis (Aguilera et al., 1995).

Moreover, SP seems to activate the noradrenergic system, an effect that may be mediated via both the NK_1 and the NK_3 receptors. ICV administrations of the NK1 peptidergic agonists [SAR(9),-Met(O(2))(11)]-SP and septide, as well as of the NK_3 peptidergic agonist senktide, have been shown to stimulate the LC and to increase noradrenaline release in the medial prefrontal cortex of guinea pigs (Jung et al., 1996; Bert et al., 2002). Further evidence for an important role of the NK_1 receptor in the mediation of this effect comes from double-immunostaining studies showing that this receptor is directly expressed on noradrenergic neurons of the LC (Ma and Bleasdale, 2002). Yet another anxiogenic-like peptide activating the noradrenergic LC is ORX-A (Walling et al., 2004).

Conversely, peptides with anxiolytic-like properties may suppress noradrenergic activity. This has been reported for a number of peptides, including END, NPY, GAL, as well as for OFQ/N. Stress-induced activation of noradrenaline release was attenuated by END in the hypothalamus, amygdala, and hippocampus (Quirarte et al., 1998; Tanaka et al., 2000). Likewise, the other opioid peptide DYN or the DYN-fragment DYN(1–13) also inhibited stimulated noradrenaline release from rabbit hippocampal slices (Jackisch et al., 1986).

A reduction of extracellular hippocampal noradrenaline was also seen in the hippocampus following ICV infusion of GAL (Yoshitake et al., 2003a, 2004), although GAL infusions directly into the PVN have been reported to increase noradrenaline levels in the PVN in rats (Kyrkouli et al., 1992). GAL is strongly co-localized with noradrenaline in the LC (Hokfelt et al., 1999; Morilak et al., 2003). At high concentrations, it causes hyperpolarization of LC noradrenergic neurons, while at low concentrations it prolongs noradrenaline-induced outward currents (Hokfelt et al., 1999), which may explain the biphasic effects reported in the literature.

Furthermore, a reduction in basal PVN noradrenaline levels was induced by ICV administration of NPY (Hastings et al., 1997). But the opposite effect of NPY, i.e., an enhanced release of noradrenaline in the PVN, was seen when noradrenaline release was stimulated with potassium (Pavia et al., 1995). This could suggest that the net effect of NPY on noradrenaline release at the level of the PVN may also be stimulatory. However, the possibly most relevant study in relation to stress and anxiety comes from Shibasaki et al. (1995), demonstrating that centrally administered NPY suppressed stress-induced noradrenaline release in the PVN in vivo. To complete the picture, it is noteworthy that NPY has also been shown to be co-located with noradrenaline in noradrenergic neurons, in particular in the nucleus of the solitary tract, while less neurons expressing both noradrenaline and NPY are seen in the LC (Pau et al., 1997), adding further evidence for potentially important interactions between this peptide and monoaminergic systems.

Finally, the basal release of noradrenaline in the basolateral nucleus of the amygdala may be under tonic inhibitory control by endogenous OFQ/N through the OFQ/N peptide receptors localized within the basolateral nucleus of the amygdala. Supporting this hypothesis, it has been shown that local infusion of OFQ/N into the basolateral amygdala with reverse microdialysis reduced noradrenaline release in that nucleus (Kawahara et al., 2004; Table 3).

IV.F. Effects of peptides on HPA axis function

Another brain system closely linked to anxiety is the HPA axis. This axis is usually activated in conjunction with an anxious reaction. Therefore, evidence showing that the HPA axis is under control of a peptidergic system may further strengthen the link between that system and anxiety.

Both CRF and AVP are key peptides activating the HPA axis, and ACTH is an integral component of this axis (Abel and Majzoub, 2005; Fulford and Harbuz, 2005). Activation of the HPA axis has also been reported by a multitude of other peptides, including CCK (Biro et al., 1993; Malendowicz et al., 2003), CGRP (Kovacs et al., 1995), GLP/1 (Larsen et al., 1997), ghrelin (Jaszberenyi et al., 2006), HCRT/ORX (Jaszberenyi et al., 2000; Al-Barazanji et al., 2001; Samson et al., 2007), MCH (Smith et al., 2006), α-MSH (Dhillo et al., 2002; Hillebrand et al., 2005), NMU (Thompson et al., 2004; Jethwa et al., 2006), NPW (Taylor et al., 2005), NPY (Wahlestedt et al., 1987; Brunton et al., 2006), and PACAP (Agarwal et al., 2005). Interestingly, CCK and CRF are co-localized in neurons of the PVN (Mezey et al., 1985), suggesting that the two peptides act synergistically in the regulation of the HPA axis.

In contrast, anxiolytic like peptides such as ANP (Wiedemann et al., 2000) and OT (Windle et al., 1997) reduce the activity of the HPA axis. However, an inhibition of basal HPA axis activity has also been reported by SP (Chowdrey et al., 1990; Jessop et al., 2000) and OFQ/N (Devine et al., 2001; Fulford and Harbuz, 2005; Leggett et al., 2006), peptides thought to have anxiogenic-like properties, while ENK and DYN(1–13) stimulated the HPA axis (Iyengar et al., 1987). Thus, the association between effects on anxiety-related behavior and actions on the HPA axis does not necessarily hold for all peptides, but in these cases there seems to be an uncoupling between effects on the HPA axis and behavioral alterations.

Table 3 summarizes the main behavioral and neurochemical findings and lists the different peptides ranked according to the weight of evidence that links a peptide system to the modulation of anxiety. CRF seems to be the peptide most strongly implicated in this type of behaviors. There is good clinical evidence and a substantial animal literature, showing prominent anxiogenic-like effects following central administration of CRF, as well as strong neurochemical evidence, supporting this notion. Based on the human literature and preclinical data, CCK is ranked second. Of course, less data have been published on more recently discovered peptides. Hence, the ranking does not just reflect the strength of the data associating a given peptide with anxiety, but also the body of literature published on this topic.

The most prominent targets for drug development within these systems are listed in Table 4. The last section of this chapter will focus on these targets.

V. Many peptide candidates: convergence onto common pathways?

From the above described interactions between the various peptide systems with GABAergic, serotonergic, and noradrenergic systems and the HPA axis it can already be concluded that these peptidergic mechanisms do not act in isolation, but that we can identify a network of peptide and other neurotransmitter systems, interacting and modulating anxiety-related behavior.

Furthermore, peptides also influence each other's activity, which may be an additional facet influencing anxiety-related behavior. As mentioned above, CCK and CRF are co-localized in neurons of the PVN (Mezey et al., 1985; Juaneda et al., 1999; Cournil et al., 2000), suggesting that the two peptides act synergistically in the regulation of the HPA axis and act in concert in response to stress. Further support for the idea that the two systems act in synergy comes from findings that the anxiogenic-like response in the rat elevated plus-maze and activation of the HPA axis induced by ICV CCK-8 was prevented by pretreatment with a CRF antiserum or the non-specific CRF receptor antagonist α-helical CRF (αhCRF) (Biro et al., 1993). ICV administration of CRF to rats reduced CCK-like immunoreactivity in the medial frontal and anterior cingulate cortices (Takamatsu et al., 1991), which may reflect compensatory mechanisms. Conversely, chronic CRF_1 receptor blockade resulted in upregulation of CCK_2 binding sites in rats (Lodge and Lawrence, 2003). This example illustrates the complex interactions not only between non-peptidergic and peptidergic systems, but also between different peptide systems, all of which could lead to fine-tuning of anxiety-related behavior. Furthermore, these types of interactions could have consequences for the long-term efficacy of pharmacological therapies to treat anxiety disorders. For example, it is conceivable that the long-term efficacy of CRF_1 antagonists could decrease due to compensatory processes in the CCK system. However, so far there is no evidence for altered anxiolytic-like activity of CRF_1 antagonism following chronic administration (Lelas et al., 2004).

Interactions have also been observed between other peptides systems, for example, between SP and CRF. In vitro, SP induced expression of the CRF_1 receptor in human astrocytoma cells via activation of the NK_1 receptor (Hamke et al., 2006). NK_1 receptor-containing dendrites radiate around neurons expressing CRF and serotonin in the dorsomedial dorsal raphe nucleus (Valentino and Commons, 2005). Thus, treatments manipulating NK_1 function, for example, NK1 antagonists, can be expected to affect anxiety-related behavior also via secondary mechanisms induced by altered CRF activity. In addition, the effects of both the CRF and the SP systems on, for example, noradrenergic mechanisms suggest that there may be important indirect interactions between these two peptide systems at this monoaminergic level. Indeed, it has been shown that CRF-induced LC cell firing is reduced following blockade of the NK_2 receptor (Steinberg et al., 2001). Thus, part of the anxiogenic-like effects of SP may be mediated via an activation of the CRF system, possibly via activation of NK_1 and/or NK_2 receptors.

Some of the arousing effects of CRF, a key component of anxiety responses, have been suggested to be due to activation of the noradrenergic system (Berridge, 2005). Another pathway through which CRF may affect arousal is via CRF_1 receptor mediated depolarization of HCRT/ORX neurons in the lateral hypothalamus (Winsky-Sommerer et al., 2005). This in turn should lead to activation of the HCRT/ORX system, thereby increasing arousal. Thus, blockade of CRF_1 receptors may in part lead to anxiolytic-like effects via inhibition of the HCRT/ORX system, besides having effects on noradrenergic and other systems. HCRT/ORX neurons in turn connect to NPY neurons (Horvath et al., 1999). This is yet another example illustrating the complex network of peptide systems that could be involved in modulating anxiety-related behavior.

As mentioned before, NPY is considered a protective stress factor, likely to also play an opposing role to the anxiogenic effects of CRF (Sajdyk et al., 2004; Valdez and Koob, 2004; Shekhar et al., 2005). Sites where the two peptides interact are the amygdala (Heilig et al., 1994; Sajdyk et al., 2004, 2006), the bed nucleus of the stria terminalis (Kash and Winder, 2006), the hypothalamus, where NPY stimulates CRF (Hastings et al., 2001), the LC (Charney, 2004) and the lateral septum, where NPY reversed the anxiogenic-like effects of CRF (Kask et al., 2001). For example, the CRF antagonist αhCRF has been shown to block the anxiogenic effects of Y$_1$ receptor blockade (Kask et al., 1997). Indirect interactions may be mediated via HCRT/ORX or other mechanisms. Ghrelin is yet another peptide being involved in the complex interactions between NPY and CRF. Axons of hypothalamic ghrelin neurons innervate NPY axons presynaptically in the hypothalamic arcuate nucleus and in the PVN, where ghrelin activates the NPY system (Cowley et al., 2003). Furthermore, ghrelin increases the rate of secretion of GABA at this level, which may lead to a further increase in the secretion of NPY. Both altered GABA and NPY release in turn modulates the activity of CRF neurons (Cowley et al., 2003). Thus, there are complex interactions between ghrelin, hypocretin, NPY, CRF, and GABA, the net effect of which may be difficult to predict. Another site where CRF, NPY, and GABA interact is the bed nucleus of the stria terminalis, where CRF increases GABAergic transmission, while GABAergic transmission is inhibited by NPY (Kash and Winder, 2006).

Another peptide considered an endogenous counterplayer to CRF is ANP (Arlt et al., 2003). ANP has been shown to decrease CRF release from the rat hypothalamus in vitro (Ibanez-Santos et al., 1990) and to counteract the sympathetic activation induced by intravenous injections of CRF in human volunteers (Arlt et al., 2003). Interestingly, the anxiogenic-like effects of CNP, another natriuretic peptide (see above), were reversed by αhCRF (Jahn et al., 2001). As discussed before, ANG II in turn is considered to be the natural counterpart of ANP. ANG II also has been shown to regulate CRF systems (Saavedra and Pavel, 2005). The AT$_1$ receptor is expressed on CRF-positive neurons in the PVN (Tsutsumi and Saavedra, 1991) and stimulation of AT$_1$ by ANG II has been suggested to activate the HPA axis, presumably by both stimulating CRF and AVP release (Saavedra and Pavel, 2005). Furthermore, it has been shown that blockade of AT$_1$ receptors could prevent stress-induced down-regulation of cortical CRF$_1$ receptors (Saavedra et al., 2006).

Clearly, these few examples indicate the interdependencies of different neuropeptide systems as well as their interaction with aminergic and monoaminergic systems. It is evident that we must consider these complex networks when discussing mechanisms involved in anxiety, and should not see single systems in isolation. Only an integrated view of the various players will eventually allow understanding why so many different systems are involved in anxiety-related processes, and will help to delineate the major players from those which play relatively minor roles in the modulation of these processes. The picture that seems to emerge, however, is that certain peptides, such as CRF, are central in the modulation of anxiety-related behavior and stress-responses.

VI. Development of small molecule, non-peptide compounds for peptidergic targets

In the preceding sections, the peptide systems thought to be of relevance for anxiety and anxiety disorders have been delineated, and possible therapeutic targets within these systems have been identified. The last part of this review will discuss the progress made in developing small molecule, non-peptide compounds acting at these targets.

A number of requirements must be met when developing drugs targeting peptidergic receptors. First, they should have drug-like properties, i.e., they should be soluble, bioavailable, metabolically stable, and brain penetrant. In general, peptidergic drugs do not fulfill these requirements. Non-peptide drugs acting at peptidergic binding sites meet some of these requirements, but often high-molecular weight, low solubility, and brain penetration remain major issues. Second, compounds should be potent and selective. Usually, this requirement is more easily achieved, at least in vitro. However, it can be a challenge to overcome these issues as the chemical diversity of small molecule, non-peptidergic compounds acting at peptidergic targets can be relatively limited – at least when compared to other psychoactive compounds acting at the classical targets.

Depending on target, some compounds should act as antagonists, while others should act as agonists, to show anxiolytic-like activity (Table 4). The discovery and development of compounds

188

acting as antagonists can be considered easier than the development of compounds acting as agonists, partly because agonistic drugs may induce fast receptor desensitization and internalization, hence leading to the development of tolerance against the compound.

Yet another issue to be considered is the side-effect profile that can be related or unrelated to the mechanism of action. Especially compounds interacting with key homeostatic mechanisms, such as compounds targeting peptide systems involved in, for example, regulation of the HPA axis, gonadotrophins, growth hormones, food intake, or salt and water balance, to name just a few, may lead to unacceptable side effects. However, these novel types of compounds also hold great potential, such as being anxiolytic without the sedative or motor side effects, and having no abuse potential characteristic of the benzodiazepines, or lacking the delayed onset of action and sexual side effects seen with the SSRIs.

VI.A. Corticotropin-releasing factor receptor 1 (CRF$_1$) antagonists

The first small molecule, non-peptide CRF$_1$ antagonists were published in a patent from Nova Pharmaceuticals (Nova Pharm. Corp., 1991). Since then a number of structurally closely related compounds with monocyclic, bicyclic, or tricyclic, often pyridine- or pyrimidine-scaffolds, coupled to an amine have been published (Steckler, 2005; Steckler and Dautzenberg, 2006).

Non-peptidergic CRF$_1$ antagonists have been published to have state-dependent anxiolytic-like properties in a wide range of animal tests, i.e., under conditions of heightened anxiety, but less so under euthymic conditions, when administered acutely (see Steckler and Holsboer, 1999; Holmes et al., 2003a; Zorrilla and Koob, 2004; Steckler, 2005; Steckler and Dautzenberg, 2006, for reviews). These states of heightened anxiety can be induced by emotional or pharmacological stressors, such as by acute stress exposure (Chaki et al., 2004; Steckler et al., 2006), acute administration of an anxiogenic compound, such as CRF itself (Zorrilla et al., 2002), during withdrawal

from alcohol (Knapp et al., 2004; Overstreet et al., 2004), or result from early trauma, such as in adult rats that underwent postnatal maternal separation (Maciag et al., 2002). However, heightened anxiety can also be genetically determined, i.e., reflect increased trait anxiety, such as in rats selectively bred for heightened anxiety-related behavior. Again, blockade of the CRF$_1$ receptor is anxiolytic-like under these conditions (Keck et al., 2001). This clearly differentiates the CRF$_1$ antagonists from "classical" anxiolytic drugs such as the benzodiazepines, which already show anxiolytic-like effects under basal conditions. Further support for the notion that CRF$_1$ antagonists and benzodiazepines differ in their central activity comes from studies showing that CRF$_1$ antagonism does not substitute for benzodiazepine cues in drug discrimination (Lelas et al., 2003).

Tolerance to the anxiolytic-like effects of CRF$_1$ antagonists does not seem to develop as anxiolytic-like properties of CRF$_1$ blockade were maintained following chronic treatment (Lelas et al., 2004), and no evidence for sedation or ataxia is observed with CRF$_1$ antagonists (Chaki et al., 2004; Li et al., 2005), which is a distinctive advantage over the benzodiazepines.

Sites where CRF$_1$ antagonists exert their anxiolytic-like properties include the central nucleus of the amygdala (Bakshi et al., 2002; Hammack et al., 2003) and the bed nucleus of the stria terminalis (Sahuque et al., 2006). LC cell firing (Schulz et al., 1996; Okuyama et al., 1999a; Steckler et al., 2006) and stress-induced prefrontal (Griebel et al., 2002) and hippocampal (Isogawa et al., 2000) noradrenaline, as well as hippocampal serotonin (Isogawa et al., 2000), release were also inhibited by CRF$_1$ receptor blockade. Furthermore, CRF$_1$ antagonism normalizes HPA axis activity following stress, but has no or only mild effects on basal HPA axis activity (Schulz et al., 1996; Steckler and Dautzenberg, 2006; Steckler et al., 2006; Ising et al., 2007), which is in line with the behavioral data.

In human, CRF$_1$ antagonism has also been shown to have anxiolytic properties. In an open label clinical study in depressed patients, beneficial effects of CRF$_1$ receptor blockade by the

CRF$_1$ antagonist R121919 was seen in both depression and anxiety scores (Zobel et al., 2000). More recently, it has been shown that another CRF$_1$ antagonist, NBI-34041, failed to alter stress-induced increases in emotionality in the Trier social stress test in healthy volunteers, but attenuated the stress-induced activation of the HPA axis (Ising et al., 2007), suggesting that resistance to psychosocial stress was enhanced.

Thus, there is good, albeit almost exclusively preclinical, evidence suggesting that CRF$_1$ antagonists could represent potent therapeutic opportunities for the treatment of anxiety disorders, especially for PTSD and panic disorder. It is of note, however, that only a few clinical data have been reported with CRF$_1$ antagonists for the last 7 years, suggesting difficulties in the development of this class of compounds. No small molecule compounds acting at CRF$_2$ receptors have been disclosed.

VI.B. Cholecystokinin receptor 2 (CCK$_2$) antagonists

Research on CCK antagonists has been conducted for about the last 20 years. CCK$_2$ antagonists have a relatively rich chemical diversity, ranging from amino acid derivatives, benzodiazepine-, benzazepine-, ureidoacetamide-, or quinazolinone-derivatives, dipeptoids, and heteroaromatic scaffolds, to name just a few (Herranz, 2003).

Preclinically, anxiolytic-like effects of CCK$_2$ receptor blockade have not always been demonstrated (Griebel, 1999; Herranz, 2003). As for CRF$_1$ receptor antagonists and the CRF system, this may be due to the fact that the CCK system first needs activation by stressful conditions in order to observe reliable anxiolytic-like effects of CCK$_2$ antagonists (Dauge and Lena, 1998), such as under conditions of alcohol withdrawal (Wilson et al., 1998). However, many CCK$_2$ antagonists also exhibit rather poor bioavailability due to low solubility and brain penetration (Chen et al., 1992). Despite these limitations, compounds have been described with potent anxiolytic-like effects in a variety of animal models, comparable to those of the benzodiazepine diazepam (Hughes et al.,

1990; Helton et al., 1996). In animals, these compounds show a number of advantages over the benzodiazepines: they lack sedation, ataxic properties, do not reduce muscle tone, and there is no development of tolerance and no withdrawal-induced increase in anxiety-related behavior – side effects characteristic for benzodiazepines (Hughes et al., 1990; Helton et al., 1996). Interestingly, and as was the case for CRF$_1$ antagonism, CCK$_2$ antagonists also failed to substitute for chlordiazepoxide in drug discrimination (Fox et al., 2001), suggesting again a dissociation between the interoceptive effects of a peptidergic mechanism and benzodiazepines.

One sites of action where CCK$_2$ antagonists affect anxiety-related and panic-like behavior in animals is the periaqueductal gray (Netto and Guimaraes, 2004; Bertoglio and Zangrossi, 2005). Part of the effects seems also mediated via interactions with the serotonergic system. CCK$_2$ antagonism was not only anxiolytic-like in guinea pigs, but also decreased basal extracellular serotonin release in the prefrontal cortex and prevented the increase in extracellular serotonin seen when guinea-pigs were exposed to a stressful situation (Rex et al., 1994).

However, the animal data did not translate into human, where CCK$_2$ antagonists showed negative or mixed results, possibly again in part due to low bioavailability. For example, initial studies with the CCK$_2$ antagonist L-365,260 suggested that the compound was able to antagonize the panic symptoms elicited by IV infusion of pentagastrin in healthy volunteers (Lines et al., 1995) or of CCK-4 in patients suffering from panic disorder (Bradwejn et al., 1994), but these initial results in panic disorder patients were not confirmed in subsequent studies (Sramek et al., 1994–1995; Kramer et al., 1995). The CCK$_2$ antagonist CI-988 was inactive in healthy volunteers following challenge with CCK-4 (Bradwejn et al., 1995), with lactate (Cowley et al., 1996), or in clinical trials in patients with generalized anxiety (Adams et al., 1995; Goddard et al., 1999) or panic disorders (Van Megen et al., 1997b; Pande et al., 1999). Thus, the therapeutic potential of CCK$_2$ antagonists for the treatment of anxiety disorders still needs to be demonstrated.

VI.C. Neurokinin (NK) antagonists

The first small molecule, non-peptide NK_1 antagonist was described in 1991 (Snider et al., 1991). Since then, numerous NK_1 antagonists with high affinity, selectivity, good solubility, and brain penetration have been developed. Initially, the development of NK_1 antagonists for the treatment of psychiatric disorders focused on depression, with conflicting results (Herpfer and Lieb, 2005; Czeh et al., 2006). However, there is increasing evidence for a role of NK_1 antagonism for the treatment of anxiety disorders and centrally active NK_1 antagonists exhibit anxiolytic-like activity in a range of animal models, such as inhibition of distress vocalizations (Kramer et al., 1998; Rupniak et al., 2000, 2001) or of stress-induced hyperthermia (Spooren et al., 2002). NK1 antagonists increase social interaction (File, 1997, 2000; Cheeta et al., 2001; Gentsch et al., 2002) and the time spent on the aversive arms of the elevated plus maze (Santarelli et al., 2001; Varty et al., 2002; but see also Rupniak et al., 2001, for negative results; see also Holmes et al., 2003a; Herpfer and Lieb, 2005; Rupniak, 2005, for reviews).

Parts of these anxiolytic-like effects of NK1 antagonists seem to be mediated at the level of the amygdala (Kramer et al., 1998; Boyce et al., 2001) and the lateral septum (Gavioli et al., 2002a). Another site where NK_1 antagonists exert their anxiolytic-like activity may be the noradrenergic LC as blockade of NK_1 receptors attenuated the stress-induced rise of extracellular noradrenaline in the rat and gerbil medial prefrontal cortex (Renoldi and Invernizzi, 2006). However, chronic, but not acute, NK_1 antagonism induced burst firing of neurons in the LC, suggesting stimulation of the noradrenergic system (Maubach et al., 2002). Moreover, NK_1 receptor blockade increased dorsal raphe neuronal firing rate in guinea pigs (Conley et al., 2002), although others have shown NK_1 antagonism to be also able to attenuate the effects of SP in the small population of rat dorsal raphe neurons that were excited by SP (Valentino et al., 2003). In mice, systemic or intraraphe NK_1 receptor blockade did not change basal cortical serotonin release, but augmented SSRI-induced serotonin release (Guiard et al., 2004).

It is also well known that affinity of NK_1 antagonists varies across species, which may in part explain the discrepant findings. However, the fact that NK1 antagonists can increase serotonergic activity is somewhat at odds with the acute anxiolytic-like effects induced by NK_1 antagonists. Furthermore, it has been reported that NK_1 inhibitors stimulate the HPA axis (Jessop et al., 2000), which is in line with the inhibitory action of SP on HPA axis function (see above and Table 3), but also does not help to explain the anxiolytic-like effects of this class of compounds.

In general, NK_1 receptor antagonists are well tolerated, and might be associated with less nausea and sexual dysfunction than SSRIs, lack sedative effects and do not impair motor function (Holmes et al., 2003a). A few studies have been reported, investigating the effects of NK_1 antagonists on anxiety in man. Kramer et al. (1998) reported anxiolytic effects of the NK_1 antagonist aprepitant (MK-869) in patients with comorbid anxiety and depression, but subsequent studies failed to reveal clear antidepressant effects in patients. A recent clinical study also reported first data with an NK_1 antagonist in patients primarily suffering from an anxiety disorder. In that study, the NK_1 antagonist GR205171 improved social phobia to comparable degree as the SSRI citalopram, and significantly more than placebo (Furmark et al., 2005). Moreover, symptom improvement was paralleled by a reduction in regional cerebral blood flow in response to public speaking in the rhinal cortex, amygdala, and parahippocampal–hippocampal regions (Furmark et al., 2005).

Finally, it should be noted that not only the NK_1 antagonists, but also NK_2 (Walsh et al., 1995; Teixeira et al., 1996; Griebel et al., 2001; Salome et al., 2006a) and NK_3 antagonists (Salome et al., 2006a) have been suggested to have anxiolytic potential. However, a recent pilot study with panic disorder patients who were responders to CCK-4 challenge failed to show any beneficial effect of the NK_3 antagonist osanetant on panic symptomatology when compared to placebo (Kronenberg et al., 2005).

VI.D. Vasopressin (AVP) antagonists

A number of small molecule, non-peptide V_{1A} antagonists (e.g., 4,4-difluorobenzazepine or 1-phenylsulfonylindoline derivatives) have been reported. Some of these compounds are orally bioavailable, but in general they suffer from poor brain penetration and some of them are also non-selective versus the V_2 receptor. Consequently, these compounds are primarily developed for peripheral indications.

Using a non-selective, peptidergic $V_{1A/B}$ receptor antagonist, anxiolytic-like effects were seen following direct infusion into the lateral septum in rats (Liebsch et al., 1996) and in rats bred for high-anxiety-related behavior following infusions into the PVN (Wigger et al., 2004). However, given the strong links between AVP and anxiety, there is a surprising paucity of pharmacological results in the literature on V_{1A} receptor manipulations and anxiety-related behavior.

There is more evidence supporting a role of blockade of the V_{1B} receptor in the modulation of anxiety-related behavior, although it should be mentioned that the data so far reported were generated with one single molecule, which is the carboxamide SSR149415. This compound has been shown to be anxiolytic-like in a number of animal paradigms and across different species (Serradeil-Le Gal et al., 2002; Griebel et al., 2003, 2005; Griebel and Serradeil-Le Gal, 2005; Salome et al., 2006a; Hodgson et al., 2007). Parts of the anxiolytic-like effects of SSR149415 are mediated through V_{1B} receptors expressed in the basolateral nucleus of the amygdala (Salome et al., 2006b), while infusions of the lateral septum with SSR149415 failed to affect anxiety-related behavior (Stemmelin et al., 2005). However, part of the anxiolytic-like effects may also be indirectly mediated via attenuation of the HPA axis as anxiolytic-like effects were absent in social interaction in hypophysectomized rats but present in control animals (Shimazaki et al., 2006). Indeed, SSR149415 has been shown to attenuate stress-induced HPA axis activation (Serradeil-Le Gal et al., 2002; Griebel and Serradeil-Le Gal, 2005), and hence could affect anxiety-related behavior via this route. Furthermore, tail pinch stress-induced (Griebel and Serradeil-Le Gal, 2005), but not pharmacological (FG7142) (Claustre et al., 2006) stress-induced cortical noradrenaline release was blocked by SSR149415. Taken together, these findings suggest that V_{1B} receptor antagonism may represent a promising mechanism for the treatment of anxiety disorders.

VI.E. Neuropeptide receptor 2 (Y_2) antagonists

Compared to the substantial literature on the effects of CRF_1 and CCK_2 antagonists, publications investigating the effects of the NPY Y_2 receptor antagonists on anxiety-related behavior are limited. Only two small molecule, non-peptide Y_2 antagonists have been described to date, namely BIIE0246 (Doods et al., 1999) and the piperidinylindoline cinnamide JNJ-5207787 (Bonaventure et al., 2004). BIIE0245 suffers from a complex structure and high-molecular weight. It likely acts at presynaptic NPY autoreceptors, thereby inhibiting the negative feedback loop on NPY release (Weiser et al., 2000). Recently, anxiolytic-like activity of BIIE0246 has been reported in rats tested on an elevated plus maze (Bacchi et al., 2006). No behavioral data have been reported with JNJ-5207787 yet.

VI.F. Melanocortin receptor 4 (MC_4) antagonists

Anxiolytic-like effects have also been reported following ICV administration of the peptidomimetic MC_4 receptor antagonist MCL0020 to previously stressed mice when they were tested in a light–dark box, as well as in rats tested in a lick suppression paradigm (Chaki et al., 2003b). Another peptidomimetic MC_4 receptor antagonist, HS014, failed to produce anxiolytic-like effects in the elevated plus maze test in rats following ICV administration when tested under baseline conditions, but enhanced the anxiolytic-like effect of alcohol and blocked the anxiogenic-like effects of alcohol withdrawal (Kokare et al., 2006). Furthermore, the non-peptide MC_4 antagonist MCL0129 reversed stress-induced anxiogenic-like effects in rats and mice after peripheral administration (Chaki et al., 2003a) and increased the interaction time in a rat social interaction paradigm following repeated oral administration (Shimazaki and Chaki, 2005).

This would suggest potentially beneficial effects of MC_4 antagonists for the treatment of anxiety disorders. However, blockade of the MC_4 receptor is a highly effective orexigenic mechanism, leading to substantial weight gain (e.g., Kask et al., 1998; Skuladottir et al., 1999), which would be a serious drawback in the treatment of patients suffering from anxiety disorders. Therefore, these types of compounds may be best suited to treat anxiety disorder patients with comorbid illness associated with anorexia or cachexia, but would be poorly tolerated in other patient groups suffering from anxiety disorders.

VI.G. Angiotensin (AT) antagonists

Evidence reviewed above suggests a role of AT_2 agonists in the modulation of anxiety, but reports on selective AT_2 receptor antagonists and their effects on anxiety-related behavior are limited. Data generated with the AT_2 antagonist PD123177 were conflicting, with one study reporting no effects (Shepherd et al., 1996), while a more recent study showed that PD123177 was able to antagonize the increase in anxiety-related behavior induced by AT II in rats (Braszko et al., 2003). As a further caveat, it should be noted that AT_2 receptors are more strongly expressed during development, while in the adult brain the predominant receptor is the AT_1 receptor (Saavedra et al., 2005).

Somewhat more information has been obtained with small molecule AT_1 antagonists, such as candesartan or losartan. Losartan exhibited anxiolytic-like properties in mice (Barnes et al., 1990; Gard et al., 2001), but was inferior to diazepam (Gard et al., 2001). In rats, peripheral treatment with losartan was also anxiolytic-like (Kaiser et al., 1992; but see Shepherd et al., 1996 for conflicting results) and the compound antagonized the increases in anxiety-related behavior induced by AT II in rats (Braszko et al., 2003). Anxiolytic-like effects of the compound were also seen following ICV administration (Kulakowska et al.,

1996), indicating that its effects are centrally mediated. Likewise, a reduction in anxiety-related behavior in rats was seen following repeated peripheral administration of the AT_1 receptor antagonist candesartan (Saavedra et al., 2005, 2006). Moreover, candesartan blocked the HPA axis activation to stress (Armando et al., 2001; Baiardi et al., 2004; Saavedra et al., 2005). More recently, it has been shown that injection of losartan directly into the dorsomedial hypothalamus in "panic-prone" rats (rats with chronic disruption of the GABA-mediated inhibition in the dorsomedial hypothalamus and additional peripheral sodium lactate infusions) blocked the panicogenic effects of sodium lactate (Shekhar et al., 2006), suggesting that AT_1 antagonists mediate at least part of their anxiolytic-like properties at the level of the dorsomedial hypothalamus and, in addition, may hold potential to treat panic disorder.

Given that AT_1 antagonists are widely used to treat hypertension, it is somewhat surprising that these drugs have not been tested in the treatment of anxiety disorders in humans. However, the blood pressure lowering effects of these compounds also represent a potential drawback as this may lead to symptomatic hypotension and may not render these compounds first line treatments for anxiety disorders.

VI.H. Galanin receptor 3 (GAL$_3$) antagonists

Although knockout data would point to a potential anxiolytic role of GAL_1 receptor agonists, no such non-peptide compounds with good in vivo potency and brain penetration have been reported. A peptidergic GAL_1 agonist, M617 [galanin(1–13)-Gln14-bradykinin(2–9)-amide], has been generated (Mazarati et al., 2006), but no effects on anxiety-related behavior have been published. Further, albeit indirect, evidence for a potential role of GAL_1 receptors in the regulation of systems modulating anxiety-related behavior comes from a study by Ma et al. (2001), showing that the mixed $GAL_{1/2}$ agonist AR-M961 [D-Ala(12)]gal(1–16)-NH(2)] has inhibitory effects on LC neurons in vitro. The selective GAL_2 agonist

AR-M1896 [Gal(2–11)-NH(2) (AR-M1896)] was less active, suggesting that it mainly is the GAL_1 receptor that mediates hyperpolarization of LC neurons.

More recently, anxiolytic-like properties were described with small-molecule GAL_3 antagonists (Swanson et al., 2005): These compounds, named SNAP37889 and SNAP398299, are orally active and both compounds enhance rat social interaction. Furthermore, SNAP 37889 reduced guinea pig vocalizations after maternal separation, attenuated stress-induced hyperthermia in mice and increased punished drinking in rats. SNAP 37889 also attenuated the inhibitory influence of GAL on serotonergic transmission at the level of the dorsal raphe nucleus (Swanson et al., 2005), which may be an important mechanism through which GAL_3 antagonists affect anxiety-related behavior.

VI.I. Bombesin receptor 1 (BB_1) antagonists

Another small molecule, non-peptide compound recently shown to have anxiolytic-like effects is the BB_1/BB_2 receptor antagonist PD176252. Central administration of PD176252 showed mild anxiolytic-like effects in the elevated plus maze task in rats (Bedard et al., 2007). Furthermore, the compound increased social interaction, attenuated separation-induced vocalizations in neonatal guinea pigs, reduced novelty-induced inhibition of food intake and fear potentiated startle (Merali et al., 2006). This effect on social interaction and a suppression of hippocampal serotonin release was also seen following direct administration into the dorsal raphe nucleus, suggesting interactions with the serotonergic system (Merali et al., 2006).

Likewise, anxiolytic-like effects were seen with the selective BB_1 antagonist BIM23127 in the elevated plus maze and in fear potentiated startle following injections into the third ventricle (Bedard et al., 2007), suggesting BB_1 antagonism to have anxiolytic potential, while a peptidergic BB_2 antagonist failed to affect fear potentiated startle (Bedard et al., 2007), suggesting that BB_1

antagonists may be of particular utility for the treatment of anxiety disorders.

VI.J. Melanin-concentrating hormone receptor 1 (MCH_1) antagonists

A seminal paper by Borowsky et al. (2002) reported anxiolytic-like properties of the non-peptide MCH_1 antagonist SNAP-7941 in rat social interaction and guinea pig maternal separation-induced vocalization. Comparable effects were reported with two other small molecule MCH_1 antagonists (Chaki et al., 2005a, b) and, more recently, anxiolytic-like properties were seen with another MCH_1 antagonist, SNAP-94847, tested acutely or chronically in mouse light–dark exploration and in novelty suppressed feeding (David et al., 2007). Furthermore, increases in anxiety-related behavior, as measured in an elevated plus maze and in HPA axis activation induced by ICV MCH, were reversed by MCH_1 receptor blockade (Smith et al., 2006). An anxiolytic effect of MCH_1 antagonism was also seen in wild-type mice exploring an elevated plus maze, but not in MCH_1 knockout mice (Smith et al., 2006), suggesting that the effect seen following treatment is indeed MCH_1 receptor mediated. However, another recent study, testing the potential anxiolytic-like effects of a number of MCH_1 antagonists used in the studies cited above, failed to see significant anxiolytic-like properties of these compounds (Basso et al., 2006), thus casting some doubts about the anxiolytic potential of this mechanism.

VI.K. Hypocretin/orexin receptor 1 (OX_1) antagonists

Data on small-molecule, non-peptide OX antagonists are sparse. However, recently is has been shown that ICV administration of an OX_1 antagonist (SB-408124) was able to block the HPA axis activation and increase in cardiovascular response induced by HCRT/ORX and of immobilization stress (Samson et al., 2007), which suggests OX_1 plays an important role in the control of stress responses and consequently could also play a role in the modulation of stress-induced alterations in anxiety-related behavior.

VI.L. Oxytocin receptor (OTR) agonists

Studies using OT suggest a role of agonists at the OT receptor to exert possible anxiolytic-like effects (see above). Further support for this hypothesis comes from reports showing that the anxiolytic-like effects of OT can be antagonized by peripheral administration of brain penetrant, but not by non-penetrant, small molecule OT antagonist (Ring et al., 2006). Recently, small molecule OT agonists have been developed and anxiolytic-like activity has been reported in the elevated zero maze, in stress-induced hyperthermia, and a four plate test in a preliminary publication (Ring et al., 2005). However, it would be relevant to exclude the possibility that these types of compounds induce lactation as OT plays a key role in this function. Furthermore, it will be relevant to show that chronic treatment with an OT agonist remains efficacious and that no tolerance develops.

VI.M. Opiate agonists

A number of non-peptide δ-opiate agonists with high potency and selectivity have been reported (e.g., Trabanco et al., 2006). The prototypical δ-opiate agonist SNC80 showed dose-dependent anxiolytic-like effects in a variety of paradigms, including the elevated plus maze, defensive burying and conditioned fear (Saitoh et al., 2004; Perrine et al., 2006). These effects were blocked by the δ-opioid antagonist naltrindole. Conversely SNC80 antagonized the anxiogenic-like effects of naltrindole and of the δ2-opioid receptor subtype antagonists naltriben on elevated plus maze behavior (Saitoh et al., 2005). Thus, there is preclinical evidence that small molecule, non-peptide δ-opiate agonists have anxiolytic potential. Anxiolytic-like effects have also been reported following peripheral treatment with small-molecule, non-peptide κ-opiate agonists in rats and mice (Kudryavtseva et al., 2004; Privette and Terrian, 1995).

A concern when dealing with opioid systems is the abuse potential of these types of drugs. SNC80 has been shown to have discriminative stimulus properties in rats (Stevenson et al. 2002). Furthermore, SNC80 substituted to a cocaine cue in monkeys (Negus et al., 1998), but did not maintain responding in monkeys trained to self-administer cocaine (Negus et al., 1998). Additional studies of the reward properties of δ-opiate agonists are required to further clarify their abuse potential. However, in general, SNC80 lacks the adverse effects seen with μ-opioid agonists, such as gastrointestinal inhibition and respiratory depression (Gallantine and Meert, 2005). On the other hand, reliable conditioned place aversion can be induced with κ-opiate agonists (Funada et al., 1993; Contarino and Papaleo, 2005), suggesting that these types of drugs may exert some aversive properties on their own.

VI.N. Orphanin FQ/nociceptin receptor 1 (OFQ_1) agonists

Anxiolytic-like effects were also demonstrated with stimulation of another member of the opioid receptors, the OFQ_1 receptor. The OFQ_1 agonist RO 64-6198 elicited anxiolytic-like effects in the rat elevated plus-maze, fear-potentiated startle and an operant conflict paradigm (Jenck et al., 2000). The compound increased punished responding in a rat conditioned lick suppression test similarly to the benzodiazepine chlordiazepoxide. This effect was attenuated by co-administration of an OFQ_1 antagonist, indicating that this effect is OFQ_1 mediated (Varty et al., 2005). In addition, RO 64-6198 reduced isolation-induced vocalizations in rat and guinea pig pups, and increased punished responding in a mouse Geller–Seifter test in wild type but not OFQ_1 knockout mice (Varty et al., 2005). In contrast to alprazolam, RO 64-6198 did not affect panic-like anxiety induced by stimulation of the periaqueductal gray (Jenck et al., 2000), suggesting possible dissociating effects of this mechanism of action on different anxiety disorders. Moreover, RO 64-6198 did not affect motor or cognitive function (Jenck et al., 2000), which also contrasts the effects of classical benzodiazepines.

As pointed out above, there are a number of other potentially interesting peptidergic targets to

Table 6. Evidence for anxiolytic properties of small molecule, non-peptide compounds acting at peptide GPCRs

GPCR	Mode of action	Proof of concept		Comment
		Animal	Human	
CRF$_1$	Antagonism	+	(+)	In depressed patients
CCK$_2$	Antagonism	+	±	Conflicting evidence in HV and patients
NK$_1$	Antagonism	+	+	In patients with social phobia
NK$_2$	Antagonism	+	Ø	
NK$_3$	Antagonism	(+)	−	In patients with panic disorder after CCK-4 challenge
Y$_2$	Antagonism	(+)	Ø	
V$_{1B}$	Antagonism	+	Ø	
MC$_4$	Antagonism	+	Ø	
AT$_1$	Antagonism	+	Ø	
AT$_2$	Antagonism	±	Ø	
GAL$_3$	Antagonism	+	Ø	
BB$_1$	Antagonism	(+)	Ø	
MCH$_1$	Antagonism	±	Ø	
OTR	Agonism	(+)	Ø	Only prelim. publication in abstract form
δ-opiate	Agonism	+	Ø	
OFQ$_1$	Agonism	+	Ø	

+, agonism; −, antagonism; ±, conflicting evidence; ( ), limited evidence; ?, indirect evidence through limited reports on the effects of ANP and CNP. See text for references.

develop novel anxiolytic drugs. However, there are no or only preliminary publications in the public domain. Table 6 summarizes the data of small molecule, non-peptide antagonists or agonists on anxiolytic-like behavior.

VII. Conclusion

Despite the relative difficulties in developing small-molecule, non-peptide ligands it can be concluded that the field has advanced substantially and a number of compounds exist that show preclinical evidence for potent anxiolytic-like effects. Some of those compounds eventually were tested in man, either in healthy volunteers and/or in patients suffering from anxiety disorders.

Characteristics that make neuropeptide systems attractive as drug targets are their generally more discrete neuroanatomical localization when compared to monoamines and GABA and their state-dependent effects, rendering antagonists more active under conditions of increased peptide release than under basal conditions. This implies that these types of compounds may normalize pathological anxiety while leaving normal anxiety responses, which may require less neuronal stimulation frequencies, relatively unaffected. This in turn opens the possibility that drugs that act on these neuropeptide systems might have a particularly low side-effect burden, because such compounds would not be expected to disrupt normal physiology in the absence of neuropeptide release.

However, it should also be recognized that at least some of these peptide systems are centrally and peripherally involved in major homeostatic mechanisms, such as the control of food intake and regulation of pituitary or cardiovascular function. Thus, it is important to not only establish therapeutic efficacy but to also closely monitor the safety and tolerability profile of drugs that target neuropeptides. Nevertheless, it can be concluded that neuropeptide-based therapeutic strategies for anxiety disorders represent a highly innovative and promising approach to treating these conditions.

References

Abel, K.B. and Majzoub, J.A. (2005) Molecular biology of the HPA axis. In: Steckler, T., Kalin, N.H. and Reul, J.M.H.M. (Eds.), Handbook of Stress and the

196

Brain, Part 1: The Neurobiology of Stress. Elsevier, Amsterdam, pp. 79–94.

Abelson, J.L., Le Melledo, J. and Bichet, D.G. (2001) Dose response of arginine vasopressin to the CCK-B agonist pentagastrin. Neuropsychopharmacology, 24: 161–169.

Abelson, J.L. and Liberzon, I. (1999) Dose response of adrenocorticotropin and cortisol to the CCK-B agonist pentagastrin. Neuropsychopharmacology, 21: 485–494.

Abelson, J.L. and Nesse, R.M. (1994) Pentagastrin infusions in patients with panic disorder. I. Symptoms and cardiovascular responses. Biol. Psychiatry, 36: 73–83.

Abelson, J.L., Khan, S., Liberzon, I. and Young, E.A. (2007) HPA axis activity in patients with panic disorder: review and synthesis of four studies. Depr. Anx., 24: 66–76.

Abelson, J.L., Nesse, R.M. and Vinik, A.I. (1994) Pentagastrin infusions in patients with panic disorder. II. Neuroendocrinology. Biol. Psychiatry, 36: 84–96.

Abramov, U., Raud, S., Koks, S., Innos, J., Kurrikoff, K., Matsui, T. and Vasar, E. (2004) Targeted mutation of CCK(2) receptor gene antagonises behavioural changes induced by social isolation in female, but not in male mice. Behav. Brain Res., 155: 1–11.

Adamantidis, A., Thomas, E., Foidart, A., Tyhon, A., Coumans, B., Minet, A., Tirelli, E., Seutin, V., Grisar, T. and Lakaye, B. (2005) Disrupting the melanin-concentrating hormone receptor 1 in mice leads to cognitive deficits and alterations of NMDA receptor function. Eur. J. Neurosci., 21: 2837–2844.

Adams, J.B., Pyke, R.E., Costa, J., Cutler, N.R., Schweizer, E., Wilcox, C.S., Wisselink, P.G., Greiner, M., Pierce, M.W. and Pande, A.C. (1995) A double-blind, placebo-controlled study of a CCK-B receptor antagonist, CI-988, in patients with generalized anxiety disorder. J. Clin. Psychopharmacol., 15: 428–434.

Agarwal, A., Halvorson, L.M. and Legradi, G. (2005) Pituitary adenylate cyclase-activating polypeptide (PACAP) mimics neuroendocrine and behavioral manifestations of stress: evidence for PKA-mediated expression of the corticotropin-releasing hormone (CRH) gene. Mol. Brain Res., 138: 45–57.

Aguiar, M.S. and Brandao, M.L. (1996) Effects of microinjections of the neuropeptide substance P in the dorsal periaqueductal gray on the behaviour of rats in the plus-maze test. Physiol. Behav., 60: 1183–1186.

Aguilera, G., Young, W.S., Kiss, A. and Bathia, A. (1995) Direct regulation of hypothalamic corticotropin-releasing-hormone neurons by angiotensin II. Neuroendocrinology, 61: 437–444.

Akiyoshi, J., Moriyama, T., Isogawa, K., Miyamoto, M., Sasaki, I., Kuga, K., Yamamoto, H., Yamada, K. and Fujii, I. (1996) CCK-4-induced calcium mobilization in T cells is enhanced in panic disorder. J. Neurochem., 66: 1610–1616.

Al-Barazanji, K.A., Wilson, S., Baker, J., Jessop, D.S. and Harbuz, M.S. (2001) Central orexin-A activates hypothalamic–pituitary–adrenal axis and stimulates hypothalamic corticotropin releasing factor and arginine vasopressin neurones in conscious rats. J. Neuroendocrinol., 13: 421–424.

Almay, B.G., Johansson, F., Von Knorring, L., Le Greves, P. and Terenius, L. (1988) Substance P in CSF of patients with chronic pain syndromes. Pain, 33: 3–9.

Amat, J., Tamblyn, J.P., Paul, E.D., Bland, S.T., Amat, P., Foster, A.C., Watkins, L.R. and Maier, S.F. (2004) Microinjection of urocortin 2 into the dorsal raphe nucleus activates serotonergic neurons and increases extracellular serotonin in the basolateral amygdala. Neuroscience, 129: 509–519.

Amico, J.A., Mantella, R.C., Vollmer, R.R. and Li, X. (2004) Anxiety and stress responses in female oxytocin deficient mice. J. Neuroendocrinol., 16: 319–324.

Andrews, N., Davis, B., Gonzalez, M.I., Oles, R., Singh, L. and McKnight, A.T. (2000) Effect of gastrin-releasing peptide on rat hippocampal extracellular GABA levels and seizures in the audiogenic seizure-prone DBA/2 mouse. Brain Res., 859: 386–389.

Appenrodt, E., Schnabel, R. and Schwarzberg, H. (1998) Vasopressin administration modulates anxiety-related behavior in rats. Physiol. Behav., 64: 543–547.

Appenrodt, E. and Schwarzberg, H. (2000) Central vasopressin administration failed to influence anxiety behavior after pinealectomy in rats. Physiol. Behav., 68: 735–739.

Arborelius, L., Owens, M.J., Plotsky, P.M. and Nemeroff, C.B. (1999) The role of corticotropin-releasing factor in depression and anxiety disorders. J. Endocrinol., 160: 1–12.

Arimura, A. (1998) Perspectives on pituitary adenylate cyclase activating polypeptide (PACAP) in the neuroendocrine, endocrine and nervous systems. Jpn. J. Physiol., 48: 301–331.

Arimura, A. and Shioda, S. (1995) Pituitary adenylate cyclase activating polypeptide (PACAP) and its receptor: neuroendocrine and endocrine interaction. Front. Neuroendocrinol., 16: 53–58.

Arlt, J., Jahn, H., Kellner, M., Strohle, A., Yassouridis, A. and Wiedemann, K. (2003) Modulation of sympathetic activity by corticotropin-releasing hormone and atrial natriuretic peptide. Neuropeptides, 37: 362–368.

Armando, I., Carranza, A., Nishimura, Y., Hoe, K.L., Barontini, M., Terron, J.A., Falcon-Neri, A., Ito, T., Juorio, A.V. and Saavedra, J.M. (2001) Peripheral administration of an angiotensin II AT(1) receptor antagonist decreases the hypothalamic–pituitary–adrenal response to isolation stress. Endocrinology, 142: 3880–3889.

Asakawa, A., Inui, A., Kaga, T., Yuzuriha, H., Nagata, T., Fujimiya, M., Katsuura, G., Makino, S., Fujino,

M.A. and Kasuga, M. (2001) A role of ghrelin in neuroendocrine and behavioral responses to stress in mice. Neuroendocrinology, 74: 143–147.

Auerbach, S. and Lipton, P. (1982) Vasopressin augments depolarization-induced release and synthesis of serotonin in hippocampal slices. J. Neurosci., 2: 477–482.

Bacchi, F., Mathe, A.A., Jimenez, P., Stasi, L., Arban, R., Gerrard, P. and Caberlotto, L. (2006) Anxiolytic-like effect of the selective neuropeptide Y Y2 receptor antagonist BIIE0246 in the elevated plus-maze. Peptides, 27: 3202–3207.

Bagdy, G., Graf, M., Anheuer, Z.E., Modos, E.A. and Kantor, S. (2001) Anxiety-like effects induced by acute fluoxetine, sertraline or m-CPP treatment are reversed by pretreatment with the 5-HT2C receptor antagonist SB-242084 but not the 5-HT1A receptor antagonist WAY-100635. Int. J. Neuropsychopharmacol., 4: 399–408.

Baiardi, G., Bregonzio, C., Jezova, M., Armando, I. and Saavedra, J.M. (2004) Angiotensin II AT1 receptor blockade prolongs the lifespan of spontaneously hypertensive rats and reduces stress-induced release of catecholamines, glucocorticoids, and vasopressin. Ann. N.Y. Acad. Sci., 1018: 131–136.

Baker, D.G., West, S.A., Nicholson, W.E., Ekhator, N.N., Kasckow, J.W., Hill, K.K., Bruce, A.B., Orth, D.N. and Geracioti Jr., T.D. (1999) Serial CSF corticotropin-releasing hormone levels and adrenocortical activity in combat veterans with posttraumatic stress disorder. Am. J. Psychiatry, 156: 585–588.

Bakshi, V.P., Smith-Roe, S., Newman, S.M., Grigoriadis, D.E. and Kalin, N.H. (2002) Reduction of stress-induced behavior by antagonism of corticotropin-releasing hormone 2 (CRH2) receptors in lateral septum or CRH1 receptors in amygdala. J. Neurosci., 22: 2926–2935.

Bale, T.L., Contarino, A., Smith, G.W., Chan, R., Gold, L.H., Sawchenko, P.E., Koob, G.F., Vale, W.W. and Lee, K.F. (2000) Mice deficient for corticotropin-releasing hormone receptor-2 display anxiety-like behaviour and are hypersensitive to stress. Nat. Genet., 24: 410–414.

Bale, T.L., Davis, A.M., Auger, A.P., Dorsa, D.M. and McCarthy, M.M. (2001) CNS region-specific oxytocin receptor expression: importance in regulation of anxiety and sex behavior. J. Neurosci., 21: 2546–2552.

Banki, C.M., Karmacsi, L., Bissette, G. and Nemeroff, C.B. (1992) Cerebrospinal fluid neuropeptides in mood disorder and dementia. J. Affect. Dis., 25: 39–45.

Bannon, A.W., Seda, J., Carmouche, M., Francis, J.M., Norman, M.H., Karbon, B. and McCaleb, M.L. (2000) Behavioral characterization of neuropeptide Y knockout mice. Brain Res., 868: 79–87.

Barnes, N.M., Costall, B., Kelly, M.E., Murphy, D.A. and Naylor, R.J. (1990) Anxiolytic-like action of

DuP753, a non-peptide angiotensin II receptor antagonist. Neuroreport, 1: 20–21.

Basso, A.M., Bratcher, N.A., Gallagher, K.B., Cowart, M.D., Zhao, C., Sun, M., Esbenshade, T.A., Brune, M.E., Fox, G.B., Schmidt, M., Collins, C.A., Souers, A.J., Iyengar, R., Vasudevan, A., Kym, P.R., Hancock, A.A. and Rueter, L.E. (2006) Lack of efficacy of melanin-concentrating hormone-1 receptor antagonists in models of depression and anxiety. Eur. J. Pharmacol., 540: 115–120.

Bedard, T., Mountney, C., Kent, P., Anisman, H. and Merali, Z. (2007) Role of gastrin-releasing peptide and neuromedin B in anxiety and fear-related behaviour. Behav. Brain Res., 179: 133–140.

Behan, D.P., Heinrichs, S.C., Troncoso, J.C., Liu, X.J., Kawas, C.H., Ling, N. and De Souza, E.B. (1995) Displacement of corticotropin releasing factor from its binding protein as a possible treatment for Alzheimer's disease. Nature, 378: 284–287.

Belcheva, I., Belcheva, S., Petkov, V.V. and Petkov, V.D. (1994) Asymmetry in behavioral responses to cholecystokinin microinjected into rat nucleus accumbens and amygdala. Neuropharmacology, 33: 995–1002.

Belfer, I., Hipp, H., McKnight, C., Evans, C., Buzas, B., Bollettino, A., Albaugh, B., Virkkunen, M., Yuan, Q., Max, M.B., Goldman, D. and Enoch, M.A. (2006) Association of galanin haplotypes with alcoholism and anxiety in two ethnically distinct populations. Mol. Psychiatry, 11: 301–311.

Belzung, C., Yalcin, I., Griebel, G., Surget, A. and Leman, S. (2006) Neuropeptides in psychiatric diseases: an overview with a particular focus on depression and anxiety disorders. CNS Neurol. Disorders Drug Targets, 5: 135–145.

Berridge, C.W. (2005) The locus coeruleus-noradrenergic system and stress: modulation of arousal state and state-dependent behavioural processes. In: Steckler, T., Kalin, N.H. and Reul, J.M.H.M. (Eds.), Handbook of Stress and the Brain, Part 1: The Neurobiology of Stress. Elsevier, Amsterdam, pp. 437–464.

Bert, L., Rodier, D., Bougault, I., Allouard, N., Le-Fur, G., Soubrie, P. and Steinberg, R. (2002) Permissive role of neurokinin NK(3) receptors in NK(1) receptor-mediated activation of the locus coeruleus revealed by SR 142801. Synapse, 43: 62–69.

Bertoglio, L.J. and Zangrossi, H. Jr. (2005) Involvement of dorsolateral periaqueductal gray cholecystokinin-2 receptors in the regulation of a panic-related behavior in rats. Brain Res., 1059: 46–51.

Bhattacharya, S.K., Bhattacharya, A.R. and Chakrabarti, A.M.I.T. (1998) Anxiogenic activity of intraventricularly administered arginine-vasopressin in the rat. Biog. Amines, 14: 367–385.

Bhattacharya, S.K., Chakrabarti, A., Sandler, M. and Glover, V. (1996) Anxiolytic activity of intraventricularly administered atrial natriuretic peptide in the rat. Neuropsychopharmacology, 15: 199–206.

Bielsky, I.F., Hu, S.B., Ren, X., Terwilliger, E.F. and Young, L.J. (2005a) The V1a vasopressin receptor is necessary and sufficient for normal social recognition: a gene replacement study. Neuron, 47: 503–513.

Bielsky, I.F., Hu, S.B., Szegda, K.L., Westphal, H. and Young, L.J. (2004) Profound impairment in social recognition and reduction in anxiety-like behavior in vasopressin V1a receptor knockout mice. Neuropsychopharmacology, 29: 483–493.

Bielsky, I.F., Hu, S.B. and Young, L.J. (2005b) Sexual dimorphism in the vasopressin system: lack of an altered behavioral phenotype in female V1a receptor knockout mice. Behav. Brain Res., 164: 132–136.

Bilkei-Gorzo, A., Racz, I., Michel, K. and Zimmer, A. (2002) Diminished anxiety- and depression-related behaviors in mice with selective deletion of the Tac1 gene. J. Neurosci., 22: 10046–10052.

Bing, O., Moller, C., Engel, J.A., Soderpalm, B. and Heilig, M. (1993) Anxiolytic-like action of centrally administered galanin. Neurosci. Lett., 164: 17–20.

Biro, E., Sarnyai, Z., Penke, B., Szabo, G. and Telegdy, G. (1993) Role of endogenous corticotropin-releasing factor in mediation of neuroendocrine and behavioral responses to cholecystokinin octapeptide sulfate ester in rats. Neuroendocrinology, 57: 340–345.

Bonaventure, P., Nepomuceno, D., Mazur, C., Lord, B., Rudolph, D.A., Jablonowski, J.A., Carruthers, N.I. and Lovenberg, T.W. (2004) Characterization of N-(1-acetyl-2,3-dihydro-1H-indol-6-yl)-3-(3-cyano-phenyl)-N-[1-(2-cyclopentyl-ethyl)-piperidin-4yl]acrylamide (JNJ-5207787), a small molecule antagonist of the neuropeptide Y Y2 receptor. J. Pharmacol. Exp. Ther., 308: 1130–1137.

Borowsky, B., Durkin, M.M., Ogozalek, K., Marzabadi, M.R., DeLeon, J., Lagu, B., Heurich, R., Lichtblau, H., Shaposhnik, Z., Daniewska, I., Blackburn, T.P., Branchek, T.A., Gerald, C., Vaysse, P.J. and Forray, C. (2002) Antidepressant, anxiolytic and anorectic effects of a melanin-concentrating hormone-1 receptor antagonist. Nat. Med., 8: 825–830.

Boulenger, J.P., Jerabek, I., Jolicoeur, F.B., Lavallee, Y.J., Leduc, R. and Cadieux, A. (1996) Elevated plasma levels of neuropeptide Y in patients with panic disorder. Am. J. Psychiatry, 153: 114–116.

Bouthillier, A. and De Montigny, C. (1988) Long-term benzodiazepine treatment reduces neuronal responsiveness to cholecystokinin: an electrophysiological study in the rat. Eur. J. Pharmacol., 151: 135–138.

Boutin, J.A., Suply, T., Audinot, V., Rodriguez, M., Beauverger, P., Nicolas, J.P., Galizzi, J.P. and Fauchere, J.L. (2002) Melanin-concentrating hormone and its receptors: state of the art. Can. J. Physiol. Pharmacol., 80: 388–395.

Boyce, S., Smith, D., Carlson, E., Hewson, L., Rigby, M., O'Donnell, R., Harrison, T. and Rupniak, N.M. (2001) Intra-amygdala injection of the substance P [NK(1) receptor] antagonist L-760735 inhibits neonatal vocalisations in guinea-pigs. Neuropharmacology, 41: 130–137.

Bradwejn, J. (1993) Neurobiological investigations into the role of cholecystokinin in panic disorder. J. Psychiatry Neurosci., 18: 178–188.

Bradwejn, J. and Koszycki, D. (2001) Cholecystokinin and panic disorder: past and future clinical research strategies. Scand. J. Clin. Lab. Invest. Suppl., 234: 19–27.

Bradwejn, J., Koszycki, D., Couetoux du Tertre, A., Van Megen, H., Den Boer, J. and Westenberg, H. (1994) The panicogenic effects of cholecystokinin-tetrapeptide are antagonized by L-365,260, a central cholecystokinin receptor antagonist, in patients with panic disorder. Arch. Gen. Psychiatry, 51: 486–493.

Bradwejn, J., Koszycki, D. and Meterissian, G. (1990) Cholecystokinin tetrapeptide induces panic-like attacks in patients with panic disorder. Can. J. Psychiatry – Rev. Can. Psychiatry, 35: 83–85.

Bradwejn, J., Koszycki, D., Paradis, M., Reece, P., Hinton, J. and Sedman, A. (1995) Effect of CI-988 on cholecystokinin tetrapeptide-induced panic symptoms in healthy volunteers. Biol. Psychiatry, 38: 742–746.

Bradwejn, J., Koszycki, D., Payeur, R., Bourin, M. and Borthwick, H. (1992) Replication of action of cholecystokinin tetrapeptide in panic disorder: clinical and behavioral findings. Am. J. Psychiatry, 149: 962–964.

Brady, K.T., Lydiard, R.B., Ballenger, J.C., Shook, J., Laraia, M. and Fossey, M. (1991) CSF opioids in panic disorder. Biol. Psychiatry, 30: 512–514.

Brambilla, F., Bellodi, L., Perna, G., Garberi, A., Panerai, A. and Sacerdote, P. (1993) Lymphocyte cholecystokinin concentrations in panic disorder. Am. J. Psychiatry, 150: 1111–1113.

Branchek, T.A., Smith, K.E., Gerald, C. and Walker, M.W. (2000) Galanin receptor subtypes. Trends Pharmacol. Sci., 21: 109–117.

Braszko, J.J., Kulakowska, A. and Winnicka, M.M. (2003) Effects of angiotensin II and its receptor antagonists on motor activity and anxiety in rats. J. Physiol. Pharmacol., 54: 271–281.

Brawman-Mintzer, O., Lydiard, R.B., Bradwejn, J., Villarreal, G., Knapp, R., Emmanuel, N., Ware, M.R., He, Q. and Ballenger, J.C. (1997) Effects of the cholecystokinin agonist pentagastrin in patients with generalized anxiety disorder. Am. J. Psychiatry, 154: 700–702.

Bremner, J.D., Licinio, J., Darnell, A., Krystal, J.H., Owens, M.J., Southwick, S.M., Nemeroff, C.B. and Charney, D.S. (1997) Elevated CSF corticotropin-releasing factor concentrations in posttraumatic stress disorder. Am. J. Psychiatry, 154: 624–629.

Bremner, J.D., Vythilingam, M., Anderson, G., Vermetten, E., McGlashan, T., Heninger, G., Rasmusson, A., Southwick, S.M. and Charney, D.S. (2003) Assessment of the hypothalamic–pituitary–adrenal axis over a 24-hour diurnal period and in response to neuroendocrine challenges in women with and without childhood sexual abuse and posttraumatic stress disorder. Biol. Psychiatry, 54: 710–718.

Brighton, P.J., Szekeres, P.G., Wise, A. and Willars, G.B. (2004) Signaling and ligand binding by recombinant neuromedin U receptors: evidence for dual coupling to Galphaq/11 and Galphai and an irreversible ligand–receptor interaction. Mol. Pharmacol., 66: 1544–1556.

Britton, K.T., Akwa, Y., Spina, M.G. and Koob, G.F. (2000) Neuropeptide Y blocks anxiogenic-like behavioral action of corticotropin-releasing factor in an operant conflict test and elevated plus maze. Peptides, 21: 37–44.

Britton, K.T., Southerland, S., Van Uden, E., Kirby, D., Rivier, J. and Koob, G. (1997) Anxiolytic activity of NPY receptor agonists in the conflict test. Psychopharmacology, 132: 6–13.

Brodin, K., Ogren, S.O. and Brodin, E. (1994) Clomipramine and clonazepam increase cholecystokinin levels in rat ventral tegmental area and limbic regions. Eur. J. Pharmacol., 263: 175–180.

Broqua, P., Wettstein, J.G., Rocher, M.N., Gauthiermartin, B. and Junien, B.L. (1995) Behavioral effects of neuropeptide Y receptor agonists in the elevated plus-maze and fear-potentiated startle procedures. Behav. Pharmacol., 6: 215–222.

Brunello, N., Blier, P., Judd, L.L., Mendlewicz, J., Nelson, C.J., Souery, D., Zohar, J. and Racagni, G. (2003) Noradrenaline in mood and anxiety disorders: basic and clinical studies. Int. Clin. Psychopharmacol., 18: 191–202.

Brunton, P.J., Bales, J. and Russell, J.A. (2006) Neuroendocrine stress but not feeding responses to centrally administered neuropeptide Y are suppressed in pregnant rats. Endocrinology, 147: 3737–3745.

Cano, V., Caicoya, E. and Ruiz-Gayo, M. (2003) Effect of peripheral cholecystokinin receptor agonists on c-Fos expression in brain sites mediating food consumption in rats. Neurosci. Lett., 343: 13–16.

Carlini, V.P., Monzon, M.E., Varas, M.M., Cragnolini, A.B., Schioth, H.B., Scimonelli, T.N. and De Barioglo, S.R. (2002) Ghrelin increases anxiety-like behavior and memory retention in rats. Biochem. Biophys. Res. Commun., 299: 739–743.

Carlini, V.P., Schioth, H.B. and de Barioglio, S.R. (2006) Melanin-concentrating hormone (MCH) reverts the behavioral effects induced by inescapable stress. Peptides, 27: 2300–2306.

Carlini, V.P., Varas, M.M., Cragnolini, A.B., Schioth, H.B., Scimonelli, T.N. and De Barioglio, S.R. (2004) Differential role of the hippocampus, amygdala, and dorsal raphe nucleus in regulating feeding, memory, and anxiety-like behavioral responses to ghrelin. Biochem. Biophys. Res. Commun., 313: 635–641.

Carr, D.B., Fishman, S.M., Kasting, N.W. and Sheehan, D.V. (1986) Vasopressin response to lactate infusion in normals and patients with panic disorder. Funct. Neurol., 1: 123–127.

Carvajal, C., Dumont, Y., Herzog, H. and Quirion, R. (2006a) Emotional behavior in aged neuropeptide Y (NPY) Y2 knockout mice. J. Mol. Neurosci., 28: 239–245.

Carvajal, C., Dumont, Y. and Quirion, R. (2006b) Neuropeptide Y: role in emotion and alcohol dependence. CNS Neurol. Dis. Drug Targets, 5: 181–195.

Carvajal, C.C., Vercauteren, F., Dumont, Y., Michalkiewicz, M. and Quirion, R. (2004) Aged neuropeptide Y transgenic rats are resistant to acute stress but maintain spatial and non-spatial learning. Behav. Brain Res., 153: 471–480.

Chaki, S., Funakoshi, T., Hirota-Okuno, S., Nishiguchi, M., Shimazaki, T., Iijima, M., Grottick, A.J., Kanuma, K., Omodera, K., Sekiguchi, Y., Okuyama, S., Tran, T.A., Semple, G. and Thomsen, W. (2005a) Anxiolytic- and antidepressant-like profile of ATC0065 and ATC0175: nonpeptidic and orally active melanin-concentrating hormone receptor 1 antagonists. J. Pharmacol. Exp. Ther., 313: 831–839.

Chaki, S., Hirota, S., Funakoshi, T., Suzuki, Y., Suetake, S., Okubo, T., Ishii, T., Nakazato, A. and Okuyama, S. (2003a) Anxiolytic-like and antidepressant-like activities of MCL0129 (1-[(S)-2-(4-fluorophenyl)-2-(4-isopropylpiperadin-1-yl)ethyl]-4-[4-(2-methoxynaphthalen-1-yl)butyl]piperazine), a novel and potent nonpeptide antagonist of the melanocortin-4 receptor. J. Pharmacol. Exp. Ther., 304: 818–826.

Chaki, S., Nakazato, A., Kennis, L., Nakamura, M., Mackie, C., Sugiura, M., Vinken, P., Ashton, D., Langlois, X. and Steckler, T. (2004) Anxiolytic- and antidepressant-like profile of a new CRF1 receptor antagonist, R278995/CRA0450. Eur. J. Pharmacol., 485: 145–158.

Chaki, S., Ogawa, S., Toda, Y., Funakoshi, T. and Okuyama, S. (2003b) Involvement of the melanocortin MC4 receptor in stress-related behavior in rodents. Eur. J. Pharmacol., 47: 95–101.

Chaki, S. and Okuyama, S. (2005) Involvement of melanocortin-4 receptor in anxiety and depression. Peptides, 26: 1952–1964.

Chaki, S., Yamaguchi, J., Yamada, H., Thomsen, W., Tran, T.A., Semple, G. and Sekiguchi, Y. (2005b) ATC0175: an orally active melanin-concentrating hormone receptor 1 antagonist for the potential treatment of depression and anxiety. CNS Durg Rev., 11: 341–352.

Charney, D.S. (2004) Psychobiological mechanisms of resilience and vulnerability: implications for successful adaptation to extreme stress. Am. J. Psychiatry, 161: 195–216.

Cheeta, S., Tucci, S., Sandhu, J., Williams, A.R., Rupniak, N.M. and File, S.E. (2001) Anxiolytic actions of the substance P (NK1) receptor antagonist L-760735 and the 5-HT1A agonist 8-OH-DPAT in the social interaction test in gerbils. Brain Res., 915: 170–175.

Chen, I.W., Dorley, J.M., Ramjit, H.G., Pitzenberger, S.M. and Lin, J.H. (1992) Physiological disposition and metabolism of L-365,260, a potent antagonist of brain cholecystokinin receptor, in laboratory animals. Drug Metab. Dispos., 20: 390–395.

Chen, L. and Huang, L.Y. (1998) Dynorphin block of *N*-methyl-D-aspartate channels increases with the peptide length. J. Pharmacol. Exp. Ther., 284: 826–831.

Chen, Q., Nakajima, A., Meacham, C. and Tang, Y.P. (2006) Elevated cholecystokininergic tone constitutes an important molecular/neuronal mechanism for the expression of anxiety in the mouse. Proc. Natl. Acad. Sci. U.S.A., 103: 3881–3886.

Chowdrey, H.S., Jessop, D.S. and Lightman, S.L. (1990) Substance P stimulates arginine vasopressin and inhibits adrenocorticotropin release in vivo in the rat. Neuroendocrinology, 52: 90–93.

Claustre, Y., Rouquier, L., Desvignes, C., Leonetti, M., Montegut, J., Aubin, N., Allouard, N., Bougault, I., Oury-Donat, F. and Steinberg, R. (2006) Effects of the vasopressin (V1b) receptor antagonist, SSR149415, and the corticotropin-releasing factor 1 receptor antagonist, SSR125543, on FG 7142-induced increase in acetylcholine and norepinephrine release in the rat. Neuroscience, 141: 1481–1488.

Cohen, H., Kaplan, Z. and Kotler, M. (1998) Inhibition of anxiety in rats by antisense to cholecystokinin precursor protein. Biol. Psychiatry, 44: 915–917.

Conley, R.K., Cumberbatch, M.J., Mason, G.S., Williamson, D.J., Harrison, T., Locker, K., Swain, C., Maubach, K., O'Donnell, R., Rigby, M., Hewson, L., Smith, D. and Rupniak, N.M. (2002) Substance P (neurokinin 1) receptor antagonists enhance dorsal raphe neuronal activity. J. Neurosci., 22: 7730–7736.

Connor, M., Bagley, E.E., Mitchell, V.A., Ingram, S.L., Christie, M.J., Humphrey, P.P. and Vaughan, C.W. (2004) Cellular actions of somatostatin on rat periaqueductal grey neurons in vitro. Brit. J. Pharmacol., 142: 1273–1280.

Contarino, A., Dellu, F., Koob, G.F., Smith, G.W., Lee, K.F., Vale, W. and Gold, L.H. (1999) Reduced anxiety-like and cognitive performance in mice lacking the corticotropin-releasing factor receptor 1. Brain Res., 835: 1–9.

Contarino, A. and Papaleo, F. (2005) The corticotropin-releasing factor receptor-1 pathway mediated the negative affective states of opiate withdrawal. Proc. Natl. Acad. Sci. U.S.A., 102: 18649–18654.

Corda, M.G., Orlandi, M. and Fratta, W. (1990) Proconflict effect of ACTH 1–24: interaction with benzodiazepines. Pharmacol. Biochem. Behav., 36: 631–634.

Coste, S.C., Kesterson, R.A., Heldwein, K.A., Stevens, S.L., Heard, A.D., Hollis, J.H., Murray, S.E., Hill, J.K., Pantely, G.A., Hohimer, A.R., Hatton, D.C., Phillips, T.J., Finn, D.A., Low, M.J., Rittenberg, M.B., Stenzel, P. and Stenzel-Poore, M.P. (2000) Abnormal adaptations to stress and impaired cardiovascular function in mice lacking corticotropin-releasing hormone receptor-2. Nat. Genet., 24: 403–409.

Cournil, I., Lafon, P., Juaneda, C., Ciofi, P., Fournier, M., Sarrieau, A. and Tramu, G. (2000) Glucocorticosteroids up-regulate the expression of cholecystokinin mRNA in the rat paraventricular nucleus. Brain Res., 877: 412–423.

Cowley, D.S., Adams, J.B., Pyke, R.E., Cook, J., Zaccharias, P., Wingerson, D. and Roy-Byrne, P.P. (1996) Effect of CI-988, a cholecystokinin-B receptor antagonist, on lactate-induced panic. Biol. Psychiatry, 40: 550–552.

Cowley, M.A., Smith, R.G., Diano, S., Tschop, M., Pronchuk, N., Grove, K.L., Strasburger, C.J., Bidlingmaier, M., Esterman, M., Heiman, M.L., Garcia-Segura, L.M., Nillni, E.A., Mendez, P., Low, M.J., Sotonyi, P., Friedman, J.M., Liu, H., Pinto, S., Colmers, W.F., Cone, R.D. and Horvath, T.L. (2003) The distribution and mechanism of action of ghrelin in the CNS demonstrates a novel hypothalamic circuit regulating energy homeostasis. Neuron, 37: 649–661.

Crawley, J.N. and Corwin, R.L. (1994) Biological actions of cholecystokinin. Peptides, 15: 731–755.

Crawley, J.N. and Moody, T.W. (1997) Anxiolytics block excessive grooming behavior induced by ACTH1–24 and bombesin. Brain Res. Bull., 10: 399–401.

Cullinan, W.E. (2000) GABA(A) receptor subunit expression within hypophysiotropic CRH neurons: a dual hybridization histochemical study. J. Comp. Neurol., 419: 344–351.

Curtis, G.C., Abelson, J.L. and Gold, P.W. (1997) Adrenocorticotropic hormone and cortisol responses to corticotropin-releasing hormone: changes in panic disorder and effects of alprazolam treatment. Biol. Psychiatry, 41: 76–85.

Czeh, B., Fuchs, E. and Simon, M. (2006) NK1 receptor antagonists under investigation for the treatment of affective disorders. Exp. Opin. Invest. Drugs, 15: 479–486.

Daniels, W.M., Richter, L. and Stein, D.J. (2004) The effects of repeated intra-amygdala CRF injections on rat behavior and HPA axis function after stress. Metabol. Brain Dis., 19: 15–23.

Dauge, V. and Lena, I. (1998) CCK in anxiety and cognitive processes. Neurosci. Biobehav. Rev., 22: 812–815.

Dauge, V., Sebret, A., Beslot, F., Matsui, T. and Roques, B.P. (2001) Behavioral profile of CCK2 receptor-deficient mice. Neuropsychopharmacology, 25: 690–698.

Dautzenberg, F.M. and Hauger, R.L. (2002) The CRF peptide family and their receptors: yet more partners discovered. Trends Pharmacol. Sci., 23: 71–77.

David, D.J., Klemenhagen, K.C., Holick, K.A., Saxe, M.D., Mendez, I., Santarelli, L., Craig, D.A., Zhong, H., Swanson, C.J., Hegde, L.G., Ping, X.I., Dong, D., Marzabadi, M.R., Gerald, C.P. and Hen, R. (2007) Efficacy of the MCHR1 antagonist N-[3-(1-{[4-(3,4-difluorophenoxy)phenyl]methyl}(4-piperidyl))-4-methylphenyl]-2-methylpropanamide (SNAP 94847) in mouse models of anxiety and depression following acute and chronic administration is independent of hippocampal neurogenesis. J. Pharmacol. Exp. Ther., 321: 237–248.

Day, H.E., Curran, E.J., Watson Jr., S.J. and Akil, H. (1999) Distinct neurochemical populations in the rat central nucleus of the amygdala and bed nucleus of the stria terminalis: evidence for their selective activation by interleukin-1beta. J. Comp. Neurol., 413: 113–128.

Day, H.E., Greenwood, B.N., Hammack, S.E., Watkins, L.R., Fleshner, M., Maier, S.F. and Campeau, S. (2004) Differential expression of 5HT-1A, alpha 1b adrenergic, CRF-R1, and CRF-R2 receptor mRNA in serotonergic, gamma-aminobutyric acidergic, and catecholaminergic cells of the rat dorsal raphe nucleus. J. Comp. Neurol., 474: 364–378.

De Groote, L., Penalva, R.G., Flachskamm, C., Reul, J.M. and Linthorst, A.C. (2005) Differential monoaminergic, neuroendocrine and behavioural responses after central administration of corticotropin-releasing factor receptor type 1 and type 2 agonists. J. Neurochem., 94: 45–56.

De Montigny, C. (1989) Cholecystokinin tetrapeptide induces panic-like attacks in healthy volunteers Preliminary findings. Arch. Gen. Psychiatry, 46: 511–517.

Deng, P.Y., Porter, J.E., Shin, H.S. and Lei, S. (2006) Thyrotropin-releasing hormone increases GABA release in rat hippocampus. J. Physiol., 577: 497–511.

Depot, M., Caille, G., Mukherjee, J., Katzman, M.A., Cadieux, A. and Bradwejn, J. (1999) Acute and chronic role of 5-HT3 neuronal system on behavioral and neuroendocrine changes induced by intravenous cholecystokinin tetrapeptide administration in humans. Neuropsychopharmacology, 20: 177–187.

Deschodt-Lanckman, M., Bui, N.D., Noyer, M. and Christophe, J. (1981) Degradation of cholecystokinin-like peptides by a crude rat brain synaptosomal fraction: a study by high pressure liquid chromatography. Regul. Pept., 2: 15–30.

Devine, D.P., Watson, S.J. and Akil, H. (2001) Nociceptin/orphanin FQ regulates neuroendocrine function of the limbic–hypothalamic–pituitary–adrenal axis. Neuroscience, 102: 541–553.

De Vries, A.C., Young III, W.S. and Nelson, R.J. (1997) Reduced aggressive behaviour in mice with targeted disruption of the oxytocin gene. J. Neuroendocrinol., 9: 363–368.

De Winter, R.F., Van Hemert, A.M., DeRijk, R.H., Zwinderman, K.H., Frankhuijzen-Sierevogel, A.C., Wiegant, V.M. and Goekoop, J.G. (2003) Anxious-retarded depression: relation with plasma vasopressin and cortisol. Neuropsychopharmacology, 28: 140–147.

Dhillo, W.S., Small, C.J., Seal, L.J., Kim, M.S., Stanley, S.A., Murphy, K.G., Ghatei, M.A. and Bloom, S.R. (2002) The hypothalamic melanocortin system stimulates the hypothalamo–pituitary–adrenal axis in vitro and in vivo in male rats. Neuroendocrinology, 75: 209–216.

Dirks, A., Fish, E.W., Kikusui, T., van der Gugten, J., Groenink, L., Olivier, B. and Miczek, K.A. (2002) Effects of corticotropin-releasing hormone on distress vocalizations and locomotion in maternally separated mouse pups. Pharmacol. Biochem. Behav., 72: 993–999.

Dockray, G.J. (1979) Cholecystokinin-like peptides in avian brain and gut. Experientia, 35: 628–630.

Doods, H., Gaida, W., Wieland, H.A., Dollinger, H., Schnorrenberg, G., Esser, F., Engel, W., Eberlein, W. and Rudolf, K. (1999) BIIE0246: a selective and high affinity neuropeptide Y Y(2) receptor antagonist. Eur. J. Pharmacol., 384: R3–R5.

Dornonville de la Cour, C., Bjorkqvist, M., Sandvik, A.K., Bakke, I., Zhao, C.M., Chen, D. and Hakanson, R. (2001) A-like cells in the rat stomach contain ghrelin and do not operate under gastrin control. Regul. Pept., 99: 141–150.

Duncan, E.A., Proulx, K. and Woods, S.C. (2005) Central administration of melanin-concentrating hormone increases alcohol and sucrose/quinine intake in rats. Alcohol. Clin. Exp. Res., 29: 958–964.

Durieux, C., Ruiz-Gayo, M. and Roques, B.P. (1991) In vivo binding affinities of cholecystokinin agonists and antagonists determined using the selective CCKB agonist [3H]pBC 264. Eur. J. Pharmacol., 209: 185–193.

Easton, A., Dwyer, E. and Pfaff, D.W. (2006) Estradiol and orexin-2 saporin actions on multiple forms of behavioral arousal in female mice. Behav. Neurosci., 120: 1–9.

Edvinsson, L. (2001) Calcitonin gene-related peptide (CGRP) and the pathophysiology of headache: therapeutic implications. CNS Drugs, 15: 745–753.

Eriksson, E., Westberg, P., Thuresson, K., Modigh, K., Ekman, R. and Widerlov, E. (1989) Increased cerebrospinal fluid levels of endorphin immunoreactivity in panic disorder. Neuropsychopharmacology, 2: 225–228.

Esclapez, M. and Houser, C.R. (1995) Somatostatin neurons are a subpopulation of GABA neurons in the rat dentate gyrus: evidence from colocalization of preprosomatostatin and glutamate decarboxylase messenger RNAs. Neuroscience, 64: 339–355.

Esler, M., Alvarenga, M., Lambert, G., Kaye, D., Hastings, J., Jennings, G., Morris, M., Schwarz, R.

202

and Richards, J. (2004) Cardiac sympathetic nerve biology and brain monoamine turnover in panic disorder. Ann. N.Y. Acad. Sci., 1018: 505–514.

Fehder, W.P., Sachs, J., Uvaydova, M. and Douglas, S.D. (1997) Substance P as an immune modulator of anxiety. Neuroimmunomodulation, 4: 42–48.

Fendt, M., Koch, M. and Schnitzler, H.U. (1996) Somatostatin in the pontine reticular formation modulates fear potentiation of the acoustic startle response: an anatomical, electrophysiological, and behavioral study. J. Neurosci., 16: 3097–3103.

Fernandez, F., Misilmeri, M.A., Felger, J.C. and Devine, D.P. (2004) Nociceptin/orphanin FQ increases anxiety-related behavior and circulating levels of corticosterone during neophobic tests of anxiety. Neuropsychopharmacology, 29: 59–71.

File, S.E. (1997) Anxiolytic action of a neurokinin1 receptor antagonist in the social interaction test. Pharmacol. Biochem. Behav., 58: 747–752.

File, S.E. (2000) NKP608, an NK1 receptor antagonist, has an anxiolytic action in the social interaction test in rats. Psychopharmacology, 152: 105–109.

File, S.E. and Clarke, A. (1980) Intraventricular ACTH reduces social interaction in male rats. Pharmacol. Biochem. Behav., 12: 711–715.

Filliol, D., Ghozland, S., Chluba, J., Martin, M., Matthes, H.W., Simonin, F., Befort, K., Gaveriaux-Ruff, C., Dierich, A., LeMeur, M., Valverde, O., Maldonado, R. and Kieffer, B.L. (2000) Mice deficient for delta- and mu-opioid receptors exhibit opposing alterations of emotional responses. Nat. Genet., 25: 195–200.

Finlay, J.M., Jedema, H.P., Rabinovic, A.D., Mana, M.J., Zigmond, M.J. and Sved, A.F. (1997) Impact of corticotropin-releasing hormone on extracellular norepinephrine in prefrontal cortex after chronic cold stress. J. Neurochem., 69: 144–150.

Forster, G.L., Feng, N., Watt, M.J., Korzan, W.J., Mouw, N.J., Summers, C.H. and Renner, K.J. (2006) Corticotropin-releasing factor in the dorsal raphe elicits temporally distinct serotonergic responses in the limbic system in relation to fear behavior. Neuroscience, 141: 1047–1055.

Fossey, M.D., Lydiard, R.B., Ballenger, J.C., Laraia, M.T., Bissette, G. and Nemeroff, C.B. (1993) Cerebrospinal fluid thyrotropin-releasing hormone concentration in patients with anxiety disorders. J. Neuropsychiatr. Clin. Neurosci., 5: 335–337.

Fossey, M.D., Lydiard, R.B., Ballenger, J.C., Laraia, M.T., Bissette, G. and Nemeroff, C.B. (1996) Cerebrospinal fluid corticotropin-releasing factor concentrations in patients with anxiety disorders and normal comparison subjects. Biol. Psychiatry, 39: 703–707.

Fox, M.A., Levine, E.S. and Riley, A.L. (2001) The inability of CCK to block (or CCK antagonists to substitute for) the stimulus effects of chlordiazepoxide. Pharmacol. Biochem. Behav., 69: 77–84.

Fraser, C.M., Cooke, M.J., Fisher, A., Thompson, I.D. and Stone, T.W. (1996) Interactions between ifenprodil and dizocilpine on mouse behaviour in models of anxiety and working memory. Eur. Neuropsychopharmacol., 6: 311–316.

Fujimoto, M., Igano, K., Watanabe, K., Irie, I., Inouye, K. and Okabayashi, T. (1985) Effects of caerulein-related peptides on cholecystokinin receptor bindings in brain and pancreas. Biochem. Pharmacol., 34: 1103–1107.

Fulford, A.J. and Harbuz, M.S. (2005) An introduction to the HPA axis. In: Steckler, T. Kalin, N.H. and Reul, J.M.H.M. (Eds.), Handbook of Stress and the Brain, Part: The Neurobiology of Stress. Elsevier, Amsterdam, pp. 43–65.

Funada, M., Suzuki, T., Narita, M., Misawa, M. and Nagase, H. (1993) Blockade of morphine reward through the activation of kappa-opioid receptors in mice. Neuropharmacology, 32: 1315–1323.

Furmark, T., Appel, L., Michelgard, A., Wahlstedt, K., Ahs, F., Zancan, S., Jacobsson, E., Flyckt, K., Grohp, M., Bergstrom, M., Pich, E.M., Nilsson, L.G., Bani, M., Langstrom, B. and Fredrikson, M. (2005) Cerebral blood flow changes after treatment of social phobia with the neurokinin-1 antagonist GR205171, citalopram, or placebo. Biol. Psychiatry, 58: 132–142.

Fuxe, K. and Agnati, L.F. (1991) Volume transmission in the brain: novel mechanisms for neural transmission. Raven Press, New York.

Gallantine, E.L. and Meert, T.F. (2005) A comparison of the antinociceptive and adverse effects of the mu-opioid agonist morphine and the delta-opioid agonist SNC80. Basic Clin. Pharmacol. Toxicol., 97: 39–51.

Gammie, S.C. and Stevenson, S.A. (2006) Intermale aggression in corticotropin-releasing factor receptor 1 deficient mice. Behav. Brain Res., 171: 63–69.

Gard, P.R., Haigh, S.J., Cambursano, P.T. and Warrington, C.A. (2001) Strain differences in the anxiolytic effects of losartan in the mouse. Pharmacol. Biochem. Behav., 69: 35–40.

Gargiulo, P.A. and Donoso, A.O. (1996) Distinct grooming patterns induced by intracerebroventricular injection of CRH, TRH and LHRH in male rats. Braz.. J. Med. Biol. Res., 29: 375–379.

Gatch, M.B., Wallis, C.J. and Lal, H. (1999) Effects of NMDA antagonists on ethanol-withdrawal induced "anxiety" in the elevated plus maze. Alcohol, 19: 207–211.

Gavioli, E.C. and Calo', G. (2006) Antidepressant- and anxiolytic-like effects of nociceptin/orphanin FQ receptor ligands. Naunyn-Schmiedebergs Arch. Pharmacol., 372: 319–330.

Gavioli, E.C., Canteras, N.S. and De Lima, T.C. (2002a) The role of lateral septal NK1 receptors in mediating anxiogenic effects induced by intracerebroventricular injection of substance P. Behav. Brain Res., 134: 411–415.

Gavioli, E.C., Rae, G.A., Calo', G., Guerrini, R. and De Lima, T.C. (2002b) Central injections of nocistatin or its C-terminal hexapeptide exert anxiogenic-like effect on behaviour of mice in the plus-maze test. Brit. J. Pharmacol., 136: 764–772.

Gehlert, D.R., Shekhar, A., Morin, S.M., Hipskind, P.A., Zink, C., Gackenheimer, S.L., Shaw, J., Fitz, S.D. and Sajdyk, T.J. (2005) Stress and central Urocortin increase anxiety-like behavior in the social interaction test via the CRF1 receptor. Eur. J. Pharmacol., 509: 145–153.

Gentsch, C., Cutler, M., Vassout, A., Veenstra, S. and Brugger, F. (2002) Anxiolytic effect of NKP608, a NK1-receptor antagonist, in the social investigation test in gerbils. Behav. Brain Res., 133: 363–368.

Goddard, A.W., Woods, S.W., Money, R., Pande, A.C., Charney, D.S., Goodman, W.K., Heninger, G.R. and Price, L.H. (1999) Effects of the CCK(B) antagonist CI-988 on responses to mCPP in generalized anxiety disorder. Psychiatry Res., 85: 225–240.

Goke, R., Larsen, P.J., Mikkelsen, J.D. and Skeikh, S.P. (1995) Distribution of GLP-1 binding sites in the rat brain: evidence that exendin is a ligand of brain GLP-1 sites. Eur. J. Neurosci., 7: 2294–2300.

Gonzalez, M.I., Vaziri, S. and Wilson, C.A. (1996) Behavioral effects of alpha-MSH and MCH after central administration in the female rat. Peptides, 17: 171–177.

Gottsch, M.L., Zeng, H., Hohmann, J.G., Weinshenker, D., Clifton, D.K. and Steiner, R.A. (2005) Phenotypic analysis of mice deficient in the type 2 galanin receptor (GALR2). Mol. Cell. Biol., 25: 4804–4811.

Gradin, K., Qadri, F., Nomikos, G.G., Hillegaart, V. and Svensson, T.H. (1992) Substance P injection into the dorsal raphe increases blood pressure and serotonin release in hippocampus of conscious rats. Eur. J. Pharmacol., 218: 363–367.

Gray, T.S. and Magnuson, D.J. (1992) Peptide immunoreactive neurons in the amygdala and the bed nucleus of the stria terminalis project to the midbrain central gray in the rat. Peptides, 13: 451–460.

Greisen, M.H., Bolwig, T.G. and Wortwein, G. (2005) Cholecystokinin tetrapeptide effects on HPA axis function and elevated plus maze behaviour in maternally separated and handled rats. Behav. Brain Res., 161: 204–212.

Griebel, G. (1999) Is there a future for neuropeptide receptor ligands in the treatment of anxiety disorders? Pharmacol. Ther., 82: 1–61.

Griebel, G., Perrault, G. and Sanger, D.J. (1999) Orphanin FQ, a novel neuropeptide with anti-stress-like activity. Brain Res., 836: 221–224.

Griebel, G., Perrault, G. and Soubrie, P. (2001) Effects of SR48968, a selective non-peptide NK2 receptor antagonist on emotional processes in rodents. Psychopharmacology, 158: 241–251.

Griebel, G. and Serradeil-Le Gal, C. (2005) Nonpeptide vasopressin V1b receptor antagonists. In: Steckler, T. Kalin, N.H. and Reul, J.M.H.M. (Eds.), Handbook of Stress and the Brain, Part 2: Integrative and Clinical Aspects. Elsevier, Amsterdam, pp. 409–421.

Griebel, G., Simiand, J., Steinberg, R., Jung, M., Gully, D., Roger, P., Geslin, M., Scatton, B., Maffrand, J.P. and Soubrie, P. (2002) 4-(2-Chloro-4-methoxy-5-methyl-phenyl)-N-[(1S)-2-cyclopropyl-1-(3-fluoro-4-methylphenyl)ethyl]5-methyl-N-(2-propynyl)-1, 3-thiazol-2-amine hydrochloride (SSR125543A), a potent and selective corticotropin-releasing factor(1) receptor antagonist. II. Characterization in rodent models of stress-related disorders. J. Pharmacol. Exp. Ther., 301: 333–345.

Griebel, G., Simiand, J., Stemmelin, J., Gal, C.S. and Steinberg, R. (2003) The vasopressin V1b receptor as a therapeutic target in stress-related disorders. Curr. Drug Targets CNS Neurol. Dis., 2: 191–200.

Griebel, G., Stemmelin, J., Gal, C.S. and Soubrie, P. (2005) Non-peptide vasopressin V1b receptor antagonists as potential drugs for the treatment of stress-related disorders. Curr. Pharmaceut. Design, 11: 1549–1559.

Grigoriadis, D.E., Pearsall, D. and De Souza, E.B. (1989) Effects of chronic antidepressant and benzodiazepine treatment on corticotropin-releasing-factor receptors in rat brain and pituitary. Neuropsychopharmacology, 2: 53–60.

Grillon, C., Levenson, J. and Pine, D.S. (2007) A single dose of the selective serotonin reuptake inhibitor citalopram exacerbates anxiety in humans: a fear-potentiated startle study. Neuropsychopharmacology, 32: 225–231.

Groenink, L., Pattij, T., De Jongh, R., Van der Gugten, J., Oosting, R.S., Dirks, A. and Olivier, B. (2003) 5-HT1A receptor knockout mice and mice overexpressing corticotropin-releasing hormone in models of anxiety. Eur. J. Pharmacol., 463: 185–197.

Guan, X.M., Yu, H., Palyha, O.C., McKee, K.K., Feighner, S.D., Sirinathsinghji, D.J., Smith, R.G., Van der Ploeg, L.H.T. and Howard, A.D. (1997) Distribution of mRNA encoding the growth hormone secretagogue receptor in brain and peripheral tissues. Mol. Brain Res., 48: 23–29.

Guiard, B.P., Przybylski, C., Guilloux, J.P., Seif, I., Froger, N., De Felipe, C., Hunt, S.P., Lanfumey, L. and Gardier, A.M. (2004) Blockade of substance P (neurokinin 1) receptors enhances extracellular serotonin when combined with a selective serotonin reuptake inhibitor: an in vivo microdialysis study in mice. J. Neurochem., 89: 54–63.

Hadjiivanova, C.H. and Georgiev, V. (1998) In vitro effect of angiotensin II on GABA release in rat hippocampus. Neuropeptides, 32: 431–434.

Hamke, M., Herpfer, I., Lieb, K., Wandelt, C. and Fiebich, B.L. (2006) Substance P induces expression of the corticotropin-releasing factor receptor 1 by activation of the neurokinin-1 receptor. Brain Res., 1102: 135–144.

Hammack, S.E., Schmid, M.J., LoPresti, M.L., Der-Avakian, A., Pellymounter, M.A., Foster, A.C., Watkins, L.R. and Maier, S.F. (2003) Corticotropin releasing hormone type 2 receptors in the dorsal raphe nucleus mediate the behavioral consequences of uncontrollable stress. J. Neurosci., 23: 1019–1025.

Han, V.K.M., Hynes, M.A., Jin, C., Towle, A.C., Lauder, J.M. and Lund, P.K. (1986) Cellular localization of proglucagon/glucagon-like peptide 1 messenger RNAs in rat brain. J. Neurosci., 16: 97–107.

Harro, J., Lang, A. and Vasar, E. (1990) Long-term diazepam treatment produces changes in cholecystokinin receptor binding in rat brain. Eur. J. Pharmacol., 180: 77–83.

Harro, J., Vasar, E. and Bradwejn, J. (1993) Cholecystokinin in animal and human research of anxiety. Trends Pharmacol. Sci., 14: 244–249.

Hasenohrl, R.U., Jentjens, O., De Souza Silva, M.A., Tomaz, C. and Huston, J.P. (1998) Anxiolytic-like action of neurokinin substance P administered systemically or into the nucleus basalis magnocellularis region. Eur. J. Pharmacol., 354: 123–133.

Hashimoto, H., Shintani, N., Tanaka, K., Mori, W., Hirose, M., Matsuda, T., Sakaue, M., Miyazaki, J., Niwa, H., Tashiro, F., Yamamoto, K., Koga, K., Tomimoto, S., Kunugi, A., Suetake, S. and Baba, A. (2001) Altered psychomotor behaviors in mice lacking pituitary adenylate cyclase-activating polypeptide (PACAP). Proc. Natl. Acad. Sci. U.S.A., 98: 13355–13360.

Hastings, J.A., McClure-Sharp, J.M. and Morris, M.J. (2001) NPY Y1 receptors exert opposite effects on corticotropin releasing factor and noradrenaline overflow from the rat hypothalamus in vitro. Brain Res., 890: 32–37.

Hastings, J.A., Pavia, J.M. and Morris, M.J. (1997) Neuropeptide Y and [Leu31,Pro34]neuropeptide Y potentiate potassium-induced noradrenaline release in the paraventricular nucleus of the aged rat. Brain Res., 750: 301–304.

Hebb, A.L. and Zacharko, R.M. (2003) Central D-Ala2-Met5-enkephalinamide mu/delta-opioid receptor activation reverses the anxiogenic-like properties of cholecystokinin on locomotor and rearing activity in CD-1 mice. Brain Res., 970: 9–19.

Heilig, M. (1995) Antisense inhibition of neuropeptide Y (NPY)-Y1 receptor expression blocks the anxiolytic-like action of NPY in amygdala and paradoxically increases feeding. Regul. Pept., 59: 201–205.

Heilig, M., Koob, G.F., Ekman, R. and Britton, K.T. (1994) Corticotropin-releasing factor and neuropeptide Y: role in emotional integration. Trends Neurosci., 17: 80–85.

Heilig, M., McLeod, S., Brot, M., Heinrichs, S.C., Menzaghi, F., Koob, G.F. and Britton, K.T. (1993) Anxiolytic-like action of neuropeptide Y: mediation by Y1 receptors in amygdala, and dissociation from food intake effects. Neuropsychopharmacology, 8: 357–363.

Heilig, M., McLeod, S., Koob, G.K. and Britton, K.T. (1992) Anxiolytic-like effect of neuropeptide Y (NPY), but not other peptides in an operant conflict test. Regul. Pept., 41: 61–69.

Heilig, M., Soderpalm, B., Engel, J.A. and Widerlov, E. (1989) Centrally administered neuropeptide Y (NPY) produces anxiolytic-like effects in animal anxiety models. Psychopharmacology, 98: 524–529.

Heinrichs, M., Baumgartner, T., Kirschbaum, C. and Ehlert, U. (2003) Social support and oxytocin interact to suppress cortisol and subjective responses to psychosocial stress. Biol. Psychiatry, 54: 1389–1398.

Heinrichs, S.C., Lapsansky, J., Lovenberg, T.W., De Souza, E.B. and Chalmers, D.T. (1997) Corticotropin-releasing factor CRF1, but not CRF2, receptors mediate anxiogenic-like behavior. Regul. Pept., 71: 15–21.

Helton, D.R., Berger, J.E., Czachura, J.F., Rasmussen, K. and Kallman, M.J. (1996) Central nervous system characterization of the new cholecystokininB antagonist LY288513. Pharmacol. Biochem. Behav., 53: 493–502.

Henry, B., Vale, W. and Markou, A. (2006) The effect of lateral septum corticotropin-releasing factor receptor 2 activation on anxiety is modulated by stress. J. Neurosci., 26: 9142–9152.

Hermus, A.R., Pieters, G.F., Smals, A.G., Benraad, T.J. and Kloppenborg, P.W. (1984) Plasma adrenocorticotropin, cortisol, and aldosterone responses to corticotropin-releasing factor: modulatory effect of basal cortisol levels. J. Clin. Endocrinol. Metabol., 58: 187–191.

Herpfer, I. and Lieb, K. (2005) Substance P receptor antagonists in psychiatry: rationale for development and therapeutic potential. CNS Drugs, 19: 275–293.

Herranz, R. (2003) Cholecystokinin antagonists: pharmacological and therapeutic potential. Med. Res. Rev., 23: 559–605.

Hervieu, G. (2003) Melanin-concentrating hormone functions in the nervous system: food intake and stress. Exp. Opin. Ther. Targets, 7: 495–511.

Hervieu, G. (2006) Further insights into the neurobiology of melanin-concentrating hormone in energy and mood balances. Exp. Opin. Ther. Targets, 10: 211–229.

Hesketh, S., Jessop, D.S., Hogg, S. and Harbuz, M.S. (2005) Differential actions of acute and chronic citalopram on the rodent hypothalamic–pituitary–adrenal axis response to acute restraint stress. J. Endocrinol., 185: 373–382.

Hillebrand, J.J., Kas, M.J. and Adan, R.A. (2005) a-MSH enhances activity-based anorexia. Peptides, 26: 1690–1696.

Hodgson, R.A., Higgins, G.A., Guthrie, D.H., Lu, S.X., Pond, A.J., Mullins, D.E., Guzzi, M.F., Parker, E.M. and Varty, G.B. (2007) Comparison of the V1b antagonist, SSR149415, and the CRF1 antagonist, CP-154,526, in rodent models of anxiety and depression. Pharmacol. Biochem. Behav., 86: 431–440.

Hokfelt, T., Bartfai, T. and Bloom, F. (2003) Neuropeptides: opportunities for drug discovery. Lancet Neurol., 2: 463–472.

Hokfelt, T., Broberger, C., Diez, M., Xu, Z.Q., Shi, T., Kopp, J., Zhang, X., Holmberg, K., Landry, M. and Koistinaho, J. (1999) Galanin and NPY, two peptides with multiple putative roles in the nervous system. Horm. Metabol. Res., 31: 330–334.

Holmes, A., Heilig, M., Rupniak, N.M.J., Steckler, T. and Griebel, G. (2003a) Neuropeptide systems as therapeutic targets for depression and anxiety disorders. Trends Pharmacol. Sci., 24: 580–588.

Holmes, A., Kinney, J.W., Wrenn, C.C., Li, Q., Yang, R.J., Ma, L., Vishwanath, J., Saavedra, M.C., Innerfield, C.E., Jacoby, A.S., Shine, J., Iismaa, T.P. and Crawley, J.N. (2003b) Galanin GAL-R1 receptor null mutant mice display increased anxiety-like behavior specific to the elevated plus-maze. Neuropsychopharmacology, 28: 1031–1044.

Holmes, A., Yang, R.J. and Crawley, J.N. (2002) Evaluation of an anxiety-related phenotype in galanin overexpressing transgenic mice. J. Mol. Neurosci., 18: 151–165.

Holsboer, F., Von Bardeleben, U., Buller, R., Heuser, I. and Steiger, A. (1987) Stimulation response to corticotropin-releasing hormone (CRH) in patients with depression, alcoholism and panic disorder. Horm. Metab. Res. Suppl., 16: 80–88.

Horinouchi, Y., Akiyoshi, J., Nagata, A., Matsushita, H., Tsutsumi, T., Isogawa, K., Noda, T. and Nagayama, H. (2004) Reduced anxious behavior in mice lacking the CCK2 receptor gene. Neuropsychopharmacology, 14: 157–161.

Horvath, T.L., Diano, S. and Van den Pol, A.N. (1999) Synaptic interaction between hypocretin (orexin) and neuropeptide Y cells in the rodent and primate hypothalamus: a novel circuit implicated in metabolic and endocrine regulations. J. Neurosci., 19: 1072–1087.

Hoyer, D., Bell, G.I., Berelowitz, M., Epelbaum, J., Feniuk, W., Humphrey, P.P., O'Carroll, A.M., Patel, Y.C., Schonbrunn, A. and Taylor, J.E., et al. (1995) Classification and nomenclature of somatostatin receptors. Trends Pharmacol. Sci., 16: 86–88.

Hughes, J., Boden, P., Costall, B., Domeney, A., Kelly, E., Horwell, D.C., Hunter, J.C., Pinnock, R.D. and Woodruff, G.N. (1990) Development of a class of selective cholecystokinin type B receptor antagonists having potent anxiolytic activity. Proc. Natl. Acad. Sci. U.S.A., 87: 6728–6732.

Husum, H., Mikkelsen, J.D., Hogg, S., Mathe, A.A. and Mork, A. (2000) Involvement of hippocampal neuropeptide Y in mediating the chronic actions of lithium, electroconvulsive stimulation and citalopram. Neuropharmacology, 39: 1463–1473.

Ibanez-Santos, J., Tsagarakis, S., Rees, L.H., Besser, G.M. and Grossman, A. (1990) Atrial natriuretic peptides inhibit the release of corticotropin-releasing factor-41 from the rat hypothalamus in vitro. J. Neuroendocrinol., 126: 223–228.

Imaki, T. and Vale, W. (1993) Chlordiazepoxide attenuates stress-induced accumulation of corticotropin-releasing factor mRNA in the paraventricular nucleus. Brain Res., 623: 223–228.

Inglefield, J.R., Bitran, D., Olschowka, J.A. and Kellogg, C.K. (1993) Selective effects on CRF neurons and catecholamine terminals in two stress-responsive regions of adult rat brain after prenatal exposure to diazepam. Brain Res. Bull., 31: 353–359.

Ising, M., Zimmermann, U.S., Kunzel, H.E., Uhr, M., Foster, A.C., Learned-Coughlin, S.M., Holsboer, F. and Grigoriadis, D.E. (2007) High-affinity CRF1 receptor antagonist NBI-34041: preclinical and clinical data suggest safety and efficacy in attenuating elevated stress response. *Neuropsychopharmacology*, 32: 1941–1949.

Isogawa, K., Akiyoshi, J., Hikichi, T., Yamamoto, Y., Tsutsumi, T. and Nagayama, H. (2000) Effect of corticotropin releasing factor receptor 1 antagonist on extracellular norepinephrine, dopamine and serotonin in hippocampus and prefrontal cortex of rats in vivo. Neuropeptides, 34: 234–239.

Isogawa, K., Akiyoshi, J., Tsutsumi, T., Kodama, K., Horinouti, Y. and Nagayama, H. (2003) Anxiogenic-like effect of corticotropin-releasing factor receptor 2 antisense oligonucleotides infused into rat brain. J. Psychopharmacol., 17: 409–413.

Iyengar, S., Kim, H.S. and Wood, P.L. (1987) Mu-, delta-, kappa- and epsilon-opioid receptor modulation of the hypothalamic-pituitary-adrenocortical (HPA) axis: subchronic tolerance studies of endogenous opioid peptides. Brain Res., 435: 220–226.

Jackisch, R., Geppert, M. and Illes, P. (1986) Characterization of opioid receptors modulating noradrenaline release in the hippocampus of the rabbit. J. Neurochem., 46: 1802–1810.

Jackson, A., Tattersall, D., Bentley, G., Rycroft, W., Bourson, A., Hargreaves, R., Tricklebank, M. and Iversen, S. (1994) An investigation into the discriminative stimulus and reinforcing properties of the CCKB-receptor antagonist, L-365,260 in rats. Neuropeptides, 26: 343–353.

Jahn, H., Montkowski, A., Knaudt, K., Strohle, A., Kiefer, F., Schick, M. and Wiedemann, K. (2001) Alpha-helical-corticotropin-releasing hormone reverses anxiogenic effects of C-type natriuretic peptide in rats. Brain Res., 893: 21–28.

Jarabek, I., Boulenger, J.P., Bradwejn, J., Lavallee, Y.J. and Jolicoeur, F.B. (1999) CCK4-induced panic in healthy subjects I: psychological and cardiovascular effects. Eur. Neuropsychopharmacol., 9: 145–155.

Jaszberenyi, M., Buidoso, E., Bagosi, Z. and Telegy, G. (2006) Mediation of the behavioural, endocrine and thermoregulatory actions of ghrelin. Horm. Behav., 50: 266–273.

Jaszberenyi, M., Bujdoso, E., Pataki, I. and Telegdy, G. (2000) Effects of orexins on the hypothalamic–pituitary–adrenal system. J. Neuroendocrinol., 12: 1174–1178.

Jenck, F., Moreau, J.L., Martin, J.R., Kilpatrick, G.J., Reinscheid, R.K., Monsma Jr., F.J., Nothacker, H.P. and Civelli, O. (1997) Orphanin FQ acts as an anxiolytic to attenuate behavioral responses to stress. Proc. Natl. Acad. Sci. U.S.A., 94: 14854–14858.

Jenck, F., Wichmann, J., Dautzenberg, F.M., Moreau, J.L., Ouagazzal, A.M., Martin, J.R., Lundstrom, K., Cesura, A.M., Poli, S.M., Roever, S., Kolczewski, S., Adam, G. and Kilpatrick, G. (2000) A synthetic agonist at the orphanin FQ/nociceptin receptor ORL1: anxiolytic profile in the rat. Proc. Natl. Acad. Sci. U.S.A., 97: 4938–4943.

Jensen, J.B., Jessop, D.S., Harbuz, M.S., Mork, A., Sanchez, C. and Mikkelsen, J.D. (1999) Acute and long-term treatments with the selective serotonin reuptake inhibitor citalopram modulate the HPA axis activity at different levels in male rats. J. Neuroendocrinol., 11: 465–471.

Jessop, D.S., Renshaw, D., Larsen, P.J., Chowdrey, H.S. and Harbuz, M.S. (2000) Substance P is involved in terminating the hypothalamo–pituitary–adrenal axis response to acute stress through centrally located neurokinin-1 receptors. Stress, 3: 209–220.

Jethwa, P.H., Smith, K.L., Small, C.J., Abbott, C.R., Darch, S.J., Murphy, K.G., Seth, A., Semjonous, N.M., Patel, S.R., Todd, J.F., Ghatei, M.A. and Bloom, S.R. (2006) Neuromedin U partially mediates leptin-induced hypothalamo–pituitary–adrenal (HPA) stimulation and has a physiological role in the regulation of the HPA axis in the rat. Endocrinology, 147: 2886–2892.

Jhamandas, J.H., MacTavish, D. and Harris, K.H. (2006) Neuropeptide FF (NPFF) control of magnocellular neurosecretory cells of the rat hypothalamic paraventricular nucleus (PVN). Peptides, 27: 973–979.

Jolkkonen, J., Lepola, U., Bissette, G., Nemeroff, C. and Riekkinen, P. (1993) CSF corticotropin-releasing factor is not affected in panic disorder. Biol. Psychiatry, 33: 136–138.

Jones, B.E. and Muhlethaler, M. (2005) Modulation of cortical activity and sleep-wake state by hypocretin/orexin. In: De Lecea, L. and Sutcliffe, J.G. (Eds.), The Hypocretins: Integrators of Physiological Systems. Springer, New York, pp. 289–301.

Jones, D.N., Kortekaas, R., Slade, P.D., Middlemiss, D.N. and Hagan, J.J. (1998) The behavioural effects of corticotropin-releasing factor-related peptides in rats. Psychopharmacology, 138: 124–132.

Jones, E.G., DeFelipe, J., Hendry, S.H. and Maggio, J.E. (1988) A study of tachykinin-immunoreactive neurons in monkey cerebral cortex. J. Neurosci., 8: 1206–1224.

Jongsma, M.E., Bosker, F.J., Cremers, T.I., Westerink, B.H. and den Boer, J.A. (2005) The effect of chronic selective serotonin reuptake inhibitor treatment on serotonin 1B receptor sensitivity and HPA axis activity. Prog. Neuro-Psychopharm. Biol. Psychiat., 29: 738–744.

Juaneda, C., Dubourg, P., Ciofi, P., Corio, M. and Tramu, G. (1999) Ultrastructural colocalization of vesicular cholecystokinin and corticoliberin in the periportal nerve terminals of the rat paraventricular nucleus. J. Neuroendocrinol., 11: 203–209.

Jung, M., Michaud, J.C., Steinberg, R., Barnouin, M.C., Hayar, A., Mons, G., Souilhac, J., Emonds-Alt, X., Soubrie, P. and Le Fur, G. (1996) Electrophysiological, behavioural and biochemical evidence for activation of brain noradrenergic systems following neurokinin NK3 receptor stimulation. Neuroscience, 74: 403–414.

Kaabi, B., Gelernter, J., Woods, S.W., Goddard, A., Page, G.P. and Elston, R.C. (2006) Genome scan for loci predisposing to anxiety disorders using a novel multivariate approach: strong evidence for a chromosome 4 risk locus. Am. J. Human Genet., 78: 543–553.

Kagamiishi, Y., Yamamoto, T. and Watanabe, S. (2003) Hippocampal serotonergic system is involved in anxiety-like behavior induced by corticotropin-releasing factor. Brain Res., 991: 212–221.

Kaiser, F.C., Palmer, G.C., Wallace, A.V., Carr, R.D., Fraser-Rae, L. and Hallam, C. (1992) Antianxiety properties of the angiotensin II antagonist, DUP 753, in the rat using the elevated plus-maze. Neuroreport, 3: 922–924.

Kamei, J., Matsunawa, Y., Miyata, S., Tanaka, S. and Saitoh, A. (2004) Effects of nociceptin on the exploratory behavior of mice in the hole-board test. Eur. J. Pharmacol., 489: 77–87.

Kanehisa, M., Akiyoshi, J., Kitaichi, T., Matsushita, H., Tanaka, E., Kodama, K., Hanada, H. and Isogawa, K. (2006) Administration of antisense DNA for ghrelin causes an antidepressant and anxiolytic response in rats. Prog. Neuro-Psychopharmacol. Biol. Psychiatry, 30: 1403–1407.

Karl, T., Burne, T.H. and Herzog, H. (2006) Effect of Y1 receptor deficiency on motor activity, exploration, and anxiety. Behav. Brain Res., 167: 87–93.

Karlsson, R.M., Holmes, A., Heilig, M. and Crawley, J.N. (2005) Anxiolytic-like actions of centrally-administered neuropeptide Y, but not galanin, in C57BL/6J mice. Pharmacol. Biochem. Behav., 80: 427–436.

Karolyi, I.J., Burrows, H.L., Ramesh, T.M., Nakajima, M., Lesh, J.S., Seong, E., Camper, S.A. and Seasholtz, A.F. (1999) Altered anxiety and weight gain in corticotropin-releasing hormone-binding protein-deficient mice. Proc. Natl. Acad. Sci. U.S.A., 96: 11595–11600.

Kasckow, J.W., Baker, D. and Geracioti, T.D. Jr. (2001) Corticotropin-releasing hormone in depression and post-traumatic stress disorder. Peptides, 22: 845–851.

Kash, T.L. and Winder, D.G. (2006) Neuropeptide Y and corticotropin-releasing factor bi-directionally modulate inhibitory synaptic transmission in the bed nucleus of the stria terminalis. Neuropharmacology, 51: 1013–1022.

Kask, A., Nguyen, H.P., Pabst, R. and Von Horsten, S. (2001) Neuropeptide Y Y1 receptor-mediated anxiolysis in the dorsocaudal lateral septum: functional antagonism of corticotropin-releasing hormone-induced anxiety. Neuroscience, 104: 799–806.

Kask, A., Rago, L. and Harro, J. (1997) Alpha-helical CRF(9–41) prevents anxiogenic-like effect of NPY Y1 receptor antagonist BIBP3226 in rats. Neuroreport, 8: 3645–3647.

Kask, A., Rago, L., Wikberg, J.E. and Schioth, H.B. (1998) Evidence for involvement of the melanocortin MC4 receptor in the effects of leptin on food intake and body weight. Eur. J. Pharmacol., 360: 15–19.

Kawahara, Y., Hesselink, M.B., van Scharrenburg, G. and Westerink, B.H. (2004) Tonic inhibition by orphanin FQ/nociceptin of noradrenaline neurotransmission in the amygdala. Eur. J. Pharmacol., 485: 197–200.

Keck, M.E., Welt, T., Muller, M.B., Uhr, M., Ohl, F., Wigger, A., Toschi, N., Holsboer, F. and Landgraf, R. (2003) Reduction of hypothalamic vasopressinergic hyperdrive contributes to clinically relevant behavioral and neuroendocrine effects of chronic paroxetine treatment in a psychopathological rat model. Neuropsychopharmacology, 28: 235–243.

Keck, M.E., Welt, T., Wigger, A., Renner, U., Engelmann, M., Holsboer, F. and Landgraf, R. (2001) The anxiolytic effect of the CRH(1) receptor antagonist R121919 depends on innate emotionality in rats. Eur. J. Neurosci., 13: 373–380.

Kehne, J.H., McCloskey, T.C., Baron, B.M., Chi, E.M., Harrison, B.L., Whitten, J.P. and Palfreyman, M.G. (1991) NMDA receptor complex antagonists have potential anxiolytic effects as measured with separation-induced ultrasonic vocalizations. Eur. J. Pharmacol., 193: 283–292.

Kehr, J., Yoshitake, T., Wang, F.H., Razani, H., Gimenez-Llort, L., Jansson, A., Yamaguchi, M. and Ogren, S.O. (2002) Galanin is a potent in vivo modulator of mesencephalic serotonergic neurotransmission. Neuropsychopharmacology, 27: 341–356.

Kela, J., Salmi, P., Rimondini-Giorgini, R., Heilig, M. and Wahlestedt, C. (2003) Behavioural analysis of melanin-concentrating hormone in rats: evidence for orexigenic and anxiolytic properties. Regul. Pept., 114: 109–114.

Kellner, M., Wiedemann, K., Yassouridis, A., Levengood, R., Guo, L.S., Holsboer, F. and Yehuda, R. (2000) Behavioral and endocrine response to cholecystokinin tetrapeptide in patients with posttraumatic stress disorder. Biol. Psychiatry, 47: 107–111.

Kellner, M., Yassouridis, A., Hubner, R., Baker, D.G. and Wiedemann, K. (2003) Endocrine and cardiovascular responses to corticotropin-releasing hormone in patients with posttraumatic stress disorder: a role for atrial natriuretic peptide? Neuropsychobiology, 47: 102–108.

Kennedy, A.R., Todd, J.F., Dhillo, W.S., Seal, L.J., Ghatei, M.A., O'Toole, C.P., Jones, M., Witty, D., Winborne, K., Riley, G., Hervieu, G., Wilson, S. and Bloom, S.R. (2003) Effect of direct injection of melanin-concentrating hormone into the paraventricular nucleus: further evidence for a stimulatory role in the adrenal axis via SLC-1. J. Neuroendocrinol., 15: 268–272.

Kennedy, J.L., Bradwejn, J., Koszycki, D., King, N., Crowe, R., Vincent, J. and Fourie, O. (1999) Investigation of cholecystokinin system genes in panic disorder. Mol. Psychiatry, 4: 284–285.

Khoshbouei, H., Cecchi, M., Dove, S., Javors, M. and Morilak, D.A. (2002) Behavioral reactivity to stress: amplification of stress-induced noradrenergic activation elicits a galanin-mediated anxiolytic effect in central amygdala. Pharmacol. Biochem. Behav., 71: 407–417.

Kikuchi, M., Komuro, R., Oka, H., Kidani, T., Hanaoka, A. and Koshino, Y. (2005) Relationship between anxiety and thyroid function in patients with panic disorder. Prog. Neuro-Psychopharmacol. Biol. Psychiatry, 29: 77–81.

Kinzig, K.P., D'Alessio, D.A., Herman, J.P., Sakai, R.R., Vahl, T.P., Figueiredo, H.F., Murphy, E.K. and Seeley, R.J. (2003) CNS glucagon-like peptide-1 receptors mediate endocrine and anxiety responses to interoceptive and psychogenic stressors. J. Neurosci., 23: 6163–6170.

Kirsch, P., Esslinger, C., Chen, Q., Mier, D., Lis, S., Siddhanti, S., Gruppe, H., Mattay, V.S., Gallhofer, B. and Meyer-Lindenberg, A. (2005) Oxytocin modulates neural circuitry for social cognition and fear in humans. J. Neurosci., 25: 11489–11493.

Kishimoto, T., Radulovic, J., Radulovic, M., Lin, C.R., Schrick, C., Hooshmand, F., Hermanson, O., Rosenfeld, M.G. and Spiess, J. (2000) Deletion of crhr2 reveals an anxiolytic role for corticotropin-releasing hormone receptor-2. Nat. Genet., 24: 415–419.

Knapp, D.J., Overstreet, D.H., Moy, S.S. and Breese, G.R. (2004) SB242084, flumazenil, and CRA1000 block ethanol withdrawal-induced anxiety in rats. Alcohol, 32: 101–111.

208

Kocorowski, L.H. and Helmstetter, F.J. (2001) Calcitonin gene-related peptide released within the amygdala is involved in Pavlovian auditory fear conditioning. Neurobiol. Learn. Mem., 75: 149–163.

Kojima, M., Hosoda, H., Date, Y., Nakazato, M., Matsuo, H. and Kangawa, K. (1999) Ghrelin is a growth-hormone-releasing acylated peptide from stomach. Nature, 402: 656–660.

Kokare, D.M., Chopde, C.T. and Subhedar, N.K. (2006) Participation of alpha-melanocyte stimulating hormone in ethanol-induced anxiolysis and withdrawal anxiety in rats. Neuropharmacology, 51: 536–545.

Kokare, D.M., Dandekar, M.P., Chopde, C.T. and Subhedar, N. (2005) Interaction between neuropeptide Y and alpha-melanocyte stimulating hormone in amygdala regulates anxiety in rats. Brain Res., 1043: 107–114.

Konig, M., Zimmer, A.M., Steiner, H., Holmes, P.W., Crawley, J.N., Brownstein, M.J. and Zimmer, A. (1996) Pain responses, anxiety and aggression in mice deficient in pre-proenkephalin. Nature, 383: 535–538.

Kosfeld, M., Heinrichs, M., Zak, P.J., Fischbacher, U. and Fehr, E. (2005) Oxytocin increases trust in humans. Nature, 435: 673–676.

Koster, A., Montkowski, A., Schulz, S., Stube, E.M., Knaudt, K., Jenck, F., Moreau, J.L., Nothacker, H.P., Civelli, O. and Reinscheid, R.K. (1999) Targeted disruption of the orphanin FQ/nociceptin gene increases stress susceptibility and impairs stress adaptation in mice. Proc. Natl. Acad. Sci. U.S.A., 96: 10444–10449.

Kovacs, A., Biro, E., Szeleczky, I. and Telegdy, G. (1995) Role of endogenous CRF in the mediation of neuroendocrine and behavioral responses to calcitonin gene-related peptide in rats. Neuroendocrinology, 62: 418–424.

Kramer, M.S., Cutler, N., Feighner, J., Shrivastava, R., Carman, J., Sramek, J.J., Reines, S.A., Liu, G., Snavely, D., Wyatt-Knowles, E., Hale, J.J., Mills, S.G., MacCoss, M., Swain, C.J., Harrison, T., Hill, R.G., Hefti, F., Scolnick, E.M., Cascieri, M.A., Chicchi, G.G., Sadowski, S., Williams, A.R., Hewson, L., Smith, D., Carlson, E.J., Hargreaves, R.J. and Rupniak, N.M. (1998) Distinct mechanism for antidepressant activity by blockade of central substance P receptors. Science, 281: 1640–1645.

Kramer, M.S., Cutler, N.R., Ballenger, J.C., Patterson, W.M., Mendels, J., Chenault, A., Shrivastava, R., Matzura-Wolfe, D., Lines, C. and Reines, S. (1995) A placebo-controlled trial of L-365,260, a CCKB antagonist, in panic disorder. Biol. Psychiatry, 37: 462–466.

Krase, W., Koch, M. and Schnitzler, H.U. (1994) Substance P is involved in the sensitization of the acoustic startle response by footshocks in rats. Behav. Brain Res., 63: 81–88.

Kronenberg, G., Berger, P., Tauber, R.F., Bandelow, B., Henkel, V. and Heuser, I. (2005) Randomized, double-blind study of SR142801 (Osanetant). A novel neurokinin-3 (NK3) receptor antagonist in panic disorder with pre- and posttreatment cholecystokinin tetrapeptide (CCK-4) challenges. Pharmacopsychiatry, 38: 25–29.

Krysiak, R., Obuchowicz, E. and Herman, Z.S. (2000) Conditioned fear-induced changes in neuropeptide Y-like immunoreactivity in rats: the effect of diazepam and buspirone. Neuropeptides, 34: 148–157.

Kubota, Y., Hattori, R. and Yui, Y. (1994) Three distinct subpopulations of GABAergic neurons in rat frontal agranular cortex. Brain Res., 649: 159–173.

Kudryavtseva, N.N., Gerrits, M.A., Avgustinovich, D.F., Tenditnik, M.V. and Van Ree, J.M. (2004) Modulation of anxiety-related behaviors by mu- and kappa-opioid receptor agonists depends on the social status of mice. Peptides, 25: 1355–1363.

Kulakowska, A., Karwowska, W., Winiewski, K. and Braszko, J.J. (1996) Losartan influences behavioural effects of angiotensin II in rats. Pharmacol. Res., 34: 109–115.

Kumar, V., Guo, D., Cassel, J.A., Daubert, J.D., Dehaven, R.N., Dehaven-Hudkins, D.L., Gauntner, E.K., Gottshall, S.L., Greiner, S.L., Koblish, M., Little, P.J., Mansson, E. and Maycock, A.L. (2005) Synthesis and evaluation of novel peripherally restricted kappa-opioid receptor agonists. Bioorg. Med. Chem. Lett., 15: 1091–1095.

Kuteeva, E., Hokfelt, T. and Ogren, S.O. (2005) Behavioural characterisation of young adult transgenic mice overexpressing galanin under the PDGF-B promoter. Regul. Pept., 125: 67–78.

Kuzmin, A., Madjid, N., Terenius, L., Ogren, S.O. and Bakalkin, G. (2006) Big dynorphin, a prodynorphin-derived peptide produces NMDA receptor-mediated effects on memory, anxiolytic-like and locomotor behavior in mice. Neuropsychopharmacology, 31: 1928–1937.

Kyrkouli, S.E., Stanley, B.G. and Leibowitz, S.F. (1992) Differential effects of galanin and neuropeptide Y on extracellular norepinephrine levels in the paraventricular hypothalamic nucleus of the rat: a microdialysis study. Life Sci., 51: 203–210.

Lacoste, B., Riad, M. and Descarries, L. (2006) Immunocytochemical evidence for the existence of substance P receptor (NK1) in serotonin neurons of rat and mouse dorsal raphe nucleus. Eur. J. Neurosci., 23: 2947–2958.

Landgraf, R. (2005) Neuropeptides in anxiety modulation. Handb. Exp. Pharmacol., 169: 335–369.

Landgraf, R. (2006) The involvement of the vasopressin system in stress-related disorders. CNS Neurol. Disorders Drug Targets, 5: 167–179.

Landgraf, R., Gerstberger, R., Montkowski, A., Probst, J.C., Wotjak, C.T., Holsboer, F. and Engelmann, M.

(1995) V1 vasopressin receptor antisense oligodeoxynucleotide into septum reduces vasopressin binding, social discrimination abilities, and anxiety-related behavior in rats. J. Neurosci., 15: 4250–4258.

Larsen, P.J., Tang-Christensen, M. and Jessop, D.S. (1997) Central administration of glucagon-like peptide-1 activates hypothalamic neuroendocrine neurons in the rat. Endocrinology, 138: 4445–4455.

Lavicky, J. and Dunn, A.J. (1993) Corticotropin-releasing factor stimulates catecholamine release in hypothalamus and prefrontal cortex in freely moving rats as assessed by microdialysis. J. Neurochem., 60: 602–612.

Leggett, J.D., Harbuz, M.S., Jessop, D.S. and Fulford, A.J. (2006) The nociceptin receptor antagonist [Nphe1, Arg14,Lys15]nociceptin/orphanin FQ-NH2 blocks the stimulatory effects of nociceptin/orphanin FQ on the HPA axis in rats. Neuroscience, 141: 2051–2057.

Lelas, S., Wong, H., Li, Y.W., Heman, K.L., Ward, K.A., Zeller, K.L., Sieracki, K.K., Polino, J.L., Godonis, H.E., Ren, S.X., Yan, X.X., Arneric, S.P., Robertson, D.W., Hartig, P.R., Grossman, S., Trainor, G.L., Taub, R.A., Zaczek, R., Gilligan, P.J. and McElroy, J.F. (2004) Anxiolytic-like effects of the corticotropin-releasing factor1 (CRF1) antagonist DMP904 [4-(3-pentylamino)-2,7-dimethyl-8-(2-methyl-4-methoxyphenyl)-pyrazolo-[1,5-a]-pyrimidine] administered acutely or chronically at doses occupying central CRF1 receptors in rats. J. Pharmacol. Exp. Ther., 309: 293–302.

Lelas, S., Zeller, K.L., Ward, K.A. and McElroy, J.F. (2003) The anxiolytic CRF(1) antagonist DMP696 fails to function as a discriminative stimulus and does not substitute for chlordiazepoxide in rats. Psychopharmacology, 166: 408–415.

Lepola, U., Jolkkonen, J., Pitkanen, A., Riekkinen, P. and Rimon, R. (1990) Cerebrospinal fluid monoamine metabolites and neuropeptides in patients with panic disorder. Ann. Med., 22: 237–239.

Lepola, U., Jolkkonen, J., Rimon, R. and Riekkinen, P. (1989) Long-term effects of alprazolam and imipramine on cerebrospinal fluid monoamine metabolites and neuropeptides in panic disorder. Neuropsychobiology, 21: 182–186.

Lewis, K., Li, C., Perrin, M.H., Blount, A., Kunitake, K., Donaldson, C., Vaughan, J., Reyes, T.M., Gulyas, J., Fischer, W., Bilezikjian, L., Rivier, J., Sawchenko, P.E. and Vale, W.W. (2001) Identification of urocortin III, an additional member of the corticotropin-releasing factor (CRF) family with high affinity for the CRF2 receptor. Proc. Natl. Acad. Sci. U.S.A., 98: 7570–7575.

Li, Y.W., Fitzgerald, L., Wong, H., Lelas, S., Zhang, G., Lindner, M.D., Wallace, T., McElroy, J., Lodge, N.J., Gilligan, P. and Zaczek, R. (2005) The pharmacology of DMP696 and DMP904, non-peptidergic CRF1 receptor antagonists. CNS Drug Rev., 11: 2–52.

Liebsch, G., Landgraf, R., Engelmann, M., Lorscher, P. and Holsboer, F. (1999) Differential behavioural effects of chronic infusion of CRH 1 and CRH 2 receptor antisense oligonucleotides into the rat brain. J. Psychiatry Res., 33: 153–163.

Liebsch, G., Landgraf, R., Gerstberger, R., Probst, J.C., Wotjak, C.T., Engelmann, M., Holsboer, F. and Montkowski, A. (1995) Chronic infusion of a CRH1 receptor antisense oligodeoxynucleotide into the central nucleus of the amygdala reduced anxiety-related behavior in socially defeated rats. Regul. Pept., 59: 229–239.

Liebsch, G., Wotjak, C.T., Landgraf, R. and Engelmann, M. (1996) Septal vasopressin modulates anxiety-related behaviour in rats. Neurosci. Lett., 217: 101–104.

Lindberg, C., Koefoed, P., Hansen, E.S., Bolwig, T.G., Rehfeld, J.F., Mellerup, E., Jorgensen, O.S., Kessing, L.V., Werge, T., Haugbol, S., Wang, A.G. and Woldbye, D.P. (2006) No association between the – 399 C > T polymorphism of the neuropeptide Y gene and schizophrenia, unipolar depression or panic disorder in a Danish population. Acta Psychiatry Scand., 113: 54–58.

Lines, C., Challenor, J. and Traub, M. (1995) Cholecystokinin and anxiety in normal volunteers: an investigation of the anxiogenic properties of pentagastrin and reversal by the cholecystokinin receptor subtype B antagonist L-365,260. Br. J. Clin. Pharmacol., 39: 235–242.

Lingueglia, E., Deval, E. and Lazdunski, M. (2006) FMRFamide-gated sodium channel and ASIC channels: a new class of ionotropic receptors for FMRFamide and related peptides. Peptides, 27: 1138–1152.

Linthorst, A.C. (2005) Interactions between corticotropin-releasing hormone and serotonin: implications for the aetiology and treatment of anxiety disorders. Handb. Exp. Pharmacol., 169: 181–204.

Linthorst, A.C., Penalva, R.G., Flachskamm, C., Holsboer, F. and Reul, J.M. (2002) Forced swim stress activates rat hippocampal serotonergic neurotransmission involving a corticotropin-releasing hormone receptor-dependent mechanism. Eur. J. Neurosci., 16: 2441–2452.

Liu, Q., Guan, X.M., Martin, W.J., McDonald, T.P., Clements, M.K., Jiang, Q., Zeng, Z., Jacobson, M., Williams Jr., D.L., Yu, H., Bomford, D., Figueroa, D., Mallee, J., Wang, R., Evans, J., Gould, R. and Austin, C.P. (2001) Identification and characterization of novel mammalian neuropeptide FF-like peptides that attenuate morphine-induced antinociception. J. Biol. Chem., 276: 36961–36969.

Llorens-Cortes, C., Giros, B., Quach, T.T. and Schwartz, J.C. (1990) Adaptative changes in two indices of enkephalin neuron activity in mouse striatum following GABAergic stimulation. Prog. Clin. Biol. Res., 328: 203–206.

Lodge, D.J. and Lawrence, A.J. (2003) The effect of chronic CRF1 receptor blockade on the central CCK systems of Fawn-Hooded rats. Peptides, 116: 27–33.

Lofberg, C., Agren, H., Harro, J. and Oreland, L. (1998) Cholecystokinin in CSF from depressed patients: possible relations to severity of depression and suicidal behaviour. Neuropsychopharmacology, 8: 153–157.

Lolait, S.J., O'Carroll, A.M., Mahan, L.C., Felder, C.C., Button, D.C., Young, W.S., III Mezey, E. and Brownstein, M.J. (1995) Extrapituitary expression of the rat V1b vasopressin receptor gene. Proc. Natl. Acad. Sci. U.S.A., 92: 6783–6787.

Lord, J.A., Waterfield, A.A., Hughes, J. and Kosterlitz, H.W. (1977) Endogenous opioid peptides: multiple agonists and receptors. Nature, 267: 495–499.

Lucas, L.R., Pompei, P. and McEwen, B.S. (1997) Effects of deoxycorticosterone acetate and diazepam on neuropeptidergic neurons in rat striatum. Neuroreport, 8: 811–816.

Lydiard, R.B., Ballenger, J.C., Laraia, M.T., Fossey, M.D. and Beinfeld, M.C. (1992) CSF cholecystokinin concentrations in patients with panic disorder and in normal comparison subjects. Am. J. Psychiatry, 149: 691–693.

Lydiard, R.B., Brewerton, T.D., Fossey, M.D., Laraia, M.T., Stuart, G., Beinfeld, M.C. and Ballenger, J.C. (1993) CSF cholecystokinin octapeptide in patients with bulimia nervosa and in normal comparison subjects. Am. J. Psychiatry, 150: 1099–1101.

Ma, Q.P. and Bleasdale, C. (2002) Modulation of brain stem monoamines and gamma-aminobutyric acid by NK1 receptors in rats. Neuroreport, 13: 1809–1812.

Ma, X., Tong, Y.G., Schmidt, R., Brown, W., Payza, K., Hodzic, L., Pou, C., Godbout, C., Hokfelt, T. and Xu, Z.Q. (2001) Effects of galanin receptor agonists on locus coeruleus neurons. Brain Res., 919: 169–174.

Maciag, C.M., Dent, G., Gilligan, P., He, L., Dowling, K., Ko, T., Levine, S. and Smith, M.A. (2002) Effects of a non-peptide CRF antagonist (DMP696) on the behavioral and endocrine sequelae of maternal separation. Neuropsychopharmacology, 26: 574–582.

Malendowicz, L.K., Spinazzi, R., Majchrzak, M., Nowak, M., Nussdorfer, G.G., Ziolkowska, A., Macchi, C. and Trejter, M. (2003) Effects of prolonged cholecystokinin administration on rat pituitary-adrenocortical axis: role of the CCK receptor subtypes 1 and 2. Int. J. Mol. Med., 12: 903–909.

Mannisto, P.T., Lang, A., Harro, J., Peuranen, E., Bradwejn, J. and Vasar, E. (1994) Opposite effects mediated by CCKA and CCKB receptors in behavioural and hormonal studies in rats. Naunyn-Schmiedebergs Arch. Pharmacol., 349: 478–484.

Mantella, R.C., Vollmer, R.R., Li, X. and Amico, J.A. (2003) Female oxytocin-deficient mice display enhanced anxiety-related behavior. Endocrinology, 144: 2291–2296.

Martinez, A. and Arilla, E. (1993) The effect of diazepam and the benzodiazepine antagonist CGS 8216 on the somatostatinergic neuronal system. Neuropharmacology, 32: 393–399.

Martinez-Ferrer, A., Boyano-Adanez, M.C., Izquierdo-Claros, R.M. and Arilla-Ferreiro, E. (2000) Diazepam attenuation of somatostatin binding and effect of somatostatin on accumulation of inositol 1,4,5-trisphosphate in the rat frontoparietal cortex. Neuropsychopharmacology, 23: 178–187.

Matto, V., Harro, J. and Allikmets, L. (1997) The effect of drugs acting on CCK receptors and rat free exploration in the exploration box. J. Physiol. Pharmacol., 48: 239–251.

Matys, T., Pawlak, R., Matys, E., Pavlides, C., McEwen, B.S. and Strickland, S. (2004) Tissue plasminogen activator promotes the effects of corticotropin-releasing factor on the amygdala and anxiety-like behavior. Proc. Natl. Acad. Sci. U.S.A., 101: 16345–16350.

Maubach, K.A., Martin, K., Chicchi, G., Harrison, T., Wheeldon, A., Swain, C.J., Cumberbatch, M.J., Rupniak, N.M. and Seabrook, G.R. (2002) Chronic substance P (NK1) receptor antagonist and conventional antidepressant treatment increases burst firing of monoamine neurones in the locus coeruleus. Neuroscience, 109: 609–617.

Mazarati, A., Lundstrom, L., Sollenberg, U., Shin, D., Langel, U. and Sankar, R. (2006) Regulation of kindling epileptogenesis by hippocampal galanin type 1 and type 2 receptors: the effects of subtype-selective agonists and the role of G-protein-mediated signaling. J. Pharmacol. Exp. Ther., 318: 700–708.

McCann, U.D., Morgan, C.M., Geraci, M., Slate, S.O., Murphy, D.L. and Post, R.M. (1997a) Effects of the 5-HT3 antagonist, ondansetron, on the behavioral and physiological effects of pentagastrin in patients with panic disorder and social phobia. Neuropsychopharmacology, 17: 360–369.

McCann, U.D., Slate, S.O., Geraci, M., Roscow-Terrill, D. and Uhde, T.W. (1997b) A comparison of the effects of intravenous pentagastrin on patients with social phobia, panic disorder and healthy controls. Neuropsychopharmacology, 16: 229–237.

McCann, U.D., Slate, S.O., Geraci, M. and Uhde, T.W. (1994–1995) Peptides and anxiety: a dose-response evaluation of pentagastrin in healthy volunteers. Anxiety, 1: 258–267.

McCarthy, M.M., McDonald, C.H., Brooks, P.J. and Goldman, D. (1996) An anxiolytic action of oxytocin is enhanced by estrogen in the mouse. Physiol. Behav., 60: 1209–1215.

McDonald, A.J. and Mascagni, F. (2002) Immunohistochemical characterization of somatostatin containing interneurons in the rat basolateral amygdala. Brain Res., 943: 237–244.

McDonald, A.J. and Pearson, J.C. (1989) Coexistence of GABA and peptide immunoreactivity in non-pyramidal neurons of the basolateral amygdala. Neurosci. Lett., 100: 53–58.

Meis, S. and Pape, H.C. (2001) Control of glutamate and GABA release by nociceptin/orphanin FQ in the rat lateral amygdala. J. Physiol., 532: 701–712.

Meis, S., Sosulina, L., Schulz, S., Hollt, V. and Pape, H.C. (2005) Mechanisms of somatostatin-evoked responses in neurons of the rat lateral amygdala. Eur. J. Neurosci., 21: 755–762.

Meloni, E.G., Gerety, L.P., Knoll, A.T., Cohen, B.M. and Carlezon, W.A. Jr. (2006) Behavioral and anatomical interactions between dopamine and corticotropin-releasing factor in the rat. J. Neurosci., 26: 3855–3863.

Merali, Z., Bedard, T., Andrews, N., Davis, B., McKnight, A.T., Gonzalez, M.I., Pritchard, M., Kent, P. and Anisman, H. (2006) Bombesin receptors as a novel anti-anxiety therapeutic target: BB1 receptor actions on anxiety through alterations of serotonin activity. J. Neurosci., 26: 10387–10396.

Merali, Z., Khan, S., Michaud, D.S., Shippy, S.A. and Anisman, H. (2004) Does amygdaloid corticotropin-releasing hormone (CRH) mediate anxiety-like behaviors? Dissociation of anxiogenic effects and CRH release. Eur. J. Neurosci., 20: 229–239.

Mezey, E., Reisine, T.D., Skirboll, L., Beinfeld, M. and Kiss, J.Z. (1985) Cholecystokinin in the medial parvocellular subdivision of the paraventricular nucleus. Co-existence with corticotropin-releasing hormone. Ann. N.Y. Acad. Sci., 448: 152–156.

Michel, M.C., Beck-Sickinger, A., Cox, H., Doods, H.N., Herzog, H., Larhammar, D., Quirion, R., Schwartz, T. and Westfall, T. (1998) XVI. International Union of Pharmacology recommendations for the nomenclature of neuropeptide Y, peptide YY, and pancreatic polypeptide receptors. Pharmacol. Rev., 50: 143–150.

Miyasaka, K., Kobayashi, S., Ohta, M., Kanai, S., Yoshida, Y., Nagata, A., Matsui, T., Noda, T., Takiguchi, S., Takata, Y., Kawanami, T. and Funakoshi, A. (2002) Anxiety-related behaviors in cholecystokinin-A, B, and AB receptor gene knockout mice in the plus-maze. Neurosci. Lett., 335: 115–118.

Moller, C., Sommer, W., Thorsell, A. and Heilig, M. (1999) Anxiogenic-like action of galanin after intra-amygdala administration in the rat. Neuropsychopharmacology, 21: 507–512.

Moller, C., Sommer, W., Thorsell, A., Rimondini, R. and Heilig, M. (2002) Anxiogenic-like action of centrally administered glucagon-like peptide-1 in a punished drinking test. Prog. Neuro-Psychopharmacol. Biol. Psychiatry, 26: 119–122.

Mollereau, C., Parmentier, M., Mailleux, P., Butour, J.L., Moisand, C., Chalon, P., Caput, D., Vassart, G. and Meunier, J.C. (1994) ORL1, a novel member of the opioid receptor family. Cloning, functional expression and localization. FEBS Lett., 341: 33–38.

Montkowski, A., Jahn, H., Strohle, A., Poettig, M., Holsboer, F. and Wiedemann, K. (1998) C-type natriuretic peptide exerts effects opposing those of atrial natriuretic peptide on anxiety-related behaviour in rats. Brain Res., 792: 358–360.

Monzon, M.E. and De Barioglio, S.R. (1999) Response to novelty after i.c.v. injection of melanin-concentrating hormone (MCH) in rats. Physiol. Behav., 67: 813–817.

Monzon, M.E., Varas, M.M. and De Barioglio, S.R. (2001) Anxiogenesis induced by nitric oxide synthase inhibition and anxiolytic effect of melanin-concentrating hormone (MCH) in rat brain. Peptides, 22: 1043–1047.

Moody, T.W. and Merali, Z. (2004) Bombesin-like peptides and associated receptors within the brain: distribution and behavioral implications. Peptides, 25: 511–520.

Morawska, D., Sieklucka-Dziuba, M. and Kleinrok, Z. (1998) Central action of glucagon. Pol. J. Pharmacol., 50: 125–133.

Moreau, J.L., Kilpatrick, G. and Jenck, F. (1997) Urocortin, a novel neuropeptide with anxiogenic-like properties. Neuroreport, 8: 1697–1701.

Morgan, C.A., III Rasmusson, A.M., Winters, B., Hauger, R.L., Morgan, J., Hazlett, G. and Southwick, S. (2003) Trauma exposure rather than posttraumatic stress disorder is associated with reduced baseline plasma neuropeptide-Y levels. Biol. Psychiatry, 54: 1087–1091.

Morilak, D.A., Cecchi, M. and Khoshbouei, H. (2003) Interactions of norepinephrine and galanin in the central amygdala and lateral bed nucleus of the stria terminalis modulate the behavioral response to acute stress. Life Sci., 73: 715–726.

Mountney, C., Sillberg, V., Kent, P., Hymie, A. and Merali, Z. (2006) The role of gastrin-releasing peptide on conditioned fear: differential cortical and amygdaloid responses in the rat. Psychopharmacology, 189: 287–296.

Muller, M.B., Zimmermann, S., Sillaber, I., Hagemeyer, T.P., Deussing, J.M., Timpl, P., Kormann, M.S., Droste, S.K., Kuhn, R., Reul, J.M., Holsboer, F. and Wurst, W. (2003) Limbic corticotropin-releasing hormone receptor 1 mediates anxiety-related behavior and hormonal adaptation to stress. Nat. Neurosci., 6: 1100–1107.

Murphy, E.K., Sved, A.F. and Finlay, J.M. (2003) Corticotropin-releasing hormone receptor blockade fails to alter stress-evoked catecholamine release in prefrontal cortex of control or chronically stressed rats. Neuroscience, 116: 1081–1087.

Negus, S.S., Gatch, M.B., Mello, N.K., Zhang, X. and Rice, K. (1998) Behavioral effects of the delta-selective opioid agonist SNC80 and related compounds in rhesus monkeys. J. Pharmacol. Exp. Ther., 286: 362–375.

Nesse, R.M., Curtis, G.C., Thyer, B.A., McCann, D.S., Huber-Smith, M.J. and Knopf, R.F. (1985) Endocrine and cardiovascular responses during phobic anxiety. Psychosom. Med., 47: 320–332.

Netto, C.F. and Guimaraes, F.S. (2004) Anxiogenic effect of cholecystokinin in the dorsal periaqueductal gray. Neuropsychopharmacology, 29: 101–107.

Newport, D.J., Heim, C., Owens, M.J., Ritchie, J.C., Ramsey, C.H., Bonsall, R., Miller, A.H. and Nemeroff, C.B. (2003) Cerebrospinal fluid corticotropin-releasing factor (CRF) and vasopressin concentrations predict pituitary response in the CRF stimulation test: a multiple regression analysis. Neuropsychopharmacology, 28: 569–576.

Nieto, M.M., Guen, S.L., Kieffer, B.L., Roques, B.P. and Noble, F. (2005) Physiological control of emotion-related behaviors by endogenous enkephalins involves essentially the delta opioid receptors. Neuroscience, 135: 305–313.

Nikolaus, S., Huston, J.P. and Hasenohrl, R.U. (1999) The neurokinin-1 receptor antagonist WIN51,708 attenuates the anxiolytic-like effects of ventralpallidal substance P injection. Neuroreport, 10: 2293–2296.

Nova Pharm. Corp., (1991) US5063245.

Nyberg, F. and Hallberg, M. (2007) Peptide conversion – a potential pathway modulating G-protein signaling. Curr. Drug Targets, 8: 147–154.

Oberto, A., Panzica, G.C., Altruda, F. and Eva, C. (2001) GABAergic and NPY-Y(1) network in the medial amygdala: a neuroanatomical basis for their functional interaction. Neuropharmacology, 41: 639–642.

Oertel, W.H., Riethmuller, G., Mugnaini, E., Schmechel, D.E., Weindl, A., Gramsch, C. and Herz, A. (1983) Opioid peptide-like immunoreactivity localized in GABAergic neurons of rat neostriatum and central amygdaloid nucleus. Life Sci., 33(Suppl. 1): 73–76.

Ogren, S.O., Schott, P.A., Kehr, J., Yoshitake, T., Misane, I., Mannstrom, P. and Sandin, J. (1998) Modulation of acetylcholine and serotonin transmission by galanin. Relationship to spatial and aversive learning. Ann. N.Y. Acad. Sci., 863: 342–363.

Okuyama, S., Chaki, S., Kawashima, N., Suzuki, Y., Ogawa, S., Nakazato, A., Kumagai, T., Okubo, T. and Tomisawa, K. (1999a) Receptor binding, behavioral, and electrophysiological profiles of nonpeptide corticotropin-releasing factor subtype 1 receptor antagonists CRA1000 and CRA1001. J. Pharmacol. Exp. Ther., 289: 926–935.

Okuyama, S., Sakagawa, T., Chaki, S., Imagawa, Y., Ichiki, T. and Inagami, T. (1999b) Anxiety-like behavior in mice lacking the angiotensin II type-2 receptor. Brain Res., 821: 150–159.

Olsson, M., Annerbrink, K., Westberg, L., Melke, J., Baghaei, F., Rosmond, R., Holm, G., Andersch, S., Allgulander, C. and Eriksson, E. (2004) Angiotensin-related genes in patients with panic disorder. Am. J. Med. Genet. B Neuropsychiatr. Genet., 127: 81–84.

Otto, C., Martin, M., Wolfer, D.P., Lipp, H.P., Maldonado, R. and Schutz, G. (2001) Altered emotional behavior in PACAP-type-I-receptor-deficient mice. Mol. Brain Res., 92: 78–94.

Ouagazzal, A.M., Moreau, J.L., Pauly-Evers, M. and Jenck, F. (2003) Impact of environmental housing conditions on the emotional responses of mice deficient for nociceptin/orphanin FQ peptide precursor gene. Behav. Brain Res., 144: 111–117.

Overstreet, D.H., Knapp, D.J. and Breese, G.R. (2004) Modulation of multiple ethanol withdrawal-induced anxiety-like behavior by CRF and CRF1 receptors. Pharmacol. Biochem. Behav., 77: 405–413.

Owens, M.J. and Nemeroff, C.B. (1993) The role of corticotropin-releasing factor in the pathophysiology of affective and anxiety disorders: laboratory and clinical studies. Ciba Found. Symp., 172: 296–308.

Page, M.E. and Abercrombie, E.D. (1999) Discrete local application of corticotropin-releasing factor increases locus coeruleus discharge and extracellular norepinephrine in rat hippocampus. Synapse, 33: 304–313.

Palamarchouk, V.S., Swiergiel, A.H. and Dunn, A.J. (2002) Hippocampal noradrenergic responses to CRF injected into the locus coeruleus of unanesthetized rats. Brain Res., 950: 31–38.

Pande, A.C., Greiner, M., Adams, J.B., Lydiard, R.B. and Pierce, M.W. (1999) Placebo-controlled trial of the CCK-B antagonist, CI-988, in panic disorder. Biol. Psychiatry, 46: 860–862.

Pau, K.Y., Ma, Y.J., Yu, J.H., Yang, S.P., Airhart, N. and Spies, H.G. (1997) Topographic comparison of the expression of norepinephrine transporter, tyrosine hydroxylase and neuropeptide Y mRNA in association with dopamine beta-hydroxylase neurons in the rabbit brainstem. Mol. Brain Res., 48: 367–381.

Pavia, J.M., Hastings, J.A. and Morris, M.J. (1995) Neuropeptide Y potentiation of potassium-induced noradrenaline release in the hypothalamic paraventricular nucleus of the rat in vivo. Brain Res., 690: 108–111.

Pelleymounter, M.A., Joppa, M., Ling, N. and Foster, A.C. (2002) Pharmacological evidence supporting a role for central corticotropin-releasing factor(2) receptors in behavioral, but not endocrine, response to environmental stress. J. Pharmacol. Exp. Ther., 302: 145–152.

Pelleymounter, M.A., Joppa, M., Ling, N. and Foster, A.C. (2004) Behavioral and neuroendocrine effects of the selective CRF2 receptor agonists urocortin II and urocortin III. Peptides, 25: 659–666.

Pennefather, J.N., Lecci, A., Candenas, M.L., Patak, E., Pinto, F.M. and Maggi, C.A. (2004) Tachykinins and tachykinin receptors: a growing family. Life Sci., 74: 1445–1463.

Perrine, S.A., Hoshaw, B.A. and Unterwald, E.M. (2006) Delta opioid receptor ligands modulate anxiety-like behaviors in the rat. Brit. J. Pharmacol., 147: 864–872.

Petrie, K.A., Schmidt, D., Bubser, M., Fadel, J., Carraway, R.E. and Deutch, A.Y. (2005) Neurotensin activates GABA ergic interneurons in the prefrontal cortex. J. Neurosci., 25: 1629–1636.

Pich, E.M., Agnati, L.F., Zini, I., Marrama, P. and Carani, C. (1993) Neuropeptide Y produces anxiolytic effects in spontaneously hypertensive rats. Peptides, 14: 909–912.

Pitkanen, A., Lepola, U., Ylinen, A. and Riekkinen, P.J. (1989) Somatostatin and beta-endorphin levels in cerebrospinal fluid of nonmedicated and medicated patients with epileptic seizures. Neuropeptides, 13: 9–15.

Pitkow, L.J., Sharer, C.A., Ren, X., Insel, T.R., Terwilliger, E.F. and Young, L.J. (2001) Facilitation of affiliation and pair-bond formation by vasopressin receptor gene transfer into the ventral forebrain of a monogamous vole. J. Neurosci., 21: 7392–7396.

Poore, L.H. and Helmstetter, F.J. (1996) The effects of central injections of calcitonin gene-related peptide on fear-related behavior. Neurobiol. Learn. Mem., 66: 241–245.

Pratt, J.A. and Brett, R.R. (1995) The benzodiazepine receptor inverse agonist FG 7142 induces cholecystokinin gene expression in rat brain. Neurosci. Lett., 184: 197–200.

Price, M.L. and Lucki, I. (2001) Regulation of serotonin release in the lateral septum and striatum by corticotropin-releasing factor. J. Neurosci., 21: 2833–2841.

Privette, T.H. and Terrian, D.M. (1995) Kappa opioid agonists produce anxiolytic-like behavior on the elevated plus-maze. Psychopharmacology, 118: 444–450.

Quirarte, G.L., Galvez, R., Roozendaal, B. and McGaugh, J.L. (1998) Norepinephrine release in the amygdala in response to footshock and opioid peptidergic drugs. Brain Res., 808: 134–140.

Radu, D., Ahlin, A., Svanborg, P. and Lindefors, N. (2003) Pentagastrin test for anxiety – psychophysiology and personality. Psychopharmacology, 166: 139–145.

Radulovic, J., Ruhmann, A., Liepold, T. and Spiess, J. (1999) Modulation of learning and anxiety by corticotropin-releasing factor (CRF) and stress: differential roles of CRF receptors 1 and 2. J. Neurosci., 19: 5016–5025.

Ragnauth, A., Schuller, A., Morgan, M., Chan, J., Ogawa, S., Pintar, J., Bodnar, R.J. and Pfaff, D.W. (2001) Female preproenkephalin-knockout mice display altered emotional responses. Proc. Natl. Acad. Sci. U.S.A., 98: 1958–1963.

Rakovska, A., Giovannini, M.G., Della Corte, L., Kalfin, R., Bianchi, L. and Pepeu, G. (1998) Neurotensin modulation of acetylcholine and GABA release from the rat hippocampus: an in vivo microdialysis study. Neurochem. Int., 33: 335–340.

Rao, T.L., Kokare, D.M., Sarkar, S., Khisti, R.T., Chopde, C.T. and Subhedar, N. (2003) GABAergic agents prevent alpha-melanocyte stimulating hormone induced anxiety and anorexia in rats. Pharmacol. Biochem. Behav., 76: 417–423.

Rapaport, M.H., Risch, S.C., Golshan, S. and Gillin, J.C. (1989) Neuroendocrine effects of ovine corticotropin-releasing hormone in panic disorder patients. Biol. Psychiatry, 26: 344–348.

Rasmusson, A.M., Hauger, R.L., Morgan, C.A., Bremner, J.D., Charney, D.S. and Southwick, S.M. (2000) Low baseline and yohimbine-stimulated plasma neuropeptide Y (NPY) levels in combat-related PTSD. Biol. Psychiatry, 47: 526–539.

Rasmusson, A.M., Lipschitz, D.S., Wang, S., Hu, S., Vojvoda, D., Bremner, J.D., Southwick, S.M. and Charney, D. (2001) Increased pituitary and adrenal reactivity in premenopausal women with posttraumatic stress disorder. Biol. Psychiatry, 12: 965–977.

Rattan, A.K. and Tejwani, G.A. (1997) Effect of chronic treatment with morphine, midazolam and both together on dynorphin(1–13) levels in the rat. Brain Res., 754: 239–244.

Raud, S., Innos, J., Abramov, U., Reimets, A., Koks, S., Soosaar, A., Matsui, T. and Vasar, E. (2005) Targeted invalidation of CCK2 receptor gene induces anxiolytic-like action in light–dark exploration, but not in fear conditioning test. Psychopharmacology, 181: 347–357.

Raud, S., Runkorg, K., Veraksits, A., Reimets, A., Nelovkov, A., Abramov, U., Matsui, T., Bourin, M., Volke, V., Koks, S. and Vasar, E. (2003) Targeted mutation of CCK2 receptor gene modifies the behavioural effects of diazepam in female mice. Psychopharmacology, 168: 417–425.

Redei, E., Rittenhouse, P.A., Revskoy, S., McGivern, R.F. and Aird, F. (1998) A novel endogenous corticotropin release inhibiting factor. Ann. N.Y. Acad. Sci., 840: 456–469.

Redrobe, J.P., Dumont, Y., Herzog, H. and Quirion, R. (2003) Neuropeptide Y (NPY) Y2 receptors mediate behaviour in two animal models of anxiety: evidence from Y2 receptor knockout mice. Behav. Brain Res., 141: 251–255.

Rehfeld, J.F. and Hansen, H.F. (1986) Characterization of preprocholecystokinin products in the porcine cerebral cortex. Evidence of different processing pathways. J. Biol. Chem., 261: 5832–5840.

Reist, C., Kauffmann, C.D., Chicz-Demet, A., Chen, C.C. and Demet, E.M. (1995) REM latency, dexamethasone suppression test, and thyroid releasing hormone stimulation test in posttraumatic stress disorder. Prog. Neuro-Psychopharmacol. Biol. Psychiatry, 19: 433–443.

Renoldi, G. and Invernizzi, R.W. (2006) Blockade of tachykinin NK1 receptors attenuates stress-induced rise of extracellular noradrenaline and dopamine in the rat and gerbil medial prefrontal cortex. J. Neurosci. Res., 84: 961–968.

Rex, A. and Fink, H. (1998) Effects of cholecystokinin-receptor agonists on cortical 5-HT release in guinea pigs on the X-maze. Peptides, 19: 519–526.

Rex, A., Fink, H. and Marsden, C.A. (1994) Effects of BOC-CCK-4 and L 365.260 on cortical 5-HT release in guinea-pigs on exposure to the elevated plus maze. Neuropharmacology, 33: 559–565.

Rex, A., Marsden, C.A. and Fink, H. (1997) Cortical 5-HT-CCK interactions and anxiety-related behaviour of guinea-pigs: a microdialysis study. Neurosci. Lett., 228: 79–82.

Reyes, T.M., Lewis, K., Perrin, M.H., Kunitake, K.S., Vaughan, J., Arias, C.A., Hogenesch, J.B., Gulyas, J., Rivier, J., Vale, W.W. and Sawchenko, P.E. (2001) Urocortin II: a member of the corticotropin-releasing factor (CRF) neuropeptide family that is selectively bound by type 2 CRF receptors. Proc. Natl. Acad. Sci. U.S.A., 98: 2843–2848.

Rezayat, M., Roohbakhsh, A., Zarrindast, M.R., Massoudi, R. and Djahanguiri, B. (2005) Cholecystokinin and GABA interaction in the dorsal hippocampus of rats in the elevated plus-maze test of anxiety. Physiol. Behav., 84: 775–782.

Rinaman, L., Hoffman, G.E., Dohanics, J., Le, W.W., Stricker, E.M. and Verbalis, J.G. (1995) Cholecystokinin activates catecholaminergic neurons in the caudal medulla that innervate the paraventricular nucleus of the hypothalamus in rats. J. Comp. Neurol., 360: 246–256.

Ring, R.H., Malberg, J., Potestio, L., Failli, A., Luo, B., Schechter, L.E., Rosenzweig-Lipson, S. and Rahman, Z. (2005) Anxiolytic-like effects of oxytocin receptor agonists in rodents. Soc. Neurosci. Abstr., 31:

Ring, R.H., Malberg, J.E., Potestio, L., Ping, J., Boikess, S., Luo, B., Schechter, L.E., Rizzo, S., Rahman, Z. and Rosenzweig-Lipson, S. (2006) Anxiolytic-like activity of oxytocin in male mice: behavioral and autonomic evidence, therapeutic implications. Psychopharmacology, 185: 218–225.

Risbrough, V.B., Hauger, R.L., Pelleymounter, M.A. and Geyer, M.A. (2003) Role of corticotropin releasing factor (CRF) receptors 1 and 2 in CRF-potentiated acoustic startle in mice. Psychopharmacology, 170: 178–187.

Roberto, M. and Siggins, G.R. (2006) Nociceptin/orphanin FQ presynaptically decreases GABAergic transmission and blocks the ethanol-induced increase of GABA release in central amygdala. Proc. Natl. Acad. Sci. U.S.A., 103: 9715–9720.

Roesler, R., Henriques, J.A. and Schwartsmann, G. (2004) Neuropeptides and anxiety disorders: bombesin receptors as novel therapeutic targets. Trends Pharmacol. Sci., 25: 241–242.

Rosenfeld, M.G., Mermod, J.J., Amara, S.G., Swanson, L.W., Sawchenko, P.E. and Rivier, J., et al. (1983) Production of a novel neuropeptide encoded by the calcitonin gene via tissue-specific RNA processing. Nature, 304: 129–135.

Roy, M., David, N.K., Danao, J.V., Baribault, H., Tian, H. and Giorgetti, M. (2006) Genetic inactivation of melanin-concentrating hormone receptor subtype 1 (MCHR1) in mice exerts anxiolytic-like behavioral effects. Neuropsychopharmacology, 31: 112–120.

Roy-Byrne, P.P., Uhde, T.W., Post, R.M., Gallucci, W., Chrousos, G.P. and Gold, P.W. (1986a) The corticotropin-releasing hormone stimulation test in patients with panic disorder. Am. J. Psychiatry, 143: 896–899.

Roy-Byrne, P.P., Uhde, T.W., Rubinow, D.R. and Post, R.M. (1986b) Reduced TSH and prolactin responses to TRH in patients with panic disorder. Am. J. Psychiatry, 143: 503–507.

Rupniak, N.M. (2005) Substance P (NK1 receptor) antagonists. In: Steckler, T. Kalin, N.H. and Reul, J.M.H.M. (Eds.), Handbook of Stress and the Brain, Part 2: Integrative and Clinical Aspects. Elsevier, Amsterdam, pp. 423–435.

Rupniak, N.M., Carlson, E.C., Harrison, T., Oates, B., Seward, E., Owen, S., de Felipe, C., Hunt, S. and Wheeldon, A. (2000) Pharmacological blockade or genetic deletion of substance P (NK(1)) receptors attenuates neonatal vocalisation in guinea-pigs and mice. Neuropharmacology, 39: 1321–1413.

Rupniak, N.M., Carlson, E.J., Webb, J.K., Harrison, T., Porsolt, R.D., Roux, S., de Felipe, C., Hunt, S.P., Oates, B. and Wheeldon, A. (2001) Comparison of the phenotype of NK1R–/– mice with pharmacological blockade of the substance P (NK1) receptor in assays for antidepressant and anxiolytic drugs. Behav. Pharmacol., 12: 497–508.

Rupniak, N.M., Schaffer, L., Siegl, P. and Iversen, S.D. (1993) Failure of intravenous pentagastrin challenge to induce panic-like effects in rhesus monkeys. Neuropeptides, 25: 115–119.

Saavedra, J.M., Ando, H., Armando, I., Baiardi, G., Bregonzio, C., Juorio, A. and Macova, M. (2005) Anti-stress and anti-anxiety effects of centrally acting angiotensin II AT1 receptor antagonists. Regul. Pept., 128: 227–238.

Saavedra, J.M., Armando, I., Bregonzio, C., Juorio, A., Macova, M., Pavel, J. and Sanchez-Lemus, E. (2006) A centrally acting, anxiolytic angiotensin II AT1 receptor antagonist prevents the isolation stress-induced decrease in cortical CRF1 receptor and benzodiazepine binding. Neuropsychopharmacology, 31: 1123–1134.

Saavedra, J.M., De Oliveira, A.M., Johren, O. and Tonelli, L. (2000) Brain endothelin and natriuretic receptors. In: Quirion, R. Bjorklund, A. and Hokfelt, T. (Eds.), Handbook of Chemical Neuroanatomy, Vol. 16: Peptide Receptors, Part 1Elsevier, Amsterdam, pp. 125–162.

Saavedra, J.M. and Pavel, J. (2005) Angiotensin II AT1 receptor antagonists inhibit the angiotensin-CRF-AVP axis and are potentially useful for the treatment of stress-related and mood disorders. Drug Dev. Res., 65: 237–269.

Sahuque, L.L., Kullberg, E.F., Mcgeehan, A.J., Kinder, J.R., Hicks, M.P., Blanton, M.G., Janak, P.H. and Olive, M.F. (2006) Anxiogenic and aversive effects of corticotropin-releasing factor (CRF) in the bed nucleus of the stria terminalis in the rat: role of CRF receptor subtypes. Psychopharmacology, 186: 122–132.

Saitoh, A., Kimura, Y., Suzuki, T., Kawai, K., Nagase, H. and Kamei, J. (2004) Potential anxiolytic and antidepressant-like activities of SNC80, a selective delta-opioid agonist, in behavioral models in rodents. J. Pharmacol. Sci., 95: 374–380.

Saitoh, A., Yoshikawa, Y., Onodera, K. and Kamei, J. (2005) Role of delta-opioid receptor subtypes in anxiety-related behaviors in the elevated plus-maze in rats. Psychopharmacology, 182: 327–334.

Sajdyk, T.J., Fitz, S.D. and Shekhar, A. (2006) The role of neuropeptide Y in the amygdala on corticotropin-releasing factor receptor-mediated behavioral stress responses in the rat. Stress, 9: 21–28.

Sajdyk, T.J., Schober, D.A. and Gehlert, D.R. (2002) Neuropeptide Y receptor subtypes in the basolateral nucleus of the amygdala modulate anxiogenic responses in rats. Neuropharmacology, 43: 1165–1172.

Sajdyk, T.J., Schober, D.A., Gehlert, D.R. and Shekhar, A. (1999a) Role of corticotropin-releasing factor and urocortin within the basolateral amygdala of rats in anxiety and panic responses. Behav. Brain Res., 100: 207–215.

Sajdyk, T.J., Shekhar, A. and Gehlert, D.R. (2004) Interactions between NPY and CRF in the amygdala to regulate emotionality. Neuropeptides, 38: 225–234.

Sajdyk, T.J., Vandergriff, M.G. and Gehlert, D.R. (1999b) Amygdalar neuropeptide Y Y1 receptors mediate the anxiolytic-like actions of neuropeptide Y in the social interaction test. Eur. J. Pharmacol., 368: 143–147.

Sakurai, T., Amemiya, A., Ishii, M., Matsuzaki, I., Chemelli, R.M., Tanaka, H., Williams, S.C., Richardson, J.A., Kozlowski, G.P., Wilson, S., Arch, J.R., Buckingham, R.E., Haynes, A.C., Carr, S.A., Annan, R.S., McNulty, D.E., Liu, W.S., Terrett, J.A., Elshourbagy, N.A., Bergsma, D.J. and Yanagisawa, M. (1998) Orexins and orexin receptors: a family of hypothalamic neuropeptides and G protein-coupled receptors that regulate feeding behavior. Cell, 92: 573–585.

Salome, N., Stemmelin, J., Cohen, C. and Griebel, G. (2006a) Selective blockade of NK2 or NK3 receptors produces anxiolytic- and antidepressant-like effects in gerbils. Pharmacol. Biochem. Behav., 83: 533–539.

Salome, N., Stemmelin, J., Cohen, C. and Griebel, G. (2006b) Differential roles of amygdaloid nuclei in the anxiolytic- and antidepressant-like effects of the V1b receptor antagonist, SSR149415, in rats. Psychopharmacology, 187: 237–244.

Samson, W.K., Bagley, S.L., Ferguson, A.V. and White, M.M. (2007) Hypocretin/orexin tye 1 receptor in brain: role in cardiovascular control and the neuroendocrine response to immobilization stress. Am. J. Physiol. Regul. Int. Comp. Physiol., 292: 382–387.

Sanchez-Fernandez, C., Gonzalez, C., Mercer, L.D., Beart, P.M., Ruiz-Gayo, M. and Fernandez-Alfonso, M.S. (2003) Cholecystokinin induces cerebral vasodilatation via presynaptic CCK2 receptors: new implications for the pathophysiology of panic. J. Cereb. Blood Flow Metabol., 23: 364–370.

Santarelli, L., Gobbi, G., Debs, P.C., Sibille, E.T., Blier, P., Hen, R. and Heath, M.J. (2001) Genetic and pharmacological disruption of neurokinin 1 receptor function decreases anxiety-related behaviors and increases serotonergic function. Proc. Natl. Acad. Sci. U.S.A., 98: 1912–1917.

Sauvage, M. and Steckler, T. (2001) Detection of corticotropin-releasing hormone receptor 1 immunoreactivity in cholinergic, dopaminergic and noradrenergic neurons of the murine basal forebrain and brainstem nuclei – potential implication for arousal and attention. Neuroscience, 104: 643–652.

Schedlowski, M., Fluge, T., Richter, S., Tewes, U., Schmidt, R.E. and Wagner, T.O. (1995) Beta-endorphin, but not substance-P, is increased by acute stress in humans. Psychoneuroendocrinology, 20: 103–110.

Schulz, C. and Lehnert, H. (1996) Activation of noradrenergic neurons in the locus coeruleus by corticotropin-releasing factor. A microdialysis study. Neuroendocrinology, 63: 454–458.

Schulz, D.W., Mansbach, R.S., Sprouse, J., Braselton, J.P., Collins, J., Corman, M., Dunaiskis, A., Faraci, S., Schmidt, A.W., Seeger, T., Seymour, P., Tingley, F.D., III Winston, E.N., Chen, Y.L. and Heym, J. (1996) CP-154,526: a potent and selective nonpeptide antagonist of corticotropin releasing factor receptors. Proc. Natl. Acad. Sci. U.S.A., 93: 10477–10482.

Seedat, S., Stein, M.B., Kennedy, C.M. and Hauger, R.L. (2003) Plasma cortisol and neuropeptide Y in female victims of intimate partner violence. Psychoneuroendocrinology, 28: 796–808.

Serradeil-Le Gal, C., Wagnon, J., Simiand, J., Griebel, G., Lacour, C., Guillon, G., Barberis, C., Brossard, G., Soubrie, P., Nisato, D., Pascal, M., Pruss, R., Scatton, B., Maffrand, J.P. and Le Fur, G. (2002) Characterization of (2S,4R)-1-[5-chloro-1-[(2,4-dimethoxyphenyl)sulfonyl]-3-(2-methoxy-phenyl)-2-oxo-2,3-dihydro-1H-indol-3-yl]-4-hydroxy-N,N-dimethyl-2-pyrrolidine carboxamide (SSR149415), a selective and orally active vasopressin V1b receptor antagonist. J. Pharmacol. Exp. Ther., 300: 1122–1130.

Shekhar, A., Johnson, P.L., Sajdyk, T.J., Fitz, S.D., Keim, S.R., Kelley, P.E., Gehlert, D.R. and DiMicco, J.A. (2006) Angiotensin-II is a putative neurotransmitter in lactate-induced panic-like responses in rats with disruption of GABAergic inhibition in the dorsomedial hypothalamus. J. Neurosci., 26: 9205–9215.

Shekhar, A., Truitt, W., Rainnie, D. and Sajdyk, T. (2005) Role of stress, corticotropin releasing factor (CRF) and amygdala plasticity in chronic anxiety. Stress, 8: 209–219.

Shepherd, J., Bill, D.J., Dourish, C.T., Grewal, S.S., McLenachan, A. and Stanhope, K.J. (1996) Effects of the selective angiotensin II receptor antagonists losartan and PD123177 in animal models of anxiety and memory. Psychopharmacology, 126: 206–218.

Shibasaki, T., Tsumori, C., Hotta, M., Imaki, T. and Demura, H. (1995) Intracerebroventricular administration of neuropeptide Y inhibits release of noradrenaline in the hypothalamic paraventricular nucleus caused by manual restraint in the rat through an opioid system. Brain Res., 688: 189–192.

Shimazaki, T. and Chaki, S. (2005) Anxiolytic-like effect of a selective and non-peptidergic melanocortin 4 receptor antagonist, MCL0129, in a social interaction test. Pharmacol. Biochem. Behav., 80: 395–400.

Shimazaki, T., Iijima, M. and Chaki, S. (2006) The pituitary mediates the anxiolytic-like effects of the vasopressin V1B receptor antagonist, SSR149415, in a social interaction test in rats. Eur. J. Pharmacol., 543: 63–67.

Shimizu, E., Hashimoto, K., Kobayashi, K., Mitsumori, M., Ohgake, S., Koizumi, H., Okamura, N., Koike, K., Kumakiri, C., Nakazato, M., Komatsu, N. and Iyo, M. (2004) Lack of association between angiotensin I-converting enzyme insertion/deletion gene functional polymorphism and panic disorder in humans. Neurosci. Lett., 363: 81–83.

Shlik, J., Aluoja, A., Vasar, V., Vasar, E., Podar, T. and Bradwejn, J. (1997) Effects of citalopram treatment on behavioural, cardiovascular and neuroendocrine response to cholecystokinin tetrapeptide challenge in patients with panic disorder. J. Psychiatry Neuroci., 22: 332–340.

Shumyatsky, G.P., Tsvetkov, E., Malleret, G., Vronskaya, S., Hatton, M., Hampton, L., Battey, J.F., Dulac, C., Kandel, E.R. and Bolshakov, V.Y. (2002) Identification of a signaling network in lateral nucleus of amygdala important for inhibiting memory specifically related to learned fear. Cell, 111: 905–918.

Singareddy, R., Uhde, T. and Commissaris, R. (2006) Differential effects of hypocretins on noise-alone versus potentiated startle responses. Physiol. Behav., 89: 650–655.

Singh, L., Lewis, A.S., Field, M.J., Hughes, J. and Woodruff, G.N. (1991) Evidence for an involvement of the brain cholecystokinin B receptor in anxiety. Proc. Natl. Acad. Sci. U.S.A., 88: 1130–1133.

Skelton, K.H., Nemeroff, C.B. and Owens, M.J. (2004) Spontaneous withdrawal from the triazolobenzodiazepine alprazolam increases cortical corticotropin-releasing factor mRNA expression. J. Neurosci., 24: 9303–9312.

Skuladottir, G.V., Jonsson, L., Skarphedinsson, J.O., Mutulis, F., Muceniece, R., Raine, A., Mutule, I., Helgason, J., Prusis, P., Wikberg, J.E. and Schioth, H.B. (1999) Long term orexigenic effect of a novel melanocortin 4 receptor selective antagonist. Br. J. Pharmacol., 126: 27–34.

Skutella, T., Probst, J.C., Renner, U., Holsboer, F. and Behl, C. (1998) Corticotropin-releasing hormone receptor (type I) antisense targeting reduces anxiety. Neuroscience, 85: 795–805.

Sloviter, R.S., Ali-Akbarian, L., Horvath, K.D. and Menkens, K.A. (2001) Substance P receptor expression by inhibitory interneurons of the rat hippocampus: enhanced detection using improved immunocytochemical methods for the preservation and colocalization of GABA and other neuronal markers. J. Comp. Neurol., 430: 283–305.

Smith, D.G., Davis, R.J., Rorick-Kehn, L., Morin, M., Witkin, J.M., McKinzie, D.L., Nomikos, G.G. and Gehlert, D.R. (2006) Melanin-concentrating hormone-1 receptor modulates neuroendocrine, behavioral, and corticolimbic neurochemical stress responses in mice. Neuropsychopharmacology, 31: 1135–1145.

Smith, G.W., Aubry, J.M., Dellu, F., Contarino, A., Bilezikjian, L.M., Gold, L.H., Chen, R., Marchuk, Y., Hauser, C., Bentley, C.A., Sawchenko, P.E., Koob, G.F., Vale, W. and Lee, K.F. (1998) Corticotropin releasing factor receptor 1-deficient mice display decreased anxiety, impaired stress response, and aberrant neuroendocrine development. Neuron, 20: 1093–1102.

Smith, M.A., Davidson, J., Ritchie, J.C., Kudler, H., Lipper, S., Chappell, P. and Nemeroff, C.B. (1989) The corticotropin-releasing hormone test in patients with posttraumatic stress disorder. Biol. Psychiatry, 26: 349–355.

Smoller, J.W., Yamaki, L.H., Fagerness, J.A., Biederman, J., Racette, S., Laird, N.M., Kagan, J., Snidman, N., Faraone, S.V., Hirshfeld-Becker, D., Tsuang, M.T., Slaugenhaupt, S.A., Rosenbaum, J.F. and Sklar, P.B. (2005) The corticotropin-releasing hormone gene and behavioral inhibition in children at risk for panic disorder. Biol. Psychiatry, 57: 1485–1492.

Snider, R.M., Constantine, J.W., Lowe, J.A., III Longo, K.P., Lebel, W.S., Woody, H.A., Drozda, S.E., Desai, M.C., Vinick, F.J. and Spencer, R.W., et al. (1991) A potent nonpeptide antagonist of the substance P (NK1) receptor. Science, 251: 435–437.

Somogyi, J., Baude, A., Omori, Y., Shimizu, H., Mestikawy, S.E., Fukaya, M., Shigemoto, R., Watanabe, M. and Somogyi, P. (2004) GABAergic basket cells expressing cholecystokinin contain vesicular glutamate transporter type 3 (VGLUT3) in their synaptic terminals in hippocampus and isocortex of the rat. Eur. J. Neurosci., 19: 552–569.

Sorensen, G., Lindberg, C., Wortwein, G., Bolwig, T.G. and Woldbye, D.P. (2004) Differential roles for neuropeptide Y Y1 and Y5 receptors in anxiety and sedation. J. Neurosci. Res., 77: 723–729.

Spiga, F., Lightman, S.L., Shekhar, A. and Lowry, C.A. (2006) Injections of urocortin 1 into the basolateral amygdala induce anxiety-like behaviour and c-fos expression in brainstem serotonergic neurons. Neuroscience, 138: 1265–1276.

Spina, M., Merlo-Pich, E., Chan, R.K., Basso, A.M., Rivier, J., Vale, W. and Koob, G.F. (1996) Appetite-suppressing effects of urocortin, a CRF-related neuropeptide. Science, 273: 1561–1564.

Spina, M.G., Merlo-Pich, E., Akwa, Y., Balducci, C., Basso, A.M., Zorrilla, E.P., Britton, K.T., Rivier, J., Vale, W.W. and Koob, G.F. (2002) Time-dependent induction of anxiogenic-like effects after central infusion of urocortin or corticotropin-releasing factor in the rat. Psychopharmacology, 160: 113–121.

Spooren, W.P., Schoeffter, P., Gasparini, F., Kuhn, R. and Gentsch, C. (2002) Pharmacological and endocrinological characterisation of stress-induced hyperthermia in singly housed mice using classical and candidate anxiolytics (LY314582, MPEP and NKP608). Eur. J. Pharmacol., 435: 161–170.

Sramek, J.J., Kramer, M.S., Reines, S.A. and Cutler, N.R. (1994–1995) Pilot study of a CCKB antagonist in patients with panic disorder: preliminary findings. Anxiety, 1: 141–143.

Stadler, T., Veltmar, A., Qadri, F. and Unger, T. (1992) Angiotensin II evokes noradrenaline release from the paraventricular nucleus in conscious rats. Brain Res., 569: 117–122.

Stahl, C.E., Redei, E., Wang, Y. and Borlongan, C.V. (2002) Behavioral, hormonal and histological stress markers of anxiety-separation in postnatal rats are reduced by prepro-thyrotropin-releasing hormone 178–199. Neurosci. Lett., 321: 85–89.

Steckler, T. (2005) CRF antagonists as novel treatment strategies for stress-related disorders. In: Steckler, T. Kalin, N.H. and Reul, J.M.H.M. (Eds.), Handbook of Stress and the Brain, Part 2: Integrative and Clinical Aspects. Elsevier, Amsterdam, pp. 373–407.

Steckler, T. and Dautzenberg, F. (2006) Corticotropin-releasing factor antagonists in affective disorders and drug dependence – an update. CNS Neurol. Disorders Drug Targets, 5: 147–165.

Steckler, T. and Holsboer, F. (1999) Corticotropin-releasing hormone receptor subtypes and emotion. Biol. Psychiatry, 46: 1480–1508.

Steckler, T., Nakazato, A., Kennis, L., Mackie, C., Nakamura, M., Vinken, P., Sugiura, M., Ashton, D., Malatynska, E., Langlois, X. and Chaki, S. (2006) CRF$_1$ antagonists – therapeutic implications for affective and mood disorders. Actualités de Chimie Thérapeutique, Société de Chimie Thérapeutique, 32: 1–19.

Stein, M.B., Hauger, R.L., Dhalla, K.S., Chartier, M.J. and Asmundson, G.J. (1996) Plasma neuropeptide Y in anxiety disorders: findings in panic disorder and social phobia. Psychiatry Res., 59: 183–188.

Stein, M.B. and Uhde, T.W. (1988) Thyroid indices in panic disorder. Am. J. Psychiatry, 145: 745–747.

Steinberg, R., Alonso, R., Griebel, G., Bert, L., Jung, M., Oury-Donat, F., Poncelet, M., Gueudet, C., Desvignes, C., Le Fur, G. and Soubrie, P. (2001) Selective blockade of neurokinin-2 receptors produces antidepressant-like effects associated with reduced corticotropin-releasing factor function. J. Pharmacol. Exp. Ther., 299: 449–458.

Stemmelin, J., Lukovic, L., Salome, N. and Griebel, G. (2005) Evidence that the lateral septum is involved in the antidepressant-like effects of the vasopressin V1b receptor antagonist, SSR149415. Neuropsychopharmacology, 30: 35–42.

Stenzel-Poore, M.P., Heinrichs, S.C., Rivest, S., Koob, G.F. and Vale, W.W. (1994) Overproduction of corticotropin-releasing factor in transgenic mice: a genetic model of anxiogenic behavior. J. Neurosci., 14: 2579–2784.

Stephens, D.N., Meldrum, B.S., Weidmann, R., Schneider, C. and Grutzner, M. (1986) Does the excitatory amino acid receptor antagonist 2-APH exhibit anxiolytic activity? Psychopharmacology, 90: 166–169.

Stevenson, G.W., Canadas, F., Gomez-Serrano, M., Ullrich, T., Zhang, X., Rice, K.C. and Riley, A.K. (2002) Delta opioid discrimination learning in the rat: assessment with the selective delta agonist SNC80. Pharmacol. Biochem. Behav., 71: 291–300.

Stoehr, J.D., Cramer, C.P. and North, W.G. (1992) Oxytocin and vasopressin hexapeptide fragments have opposing influences on conditioned freezing behavior. Psychoneuroendocrinology, 17: 267–271.

Stout, S.C., Owens, M.J., Lindsey, K.P., Knight, D.L. and Nemeroff, C.B. (2001) Effects of sodium valproate on corticotropin-releasing factor systems in rat brain. Neuropsychopharmacology, 24: 624–631.

Strohle, A., Jahn, H., Montkowski, A., Liebsch, G., Boll, E., Landgraf, R., Holsboer, F. and Wiedemann, K. (1997) Central and peripheral administration of atriopeptin is anxiolytic in rats. Neuroendocrinology, 65: 210–215.

Strohle, A., Kellner, M., Holsboer, F. and Wiedemann, K. (2001) Anxiolytic activity of atrial natriuretic peptide in patients with panic disorder. Am. J. Psychiatry, 158: 1514–1516.

Sutton, S.W., Bonaventure, P., Kuei, C., Roland, B., Chen, J., Nepomuceno, D., Lovenberg, T.W. and Liu, C. (2004) Distribution of G-protein-coupled receptor (GPCR)135 binding sites and receptor mRNA in the rat brain suggests a role for relaxin-3 in neuroendocrine and sensory processing. Neuroendocrinology, 80: 298–307.

Suzuki, M., Beuckmann, C.T., Shikata, K., Ogura, H. and Sawai, T. (2005) Orexin-A (hypocretin-1) is possibly involved in generation of anxiety-like behavior. Brain Res., 1044: 116–121.

218

Swanson, C.J., Blackburn, T.P., Zhang, X., Zheng, K., Xu, Z.Q., Hokfelt, T., Wolinsky, T.D., Konkel, M.J., Chen, H., Zhong, H., Walker, M.W., Craig, D.A., Gerald, C.P. and Branchek, T.A. (2005) Anxiolytic- and antidepressant-like profiles of the galanin-3 receptor (Gal3) antagonists SNAP 37889 and SNAP 398299. Proc. Natl. Acad. Sci. U.S.A., 102: 17489–17494.

Takamatsu, Y., Yamamoto, H., Ogunremi, O.O., Matsuzaki, I. and Moroji, T. (1991) The effects of corticotropin-releasing hormone on peptidergic neurons in the rat forebrain. Neuropeptides, 20: 255–265.

Tanaka, J., Hayashi, Y., Nomura, S., Miyakubo, H., Okumura, T. and Sakamaki, K. (2001) Angiotensinergic and noradrenergic mechanisms in the hypothalamic paraventricular nucleus participate in the drinking response induced by activation of the subfornical organ in rats. Behav. Brain Res., 118: 117–122.

Tanaka, M., Iijima, N., Miyamoto, Y., Fukusumi, S., Itoh, Y., Ozawa, H. and Ibata, Y. (2005) Neurons expressing relaxin 3/INSL 7 in the nucleus incertus respond to stress. Eur. J. Neurosci., 21: 1659–1670.

Tanaka, M., Yoshida, M., Emoto, H. and Ishii, H. (2000) Noradrenaline systems in the hypothalamus, amygdala and locus coeruleus are involved in the provocation of anxiety: basic studies. Eur. J. Pharmacol., 405: 397–406.

Tanaka, S. and Tsujimoto, A. (1981) Somatostatin facilitates the serotonin release from rat cerebral cortex, hippocampus and hypothalamus slices. Brain Res., 208: 219–222.

Tao, R., Ma, Z., McKenna, J.T., Thakkar, M.M., Winston, S., Strecker, R.E. and McCarley, R.W. (2006) Differential effect of orexins (hypocretins) on serotonin release in the dorsal and median raphe nuclei of freely behaving rats. Neuroscience, 141: 1101–1105.

Taylor, M.M., Yuill, E.A., Baker, J.R., Ferri, C.C., Ferguson, A.V. and Samson, W.K. (2005) Actions of neuropeptide W in paraventricular hypothalamus: implications for the control of stress hormone secretion. Am. J. Physiol. Reg. Integr. Comp. Physiol., 288: R270–R275.

Teixeira, R.M. and De Lima, T.C. (2003) Involvement of tachykinin NK1 receptor in the behavioral and immunological responses to swimming stress in mice. Neuropeptides, 37: 307–315.

Teixeira, R.M., Duarte, F.S. and De Lima, T.C. (2004) Behavioral and immunological effects of substance P in female and male mice. Pharmacol. Biochem. Behav., 79: 1–9.

Teixeira, R.M., Santos, A.R., Ribeiro, S.J., Calixto, J.B., Rae, G.A. and De Lima, T.C. (1996) Effects of central administration of tachykinin receptor agonists and antagonists on plus-maze behavior in mice. Eur. J. Pharmacol., 311: 7–14.

Tezval, H., Jahn, O., Todorovic, C., Sasse, A., Eckart, K. and Spiess, J. (2004) Cortagine, a specific agonist of corticotropin-releasing factor receptor subtype 1, is anxiogenic and antidepressive in the mouse model. Proc. Natl. Acad. Sci. U.S.A., 101: 9468–9473.

Thompson, E.L., Murphy, K.G., Todd, J.F., Martin, N.M., Small, C.J., Ghatei, M.A. and Bloom, S.R. (2004) Chronic administration of NMU into the paraventricular nucleus stimulates the HPA axis but does not influence food intake or body weight. Biochem. Biophys. Res. Comm., 323: 65–71.

Thorsell, A., Michalkiewicz, M., Dumont, Y., Quirion, R., Caberlotto, L., Rimondini, R., Mathe, A.A. and Heilig, M. (2000) Behavioral insensitivity to restraint stress, absent fear suppression of behavior and impaired spatial learning in transgenic rats with hippocampal neuropeptide Y overexpression. Proc. Natl. Acad. Sci. U.S.A., 97: 12852–12857.

Timpl, P., Spanagel, R., Sillaber, I., Kresse, A., Reul, J.M., Stalla, G.K., Blanquet, V., Steckler, T., Holsboer, F. and Wurst, W. (1998) Impaired stress response and reduced anxiety in mice lacking a functional corticotropin-releasing hormone receptor 1. Nat. Genet., 19: 162–166.

To, C.T. and Bagdy, G. (1999) Anxiogenic effect of central CCK administration is attenuated by chronic fluoxetine or ipsapirone treatment. Neuropharmacology, 38: 279–282.

Trabanco, A.A., Pullan, S., Alonso, J.M., Alvarez, R.M., Andres, J.I., Boeckx, I., Fernandez, J., Gomez, A., Iturrino, L., Janssens, F.E., Leenaerts, J.E., De Lucas, A.I., Matesanz, E., Meert, T. and Steckler, T. (2006) 4-Phenyl-4-[1H-imidazol-2-yl]-piperidine derivatives, a novel class of selective delta-opioid agonists. Bioorg. Med. Chem. Lett., 16: 146–149.

Tschenett, A., Singewald, N., Carli, M., Balducci, C., Salchner, P., Vezzani, A., Herzog, H. and Sperk, G. (2003) Reduced anxiety and improved stress coping ability in mice lacking NPY-Y2 receptors. Eur. J. Neurosci., 18: 143–148.

Tschop, M., Smiley, D.L. and Heiman, M.L. (2000) Ghrelin induces adiposity in rodents. Nature, 407: 908–991.

Tsuda, M., Suzuki, T., Misawa, M. and Nagase, H. (1996) Involvement of the opioid system in the anxiolytic effect of diazepam in mice. Eur. J. Pharmacol., 307: 7–14.

Tsutsumi, K. and Saavedra, J.M. (1991) Characterization and development of angiotensin II receptor subtypes (AT1 and AT2) in rat brain. Am. J. Physiol., 261: R209–R216.

Tsutsumi, T., Akiyoshi, J., Hikichi, T., Kiyota, A., Kohno, Y., Katsuragi, S., Yamamoto, Y., Isogawa, K. and Nagayama, H. (2001) Suppression of conditioned fear by administration of CCKB receptor antisense oligodeoxynucleotide into the lateral ventricle. Pharmacopsychiatry, 34: 232–237.

Unger, T., Carolus, S., Demmert, G., Ganten, D., Lang, R.E., Maser-Gluth, C., Steinberg, H. and Veelken, R.

(1988) Substance P induces a cardiovascular defense reaction in the rat: pharmacological characterization. Circ. Res., 63: 812–820.

Uvnas-Moberg, K., Ahlenius, S., Hillegaart, V. and Alster, P. (1994) High doses of oxytocin cause sedation and low doses cause an anxiolytic-like effect in male rats. Pharmacol. Biochem. Behav., 49: 101–106.

Valdez, G.R., Inoue, K., Koob, G.F., Rivier, J., Vale, W. and Zorrilla, E.P. (2002) Human urocortin II: mild locomotor suppressive and delayed anxiolytic-like effects of a novel corticotropin-releasing factor related peptide. Brain Res., 943: 142–150.

Valdez, G.R. and Koob, G.F. (2004) Allostasis and dysregulation of corticotropin-releasing factor and neuropeptide Y systems: implications for the development of alcoholism. Pharmacol. Biochem. Behav., 79: 671–689.

Valdez, G.R., Zorrilla, E.P., Rivier, J., Vale, W.W. and Koob, G.F. (2003) Locomotor suppressive and anxiolytic-like effects of urocortin 3, a highly selective type 2 corticotropin-releasing factor agonist. Brain Research 980: 206–212.

Valentino, R.J., Bey, V., Pernar, L. and Commons, K.G. (2003) Substance P acts through local circuits within the rat dorsal raphe nucleus to alter serotonergic neuronal activity. J. Neurosci., 23: 155–159.

Valentino, R.J. and Commons, K.G. (2005) Peptides that fine-tune the serotonin system. Neuropeptides, 39: 1–8.

Vanderah, T.W., Schteingart, C.D., Trojnar, J., Junien, J.L., Lai, J. and Riviere, P.J. (2004) FE200041 (D-Phe-D-Phe-D-Nle-D-Arg-NH$_2$): a peripheral efficacious kappa opioid agonist with unprecedented selectivity. J. Pharmacol. Exp. Ther., 310: 326–333.

Van Gaalen, M.M., Stenzel-Poore, M.P., Holsboer, F. and Steckler, T. (2002) Effects of transgenic over-production of CRH on anxiety-like behaviour. Eur. J. Neurosci., 15: 2007–2015.

Van Megen, H.J., Westenberg, H.G., Den Boer, J.A., Haigh, J.R. and Traub, M. (1994) Pentagastrin induced panic attacks: enhanced sensitivity in panic disorder patients. Psychopharmacology, 114: 449–455.

Van Megen, H.J., Westenberg, H.G., Den Boer, J.A. and Kahn, R.S. (1996) Cholecystokinin in anxiety. Eur. J. Neuropsychopharmacol., 6: 263–280.

Van Megen, H.J., Westenberg, H.G., Den Boer, J.A., Slaap, B. and Scheepmakers, A. (1997a) Effect of the selective serotonin reuptake inhibitor fluvoxamine on CCK-4 induced panic attacks. Psychopharmacology, 129: 357–364.

Van Megen, H.J., Westenberg, H.G., Den Boer, J.A., Slaap, B., Van Es-Radhakishun, F. and Pande, A.C. (1997b) The cholecystokinin-B receptor antagonist CI-988 failed to affect CCK-4 induced symptoms in panic disorder patients. Psychopharmacology, 129: 243–248.

Van Rossum, D., Hanisch, U.K. and Quirion, R. (1997) Neuroanatomical localization, pharmacological characterization and functions of CGRP, related peptides and their receptors. Neurosci. Biobehav. Rev., 21: 649–678.

Van Vliet, I.M., Westenberg, H.G., Slaap, B.R., Den Boer, J.A. and Ho Pian, K.L. (1997) Anxiogenic effects of pentagastrin in patients with social phobia and healthy controls. Biol. Psychiatry, 42: 76–78.

Varty, G.B., Cohen-Williams, M.E., Morgan, C.A., Pylak, U., Duffy, R.A., Lachowicz, J.E., Carey, G.J. and Coffin, V.L. (2002) The gerbil elevated plus-maze II: anxiolytic-like effects of selective neurokinin NK1 receptor antagonists. Neuropsychopharmacology, 27: 371–379.

Varty, G.B., Hyde, L.A., Hodgson, R.A., Lu, S.X., McCool, M.F., Kazdoba, T.M., Del Vecchio, R.A., Guthrie, D.H., Pond, A.J., Grzelak, M.E., Xu, X., Korfmacher, W.A., Tulshian, D., Parker, E.M. and Higgins, G.A. (2005) Characterization of the nociceptin receptor (ORL-1) agonist, Ro64-6198, in tests of anxiety across multiple species. Psychopharmacology, 182: 132–143.

Vaughan, J., Donaldson, C., Bittencourt, J., Perrin, M.H., Lewis, K., Sutton, S., Chan, R., Turnbull, A.V., Lovejoy, D. and Rivier, C., et al. (1995) Urocortin, a mammalian neuropeptide related to fish urotensin I and to corticotropin-releasing factor. Nature, 378: 287–292.

Veltmar, A., Culman, J., Qadri, F., Rascher, W. and Unger, T. (1992) Involvement of adrenergic and angiotensinergic receptors in the paraventricular nucleus in the angiotensin II-induced vasopressin release. J. Pharmacol. Exp. Ther., 263: 1230–1260.

Venihaki, M., Sakihara, S., Subramanian, S., Dikkes, P., Weninger, S.C., Liapakis, G., Graf, T. and Majzoub, J.A. (2004) Urocortin III, a brain neuropeptide of the corticotropin-releasing hormone family: modulation by stress and attenuation of some anxiety-like behaviours. J. Neuroendocrinol., 16: 411–422.

Viollet, C., Vaillend, C., Videau, C., Bluet-Pajot, M.T., Ungerer, A., L'Heritier, A., Kopp, C., Potier, B., Billard, J., Schaeffer, J., Smith, R.G., Rohrer, S.P., Wilkinson, H., Zheng, H. and Epelbaum, J. (2000) Involvement of sst2 somatostatin receptor in locomotor, exploratory activity and emotional reactivity in mice. Eur. J. Neurosci., 12: 3761–3770.

Vitale, G., Arletti, R., Ruggieri, V., Cifani, C. and Massi, M. (2006) Anxiolytic-like effects of nociceptin/orphanin FQ in the elevated plus maze and in the conditioned defensive burying test in rats. Peptides, 27: 2193–2200.

Voigt, J.P., Hortnagl, H., Rex, A., van Hove, L., Bader, M. and Fink, H. (2005) Brain angiotensin and anxiety-related behavior: the transgenic rat TGR(AS-rAOGEN)680. Brain Res., 1046: 145–156.

Von Bardeleben, U. and Holsboer, F. (1988) Human corticotropin releasing hormone: clinical studies in patients with affective disorders, alcoholism, panic disorder and in normal controls. Prog. Neuro-Psycho-pharmacol. Biol. Psychiatry, 12(Suppl.): S165–S187.

Wahlestedt, C., Pich, E.M., Koob, G.F., Yee, F. and Heilig, M. (1993) Modulation of anxiety and neuro-peptide Y-Y1 receptors by antisense oligodeoxynu-cleotides. Science, 259: 528–531.

Wahlestedt, C., Skagerberg, G., Ekman, R., Heilig, M., Sundler, F. and Hakanson, R. (1987) Neuropeptide Y (NPY) in the area of the hypothalamic paraventricular nucleus activates the pituitary-adrenocortical axis in the rat. Brain Res., 417: 33–38.

Walling, S.G., Nutt, D.J., Lalies, M.D. and Harley, C.W. (2004) Orexin-A infusion in the locus ceruleus triggers norepinephrine (NE) release and NE-induced long-term potentiation in the dentate gyrus. J. Neurosci., 24: 7421–7424.

Walsh, D.M., Stratton, S.C., Harvey, F.J., Beresford, I.J. and Hagan, R.M. (1995) The anxiolytic-like activity of GR159897, a non-peptide NK2 receptor antagonist, in rodent and primate models of anxiety. Psychopharmacology, 121: 186–191.

Walther, T., Voigt, J.P., Fukamizu, A., Fink, H. and Bader, M. (1999) Learning and anxiety in angiotensin-deficient mice. Behav. Brain Res., 100: 1–4.

Wang, Z., Valdes, J., Noyes, R., Jr. Zoega, T. and Crowe, R.R. (1998) Possible association of a chole-cystokinin promoter polymorphism (CCK-36CT) with panic disorder. Am. J. Med. Genet., 81: 228–234.

Waselus, M., Galvez, J.P., Valentino, R.J. and Van Bockstaele, E.J. (2006) Differential projections of dorsal raphe nucleus neurons to the lateral septum and striatum. J. Chem. Neuroanat., 31: 233–242.

Weiser, T., Wieland, H.A. and Doods, H.N. (2000) Effects of the neuropeptide Y Y(2) receptor antagonist BIIE0246 on presynaptic inhibition by neuropeptide Y in rat hippocampal slices. Eur. J. Pharmacol., 404: 133–136.

Weiss, D.W., Hirt, R., Tarcic, N., Berzon, Y., Ben-Zur, H., Breznitz, S., Glaser, B., Grover, N.B., Baras, M. and O'Dorisio, T.M. (1996) Studies in psychoneur-oimmunology: psychological, immunological, and neuroendocrinological parameters in Israeli civilians during and after a period of Scud missile attacks. Behav. Med., 22: 5–14.

Welt, T., Engelmann, M., Renner, U., Erhardt, A., Muller, M.B., Landgraf, R., Holsboer, F. and Keck, M.E. (2006) Temazepam triggers the release of vasopressin into the rat hypothalamic paraventricular nucleus: novel insight into benzodiazepine action on hypothalamic-pituitary-adrenocortical system activity during stress. Neuropsychopharmacology, 31: 2573–2579.

Wemmie, J.A., Askwith, C.C., Lamani, E., Cassell, M.D., Freeman, J.H. Jr. and Welsh, M.J. (2003) Acid-sensing ion channel 1 is localized in brain regions with high synaptic density and contributes to fear con-ditioning. J. Neurosci., 23: 5496–5502.

Wichniak, A., Brunner, H., Ising, M., Pedrosa Gil, F., Holsboer, F. and Friess, E. (2004) Impaired hypotha-lamic-pituitary-adrenocortical (HPA) system is related to severity of benzodiazepine withdrawal in patients with depression. Psychoneuroendocrinology, 29: 1101–1108.

Wiedemann, K., Jahn, H. and Kellner, M. (2000) Effects of natriuretic peptides upon hypothalamo-pituitary-adrenocortical system activity and anxiety behaviour. Exp. Clin. Endocrinol. Diab., 108: 5–13.

Wiedemann, K., Jahn, H., Yassouridis, A. and Kellner, M. (2001) Anxiolyticlike effects of atrial natriuretic peptide on cholecystokinin tetrapeptide-induced panic attacks: preliminary findings. Arch. Gen. Psychiatry, 58: 371–377.

Wigger, A., Sanchez, M.M., Mathys, K.C., Ebner, K., Frank, E., Liu, D., Kresse, A., Neumann, I.D., Holsboer, F., Plotsky, P.M. and Landgraf, R. (2004) Alterations in central neuropeptide expression, release, and receptor binding in rats bred for high anxiety: critical role of vasopressin. Neuropsycho-pharmacology, 29: 1–14.

Wilson, J., Watson, W.P. and Little, H.J. (1998) CCK(B) antagonists protect against anxiety-related behaviour produced by ethanol withdrawal, measured using the elevated plus maze. Psychopharmacology, 137: 120–131.

Wilson, M.A., Biscardi, R., Smith, M.D. and Wilson, S.P. (1996a) Effects of benzodiazepine agonist expo-sure on corticotropin-releasing factor content and hormonal stress responses: divergent responses in male and ovariectomized female rats, J. Pharmacol. Exp. Ther., 278: 1073–1082.

Wilson, W., Voigt, P., Bader, M., Marsden, C.A. and Fink, H. (1996b) Behaviour of the transgenic (mREN2)27 rat. Brain Res., 729: 1–9.

Windle, R.J., Shanks, N., Lightman, S.L. and Ingram, C.D. (1997) Central oxytocin administration reduces stress-induced corticosterone release and anxiety behavior in rats. Endocrinology, 138: 2829–2834.

Winsky-Sommerer, R., Boutrel, B. and De Lecea, L. (2005) Stress and arousal-the corticotropin-releasing factor/hypocretin circuitry. Mol. Neurobiol., 32: 285–294.

Winslow, J.T., Hearn, E.F., Ferguson, J., Young, L.J., Matzuk, M.M. and Insel, T.R. (2000) Infant vocaliza-tion, adult aggression, and fear behavior of an oxytocin null mutant mouse. Horm. Behav., 37: 145–155.

Wittmann, W., Loacker, S., Kapeller, I., Herzog, H. and Schwarzer, C. (2005) Y1-receptors regulate the expres-sion of Y2-receptors in distinct mouse forebrain areas. Neuroscience, 136: 241–250.

Wotjak, C.T., Ludwig, M., Ebner, K., Russell, J.A., Singewald, N. and Landgraf, R., et al. (2002) Vasopressin from hypothalamic magnocellular neu-rons has opposite actions at the adenohypophysis and in the supraoptic nucleus on ACTH secretion. Eur. J. Neurosci., 16: 477–485.

Wright, J.W. and Harding, J.W. (1992) Regulatory role of brain angiotensins in the control of physiological and behavioral responses. Brain Res. Rev., 17: 227–262.

Wynn, P.C., Harwood, J.P., Catt, K.J. and Aguilera, G. (1988) Corticotropin-releasing factor (CRF) induces desensitization of the rat pituitary CRF receptor-adenylate cyclase complex. Endocrinology, 122: 351–358.

Xu, Y.L., Gall, C.M., Jackson, V.R., Civelli, O. and Reinscheid, R.K. (2007) Distribution of neuropeptide S receptor mRNA and neurochemical characteristics of neuropeptide S-expressing neurons in the rat brain. J. Comp. Neurol., 500: 84–102.

Xu, Y.L., Reinscheid, R.K., Huitron-Resendiz, S., Clark, S.D., Wang, Z., Lin, S.H., Brucher, F.A., Zeng, J., Ly, N.K., Henriksen, S.J., de Lecea, L. and Civelli, O. (2004) Neuropeptide S: a neuropeptide promoting arousal and anxiolytic-like effects. Neuron, 43: 487–497.

Yamada, K., Santo-Yamada, Y. and Wada, K. (2003) Stress-induced impairment of inhibitory avoidance learning in female neuromedin B receptor-deficient mice. Physiol. Behav., 78: 303–309.

Yamada, K., Santo-Yamada, Y., Wada, E. and Wada, K. (2002) Role of bombesin (BN)-like peptides/receptors in emotional behavior by comparison of three strains of BN-like peptide receptor knockout mice. Mol. Psychiatry, 7: 113–117.

Yamada, K., Wada, E. and Wada, K. (2000) Male mice lacking the gastrin-releasing peptide receptor (GRP-R) display elevated preference for conspecific odors and increased social investigatory behaviors Brain Res., 870: 20–26.

Yamano, M., Ogura, H., Okuyama, S. and Ohki-Hamazaki, H. (2002) Modulation of 5-HT system in mice with a targeted disruption of neuromedin B receptor. J. Neurosci. Res., 68: 59–64.

Yehuda, R., Brand, S. and Yang, R.K. (2006) Plasma neuropeptide Y concentrations in combat exposed veterans: relationship to trauma exposure, recovery from PTSD, and coping. Biol. Psychiatry, 59: 660–663.

Yehuda, R., Giller, E.L., Southwick, S.M., Lowry, M.T. and Mason, J.W. (1991) Hypothalamic–pituitary–adrenal dysfunction in posttraumatic stress disorder. Biol. Psychiatry, 30: 1031–1048.

Yoshitake, T., Reenila, I., Ogren, S.O., Hokfelt, T. and Kehr, J. (2003a) Galanin attenuates basal and antidepressant drug-induced increase of extracellular serotonin and noradrenaline levels in the rat hippocampus. Neurosci. Lett., 339: 239–242.

Yoshitake, T., Wang, F.H., Kuteeva, E., Holmberg, K., Yamaguchi, M., Crawley, J.N., Steiner, R., Bartfai, T., Ogren, S.O., Hokfelt, T. and Kehr, J. (2004) Enhanced hippocampal noradrenaline and serotonin release in galanin-overexpressing mice after repeated forced swimming test. Proc. Natl. Acad. Sci. U.S.A., 101: 354–359.

Yoshitake, T., Yoshitake, S., Yamaguchi, M., Ogren, S.O. and Kehr, J. (2003b) Activation of 5-HT(1A) autoreceptors enhances the inhibitory effect of galanin on hippocampal 5-HT release in vivo. Neuropharmacology, 44: 206–231.

Zanoveli, J.M., Netto, C.F., Guimaraes, F.S. and Zangrossi, H. Jr. (2004) Systemic and intra-dorsal periaqueductal gray injections of cholecystokinin sulfated octapeptide (CCK-8s) induce a panic-like response in rats submitted to the elevated T-maze. Peptides, 25: 1935–1941.

Zedkova, L., Coupland, N.J., Man, G.C., Dinsa, G. and Sanghera, G. (2003) Panic-related responses to pentagastrin, flumazenil, and thyrotropin-releasing hormone in healthy volunteers. Depress. Anxiety, 17: 78–87.

Zobel, A.W., Nickel, T., Kunzel, H.E., Ackl, N., Sonntag, A., Ising, M. and Holsboer, F. (2000) Effects of the high-affinity corticotropin-releasing hormone receptor 1 antagonist R121919 in major depression: the first 20 patients treated. J. Psychiatry Res., 34: 171–181.

Zorrilla, E.P. and Koob, G.F. (2004) The therapeutic potential of CRF1 antagonists for anxiety. Exp. Opin. Invest. Drugs, 13: 799–828.

Zorrilla, E.P., Valdez, G.R., Nozulak, J., Koob, G.F. and Markou, A. (2002) Effects of antalarmin, a CRF type 1 receptor antagonist, on anxiety-like behavior and motor activation in the rat. Brain Res., 952: 188–199.

Zwanzger, P., Eser, D., Aicher, S., Schule, C., Baghai, T.C., Padberg, F., Ella, R., Moller, H.J. and Rupprecht, R. (2003) Effects of alprazolam on cholecystokinin-tetrapeptide-induced panic and hypothalamic–pituitary–adrenal-axis activity: a placebo-controlled study. Neuropsychopharmacology, 28: 979–984.

CHAPTER 4.2

Subtype-selective GABA$_A$/benzodiazepine receptor ligands for the treatment of anxiety disorders

James K. Rowlett[*]

Harvard Medical School, New England Primate Research Center, Southborough, MA, USA

Abstract: Anxiety disorders can be treated successfully with benzodiazepines, which act by binding to a site on the γ-aminobutyric acid type A (GABA$_A$) receptor and potentiating the inhibitory effects of GABA. In addition to anxiolytic effects, benzodiazepines also induce unwanted side effects, including motor coordination deficits, sedation, memory impairments, and abuse liability. In recent years, the discovery of subtypes of the GABA$_A$ receptor associated with specific effects of benzodiazepines has led to the hope of improved anxiolytic drugs. In this regard, experiments with transgenic mice and novel ligands have implicated GABA$_A$ receptors containing $\alpha2$ and/or $\alpha3$ subunits as playing a key role in the anxiolytic effects of benzodiazepines, but not other effects such as sedation. This review summarizes current research supporting a role for $\alpha2$ and $\alpha3$ subunit-containing GABA$_A$ receptors in anxiolysis, with an emphasis on the pharmacology of recently developed compounds displaying subtype selectivity. Ultimately, the identification of specific receptor subtypes associated with anxiolysis will hopefully shed light onto how the brain systems that regulate anxiety work in the absence of a pharmacological intervention. This information, in turn, should help in identifying, and ultimately treating, the underlying pathological states associated with anxiety disorders.

Keywords: GABA$_A$ receptor; benzodiazepine; anxiolysis; sedation; intrinsic efficacy

I. Introduction

Anxiety disorders are considered to be the most prevalent of psychiatric disorders, with estimates in the United States alone of approximately 20–40 million adults aged 18 and older diagnosed with at least one of these disorders (Kessler et al., 2005). Anxiety disorders include panic disorder, obsessive-compulsive disorder, post-traumatic stress disorder, generalized anxiety disorder, and phobias (see Table 1 for descriptions). These disorders frequently co-occur with depressive disorders or substance abuse, and many people with one anxiety disorder also have another anxiety disorder (Kessler et al., 2005). Treatment of anxiety disorders includes medication (i.e., anxiety-reducing, or "anxiolytic" drugs), psychotherapy, or both.

While there are numerous anxiolytic drugs on the market, there remains much room for improvement. Drugs based on enhancing the action of the neurotransmitter γ-aminobutyric acid (GABA) have the advantage of good clinical efficacy, but also induce unwanted side effects ranging from motor coordination deficits to cognitive impairment (Nutt, 2005). At present,

*Corresponding author.
E-mail: james_rowlett@hms.harvard.edu

R.J. Blanchard, D.C. Blanchard, G. Griebel and D. Nutt (Eds.)
Handbook of Anxiety and Fear, Vol. 17
ISBN 978-0-444-53065-3

223

DOI: 10.1016/S1569-7339(07)00011-2

Table 1. The primary anxiety disorders

Disorder	Descriptions
Generalized anxiety disorder (GAD)	Characterized by excessive, unrealistic worry that lasts for 6 months or more; also may include trembling, muscular aches, insomnia, abdominal upsets, dizziness, and irritability.
Obsessive-compulsive disorder (OCD)	Individuals are plagued by persistent, recurring thoughts (obsessions) that reflect exaggerated anxiety or fears. The obsessions may lead an individual to perform a ritual or routine (compulsions) – such as washing hands, repeating phrases, or hoarding – to relieve the anxiety caused by the obsession.
Panic disorder	Characterized by severe attacks of panic – which may resemble a heart attack or induce individuals to feel that they are "going crazy" – for no apparent reason. Symptoms include heart palpitations, chest pain, or discomfort, sweating, trembling, tingling sensations, feeling of choking, fear of dying, fear of losing control, and feelings of unreality. Panic disorder often occurs with agoraphobia in which people are afraid of having a panic attack in a place from which escape would be difficult, so they avoid these places.
Post-traumatic stress disorder (PTSD)	PTSD can follow an exposure to a traumatic event such as a sexual or physical assault, witnessing a death, the unexpected death of a loved one, or natural disaster. The main symptoms include: "reliving" of the traumatic event (such as flashbacks and nightmares), avoidance behaviors (such as avoiding places related to the trauma) and emotional numbing (detachment from others), and physiological arousal such as difficulty sleeping, irritability, or poor concentration.
Social anxiety disorder (Social phobia)	Characterized by extreme anxiety about being judged by others or behaving in a way that might cause embarrassment or ridicule. This intense anxiety may lead to avoidance behavior. Physical symptoms associated with this disorder include heart palpitations, faintness, blushing, and profuse sweating.
Specific phobias	People with specific phobias suffer from an intense fear reaction to a specific object or situation (such as spiders, dogs, or heights); the level of fear is usually inappropriate to the situation, and is recognized by the sufferer as being irrational. This inordinate fear can lead to the avoidance of common, everyday situations.

Source: Adapted from the DSM-IV (American Psychiatric Association, 2000).

compounds based on a GABAergic mechanism of action consist of the benzodiazepines, but in the past consisted of barbiturates and meprobamate. The second major class of anxiolytic drugs exerts their action via the neurotransmitter serotonin, or 5-hydroxytryptamine (5-HT), either by blockade of serotonin uptake or by binding to a specific subtype of serotonin receptor (5-HT1$_A$ subtype; for review see Nutt, 2005). Serotonergic compounds lack many of the side effects of GABAergic compounds, but have issues of their own. For example, serotonergic compounds are associated with "therapeutic lag" in which anxiolytic effects are not apparent for several weeks after initiation of treatment (Nutt, 2005). Acute treatment with some 5-HT-based compounds actually can induce anxiety, creating serious compliance issues. Due to the shortcomings of current anxiolytic therapeutics, combined with the large number of patients with anxiety disorders, development of improved therapeutics is an important and robust area of research and development efforts.

II. A brief history of anxiolytic development and use

The first major class of anxiolytic drugs was the barbiturates, with the first compound available for clinicians being barbital, introduced in 1903 (Guillen Sans and Guzman Chozas, 1988). Clinical experience with the barbiturates soon revealed that for day-to-day treatment, these compounds were effective but also relatively toxic, as well as prone to inducing abuse and dependence. A turning point in psychiatric medicine was the debut of meprobamate (Miltown, Wallace Laboratories) in 1955 (Tone, 2005). Meprobamate was originally thought to be safer than the barbiturates, and this drug was by all accounts a success, spurring the interest in the development of novel anxiolytic drugs (Tone, 2005).

The apex of early anxiolytic drug development was reached in 1960 with the introduction of chlordiazepoxide (Librium) and in 1963 of diazepam (Valium) by the Swiss company F. Hoffman-La Roche. The popularity of diazepam has been well-documented, with this compound becoming the most widely prescribed drug irrespective of therapeutic use in the US and Europe between 1968 and 1987 (Speaker, 1997). But by as early as 1967, reports in the popular media were warning of the potential for illicit use and abuse, particularly by youth and the counterculture (Speaker, 1997; Tone, 2005). Use of benzodiazepines in fact entered the popular culture, as typified by the Rolling Stone's song "Mother's Little Helper," referring to a street name associated with the perceived widespread use of diazepam (and other anxiolytics) by middle class housewives (similarly, "Executive Excedrin" was a street name associated with the popular use of benzodiazepines and related anxiolytics by business executives). By the 1970s, the lurid accounts of abuse and dependence had escalated (a popular example was the best-selling non-fiction novel "I'm Dancing as Fast as I Can," published by Gordon in 1979), and in 1979, the US Congress initiated hearings on the "Valium Scare" (US Committee on Labor and Human Resources, 1979).

As a consequence of the 1979 Congressional hearings, benzodiazepines currently are regulated in the US by the Drug Enforcement Agency (DEA) and by comparable regulatory agencies worldwide. Benzodiazepine-type drugs are categorized as Schedule IV,[1] which in regulatory terms reflects

---

[1] The DEA categorizes drugs into five schedules based on medical use and relative abuse liability. Schedule I and II drugs are considered to have high abuse liability, but those in Schedule I are not approved for medical use in the U.S. Schedules III, IV, and V have medical use and abuse liability in descending degree of probability, with Schedule V available over-the-counter in some cases.

the idea that the abuse potential of these drugs is considered low relative to other drugs of abuse (Ator, 2005). The consequence of this scheduling in the US and other nations primarily is restrictions on how long a benzodiazepine-type drug can be prescribed.

Largely as a result of the DEA scheduling and the associated bad press, clinical use of benzodiazepines declined during the 1980s and 1990s, with drug discovery efforts shifting over to non-GABAergic mechanisms of action. However, at the beginning of the new millennium, several insights into benzodiazepine pharmacology, both from the fields of molecular genetics and drug discovery/medicinal chemistry, have heralded a new era of understanding the various effects – both the good and the bad – of this important class of compounds.

III. Benzodiazepines and GABA$_A$ receptor heterogeneity

The type A GABA receptors (GABA$_A$ receptors) have received considerable attention as the site of action for drugs that act not only as anxiolytics, but as sedatives, anti-convulsants, and muscle relaxants. All of these clinically beneficial effects are exhibited by the benzodiazepine-type drugs, which act by allosterically binding to GABA$_A$ receptors and enhancing the ability of GABA to increase chloride conductance. Thus, benzodiazepines are positive allosteric modulators of GABA, with an absolute requirement of GABA binding to the receptor to have an effect (a requirement often postulated to be the basis of the remarkable safety of benzodiazepine-type compounds). Discovery of a specific "benzodiazepine site" on GABA$_A$ receptors did not occur until the mid-1970s (some 15 years after the introduction of benzodiazepines to clinical practice), and identification of heterogeneity of the GABA$_A$ receptor and subsequent functional ramifications has occurred only in the last 5–10 years (meaning, of course, that there is still much work to be done).

The GABA$_A$ receptors in the central nervous system are pentamers constituted from structurally

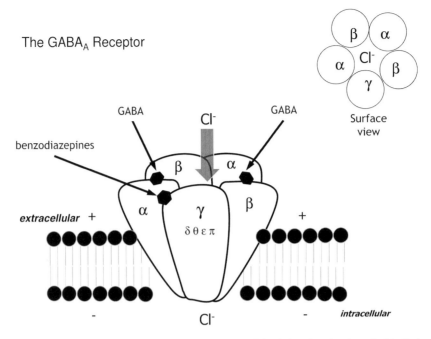

Fig. 1. Representation of the GABA$_A$ receptor. Adapted from original drawing by Angela N. Duke.

distinct proteins, with each protein family consisting of different subunits (Fig. 1). The majority of GABA$_A$ receptors consist of α, β, and γ subunit families, with the stoichiometry of two α subunits, two β subunits, and one γ subunit, arranged in the sequence αβαβγ as viewed from "above" the synapse (Fig. 1). When two GABA molecules bind to sites at the interfaces of the α and β subunits, chloride moves into the channel resulting in miniature inhibitory post-synaptic potentials (mIPSPs) and consequent reduction of cell membrane potential (for review, see Möhler, 2006).

Benzodiazepine action appears to be determined predominantly by the presence of particular α subunits. Benzodiazepine-type drugs bind to a site on the native GABA$_A$ receptor that occurs at the interface of the γ2 subunit with either α1, α2, α3, or α5 subunits, whereas most of these drugs are inactive at corresponding α4 and α6 subunit-containing receptors. Benzodiazepine occupation of its site facilitates the action of GABA by increasing the frequency of channel opening (as well as enhancing affinity of GABA site for

the neurotransmitter). Greater than 90% of the GABA$_A$ receptors in the brain contain α1, α2, and α3 subunits (McKernan and Whiting, 1996), and GABA$_A$ receptors containing α1 subunits make up ~50% of the total GABA$_A$ receptors in the brain (specifically, the α1β2γ2 configuration; McKernan and Whiting, 1996).

Based on sheer numbers, the α1 subunit-containing GABA$_A$ receptor clearly is a major player in the action of benzodiazepine-type drugs. In fact, the α1 subunit-containing receptors are promiscuously distributed throughout the mammalian brain, associated with GABA interneurons that exist in virtually all neural circuits (for review, see Möhler, 2006). However, the anatomical distribution of the other benzodiazepine-sensitive GABA$_A$ receptors raises intriguing possibilities for functional specificity. In this regard, the α2 subunit-containing GABA$_A$ receptor is found in limbic areas (regulation of emotion and motivated behavior); the α3 subunit-containing GABA$_A$ receptor is found on monoaminergic neurons (modulation of many behavioral effects, including motor function); and the α5 subunit-containing GABA$_A$ receptor is found at high densities in the hippocampus (associated primarily with cognition, including spatial memory).

IV. Subtype-dependent effects of benzodiazepines: evidence from transgenic mice

Although findings of subunit heterogeneity and anatomical specificity raised intriguing possibilities about different behavioral effects being associated with different GABA$_A$ receptor subtypes, direct evidence for this was not available until the late 1990s and the early 2000s, through a series of studies published by Hanns Möhler and colleagues. These researchers exploited the fact that benzodiazepine-sensitive α1, α2, α3, and α5 subunits differ from benzodiazepine-insensitive α6 subunits by a single amino acid (Wieland et al., 1992; Kleingoor et al., 1993; Benson et al., 1999). Using this single substitution (histidine to arginine), mice were created in which point mutations of α1, α2, α3, or α5 subunits rendered these GABA$_A$ receptors insensitive to diazepam (Rudolph et al., 1999; Löw et al., 2000; McKernan et al., 2000). A key feature of these "knock-in" mice is that the action of GABA at the GABA$_A$ receptor is not affected by the point mutation, resulting in mice that by – and – large are similar to wild-type mice (but see Crestani et al., 2002; Morris et al., 2006).

The basic strategy of these studies with transgenic mice was to administer diazepam and compare the characteristic behavioral effects induced by this benzodiazepine in wild-type mice to the effects of the drug in knock-in mice. In the first published paper, Rudolph et al. (1999) showed that the anxiolytic-like effects of diazepam were spared in α1 subunit knock-in mice; however, locomotor activity-reducing effects of diazepam were absent. Subsequently, Löw et al. (2000) demonstrated that anxiolytic-like effects of diazepam were absent in α2 subunit knock-in mice, but not α3 subunit knock-in mice; and a later report also showed lack of anxiolytic-like effects of diazepam for α5 subunit knock-in mice (Crestani et al., 2002). Altogether, the research with

transgenic mice provides a compelling case for a key role of the α2 subunit-containing GABA$_A$ receptor in the anxiolytic effects of diazepam and related benzodiazepine-type drugs (for reviews, see Möhler, 2006; Whiting, 2006).

V. Subtype-dependent effects of benzodiazepines: recent findings with subtype-selective ligands

The search for benzodiazepine-site ligands that bind to multiple subtypes predates the discovery of GABA$_A$ receptor subtypes. In the absence of direct evidence for receptor subtypes, a logical approach to identifying receptor subtype heterogeneity is characterization of ligands with novel structures that induce functional effects that differ from standard compounds. Prior to its identification in vitro as a drug selective for α1 subunit-containing GABA$_A$ receptors, zolpidem was often reported to exert behavioral effects that differed, oftentimes strikingly, from conventional benzodiazepines (Griebel et al., 1999).

V.A. Compounds with selective efficacy: mixtures of antagonist and agonist activity

Investigations into the role of GABA$_A$ receptor subtypes in the anxiolytic effects of benzodiazepine-type drugs took a major step forward with the development of the compound L-838,417 (McKernan et al., 2000; see also Dawson et al., 2005). L-838,417 binds with near-equal affinity at all benzodiazepine-sensitive GABA$_A$ receptor subtypes but exerts different levels of intrinsic efficacy, as measured by the ability to potentiate GABA-mediated chloride currents (McKernan et al., 2000). In this regard, L-838,417 is a partial agonist at α2, α3, and α5 subunit-containing GABA$_A$ receptors but essentially lacks intrinsic efficacy at α1 subunit-containing GABA$_A$ receptors. Assuming that very low efficacy at a subtype relative to full agonists translates to a lack of effects in vivo, L-838,417 can be said to have "selective efficacy" for α2, α3, and α5 subunit-containing GABA$_A$ receptors (Fig. 2), which differs from the more

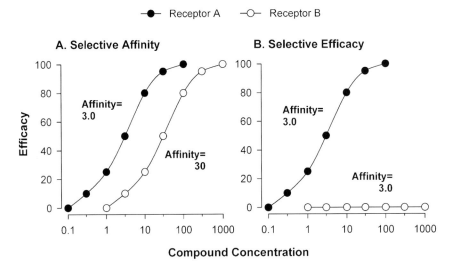

Fig. 2. Hypothetical results for compounds with (A) selective affinity or (B) selective efficacy. For benzodiazepine-type compounds, efficacy is determined by potentiation of GABA-mediated chloride currents. Affinity refers to dissociation constants (K_i) for the individual receptors determined via radioligand-binding experiments.

conventional conceptualization of pharmacological selectivity based on binding affinity differences (referred to as "selective affinity," Fig. 2). The importance of selective efficacy as an approach to the development of subtype-selective ligands is that α subunits differ only slightly (often by a single amino acid), raising the possibility that the subunits are too similar in structure to facilitate the development of "traditional" selective affinity ligands (e.g., ligands with 100-fold or greater selectivity for a subtype based on binding affinity differences).

When evaluated in preclinical behavioral models assessing anxiolytic-like effects and motor responses, L-838,417 shows a pattern of effects concordant with the findings from transgenic mouse research. In this regard, L-838,417 was shown to be effective in the elevated plus maze and fear-potentiated startle tests of anxiety in rats (McKernan et al., 2000). Moreover, L-838,417 was effective in a primate conflict model of the anxiolytic-like effects of benzodiazepines (Rowlett et al., 2005b). Importantly, L-838,417 was ineffective when evaluated for impairment of motor function (e.g., chain-pulling procedure in rodents and quantitative observational procedures in

monkeys). The importance of these findings is that they corroborate the results from transgenic mice in organisms that were not genetically modified, suggesting a high potential for these results to translate into the clinic.

Since the introduction of L-838,417 in 2000, several other compounds with selective efficacy have been described (Table 2 and Fig. 3). Examples of specific compounds are shown in Fig. 3, which also depicts the reported maximum efficacies for each compound at the different GABA$_A$ receptor subtypes. As is evident from the figure, compounds with various "configurations" of efficacies have been developed, offering intriguing possibilities for both preclinical research as well as drug development. A few general comments can be made. First, at the time of this chapter's preparation, only one compound has been reported to have relatively unambiguous selective efficacy for a single subtype (TP003; Dias et al., 2005). Second, many compounds vary not only with respect to selective efficacy; it often is the case that the degree of efficacy (from partial to full) varies considerably within a compound for different subtypes. Finally, a particularly

Table 2. Examples of compounds with selective efficacy or selective affinity for $GABA_A$ receptor subtypes

Compound	Subtype ($\alpha \times \beta2/3\gamma2$)				Reference
	$\alpha1$	$\alpha2$	$\alpha3$	$\alpha5$	
Selective efficacy, antagonist at one or more subtypes[a]					
L-838,417	Zero	Partial	Partial	Partial	McKernan et al. (2000)
TPA023	Zero	Partial	Partial	Zero	Atack et al. (2006)
TP003	Zero	Zero	Full	Zero	Dias et al. (2005)
Compound 4	Zero	Full	N.A.	n.a.	Johnstone et al. (2004)
Selective efficacy, mixed full and partial agonist[a]					
SL651498	Partial	Full	Full	Partial	Griebel et al. (2001)
Ocinaplon	Full	Partial	Partial	Partial	Lippa et al. (2005)
DOV 51,982	Full	Partial	Partial	Full	Popik et al. (2006)
Pagoclone	Partial	Partial	Full	Partial	Atack et al. (2006)
Selective affinity[b]					
Zolpidem	High	Moderate	Moderate	Zero	Dämgen and Lüddens (1999)
Zaleplon	High	Moderate	Moderate	Low	Dämgen and Lüddens (1999)
Indiplon	High	Moderate	Moderate	Moderate	Foster et al. (2004)
ELB139	Moderate	Moderate	High	Moderate	Rabe et al. (2006)

[a]Efficacy was determined with electrophysiological studies in cloned $GABA_A$ receptors: zero, no potentiation of GABA-mediated chloride current; partial, potentiation of GABA-mediated chloride current less than observed with a full agonist; full, potentiation of GABA-mediated chloride current equal to or greater than a full agonist; n.a., data not available. [b]Affinity was determined by radioligand-binding studies in cloned receptors, except for ELB139, in which potencies to potentiate GABA-mediated chloride currents were used: zero, no binding; low K_i values $>1,000$ nM; moderate, K_i values $100-1,000$ nM; high, $1-100$ nM.

noteworthy absence from the $GABA_A$ pharmacopeia is a compound with any degree of selective efficacy (or selective affinity) for $\alpha2$ subunit-containing $GABA_A$ receptors.

In addition to L-838,417, a particularly interesting compound is TP003 (Dias et al., 2005), a compound with nanomolar affinity for benzodiazepine-sensitive $GABA_A$ receptors that exhibits efficacy at only $\alpha3$ subunit-containing $GABA_A$ receptors (Fig. 3). Based on the findings from transgenic mouse studies, this compound would not be expected to induce anxiolytic-like effects. However, TP003 has been shown to engender anxiolytic-like effects in rodent models (including elevated plus maze) as well as primate models (conditioned emotional response; see Dias et al., 2005). These effects are as robust as those exhibited by conventional benzodiazepines. This observation supports an earlier report that showed anxiogenic-like effects from a partial agonist with selectivity for $\alpha3$ subunit-containing receptors (Atack et al., 2005). These findings are, of course,

contradictory to the genetic mouse research and suggest an important role for $\alpha3$ subunit-containing $GABA_A$ receptors in the anxiolytic action of benzodiazepine-type compounds.

The second important compound from the Merck laboratories is TPA023, a relatively weak partial agonist of $\alpha2$ and $\alpha3$ subunit-containing $GABA_A$ receptors with no activity at $\alpha1$ and $\alpha5$ subunit-containing receptors (Atack et al., 2006). Despite the only 12–33% maximum efficacy exhibited by this compound, it is not without pharmacological activity. Thus, TPA023 was active in the elevated plus maze, fear-potentiated startle, and conditioned suppression of drinking tests in rodents and the conditioned emotional response tests in monkeys (Atack et al., 2006). TPA023 was initiated into Phase II clinical trials, but the trials were halted for unspecified reasons, and at this time, the efficacy of the compound for reducing anxiety in humans is unknown. Regarding mechanism of action, TPA023's highest degree of efficacy was at the $\alpha3$ subunit-containing receptor,

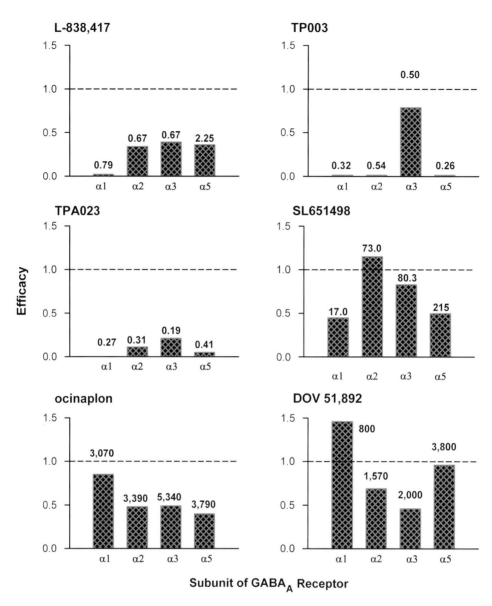

Fig. 3. Summary of maximum efficacy (potentiation of GABA-mediated chloride currents) for recently developed compounds. Horizontal lines represent maximum potentiation by full agonists (diazepam, chlordiazepoxide). Numbers above bars are affinity values (K_i, nM) for L-838,417, TP003, TPA023, and SL651498; and IC_{50} values (concentration [nM] resulting in 50% of maximum effect in electrophysiology experiments) for ocinaplon and DOV 51,892. Data are adapted from McKernan et al. (2000), Dias et al. (2005); Lippa et al. (2005), Atack et al. (2006), and Popik et al. (2006).

although the difference between this subtype and the $\alpha 2$ subunit-containing receptor was slight. Irrespective of receptor subtype, the work with TPA023 suggests that only a very small degree of efficacy is needed for anxiolytic-like effects.

V.B. Compounds with selective efficacy: mixtures of partial and full agonist activity

Another general type of compound is illustrated in Fig. 3 and consists of compounds that do not have subtypes for which they are inactive, but instead are characterized by varying degrees of efficacy at the different subtypes. These include SL651498, which has full or near-full agonist efficacy at $\alpha2$ and $\alpha3$ subunit-containing receptors but only partial activity at $\alpha1$ and $\alpha5$ subunit-containing GABA$_A$ receptors (Fig. 3; Griebel et al., 2001). This compound has been shown to induce anxiolytic-like activity in rodents and monkeys (Griebel et al., 2001, 2003; Licata et al., 2005). The primary difference between this compound and the Merck ligands is that effects presumably mediated via $\alpha1$ subunit-containing receptors, for example, ataxia, are evident at the highest dose levels of the compound (Licata et al., 2005), consistent with near 50% efficacy at this subtype. Nevertheless, these findings provide additional support for $\alpha2$ and/or $\alpha3$ subunit-containing GABA$_A$ receptors as playing a key role in mediating the anxiolytic effects of benzodiazepine-type compounds.

Recently, a somewhat different approach to development of anxiolytic compounds was introduced by DOV Pharmaceutical, Inc. (Lippa et al., 2005; Popik et al., 2006). To date, two compounds have been reported from DOV's efforts: ocinaplon and DOV 51,892 (Fig. 3). Two features of these compounds are noteworthy, the most striking being that both Lippa et al. (2005) and Popik et al. (2006) have noted that while the two compounds appear to be preferentially anxiolytic, they have a degree of functional selectivity for $\alpha1$ subunit-containing GABA$_A$ receptors. Thus, at least on the surface, the results with these compounds appear to be contrary to both experiments with transgenic mice and other compounds with selective efficacy. A particularly compelling finding from DOV's research program is the report that ocinaplon significantly reduced Hamilton Anxiety Scale (HAM-A) scores in patient with generalized anxiety disorder (Lippa et al., 2005). To date, these are the only data from human subjects published for any of the newer compounds (ocinaplon reached Phase III clinical trials, but was halted for reasons purportedly not related to efficacy according to DOV's Web site).

The second noteworthy feature of these compounds is that they have relatively weak, micromolar binding affinity for GABA$_A$ receptors (Fig. 3, note that potencies are IC$_{50}$s from electrophysiological studies rather than K_i values from binding studies). The observation of relatively weak binding might complicate the interpretation of selective efficacy for $\alpha1$ subunit-containing receptors conferring a mostly anxiolytic profile. In this regard, selective efficacy for these compounds is concluded based on the maximum efficacy obtained (E_{max}); however, due to weak binding, levels of compound sufficient to reach E_{max} may not be obtainable due to limitations in bioavailability. Some evidence counter to this possibility was provided by Popik et al. (2006), who showed that doses of DOV 51,892 that engendered anxiolytic-like effects in rats resulted in whole-brain levels of the compound of approximately 5,600 nM, clearly above the range of IC$_{50}$ values and in the range of concentrations for this compound's E_{max} values (see Fig. 1 in Popik et al., 2006). This conclusion must be tempered due to the fact that it is not known if whole-brain concentrations of a compound accurately reflect the concentration of compound available for the receptors in synapses. At present, the extent to which the DOV compounds' preferential anxiolytic effects are due to selective efficacy or simply partial agonist profiles is not resolved.

VI. Reducing anxiety selectively: how might this work?

A key to the development of the elusive "anxioselective" benzodiazepine-type compound, that is, a compound that has anxiolytic activity and no other effects, is a more complete understanding of the relationship of receptor mechanisms to in vivo benzodiazepine effects. Prior to the discovery of the involvement of GABA$_A$ receptor subtypes in the effects of benzodiazepine-type compounds, differences in the ability of these compounds to induce diverse behavioral effects was attributed primarily to intrinsic efficacy (Facklam et al., 1992; Haefely et al., 1993). During the 1980s and 1990s, development of non-selective partial agonists was a primary approach to the development of anxioselective drugs, albeit to varying degrees of success (for review, see Atack, 2005).

Intrinsic Efficacy as a Determinant of Effect *Type*

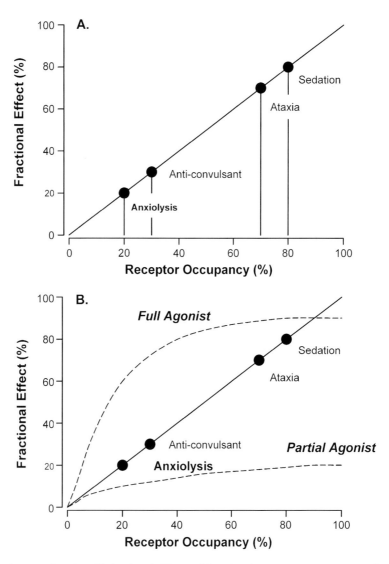

Fig. 4. Relationship between fractional behavioral effect and fractional receptor occupancy, as determined by intrinsic efficacy. Note that "fractional behavioral effect" refers to the *types* of behavioral effect that is part of the whole, rather than the *degree* or *intensity* of behavioral effects. (A) Representation of thresholds for four behavioral effects of benzodiazepine-type drugs, that is, degree of receptor occupancy required for emergence of each behavioral effect. (B) Definitions of full agonist and partial agonist based on intrinsic efficacy model.

To explain the relationship between behavioral effect and intrinsic efficacy, the model depicted in Fig. 4A was proposed. This simplified version of the original model described by Haefely and colleagues (e.g., Facklam et al., 1992) shows that as receptor occupancy of a compound increases, the *type* of behavioral effect changes. This is represented by the concept "fractional effect," which refers not to a quantitative increase in effect intensity, but rather to an accumulation of qualitatively different effects that make up the whole benzodiazepine behavioral profile. Thus, for a full agonist, as the receptor occupancy increases, the type of behavior changes from anxiolysis at the lowest levels of receptor occupancy to sedation at the highest levels of occupancy (Fig. 4B). For partial agonists, the relationship between fractional effect and receptor occupancy is a shallow curve, resulting in occupancy sufficient to reach the requirement for anxiolysis but not other effects for which the requirements are much higher (Fig. 4B).

Based on the findings reviewed above on the role of GABA$_A$ receptor subtypes in mediating different behavioral effects of benzodiazepine-type

Receptor Selectivity as a Determinant of Effect *Type*

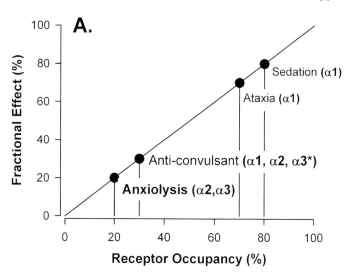

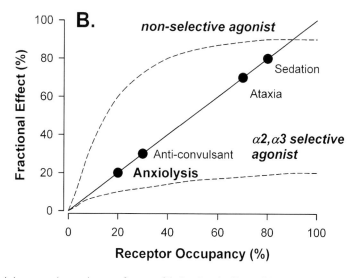

Fig. 5. Receptor selectivity as a determinant of type of behavioral effect. (A) Representation of thresholds based on putative specific roles for receptor subtypes (in parentheses). (B) Predicted behavioral effects based on receptor selectivity. Anti-convulsant activity may involve an interaction of the 3 receptor subtypes (Fradley et al., 2007).

ligands, it appears possible that subtype selectivity can provide an alternative hypothesis to one based solely on intrinsic efficacy. One conceptualization of this idea is shown in Fig. 5A, B. In this model, increases in occupancy would be directly related to the subtype being occupied, based primarily on the assumption that $\alpha2$ and $\alpha3$ subunit-containing receptors are sufficiently activated at low levels of overall receptor occupancy (Fig. 5A). In other words, the observation that anxiolysis typically occurs at relatively low doses of benzodiazepine-type drugs might be due to occupation of $\alpha2$ and $\alpha3$ subunit-containing receptors at low levels of overall receptor occupancy. Importantly, there is no direct evidence for this assumption, although an anxiolytic dose of a non-selective benzodiazepine has been shown to occupy very low levels (<10%) of binding sites in human brain (Lingford-Hughes et al., 2005). Nevertheless, this model accounts for the diverse effects of many benzodiazepine-type compounds. For example, agonists with selective efficacy for $\alpha2$ and/or $\alpha3$ subunit-containing GABA$_A$ receptors induce anxiolysis and anti-convulsant effects due primarily to targeting these effect-specific subtypes, whereas a non-selective agonist induces all effects associated with GABA$_A$ receptors due simply to binding at

all subtypes (Fig. 5B). An important, and largely untested, assumption of this model is that different levels of total receptor occupancy are required for activation of different receptor subtypes.

A prediction of this subtype-based model is that a non-selective partial agonist might be expected to engender a degree of ataxia and sedation, by virtue of binding to $\alpha1$ subunit-containing receptors, albeit with weak efficacy. Although the preponderance of preclinical data suggest that non-selective partial agonists should not induce impairment of motor coordination or sedative effects, clinical results have suggested that sedation does occur for at least one of the non-selective partial agonists, bretazenil (for review, see Atack, 2005). A complicating factor regarding bretazenil, however, is this compound's strong agonist action at $\alpha4$ subunit-containing GABA$_A$ receptors, which recently have been identified as targets for sleep-promoting drugs (e.g., Chandra et al., 2006).

Both models described above provide satisfactory accounts of the effects of many compounds, including in some cases compounds with selectivity for $\alpha1$ subunit-containing GABA$_A$ receptors. As shown in Fig. 6, a compound with either selective affinity or selective efficacy can be depicted by assuming a very steep dose–response

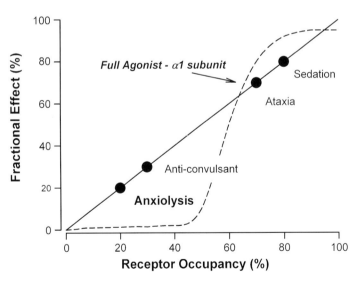

Fig. 6. Steep dose–response function as a possible explanation for the lack of anxiolytic effects of agonists selective for $\alpha1$ subunit-containing GABA$_A$ receptors.

235

function, such that the range of doses that induce anxiolysis versus sedation is narrow. Empirically, data are available for compounds with selective affinity for α1 subunit-containing GABA_A receptors, including zolpidem, zaleplon, and indiplon. A characteristic finding in preclinical models with these compounds is that they engender either relatively weak or no effects in tests for anxiolytic activity; and when anxiolytic-like effects are observed, they typically are at doses that also induce sedative effects (e.g., Griebel et al. 1999; Foster et al., 2004; Rowlett et al., 2005b). However, it is not entirely clear how a compound

with selective efficacy for α1 subunit-containing GABA_A receptors would fit in this model, particularly one that has essentially zero efficacy at other GABA_A receptor subtypes.

An important consideration that arises from examining the relationship between benzodiazepine-like effect and receptor occupancy is the extent to which each individual subtype might have occupancy and efficacy requirements for fractional effects. Adding this factor to the models discussed above is difficult when using a two-dimensional plot; therefore, a third model is shown in Fig. 7A–D that shows the relevant

A. **Non-selective, full agonist**

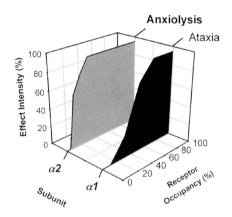

B. **Non-selective, partial agonist**

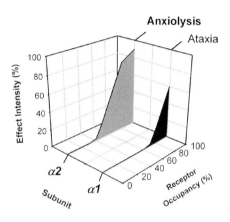

C. **Selective efficacy, partial agonist**

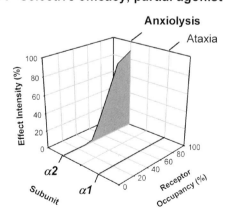

D. **Selective affinity, full agonist**

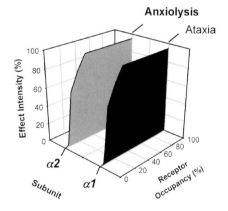

Fig. 7. Model of benzodiazepine action based on selectivity and efficacy. Only two behavioral effects (anxiolysis, ataxia) are shown for clarity. Data are hypothetical.

variables in three-dimensional plots. For the sake of simplicity, only two of the behavioral effects of benzodiazepine-type compounds are shown: anxiolysis and ataxia. As with the models described above, an assumption is that anxiolytic effects require a relatively low degree of receptor occupancy compared to ataxic effects. A second assumption is that all effects can occur at maximum intensity, and the difference between a partial and full agonist is the degree of receptor occupancy required to induce maximum effects (Facklam et al., 1992). By separating out receptor occupancy and type of effect, the primary dependent measure for this model becomes *intensity* of effect rather than fractional effect.

Four examples are shown in Fig. 7. In graph A, the predicted results for a standard benzodiazepine are shown. In this case, anxiolysis occurs because relatively low levels of occupancy of $\alpha2$ subunit-containing $GABA_A$ receptors are required to engender a maximal effect. At higher levels of occupancy of $\alpha2$ subunit-containing receptors, anxiolysis occurs along with ataxia, which emerges with the occupancy of $\alpha1$ subunit-containing $GABA_A$ receptors. In graph B, the profile of a non-selective partial agonist is similar to a non-selective full agonist, except that both effects require higher levels of receptor occupancy. Thus, this model predicts that the latter type of compound can engender near maximum levels of anxiolysis with relatively weak ataxic effects. Hypothetical results for selective compounds are shown in graphs C and D. Graph C depicts a compound that is a partial agonist at $\alpha2$ subunit-containing receptors and an antagonist at $\alpha1$ subunit-containing receptors. Because a partial agonist may induce maximum effects depending on the degree of receptor occupancy obtained and due to the fact that no ataxic effects are present due to lack of efficacy at $\alpha1$ subunit-containing receptors; the profile of this compound is predicted to be anxioselective. Finally, graph D shows effects based on a compound with high efficacy but selectivity for $\alpha1$ subunit-containing receptors (e.g., zolpidem). In this case, ataxia occurs at lower levels of occupancy due to binding affinity differences. In this case, anxiolysis still arises at low levels of occupancy, suggesting that an increase in binding affinity at one receptor might be overshadowed by a low occupancy requirement in another receptor. Importantly, the expression of anxiolysis in an experimental context likely is masked by ataxic effects inhibiting the ability of the organism to respond.

Although this presentation of interdependent effects of effect type, intensity, and occupancy is admittedly simplistic in that only two behaviors and two subtypes are represented, the intent is to provide a conceptual framework for conducting comprehensive evaluation of the relationships between behavioral effect and occupancy of a specific subtype and, eventually, dose of the compound. Of course, this type of analysis would also require complete information of pharmacokinetics for a given compound. This type of approach ultimately may provide a conceptual platform for developing selective anxiolytic drugs lacking undesired side effects.

VII. Controversies and comments: points of contention between (and within) the "old" and the "new" benzodiazepine pharmacology

Although our knowledge of anxiolytic pharmacology based on the benzodiazepine site on $GABA_A$ receptors has advanced dramatically in the past decade, there clearly remain unresolved issues. One issue in particular that stands out is the lack of concordance between transgenic mouse and pharmacological studies in the extent to which anxiolysis involves $\alpha2$ subunit-containing versus $\alpha3$ subunit-containing $GABA_A$ receptors. Several possibilities for reconciliation of these findings have been suggested, for example, Atack et al. (2006) speculated that different types of anxiety might be associated with the two receptor subtypes (cf., Morris et al., 2006). As an alternate explanation, Möhler (2006) noted that while TP003 was a full agonist in vitro, it induced anxiolytic-like effects only at high levels of occupancy of $\alpha3$ subunit-containing receptors. Because the anxiolytic effects of benzodiazepines in general is associated with therapeutic doses resulting in relatively low levels of receptor occupancy, Möhler (2006) suggested that for benzodiazepine-type drugs, α3 subunit-mediated anxiolysis might be a secondary effect to anxiolysis mediated by α2 subunit-containing receptors (and conceivably might play no role whatsoever in the anxiolytic effects of benzodiazepines at therapeutic doses). This possibility, however, must be tempered by the fact that TP003 is the only compound with selectivity for α3 subunit-containing receptors for which data are available; thus, it is not clear that the receptor occupancy requirements for anxiolysis are uniquely high for the α3 subunit-containing receptor in general, or simply due to unique physicochemical properties of TP003. Regardless of these issues, the key to understanding this interesting debate is the availability of a compound with selectivity for α2 subunit-containing GABA$_A$ receptors, which has yet to materialize.

A final point that has not been resolved completely is a role, if any, for the α1 subunit-containing GABA$_A$ receptor in mediating anxiolysis. As mentioned earlier, ocinaplon and DOV 51,892 have a degree of functional selectivity for α1 subunit-containing receptors yet induce anxiolytic effects with minimal sedative–motor side effects. That this profile of effects has been shown in human subjects with ocinaplon is particularly striking. According to the model depicted in Fig. 7A–D, however, both compounds might fit the profile of graph B (non-selective partial agonist), and because anxiolysis occurs with relatively low levels of receptor occupancy, the modest functional selectivity for α1 subunit-containing receptors might be irrelevant. Regardless, other support for a role of the α1 subunit-containing GABA$_A$ receptor in mediating anxiolysis exists in the extant literature. This support comes from studies with the compound β-carboline-3-carboxylate-*t*-butyl ester (βCCT), an antagonist with selective affinity for the α1 subunit-containing receptor (reviewed by Rowlett et al., 2005a). βCCT has been shown to block the effects of non-selective benzodiazepines in rodent and primate models of anxiolysis (Shannon et al., 1984; Griebel et al., 1999; Belzung et al., 2000; Rowlett et al., 2005a) and for the rodent models, this blockage occurs at doses shown to primarily occupy α1 subunit-containing receptors (Griebel et al., 1999). Overall,

these findings suggest that a role for the α1 subunit-containing subtype in mediating anxiolysis cannot yet be discounted completely (for transgenic mouse evidence of a role for α1 subunit-containing receptors in the "anti-stress" action of diazepam, see Crestani et al., 2000; McKernan et al., 2000).

βCCT exhibits the lowest degree of selectivity for α1 subunit-containing receptors versus α2 and α3 subunit-containing receptors (~ 20-fold), raising the possibility that blockade of anxiolytic-like effects is due to relatively high doses of βCCT binding non-selectively. However, βCCT has been shown to be ineffective in blocking the muscle relaxant effects of benzodiazepines, an effect that appears to involve both α2 and α3 subunit-containing receptors (Crestani et al., 2002; Licata et al., 2005; Rowlett et al., 2005a,b). Although speculative, a possible explanation may lie with the amount of receptor occupancy required for anxiolysis versus muscle relaxation. Anxiolytic effects characteristically occur at lower levels of GABA$_A$ receptor occupancy than muscle relaxant effects (Facklam et al., 1992); therefore, it may require less βCCT to block anxiolytic effects at α2 and/or α3 subunit-containing receptors than muscle relaxant effects. Evaluation of this possibility, as well as others (including the possibility that α1 subunit-containing GABA$_A$ receptors are involved in anxiolysis in some as yet uncharacterized fashion), awaits further investigation.

VIII. Where do we go from here?

Understanding of mechanisms underlying the anxiolytic effects of benzodiazepines has advanced considerably since the late 1990s due to both transgenic mouse research and the development of unique pharmacological tools. Based on this work, several conclusions can be reached with a fair degree of confidence: (1) the different behavioral effects of benzodiazepines can be associated with action at distinct GABA$_A$ receptor subtypes, (2) the phenomenon of anxiolysis at lower doses than sedative–motor effects likely reflects unique sensitivity of α2 and/or α3 subunit-containing GABA$_A$ receptors compared to α1 subunit-containing

GABA$_A$ receptors, and (3) the potential for the clinical development of an anxioselective medication for treating anxiety disorders is real.

As mentioned in the beginning, however, there still clearly is work to be done. The need for a compound selective for α2 subunit-containing receptors for both basic research and preclinical discovery efforts cannot be overemphasized. And while the scheme shown in Fig. 7A–D fits existing data, the real value of these concepts in predicting a profile of behavioral effects for a subtype-selective compound will be evident only after empirical validation of the assumptions. In this respect, the idea of sufficient receptor occupancy associated with specific behavioral effects that are, in turn, associated with a specific receptor subtype needs to be determined experimentally and expanded to other effects of benzodiazepines (e.g., abuse potential).

In a broader conceptual context, research on benzodiazepine pharmacology over the past several decades has cemented into the overarching theoretical perspective on anxiety, a key role for the GABAergic system. Ultimately, the identification of specific receptor subtypes associated with anxiolysis will hopefully shed light onto how the brain systems that regulate anxiety work in the absence of a pharmacological intervention. This information, in turn, should help in identifying the underlying pathological states associated with anxiety disorders.

Acknowledgments

I wish to thank Dr. D.M. Platt for comments on an early version of this manuscript, and for G. Platt for assistance with preparation. I also wish to thank Dr. G.R. Dawson, Dr. R.M. McKernan, and Dr. J.R. Atack for invaluable discussions and support over the years. This manuscript was prepared with support from USPHS grants DA11792 and RR00168.

References

American Psychiatric Association (2000) Diagnostic and Statistical Manual of Mental Disorders DSM-IV-TR Fourth Edition (Text Revision). Prepared by the Task Force on DSM-IV and other committees and work groups of the American Psychiatric Association, Office of Publishing Operations, American Psychiatric Association.

Atack, J.R. (2005) The benzodiazepine binding site of GABA$_A$ receptors as a target for the development of novel anxiolytics. Expert. Opin. Investig. Drugs, 14: 601–618.

Atack, J.R., Hutson, P.H., Collinson, N., Marshall, G., Bentley, G., Moyes, C., Cook, S.M., Collins, I., Wafford, K., McKernan, R.M. and Dawson, G.R. (2005) Anxiogenic properties of an inverse agonist selective for α3 subunit-containing GABA$_A$ receptors. Br. J. Pharmacol., 144: 357–366.

Atack, J.R., Wafford, K.A., Tye, S.J., Cook, S.M., Sohal, B., Pike, A., Cur, C., Melillo, D., Bristow, L., Bromidge, F., Ragan, I., Kerby, J., Street, L., Carling, R., Castro, J.L., Whiting, P., Dawson, G.R. and McKernan, R.M. (2006) TPA023 [7-(1,1-dimethylethyl)-6-(2-ethyl-2H-1,2,4-triazol-3-ylmethoxy)-3-(2-fluorophenyl)-1,2,4-triazolo[4,3-b]pyridazine], an agonist selective for α2 and α3-containing GABA$_A$ receptors, is a nonsedating anxiolytic in rodents and primates. J. Pharmacol. Exp. Ther., 316: 410–422.

Ator, N.A. (2005) Contributions of GABA$_A$ receptor subtype selectivity to abuse liability and dependence potential of pharmacological treatments for anxiety and sleep disorders. CNS Spectrosc., 10: 31–39.

Belzung, C., Le Guisquet, A.M. and Griebel, G. (2000) Beta-CCT, a selective BZ-omega1 receptor antagonist, blocks the anti-anxiety but not the amnestic effects of chlordiazepoxide in mice. Behav. Pharmacol., 11: 125–131.

Benson, J.A., Löw, K., Keist, R., Möhler, H. and Rudolph, U. (1999) Pharmacology of recombinant γ-aminobutyric acid$_A$ receptors rendered diazepam-insensitive by point-mutated α-subunits. FEBS Lett., 431: 400–404.

Chandra, D., Jia, F., Liang, J., Peng, Z., Suryanarayanan, A., Werner, D.F., Spigelman, I., Houser, C.R., Olsen, R.W., Harrison, N.L. and Homanics, G.E. (2006) GABA$_A$ receptor α4 subunits mediate extrasynaptic inhibition in thalamus and dentate gyrus and the action of gaboxadol. Proc. Natl. Acad. Sci. USA, 103: 15230–15235.

Crestani, F., Keist, R., Fritschy, J.-M., Benke, D., Vogt, K., Prut, L., Blüthmann, H., Möhler, H. and Rudolph, U. (2002) Trace fear conditioning involves hippocampal α_5 GABA$_A$ receptors. Proc. Natl. Acad. Sci. USA, 99: 8980–8985.

Crestani, F., Martin, J.R., Möhler, H. and Rudolph, U. (2000) Resolving differences in GABA$_A$ receptor mutant mouse studies. Nat. Neurosci., 3: 1059.

Dämgen, K. and Lüddens, H. (1999) Zaleplon displays a selectivity to recombinant GABA$_A$ receptors different from zolpidem, zopiclone and benzodiazepines. Neurosci. Res. Comm., 25: 139–148.

Dawson, G.R., Collinson, N. and Atack, J.R. (2005) Development of subtype selective GABA_A modulators. CNS Spectrosc., 10: 21–27.

Dias, R., Sheppard, W.F., Fradley, R.L., Garrett, E.M., Stanley, J.L., Tye, S.J., Goodacre, S., Lincoln, R.J., Cook, S.M., Conley, R., Hallett, D., Humphries, A.C., Thompson, S.A., Wafford, K.A., Street, L.J., Castro, J.L., Whiting, P.J., Rosahl, T.W., Atack, J.R., McKernan, R.M., Dawson, G.R. and Reynolds, D.S. (2005) Evidence for a significant role of alpha 3-containing GABA_A receptors in mediating the anxiolytic effects of benzodiazepines. J. Neurosci., 25: 10682–10688.

Facklam, M., Schoch, P., Bonetti, E.P., Jenck, F., Martin, J.R., Moreau, J.-L. and Haefely, W. (1992) Relationship between benzodiazepine receptor occupancy and functional effects in vivo of four ligands of differing intrinsic efficacies. J. Pharmacol. Exp. Ther., 261: 1113–1121.

Foster, A.C., Pelleymounter, M.A., Cullen, M.J., Lewis, D., Joppa, M., Chen, T.K., Bozigian, H.P., Gross, R.S. and Gogas, K.R. (2004) In vivo pharmacological characterization of indiplon, a novel pyrazolopyrimidine sedative-hypnotic. J. Pharmacol. Exp. Ther., 311: 547–559.

Fradley, R.L., Guscott, M.R., Bull, S., Hallett, D.J., Goodacre, S.C., Wafford, K.A., Garrett, E.M., Newman, R.J., O'Meara, G.F., Whiting, P.J., Rosahl, T.W., Dawson, G.R., Reynolds, D.S., and Atack, J.R. (2007) Differential contribution of GABA_A receptor subtypes to the anticonvulsant efficacy of benzodiazepine site ligands. J. Psychopharmacol. 21: 384–391.

Gordon, B. (1979) I'm Dancing as Fast as I Can. Harper & Row, New York, NY.

Griebel, G., Perrault, G., Letang, V., Granger, P., Avenet, P., Schoemaker, H. and Sanger, D.J. (1999) New evidence that the pharmacological effects of benzodiazepine receptor ligands can be associated with activities at different BZ (ω) receptor subtypes. Psychopharmacology, 146: 205–213.

Griebel, G., Perrault, G., Simiand, J., Cohen, C., Granger, P., Decobert, M., Francon, D., Avenet, P., Depoortere, H., Tan, S., Oblin, A., Schoemaker, H., Evanno, Y., Sevrin, M., George, P. and Scatton, B. (2001) SL651498: an anxioselective compound with functional selectivity for alpha2- and alpha3-containing gamma-aminobutyric acid_A (GABA_A) receptors. J. Pharmacol. Exp. Ther., 298: 753–768.

Griebel, G., Perrault, G., Simiand, J., Cohen, C., Granger, P., Depoortere, H., Francon, D., Avenet, P., Schoemaker, H., Evanno, Y., Sevrin, M., George, P. and Scatton, B. (2003) SL651498, a GABA_A receptor agonist with subtype-selective efficacy, as a potential treatment for generalized anxiety disorder and muscle spasms. CNS Drug Rev., 9: 3–20.

Guillen Sans, R. and Guzman Chozas, M. (1988) Historical aspects and applications of barbituric acid derivatives. A review. Pharmazie, 43: 827–829.

Haefely, W.E., Martin, J.R., Richards, J.G. and Schoch, P. (1992) The multiplicity of actions of benzodiazepine receptor ligands. Can. J. Psychiatry, 4: S102–S108.

Johnstone, T.B.C., Hogenkamp, D.J., Coyne, L., Su, J., Halliwell, R.F., Tran, M.B., Yoshimura, R.F., Li, W.-Y., Wang, J. and Gee, K.W. (2004) Modifying quinolone antibiotics yields new anxiolytics. Nat. Med., 10: 31–32.

Kessler, R.C., Chiu, W.T., Demler, O. and Walters, E.E. (2005) Prevalence, severity, and comorbidity of twelve-month DSM-IV disorders in the National Comorbidity Survey Replication (NCS-R). Arch. Gen. Psychiatry, 62: 617–627.

Kleingoor, C., Weiland, H.A., Korpi, E.R., Seeburg, P.H. and Kettenmann, H. (1993) Current potentiation by diazepam but not GABA sensitivity is determined by a single histidine residue. Neuroreport, 4: 187–190.

Licata, S.C., Platt, D.M., Cook, J.M., Sarma, P.V.V.S., Griebel, G. and Rowlett, J.K. (2005) Contribution of GABA_A receptor subtypes to the anxiolytic-like, motor, and discriminative stimulus effects of benzodiazepines: Studies with the functionally-selective ligand SL 651498. J. Pharmacol. Exp. Ther., 313: 1118–1125.

Lingford-Hughes, A., Wilson, S.J., Feeney, A., Grasby, P.G. and Nutt, D.J. (2005) A proof-of-concept study using [^{11}C]flumazenil PET to demonstrate that pagoclone is a partial agonist. Psychopharmacology, 180: 789–791.

Lippa, A., Czobor, P., Stark, J., Beer, B., Kostakis, E., Gravielle, M., Bandyopadhyay, S., Russek, S.J., Gibbs, T.T., Farb, D.H. and Skolnick, P. (2005) Selective anxiolysis produced by ocinaplon, a GABA_A receptor modulator. Proc. Natl. Acad. Sci. USA, 102: 7380–7385.

Löw, K., Crestani, F., Keist, R., Benke, D., Brünig, I., Benson, J.A., Fritschy, J.-M., Rülicke, T., Bluethmann, H., Möhler, H. and Rudolph, W. (2000) Molecular and neuronal substrate for the selective attenuation of anxiety. Science, 290: 131–134.

McKernan, R.M., Rosahl, T.W., Reynolds, D.S., Sur, C., Wafford, K.A., Atack, J.R., Farrar, S., Myers, J., Cook, G. and Ferris, P. (2000) Sedative but not anxiolytic properties of benzodiazepines are mediated by the GABA_A receptor alpha1 subtype. Nat. Neurosci., 3: 587–592.

McKernan, R.M. and Whiting, P.J. (1996) Which GABA_A-receptor subtypes really occur in the brain?. Trends Pharmacol. Sci., 19: 139–143.

Möhler, H. (2006) GABA_A receptor diversity and pharmacology. Cell Tissue Res., 326: 505–516.

Morris, H.V., Dawson, G.R., Reynolds, D.S., Atack, J.R. and Stephens, D.N. (2006) Both α2 and α3

GABA$_A$ receptor subtypes mediate the anxiolytic properties of benzodiazepine site ligands in the conditioned emotional response paradigm. Eur. J. Neurosci., 23: 2495–2504.

Nutt, D.J. (2005) Overview of diagnosis and drug treatments of anxiety disorders. CNS Spectrosc., 10: 49–56.

Popik, P., Kostakis, E., Krawczyk, M., Nowak, G., Szewczyk, B., Krieter, P., Chen, Z., Russek, S.J., Gibbs, T.T., Farb, D.H., Skolnick, P., Lippa, A.S. and Basile, A.S. (2006) The anxioselective agent 7-(2-chloropyridin-4-yl)pyrazolo-[1,5-a]-pyrimidin-3-yl](pyridine-2-yl)methanone (DOV 51892) is more efficacious than diazepam at enhancing GABA-gated currents at α1 subunit-containing GABA$_A$ receptors. J. Pharmacol. Exp. Ther., 319: 1244–1252.

Rabe, H., Kronbach, C., Rundfeldt, C. and Lüddens, H. (2006) The novel anxiolytic ELB139 displays selectivity to recombinant GABA$_A$ receptors different from diazepam. Neuropharmacology, 52: 796–801.

Rowlett, J.K., Cook, J.M., Duke, A.N. and Platt, D.M. (2005a) Selective antagonism of GABA$_A$ receptor subtypes: an in vivo approach to exploring the therapeutic and side effects of benzodiazepine-type drugs. CNS Spectrosc., 10: 40–48.

Rowlett, J.K., Platt, D.M., Lelas, S., Atack, J.R. and Dawson, G.R. (2005b) Different GABA$_A$ receptor subtypes mediate the anxiolytic, abuse-related, and motor effects of benzodiazepine-like drugs in primates. Proc. Natl. Acad. Sci. USA, 102: 915–920.

Rudolph, U., Crestani, F., Benke, D., Brünig, I., Benson, J., Fritschy, J.M., Martin, J.R., Bluethmann, H. and Möhler, H. (1999) Benzodiazepine actions mediated by specific γ-aminobutyric acid$_A$ receptor subtypes. Nature, 401: 796–800.

Shannon, H.E., Guzman, F. and Cook, J.M. (1984) Beta-carboline-3-carboxylate-t-butyl ester: a selective BZ1 benzodiazepine receptor antagonist. Life Sci., 35: 2227–2236.

Speaker, S. (1997) From "happiness pills" to "national nightmare": changing cultural assessment of minor tranquilizers in America, 1955–1980. J. Hist. Med. Allied Sci., 52: 338–376.

Tone, A. (2005) Listening to the past: history, psychiatry, and anxiety. Can. J. Psychiatry, 50: 373–380.

US Committee on Labor and Human Resources. (1979) Use and misuse of benzodiazepines. US Government Printing Office, Washington, DC.

Whiting, P.J. (2006) GABA-A receptors: a viable target for novel anxiolytics? Curr. Opin. Pharmacol., 6: 24–29.

Wieland, H.A., Lüddens, H. and Seeburg, P.H. (1992) A single histidine in GABA$_A$ receptors is essential for benzodiazepine agonist binding. J. Biol. Chem., 267: 1426–1429.

CHAPTER 4.3

Modulation of anxiety behaviors by 5-HT-interacting drugs

Francisco Silveira Guimarães[1],[*], Antonio Pádua Carobrez[2] and
Frederico Guilherme Graeff[3]

[1]*Department of Pharmacology, Faculdade de Medicina de Ribeirão Preto, Universidade de São Paulo,
Ribeirão Preto, SP, Brazil*
[2]*Department of Pharmacology, CCB, Universidade Federal de Santa Catarina, Campus Universitário-Trindade,
Florianópolis, SC, Brazil*
[3]*Department of Neurology, Psychiatry and Medical Psychology, Hospital das Clínicas da Faculdade de Medicina de
Ribeirão Preto, Universidade de São Paulo, Ribeirão Preto, SP, Brazil*

Abstract: Results gathered in the last 35 years clearly show that serotonin (5-HT) is involved in anxiety. In agreement with this proposal, serotonin selective reuptake inhibitors (SSRIs) are the main drug treatment for anxiety disorders. However, the precise role of 5-HT in these disorders and the mechanisms responsible for the SSRIs therapeutic effects remain incompletely understood due to factors, such as the anatomical and neurochemical complexity of the 5-HT system, the lack of specificity of several available drugs, the adaptive neural changes caused by repeated drug administration and/or exposure to aversive stimuli and difficulties in interpreting results as cause or consequence of pathological anxiety and/or drug treatment. More recent ethological studies have shown that specific classes of threatening stimuli trigger particular defensive responses, probably reflecting discrete contributions of an interconnected and diffuse neural defensive system. As it will be discussed below, several pieces of evidence indicate that 5-HT exerts distinct modulator roles in specific areas of this network, which could help to explain the therapeutic effects of SSRIs in several anxiety disorders.

Keywords: serotonin; anxiety; panic; anxiolytics; antidepressants; periaqueductal gray; amygdala; hippocampus

I. Introduction

The first animal models of anxiety were developed before the elaboration of the DSM classifications of psychiatric disorders, and were aimed at modeling anxiety in general. They had been designed within the conceptual framework of the experimental psychology of the 1950s and 60s, which was mainly focused on learning through conditioning procedures. These animal models of anxiety rely on either inhibition of ongoing behavior elicited by conditioned stimuli that predict unavoidable electric shock or on suppression of rewarded responding by electric-shock punishment. The first type is based on associative or Pavlovian conditioning, comprising the so-called conditional emotional response (CER) and the conditioned suppression of lever pressing (Estes and Skinner, 1941; Millenson and Leslie 1974). In contrast, the punishment model is based on instrumental or operant conditioning, and

*Corresponding author. E-mail: fsguimar@fmrp.usp.br

R.J. Blanchard, D.C. Blanchard, G. Griebel and D. Nutt (Eds.)
Handbook of Anxiety and Fear, Vol. 17
ISBN 978-0-444-53065-3

241

DOI: 10.1016/S1569-7339(07)00012-4

involves an approach–avoidance conflict. For this reason, these models of anxiety are also named conflict tests.

Early pharmacological analysis had shown that conflict tests had higher predictive value of drug response than conditioned suppression in regard to clinical anxiety (Kelleher and Morse, 1968). As a result, punishment tests became widely used for assaying anti-anxiety drugs, represented by benzodiazepine and barbiturate derivatives, which primarily affect GABA-mediated neurotransmission.

Punishment tests have been historically important for the formulation of the concept that serotonin (5-HT) plays a key role in anxiety, as shortly described below. Using a widely used rat conflict test (Geller and Seifter, 1960), Robichaud and Sledge (1969) have shown that the selective inhibitor of 5-HT synthesis *para*-chlorophenylalanine (PCPA) increases bar pressing rates maintained by sweetened milk presentation, simultaneously suppressed by response-contingent foot-shock. Shortly thereafter, Graeff and Schoenfeld (1970) observed that the non-selective 5-HT receptor antagonists methysergide and bromolysergic acid (BOL) increased key-pecking rates that were maintained by food presentation, concurrently suppressed by response-contingent electric shocks; to the opposite direction, the receptor agonist α-methyltryptamine further suppressed punished responding. On the basis of these results, it has been suggested that tryptaminergic mechanisms in the brain mediate the response suppression determined by punishment.

In the years that followed these initial findings, a large body of experimental evidence has supported the involvement of serotonin in defensive mechanisms. However, its precise role is still unclear, with several conflicting proposals. For example, two completely opposite hypothesis to explain the involvement of 5-HT in panic disorder (PD) have been proposed. Whereas some researchers advocate an over activity of the 5-HT system (due to either increased neurotransmitter release or postsynaptic receptor supersensitivity) others endorse a contrary view, suggesting an impaired serotonergic neurotransmission (for review, see Maron and Shlik, 2006).

As discussed below, a number of factors may have contributed to these contradictions. For example, the anatomical and neurochemical complexity of the 5-HT system (Lowry et al., 2005), the lack of specificity of several available drugs for basic and clinical studies, the adaptive neural changes caused by repeated drug administration and/or exposure to aversive stimuli (Maier and Watkins, 2005), and difficulties in interpreting results as either cause or consequence of pathological anxiety and/or drug treatment. Moreover, careful ethological studies carried out in the last 25 years have clearly shown that particular defensive responses are triggered by specific classes of threatening stimuli (Blanchard et al., 2003). Humans faced with threatening situations also utilize specific behavioral strategies, including flight, hiding, freezing, defensive threat/attack, and risk assessment, similar to those described in rodents (Blanchard et al., 2001). These responses probably reflect discrete contributions of an interconnected and diffuse neural defensive system. As will be discussed below, several pieces of evidence indicate that 5-HT exerts distinct modulatory roles in specific areas of this network.

II. The serotonin system in the central nervous system

The monoamine serotonin was identified in 1945 by Irving Page's group as a serum vasoconstrictor released by platelet breakdown and further characterized as 5-hydroxytryptamine (5-HT; Rapport, 1949). The enzymatic cascade that synthesizes 5-HT begins with the amino acid tryptophan being hydroxylized by a rate-limiting enzyme tryptophan hydroxylase (TH), followed by a decarboxylase which will form 5-HT. The enzyme TH is not fully saturated in physiological conditions and therefore, additional quantity of tryptophan can eventually increase the amount of 5-HT (Green, 2006). On the other hand, systemic administration of the TH-inhibitor PCPA is capable of decreasing 5-HT content by 80% (Koe and Weissman, 1966). After being released from the nerve terminal, either by a Ca^{++}-mediated exocytosis of vesicles or by a Na^+-dependent carrier-mediated release from a non-vesicular pool of 5-HT (Levi and Raiteri, 1993), the transmitter will bind to several types of pre and postsynaptic 5-HT receptors (for reviews, see Hoyer et al., 2002; Green, 2006).The present 5-HT receptor classification (Hoyer et al., 2002) considers the existence of seven 5-HT receptor classes, one ionotropic, linked directly to an ion channel and six metabotropic-types, coupled to G proteins and second messengers' systems. The 5-HT$_1$-class is formed by five receptor subtypes (5-HT$_{1A}$, 5-HT$_{1B}$, 5-HT$_{1D}$, 5-ht$_{1E}$, 5-ht$_{1F}$), coupled to a G$_{i/0}$ protein that preferentially inhibits adenylate cyclase, reducing the formation of cAMP (Peroutka, 1988). Their sub-cellular location was found both at presynaptic membranes, mainly in somatodendritic processes of the raphé nucleus complex, for the 1A and 1D subtypes, and in fiber terminals, for the 1B and 1D subtypes (Piñeyro and Blier, 1999), or at postsynaptic membranes (Kia et al., 1996a, b). Although present in several postsynaptic brain areas, the 5-HT$_1$receptor class also controls 5-HT transmission through its location in somatodendritic raphé cell bodies. Due to its negative coupling to adenylate cyclase and location, 5-HT$_{1A}$ and 5-HT$_{1D}$ receptors can reduce the amount of 5-HT released from fibers' terminals in the projection areas. Another important role for this receptor class is the immediate control of 5-HT release in the presynaptic region exerted by the 5-HT$_{1B}$ or 5-HT$_{1D}$ receptors (see Piñeyro and Blier, 1999, for an extensive review). The 5-HT$_2$-class comprises three receptor subtypes (5-HT$_{2A}$, 5-HT$_{2B}$, 5-HT$_{2C}$), coupled to a Gq protein that preferentially increases the hydrolysis of inositol phosphates, and elevates cytosolic Ca^{++} (Conn and Sanders-Bush, 1986). The ionotropic 5-HT$_3$-class (5-HT$_{3A}$, 5-HT$_{3B}$, 5-ht$_{3C}$) has a pentameric structure, with the five subunits forming a central non-selective cation (Na$^+$, Ca^{++}, K$^+$) channel (Boess et al., 1995). The metabotropic receptors 5-HT$_4$, 5-ht$_6$, and 5-HT$_7$ are preferentially coupled to the G$_s$ protein, promoting cAMP formation. Finally, the putative metabotropic 5-ht$_5$ receptor comprises two subtypes (5-ht$_{5A}$, 5-ht$_{5B}$) preferentially either positively or negatively coupled to the G-protein involved in the formation of cAMP (Francken et al., 1998; Grailhe et al., 2001).

The effects of 5-HT are terminated following its removal from the synaptic cleft by a high-affinity selective Na$^+$–Cl$^-$-dependent transporter, which will increase the amount of 5-HT in the cytosol, where it can be either transported into the cytoplasmic vesicle or serve as substrate for the enzyme monoaminoxidase (MAO), being inactivated to the metabolite 5-hydroxyindoleacetic acid (Piñeyro and Blier, 1999).

Quantitative autoradiographic studies have shown a widespread distribution of 5-HT receptors in the brain (Pazos and Palacios, 1985; Barnes and Sharp, 1999). Relevant for fear and anxiety are some of the ascending projections originating in the raphé nuclei, mainly in the dorsal (DRN) and/or in the median (MRN) raphé nucleus. Ascending projections from the MRN include the dorsal hippocampus, the entorhinal cortex, the medial septum and the anterior hypothalamus. Axons originating in the DRN innervate the prefrontal cortex, the lateral septum, the amygdala, the dorsal striatum, the entorhinal cortex, the ventral hippocampus, and the dorsal periaqueductal gray (Palkovits et al., 1974; Pazos and Palacios, 1985; Barnes and Sharp, 1999; Hensler, 2006). However, it is now clear that the DRN shows a high degree of heterogeneity, with distinct receptor expression and functional properties along its axis (Clark et al., 2006). For example, recent findings indicate that the projections to cortical and limbic structures arise from neurons located in a specific part of the caudal DRN. These neurons are particularly sensitive to stressful stimuli, and their projections are thought to constitute a mesocorticolimbic 5-HT system related to anxiety, like the dopamine mesocorticolimbic system in relation to reward (for review see Lowry et al., 2005).

III. Human findings: serotonin and pathological anxiety

Although imipramine has later been shown to be effective in patients with generalized anxiety disorder (GAD) (Kahn et al., 1986), the discovery of its beneficial effect in panic patients was decisive for the recognition of PD as a distinct nosological entity (Klein and Flink, 1962). Subsequently, buspirone, a partial 5-HT$_{1A}$ receptor agonist, has also been found to be effective in treating patients with GAD (Goldberg and Finnerty, 1979). In the following years, a few other 5-HT-related drugs have also been tested in patients with anxiety disorders, but the results have been far from encouraging. For example, ritanserin, a $5HT_{2A/2C}$ receptor antagonist, has been reported to be as effective as lorazepam in patients with GAD (Ceulemans et al., 1985). However, it has no effect or even impairs PD (den Boer and Westenberg, 1990). Antagonists of $5-HT_3$ receptors (ondansetron and tropisetron) have also been investigated in patients with anxiety disorders with mixed results (Romach et al., 1998; Lecrubier et al., 1999; Hewlett et al., 2003). Finally, regarding the effects of 5-HT agonists in patients with anxiety disorders, d-fenfluramine, a 5-HT releaser, was reported to ameliorate panic patients resistant to traditional treatments (Solyom, 1994; Hetem, 1996). However, flesinoxan, a $5-HT_{1A}$ agonist,

failed to improve these patients in pilot studies (van Vliet et al., 1996a, b).

Despite these findings, the discovery that SSRIs are effective in treating panic, generalized anxiety, obsessive-compulsive, social anxiety, and post-traumatic stress disorders (PSTDs) (Baldwin et al., 2005) has boosted the research on the role of 5-HT in anxiety along the last two decades.

IV. Human findings: experimental studies with patients

Several chemical compounds have been used to elicit anxiety symptoms, particularly panic attacks in patients with anxiety disorders (see Table 1). Similar to their clinical effects, drugs that facilitate 5-HT-mediated neurotransmission, such as SSRIs, tricyclic antidepressants (TCAs) or l-5-hydroxy-tryptophan, decrease anxiety symptoms, whereas

Table 1. Main reported findings on chemically induced anxiety in patients with anxiety disorders receiving 5-HT-related compounds

Anxiogenic/ panicogenic compound	Patients	5-HT-related drug	Results	References
Cholecystokinin-4 (CCK-4)	PD	SSRI	↓	Van Megen et al. (1997)
		l-5-hydroxytryptophan	(↓)	Maron et al., 2004a, b
		Tryptophan depletion	0	Koszycki et al. (1996)
CO_2	PD	SSRI, TCA	↓	Perna et al. (2002)
		l-5-hydroxytryptophan	↓	Schruers et al. (2002)
		d-fenfluramine	↓ panic attack ↑ anticipatory anxiety	Mortimore and Anderson (2000)
		Tryptophan depletion	↑	Miller et al. (2000)
		Metergoline	↑	Ben-Zion et al. (1999)
MCPP	PD		↑	Germine et al. (1994)
	PTSD		↑	Southwick et al. (1997)
	OCD		↑ or 0	Goodman et al. (1995), Erzegovesi et al. (2001)
Tryptophan depletion	Social anxiety	SSRI	↑ (reverses the SSRI effect)	Argyropoulos et al. (2004)
	OCD	SSRI	0 (↑distress on symptom provocation)	Berney et al. (2006)
Flumazenil	PD	SSRI + tryptophan depletion	↑	Bell et al. (2002)
Metergoline	OCD	TCA	↑	Murphy et al. (1989)
Sumatriptan	PD		↑	Amital et al. (2005)
Yohimbine	PD	SSRI	↓	Goddard et al. (1993)

Note: PD, panic disorder; PTSD, post-traumatic stress disorder; OCD, obsessive compulsive disorder; SSRI, serotonin selective reuptake inhibitors; TCA, tricyclic antidepressant. ↑, increase; ↓, decrease, (↓) decrease in females.

treatment that impair its functioning has the opposite effect (or reverse the therapeutic effect of SSRIs). Most studies, however, have been performed with panic or obsessive compulsive patients, what prevent conclusions regarding the effects of this approach in other forms of pathological anxiety.

Results obtained with two drugs that facilitate 5-HT neurotransmission, d-fenfluramine and mCPP, have apparently produced conflicting results. Corroborating findings obtained in healthy subjects submitted to experimental anxiety models (see below), d-fenfluramine produced a dual effect, attenuating panic attacks induced by 7% CO_2, but increasing anticipatory anxiety symptoms and arousal (Mortimore and Anderson, 2000). This result can help to explain the original claim that this drug was "panicogenic", whereas, in reality, it seems to ameliorate panic patients (Solyom, 1994; Hetem, 1996). However, results with mCPP, a 5-HT$_2$ agonist, in PD, PSTD, and obsessive compulsive disorder (OCD) patients, are more difficult to understand. Although the panicogenic and anxiogenic effects of this drug have usually been interpreted as indicating 5-HT$_{2C}$ supersensitivity in anxiety disorders, mCPP has several other pharmacological effects. For example, at the nanomolar range, it shows affinity for 5-HT$_{1A}$, 5-HT$_{1B}$, 5-HT$_{2A/B/C}$, 5HT$_3$, and even 5-HT$_7$ receptors. Moreover, it produces peripheral symptoms that could act as confounding variables. This is particularly true for PD, where these symptoms can secondarily lead to panic attacks due to a "catastrophic" interpretation (Nutt, 1990).

V. Neuroendocrine studies

Another clinical insight into central serotonergic activity has been achieved by measuring drug-induced hormonal changes, particularly increases in prolactin and cortisol levels induced by facilitation of 5-HT-mediated neurotransmission. A summary of the main findings in patients with anxiety disorders regarding these two hormones can be seen in Table 2. The results suggest the presence of distinct central serotonergic dysfunctions in specific anxiety disorders. For example, whereas a decreased sensitivity of 5-HT$_{1A}$-mediated neurotransmission in PD has been indicated by several studies, no change in neuroendocrine responses to ipsapirone or fenfluramine has been found in OCD. On the other hand, results with 5-HT$_2$ agonists suggest an increased sensitivity in PD and PTSD, but a decreased sensitivity in OCD. In PD and OCD, however, a blunted response to d-fenfluramine has been found (Table 2), raising the possibility that the increased sensitivity to mCPP reflects a compensatory up-regulation of 5-HT$_{2C}$ receptors due to a decrease in 5-HT neurotransmission.

Table 2. Cortisol and/or prolactin responses to 5-HT-interacting drugs in patients with anxiety disorders compared to healthy controls

Anxiety disorder	Drug	Results	Reference
PD	5-HT$_{1A}$ agonist (ipsapirone)	↓	Broocks et al. (2000), Lesch et al. (1992)
PD	5-HT$_2$ agonist (mCPP)	↑ (with mCPP)	Broocks et al. (2000)
PD	5-HT precursor (5-HTP, tryptophan)	No main difference	van Vliet et al., 1996a, b, Charney and Heninger (1986)
PD	5-HT releaser (d-fenfluramine)	↓ (severe PD)	Mortimore and Anderson (2000)
OCD	5-HT$_{1A}$ agonist (ipsapirone)	No main difference	Lesch et al. (1991)
OCD	5-HT$_2$ agonist (MK-212)	↓	Bastani et al. (1990)
OCD	5-HT releaser (fenfluramine)	No main difference	McBride et al. (1992)
PSTD	5-HT releaser (fenfluramine)	No main difference	Southwick et al. (1999)
PSTD	5-HT$_2$ agonist (mCPP)	↑	Southwick et al. (1999)
SAD	SSRI (citalopram)	No main difference	Shlik et al. (2004)

Note: 5-HTP, 5-hydroxytryptophan; ↑, increased response; ↓, blunted response. For further specifications see Table 1.

VI. Human findings: experimental studies with healthy volunteers

Experimental anxiety in healthy volunteers represents a useful bridge between animal models and clinical disorders. Anxiety symptoms can be induced by either chemical (e.g., caffeine, penthylenetetrazol, yohimbine, CO_2 inhalation) or psychological means. Among psychological models, as far as 5-HT related drugs are concerned, the main tests have been the aversive conditioning to tones and the simulated public speaking (SPS) test (for review, see Graeff et al., 2003).

Classical conditioning plays a fundamental role in most theories of anxiety, explaining how initially neutral stimuli or contexts acquire the ability to elicit fear after being paired with painful and/or unpleasant stimuli. Deakin and co-workers tested several 5-HT related drugs in a conditioned fear model that measures skin conductance responses (SCRs) elicited by a tone before and after its pairing with a loud white noise. SCRs have been considered as an index of activation of Gray's "brain inhibition system" (Fowles, 2000), which has been related to anxiety (Gray and McNaughton, 2000). Like diazepam, buspirone has facilitated both the habituation to the neutral tone and the extinction of the conditioned responses, while ritanserin has affected extinction, but did not change habituation. On the contrary, mCPP and d-fenfluramine have tended to facilitate conditioning (Table 3). Together, these results indicate that facilitation of 5-HT$_{1A}$ or antagonism of 5-HT$_{2A/C}$-mediated neurotransmission decrease conditioned anxiety whereas facilitation of the latter has the opposite effect (see Graeff et al., 2003).

The SPS test was first proposed by McNair et al. (1982) and further modified by Guimarães et al. (1987). In this test, the subject is requested to prepare a speech, and then speak in front of a video camera, the performance being recorded on videotape. The SPS test has been proposed to mobilize species-specific, unconditioned fear mechanisms, since it is highly prevalent among all

Table 3. Effects of 5HT-interacting drugs on experimental anxiety in healthy volunteers (based on Graeff et al., 2003)

Mechanism	Drug	Test phase		Observation
		Habituation	Extinction	
Aversive conditioning to tones (ACT)				
5-HT antagonist	Ritanserin	0	↓	5-HT$_2$ antagonist
5-HT agonist	Buspirone	↓	↓	5-HT$_{1A}$ partial agonist
	mCPP	0	(↑)	Tended to enhance responses
5-HT releaser	d-fenfluramine	0	(↑)	Tended to enhance responses
Serotonin reuptake inhibitor	Fluvoxamine	↓	↓	Only in females

Mechanism	Drug	Test phase			Observation
		Before	During	After	
Simulated public speaking test					
5-HT antagonist	Metergoline	↑	0	0	Non-selective 5-HT antagonist
	Ritanserin	0	0	↑	5-HT$_2$ antagonist
Tryptophan depletion		0	↑	0	Only in females
5-HT releaser	d-fenfluramine	0	↓	↓	
5-HT agonist	Buspirone	0	0	0	5-HT$_{1A}$ partial agonist
	Ipsapirone	0	↓	0	5-HT$_{1A}$ partial agonist
	mCPP	0	0	0	Non-selective 5-HT$_2$ agonist
Serotonin reuptake inhibitor	Clomipramine	0	↑	0	5-HT$_2$ antagonist
	Nefazodone	0	↑	0	5-HT$_2$ antagonist

Note: ↑, increased subjective anxiety (SPS) or skin conductance response (ACT); ↓, decreased subjective anxiety or skin conductance responses (ACT); 0, no change.

kinds of people, and provokes anxiety in healthy volunteers, irrespective of trait anxiety level (Graeff et al., 2003). Although benzodiazepine anxiolytics have consistently decreased basal anxiety (pre-stress measurement) in this test, compounds that act primarily on serotonergic neurotransmission usually have not changed pre-stress anxiety (Table 3). In contrast, drugs that either facilitate or inhibit 5-HT-mediated neurotransmission, respectively decrease or increase speech-induced fear. Therefore, the serotonergic system seems to exert a phasic rather than a tonic modulator control over this kind of fear. In addition, the results go to an opposite direction than those obtained in the conditioned SCR model. This agrees with the suggestion that, different from basal and conditioned anxiety, SPS induces a distinct type of emotion, possibly related to unconditioned fear.

VII. Human studies: neuroimaging

The use of techniques such as single-photon emission computed tomography (SPECT), positron emission tomography (PET), and functional magnetic resonance (fMRI) has detected several changes in 5-HT-mediated neurotransmission in patients with anxiety disorders. In addition, these techniques have also been used to investigate neurobiological and genetic aspects related to anxiety.

VII.A. Serotonin transporters (5-HTT)

Individuals with one or two copies of the short (SLC6A4) allele of the serotonin transporter (5-HTT) promoter polymorphism exhibit greater amygdala neuronal activity in response to fearful stimuli compared with individuals homozygous for the long allele. This polymorphism has been associated with reduced 5-HTT expression and function, and has increased depressive and anxiety symptoms (Hariri et al., 2002). It may be related to a susceptibility factor for affective disorders, by biasing the functional reactivity of the human amygdala in the context of stressful life experiences (Hariri et al., 2005). So far, however, studies comparing the presence of the short allele in anxiety disorders, such as OCD or GAD, have

produced mainly negative results (Hesse et al., 2004; Maron et al., 2004a, b), although an inverse correlation between 5HTT binding and subjective anxiety has been reported (Maron et al., 2004a, b). Nevertheless, social anxiety disorder (SAD) patients with one or two copies of the short allele in the promoter region of the 5-HTT gene have increased levels of anxiety-related traits, state anxiety, and enhanced right amygdala responding to anxiety provocation (Furmark et al., 2004). In these patients successful treatment with citalopram reduced activity in the anterior and lateral part of the left temporal cortex; the anterior, lateral, and posterior part of the left mid frontal cortex; and the left cingulum (Van der Linden et al., 2000). This was accompanied by a decreased rCBF-response to public speaking in the amygdala, hippocampus, and the periamygdaloid, rhinal, and parahippocampal cortices, bilaterally (Furmark et al, 2002).

Individuals with two copies of the short allele also show significantly lower hippocampal (NAA) concentration, as compared to those with the l/l genotype. Hippocampal NAA concentration has negatively been correlated with trait anxiety scores (Gallinat et al., 2005). Despite these pieces of evidence linking changes in 5-HTT expression and emotional processing in the amygdala, the functional consequences of these variations on 5-HT-mediated neurotransmission is still unclear. A decrease in 5-HT transporters would increase synaptic 5-HT. However, this has been difficult to prove. On the contrary, evidence exists that this polymorphism is associated with blunted 5-HT function (Reist et al., 2001). Moreover, it is possible that this genetic trait interferes with neuronal development, having long-term effects that go beyond a simple change in 5-HT availability (see below). Corroborating this possibility, individuals with two copies of the short allele have reduced gray matter volume in limbic regions related to the processing of negative emotion, particularly perigenual cingulate and amygdala (Pezawas et al., 2005).

VII.B. Serotonin receptors

A PET study with healthy volunteers has shown a significant negative correlation between 5-HT$_{1A}$

binding potential and anxiety in four regions: the dorsolateral prefrontal, anterior cingulate, parietal, and occipital cortices (Tauscher et al., 2001). Reduced $5-HT_{1A}$ binding in areas which have been shown to be correlated with anxiety/depressive symptoms, such as the amygdala, anterior cingulate, insula, lateral temporal cortex, and raphe nuclei, has also been found in schizophrenics and patients with temporal lobe epilepsy (Savic et al., 2004; Yasuno et al., 2004). In addition to $5-HT_{1A}$ receptors, one recent study has shown that a single polymorphism in the regulatory region of the $5-HT_3$ gene (HTR3A) is associated with greater reactivity in the amygdala and dorsal and medial PFC (Iidaka et al., 2005).

In patients with anxiety disorders, individuals with PD have a lower number of $5-HT_{1A}$ receptors in the anterior cingulate, posterior cingulate, and raphe (Neumeister et al., 2004). A reduction of these receptors in limbic and paralimbic areas, particularly the amygdala, has also been recently reported in patients with SAD (Lanzenberger et al., 2007). Although no change in 5-HT receptors has been reported in PSTD or GAD (Bonne et al., 2005), successful treatment with SSRIs has been able to normalize activity changes during symptom provocation in these patients, in the insula, prefrontal, and inferior frontal cortices (Fernandez et al., 2001; Hoehn-Saric et al., 2004). Also, the activation of the anterolateral orbito-frontal cortex (OFC), caudate nucleus, thalamus, and temporal regions, which is usually found in OCD patients, is attenuated by chronic treatment with SSRIs (Carey et al., 2004).

VIII. Summary of clinical studies

The therapeutic efficacy of 5-HT-interacting compounds clearly points to an involvement of this neurotransmitter in anxiety disorders (Gordon and Hen, 2004). In spite of being a relatively new field, neuroimaging studies have provided important data regarding the role of 5-HT in anxiety. Physiological links have been established between functional genetic polymorphisms and differences in information processing within distinct brain regions and circuits related to anxiety (Hariri

et al., 2005). Other consistent finding is a negative correlation between $5-HT_{1A}$ receptor binding and anxiety in healthy volunteers, a result that is supported by the observation of reduced binding to these receptors in panic patients.

Experimental studies in healthy volunteers and patients with anxiety disorders indicate that 5-HT exerts a rather complex, sometimes opposite, control over defensive responses, suggesting the presence of distinct central serotonergic dysfunctions in specific anxiety disorders.

IX. Serotonin and defensive behavior in animal models

Studies with animal models of anxiety can potentially overcome some limitations of clinical investigations. These studies can address the questions of whether 5-HT is anxiolytic or anxiogenic, where it exerts such effects, and through what type of receptor.

There are excellent reviews in the literature on the effects of 5-HT-related drugs in animal models of anxiety (e.g. Griebel, 1995; Blanchard et al., 2003; Bourin and Hascoet, 2003; Millan, 2003; Olivier et al., 2003; Prut and Belzung, 2003; Sanchez, 2003). As with clinical data, highly variable results have been obtained (Belzung, 2001). In the following sessions we will mainly focus on results obtained with conflict tests, aversive brain electrical stimulation, and elevated mazes.

IX.A. Serotonin and punished behavior

Two years after the initial reports showing the anti-punishment effect of impairment of 5-HT neurotransmission (Robichaud and Sledge, 1969, Graeff and Schoenfeld, 1970), Wise et al. (1972) reported that the benzodiazepine anxiolytic oxazepam decreased 5-HT turnover in the rat midbrain at the same dose that released punished responding in the Geller–Seifter procedure. Summing up the available neurochemical and anatomical evidence, they suggested that the ascending 5-HT pathways that originate in the midbrain raphe nuclei would facilitate the effects of punishment by acting on limbic forebrain and midbrain structures that suppress ongoing behavior; benzo-diazepine anxiolytics would reduce anxiety by decreasing 5-HT release in these brain areas. Although later evidence has shown that the anxiolytic action of benzodiazepines is largely independent of 5-HT, the implicit idea that 5-HT generally increases anxiety has become widely accepted (Gardner, 1986; Chopin and Briley, 1987).

The suggestion that 5-HT increases the effects of punishment by acting on the forebrain (Wise et al., 1972) got strong support from the results reported by Tye et al. (1977) using the neurotoxin 5,7-dihydroxytryptamine (5,7-DHT), which selectively destroys 5-HT neurons. They found that micro-injection of 5,7-DHT into the ventromedial tegmentum of the rat midbrain, causing 70% depletion of cortical 5-HT, prevented the acquisition of response suppression induced by foot-shock in a modified Geller–Seifter procedure. As complementary evidence, Graeff and Silveira Filho (1978) found that electrical stimulation of the median raphe nucleus (MRN) inhibited ongoing lever-pressing behavior maintained by a variable interval schedule of water presentation, as well as induced defecation, urination, piloerection, teeth clattering, and exophthalmos. Thus, electrical stimulation of the MRN suppressed ongoing lever-pressing behavior while pretreatment with PCPA reduced the effect of MRN electrical stimulation, suggesting a 5-HT mediation of the response suppression. Since MRN 5-HT neurons project mainly to the dorsal hippocampus (Azmitia and Segal, 1978), the latter results are in agreement with Gray's (1982) proposal that anxiety is due to activation of the septo-hippocampal system. In the same direction, Schoenfeld (1976) reported that the hallucinogens LSD and mescaline released punished licking in the rat, and suggested that this effect may be due to decreased activity of ascending serotonergic neurons.

Early results also implicate the amygdala in the mediation of the suppressant action of 5-HT on punished responding. Thus, microinjection of 5-HT antagonists into the basolateral amygdala has been shown to release water licking suppressed by electric shock punishment (Petersen and Scheel-Krüger, 1984, Fig. 1). As a counterpart, microinjection of 5-HT into the same amygdala

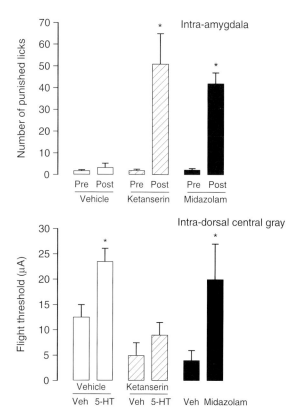

Fig. 1. Opposite roles of 5-HT in the amygdala and dorsal periaqueductal gray. Whereas in the former brain region 5-HT$_2$ antagonism releases punished behavior, in the latter the same treatment prevents 5-HT-induced antiaversive effects (modified from Audi and Graeff, 1984; Petersen and Scheel-Krüger, 1984; Schütz et al. 1985, with kind permission of Springer Science and Business Media and Elsevier). Results obtained with midazolam in the two models are presented as positive control.

region has been reported to further decrease punished lever pressing in a modified Geller–Seifter procedure (Hodges et al., 1987). In this regard, a large body of evidence highlights the importance of the amygdala in the learning and expression of conditioned fear and anxiety (e.g., Davis, 1992; LeDoux, 1993).

IX.B. Serotonin and escape

Although the evidence reviewed above agrees with the suggestion that 5-HT enhances anxiety by acting in forebrain structures, such as the septo-hippocampal system and the amygdala, the additional proposal by Wise et al. (1972) that 5-HT similarly enhances anxiety in the periaqueductal gray matter (PAG) of the midbrain has not been supported by experimental evidence, as described below.

Early results have shown that manipulations that result in less 5-HT action, such as the injection of PCPA or of the non-selective 5-HT receptor blocker cyproheptadine, increase lever-pressing that switches off PAG electrical stimulation in the rat. In the opposite direction, drug treatment that enhances 5-HT action, such as administration of the synthesis precursor 5-hydroxitryptophan and of the 5-HT reuptake inhibitor clomipramine, reduce this switch-off responding (Kiser and Lebovitz, 1975; Kiser et al., 1978a, b; Schenberg and Graeff, 1978).

Using a different procedure, in which rats were trained to jump over a ridge separating the two compartments of a shuttle box in order to switch off PAG electrical stimulation, Jenck and coworkers have similarly found that the non-selective 5-HT receptor antagonists metergoline and mianserin, facilitate PAG-induced escape, whereas two 5-HT reuptake inhibitors, fluvoxamine and sertraline, impair escape performance (Jenck et al., 1989, 1990). However, results reported by the same authors with the selective 5-HT$_2$-receptor antagonist ketanserin, as well as with the selective 5-HT$_{1A}$ receptor agonist 8-OH-DPAT were incompatible with the idea that 5-HT inhibits aversion in the PAG (Jenck et al., 1989).

To explore the mode of action of 5-HT on the PAG more directly, a series of experiments has been conducted by Graeff and coworkers using intra-cerebral drug administration combined with electrical stimulation by means of a chemitrode implanted inside the dorsal PAG. For determining the aversive threshold, rats are placed inside one of the two compartments of a shuttle box, and electrical current is applied to the PAG with gradually increasing intensity until the rat runs toward the opposite compartment of the box, switching off the brain stimulation. The results of these studies are consistent with an anti-aversive role of 5-HT in the PAG, since they have shown

that 5-HT$_1$ and/or 5-HT$_2$ receptor agonists, including 5-HT itself, inhibit escape from PAG electrical stimulation, and that this effect is antagonized by local pretreatment with 5-HT$_1$ and 5-HT$_2$ receptor blockers (Schütz et al., 1985; Nogueira and Graeff, 1995, Fig. 1). Accordingly, Beckett and Marsden, 1997 have reported that intra-PAG injection of 8-OH-DPAT decreases running behavior (flight) elicited by microinjection of the excitatory amino acid L-homocysteic acid (LHA) into the same PAG. Additional results obtained by the same research group have shown that the selective 5-HT$_{1A}$-receptor blocker WAY 100635 antagonizes the anti-aversive effect of 8-OH-DPAT, whereas the preferential 5-HT$_{2C}$-receptor agonist mCPP facilitates running induced by intra-DPAG injection of LHA (Beckett et al., 1992; Beckett and Marsden, 1997). The last result ascribes a pro-aversive role to 5-HT$_{2C}$ receptors in the PAG.

It is worth remarking that in the study by Schütz et al. (1985) intra-PAG administration of the 5-HT reuptake inhibitor zimelidine not only has potentiated the anti-aversive effect of subsequently injected 5-HT, but has also had an anti-aversive effect of its own. This implies the existence of 5-HT nerve fibers in the PAG that physiologically inhibit aversion. This view is strengthened by further experimental evidence showing that blockade with isamoltane of pre-synaptic 5-HT$_{1B}$ receptors that inhibit the release of 5-HT raises the aversive threshold of PAG electrical stimulation (Nogueira and Graeff, 1991). A recent study has also shown that a 21-day treatment with imipramine enhances the effect intra-PAG injection of 8-OH-DPAT and of the 5-HT$_{2A/2C}$ agonist DOI, indicating sensitization of postsynaptic 5-HT$_{1A}$ and 5-HT$_{2A/2C}$ receptors. This action has been related to the anti-panic effect of this drug regimen, as it will be discussed latter.

Another interesting issue is that intra-PAG administration of 5-HT receptor antagonists alone has no effect on the aversive threshold measured in the shuttle box (Schütz et al., 1985; Nogueira and Graeff, 1991). This finding contrasts with the major aversive effects caused by compounds like bicuculline, which block γ-amino-butyric acid type

A (GABA$_A$) receptors in the PAG (Brandão et al., 1982). It may be concluded that while GABAergic terminals tonically inhibit the PAG neurons that control defensive behavior, serotonergic fibers seem to exert a phasic inhibition. It has been further suggested that the modulatory influence of 5-HT on PAG functioning would be manifested only under environmental conditions that engage the 5-HT systems, chiefly the stressful ones (Deakin and Graeff, 1991).

Unlike punished behavior, escape and avoidance do not involve conflict, and are resistant to benzodiazepine anxiolytics, unless high sedative doses are used (Kelleher and Morse, 1968). Therefore, these tasks do not qualify as models of anxiety.

X. Dual role of serotonin

The introduction of new agents that act primarily on 5-HT neurotransmission, such as buspirone, ritanserin, mCPP, TFMPP, and others, have resulted in inconsistent results in conflict tests (for an extensive review, see Griebel, 1995), undermining the general confidence in these procedures, at least in their original paradigms, as reliable models of anxiety.

As these developments were taking place in basic research, classifications of anxiety disorders based on symptom clusters, time course, and therapeutic response have been elaborated. The proposal that each class of anxiety disorder engages a particular set of neurobiological systems has led to the conclusion that animal models should address anxiety disorders specifically. Therefore, a given animal model is expected to have a pharmacological profile that correlates with the clinical drug response of the disorder it is intended to represent. Following this line of reasoning, the results obtained with PAG stimulation have led to the proposal that conflict and escape models refer to different psychobiological processes, namely anxiety and panic, respectively. Serotonin would enhance the former while inhibiting the latter (Deakin and Graeff, 1991).

At about the same time these ideas were being conceived, several ethologically based models

aimed at mimicking anxiety disorders were being developed to replace the classical punishment tests. One of these new models, the elevated "X" or "plus" maze (EPM), has become the most widely used animal model of anxiety in the last two decades (Handley and Mithani 1984; Pellow et al. 1985; Carobrez and Bertoglio, 2005). However, results obtained with numerous 5-HT-related drugs assayed in this model have also produced contradictory or inconclusive results (Handley et al., 1993; Griebel 1995, Table 4).

Trying to explain these inconsistencies, the British psychologist Sheila Handley, who conceived the idea of the crossed elevated maze, has argued that the elevated X and plus mazes are in fact, mixed models, in the sense that the rat displays different strategies of defense while exploring them, which could be influenced in opposite directions by 5-HT (Handley et al., 1993). At least two strategies may be easily observed: (1) avoidance of open arms when the rat is in one of the closed arms, and (2) escape from an open arm to enter a safer, enclosed arm. This observation has led to the idea of separating these behavioral tasks: inhibitory avoidance and one-way escape, a goal that has been achieved by building the elevated T-maze (ETM, Graeff et al., 1993, Table 4).

This model was obtained by closing the entrance of one of the enclosed arms of the elevated plus-maze. For the inhibitory avoidance task, the rat is placed at the end of the remaining enclosed arm, and the latency to withdraw from this arm with the four paws is recorded in three successive trials made at 30-s intervals. Learning is indicated by the increase in withdrawal latency along the trials. For the escape task, which initiates 30 s after the completion of the avoidance training, the rat is placed at the end of one of the open arms, and the withdrawal latency from this arm is similarly recorded. Pre-exposure to the open arm for 30 min, 24 h before the test, has been found to decrease de first withdrawal latency from the open arm, and to increase the drug sensitivity of the escape task (Teixeira et al., 2000; Zanoveli et al., 2003). As expected, diazepam has been found to impair inhibitory avoidance, while one-way escape remained unaffected (Graeff et al., 1993). In

Table 4. Comparative effects of 5-HT-interacting drugs on rat behavior in elevated mazes

Drug action	T-maze		Plus or X-maze	Clinical effects	
	Inhibitory avoidance	One-way escape	Open-arm avoidance	GAD	PD
Mixed (NA/5-HT) reuptake inhibitors (imipramine, sibutramine)	↑ or ↓[a] ↓[b]	= or ↓[a] ↓[b]	=[a] Not tested[b]	=[a] ↓[b]	↑[a] ↓[b]
SSRIs (clomipramine, fluoxetine, paroxetine, zimelidine, fluvoxamine, citolapram, cianopramine)	↑ or =[a] = or ↓[b]	=[a] ↓[b]	= or ↑[a] ↓ = or ↑[b]	=[a] ↓[b]	↑[a] ↓[b]
5-HT releaser (fenfluramine)	↑	↓	Not tested	↑	↓
5-HT$_{1/2}$ agonist (5-MeODMT, RU 24969)	Not tested	Not tested	↑	Not tested	Not tested
5-HT$_{1A}$ agonist (8-OH-DPAT, BAY R 1521, flesinoxan)	Not tested	Not tested	↑ or ↓ or =	Not tested	=
5-HT$_{1A}$ partial agonist (buspirone, ipsapirone, gepirone)	↓ or =	=		↓ (chronic treatment)	=**
5-HT$_{1A}$ partial agonist /5-HT$_{1B}$ antagonist (yohimbine*)	↑	=	↑	↑	↑
5-HT$_{1A/B}$ antagonist (propranolol, pindolol)	Not tested	Not tested	↑ or = or ↓	=	=
5-HT$_{1A}$ antagonist (WAY 100635, MDL 73005EF)	Not tested	Not tested	= or ↓	Not tested	Not tested
5-HT$_{1B/2C}$ agonist (mCPP, TFMPP)	↑	↓	↑ or =	↑	↑
5-HT$_{2A/2C}$ agonist (DOI)	=	=	=	Not tested	Not tested
5-HT$_{2A/C}$ antagonist (mianserin, ritanserin, ketanserin, seganserin, pirenperone)	Not tested	Not tested	↑ or ↓ or =	↓	↑ (ritanserin)
5-HT$_{2A}$ antagonist (SR 46349B, RP 62203)	↓ or =	=	Not tested	Not tested	Not tested
5-HT$_{2B/C}$ antagonist (SB 200646A, SER 082)	↓	Unchanged	Not tested	Not tested	Not tested
5-HT$_{2C}$ antagonist (SB-242084)	Not tested	Not tested	↓	Not tested	Not tested
5-HT$_3$ antagonists (ondansetron, zacopride, ICS 205-9307, MDL72222, BRL 4670)	Not tested	Not tested	=	↓ or =	= ?

Note: 5-HT, serotonin; NA, noradrenaline; SSRIs, serotonin selective reuptake inhibitors; ↑, increase; ↓, decrease; =, no change; * also α_2 antagonist, ** report of antipanic effect for gepirone. [a]acute administration, [b]repeated administration. Beijamini and Andreatini (2003), Chaouloff et al. (1997), Critchley and Handley (1987), Critchley et al. (1992), Gibson et al. (1994), Graeff et al. (1998), Griebel et al. (1994, 1997, 1999), Jorge et al. (2004), Koks et al. (2001), Martin et al. (2002), McBlane and Handley (1994), Mora et al. (1997), Moser et al. (1990), Motta et al. (1992), Munjack et al. (1989), Pinheiro et al. (2007), Poltronieri et al. (2003), Rickels et al. (1993), Setem et al. (1999), Silva and Brandão (2000), Silva et al. (1999), Teixeira et al. (2000), Zanoveli et al. (2005).
The clinical effects of these drugs in patients with generalized anxiety disorder (GAD) and panic disorder (PD) were also included in the table.

contrast, further results have shown that escape is decreased by chronic treatment with antidepressants that are used to treat PD (Teixeira et al., 2000; Poltronieri et al., 2003, Table 4) and is enhanced by the panicogenic agent cholecystokinin (Zanoveli et al., 2004). Therefore, the ETM may be modeling two different anxiety disorders, respectively GAD and PD (Table 4).

However, even with these more neurobiological orientated models, discrepant results have been found. For example, the mouse defense test battery is another animal model where particular defensive behaviors, in this case flight and risk assessment behavior, are proposed to model some aspects of panic and GADs, respectively (Blanchard et al., 2003). Accordingly, chronic, but not acute, treatment with SSRIs is able to decrease both flight and risk assessment responses. Results with other 5-HT-acting compounds, however, have not produced such clear results, although systemic administration of 5-HT$_{1A}$ antagonists had clear anxiolytic-like effects (Blanchard et al., 2003). Since these drugs do not differentiate between pre and postsynaptic receptors, they determine complex effects, antagonizing 5-HT$_{1A}$ post-synaptic neurotransmission, but facilitating other

5-HT-receptor mediated behaviors, by increasing the activity of 5-HT neurons.

Intracerebral drug administration can potentially overcome some of the problems faced by studies using systemic injections, helping to clarify the role of 5-HT in specific areas related to defensive behaviors. Using this approach to verify whether 5-HT influences the two tasks performed by the rat in the ETM, a series of experiments has been conducted in which drugs have been injected into the DRN. Since 5-HT neurons that lie in this nucleus send terminals to both the amygdala and the PAG (Azmitia and Segal, 1978, see above), manipulation of 5-HT neurotransmission is expected to affect both the avoidance (controlled by the amygdala) and the escape (controlled by the PAG) tasks. Consistent with the hypothesis that 5-HT enhances anxiety in the amygdala and inhibits panic in the PAG (Deakin and Graeff, 1991), results obtained in Hélio Zangrossi's laboratory have shown that stimulating autosomic 5-HT$_{1A}$ receptors with 8-OH-DPAT impairs avoidance (like systemic diazepam) while enhancing escape (Sena et al., 2003), whereas blockade of the same receptors with WAY-100635 has opposite effects (Pobbe and Zangrossi, 2005, Fig. 2). Consistently, destruction of 5-HT neurons with the neurotoxin 5,7-DHT mimicked the effects of

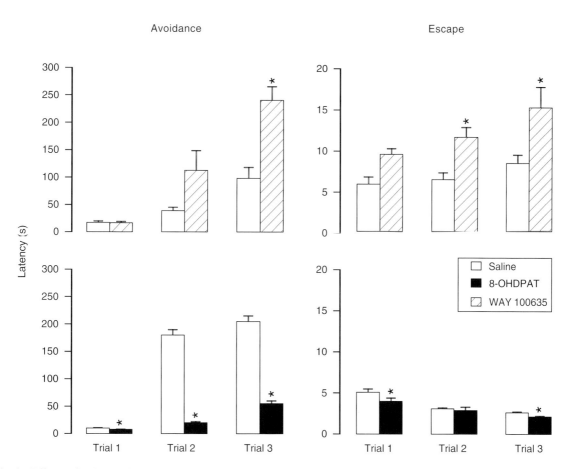

Fig. 2. Effects of 8-OHDPAT (8 nmol) or WAY 100635 (0.37 nmol) microinjected into the dorsal raphe nucleus of rats submitted to the elevated T-maze. Whereas 8-OHDPAT significantly decreased avoidance and facilitated escape from the open arms, WAY 100635 produced the opposite effect. Neither of the drugs affected locomotor behavior measured in an open arena (modified from Sena et al., 2003 and Pobbe and Zangrossi, 2005, with kind permission of Springer Science and Business Media and Elsevier).

8-OH-DPAT (Sena et al., 2003), and direct stimulation of 5-HT neurons (among others) with kainite, those of WAY-100635 (Graeff et al., 1997). Microdialysis experiments have shown that the same dose of intra-DRN kainate increases extra-neuronal levels of 5-HT both in the amygdala and in the PAG of wakeful rats (Viana et al., 1997).

Although the above results with interventions in the DRN are entirely consistent with the idea that 5-HT enhances anxiety (avoidance) in the amygdala and inhibits panic (escape) in the PAG, the results obtained so far with drugs injected into the PAG and the amygdala have drawn a more complex picture. For instance, a study conducted by Zanoveli et al. (2003) has evidenced that 5-HT, 8-OH-DPAT, DOI, and mCPP, all injected into the dorsal PAG impair one-way escape. The impairment of escape caused by mCPP is disturbing in terms of clinical correlation, since this drug is anxiogenic. In addition, inhibitory avoidance has been reduced by three of these drugs, only DOI being ineffective. According to Deakin-Graeff (1991), the PAG would control escape, while inhibitory avoidance would be dependent on the amygdala. For that reason, the changes in inhibitory avoidance verified after local administration of drugs into the PAG are unexpected. Furthermore, H. Zangrossi Jr. and C.V. Strauss (unpublished) have shown impairment of one-way escape caused by microinjection of either the GABA$_A$ receptor agonist muscimol or the modulator of GABA$_A$ receptors midazolam into the medial amygdala, without any change in inhibitory avoidance. Therefore, GABA$_A$ receptors in the medial amygdala seem to participate in the mediation of panic-related, but not GAD-related responses. In contrast, bilateral injection of either midazolam or 8-OH-DPAT into the basolateral amygdala has impaired avoidance without affecting escape in the ETM (Zangrossi et al., 1999). Considering that the basolateral amygdala has been proposed to assign emotional salience to both rewarding and aversive stimuli, the contradictory findings found after direct injections of 5-HT related compounds may involve a complex interference on both approach and avoidance behaviors (Lowry et al., 2005). Anyway, the last results question the rostro-caudal hierarchy suggested by Deakin and Graeff (1991). Instead, they point to two parallel, longitudinally organized systems controlling anxiety and panic, respectively, as suggested by McNaughton and Corr (2004).

XI. Serotonin and the hippocampus

In addition to the PAG and amygdala, the septohippocampal formation is another brain structure related to defensive reactions that receives an important 5-HT input. It plays a central role in Gray's theory on the neurobiology of anxiety (Gray and McNaughton, 2000). Several studies show anxiolytic-like effects of 5-HT$_{1A}$ agonists injected into the hippocampus. However, conflicting results also exist (for review, see Gordon and Hen, 2004). For example, unlike the DRN, the MRN sends ascending 5-HT-containing nerve fibers mainly to the dorsal hippocampus (see above). Either local injection of 8-OH-DPAT or the 5,7-DHT lesion of the MRN have impaired avoidance without affecting escape in the ETM, suggesting that the MRN-hippocampal pathway plays an anxiogenic role (Andrade et al., 2000, 2004). Complex effects on different 5-HT receptor sub-types could help to explain these results. Even though 5-HT can depolarize pyramidal neurons in the hippocampus acting on 5-HT$_4$ receptors (provided 5-HT$_{1A}$ receptors are blocked), the predominant effect is inhibitory, mediated by direct hyperpolarization through postsynaptic 5-HT$_{1A}$ receptors activation. Helping this inhibitory action, 5-HT can also excite GABA-inhibitory interneurons by acting on 5-HT$_2$ and 5-HT$_3$ receptors (Gordon and Hen, 2004). A serotonin-mediated effect on hippocampal plasticity is an additional possibility to explain the anxiolytic effects of SSRIs. Chronic treatment with these compounds facilitates neurogenesis in the dentate gyrus, an effect that involves activation of hippocampal 5-HT$_{1A}$ receptors. Neurogenesis inhibition prevents anxiolytic-like effects induced by these drugs (Santarelli et al., 2003).

XII. Genetic manipulations of the 5-HT system

In the last couple of decades several studies, using either gene deletion or selection of inbred animals, have tried to link specific genes to behavior changes observed in anxiety models. Most of these models, however, rely on normal defensive behavior, somehow limiting their use to understand pathological anxiety. Gene targeting manipulation may help to investigate the biological vulnerability that underlies "traits" of fear/anxiety related to clinical disorders (for comprehensive reviews, see Gottesman and Gould, 2003; Holmes et al., 2005; Lesch, 2005; Hariri and Holmes, 2006; Leonardo and Hen, 2006; Wrase et al., 2006). In relation to 5-HT, several studies have focused on the deletion of genes coding for 5-HT receptors, 5-HT-related enzymes and the 5-HT transporter (5-HTT). Inactivation of several of these specific points in knockout (KO) mice has either confirmed the results of pharmacological studies or has been able to change our views on the role played by 5-HT in brain development underlying emotionality (Lesch, 2005).

XII.A. 5-HT$_{1A}$ receptor

As mentioned in previous sections, several pieces of evidence suggest the participation of 5-HT$_{1A}$ receptors in anxiety disorders. 5-HT$_{1A}$-KO mice exhibit increased anxiety related behavior in the open field, elevated zero-maze, EPM, and novelty-suppressed feeding tests (Heisler et al., 1998; Parks et al., 1998; Ramboz et al., 1998). Genetic inactivation of the 5-HT$_{1A}$ receptor results in several intra- and inter-synaptic compensatory mechanisms which include an upregulation of 5-HT$_{1B}$- autoreceptors and a downregulation of α-GABA-A receptor subunits. These animals have normal or increased basal levels of serotonin and their metabolites, but show a benzodiazepine-resistant anxiety as a consequence of reduced GABA-A receptor binding in the basolateral and central amygdala (Ramboz et al., 1998; Sibille et al., 2000).

Since 5-HT$_{1A}$ receptors can occur both as autoreceptors in raphe nuclei and as postsynaptic heteroreceptors in the forebrain and the midbrain, these initial experiments have not been able to discriminate which brain region would be more important for the anxiogenic action of the gene deletion. More recently, Gross et al. (2002), in a landmark study, used a tissue-specific conditional rescue strategy to investigate this issue. Results obtained with double transgenic mice engineered to exhibit constitutive KO 5-HT$_{1A}$-receptor binding sites restricted to the raphe nuclei and temporally normal expression of the receptor in forebrain structures have suggested that 5HT$_{1A}$ receptors present in forebrain structures, but not the autoreceptors in the raphe nuclei, were related to anxiety (Gross et al., 2002). The authors were also able to demonstrate that forebrain 5-HT$_{1A}$ receptors are necessary, between the 5th and the 21st postnatal day, for the development of brain mechanisms underlying normal adult anxiety-like behavior (Gross et al., 2002; Leonardo and Hen, 2006). 5-HT$_{1A}$ KO mice also show a reduced immobility time in the forced swim and the tail suspension tests (Heisler et al., 1998; Parks et al., 1998; Ramboz et al., 1998), suggesting that the gene deletion might have resulted in a compensatory increase of monoaminergic activity. Although these results do not fully explain the opposite results obtained with 5-HT$_{1A}$ compounds in adult animals submitted to animal models of anxiety (De Vry, 1995; Cao and Rodgers, 1997), they are consistent with clinical data showing reduced 5-HT$_{1A}$ receptor binding, as well as 5-HT-mediated hypothermia and ACTH/cortisol activation in either PD or depressed patients (Lesch et al., 1992; Drevets et al., 1999; Neumeister et al., 2004, see above).

XII.B. 5-HT$_{2A}$ receptors

Different from 5-HT$_{1A}$ KO, genetically modified mice with a global disruption of 5-HT$_{2A}$ receptor signaling show decreased anxiety in models involving conflict, such as elevated plus-maze, dark/light exploration, and novelty suppressed feeding. This change disappears after selective restoration of 5-HT$_{2A}$ signaling, in the cortex (Weisstaub et al., 2006). Anxiolytic effects have also been reported after reduction of this neurotransmission with repeated antisense treatment (Cohen, 2005).

XII.C. 5-HT transporter

The 5-HTT appears to be a suitable genetic engineering tool to understand the role of 5-HT in anxiety, since (1) it plays a major role in synaptic functioning (Piñeyro and Blier, 1999); (2) chronic treatment with 5-HTT-inhibitors (SSRIs) induces anxiolytic and antidepressant effects (Blier and Abbott, 2001; Millan, 2006a); and (3) a genetic polymorphism in the human 5-HTT gene related to anxiety and/or depression has been described (Heils et al., 1996; Lesch et al., 1996; Ogilvie et al., 1996).

After its first appearance in 1998 (Bengel et al., 1998), the mice 5-HTT KO, either homozygous (5-HTT$^{-/-}$) or heterozygous (5-HTT$^{+/-}$) have been tested in a great variety of behavioral and biochemical conditions (for review see Lesch et al., 2003; Hariri and Holmes, 2006). 5-HTT$^{-/-}$ mice display increased anxiety-like behavior, as detected in the EPM, open field and light/dark exploration tests (Holmes et al., 2003a, b). In addition, 5-HTT KO mice exhibit a failure in the capacity to cope with stress, an important feature for the risk of developing emotional disorders (Adamec et al., 2006; Hariri and Holmes, 2006).

Neuroadaptive compensatory mechanisms found in the 5-HTT KO mice depend on the brain region and gender. They include enhanced 5-HT synthesis and turnover, increased extracellular and decreased intracellular levels of 5-HT (Bengel et al., 1998; Mathews et al., 2004; Kim et al., 2005). These animals also show down-regulated 5-HT$_{1A}$-receptors in the dorsal raphe and at forebrain targets, such as the hypothalamus, amygdala and septum, but not in the hippocampus or frontal cortex (Li et al., 1999, 2000; Gobbi et al., 2001), as well as down-regulated 5-HT$_{1B}$ receptors (Fabre et al., 2000). In addition, 5-HTT KO mice also exhibit up-regulated 5-HT$_{2A}$ (ventral medium and lateral hypothalamus, lateral septum, intermediate and lambdoid septal zone), 5-HT$_{2C}$ (lateral, medial, basolateral and basomedial amygdaloid nuclei), and 5-HT$_3$ receptors (frontal and parietal cortex and hippocampal CA3 area) (Rioux et al., 1999; Li et al., 2003; Mössner et al., 2004; Hariri and Holmes, 2006). Besides possible interactions among different neurotransmitter systems, the compensatory rearrangements in the 5-HT systems could explain part of the increased anxiety-like behavior in the 5-HTT null mice. Desensitized 5-HT$_{1A}$ and 5-HT$_{1B}$-autoreceptors (Kim et al.,

2005) would increase 5-HT release on either unchanged (hippocampus, frontal cortex) or downregulated (hypothalamus, amygdala, and septum) postsynaptic 5-HT$_{1A}$ receptors, and on upregulated 5-HT$_3$, 5-HT$_{2A}$, and 5-HT$_{2C}$ receptors present in the hippocampal formation, medial hypothalamic area and in septal regions, and in the amygdala, respectively. All these structures participate in the mediation of defensive behavior (for reviews, see Canteras, 2002; Graeff, 2004), and interference with these receptors have been shown to produce either anxiolytic or anxiogenic-like effects (Hodges et al., 1987; Costall et al., 1989; Higgins et al., 1991; Holmes et al., 2003b).

The possible influence of the 5-HTT blockade during development, was assessed by treating normal and 5-HTT KO mice with fluoxetine between postnatal days 4 and 21 (Ansorge et al., 2004). Whereas the antidepressant was not able to interfere with the behavioral performance of 12-weeks-old 5-HTT$^{-/-}$ mice tested in the open field and in the EPM, a reduced exploratory behavior in those models was found in 5-HTT$^{+/+}$ and 5-HTT$^{+/-}$ mice pre-treated with fluoxetine. An increased anxiety-like behavior in the novelty-suppressed feeding paradigm, and a maladaptive stress response in the shock-escape paradigm has also been detected in 5-HTT$^{+/+}$ and 5-HTT$^{+/-}$ mice treated with fluoxetine, when compared to controls pretreated with vehicle or to 5-HTT$^{-/-}$ mice (Ansorge et al., 2004). Therefore, similar to 5-HT$_{1A}$ KO, interference with the 5-HT system during the first three weeks of life seems critical for emotional reactions exhibited later, in adult life, suggesting that the 5-HT neurotransmission plays a pivotal role in shaping and preparing the brain to cope with aversive or traumatic events.

The increased anxiety-like behavior found in the 5-HTT mutant mice is compatible with the behavioral changes found in humans and other mammals carrying the S allele 5-HTT gene polymorphism (see above). These subjects, when confronted with traumatic events, such as social isolation stress (Bennett et al., 2002; Barr et al., 2004), predator odor (Adamec et al., 2006), or stressful life events (Caspi et al., 2003), express a high risk for developing anxiety-like behavior and/or negative mood states. In humans this polymorphism has been shown to produce a reduced 5-HTT binding and 5-HT re-uptake in the dorsal raphe (Malison et al., 1998; Arango et al., 2001). However, its impact on other regions and on brain development is still largely unclear. As described above, subjects carrying this polymorphism present an increased functional reactivity of the amygdala in response to aversive stimuli (Hariri et al., 2005).

The presence of the S allele could also contribute to the fact that around 30% of depressed patients are refractory to antidepressants (Yu et al., 2002; Smits et al., 2004; Kim et al., 2006; Millan, 2006a). Using 5-HTT KO mice, Holmes et al. (2002) have shown that 5-HTT$^{-/-}$ mice (but not the control 5-HTT$^{+/+}$ or heterozigous 5-HTT$^{+/-}$ mice) are resistant to fluoxetine but not to desipramine (a selective noradrenergic transporter inhibitor) or to imipramine (a non-selective noradrenaline/5HT transporter inhibitor) treatment in the tail suspension test (Holmes et al., 2002).

Still at its early age, studies using genetic manipulations clearly unfold the complex neuroadaptations shown by 5-HT-related KO mice. The impact of these changes on glutamatergic, GABAergic, cathecolaminergic, and peptidergic systems is just one side of the enormous challenge to explain the contradictory results in the literature. According to Lesch (2005), future research in this field should focus in investigating further points of the 5-HTmediated neurotransmission such as: (1) 5-HT$_{1B}$ receptors; (2) TH 2; (3) monoamine oxidase A; (4) signal transduction, including calcium-stimulated adenyl cyclase type VIII (AC VIII), calcium-calmodulin kinase II (CamKII), G protein-activated inward rectifying potassium 2 (GIRK2) and neuronal nitric oxide synthase (nNOS); and (5) developmental factors, such as neural cell adhesion molecule (NCAM), transcription factor Pet1 and brain-derived neurotrophic factor (BDNF). Nevertheless, data obtained from 5-HT-related KO mice has once more drawn attention to the important role of this neurotransmitter in modulating fear and anxiety (Griebel, 1995). They have also highlighted the complexity of this role.

XIII. Plasticity of the 5-HT systems and anxiety

Exposure to stressful stimuli has been closely associated with the development and/or time course of anxiety disorders. Several neurotransmitters, including glutamate, noradrenaline, corticotropin releasing hormone (CRH), and serotonin, have been related to these changes. The latter has received particular attention by Maier and co-workers (see Maier and Watkins, 2005). They have shown that exposure to inescapable and uncontrollable stress (IS) induces delayed behavioral changes that include a reduction in fight/flight defensive responses and a facilitation of fear/anxiety-related behavior. Based on a large body of experimental evidence, they have proposed that the intense activation of caudal DRN 5-HT neurons caused by IS (and involving activation of CRH$_2$, α_1-noradrenergic, and glutamate receptors) would desensitize 5-HT$_{1A}$ inhibitory autoreceptors, by releasing large amounts of 5-HT, locally. As a consequence, for at least a period of time, 5-HT neurons would become sensitized to further aversive stimuli. In agreement with the proposal of a dual role of 5-HT in anxiety, Maier and co-workers have suggested that an increased release of 5-HT would potentiate fear conditioning in the amygdala while inhibiting the escape response in the PAG. Therefore, 5-HT would not be mediating normal defensive responses, but only potentiating them whenever they are activated.

XIV. Mechanisms of the anxiolytic effects of SSRIs and buspirone

After repeated administration, the clinical efficacy of the SSRIs has been proposed to rely largely on their capacity to attenuate the function of 5-HT$_{1A}$ presynaptic receptors, without affecting 5-HT$_{1A}$ postsynaptic function (Blier and Abbott, 2001). This would lead to increased 5-HT-mediated neurotransmission in projection areas. However, the question concerning which areas and receptors are involved in the distinct anxiety disorders that respond to this class of drugs remains. As discussed above, 5-HT$_{1A}$ postsynaptic receptors located in the hippocampus, amygdala, and other limbic areas may be likely candidates. Both TCAs and electroconvulsive shocks (ECS) sensitize these receptors, without changing the presynaptic 5-HT$_{1A}$ receptor (Gordon and Hen, 2004). The reason why pre and postsynaptic 5-HT$_{1A}$ receptors respond differently to these treatments (SSRIs, TCAs and ECS) is unclear, since both are coded by the same gene. It has been proposed that different configurations of the receptor site on the membrane and/or distinct coupling to transduction mechanisms may be involved (Blier and Abbott, 2001). The existence of such differences has received support from experiments conducted in human subjects showing that pindolol binds preferentially to presynaptic, instead of postsynaptic, 5-HT$_{1A}$ receptors (Rabiner et al., 2000).

Effects on 5-HT$_2$ receptors after repeated treatment have also been reported. However, as with the 5-HT$_{1A}$ receptor, the obtained results are difficult to interpret. TCAs have been consistently reported to decrease cortical 5-HT$_2$ binding sites, but seem to increase their electrophysiological responsiveness; diverse 5-HT$_2$ receptor subtypes (2A and 2C) may explain these conflicting results (Blier and Abbott, 2001). Actually, downregulation of 5-HT$_{2C}$ receptors in limbic areas, an effect shared by several classes of antidepressants after long-term treatment, has been proposed as a major mechanism of their clinical efficacy (Millan, 2006b). Based on findings that 5-HT$_{2C}$ receptors could be constitutively active whereas postsynaptic 5-HT$_{1A}$ receptors require spontaneous release of 5-HT, Millan (2006b) has suggested that 5-HT$_{2C}$ receptors exert a negative control on mood that is opposed by postsynaptic 5-HT$_{1A}$ receptors. A general decrease in 5-HT mediated neurotransmission would, therefore, change the balance towards 5-HT$_{2C}$-mediated effects. SSRIs would cause the initial anxiogenic response reported by some patients, by acutely increasing 5-HT$_{2C}$ neurotransmission. With repeated treatment, the downregulation of these receptors in limbic areas, such as the amygdala, together with increased postsynaptic 5-HT$_{1A}$-mediated neurotransmission, would decrease anxiety.

Disruption of 5-HT$_{2A}$ receptor signaling produces anxiolytic effects (see above, Cohen, 2005; Weisstaub et al., 2006), suggesting that chronic downregulation of 5-HT$_{2A}$-mediated neurotransmission, usually found after repeated antidepressant or buspirone treatment (Millan, 2003), could be at least partially responsible for the anxiolytic effects of these drugs (Weisstaub et al., 2006). However, acute administration of 5-HT$_{2A}$ antagonists has produced conflicting results in animal models (Griebel, 1995). In mice, although there are also opposite results (Peng et al., 2004), 5-HT$_{2A}$ agonists are anxiolytic and potentiate the anxiolytic effects of SSRIs and benzodiazepines (Dhonnchadha et al., 2005, Massé et al., 2007). Studies in rats, however, have not produced so clear results (see Table 4). Together, these data suggest that modifications of 5-HT$_{2A}$-mediated neurotransmission could also be related to the anxiolytic effects of SSRIs, but further studies are needed to conciliate these contradictory results.

The question remains on how to explain the antipanic effects of SSRIs. Several pieces of evidence have related a facilitation of 5-HT-mediated neurotransmission in the PAG to these effects. In this case, a general downregulation of 5-HT$_{2C}$ receptors induced by SSRIs would be expected to facilitate panic symptoms. However, in addition to the possible involvement of other 5-HT receptors in the PAG (5-HT$_{2A}$, 5-HT$_{1A}$), as discussed above, several isoforms of 5-HT$_{2C}$ receptors have been described. They may show distinct pharmacological characteristics and coupling mechanisms in, for example, the amygdala and the PAG (Millan, 2006b). Actually, recent results support this view. Repeated treatment with imipramine or fluoxetine enhances the inhibitory effect of intra-dlPAG injection of 5-HT$_{1A}$ or 5-HT$_2$ agonists on escape responses either induced by local electrical stimulation or measured in the elevated T-maze (Zanoveli et al., 2005; de Bortoli et al., 2006).

Buspirone and other azapirones (ipsapirone, gepirone) are 5-HT$_{1A}$ partial agonists at postsynaptic receptors, but act as full agonists presynaptically, in the raphe nuclei. The acute administration of these compounds inhibits the firing of 5-HT neurons. However, the activity of these neurons plays a more important role on 5-HT release in brain areas innervated by the DRN than by the MRN (Blier and Ward, 2003).

The presynaptic inhibitory effect disappears after repeated administration of these drugs, which could help to explain the clinical delay of their therapeutic action. Since no such effect occurs at postsynaptic 5-HT_{1A} receptors, it has been proposed that, under repeated administration, activation of these receptors is significantly increased (Blier and Ward, 2003). However, differently than SSRIs, buspirone failed to enhance the inhibitory effects of 5-HT_{1A} or 5-HT2 agonists on escape responses mediated by the dlPAG (Zanoveli et al., 2005; de Bortoli et al., 2006), what could explain its lack of therapeutic efficacy in PD.

An alternative and opposite proposal to explain the anxiolytic effects of buspirone is that GAD patients have an excess of 5-HT neurotransmission at postsynaptic 5-HT_{1A} receptors, that would be attenuated by the partial agonist activity of this drug. This proposal, however, fails to explain several observations, such as the delayed onset of the anxiolytic effects of buspirone (Blier and Ward, 2003), the inverse relationship found in patients between postsynaptic 5-HT_{1A} binding and anxious symptoms or the anxious behavior displayed by genetically modified mice with attenuated 5-HT_{1A}-mediated neurotransmission.

The desensitization of inhibitory presynaptic 5-HT_{1D} receptors by SSRIs, leading to an enhanced release of 5-HT in the OFC has been related to their anti-obsessional properties (Blier and Abbott, 2001). Since this therapeutic effect requires longer periods of repeated administration, it can explain the more delayed therapeutic action of SSRIs in OCD, as compared to depression or PD. In addition, the responsiveness of 5-HT_2 postsynaptic receptor in this region is not changed by SSRIs, whereas 5-HT_{1A}-mediated responses are attenuated. This suggests that the final effect of 5-HT in OCD is mediated by 5-HT_2 receptors. Metergoline, a 5-HT_2 receptor antagonist, has been shown to exacerbate OCD symptoms after 4 days of treatment. However, due to the complex role of 5-HT_2 receptors in this disorder, patients with OCD may experience remission of symptoms during intoxication with psychedelic drugs that have potent $5\text{-HT}_{2A/2C}$ agonist activity (Delgado and Moreno, 1998). These conflicting results may involve some unique pharmacological properties of 5-HT_2 receptors in the OFC. For example, low doses of risperidone, reported to ameliorate OCD patients, block 5-HT_2 mediated responses in the medial prefrontal cortex, but not in the OFC. On the other hand, high doses of the same drug, which exacerbate OCD symptoms, are able to antagonize 5-HT_2 receptors in the OFC (Mansari and Blier, 2006).

XV. Conclusions

Serotonin is clearly involved in anxiety and in the therapeutic effects of SSRIs. Its precise role, however, remains incompletely understood. Converging evidence, gathered in the last years from studies with laboratory animals, normal volunteers, and patients with anxiety disorders, strongly indicates that serotonin plays a multifaceted, probably dual role, on defensive behaviors and pathological anxiety. Although major points still need to be clarified, we have traveled a long way since the original proposal by Stein and co-workers (Wise et al., 1972) on the role of 5-HT in anxiety. It is clear now that 5-HT plays a much more intricate role than originally proposed. Hopefully, future studies combining the traditional approaches (behavioral, pharmacological, anatomical, and electrophysiological) with the new molecular genetic and functional imaging analysis techniques will help us to further unveil the complex role of this neurotransmitter in anxiety.

References

Adamec, R., Burton, P., Blundell, J., Murphy, D.L. and Holmes, A. (2006) Vulnerability to mild predator stress in serotonin transporter knockout mice. Behav. Brain Res., 170: 126–140.

Amital, D., Fostick, L., Sasson, Y., Kindler, S., Amital, H. and Zohar, J. (2005) Anxiogenic effects of sumatriptan in panic patients: a double-blind, placebo-controlled study. Eur. Neuropsychopharmacol., 15: 279–282.

Andrade, T.G.C.S., Macedo, C.E.A., Zangrossi, H. Jr. and Graeff, F.G. (2000) Role of the median raphe nucleus in the modulation of two types of fear/anxiety responses in rats submitted to the elevated T-maze. J. Psychopharmacol., 14(Suppl.): A38.

Andrade, T.G.C.S., Macedo, C.E.A., Zangrossi, H. Jr. and Graeff, F.G. (2004) Anxiolytic-like effects of median raphe nucleus lesion in the elevated T-maze. Behav. Brain Res., 153: 55–60.

Ansorge, M.S., Zhou, M., Lira, A., Hen, R. and Gingrich, J.A. (2004) Early-life blockade of the 5-HT transporter alters emotional behavior in adult mice. Science, 306: 879–881.

Arango, V., Underwood, M.D., Boldrini, M., Tamir, H., Kassir, S.A., Hsiung, S., Chen, J.J. and Mann, J.J. (2001) Serotonin 1A receptors, serotonin transporter binding and serotonin transporter mRNA expression in the brainstem of depressed suicide victims. Neuropsychopharmacology, 25: 892–903.

Argyropoulos, S.V., Hood, S.D., Adrover, M., Bell, C.J., Rich, A.S., Nash, J.R., Rich, N.C., Witchel, H.J. and Nutt, D.J. (2004) Tryptophan depletion reverses the therapeutic effect of selective serotonin reuptake inhibitors in social anxiety disorder. Biol. Psychiatry, 56: 503–509.

Audi, E.A. and Graeff, F.G. (1984) Benzodiazepine receptors in the periaqueductal gray mediate anti-aversive drug action. Eur. J. Pharmacol., 103: 279–285.

Azmitia, E.C. and Segal, M. (1978) An autodiographic analysis of the differential ascending projections of the dorsal and median raphe nuclei in the rat. J. Comp. Neurol., 179: 641–688.

Baldwin, D.S., Anderson, I.M., Nutt, D.J., Bandelow, B., Bond, A., Davidson, J.R.T., den Boer, J.A., Fineberg, N.A., Knapp, M., Scott, J. and Wittchen, H.U. (2005) Evidence-based guidelines for the pharmacological treatment of anxiety disorders: recommendations from the British Association for Psychopharmacology. J. Psychopharmacol., 19: 567–596.

Barnes, N. and Sharp, T. (1999) A review of central 5-HT receptors and their function. Neuropharmacology, 38: 1083–1152.

Barr, C.S., Newman, T.K., Shannon, C., Parker, C., Dvoskin, R.L., Becker, M.L., Schwandt, M., Champoux, M., Lesch, K.P., Goldman, D., Suomi, S.J. and Higley, J.D. (2004) Rearing condition and rh5-HTTLPR interact to influence limbic–hypothalamic–pituitary–adrenal axis response to stress in infant macaques. Biol. Psychiatry, 55: 733–738.

Bastani, B., Nash, J.F. and Meltzer, H.Y. (1990) Prolactin and cortisol responses to MK-212, a serotonin agonist, in obsessive-compulsive disorder. Arch. Gen. Psychiatry, 47: 833–839.

Beckett, S. and Marsden, C.A. (1997) The effect of central and systemic injection of the 5-HT$_{1A}$ receptor agonist 8-OHDPAT and the 5-HT$_{1A}$ receptors antagonist WAY 100635 on periaqueductal grey-induced defence behaviour. J. Psychopharmacol., 11: 35–40.

Beckett, S.R.G., Lawrence, A.J., Marsden, C.A. and Marshal, P.W. (1992) Attenuation of chemically induced defence response by 5-HT$_1$ receptor agonists administered into the periaqueductal gray. Psychopharmacology, 108: 110–114.

Beijamini, V. and Andreatini, R. (2003) Effects of Hypericum perforatum and paroxetine on rat performance in the elevated T-maze. Pharmacol. Res., 48: 199–207.

Bell, C., Forshall, S., Adrover, M., Nash, J., Hood, S., Argyropoulos, S., Rich, A. and Nutt, D.J. (2002) Does 5-HT restrain panic? A tryptophan depletion study in panic disorder patients recovered on paroxetine. J. Psychopharmacol., 16: 5–14.

Belzung, C. (2001) Rodent models of anxiety-like behaviors: are they predictive for compounds acting via non-benzodiazepine mechanisms? Curr. Opin. Investig. Drugs, 2: 1108–1111.

Bengel, D., Murphy, D.L., Andrews, A.M., Wichems, C.H., Feltner, D., Heils, A., Mossner, R., Westphal, H. and Lesch, K.P. (1998) Altered brain serotonin homeostasis and locomotor insensitivity to 3,4-methylenedioxymethamphetamine ("Ecstasy") in serotonin transporter-deficient mice. Mol. Pharmacol., 53: 649–655.

Bennett, A.J., Lesch, K.-P., Heils, A., Long, J.C., Lorenz, J.G., Shoaf, S.E., Champoux, M., Suomi, S.J., Linnoila, M.V. and Higley, J.D. (2002) Early experience and serotonin transporter gene variation interact to influence primate CNS function. Mol. Psychiatry, 7: 118–122.

Ben-Zion, I.Z., Meiri, G., Greenberg, B.D., Murphy, D.L. and Benjamin, J. (1999) Enhancement of CO$_2$-induced anxiety in healthy volunteers with the serotonin antagonist metergoline. Am. J. Psychiatry, 156: 1635–1637.

Berney, A., Sookman, D., Leyton, M., Young, S.N. and Benkelfat, C. (2006) Lack of effects on core obsessive-compulsive symptoms of tryptophan depletion during symptom provocation in remitted obsessive-compulsive disorder patients. Biol. Psychiatry, 59: 853–857.

Blanchard, D.C., Griebel, G. and Blanchard, R.J. (2003) The mouse defense test battery: pharmacological and behavioral assay for anxiety and panic. Eur. J. Pharmacol., 463: 97–116.

Blanchard, D.C., Hynd, A.L., Minke, K.A., Minemoto, T. and Blanchard, R.J. (2001) Human defensive behaviors to threat scenarios show parallels to fear- and anxiety-related defense patterns on non-human mammals. Neurosci. Biobehav. Rev., 25: 761–770.

Blier, P. and Abbott, F.V. (2001) Putative mechanisms of action of antidepressant drugs in affective and anxiety disorders and pain. J. Psychiatry Neurosci., 26: 37–43.

Blier, P. and Ward, N.M. (2003) Is there a role for 5-HT$_{1A}$ agonists in the treatment of depression?. Biol. Psychiatry, 53: 193–203.

Boess, F.G., Beroukhim, R. and Martin, I.L. (1995) Ultrastructure of the 5-hydroxytryptamine 3 receptor. J. Neurochem., 64: 1401–1405.

Bonne, O., Bain, E., Neumeister, A., Nugent, A.C., Vythilingam, M., Carson, R.E., Luckenbaugh, D.A., Eckelman, W., Herscovitch, P., Drevets, W.C. and Charney, D.S. (2005) No change in serotonin type 1A receptor binding in patients with posttraumatic stress disorder. Am. J. Psychiatry, 162: 383–385.

Bourin, M. and Hascoet, M. (2003) The mouse light/dark box test. Eur. J. Pharmacol., 463: 55–65.

Brandão, M.L., de Aguiar, J.C. and Graeff, F.G. (1982) GABA mediation of the anti-aversive action of minor tranquilizers. Pharmacol. Biochem. Behav., 16: 397–402.

Broocks, A., Bandelow, B., George, A., Jestrabeck, C., Opitz, M., Bartmann, U., Gleiter, C.H., Meineke, I., Roed, I.S., Ruther, E. and Hajak, G. (2000) Increased psychological responses and divergent neuroendocrine responses to m-CPP and ipsapirone in patients with panic disorder. Int. Clin. Psychopharmacol., 15: 153–161.

Canteras, N.S. (2002) The medial hypothalamic defensive system: hodological organization and functional implications. Pharmacol. Biochem. Behav., 71: 481–491.

Cao, B.J. and Rodgers, R.J. (1997) Influence of 5-HT$_{1A}$ receptor antagonism on plus-maze behaviour in mice. II. WAY 100635, SDZ 216-525 and NAN-190. Pharmacol. Biochem. Behav., 58: 593–603.

Carey, P.D., Warwick, J., Niehaus, D.J., van der Linden, G., van Heerden, B.B., Harvey, B.H., Seedat, S. and Stein, D.J. (2004) Single photon emission computed tomography (SPECT). B.M.C. Psychiatry, 4: 30.

Carobrez, A.P. and Bertoglio, L.J. (2005) Ethological and temporal analyses of anxiety-like behavior: the elevated plus-maze model 20 years on. Neurosci. Biobehav. Rev., 29: 1193–1205.

Caspi, A., Sugden, K., Moffitt, T.E., Taylor, A., Craig, I.W., Harrington, H., McClay, J., Mill, J., Martin, J., Braithwaite, A. and Poulton, R. (2003) Influence of life stress on depression: moderation by a polymorphism in the 5-HTT gene. Science, 301: 386–389.

Ceulemans, D.L.S., Hoppenbrowers, M.L.J.A., Gelders, Y.G. and Reyntjens, A.J.M. (1985) The influence of ritanserin, a serotonin antagonist, in anxiety disorders: a double-blind, placebo-controlled study versus lorazepam. Pharmacopsychiatry, 18: 303–305.

Chaouloff, F., Kulikov, A. and Mormède, P. (1997) Repeated DOI and SR46349B treatments do not affect elevated plus-maze anxiety despite opposite effects on cortical 5-HT$_{2A}$ receptors. Eur. J. Pharmacol., 334: 25–29.

Charney, D.S. and Heninger, G.R. (1986) Serotonin function in panic disorders. The effect of intravenous tryptophan in healthy subjects and patients with panic disorder before and during alprazolam treatment. Arch. Gen. Psychiatry, 43: 1059–1065.

Chopin, P. and Briley, M. (1987) Animal models of anxiety: the effect of compounds that modify 5-HT neurotransmission. Trends Pharmacol. Sci., 8: 383–388.

Clark, M.S., McDevitt, R.A. and Neumaier, J.F. (2006) Quantitative mapping of tryptophan hydroxilase-2, 5-HT$_{1A}$, 5-HT$_{1B}$, and serotonin transporter expression across the anteroposterior axis of the rat dorsal and median raphe nuclei. J. Comp. Neurol., 498: 611–623.

Cohen, H. (2005) Anxiolytic effect and memory improvement in rats by antisense oligodeoxynucleotide to 5-hydroxytryptamine-2A precursor protein. Depress. Anxiety, 22: 84–93.

Conn, P.J. and Sanders-Bush, E. (1986) Regulation of serotonin stimulated phosphoinositide hydrolysis: relation to the serotonin 5-HT$_2$ binding site. J. Neurosci., 6: 3669–3675.

Costall, B., Kelly, M.E., Naylor, R.J., Onaivi, E.S. and Tyers, M.B. (1989) Neuroanatomical sites of action of 5-HT$_3$ receptor agonists and antagonists for alteration of aversive behaviour in the mouse. Br. J. Pharmacol., 96: 325–332.

Critchley, M.A. and Handley, S.L. (1987) Effects in the X-maze anxiety model of agents acting at 5-HT$_1$ and 5-HT$_2$ receptors. Psychopharmacology, 93: 502–506.

Critchley, M.A., Njung'e, K. and Handley, S.L. (1992) Actions and some interactions of 5-HT$_{1A}$ ligands in the elevated X-maze and effects of dorsal raphe lesions. Psychopharmacology, 106: 484–490.

Davis, M. (1992) The role of the amygdala in fear and anxiety. Annu. Rev. Neurosci., 15: 353–375.

De Bortoli, V.C., Nogueira, R.L. and Zangrossi, H. Jr. (2006) Effects of fluoxetine and buspirone on the panicolytic-like response induced by the activation of 5-HT$_{1A}$ and 5-HT$_{2A}$ receptors in the rat dorsal periaqueductal gray. Psychopharmacology, 183: 422–428.

De Vry, J. (1995) 5-HT$_{1A}$ receptor agonists: recent developments and controversial issues. Psychopharmacology, 121: 1–26.

Deakin, J.F.W. and Graeff, F.G. (1991) 5-HT and mechanisms of defence. J. Psychopharmacol., 5: 305–315.

Delgado, P.L. and Moreno, F.A. (1998) Different roles for serotonin in anti-obsessional drug action and the pathophysiology of obsessive-compulsive disorder. Br. J. Psychiatry Suppl., 35: 21–25.

den Boer, J.A. and Westenberg, H.G.M. (1990) Serotonin function in panic disorder: a double blind placebo controlled study with fluvoxamine and ritanserin. Psychopharmacology, 102: 85–94.

Dhonnchadha, B.A.N., Ripoll, N., Clénet, F., Hascoët, M. and Bourin, M. (2005) Implication of 5-HT$_2$ receptors subtypes in the mechanism of action of antidepressants in the four plates test. Psychopharmacology, 179: 418–429.

Drevets, W.C., Frank, E., Price, J.C., Kupfer, D.J., Holt, D., Greer, P.J., Huang, Y., Gautier, C. and Mathis, C. (1999) PET imaging of serotonin 1A receptor binding in depression. Biol. Psychiatry, 46: 1375–1387.

Erzegovesi, S., Martucci, L., Henin, M. and Bellodi, L. (2001) Low versus standard dose mCPP challenge in obsessive-compulsive patients. Neuropsychopharmacology, 24: 31–36.

Estes, W.K. and Skinner, F.B. (1941) Some quantitative properties of anxiety. J. Exp. Psychol., 29: 390–400.

Fabre, V., Beaufour, C., Evrard, A., Rioux, A., Hanoun, N., Lesch, K.P., Murphy, D.L., Lanfumey, L., Hamon, M. and Martres, M.P. (2000) Altered expression and functions of serotonin 5-HT$_{1A}$ and 5-HT$_{1B}$ receptors in knock-out mice lacking the 5-HT transporter. Eur. J. Neurosci., 12: 2299–2310.

Fernandez, M., Pissiota, A., Frans, O., von Knorring, L., Fischer, H. and Fredrikson, M. (2001) Brain function in a patient with torture related posttraumatic stress disorder before and after fluoxetine treatment: a positron emission tomography provocation study. Neurosci. Lett., 297: 101–104.

Fowles, D.C. (2000) Electrodermal hyporeactivity and antisocial behavior: does anxiety mediate the relationship? J. Affect. Disord., 61: 177–189.

Francken, B.J.B., Jurzak, M., Vanhauwe, J.F.M., Luyten, W.H.M.L. and Leysen, J.E. (1998) The human 5-ht5A receptor couples to Gi/Go proteins and inhibits adenylate cyclase in HEK-293 cells. Eur. J. Pharmacol., 361: 299–309.

Furmark, T., Tillfors, M., Garpenstrand, H., Marteinsdottir, I., Langstrom, B., Oreland, L. and Fredrikson, M. (2004) Serotonin transporter polymorphism related to amygdala excitability and symptom severity in patients with social phobia. Neurosci. Lett., 362: 189–192.

Furmark, T., Tillfors, M., Marteinsdottir, I., Fischer, H., Pissiota, A., Langstrom, B. and Fredrikson, M. (2002) Common changes in cerebral blood flow in patients with social phobia treated with citalopram or cognitive-behavioral therapy. Arch. Gen. Psychiatry, 59: 425–433.

Gallinat, J., Strohle, A., Lang, U.E., Bajbouj, M., Kalus, P., Montag, C., Seifert, F., Wernicke, C., Rommelspacher, H., Rinneberg, H. and Schubert, F. (2005) Association of human hippocampal neurochemistry, serotonin transporter genetic variation, and anxiety. Neuroimage, 26: 123–131.

Gardner, C.R. (1986) Recent developments in 5HT-related pharmacology of animal models of anxiety. Pharmacol. Biochem. Behav., 24: 1479–1485.

Geller, I. and Seifter, J. (1960) The effects of meprobamate, barbiturates, d-amphetamine and promazine on experimentally induced conflict in the rat. Psychopharmacologia, 1: 482–492.

Germine, M., Goddard, A.W., Sholomskas, D.E., Woods, S.W., Charney, D.S. and Heninger, G.R. (1994) Response to meta-chlorophenylpiperazine in panic disorder patients and healthy subjects: influence of reduction in intravenous dosage. Psychiatry Res., 54: 115–133.

Gibson, E.L., Barnfield, A.M. and Curzon, G. (1994) Evidence that mCPP-induced anxiety in the plus-maze is mediated by postsynaptic 5-HT$_{2C}$ receptors but not by sympathomimetic effects. Neuropharmacology, 33: 457–465.

Gobbi, G., Murphy, D.L., Lesch, K. and Blier, P. (2001) Modifications of the serotonergic system in mice lacking serotonin transporters: an in vivo electrophysiological study. J. Pharmacol. Exp. Ther., 296: 987–995.

Goddard, A.W., Woods, S.W., Sholomskas, D.E., Goodman, W.K., Charney, D.S. and Heninger, G.R. (1993) Effects of the serotonin reuptake inhibitor fluvoxamine on yohimbine-induced anxiety in panic disorder. Psychiatry Res., 48: 119–133.

Goldberg, H.L. and Finnerty, R.J. (1979) The comparative efficacy of buspirone and diazepam in the treatment of anxiety. Am. J. Psychiatry, 136: 1184–1187.

Goodman, W.K., McDougle, C.J., Price, L.H., Barr, L.C., Hills, O.F., Caplik, J.F., Charney, D.S. and Heninger, G.R. (1995) m-Chlorophenylpiperazine in patients with obsessive-compulsive disorder: absence of symptom exacerbation. Biol. Psychiatry, 38: 138–149.

Gordon, J.A. and Hen, R. (2004) The serotonergic system and anxiety. Neuromolecular Med., 5: 27–40.

Gottesman, I.I. and Gould, T.D. (2003) The endophenotype concept in psychiatry: etymology and strategic intentions. Am. J. Psychiatry, 160: 636–645.

Graeff, FG. (2004) Serotonin, the periaqueductal gray and panic. Neurosci. Biobehav. Rev., 28: 239–259.

Graeff, F.G., Netto, C.F. and Zangrossi, H. Jr. (1998) The elevated T-maze as an experimental model of anxiety. Neurosci. Biobehav. Rev., 23: 237–246.

Graeff, F.G., Parente, A., Del-Ben, C.M. and Guimarães, F.S. (2003) Pharmacology of human experimental anxiety. Braz. J. Med. Biol. Res., 36: 421–432.

Graeff, F.G. and Schoenfeld, R.I. (1970) Tryptaminergic mechanisms in punished and nonpunished behavior. J. Pharmacol. Exp. Ther., 173: 277–283.

Graeff, F.G. and Silveira Filho, N.G. (1978) Behavioral inhibition induced by electrical stimulation of the median raphe nucleus of the rat. Physiol. Behav., 21: 477–484.

Graeff, F.G., Viana, M.B. and Mora, P. (1997) Dual role of 5-HT in defense and anxiety. Neurosci. Biobehav. Rev., 21: 791–799.

Graeff, F.G., Viana, M.B. and Tomaz, C. (1993) The elevated T maze, a new experimental model of anxiety and memory: effect of diazepam. Braz. J. Med. Biol. Res., 26: 67–70.

Grailhe, R., Grabtree, G.W. and Hen, R. (2001) Human 5-HT$_5$ receptors: the 5-HT$_{5A}$ receptor is functional but the 5-HT$_{5B}$ receptor was lost during mammalian evolution. Eur. J. Pharmacol., 418: 15–167.

Gray, J.A. (1982) The neuropsychology of anxiety. Oxford University Press, New York, NY.

Gray, J.A. and McNaughton, N. (2000) The neuropsychology of anxiety, 2nd edn. Oxford University Press, New York, NY.

Green, A.R. (2006) Neuropharmacology of 5-hydroxytryptamine. Br. J. Pharmacol., 147: S145–S152.

Griebel, G. (1995) 5-Hydroxytryptamine-interacting drugs in animal models of anxiety disorders: more than 30 years of research. Pharmacol. Ther., 65: 319–395.

Griebel, G., Cohen, C., Perrault, G. and Sanger, D.J. (1999) Behavioral effects of acute and chronic fluoxetine in Wistar-Kyoto rats. Physiol. Behav., 67: 315–320.

Griebel, G., Moreau, J.L., Jenck, F., Mutel, V., Martin, J.R. and Misslin, R. (1994) Evidence that tolerance to the anxiogenic-like effects of mCPP does not involve alteration in the function of 5-HT$_{2C}$ receptors in the rat choroid plexus. Behav. Pharmacol., 5: 642–645.

Griebel, G., Rodgers, R.J., Perrault, G. and Sanger, D.J. (1997) Risk assessment behaviour: evaluation of utility in the study of 5-HT-related drugs in the rat elevated plus-maze test. Pharmacol. Biochem. Behav., 57: 817–827.

Gross, C., Zhuang, X., Stark, K., Ramboz, S., Oosting, R., Kirby, L., Santarelli, L., Beck, S. and Hen, R. (2002) Serotonin1A receptor acts during development to establish normal anxiety-like behaviour in the adult. Nature, 416: 396–400.

Guimarães, F.S., Zuardi, A.W. and Graeff, F.G. (1987) Effect of chlorimipramine and maprotiline on experimental anxiety in humans. J. Psychopharmacol., 1: 184–192.

Handley, S.L., McBlane, J.W., Critchley, M.A.E. and Njung'e, K. (1993) Multiple serotonin mechanisms in animal models of anxiety: environmental, emotional and cognitive factors. Behav. Brain Res., 58: 203–210.

Handley, S.L. and Mithani, S. (1984) Effects of alpha-adrenoceptor agonists in a maze-exploration model of "fear"-motivated behaviour. Naunyn-Schmiedeberg's Arch. Pharmacol., 327: 1–5.

Hariri, A.R., Drabant, E.M., Munoz, K.E., Kolachana, B.S., Mattay, V.S., Egan, M.F. and Weinberger, D.R. (2005) A susceptibility gene for affective disorders and the response of the human amygdala. Arch. Gen. Psychiatry, 62: 146–152.

Hariri, A.R. and Holmes, A. (2006) Genetics of emotional regulation: the role of the serotonin transporter in neural function. Trends Cogn. Sci., 10: 182–191.

Hariri, A.R., Mattay, V.S., Tessitore, A., Kolachana, B., Fera, F., Goldman, D., Egan, M.F. and Weinberger, D.R. (2002) Serotonin transporter genetic variation and the response of the human amygdala. Science, 297: 400–403.

Heils, A., Teufel, A., Petri, S., Stober, G., Riederer, P., Bengel, D. and Lesch, K.P. (1996) Allelic variation of human serotonin transporter gene expression. J. Neurochem., 66: 2621–2624.

Heisler, L.K., Chu, H.M., Brennan, T.J., Danao, J.A., Bajwa, P., Parsons, L.H. and Tecott, L.H. (1998) Elevated anxiety and antidepressant-like responses in serotonin 5-HT$_{1A}$ receptor mutant mice. Proc. Natl. Acad. Sci. USA, 95: 15049–15054.

Hensler, J.G. (2006) Serotonergic modulation of the limbic system. Neurosci. Biobehav. Rev., 30: 203–214.

Hesse, S., Barthel, H., Schwarz, J., Sabri, O. and Müller, U. (2004) Advances in in vivo imaging of serotonergic neurons in neuropsychiatric disorders. Neurosci. Biobehav. Rev., 28: 547–563.

Hetem, L.A. (1996) Addition of d-fenfluramine to benzodiazepines produces a marked improvement in refractory panic disorder—a case report. J. Clin. Psychopharmacol., 16: 77–78.

Hewlett, W.A., Schmid, S.P. and Salomon, R.M. (2003) Pilot trial of ondansetron in the treatment of 8 patients with obsessive-compulsive disorder. J. Clin. Psychiatry, 64: 1025–1030.

Higgins, G.A., Jones, B.J., Oakley, N.R. and Tryers, M.B. (1991) Evidence that the amygdala is involved in the disinhibitory effects of 5-HT$_3$ receptor antagonists. Psychopharmacology, 104: 545–551.

Hodges, H., Green, S. and Glenn, B. (1987) Evidence that the amygdala is involved in benzodiazepine and serotonergic effects on punished responding but not in discrimination. Psychopharmacology, 92: 491–504.

Hoehn-Saric, R., Schlund, M.W. and Wong, S.H. (2004) Effects of citalopram on worry and brain activation in patients with generalized anxiety disorder. Psychiatry Res., 131: 11–21.

Holmes, A., le Guisquet, A.M., Vogel, E., Millstein, R.A., Leman, S. and Belzung, C. (2005) Early life genetic, epigenetic and environmental factors shaping emotionality in rodents. Neurosci. Biobehav. Rev., 29: 1335–1346.

Holmes, A., Lit, Q., Murphy, D.L., Gold, E. and Crawley, J.N. (2003a) Abnormal anxiety-related behavior in serotonin transporter null mutant mice: the influence of genetic background. Genes Brain Behav., 2: 365–380.

Holmes, A., Yang, R.J., Lesch, K.P., Crawley, J.N. and Murphy, D.L. (2003b) Mice lacking the serotonin transporter exhibit 5-HT$_{1A}$ receptor-mediated abnormalities in tests for anxiety-like behavior. Neuropsychopharmacology, 28: 2077–2088.

Holmes, A., Yang, R.J., Murphy, D.L. and Crawley, J.N. (2002) Evaluation of antidepressant-related behavioral responses in mice lacking the serotonin transporter. Neuropsychopharmacology, 27: 914–923.

Hoyer, D., Hannon, J.P. and Martin, G.R. (2002) Molecular, pharmacological and functional diversity of 5-HT receptors. Pharmacol. Biochem. Behav., 71: 533–554.

Iidaka, T., Ozaki, N., Matsumoto, A., Nogawa, J., Kinoshita, Y., Suzuki, T., Iwata, N., Yamamoto, Y.,

Okada, N. and Sadato, N. (2005) A variant C178 T in the regulatory region of the serotonin receptor gene HTR_{3A} modulates neural activation in the human amygdala. J. Neurosci., 25: 6460–6466.

Jenck, F., Broekkamp, C.L.E. and van Delft, A.M.L. (1989) Opposite control mediated by central $5HT_{1A}$ and non-$5HT_{1A}$ ($5HT_{1B}$ or $5H_{1C}$) receptors on periaqueductal gray aversion. Eur. J. Pharmacol., 161: 219–221.

Jenck, F., Broekkamp, C.L.E. and van Delft, A.M.L. (1990) The effect of antidepressants on aversive PAG stimulation. Eur. J. Pharmacol., 177: 201–204.

Jorge, S.D., Pobbe, R.L., De Paula, V.S., Oliveira, A.M. and Zangrossi, H. Jr. (2004) Effects of sibutramine on anxiety-related behaviours in rats. Pharmacol. Res., 50: 517–522.

Kahn, R.J., McNair, D.M., Lipman, R.S., Covi, L., Rickels, K., Downing, R., Fisher, S. and Frankenthaler, L.M. (1986) Imipramine and chlordiazepoxide in depressive and anxiety disorders. II Efficacy in anxious outpatients. Arch. Gen. Psychiatry, 43: 79–85.

Kelleher, R.T. and Morse, W.H. (1968) Determinants of the specificity of behavioral effects of drugs. Ergeb. Physiol., 60: 1–56.

Kia, H.K., Brisorgueil, M.J., Hamon, M., Calas, A. and Verge, D. (1996) Ultrastructural localization of 5-hydroxytryptamine1A receptors in the rat brain. J. Neurosci. Res., 46: 697–708.

Kia, H.K., Miquel, M.C., Brisorgueil, M.J., Daval, G., Riad, M., El Mestikawy, S., Hamon, M. and Verge, D. (1996) Immunocytochemical localization of serotonin1A receptors in the rat central nervous system. J. Comp. Neurol., 365: 289–305.

Kim, D.K., Tolliver, T.J., Huang, S.J., Martin, B.J., Andrews, A.M., Wichems, C., Holmes, A., Lesch, K.P. and Murphy, D.L. (2005) Altered serotonin synthesis, turnover and dynamic regulation in multiple brain regions of mice lacking the serotonin transporter. Neuropharmacology, 49: 798–810.

Kim, H., Lim, S.W., Kim, S., Kim, J.W., Chang, Y.H., Carroll, B.J. and Kim, D.K. (2006) Monoamine transporter gene polymorphisms and antidepressant response in koreans with late-life depression. J. Am. Med. Assoc., 296: 1609–1618.

Kiser, R.S., German, D.C. and Lebovitz, R.M. (1978a) Serotonergic reduction of dorsal central gray area stimulation-produced aversion. Pharmacol. Biochem. Behav., 9: 27–31.

Kiser, R.S. Jr. and Lebovitz, R.M. (1975) Monoaminergic mechanisms in aversive brain stimulation. Physiol. Behav., 15: 47–53.

Kiser, R.S., Lebovitz, R.M. and German, D.C. (1978b) Anatomic and pharmacologic differences between two types of aversive midbrain stimulation. Brain Res., 155: 331–342.

Klein, F.F. and Flink, M. (1962) Psychiatric reaction patterns to imipramine. Am. J. Psychiatry, 119: 432–438.

Koe, B.K. and Weissman, A. (1966) p-Chlorophenylalanine: a specific depletor of brain serotonin. J. Pharmacol. Exp. Ther., 154: 499–516.

Koks, S., Beljajev, S., Koovit, I., Abramov, U., Bourin, M. and Vasar, E. (2001) 8-OH-DPAT, but not deramciclane, antagonizes the anxiogenic-like action of paroxetine in an elevated plus-maze. Psychopharmacology, 153: 365–372.

Koszycki, D., Zacharko, R.M., Le Melledo, J.M., Young, S.N. and Bradwejn, J. (1996) Effect of acute tryptophan depletion on behavioral, cardiovascular, and hormonal sensitivity to cholecystokinin–tetrapeptide challenge in healthy volunteers. Biol. Psychiatry, 40: 648–655.

Lanzenberger, R.R, Mitterhauser, M., Spindelegger, C., Wadsak, W., Klein, N., Mien, L.-K., Holik, A., Attarbaschi, T., Mossaheb, N., Sacher, J., Geiss-Granadia, T., Kletter, K., Kasper, S. and Tauscher, J. (2007) Reduced serotonin-1A receptor binding in social anxiety disorder. *Biol. Psychiatry*, 61: 1081–1089.

Lecrubier, Y., Pucch, A.J., Azeona, A., Bailey, P.E. and Lataste, X. (1999) A randomized double-blind placecontrolled study of tropisetron in the treatment of outpatients with generalized anxiety disorder. Psychopharmacology, 112: 129–133.

LeDoux, J.E. (1993) Emotional memory systems in the brain. Behav. Brain Res., 58: 69–79.

Leonardo, E.D. and Hen, R. (2006) Genetics of affective and anxiety disorders. Annu. Rev. Psychol., 57: 117–137.

Lesch, K.P. (2005) Genetic alterations of the murine serotonergic gene pathway: the neurodevelopmental basis of anxiety. Handb. Exp. Pharmacol., 169: 71–112.

Lesch, K.P., Bengel, D., Heils, A., Sabol, S.Z., Greenberg, B.D., Petri, S., Benjamim, J., Müller, C.R., Hamer, D.H. and Murphy, D.L. (1996) Association of anxiety-related traits with a polymorphism in the serotonin transporter gene regulatory region. Science, 274: 1527–1531.

Lesch, K.P., Hoh, A., Disselkamp-Tietze, J., Wiesmann, M., Osterheider, M. and Schulte, H.M. (1991) 5-Hydroxytryptamine1A receptor responsivity in obsessive-compulsive disorder. Comparison of patients and controls. Arch. Gen. Psychiatry, 48: 540–547.

Lesch, K.P., Wiesmann, M., Hoh, A., Muller, T., Disselkamp-Tietze, J., Osterheider, M. and Schulte, H.M. (1992) 5-HT_{1A} receptor–effector system responsivity in panic disorder. Psychopharmacology, 106: 111–117.

Lesch, K.P., Zeng, Y., Reif, A. and Gutknecht, L. (2003) Anxiety-related traits in mice with modified genes of the serotonergic pathway. Eur. J. Pharmacol., 480: 185–204.

Levi, G. and Raiteri, M. (1993) Carrier-mediated release of neurotransmitters. Trends Neurol. Sci., 16: 415–419.

Li, Q., Wichems, C., Heils, A., Lesch, K.P. and Murphy, D.L. (2000) Reduction in the density and expression, but not G-protein coupling, of serotonin receptors (5-HT$_{1A}$) in 5-HT transporter knock-out mice: gender and brain region differences. J. Neurosci., 20: 7888–7895.

Li, Q., Wichems, C., Heils, A., Van De Kar, L.D., Lesch, K.P. and Murphy, D.L. (1999) Reduction of 5-hydroxytryptamine (5-HT$_{1A}$)-mediated temperature and neuroendocrine responses and 5-HT$_{1A}$ binding sites in 5-HT transporter knockout mice. J. Pharmacol. Exp. Ther., 291: 999–1007.

Li, Q., Wichems, C., Ma, L., Van de Kar, L.D., Garcia, F. and Murphy, D.L. (2003) Brain region-specific alterations of 5-HT$_{2A}$ and 5-HT$_{2C}$ receptors in serotonin transporter knockout mice. J. Neurochem., 84: 1256–1265.

Lowry, C.A., Johnson, P.L., Hay-Schmidt, A., Mikkelsen, J. and Shekhar, A. (2005) Modulation of anxiety circuits by serotonergic systems. Stress, 8: 233–246.

Maier, S.F. and Watkins, L.R. (2005) Stressor controllability and learned helplessness: the roles of the dorsal raphe nucleus, serotonin, and corticotropin-releasing factor. Neurosci. Biobehav. Rev., 29: 829–841.

Malison, R.T., Price, L.H., Berman, R., van Dyck, C.H., Pelton, G.H., Carpenter, L., Sanacora, G., Owens, M.J., Nemeroff, C.B., Rajeevan, N., Baldwin, R.M., Seibyl, J.P., Innis, R.B. and Charney, D.S. (1998) Reduced brain serotonin transporter availability in major depression as measured by [^{123}I]-2 beta-carbomethoxy-3 beta-(4-iodophenyl)tropane and single photon emission computed tomography. Biol. Psychiatry, 44: 1090–1098.

Mansari, M.E. and Blier, P. (2006) Mechanism of action of current and potential pharmacotherapies of obsessive-compulsive disorder. Progress Neuro-Psychopharmacol. Biol. Psychiatry, 30: 362–373.

Maron, E., Kuikka, J.T., Ulst, K., Tiihonen, J., Vasar, V. and Shlik, J. (2004) SPECT imaging of serotonin transporter binding in patients with generalized anxiety disorder. Eur. Arch. Psychiatry Clin. Neurosci., 254: 392–396.

Maron, E. and Shlik, J. (2006) Serotonin function in panic disorder: important, but why? Neuropsychopharmacology, 31: 1–11.

Maron, E., Toru, I., Vasar, V. and Shlik, J. (2004b) The effect of 5-hydroxytryptophan on cholecystokinin-4-induced panic attacks in healthy volunteers. J. Psychopharmacol., 18: 194–199.

Martin, J.R., Ballard, T.M. and Higgins, G.A. (2002) Influence of the 5-HT$_{2C}$ receptor antagonist, SB-242084, in tests of anxiety. Pharmacol. Biochem. Behav., 71: 615–625.

Massé, F., Aïne, B., Dhonnchadha, N., Ascote, M. and Bourin, M. (2007) Anxiolytic-like effect of 5-HT$_2$ ligands on benzodiazepines co-administration: comparison of two animal models of anxiety (the tour-plate test and the elevated plus maze). Behav. Brain Res., 177: 214–226.

Mathews, T.A., Fedele, D.A., Coppelli, F.M., Avila, A.M., Murphy, D.L. and Andrews, A.M. (2004) Gene dose-dependent alterations in extraneuronal serotonin but not dopamine in mice with reduced serotonin transporter expression. J. Neurosci. Meth., 140: 169–181.

Mcblane, J.W. and Handley, S.L. (1994) Effects of two stressors on behavior in the elevated X-maze: preliminary investigation of their interaction with 8-OH-DPAT. Psychopharmacology, 116: 173–182.

McBride, P.A., DeMeo, M.D., Sweeney, J.A., Halper, J., Mann, J.J. and Shear, M.K. (1992) Neuroendocrine and behavioral responses to challenge with the indirect serotonin agonist dl-fenfluramine in adults with obsessive-compulsive disorder. Biol. Psychiatry, 31: 19–34.

McNair, D.M., Frankenthaler, L.M., Czerlinsky, T., White, T.W., Sasson, S. and Fisher, S. (1982) Simulated public speaking as a model of clinical anxiety. Psychopharmacology, 77: 7–10.

McNaughton, N. and Corr, P.J. (2004) A two-dimensional neuropsychology of defense: fear/anxiety and defensive distance. Neurosci. Biobehav. Rev., 28: 285–305.

Millan, M.J. (2003) The neurobiology and control of anxious states. Prog. Neurobiol., 70: 53–244.

Millan, M.J. (2006a) Multi-target strategies for the improved treatment of depressive states: conceptual foundations and neuronal substrates, drug discovery and therapeutic application. Pharmacol. Ther., 110: 135–370.

Millan, M.J. (2006b) Serotonin 5-HT$_{2C}$ receptors as a target for the treatment of depressive and anxious states: focus on novel therapeutic strategies. Therapie, 60: 441–460.

Millenson, J.R. and Leslie, J. (1974) The conditioned emotional response (CER) as a baseline for the study of anti-anxiety drugs. Neuropharmacology, 13: 1–9.

Miller, H.E., Deakin, J.F. and Anderson, I.M. (2000) Effect of acute tryptophan depletion on CO$_2$-induced anxiety in patients with panic disorder and normal volunteers. Br. J. Psychiatry, 176: 182–188.

Mora, P.O., Netto, C.F. and Graeff, F.G. (1997) Role of 5-HT$_{2A}$ and 5-HT$_{2C}$ receptors subtypes in the two types of fear generated by the elevated T-maze. Pharmacol. Biochem. Behav., 58: 1051–1057.

Mortimore, C. and Anderson, I.M. (2000) d-Fenfluramine in panic disorder: a dual role for 5-hydroxytryptamine. Psychopharmacology, 149: 251–258.

Moser, P.C., Tricklebank, M.D., Middlemiss, D.N., Mir, A.K., Hibert, M.F. and Fozard, J.R. (1990) Characterization of MDL 73005EF as a 5-HT$_{1A}$ selective ligand and its effects in animal models of anxiety: comparison with buspirone, 8-OH-DPAT and diazepam. Br. J. Pharmacol., 99: 343–349.

Mössner, R., Schmitt, A., Hennig, T., Benninghoff, J., Gerlach, M., Riederer, P., Deckert, J. and Lesch, K.P. (2004) Quantification of 5HT$_3$ receptors in forebrain of serotonin transporter deficient mice. J. Neural Transm., 111: 27–35.

Motta, V., Maisonette, S., Morato, S., Castrechini, P. and Brandão, M.L. (1992) Effects of blockade of 5-HT$_2$ receptors and activation of 5-HT$_{1A}$ receptors on the exploratory activity of rats in the elevated plus-maze. Psychopharmacology, 107: 135–139.

Munjack, D.J., Crocker, B., Cable, D., Brown, R., Usigli, R., Zulueta, A., McManus, M., McDowell, D., Palmer, R. and Leonard, M. (1989) Alprazolam, propranolol, and placebo in the treatment of panic disorder and agoraphobia with panic attacks. Clin. Psychopharmacol., 9: 22–27.

Murphy, D.L., Zohar, J., Benkelfat, C., Pato, M.T., Pigott, T.A. and Insel, T.R. (1989) Obsessive-compulsive disorder as a 5-HT subsystem-related behavioural disorder. Br. J. Psychiatry Suppl., 8: 15–24.

Neumeister, A., Bain, E., Nugent, A.C., Carson, R.E., Bonne, O., Luckenbaugh, D.A., Eckelman, W., Herscovitch, P., Charney, D.S. and Drevets, W.C. (2004) Reduced serotonin type 1A receptor binding in panic disorder. J. Neurosci., 24: 589–591.

Nogueira, R.L. and Graeff, F.G. (1991) Mediation of the antiaversive effect of isamoltane injected into the dorsal periaqueductal grey. Behav. Pharmacol., 2: 73–77.

Nogueira, R.L. and Graeff, F.G. (1995) Role of 5-HT receptor subtypes in the modulation of aversion generated in the dorsal periaqueductal gray. Pharmacol. Biochem. Behav., 52: 1–6.

Nutt, D.J. (1990) The pharmacology of human anxiety. Pharmacol. Ther., 47: 233–266.

Ogilvie, A.D., Battersby, S., Bubb, V.J., Fink, G., Harmar, A.J., Goodwim, G.M. and Smith, C.A. (1996) Polymorphism in serotonin transporter gene associated with susceptibility to major depression. Lancet, 347: 731–733.

Olivier, B., Zethof, T., Parttij, T., van Boogaert, M., van Oorschot, R., Leahy, C., Oosting, R., Bouwknecht, A., Veening, J., van der Gugten, J. and Groenink, L. (2003) Stress-induced hyperthermia and anxiety: pharmacological validation. Eur. J. Pharmacol., 463: 117–132.

Palkovits, M., Brownstein, M. and Saavedra, J.M. (1974) Serotonin content of the brain stem nuclei in the rat. Brain Res., 80: 237–249.

Parks, C.L., Robinson, P.S., Sibille, E., Shenk, T. and Toth, M. (1998) Increased anxiety of mice lacking the serotonin1A receptor. Proc. Natl. Acad. Sci. USA, 95: 10734–10739.

Pazos, A. and Palacios, J.M. (1985) Quantitative autoradiographic mapping of serotonin receptors in the rat brain. I. Serotonin-1 receptors. Brain Res., 346: 205–230.

Pellow, S., Chopin, P., File, S.E. and Briley, M. (1985) Validation of open:closed arm entries in the elevated plus-maze as a measure of anxiety in the rat. J. Neurosci. Meth., 14: 149–167.

Peng, W.H., Wu, C.R., Chen, C.S., Chen, C.F., Leu, Z.C. and Hsieh, M.T. (2004) Anxiolytic effect of berberine on exploratory activity of the mouse in two experimental anxiety models: interaction with drugs acting at 5-HT receptors. Life Sci., 75: 2451–2462.

Perna, G., Bertani, A., Caldirola, D., Gabriele, A., Cocchi, S. and Bellodi, L. (2002) Antipanic drug modulation of 35% CO$_2$ hyperreactivity and short-term treatment outcome. J. Clin. Psychopharmacol., 22: 300–308.

Peroutka, S.J. (1988) 5-hydroxytryptamine receptor subtypes: molecular, biochemical and physiological characterization. Trends Neurosci., 11: 496–500.

Petersen, E.N. and Scheel-Krüger, J. (1984) Anticonflict effects of 5-HT antagonists by intraamygdaloid injection. *Abstracts of the 14th CINP Congress*, pp. 654.

Pezawas, L., Meyer-Lindenberg, A., Drabant, E.M., Verchinski, B.A., Munoz, K.E., Kolachana, B.S., Egan, M.F., Mattay, V.S., Hariri, A.R. and Weinberger, D.R. (2005) 5-HTTLPR polymorphism impacts human cingulate–amygdala interactions: a genetic susceptibility mechanism for depression. Nat. Neurosci., 8: 828–834.

Piñeyro, G. and Blier, P. (1999) Autoregulation of serotonin neurons: role in antidepressant drug action. Pharmacol. Rev., 51: 534–591.

Pinheiro, S.N., Zangrossi, H. Jr., Del-Ben, C.M. and Graeff, F.G. (2007) Elevated mazes as animal models of anxiety: effects of serotonergic agents. *An. Acad. Bras. Cienc.*, 79: 71–85.

Pobbe, R.L. and Zangrossi, H. Jr. (2005) 5-HT$_{1A}$ and 5-HT$_{2A}$ receptors in the rat dorsal periaqueductal gray mediate the antipanic-like effect induced by the stimulation of serotonergic neurons in the dorsal raphe nucleus. Psychopharmacology, 183: 314–321.

Poltronieri, S.C., Zangrossi, H. Jr. and Viana, M.B. (2003) Antipanic-like effect of serotonin reuptake inhibitors in the elevated T-maze. Behav. Brain Res., 147: 185–192.

Prut, L. and Belzung, C. (2003) The open field as a paradigm to measure the effects of drugs on anxiety-like behaviors: a review. Eur. J. Pharmacol., 463: 3–33.

Rabiner, E.A., Gun, R.N., Wilkins, M.R., Sargent, P.A., Mocaer, E., Sedman, E., Cowen, P.J. and Grasby, P.M. (2000) Drug action at the 5-HT$_{1A}$ receptor in vivo: autoreceptor and postsynaptic receptor occupancy examined with PET and [carbonyl-(11)C]WAY-100635. Nucl. Med. Biol., 27: 509–513.

Ramboz, S., Oosting, R., Amara, D.A., Kung, H.F., Blier, P., Mendelsohn, M., Mann, J.J., Brunner, D. and Hen, R. (1998) Serotonin receptor 1A knockout: an animal model of anxiety-related disorder. Proc. Natl. Acad. Sci. USA, 95: 14476–14481.

Rapport, M.M. (1949) Serum vasoconstrictor (serotonin). V. The presence of creatinine in the complex: a proposed structure of the vasoconstrictor principle. J. Biol. Chem., 180: 961–969.

Reist, C., Mazzanti, C., Vu, R., Tran, D. and Goldman, D. (2001) Serotonin transporter promoter polymorphism is associated with attenuated prolactin response to fenfluramine. Am. J. Med. Genet., 105: 363–368.

Rickels, K., Downing, R., Scweizer, E. and Hassman, H. (1993) Antidepressants for the treatment of generalized anxiety disorder. A placebo-controlled comparison of imipramine, trazodone, and diazepam. Arch. Gen. Psychiatry, 50: 884–895.

Rioux, A., Fabre, V., Lesch, K.P., Moessner, R., Murphy, D.L., Lanfumey, L., Hamon, M. and Martres, M.P. (1999) Adaptive changes of serotonin 5-HT$_{2A}$ receptors in mice lacking the serotonin transporter. Neurosci. Lett., 262: 113–116.

Robichaud, R.C. and Sledge, K.L. (1969) The effects of p-chlorophenylalanine on experimentally induced conflict in the rat. Life Sci., 8: 965–969.

Romach, M.K., Kaplan, H.L., Busto, U.E., Somer, G. and Sellers, E.M. (1998) A controlled trial of ondansetran, a 5HT$_3$ antagonist, in benzodiazepine discontinuation. J. Clin. Psychopharmacol., 18: 121–131.

Sanchez, C. (2003) Stress-induced vocalization in adult animals. A valid model of anxiety? Eur. J. Pharmacol., 463: 133–143.

Santarelli, L., Saxe, M., Gross, C., Surget, A., Battaglia, F., Dulawa, S., Weisstaub, N., Lee, J., Duman, R., Arancio, O., Belzung, C. and Hen, R. (2003) Requirement of hippocampal neurogenesis for the behavioral effects of antidepressants. Science, 301: 805–809.

Savic, I., Lindstrom, P., Gulyas, B., Halldin, C., Andree, B. and Farde, L. (2004) Limbic reductions of 5-HT$_{1A}$ receptor binding in human temporal lobe epilepsy. Neurology, 62: 1343–1351.

Schenberg, L.C. and Graeff, F.G. (1978) Role of the periaqueductal gray substance in the antianxiety action of benzodiazepines. Pharmacol. Biochem. Behav., 9: 287–295.

Schoenfeld, R.I. (1976) Lysergic acid diethylamide- and mescaline-induced attenuation of the effect of punishment in the rat. Science, 192: 801–803.

Schruers, K., van Diest, R., Overbeek, T. and Griez, E. (2002) Acute L-5-hydroxytryptophan administration inhibits carbon dioxide-induced panic in panic disorder patients. Psychiatry Res., 113: 237–243.

Schütz, M.T.B., de Aguiar, J.C. and Graeff, F.G. (1985) Anti-aversive role of serotonin on the dorsal periaqueductal grey matter. Psychopharmacology, 85: 340–345.

Sena, L.M., Bueno, C., Pobbe, R.L., Andrade, T.G., Zangrossi, H. and Viana, M.B. (2003) The dorsal raphe nucleus exerts opposed control on generalized anxiety and panic-related defensive responses in rats. Behav. Brain Res., 142: 125–133.

Setem, J., Pinheiro, A.P., Motta, V.A., Morato, S. and Cruz, A.P. (1999) Ethopharmacological analysis of 5-HT ligands on the rat elevated plus-maze. Pharmacol. Biochem. Behav., 62: 515–521.

Shlik, J., Maron, E., Tru, I., Aluoja, A. and Vasar, V. (2004) Citalopram challenge in social anxiety disorder. Int. J. Neuropsychopharmacol., 7: 177–182.

Sibille, E., Pavlides, C., Benke, D. and Toth, M. (2000) Genetic inactivation of the serotonin(1A) receptor in mice results in downregulation of major GABA(A) receptor alpha subunits, reduction of GABA(A) receptor binding, and benzodiazepine-resistant anxiety. J. Neurosci., 20: 2758–2765.

Silva, R.C. and Brandão, M.L. (2000) Acute and chronic effects of gepirone and fluoxetine in rats tested in the elevated plus-maze: an ethological analysis. Pharmacol. Biochem. Behav., 65: 209–216.

Smits, K.M., Smits, L.J., Schouten, J.S., Stelma, F.F., Nelemans, P. and Prins, M.H. (2004) Influence of SERTPR and STin2 in the serotonin transporter gene on the effect of selective serotonin reuptake inhibitors in depression: a systematic review. Mol. Psychiatry, 9: 433–441.

Solyom, L. (1994) Controlling panic attacks with fenfluramine. Am. J. Psychiatry, 151: 621–622.

Southwick, S.M., Krystal, J.H., Bremner, J.D., Morgan, C.A., 3rd Nicolaou, A.L., Nagy, L.M., Johnson, D.R., Heninger, G.R. and Charney, D.S. (1997) Noradrenergic and serotonergic function in posttraumatic stress disorder. Arch. Gen. Psychiatry, 54: 749–758.

Southwick, S.M., Paige, S., Morgan, C.A., 3rd Bremner, J.D., Krystal, J.H. and Charney, D.S. (1999) Neurotransmitter alterations in PTSD: catecholamines and serotonin. Semin. Clin. Neuropsychiatry, 4: 242–248.

Tauscher, J., Bagby, R.M., Javanmard, M., Christensen, B.K., Kasper, S. and Kapur, S. (2001) Inverse relationship between serotonin 5-HT$_{1A}$ receptor binding and anxiety: a[(11)C]WAY-100635 PET investigation in healthy volunteers. Am. J. Psychiatry, 158: 1326–1328.

Teixeira, R.C., Zangrossi, H. Jr. and Graeff, F.G. (2000) Behavioral effects of acute and chronic imipramine in the elevated T-maze model of anxiety. Pharmacol. Biochem. Behav., 65: 571–576.

Tye, N.C., Everitt, B.J. and Iversen, S.D. (1977) 5-Hydroxytryptamine and punishment. Nature, 268: 741–742.

Van der Linden, G., van Heerden, B., Warwick, J., Wessels, C., van Kradenburg, J., Zungu-Dirwayi, N. and Stein, D.J. (2000) Functional brain imaging and pharmacotherapy in social phobia: single photon emission computed tomography before and after treatment with the selective serotonin reuptake inhibitor citalopram. Prog. Neuropsychopharmacol. Biol. Psychiatry, 24: 419–438.

van Megen, H.J., Westenberg, H.G., den Boer, J.A., Slaap, B. and Scheepmakers, A. (1997) Effect of the selective serotonin reuptake inhibitor fluvoxamine on CCK-4 induced panic attacks. Psychopharmacology, 129: 357–364.

van Vliet, I.M., Slaap, B.R., Westenberg, H.G. and Den Boer, J.A. (1996a) Behavioral, neuroendocrine and biochemical effects of different doses of 5-HTP in panic disorder. Eur. Neuropsychopharmacol., 6: 103–110.

van Vliet, I.M., Westenberg, H.G. and den Boer, J.A. (1996b) Effects of the 5HT$_{1A}$ receptor agonist flesinoxan in panic disorder. Psychopharmacology, 127: 174–180.

Viana, M.B., Graeff, F.G. and Löschmann, P.-A. (1997) Kainate microinjection into the dorsal raphe nucleus induces 5-HT release in the amygdala and periaqueductal gray. Pharmacol. Biochem. Behav., 58: 167–172.

Weisstaub, N.V., Zhou, M., Lira, A., Gonzalez-Maeso, J., Hornung, J.-P., Sibille, E., Underwood, M., Itohara, S., Dauer, W.T., Ansorge, M.S., Morelli, E., Mann, J.J., Toth, M., Aghajanian, G., Sealfon, S.C., Hen, R. and Gingrich, J.A. (2006) Cortical 5-HT$_{2A}$ receptor signiling modulates anxiety-like behaviors in mice. Science, 313: 536–540.

Wise, C.D., Berger, B.D. and Stein, L. (1972) Benzodiazepines: anxiety-reducing activity by reduction of serotonin turnover in the brain. Science, 177: 180–183.

Wrase, J., Reimold, M., Puls, I., Kienast, T. and Heinz, A. (2006) Serotonergic dysfunction: brain imaging and behavioral correlates. Cogn. Affect. Behav. Neurosci., 6: 53–61.

Yasuno, F., Suhara, T., Ichimiya, T., Takano, A., Ando, T. and Okubo, Y. (2004) Decreased 5-HT$_{1A}$ receptor binding in amygdala of schizophrenia. Biol. Psychiatry, 55: 439–444.

Yu, Y.W., Tsai, S.J., Chen, T.J., Lin, C.H. and Hong, C.J. (2002) Association study of the serotonin transporter promoter polymorphism and symptomatology and antidepressant response in major depressive disorders. Mol. Psychiatry, 7: 1115–1119.

Zangrossi, H., Jr. Viana, M.B. and Graeff, F.G. (1999) Anxiolytic effect of intra-amygdala injection of midazolam and 8-hydroxy-2(di-n-propylamino)tetralin in the elevated T-maze. Eur. J. Pharmacol., 369: 267–270.

Zanoveli, J.M., Netto, C.F., Guimarães, F.S. and Zangrossi, H. Jr. (2004) Systemic and intra-dorsal periaqueductal gray injections of cholecystokinin sulfated octapeptide (CCK-8 s) induce a panic-like response in rats submitted to the elevated T-maze. Peptides, 25: 1935–1941.

Zanoveli, J.M., Nogueira, R.L. and Zangrossi, H. Jr. (2003) Serotonin in the dorsal periaqueductal gray modulates inhibitory avoidance and one-way escape behaviors in the elevated T-maze. Eur. J. Pharmacol., 473: 153–161.

Zanoveli, J.M., Nogueira, R.L. and Zangrossi, H. Jr. (2005) Chronic imipramine treatment sensitizes 5-HT$_{1A}$ and 5-HT$_{2A}$ receptors in the dorsal periaqueductal gray matter: evidence from the elevated T-maze test of anxiety. Behav. Pharmacol., 16: 543–552.

CHAPTER 4.4

The glutamatergic system as a potential therapeutic target for the treatment of anxiety disorders

John F. Cryan[1,*] and Kumlesh K. Dev[2]

[1]School of Pharmacy, Department of Pharmacology and Therapeutics, Alimentary Pharmabiotic Centre, University College Cork, Cork, Ireland
[2]Department of Anatomy, Biosciences Institute, University College Cork, Cork, Ireland

Abstract: Glutamate is the major excitatory neurotransmitter in the adult central nervous system. Its fast actions are mediated by ionotropic receptors (NMDA, AMPA and kainate receptors). In addition, three groups comprised of eight G-protein coupled metabotropic glutamate receptors (mGluR) mediate slower modulatory actions of glutamate on neurotransmitter release and cell excitability. In recent years, there has been an accumulation of evidence that selective targeting of glutamate receptors may be a useful strategy for the treatment of anxiety disorders. Such evidence has been contingent on the availability of predictive animal models, and is largely driven by the development of selective, potent and orally bioavailable tools for distinct glutamate receptors and receptor binding sites in the brain. Moreover, the availability of genetically modified mice is also adding to the armamentarium, researchers have to dissect the role of glutamate in brain circuits relevant to anxiety. Clinical validation of the anxiolytic effects derived from preclinical models is now warranted.

Keywords: glutamate; fear; animal model; NMDA; mGluR; AMPA

I. Introduction

Anxiety disorders are among the most commonly occurring of the psychiatric illnesses affecting approximately 19 million American adults (http://www.nimh.nih.gov/publicat/anxiety.cfm) with an immense economic cost (Kessler and Greenberg, 2002). Recent European studies have shown that anxiety disorders have the highest prevalence of all brain disorders affecting over 41 million people (Andlin-Sobocki et al., 2005). Hence, the burden placed on health systems around the world by anxiety is immense. The hallmark of anxiety

disorders is a 'marked, persistent and excessive or unreasonable fear' that is experienced to such a degree that it significantly interferes with everyday life (American Psychiatric Association, 1994; Cryan and Holmes, 2005). The diagnostic and statistical manual of the American Psychiatric Association (DSM-IV) classification of clinical anxiety distinguishes between numerous sub-disorders of anxiety, the most common being (i) generalised anxiety disorder, (ii) panic disorder (diagnosed with or without agoraphobia), (iii) specific phobia, (iv) social phobia, (v) obsessive-compulsive disorder (OCD) and (vi) post-traumatic stress disorder. These disorders are largely distinguished from one another by the nature of the stimulus provoking the anxiety. Moreover, while there is

*Corresponding author. E-mail: j.cryan@ucc.ie

R.J. Blanchard, D.C. Blanchard, G. Griebel and D. Nutt (Eds.)
Handbook of Anxiety and Fear, Vol. 17
ISBN 978-0-444-53065-3

DOI: 10.1016/S1569-7339(07)00013-6

epidemiological co-morbidity between anxiety sub-disorders, they are to some degree differentially responsive to different classes of anxiolytic drug treatments, suggesting discrete neurobiological and genetic aetiologies (American Psychiatric Association, 1994).

The introduction of the benzodiazepines in the late 1950s, which were better tolerated and had a superior safety profile than previously used barbiturates, revolutionised the treatment of anxiety (Sandford et al., 2000; Nemeroff, 2003). However, over the ensuing decades, it has become clear that there are many unwanted side effects associated with benzodiazepine usage. These include short-term memory impairments, interactions with alcohol, psychomotor impairments in addition to concerns about dependence and pharmacological tolerance (Gorman et al., 2002). This has propelled research into the development of anxiolytics with a better safety profile, which are equally efficacious. Treatments that increase activity of the serotonergic neurotransmitter system by selectively inhibiting serotonin reuptake (serotonin reuptake inhibitors, SSRIs) or activating the 5-HT1A receptor (5-HT1A receptor agonists, e.g. buspirone) have emerged. However, these drugs may have a slow onset of action, are of limited efficacy in a significant proportion of patients and are associated with troublesome side effects that reduce compliance. Thus, there remains a greater than ever impetus to develop novel anxiolytic medications devoid of side effects. Recent studies suggest that selectively targeting the glutamate system may give rise to a suitable and novel therapies for anxiety (Bergink et al., 2004; Cortese and Phan, 2005; Swanson et al., 2005; Simon and Gorman, 2006). In this article, we review the evidence of such propositions.

II. Glutamate receptor diversity

More than half a century has passed since the excitatory effects of L-glutamate were first observed in neurons of the spinal cord (Curtis and Watkins, 1961). Since then, it has been widely demonstrated that L-glutamate is the predominant excitatory neurotransmitter in the central nervous system (CNS) mediating neurotransmission at an overwhelming majority of synapses. Both ligand-gated ion channel (ionotropic) and G-protein coupled (metabotropic) types of glutamate receptors have been characterized. Ionotropic glutamate receptors are responsible for the fast component of synaptic excitatory neurotransmission whereas activation of metabotropic receptors leads to more sustained intracellular signalling. These glutamate receptors are differentially distributed in the mammalian brain and can be localised extra-, pre- and/or post-synaptically.

In the mammalian CNS, there are three distinct classes of ionotropic glutamate receptors named according to their sensitivity to the agonists N-methyl-D-aspartate (NMDA), α-amino-3-hydroxy-5-methylisoxazole-4-propionate (AMPA) and kainate (KA) (Henley, 1994; Hollmann and Heinemann, 1994; Bettler and Mulle, 1995). Each subgroup comprise a set of distinct subunits such that NMDA receptors are encoded by NR1, 2A-D, 3A-B, the AMPA receptors are encoded by GluR1–4, and KA receptors are encoded by GluR5–7 and KA1–2 (see Fig. 1). Each of these subunits are approximately 900 amino acids long. Sequence identity may be close to 70% within each receptor subgroup and around 30% with other glutamate receptor subunits (Bettler and Mulle, 1995).

The metabotropic glutamate (mGluR) receptor family mediates its effects on second messenger systems via G proteins (Nakanishi, 1994; Pin and Duvoisin, 1995). The eight subtypes mGluR1–mGluR8 (and the splice variants) have been split into three distinct subgroups (see Fig. 1). Group I comprises mGluR1$_{(a-d)}$ and mGluR5$_{(a-b)}$ and are coupled to Gq proteins. Receptor activation leads to stimulation of phospholipase C (PLC) and protein kinase C (PKC) and causes the release of Ca^{2+} from intracellular stores. Group II (mGluR2 and mGluR3) and Group III (mGluR4$_{(a-b)}$, mGluR6, mGluR7$_{(a-b)}$ and mGluR8$_{(a-b)}$) receptors are coupled to Gi proteins and inhibit adenylyl cyclase activity (Pin and Acher, 2002; Kew and Kemp, 2005).

Both ionotropic and metabotropic glutamate receptor (mGluR) subunits and subtypes can also undergo alternative splicing and RNA editing (e.g. see, Seeburg, 1996). These molecular

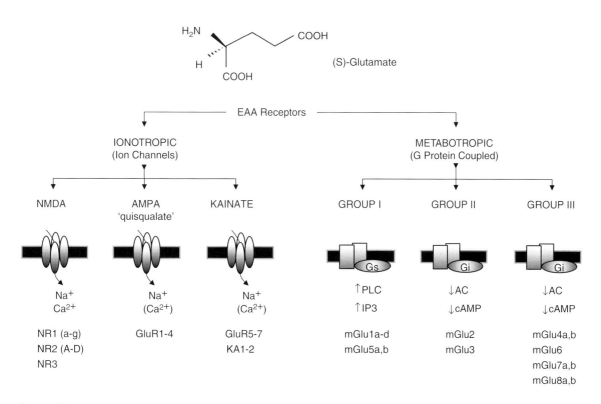

Fig. 1. Glutamate receptor classification and signalling pathways. Ionotropic glutamate receptors are divided into NMDA, AMPA, and kainate. The subunits that heterodimerise to form the ion channels are indicated. Metabotropic receptors are divided into Groups I, II and III. While Group I mGlu receptors stimulation PLC, the Groups II and III mGlu receptors inhibit AC.

mechanisms may alter receptor function by changing ion gating properties, intracellular coupling efficiencies, receptor desensitisation rates, pharmacological profiles and/or trafficking to synaptic membranes. The mRNAs and proteins encoding glutamate receptors differentially spread throughout the CNS creating further diversity at the level of temporal and spatial expression. At a subcellular level glutamate receptors may be found within cell bodies, axons, dendrites and spines and can be clustered at pre-, post- and/or extra-synaptic sites. As an example Group I mGluRs are located post-synaptically whereas Groups II and III mGluRs are mainly pre-synaptic (Cartmell and Schoepp, 2000; Ferraguti and Shigemoto, 2006). Furthermore a proportion of glutamate receptors are thought to be located in intracellular pools ready for delivery to the synaptic membrane (e.g. see, Henley, 1994).

III. Glutamate receptor structure

Ionotropic glutamate receptors are oligomeric membrane proteins assembled around a central ion-conducting pore (Bettler and Mulle, 1995). These receptors are considered to be teteromeric assemblies comprising more than one type of subunit (Kew and Kemp, 2005). While the subunits of NMDA, AMPA and kainite do not interact outside their own subgroups, they do homo- or hetero-dimerise within each group. NMDA, AMPA and KA receptors can form ion channels with multiple subunit combinations where the subunit composition can alter the ion gating and pharmacological properties. The subunit composition of ionotropic glutamate receptors varies depending on development stage, brain area and brain cell type (Sommer and Seeburg,

1992; Hollmann and Heinemann, 1994; Nakanishi and Masu, 1994).

NMDA receptors that comprise NR1 and NR2 gate Na^{2+} and Ca^{2+} ions, but the presence of NR3 subunits suppresses NMDA channel conductance and Ca^{2+} permeability. The NR1 subunit is essential for channel function, whereas the NR2 subunit regulates channel gating and Mg^{2+} dependency (Monyer et al., 1992). In adult forebrain, regions such as the hippocampus and cortex express NR2A and NR2B subunits which are available to form an NMDA receptor complex with the NR1 subunit. The recombinant NR1–NR2B complex in vitro shows longer excitatory post-synaptic potentials (EPSPs) than does the NR1–NR2A complex (Monyer et al., 1994). Interestingly, NR2B expression is downregulated during transition from juvenile to adult (Sheng et al., 1994; Okabe et al., 1998) correlating with the gradual shortening of EPSP duration of the NMDA channel (Carmignoto and Vicini, 1992; Hestrin, 1992). This lack of NR2B could decrease NMDA-mediated plasticity, and perhaps explains the decreased memory performance in adult animals including humans (Tang et al., 1999).

AMPA receptors can also gate Na^{2+} and Ca^{2+} ions. However, the presence of a GluR2 subunit (an arginine edited version) found in a majority of AMPA receptors prevents permeability to Ca^{2+} (Seeburg, 1996). AMPA receptors lacking edited GluR2, with high Ca^{2+} permeability, are found in inhibitory interneurones of the hippocampus and amygdale (Burnashev, 1996). KA receptors also gate Na^{2+} and may allow flow of Ca^{2+}, again dependent on the subunit composition of the receptor. The composition of native KA receptors remain unclear, however, it is known that GluR5, 6 and 7 subunits can form functional homomeric receptors. In contrast, KA1 and KA2 subunits do not form functional homomeric receptors; however, the addition of these subunits alters pharmacological properties increasing affinity for KA, possibly indicating high affinity binding sites on these particular subunits.

In contrast to AMPA and KA receptors, the NMDA receptor requires the binding of glycine in addition to the binding of glutamate for activation. In the NMDA receptor complex, the binding of glycine occurs to NR1 subunits and binding of glutamate to NR2 subunits. It is thought that NMDA receptor activation requires occupation of a total of two glycine and two glutamate molecules such that an NMDA receptor is likely composed of at least two NR1 and two NR2 subunits that assemble in a tetramer.

The classical four trans-membrane domain (T-MD) model characterized previously for nicotinic acetylcholine and γ-amino-n-butyric acid (GABA$_A$) receptor subunits has proved inconsistent for glutamate ionotropic receptors (Hollmann et al., 1989; Keinanen et al., 1990). Ionotropic glutamate receptors subunits have three T-MDs with a second re-entrant membrane domain not crossing the membrane but rather lining the membrane close to the intracellular surface. Importantly, an odd number of trans-membrane crossings places the C-terminus intracellularly (see Fig. 2). This allows the C-terminus to be phosphorylated by a variety of kinases, act as a protein–protein interaction motif and play an important role in receptor signalling and trafficking (Dev et al., 2004).

The mGluRs subfamily have a large extracellular N-terminus that creates a glutamate binding pocket, an extracellular cysteine rich region, seven transmembrane domains and an intracellular C-terminus domain, see Fig. 2 (Pin and Acher, 2002; Kew and Kemp, 2005). Similar to ionotropic receptors the C-terminus is phosphorylated by a variety of kinases and plays a role in protein–protein interaction, signalling and receptor cycling (Dev et al., 2001). mGluRs are know to homodimerise and it is thought that agonist binding induces homodimerisation which triggers intracellular signalling (Jingami, 2005) where the occupation of both glutamate binding pockets in a homodimer is required for full activity (Kniazeff et al., 2004).

IV. Advancing glutamate receptor research in anxiety: selective molecules and mutant animals

As glutamate is key to orchestrating fast synaptic neurotransmission, there has been traditionally a reluctance to target glutamate neurotransmission for the chronic treatment of psychiatric disorders

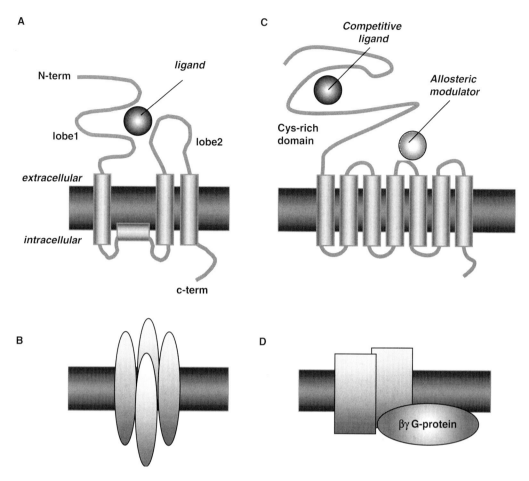

Fig. 2. Structure and assembly of glutamate receptors. Ionotropic glutamate receptors are three transmembrane proteins with a re-entrant loop (A) that homo- or hetero-dimerise to from a ion gated ligand channel (B). Metabotropic receptors are seven transmembrane proteins (C) that dimerise on ligand binding to activate intracellular signals via G-proteins (D).

due to feasibility and safety concerns (Holden, 2003). However, given the diversity of the iono-tropic and mGluRs, it is becoming clear that manipulation of this system by selective activation or antagonism may have potential to modify anxiety responses. Moreover, the characterisation of modulatory sites on ionotropic glutamate receptors and identification of metabotropic receptors has suggested many potential targets for drug development. The availability of selective, systemically active pharmacological tools for NMDA, AMPA and KA receptors in addition to Group I, and Group II receptors and more recently Group III metabotropic receptors

(see Tables 1 and 2) has been a major facilitator in the process of dissecting the relative contribution of various glutamate receptor and receptor subunits in anxiety (Schoepp, 2001; Spooren et al., 2003). Given the success of allosteric modulators for the $GABA_A$ receptor, that is benzodiazepines, it is not surprising that discovery of allosteric sites on NMDA, AMPA and KA receptors has been pursued. Allosteric modulators both positive and negative differ from full agonists/antagonists, in that they only operate under tonic control of glutamate, in a use-dependent manner. Hence it is widely thought they will have much lower side-effect liability and potentially avoid receptor

Table 1. Pharmacology of ionotropic glutamate receptors

Drug action	Receptor	Drug name	Reference
NMDA			
Agonists	NR1 glycine site	D-serine	
	NR2 glutamate site	NMDA	
Antagonists	NR1 glycine site	Kynurenic acid	Jane et al. (1994)
	NR2 glutamate site	DAP5	
	NR2B selective	Ifenprodil	Williams (1993)
	NR2A selective	PEAQX	Auberson et al. (2002)
Channel blockers	Ketamine, phencyclidine, dizocilpine (MK-801)		Wong et al. (1986)
Positive modulators	Polyamines (spermine, spermidine)		Ransom and Stec (1988)
	Pregnenolone		Malayev et al. (2002)
AMPA			
Agonists	5-Fluorowillardiine		Wong et al. (1994)
Antagonists	CNQX		Drejer and Honore (1988)
	NBQX		Sheardown et al. (1990)
Non-competitive antagonist	GYKI53773		Ruel et al. (2002)
Positive modulators	Cyclothiazide		Partin et al. (1993)
	Aniracetam		Ito et al. (1990)
Kainate			
Agonists	ATPA		Clarke et al. (1997)
	(S)-5-iodowillardiine		Swanson et al. (1998)
Antagonists	UBP296		More et al. (2004)
	NS3763		Christensen et al. (2004)
Positive modulators	Concanavalin A		Lerma et al. (2001)

Key compounds for NMDA, AMPA and kainate receptors are listed. Some compounds may be highly selective whereas others show pan-receptor activity. For example CNQX is an inhibitor of both AMPA and kainite receptors, with only fivefold selectivity toward AMPA receptors. Compounds such as cyclothiazide, the GYKI compounds and aniracetam may show further selectivity toward particular subunits and splice isoforms.

Abbreviations: DAP5: (R)-2-amino-5-phosphonopentanoate; CNQX: cyano-7-nitroquinoxaline-2,3-dione; NBQX: 6-nitro-7-sulphamoylbenzo (f) quinoxaline-2-3-dione; GYKI 53773/LY300164: (R)-7-acetyl-5-(4-aminophenyl)-8,9-dihydro-8-methyl-7H-1,3-dioxolo (4,5-h) (2,3) benzodiazepine; ATPA: 5-*tert*-butyl-4-isoxazolepropionic acid; UBP296: (R,S)-3-(2-carboxybenzyl) willardiine; NS3763: 5-carboxyl-2,4-di-benzamidobenzoic acid.

desensitisation, and loss of the neuronal activity dependence of receptor activation by pulsatile release of neurotransmitter. In glutamate research, this is one of the most exciting areas in drug development today for the treatment of chronic disorders such as anxiety (Foster and Kemp, 2006; Marino and Conn, 2006). Indeed, the NR2B antagonists appear to act as negative allosteric modulators (Gogas, 2006). Negative allosteric modulators for the AMPA receptor have also been discovered, for example GYKI 52466 (Ruel et al., 2002). However, it is allosteric modulation of metabotropic receptors that has emerged as one of the most promising areas for the development of novel therapeutics (Gasparini et al., 2002; Kew,

2004; Marino and Conn, 2006). Translating such advances in medicinal chemistry and molecular pharmacology into potential drug treatments relies entirely on the availability of suitable anxiety models predictive of anxiolytic function.

In the past decade, there has been an explosion in the use of mice in neuropsychiatric research. The major driving force behind this trend has been the development and application of novel molecular technologies, such as gene targeting, which enable researchers to engineer precise genetic alterations to study the neural basis of behaviour (Crawley, 2000; Tecott, 2003; Holmes et al., 2004; Cryan and Holmes, 2005). Surprisingly, data does not exist in the public domain for potential anxiety

Table 2. Pharmacology of metabotropic glutamate receptors

Drug action	Receptor	Drug name	Reference
Group I mGluR			
Agonists	Non-selective	DHPG	Schoepp et al. (1994)
	mGluR5	CHPG	Doherty et al. (1997)
Antagonists	mGluR1	4CPG	Thomsen et al. (1994)
Negative modulator	mGluR1	CPCCOEt	Annoura et al. (1996)
	mGluR5	MPEP	Gasparini et al. (1999b)
		MTEP	Cosford et al. (2003)
Positive modulator	mGluR1	Ro 67-7476	Knoflach et al. (2001)
	mGluR5	DFB	O'Brien et al. (2003)
		CPPHA	O'Brien et al. (2004)
Group II mGluR			
Agonists	mGluR2 and 3	LY354740	Monn et al. (1997)
Antagonists	mGluR2 and 3	LY341495	Kingston et al. (1998)
Positive modulator	mGluR2	LY487379	Johnson et al. (2003)
Group III mGluR			
Agonists	mGluR4, 6 and 8	S-AP4	Schoepp et al. (1999)
	mGluR6	S-homo-AMPA	Ahmadian et al. (1997)
	mGluR7	AMN082	Mitsukawa et al. (2005)
	mGluR8	PPG	Gasparini et al. (1999a)
	mGluR8	DCPG	Thomas et al. (2001)
Antagonists		CPPG, MSOP	Schoepp et al. (1999)
Positive modulators	mGluR4	PHCCC	Maj et al. (2003)

Listed are some of drugs which have helped to define the function of Group I–III metabotropic glutamate receptors. Some compounds listed are highly selective whereas others show only tenfold selectivity against other family members. For example, LY341495 is also an antagonist at Group I and Group III mGluRs (Kingston et al., 1998) DFB and CPPHA are also weak antagonists at both mGluR4 and mGluR8 (O'Brien et al., 2003, 2004). PHCCG is also a weak antagonist at mGluR1 (Annoura et al., 1996) and MPEP at relatively high doses has been reported to be a positive modulator of mGluR4 (Mathiesen et al., 2003).

Abbreviations: (S)-DHPG: (S)-3,5-dihydroxyphenylglycine; CHPG: (R,S)-2-chloro-5-hydroxyphenylglycine; (S)-4CPG: (S)-4-carboxyphenylglycine; CPCCOEt: 7-hydroxyiminocyclopropan[b]chromen-1a-carboxylic acid ethyl ester; MPEP: 2-methyl-6-(phenylethynyl)-pyridine; MTEP: 3-[2-methyl-1, 3-thiazol-4-yl)ethynyl]pyridine; Ro 67-7476: (S)-2-(4-fluoro-phenyl)-1-(toluene-4-sulfonyl)-pyrrolidine; DFB: 3,3'-difluorobenzaldazine; CPPHA: N-{4-chloro-2-[(1,3-dioxo-1,3-dihydro-2H-isoindol-2-yl)methyl]phenyl}-2-hydroxybenzamide; LY354740: (1S,2S,5R,6S)-2-amino-bicyclo[3.1.0]hexane-2, 6-di-carboxylic acid; LY341495: 2S-2-amino-2-(1S,2S-2-carboxycycloprop-1-yl)-3-(xanth-9-yl) propanoic acid; Ro 67-6221: 3-(4-oxo-7-phenylethynyl-4, 5-dihydro-3H-benzo[b][1,4]diazepin-2-yl)-benzonitrile; LY487379: N-(4-(2-methoxyphenoxy) phenyl)-N-(2,2,2-trifluoroethylsulfonyl)prid-3-ylmethylamine; S-AP4: (S)-4-Phosphono-2-aminobutyric acid; S-homo-AMPA: (S)-2-amino-4-(3-hydroxy-5-methylisoxazol-4-yl)butyric acid; PPG: (R,S)-4-phospho-nophenylglycine; DCPG: (S)-3,4-dicarboxyphenylglycine; CPPG: (R,S)-α-cyclopropyl-4-phosphonophenylglycine; MSOP: (R,S)-α-methylserine-O-phosphate; (−)-PHCCC: (−)-N-Phenyl-7-(hydroximino)-cyclopropa-[b]-chromen-1a-carboxamide.

phenotypes of all of the glutamate receptors. However, given the rich pharmacology of glutamate receptors, genetically modified mice have largely focused on receptors and receptor subtypes where no distinct antagonist pharmacological tool exists. That said there are major caveats which arise when using knockout animals. Behavioural analysis of genetically modified mice can uncover unexpected compensations, effects on other gene products, altered endocrine and neuronal feedback loops, as there is a lack of control over the temporal and spatial impact of the genetic manipulation (Crawley, 2000; Pfaff, 2001; Cryan and Mombereau, 2004). Epigenetic and environmental factors may result in ectopic expression of other proteins which may markedly influence behaviour. Thus, it is also possible that the direction of a behavioural change in a conventional mutant animal may not be in agreement with acute pharmacological manipulation of the very same protein. This is especially pertinent to studies investigating genetic alterations in the glutamatergic system which is so important for many aspects of neurotransmission. One example of this occurs in the schizophrenia field where mice lacking mGluR5 receptors have marked behavioural deficits in prepulse inhibition of the startle reflex which is not recapitulated by mGluR5 antagonists (Brody et al., 2004; Brody and Geyer, 2004). Thus there has been a strong impetus to develop methods for knocking down genes in the brain in adult animals. Short interfering RNA (siRNA) technology has emerged as a potentially exciting method to overcome such problems (Thakker et al., 2006; Cryan et al., 2007). We have recently developed a method for widespread siRNA-induced knockdown in the adult mouse brain (Thakker et al., 2004). Moreover, we have applied it successfully to the behavioural analysis of animals with knockdown of a variety of genes (Thakker et al., 2004, 2005; Senechal et al., 2007) including those for the Group III mGluR7 (Fendt et al., 2007).

It should also be noted that anxiety phenotypes are not always bidirectional. Mice deficient in mGluR2 do not have an anxiety phenotype in the elevated plus maze and thus if one relied only on such evidence for target validation there is a risk of generating false negative results. The same also applies to pharmacology as mGluR2 antagonists are without effect in this test too, although agonists have anxiolytic effects.

There is no scope in this article to focus in any depth on the individual animal models that are widely used to assess different aspects of anxiety. The variety of knockout animals for glutamate receptors that have been tested in anxiety related tasks is highlighted in Table 3. The reader is also refereed to recent review articles on this topic (Belzung and Griebel, 2001; Holmes, 2001; Shekhar et al., 2001; Graeff and Zangrossi, 2002; Finn et al., 2003; Cryan and Holmes, 2005).

V. Animal models of anxiety

In general, many animal models of anxiety disorders, used in glutamate research today, take advantage of the natural behavioural patterns of rats and mice to develop ethologically based behavioural tasks (Rodgers et al., 1997). Most popular among these are the so-called exploratory 'approach-avoidance' tasks (Cryan and Holmes, 2005). Small rodents have an innate aversion to exposed, well-lit spaces yet they also are naturally foraging, exploratory species and exploration-based tasks exploit the conflicting tendencies to approach versus avoid a potentially dangerous area. The aversive area takes different forms in different tests, including: (i) open, elevated arms (elevated plus-maze), (ii) open, elevated quadrants (elevated zero-maze), (iii) a light compartment/arena (light/dark exploration test, dark/light emergence test), (iv) a staircase (staircase test) or (v) the central area of a brightly-lit open field (open field test) (for a fuller description of these tests (see Belzung and Griebel, 2001; Holmes, 2001; Cryan and Holmes, 2005). Avoidance behaviours are reduced by treatment with clinically efficacious anxiolytics, although principally the benzodiazepines which include diazepam (Rodgers, 1997). The same logic is extended to the interpretation of phenotypic abnormalities in mutant mice on these tests. For example, a decreased avoidance of threatening areas in the apparatus, where mutant mice spend more time (compared to control mice) in the open arms of the elevated plus-maze is interpreted as a reduced anxiety-like behaviour or an anxiolytic-like phenotype. In addition, because avoidance behaviour can be augmented by drugs with pro-anxiety effects in humans, these tests are also used to assess heightened anxiety-like phenotypes following genetic or pharmacological manipulations.

Punishment-based conflict procedures in rats have been employed for over 40 years in the identification and characterisation of anxiolytic agents (Geller and Seifter, 1960) and have been among the first employed to assess the role of glutamate in anxiety. The punished drinking test originated by Vogel and colleagues is among the most widely used and is particular sensitive to glutamatergic manipulations (Millan and Brocco, 2003). In this test, rodents are provided with a drinking spout that delivers a mild shock after every 20 licks (Vogel et al., 1971). Reference anxiolytics, attenuate the shock-induced suppression of drinking (Vogel et al., 1971). In addition, defensive burying tests, either of shock probes or marbles, are often used to assess potential anxiolytic

Table 3. Anxiety in glutamate receptor mutant mice

Mouse	Effect on anxiety	Tests used	Reference
Ionotropic receptors			
NR2A	Decreased anxiety	Light–dark test	Boyce-Rustay and Holmes (2006)
NR2A	Decreased anxiety	Elevated plus maze	Boyce-Rustay and Holmes (2006)
NR2A	Decreased anxiety	Open field test	Boyce-Rustay and Holmes (2006)
NR2A	No effect	Elevated plus maze	Moriya et al. (2000)
NR2A	No effect	Open field test	Moriya et al. (2000)
NR2C	No effect	Elevated plus maze	Moriya et al. (2000)
NR2C	No effect	Open field test	Moriya et al. (2000)
NR2A/NR2C	No effect	Elevated plus maze	Moriya et al. (2000)
NR2A/NR2C	No effect	Open field test	Moriya et al. (2000)
NR2C-2B mutant mice[a]	Increased anxiety	Elevated plus maze	De Souza Silva et al. (2006)
GluR1	Increased anxiety	Elevated plus maze	Mead et al. (2006)
GluR1	Increased anxiety	Novelty suppressed drinking	Bannerman et al. (2004)
GluR1	Increased anxiety	Light–dark test	Bannerman et al. (2004)
GluR2	Decreased anxiety	Elevated plus maze	Mead et al. (2006)
Metabotropic receptors			
mGluR2	No effect	Elevated plus maze	Linden et al. (2005b)
mGluR3	No effect	Elevated plus maze	Linden et al. (2005b)
mGluR5	Decreased anxiety	Stress-induced hyperthermia	Brodkin et al. (2002a)
mGluR7	Decreased anxiety	Elevated plus maze	Cryan et al. (2003) and Callaerts-Vegh et al. (2006)
mGluR7	Decreased anxiety	Light–dark test	Cryan et al. (2003)
mGluR7	Decreased anxiety	Stress-induced hyperthermia	Cryan et al. (2003)
mGluR7	Decreased anxiety	Staircase test	Cryan et al. (2003)
mGluR7	Decreased anxiety	Marble burying	Callaerts-Vegh et al. (2006)
mGluR8	Increased anxiety	Elevated plus maze	Linden et al. (2002), Duvoisin et al. (2005) and Robbins et al. (2007)
mGluR8	Increased anxiety	Open field test	Duvoisin et al. (2005) and Robbins et al. (2007)
Others: glutamatergic system			
Grin1D481N	Decreased anxiety	Light–dark test	Kew et al. (2000)
VGluT1 +/−	Increased anxiety	Light–dark test	Tordera et al. (2007)
VGluT1 +/−	No effect	Elevated plus maze	Tordera et al. (2007)

[a]These mice have been modified to have NR2C replaced by NR2B during development.

agents. In these tests the animals who are more anxious must engage in active behaviours, such as defensive burying which is in contrast to that in approach avoidance tasks where anxious animals engage in passive behaviours to avoid anxiogenic stimuli (e.g. avoid open arms of elevated plus maze) (Jacobson et al., 2007).

Two other naturalistic tests for mouse anxiety-like behaviour have been widely used in testing glutamatergic manipulations. Adult rodents hear and emit ultrasound vocalisations (USVs) above the audible frequency range and, interestingly, fear and anxiety-like responses have been related to certain characteristic ultrasonic vocalisation frequencies (typically 20–30 kHz) (Miczek et al., 1995; Sanchez, 2003; Litvin et al., 2006). In rats, stressful/anxiety-provoking manipulations can induce such USVs in an anxiolytic-reversible manner (Miczek et al., 1995; Sanchez, 2003). Moreover, separation of young mouse pups from their mother also evokes USVs. These USVs can be attenuated by modulators of glutamatergic neurotransmission (e.g. Kehne et al., 1991).

Another innate response shown by mice that has potential applicability as a quantifiable assay for anxiety-related phenotypes is the increase in core body temperature and autonomic arousal following exposure to stress. Methods have been successfully developed for assessing autonomic responses to fear- and anxiety-provoking stimuli via radiotelemetry (Salas et al., 2003; Adriaan Bouwknecht et al., 2007). Radiotelemetry uses radiowaves to assess a variety of physiologiocal parameters online and in real time. Less technically-demanding, the stress-induced hyperthermia (SIH) paradigm, quantifies the degree of hyperthermia elicited by an acute mild stress, namely, the rectal insertion of temperature probe (Adriaan Bouwknecht et al., 2007). The degree of SIH is attenuated by anxiolytics (Adriaan Bouwknecht et al., 2007).

VI. Modelling cognitive dysfunction in anxiety

The use of models that focus on the cognitive dysfunctions in anxiety has increased over the past decade. This work has been fuelled by realisation from neuroimaging studies in humans which demonstrate that the neural mechanisms and structures underlying these processes in rodents have been in part evolutionary conserved and include brain areas such as the amygdala, hippocampus and prefrontal cortex (LeDoux, 2000; Cryan and Holmes, 2005). Cognitive disturbances including misappraisal and over-attention to threatening stimuli are seen in panic disorder, generalised anxiety disorder and phobias, while traumatic memories are a major feature of post-traumatic stress disorder (American Psychiatric Association, 1994; Lang et al., 2000). Glutamatergic neurotransmission underlies synaptic plasticity associated with learning and memory (Day et al., 2003; Riedel et al., 2003), so it comes as no surprise that much efforts are focused on unravelling its role in cognitive tasks relevant to anxiety.

Insights into emotional cognition in rodents has centred on certain well-established paradigms such as Pavlovian fear conditioning (Davis, 1990; Fendt and Fanselow, 1999; Maren, 2001) based on the classical work of Pavlov (1927). This model measures fear-related behaviours induced by exposure to a previously innocuous stimulus (e.g. auditory tone) that has been associated through repeated pairings with an innately aversive stimulus (e.g. footshock). Evolution has favoured this form of learning as a means to rapidly learn about environmental stimuli that signal danger, and it is an essential component of many mammalian defensive behaviour systems (Maren, 2001). In the laboratory, the degree of conditioned fear can be readily quantified via a variety of behaviours, such as freezing, startle, tachycardia, defensive burying and ultrasonic vocalisation (Davis, 1990; Fendt and Fanselow, 1999; Maren, 2001; Stiedl et al., 2005). Failure to extinguish learned fear responses is another major feature of post-traumatic stress disorder, phobias and other anxiety disorders, which is readily studied (Barad, 2005; Davis et al., 2006a, b; Myers and Davis, 2007). Supporting the strong potential of fear extinction as a translational model of anxiety, Davis and colleagues have recently shown that drugs which activate the glycine cite of NMDA receptors (D-cycloserine) receptors, can facilitate extinction leaning in mice and also promote the extinction of phobias in a clinical population (Ressler et al., 2004; Ledgerwood et al., 2005). It is also becoming evident that selective targeting of other glutamate receptors (e.g. mGluR7) will play a role in facilitating fear extinction and thus potentially have utility as an adjunct to psychotherapy for a variety of anxiety disorders (Fendt et al., 2007).

VII. Pharmacology of glutamate in animal models of anxiety

Tables 4 and 5 collates studies which have used glutamatergic ligands in a variety of animal models for assessing anxiolytic activity over the past 25 years (1982–April 2007), while every effort has been made to make these tables as complete as possible we cannot exclude the possibility that some studies are inadvertently overlooked and

Table 4. Ionotropic glutamate receptor drugs in anxiety models

Drug name	Effect	Tests used	Reference
NMDA receptor competitive antagonists			
CPP	Anxiolytic	Punished responding in pigeons	Koek and Colpaert (1991)
CPP	Anxiolytic	Fear potentiated startle	Anthony and Nevins (1993)
CGS 19755	Anxiolytic	Punished responding in pigeons	Koek and Colpaert (1991)
CGP 37849	Anxiolytic	Vogel test	Plaznik et al. (1994) and Przegalinski et al. (1996)
CGP 37849	Anxiolytic	Open field test	Plaznik et al. (1994)
CGP 39551	Anxiolytic	Vogel test	Plaznik et al. (1994)
CGP 39551	No effect	Open field test	Plaznik et al. (1994)
NPC 12626	Anxiolytic	Geller–Seifter test	Wiley et al. (1992)
NPC 17742	Anxiolytic	Elevated plus maze	Wiley et al. (1995)
AP-7	Anxiolytic	4-Plate test; Elevated plus maze	Stephens et al. (1986)
AP-7	Anxiolytic	Vogel test	Plaznik et al. (1994)
AP7	Anxiolytic	Open field test	Plaznik et al. (1994)
AP7	Anxiolytic	Fear potentiated startle	Anthony and Nevins (1993)
AP7 (intra-dlPAG)	Anxiolytic	Elevated plus maze	Guimaraes et al. (1991)
AP7 (intra-dlPAG)	Anxiolytic	Vogel test	Molchanov and Guimaraes (2002)
AP5	Anxiolytic	Separation-induced vocalisations	Kehne et al. (1991)
AP5 (intra-BLA)	Anxiolytic	Social interaction	Sajdyk and Shekhar (1997)
AP5 (intra-DMH)	Anxiolytic	Panic-induced social interaction	Johnson and Shekhar (2006)
MDL 100,453	Anxiolytic	Separation-induced vocalisations	Kehne et al. (1991)
LY235959	Anxiolytic	Stress-induced hyperthermia	Rorick-Kehn et al. (2005)
NMDA receptor non-competitive antagonists			
PCP	No effect	Punished responding in pigeons	Koek and Colpaert (1991)
PCP	Anxiolytic	Geller–Seifter test	Wiley et al. (1992)
Ketamine	No effect	Punished responding in pigeons	Koek and Colpaert (1991)
Ketamine	No effect	Elevated plus maze	Becker et al. (2003)
Ketamine	Anxiolytic	Conditioned freezing	Pietersen et al. (2006)
MK-801	Anxiolytic	Conditioned emotional response	Clineschmidt (1982) and Clineschmidt et al. (1982)
MK-801	Anxiolytic	Vogel test	Clineschmidt (1982) and Clineschmidt et al. (1982)
MK 801	No effect	Punished responding in pigeons	Koek and Colpaert (1991)
MK 801	Anxiolytic	Separation induced vocalisations	Kehne et al. (1991)
MK 801	Anxiolytic	Vogel test	Plaznik et al. (1994)
NMDA (Intra-dlPAG)	Anxiogenic	Elevated T-maze	Bertoglio and Zangrossi (2006)
Kynurenic acid	No effect	Punished responding in pigeons	Koek and Colpaert (1991)
NMDA receptor glycine site			
MRZ21576	No effect	Vogel test	Karcz-Kubicha et al. (1997)
MRZ21576	No effect	Elevated plus maze	Karcz-Kubicha et al. (1997)
D-cycloserine	No effect	Stress-induced hyperthermia	Rorick-Kehn et al. (2005)
D-cycloserine	Anxiolytic	Elevated plus maze	Karcz-Kubicha et al. (1997)
D-cycloserine	Anxiolytic	Fear potentiated startle	Anthony and Nevins (1993)
L-701,324	No effect	Vogel test	Karcz-Kubicha et al. (1997)
L-701,324	Anxiolytic	Elevated plus maze	Karcz-Kubicha et al. (1997)
(+R)-HA-966	Anxiolytic	Elevated plus maze	Karcz-Kubicha et al. (1997)
(+R)-HA-966	Anxiolytic	Fear potentiated startle	Anthony and Nevins (1993)
SSR504734	Anxiolytic	Separation induced vocalisations	Depoortere et al. (2005)
7-Chlorokynurenate	No effect	Punished responding in pigeons	Koek and Colpaert (1991)
7-Chlorokynurenate	Anxiolytic	Fear potentiated startle	Anthony and Nevins (1993)
ACPC	No effect	Vogel test	Karcz-Kubicha et al. (1997)
ACPC	Anxiolytic	Elevated plus maze	Trullas et al. (1989)

Table 4 (*continued*)

Drug name	Effect	Tests used	Reference
ACPC	Anxiolytic	Vogel test	Chojnacka-Wojcik et al. (1996) and Przegalinski et al. (1996, 1999)
ACPC	Anxiolytic	Fear potentiated startle	Anthony and Nevins (1993)
ACPC	No effect	Punished responding in pigeons	Koek and Colpaert (1991)
5,7-Dichlorokynurenic acid	Anxiolytic	Separation-induced vocalisations	Kehne et al. (1991)
5,7-Dichlorokynurenic acid	Anxiolytic	Vogel test	Plaznik et al. (1994)
NMDA-R magnesium site			
Mg^{2+}	Anxiolytic	Elevated plus maze	Poleszak et al. (2004)
NMDA-R polyamine site			
Ifenprodil	No effect	Punished responding in pigeons	Koek and Colpaert (1991)
Ifenprodil	No effect	Light–dark box	Mikolajczak et al. (2003)
Ifenprodil	No effect	Graded anxiety test	Dere et al. (2003)
Ifenprodil	Anxiolytic	Light–dark box	Fraser et al. (1996)
Eliprodil	No effect	Geller–Seifter test	Wiley et al. (1998)
AMPA receptor agonists			
LY451646	No effect	Stress-induced hyperthermia	Rorick-Kehn et al. (2005)
CX546	No effect	Stress-induced hyperthermia	Iijima et al. (2007)
AMPA/kainate receptor antagonist			
S-AMPA (icv)	No effect	Vogel test	Czlonkowska et al. (1997)
LY293558	Anxiolytic	Vogel test	Alt et al. (2006)
LY293558	Anxiolytic	Punished responding in pigeons	Benvenga et al. (1995)
LY326325	Anxiogenic	Elevated plus maze	Alt et al. (2006)
LY326325 (intra-PAG)	Anxiolytic	Vogel test	Kotlinska and Liljequist (1998)
LY326325	Anxiolytic	Elevated plus maze	Kotlinska and Liljequist (1998)
GYKI 52466	No effect	Vogel test	Czlonkowska et al. (1997)
GYKI 52466	Anxiolytic	Stress-induced hyperthermia	Rorick-Kehn et al. (2005)
GYKI 53655	No effect	Vogel test	Alt et al. (2006)
CNQX (intra-BLA)	Anxiolytic	Social interaction	Sajdyk and Shekhar (1997)
CNQX (intra-Septal)	Anxiolytic	Elevated plus maze	Menard and Treit (2000)
CNQX (intra-Septal)	Anxiolytic	Defensive Probe burying	Menard and Treit (2000)
CNQX (intra-DMH)	No effect	Panic-induced social interaction	Johnson and Shekhar (2006)
CNQX (intra-PAG)	Anxiolytic	Elevated plus maze	Matheus and Guimaraes (1997)
CNQX (intra-amygdala)	Anxiolytic	Fear potentiated startle	Kim et al. (1993)
CNQX	No effect	Vogel test	Czlonkowska et al. (1997)
DNQX	No effect	Vogel test	Czlonkowska et al. (1997)
NBQX	Anxiolytic	4-Plate test	Turski et al. (1992)
NBQX	No effect	Vogel test	Czlonkowska et al. (1997)
LY382884 (GLURk5 antagonist)	Anxiolytic	Vogel test	Alt et al. (2007)
LY382884	No effect	Stress-induced hyperthermia	Rorick-Kehn et al. (2005)

apologise in advance. On first inspection two facts emerge: the vast number of different ligands, which target different aspects of glutamatergic neurotransmission, with anxiolytic potential is quite astounding. Secondly, there are limited reports of glutamate ligands that actually increase anxiety. Thirdly, there appears to be many discrepancies; whereas some studies suggest a role for a given receptor in anxiety behaviour others fail to do so. With regard to the first two points

Table 5. Metabotropic glutamate receptor drugs in anxiety models

Selective compounds			
Drug name	Effect	Tests used	Reference
MGluR 1 antagonist			
AIDA	Anxiolytic	Elevated plus maze	Klodzinska et al. (2004b)
AIDA	Anxiolytic	Vogel test	Klodzinska et al. (2004b)
CPCCOEt (intra-amygdala)	No effect	Vogel test	Stachowicz et al. (2004)
CPCCOEt (intra-hippocampal)	Anxiolytic	Vogel test	Tatarczynska et al. (2001b)
(s)-4CPG (intra-hippocampal)	Anxiolytic	Vogel test	Tatarczynska et al. (2001b)
LY456236	Anxiolytic	Vogel test	Varty et al. (2005)
LY456236	Anxiolytic	Stress-induced hyperthermia	Rorick-Kehn et al. (2005)
LY456236	Anxiolytic	Conditioned lick suppression	Varty et al. (2005)
JNJ16259685	Anxiolytic	Lick suppression	Steckler et al. (2005a)
JNJ16259685	No effect	Elevated zero maze	Steckler et al. (2005a)
EMQMCM	Anxiolytic	Contextual freezing	Pietraszek et al. (2005)
EMQMCM	Anxiolytic	Fear potentiated startle	Pietraszek et al. (2005)
EMQMCM	No effect	Elevated plus maze	Pietraszek et al. (2005)
EMQMCM	No effect	Geller–Seifter conflict test	Pietraszek et al. (2005)
MGluR2 agonist			
LY354740	Anxiolytic	Elevated plus maze	Monn et al. (1997) and Helton et al. (1998)
LY354740	Anxiolytic	Stress-induced hyperthermia	Rorick-Kehn et al. (2005)
LY354740	Anxiolytic	Fear potentiated startle	Helton et al. (1998)
LY354740	Anxiolytic	Vogel test	Klodzinska et al. (1999)
LY354740	Anxiolytic	Panic-induced social interaction test	Shekhar and Keim (2000)
LY354740	No effect	Marble burying	Shimazaki et al. (2004)
LY354740 (intra-hippocampal)	Anxiolytic	Vogel test	Tatarczynska et al. (2001b)
LY314582	Anxiolytic	Stress-induced hyperthermia	Spooren et al. (2002)
(2S,1′S,2′S,3′R)-2-(2′-carboxy-3′-methylcyclopropyl) glycine	Anxiolytic	Fear potentiated startle	Collado et al. (2004)
L-CCG-I (intra-hippocampal)	Anxiolytic	Elevated plus maze	Smialowska et al. (2006)
L-CCG-I (intra-hippocampal)	Anxiolytic	Vogel test	Tatarczynska et al. (2001b)
LY404039	Anxiolytic	Fear potentiated startle	Rorick-Kehn et al. (2007)
LY404039	Anxiolytic	Marble burying	Rorick-Kehn et al. (2007)
4-APPES	Anxiolytic	Fear potentiated startle	Johnson et al. (2005)
4-MPPTS	Anxiolytic	Fear potentiated startle	Johnson et al. (2005)
CBiPES	Anxiolytic	Stress-induced hyperthermia	Johnson et al. (2005)
MGS0008	No effect	Stress-induced hyperthermia	Iijima et al. (2007)
LY544344	Anxiolytic	Stress-induced hyperthermia	Rorick-Kehn et al. (2006)
LY544344	Anxiolytic	Fear-induced suppression of operant behavior	Rorick-Kehn et al. (2006)
BINA	Anxiolytic	Stress-induced hyperthermia	Galici et al. (2006)
BINA	Anxiolytic	Elevated plus maze	Galici et al. (2006)

Table 5 (*continued*)

	Selective compounds		
Drug name	Effect	Tests used	Reference
LY566332	Anxiolytic	Stress-induced hyperthermia	Rorick-Kehn et al. (2005)
mGluR2 antagonist			
MGS0039	Anxiolytic	Marble-burying test	Shimazaki et al. (2004)
MGS0039	Anxiolytic	Conditioned fear stress	Yoshimizu et al. (2006)
MGS0039	Anxiolytic	Stress-induced hyperthermia	Iijima ct al. (2007)
MGS0039	Anxiolytic	Stress-induced hyperthermia	Iijima et al. (2007)
MGS0039	No effect	Elevated plus-maze	Chaki et al. (2004)
MGS0039	No effect	Social interaction test	Chaki et al. (2004)
LY341495	No effect	Stress-induced hyperthermia	Galici et al. (2006)
LY341495	Anxiolytic	Marble-burying behavior test	Shimazaki et al. (2004)
mGluR4 agonist			
PHCCC (intra-amygdala)	Anxiolytic	Vogel test	Stachowicz et al. (2004)
mGluR5 antagonist			
MPEP	Anxiolytic	Geller–Seifter conflict model	Spooren et al. (2000) and Ballard et al. (2005)
MPEP	Anxiolytic	Elevated plus maze	Spooren et al. (2000)
MPEP	Anxiolytic	Social interaction	Spooren et al. (2000)
MPEP	Anxiolytic	Marble Burying	Spooren et al. (2000)
MPEP	Anxiolytic	Stress-induced hyperthermia	Spooren et al. (2000), Spooren et al. (2002) and Rorick-Kehn et al. (2005)
MPEP	Anxiolytic	Vogel test	Tatarczynska et al. (2001a)
MPEP	Anxiolytic	4-Plate test	Tatarczynska et al. (2001a)
MPEP	Anxiolytic	Ultrasonic vocalisations	Brodkin et al. (2002b)
MPEP	Anxiolytic	Conditioned emotional response	Ballard et al. (2005)
MPEP (intra-amygdala)	Anxiolytic	Shock-probe burying test	Perez de la Mora et al. (2006)
MPEP (intra-amygdala)	Anxiolytic	Elevated plus maze	Perez de la Mora et al. (2006)
MPEP (intra-amygdala)	Anxiolytic	Light–dark box test	Perez de la Mora et al. (2006)
MPEP	Anxiolytic	Conditioned lick suppression	Varty et al. (2005)
MTEP	Anxiolytic	Fear potentiated startle	Cosford et al. (2003)
MTEP	Anxiolytic	Vogel test	Klodzinska et al. (2004a)
MTEP	Anxiolytic	Elevated plus maze	Busse et al. (2004)
MTEP	Anxiolytic	Geller–Seifter conflict model	Busse et al. (2004)
MTEP	Anxiolytic	Conditioned lick suppression	Varty et al. (2005)
MTEP (intra-lateral septal)	Anxiolytic	Elevated plus maze	Molina-Hernandez et al. (2006)
5-[(2-Methyl-1,3-thiazol-4-yl)ethynyl]-2,3′-bipyridine	Anxiolytic	FPS	Roppe et al. (2004)
5-[(2-Methyl-1,3-thiazol-4-yl)ethynyl]-2,3′-bipyridine	Anxiolytic	Stress-induced hyperthermia	Porter et al. (2005)
Fenobam	Anxiolytic	Vogel conflict test	Porter et al. (2005)

Table 5 (*continued*)

Selective compounds			
Drug name	Effect	Tests used	Reference
Fenobam	Anxiolytic	Geller–Seifter conflict test	Porter et al. (2005)
Fenobam	Anxiolytic	Conditioned emotional response	Porter et al. (2005)
mGluR8 agonist			
(S)-3,4-DCPG (intra-hippocampus)	No effect	Vogel test	Stachowicz et al. (2005)
(S)-3,4-DCPG	Anxiolytic	Stress-induced hyperthermia	Rorick-Kehn et al. (2005)
Non-selective compounds			
Non-selective			
ABHxD-I	No effect	Vogel test	Tatarczynska et al. (2001b)
Group III mGluR agonists			
ACPT-I (intra-hippocampal)	Anxiolytic	Vogel test	Palucha et al. (2004)
HomoAMPA, (intra-hippocampal)	Anxiolytic	Vogel test	Palucha et al. (2004)
L-SOP (intra-hippocampal)	Anxiolytic	Vogel test	Tatarczynska et al. (2001b)
Group III mGluR antagonists			
MSOP (intra-hippocampal)	Anxiolytic	Vogel test	Chojnacka-Wojcik et al. (1997)
CPPG (intra-hippocampal)	No effect	Vogel test	Palucha et al. (2004)
CPPG	Anxiolytic	Vogel test	Stachowicz et al. (2007)
Other glutamate drugs			
Riluzole	No effect	Geller–Seifter test	Stutzmann et al. (1989)
Riluzole	No effect	Punished responding in pigeons	Koek and Colpaert (1991)
Memantine	No effect	Vogel test	Karcz-Kubicha et al. (1997)
Memantine	No effect	Elevated plus maze	Karcz-Kubicha et al. (1997)
Memantine	Anxiolytic	Elevated plus maze	Talalaenko et al. (2003)
MS-153	Anxiolytic	Conditioned fear response	Li et al. (2004)

raised, caution is needed as there tends to be a tendency for publication bias towards positive data. This is apparent in all aspects of behavioural pharmacology, and scientific literature in general. However, as more selective and potent orally bioavailable compounds emerge it is hoped that over the coming years that a clear picture of the distinct roles of given glutamate compounds in anxiety will emerge. In the next sections, we will synthesise the main findings that emerge from pharmacological studies to date.

VIII. NMDA receptors

A clear picture emerges with regard to the effects of competitive NMDA antagonists across a variety models, which tap into different aspects of the anxiety domain from approach avoidance tasks to conflict models, to learned fear assays. Overall, these studies, beginning with those of Clineschmidt and colleagues in the early 1980s (Clineschmidt, 1982; Clineschmidt et al., 1982) show that blocking NMDA receptors induces an anxiolytic effect. This is in agreement with a growing corpus of data which suggests that NMDA receptors are crucial for regulation of anxious states (Millan, 2003). Firstly, NMDA receptor are highly localised in key corticolimbic regions involved in the control of emotion and stress responses (Millan, 2003). Neurochemical studies have shown that exposure to stressful environments produces a robust increase in glutamate release in locus coeruleus, hippocampus and prefrontal cortex (Moghaddam, 1993; Moghaddam et al., 1994; Singewald et al., 1995, 1996). Additionally, exposure to stress increases NMDA receptor expression and mRNA levels in the rat ventral tegmental area and hippocampus (Bartanusz et al., 1995; Fitzgerald et al., 1996). Secondly, as referred to previously current theories indicating that learned aspects of fear plays a role in anxiety and seminal work from Davis and colleagues have demonstrated that NMDA receptors within the amygdala are crucial for many aspects of fear learning including acquisition and extinction (Miserendino et al., 1990; Campeau et al., 1992; Falls et al., 1992; Sananes and Davis, 1992; Liang et al., 1994; Gewirtz and Davis, 1997; Walker and Davis, 2000, 2004). Although both NMDA and non-NMDA glutamate receptors are involved in synaptic plasticity in the amygdala (Shekhar et al., 2005), most studies support the role of the NMDA receptors in the initiation of synaptic plasticity relevant to anxiety and fear learning (Miserendino et al., 1990; Gewirtz and Davis, 1997; Rogan et al., 1997; Adamec, 1998; Maren, 1999; Rainnie et al., 2004). Further evidence for a role of NMDA receptors in anxiety emerges from studies which demonstrate the anxiogenic neuropeptide corticotrophin releasing factor (CRF) is released under the control of NMDA activation (Joanny et al., 1997; Cratty and Birkle, 1999), as is the CRF receptor agonist urocortin II (Rainnie et al., 2004). Thus it is possible that the anxiolytic effects of competitive NMDA antagonists may be due to their ability to downregulate CRF neurotransmission.

Regarding non-competitive NMDA antagonists the data collated in Table 4 fails to give any consensus on whether they have anxiolytic effects or not in animal models. The fact that compounds such as PCP and ketamine are known to cause perceptual distortions, which are not easily assessed in animals, make it also possible that these drugs prevented proper sensory encoding of certain anxiety stimuli. Moreover, the ataxic and anaesthetic effects of such drugs necessitate very controlled dose titration which may also contribute to the inconsistent findings between labs. In line with this fact, marked differences between competitive and non-competitive NMDA

antagonist occur across many behavioural domains (Schmidt, 1994).

While the data in animal models are relative supportive there is still a general lack of enthusiasm for the development of NMDA antagonists for anxiety disorders largely due to the experience of such compounds for the treatment of stroke and traumatic brain injury. Based on very positive, if in hindsight misleading (Gladstone et al., 2002), preclinical data where NMDA antagonists proved to be very effective neuroprotective drugs in vitro and in animal models of stroke, traumatic brain injury and spinal-cord injury, clinical trials of NMDA antagonists were initiated. However, sequentially the clinical trials were terminated based on efficacy and side effects (Ikonomidou and Turski, 2002; Kemp and McKernan, 2002; Muir, 2006). Failure maybe due to deficient pharmacokinetics with the plasma levels achieved in studies consistently below those needed for maximal neuroprotection in animal models (Kemp and McKernan, 2002). Moreover, NMDA antagonists have a number of mechanism-based adverse CNS effects, including hallucinations, a centrally mediated increase in blood pressure and, at high doses, catatonia which have limited the doses used clinically (Kemp and McKernan, 2002). Together, it seems unlikely that non-selective channel blockers will ever pass the safety hurdles to receive approval for widespread use (Ikonomidou and Turski, 2002; Kemp and McKernan, 2002; Muir, 2006). It is widely considered that the development of ligands selective for specific NMDA receptor subtypes may be an exciting avenue for the development of novel anxiolytic therapies. Current literature on the NR2B selective antagonist ifenopridol do not provide a robust rationale for that receptors involvement in anxiety (Koek and Colpaert, 1991; Wiley et al., 1998; Dere et al., 2003; Mikolajczak et al., 2003; but see also Fraser et al., 1996). Although some studies in genetically modified mice indicate a role for the NR2A receptor in anxiety (Boyce-Rustay and Holmes, 2006; but see also Moriya et al., 2000), these mice are also burdened with deficits in certain forms of synaptic plasticity and learning and memory performance (Sakimura et al., 1995; Kishimoto et al., 1997; Kiyama et al., 1998) which, if recapitulated by pharmacological agents may negate their overall utility.

Another conundrum in NMDA pharmacology is that there are anxiolytic effects of both positive (e.g. D-cycloserine) and negative (competitive antagonists) modulators of NMDA receptors in animal models. Clinical investigations are however, pointing to a possible understanding that positive NMDA modulators are effective as adjunctive anxiety therapy largely due to their cognitive enhancement properties (Ressler et al., 2004; Gillespie and Ressler, 2005; Kushner et al., 2007). Thus the facilitation of new learning can be a useful aspect of anxiety management. On the other hand, anxiolytic-effects of NMDA antagonists may be due to their ability to impair learning and memories of specific cues and situations (Gillespie and Ressler, 2005).

IX. AMPA receptors

Pharmacological data also supports a role for AMPA receptors in the control of anxious states (Table 5; Millan, 2003), which is in line with their ubiquitous role in the CNS in mediating fast excitatory transmission. AMPA receptors are localised in high concentrations in key brain regions involved in anxiety including monoaminergic cell clusters, and in the PAG, amygdala, septum and hippocampus (Ozawa et al., 1998; Lees, 2000). Acute and prolonged stress have been shown to elicit alterations in AMPA receptor expression in the hippocampus and cortex, though no consensus has as yet been reached as concerns the precise nature of these changes (Krugers et al., 1993; Fitzgerald et al., 1996; Schwendt and Jezova, 2000; Rosa et al., 2002; Pickering et al., 2006). Moreover, while the corticolimbic regions responsible for integrating the anxiolytic actions of AMPA antagonists remain to be definitively identified, it is clear from studies utilising focal injections that the hippocampus, PAG, septum and amygdala are likely candidates (see Table 5; Millan, 2003). Millan suggests that the anxiolytic effects of AMPA antagonists more than likely are due to the suppression of stress-induced activation of raphe-derived serotonergic projections,

VTA-derived dopaminergic neurones and LC-derived noradrenergic pathway. Moreover, a reinforcement of GABAergic transmission in limbic structures is probably also of significance in manifestation of anxiolysis (Millan, 2003).

Perhaps one of the reasons that interest in AMPA receptors for anxiety has been growing steadily, comes from the fact that AMPA receptor antagonists are being developed as antiepileptic agents (Rogawski and Donevan, 1999; De Sarro et al., 2005). Accumulating evidence from both clinical and animal studies suggest that anticonvulsant agents from a variety of classes may have anxiolytic-like potential across the spectrum of anxiety disorders (Gorman et al., 2002; Stahl, 2004a, b). Thus if AMPA antagonists do emerge as safe anticonvulsants it will be of interest to see if anxiolytic effects cross-generalise.

X. mGluRs

One of the most exciting developments in recent years has been the discovery that selective ligands of mGluRs have distinct anxiolytic effects. Initial studies with antagonists of Group I mGluRs (mGluR1 and mGluR5) have indeed been promising, yet it is becoming clear that mGluR5 may prove to be the more beneficial target (see Table 5). mGlu1 antagonists appear to have more limited, task-dependent effects in anxiety models (see e.g. Steckler et al., 2005a) whereas the effects of mGluR5 antagonists appear to be much more robust and generalize across many anxiety domains (Spooren et al., 2003; Spooren and Gasparini, 2004). Both receptors share same transduction mechanism, that is activation of phosphoinositol hydrolysis, and can act in a functionally synergistic manner (Rae and Irving, 2004). However, although their distribution within the brain shares some overlap, marked differences in some brain regions are evident, for example mGlu1 receptors are most dense in the cerebellum where mGlu5 receptors are nearly absent, and reverse is true for the cerebral cortex (Shigemoto et al., 1997). Moreover, accumulating in vitro studies indicate that mGlu1 and mGlu5 receptors have different functions (Mannaioni et al., 2001; Valenti et al., 2002). It is of interest that both mGlu1 and mGlu5 receptors can be physically and functionally connected with NMDA receptors, the mode of this interaction may be different; mGluR5 via G-protein activation whereas mGluR1's potentiation of NMDA currents in G-Protein independent (Benquet et al., 2002). Together, these differences may play a role in the differential effects of mGluR5 and mGluR1 antagonist in animal models of anxiety. The fact that Group I mGluR antagonists can intracellularly and functionally downregulate NMDA receptor function, brings about concerns that these ligands may have side effects similar to NMDA antagonists. This is supported by data in mGluR5 deficient mice which have marked spatial learning deficits, deficits in LTP (Lu et al., 1997) and prepulse inhibition deficits (Brody et al., 2004). However, although some studies have shown that cognitive deficits have emerged following administration of mGluR5 antagonists (Balschun and Wetzel, 2002; Schachtman et al., 2003; Campbell et al., 2004; Homayoun et al., 2004; Naie and Manahan-Vaughan, 2004; Steckler et al., 2005b) they tend to emerge only following high doses and are therapeutically less marked than that of benzodiazepines or mGluR1 antagonists (Petersen et al., 2002; Naie and Manahan-Vaughan, 2004; Ballard et al., 2005; Steckler et al., 2005b; Car et al., 2007). Fear conditioning learning depends on mGluR5 function and the receptor is upregulated in the hippocampus following fear learning (Riedel et al., 2000). On the other hand, LTP at thalamic input synapses to the lateral amygdala is impaired by bath application of a specific mGluR5 MPEP in vitro (Rodrigues et al., 2002). Moreover, intra-amygdala administration of MPEP dose-dependently impairs the acquisition of auditory and contextual fear conditioning (Rodrigues et al., 2002) which is in line with studies indicating that systemic administration of mGluR5 antagonists also blocks conditioned fear learning (Schulz et al., 2001). mGluR5 antagonists, like benzodiazepine anxiolytics (Finlay et al., 1995), have also been shown to interact with the noradrenergic system with both MPEP and MTEP lowering basal noradrenaline levels and blocking stress-induced increases in the monoamine in the frontal cortex (Page et al., 2005). Together, mGluR5 antagonists

appear to be inducing effects at multiple sites in the brain which is involved in the manifestation of fear and stress responses. The clinical validation of mGluR5 antagonists is now awaited. The recent development of a selective radiotracer for mGluR5 (Ametamey et al., 2006, 2007; Hintermann et al., 2007) will assist no-end, not only in both the dose-finding and pharmacokinetic aspects of such clinical trials, but also in examining mGluR5 function in patients with various anxiety disorders.

Group II mGluRs (mGluR2 and mGluR3) are widely distributed throughout the CNS in brain regions that are commonly associated with anxiety disorders, including the hippocampus, prefrontal cortex and amygdala (Ohishi et al., 1993a, b; Ohishi et al., 1998). The mGlu2 receptors are generally expressed at extrasynaptic sites on neuronal terminals, where they have been shown to suppress excitatory amino-acid neurotransmission at a number of synapses (Cartmell and Schoepp, 2000; Swanson et al., 2005). By contrast, mGlu3 receptors have both pre- and post-synaptic localisation on neurons, as well as more widespread localisation on certain glial cells (Tamaru et al., 2001). Differentiation between the two receptors has been difficult to date due to lack of pharmacological tools. More recently genetically modified mice have been used to investigate if the effects of certain group two agonists are selectively due to either mGluR2 or mGluR3 (Linden et al., 2005b, 2006). These data indicate that most of the anxiolytic effects rely on mGluR2 (Linden et al., 2005b, 2006) yet mGluR3 does play some role in anxiety-related behaviours, as the behavioural effects of LY354740 in the elevated plus maze (Linden et al., 2005b). The recent development of selective mGluR2 positive modulators (Johnson et al., 2005), which are devoid of activity at mGluR3 receptors has further strengthened the proposition that mGluR2 is the key Group II mGluR in anxiety (Johnson et al., 2005; Swanson et al., 2005). The mechanism of action of mGluR2 agonists is not fully understood but is thought that by altering presynaptic glutamate release in various limbic regions including hippocampus and amygdala, mGluR2 agonists might dampen excitation that leads to exaggerated anxious responses (Cartmell and Schoepp, 2000; Swanson et al., 2005).

This is supported by c-Fos immunohistochemstry labelling studies which demonstrate that mGluR2 agonists act through regulation of excitation of GABAergic interneurons innervating the central amygdala (Linden et al., 2004, 2005a, b). Interestingly, mGluR2 antagonists have been shown to have anxiolytic properties in a number (Shimazaki et al., 2004; Yoshimizu et al., 2006; Iijima et al., 2007), but not all (Chaki et al., 2004) behavioural assays examined. Reasons for these paradoxical findings are currently unclear. mGluR2 receptor antagonists have been shown to have antidepressant-like properties (Chaki et al., 2004) in addition to having pro-cognitive benefits (Higgins et al., 2004). Therefore, it is possible that, given the role of altered mood and learning dysfunction in anxiety disorders, mGluR2 receptor antagonist may have distinct roles in certain aspects of anxiety. Further investigations into how such effects of such antagonists are manifested at a circuit level are required. Of all mGluRs, Group II agonists have advanced the furthest in clinical trials with LY354740 and more recently its prodrug LY544344 progressing into Phase II clinical trials for anxiety disorders with encouraging data emerging in some (Grillon et al., 2003; Kellner et al., 2005) but not all studies (Bergink and Westenberg, 2005).

The development of systemically active Group III mGluR subtype-selective agents is lagging behind that of other mGluRs and thus less is known about the roles of these subtypes in brain function and disease. Group III mGluRs are typically presynaptic, inhibit neurotransmitter release and are localized to key limbic-system nuclei. Group III mGluRs modulate excitatory neurotransmission in the nucleus locus coeruleus (Dube and Marshall, 1997), and regulate a variety of other non-glutamatergic neurotransmitters directly or indirectly (reviewed in Cartmell and Schoepp, 2000). For example, they have been associated with inhibition of glutamate and/or GABA within the hippocampus and hypothalamus (Schrader and Tasker, 1997a, b; Semyanov and Kullmann, 2000) To date there is some, albeit limited, evidence that mGluR4 and mGluR8 agonists may have some anxiolytic potential (Stachowicz et al., 2004; Rorick-Kehn et al.,

2005). Activation of mGluR7 on the other hand, facilitates the extinction of learned aversive memories. However, such activators can also block the acquisition of fear potentiated startle (Fendt et al., 2007). In line with the latter, animals deficient in mGluR7 or who have administered siRNA targeting mGluR7 have deficits in fear extinction (Callaerts-Vegh et al., 2006; Fendt et al., 2007). As stated earlier this the development of fear extinction facilitators is an exciting avenue being pursued so as to get novel therapies for certain anxiety disorders.

Growing evidence supports a role for Group III mGluRs in regulation of the neuroendocrine response to stress. Although ionotropic receptors are long known to regulate stress hormone concentrations (Pechnick et al., 1987; Farah et al., 1991; Yousef et al., 1994) more recent evidence points to an involvement of Group I and possibly Group II mGluRs (Johnson et al., 2001; Johnson and Chamberlain, 2002; Bradbury et al., 2003; Scaccianoce et al., 2003). Additionally, it also has been demonstrated that i.c.v. administration of the non-selective Group III mGluR agonists L-AP$_4$ and L-SOP activates the hypothalamic–pituitary–adrenal (HPA) axis (Johnson et al., 2001) as does a selective mGluR7 activator AMN082 (Mitsukawa et al., 2005). Currently, it is unclear if there is any link between such a regulation and behavioural effects in animal models of anxiety. Interestingly, mice deficient in mGluR7 have an anxiolytic-phenotype which is coupled with dysregulation of the HPA axis and increased levels of glucocorticoid receptors in the hippocampus. Future studies must investigate if these effects are causally related.

XI. Conclusions and future directions

The quest for new anxiolytic agents with a better side-effect profile has lead investigators to exploit the pharmacology of the glutamate system. These side effects include short-term memory impairments, interactions with alcohol, psychomotor impairments/sedation in addition to concerns about dependence and the development of tolerance (Gorman et al., 2002). Promising data has emerged with regard to NMDA antagonists, mGluR2 agonists and mGluR5 antagonists in animal models. While development of competitive NMDA antagonists does not appear to be progressing due to side effect concerns discussed above, mGluR2 agonists and mGluR5 antagonists, based on their excellent profile in preclinical models are being advanced as potential anxiolytics by a number of pharmaceutical companies. It is still unclear whether such drug targets can be effective clinically without-inducing glutamate-related behavioural side effects. Of those side-by-side comparisons of mGluR ligands carried out within the published literature, especially mGluR5 antagonists, it is clear that they have favourable side effect profile in comparison with benzodiazepine anxiolytics especially in relation to sedation and cognitive side effects (Ballard et al., 2005). One of the big remaining issues with mGluR ligands is their ability to develop tolerance. There are some reports of rapid tolerance emerging to the anxiolytic effect of mGluR5 antagonists in some (Busse et al., 2004) but not all animal models (Pilc et al., 2002; Klodzinska et al., 2004a; Steckler et al., 2005a; Nordquist et al., 2007). Moreover, tolerance has also been reported to selective behavioural effects of mGluR2 agonists (Cartmell et al., 2000). This reinforces the point that there is a paucity of studies investigating the long-term use of glutamatergic ligands in animal models of anxiolytic efficacy and their side effect potential.

There is still much chemical 'mining' to do in terms of developing subtype selective allosteric modulators of either ionotropic or metabotropic receptors. Although much data has emerged over the past 25 years, it is still too premature to be able to develop a consensus as to which subunits of ionotropic receptors will provide the best target for developing novel therapies. Animal models will continue to play a key role in investigation of such effects and it is hoped that efforts in translational medicine will also be increased to develop analogous models in the human experimental setting. While current animal models are relatively predictive of clinical efficacy in anxiety disorders, they are particularly primed to detect drugs affecting GABAergic neurotransmission (Belzung, 2001),

and are for instance, insensitive in many cases to the anxiolytic effects of chronic SSRIs (Borsini et al., 2002). A case in point regarding the glutamatergic system is the drug riluzole, which is a presynaptic glutamate release inhibitor, approved by the US Food and Drug Administration for the treatment of amyotrophic lateral sclerosis. It has been shown to be without effect in conflict based models (see Table 5) yet recent, albeit small, studies indicates that it has anxiolytic effects in both generalised anxiety and OCD patients (Coric et al., 2005; Mathew et al., 2005). Therefore, animal models of specific endophenotypes of anxiety syndrome need to be refined and new ones developed. The burgeoning use of neuroimaging techniques in humans is helping to vastly increase our knowledge of the circuitry underlying anxiety at baseline and in a fear provoked state (Cannistraro and Rauch, 2003; Kugaya and Sanacora, 2005; Phelps and LeDoux, 2005). Further, it is hopped that such techniques will allow in the future a better understanding of the glutamatergic circuits which are dysfunctional in anxiety disorders (Kugaya and Sanacora, 2005) and which are amenable to reversal by novel, selective pharmacological agents targeting ionotropic or metabotropic receptors. Overall we have come a long way in the past 25 years in our understanding the behavioural pharmacology of glutamate in anxiety. It is hoped that the coming years will see glutamatergic drugs emerge as novel effective treatments for anxiety disorders with lower side-effect profile than current drugs as this will fulfil a large unmet medical need.

References

Adamec, R.E. (1998) Evidence that NMDA-dependent limbic neural plasticity in the right hemisphere mediates pharmacological stressor (FG-7142)-induced lasting increases in anxiety-like behavior. Study 1 – Role of NMDA receptors in efferent transmission from the cat amygdala. J. Psychopharmacol., 12: 122–128.

Adriaan Bouwknecht, J., Olivier, B. and Paylor, R.E. (2007) The stress-induced hyperthermia paradigm as a physiological animal model for anxiety: a review of pharmacological and genetic studies in the mouse. Neurosci. Biobehav. Rev., 31: 41–59.

Ahmadian, H., Nielsen, B., Brauner-Osborne, H., Johansen, T.N., Stensbol, T.B., Slok, F.A., Sekiyama, N., Nakanishi, S., Krogsgaard-Larsen, P. and Madsen, U. (1997) (S)-homo-AMPA, a specific agonist at the mGlu6 subtype of metabotropic glutamic acid receptors. J. Med. Chem., 40: 3700–3705.

Alt, A., Weiss, B., Ogden, A.M., Li, X., Gleason, S.D., Calligaro, D.O., Bleakman, D. and Witkin, J.M. (2006) In vitro and in vivo studies in rats with LY293558 suggest AMPA/kainate receptor blockade as a novel potential mechanism for the therapeutic treatment of anxiety disorders. Psychopharmacology (Berlin), 185: 240–247.

Alt, A., Weiss, B., Ornstein, P.L., Gleason, S.D., Bleakman, D., Stratford, R.E. Jr. and Witkin, J.M. (2007) Anxiolytic-like effects through a GLU(K5) kainate receptor mechanism. Neuropharmacology, 52: 1482–1487.

American Psychiatric Association. (1994) Diagnostic and Statistical Manual of Mental Disorders, 4th edn. American Psychiatric Press, Washington, DC.

Ametamey, S.M., Kessler, L.J., Honer, M., Wyss, M.T., Buck, A., Hintermann, S., Auberson, Y.P., Gasparini, F. and Schubiger, P.A. (2006) Radiosynthesis and preclinical evaluation of 11C-ABP688 as a probe for imaging the metabotropic glutamate receptor subtype 5. J. Nucl. Med., 47: 698–705.

Ametamey, S.M., Treyer, V., Streffer, J., Wyss, M.T., Schmidt, M., Blagoev, M., Hintermann, S., Auberson, Y., Gasparini, F., Fischer, U.C. and Buck, A. (2007) Human PET studies of metabotropic glutamate receptor subtype 5 with 11C-ABP688. J. Nucl. Med., 48: 247–252.

Andlin-Sobocki, P., Jonsson, B., Wittchen, H.U. and Olesen, J. (2005) Cost of disorders of the brain in Europe. Eur. J. Neurol., 12(Suppl. 1): 1–27.

Annoura, H., Fukunaga, A., Uesugi, M., Tatsuoka, T. and Horikawa, Y. (1996) A novel class of antagonist for metabotropic glutamate receptors, 7-(hydroxyimino)-cyclopropachromen-1a-carboxylates. Bioorg. Med. Chem., 6: 763–766.

Anthony, E.W. and Nevins, M.E. (1993) Anxiolytic-like effects of N-methyl-D-aspartate-associated glycine receptor ligands in the rat potentiated startle test. Eur. J. Pharmacol., 250: 317–324.

Auberson, Y.P., Allgeier, H., Bischoff, S., Lingenhoehl, K., Moretti, R. and Schmutz, M. (2002) 5-Phosphonomethylquinoxalinediones as competitive NMDA receptor antagonists with a preference for the human 1A/2A, rather than 1A/2B receptor composition. Bioorg. Med. Chem. Lett., 12: 1099–1102.

Ballard, T.M., Woolley, M.L., Prinssen, E., Huwyler, J., Porter, R. and Spooren, W. (2005) The effect of the mGlu5 receptor antagonist MPEP in rodent tests of anxiety and cognition: a comparison. Psychopharmacology (Berlin), 179: 218–229.

Balschun, D. and Wetzel, W. (2002) Inhibition of mGluR5 blocks hippocampal LTP in vivo and spatial learning in rats. Pharmacol. Biochem. Behav., 73: 375–380.

Bannerman, D.M., Deacon, R.M., Brady, S., Bruce, A., Sprengel, R., Seeburg, P.H. and Rawlins, J.N. (2004) A comparison of GluR-A-deficient and wild-type mice on a test battery assessing sensorimotor, affective, and cognitive behaviors. Behav. Neurosci., 118: 643–647.

Barad, M. (2005) Fear extinction in rodents: basic insight to clinical promise. Curr. Opin. Neurobiol., 15: 710–715.

Bartanusz, V., Aubry, J.M., Pagliusi, S., Jezova, D., Baffi, J. and Kiss, J.Z. (1995) Stress-induced changes in messenger RNA levels of N-methyl-D-aspartate and AMPA receptor subunits in selected regions of the rat hippocampus and hypothalamus. Neuroscience, 66: 247–252.

Becker, A., Peters, B., Schroeder, H., Mann, T., Huether, G. and Grecksch, G. (2003) Ketamine-induced changes in rat behaviour: a possible animal model of schizophrenia. Prog. Neuropsychopharmacol. Biol. Psychiatry, 27: 687–700.

Belzung, C. (2001) Rodent models of anxiety-like behaviors: are they predictive for compounds acting via non-benzodiazepine mechanisms? Curr. Opin. Investig. Drugs., 2: 1108–1111.

Belzung, C. and Griebel, G. (2001) Measuring normal and pathological anxiety-like behaviour in mice: a review. Behav. Brain. Res., 125: 141–149.

Benquet, P., Gee, C.E. and Gerber, U. (2002) Two distinct signaling pathways upregulate NMDA receptor responses via two distinct metabotropic glutamate receptor subtypes. J. Neurosci., 22: 9679–9686.

Benvenga, M.J., Ornstein, P.L. and Leander, J.D. (1995) Schedule-controlled behavioral effects of the selective 2-amino-3-(5-methyl-3-hydroxyisoxazol-4-yl)propanoic acid antagonist LY293558 in pigeons. J. Pharmacol. Exp. Ther., 275: 164–170.

Bergink, V. and Westenberg, H.G. (2005) Metabotropic glutamate II receptor agonists in panic disorder: a double blind clinical trial with LY354740. Int. Clin. Psychopharmacol., 20: 291–293.

Bergink, V., van Megen, H.J. and Westenberg, H.G. (2004) Glutamate and anxiety. Eur. Neuropsychopharmacol., 14: 175–183.

Bertoglio, L.J. and Zangrossi, H. Jr. (2006) Involvement of dorsolateral periaqueductal gray N-methyl-D-aspartic acid glutamate receptors in the regulation of risk assessment and inhibitory avoidance behaviors in the rat elevated T-maze. Behav. Pharmacol., 17: 589–596.

Bettler, B. and Mulle, C. (1995) Review: neurotransmitter receptors. II. AMPA and kainate receptors. Neuropharmacology, 34: 123–139.

Borsini, F., Podhorna, J. and Marazziti, D. (2002) Do animal models of anxiety predict anxiolytic-like effects of antidepressants? Psychopharmacology (Berlin), 163: 121–141.

Boyce-Rustay, J.M. and Holmes, A. (2006) Genetic inactivation of the NMDA receptor NR2A subunit has anxiolytic- and antidepressant-like effects in mice. Neuropsychopharmacology, 31: 2405–2414.

Bradbury, M.J., Giracello, D.R., Chapman, D.F., Holtz, G., Schaffhauser, H., Rao, S.P., Varney, M.A. and Anderson, J.J. (2003) Metabotropic glutamate receptor 5 antagonist-induced stimulation of hypothalamic–pituitary–adrenal axis activity: interaction with serotonergic systems. Neuropharmacology, 44: 562–572.

Brodkin, J., Bradbury, M., Busse, C., Warren, N., Bristow, L.J. and Varney, M.A. (2002a) Reduced stress-induced hyperthermia in mGluR5 knockout mice. Eur. J. Neurosci., 16: 2241–2244.

Brodkin, J., Busse, C., Sukoff, S.J. and Varney, M.A. (2002b) Anxiolytic-like activity of the mGluR5 antagonist MPEP a comparison with diazepam and buspirone. Pharmacol. Biochem. Behav., 73: 359–366.

Brody, S.A., Dulawa, S.C., Conquet, F. and Geyer, M.A. (2004) Assessment of a prepulse inhibition deficit in a mutant mouse lacking mGlu5 receptors. Mol. Psychiatry, 9: 35–41.

Brody, S.A. and Geyer, M.A. (2004) Interactions of the mGluR5 gene with breeding and maternal factors on startle and prepulse inhibition in mice. Neurotox. Res., 6: 79–90.

Burnashev, N. (1996) Calcium permeability of glutamate-gated channels in the central nervous system. Curr. Opin. Neurobiol., 6: 311–317.

Busse, C.S., Brodkin, J., Tattersall, D., Anderson, J.J., Warren, N., Tehrani, L., Bristow, L.J., Varney, M.A. and Cosford, N.D. (2004) The behavioral profile of the potent and selective mGlu5 receptor antagonist 3-[(2-methyl-1,3-thiazol-4-yl)ethynyl]pyridine (MTEP) in rodent models of anxiety. Neuropsychopharmacology, 29: 1971–1979.

Callaerts-Vegh, Z., Beckers, T., Ball, S.M., Baeyens, F., Callaerts, P.F., Cryan, J.F., Molnar, E. and D'Hooge, R. (2006) Concomitant deficits in working memory and fear extinction are functionally dissociated from reduced anxiety in metabotropic glutamate receptor 7-deficient mice. J. Neurosci., 26: 6573–6582.

Campbell, U.C., Lalwani, K., Hernandez, L., Kinney, G.G., Conn, P.J. and Bristow, L.J. (2004) The mGluR5 antagonist 2-methyl-6-(phenylethynyl)-pyridine (MPEP) potentiates PCP-induced cognitive deficits in rats. Psychopharmacology (Berlin), 175: 310–318.

Campeau, S., Miserendino, M.J. and Davis, M. (1992) Intra-amygdala infusion of the N-methyl-D-aspartate receptor antagonist AP5 blocks acquisition but not expression of fear-potentiated startle to an auditory conditioned stimulus. Behav. Neurosci., 106: 569–574.

Cannistraro, P.A. and Rauch, S.L. (2003) Neural circuitry of anxiety: evidence from structural and functional neuroimaging studies. Psychopharmacol. Bull., 37: 8–25.

Car, H., Stefaniuk, R. and Wisniewska, R.J. (2007) Effect of MPEP in Morris water maze in adult and old rats. Pharmacol. Rep., 59: 88–93.

Carmignoto, G. and Vicini, S. (1992) Activity-dependent decrease in NMDA receptor responses during development of the visual cortex. Science, 258: 1007–1011.

Cartmell, J., Monn, J.A. and Schoepp, D.D. (2000) Tolerance to the motor impairment, but not to the reversal of PCP-induced motor activities by oral administration of the mGlu2/3 receptor agonist, LY379268. Naunyn Schmiedebergs Arch. Pharmacol., 361: 39–46.

Cartmell, J. and Schoepp, D.D. (2000) Regulation of neurotransmitter release by metabotropic glutamate receptors. J. Neurochem., 75: 889–907.

Chaki, S., Yoshikawa, R., Hirota, S., Shimazaki, T., Maeda, M., Kawashima, N., Yoshimizu, T., Yasuhara, A., Sakagami, K., Okuyama, S., Nakanishi, S. and Nakazato, A. (2004) MGS0039: a potent and selective group II metabotropic glutamate receptor antagonist with antidepressant-like activity. Neuropharmacology, 46: 457–467.

Chojnacka-Wojcik, E., Tatarczynska, E. and Deren-Wesolek, A. (1996) Effect of glycine on antidepressant- and anxiolytic-like action of 1-aminocyclopropanecarboxylic acid (ACPC) in rats. Pol. J. Pharmacol., 48: 627–629.

Chojnacka-Wojcik, E., Tatarczynska, E. and Pilc, A. (1997) The anxiolytic-like effect of metabotropic glutamate receptor antagonists after intrahippocampal injection in rats. Eur. J. Pharmacol., 319: 153–156.

Christensen, J.K., Varming, T., Ahring, P.K., Jorgensen, T.D. and Nielsen, E.O. (2004) In vitro characterization of 5-carboxyl-2,4-di-benzamidobenzoic acid (NS3763), a noncompetitive antagonist of GLUK5 receptors. J. Pharmacol. Exp. Ther., 309: 1003–1010.

Clarke, V.R., Ballyk, B.A., Hoo, K.H., Mandelzys, A., Pellizzari, A., Bath, C.P., Thomas, J., Sharpe, E.F., Davies, C.H., Ornstein, P.L., Schoepp, D.D., Kamboj, R.K., Collingridge, G.L., Lodge, D. and Bleakman, D. (1997) A hippocampal GluR5 kainate receptor regulating inhibitory synaptic transmission. Nature, 389: 599–603.

Clineschmidt, B.V. (1982) Effect of the benzodiazepine receptor antagonist Ro 15-1788 on the anticonvulsant and anticonflict actions of MK-801. Eur. J. Pharmacol., 84: 119–121.

Clineschmidt, B.V., Williams, M., Witoslawski, J.J., Bunting, P.R., Risley, E.A. and Totaro, J.A. (1982) Restoration of shock-suppressed behavior by treatment with (+)-5-methyl-10,11-dihydro-5H-dibenzo[a, d]cyclohepten-5, 10-imine (MK-801), a substance with potent anticonvulsant, central sympathomimetic, and apparent anxiolytic properties. Drug Develop. Res., 2: 147–163.

Collado, I., Pedregal, C., Bueno, A.B., Marcos, A., Gonzalez, R., Blanco-Urgoiti, J., Perez-Castells, J., Schoepp, D.D., Wright, R.A., Johnson, B.G., Kingston, A.E., Moher, E.D., Hoard, D.W., Griffey, K.I. and Tizzano, J.P. (2004) (2S,1'S,2'R,3'R)-2-(2'-carboxy-3'-hydroxymethylcyclopropyl) glycine is a highly potent group 2 and 3 metabotropic glutamate receptor agonist with oral activity. J. Med. Chem., 47: 456–466.

Coric, V., Taskiran, S., Pittenger, C., Wasylink, S., Mathalon, D.H., Valentine, G., Saksa, J., Wu, Y.T., Gueorguieva, R., Sanacora, G., Malison, R.T. and Krystal, J.H. (2005) Riluzole augmentation in treatment-resistant obsessive-compulsive disorder: an open-label trial. Biol. Psychiatry, 58: 424–428.

Cortese, B.M. and Phan, K.L. (2005) The role of glutamate in anxiety and related disorders. CNS Spectrosc., 10: 820–830.

Cosford, N.D., Tehrani, L., Roppe, J., Schweiger, E., Smith, N.D., Anderson, J., Bristow, L., Brodkin, J., Jiang, X., McDonald, I., Rao, S., Washburn, M. and Varney, M.A. (2003) 3-[(2-Methyl-1,3-thiazol-4-yl)ethynyl]-pyridine: a potent and highly selective metabotropic glutamate subtype 5 receptor antagonist with anxiolytic activity. J. Med. Chem., 46: 204–206.

Cratty, M.S. and Birkle, D.L. (1999) N-methyl-D-aspartate (NMDA)-mediated corticotropin-releasing factor (CRF) release in cultured rat amygdala neurons. Peptides, 20: 93–100.

Crawley, J.N. (2000) Whats Wrong with my mouse? Behavioral Phenotyping of Transgenic and Knockout Mice. Wiley-Liss, New York.

Cryan, J.F. and Holmes, A. (2005) The ascent of mouse: advances in modelling human depression and anxiety. Nat. Rev. Drug Discov., 4: 775–790

Cryan, J.F., Kelly, P.H., Neijt, H.C., Sansig, G., Flor, P.J. and Van Der Putten, H. (2003) Antidepressant and anxiolytic-like effects in mice lacking the group III metabotropic glutamate receptor mGluR7. Eur. J. Neurosci., 17: 2409–2417.

Cryan, J.F. and Mombereau, C. (2004) In search of a depressed mouse: utility of models for studying depression-related behavior in genetically modified mice. Mol. Psychiatry, 9: 326–357.

Cryan, J.F., Thakker, D.R. and Hoyer, D. (2007) Emerging use of non-viral RNA interference in the brain. Biochem. Soc. Trans., 35: 411–415.

Curtis, D.R. and Watkins, J.C. (1961) Analogues of glutamic and gamma-amino-n-butyric acids having potent actions on mammalian neurones. Nature, 191: 1010–1011.

Czlonkowska, A., Siemiatkowski, M. and Plaznik, A. (1997) Some behavioral effects of AMPA/kainate receptor agonist and antagonists. J. Physiol. Pharmacol., 48: 479–488.

Davis, M. (1990) Animal models of anxiety based on classical conditioning: the conditioned emotional response (CER) and the fear-potentiated startle effect. Pharmacol. Ther., 47: 147–165.

Davis, M., Myers, K.M., Chhatwal, J. and Ressler, K.J. (2006a) Pharmacological treatments that facilitate extinction of fear: relevance to psychotherapy. NeuroRx, 3: 82–96.

Davis, M., Ressler, K., Rothbaum, B.O. and Richardson, R. (2006b) Effects of D-cycloserine on extinction: translation from preclinical to clinical work. Biol. Psychiatry, 60: 369–375.

Day, M., Langston, R. and Morris, R.G. (2003) Glutamate-receptor-mediated encoding and retrieval of paired-associate learning. Nature, 424: 205–209.

De Sarro, G., Gitto, R., Russo, E., Ibbadu, G.F., Barreca, M.L., De Luca, L. and Chimirri, A. (2005) AMPA receptor antagonists as potential anticonvulsant drugs. Curr. Top. Med. Chem., 5: 31–42.

De Souza Silva, M.A., Marchetti, L., Eisel, U.L., Huston, J.P. and Dere, E. (2007) NR2C by NR2B subunit exchange in juvenile mice affects emotionality and 5-HT in the frontal cortex. Genes Brain. Behav., 6: 465–472.

Depoortere, R., Dargazanli, G., Estenne-Bouhtou, G., Coste, A., Lanneau, C., Desvignes, C., Poncelet, M., Heaulme, M., Santucci, V., Decobert, M., Cudennec, A., Voltz, C., Boulay, D., Terranova, J.P., Stemmelin, J., Roger, P., Marabout, B., Sevrin, M., Vige, X., Biton, B., Steinberg, R., Francon, D., Alonso, R., Avenet, P., Oury-Donat, F., Perrault, G., Griebel, G., George, P., Soubrie, P. and Scatton, B. (2005) Neurochemical, electrophysiological and pharmacological profiles of the selective inhibitor of the glycine transporter-1 SSR504734, a potential new type of antipsychotic. Neuropsychopharmacology, 30: 1963–1985.

Dere, E., Topic, B., De Souza Silva, M.A., Fink, H., Buddenberg, T. and Huston, J.P. (2003) NMDA-receptor antagonism via dextromethorphan and ifenprodil modulates graded anxiety test performance of C57BL/6 mice. Behav. Pharmacol., 14: 245–249.

Dev, K.K., Nakanishi, S. and Henley, J.M. (2001) Regulation of mglu(7) receptors by proteins that interact with the intracellular C-terminus. Trends Pharmacol. Sci., 22: 355–361.

Dev, K.K., Nakanishi, S. and Henley, J.M. (2004) The PDZ domain of PICK1 differentially accepts protein kinase C-alpha and GluR2 as interacting ligands. J. Biol. Chem., 279: 41393–41397.

Doherty, A.J., Palmer, M.J., Henley, J.M., Collingridge, G.L. and Jane, D.E. (1997) (RS)-2-chloro-5-hydroxyphenylglycine (CHPG) activates mGlu5, but no mGlu1, receptors expressed in CHO cells and potentiates NMDA responses in the hippocampus. Neuropharmacology, 36: 265–267.

Drejer, J. and Honore, T. (1988) New quinoxalinediones show potent antagonism of quisqualate responses in cultured mouse cortical neurons. Neurosci. Lett., 87: 104–108.

Dube, G.R. and Marshall, K.C. (1997) Modulation of excitatory synaptic transmission in locus coeruleus by multiple presynaptic metabotropic glutamate receptors. Neuroscience, 80: 511–521.

Duvoisin, R.M., Zhang, C., Pfankuch, T.F., O'Connor, H., Gayet-Primo, J., Quraishi, S. and Raber, J. (2005) Increased measures of anxiety and weight gain in mice lacking the group III metabotropic glutamate receptor mGluR8. Eur. J. Neurosci., 22: 425–436.

Falls, W.A., Miserendino, M.J. and Davis, M. (1992) Extinction of fear-potentiated startle: blockade by infusion of an NMDA antagonist into the amygdala. J. Neurosci., 12: 854–863.

Farah, J.M., Jr. Rao, T.S., Mick, S.J., Coyne, K.E. and Iyengar, S. (1991) N-methyl-D-aspartate treatment increases circulating adrenocorticotropin and luteinizing hormone in the rat. Endocrinology, 128: 1875–1880.

Fendt, M. and Fanselow, M.S. (1999) The neuroanatomical and neurochemical basis of conditioned fear. Neurosci. Biobehav. Rev., 23: 743–760.

Fendt, M., Schmid, S., Thakker, D.R., Jacobson, L.H., Yamamota, R., Mitsukawa, K., Maier, R., McAllister, K.H., Hoyer, D., van der Putten, H., Cryan, J.F. and Flor, P.J. (2007) Activation of mGluR7 alters amygdala plasticity and facilitates extinction of fear memories. Mol. Psychiatry (in press).

Ferraguti, F. and Shigemoto, R. (2006) Metabotropic glutamate receptors. Cell Tissue Res., 326: 483–504.

Finlay, J.M., Zigmond, M.J. and Abercrombie, E.D. (1995) Increased dopamine and norepinephrine release in medial prefrontal cortex induced by acute and chronic stress: effects of diazepam. Neuroscience, 64: 619–628.

Finn, D.A., Rutledge-Gorman, M.T. and Crabbe, J.C. (2003) Genetic animal models of anxiety. Neurogenetics, 4: 109–135.

Fitzgerald, L.W., Ortiz, J., Hamedani, A.G. and Nestler, E.J. (1996) Drugs of abuse and stress increase the expression of GluR1 and NMDAR1 glutamate receptor subunits in the rat ventral tegmental area: common adaptations among cross-sensitizing agents. J. Neurosci., 16: 274–282.

Foster, A.C. and Kemp, J.A. (2006) Glutamate- and GABA-based CNS therapeutics. Curr. Opin. Pharmacol., 6: 7–17.

Fraser, C.M., Cooke, M.J., Fisher, A., Thompson, I.D. and Stone, T.W. (1996) Interactions between ifenprodil and dizocilpine on mouse behaviour in models of anxiety and working memory. Eur. Neuropsychopharmacol., 6: 311–316.

Galici, R., Jones, C.K., Hemstapat, K., Nong, Y., Echemendia, N.G., Williams, L.C., de Paulis, T. and Conn, P.J. (2006) Biphenyl-indanone A, a positive allosteric modulator of the metabotropic glutamate receptor subtype 2, has antipsychotic- and anxiolytic-like effects in mice. J. Pharmacol. Exp. Ther., 318: 173–185.

Gasparini, F., Bruno, V., Battaglia, G., Lukic, S., Leonhardt, T., Inderbitzin, W., Laurie, D., Sommer, B., Varney, M.A., Hess, S.D., Johnson, E.C., Kuhn, R., Urwyler, S., Sauer, D., Portet, C., Schmutz, M., Nicoletti, F. and Flor, P.J. (1999a) (R,S)-4-phosphonophenylglycine, a potent and selective group III metabotropic glutamate receptor agonist, is anticonvulsive and neuroprotective in vivo. J. Pharmacol. Exp. Ther., 289: 1678–1687.

Gasparini, F., Kuhn, R. and Pin, J.P. (2002) Allosteric modulators of group I metabotropic glutamate receptors: novel subtype-selective ligands and therapeutic perspectives. Curr. Opin. Pharmacol., 2: 43–49.

Gasparini, F., Lingenhöhl, K., Stoehr, N., Flor, P.J., Heinrich, M., Vranesic, I., Biollaz, M., Allgeier, H., Heckendorn, R., Urwyler, S., Varney, M.A., Johnson, E.C., Hess, S.D., Rao, S.P., Sacaan, A.I., Santori, E.M., Velicelebi, G. and Kuhn, R. (1999b) 2-Methyl-6-(phenylethynyl)-pyridine (MPEP), a potent, selective and systemically active mGlu5 receptor antagonist. Neuropharmacology, 38: 1493–1503.

Geller, I. and Seifter, S. (1960) The effects of meprobamate, barbiturate, D-amphetamine and promazine on experimentally induced conflict in the rat. Psychopharmacologia, 1: 482–492.

Gewirtz, J.C. and Davis, M. (1997) Second-order fear conditioning prevented by blocking NMDA receptors in amygdala. Nature, 388: 471–474.

Gillespie, C.F. and Ressler, K.J. (2005) Emotional learning and glutamate: translational perspectives. CNS Spectrosc., 10: 831–839.

Gladstone, D.J., Black, S.E. and Hakim, A.M. (2002) Toward wisdom from failure: lessons from neuroprotective stroke trials and new therapeutic directions. Stroke, 33: 2123–2136.

Gogas, K.R. (2006) Glutamate-based therapeutic approaches: NR2B receptor antagonists. Curr. Opin. Pharmacol., 6: 68–74.

Gorman, J.M., Kent, J.M. and Coplan, J.D. (2002) Current and emerging therapeutics of anxiety and stress disorders. In: Davis, K.L. Charney, D.S. and Nemeroff, C.B. (Eds.), Neuropschopharmacology: The Fifth Generation of Progress. Lipincott Williams and Wilkins, Philadelphia, pp. 967–980.

Graeff, F. and Zangrossi, H. Jr. (2002) Animal Models of Anxiety Disorders. In: D'haene, H. den Boer, J.A. and Willner, P. (Eds.), Biological Psychiatry. Wiley Brothers, London, pp. 877–893.

Grillon, C., Cordova, J., Levine, L.R. and Morgan, C.A. III (2003) Anxiolytic effects of a novel group II metabotropic glutamate receptor agonist (LY354740) in the fear-potentiated startle paradigm in humans. Psychopharmacology (Berlin), 168: 446–454.

Guimaraes, F.S., Carobrez, A.P., De Aguiar, J.C. and Graeff, F.G. (1991) Anxiolytic effect in the elevated plus-maze of the NMDA receptor antagonist AP7 microinjected into the dorsal periaqueductal grey. Psychopharmacology (Berlin), 103: 91–94.

Helton, D.R., Tizzano, J.P., Monn, J.A., Schoepp, D.D. and Kallman, M.J. (1998) Anxiolytic and side-effect profile of LY354740: a potent, highly selective, orally active agonist for group II metabotropic glutamate receptors. J. Pharmacol. Exp. Ther., 284: 651–660.

Henley, J.M. (1994) Kainate-binding proteins: phylogeny, structures and possible functions. Trends Pharmacol. Sci., 15: 182–190.

Hestrin, S. (1992) Developmental regulation of NMDA receptor-mediated synaptic currents at a central synapse. Nature, 357: 686–689.

Higgins, G.A., Ballard, T.M., Kew, J.N., Richards, J.G., Kemp, J.A., Adam, G., Woltering, T., Nakanishi, S. and Mutel, V. (2004) Pharmacological manipulation of mGlu2 receptors influences cognitive performance in the rodent. Neuropharmacology, 46: 907–917.

Hintermann, S., Vranesic, I., Allgeier, H., Brulisauer, A., Hoyer, D., Lemaire, M., Moenius, T., Urwyler, S., Whitebread, S., Gasparini, F. and Auberson, Y.P. (2007) ABP688, a novel selective and high affinity ligand for the labeling of mGlu5 receptors: identification, in vitro pharmacology, pharmacokinetic and biodistribution studies. Bioorg. Med. Chem., 15: 903–914.

Holden, C. (2003) Psychiatric drugs. Excited by glutamate. Science, 300: 1866–1868.

Hollmann, M. and Heinemann, S. (1994) Cloned glutamate receptors. Annu. Rev. Neurosci., 17: 31–108.

Hollmann, M., O'Shea-Greenfield, A., Rogers, S.W. and Heinemann, S. (1989) Cloning by functional expression of a member of the glutamate receptor family. Nature, 342: 643–648.

Holmes, A. (2001) Targeted gene mutation approaches to the study of anxiety-like behavior in mice. Neurosci. Biobehav. Rev., 25: 261–273.

Holmes, A., Lachowicz, J.E. and Sibley, D.R. (2004) Phenotypic analysis of dopamine receptor knockout mice; recent insights into the functional specificity of dopamine receptor subtypes. Neuropharmacology, 47: 1117–1134.

Homayoun, H., Stefani, M.R., Adams, B.W., Tamagan, G.D. and Moghaddam, B. (2004) Functional interaction between NMDA and mGlu5 receptors: effects on working memory, instrumental learning, motor behaviors, and dopamine release. Neuropsychopharmacology, 29: 1259–1269.

Iijima, M., Shimazaki, T., Ito, A. and Chaki, S. (2007) Effects of metabotropic glutamate 2/3 receptor antagonists in the stress-induced hyperthermia test in singly housed mice. Psychopharmacology (Berlin), 190: 233–239.

Ikonomidou, C. and Turski, L. (2002) Why did NMDA receptor antagonists fail clinical trials for stroke and traumatic brain injury? Lancet Neurol., 1: 383–386.

Ito, I., Tanabe, S., Kohda, A. and Sugiyama, H. (1990) Allosteric potentiation of quisqualate receptors by a nootropic drug aniracetam. J. Physiol., 424: 533–543.

Jacobson, L.H., Bettler, B., Kaupmann, K. and Cryan, J.F. (2007) Behavioral evaluation of mice deficient in GABA(B(1)) receptor isoforms in tests of unconditioned anxiety. Psychopharmacology (Berlin), 190: 541–553.

Jane, D.E., Jones, P.L., Pook, P.C., Tse, H.W. and Watkins, J.C. (1994) Actions of two new antagonists showing selectivity for different sub-types of metabotropic glutamate receptor in the neonatal rat spinal cord. Br. J. Pharmacol., 112: 809–816.

Jingami, H. (2005) Structural and biochemical views of metabotropic glutamate receptor activation. J. Mol. Neurosci., 26: 123–124.

Joanny, P., Steinberg, J., Oliver, C. and Grino, M. (1997) Glutamate and N-methyl-D-aspartate stimulate rat hypothalamic corticotropin-releasing factor secretion in vitro. J. Neuroendocrinol., 9: 93–97.

Johnson, M.P., Baez, M., Jagdmann, G.E., Jr. Britton, T.C., Large, T.H., Callagaro, D.O., Tizzano, J.P., Monn, J.A. and Schoepp, D.D. (2003) Discovery of allosteric potentiators for the metabotropic glutamate 2 receptor: synthesis and subtype selectivity of N-(4-(2-methoxyphenoxy)phenyl)-N-(2,2,2-trifluoroethylsulfonyl)pyrid 3 ylmethylamine. J. Med. Chem., 46: 3189–3192.

Johnson, M.P., Barda, D., Britton, T.C., Emkey, R., Hornback, W.J., Jagdmann, G.E., McKinzie, D.L., Nisenbaum, E.S., Tizzano, J.P. and Schoepp, D.D. (2005) Metabotropic glutamate 2 receptor potentiators: receptor modulation, frequency-dependent synaptic activity, and efficacy in preclinical anxiety and psychosis model(s). Psychopharmacology (Berlin), 179: 271–283.

Johnson, M.P. and Chamberlain, M. (2002) Modulation of stress-induced and stimulated hyperprolactinemia with the group II metabotropic glutamate receptor selective agonist, LY379268. Neuropharmacology, 43: 799–808.

Johnson, M.P., Kelly, G. and Chamberlain, M. (2001) Changes in rat serum corticosterone after treatment with metabotropic glutamate receptor agonists or antagonists. J. Neuroendocrinol., 13: 670–677.

Johnson, P.L. and Shekhar, A. (2006) Panic-prone state induced in rats with GABA dysfunction in the dorsomedial hypothalamus is mediated by NMDA receptors. J. Neurosci., 26: 7093–7104.

Karcz-Kubicha, M., Jessa, M., Nazar, M., Plaznik, A., Hartmann, S., Parsons, C.G. and Danysz, W. (1997) Anxiolytic activity of glycine-B antagonists and partial agonists – no relation to intrinsic activity in the patch clamp. Neuropharmacology, 36: 1355–1367.

Kehne, J.H., McCloskey, T.C., Baron, B.M., Chi, E.M., Harrison, B.L., Whitten, J.P. and Palfreyman, M.G. (1991) NMDA receptor complex antagonists have potential anxiolytic effects as measured with separation-induced ultrasonic vocalizations. Eur. J. Pharmacol., 193: 283–292.

Keinanen, K., Wisden, W., Sommer, B., Werner, P., Herb, A., Verdoorn, T.A., Sakmann, B. and Seeburg, P.H. (1990) A family of AMPA-selective glutamate receptors. Science, 249: 556–560.

Kellner, M., Muhtz, C., Stark, K., Yassouridis, A., Arlt, J. and Wiedemann, K. (2005) Effects of a metabotropic glutamate(2/3) receptor agonist (LY544344/LY354740) on panic anxiety induced by cholecystokinin tetrapeptide in healthy humans: preliminary results. Psychopharmacology (Berlin), 179: 310–315.

Kemp, J.A. and McKernan, R.M. (2002) NMDA receptor pathways as drug targets. Nat. Neurosci., 5(Suppl.): 1039–1042.

Kessler, R.C. and Greenberg, P.E. (2002) The economic burden of anxiety and stress disorders. In: Davis, K. Charney, D. Coyle, J. and Nemeroff, C. (Eds.), Neuropschopharmacology: The Fifth Generation of Progress. Lipincott Williams and Wilkins, Philadelphia, pp. 981–992.

Kew, J.N. (2004) Positive and negative allosteric modulation of metabotropic glutamate receptors: emerging therapeutic potential. Pharmacol. Ther., 104: 233–244.

Kew, J.N. and Kemp, J.A. (2005) Ionotropic and metabotropic glutamate receptor structure and pharmacology. Psychopharmacology (Berlin), 179: 4–29.

Kew, J.N., Koester, A., Moreau, J.L., Jenck, F., Ouagazzal, A.M., Mutel, V., Richards, J.G., Trube, G., Fischer, G., Montkowski, A., Hundt, W., Reinscheid, R.K., Pauly-Evers, M., Kemp, J.A. and Bluethmann, H. (2000) Functional consequences of reduction in NMDA receptor glycine affinity in mice carrying targeted point mutations in the glycine binding site. J. Neurosci., 20: 4037–4049.

Kim, M., Campeau, S., Falls, W.A. and Davis, M. (1993) Infusion of the non-NMDA receptor antagonist CNQX into the amygdala blocks the expression of fear-potentiated startle. Behav. Neural. Biol., 59: 5–8.

Kingston, A.E., Ornstein, P.L., Wright, R.A., Johnson, B.G., Mayne, N.G., Burnett, J.P., Belagaje, R., Wu, S. and Schoepp, D.D. (1998) LY341495 is a nanomolar potent and selective antagonist of group II metabotropic glutamate receptors. Neuropharmacology, 37: 1–12.

Kishimoto, Y., Kawahara, S., Kirino, Y., Kadotani, H., Nakamura, Y., Ikeda, M. and Yoshioka, T. (1997) Conditioned eyeblink response is impaired in mutant mice lacking NMDA receptor subunit NR2A. Neuroreport, 8: 3717–3721.

Kiyama, Y., Manabe, T., Sakimura, K., Kawakami, F., Mori, H. and Mishina, M. (1998) Increased thresholds for long-term potentiation and contextual learning in mice lacking the NMDA-type glutamate receptor epsilon1 subunit. J. Neurosci., 18: 6704–6712.

Klodzinska, A., Chojnacka-Wojcik, E., Palucha, A., Branski, P., Popik, P. and Pilc, A. (1999) Potential anti-anxiety, anti-addictive effects of LY 354740, a selective group II glutamate metabotropic receptors agonist in animal models. Neuropharmacology, 38: 1831–1839.

Klodzinska, A., Tatarczynska, E., Chojnacka-Wojcik, E., Nowak, G., Cosford, N.D. and Pilc, A. (2004a) Anxiolytic-like effects of MTEP, a potent and selective mGlu5 receptor agonist does not involve GABA(A) signaling. Neuropharmacology, 47: 342–350.

Klodzinska, A., Tatarczynska, E., Stachowicz, K. and Chojnacka-Wojcik, E. (2004b) The anxiolytic-like activity of AIDA (1-aminoindan-1,5-dicarboxylic acid), an mGLu 1 receptor antagonist. J. Physiol. Pharmacol., 55: 113–126.

Kniazeff, J., Bessis, A.S., Maurel, D., Ansanay, H., Prezeau, L. and Pin, J.P. (2004) Closed state of both binding domains of homodimeric mGlu receptors is required for full activity. Nat. Struct. Mol. Biol., 11: 706–713.

Knoflach, F., Mutel, V., Jolidon, S., Kew, J.N., Malherbe, P., Vieira, E., Wichmann, J. and Kemp, J.A. (2001) Positive allosteric modulators of metabotropic glutamate 1 receptor: characterization, mechanism of action, and binding site. Proc. Natl. Acad. Sci. USA, 98: 13402–13407.

Koek, W. and Colpaert, F.C. (1991) Use of a conflict procedure in pigeons to characterize anxiolytic drug activity: evaluation of N-methyl-D-aspartate antagonists. Life Sci., 49: PL37–PL42.

Kotlinska, J. and Liljequist, S. (1998) The putative AMPA receptor antagonist, LY326325, produces anxiolytic-like effects without altering locomotor activity in rats. Pharmacol. Biochem. Behav., 60: 119–124.

Krugers, H.J., Koolhaas, J.M., Bohus, B. and Korf, J. (1993) A single social stress-experience alters glutamate receptor-binding in rat hippocampal CA3 area. Neurosci. Lett., 154: 73–77.

Kugaya, A. and Sanacora, G. (2005) Beyond monoamines: glutamatergic function in mood disorders. CNS Spectrosc., 10: 808–819.

Kushner, M.G., Kim, S.W., Donahue, C., Thuras, P., Adson, D., Kotlyar, M., McCabe, J., Peterson, J. and Foa, E.B. (2007) D-cycloserine augmented exposure therapy for obsessive-compulsive disorder. Biol. Psychiatry, 62: 835–838.

Lang, P.J., Davis, M. and Ohman, A. (2000) Fear and anxiety: animal models and human cognitive psychophysiology. J. Affect. Disord., 61: 137–159.

Ledgerwood, L., Richardson, R. and Cranney, J. (2005) D-cycloserine facilitates extinction of learned fear: effects on reacquisition and generalized extinction. Biol. Psychiatry, 57: 841–847.

LeDoux, J.E. (2000) Emotion circuits in the brain. Annu. Rev. Neurosci., 23: 155–184.

Lees, G.J. (2000) Pharmacology of AMPA/kainate receptor ligands and their therapeutic potential in neurological and psychiatric disorders. Drugs, 59: 33–78.

Lerma, J., Paternain, A.V., Rodriguez-Moreno, A. and Lopez-Garcia, J.C. (2001) Molecular physiology of kainate receptors. Physiol. Rev., 81: 971–998.

Li, X., Inouei, T., Abekawai, T., YiRui, F. and Koyama, T. (2004) Effect of MS-153 on the acquisition and expression of conditioned fear in rats. Eur. J. Pharmacol., 505: 145–149.

Liang, K.C., Hon, W. and Davis, M. (1994) Pre- and posttraining infusion of N-methyl-D-aspartate receptor antagonists into the amygdala impair memory in an inhibitory avoidance task. Behav. Neurosci., 108: 241–253.

Linden, A.M., Baez, M., Bergeron, M. and Schoepp, D.D. (2006) Effects of mGlu2 or mGlu3 receptor deletions on mGlu2/3 receptor agonist (LY354740)-induced brain c-Fos expression: specific roles for mGlu2 in the amygdala and subcortical nuclei, and mGlu3 in the hippocampus. Neuropharmacology, 51: 213–228.

Linden, A.M., Bergeron, M. and Schoepp, D.D. (2005a) Comparison of c-Fos induction in the brain by the mGlu2/3 receptor antagonist LY341495 and agonist LY354740: evidence for widespread endogenous tone at brain mGlu2/3 receptors in vivo. Neuropharmacology, 49(Suppl. 1): 120–134.

Linden, A.M., Greene, S.J., Bergeron, M. and Schoepp, D.D. (2004) Anxiolytic activity of the MGLU2/3 receptor agonist LY354740 on the elevated plus maze is associated with the suppression of stress-induced c-Fos in the hippocampus and increases in c-Fos induction in several other stress-sensitive brain regions. Neuropsychopharmacology, 29: 502–513.

Linden, A.M., Johnson, B.G., Peters, S.C., Shannon, H.E., Tian, M., Wang, Y., Yu, J.L., Koster, A., Baez, M. and Schoepp, D.D. (2002) Increased anxiety-related behavior in mice deficient for metabotropic glutamate 8 (mGlu8) receptor. Neuropharmacology, 43: 251–259.

Linden, A.M., Shannon, H., Baez, M., Yu, J.L., Koester, A. and Schoepp, D.D. (2005b) Anxiolytic-like activity of the mGLU2/3 receptor agonist LY354740 in the elevated plus maze test is disrupted in metabotropic glutamate receptor 2 and 3 knock-out mice. Psychopharmacology (Berlin), 179: 284–291.

Litvin, Y., Blanchard, D.C. and Blanchard, R.J. (2007) Rat 22kHz ultrasonic vocalizations as alarm cries. Behav. Brain. Res., 182: 166–172.

Lu, Y.M., Jia, Z., Janus, C., Henderson, J.T., Gerlai, R., Wojtowicz, J.M. and Roder, J.C. (1997) Mice lacking metabotropic glutamate receptor 5 show impaired learning and reduced CA1 long-term potentiation (LTP) but normal CA3 LTP. J. Neurosci., 17: 5196–5205.

Maj, M., Bruno, V., Dragic, Z., Yamamoto, R., Battaglia, G., Inderbitzin, W., Stoehr, N., Stein, T., Gasparini, F., Vranesic, I., Kuhn, R., Nicoletti, F. and Flor, P.J. (2003) (–)-PHCCC, a positive allosteric modulator of mGluR4: characterization, mechanism of action, and neuroprotection. Neuropharmacology, 45: 895–906.

Malayev, A., Gibbs, T.T. and Farb, D.H. (2002) Inhibition of the NMDA response by pregnenolone sulphate reveals subtype selective modulation of NMDA receptors by sulphated steroids. Br. J. Pharmacol., 135: 901–909.

Mannaioni, G., Marino, M.J., Valenti, O., Traynelis, S.F. and Conn, P.J. (2001) Metabotropic glutamate receptors 1 and 5 differentially regulate CA1 pyramidal cell function. J. Neurosci., 21: 5925–5934.

Maren, S. (1999) Long-term potentiation in the amygdala: a mechanism for emotional learning and memory. Trends Neurosci., 22: 561–567.

Maren, S. (2001) Neurobiology of Pavlovian fear conditioning. Annu. Rev. Neurosci., 24: 897–931.

Marino, M.J. and Conn, P.J. (2006) Glutamate-based therapeutic approaches: allosteric modulators of metabotropic glutamate receptors. Curr. Opin. Pharmacol., 6: 98–102.

Matheus, M.G. and Guimaraes, F.S. (1997) Antagonism of non-NMDA receptors in the dorsal periaqueductal grey induces anxiolytic effect in the elevated plus maze. Psychopharmacology (Berlin), 132: 14–18.

Mathew, S.J., Amiel, J.M., Coplan, J.D., Fitterling, H.A., Sackeim, H.A. and Gorman, J.M. (2005) Open-label trial of riluzole in generalized anxiety disorder. Am. J. Psychiatry, 162: 2379–2381.

Mathiesen, J.M., Svendsen, N., Brauner-Osborne, H., Thomsen, C. and Ramirez, M.T. (2003) Positive allosteric modulation of the human metabotropic glutamate receptor 4 (hmGluR4) by SIB-1893 and MPEP. Br. J. Pharmacol., 138: 1026–1030.

Mead, A.N., Morris, H.V., Dixon, C.I., Rulten, S.L., Mayne, L.V., Zamanillo, D. and Stephens, D.N. (2006) AMPA receptor GluR2, but not GluR1, subunit deletion impairs emotional response conditioning in mice. Behav. Neurosci., 120: 241–248.

Menard, J. and Treit, D. (2000) Intra-septal infusions of excitatory amino acid receptor antagonists have differential effects in two animal models of anxiety. Behav. Pharmacol., 11: 99–108.

Miczek, K.A., Weerts, E.M., Vivian, J.A. and Barros, H.M. (1995) Aggression, anxiety and vocalizations in animals: GABAA and 5-HT anxiolytics. Psychopharmacology (Berlin), 121: 38–56.

Mikolajczak, P., Okulicz-Kozaryn, I., Kaminska, E., Szulc, M., Dyr, W. and Kostowski, W. (2003) Lack of ifenprodil anxiolytic activity after its multiple treatment in chronically ethanol-treated rats. Alcohol, 38: 310–315.

Millan, M.J. (2003) The neurobiology and control of anxious states. Prog. Neurobiol., 70: 83–244.

Millan, M.J. and Brocco, M. (2003) The Vogel conflict test: procedural aspects, gamma-aminobutyric acid, glutamate and monoamines. Eur. J. Pharmacol., 463: 67–96.

Miserendino, M.J., Sananes, C.B., Melia, K.R. and Davis, M. (1990) Blocking of acquisition but not expression of conditioned fear-potentiated startle by NMDA antagonists in the amygdala. Nature, 345: 716–718.

Mitsukawa, K., Yamamoto, R., Ofner, S., Nozulak, J., Pescott, O., Lukic, S., Stoehr, N., Mombereau, C., Kuhn, R., McAllister, K.H., van der Putten, H., Cryan, J.F. and Flor, P.J. (2005) A selective metabotropic glutamate receptor 7 agonist: activation of receptor signaling via an allosteric site modulates stress parameters in vivo. Proc. Natl. Acad. Sci. USA, 102: 18712–18717.

Moghaddam, B. (1993) Stress preferentially increases extraneuronal levels of excitatory amino acids in the prefrontal cortex: comparison to hippocampus and basal ganglia. J. Neurochem., 60: 1650–1657.

Moghaddam, B., Bolinao, M.L., Stein-Behrens, B. and Sapolsky, R. (1994) Glucocorticoids mediate the stress-induced extracellular accumulation of glutamate. Brain Res., 655: 251–254.

Molchanov, M.L. and Guimaraes, F.S. (2002) Anxiolytic-like effects of AP7 injected into the dorsolateral or ventrolateral columns of the periaqueductal gray of rats. Psychopharmacology (Berlin), 160: 30–38.

Molina-Hernandez, M., Tellez-Alcantara, N.P., Perez-Garcia, J., Olivera-Lopez, J.I. and Jaramillo, M.T. (2006) Antidepressant-like and anxiolytic-like actions of the mGlu5 receptor antagonist MTEP, microinjected into lateral septal nuclei of male Wistar rats. Prog. Neuropsychopharmacol. Biol. Psychiatry, 30: 1129–1135.

Monn, J.A., Valli, M.J., Massey, S.M., Wright, R.A., Salhoff, C.R., Johnson, B.G., Howe, T., Alt, C.A., Rhodes, G.A., Robey, R.L., Griffey, K.R., Tizzano, J.P., Kallman, M.J., Helton, D.R. and Schoepp, D.D. (1997) Design, synthesis, and pharmacological characterization of (+)-2-aminobicyclo[3.1.0]hexane-2,6-dicarboxylic acid (LY354740): a potent, selective, and orally active group 2 metabotropic glutamate receptor agonist possessing anticonvulsant and anxiolytic properties. J. Med. Chem., 40: 528–537.

Monyer, H., Burnashev, N., Laurie, D.J., Sakmann, B. and Seeburg, P.H. (1994) Developmental and regional expression in the rat brain and functional properties of four NMDA receptors. Neuron, 12: 529–540.

Monyer, H., Sprengel, R., Schoepfer, R., Herb, A., Higuchi, M., Lomeli, H., Burnashev, N., Sakmann, B. and Seeburg, P.H. (1992) Heteromeric NMDA receptors: molecular and functional distinction of subtypes. Science, 256: 1217–1221.

More, J.C., Nistico, R., Dolman, N.P., Clarke, V.R., Alt, A.J., Ogden, A.M., Buelens, F.P., Troop, H.M.,

Kelland, G.L., Pilato, F., Bleakman, D., Bortolotto, Z.A., Collingridge, G.L. and Jane, D.E. (2004) Characterisation of UBP296: a novel, potent and selective kainate receptor antagonist. Neuropharmacology, 47: 46–64.

Moriya, T., Kouzu, Y., Shibata, S., Kadotani, H., Fukunaga, K., Miyamoto, E. and Yoshioka, T. (2000) Close linkage between calcium/calmodulin kinase II alpha/beta and NMDA-2A receptors in the lateral amygdala and significance for retrieval of auditory fear conditioning. Eur. J. Neurosci., 12: 3307–3314.

Muir, K.W. (2006) Glutamate-based therapeutic approaches: clinical trials with NMDA antagonists. Curr. Opin. Pharmacol., 6: 53–60.

Myers, K.M. and Davis, M. (2007) Mechanisms of fear extinction. Mol. Psychiatry, 12: 120–150.

Naie, K. and Manahan-Vaughan, D. (2004) Regulation by metabotropic glutamate receptor 5 of LTP in the dentate gyrus of freely moving rats: relevance for learning and memory formation. Cereb. Cortex, 14: 189–198.

Nakanishi, S. (1994) Metabotropic glutamate receptors: synaptic transmission, modulation, and plasticity. Neuron, 13: 1031–1037.

Nakanishi, S. and Masu, M. (1994) Molecular diversity and functions of glutamate receptors. Annu. Rev. Biophys. Biomol. Struct., 23: 319–348.

Nemeroff, C.B. (2003) Anxiolytics: past, present, and future agents. J. Clin. Psychiatry, 64(Suppl. 3): 3–6.

Nordquist, R.E., Durkin, S., Jaeschke, G. and Spooren, W. (2007) Stress-induced hyperthermia: Effects of acute and repeated dosing of MPEP. Eur. J. Pharmacol., 568: 198–202.

O'Brien, J.A., Lemaire, W., Chen, T.B., Chang, R.S., Jacobson, M.A., Ha, S.N., Lindsley, C.W., Schaffhauser, H.J., Sur, C., Pettibone, D.J., Conn, P.J. and Williams, D.L. Jr. (2003) A family of highly selective allosteric modulators of the metabotropic glutamate receptor subtype 5. Mol. Pharmacol., 64: 731–740.

O'Brien, J.A., Lemaire, W., Wittmann, M., Jacobson, M.A., Ha, S.N., Wisnoski, D.D., Lindsley, C.W., Schaffhauser, H.J., Rowe, B., Sur, C., Duggan, M.E., Pettibone, D.J., Conn, P.J. and Williams, D.L. Jr. (2004) A novel selective allosteric modulator potentiates the activity of native metabotropic glutamate receptor subtype 5 in rat forebrain. J. Pharmacol. Exp. Ther., 309: 568–577.

Ohishi, H., Neki, A. and Mizuno, N. (1998) Distribution of a metabotropic glutamate receptor, mGluR2, in the central nervous system of the rat and mouse: an immunohistochemical study with a monoclonal antibody. Neurosci. Res., 30: 65–82.

Ohishi, H., Shigemoto, R., Nakanishi, S. and Mizuno, N. (1993a) Distribution of the messenger RNA for a metabotropic glutamate receptor, mGluR2, in the central nervous system of the rat. Neuroscience, 53: 1009–1018.

Ohishi, H., Shigemoto, R., Nakanishi, S. and Mizuno, N. (1993b) Distribution of the mRNA for a metabotropic glutamate receptor (mGluR3) in the rat brain: an in situ hybridization study. J. Comp. Neurol., 335: 252–266.

Okabe, S., Collin, C., Auerbach, J.M., Meiri, N., Bengzon, J., Kennedy, M.B., Segal, M. and McKay, R.D. (1998) Hippocampal synaptic plasticity in mice overexpressing an embryonic subunit of the NMDA receptor. J. Neurosci., 18: 4177–4188.

Ozawa, S., Kamiya, H. and Tsuzuki, K. (1998) Glutamate receptors in the mammalian central nervous system. Prog. Neurobiol., 54: 581–618.

Page, M.E., Szeliga, P., Gasparini, F. and Cryan, J.F. (2005) Blockade of the mGlu5 receptor decreases basal and stress-induced cortical norepinephrine in rodents. Psychopharmacology (Berlin), 179: 240–246.

Palucha, A., Tatarczynska, E., Branski, P., Szewczyk, B., Wieronska, J.M., Klak, K., Chojnacka-Wojcik, E., Nowak, G. and Pilc, A. (2004) Group III mGlu receptor agonists produce anxiolytic- and antidepressant-like effects after central administration in rats. Neuropharmacology, 46: 151–159.

Partin, K.M., Patneau, D.K., Winters, C.A., Mayer, M.L. and Buonanno, A. (1993) Selective modulation of desensitization at AMPA versus kainate receptors by cyclothiazide and concanavalin A. Neuron, 11: 1069–1082.

Pavlov, I.P. (1927) Conditioned reflexes: an investigation of the physiological activity of the cerebral cortex. Oxford University Press, London.

Pechnick, R.N., George, R. and Poland, R.E. (1987) MK-801 stimulates the release of adrenocorticotrophin but not does affect the release of prolactin in the rat. Eur. J. Pharmacol., 141: 323–324.

Perez de la Mora, M., Lara-Garcia, D., Jacobsen, K.X., Vazquez-Garcia, M., Crespo-Ramirez, M., Flores-Gracia, C., Escamilla-Marvan, E. and Fuxe, K. (2006) Anxiolytic-like effects of the selective metabotropic glutamate receptor 5 antagonist MPEP after its intra-amygdaloid microinjection in three different non-conditioned rat models of anxiety. Eur. J. Neurosci., 23: 2749–2759.

Petersen, S., Bomme, C., Baastrup, C., Kemp, A. and Christoffersen, G.R. (2002) Differential effects of mGluR1 and mGlur5 antagonism on spatial learning in rats. Pharmacol. Biochem. Behav., 73: 381–389.

Pfaff, D. (2001) Precision in mouse behavior genetics. Proc. Natl. Acad. Sci. USA, 98: 5957–5960.

Phelps, E.A. and LeDoux, J.E. (2005) Contributions of the amygdala to emotion processing: from animal models to human behavior. Neuron, 48: 175–187.

Pickering, C., Gustafsson, L., Cebere, A., Nylander, I. and Liljequist, S. (2006) Repeated maternal separation of male Wistar rats alters glutamate receptor expression in the hippocampus but not the prefrontal cortex. Brain Res., 1099: 101–108.

Pietersen, C.Y., Bosker, F.J., Postema, F., Fokkema, D.S., Korf, J. and den Boer, J.A. (2006) Ketamine administration disturbs behavioural and distributed neural correlates of fear conditioning in the rat. Prog. Neuropsychopharmacol. Biol. Psychiatry, 30: 1209–1218.

Pietraszek, M., Sukhanov, I., Maciejak, P., Szyndler, J., Gravius, A., Wislowska, A., Plaznik, A., Bespalov, A.Y. and Danysz, W. (2005) Anxiolytic-like effects of mGlu1 and mGlu5 receptor antagonists in rats. Eur. J. Pharmacol., 514: 25–34.

Pilc, A., Klodzinska, A., Branski, P., Nowak, G., Palucha, A., Szewczyk, B., Tatarczynska, E., Chojnacka-Wojcik, E. and Wieronska, J.M. (2002) Multiple MPEP administrations evoke anxiolytic- and antidepressant-like effects in rats. Neuropharmacology, 43: 181–187.

Pin, J.P. and Acher, F. (2002) The metabotropic glutamate receptors: structure, activation mechanism and pharmacology. Curr. Drug Targets CNS Neurol. Disord., 1: 297–317.

Pin, J.P. and Duvoisin, R. (1995) The metabotropic glutamate receptors: structure and functions. Neuropharmacology, 34: 1–26.

Plaznik, A., Palejko, W., Nazar, M. and Jessa, M. (1994) Effects of antagonists at the NMDA receptor complex in two models of anxiety. Eur. Neuropsychopharmacol., 4: 503–512.

Poleszak, E., Szewczyk, B., Kedzierska, E., Wlaz, P., Pilc, A. and Nowak, G. (2004) Antidepressant- and anxiolytic-like activity of magnesium in mice. Pharmacol. Biochem. Behav., 78: 7–12.

Porter, R.H., Jaeschke, G., Spooren, W., Ballard, T.M., Buttelmann, B., Kolczewski, S., Peters, J.U., Prinssen, E., Wichmann, J., Vieira, E., Muhlemann, A., Gatti, S., Mutel, V. and Malherbe, P. (2005) Fenobam: a clinically validated nonbenzodiazepine anxiolytic is a potent, selective, and noncompetitive mGlu5 receptor antagonist with inverse agonist activity. J. Pharmacol. Exp. Ther., 315: 711–721.

Przegalinski, E., Tatarczynska, E., Deren-Wesolek, A. and Chojnacka-Wojcik, E. (1996) Anticonflict effects of a competitive NMDA receptor antagonist and a partial agonist at strychnine-insensitive glycine receptors. Pharmacol. Biochem. Behav., 54: 73–77.

Przegalinski, E., Tatarczynska, E., Klodzinska, A. and Chojnacka-Wojcik, E. (1999) Tolerance to anxiolytic- and antidepressant-like effects of a partial agonist of glycineB receptors. Pharmacol. Biochem. Behav., 64: 461–466.

Rae, M.G. and Irving, A.J. (2004) Both mGluR1 and mGluR5 mediate Ca^{2+} release and inward currents in hippocampal CA1 pyramidal neurons. Neuropharmacology, 46: 1057–1069.

Rainnie, D.G., Bergeron, R., Sajdyk, T.J., Patil, M., Gehlert, D.R. and Shekhar, A. (2004) Corticotrophin releasing factor-induced synaptic plasticity in the amygdala translates stress into emotional disorders. J. Neurosci., 24: 3471–3479.

298

Ransom, R.W. and Stec, N.L. (1988) Cooperative modulation of [3H]MK-801 binding to the *N*-methyl-D-aspartate receptor-ion channel complex by L-glutamate, glycine, and polyamines. J. Neurochem., 51: 830–836.

Ressler, K.J., Rothbaum, B.O., Tannenbaum, L., Anderson, P., Graap, K., Zimand, E., Hodges, L. and Davis, M. (2004) Cognitive enhancers as adjuncts to psychotherapy: use of D-cycloserine in phobic individuals to facilitate extinction of fear. Arch. Gen. Psychiatry, 61: 1136–1144.

Riedel, G., Casabona, G., Platt, B., Macphail, E.M. and Nicoletti, F. (2000) Fear conditioning-induced time- and subregion-specific increase in expression of mGlu5 receptor protein in rat hippocampus. Neuropharmacology, 39: 1943–1951.

Riedel, G., Platt, B. and Micheau, J. (2003) Glutamate receptor function in learning and memory. Behav. Brain Res., 140: 1–47.

Robbins, M.J., Starr, K.R., Honey, A., Soffin, E.M., Rourke, C., Jones, G.A., Kelly, F.M., Strum, J., Melarange, R.A., Harris, A.J., Rocheville, M., Rupniak, T., Murdock, P.R., Jones, D.N., Kew, J.N. and Maycox, P.R. (2007) Evaluation of the mGlu8 receptor as a putative therapeutic target in schizophrenia. Brain Res., 1152: 215–227.

Rodgers, R.J. (1997) Animal models of 'anxiety': where next? Behav. Pharmacol., 8: 477–496. discussion 497–504.

Rodgers, R.J., Cao, B.J., Dalvi, A. and Holmes, A. (1997) Animal models of anxiety: an ethological perspective. Braz. J. Med. Biol. Res., 30: 289–304.

Rodrigues, S.M., Bauer, E.P., Farb, C.R., Schafe, G.E. and LeDoux, J.E. (2002) The group I metabotropic glutamate receptor mGluR5 is required for fear memory formation and long-term potentiation in the lateral amygdala. J. Neurosci., 22: 5219–5229.

Rogan, M.T., Staubli, U.V. and LeDoux, J.E. (1997) Fear conditioning induces associative long-term potentiation in the amygdala. Nature, 390: 604–607.

Rogawski, M.A. and Donevan, S.D. (1999) AMPA receptors in epilepsy and as targets for antiepileptic drugs. Adv. Neurol., 79: 947–963.

Roppe, J.R., Wang, B., Huang, D., Tehrani, L., Kamenecka, T., Schweiger, E.J., Anderson, J.J., Brodkin, J., Jiang, X., Cramer, M., Chung, J., Reyes-Manalo, G., Munoz, B. and Cosford, N.D. (2004) 5-[(2-Methyl-1,3-thiazol-4-yl)ethynyl]-2,3′-bipyridine: a highly potent, orally active metabotropic glutamate subtype 5 (mGlu5) receptor antagonist with anxiolytic activity. Bioorg. Med. Chem. Lett., 14: 3993–3996.

Rorick-Kehn, L.M., Hart, J.C. and McKinzie, D.L. (2005) Pharmacological characterization of stress-induced hyperthermia in DBA/2 mice using metabotropic and ionotropic glutamate receptor ligands. Psychopharmacology (Berlin), 183: 226–240.

Rorick-Kehn, L.M., Johnson, B.G., Knitowski, K.M., Salhoff, C.R., Witkin, J.M., Perry, K.W., Griffey, K.I., Tizzano, J.P., Monn, J.A., McKinzie, D.L. and Schoepp, D.D. (2007) In vivo pharmacological characterization of the structurally novel, potent, selective mGlu2/3 receptor agonist LY404039 in animal models of psychiatric disorders. Psychopharmacology (Berlin), 193: 121–136.

Rorick-Kehn, L.M., Perkins, E.J., Knitowski, K.M., Hart, J.C., Johnson, B.G., Schoepp, D.D. and McKinzie, D.L. (2006) Improved bioavailability of the mGlu2/3 receptor agonist LY354740 using a prodrug strategy: in vivo pharmacology of LY544344. J. Pharmacol. Exp. Ther., 316: 905–913.

Rosa, M.L., Guimaraes, F.S., Pearson, R.C. and Del Bel, E.A. (2002) Effects of single or repeated restraint stress on GluR1 and GluR2 flip and flop mRNA expression in the hippocampal formation. Brain Res. Bull., 59: 117–124.

Ruel, J., Guitton, M.J. and Puell, J.L. (2002) Negative allosteric modulation of AMPA-preferring receptors by the selective isomer GYKI 53784 (LY303070), a specific non-competitive AMPA antagonist. CNS Drug Rev., 8: 235–254.

Sajdyk, T.J. and Shekhar, A. (1997) Excitatory amino acid receptors in the basolateral amygdala regulate anxiety responses in the social interaction test. Brain Res., 764: 262–264.

Sakimura, K., Kutsuwada, T., Ito, I., Manabe, T., Takayama, C., Kushiya, E., Yagi, T., Aizawa, S., Inoue, Y. and Sugiyama, H. (1995) Reduced hippocampal LTP and spatial learning in mice lacking NMDA receptor epsilon 1 subunit. Nature, 373: 151–155.

Salas, R., Pieri, F., Fung, B., Dani, J.A. and De Biasi, M. (2003) Altered anxiety-related responses in mutant mice lacking the beta4 subunit of the nicotinic receptor. J. Neurosci., 23: 6255–6263.

Sananes, C.B. and Davis, M. (1992) *N*-methyl-D-aspartate lesions of the lateral and basolateral nuclei of the amygdala block fear-potentiated startle and shock sensitization of startle. Behav. Neurosci., 106: 72–80.

Sanchez, C. (2003) Stress-induced vocalisation in adult animals. A valid model of anxiety? Eur. J. Pharmacol., 463: 133–143.

Sandford, J.J., Argyropoulos, S.V. and Nutt, D.J. (2000) The psychobiology of anxiolytic drugs. Part 1: basic neurobiology. Pharmacol. Ther., 88: 197–212.

Scaccianoce, S., Matrisciano, F., Del Bianco, P., Caricasole, A., Di Giorgi Gerevini, V., Cappuccio, I., Melchiorri, D., Battaglia, G. and Nicoletti, F. (2003) Endogenous activation of group-II metabotropic glutamate receptors inhibits the hypothalamic–pituitary–adrenocortical axis. Neuropharmacology, 44: 555–561.

Schachtman, T.R., Bills, C., Ghinescu, R., Murch, K., Serfozo, P. and Simonyi, A. (2003) MPEP, a selective metabotropic glutamate receptor 5 antagonist, attenuates conditioned taste aversion in rats. Behav. Brain Res., 141: 177–182.

Schmidt, W.J. (1994) Behavioural effects of NMDA-receptor antagonists. J. Neural Transm. Suppl., 43: 63–69.

Schoepp, D.D. (2001) Unveiling the functions of presynaptic metabotropic glutamate receptors in the central nervous system. J. Pharmacol. Exp. Ther., 299: 12–20.

Schoepp, D.D., Goldsworthy, J., Johnson, B.G., Salhoff, C.R. and Baker, S.R. (1994) 3,5-dihydroxyphenylglycine is a highly selective agonist for phosphoinositide-linked metabotropic glutamate receptors in the rat hippocampus. J. Neurochem., 63: 769–772.

Schoepp, D.D., Jane, D.E. and Monn, J.A. (1999) Pharmacological agents acting at subtypes of metabotropic glutamate receptors. Neuropharmacology, 38: 1431–1476.

Schrader, L.A. and Tasker, J.G. (1997a) Modulation of multiple potassium currents by metabotropic glutamate receptors in neurons of the hypothalamic supraoptic nucleus. J. Neurophysiol., 78: 3428–3437.

Schrader, L.A. and Tasker, J.G. (1997b) Presynaptic modulation by metabotropic glutamate receptors of excitatory and inhibitory synaptic inputs to hypothalamic magnocellular neurons. J. Neurophysiol., 77: 527–536.

Schulz, B., Fendt, M., Gasparini, F., Lingenhohl, K., Kuhn, R. and Koch, M. (2001) The metabotropic glutamate receptor antagonist 2-methyl-6-(phenylethynyl)-pyridine (MPEP) blocks fear conditioning in rats. Neuropharmacology, 41: 1–7.

Schwendt, M. and Jezova, D. (2000) Gene expression of two glutamate receptor subunits in response to repeated stress exposure in rat hippocampus. Cell Mol. Neurobiol., 20: 319–329.

Seeburg, P.H. (1996) The role of RNA editing in controlling glutamate receptor channel properties. J. Neurochem., 66: 1–5.

Semyanov, A. and Kullmann, D.M. (2000) Modulation of GABAergic signaling among interneurons by metabotropic glutamate receptors. Neuron, 25: 663–672.

Senechal, Y., Kelly, P.H., Cryan, J.F., Natt, F. and Dev, K.K. (2007) Amyloid precursor protein knockdown by siRNA impairs spontaneous alternation in adult mice. J. Neurochem., 102: 1928–1940.

Sheardown, M.J., Nielsen, E.O., Hansen, A.J., Jacobsen, P. and Honore, T. (1990) 2,3-Dihydroxy-6-nitro-7-sulfamoyl-benzo(F)quinoxaline: a neuroprotectant for cerebral ischemia. Science, 247: 571–574.

Shekhar, A. and Keim, S.R. (2000) LY354740, a potent group II metabotropic glutamate receptor agonist prevents lactate-induced panic-like response in panic-prone rats. Neuropharmacology, 39: 1139–1146.

Shekhar, A., McCann, U.D., Meaney, M.J., Blanchard, D.C., Davis, M., Frey, K.A., Liberzon, I., Overall, K.L., Shear, M.K., Tecott, L.H. and Winsky, L. (2001) Summary of a National Institute of Mental Health workshop: developing animal models of anxiety disorders. Psychopharmacology (Berlin), 157: 327–339.

Shekhar, A., Truitt, W., Rainnie, D. and Sajdyk, T. (2005) Role of stress, corticotrophin releasing factor (CRF) and amygdala plasticity in chronic anxiety. Stress, 8: 209–219.

Sheng, M., Cummings, J., Roldan, L.A., Jan, Y.N. and Jan, L.Y. (1994) Changing subunit composition of heteromeric NMDA receptors during development of rat cortex. Nature, 368: 144–147.

Shigemoto, R., Kinoshita, A., Wada, E., Nomura, S., Ohishi, H., Takada, M., Flor, P.J., Neki, A., Abe, T., Nakanishi, S. and Mizuno, N. (1997) Differential presynaptic localization of metabotropic glutamate receptor subtypes in the rat hippocampus. J. Neurosci., 17: 7503–7522.

Shimazaki, T., Iijima, M. and Chaki, S. (2004) Anxiolytic-like activity of MGS0039, a potent group II metabotropic glutamate receptor antagonist, in a marble-burying behavior test. Eur. J. Pharmacol., 501: 121–125.

Simon, A.B. and Gorman, J.M. (2006) Advances in the treatment of anxiety: targeting glutamate. NeuroRx, 3: 57–68.

Singewald, N., Zhou, G.Y., Chen, F. and Philippu, A. (1996) Corticotropin-releasing factor modulates basal and stress-induced excitatory amino acid release in the locus coeruleus of conscious rats. Neurosci. Lett., 204: 45–48.

Singewald, N., Zhou, G.Y. and Schneider, C. (1995) Release of excitatory and inhibitory amino acids from the locus coeruleus of conscious rats by cardiovascular stimuli and various forms of acute stress. Brain Res., 704: 42–50.

Smialowska, M., Wieronska, J.M., Domin, H. and Zieba, B. (2006) The effect of Intrahippocampal Injection of Group II and III metobotropic glutamate receptor agonists on anxiety; the role of neuropeptide Y. Neuropsychopharmacology, 32: 1242–1250.

Sommer, B. and Seeburg, P.H. (1992) Glutamate receptor channels: novel properties and new clones. Trends Pharmacol. Sci., 13: 291–296.

Spooren, W., Ballard, T., Gasparini, F., Amalric, M., Mutel, V. and Schreiber, R. (2003) Insight into the function of Group I and Group II metabotropic glutamate (mGlu) receptors: behavioural characterization and implications for the treatment of CNS disorders. Behav. Pharmacol., 14: 257–277.

Spooren, W. and Gasparini, F. (2004) mGlu5 receptor antagonists: a novel class of anxiolytics? Drug News Perspect., 17: 251–257.

Spooren, W.P., Schoeffter, P., Gasparini, F., Kuhn, R. and Gentsch, C. (2002) Pharmacological and

300

endocrinological characterisation of stress-induced hyperthermia in singly housed mice using classical and candidate anxiolytics (LY314582, MPEP and NKP608). Eur. J. Pharmacol., 435: 161–170.

Spooren, W.P., Vassout, A., Neijt, H.C., Kuhn, R., Gasparini, F., Roux, S., Porsolt, R.D. and Gentsch, C. (2000) Anxiolytic-like effects of the prototypical metabotropic glutamate receptor 5 antagonist 2-methyl-6-(phenylethynyl)pyridine in rodents. J. Pharmacol. Exp. Ther., 295: 1267–1275.

Stachowicz, K., Chojnacka-Wojcik, E., Klak, K. and Pilc, A. (2007) Anxiolytic-like effect of group III mGlu receptor antagonist is serotonin-dependent. Neuropharmacology, 52: 306–312.

Stachowicz, K., Klak, K., Klodzinska, A., Chojnacka-Wojcik, E. and Pilc, A. (2004) Anxiolytic-like effects of PHCCC, an allosteric modulator of mGlu4 receptors, in rats. Eur. J. Pharmacol., 498: 153–156.

Stachowicz, K., Klak, K., Pilc, A. and Chojnacka-Wojcik, E. (2005) Lack of the antianxiety-like effect of (S)-3, 4-DCPG, an mGlu8 receptor agonist, after central administration in rats. Pharmacol. Rep., 57: 856–860.

Stahl, S.M. (2004a) Anticonvulsants as anxiolytics, part 1: tiagabine and other anticonvulsants with actions on GABA. J. Clin. Psychiatry, 65: 291–292.

Stahl, S.M. (2004b) Anticonvulsants as anxiolytics, part 2: pregabalin and gabapentin as alpha(2)delta ligands at voltage-gated calcium channels. J. Clin. Psychiatry, 65: 460–461.

Steckler, T., Lavreysen, H., Oliveira, A.M., Aerts, N., Van Craenendonck, H., Prickaerts, J., Megens, A. and Lesage, A.S. (2005a) Effects of mGlu1 receptor blockade on anxiety-related behaviour in the rat lick suppression test. Psychopharmacology (Berlin), 179: 198–206.

Steckler, T., Oliveira, A.F., Van Dyck, C., Van Craenendonck, H., Mateus, A.M., Langlois, X., Lesage, A.S. and Prickaerts, J. (2005b) Metabotropic glutamate receptor 1 blockade impairs acquisition and retention in a spatial Water maze task. Behav. Brain Res., 164: 52–60.

Stephens, D.N., Meldrum, B.S., Weidmann, R., Schneider, C. and Grutzner, M. (1986) Does the excitatory amino acid receptor antagonist 2-APH exhibit anxiolytic activity? Psychopharmacology (Berlin), 90: 166–169.

Stiedl, O., Meyer, M., Jahn, O., Ogren, S.O. and Spiess, J. (2005) Corticotropin-releasing factor receptor 1 and central heart rate regulation in mice during expression of conditioned fear. J. Pharmacol. Exp. Ther., 312: 905–916.

Stutzmann, J.M., Cintrat, P., Laduron, P.M. and Blanchard, J.C. (1989) Riluzole antagonizes the anxiogenic properties of the beta-carboline FG 7142 in rats. Psychopharmacology (Berlin), 99: 515–519.

Swanson, C.J., Bures, M., Johnson, M.P., Linden, A.M., Monn, J.A. and Schoepp, D.D. (2005) Metabotropic glutamate receptors as novel targets for anxiety and stress disorders. Nat. Rev. Drug Discov., 4: 131–144.

Swanson, G.T., Green, T. and Heinemann, S.F. (1998) Kainate receptors exhibit differential sensitivities to (S)-5-iodowillardiine. Mol. Pharmacol., 53: 942–949.

Talalaenko, A.N., Pankrat'ev, D.V. and Goncharenko, N.V. (2003) Neurochemical characteristics of the ventromedial hypothalamus in mediating the anti-aversive effects of anxiolytics in different models of anxiety. Neurosci. Behav. Physiol., 33: 255–261.

Tamaru, Y., Nomura, S., Mizuno, N. and Shigemoto, R. (2001) Distribution of metabotropic glutamate receptor mGluR3 in the mouse CNS: differential location relative to pre- and postsynaptic sites. Neuroscience, 106: 481–503.

Tang, Y.P., Shimizu, E., Dube, G.R., Rampon, C., Kerchner, G.A., Zhuo, M., Liu, G. and Tsien, J.Z. (1999) Genetic enhancement of learning and memory in mice. Nature, 401: 63–69.

Tatarczynska, E., Klodzinska, A., Chojnacka-Wojcik, E., Palucha, A., Gasparini, F., Kuhn, R. and Pilc, A. (2001a) Potential anxiolytic- and antidepressant-like effects of MPEP, a potent, selective and systemically active mGlu5 receptor antagonist. Br. J. Pharmacol., 132: 1423–1430.

Tatarczynska, E., Klodzinska, A., Kroczka, B., Chojnacka-Wojcik, E. and Pilc, A. (2001b) The antianxiety-like effects of antagonists of group I and agonists of group II and III metabotropic glutamate receptors after intrahippocampal administration. Psychopharmacology (Berlin), 158: 94–99.

Tecott, L.H. (2003) The genes and brains of mice and men. Am. J. Psychiatry, 160: 646–656.

Thakker, D.R., Hoyer, D. and Cryan, J.F. (2006) Interfering with the brain: use of RNA interference for understanding the pathophysiology of psychiatric and neurological disorders. Pharmacol. Ther., 109: 413–438.

Thakker, D.R., Natt, F., Husken, D., Maier, R., Muller, M., van der Putten, H., Hoyer, D. and Cryan, J.F. (2004) Neurochemical and behavioral consequences of widespread gene knockdown in the adult mouse brain by using nonviral RNA interference. Proc. Natl. Acad. Sci. USA, 101: 17270–17275.

Thakker, D.R., Natt, F., Husken, D., van der Putten, H., Maier, R., Hoyer, D. and Cryan, J.F. (2005) siRNA-mediated knockdown of the serotonin transporter in the adult mouse brain. Mol. Psychiatry, 10: 782–789.

Thomas, N.K., Wright, R.A., Howson, P.A., Kingston, A.E., Schoepp, D.D. and Jane, D.E. (2001) (S)-3, 4-DCPG, a potent and selective mGlu8a receptor agonist, activates metabotropic glutamate receptors on primary afferent terminals in the neonatal rat spinal cord. Neuropharmacology, 40: 311–318.

Thomsen, C., Boel, E. and Suzdak, P.D. (1994) Actions of phenylglycine analogs at subtypes of the metabotropic glutamate receptor family. Eur. J. Pharmacol., 267: 77–84.

Tordera, R.M., Totterdell, S., Wojcik, S.M., Brose, N., Elizalde, N., Lasheras, B. and Del Rio, J. (2007) Enhanced anxiety, depressive-like behaviour and impaired recognition memory in mice with reduced expression of the vesicular glutamate transporter 1 (VGLUT1). Eur. J. Neurosci., 25: 281–290.

Trullas, R., Jackson, B. and Skolnick, P. (1989) Anxiolytic properties of 1-aminocyclopropanecarboxylic acid, a ligand at strychnine-insensitive glycine receptors. Pharmacol. Biochem. Behav., 34: 313–316.

Turski, L., Jacobsen, P., Honore, T. and Stephens, D.N. (1992) Relief of experimental spasticity and anxiolytic/anticonvulsant actions of the alpha-amino-3-hydroxy-5-methyl-4-isoxazolepropionate antagonist 2,3-dihydroxy-6-nitro-7-sulfamoyl-benzo(F)quinoxaline. J. Pharmacol. Exp. Ther., 260: 742–747.

Valenti, O., Conn, P.J. and Marino, M.J. (2002) Distinct physiological roles of the Gq-coupled metabotropic glutamate receptors Co-expressed in the same neuronal populations. J. Cell Physiol., 191: 125–137.

Varty, G.B., Grilli, M., Forlani, A., Fredduzzi, S., Grzelak, M.E., Guthrie, D.H., Hodgson, R.A., Lu, S.X., Nicolussi, E., Pond, A.J., Parker, E.M., Hunter, J.C., Higgins, G.A., Reggiani, A. and Bertorelli, R. (2005) The antinociceptive and anxiolytic-like effects of the metabotropic glutamate receptor 5 (mGluR5) antagonists, MPEP and MTEP, and the mGluR1 antagonist, LY456236, in rodents: a comparison of efficacy and side-effect profiles. Psychopharmacology (Berlin), 179: 207–217.

Vogel, J.R., Beer, B. and Clody, D.E. (1971) A simple and reliable conflict procedure for testing anti-anxiety agents. Psychopharmacologia, 21: 1–7.

Walker, D.L. and Davis, M. (2000) Involvement of NMDA receptors within the amygdala in short- versus long-term memory for fear conditioning as assessed with fear-potentiated startle. Behav. Neurosci., 114: 1019–1033.

Walker, D.L. and Davis, M. (2004) Are fear memories made and maintained by the same NMDA receptor-dependent mechanisms? Neuron, 41: 680–682.

Wiley, J.L., Compton, A.D., Holcomb, J.D., McCallum, S.E., Varvel, S.A., Porter, J.H. and Balster, R.L. (1998) Effects of modulation of NMDA neurotransmission on response rate and duration in a conflict procedure in rats. Neuropharmacology, 37: 1527–1534.

Wiley, J.L., Cristello, A.F. and Balster, R.L. (1995) Effects of site-selective NMDA receptor antagonists in an elevated plus-maze model of anxiety in mice. Eur. J. Pharmacol., 294: 101–107.

Wiley, J.L., Porter, J.H., Compton, A.D. and Balster, R.L. (1992) Antipunishment effects of acute and repeated administration of phencyclidine and NPC 12626 in rats. Life Sci., 50: 1519–1528.

Williams, K. (1993) Ifenprodil discriminates subtypes of the N-methyl-D-aspartate receptor: selectivity and mechanisms at recombinant heteromeric receptors. Mol. Pharmacol., 44: 851–859.

Wong, E.H., Kemp, J.A., Priestley, T., Knight, A.R., Woodruff, G.N. and Iversen, L.L. (1986) The anticonvulsant MK-801 is a potent N-methyl-D-aspartate antagonist. Proc. Natl. Acad. Sci. USA, 83: 7104–7108.

Wong, L.A., Mayer, M.L., Jane, D.E. and Watkins, J.C. (1994) Willardiines differentiate agonist binding sites for kainate- versus AMPA-preferring glutamate receptors in DRG and hippocampal neurons. J. Neurosci., 14: 3881–3897.

Yoshimizu, T., Shimazaki, T., Ito, A. and Chaki, S. (2006) An mGluR2/3 antagonist, MGS0039, exerts antidepressant and anxiolytic effects in behavioral models in rats. Psychopharmacology (Berlin), 186: 587–593.

Yousef, K.A., Tepper, P.G., Molina, P.E., Abumrad, N.N. and Lang, C.H. (1994) Differential control of glucoregulatory hormone response and glucose metabolism by NMDA and kainate. Brain Res., 634: 131–140.

CHAPTER 4.5

The endocannabinoid system and anxiety responses

Marco Bortolato[1],* and Daniele Piomelli[2],*

[1]*Department of Cardiovascular and Neurological Sciences, Policlinico Universitario, University of Cagliari, Monserrato, CA, Italy*
[2]*Department of Pharmacology and Center for Drug Discovery, 3101 Gillespie Neuroscience Facility, University of California, Irvine, CA, USA*

Abstract: The main psychoactive ingredient of *Cannabis sativa*, Δ^9-tetrahydrocannabinol (THC) produces complex modulatory effects on emotional states in humans and laboratory animals. The characterization of the receptors activated by THC and their endogenous ligands (endocannabinoids) has initiated numerous studies exploring the functions of the endocannabinoid system and its impact on anxiety-related and emotional responses. These studies, which have been facilitated by the development of selective pharmacological tools and genetically engineered mice, have led to recognize that the endocannabinoid system plays an important role in the regulation of emotional states. However, its impact on anxiety-related behaviors is highly variable, probably depending on the involvement of different receptors, brain regions and neurotransmitter systems. Furthermore, numerous factors contribute to modulate the role of endocannabinoids on anxiety, such as genetic background, age, sex and situational context. Under specific environmental circumstances, pharmacological enhancement of endocannabinoid signaling has indeed been shown to produce anxiolytic-like and mood-enhancing functions in rodents, without causing the wide spectrum of untoward behavioral responses induced by THC and other cannabinoid agonists. Thus, endocannabinoid system might be a novel pharmacological target for anti-anxiety therapy. Here we provide a comprehensive overview on the current state of knowledge of the involvement of endocannabinoid system in anxiety-related responses and highlight the present challenges of research in this field as well as the novel perspectives offered by this system in the therapy of anxiety disorders.

Keywords: endocannabinoids; anxiety; CB; receptor; anandamide; 2-AG; URB597; rimonabant

I. Introduction

Anxiety is an integrative constellation of behavioral responses directed at alerting the organism to a potential danger and carrying out a defensive strategy. Not surprisingly, this complex phenomenon – encompassing sensory, motor, emotional

and cognitive processes – is underpinned by multiple neuromodulatory neurotransmitter systems in the brain. Emerging evidence indicates that one such system is constituted by the receptors engaged by the psychoactive ingredient of marijuana (*Cannabis sativa*) and their endogenous ligands. In the present chapter, we illustrate clinical and pre-clinical findings that suggest a role for the endogenous cannabinoid system in anxiety. Moreover, we highlight the conceptual challenges and novel therapeutic perspectives offered by this system in the treatment of anxiety disorders.

---

*Corresponding authors.
E-mail: marco.bortolato@inwind.it (Bortolato) and piomelli@uci.edu (Piomelli)

R.J. Blanchard, D.C. Blanchard, G. Griebel and D. Nutt (Eds.)
Handbook of Anxiety and Fear, Vol. 17
ISBN 978-0-444-53065-3

303

DOI: 10.1016/S1569-7339(07)00014-8

II. The endocannabinoid system

Although the psychotropic properties of cannabis have been known for thousands of years, its mechanisms of action remained unclear until relatively recent times. After decades of research (Adams et al., 1941), an important breakthrough in cannabinoid research came in the 1960s, with the definitive identification of Δ^9-tetrahydrocannabinol (THC) as the major psychoactive component in cannabis (Gaoni and Mechoulam, 1964). This discovery gave impetus to a number of experiments aimed at elucidating the molecular and cellular substrates activated by cannabis in the brain, as well as the development of synthetic analogs of THC (summarized in Table 1). In particular, the utilization of radiolabeled agonists led to the identification of a high-affinity cannabinoid binding site in brain membranes (Devane et al., 1988). In the following years, this novel site was identified as a G-protein-coupled receptor and eventually named CB_1 (Matsuda et al., 1990). Moreover, a peripheral CB_2 receptor was also described in human promyelocytic leukemia cells (Munro et al., 1993). Although CB_1 and CB_2 receptors are both primarily coupled to $G_{i/o}$ proteins (Howlett, 2002), they share only about 44% sequence homology at the protein level, suggesting that they might have followed different evolutionary pathways (Ameri, 1999). Anatomical studies have shown that CB_1 and CB_2 display very different distributions in the organism: CB_1 receptors are very abundant in the brain (Herkenham et al., 1990), but they are also localized, at much lower concentrations, in peripheral tissues. Conversely, CB_2 receptors are mostly expressed in immune cells, although recent studies have also revealed their expression in the brainstem (Van Sickle et al., 2005). Accurate descriptions of the anatomic localization of CB receptors have been presented in several reviews (see Matsuda et al., 1992; Freund et al., 2003; Mackie, 2005).

In addition to CB_1 and CB_2, recent evidence suggests the existence of other, as-yet-uncharacterized cannabinoid receptors (Begg et al., 2005). Indeed, various cannabinoid agents have been shown to exert pharmacological effects in mice with a genetic ablation of CB_1 receptors (Jarai et al., 1999; Breivogel et al., 2001; O'Sullivan et al., 2004). Furthermore, studies indicate that the GPR55 orphan receptor is bound by various cannabinoid agonists (Sjögren et al., 2005).

The research on CB receptors has been greatly powered by the development of selective ligands (see Table 2), such as the prototypical CB_1 antagonist rimonabant (formerly called SR141716A) (Rinaldi-Carmona et al., 1994), recently approved by the European Commission for the treatment of obesity.

Another critical step in the characterization of the endocannabinoid system was the identification of CB receptor endogenous ligands. In 1992, Devane et al. (1992) described the isolation of arachidonoylethanolamide, a N-acylethanolamine derived from arachidonic acid, from porcine brain samples. The compound, which bound to brain CB_1 receptors with high affinity and elicited cannabinergic responses in vivo, was suggestively termed *anandamide*, after the Sanskrit word for bliss. A few years later, another arachidonic acid derivative, 2-arachidonoylglycerol (2-AG) was reported to engage cannabinoid receptors (Mechoulam et al., 1995; Sugiura et al., 1995; Stella et al., 1997). 2-AG has a lower affinity for CB_1, but is about 200 times more abundant in the brain than anandamide (Stella et al., 1997). Other putative endocannabinoids have been reported (for a review, see Bradshaw and Walker, 2005), but their metabolism and physiological function are still poorly understood.

Unlike other classical and peptidic neurotransmitters, endocannabinoids are not released by exocytosis, but are synthesized upon demand through enzymatic cleavage of membrane lipid precursors, and then immediately released into the synaptic space (Di Marzo et al., 1994; Cadas et al., 1997; Giuffrida et al., 1999).

The best-characterized mechanism of anandamide biosynthesis occurs through a two-step reaction, illustrated in Fig. 1. First, arachidonic acid is transferred by an N-acyltransferase (NAT) from a membrane phospholipid precursor to phosphatidyl ethanolamine, in a Ca^{2+}-dependent manner, forming N-arachidonoylphosphatidyl ethanolamine (NAPE) (Di Marzo et al., 1994;

Table 1. Synopsis of the effects of cannabinoid agonists on anxiety responses in experimental animals

Drugs	Doses (mg/kg, i.p.)	Models	Species		Effects	References
Δ^9-THC	0.3	Light/dark choice task	Mice (CD1)	(−)	Increased time spent in light compartment	Berrendero and Maldonado (2002
	0.075–0.75	Elevated plus-maze	Rats (SD)	(−)	Increased time spent in open arms	Braida et al. (2007)
	0.03–5	Light/dark choice task	Mice (CD1)	(−)	Increased time spent in light compartment	Valjent et al. (2002)
	0.3	Open field test	Mice (CD1)	(−)	Decreased anxiety	Valjent et al. (2002)
	0.2–7.5	Elevated plus-maze; light/dark choice task	Mice	(+;−)	Dose-dependent anxiolytic – (low doses) and anxiogenic – (high doses) like effects	Celerier et al. (2006)
	0.4	Elevated plus-maze	Rats	(+;−)	Dose-dependent anxiolytic – (low doses) and anxiogenic – (high doses) like effects	Marco et al. (2004)
	1–10	Elevated plus-maze	Rats (SD)	(+)	Decreased time spent in open arms	Onaivi et al. (1990)
	10–20	Elevated plus-maze	Mice (ICR)	(+)	Decreased time spent in open arms	Onaivi et al. (1990)
	0.25–10	Elevated plus-maze	Mice	(+)	Decreased time spent in open arms	Patel and Hillard (2006)
	2.5	Social interaction test	Rats (W)	(0)	No effects on the social interaction test	Morley et al. (2004)
(+)-WIN55212-2	0.3–10	Elevated plus-maze	Mice (ICR)	(−)	Increased time spent in open arms	Patel and Hillard (2006)
	1–3	Elevated plus-maze	Mice	(−)	Increased time spent in open arms	Haller et al. (2004)
	1–3	Conditioned fear response	Mice	(+)	Increased conditioned fear response	Mikics et al. (2006)
	1–5	Light/dark choice task	Mice	(+)	Increased time spent in light compartment	Rutkowska et al. (2006)
	1.2	Open field test	Rats	(+)	Increased anxiety	Schneider et al. (2005)
	5	Conditioned fear response	Mice	(0)	No effect; enhancement of extinction	Chhatwal et al. (2005)
CP55,940	0.001–0.3	Elevated plus-maze	Mice	(−)	Increased time spent in open arms	Patel and Hillard (2006)
	0.01–0.05	Elevated plus-maze	Rats	(+;−)	Dose-dependent anxiolytic – (low doses) and anxiogenic – (high doses) like effects	Marco et al. (2004)
	0.01–0.04	Social interaction test	Rats	(+)	Decreased the time spent in social interaction	Genn et al. (2004)
	0.15–0.3	Social interaction test	Rats	(+)	Decreased the time spent in social interaction	O'Shea et al. (2006)
HU-210	10–50	Chronic unpredictable stress-effects on elevated plus-maze	Rats	(−)	Prior stress eliminated the low dose anxiolytic-like effects of HU-210	Hill and Gorzalka (2004)

Table 1 (*continued*)

Drugs	Doses (mg/kg, i.p.)	Models	Species		Effects	References
	0.01	Defensive withdrawal	Rats	(+;−)	Dose-dependent anxiolytic- and anxiogenic-like effects	Rodriguez De Fonseca et al. (1996)
	3	Open field test	Rats	(+)	Increased anxiety	
	0.025–0.1	Elevated plus-maze	Rats	(0)	No effects	Giuliani et al. (2000)

Table 2. Synopsis of the effects of rimonabant on anxiety responses in experimental animals

Drugs	Doses (mg/kg, i.p.)	Models	Species		Effects	References
Rimonabant	0.3–3	Light/dark choice task	Mice	(−)	Anxiolysis dependent on mouse strain	Akinshola et al. (1999)
	0.15–5	Conditioned fear response	Mice	(−)	Decreased extinction. Comparable effect to CB_1 receptor deletion	Chhatwal et al. (2005)
	3–10	Defensive burying	Mice	(−)	Decreased burying and reduced probe contacts. Comparable to the effects to CB_1 receptor deletion	Degroot and Nomikos (2004)
	0.3–3	Elevated plus-maze	Rats	(−)	Increased open arm time like diazepam	Griebel et al. (2005)
	0.3–3	Vogel conflict	Rats	(−)	Increased punished responses like diazepam	Griebel et al. (2005)
	0.1–3	Elevated plus-maze	Mice	(−)	Increased open arm time. Effect persists with CB_1 receptor deletion	Haller et al. (2002)
	3–5.6	Open field test	Rats	(−)	Improved ambulation	Jarbe et al. (2004)
	1–3	Elevated plus-maze	Mice	(−)	Reduction of anxiety-like responses in maze-experienced animals	Rodgers et al. (2003)
	0.5	Light/dark choice task	Mice	(+)	Blocks the anxiolytic-like response induced by THC	Berrendero and Maldonado (2002)
	0.1–3	Elevated plus-maze	Rats	(+)	Decreased open arm time	Navarro et al. (1997)
	0.1–3	Defensive withdrawal	Rats	(+)	Increased withdrawal latency	Navarro et al. (1997)
	3	Defensive withdrawal	Rats	(+)	Increased withdrawal latency	Rodriguez de Fonseca et al. (1997)
	0.1	Elevated plus-maze	Rats	(0)	No intrinsic effect on time spent into open compartments	Arevalo et al. (2001)
	1	Elevated plus-maze	Rats	(0)	No intrinsic effect on time spent into open compartments	Bortolato et al. (2006)

Table 2 (*continued*)

Drugs	Doses (mg/kg, i.p.)	Models	Species		Effects	References
	1	Isolation-induced ultrasonic emission	Rats	(0)	No intrinsic effect in ultrasonic calls	Bortolato et al. (2006)
	1	Defensive withdrawal	Rats	(0)	No intrinsic effect on withdrawal latency	Bortolato et al. (2006)
	2.0	Elevated zero-maze	Rats	(0)	No intrinsic effect on time spent into open compartments	Kathuria et al. (2003)
	2.0	Isolation-induced ultrasonic emission	Rats	(0)	No intrinsic effect in ultrasonic calls	Kathuria et al. (2003)
	0.5–2.0	Elevated plus-maze	Mice	(0)	No changes in locomotion or anxiety levels	Takahashi et al. (2005)
AM 251	0.3–3	Elevated plus-maze	Mice	(+)	Decreased open arm time. Effect absent with CB_1 receptor deletion	Haller et al. (2004)
	0.3–3	Conditioned fear response	Mice	(+)	Decreased the conditioned fear response	Mikics et al. (2006)
	1–10	Elevated plus-maze	Mice	(+)	Decreased open arm time dose related	Patel and Hillard (2006)
	1.5–3	Elevated plus-maze	Mice	(+)	Decreased open arm time in plus-maze-naive and plus-maze-experienced mice	Rodgers et al. (2005)
AM 281	1–4	Light/dark choice task	Mice	(0)	No effects	Rutkowska et al. (2006)

Cadas et al., 1997). This compound is then hydrolyzed to anandamide and phosphatidic acid by NAPE-PLD, a D-type phospholipase (Okamoto et al., 2004; for a review see Freund et al., 2003). The recent finding that anandamide levels are unaffected in NAPE-PLD knockout mice, in comparison to wild-type animals, raises the possibility of the existence of other parallel biosynthetic pathways, involving PLA_2 (Sun et al., 2004) or phospholipase C (PLC) (Liu et al., 2006).

Although 2-AG can be synthesized by several different mechanisms (Piomelli, 2003), the best-known pathway to date is the hydrolysis of membrane phosphoinositides, mediated by PLC and producing 1,2-diacylglycerol (DAG) (Stella et al., 1997). DAG is further cleaved to 2-AG by specific DAG lipases (DGL) (Bisogno et al., 2003). Alternatively, 2-AG might be produced through

action of different enzymes, such as phospholipase A_1 (PLA_1) (Piomelli, 2003).

After release and activation of CB receptors, endocannabinoids are rapidly removed from the synaptic space by a high-affinity transport system (Di Marzo et al., 1994; Beltramo et al., 1997; Hillard et al., 1997). Although the molecular structure of this carrier is still unknown, the development of several pharmacological inhibitors, such as AM404 and UCM707 (Beltramo et al., 1997; Piomelli et al., 1999; de Lago et al., 2002) has allowed the characterization of its functional properties; these include independence from ion gradients or ATP, saturation at $37°C$ and stereo-selective substrate recognition (for review, see Hillard and Jarrahian, 2003). After internalization, the two endocannabinoids follow distinct metabolic pathways. Anandamide is mainly hydrolyzed by

308

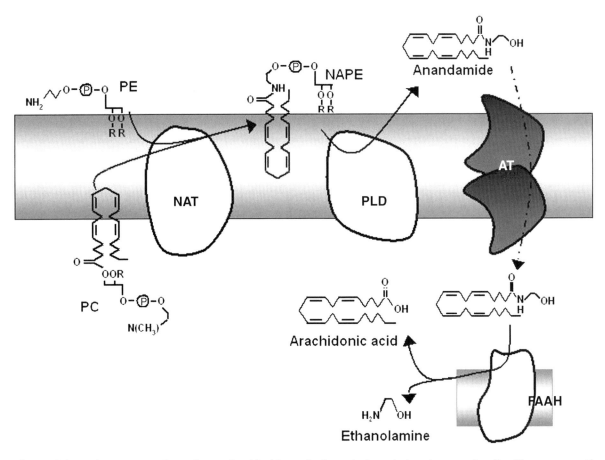

Fig. 1. Schematic representation of anandamide biosynthesis and degradation in neural cells. The enzyme *N*-acyltransferase (NAT) catalyzes the production of *N*-arachidonoyl-phosphatidylethanolamine (NAPE) from phosphatidylethanolamine (PE) and phosphatidylcholine (PC); NAPE is then hydrolyzed into anandamide by phospholipase D (PLD). After engaging CB receptors, anandamide is internalized through a high-affinity transporter (AT) and finally hydrolyzed by fatty-acid amide hydrolase (FAAH). For more details, see text.

fatty-acid amide hydrolase (FAAH), a membrane-bound intracellular serine enzyme (Desarnaud et al., 1995; Hillard et al., 1995; Ueda et al., 1995; Cravatt et al., 1996) (Fig. 1). Notably, several potent inhibitors of FAAH activity have been recently developed, like URB597 and OL-135 (Kathuria et al., 2003; Lichtman et al., 2004a, b; for a review, see Piomelli, 2005). In contrast, 2-AG is hydrolyzed by monoglyceride lipase (MGL), a cytosolic serine hydrolase abundantly expressed in many brain areas rich in CB_1 receptors, such as hippocampus, cortex and cerebellum (Dinh et al., 2002b). This enzyme converts 2-AG into arachidonic acid and glycerol

(Dinh et al., 2002a; Saario et al., 2004). Inhibitors of this enzymatic process, such as URB602, have been developed (Hohmann et al., 2005). Of note, evidence points also to a role of other enzymes in endocannabinoid metabolism, such as cyclooxygenase-2 and lipoxygenase (Kozak and Marnett, 2002; Fowler, 2004; for review see Kozak et al., 2004).

III. Effects of cannabinoids on anxiety

Clinical observations have shown that the effects of cannabis on mood and anxiety are highly variable, ranging from euphoria, enhanced sociability, relaxation and anxiolysis to anxious and dysphoric reactions following marijuana use (Hollister, 1986; Hall and Solowij, 1998; Patton et al., 2002; Green et al., 2003; Dannon et al., 2004). Unfortunately, most clinical evidence on the impact of cannabinoids on anxiety and mood is anecdotal and suffers from numerous methodological shortcomings (Robson, 2005). Indeed, depression and anxiety are frequently comorbid with long-term cannabis consumption (Degenhardt et al., 2001). To explain this phenomenon, several surveys endorse the "self-medication hypothesis", which posits that cannabis is consumed to ameliorate depressive or anxiety symptoms (Swift et al., 2005). In support of this possibility, early clinical trials have revealed that nabilone – a cannabinoid analog approved in United Kingdom as an antiemetic treatment – produces dose-dependent improvements in anxiety scores over placebo-treated patients (Glass et al., 1980; Fabre and McLendon, 1981; Ilaria et al., 1981). These findings are at variance, however, with recent cross-sectional and prospective epidemiological studies, which suggest that initiation of cannabis consumption is not significantly related to current depressive or anxiety symptoms (Arseneault et al., 2002; Patton et al., 2002). Furthermore, several authors have reported that adolescents develop mood, personality and anxiety disorders after prolonged cannabis use (Fergusson et al., 2002; Patton et al., 2002; Rey et al., 2002; for contrasting results see Arseneault et al., 2002).

The wide variability of response to cannabis use across subjects is often interpreted to reflect differences in situational elements (Stark-Adamec et al., 1981; Davidson and Schenk, 1994) and/or biological factors such as age, gender, genetic vulnerability and, of course, level of exposure (Grant and Pickering, 1998; Fergusson et al., 2002; Milani et al., 2004; Henquet et al., 2005a, b; Hopfer et al., 2006). For example, only a subset of marijuana smokers develop cannabis dependence, probably in relation to CB_1 receptor haplotype polymorphisms (Hopfer et al., 2006). Notably, the withdrawal symptoms following discontinuation of cannabis in those patients typically include intense anxiety and emotional lability (Haney, 2005).

Finally, it is important to remark that the impact of cannabis on behavior may also depend on the relative composition in cannabinoid compounds (Fadda et al., 2004), in view of the anxiolytic and sleep-enhancing properties of cannabidiol (CBD), a component of cannabis that does not activate CB_1 receptors (Pertwee, 1993; Zuardi et al., 1993).

In congruence with human data, animal findings show a dose-related bidirectional effect of cannabinoid agonists on anxiety-like behavioral responses. In rodents, most evidence indicates that low doses of CB_1 agonists produce anxiolytic-like effects (Onaivi et al., 1990; Rodriguez de Fonseca et al., 1997; Berrendero and Maldonado, 2002; Genn et al., 2004), while moderate to high doses elicit anxiogenesis (Rodriguez de Fonseca et al., 1996; Arevalo et al., 2001; Genn et al., 2004; Marin et al., 2003). The biphasic effects of cannabinoids on anxiety parallel similar responses in other behavioral and physiological functions, such as locomotion, exploration and reward (McGregor et al., 1998; Chaperon and Thiebot, 1999; Marin et al., 2003; Genn et al., 2004). Nevertheless, dosage is not the only factor governing the variability in behavioral outcomes produced by cannabinoid agents.

Strain differences play a key role on the impact of cannabinoid ligands on anxiety-like behaviors (Akinshola et al., 1999), as well as on other behavioral and neuroendocrine responses (Mokler et al., 1986; Parker and Gillies, 1995; Deiana et al., 2006). Additionally, age influences anxiety-like responses to cannabinoids. Adolescent, but not adult rats exhibit reduced social interaction several weeks after discontinuation of a chronic treatment with a cannabinoid agonist (O'Shea et al., 2004, 2006). However, the authors of these studies also reported that adolescent rats under the same experimental conditions exhibited also a modest reduction in anxiety in an emergence test (O'Shea et al., 2006), plausibly suggesting that cannabinoids might impact different aspects of anxiety in a multi-faceted way, at least before adulthood. This interpretation might also partially account for some contrasting results on the effects of cannabinoid agonists in anxiety-related behaviors in immature rats (McGregor et al., 1998; Romero et al., 2002).

Finally, recent studies have evidenced sex-dependent differences in the anxiogenic effects of a CB_1 receptor agonist in rats chronically treated with nicotine (Marco et al., 2006), underscoring the possibility that gender might also influence the modulatory role of cannabinoids in anxiety.

IV. Role of the endocannabinoid system in anxiety

The evidence on the impact of cannabinoid agents on anxiety-related responses in humans parallels findings on the implication of the endocannabinoid system in the regulation of emotional behaviors and the modulation of anxiety-related responses in rodents. Evidence indicates that stressful events affect endocannabinoid levels in the major brain areas involved in the regulation of emotional behavior in rodents. For example, a single electric shock to the paw elevates anandamide and 2-AG levels in the midbrain (Hohmann et al., 2005). In contrast, physical restraint decreases anandamide and increases 2-AG content in the amygdala (Patel et al., 2004, 2005a, b).

CB_1 receptors are abundantly expressed in all the key brain regions known to govern anxiety and mood, including the amygdaloid complex, the septo-hippocampal system, the anterior cingulate cortex, the prefrontal cortex and the periacqueductal gray matter (Herkenham et al., 1990, 1991a–c; Katona et al., 2001; Hàjos and Freund, 2002). Genetic deletion of CB_1 receptors in mice conduces to the expression of a phenotype with hypersensitivity to stressful stimuli, with reduced corticosterone secretion, decreased sociability, increased aggressive and anxiety-like behaviors and disrupted response to anxiolytic agents (Haller et al., 2002; Martin et al., 2002; Uriguen et al., 2004). However, some studies reported CB_1 knockout mice as displaying normal (Marsicano et al., 2002a, b) or even anxiolytic-like behaviors (DeGroot and Nomikos, 2004; Griebel et al., 2005). Another remarkable feature of these genetically engineered animals is their inability to extinguish fear conditioning, in contrast to an otherwise intact mnemonic profile (Marsicano et al., 2002a, b). This finding points to an inhibitory role for the endocannabinoids in the retention of aversive

memories (Chhatwal et al., 2005), and is in line with epidemiological data showing a high prevalence of cannabis abuse in patients affected by post-traumatic stress disorder (Koenen et al., 2003; Okulate and Jones, 2006). The expression of behavioral responses in CB_1 knockout mice is also modulated by strain and age differences. Indeed, most behavioral changes are consistently observed in the CD1 background, but not in others (Griebel et al., 2005), and were shown to decrease with age (Maccarone et al., 2002a–d).

Most behavioral studies on the effects of pharmacological blockade of CB_1 receptors have been performed with rimonabant (SR141716A). The majority of studies suggest that this compound is anxiogenic at high doses (McGregor et al., 1998; Rodriguez de Fonseca et al., 1996; Navarro et al., 1997; Arevalo et al., 2001) and ineffective at low doses (Patel et al., 2005a, b; Bortolato et al., 2006). However, anxiolytic effects of rimonabant have been reported by several investigators (Akinshola et al., 1999; Haller et al., 2002; Rodgers et al., 2003; Griebel et al., 2005). Although this variability may reflect methodological differences in testing multidimensional aspects of anxiety (see below), recent findings suggest that the anxiolytic properties of rimonabant might be related to a receptor other than CB_1. Indeed, this drug fails to block the anxiogenic effects of a CB receptor agonist in the plus-maze (Arevalo et al., 2001) and retains anxiolytic efficacy in CB_1 knockout mice (Haller et al., 2002). In agreement with the hypothesis that rimonabant acts on multiple receptors, recent studies in rodents have demonstrated anxiogenic-like effects for AM251 (Haller et al., 2004; Rodgers et al., 2005), a CB_1 antagonist with slightly higher affinity for CB_1 receptors than rimonabant (Gatley et al., 1996, 1997). The anxiogenic properties of CB_1 antagonists are also supported by human data on increased incidence of anxiety and depression in obese patients treated with rimonabant (Van Gaal et al., 2005; Gelfand and Cannon, 2006; Pi-Sunyer et al., 2006).

A third line of evidence on the endocannabinoid role in anxiety stems from the research on the behavioral effects of anandamide degradation inhibitors (Table 3). Our group and others have shown that the highly selective FAAH inhibitor URB597 produces anxiolytic-like effects in the elevated zero-maze in adult rats, and in the isolation-induced ultrasonic vocalization test in rat pups. Both effects were paralleled by increased anandamide brain levels and were reversed by a non-anxiogenic dose of rimonabant, suggesting that the anxiolytic-like effects of URB597 reflect enhanced anandamide signaling at CB_1 receptors (Kathuria et al., 2003; Patel et al., 2004; Patel and Hillard, 2006). The impact of anandamide on anxiety has been further confirmed by investigations on the behavioral outcomes of the endocannabinoid transport inhibitor AM404. Recent studies have shown that systemic administration of this compound elicits anxiolytic-like behaviors in the elevated plus-maze and defensive withdrawal in adult rats, as well as an attenuation of ultrasonic vocalizations in rat pups (Bortolato et al., 2006). Such behavioral changes are accompanied by dose-dependent enhancements of anandamide levels in select brain regions (cortex, hippocampus and thalamus) which were implicated in the regulation of stress and emotion (Cahill and McGaugh, 1998; Nestler et al., 2002).

Table 3. Synopsis of the effects of endocannabinoid deactivation inhibitors on anxiety responses in experimental animals

Drugs		Doses (mg/kg, i.p.)	Models	Species		Effects	References
Anandamide transport inhibitors	AM404	1–5	Elevated plus-maze	Rats (SD)	(+)	Increased time spent in the open arms and reduced other anxiety parameters	Bortolato et al. (2006); Braida et al. (2007)
		1–5	Defensive withdrawal	Rats	(+)	Decreased withdrawal latency	Bortolato et al. (2006)
		1–5	Isolation-induced ultrasonic emission	Rats	(+)	Reduced ultrasonic calls	Bortolato et al. (2006)
		0.3–10	Elevated plus-maze	Mice	(+)	Increased time spent in the open arms	Patel and Hillard (2006)
		1–4	Light/dark box	Mice	(0)	No effects	Rutkowska et al. (2006)
FAAH inhibitors	URB597	0.05–0.1	Elevated zero-maze	Rats	(+)	Increased time spent into open compartments	Kathuria et al. (2003)
		0.1	Isolation-induced ultrasonic emission	Rats	(+)	Reduced ultrasonic calls	Kathuria et al. (2003)
	URB532	0.1–10	Elevated zero-maze	Rats	(+)	Increased time spent into open compartments	Kathuria et al. (2003)
		1–5	Isolation-induced ultrasonic emission	Rats	(+)	Reduced ultrasonic calls	Kathuria et al. (2003)

V. Methodological issues in the study of endocannabinoids in anxiety

As discussed above, animal studies on the role of the endocannabinoid system in anxiety have yielded inconsistent results. While several biological and pharmacological factors certainly contribute to these discrepancies, it is also important to highlight a number of methodological and theoretical issues on the impact of cannabinoid agents on anxiety-like behaviors in rodent models that might help reframe and interpret present uncertainties.

Like other nosographic categories in psychiatry, the classification of anxiety disorders is currently based on descriptive criteria and not on a pathophysiological perspective. The very definition of anxiety is a broad rubric encompassing a number of heterogeneous nosological entities. In the absence of a detailed etiological and neurobiological framework that may allow us to capture differences between such disorders, the validation of animal paradigms as anxiety models must rely on the simulation of specific aspects of the disorder or on the pharmacological isomorphism with respect to known anxiolytic therapeutic agents (Koob et al., 1998; Nestler et al., 2002). Although this approach has been greatly helpful in the process of identification and standardization of novel animal models of anxiety, it has also raised a number of criticisms. Current anxiety models cannot efficiently discriminate between different clinical syndromes, although they might measure diverse facets of anxiety (Rodgers, 1997; Ramos and Mormede, 1998) and have different neural substrates (File, 1992; Gonzalez et al., 1996). Moreover, since most of the classical animal models of anxiety have been validated pharmacologically using benzodiazepine-related drugs, they might have limited utility for the identification of novel compounds with potential therapeutic usefulness, but different pharmacological properties (Belzung, 2001). A remarkable example in this respect is the lack of acute effects of selective serotonin reuptake inhibitors (SSRI) in most animal models of anxiety, despite their clinical efficacy in anxious patients (for a review, see Griebel, 1995). Concerns about the predictive validity of anxiety models seem to be particularly relevant in the analysis of neuromodulatory agents, such as endocannabinoids or neuropeptides. Indeed, the impact of several neuropeptides – such as corticotropin-releasing factor (CRF), cholecystokinin (CCK) and atrial natriuretic peptide (ANP) – in anxiety models has been the center of controversy and debate.

For example, early evidence on the anxiolytic-like properties of CCK_B receptor antagonists in rodents, in the elevated plus-maze and zero-maze (Chopin and Briley, 1993; Bickerdike et al., 1994) was later challenged by groups reporting negative findings in the same models (Dawson et al., 1995; Charrier et al., 1995; for a general review, see van Megen et al., 1996). Similar concerns have been raised for CRF receptor antagonists. While many authors have reported anxiolytic-like effects of these agents in animal models (Adamec, 1997), others have found these drugs to be ineffective (Conti et al., 1994; for a review see Griebel, 1999). Another case of inconsistent responses across anxiety models is provided by ANP. Intracerebroventricular administration of this peptide increases the time spent by rats in the open arms of an elevated plus-maze (Biro et al., 1995; Bhattacharya et al., 1996) but has no effect in the Geller–Seifter conflict test (Heilig et al., 1992).

These premises suggest that some of the inconsistencies on the role of endocannabinoids may be ascribed to inherent limits in sensitivity of the traditional anxiety protocols in rodents. A possibility to obviate this pitfall might come from the adjustment of behavioral protocols in relation to the factors that influence pharmacological responses to cannabinoid-based agents. In parallel, recent research has shown that the anxiolytic properties of CRF receptor antagonists are better detected under specific conditions of environmental stress or in strains with high susceptibility to stress (Menzaghi et al., 1994a–c; Conti et al., 1994; Griebel et al., 1998). In a similar manner, the endocannabinoids might reveal full anxiolytic potential in the presence of certain experimental settings that alter contextual stress – for example, light levels in the elevated plus-maze, or environment familiarity in the social interaction test. The context dependence of endocannabinoid action has been suggested by experiments on CB_1

313

knockout mice, which display anxiogenesis only in presence of environmental stress (Haller et al., 2004). Similarly, endocannabinoid signaling modulates the function of HPA axis in a context-dependent manner (Patel et al., 2004). These factors might explain the inconsistent results obtained with the FAAH inhibitor URB597 across labs (Kathuria et al., 2003; Durham et al., 2006).

Unpublished experiments conducted in our lab might contribute to the ongoing discussion on these important issues. We have studied the differential impact of URB597 on plus-maze anxiety in rats under different conditions of light and familiarity with the investigator. Adult Wistar rats were placed in an elevated plus-maze and tested for 5 min. Two variables were varied across the experiments: the light of the experimental room (full or dim) and the animal handling (brief, 1 min the day before the test; or long, 5 min daily for 3 days before the test). Behavior was then video recorded and measured by a custom software package. As shown in Fig. 2, URB597 exhibited anxiolytic-like properties under conditions of either high light or low familiarity with the experimenter, but not after long handling and in presence of dim light. Although other variables, such as age and strain, were not considered, the present results confirm the importance of context and baseline stress in the anxiolytic properties of anandamide and encourage further research on the influence of contextual parameters on the role of endocannabinoid on anxiety-related behaviors.

VI. Mechanisms for the endocannabinoid role in anxiety

The complex role of the endocannabinoids in anxiety likely reflects the modulatory functions served by these mediators in brain regions that govern emotional behavior and anxiety-related responses. Such regions, including the septo-hippocampal system, the amygdaloid complex, the anterior cingulate cortex, the prefrontal cortex and the periacqueductal gray matter of the midbrain (Herkenham et al., 1990, 1991a–c; Charney and Deutch 1996; Glass et al., 1997; Katona et al., 2001;

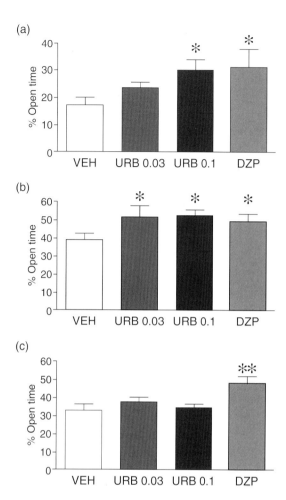

Fig. 2. Effects of vehicle (VEH), URB597 (0.03–0.1 mg/kg, i.p.) and diazepam (DZP, 1 mg/kg, i.p.) in the rat elevated plus-maze under different levels of manipulation and experimental conditions: (a) Wistar rats underwent intensive handling (5 min/day each, throughout the 5 days prior to the experiment) and were tested in a room with intense light (about 300 lux); (b) Wistar rats were briefly handled (1 min each) on the day before the experiment and performed the elevated plus-maze test in a dimly lit room (about 100 lux); (c) Wistar rats were subject to intensive handling and were tested under dim light (about 100 lux). Animals were tested 1 h after treatment, for 5 min each. Each rat was used only once, under one experimental condition. Values represent mean ± SEM for each treatment. %Open time: time spent in the open arms of the maze/total time in the maze; n = 8–12 per treatment group. Statistical analyses were performed by ANOVA, followed by Tukey's test for post hoc comparison of the means. *p < 0.05 compared with VEH-treated animals; **p < 0.01 compared with VEH-treated animals.

314

Hàjos and Freund, 2002), process different, and sometimes contrasting aspects of the anxious response. For example, the hippocampus is thought to elaborate context-related information and adjust the behavioral response to environmental inputs, while the amygdala produces emotional reactions to fearful stimuli and the cortex shapes the phenotypic expression of anxiety. The endocannabinoid system might plausibly regulate the interplay of these areas to adjust the modality and intensity of anxious reactions to specific contextual situations.

The organization of the anxious response involves multiple neurotransmitter systems. It is generally accepted that GABAergic and glutamatergic signaling in the amygdala and hippocampus affects anxiety-related responses in an opposite fashion. Glutamatergic activation in the basolateral amygdala improves aversive conditioning, while its decrease produces anxiolytic effects (Miserendino et al., 1990; Kim and McGaugh, 1992; LeDoux, 1994; Maren, 1996). Conversely, activation of GABA signaling retards aversive conditioning and produces anxiolytic effects by decreasing excitability of neurons in the amygdala (Davis et al., 1994; Nemeroff, 2003). The balance between these two systems is therefore critical for the shaping of the behavioral response (Sajdyk and Shekhar, 1997). Endocannabinoids have been shown to modulate negatively the release of both glutamate and GABA through retrograde activation of presynaptic CB_1 receptors (Morishita and Alger, 1999; Wilson and Nicoll, 2001; Ohno-Shosaku et al., 2001; Varma et al., 2001). Thus, endocannabinoid activation may affect anxiety-related reactions differently, depending on the predominant balance of signaling caused in amygdala and hippocampus by a given situational context. Furthermore, anandamide and 2-AG might subserve different mechanisms of anxiety regulation, by exerting their actions on different terminals and neurotransmitter systems. There is evidence that 2-AG is a retrograde mediator of long-term plasticity at glutamatergic synapses (Gerdeman et al., 2002; Robbe et al., 2002a, b; Sjostrom et al., 2003; Jung et al., 2005); moreover, functional studies have revealed that 2-AG, but not anandamide, acts as a retrograde messenger to silence GABAergic signaling in the hippocampus

(Kim and Alger, 2004; Makara et al., 2005). This result is in agreement with previous findings highlighting the role of 2-AG in hippocampal synaptic plasticity (Stella et al., 1997).

Conversely, recent evidence indicates that anandamide may be involved in the regulation of monoaminergic transmission, which is known to play a key role in anxiety (Selden et al., 1991; Stein et al., 2002; Millan, 2003). The administration of dopamine D_2-like agonists increases anandamide, but not 2-AG release in dorsal striatum and other brain regions (Giuffrida et al., 1999), suggesting that anandamide may act as an activity-dependent modulator of dopaminergic transmission. This concept is further supported by the finding that anandamide levels in the cerebrospinal fluid of antipsychotic-naïve paranoid schizophrenics are increased eightfolds in comparison to controls, and that this alteration is absent in schizophrenics treated with typical antipsychotics, which block D_2 receptors (Giuffrida et al., 2004). Likewise, functional and morphological evidence supports the involvement of anandamide in the modulation of noradrenergic and serotonergic signaling. Thus, acute and subchronic treatment with URB597 increases the spontaneous firing of serotonergic and noradrenergic neurons in the midbrain, and enhances serotonin levels in the hippocampus, in a rimonabant-sensitive manner (Gobbi et al., 2005). This evidence is in agreement with previous findings on the ability of CB_1 agonists to affect norepinephrine release and signaling (Schlicker et al., 1998) or to mediate anxiogenic effects through $5\text{-}HT_{1A}$ receptors (Arevalo et al., 2001; Marco et al., 2004).

A complementary line of evidence points to possible interaction of endocannabinoids and neuropeptides, such as CRF, CCK or opioid peptides, in the regulation of anxiety. CRF is hypothesized to facilitate anxiogenic mechanisms by activation of the central nucleus of the amygdala (Shepard et al., 2000). Cannabinoids are known to activate the HPA axis in rodents, probably through a dose-dependent effect on CRF release (Weidenfeld et al., 1994; Martin-Calderon et al., 1998; Manzanares et al., 1999; Romero et al., 2002; Marin et al., 2003; Marco et al., 2004). Moreover, blockade of CRF receptors counters the anxiety-like behavior induced by high doses of the cannabinoid agonist HU-210 (Rodriguez de Fonseca et al., 1996).

CB$_1$ receptor activation in the hippocampus may block K$^+$-evoked release of CCK in the hippocampus (Beinfeld and Connolly, 2001), and this action might be partially responsible for the control of anxiety-related responses mediated by endocannabinoids.

Interactions between the opioid and the cannabinoid system have been extensively demonstrated in rodents (Manzanares et al., 1999; Welch and Eads, 1999; Valverde et al., 2000, 2001; Ghozland et al., 2002). In particular, evidence suggests that cannabinoid-mediated anxiolysis might involve the activation of mu and delta opioid receptors (Berrendero and Maldonado, 2002), while dynorphins and kappa opioid receptors might be implicated in the aversive, dysphoric and anxiogenic actions of high doses of cannabinoid agonists (Zimmer et al., 2001; Ghozland et al., 2002; Marin et al., 2003).

VII. Endocannabinoids as a pharmacological target for anxiety treatment

Research on the endocannabinoid system has generated a great deal of interest in the potential of this signaling system as a therapeutic target. However, clinical applications of cannabinoid receptor agonists are hindered by the numerous side effects of these drugs, and particularly by the inaddictive properties. To date, the only two cannabinoid agonists that have been approved for human use are nabilone (in the UK), for its antiemetic properties, and dronabinol (in the USA), as an orexigenic treatment for nausea and wasting syndrome associated with AIDS and anticancer chemotherapy. Several preliminary clinical trials indicate that the activation of cannabinoid receptors may also find clinical applications in the treatment of a number of other disorders, ranging from anorexia to cancer. In particular, initial studies suggest that the endocannabinoid system may be a putative therapeutic target in the treatment of neuropathic and inflammatory pain, neurotoxicity, stroke, sleep disorders, epilepsy,

multiple sclerosis, spinal cord injury and movement disorders (such as Parkinson's disease, Tourette's disease and Huntington's disease) (for a general review, see Pacher et al., 2006). The results outlined in this overview also support the possibility that cannabinoid-related agents might be useful in the treatment of anxiety and mood disorders.

An intriguing strategy to trigger anxiolysis by activation of cannabinoid receptors with limited side effects may be offered by endocannabinoid degradation inactivators, such as anandamide transport or FAAH inhibitors. Indeed, we and others have shown that URB597, in addition to its anxiolytic-like properties, exerts also antidepressant-like effects in several animal models, such as the forced swim test, the tail suspension test, the restraint-induced enhancement in corticosterone and the chronic mild stress paradigm (Patel et al., 2004; Gobbi et al., 2005; Bortolato et al., 2007). Moreover, this compound elicits analgesic effects in animal models of inflammatory and neuropathic pain (Holt et al., 2005; Jayamanne et al., 2006; Chang et al., 2006; Jhaveri et al., 2006). Notably, these effects are not paralleled by either classical cannabimimetic properties, such as the ability to induce catalepsy, hyperthermia and hyperphagia (Fegley et al., 2004; Piomelli et al., 2006), or by abuse liability, as suggested by the inability of this drug to mimic the hedonic and interoceptive states induced by direct-acting cannabinoid agonists (Gobbi et al., 2005). Recent studies have also shown that URB597 is orally available, and does not produce toxicity in rodents and monkeys after sub-chronic treatment (Piomelli et al., 2006). Furthermore, acute treatment with URB597 does not produce motor deficits in the rat rotarod test (Piomelli et al., 2006). These data suggest that URB597 and other FAAH inhibitors may be promising tools in the therapy of anxiety and related mood disorders with a safer profile than cannabinoid direct agonists. In particular, they may be particularly indicated in the therapy of disturbances associated with inappropriate retention of aversive memories, such as post-traumatic stress disorders (Marsicano et al., 2002a, b; Haller et al., 2004; Varvel et al., 2007).

VIII. Conclusions

In recent years, the relationship between cannabinoids and anxiety has been described and established in animal models as well as in humans. Our studies and those of others have shown anxiolytic-like and antidepressant-like properties of URB597 in several animal models, highlighting the therapeutic potential of this drug that comes without the major side effects of cannabinoid receptor agents. Although the neural mechanisms underlying these effects are not fully understood, emerging evidence points to the endocannabinoid system as a promising new target for the treatment of anxiety and mood disorders. Hopefully future human studies will provide better insights on the role of endocannabinoids in anxiety and the therapeutic potential of endocannabinoid-activating agents.

Acknowledgments

This work was supported by grants from the National Institute on Drug Abuse (NIDA) DA12413, DA12447, DA009158 and the National Alliance for Research on Schizophrenia and Depression (NARSAD) (to Daniele Piomelli). Marco Bortolato was a 2004 NIDA INVEST fellow.

References

Adamec, R.E. (1997) Transmitter systems involved in neural plasticity underlying increased anxiety and defense – implications for understanding anxiety following traumatic stress. Neurosci. Biobehav. Rev., 21: 755–765.

Adams, R., Loewe, S., Jelinek, C. and Wolff, H. (1941) Tetrahydrocannabinol homologs with marihuana activity. J. Am. Chem. Soc., 63: 1–1973.

Akinshola, B.E., Chakrabarti, A. and Onaivi, E.S. (1999) In-vitro and in-vivo action of cannabinoids. Neurochem. Res., 24: 1233–1240.

Ameri, A. (1999) The effects of cannabinoids on the brain. Prog. Neurobiol., 58: 315–348.

Arevalo, C., De Miguel, R. and Hernandez-Tristan, R. (2001). Cannabinoid effects on anxiety-related behaviours and hypothalamic neurotransmitters. Pharmacol. Biochem. Behav., 70: 123–131.

Arseneault, L., Cannon, M., Poulton, R., Murray, R., Caspi, A. and Moffitt, T.E. (2002) Cannabis use in adolescence and risk for adult psychosis: longitudinal prospective study. BMJ, 325: 1212–1213.

Begg, M., Pacher, P., Batkai, S., Osei-Hyiaman, D., Offertaler, L., Mo, F.M., Liu, J. and Kunos, G. (2005) Evidence for novel cannabinoid receptors. Pharmacol. Ther., 106: 133–145.

Beinfeld, M.C. and Connolly, K. (2001) Activation of CB1 cannabinoid receptors in rat hippocampal slices inhibits potassium-evoked cholecystokinin release, a possible mechanism contributing to the spatial memory defects produced by cannabinoids. Neurosci. Lett., 301: 69–71.

Beltramo, M., Stella, N., Calignano, A., Lin, S.Y., Makriyannis, A. and Piomelli, D. (1997) Functional role of high-affinity anandamide transport, as revealed by selective inhibition. Science, 277: 1094–1097.

Belzung, C. (2001) Rodent models of anxiety-like behaviors: are they predictive for compounds acting via non-benzodiazepine mechanisms? Curr. Opin. Investig. Drugs, 2: 1108–1111.

Berrendero, F. and Maldonado, R. (2002) Involvement of the opioid system in the anxiolytic-like effects induced by delta(9)-tetrahydrocannabinol. Psychopharmacology, 163: 111–117.

Bhattacharya, S.K., Chakrabarti, A., Sandler, M. and Glover, V. (1996) Effects of some anxiogenic agents on rat brain monoamine oxidase (MAO) A and B inhibitory (tribulin) activity. Indian J. Exp. Biol., 34: 1190–1193.

Bickerdike, M.J., Marsden, C.A., Dourish, C.T. and Fletcher, A. (1994) The influence of 5- hydroxytryptamine re-uptake blockade on CCK receptor antagonist effects in the rat elevated zero-maze. Eur. J. Pharmacol., 271: 403–411.

Biro, E., Toth, G. and Telegdy, G. (1995) Involvement of neurotransmitters in the 'anxiolytic-like' action of atrial natriuretic peptide in rats. Neuropeptides, 29: 215–220.

Bisogno, T., Howell, F., Williams, G., Minassi, A., Cascio, M.G., Ligresti, A., Matias, I., Schiano-Moriello, A., Paul, P., Williams, E.J., Gangadharan, U., Hobbs, C., Di Marzo, V. and Doherty, P. (2003) Cloning of the first sn1-DAG lipases points to the spatial and temporal regulation of endocannabinoid signaling in the brain. J. Cell Biol., 163: 463–468.

Bortolato, M., Campolongo, P., Mangieri, R.A., Scattoni, M.L., Frau, R., Trezza, V., La Rana, G., Russo, R., Calignano, A., Gessa, G.L., Cuomo, V. and Piomelli, D. (2006) Anxiolytic-like properties of the anandamide transport inhibitor AM404. Neuropsychopharmacology, 31: 2652–2659.

Bortolato, M., Mangieri, R.A., Fu, J., Kim, J.H., Arguello, O., Duranti, A., Tontini, A., Mor, M.,

Tarzia, G. and Piomelli, D. (2007) Antidepressant-like activity of the fatty acid amide hydrolase inhibitor URB597 in a rat model of chronic mild stress. *Biol. Psychiatry*, 62: 1103–1110.

Bradshaw, H.B. and Walker, J.M. (2005) The expanding field of cannabimimetic and related lipid mediators. Br. J. Pharmacol., 144: 459–465.

Braida, D., Limonta, V., Malabarba, L., Zani, A. and Sala, M. (2007) 5-HT(1A) receptors are involved in the anxiolytic effect of Delta(9)-tetrahydrocannabinol and AM 404, the anandamide transport inhibitor, in Sprague-Dawley rats. Eur. J. Pharmacol., 555: 156–163.

Breivogel, C.S., Griffin, G., Di Marzo, V. and Martin, B.R. (2001) Evidence for a new G protein-coupled cannabinoid receptor in mouse brain. Mol. Pharmacol., 60: 155–163.

Cadas, H., di Tomaso, E. and Piomelli, D. (1997) Occurrence and biosynthesis of endogenous cannabinoid precursor, N-arachidonoyl phosphatidylethanolamine, in rat brain. J. Neurosci., 17: 1226–1242.

Cahill, L. and McGaugh, J.L. (1998) Mechanisms of emotional arousal and lasting declarative memory. Trends Neurosci., 21: 294–299.

Celerier, E., Ahdepil, T., Wikander, H., Berrendero, F., Nyberg, F. and Maldonado, R. (2006) Influence of the anabolic-androgenic steroid nandrolone on cannabinoid dependence. Neuropharmacology, 50: 788–806.

Chang, L., Luo, L., Palmer, J.A., Sutton, S., Wilson, S.J., Barbier, A.J., Breitenbucher, J.G., Chaplan, S.R. and Webb, M. (2006) Inhibition of fatty acid amide hydrolase produces analgesia by multiple mechanisms. Br. J. Pharmacol., 148: 102–113.

Chaperon, F. and Thiebot, M.H. (1999) Behavioral effects of cannabinoid agents in animals. Crit. Rev. Neurobiol., 13: 243–281.

Charney, D.S. and Deutch, A. (1996) A functional neuroanatomy of anxiety and fear: implications for the pathophysiology and treatment of anxiety disorders. Crit. Rev. Neurobiol., 10: 419–446.

Charrier, D., Dangoumau, L., Puech, A.J., Hamon, M. and Thiebot, M.H. (1995) Failure of CCK receptor ligands to modify anxiety-related behavioural suppression in an operant conflict paradigm in rats. Psychopharmacology, 121: 127–134.

Chhatwal, J.P., Davis, M., Maguschak, K.A. and Ressler, K.J. (2005) Enhancing cannabinoid neurotransmission augments the extinction of conditioned fear. Neuropsychopharmacology, 30: 516–524.

Chopin, P. and Briley, M. (1993) The benzodiazepine antagonist flumazenil blocks the effects of CCK receptor agonists and antagonists in the elevated plus-maze. Psychopharmacology, 110: 409–414.

Conti, L.H., Costello, D.G., Martin, L.A., White, M.F. and Abreu, M.E. (1994) Mouse strain differences in the behavioral effects of corticotropin-releasing factor (CRF) and the CRF antagonist alpha-helical CRF9-41. Pharmacol. Biochem. Behav., 48: 497–503.

Cravatt, B.F., Giang, D.K., Mayfield, S.P., Boger, D.L., Lerner, R.A. and Gilula, N.B. (1996) Molecular characterization of an enzyme that degrades neuromodulatory fatty-acid amides. Nature, 384: 83–87.

Dannon, P.N., Lowengrub, K., Amiaz, R., Grunhaus, L. and Kotler, M. (2004) Comorbid cannabis use and panic disorder: short term and long term follow-up study. Hum. Psychopharmacol., 19: 97–101.

Davidson, E.S. and Schenk, S. (1994) Variability in subjective responses to marijuana: initial experiences of college students. Addict. Behav., 19: 531–538.

Davis, M., Rainnie, D. and Cassell, M. (1994) Neurotransmission in the rat amygdala related to fear and anxiety. Trends Neurosci., 17: 208–214.

Dawson, G.R., Rupniak, N.M., Iversen, S.D., Curnow, R., Tye, S., Stanhope, K.J. and Tricklebank, M.D. (1995) Lack of effect of *CCKB* receptor antagonists in ethological and conditioned animal screens for anxiolytic drugs. Psychopharmacology, 121: 109–117.

De Lago, E., Fernandez-Ruiz, J., Ortega-Gutierrez, S., Viso, A., Lopez-Rodriguez, M.L. and Ramos, J.A. (2002) UCM707, a potent and selective inhibitor of endocannabinoid uptake, potentiates hypokinetic and antinociceptive effects of anandamide. Eur. J. Pharmacol., 449: 99–103.

Degenhardt, L., Hall, W. and Lynskey, M. (2001) The relationship between cannabis use, depression and anxiety among Australian adults: findings from the National Survey of Mental Health and Well-Being. Soc. Psychiatry Psychiatr. Epidemiol., 36: 219–227.

Degroot, A. and Nomikos, G.G. (2004) Genetic deletion and pharmacological blockade of CB1 receptors modulates anxiety in the shock probe burying test. Eur. J. Neurosci., 20: 1059–1064.

Deiana, S., Fattore, L., Spano, M.S., Cossu, G., Porcu, E., Fadda, P. and Fratta, W. (2006) Strain and schedule-dependent differences in the acquisition, maintenance and extinction of intravenous cannabinoid self-administration in rats. *Neuropharmacology*, 52: 646–654.

Desarnaud, F., Cadas, H. and Piomelli, D. (1995) Anandamide amidohydrolase activity in rat brain microsomes. Identification and partial characterization. J. Biol. Chem., 270: 6030–6035.

Devane, W.A., Dysarz, F.A., III Johnson, M.R., Melvin, L.S. and Howlett, A.C. (1988) Determination and characterization of a cannabinoid receptor in rat brain. Mol. Pharmacol., 34: 605–613.

Devane, W.A., Hanus, L., Breuer, A., Pertwee, R.G., Stevenson, L.A., Griffin, G., Gibson, D., Mandelbaum, A., Etinger, A. and Mechoulam, R. (1992) Isolation and structure of a brain constituent that binds to the cannabinoid receptor. Science, 258: 1946–1949.

Di Marzo, V., Fontana, A., Cadas, H., Schinelli, S., Cimino, G., Schwartz, J.C. and Piomelli, D. (1994)

Formation and inactivation of endogenous cannabinoid anandamide in central neurons. Nature, 372: 686–691.

Dinh, T.P., Carpenter, D., Leslie, F.M., Freund, T.F., Katona, I., Sensi, S.L., Kathuria, S. and Piomelli, D. (2002a) Brain monoglyceride lipase participating in endocannabinoid inactivation. Proc. Natl. Acad. Sci. USA, 99: 10819–10824.

Dinh, T.P., Freund, T.F. and Piomelli, D. (2002b) A role for monoglyceride lipase in 2-arachidonoylglycerol inactivation. Chem. Phys. Lipids, 121: 149–158.

Durham, R.A., Li, W., Bhattacharya, K., Kinsora, J., Snyder, B., Lotarski, S., Sadagopan, N., Johnson, D.S. and Ahn, K. (2006) Inhibition of fatty acid amide hydrolase: the search for an anxiolytic or antidepressant indication. Program No. 830.3. 2006 Neuroscience Meeting Planner. Atlanta, GA: Society for Neuroscience, 2006. Online.

Fabre, L.F. and McLendon, D. (1981) The efficacy and safety of nabilone (a synthetic cannabinoid) in the treatment of anxiety. J. Clin. Pharmacol., 21: 377S–382S.

Fadda, P., Robinson, L., Fratta, W., Pertwee, R.G. and Riedel, G. (2004) Differential effects of THC- or CBD-rich cannabis extracts on working memory in rats. Neuropharmacology, 47: 1170–1179.

Fegley, D., Gaetani, S., Duranti, A., Tontini, A., Mor, M., Tarzia, G. and Piomelli, D. (2004) Characterization of the fatty acid amide hydrolase inhibitor cyclohexyl carbamic acid 3′-carbamoyl-biphenyl-3-yl ester (URB597): effects on anandamide and oleoylethanolamide deactivation. J. Pharmacol. Exp. Ther., 313: 352–358.

Fergusson, D.M., Horwood, L.J. and Swain-Campbell, N. (2002) Cannabis use and psychosocial adjustment in adolescence and young adulthood. Addiction, 97: 1123–1135.

File, S.E. (1992) Behavioural detection of anxiolytic action. In: Elliot, J.M. Heal, D.J. and Marsden, C.A. (Eds.), Experimental Approaches to Anxiety and Depression. Wiley, New York, pp. 25–44.

Fowler, C.J. (2004) Possible involvement of the endocannabinoid system in the actions of three clinically used drugs. Trends Pharmacol. Sci., 25: 59–61.

Freund, T.F., Katona, I. and Piomelli, D. (2003) Role of endogenous cannabinoids in synaptic signaling. Physiol. Rev., 83: 1017–1066.

Gaoni, Y. and Mechoulam, R. (1964) Isolation, structure and partial synthesis of an active constituent of hashish. J. Am. Chem. Soc., 86: 1646.

Gatley, S.J., Gifford, A.N., Volkow, N.D., Lan, R. and Makriyannis, A. (1996) 123I-labeled AM251: a radioiodinated ligand which binds in vivo to mouse brain cannabinoid CB1 receptors. Eur. J. Pharmacol., 307: 331–338.

Gatley, S.J., Lan, R., Pyatt, B., Gifford, A.N., Volkow, N.D. and Makriyannis, A. (1997) Binding of the nonclassical cannabinoid CP 55,940, and the diarylpyrazole AM251 to rodent brain cannabinoid receptors. Life Sci., 61: 191–197.

Gelfand, E.V. and Cannon, C.P. (2006) Rimonabant: a selective blocker of the cannabinoid CB1 receptors for the management of obesity, smoking cessation and cardiometabolic risk factors. Expert Opin. Invest. Drugs, 15: 307–315.

Genn, R.F., Tucci, S., Marco, E.M., Viveros, M.P. and File, S.E. (2004) Unconditioned and conditioned anxiogenic effects of the cannabinoid receptor agonist CP 55,940 in the social interaction test. Pharmacol. Biochem. Behav., 77: 567–573.

Gerdeman, G.L., Ronesi, J. and Lovinger, D.M. (2002) Postsynaptic endocannabinoid release is critical to long-term depression in the striatum. Nat. Neurosci., 5: 446–451.

Ghozland, S., Matthes, H.W., Simonin, F., Filliol, D., Kieffer, B.L. and Maldonado, R. (2002) Motivational effects of cannabinoids are mediated by mu-opioid and kappa-opioid receptors. J. Neurosci., 22: 1146–1154.

Giuffrida, A., Leweke, F.M., Gerth, C.W., Schreiber, D., Koethe, D., Faulhaber, J., Klosterkotter, J. and Piomelli, D. (2004) Cerebrospinal anandamide levels are elevated in acute schizophrenia and are inversely correlated with psychotic symptoms. Neuropsychopharmacology, 29: 2108–2114.

Giuffrida, A., Parsons, L.H., Kerr, T.M., Rodriguez de Fonseca, F., Navarro, M. and Piomelli, D. (1999) Dopamine activation of endogenous cannabinoid signaling in dorsal striatum. Nat. Neurosci., 2: 358–363.

Giuliani, D., Ferrari, F. and Ottani, A. (2000) The cannabinoid agonist HU 210 modifies rat behavioural responses to novelty and stress. Pharmacol. Res., 41: 47–53.

Glass, M., Faull, R.L.M. and Dragunow, M. (1997) Cannabinoid receptors in the human brain: a detailed anatomical and quantitative autoradiographic study on the fetal, neonatal and adult human brain. Neuroscience, 77: 299–318.

Glass, R.M., Uhlenhuth, E.H., Hartel, F.W., Schuster, C.R. and Fischman, M.W. (1980) A single dose study of nabilone, a synthetic cannabinoid. Psychopharmacology, 71: 137–142.

Gobbi, G., Bambico, F.R., Mangieri, R., Bortolato, M., Campolongo, P., Solinas, M., Cassano, T., Morgese, M.G., Debonnel, G., Duranti, A., Tontini, A., Tarzia, G., Mor, M., Trezza, V., Goldberg, S.R., Cuomo, V. and Piomelli, D. (2005) Antidepressant-like activity and modulation of brain monoaminergic transmission by blockade of anandamide hydrolysis. Proc. Natl. Acad. Sci. USA, 102: 18620–18625.

Gonzalez, L.E., Andrews, N. and File, S.E. (1996) 5-HT1A and benzodiazepine receptors in the basolateral amygdala modulate anxiety in the social interaction test, but not in the elevated plus-maze. Brain. Res., 732: 145–153.

Grant, B.F. and Pickering, R. (1998) The relationship between cannabis use and DSM-IV cannabis abuse and dependence: results from the National Longitudinal Alcohol Epidemiologic Survey. J. Subst. Abuse, 10: 255–264.

Green, B., Kavanagh, D. and Young, R. (2003) Being stoned: a review of self-reported cannabis effects. Drug Alcohol Rev., 22: 453–460.

Griebel, G. (1995) 5-Hydroxytryptamine-interacting drugs in animal models of anxiety disorders: more than 30 years of research. Pharmacol. Ther., 65: 319–395.

Griebel, G. (1999) Is there a future for neuropeptide receptor ligands in the treatment of anxiety disorders? Pharmacol. Ther., 82: 1–61.

Griebel, G., Perrault, G. and Sanger, D.J. (1998) Characterization of the behavioral profile of the non-peptide CRF receptor antagonist CP-154,526 in anxiety models in rodents. Comparison with diazepam and buspirone. Psychopharmacology, 138: 55–66.

Griebel, G., Stemmelin, J. and Scatton, B. (2005) Effects of the cannabinoid CB1 receptor antagonist rimonabant in models of emotional reactivity in rodents. Biol. Psychiatry, 57: 261–267.

Hajos, N. and Freund, T.F. (2002) Pharmacological separation of cannabinoid sensitive receptors on hippocampal excitatory and inhibitory fibers. Neuropharmacology, 43: 503–510.

Hall, W. and Solowij, N. (1998) Adverse effects of cannabis. Lancet, 352: 1611–1616.

Haller, J., Bakos, N., Szirmay, M., Ledent, C. and Freund, T.F. (2002) The effects of genetic and pharmacological blockade of the CB1 cannabinoid receptor on anxiety. Eur. J. Neurosci., 16: 1395–1398.

Haller, J., Varga, B., Ledent, C. and Freund, T.F. (2004) CB1 cannabinoid receptors mediate anxiolytic effects: convergent genetic and pharmacological evidence with CB1-specific agents. Behav. Pharmacol., 15: 299–304.

Haney, M. (2005) The marijuana withdrawal syndrome: diagnosis and treatment. Curr. Psychiatry Rep., 7: 360–366.

Heilig, M., McLeod, S., Koob, G.K. and Britton, K.T. (1992) Anxiolytic-like effect of neuropeptide Y (NPY), but not other peptides in an operant conflict test. Regul. Pept., 41: 61–69.

Henquet, C., Krabbendam, L., Spauwen, J., Kaplan, C., Lieb, R., Wittchen, H.U. and van Os, J. (2005a) Prospective cohort study of cannabis use, predisposition for psychosis, and psychotic symptoms in young people. BMJ, 330: 11.

Henquet, C., Murray, R., Linszen, D. and van Os, J. (2005b) The environment and schizophrenia: the role of cannabis use. Schizophr. Bull., 31: 608–612.

Herkenham, M., Groen, B.G., Lynn, A.B., De Costa, B.R. and Richfield, E.K. (1991a) Neuronal localization of cannabinoid receptors and second messengers in mutant mouse cerebellum. Brain Res., 552: 301–310.

Herkenham, M., Lynn, A.B., de Costa, B.R. and Richfield, E.K. (1991b) Neuronal localization of cannabinoid receptors in the basal ganglia of the rat. Brain Res., 547: 267–274.

Herkenham, M., Lynn, A.B., Johnson, M.R., Melvin, L.S., de Costa, B.R. and Rice, K.C. (1991c) Characterization and localization of cannabinoid receptors in rat brain: a quantitative in vitro autoradiographic study. J. Neurosci., 11: 563–583.

Herkenham, M., Lynn, A.B., Little, M.D., Johnson, M.R., Melvin, L.S., de Costa, B.R. and Rice, KC. (1990) Cannabinoid receptor localization in brain. Proc. Natl. Acad. Sci. USA, 87: 1932–1936.

Hill, M.N. and Gorzalka, B.B. (2004) Enhancement of anxiety-like responsiveness to the cannabinoid CB(1) receptor agonist HU-210 following chronic stress. Eur. J. Pharmacol., 499: 291–295.

Hillard, C.J., Edgemond, W.S., Jarrahian, A. and Campbell, W.B. (1997) Accumulation of N-arachidonoylethanolamine (anandamide) into cerebellar granule cells occurs via facilitated diffusion. J. Neurochem., 69: 631–638.

Hillard, C.J. and Jarrahian, A. (2003) Cellular accumulation of anandamide: consensus and controversy. Br. J. Pharmacol., 140: 802–808.

Hillard, C.J., Wilkison, D.M., Edgemond, W.S. and Campbell, W.B. (1995) Characterization of the kinetics and distribution of N-arachidonylethanolamine (anandamide) hydrolysis by rat brain. Biochem. Biophys. Acta, 1257: 249–256.

Hohmann, A.G., Suplita, R.L., Bolton, N.M., Neely, M.H., Fegley, D., Mangieri, R., Krey, J.F., Walker, J.M., Holmes, P.V., Crystal., J.D., Duranti, A., Tontini, A., Mor, M., Tarzia, G. and Piomelli, D. (2005) An endocannabinoid mechanism for stress-induced analgesia. Nature, 435: 1108–1112.

Hollister, L.E. (1986) Health aspects of cannabis. Pharmacol. Rev., 38: 1–20.

Holt, S., Comelli, F., Costa, B. and Fowler, C.J. (2005) Inhibitors of fatty acid amide hydrolase reduce carrageenan-induced hind paw inflammation in pentobarbital-treated mice: comparison with indomethacin and possible involvement of cannabinoid receptors. Br. J. Pharmacol., 146: 467–476.

Hopfer, C.J., Young, S.E., Purcell, S., Crowley, T.J., Stallings, M.C., Corley, R.P., Rhee, S.H., Smolen, A., Krauter, K., Hewitt, J.K. and Ehringer, M.A. (2006) Cannabis receptor haplotype associated with fewer cannabis dependence symptoms in adolescents. Am. J. Med. Genet. B Neuropsychiatr. Genet., 141: 895–901.

Howlett, A.C. (2002) The cannabinoid receptors. Prostaglandins Other Lipid Mediat., 68–69: 619–631.

Ilaria, R.L., Thornby, J.I. and Fann, W.E. (1981) Nabilone, a cannabinol derivative, in the treatment of anxiety neurosis. Curr. Ther. Res., 29: 943–949.

Jarai, Z., Wagner, J.A., Varga, K., Lake, K.D., Compton, D.R., Martin, B.R., Zimmer, A.M., Bonner, T.I.,

Buckley, G., Mezey, E., Razdan, R.K., Zimmer, A. and Kunos, G. (1999) Cannabinoid-induced mesenteric vasodilation through an endothelial site distinct from CB1 or CB2 receptors. Proc. Natl. Acad. Sci. USA, 96: 14136–14141.

Jarbe, T.U., DiPatrizio, N.V., Lu, D. and Makriyannis, A. (2004) (-)-Adamantyl-delta8-tetrahydrocannabinol (AM-411), a selective cannabinoid CB1 receptor agonist: effects on open-field behaviors and antagonism by SR-141716 in rats. Behav. Pharmacol., 15: 517–521.

Jayamanne, A., Greenwood, R., Mitchell, V.A., Aslan, S., Piomelli, D. and Vaughan, C.W. (2006) Actions of the FAAH inhibitor URB597 in neuropathic and inflammatory chronic pain models. Br. J. Pharmacol., 147: 281–288.

Jhaveri, M.D., Richardson, D., Kendall, D.A., Barrett, D.A. and Chapman, V. (2006) Analgesic effects of fatty acid amide hydrolase inhibition in a rat model of neuropathic pain. J. Neurosci., 26: 13318–13327.

Jung, K.M., Mangieri, R., Stapleton, C., Kim, J., Fegley, D., Wallace, M., Mackie, K. and Piomelli, D. (2005) Stimulation of endocannabinoid formation in brain slice cultures through activation of group I metabotropic glutamate receptors. Mol. Pharmacol., 68: 1196–1202.

Kathuria, S., Gaetani, S., Fegley, D., Valino, F., Duranti, A., Tontini, A., Mor, M., Tarzia, G., La Rana, G., Calignano, A., Giustino, A., Tattoli, M., Palmery, M., Cuomo, V. and Piomelli, D. (2003) Modulation of anxiety through blockade of anandamide hydrolysis. Nat. Med., 9: 76–81.

Katona, I., Rancz, E.A., Acsady, L., Ledent, C., Mackie, K., Hajos, N. and Freund, TF. (2001) Distribution of CB1 cannabinoid receptors in the amygdala and their role in the control of GABAergic transmission. J. Neurosci., 21: 9506–9518.

Kim, J. and Alger, B.E. (2004) Inhibition of cyclooxygenase-2 potentiates retrograde endocannabinoid effects in hippocampus. Nat. Neurosci., 7: 697–698.

Kim, M. and McGaugh, J.L. (1992) Effects of intra-amygdala injections of NMDA receptor antagonists on acquisition and retention of inhibitory avoidance. Brain Res., 585: 35–48.

Koenen, K.C., Lyons, M.J., Goldberg, J., Simpson, J., Williams, W.M., Toomey, R., Eisen, S.A., True, W. and Tsuang, M.T. (2003) Co-twin control study of relationships among combat exposure, combat-related PTSD, and other mental disorders. J. Trauma Stress, 16: 433–438.

Koob, G.F., Sanna, P.P. and Bloom, F.E. (1998) Neuroscience of addiction. Neuron, 21: 467–476.

Kozak, K.R. and Marnett, L.J. (2002) Oxidative metabolism of endocannabinoids. Prostaglandins Leukot. Essent. Fatty Acids, 66: 211–220.

Kozak, K.R., Prusakiewicz, J.J. and Marnett, L.J. (2004) Oxidative metabolism of endocannabinoids by COX-2. Curr. Pharm. Des., 10: 659–667.

LeDoux, J.E. (1994) Emotion, memory and the brain. Sci. Am., 270: 50–57.

Lichtman, A.H., Leung, D., Shelton, C.C., Saghatelian, A., Hardouin, C., Boger, D.L. and Cravatt, B.F. (2004a) Reversible inhibitors of fatty acid amide hydrolase that promote analgesia: evidence for an unprecedented combination of potency and selectivity. J. Pharmacol. Exp. Ther., 311: 441–448.

Lichtman, A.H., Shelton, C.C., Advani, T. and Cravatt, B.F. (2004b) Mice lacking fatty acid amide hydrolase exhibit a cannabinoid receptor-mediated phenotypic hypoalgesia. Pain, 109: 319–327.

Liu, J., Wang, L., Harvey-White, J., Osei-Hyiaman, D., Razdan, R., Gong, Q., Chan, A.C., Zhou, Z., Huang, B.X., Kim, H.Y. and Kunos, G. (2006) A biosynthetic pathway for anandamide. Proc. Natl. Acad. Sci., USA, 103: 13345–13350.

Maccarone, M., Bari, M., Battista, N. and Finazzi-Agro, A. (2002a) Estrogen stimulates arachidonoyl-ethanolamide release from human endothelial cells and platelet activation. Blood, 100: 4040–4048.

Maccarone, M., Bari, M. and Finazzi-Agro, A. (2002b) Quantification of anandamide content in animal cells and tissues: the normalization makes the difference. Lipids Health Dis., 1: 4.

Maccarone, M., Del Principe, D. and Finazzi-Agro, A. (2002c) Endocannabinoids: new physiological (co-) agonists of human platelets. Thromb. Haemost., 88: 165–166.

Maccarone, M., Falciglia, K., Di Rienzo, M. and Finazzi-Agro, A. (2002d) Endocannabinoids, hormone-cytokine networks and human fertility. Prostaglandins Leukot. Essent. Fatty Acids, 66: 309–317.

Mackie, K. (2005) Distribution of cannabinoid receptors in the central and peripheral nervous system. Handb. Exp. Pharmacol., 168: 299–325.

Makara, J.K., Mor, M., Fegley, D., Szabo, S.I., Kathuria, S., Astarita, G., Duranti, A., Tontini, A., Tarzia, G., Rivara, S., Freund, T.F. and Piomelli, D. (2005) Selective inhibition of 2-AG hydrolysis enhances endocannabinoid signaling in hippocampus. Nat. Neurosci., 8: 1139–1141.

Manzanares, J., Corchero, J., Romero, J., Fernandez-Ruiz, J.J., Ramos, J.A. and Fuentes, J.A. (1999) Pharmacological and biochemical interactions between opioids and cannabinoids. Trends Pharmacol. Sci., 20: 287–294.

Marco, E.M., Granstrem, O., Moreno, E., Llorente, R., Adriani, W., Laviola, G. and Viveros, M.P. (2006) Subchronic nicotine exposure in adolescence induces long-term effects on hippocampal and striatal cannabinoid-CB(1) and mu-opioid receptors in rats. Eur. J. Pharmacol., 172: 46–53.

Marco, E.M., Perez-Alvarez, L., Borcel, E., Rubio, M., Guaza, C., Ambrosio, E., File, S.E. and Viveros, M.P. (2004) Involvement of 5-HT1A receptors in behavioural effects of the cannabinoid receptor agonist CP 55,940 in male rats. Behav. Pharmacol., 15: 21–27.

Maren, S. (1996) Synaptic transmission and plasticity in the amygdala, an emerging physiology of fear conditioning circuits. Mol. Neurobiol., 13: 1–22.

Marin, S., Marco, E., Biscaia, M., Fernandez, B., Rubio, M., Guaza, C., Schmidhammer, H. and Viveros, M.P. (2003) Involvement of the kappa-opioid receptor in the anxiogenic-like effect of CP 55,940 in male rats. Pharmacol. Biochem. Behav., 74: 649–656.

Marsicano, G., Moosmann, B., Hermann, H., Lutz, B. and Behl, C. (2002a) Neuroprotective properties of cannabinoids against oxidative stress: role of the cannabinoid receptor CB1. J. Neurochem., 80: 448–456.

Marsicano, G., Wotjak, C.T., Azad, S.C., Bisogno, T., Rammes, G., Cascio, M.G., Hermann, H., Tang, J., Hofmann, C., Zieglgansberger, W., Di Marzo, V. and Lutz, B. (2002b) The endogenous cannabinoid system controls extinction of aversive memories. Nature, 418: 530–534.

Martin, M., Ledent, C., Parmentier, M., Maldonado, R. and Valverde, O. (2002) Involvement of CB1 cannabinoid receptors in emotional behaviour. Psychopharmacology, 159: 379–387.

Matsuda, L.A., Bonner, T.I. and Lolait, S.J. (1992) Cannabinoid receptors: which cells, where, how, and why? NIDA Res. Monogr., 126: 48–56.

Matsuda, L.A., Lolait, S.J., Brownstein, M.J., Young, A.C. and Bonner, T.I. (1990) Structure of a cannabinoid receptor and functional expression of the cloned cDNA. Nature, 346: 561–564.

McGregor, C., Darke, S., Ali, R. and Christie, P. (1998) Experience of non-fatal overdose among heroin users in Adelaide, Australia: circumstances and risk perceptions. Addiction, 93: 701–711.

Mechoulam, R., Ben-Shabat, S., Hanus, L., Ligumsky, M., Kaminski, N.E., Schatz, A.R., Gopher, A., Almog, S., Martin, B.R. and Compton, D.R. (1995) Identification of an endogenous 2-monoglyceride, present in canine gut, that binds to cannabinoid receptors. Biochem. Pharmacol., 50: 83–90.

Menzaghi, F., Heinrichs, S.C., Merlo-Pich, E., Tilders, F.J. and Koob, G.F. (1994a) Involvement of hypothalamic corticotropin-releasing factor neurons in behavioral responses to novelty in rats. Neurosci. Lett., 168: 139–142.

Menzaghi, F., Howard, R.L., Heinrichs, S.C., Vale, W., Rivier, J. and Koob, G.F. (1994b) Characterization of a novel and potent corticotropin-releasing factor antagonist in rats. J. Pharmacol. Exp. Ther., 269: 564–572.

Menzaghi, F., Rassnick, S., Heinrichs, S., Baldwin, H., Pich, E.M., Weiss, F. and Koob, G.F. (1994c) The role of corticotropin-releasing factor in the anxiogenic effects of ethanol withdrawal. Ann. N.Y. Acad. Sci., 739: 176–184.

Mikics, E., Dombi, T., Barsvari, B., Varga, B., Ledent, C., Freund, T.F. and Haller, J. (2006) The effects of cannabinoids on contextual conditioned fear in CB1 knockout and CD1 mice. Behav. Pharmacol., 17: 223–230.

Millan, M.J. (2003) The neurobiology and control of anxious states. Prog. Neurobiol., 70: 83–244.

Milani, R.M., Parrott, A.C., Turner, J.J. and Fox, H.C. (2004) Gender differences in self-reported anxiety, depression, and somatization among ecstasy/MDMA polydrug users, alcohol/tobacco users, and nondrug users. Addict. Behav., 29: 965–971.

Miserendino, M.J., Sananes, C.B., Melia, K.R. and Davis, M. (1990) Blocking of acquisition but not expression of conditioned fear-potentiated startle by NMDA antagonists in the amygdala. Nature, 345: 716–718.

Mokler, D.J., Robinson, S.E., Johnson, J.H., Hong, J.S. and Rosecrans, J.A. (1986) Effects of postweaning administration of delta-9-tetrahydrocannabinol (THC) on adult behavioral and neuroendocrine function in Sprague-Dawley and Fischer-344 rats. Neurobehav. Toxicol. Teratol., 8: 407–413.

Morishita, W. and Alger, B.E. (1999) Evidence for endogenous excitatory amino acids as mediators in DSI of GABA(A)ergic transmission in hippocampal CA1. J. Neurophysiol., 82: 2556–2564.

Morley, K.C., Li, K.M., Hunt, G.E., Mallet, P.E. and McGregor, I.S. (2004) Cannabinoids prevent the acute hyperthermia and partially protect against the 5-HT depleting effects of MDMA ("Ecstasy") in rats. Neuropharmacology, 46: 954–965.

Munro, S., Thomas, K.L. and Abu-Shaar, M. (1993) Molecular characterization of a peripheral receptor for cannabinoids. Nature, 365: 61–65.

Navarro, M., Hernandez, E., Munoz, R.M., del Arco, I., Villanua, M.A., Carrera, M.R. and Rodriguez de Fonseca, F. (1997) Acute administration of the CB1 cannabinoid receptor antagonist SR 141716A induces anxiety-like responses in the rat. Neuroreport, 8: 491–496.

Nemeroff, C.B. (2003) The role of GABA in the pathophysiology and treatment of anxiety disorders. Psychopharmacol. Bull., 37: 133–146.

Nestler, E.J., Gould, E., Manji, H., Buncan, M., Duman, R.S., Greshenfeld, H.K., Hen, R., Koester, S., Lederhendler, I., Meaney, M., Robbins, T., Winsky, L. and Zalcman, S. (2002) Preclinical models: status of basic research in depression. Biol. Psychiatry, 52: 503–528.

O'Shea, M., McGregor, I.S. and Mallet, P.E. (2006) Repeated cannabinoid exposure during perinatal, adolescent or early adult ages produces similar long-lasting deficits in object recognition and reduced social interaction in rats. Psychopharmacology, 20: 611–621.

O'Shea, M., Singh, M.E., McGregor, I.S. and Mallet, P.E. (2004) Chronic cannabinoid exposure produces lasting memory impairment and increased anxiety in adolescent but not adult rats. J. Psychopharmacol., 18: 502–508.

O'Sullivan, S.E., Kendall, D.A. and Randall, M.D. (2004) Heterogeneity in the mechanisms of vasorelaxation to anandamide in resistance and conduit rat mesenteric arteries. Br. J. Pharmacol., 142: 435–442.

Ohno-Shosaku, T., Maejima, T. and Kano, M. (2001) Endogenous cannabinoids mediate retrograde signals from depolarized postsynaptic neurons to presynaptic terminals. Neuron, 29: 729–738.

Okamoto, Y., Morishita, J., Tsuboi, K., Tonai, T. and Ueda, N. (2004) Molecular characterization of a phospholipase D generating anandamide and its congeners. J. Biol. Chem., 279: 5298–5305.

Okulate, G.T. and Jones, O.B. (2006) Post-traumatic stress disorder, survivor guilt and substance use–a study of hospitalised Nigerian army veterans. S. Afr. Med. J., 96: 144–146.

Onaivi, E.S., Green, M.R. and Martin, B.R. (1990) Pharmacological characterization of cannabinoids in the elevated plus maze. J. Pharmacol. Exp. Ther., 253: 1002–1009.

Pacher, P., Batkai, S. and Kunos, G. (2006) The endocannabinoid system as an emerging target of pharmacotherapy. Pharmacol. Rev., 58: 389–462.

Parker, L.A. and Gillies, T. (1995) THC-induced place and taste aversions in Lewis and Sprague-Dawley rats. Behav. Neurosci., 109: 71–78.

Patel, S., Cravatt, B.F. and Hillard, C.J. (2005a) Synergistic interactions between cannabinoids and environmental stress in the activation of the central amygdala. Neuropsychopharmacology, 30: 497–507.

Patel, S. and Hillard, C.J. (2006) Pharmacological evaluation of cannabinoid receptor ligands in a mouse model of anxiety: further evidence for an anxiolytic role for endogenous cannabinoid signaling. J. Pharmacol. Exp. Ther., 318: 304–311.

Patel, S., Roelke, C.T., Rademacher, D.J., Cullinan, W.E. and Hillard, C.J. (2004) Endocannabinoid signaling negatively modulates stress-induced activation of the hypothalamic-pituitary-adrenal axis. Endocrinology, 145: 5431–5438.

Patel, S., Roelke, C.T., Rademacher, D.J. and Hillard, C.J. (2005b) Inhibition of restraint stress-induced neural and behavioural activation by endogenous cannabinoid signalling. Eur. J. Neurosci., 21: 1057–1069.

Patton, G.C., Coffey, C., Carlin, J.B., Degenhardt, L., Lynskey, M. and Hall, W. (2002) Cannabis use and mental health in young people: cohort study. BMJ, 325: 1195–1198.

Pertwee, R. (1993) The evidence for the existence of cannabinoid receptors. Gen. Pharmacol., 24: 811–824.

Piomelli, D. (2003) The molecular logic of endocannabinoid signalling. Nat. Rev. Neurosci., 4: 873–884.

Piomelli, D. (2005) The endocannabinoid system: a drug discovery perspective. Curr. Opin. Investig. Drugs, 6: 672–679.

Piomelli, D., Beltramo, M., Glasnapp, S., Lin, S.Y., Goutopoulos, A., Xie, X.Q. and Makriyannis, A. (1999) Structural determinants for recognition and translocation by the anandamide transporter. Proc. Natl. Acad. Sci. USA, 96: 5802–5807.

Piomelli, D., Tarzia, G., Duranti, A., Tontini, A., Mor, M., Compton, T.R., Dasse, O., Monaghan, E.P., Parrott, J.A. and Putman, D. (2006) Pharmacological profile of the selective FAAH inhibitor DS-4103 (URB597). CNS Drug Rev., 12: 21–38.

Pi-Sunyer, F.X., Aronne, L.J., Heshmati, H.M., Devin, J. and Rosenstock, J., RIO-North America Study Group. (2006) Effect of rimonabant, a cannabinoid-1 receptor blocker, on weight and cardiometabolic risk factors in overweight or obese patients: RIO-North America: a randomized controlled trial. JAMA, 295: 761–775.

Ramos, A. and Mormede, P. (1998) Stress and emotionality: a multidimensional and genetic approach. Neurosci. Biobehav. Rev., 22: 33–57.

Rey, J.M., Sawyer, M.G., Raphael, B., Patton, G.C. and Lynskey, M. (2002) Mental health of teenagers who use cannabis. Results of an Australian survey. Br. J. Psychiatry, 180: 216–221.

Rinaldi-Carmona, M., Barth, F., Heaulme, M., Shire, D., Calandra, B., Congy, C., Martinez, S., Maruani, J., Neliat, G. and Caput, D. (1994) SR141716A, a potent and selective antagonist of the brain cannabinoid receptor. FEBS Lett., 350: 240–244.

Robbe, D., Alonso, G., Chaumont, S., Bockaert, J. and Manzoni, O.J. (2002a) Role of p/q-Ca2+ channels in metabotropic glutamate receptor 2/3-dependent presynaptic long-term depression at nucleus accumbens synapses. J. Neurosci., 22: 4346–4356.

Robbe, D., Bockaert, J. and Manzoni, O.J. (2002b) Metabotropic glutamate receptor 2/3-dependent long-term depression in the nucleus accumbens is blocked in morphine withdrawn mice. Eur. J. Neurosci., 16: 2231–2235.

Robson, P. (2005) Therapeutic aspects of cannabis and cannabinoids. Br. J. Psychiatry, 178: 107–115.

Rodgers, R.J. (1997) Animal models of 'anxiety': where next? Behav. Pharmacol., 8: 477–496.

Rodgers, R.J., Evans, P.M. and Murphy, A. (2005) Anxiogenic profile of AM-251, a selective cannabinoid CB1 receptor antagonist, in plus-maze-naive and plus-maze-experienced mice. Behav. Pharmacol., 16: 405–413.

Rodgers, R.J., Haller, J., Halasz, J. and Mikics, E. (2003) 'One-trial sensitization' to the anxiolytic-like effects of cannabinoid receptor antagonist SR141716A in the mouse elevated plus-maze. Eur. J. Neurosci., 17: 1279–1286.

Rodriguez de Fonseca, F., Carrera, M.R., Navarro, M., Koob, G.F. and Weiss, F. (1997) Activation of corticotropin-releasing factor in the limbic system during cannabinoid withdrawal. Science, 276: 2050–2054.

Rodriguez de Fonseca, F., Rubio, P., Menzaghi, F., Merlo-Pich, E., Rivier, J., Koob, G.F. and Navarro, M. (1996) Corticotropin-releasing factor (CRF) antagonist [D-Phe12,Nle21,38,C alpha MeLeu37]CRF attenuates the acute actions of the highly potent cannabinoid receptor agonist HU-210 on defensive-withdrawal behavior in rats. J. Pharmacol. Exp. Ther., 276: 56–64.

Romero, E.M., Fernandez, B., Sagredo, O., Gomez, N., Uriguen, L., Guaza, C., De Miguel, R., Ramos, J.A. and Viveros, M.P. (2002) Antinociceptive, behavioural and neuroendocrine effects of CP 55,940 in young rats. Brain Res. Dev. Brain. Res., 136: 85–92.

Rutkowska, M., Jamontt, J. and Gliniak, H. (2006) Effects of cannabinoids on the anxiety-like response in mice. Pharmacol. Rep., 58: 200–206.

Saario, S.M., Savinainen, J.R., Laitinen, J.T., Jarvinen, T. and Niemi, R. (2004) Monoglyceride lipase-like enzymatic activity is responsible for hydrolysis of 2-arachidonoylglycerol in rat cerebellar membranes. Biochem. Pharmacol., 67: 1381–1387.

Sajdyk, T.J. and Shekhar, A. (1997) Excitatory amino acid receptor antagonists block the cardiovascular and anxiety responses elicited by gamma-aminobutyric acid A receptor blockade in the basolateral amygdala of rats. J. Pharmacol. Exp. Ther., 283: 969–977.

Schlicker, E., Timm, J., Zentner, J. and Gothert, M. (1998) Cannabinoid CB1 receptor-mediated inhibition of noradrenaline release in the human and guinea-pig hippocampus. Naunyn Schmiedebergs Arch. Pharmacol., 356: 583–589.

Schneider, M., Drews, E. and Koch, M. (2005) Behavioral effects in adult rats of chronic prepubertal treatment with the cannabinoid receptor agonist WIN 55,212-2. Behav. Pharmacol., 16: 447–454.

Selden, N.R., Everitt, B.J. and Robbins, T.W. (1991) Telencephalic but not diencephalic noradrenaline depletion enhances behavioural but not endocrine measures of fear conditioning to contextual stimuli. Behav. Brain Res., 43: 139–154.

Shepard, J.D., Barron, K.W. and Myers, D.A. (2000) Corticosterone delivery to the amygdala increases corticotropin-releasing factor mRNA in the central amygdaloid nucleus and anxiety-like behavior. Brain Res., 861: 288–295.

Sjögren, S., Ryberg, E., Lindblom, A., Larsson, N., Astrand, A., Hjorth, S., Andersson, A., Groblewski, T. and Greasley, P. (2005) A new receptor for cannabinoid ligands. Symposium on the Cannabinoids. International Cannabinoid Research Society, Burlington, VT.

Sjostrom, P.J., Turrigiano, G.G. and Nelson, S.B. (2003) Neocortical LTD via coincident activation of presynaptic NMDA and cannabinoid receptors. Neuron, 39: 641–654.

Stark-Adamec, C., Adamec, R.E. and Pihl, R.O. (1981) The subjective marijuana experience: great expectations. Int. J. Addict., 16: 1169–1181.

Stein, D.J., Westenberg, H.G. and Liebowitz, M.R. (2002) Social anxiety disorder and generalized anxiety disorder: serotonergic and dopaminergic neurocircuitry. J. Clin. Psychiatry, 63: 12–19.

Stella, N., Schweitzer, P. and Piomelli, D. (1997) A second endogenous cannabinoid that modulates long-term potentiation. Nature, 388: 773–778.

Sugiura, T., Kondo, S., Sukagawa, A., Nakane, S., Shinoda, A., Itoh, K., Yamashita, A. and Waku, K. (1995) 2-Arachidonoylglycerol: a possible endogenous cannabinoid receptor ligand in brain. Biochem. Biophys. Res. Commun., 215: 89–97.

Sun, Y.X., Tsuboi, K., Okamoto, Y., Tonai, T., Murakami, M., Kudo, I. and Ueda, N. (2004) Biosynthesis of anandamide and N-palmitoylethanolamine by sequential actions of phospholipase A2 and lysophospholipase D. Biochem. J., 380: 749–756.

Swift, W., Gates, P. and Dillon, P. (2005) Survey of Australians using cannabis for medical purposes. Harm Reduct. J., 2: 18.

Takahashi, R.N., Pamplona, F.A. and Fernandes, M.S. (2005) The cannabinoid antagonist SR141716A facilitates memory acquisition and consolidation in the mouse elevated T-maze. Neurosci. Lett., 380: 270–275.

Ueda, N., Kurahashi, Y., Yamamoto, S. and Tokunaga, T. (1995) Partial purification and characterization of the porcine brain enzyme hydrolyzing and synthesizing anandamide. J. Biol. Chem., 270: 23823–23827.

Uriguen, L., Perez-Rial., S., Ledent, C., Palomo, T. and Manzanares, J. (2004) Impaired action of anxiolytic drugs in mice deficient in cannabinoid CB1 receptors. Neuropharmacology, 46: 966–973.

Valjent, E., Mitchell, J.M., Besson, M.J., Caboche, J. and Maldonado, R. (2002) Behavioural and biochemical evidence for interactions between Delta 9-tetrahydrocannabinol and nicotine. Br. J. Pharmacol., 135: 564–578.

Valverde, O., Ledent, C., Beslot, F., Parmentier, M. and Roques, B.P. (2000) Reduction of stress-induced analgesia but not of exogenous opioid effects in mice lacking CB1 receptors. Eur. J. Neurosci., 12: 533–539.

Valverde, O., Noble, F., Beslot, F., Dauge, V., Fournie-Zaluski, B.P. and Roques, B.P. (2001)

324

Delta9-tetrahydrocannabinol releases and facilitates the effects of endogenous enkephalins: reduction in morphine withdrawal syndrome without change in rewarding effect. Eur. J. Neurosci., 13: 1816–1824.

Van Gaal, L.F., Rissanen, A.M., Scheen, A.J., Ziegler, O. and Rossner, S., RIO-Europe Study Group. (2005) Effects of the cannabinoid-1 receptor blocker rimonabant on weight reduction and cardiovascular risk factors in overweight patients: 1-year experience from the RIO-Europe study. Lancet, 365: 1389–1397.

Van Megen, H.J., Westenberg, H.G., den Boer, J.A. and Kahn, R.S. (1996) Cholecystokinin in anxiety. Eur. Neuropsychopharmacol., 6: 263–280.

Van Sickle, M.D., Duncan, M., Kingsley, P.J., Mouihate, A., Urbani, P., Mackie, K., Stella, N., Makriyannis, A., Piomelli, D., Davison, J.S., Marnett, L.J., Di Marzo, V., Pittman, Q.J., Patel, K.D. and Sharkey, K.A. (2005) Identification and functional characterization of brainstem cannabinoid CB2 receptors. Science, 310: 329–332.

Varma, N., Carlson, G.C., Ledent, C. and Alger, B.E. (2001) Metabotropic glutamate receptors drive the endocannabinoid system in hippocampus. J. Neurosci., 21: RC188.

Varvel, S.A., Wise, L.E., Niyuhire, F., Cravatt, B.F. and Lichtman, A.H. (2007) Inhibition of fatty-acid amide hydrolase accelerates acquisition and extinction rates in a spatial memory task. *Neuropsychopharmacology*, 32: 1032–1041.

Weidenfeld, J., Feldman, S. and Mechoulam, R. (1994) Effect of the brain constituent anandamide, a cannabinoid receptor agonist, on the hypothalamo-pituitary-adrenal axis in the rat. Neuroendocrinology, 59: 110–122.

Welch, S.P. and Eads, M. (1999) Synergistic interactions of endogenous opioids and cannabinoid systems. Brain Res., 848: 183–190.

Wilson, R.I. and Nicoll, R.A. (2001) Endogenous cannabinoids mediate retrograde signalling at hippocampal synapses. Nature, 410: 588–592.

Zimmer, A., Valjent, E., Konig, M., Zimmer, A.M., Robledo, P., Hahn, H., Valverde, O. and Maldonado, R. (2001) Absence of delta-9-tetrahydrocannabinol dysphoric effects in dynorphin-deficient mice. J. Neurosci., 21: 9499–9505.

Zuardi, A.W., Guimaraes, F.S. and Moreira, A.C. (1993) Effect of cannabidiol on plasma prolactin, growth hormone and cortisol in human volunteers. Braz. J. Med. Biol. Res., 26: 213–217.

CHAPTER 4.6

Genetic factors underlying anxiety-behavior: a meta-analysis of rodent studies involving targeted mutations of neurotransmission genes

Catherine Belzung[1,*], Samuel Leman[1] and Guy Griebel[2]

[1]EA3248 Psychobiologie des Emotions, Université François Rabelais, UFR Sciences et Techniques,
Parc Grandmont, Tours, France
[2]Sanofi-Aventis, Psychopharmacology Department, Bagneux, France

Abstract: This paper aimed at reviewing publications investigating the involvement of genetic factors in anxiety behavior, using a meta-analysis of rodent studies involving targeted mutations of neurotransmission genes. We summarized 311 experiments investigating the involvement of GABAergic, serotoninergic, glutamatergic, and neuropeptidergic targets, and then analyzed these tables according several questions such as: Are some particular behavioral tests used in these studies? Which genetic method has been used? Which phenotypes are observed? Can these results be explained by the species or the strain used? Did this strategy enable to precise the brain area involved in these processes? Is the contribution of the genetic factor limited to the developmental period? Do the effects of the mutation correlate with the results of pharmacological challenge? Does the mutation modify the response to anxiolytic or anxiogenic agents? We propose some conclusions on the genes involved in normal and pathological anxiety behavior.

Keywords: anxiety; genetic; serotonin; glutamate; GABA-neuropeptide

I. Introduction

Anxiety is an all day experience of most people, corresponding to an adaptive reaction to potential threats. The probability of the occurrence of this reaction as well as its intensity may vary among subjects, depending on genetic as well as epigenetic factors. In some subjects, the frequency and intensity of this reaction can become excessive and maladapted: this can correspond to anxiety disorders, such as panic, post-traumatic stress, generalized anxiety, or obsessive-compulsive disorder. In humans, several studies have tried to identify the

genetic factors involved either in normal anxiety or in pathological anxiety states. Such a research is mainly based on polymorphism studies. However, polymorphism has not been described for all genes of interest, which limits the progress of human studies. Recently (Belzung and Philippot, 2007), we have shown that rodents are excellent species to study anxiety-related behaviors, as they display most (but not all) of the cognitive processes necessary to human anxiety. Further, targeted genetic modification tools have been particularly well developed in rodents, especially in mice, enabling progress in the study of the genetic factors involved in anxiety using such species.

This paper aimed at reviewing publications that investigated the involvement of genetic factors in anxiety-related behaviors in rodents. Indeed,

*Corresponding author.
E-mail: catherine.belzung@univ-tours.fr

R.J. Blanchard, D.C. Blanchard, G. Griebel and D. Nutt (Eds.)
Handbook of Anxiety and Fear, Vol. 17
ISBN 978-0-444-53065-3

DOI: 10.1016/S1569-7339(07)00015-X

several arguments indicate that genetic factors may be involved in anxiety behavior. First, the polymorphism of several genes is associated with human anxiety. For example, the Met88Val diazepam binding inhibitor gene polymorphism (Thoeringer et al., 2007), the serotonin transporter promotor region polymorphism (Mazzanti et al., 1999; Hariri et al., 2002; Pezawas et al., 2005; Brocke et al., 2006; Gonda et al., 2007; Hayden et al., 2007; Stein et al., 2007), or the *BDNF* Val66Met polymorphism (Jiang et al., 2005; Lang et al., 2005; Chen et al., 2006b; Hashimoto, 2007; Hunnerkopf et al., 2007) are associated with modifications in anxiety-related phenotypes, suggesting an involvement of genetic factors on these traits. Second, excessive anxiety can be treated by various pharmacological agents targeting specific neurotransmitter systems (see e.g., Millan, 2003 for a review), suggesting that anxiety traits may be related to dysfunctions of these neurotransmitter systems. This indicates that the genes coding for the proteins involved in the secretion, the regulation, or the binding of these molecules may be involved in anxiety processes.

As a huge amount of data is available on genes involved in the anxiety phenotype, we will focus on the results of targeted invalidation or over-expression studies. Other experimental strategies (such as QTL, selected lines, or multiple marker strains) are available, but an exhaustive review of all these studies is not possible in such a limited space. Further, genetic factors can exert their action at two different time points: they can act during the developmental period, modifying the development of the brain (e.g., neurotrophic factors) or act once the animals are adults, interfering either with non-specific processes (such as perception, motricity, pain) or with neurotransmission. We will focus on the second ones, because this may allow comparing the results with the ones obtained using pharmacological activation or in-activation of the proteins that result from the targeted genes (e.g., neurotransmitter receptors). To do that, we will present several tables, which present in an exhaustive way the studies that were undertaken in this field with a focus on the following systems: serotonin (Table 1), glutamate (Table 2), GABA (Table 3), endocannabinoids

(Table 4) and a variety of neuroactive peptides (Table 4). In each table, we describe the following parameters: gene involved, genetic method used (knock out, knock in, over-expression), species studied, strain used, experimental device as well as the observed phenotype. For practical reasons, each line of a given table corresponds to an experiment, and not to a published paper. A paper can correspond to several experiments. A total number of 311 experiments have been analyzed in this meta-analysis.

The principal focus of this paper is to analyze these tables, according several questions such as: Are some particular behavioral tests used in these studies? Which genetic method has been used? Was there any particular choice of construction (knock-in, knock-out, and over-expressed models) made for each of the neurotransmission systems? Which phenotypes are observed? Can these results be explained by the species or the strain used? Did this strategy enable to precise the brain area involved in these processes? Is the contribution of the genetic factor limited to the developmental period? Do the effects of the mutation correlate with the results of pharmacological challenge? Does the mutation modify the response to anxiolytic or anxiogenic agents? What do these findings tell us about the link between neurotransmitter systems and anxiety? Do these studies provide useful information about the role played by the various GABAergic, serotoninergic, glutamatergic, and neuropeptidergic targets in anxiety behavior? The response to these questions will enable us to propose some conclusions about the genes involved in normal and pathological anxiety behaviors.

II. Are some particular behavioral tests used in these studies?

Several test situations have been used to assess anxiety behavior, including elevated plus-maze, light/dark test, open-field, free exploration, stress-induced hyperthermia, novelty-induced suppression of feeding, mouse defense test battery, acoustic startle, conditioned fear, Vogel conflict, and cat odor presentation. In these situations, the

Table 1. Effect of targeted mutation of serotonin-related genes on rodents in anxiety tests

Model	Test	Animal	Effects	Reference
5-HT1A KO mice	Open-field	Swiss-Webster/12^{SV} mice	Anxiogenic	Parks et al. (1998)
5-HT1A KO mice	Open-field Elevated plus-maze	n/a	Anxiogenic	Toth and Sibille (1998)
5-HT1A KO mice + diazepam (0.1–1 mg/kg)	Open-field Elevated plus-maze	129/Sv × Swiss-Webster background mice	Diazepam lost its ability to produce anxiolytic-like activity Diazepam lost its ability to produce anxiolytic-like activity	Sibille et al. (2000)
5-HT1A KO mice	Open-field Elevated plus-maze	Male and female C57BL/6J × 129/Sv mice	Anxiogenic Anxiogenic	Ramboz et al. (1998)
5-HT1A KO mice + WAY100635 (0.03–0.3 mg/kg)	Open-field		No effect when compared to vehicle-treated −/− mice	
5-HT1A KO mice + 8-OH-DPAT (0.1–1 mg/kg)				
5-HT1A KO mice + buspirone (0.05–2.5 mg/kg)				
5-HT1A KO mice	Open-field Elevated zero-maze Responses to a novel object	129/Sv × C57BL/6J mice	Anxiogenic Anxiogenic Anxiogenic	Heisler et al. (1998)
5-HT1A KO mice + flesinoxan (0.3–3 mg/kg)	Stress-induced hyperthermia	129/Sv-ter background mice	The anxiolytic-like activity seen in WT mice was lost in KO animals	Pattij et al. (2000)
5-HT1A KO mice	Stress-induced hyperthermia		KO animals were more anxious than WT mice	
5-HT1A KO mice + mCPP (0.3–3 mg/kg)	Stress-induced hyperthermia		WT animals and KO mice displayed similar phenotype	
5-HT1A KO mice + diazepam (1–4 mg/kg)	Stress-induced hyperthermia		The anxiolytic-like activity seen in WT mice was still present in KO animals	
5-HT1A KO mice	Elevated plus-maze	Female and male 129/Sv × C57BL/6J mice (8–10-week-old)	KO animals were more anxious than WT mice	Gross et al. (2002)
5-HT1A KO rescue transgenic mice		Female and male 129/Sv × C57BL/6J mice (18–20-week-old)	Anxious phenotype of 5-HT1A KO mice was no longer seen	
5-HT1A KO mice	Open-field test	Female and male 129/Sv × C57BL/6J mice (8–10-week-old)	KO animals were more anxious than WT mice	
5-HT1A KO rescue transgenic mice		Female and male 129/Sv × C57BL/6J mice (18–20-week-old)	Anxious phenotype of 5-HT1A KO mice was no longer seen	
5-HT1A KO mice	Novelty-induced suppression of feeding	Female and male 129/Sv × C57BL/6J mice (8–10-week-old)	KO animals were more anxious than WT mice	
5-HT1A KO rescue transgenic mice		Female and male 129/Sv × C57BL/6J mice (18–20-week-old)	Anxious phenotype of 5-HT1A KO mice was no longer seen	
5-HT1A KO mice + doxycycline (for 2 months)	Novelty-induced suppression of feeding		KO animals were more anxious than WT mice	

Table 1 (*continued*)

Model	Test	Animal	Effects	Reference
5-HT1A KO rescue transgenic mice + doxycycline (for 2 months)		Female and male 129/Sv × C57BL/6J mice (80–140-day-old)	Anxious phenotype of 5-HT1A KO mice was no longer seen despite 5-HT1A turning off	Gross et al. (2002)
5-HT1A KO mice + doxycycline (during development) 5-HT1A KO rescue transgenic mice + doxycycline (during development)			KO animals were more anxious than WT mice Reversal of anxious phenotype of 5-HT1A KO mice was no longer seen	
5-HT1A KO mice + doxycycline (for 2 months) 5-HT1A KO rescue transgenic mice + doxycycline (for 2 months)	Open-field test	Female and male 129/Sv × C57BL/6J mice (80–140-day-old)	KO animals were more anxious than WT mice Anxious phenotype of 5-HT1A KO mice was no longer seen despite 5-HT1A turning off	
5-HT1A KO mice + doxycycline (during development) 5-HT1A KO rescue transgenic mice + doxycycline (during development)			KO animals were more anxious than WT mice Reversal of anxious phenotype of 5-HT1A KO mice was no longer seen	
5-HT1A KO mice + doxycycline (for 2 months) 5-HT1A KO rescue transgenic mice + doxycycline (for 2 months)	Elevated plus-maze		KO animals were more anxious than WT mice Anxious phenotype of 5-HT1A KO mice was no longer seen despite 5-HT1A turning off	
5-HT1A KO mice + doxycycline (during development) 5-HT1A KO rescue transgenic mice + doxycycline (during development)			KO animals were more anxious than WT mice Reversal of anxious phenotype of 5-HT1A KO mice was no longer seen	
5-HT1A KO mice	Acoustic startle reflex	Mixed 129/Sv background	(1) No difference between genotypes; (2) 85–120 dB were used	Dirks et al. (2001)
	Footshock-induced sensitization in acoustic startle reflex		No difference between genotypes	
5-HT1B KO mice	Acoustic startle reflex		(1) Reduced reactivity in KO; (2) 85–120 dB were used	
	Footshock-induced sensitization in acoustic startle reflex		Sensitization was reduced in KO	
5-HT1A KO mice	Open-field test Light/dark test Stress-induced hyperthermia Stress-induced physiological changes Stress-induced physiological changes	Mixed 129/Sv background	No difference between genotypes No difference between genotypes No difference between genotypes (1) KO mice displayed higher stress response; (2) injection stress was used (1) KO mice displayed higher stress response; (2) novel cage exposure stress was used	Pattij and Olivier (2001)

Genotype / treatment	Test	Background	Result	Reference
5-HT1A KO mice	Stress-induced hyperthermia; Elevated plus-maze	129/Sv background	No difference between genotypes	Pattij et al. (2002b)
5-HT1A KO mice + alprazolam (1–3 mg/kg); 5-HT1A KO mice + flumazenil (3–30 mg/kg)	Stress-induced hyperthermia		The anxiolytic-like activity seen in WT mice was still present in KO animals; No difference between genotypes	
5-HT1A KO mice + alcohol (2–4 g/kg); 5-HT1A KO mice + pentylenetetrazole (7.5–30 mg/kg)			The anxiolytic-like activity seen in WT mice was still present in KO animals; No difference between genotypes	
5-HT1A KO mice + diazepam (1 mg/kg)	Elevated plus-maze		The anxiolytic-like activity seen in WT mice was still present in KO animals	Pattij et al. (2002a)
5-HT1A KO mice	Injection stress-induced tachycardia; Rectal temperature procedure-induced hyperthermia	129/Sv background (12-week-old)	KO mice displayed higher stress response; No difference between genotypes	
5-HT1A KO mice + diazepam (4 mg/kg)	Injection stress-induced hyperthermia and tachycardia		Anxiolytic	
5-HT1A KO mice	Novelty stress-induced hyperthermia and tachycardia		KO mice displayed higher stress response	
5-HT1A KO mice	Elevated plus-maze; Open-field test	Swiss background mice (2–5-month-old); C57BL/6J background mice (2–5-month-old)	KO animals were more anxious than WT mice	Bailey and Toth (2004)
5-HT1A KO mice + diazepam	Elevated plus-maze; Open-field test	Swiss background mice (2–5-month-old)		
5-HT1A KO mice + diazepam (0.2–1 mg/kg); 5-HT1A KO mice + diazepam (1 mg/kg); 5-HT1A KO mice + diazepam (0.2–1 mg/kg)	Elevated plus-maze	C57BL/6J background mice (2–5-month-old); Swiss/B6 background mice (2–5-month-old)	The anxiolytic-like activity seen in WT mice was lost in KO animals; The anxiolytic-like activity seen in WT mice was still present in KO animals; The anxiolytic-like activity seen in WT mice was lost in KO animals	
5-HT1A KO mice	Elevated plus-maze	Female C57BL/6J background mice (5–8-month-old)	KO mice displayed increased anxiety-like behavior	Li et al. (2004)
5-HT1A KO mice + Ad-1AP sense			KO mice displayed increased anxiety-like behavior despite 5-HT1A receptor restoration in the hypothalamus	
5-HT1A KO mice	Light/dark test; Vogel conflict test; Conditioned fear stress	129/Sv × C57BL/6J mice (8–10-week-old)	KO animals were more anxious than WT mice; No difference between genotypes; Freezing response of KO mice did not decrease when placed in an ambiguous environment	Klemenhagen et al. (2006)
5-HT1A receptor overexpression transgenic mice	Elevated plus-maze; Open-field test; Free-exploration test	Male and female NMRI mice (15-week-old)	Mice displayed reduced anxiety-like behavior; No phenotypic differences; Mice displayed reduced anxiety-like behavior	Kusserow et al. (2004)
5-HT2A KO mice	Open-field test; Light/dark test; Elevated plus-maze; Novelty-induced suppression of feeding	n/a	KO animals appeared less anxious than WT mice	Weisstaub et al. (2006)

Table 1 (continued)

Model	Test	Animal	Effects	Reference
5-HT2A KO mice + Emx1-Cre	Open-field test; Light/dark test; Novelty-induced suppression of feeding	n/a	(1) Emx1-Cre restored 5-HT$_{2A}$ function in the cortex; (2) anxiolytic-like phenotype was lost	
5-HT2C KO mice	Open-field; Elevated plus-maze; Novel object-induced anxiety	n/a	Anxiolytic	Heisler et al. (1998)
5-HT3 KO mice	Elevated plus-maze; Open-field test; Light/dark test; Conditioned fear stress	C57BL/6J × 129 background (7–20-week-old)	KO animals were less anxious than WT mice; No difference between genotypes; No difference between genotypes; KO mice displayed enhancing freezing	Bhatnagar et al. (2004b)
5-HT3 KO mice	Defensive withdrawal; Defensive withdrawal	C57BL/6J background (5–7-month-old); Female C57BL/6J background (5–7-month-old)	KO animals appeared more anxious than WT mice; KO animals appeared less anxious than WT mice	Bhatnagar et al. (2004a)
5-HT3 KO mice	Light/dark test; Elevated plus-maze	C57BL/6J × 129 background (90–120-day-old)	KO animals were less anxious than WT mice	Kelley et al. (2003)
5-HT4 KO mice	Restraint stress-induced hypophagia; Open-field test	Mixed 129/Sv × C57BL/6J × B6CBAF1/J background mice	Hypophagia was reduced in KO mice	Compan et al. (2004)
5-HT5A KO mice	Open-field; Novel object test	C57BL/6J mice	KO mice were less anxious; Increase in exploratory activity; Increase in exploratory activity and curiosity; No effect; Shock of 0.15 mA; Bursts of 120 dB	Grailhe et al. (1999)
5-HT1B KO mice	Elevated plus-maze; Shock-probe burying test; Acoustic startle test; Ultrasonic 'distress' vocalization; Elevated plus-maze	Male and female mice from 129/Sv strain	Anxiolytic; Weak decrease in anxiety-related behaviors	Brunner et al. (1999)
5-HT1B KO mice	Elevated plus-maze; Object exploration	Male and female mice from 129/Sv strain	No effect; Anxiolytic	Malleret et al. (1999)
5-HT1B KO mice	Elevated plus-maze; Burying behavior	Mice from 129/Sv strain (20–30 g)	No difference between genotypes; KO animals were less anxious than WT mice	Lopez-Rubalcava et al. (2000)
5-HT1B overexpression (in the dorsal raphe nucleus) transgenic rats (3 days)	Open-field test; Open-field test following restraint stress; Elevated plus-maze following restraint stress	Sprague–Dawley rats (180–250 g)	Anxiolytic (overexpression was achieved by using herpes simplex virus gene transfer); Anxiogenic (overexpression was achieved by using herpes simplex virus gene transfer); Anxiogenic (overexpression was achieved by using herpes simplex virus gene transfer)	Clark et al. (2002)

Treatment	Strain	Test	Result	Reference
5-HT transporter KO mice	Female and male 129S6/SvEv background mice	Open-field test; Elevated plus-maze; Novelty-induced suppression of feeding	No difference between genotypes; No difference between genotypes; KO mice showed an increase in latency to feed	Lira et al. (2003)
5-HT transporter KO mice	Female and male C57BL/6J background mice (3–7-month-old)	Elevated plus-maze; Light/dark test; Emergence test; Open-field test	5-HTT−/− mice showed increased anxiety-like behavior; 5-HTT−/− mice showed increased anxiety-like behavior; 5-HTT−/− mice showed increased anxiety-like behavior; 5-HTT−/− mice showed increased anxiety-like behavior	Holmes et al. (2003)
5-HT transporter KO mice + WAY100635 (0.05–0.3 mg/kg)	Female C57BL/6J background mice (3–7-month-old)	Elevated plus-maze	Anxiolytic	
5-HT transporter overexpression transgenic mice	CBA × C57BL/6J background mice (3–6-month-old)	Elevated plus-maze	Transgenic mice displayed reduced anxiety-related behaviors	Jennings et al. (2006)
5-HT transporter overexpression transgenic mice		Hyponeophagia	Transgenic mice displayed reduced anxiety-related behaviors	
5-HT transporter overexpression transgenic mice + paroxetine (10 mg/kg)		Elevated plus-maze	Paroxetine normalized low anxiety in transgenic mice	

Table 2. Effect of targeted mutation of glutamate-related genes on rodents in anxiety tests

Model	Test	Animal strain	Effects	Reference
mGluR5 KO mice	Stress-induced hyperthermia	B6/129 background mice (25–35 g)	(1) Mice displayed an anxiolytic-like phenotype; (2) the stressor was the rectal probing	Brodkin et al. (2002)
			(1) Mice displayed an anxiolytic-like phenotype; (2) the stressor was an intruder	
			(1) Mice displayed an anxiolytic-like phenotype; (2) the stressor was an injection	
mGluR5 KO mice + mGluR5 antagonist (MTEP (16 mg/kg, sc))			(1) The anxiolytic-like activity of MTEP was lost; (2) the stressor was an injection	
mGluR5 KO mice	Conditioned fear	129Sv/C57BL/6 background mice (8–12-week-old)	No difference between both genotypes	Ko et al. (2005)
mGluR6 KO mice			KO mice showed reduced fear memory when tested 3, 7, or 14 days after training	
mGluR7 KO mice	Open-field	Male and female C57BL/6 background mice (8–10-week-old)	No difference between both genotypes	Callaerts-Vegh et al. (2006)
	Elevated plus-maze		KO mice showed decreased anxiety-like behavior	
	Marble burying		KO mice showed decreased anxiety-like behavior	
	Passive-avoidance		(1) KO mice had a reduced latency to enter the unknown dark compartment; (2) electric shocks of 0.2 mA/2 s were applied	
	Conditioned emotional response		(1) KO animals had a higher resistance to extinction of fear-elicited response suppression; (2) A VI-30s schedule was used	
mGluR7 KO mice	Elevated plus-maze	129/Ola × C57BL/6 background mice (10–14-week-old)	KO mice showed decreased anxiety-like behavior	Cryan et al. (2003)
	Light/dark test			
	Staircase test			
	Stress-induced hyperthermia			
mGluR8 KO mice	Open-field	C57BL/6 background mice (6-month-old)	KO mice showed increased anxiety-like behavior	Duvoisin et al. (2005)
	Elevated plus-maze	ICR background mice (12-week-old)		
mGluR8 KO mice	Elevated plus-maze	ICR background mice (24-week-old)	KO mice showed increased anxiety-like behavior	Linden et al. (2002)
		ICR background mice (12-week-old)	(1) No difference between both genotypes; (2) animals were tested under fluorescent light conditions	
			(1) No difference between both genotypes; (2) animals were submitted to restraint stress	
NR2A KO mice	Elevated plus-maze	Male and female C57BL/6 × CBA background mice (at least 10-week-old)	KO mice showed decreased anxiety-like behavior	Boyce-Rustay and Holmes (2006)
	Light/dark test			
	Open-field			

Table 3. Effect of targeted mutation of GABA-related genes on rodents in anxiety tests

Model	Test	Animal strain	Effects	Reference
GABA$_A$ alpha1 subunit KO mice	Contextual fear conditioning	129S1/X1 × FVB/N	Anxiogenic	Sonner et al. (2005)
GABA$_A$ alpha1 subunit KO mice + isoflurane			EC50 for isofluorane increased in mutants	
GABA$_A$ alpha1 subunit conditional KO mice in forebrain (amygdala, hippocampus, cortex)			No effect	
GABA$_A$ alpha1 subunit conditional KO mice in forebrain (amygdala, hippocampus, cortex) + isoflurane			EC50 for isofluorane increased in mutants	
GABA$_A$ alpha1 subunit conditional KO mice in forebrain (amygdala, hippocampus, cortex)	Tone fear conditioning		No effect	
GABA$_A$ alpha1 subunit conditional KO mice in forebrain (amygdala, hippocampus, cortex) + isoflurane			EC50 for isofluorane increased in mutants	
GABA$_A$ alpha1 subunit KO mice	Elevated plus-maze	C57BL/6J × 129Sv/SvJ	No effect	Kralic et al. (2003)
GABA$_A$ alpha1 subunit KO mice + ethanol 0.75–1.5 g/kg			No effect (KO more sensitive to the locomotor stimulating effects of ethanol)	
GABA$_A$ alpha1 subunit KO mice	Open-field		No effect	
GABA$_A$ alpha1 subunit KO mice + ethanol 0.75–1.5 g/kg			No effect	
GABA$_A$ alpha1 subunit KO mice	Elevated plus-maze	n/a	No effect	Kralic et al. (2002)
GABA$_A$ alpha1 subunit KO mice + diazepam 0.3–1 mg/kg			Mutants more sensitive to Diazepam: anxiolytic at a 0.6 mg/kg in mutants and at a 1 mg/kg dose in WT	
GABA$_A$ alpha1 H101R point mutation knock-in mice + diazepam 0.5–2 mg/kg	Elevated plus-maze	129/svJ × C57BL/6J	No effect of mutation	Rudolph et al. (1999)
GABA$_A$ alpha1 H101R point mutation knock-in mice + diazepam 1–3 mg/kg	Light/dark		No effect of mutation	

Table 3 (*continued*)

Model	Test	Animal strain	Effects	Reference
GABA$_A$ alpha1 S270H/L27 mutation knock-in mice	Elevated plus-maze	C57BL/6J × 129/SvJ	No effect of mutation	Werner et al. (2006)
GABA$_A$ alpha1 S270H/L277A point mutation knock-in mice + ethanol 0.75 g/kg			Effects of ethanol increased	
GABA$_A$ alpha3 H126R point mutation knock-in mice	Elevated plus-maze	n/a	No effect of mutation	Low et al. (2000)
GABA$_A$ alpha2 H101R mutation knock-in mice	Light/dark		No effect of diazepam in mutants	
GABA$_A$ alpha3 H126R point mutation knock-in mice	Elevated plus-maze		No effect of mutation	
GABA$_A$ alpha2 H101R point mutation knock-in mice	Light/dark		No effect of diazepam in mutants	
GABA$_A$ alpha5 H105R point mutation knock-in	Light/dark	129/SvJ	No difference in diazepam-induced effects	Crestani et al. (2002)
GABA$_A$ alpha5 H105R point mutation knock-in mice + diazepam 1 mg/kg, p.o.	Elevated plus-maze		No difference in diazepam-induced effects	
GABA$_A$ alpha5 H105R point mutation knock-in mice	Trace fear conditioning		Facilitation in mutant mice	
	Delay fear conditioning		No effect	
	Context fear conditioning		No effect	
GABA$_A$ alpha5 subunit KO mice	Elevated plus-maze	C57BL6 × 129SvEv	No effect	Collinson et al. (2002)
GABA$_A$ alpha5 subunit KO mice + chlordiazepoxide 10 mg/kg				
GABA$_A$ beta3 subunit KO mice	Elevated plus-maze	C57BL6 × 129SvSvJ	Slightly anxiogenic (increased time spent in closed arm)	Liljelund et al. (2005)
GABA$_A$ beta3 subunit KO mice + diazepam 1.5 mg/kg first post-natal week			No effect	
GABA$_A$ beta3 subunit KO mice + diazepam 1.5 mg/kg second post-natal week			Anxiolytic in mutants but not in WT	
GABA$_A$ delta subunit KO mice	Elevated plus-maze	C57BL/6J × 129Sv/SvJ	No effect	Mihalek et al. (1999)
GABA$_A$ delta subunit KO mice + ganaxolone 10 mg/kg i.p.			No effect of ganaxolone in mutants	
GABA$_A$ delta subunit KO mice	Context fear conditioning		No effect	
	Cued fear conditioning		No effect	

Mice / treatment	Test	Strain	Result	Reference
GABA$_A$ delta subunit KO mice + THP 10 mg/kg	Elevated plus-maze	Mutants compared to C57BL6	No effect (comparisons probably not made with littermates)	Smith et al. (2006b)
GABA$_A$ delta subunit KO mice + THP 10 mg/kg	Elevated plus-maze after shock		Anxiolytic effect of THP lost in mutants (comparisons probably not made with littermates)	
GABA$_A$ delta subunit KO mice + THP 10 mg/kg + finasteride 50 mg/kg	Elevated plus-maze		Anxiogenic effect lost in mutants (comparisons probably not made with littermates)	
GABA$_A$ delta subunit KO mice + THP 10 mg/kg + finasteride 50 mg/kg	Elevated plus-maze after shock		No effect (comparisons probably not made with littermates)	
GABA$_A$ delta subunit KO mice + lorazepam 0.1 mg/kg			No effect (comparisons probably not made with littermates)	
GABA$_A$ delta subunit KO mice + THP 10 mg/kg + finasteride 50 mg/kg + lorazepam 0.1 mg/kg			No effect (comparisons probably not made with littermates)	
GABA$_A$ delta subunit KO mice + THIP 3 mg/kg	Elevated plus-maze		Anxiolytic effect of THIP lost (comparisons probably not made with littermates)	
GABA$_A$ delta subunit KO mice + THP 10 mg/kg + finasteride 50 mg/kg + THIP 3 mg/kg			Effect lost (comparisons probably not made with littermates)	
GABA$_A$ delta subunit KO mice + flumazenil 2 mg/kg	Elevated plus-maze after shock		No effect (comparisons probably not made with littermates)	
GABA$_A$ delta subunit KO mice + flumazenil 7 mg/kg			No effect (comparisons probably not made with littermates)	
GABA$_A$ delta subunit KO mice + THP 10 mg/kg + finasteride 50 mg/kg + flumazenil 2 mg/kg			Anxiogenic in WT, anxiolytic in mutants (comparisons probably not made with littermates)	
GABA$_A$ delta subunit KO mice + THP 10 mg/kg + finasteride 50 mg/kg + flumazenil 7 mg/kg			Amplitude of anxiolytic effect reduced (comparisons probably not made with littermates)	
GABA$_A$ gamma2L overexpression transgenic mice	Elevated plus-maze, Light/dark, Mirrored chamber, Y maze, Open-field	C57BL/6J × DBA/2	No effect of mutation	Wick et al. (2000)
GABA$_A$ gamma2L null allele KO mice	Elevated plus-maze	C57BL/6J × 129/Sv/SvJ	Anxiogenic	Homanics et al. (1999)
GABA$_A$ gamma2L null allele KO mice + ethanol 1.5 g/kg			No difference between genotypes	
GABA$_A$ gamma2 KO mice (heterozygote)	Free exploration, Light/dark, Elevated plus-maze	129/SvJ × C57BL/6J	Anxiogenic in mutants	Crestani et al. (1999)

Table 3 (*continued*)

Model	Test	Animal strain	Effects	Reference
GABA$_A$ gamma2 KO mice (heterozygote) + diazepam 0.3 mg/kg	Free exploration	129/SvJ × C57BL/6J	Anxiogenic in mutants, reversed by diazepam. Diazepam ineffective in WT	
	Light/dark		Anxiogenic in mutants, reversed by diazepam. Diazepam ineffective in WT	
	Elevated plus-maze		Anxiogenic in mutants, reversed by diazepam. Diazepam ineffective in WT	
GABA$_A$ gamma2 KO mice (heterozygote)	Contextual fear conditioning	129/SvJ × C57BL/6J	No effect	Chandra et al. (2005)
	Delay fear conditioning		No effect	
	Trace fear conditioning		Freezing increased in mutants	
	Fear conditioning to an ambiguous stimulus		Freezing increased in mutants (interpreted as a cognitive bias for anxiogenic stimuli)	
GABA$_A$ gamma2 knock-down mice	Elevated plus-maze Open-field	C57BL/6J	Anxiogenic Anxiogenic (less distance traveled)	Mombereau et al. (2005)
GABA$_{B1}$ subunit KO mice GABA$_{B2}$ subunit KO mice	Light/dark Light/dark	BALB/c	Anxiogenic	Mombereau et al. (2004b)
GABA$_{B1}$ KO mice + chlordiazepoxide (10 mg/kg, p.o.) GABA$_{B1}$ KO mice + diazepam (7.5 mg/kg, p.o.)	Light/dark	BALB/c	Anxiolytic effect of the benzodiazepine was lost	
GABA$_{B1}$ subunit KO mice	Light/dark Staircase	BALB/c	Anxiogenic	Mombereau et al. (2004a)

Table 4. Effect of targeted mutation of endocannabinoid- neuropeptide-related genes on rodents in anxiety tests

Model	Test	Animal strain	Effects	Reference
Corticotropin-releasing factor (CRF) and Urocortin				
CRF overproduction transgenic mice	Elevated plus-maze	CRH-Tg$^+$	Animals showed a marked reduction in open arm activity compared with control animals	Stenzel-Poore et al. (1996)
	Open-field		Animals showed a marked reduction in locomotor activity compared with control animals	
CRF overproduction transgenic mice	Exploration tests	n/a	Anxiogenic	Koob and Gold (1997)
CRF overproduction transgenic mice	Acoustic startle reflex	Mice	Not different from wild-type animals	Dirks et al. (1999)
CRF inhibition transgenic mice	n/a	n/a	No behavioral differences were observed between mutant and wild-type mice	Miczek (1997)
CRF-binding protein KO mice	Elevated plus-maze	C57BL/6J × SJL and CD1 mice	Weak anxiolytic effects	Burrows et al. (1998)
CRF-binding protein KO mice	Elevated plus-maze Defensive-withdrawal	C57BL/6J-based mice (2–7 months)	Anxiogenic	Karolyi et al. (1999)
CRF-binding protein KO mice	Elevated plus-maze Open-field	n/a	Anxiogenic	Ramesh et al. (1998)
CRF1 KO mice	Light/dark test	129/Ola or CD1 mice	Anxiolytic	Timpl et al. (1998)
CRF1 KO mice + ethanol withdrawal				
CRF1 KO mice	Elevated plus-maze Light/dark test	C57BL/6J mice	Anxiolytic	Smith et al. (1998)
CRF1 KO mice	Elevated plus-maze Light/dark test	n/a	Anxiolytic	Contarino et al. (1998)
CRF1 KO mice	Exploratory behavior	n/a	Anxiolytic	Kresse et al. (1998)
CRF1 KO mice + ethanol withdrawal			Anxiogenesis-like activity of ethanol withdrawal was lost in KO mice	
CRF1 KO mice	Elevated plus-maze Light/dark test	C57BL/6J × 129 genetic background	Animals showed reduced anxiety-related responses	Contarino et al. (1999)
CRF1 KO mice	Elevated plus-maze	C57BL/6 background mice (about 50 day-old)	KO mice showed reduced anxiety-like behaviors compared to WT animals	Gammie and Stevenson (2006)
CRF1 conditional KO mice restricted to forebrain	Elevated plus-maze Light/dark test	129/Sv × C57BL/6J	Anxiolytic	Muller et al. (2003)
CRF KO mice	Multicompartment chamber Multicompartment chamber+restraint stress Elevated plus-maze Elevated plus-maze+restraint stress Startle reflex after air puff Conditioned fear stress	129SVJ/C57BL6-based mice	Not different from wild-type animals	Weninger et al. (1999)

Table 4 (*continued*)

Model	Test	Animal strain	Effects	Reference
CRF KO mice	Multicompartment chamber, Elevated plus-maze	n/a	Not different from wild-type animals	Dunn and Swiergiel (1999)
CRF$_2$ receptor KO mice	Elevated plus-maze, Light/dark emergence task, Open-field	Male and female 129SVJ/C57BL6J-based mice	Mutant males (not females) mice showed increased anxiety-like behavior	Kishimoto et al. (2000)
CRF$_2$ receptor KO mice + α-hel CRF9–41 (1 μg)	Elevated plus-maze	129SVJ/C57BL6J-based mice	No blockade of anxiety-like behavior	
CRF$_2$ receptor KO mice	Elevated plus-maze, Open-field	129SVJ/C57BL6J-based mice	No effect; Weak increase in anxiety-related behavior (i.e., time in the center)	Coste et al. (2000)
CRF$_2$ receptor KO mice	Elevated plus-maze, Light/dark test, Open-field	Male and female 129SVJ/C57BL6J-based mice	Anxiogenic; No effect; Anxiogenic	Bale et al. (2000)
Urocortin KO mice	Acoustic startle reflex; Open-field, Elevated plus-maze, Light/dark test	Male and female 129S7/C57BL/6 (10–14-week-old)	Startle response was impaired: lower to loud sound and more sensitive to low sound levels; No effect	Wang et al. (2002)
Nociceptin/orphanin FQ Nociceptin-deficient KO mice	Acoustic startle	Male and female 129/Ola × C57BL/6J mice; Male and female 129/Ola × C57BL/6J mice	No effect (animals were housed individually); (1) Mutant mice displayed increased anxiety-like behaviors; (2) they were housed in groups and females were submitted to restraint stress	Ouagazzal et al. (2003)
	Light/dark test	Male and female 129/Ola × C57BL/6J mice; 129/Ola × C57BL/6J mice; Female 129/Ola × C57BL/6 mice	No effect (animals were housed individually); (1) Mutant mice displayed increased anxiety-like behaviors; (2) they were housed in groups; No effect (animals were housed in groups and subjected to restraint stress)	
Vasopressin V$_{1a}$ reexpression in V$_{1a}$ KO mice	Elevated plus-maze, Open-field, Light/dark test	C57BL/6J-129/SvJ background mice (2–5-month-old)	Animals treated with LacZ virus were not different from V$_{1a}$ KO mice	Bielsky et al. (2005)
V$_{1a}$ overexpression transgenic mice	Light/dark test	C57BL/6J-129/SvJ background mice (2–5-month-old)	Mice treated with NSE-V$_{1a}$ viral vector showed increased anxiety-related behaviors	
V$_{1a}$ KO mice	Open-field, Light/dark test	Female C57BL/6J-129 SvJ background mice (2–5-month-old)	V$_{1a}$ KO mice performed normally	

Mice/Model	Test	Background	Result	Reference
V$_{1b}$ KO mice	Light/dark test; Elevated plus-maze	C57BL/6J-129/SvJ background mice (3–7-month-old)	No phenotypic difference between WT and KO mice	Egashira et al. (2005)
Neurokinin (NK)				
NK$_1$ receptor disruption transgenic mice	Elevated plus-maze	J129/C57 hybrid mouse pups (20–30 g)	Anxiety-related behavior was decreased in −/− animals	Rupniak et al. (2001)
NK$_1$ receptor disruption transgenic mice	Elevated plus-maze; Novelty-suppressed feeding; Maternal separation-induced vocalizations	129/SvEv background mice (12–20-week-old) 129/SvEv background mice (8-day-old)	Anxiety-related behavior was decreased in −/− animals	Santarelli et al. (2001)
Neuropeptide Y (NPY)				
NPY overexpression transgenic rats	Elevated plus-maze; Elevated plus-maze	Sprague–Dawley background rats (5-month-old; 325–375 g)	No effect; Anxiolytic (animals were subjected to restraint stress prior to the test); Anxiolytic	Thorsell et al. (2000)
NPY overexpression transgenic rats	Vogel conflict test; Elevated plus-maze	Sprague–Dawley background rats (1-year-old)	Anxiolytic (animals were subjected to restraint stress prior to the test); No effect; Transgenic rats appeared less anxious than their WT counterparts	Carvajal et al. (2004)
NPY KO mice	Elevated plus-maze; Open-field; Acoustic startle reflex	129/sv-C57BL6 background mice	KO mice displayed increased anxiety-like behavior	Bannon et al. (2000)
Y$_1$ KO mice	Open-field; Elevated plus-maze; Light/dark test	C57BL/6-129svJ background mice	Y$_1$ −/− mice showed reduced anxiety-like behaviors when tested during the light phase or after restraint stress; Y$_1$ −/− mice showed reduced anxiety-like behaviors when tested after restraint stress; Y$_1$ −/− mice showed increased anxiety-like behaviors when tested during the light phase	Karl et al. (2006)
Y$_2$ KO mice	Elevated plus-maze; Open-field; Light/dark test	C57BL/6-129svJ background mice	Y$_2$ −/− mice showed reduced anxiety-like behaviors	Tschenett et al. (2003)
Y$_2$ KO mice	Elevated plus-maze; Open-field	C57BL/6-129svJ background mice (28–30 g)	Y$_2$ −/− mice showed reduced anxiety-like behaviors	Redrobe et al. (2003)
Y$_2$ KO mice	Elevated plus-maze; Open-field	C57BL/6-129svJ background mice (24-month-old)	Y$_2$ −/− mice showed decreased anxiety-like behaviors	Carvajal et al. (2006)
Cannabinoid (CB)				
CB$_1$ KO mice	Mouse defense test battery	C57BL/6 × 129/Ola background mice (10-week-old)	KO mice displayed reduced defensive aggression responses	Griebel et al. (2005)
CB$_1$ KO mice	Light/dark test	CD1 background mice	KO mice displayed increased anxiety-like behavior	Martin et al. (2002)

Table 4 (continued)

Model	Test	Animal strain	Effects	Reference
CB$_1$ KO mice	Conditioned fear	C57BL/6NCrl background mice (6–14-week-old)	KO mice were impaired in within-session extinction and adaptation, but not in acquisition of conditioned and sensitized fear	Kamprath et al. (2006)
	Conditioned fear		CB1 deficiency impaired both within-session and long-term adaptation of sensitized fear	
CB$_1$ KO mice	Open-field Light/dark test	CD1 background mice (4-month-old, 28–30 g)	Mice exhibited a mild anxiety-like behavior	Maccarrone et al. (2002)
Melanin-concentrating hormone (MCH)				
MCH1 KO mice	Elevated plus-maze Stress-induced hyperthermia	129/SvJ × C57BL/6J background mice (25–35 g)	No phenotypic differences KO mice showed attenuated stress response compared to WT animals	Smith et al. (2006a)
MCH1 KO mice	Elevated plus-maze Open-field Stress-induced hyperthermia	129SvJ × C57BL/6J background mice (3–10-month-old)	KO mice showed attenuated anxiety-like behaviors compared to WT animals KO mice are protected against stress-induced hyperthermia	Roy et al. (2006)
	Social interaction		KO mice showed attenuated anxiety-like behaviors compared to WT animals	
Cholecystokinin (CCK)				
CCK1 receptor gene transgenic rats	Open-field	OLETF and LETO rats (4 weeks)	Rats lacking CCK1 receptors displayed reduced locomotor and rearing activities	Kobayashi et al. (1996)
CCK1 mutant rats (OLETF)	Elevated plus-maze Light/dark test	OLETF and LETO rats (7–9-week-old)	OLETF rats were more anxious than LETO rats	Yamamoto et al. (2000)
CCK1 mutant rats (OLETF)	Elevated plus-maze	OLETF and LETO rats (4-week-old)	Motor activity was reduced	Li et al. (2002)
CCK1 KO mice	Elevated plus-maze	C57BL/6J background mice (7-month-old)	No difference in anxiety between WT and KO mice	Miyasaka et al. (2002)
CCK2 KO mice CCK1/2 KO mice			Anxious phenotype No difference in anxiety between WT and KO mice	
CCK2 KO mice	Elevated plus-maze	Female 129sv/C57BL6 background mice Male 129sv/C57BL6 background mice	Homozygotes showed increased anxiety No difference in anxiety between genotypes	Vasar et al. (2000)
CCK2 KO mice	Elevated plus-maze Open-field Motility conditioned suppression test	Male and female 129sv/C57BL/6 background mice	No difference in anxiety between genotypes	Dauge et al. (2001)
CCK2 KO mice	Elevated plus-maze Light/dark test	Male 129sv/C57BL6 background mice	Homozygotes showed decreased anxiety	Horinouchi et al. (2004)
CCK2 KO mice	Light/dark test	Female 129sv/C57BL6 background mice	Homozygotes showed decreased anxiety	Raud et al. (2005)
	Fear conditioned test		No difference in phenotype	

Model/treatment	Test	Animal	Findings	Reference
CCK2 KO mice + DMCM (0.25–1 mg/kg)	Light/dark test		DMCM produced anxiogenic-like effects in −/− but not in +/+ mice	
CCK2 KO mice + diazepam (0.5–2 mg/kg)			No influence of mutation on the effects of diazepam	
CCK2 KO mice	Elevated plus-maze	Female 129sv/C57BL6 background mice	Homozygotes showed decreased anxiety	Areda et al. (2006)
	Elevated plus-maze		(1) Mice were exposed to a cat odor prior to testing; (2) no phenotypic differences	
	Cat odor		No phenotypic differences	
CCK2 overexpression (in forebrain) transgenic mice	Open-field / Social interaction test / Conditioned fear	IF-CCKR-2 mice (2-4-month-old)	Transgenic mice showed increased anxiety-related behaviors / (1) Transgenic mice showed increased anxiety-related behaviors; (2) electric shocks of 0.4 mA were applied	Chen et al. (2006a)
CCK2 overexpression (in forebrain) transgenic mice + doxycycline	Open-field		The drug, which inhibits the transgene, abolished the anxious phenotype	
CCK2 overexpression (in forebrain) transgenic mice	Social interaction test			
CCK2 overexpression (in forebrain) transgenic mice + diazepam (0.5 mg/kg)	Open-field / Conditioned fear		The drug abolished the anxious phenotype / (1) The drug abolished the anxious phenotype; (2) electric shocks of 0.4 mA were applied	

anxiety-like response is triggered off by different kind of stressors such as suddenness (acoustic startle), forced confrontation with novel space (elevated plus-maze, open-field, light/dark choice test, novelty-induced suppression of feeding), or predator-related stimulus (mouse defense test battery, cat odor), association with a fearful stimulus after conditioning (Vogel test, fear conditioning). The observed response can be a reflex (startle), an avoidance response (cat odor), a freezing response (in the fear conditioning test), a preference for the protected regions of the device (the peripheral part of the open-field, the closed arms of the elevated plus-maze, the dark compartment of the light/dark test), or a decrease of consummatory behavior in the situation associated with stressful events (decrease of drinking when associated with an electric shock in the Vogel test, decrease of feeding in novel space in the novelty-induced suppression of feeding test). These responses are adaptative ones, as they enable the subject to cope with the situation when faced to a danger or a stressful situation. However, in humans suffering from some forms of pathological anxiety such as generalized anxiety, panic, phobia, obsessive-compulsive disorder, or post-traumatic stress disorder, the response toward stimulus from the external world can sometimes be maladapted: these people may display an anxious response in non-stressful situation (excessive trait anxiety in generalized anxiety disorder or excessive autonomous system activation of panic patients in non-stressful environments) or, when faced with some specific threat, they may display an excessive response (e.g., in post-traumatic stress disorder when the patients are faced with stimulus related to the trauma, in obsessive-compulsive disorders when the persons are faced with the stimulus inducing the compulsions, in phobic patients when faced the specific stimulus inducing the phobic response). In rodents, specific experimental situations have been described that may enable to model some of these forms of anxiety: for example, trait anxiety can be assessed using a free exploration situation (Griebel et al., 1993; Belzung and Berton, 1997; Belzung and Griebel, 2001), while the mouse defense test battery has been

suggested to model some aspects of panic disorder (Griebel et al., 1995).

A first aspect that can be discussed is the apparent target-related variation in the device used. For example, 26% of the studies assessing the effects of mutations targeting the serotoninergic system used the open-field, while only 5% of the studies assessing GABAergic-related mutations used this situation. Such variation may have occurred by chance, or be related to availability of a given device in the laboratories doing such research. However, it is also possible that this means that some experimental situations are more adapted to reveal anxiolytic or anxiogenic effects of a given neurotransmitter system than others. For example, it can be mentioned that the open-field is more adapted to assess effects of genetic studies targeting the serotoninergic system. In this case, the different tests may not assess equivalent features of anxiety behavior, but measure some particular aspects of this behavior, related to a particular system.

Further, it is obvious that most experiments described in our tables (71%) used forced exploration (38% used elevated plus-maze, 18% used open-field, and 15% used light/dark test) to induce an anxiety-like state and to measure the resulting behavioral phenotype. Forced exploration is known to be stressful in these species (Misslin and Cigrang, 1986) so that these studies investigated an anxious phenotype related to a stressful situation, exacerbating or reducing a normal response. Thus, these studies did not investigate genes involved in the pathological forms of anxiety. Indeed, from our tables, it seems that very few studies used devices related to anxiety disorders: only three used free exploration (less then 1%) and only one used the mouse defense test battery. This is an important point to highlight here. Indeed, one may argue that targeted genetic alteration should induce a pathological phenotype, rather then a normal one. As suggested by Canguilhelm (1943), the factors underlying normal processes may not be the same as the ones involved in pathological processes. Therefore, in order to assess the genetic factors involved in the anxiety disorders, it would be necessary to study the effects of the genetic alteration using situations modeling normal as well as pathological aspects of anxiety.

III. Which genetic method has been used?

Most studies (85%) involved genetic invalidation of a given gene. This means that the function of a given gene was studied in its absence. This method has been much criticized elsewhere (see e.g., Gerlai, 1996; Wolfer et al., 2002; Crusio, 2004). For example, it is possible that the behavioral alterations that were observed are related to compensation, rather than to the absence of the gene per se. Another point that should be mentioned here is that this strategy has poor significance for clinical research, as very few human behavioral alterations or psychiatric disorders are caused by the absence of a gene. In general, such disease or abnormalities are rather related to modifications of the functioning of a given gene, for example, when a polymorphism has been observed. Such polymorphism can then induce reduction of the expression of a particular gene product. Thus, one may suggest that the development of targeted insertion of a transgene (knock-in strategies) may enable to mimic some features of human polymorphism and would thus have higher isomorphic value and relevance for the study on genetic involvement in a particular anxiety disorder.

Another point to be mentioned here is that most (85%) of the animal models that have been proposed are based on targeting of receptors' genes (serotonin receptors, CRF receptors, GABA$_B$ receptors, cannabinoid receptors) or of subunits (e.g., GABA$_A$ receptors subunits) of receptors of specific neurotransmitters. The remaining studies concerned some transporters (e.g., the serotonin transporter), neuropeptides (e.g., nociceptine), or binding proteins of some neuropeptides (e.g., the CRF binding protein). Very few studies concerned genes involved in the synthesis of a given neurotransmitter. Parallels to the fact that most pharmacological agents used to alter anxiety behavior target specific receptors; which enable to act on specific brain areas (when a given receptor is located in particular brain regions) or on specific intracellular signaling cascades.

IV. Was there any particular choice of construction (knock-in, knock-out, and over-expressed models) made for each neurotransmission system?

It can be observed that particular choices of construction were made, depending on the neurotransmitter system that was targeted. Indeed, for the serotoninergic system, the main strategy used was the genetic invalidation: from Table 1, one can observe that 10 different models were used, 8 of which were knock-outs (of the 5HT$_{1A}$, the 5HT$_{1B}$, the 5-HT$_{2A}$, the 5HT$_{2C}$, the 5HT$_3$, the 5HT$_4$, and the 5HT$_{5A}$ receptors and of the serotonin transporter), the two remaining ones using the over-expression construction (over-expression of the 5HT$_{1A}$ and of the 5HT$_{1B}$ receptors). On the contrary, in research on the GABA$_A$ receptors, many studies were made using the knock-in strategy. Among the 14 different models, 5 used the knock-in strategy (of various alpha subunits), 7 used the knock-out construction (for various alpha, beta, gamma, and delta subunit). The over-expression and the knock-down strategy were also used in the field of research on involvement of GABA$_A$ receptors in anxiety. In the field of glutamate research, all constructions were based on genetic invalidation. Finally, when targeting neuropeptidergic systems, the knock-out strategy was used in 15 cases, and over-expression in 4 cases. So, one can see that the knock-in and the knock-down strategies were exclusively used in the field of GABA research, while the other strategies (knock-out and over-expression constructions) are found throughout all neurotransmitter system research. This particularity is related to spectacular findings concerning the role of some point mutations in the properties of some specific alpha subunit of the GABA$_A$ pentamer regarding their ability to bind and to react to benzodiazepines. Such precise properties regarding the function of precise amino acids in the binding capacities of the receptors of other neurotransmitter systems have not been described, which may explain the lack of such studies concerning serotonin, GABA, or neuropeptides.

V. Which phenotypes are observed?

It can be observed that 32% of the studies showed increased anxiety behavior while 25% showed the contrary. This indicates that the procedure used enables to observe both phenotypes, in an equiprobable manner. This applies more or less to each device. For example, in the elevated plus-maze or in the elevated zero-maze, an anxiogenic effect was seen in 35% of the studies, an anxiolytic effect in 35% of the studies while 30% of them did not detect any change. Further, in the light/dark test, 36% of the studies obtained anxiogenesis, 27% anxiolysis, and 36% found no effect; in the novelty-induced suppression of feeding half of the studies observed increased anxiety and the other half showed decreased anxiety. There are some exceptions: in the open-field, an anxiogenesis is observed more frequently (48%) than an anxiolysis (25%) while in the stress-induced hypethermia test, the contrary was observed: anxiolysis in 55% of the studies and anxiogenesis in only 11% of them. However, this does not necessarily mean that the open-field is more pertinent to detect anxiogenesis or that the stress-induced hyperthermia test would be more appropriate to detect anxiolysis; indeed, the number of studies is too small to bring to satisfactory conclusion. Further, a more detailed analysis would be necessary in order to check if, in each particular test, the experimental conditions used (lighting of the device, noise, strains used, etc.) enabled the assessment of anxiolytic as well as anxiogenic effects. Indeed, in some particular cases, this was not fulfilled as ceiling effects were present.

VI. Can these results be explained by the species or the strain used?

Most studies used mice (only 2.9% used rats). Among the mouse strains, very few different genetic backgrounds were used in the different studies. Indeed, 5.1% used outbred strains, 15.4% used C57BL/6 mice, 13.8% used 129 strains, 45.6% used an intercross between C57BL/6 and 129 mice while the remaining ones used an inter-cross between C57BL/6 or 129 and another strain. So, a large majority of the studies were undertaken in C57BL/6 or 129 genetic backgrounds. It is to be observed that these strains do not exhibit elevated anxiety in inter-strain comparisons, suggesting that they would be more adapted to assess anxiogenic effects. However, this has probably not influenced very much the results of the various studies as anxiogenic phenotypes have been observed as well as anxiolytic ones. One may also observe that most targeted invalidation or over-expression studies were done in only one genetic background. In studies phenotyping other aspects of behavior, such as aggression or learning and memory, it has been shown that some behavioral effects of the mutations were observed in one strain, and not in another strain. It would be useful to undertake also this type of study in research on genetic factors involved in anxiety behavior, as a large inter-strain variation has been documented. This could be very easily done; it may just need several backcrosses.

Another point that should be mentioned is that most studies (65.7%) used an F5-F8 generation intercross between 129 mice and mice from another strain (e.g., C57BL/6). One has to remember that in such a population, recombinant genotypes derived from the two parental mouse strains may be expressed so that that knock-out mice can be genetically different from their control littermates not only at the locus of interest but also at other loci (Gerlai, 1996). Further, in many case, the targeted mutation has been undertaken in embryonic stem (ES) cells from mice belonging to the 129 strain, so that the chromosome with the targeted locus will carry alleles of genes of 129-type. As the probability of genetic recombination is generally inversely related to the distance between the loci of the genes, the 129-type alleles of the genes whose loci are close to the locus of the mutated gene will remain associated with the mutated allele of the gene of interest (Gerlai, 1996). Consequently, the behavioral differences observed between mutants and their wild-type littermates of the hybrid genetic origin might be due to the targeted mutation as well as to the 129 background genes linked to the targeted locus, inducing false-positive results. This point should be addressed in further studies.

VII. Did this strategy enable to precise the brain area involved in these processes?

Some genes may be pleiotropic, thus exerting multiple effects. This can, for example, be related to the fact that a gene can be expressed in different tissues of the body (e.g., heart, liver, brain) or in different brain areas. Many studies have shown that anxiety-behavior is mostly related to specific brain structures, particularly to limbic ones (amygdala, hippocampus, cortex). These regions are all located in the anterior forebrain. Therefore, when assessing the effect of targeted mutations on anxiety behavior, it would be useful to restrict the targeted mutation to the limbic areas. This can be done using the Cre/LoxP system for generating tissue-specific mutants in which Cre recombinase is expressed under the control of the forebrain specific CaMKII promoter, thus generating mice with forebrain-specific disruption of the gene of interest and Cre-negative littermate controls. This strategy has been used in anxiety research as several mutants of this type have been generated, including knock-out mice for the 5-HT$_{2A}$ receptors, knock-out mice of the GABA$_A$ alpha1 subunit, and knock-out of the CRF$_1$ receptor. Results confirmed the impact of regions of the anterior forebrain in the effects of these genes and thus the involvement of these brain regions in anxiety-behavior.

VIII. Is the contribution of the genetic factor limited to the developmental period?

Some studies used agents inhibiting expression of the transgene at a given time point (e.g., doxycyline), thus enabling to distinguish the involvement of a gene on anxiety behavior during the developmental period from its impact at a precise time point once adults. This has been done in mice with deletion of the 5-HT$_{1A}$ receptor, showing the crucial importance of this gene during the developmental period. It can be that different patterns of the development of limbic areas may modify in a durable way anxiety-related behaviors. Some genetic factors may thus be involved in the developmental pattern of limbic areas, modifying in an enduring way anxiety behavior and thus affecting trait anxiety. Other genes may be involved in the secretion or in the release of proteins expressed at a particular time point, for example, during stressful situations, thus affecting state anxiety. One may suggest that new pharmacological tools should act rather on proteins related to the second process because its injection in adults cannot modify developmental features.

IX. Do the effects of the mutation correlate with the results of pharmacological challenge?

Do the knock-out mice for a given gene display the same behavior as wild-type mice that have been treated with an antagonist or an inverse agonist of the receptor? Does the over-expression of a gene elicit the same phenotype as the injection of an agonist of the corresponding protein? A correlation is sometimes observed. For example, knock-out of the γ2 subunit of the GABA$_A$ receptor elicits a 30% decrease of benzodiazepine receptors and an anxiogenic phenotype in the heterozygotous mice, an effect that is identical to the ones elicited by benzodiazepine receptor inverse agonists. Another example can be found with the CRF$_1$ receptor, as the CRF$_1$ receptor knock-out mice display anxiolysis, an effect which is identical to the one induced by CRF$_1$ receptor antagonists. However, counter-examples can also be found. For example, targeted invalidation of the 5-HT$_{1A}$ receptor induces anxiogenesis while over-expression of the same receptor elicits anxiolysis; conversely, in most pharmacological experiments, 5-HT$_{1A}$ receptor agonists such as buspirone or flesinoxan induce anxiolysis. In most cases, no specific ligands exist for the different target, so that it is not possible to check this point in an exhaustive way. The reasons for discrepancies between genetic and pharmacological data can be related either to the fact that a given target may be important in development (see previous paragraph) or to the fact that some pharmacological agents lack specificity, thus eliciting other effects that the ones related to the target.

X. Does the mutation modify the response to anxiolytic or anxiogenic agents?

In some studies, the effects of pharmacological agents were investigated. Sometimes, the pharmacological agent was a ligand of the protein whose expression was reduced or deleted (e.g., 5-HT$_{1A}$ receptors ligands were studied in 5-HT$_{1A}$ receptor knock-out mice) and sometimes this was not the case (e.g., when benzodiazepines were studied in 5-HT$_{1A}$ receptor knock-out mice). This strategy was not only used in knock-out mice but also in knock-in mice of the GABAergic system (e.g., knock-in of the alpha1, alpha 2, or alpha3 subunits of the GABA$_A$ receptor). In this case, it enabled to assess the effects of single point mutations on the ability of a given compound to interact with the target protein. It is important here to distinguish the effects of a targeted mutation on anxiety from the effects of a given mutation on the effects of anxiolytic compounds. These two processes are not identical. Indeed, our tables show that in some case, a null mutation can alter the response of mice to anxiogenic situations (this is, e.g., the case with the 5-HT$_{1A}$ null mutation) as well as their response to a pharmacological challenge, while in other case, the mutation has no action on anxiety behavior, but modifies the response of ligands of the receptor whose expression has been modified by the mutation.

XI. What do these findings tell us about the link between neurotransmitter systems and anxiety? Do these studies provide useful information about the role played by the various GABAergic, serotoninergic, glutamatergic, and neuropeptidergic targets in the anxiety behavior?

Table 1 summarizes data on serotonin neurotransmission. It is clear that alteration in genes coding for proteins that control serotonin reuptake or modulating 5-HT receptor-mediated signal transduction is involved in anxiety. The role of the serotonin system in establishing normal anxiety levels seems crucial during development, as ablation of the 5HT$_{1A}$ gene during the developmental period induces permanent modifications of the anxiety level in the animals once adults, even if the gene has been "turned on" when the mice reached adult age. This indicates a role of this protein in developing the brain circuitry that is essential to display a normal reaction to threat. This is coherent with the observation that serotonin plays a role in development before it acts as a neurotransmitter. However, the role of serotonin is not limited to the developmental period. One can also observe that most serotonin receptors control the anxiety level. Indeed, ablation of most serotonin receptors (5HT$_{2A}$, 5HT$_{2C}$, 5HT$_3$, 5HT$_4$, 5HT$_{5A}$) induces anxiolysis, with the exception of the 5HT$_{1A}$ receptor whose ablation is anxiogenic. The involvement of the 5HT$_{2A}$ receptor seems related to a cortical site, as ablation of this receptor in this precise region is sufficient to induce the phenotype. This receptor may thus control the cortical-related process associated with the anxiety response. Further, the fact that ablation of a given receptor induces either anxiolysis or anxiogenesis is not related to the intracellular events that are associated with the receptor: indeed, deletion of the 5HT$_{1A}$ receptor, which is negatively coupled to adenylate cyclase, induces anxiogenesis, while ablation of the 5HT$_4$ receptor that is positively coupled to adenylate cyclase and of the 5HT$_{5A}$ receptor that is negatively coupled to adenytate cyclase both elicit anxiolysis. Unfortunately, few of these studies investigated the level of serotonin in the mutant mice. One can mention the study of Parsons et al. (2001) that showed, using microdialysis, that 5HT$_{1A}$ knock-out mice displayed an increased level of serotonin in the hippocampus and the cortex. This suggests that high serotonin level might be associated with elevated anxiety. However, a systematic study of the serotonin level of the different mutant would enable to propose more strong conclusions about the relationship between serotonin and anxiety.

Glutamate is the most widespread excitatory neurotransmitter in brain. It binds to two classes of receptors: the ionotropic and the metabotropic one. Among the ionotropic receptors, three subtypes have been described: the AMPA, the NMDA, and the kainate receptors. Different functional subunits assemble together in heteromultimeric complexes to form these receptors: one can mention the NR1, NR2A-NR2D, and NR3 for the NMDA receptors. On the other side, the metabotropic glutamate receptors can be subdivided in three groups: group I (mGluR1, mGluR5), group II (mGluR2, mGluR3), and group III (mGluR4, mGluR6, mGluR7, and mGluR8). Table 2 presents the phenotype of different glutamate receptor knock-out mice. The genetic invalidation studies that have been undertaken to alter the glutamatergic neurotransmission targeted the NR2A subunit, the mGluR5, the mGluR6, the mGluR7, and the mGluR8 receptors. These mutations, therefore, altered either the NMDA receptors, or the group I or III metabotropic receptors. All mutations induced anxiolysis, except the mGluR8 invalidation that rather induced anxiogenesis. Again, no relationship can be made with intracellular cascades as the mGluR6, the mGluR7, and the mGluR8 receptors are all negatively coupled with adenylate cyclase. Few data are available on the level of glutamate in these mutants, so that it is not really possible to associate the anxiolytic profile of these mutants with glutamatergic activity.

The data on targeted genetic manipulation on GABAergic targets confirms the involvement of this neurotransmitter in anxiety (Table 3). This is not surprising as GABA is the most abundant inhibitory neurotransmitter in the brain. It binds to two classes of receptors: the $GABA_A$ receptor, which is composed of five subunits, and the $GABA_B$ receptor, that includes two subcategories, the $GABA_{B1}$ and the $GABA_{B2}$ receptors. The subunit composition of $GABA_A$ receptors determines the receptor pharmacology and the density of benzodiazepine receptors. When the number of these benzodiazepine sites is decreased, an anxious phenotype appears. For example, the gamma2 null mutant heterozygotous mice, which display a reduction of approximately 30% of the number of benzodiazepine receptors, display increased anxiety. Generally, the number of benzodiazepine receptors is not modified in the various alpha subunit knock-in mice, so that no anxious phenotype appears in these mice. However, they display modifications in their response to anxiolytic agents. As to the $GABA_B$ receptor, genetic invalidation of the $GABA_{B1}$ as well as of the $GABA_{B2}$ receptor induce anxiogenic effects.

Finally, the effects of mutations involving neuropeptidergic or endocannabinoid targets confirm the implication of these molecules in anxiety behavior (Table 4). Logically, stress peptides such as CRF are involved in this behavior: invalidation of the CRF_2 receptor is anxiogenic while inhibition of the CRF_1 receptor is anxiolytic; this last effect being mediated by the forebrain. Surprisingly, inhibition as well as over-expression of CRF does not elicit main effects on anxiety. Another stress-related peptide, vasopressine, is also involved in anxiety as over-expression of the V_{1B} receptor is anxiogenic. However, a symmetrical effect is not found when invalidating this receptor: no phenotype is seen in the V_{1B} receptor knockouts. Genetic invalidation studies also focuses on the involvement of cannabinoid targets and showed that invalidation of the CB_1 receptors elicits an anxiogenic effect.

XII. Conclusion and perspectives

In summary, these studies precise the involvement of neurotransmitter genes expressed in normal anxiety. These genes can act either by modifying brain development or by interfering with neurotransmission at a particular moment.

Did this research on targeted genes involved in anxiety really enable to improve treatments of anxiety disorders? To our knowledge, this is unfortunately not really the case. For example, much research focused on the involvement of genes coding for subunits of $GABA_A$ receptors, but no pharmacological treatments binding on specific subunits are available. The same is true for serotoninergic targets. The probability that research on targeted mutations will enable the discovery of new pharmacological tools in the future is also very low because most genes involved in anxiety behavior are in fact non-neurotransmitter genes such as those involved in brain development (e.g., BDNF): such a developmental pattern elicited by particular genes cannot be counteracted by pharmacological treatments applied to the subject once adult. Further, many epigenetic factors have been involved in anxiety, including maternal care (Calatayud and Belzung, 2001; Meaney, 2001 Calatayud et al., 2004). These factors modify the expression of particular genes such as glucocorticoid receptors via different mechanisms including DNA methylation (Meaney and Szyf, 2005; Weaver et al., 2005, 2006). Therefore, some anxiety-related phenotypes may be related to DNA methylation defects inducing decreased transcription of a given gene, rather than to the absence of a gene. Such mechanisms are completely ignored in targeted gene research and should be considered when aiming at discovering new treatments of anxiety.

References

Areda, T., Raud, S., Philips, M.A., Innos, J., Matsui, T., Koks, S., Vasar, E., Karis, A. and Asser, T. (2006) Cat odour exposure decreases exploratory activity and alters neuropeptide gene expression in CCK(2) receptor deficient mice, but not in their wild-type littermates. Behav. Brain Res., 169: 212–219.

Bailey, S.J. and Toth, M. (2004) Variability in the benzodiazepine response of serotonin 5-HT1A receptor null mice displaying anxiety-like phenotype: evidence for genetic modifiers in the 5-HT-mediated regulation of GABA(A) receptors. J. Neurosci., 24: 6343–6351.

Bale, T.L., Contarino, A., Smith, G.W., Chan, R., Gold, L.H., Sawchenko, P.E., Koob, G.F., Vale, W.W. and Lee, K.F. (2000) Mice deficient for corticotropin-releasing hormone receptor-2 display anxiety-like behaviour and are hypersensitive to stress. Nat. Genet., 24: 410–414.

Bannon, A.W., Seda, J., Carmouche, M., Francis, J.M., Norman, M.H., Karbon, B. and McCaleb, M.L. (2000) Behavioral characterization of neuropeptide Y knockout mice. Brain Res., 868: 79–87.

Belzung, C. and Berton, F. (1997) Further pharmacological validation of the Balb/c neophobia in the free exploratory paradigm as an animal model of trait anxiety. Behav. Pharmacol., 8: 541–548.

Belzung, C. and Griebel, G. (2001) Measuring normal and pathological anxiety-like behaviour in mice: a review. Behav. Brain Res., 125: 141–149.

Belzung, C. and Philippot, P. (2007) Anxiety from a phylogenetic perspective: is there a qualitative difference between human and animal anxiety? Neural Plasticity, ID 59676.

Bhatnagar, S., Nowak, N., Babich, L. and Bok, L. (2004a) Deletion of the 5-HT3 receptor differentially affects behavior of males and females in the Porsolt forced swim and defensive withdrawal tests. Behav. Brain Res., 153: 527–535.

Bhatnagar, S., Sun, L.M., Raber, J., Maren, S., Julius, D. and Dallman, M.F. (2004b) Changes in anxiety-related behaviors and hypothalamic–pituitary–adrenal activity in mice lacking the 5-HT-3A receptor. Physiol Behav., 81: 545–555.

Bielsky, I.F., Hu, S.B., Ren, X., Terwilliger, E.F. and Young, L.J. (2005) The V1a vasopressin receptor is necessary and sufficient for normal social recognition: a gene replacement study. Neuron, 47: 503–513.

Boyce-Rustay, J.M. and Holmes, A. (2006) Genetic inactivation of the NMDA receptor NR2A subunit has anxiolytic- and antidepressant-like effects in mice. Neuropsychopharmacology, 31: 2405–2414.

Brocke, B., Armbruster, D., Muller, J., Hensch, T., Jacob, C.P., Lesch, K.P., Kirschbaum, C. and Strobel, A. (2006) Serotonin transporter gene variation impacts innate fear processing: Acoustic startle response and emotional startle. Mol. Psychiatry, 11: 1106–1112.

Brodkin, J., Bradbury, M., Busse, C., Warren, N., Bristow, L.J. and Varney, M.A. (2002) Reduced stress-induced hyperthermia in mGluR5 knockout mice. Eur. J. Neurosci., 16: 2241–2244.

Brunner, D., Buhot, M.C., Hen, R. and Hofer, M. (1999) Anxiety, motor activation, and maternal-infant interactions in 5HT1B knockout mice. Behav. Neurosci., 113: 587–601.

Burrows, H.L., Nakajima, M., Lesh, J.S., Goosens, K.A., Samuelson, L.C., Inui, A., Camper, S.A. and Seasholtz, A.F. (1998) Excess corticotropin releasing hormone-binding protein in the hypothalamic–pituitary–adrenal axis in transgenic mice. J. Clin. Invest., 10: 1439–1447.

Calatayud, F. and Belzung, C. (2001) Emotional reactivity in mice, a case of nongenetic heredity? Physiol. Behav., 74: 355–362.

Calatayud, F., Coubard, S. and Belzung, C. (2004) Emotional reactivity in mice may not be inherited but influenced by parents. Physiol. Behav., 80: 465–474.

Callaerts-Vegh, Z., Beckers, T., Ball, S.M., Baeyens, F., Callaerts, P.F., Cryan, J.F., Molnar, E. and D'Hooge, R. (2006) Concomitant deficits in working memory and fear extinction are functionally dissociated from reduced anxiety in metabotropic glutamate receptor 7-deficient mice. J. Neurosci., 26: 6573–6582.

Canguilhelm, G. (1943) Le normal et le pathologique. Paris, PUF. Trad. On the Normal and the Pathological, Dordrecht: Reidal, 1978.

Carvajal, C., Dumont, Y., Herzog, H. and Quirion, R. (2006) Emotional behavior in aged neuropeptide Y (NPY) Y2 knockout mice. J. Mol. Neurosci., 28: 239–245.

Carvajal, C.C., Vercauteren, F., Dumont, Y., Michalkiewicz, M. and Quirion, R. (2004) Aged neuropeptide Y transgenic rats are resistant to acute stress but maintain spatial and non-spatial learning. Behav. Brain Res., 153: 471–480.

Chandra, D., Korpi, E.R., Miralles, C.P., De Blas, A.L. and Homanics, G.E. (2005) GABAA receptor gamma 2 subunit knockdown mice have enhanced anxiety-like behavior but unaltered hypnotic response to benzodiazepines. BMC. Neurosci., 6: 30.

Chen, Q., Nakajima, A., Meacham, C. and Tang, Y.P. (2006a) Elevated cholecystokininergic tone constitutes an important molecular/neuronal mechanism for the expression of anxiety in the mouse. Proc. Natl. Acad. Sci. USA, 103: 3881–3886.

Chen, Z.Y., Jing, D., Bath, K.G., Ieraci, A., Khan, T., Siao, C.J., Herrera, D.G., Toth, M., Yang, C., McEwen, B.S., Hempstead, B.L. and Lee, F.S. (2006b) Genetic variant BDNF (Val66Met) polymorphism alters anxiety-related behavior. Science, 314: 140–143.

Clark, M.S., Sexton, T.J., McClain, M., Root, D., Kohen, R. and Neumaier, J.F. (2002) Overexpression of 5-HT1B receptor in dorsal raphe nucleus using Herpes Simplex Virus gene transfer increases anxiety behavior after inescapable stress. J. Neurosci., 22: 4550–4562.

Collinson, N., Kuenzi, F.M., Jarolimek, W., Maubach, K.A., Cothliff, R., Sur, C., Smith, A., Otu, F.M., Howell, O., Atack, J.R., McKernan, R.M., Seabrook, G.R., Dawson, G.R., Whiting, P.J. and Rosahl, T.W. (2002) Enhanced learning and memory and altered GABAergic synaptic transmission in mice lacking the alpha 5 subunit of the GABAA receptor. J. Neurosci., 22: 5572–5580.

Compan, V., Zhou, M., Grailhe, R., Gazzara, R.A., Martin, R., Gingrich, J., Dumuis, A., Brunner, D., Bockaert, J. and Hen, R. (2004) Attenuated response to stress and novelty and hypersensitivity to seizures in 5-HT4 receptor knock-out mice. J. Neurosci., 24: 412–419.

Contarino, A., Dellu, F., Koob, G.F., Smith, G.W., Lee, K.F., Vale, W. and Gold, L.H. (1998) Anxiety-like and cognitive behavioral phenotypes in mice lacking the corticotropin-releasing factor receptor. Soc. Neurosci. Abstr., 24: 201.

Contarino, A., Dellu, F., Koob, G.F., Smith, G.W., Lee, K.F., Vale, W. and Gold, L.H. (1999) Reduced anxiety-like and cognitive performance in mice lacking the corticotropin-releasing factor receptor 1. Brain Res., 835: 1–9.

Coste, S.C., Kesterson, R.A., Heldwein, K.A., Stevens, S.L., Heard, A.D., Hollis, J.H., Murray, S.E., Hill, J.K., Pantely, G.A., Hohimer, A.R., Hatton, D.C., Phillips, T.J., Finn, D.A., Low, M.J., Rittenberg, M.B., Stenzel, P. and Stenzel-Poore, M.P. (2000) Abnormal adaptations to stress and impaired cardiovascular function in mice lacking corticotropin-releasing hormone receptor-2. Nat. Genet., 24: 403–409.

Crestani, F., Keist, R., Fritschy, J.M., Benke, D., Vogt, K., Prut, L., Bluthmann, H., Mohler, H. and Rudolph, U. (2002) Trace fear conditioning involves hippocampal alpha5 GABA(A) receptors. Proc. Natl. Acad. Sci. USA, 99: 8980–8985.

Crestani, F., Lorez, M., Baer, K., Essrich, C., Benke, D., Laurent, J.P., Belzung, C., Fritschy, J.M., Luscher, B. and Mohler, H. (1999) Decreased GABAA-receptor clustering results in enhanced anxiety and a bias for threat cues. Nat. Neurosci., 2: 833–839.

Crusio, W.E. (2004) Flanking gene and genetic background problems in genetically manipulated mice. Biol. Psychiatry, 56: 381–385.

Cryan, J.F., Kelly, P.H., Neijt, H.C., Sansig, G., Flor, P.J. and van der, P.H. (2003) Antidepressant and anxiolytic-like effects in mice lacking the group III metabotropic glutamate receptor mGluR7. Eur. J. Neurosci., 17: 2409–2417.

Dauge, V., Sebret, A., Beslot, F., Matsui, T. and Roques, B.P. (2001) Behavioral profile of CCK2 receptor-deficient mice. Neuropsychopharmacology, 25: 690–698.

Dirks, A., Pattij, T., Bouwknecht, J.A., Westphal, T.T., Hijzen, T.H., Groenink, L., van der, G.J., Oosting, R.S., Hen, R., Geyer, M.A. and Olivier, B. (2001) 5-HT1B receptor knockout, but not 5-HT1A receptor knockout mice, show reduced startle reactivity and footshock-induced sensitization, as measured with the acoustic startle response. Behav. Brain Res., 118: 169–178.

Dirks, A., Veening, J.G., Dederen, P.J.W.C., Ronken, E., Oosting, R., Bouwknecht, J.A., Hijzen, T.H., Van der Gugten, J. and Olivier, B. (1999) Histological, physiological and behavioral characterization of CRH overexpressing mice. Soc. Neurosci. Abstr., 25: 64.

Dunn, A.J. and Swiergiel, A.H. (1999) Behavioral responses to stress are intact in CRF-deficient mice. Brain Res., 845: 14–20.

Duvoisin, R.M., Zhang, C., Pfankuch, T.F., O'Connor, H., Gayet-Primo, J., Quraishi, S. and Raber, J. (2005) Increased measures of anxiety and weight gain in mice lacking the group III metabotropic glutamate receptor mGluR8. Eur. J. Neurosci., 22: 425–436.

Egashira, N., Tanoue, A., Higashihara, F., Fuchigami, H., Sano, K., Mishima, K., Fukue, Y., Nagai, H., Takano, Y., Tsujimoto, G., Stemmelin, J., Griebel, G., Iwasaki, K., Ikeda, T., Nishimura, R. and Fujiwara, M. (2005) Disruption of the prepulse inhibition of the startle reflex in vasopressin V1b receptor knockout mice: reversal by antipsychotic drugs. Neuropsychopharmacology, 30: 1996–2005.

Gammie, S.C. and Stevenson, S.A. (2006) Intermale aggression in corticotropin-releasing factor receptor 1 deficient mice. Behav. Brain Res., 171: 63–69.

Gerlai, R. (1996) Gene-targeting studies of mammalian behavior: is it the mutation or the background genotype? Trends Neurosci., 19: 177–181.

Gonda, X., Rihmer, Z., Juhasz, G., Zsombok, T. and Bagdy, G. (2007) High anxiety and migraine are associated with the s allele of the 5HTTLPR gene polymorphism. Psychiatry Res., 149: 261–266.

Grailhe, R., Waeber, C., Dulawa, S.C., Hornung, J.P., Zhuang, X., Brunner, D., Geyer, M.A. and Hen, R. (1999) Increased exploratory activity and altered response to LSD in mice lacking the 5-HT(5A) receptor. Neuron, 22: 581–591.

Griebel, G., Belzung, C., Misslin, R. and Vogel, E. (1993) The free-exploratory paradigm: an effective method for measuring neophobic behaviour in mice and testing potential neophobia-reducing drugs. Behav. Pharmacol., 4: 637–644.

Griebel, G., Blanchard, D.C., Jung, A., Lee, J.C., Masuda, C.K. and Blanchard, R.J. (1995) Further evidence that the mouse defense test battery is useful for screening anxiolytic and panicolytic drugs: effects of acute and chronic treatment with alprazolam. Neuropharmacology, 34: 1625–1633.

Griebel, G., Stemmelin, J. and Scatton, B. (2005) Effects of the cannabinoid CB1 receptor antagonist rimonabant in models of emotional reactivity in rodents. Biol. Psychiatry, 57: 261–267.

Gross, C., Zhuang, X., Stark, K., Ramboz, S., Oosting, R., Kirby, L., Santarelli, L., Beck, S. and Hen, R. (2002) Serotonin1A receptor acts during development to establish normal anxiety-like behaviour in the adult. Nature, 416: 396–400.

Hariri, A.R., Mattay, V.S., Tessitore, A., Kolachana, B., Fera, F., Goldman, D., Egan, M.F. and Weinberger, D.R. (2002) Serotonin transporter genetic variation and the response of the human amygdala. Science, 297: 400–403.

Hashimoto, K. (2007) BDNF variant linked to anxiety-related behaviors. Bioessays, 29: 116–119.

Hayden, E.P., Dougherty, L.R., Maloney, B., Emily Durbin, C., Olino, T.M., Nurnberger, J.I., Jr. Lahiri, D.K. and Klein, D.N. (2007) Temperamental fearfulness in childhood and the serotonin transporter promoter region polymorphism: a multimethod association study. Psychiatr Genet., 17: 135–142.

Heisler, L.K., Chu, H.M., Brennan, T.J., Danao, J.A., Bajwa, P., Parsons, L.H. and Tecott, L.H. (1998) Elevated anxiety and antidepressant-like responses in serotonin 5-HT1A receptor mutant mice. Proc. Natl. Acad. Sci. USA, 95: 15049–15054.

Holmes, A., Yang, R.J., Lesch, K.P., Crawley, J.N. and Murphy, D.L. (2003) Mice lacking the serotonin transporter exhibit 5-HT(1A) receptor-mediated abnormalities in tests for anxiety-like behavior. Neuropsychopharmacology, 28: 2077–2088.

Homanics, G.E., Harrison, N.L., Quinlan, J.J., Krasowski, M.D., Rick, C.E., De Blas, A.L., Mehta, A.K., Kist, F., Mihalek, R.M., Aul, J.J. and Firestone, L.L. (1999) Normal electrophysiological and behavioral responses to ethanol in mice lacking the long splice variant of the gamma2 subunit of the gamma-aminobutyrate type A receptor. Neuropharmacology, 38: 253–265.

Horinouchi, Y., Akiyoshi, J., Nagata, A., Matsushita, H., Tsutsumi, T., Isogawa, K., Noda, T. and Nagayama, H. (2004) Reduced anxious behavior in mice lacking the CCK2 receptor gene. Eur. Neuropsychopharmacol., 14: 157–161.

Hunnerkopf, R., Strobel, A., Gutknecht, L., Brocke, B. and Lesch, K.P. (2007) Interaction between BDNF Val66Met and dopamine transporter gene variation influences anxiety-related traits. Neuropsychopharmacology (in press).

Jennings, K.A., Loder, M.K., Sheward, W.J., Pei, Q., Deacon, R.M., Benson, M.A., Olverman, H.J., Hastie, N.D., Harmar, A.J., Shen, S. and Sharp, T. (2006) Increased expression of the 5-HT transporter confers a low-anxiety phenotype linked to decreased 5-HT transmission. J. Neurosci., 26: 8955–8964.

Jiang, X., Xu, K., Hoberman, J., Tian, F., Marko, A.J., Waheed, J.F., Harris, C.R., Marini, A.M., Enoch, M.A. and Lipsky, R.H. (2005) BDNF variation and mood disorders: a novel functional promoter polymorphism and Val66Met are associated with anxiety but have opposing effects. Neuropsychopharmacology, 30: 1353–1361.

Kamprath, K., Marsicano, G., Tang, J., Monory, K., Bisogno, T., Di, M.V., Lutz, B. and Wotjak, C.T. (2006) Cannabinoid CB1 receptor mediates fear extinction via habituation-like processes. J. Neurosci., 26: 6677–6686.

Karl, T., Burne, T.H. and Herzog, H. (2006) Effect of Y1 receptor deficiency on motor activity, exploration, and anxiety. Behav. Brain Res., 167: 87–93.

Karolyi, I.J., Burrows, H.L., Ramesh, T.M., Nakajima, M., Lesh, J.S., Seong, E., Camper, S.A. and Seasholtz, A.F. (1999) Altered anxiety and weight gain in corticotropin-releasing hormone-binding protein-deficient mice. Proc. Natl. Acad. Sci. USA, 96: 11595–11600.

Kelley, S.P., Bratt, A.M. and Hodge, C.W. (2003) Targeted gene deletion of the 5-HT3A receptor subunit produces an anxiolytic phenotype in mice. Eur. J. Pharmacol., 461: 19–25.

Kishimoto, T., Radulovic, J., Radulovic, M., Lin, C.R., Schrick, C., Hooshmand, F., Hermanson, O., Rosenfeld, M.G. and Spiess, J. (2000) Deletion of crhr2 reveals an anxiolytic role for corticotropin-releasing hormone receptor-2. Nat. Genet., 24: 415–419.

Klemenhagen, K.C., Gordon, J.A., David, D.J., Hen, R. and Gross, C.T. (2006) Increased fear response to contextual cues in mice lacking the 5-HT1A receptor. Neuropsychopharmacology, 31: 101–111.

Ko, S., Zhao, M.G., Toyoda, H., Qiu, C.S. and Zhuo, M. (2005) Altered behavioral responses to noxious stimuli and fear in glutamate receptor 5 (GluR5)- or GluR6-deficient mice. J. Neurosci., 25: 977–984.

Kobayashi, S., Ohta, M., Miyasaka, K. and Funakoshi, A. (1996) Decrease in exploratory behavior in naturally occurring cholecystokinin (CCK)-A receptor gene knockout rats. Neurosci. Lett., 214: 61–64.

Koob, G.F. and Gold, L.H. (1997) Molecular biological approaches in the behavioural pharmacology of anxiety and depression. Behav. Pharmacol., 8: 652.

Kralic, J.E., O'Buckley, T.K., Khisti, R.T., Hodge, C.W., Homanics, G.E. and Morrow, A.L. (2002) GABA(A) receptor alpha-1 subunit deletion alters receptor subtype assembly, pharmacological and behavioral responses to benzodiazepines and zolpidem. Neuropharmacology, 43: 685–694.

Kralic, J.E., Wheeler, M., Renzi, K., Ferguson, C., O'Buckley, T.K., Grobin, A.C., Morrow, A.L. and Homanics, G.E. (2003) Deletion of GABAA receptor alpha 1 subunit-containing receptors alters responses to ethanol and other anesthetics. J. Pharmacol. Exp. Ther., 305: 600–607.

Kresse, A.E., Timpl, P., Sillaber, I., Spanagel, R., Reul, J.M.H.M., Dtalla, G.K., Blanquet, V., Steckler, T., Holsboer, F. and Wurst, W. (1998) Neuroendocrine and behavioral analysis of mice lacking the cortico-tropin-releasing hormone receptor 1 (CRHR1). Soc. Neurosci. Abstr., 24: 617.

Kusserow, H., Davies, B., Hortnagl, H., Voigt, I., Stroh, T., Bert, B., Deng, D.R., Fink, H., Veh, R.W. and Theuring, F. (2004) Reduced anxiety-related behaviour in transgenic mice overexpressing serotonin 1A receptors. Brain Res. Mol. Brain Res., 129: 104–116.

Lang, U.E., Hellweg, R., Kalus, P., Bajbouj, M., Lenzen, K.P., Sander, T., Kunz, D. and Gallinat, J. (2005) Association of a functional BDNF polymorphism and anxiety-related personality traits. Psycho-pharmacology, 180: 95–99.

Li, Q., Holmes, A., Ma, L., Van de Kar, L.D., Garcia, F. and Murphy, D.L. (2004) Medial hypothalamic 5-hydroxytryptamine (5-HT)1A receptors regulate neuroendocrine responses to stress and exploratory locomotor activity: application of recombinant adenovirus containing 5-HT1A sequences. J. Neurosci., 24: 10868–10877.

Li, X.L., Aou, S., Hori, T. and Oomura, Y. (2002) Spatial memory deficit and emotional abnormality in OLETF rats. Physiol Behav., 75: 15–23.

Liljelund, P., Ferguson, C., Homanics, G. and Olsen, R.W. (2005) Long-term effects of diazepam treatment of epileptic GABAA receptor beta3 subunit knockout mouse in early life. Epilepsy Res., 66: 99–115.

Linden, A.M., Johnson, B.G., Peters, S.C., Shannon, H.E., Tian, M., Wang, Y., Yu, J.L., Koster, A., Baez, M. and Schoepp, D.D. (2002) Increased anxiety-related behavior in mice deficient for metabotropic glutamate 8 (mGlu8) receptor. Neuropharmacology, 43: 251–259.

Lira, A., Zhou, M., Castanon, N., Ansorge, M.S., Gordon, J.A., Francis, J.H., Bradley-Moore, M., Lira, J., Underwood, M.D., Arango, V., Kung, H.F., Hofer, M.A., Hen, R. and Gingrich, J.A. (2003) Altered depression-related behaviors and functional changes in the dorsal raphe nucleus of serotonin transporter-deficient mice. Biol. Psychiatry, 54: 960–971.

Lopez-Rubalcava, C., Hen, R. and Cruz, S.L. (2000) Anxiolytic-like actions of toluene in the burying behavior and plus-maze tests: differences in sensitivity between 5-HT(1B) knockout and wild-type mice. Behav. Brain Res., 115: 85–94.

Low, K., Crestani, F., Keist, R., Benke, D., Brunig, I., Benson, J.A., Fritschy, J.M., Rulicke, T., Bluethmann, H., Mohler, H. and Rudolph, U. (2000) Molecular and neuronal substrate for the selective attenuation of anxiety. Science, 290: 131–134.

Maccarone, M., Valverde, O., Barbaccia, M.L., Castane, A., Maldonado, R., Ledent, C., Parmentier, M. and Finazzi-Agro, A. (2002) Age-related changes of anandamide metabolism in CB1 cannabinoid receptor knockout mice: correlation with behaviour. Eur. J. Neurosci., 15: 1178–1186.

Malleret, G., Hen, R., Guillou, J.L., Segu, L. and Buhot, M.C. (1999) 5-HT1B receptor knock-out mice exhibit increased exploratory activity and enhanced spatial memory performance in the Morris water maze. J. Neurosci., 19: 6157–6168.

Martin, M., Ledent, C., Parmentier, M., Maldonado, R. and Valverde, O. (2002) Involvement of CB1 cannabinoid receptors in emotional behaviour. Psychopharmacology (Berlin), 159: 379–387.

Mazzanti, C.M., Lappalainen, J., Long, J.C., Bengel, D., Naukkarinen, H., Eggert, M., Virkkunen, M., Linnoila, M. and Goldman, D. (1999) Role of the serotonin transporter promoter polymorphism in anxiety-related traits. Arch. Gen. Psychiatry, 55: 936–940.

Meaney, M.J. (2001) Maternal care, gene expression, and the transmission of individual differences in stress reactivity across generations. Annu. Rev. Neurosci., 24: 1161–1192.

Meaney, M.J. and Szyf, M. (2005) Maternal care as a model for experience-dependent chromatin plasticity? Trends Neurosci., 28: 456–463.

Miczek, K.A. (1997) Genetic approaches to anxiety and depression. Behav. Pharmacol., 8: 657–658.

Mihalek, R.M., Banerjee, P.K., Korpi, E.R., Quinlan, J.J., Firestone, L.L., Mi, Z.P., Lagenaur, C., Tretter, V., Sieghart, W., Anagnostaras, S.G., Sage, J.R., Fanselow, M.S., Guidotti, A., Spigelman, I., Li, Z., DeLorey, T.M., Olsen, R.W. and Homanics, G.E. (1999) Attenuated sensitivity to neuroactive steroids in gamma-aminobutyrate type A receptor delta subunit knockout mice. Proc. Natl. Acad. Sci. USA, 96: 12905–12910.

Millan, M.J. (2003) The neurobiology and control of anxious states. Prog Neurobiol., 70: 83–244.

Misslin, R. and Cigrang, M. (1986) Does neophobia necessarily imply fear or anxiety? Behavioural Process, 12: 45–50.

Miyasaka, K., Kobayashi, S., Ohta, M., Kanai, S., Yoshida, Y., Nagata, A., Matsui, T., Noda, T., Takiguchi, S., Takata, Y., Kawanami, T. and Funakoshi, A. (2002) Anxiety-related behaviors in cholecystokinin-A, B, and AB receptor gene knockout mice in the plus-maze. Neurosci. Lett., 335: 115–118.

Mombereau, C., Kaupmann, K., Froestl, W., Sansig, G., van der, P.H. and Cryan, J.F. (2004a) Genetic and pharmacological evidence of a role for GABA(B) receptors in the modulation of anxiety- and anti-depressant-like behavior. Neuropsychopharmacology, 29: 1050–1062.

Mombereau, C., Kaupmann, K., Gassmann, M., Bettler, B., van der, P.H. and Cryan, J.F. (2005) Altered anxiety and depression-related behaviour in mice lacking GABAB(2) receptor subunits. Neuroreport, 16: 307–310.

Mombereau, C., Kaupmann, K., van der, P.H. and Cryan, J.F. (2004b) Altered response to benzodiazepine anxiolytics in mice lacking GABA B(1) receptors. Eur. J. Pharmacol., 497: 119–120.

Muller, M.B., Zimmermann, S., Sillaber, I., Hagemeyer, T.P., Deussing, J.M., Timpl, P., Kormann, M.S., Droste, S.K., Kuhn, R., Reul, J.M., Holsboer, F. and Wurst, W. (2003) Limbic corticotropin-releasing hormone receptor 1 mediates anxiety-related behavior and hormonal adaptation to stress. Nat. Neurosci., 6: 1100–1107.

Ouagazzal, A.M., Moreau, J.L., Pauly-Evers, M. and Jenck, F. (2003) Impact of environmental housing conditions on the emotional responses of mice deficient for nociceptin/orphanin FQ peptide precursor gene. Behav. Brain Res., 144: 111–117.

Parks, C.L., Robinson, P.S., Sibille, E., Shenk, T. and Toth, M. (1998) Increased anxiety of mice lacking the serotonin1A receptor. Proc. Natl. Acad. Sci. USA, 95: 10734–10739.

Parsons, L.H., Kerr, T.M. and Tecott, L.H. (2001) 5-HT(1A) receptor mutant mice exhibit enhanced tonic, stress-induced and fluoxetine-induced serotonergic neurotransmission. J. Neurochem., 77: 607–617.

Pattij, T., Groenink, L., Hijzen, T.H., Oosting, R.S., Maes, R.A., van der, G.J. and Olivier, B. (2002a) Autonomic changes associated with enhanced anxiety in 5-HT(1A) receptor knockout mice. Neuropsychopharmacology, 27: 380–390.

Pattij, T., Groenink, L., Oosting, R.S., van der, G.J., Maes, R.A. and Olivier, B. (2002b) GABA(A)-benzodiazepine receptor complex sensitivity in 5-HT(1A) receptor knockout mice on a 129/Sv background. Eur. J. Pharmacol., 447: 67–74.

Pattij, T. and Olivier, B. (2001) Serotonin 1A receptor knockout mice are paradigm-dependent more anxious. Behav. Pharmacol., 12: S75.

Pattij, T., Sarnyai, Z., Brunner, D. and Olivier, B. (2000) Does the 5-HT$_{1A}$ receptor knockout mouse have an anxious phenotype?. Int. J. Neuropsychopharmacol., 3: S275.

Pezawas, L., Meyer-Lindenberg, A., Drabant, E.M., Verchinski, B.A., Munoz, K.E., Kolachana, S., Egan, M.F., Mattay, V.S., Hariri, A.R. and Weinberger, D.R. (2005) 5-HTTLPR polymorphism impacts human cingulate–amygdala interactions: a genetic susceptibility mechanism for depression. Nat. Neurosci., 8: 828–834.

Ramboz, S., Oosting, R., Amara, D.A., Kung, H.F., Blier, P., Mendelsohn, M., Mann, J.J., Brunner, D. and Hen, R. (1998) Serotonin receptor 1A knockout: an animal model of anxiety-related disorder. Proc. Natl. Acad. Sci. USA, 95: 14476–14481.

Ramesh, T.M., Karolyi, I.J., Nakajima, M., Camper, S.A. and Seasholtz, A.F. (1998) Altered physiological and behavioral responses in CRH-binding protein deficient mice. Soc. Neurosci. Abstr., 24: 505.

Raud, S., Innos, J., Abramov, U., Reimets, A., Koks, S., Soosaar, A., Matsui, T. and Vasar, E. (2005) Targeted invalidation of CCK2 receptor gene induces anxiolytic-like action in light–dark exploration, but not in fear conditioning test. Psychopharmacology (Berlin), 181: 347–357.

Redrobe, J.P., Dumont, Y., Herzog, H. and Quirion, R. (2003) Neuropeptide Y (NPY) Y2 receptors mediate behaviour in two animal models of anxiety: evidence from Y2 receptor knockout mice. Behav. Brain Res., 141: 251–255.

Roy, M., David, N.K., Danao, J.V., Baribault, H., Tian, H. and Giorgetti, M. (2006) Genetic inactivation of melanin-concentrating hormone receptor subtype 1 (MCHR1) in mice exerts anxiolytic-like behavioral effects. Neuropsychopharmacology, 31: 112–120.

Rudolph, U., Crestani, F., Benke, D., Brunig, I., Benson, J.A., Fritschy, J.M., Martin, J.R., Bluethmann, H. and Mohler, H. (1999) Benzodiazepine actions mediated by specific gamma-aminobutyric acid(A) receptor subtypes. Nature, 401: 796–800.

Rupniak, N.M., Carlson, E.J., Webb, J.K., Harrison, T., Porsolt, R.D., Roux, S., de, F.C., Hunt, S.P., Oates, B. and Wheeldon, A. (2001) Comparison of the phenotype of NK1R–/– mice with pharmacological blockade of the substance P (NK1) receptor in assays for antidepressant and anxiolytic drugs. Behav. Pharmacol., 12: 497–508.

Santarelli, L., Gobbi, G., Debs, P.C., Sibille, E.T., Blier, P., Hen, R. and Heath, M.J. (2001) Genetic and pharmacological disruption of neurokinin 1 receptor function decreases anxiety-related behaviors and increases serotonergic function. Proc. Natl. Acad. Sci. USA, 98: 1912–1917.

Sibille, E., Pavlides, C., Benke, D. and Toth, M. (2000) Genetic inactivation of the Serotonin(1A) receptor in mice results in downregulation of major GABA(A) receptor alpha subunits, reduction of GABA(A) receptor binding, and benzodiazepine-resistant anxiety. J. Neurosci., 20: 2758–2765.

Smith, D.G., Davis, R.J., Rorick-Kehn, L., Morin, M., Witkin, J.M., McKinzie, D.L., Nomikos, G.G. and Gehlert, D.R. (2006a) Melanin-concentrating hormone-1 receptor modulates neuroendocrine, behavioral, and corticolimbic neurochemical stress responses in mice. Neuropsychopharmacology, 31: 1135–1145.

Smith, G.W., Aubry, J.M., Dellu, F., Contarino, A., Bilezikjian, L.M., Gold, L.H., Chen, R., Marchuk, Y., Hauser, C., Bentley, C.A., Sawchenko, P.E., Koob, G.F., Vale, W. and Lee, K.F. (1998) Corticotropin releasing factor receptor 1-deficient mice display decreased anxiety, impaired stress response, and aberrant neuroendocrine development. Neuron, 20: 1093–1102.

Smith, S.S., Ruderman, Y., Frye, C., Homanics, G. and Yuan, M. (2006b) Steroid withdrawal in the mouse results in anxiogenic effects of 3alpha,5beta-THP: a possible model of premenstrual dysphoric disorder. Psychopharmacology (Berlin), 186: 323–333.

Sonner, J.M., Cascio, M., Xing, Y., Fanselow, M.S., Kralic, J.E., Morrow, A.L., Korpi, E.R., Hardy, S., Sloat, B., Eger, E.I. and Homanics, G.E. (2005) Alpha 1 subunit-containing GABA type A receptors in forebrain contribute to the effect of inhaled anesthetics on conditioned fear. Mol. Pharmacol., 68: 61–68.

Stein, M.B., Schork, N.J. and Gelernter, J. (2007) Gene-by-environment (serotonin transporter and childhood maltreatment) interaction for anxiety sensitivity, an intermediate phenotype for anxiety disorders. Neuropsychopharmacology (in press).

Stenzel-Poore, M.P., Duncan, J.E., Rittenberg, M.B., Bakke, A.C. and Heinrichs, S.C. (1996) CRH overproduction in transgenic mice: behavioral and immune system modulation. Ann. NY Acad. Sci., 780: 36–48.

Thoeringer, C.K., Binder, E.B., Salyakina, D., Erhardt, A., Ising, M., Unschuld, P.G., Kern, N., Lucae, S., Brueckl, T.M., Muelle, M.B., Fuchs, B., Puetz, B., Lieb, R., Uhr, M., Holsboer, F., Mueller-Myhsok, B. and Keck, M.E. (2007) Association of a Met88Val diazepam binding inhibitor (DBI) gene polymorphism and anxiety disorders with panic attacks. J. Psychiatr. Res., 41: 579–584.

Thorsell, A., Michalkiewicz, M., Dumont, Y., Quirion, R., Caberlotto, L., Rimondini, R., Mathe, A.A. and Heilig, M. (2000) Behavioral insensitivity to restraint stress, absent fear suppression of behavior and impaired spatial learning in transgenic rats with hippocampal neuropeptide Y overexpression. Proc. Natl. Acad. Sci. USA, 97: 12852–12857.

Timpl, P., Spanagel, R., Sillaber, I., Kresse, A., Reul, J.M., Stalla, G.K., Blanquet, V., Steckler, T., Holsboer, F. and Wurst, W. (1998) Impaired stress response and reduced anxiety in mice lacking a functional corticotropin-releasing hormone receptor 1. Nat. Genet., 19: 162–166.

Toth, M. and Sibille, E. (1998) Genetic inactivation of the serotonin$_{1A}$ receptor reveals its essential role in the anxiolytic effect of benzodiazepines. Soc. Neurosci. Abstr., 24: 600.

Tschenett, A., Singewald, N., Carli, M., Balducci, C., Salchner, P., Vezzani, A., Herzog, H. and Sperk, G. (2003) Reduced anxiety and improved stress coping ability in mice lacking NPY-Y2 receptors. Eur. J. Neurosci., 18: 143–148.

Vasar, E., Koks, S., Beljajev, S., Abramov, U., Koovit, I. and Matsui, T. (2000) CCK$_B$ receptor knockout mice: gender related behavioural differences. Eur. Neuropsychopharmacol., 10: S69.

Wang, X., Su, H., Copenhagen, L.D., Vaishnav, S., Pieri, F., Shope, C.D., Brownell, W.E., De, B.M., Paylor, R. and Bradley, A. (2002) Urocortin-deficient mice display normal stress-induced anxiety behavior and autonomic control but an impaired acoustic startle response. Mol. Cell Biol., 22: 6605–6610.

Weaver, I.C., Champagne, F.A., Brown, S.E., Dymov, S., Sharma, S., Meaney, M.J. and Szyf, M. (2005) Reversal of maternal programming of stress responses in adult offspring through methyl supplementation: altering epigenetic marking later in life. J. Neurosci., 25: 11045–11054.

Weaver, I.C., Meaney, M.J. and Szyf, M. (2006) Maternal care effects on the hippocampal transcriptome and anxiety-mediated behaviors in the offspring that are reversible in adulthood. Proc. Natl. Acad. Sci. USA, 103: 3480–3485.

Weisstaub, N.V., Zhou, M., Lira, A., Lambe, E., Gonzalez-Maeso, J., Hornung, J.P., Sibille, E., Underwood, M., Itohara, S., Dauer, W.T., Ansorge, M.S., Morelli, E., Mann, J.J., Toth, M., Aghajanian, G., Sealfon, S.C., Hen, R. and Gingrich, J.A. (2006) Cortical 5-HT2A receptor signaling modulates anxiety-like behaviors in mice. Science, 313: 536–540.

Weninger, S.C., Dunn, A.J., Muglia, L.J., Dikkes, P., Miczek, K.A., Swiergiel, A.H., Berridge, C.W. and Majzoub, J.A. (1999) Stress-induced behaviors require the corticotropin-releasing hormone (CRH) receptor, but not CRH. Proc. Natl. Acad. Sci. USA, 96: 8283–8288.

354

Werner, D.F., Blednov, Y.A., Ariwodola, O.J., Silberman, Y., Logan, E., Berry, R.B., Borghese, C.M., Matthews, D.B., Weiner, J.L., Harrison, N.L., Harris, R.A. and Homanics, G.E. (2006) Knockin mice with ethanol-insensitive alpha1-containing gamma-aminobutyric acid type A receptors display selective alterations in behavioral responses to ethanol. J. Pharmacol. Exp. Ther., 319: 219–227.

Wick, M.J., Radcliffe, R.A., Bowers, B.J., Mascia, M.P., Luscher, B., Harris, R.A. and Wehner, J.M. (2000) Behavioural changes produced by transgenic overexpression of gamma2L and gamma2S subunits of the GABAA receptor. Eur. J. Neurosci., 12: 2634–2638.

Wolfer, D.P., Crusio, W.E. and Lipp, H.P. (2002) Knockout mice: simple solutions to the problems of genetic background and flanking genes. Trends Neurosci., 25: 336–340.

Yamamoto, Y., Akiyoshi, J., Kiyota, A., Katsuragi, S., Tsutsumi, T., Isogawa, K. and Nagayama, H. (2000) Increased anxiety behavior in OLETF rats without cholecystokinin-A receptor. Brain Res. Bull., 53: 789–792.

CHAPTER 4.7

The pharmacology of anxiolysis

Andrew Holmes[*]

Section on Behavioral Science and Genetics, Laboratory for Integrative Neuroscience, National Institute on Alcohol Abuse and Alcoholism, National Institute of Mental Health, Rockville, MD, USA

Abstract: Anxiety disorders are a diverse class of psychiatric conditions that are proliferating but inadequately treated by existing therapeutics. The development of novel anxiolytic mediations is a very active field of research in academia and the pharmaceutical industry. This chapter provides a précis of five preceding chapters that review research on some of the major neural systems implicated in anxiety disorders and targeted as novel anxiolytic mediations: cannabinoid, glutamate, serotonin, GABA/ benzodiazepine, and neuropeptides. A survey of this rich literature indicates that there are many promising developments in the study of the pharmacology of anxiolysis, but still many hurdles to overcome.

Keywords: anxiety; anxiolytic; drug; medication; cannabinoid; glutamate; serotonin; GABA; benzodiazepine; neuropeptide

I. Introduction

The major diagnostic manuals (American Psychiatric Association, 1994; World Health Organisation, 1994) currently divide anxiety into multiple subdisorders, the most frequently diagnosed being generalized anxiety disorder, posttraumatic stress disorder, panic disorder (with and without agoraphobia), social anxiety disorder, specific phobias, and obsessive-compulsive disorder. A description of the specific clinical profile of each subdisorder can be found in Rowlett (2007). The feature common to all subdisorders is the presence of anxiety that persistently interferes with the ability to live a normal life.

Sadly, the incidence of anxiety disorders is proliferating throughout the world and available therapeutic interventions, including anxiolytic medications, are useful but far from optimal due to delayed or inadequate efficacy and poor tolerability (Holmes et al., 2003). As such, there

is a major need for better understanding of the pathophysiology of anxiety disorders and for better treatment. The subsequent chapters provide a state-of-the-field review of five major neural systems that are implicated in anxiety disorders and targets for novel anxiolytic mediations (cannabinoid, glutamate, serotonin, GABA/benzodiazepine, neuropeptides). This chapter provides a brief précis of each of the preceding reviews.

II. Recent developments and emerging targets

II.A. Cannabinoid: a new kid on the block

Understanding of the role of the endocannabinoid system in mediating various forms of higher-order behaviors has grown dramatically in recent years, and there is intense interest in the therapeutic potential for targeting this system for disorders ranging from obesity to drug addiction. Some of the most striking breakthroughs have been attained in the field of anxiety research, as discussed by Bortolato and Piomelli in Chapter 4.5 (Bortolato

---

[*]Corresponding author. E-mail: holmesan@mail.nih.gov

R.J. Blanchard, D.C. Blanchard, G. Griebel and D. Nutt (Eds.)
Handbook of Anxiety and Fear, Vol. 17
ISBN 978-0-444-53065-3

DOI: 10.1016/S1569-7339(07)00016-1

and Piomelli, 2007). As these authors discuss, research to date has focused on endocannabinoid actions at the CB1 receptor subtype, which is densely localized in brain regions linked to anxiety (Herkenham et al., 1990). There have been two main lines of investigation: (1) studies of the effects of CB1 receptor agonists (e.g., WIN 55,212-2) and antagonists (e.g., SR141716A, rimonabant) or CB1 'knockout' in rodents, and (2) studies of the compounds (e.g., AM404, URB547) that prevent either the deactivation or reuptake of endocannabinoids (e.g., anandamide).

The effects of cannabis sativa on human anxiety are complex and variable. Bortolato and Piomelli note that the available preclinical evidence demonstrates anxiolytic-like effects following administration of low doses of CB1 agonists, but pro-anxiety-like effects at higher doses. The anxiety-related effects of CB1 antagonists and anxiety-related phenotype of CB1 knockout mice are also reported to vary across studies, and may reflect interactions of this system with environmental (test conditions) and organism (genotype, sex) factors. Notwithstanding, a prominent phenotypic feature of CB1 knockout mice was an impairment in fear extinction (Marsicano et al., 2002; see also Kamprath et al., 2006). Fear extinction is an active form of learning that serves to reduce learned fear responses in animals and humans, and has created much recent interest as a potential model for learned fear and its therapeutic alleviation in anxiety disorders (Barad, 2005; Myers and Davis, 2007). These findings have substantiated the hypothesis that stimulating the cannabinoid system may promote fear extinction. In the context of data showing that stress impairs fear extinction (Izquierdo et al., 2006), it is interesting to note recent data indicating that increasing endocannabinoid levels with URB547 or AM404 has not only extinction facilitating effects (Chhatwal and Ressler, 2007) but also anxiolytic-like and anti-stress properties (Bortolato and Piomelli, 2007). Thus, drugs targeting the cannabinoid system may have effects on multiple symptomatic features of anxiety disorders. Clearly, however, this is a very complex neuromodulatory system and more work needs to be done at both the preclinical and clinical levels to elucidate it precise role in anxiety.

II.B. Glutamate: excitement about modifying excitation

The actions of L-glutamate, the predominant excitatory neurotransmitter in the central nervous system, are mediated by a diverse array of receptors classified into different families (ionotropic, metabotropic), classes (N-methyl-D-aspartate (NMDA), α-amino-3-hydroxy-5-methylisoxazole-4-propionate (AMPA), kainate), and subtypes (NR1, NR2A–D, NR3, GluR1–4, GluR5–7, KA1–2, mGluR1–8). In Chapter 4.4, Cryan and Dev discuss how advances in the characterization of the physiological properties of glutamate and its receptors has stimulated interest in the potential for selectively targeting the glutamatergic system as a means to develop novel anxiolytics (Cryan and Dev, 2007).

Preclinical research on this topic is a very active field with investigators using a combination of research tools including receptor subtype specific pharmacological compounds, gene mutant mice, and more novel techniques such as a short interfering RNA. As Cryan and Dev review and discuss, the available data is still far from definitive. Thus, there is evidence of anxiolytic activity following NMDA, AMPA, Group I mGlu receptor blockade, or Group II mGlu receptor activation but this literature still needs to be refined and replicated before a strong case for clinical evaluation can be made. Compelling preclinical evidence is particularly important for glutamate-acting targets given the potential for side effects such as memory impairment and psychomimesis.

An important development in this regard is the generation of compounds that might be able to bypass side effect, such as the allosteric modulators of glutamate receptors which modify the actions of endogenously released glutamate rather than artificially driving glutamatergic neurotransmission (Marino and Conn, 2006). Another promising development, given the well-described role of glutamate in cognition (Malinow and Malenka, 2002), is the potential for glutamate-acting drugs to alleviate cognitive dysfunction in anxiety disorders, which until recently has been a neglected aspect of anxiolytic medication.

Interestingly, recent evidence that the NMDA receptor partial agonist D-cycloserine facilitates extinction in patients and preclinical subjects (Ressler et al., 2004). Thus, further work on the anxiolytic potential of targeting the glutamate system is eagerly awaited.

II.C. GABA/benzodiazepine: an old dog with new tricks

The Yin to glutamate's Yang, γ-aminobutyric acid (GABA) is the brain's primary inhibitory neurotransmitter system. Activation of the benzodiazepine receptor, an allosteric modulatory site on the GABA$_A$ receptor subtype, by treatment with drugs such as diazepam is highly effective at reducing anxiety. Unfortunately, and consistent with GABA's ubiquitous role in mediating brain functions, benzodiazepine agonists are also effective at producing motor incoordination, sedation, cognitive impairment, and psychological dependence, which dampened their enormous popularity as anxiolytics. However, as discussed by Rowlett in Chapter 4.2, new insights into the molecular pharmacology of the GABA$_A$ receptor has reignited interest in the possibility of manufacturing a new generation of GABA-acting drugs that have good anxiolytic activity without the unwanted side-effects (Atack, 2005; Rudolph and Mohler, 2006; Rowlett, 2007).

GABA$_A$ receptors are pentamers made up of multiple subunits, predominantly those of the α, β, and γ families (McKernan and Whiting, 1996). With the exception of α4, the subunits within the α family are all benzodiazepine-sensitive. However, while α1 is expressed widely throughout brain, while the distribution of α2, α3, and α5 is more restricted to regions associated with anxiety. The relative roles of each subunit to anxiety have been studied employing an elegant 'knockin' technique in which mutant mice were generated with α1, α2, α3, or α5 rendered benzodiazepine-insensitive. The results of these studies suggested a necessary contribution of α2 or α5 but not α3 to benzodiazepine-mediated anxiolysis, although recent pharmacological studies indicate that a role for α3 cannot be excluded (Dias et al., 2005). Subsequent

development and preclinical investigation of novel compounds with full or partial agonist activity at α2 and α3 (not α1 and/or α5) subunit-containing GABA$_A$ receptors (e.g., L-838,417, TPA023, SL651498) provided evidence for anti-anxiety effects without concomitant ataxia or sedation at the same dose range. However, as discussed by Rowlett, other compounds with less clear pharmacology (e.g., ocinaplon) also demonstrate anxioselectivity in preclinical tests (Lippa et al., 2005).

In sum, while the delineation of subunits to be targeted to produce anxioselectivity is far from settled, novel GABA-acting drugs developed from these insights would seem to have great clinical potential. However, given the recent termination of clinical trials for some of the drugs from this new class, the jury is still out on whether this old dog can learn some new tricks.

II.D. Serotonin: still waiting for the next generation

Along with the benzodiazepines, drugs such as the serotonin reuptake inhibitors (SRIs) that target the serotonin system (by blocking transporter-mediated reuptake) have become the most commonly prescribed class of anxiolytic medications. SRIs are, however, associated with poor efficacy in a proportion of patients, a delayed onset of therapeutic action and various side effects that reduce tolerability (e.g., sexual dysfunction, nausea, jitteriness, and changes in body weight). There is also considerable debate about the precise contribution of serotonin to the therapeutic actions of these drugs (Manji et al., 2001; Duman, 2002). As pointed out by Guimarães et al. in Chapter 4.6 (Guimarães et al., 2007), the fact that no clear conclusions have been drawn speaks to the incredible complexity of serotonergic modulation of anxiety.

The richness of serotonin system is reflected in the 14 or more serotonin receptor subtypes found in brain (Hoyer et al., 2002). Such diversity hints at the possibility of differential functional roles for receptor subtypes, and hence the potential for targeting specific subtypes to produce a new generation of selective anxiolytics that lack the burdensome side effects of SRIs. A great deal of preclinical and clinical research has been undertaken to identify such a target (Griebel, 1995; Millan, 2003). However, as Guimarães et al. discuss, the results of these efforts have been disappointing. With the exception of the 5-HT1A receptor partial agonist buspirone, which was introduced for generalized anxiety disorder in 1985, no anxiolytic targeting a serotonin receptor subtype has demonstrated robust efficacy in the clinic. This has been particularly disappointing in the case of 5-HT2A and 5-HT2C receptor antagonists, given persuasive evidence of functional abnormalities in these subtypes in anxiety disorders (Zohar et al., 1987).

The reasons for the failure to make a breakthrough are far from clear; although it should be noted that attempts to dissect the 'dirty pharmacology' of other monoaminergic psychotropic medications, for example, antipsychotics, to produce the magic bullet have also been harder to achieve in practice than in principle. Solutions to help move things forward are no easier to discern. One salient issue is the development of preclinical behavioral assays that are better able to detect anxiety-related effects of serotonergic drugs. Indeed, the reliance on exploration-based conflict tests of rodent anxiety-like behavior that are principally validated for sensitivity to GABA/benzodiazepine agonists is a major issue in the field (Cryan and Holmes, 2005). This issue is repeatedly raised by a number of authors of the following chapters in the context of the ability of existing behavioral tests to detect truly novel mechanisms of action (Bortolato and Piomelli, 2007; Guimarães et al., 2007).

As Guimarães et al. discuss, one approach to finding better assays is to better define the nature of the behaviors being tested (e.g., whether conflict- or escape-related). Another approach that has gained recent currency has been to employ gene-targeting techniques to generate mice with functional mutations in components of the serotonin system, including receptor subtypes and the reuptake-mediating transporter. This has provided some intriguing insights into the neurobiology of serotonergic modulation of anxiety, including evidence that pharmacological manipulations of this system may have very different effects in developing or juvenile animals than in adults (Ansorge et al., 2004; Gross and Hen, 2004; Hariri and Holmes, 2006). These emerging findings further add to an already complex picture.

II.E. Neuropeptides: modulators without the side effects?

Neuropeptides are a diverse class of substances in the brain that often differ from the classical neurotransmitters in terms of biochemical regulation and neurophysiological actions. As discussed in Chapter 4.1 by Steckler (Steckler, 2007), neuropeptides are attractive targets for anxiolytics for anxiety disorders (see also Griebel, 1999; Hokfelt et al., 2003; Holmes et al., 2003; Belzung et al., 2006). First, the largely modulatory action of neuropeptides in the brain could mean that pharmacologically manipulating them would have less marked effects on the type of essential neurophysiological functions (e.g., motor) mediated by classical neurotransmitters and, therefore, have fewer side effects. Moreover, neuropeptides are thought to be preferentially released and recruited by the neural systems mediating anxiety when neuronal activity is high, as in disease-related overactivity (reviewed by Steckler, 2007) or during exposure to stress. This is another putative reason why neuropeptide-targeting anxiolytics could potentially mitigate the symptoms of anxiety while being otherwise 'silent' or at least better tolerated than existing drugs.

Of the various neuropeptides that have been assessed for their anxiolytic potential, corticotropin-releasing factor (CRF), opioid peptides such as enkephalin, neuropeptide Y (NPY), cholecystokinin (CCK), vasopressin (AVP), substance P, and galanin have received most attention. As comprehensively reviewed by Steckler, this has generated a large corpus of preclinical data investigating the effects of pharmacological manipulations or engineered gene mutations in these and other peptides. This literature is complex, reflecting the richness and neurobiological diversity of neuropeptides, as well as the technical caveats associated with studying these systems. However, evidence has supported the hypothesis that the actions of neuropeptides in rodents models are predominant seen under conditions in which a high level of experimental anxiety is elicited (i.e., on putatively stressful anxiety tests, or following pre-exposure to a stressor). Preclinical work also demonstrates strong interactions of peptides with other peptides and with neurotransmitters such as GABA, noradrenaline, and 5-HT that are implicated in the action of existing anxiolytics (Steckler, 2007).

While the preclinical literature offers encouraging although still far from definitive support for targeting neuropeptides, there are considerable challenges in making neuropeptide targets druggable. These include, for example, poor bioavailability and brain penetration when orally administered and the development of tolerance with chronic use. These issues have contributed to the rather slow progress in taking neuropeptide targets from the laboratory to the clinic. Those compounds that have been tested for anxiolytic potential in clinical populations (e.g., CRF R1 receptor antagonists, NK1 receptor antagonists) have not demonstrated clear efficacy and require further evaluation. Thus, while neuropeptides remain a very promising class of novel anxiolytics, they have not yet been able to fulfill that promise.

III. Concluding remarks and future directions

While there is a strong case for each of the neural systems discussed above to provide new, efficacious anxiolytics, this does not necessarily mean that targeting any one system will provide the anxiolytic panacea. Different anxiety disorders likely differ considerably from one another in neuropathophysiology and pharmacology and a certain type of mediation may turn out to be best suited to a specific anxiety disorder. Even within a subdisorder, finding the best anxiolytic may in part depend on an individual's genetic make-up. While we are still at an early stage of identifying genetic variants that affect pathophysiology and treatment responses, recent studies indicate that common polymorphisms, for example, in the gene encoding the serotonin transporter, can influence

both the efficacy or tolerability of anxiolytics (Hariri and Holmes, 2006; Serretti et al., 2006). Understanding the pharmacogenomics of anxiolytics will be one important issue for the field.

Of course, pharmacology is not the only way to treat anxiety. There is in fact considerable potential for drugs to serve primarily as adjuncts to psychological interventions (Davis et al., 2006). This has been recently illustrated by the efficacy of the NMDA receptor partial agonist D-cycloserine when used during cognitive behavioral therapy in patients with phobias (Ressler et al., 2004). This represents an interesting approach, because it suggests that that drugs that might have little discernible effect on anxiety symptoms while in the patient's system might nonetheless produce long-lasting therapeutic benefit by facilitating new learning 'about not being anxious' (Barad, 2005; Myers and Davis, 2007).

Clearly, there are many promising developments in the study of the pharmacology of anxiolysis. The field is at critical juncture.

References

American Psychiatric Association (1994) Diagnostic and Statistical Manual of Mental Disorders (DSM-IV), 4th edn. American Psychiatric Association.

Ansorge, M.S., Zhou, M., Lira, A., Hen, R. and Gingrich, J.A. (2004) Early-life blockade of the 5-HT transporter alters emotional behavior in adult mice. Science, 306: 879–881.

Atack, J.R. (2005) The benzodiazepine binding site of GABA(A) receptors as a target for the development of novel anxiolytics. Expert. Opin. Investig. Drugs, 14: 601–618.

Barad, M. (2005) Fear extinction in rodents: basic insight to clinical promise. Curr. Opin. Neurobiol. 15: 710–715.

Belzung, C., Yalcin, I., Griebel, G., Surget, A. and Leman, S. (2006) Neuropeptides in psychiatric diseases: an overview with a particular focus on depression and anxiety disorders. CNS Neurol. Disord. Drug Targets, 5: 135–145.

Bortolato, M. and Piomelli, D. (2007) The endocannabinoid system and anxiety responses. In: Blanchard, R.J. Blanchard, D.C. and Nutt, D.J. (Eds.), Handbook of Anxiety and Fear. (this volume).

Chhatwal, J.P. and Ressler, K.J. (2007) Modulation of fear and anxiety by the endogenous cannabinoid system. CNS Spectrosc., 12: 211–220.

Cryan, J.F. and Dev, K.K. (2007) The glutamatergic system as a potential therapeutic target for the treatment of anxiety disorders. In: Blanchard, R.J. Blanchard, D.C. and Nutt, D.J. (Eds.), Handbook of Anxiety and Fear. (this volume).

Cryan, J.F. and Holmes, A. (2005) The ascent of mouse: advances in modelling human depression and anxiety. Nat. Rev. Drug Discov., 4: 775–790.

Davis, M., Barad, M., Otto, M. and Southwick, S. (2006) Combining pharmacotherapy with cognitive behavioral therapy: traditional and new approaches. J. Trauma Stress., 19: 571–581.

Dias, R., Sheppard, W.F., Fradley, R.L., Garrett, E.M., Stanley, J.L., Tye, S.J., Goodacre, S., Lincoln, R.J., Cook, S.M., Conley, R., Hallett, D., Humphries, A.C., Thompson, S.A., Wafford, K.A., Street, L.J., Castro, J.L., Whiting, P.J., Rosahl, T.W., Atack, J.R., McKernan, R.M., Dawson, G.R. and Reynolds, D.S. (2005) Evidence for a significant role of alpha 3-containing GABAA receptors in mediating the anxiolytic effects of benzodiazepines. J. Neurosci., 25: 10682–10688.

Duman, R.S. (2002) Synaptic plasticity and mood disorders. Mol. Psychiatry, 7(Suppl. 1): 29–34.

Griebel, G. (1995) 5-Hydroxytryptamine-interacting drugs in animal models of anxiety disorders: more than 30 years of research. Pharmacol. Ther., 65: 319–395.

Griebel, G. (1999) Is there a future for neuropeptide receptor ligands in the treatment of anxiety disorders? Pharmacol. Ther., 82: 1–61.

Gross, C. and Hen, R. (2004) The developmental origins of anxiety. Nat. Rev. Neurosci., 5: 545–552.

Guimarães, F.S., Carobrez, A.P. and Graeff, F.G. (2007) Modulation of anxiety behaviors by 5-HT-interacting drugs. In: Blanchard, R.J., Blanchard, D.C. and Nutt, D.J. (Eds.), Handbook of Anxiety and Fear (this volume).

Hariri, A.R. and Holmes, A. (2006) Genetics of emotional regulation: the role of the serotonin transporter in neural function. Trends Cogn. Sci., 10: 182–191.

Herkenham, M., Lynn, A.B., Little, M.D., Johnson, M.R., Melvin, L.S., de Costa, B.R. and Rice, K.C. (1990) Cannabinoid receptor localization in brain. Proc. Natl. Acad. Sci. USA, 87: 1932–1936.

Hokfelt, T., Bartfai, T. and Bloom, F. (2003) Neuropeptides: opportunities for drug discovery. Lancet Neurol., 2: 463–472.

Holmes, A., Heilig, M., Rupniak, N.M., Steckler, T. and Griebel, G. (2003) Neuropeptide systems as novel therapeutic targets for depression and anxiety disorders. Trends Pharmacol. Sci., 24: 580–588.

Hoyer, D., Hannon, J.P. and Martin, G.R. (2002) Molecular, pharmacological and functional diversity of 5-HT receptors. Pharmacol. Biochem. Behav., 71: 533–554.

Izquierdo, A., Wellman, C.L. and Holmes, A. (2006) Brief uncontrollable stress causes dendritic retraction in infralimbic cortex and resistance to fear extinction in mice. J. Neurosci., 26: 5733–5738.

Kamprath, K., Marsicano, G., Tang, J., Monory, K., Bisogno, T., Di Marzo, V., Lutz, B. and Wotjak, C.T. (2006) Cannabinoid CB1 receptor mediates fear extinction via habituation-like processes. J. Neurosci., 26: 6677–6686.

Lippa, A., Czobor, P., Stark, J., Beer, B., Kostakis, E., Gravielle, M., Bandyopadhyay, S., Russek, S.J., Gibbs, T.T., Farb, D.H. and Skolnick, P. (2005) Selective anxiolysis produced by ocinaplon, a GABA(A) receptor modulator. Proc. Natl. Acad. Sci. USA, 102: 7380–7385.

Malinow, R. and Malenka, R.C. (2002) AMPA receptor trafficking and synaptic plasticity. Annu. Rev. Neurosci., 25: 103–126.

Manji, H.K., Drevets, W.C. and Charney, D.S. (2001) The cellular neurobiology of depression. Nat. Med., 7: 541–547.

Marino, M.J. and Conn, P.J. (2006) Glutamate-based therapeutic approaches: allosteric modulators of metabotropic glutamate receptors. Curr. Opin. Pharmacol., 6: 98–102.

Marsicano, G., Wotjak, C.T., Azad, S.C., Bisogno, T., Rammes, G., Cascio, M.G., Hermann, H., Tang, J., Hofmann, C., Zieglgansberger, W., Di Marzo, V. and Lutz, B. (2002) The endogenous cannabinoid system controls extinction of aversive memories. Nature, 418: 530–534.

McKernan, R.M. and Whiting, P.J. (1996) Which GABAA-receptor subtypes really occur in the brain? Trends Neurosci., 19: 139–143.

Millan, M.J. (2003) The neurobiology and control of anxious states. Prog. Neurobiol., 70: 83–244.

Myers, K.M. and Davis, M. (2007) Mechanisms of fear extinction. Mol. Psychiatry, 12: 120–150.

Ressler, K.J., Rothbaum, B.O., Tannenbaum, L., Anderson, P., Graap, K., Zimand, E., Hodges, L. and Davis, M. (2004) Cognitive enhancers as adjuncts to psychotherapy: use of D-cycloserine in phobic individuals to facilitate extinction of fear. Arch. Gen. Psychiatry, 61: 1136–1144.

Rowlett, J.K. (2007) Subtype-selective GABAA/benzodiazepine receptor ligands for the treatment of anxiety disorders. In: Blanchard, R.J. Blanchard, D.C. and Nutt, D.J. (Eds.), Handbook of Anxiety and Fear. (this volume).

Rudolph, U. and Mohler, H. (2006) GABA-based therapeutic approaches: GABAA receptor subtype functions. Curr. Opin. Pharmacol., 6: 18–23.

Serretti, A., Kato, M., De Ronchi, D. and Kinoshita, T. (2006) Meta-analysis of serotonin transporter gene promoter polymorphism (5-HTTLPR) association with selective serotonin reuptake inhibitor efficacy in depressed patients. Mol. Psychiatry, 12: 247–257.

Steckler, T. (2007) Peptide receptor ligands to treat anxiety disorders. In: Blanchard, R.J. Blanchard, D.C.

and Nutt, D.J. (Eds.), Handbook of Anxiety and Fear. (this volume).

World Health Organisation (1994) International Classification of Diseases (ICD-10). World Health Organisation.

Zohar, J., Mueller, E.A., Insel, T.R., Zohar-Kadouch, R.C. and Murphy, D.L. (1987) Serotonergic responsivity in obsessive-compulsive disorder. Comparison of patients and healthy controls. Arch. Gen. Psychiatry, 44: 946–951.

SECTION 5

Handbook of Fear and Anxiety: Clinical and Experimental Considerations

CHAPTER 5.1

Phenomenology of anxiety disorders

David Nutt[1,*], Berta Garcia de Miguel[1] and Simon J.C. Davies[2]

[1]*Psychopharmacology Unit, University of Bristol, Bristol, UK*
[2]*Academic Unit of Psychiatry, University of Bristol, Bristol, UK*

Abstract: Anxiety disorders are common, very disabling and have high personal and social costs. We aim to describe and discuss in this chapter the main phenomenological features of the five main anxiety syndromes/disorders: panic disorder, obsessive-compulsive disorder, social anxiety disorder, post-traumatic stress disorder and generalized anxiety disorder, taking the position that some of these features are shared between them – both phenomenological and aetiological. We specifically aim to focus on diagnostic criteria, prevalence and phenomenology of anxiety disorders.

Keywords: anxiety; phenomenology; SAnD; OCD; PD; PTSD; GAD

I. Anxiety disorders: clinical features

Anxiety disorders are common, very disabling and have high personal and social costs. In this chapter, we discuss the five main anxiety syndromes/disorders, panic disorder (PD), obsessive-compulsive disorder (OCD), social anxiety disorder (SanD), post-traumatic stress disorder (PTSD) and generalized anxiety disorder (GAD) according to the conceptual framework or approach shown in Fig. 1.

This figure shows each of the five disorders as separate diagnostic entities, and in each circle is the key feature that discriminates each disorder with the specific cognitions that are associated with each. We take the position that all anxiety disorders show shared features such as anxiety, certain physiological features and behavioural changes, and these are represented by the circle of overlap in the centre. These central features are also present in and indeed form the core of the other anxiety disorder-specific phobia. We believe this conceptual framework helps explain both the differences in phenomenological presentations in anxiety disorders and the overlap in basic physiological symptoms and the resulting interference with performance and behaviour, such as escape behaviours, avoidance and long-lasting fearful memories. An implication of this approach is that it may help explain why certain drugs, e.g. the SSRIs, act across such a wide range of anxiety disorders, but it also raises important challenges to those developing animal models of anxiety disorders, as many of the discrete diagnostic features of the human disorders are not easily assessed in animals.

The categorization of all disorders is constantly evolving and latest developments in psychiatry reflect a drive towards an empirically based classification system as proposed for the forthcoming DSM-V, reflecting the knowledge base for aetiology, genetic associations and phenotypic evidence. This chapter attempts to provide a description of the phenomenology of anxiety disorders, discussing past, current and future classifications.

I.A. Normal versus pathological anxiety

Anxiety is a normal experience and often provides appropriate motivation for action. If at some

---

*Corresponding author. E-mail: david.j.nutt@bristol.ac.uk

R.J. Blanchard, D.C. Blanchard, G. Griebel and D. Nutt (Eds.)
Handbook of Anxiety and Fear, Vol. 17
ISBN 978-0-444-53065-3

365

DOI: 10.1016/S1569-7339(07)00017-3

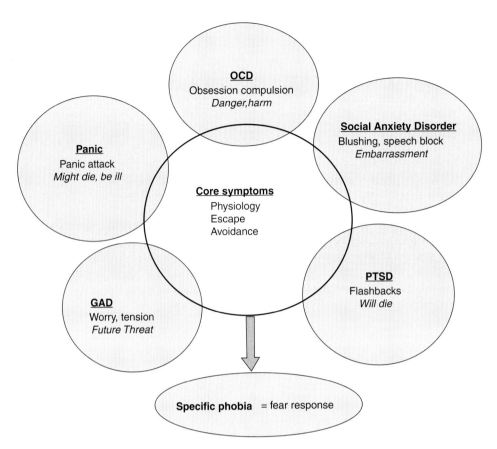

Fig. 1. The shared core and specific features of anxiety disorders (symptoms in normal type and cognitions in italics).

point anxiety becomes either so severe or so enduring that it significantly impairs function that is when it fulfils the criteria as a category of disorder or illness.

The question whether categorical or dimensional models should be used is being actively discussed. Since initial classification systems were established, the prevailing diagnostic criteria have been revised several times. The forthcoming DSM-V will try to improve structural concepts about anxiety disorders, as there are controversies in classification, both in individual anxiety disorders and in their co-morbidity with affective disorders. However, future reconsiderations about classifications require considerable caution. In addition to a true understanding of the core phenomenology of each disorder, aetiology,

genetic associations, subtypes, symptom overlap and co-morbidity must be considered.

In this review, we aim to examine the existing evidence base relating to anxiety disorders in all of these domains.

II. Social anxiety disorder (SAnD)

II.A. Introduction

The vast majority of individuals will experience mild anxiety on perceived scrutiny in public situations. However, symptoms in SAnD are extreme and associated with severe consequences. SAnD is a prevalent and commonly a debilitating personal problem.

II.B. Clinical features

Symptoms in SAnD belong to three different clusters, both in DSM-IV and in ICD-10 classifications: the existence of fear in one or more social situations (impairment in cognition), anxiety provoked by exposure to the feared conditions (cognitions and body sensations) and avoidance and anxious anticipation (impairment in behaviour).

II.B.1. The phenomenology of social anxiety disorder

II.B.1.a. Feared situations. The extent of the feared situations can vary from a specific social setting to all interpersonal contacts. Social situations include those where the individual may become the focus of attention of others, especially where performance might be assessed. These include common situations such as being engaged in a conversation, undertaking public presentations, being watched at work, meeting people or having interviews. Public speaking is the most common feared situation, both in specific SAnD and in generalized SAnD (Turner et al., 1992; Faravelli et al., 2000). In any case, the interference of the fear disrupts daily routines, occupational functioning and social life, and fear can appear both when imagining social situations and when being present in any of them.

The two different subtypes of SAnD are based on the number of social situations feared – if fears are limited to one or two situations (e.g. public speaking), then it is considered non-generalized SAnD – but if they occur in most circumstances, it is considered generalized SAnD (see below).

II.B.1.b. Feared cognitions. Cognitions in SAnD are based on interpersonal evaluation. Social phobic fear may be based on three factors: the inherent criticism of others, the likelihood of being negatively evaluated and the insecurity regarding the individual's ability to give a favourable impression of themselves to others. Many authors have suggested that the main concerns related to real-life situations in SAnD are being speechless, visibly distressed and socially awkward (Rapee and Heimberg, 1997) (Fig. 2).

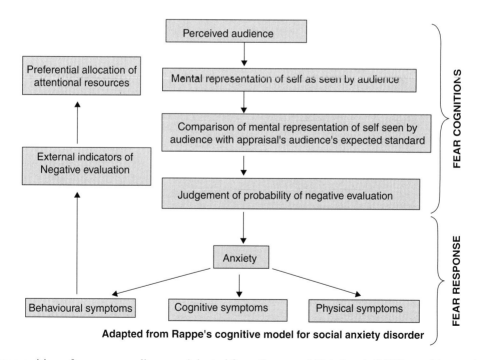

Fig. 2. Fear cognitions–fear response diagram. Adapted from Rapee and Heimberg's (1997) cognitive model for social anxiety disorder.

The literature has focused on four major approaches to describe the aetiology of social anxiety cognitions: the skills deficit model, the cognitive self-evaluation model, the classical conditioning model and the personality trait approach (Schlenker and Leary, 1982). There may be a basic bias in information processing in SAnD (Rapee and Lim, 1992); some authors have focused on the probability and cost estimates for outcomes in social situations and the threat posed by ambiguous and mildly negative social information (Hirsch and Clark, 2004).

II.B.1.c. Fear response.
Symptoms in SAnD can be divided into somatic and behavioural symptoms.

Somatic symptoms. Most patients with SAnD experience several somatic symptoms. Symptoms that are visible to others are more frequent among social phobic individuals when they are compared with those found in patients with PD. Blushing, twitching and stammering are more common, dizziness and dyspnoea are less common and other symptoms such as palpitations, sweating, trembling, muscle tension and GI symptoms are similar in both groups (Amies et al., 1983). However, the common feature is that all these symptoms are related to a definitive social or performance situation, or to the recollection or anticipation of such situations.

Avoidance and anxious anticipation. Behavioural manifestations of SAnD are avoidance, anxious anticipation and safety behaviours, avoidance being the greatest source of impairment (Nutt and Ballenger, 2005). Avoidance expression can range from avoiding any eye contact to minimizing all social contact outside the patient's immediate family. It has been considered that all these reactions prevent exposure to feared situations so that individuals with SAnD do not learn to overcome their fears (Clark and Wells, 1995).

Different models have proposed that anxious individuals are hypervigilant to threat (for review, see Mogg and Bradley, 1998). The vigilance–avoidance hypothesis by Mogg and Bradley (1998) suggests that hypervigilance is followed by avoidance of the threat stimulus, and all this process acts as a defensive function. It has been proposed that regarding social situations, hypervigilance–avoidance may result in the initial enhanced processing of threatening stimuli, yet the opportunity to habituate to, or to reappraise the stimulus as non-threatening is limited. In this case, the threat stimuli keep the capacity to produce anxiety and to be interpreted as threatening (for a review, see Bogels and Mansell, 2004).

Other models give support to the existence of an increased self-focused attention, and they explain that in social interactions, SAnD individuals divert much attention to themselves, therefore, having little attention for their task, to other individuals and their environment. As a result of this internal focus, they are assumed to engage in self-evaluation and become inconveniently aware of their fear and arousal and of possible flaws in their behaviour. These models also state that a lack of outward directed attention might result in actually impaired behaviour (for a review, see Clark and Wells, 1995; Rapee and Heimberg, 1997).

II.B.2. Subtypes of the disorder
Despite research identifying subtypes of social anxiety disorder, the topic remains controversial (Vriends et al., 2007). Currently, only two subtypes of SAnD have been distinguished: the generalized and non-generalized SAnD. In the generalized subtype of SAnD, individuals fear most social situations, while in non-generalized SAnD, one or two situations are feared but not the majority of situations. This distinction appears both in ICD-10 and DSM-IV classifications. However, it has yet to be proven that the course and response to treatment differs between the two types.

II.B.2.a. Generalized social anxiety.
In this subtype, most social situations are feared. There are usually more symptoms, and individuals have higher severity than in non-generalized SAnD. Individuals may also have greater impairment, an earlier age of onset and greater lifetime co-morbidity, especially with other anxiety disorders and depression (Stein and Chavira, 1998).

II.B.2.b. Non-generalized social anxiety. This is the more common of the two subtypes. As described before, it is usually related to a fear of one or two particular situations, public speaking being the most common one (Faravelli et al., 1989). It is considered to be not globally disabling, but patients can be substantially impaired, leading to an underachievement at work or school. It usually does not require medical help, but self-help programs that teach public skills are used and helpful (Stein, 1996).

After DSM-III-R included a 'generalized subtype' in SAnD, some researchers understood the term to be a quantitative dimension, meaning that it was based on the number of feared situations, while others provided a qualitative explanation in relation to most social situations, on the basis of the type of feared social situations (Turner et al., 1992).

The National Co-morbidity Survey (NCS) and other studies brought an epidemiological perspective to the clinical observation of subtypes of SAnD and even supported the existence of a specific public-speaking subtype, although this has not been supported elsewhere (Kessler et al., 1994; Stein et al., 1996).

II.B.3. Child and adolescent considerations

Although mild to moderate levels of social anxiety are usual (and probably necessary) in effective social functioning and developmental growth in children, SAnD is considered an extreme of this spectrum. SAnD phenomenology in children may differ markedly from adults (Velting and Albano, 2001).

II.B.3.a. Criteria consideration. Whereas ICD-10 does not mention paediatric populations, DMS-IV emphasizes developmental considerations in SAnD. Children must be capable of establishing social relationships with familiar people; thus, anxiety should be limited to certain contexts, not just to adults. In general, as children may experience transient periods of shyness during developmental periods, the duration of impairment of at least 6 months in people younger than 18 is required. Moreover, it is not necessary that they recognize the excessiveness or unreasonableness of their fear because of their cognitive limitations.

II.B.3.b. Phenomenology. SAnD symptoms in children include crying, tantrums, freezing, clinging or staying close to a familiar person as well as inhibited interactions manifesting as elective mutism. Common behaviours are refusing to participate in group play and staying on the periphery of social activities. However, over the past decades, little research has examined the psychopathology of SAnD in adolescents (Essau et al., 1999a, b) and children (Beidel et al., 1999). Moreover, most of the clinical and epidemiological childhood studies include data combining samples of children and adolescents even with different disorders, despite presentation symptoms varying by age group. In this case, results based on pre-adolescent samples may not be relevant for an adolescent population and vice versa.

Comparisons between younger versus older children have rarely been performed; a recent study by Alfano et al. (2006) comparing group differences in their clinical presentation stated that the presence of negative cognitions during social interaction tasks were only present in the adolescent group. Another study by Rao et al. (2007) also compared these subgroups concluding equivalent moderate levels of social distress and impairment for both children and adolescents. However, they found that adolescents presented a broader pattern of fear and avoidance when compared to younger children, resulting in increased social avoidance, fewer friendships and a stronger feeling of social isolation.

II.B.3.c. Behaviour inhibition, elective mutism and SAnD. Some authors support that early behavioural inhibition (BI) is a risk factor for the development of SAnD. BI describes a child with uncertain and reticent response to the presence of unfamiliar adults, peers and novel objects and events. Specific impairment in behaviourally inhibited children includes being slow to verbalize and approach others, keeping very close to the mother and a lack of spontaneity of comments and smiles directed at any examiner, and includes both behavioural and physiological reactions (for a review, see Kagan et al., 1988). In an attempt to explain this relation, social wariness is suggested to evolve into an extreme fear of social situations in those who develop SAnD (Schwartz et al., 1999; Velting and Albano, 2001).

II.B.4. Personality considerations

Avoidant personality disorder (APD) and SAnD were classified in two different axes in DSM-IV. However, on the basis of their overlap, many authors have questioned whether they are genuinely different, as there is great evidence of co-morbidity between them.

It may be that the only difference between them is the severity of the social anxiety and the social functioning, particularly that poor social skills distinguish APD patients from those with SAnD alone (Holt et al., 1992; Turner et al., 1992).

II.C. Clinical course

II.C.1. Age of onset

SAnD is an early-onset disorder in the majority of cases. The average age of onset is reported in between 12 and 16.6 years (Faravelli et al., 2000; Wittchen and Fehm, 2003; Fehm et al., 2005). There may be two peaks of incidence: before 5 and around 15, and onset appears to be earlier for the generalized subtype (Kessler et al., 1994; Wittchen and Fehm, 2003). Studies have shown that it is relatively rare for it to begin in adulthood, with incidence rates of 4–5 per 1,000 per year, and that these new cases are often secondary to other disorders, as panic disorder or depression.

II.C.2. Clinical course of the disorder

SAnD is generally regarded as a chronic condition. Fehm et al. (2005) reported in a recent epidemiological review a mean duration of 10 or more years, although high variability in the course was found. Nearly 80% of the individuals of their sample with SAnD received no treatment, and the mean age at first treatment was 27.2 years.

SAnD has on an average been associated with substantial unremitting course, especially as it often goes untreated, underscoring the need for healthcare initiatives designed to increase recognition and treatment. Its course seems to oscillate

around the diagnostic threshold and its remission has been shown to be the lowest of all the major anxiety disorders (Fehm et al., 2005).

II.D. Epidemiology and social impact

II.D.1. Prevalence

The key limitation of epidemiological studies in SAnD is its under-recognition, as patients are felt to be 'shy'. This may account for differences in estimated prevalence. In addition, differences between surveys in definitions and methods, including differences between ICD and DSM-IV criteria, may contribute to variation in prevalence estimates.

II.D.1.a. General population. Studies using instruments consistent with DSM-III-R and DSM-IV criteria suggested lifetime prevalence rates for SAnD ranging between 4.1 (Lepine and Lellouch, 1995) and 16%.

The most frequently cited international DSM-III-R prevalence estimate has been 13.3%, as determined by the NCS for the US adult population, making SAnD the most common anxiety disorder and the third most common psychiatric disorder (Kessler et al., 1994). The lifetime prevalence in adults in different countries has been assessed and it ranges from 3.9 to 13.7%; the median was 6.65%. Twelve-month prevalence ranged from 0.6 (Spain) to 7.9% (Norway), and the median was 2.0% (Fehm et al., 2005).

Epidemiological studies have shown a greater prevalence of SAnD in females. In general, the female-to-male ratio for the lifetime prevalence of SAnD varies between 1.5 and 2 females for 1 male, although in clinical setting the incidence seems to be roughly equal (Yonkers et al., 2001; Neal and Edelmann, 2003). This discrepancy has been interpreted to reflect that SAnD causes greater impact on the lives of males.

II.D.1.b. Children. Recent prevalence rates of SAnD in children and adolescents range from 0.5 to 4.0% (Chavira and Stein, 2000). As in adults, social anxiety in childhood has very high rates of co-morbidity.

II.D.1.c. Elderly. A recent study using data drawn from a large nationally representative sample of older adults from Canada ($N = 12,792$) estimated a lifetime and 12-month prevalence of SAnD of 4.94 and 1.32%, respectively. Current 12-month prevalence of SAnD declined with age and the disorder was more common in individuals with other psychiatric disorders (Cairney et al., 2007).

II.D.2. Social impact considerations

SAnD is a persistent condition that reduces quality of life considerably. Epidemiological data show its negative outcome in social functioning (family life and close relationships) and occupational (engaging jobs below the individual's level of qualification and higher risk of being unemployed) and educational domains (lower educational attainment, early leaving of school) (Schneier et al., 1994; Fehm et al., 2005). An increased suicide risk has also been found (Sareen et al., 2005).

The sequelae of SAnD in children include high levels of dysphoria, loneliness and generalized anxiety. Adolescents are reported to have poorer social functioning (less support from classmates, less social acceptance), fewer friendships, less intimacy or companionship and less support in their close friendships, with particular interference in the development of interpersonal relationships (La Greca and Lopez, 1998).

In a recent clinical study, Pelissolo et al. (2000) analysed 771 patients with DSM-IV SAnD, showing that a professional, social and medical burden could be specifically attributed to this disorder, independently of co-morbid disorders.

II.D.3. Specific considerations

Cultural variations in SAnD nature are seen when comparing different societies, with some extremely low and high rates reported (0–54%) (Fehm et al., 2005). Moreover, there are culturally distinct syndromes, e.g. in Japan, a syndrome named 'tajin kyofusho' is described, which is the fear that one's anxious behaviour may cause distress in others (Suzuki et al., 2003).

II.E. Conclusion

Initial indifference to SAnD led it to be called the 'neglected anxiety disorder' once. However, although there are difficulties in delineating SAnD from sub-syndromal social anxiety or shyness, SAnD is a common disorder, even when narrowly defined. Thus, it is essential to minimize its under-recognition and under-treatment, increasing early detection, especially among children.

III. Obsessive-compulsive disorder

III.A. Introduction

The key rationale to categorize OCD as an anxiety disorder has been for a long time the central role anxiety plays in OCD, reflected in obsessions and behavioural or cognitive compulsions. However, there is still controversy about this symptom-focused reasoning (Tynes et al., 1990; Bartz and Hollander, 2006). Until further research is done, DSM-IV and ICD-10 currently rate the phenomenology of OCD similarly (see Nutt and Malizia, 2006).

III.B. Clinical features

III.B.1. The phenomenology of OCD

The essential symptoms in OCD are both obsessions and compulsions. Symptom shifting is frequent and many individuals may present with different combinations of symptoms despite the predominance of one of them. Many authors suggest that obsessions may be the primary phenomena in OCD while compulsions could be a repeated behaviour present in other disorders.

Individuals need to recognize the unreasonable or excessive nature of either obsessions or compulsions at some point of the illness. Symptoms must cause marked distress and be time-consuming (more than 1 h a day) or significantly interfere with the person's normal routine, and the specific temporal criteria of 2 weeks are needed in ICD-10 classification.

III.B.1.a. Obsessions

Description. Obsessive symptoms include ideas, thoughts, impulses and images. The term obsession only relates to the recurrent, persistent and intrusive nature of the thought, which was once named 'ego-dystonic', meaning that the individual feels upset or repelled by them though they recognize them as emanating from themselves (i.e. not being imposed from outside as it happens in schizophrenia).

Types. Obsessions are remarkably limited and stereotypical, making it possible to establish different subcategories. Common obsessions are described below in frequency order.

Contamination. This may be the most prevalent obsession. Repetitive thoughts about dirt and germs are present. Individuals avoid sources of contamination which can differ considerably, as doorknobs, electric switches or newspapers. It often leads to excessive cleanliness, as repetitive hand washing.

Pathological doubt. This obsession is also very prevalent, perhaps even the most prevalent. Doubt is frequently associated with the feeling of guilt. Although doubts can be about concrete, possibly dangerous situations, some individuals may not even be sure why they doubt, it then becomes a form of free-floating anxiety.

Aggression or harm. The content of this obsession involves fear to harm people around, as harm and aggressive impulses are present. Frequently, they are directed at the one person most valuable to the patient. These thoughts have a different nature than violent thoughts occurring in psychopathic individuals (Heyman et al., 2006).

Sexuality. This subtype may focus on various forbidden or perverse sexual thoughts, images and impulses: unwanted sexual content involving friends, family or children; violent sexual behaviour content; content related to homosexual activity and sex content with animals. These are always reprehensible thoughts. Rates of sexual obsessions among subjects with OCD vary, up to

reports of 24% (Foa et al., 1995). Sexual obsessions are thought to be more common in men (Lensi et al., 1996). They are associated with poorer insight and treatment response.

Religion. These convictions become sometimes a problem to clinicians, as it is difficult to draw the line between devotion and obsession. Such thoughts may be experienced as blasphemous, leading to repetitive silent prayer or confessions.

Need for symmetry/precision/order. Having objects or events in a certain order or in a perfectly symmetrical position. The associated compulsions to perform certain actions over and over again may mean that a large amount of time is required to complete a simple task. Thus the obsessions in this subtype often lead to a disabling slowness in achieving daily goals of living.

III.B.1.b. Compulsions

Description. Compulsions are stereotyped behaviours whose function is either to reduce the distress caused by the obsession or to prevent an unlikely event linked to it.

Types. Certain compulsions relate commonly to particular obsessions, like checking and needing to ask questions in pathological doubt, washing and cleaning in contamination obsessions, and creating symmetry or order and needing to be precise in the symmetry obsession. Often compulsions are performed a specific number of times, as patients often have their own specific number.

Common compulsions are listed below in order of frequency.

Checking. Individuals need to check especially that switches are off, doors and gas taps are locked, timetables read and re-read, passport is where it should be, etc. The attempt to resist or refrain from checking leads to difficulty in concentrating and to endless intrusion of anxiety and uncertainties, finally resulting in giving in and checking again.

Washing. This is seen especially in relation with contaminating thoughts and commonly, individuals have the need to ensure they are not contaminated or dirty. They often spend several hours showering, cleaning or washing hands and typically tend to avoid common sources of contamination such as newspapers or handshakes with other individuals.

Counting. A less specific compulsion, individuals here can count different items and different number of times. This compulsion is frequently used to neutralize aggressive and sexual obsessions.

Need to ask or confess. Individuals confess events or feelings. Commonly, individuals later regret their confessions.

Symmetry and precision. This compulsion relates to order obsession. Individuals spend long time keeping objects in a very precise and symmetric way. At work, they may take several hours to organize their desk each day and take a long time to organize routine activities.

Hoarding. This is a complex compulsive behaviour where individuals may refuse to throw out their old stuff, as they fear throwing away important things in the process.

Fig. 3 shows how obsessions and compulsions may interrelate.

III.B.1.c. Avoidance behaviour. Because of the powerful role obsessions and compulsions play in a person's life, individuals with OCD often avoid events or situations that trigger their obsessive or compulsive behaviours; thus, avoidance behaviour

is also a central feature of OCD (Wood and Tolin, 2002).

III.B.2. Anxiety considerations

Many authors have claimed that OCD anxiety symptoms are secondary, but clinical experience suggests that this is not always the case, suggesting that anxiety in OCD can be both primary (i.e. precede or occur simultaneously with the disorder) or secondary (occurring as a consequence of interruption of rituals or from obsessional thoughts).

One way of conceptualizing the relation of anxiety to OCD is considering that there may be two primary sources of anxiety – danger-related and desire-related, shown in Fig. 4 by Nutt and Malizia (2006). It is suggested that in danger-related anxiety, primary anxiety is associated with the fear evoked by thoughts, and it possibly emerges from an intolerability of uncertainty relating to safety of self or others, similar to the symptom of worry in GAD. Nevertheless, the secondary anxiety exists, as behaviours are anxiety-reducing because they remove the danger threat and are part of primitive rituals. Therefore, we take the position that in danger-related OCD, anxiety is both primary and secondary (Nutt and Malizia, 2006).

Desire-related anxiety is present when internal impulses appear. Sufferers feel that they have to resist them and are anxious that they may not be able to control them. OCD is, therefore, a complex mixture of anxiety, behaviours and habits, each of which may be amenable to specific treatments that might differ at different stages in the evolution of the disorder.

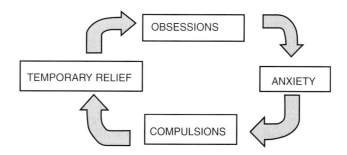

Fig. 3. Schematic representation of the inter-relation of obsessions and compulsions in Obsessive-Compulsive disorder.

374

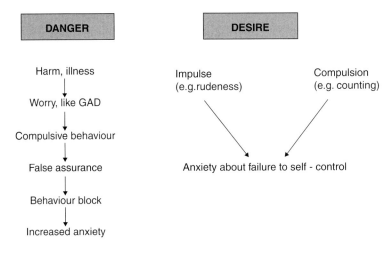

Adapted from Nutt and Malizia

Fig. 4. Anxious thought content. Adapted from Nutt and Malizia (2006).

III.B.3. Personality considerations

Obsessive-compulsive personality disorder (OCPD) is a differential diagnosis for OCD and may be a precursor stage. However, some authors suggest that OCD patients are also more likely to have a Cluster C personality disorder in general than personality disorders from Cluster A or Cluster B, and that OCPD is not necessarily the most common one (Wu et al., 2006).

III.B.4. Subtypes of the disorder: a current dimensional approach

There have been different attempts to delimitate subcategories in OCD, either following patterns of genetic transmission, neurobiological variables or treatment response.

III.B.4.a. Clinical features approach. Three of the most interesting cluster approaches to subdivide OCD have been the age of onset, a positive family history of OCD and the presence of co-morbid tic disorder (for a review, see Miguel et al., 2005).

Early-onset OCD has been associated with higher male OCD rate, a greater prevalence of tic disorder and trichotillomania and increased family OCD (Hemmings et al., 2004). Individuals with co-morbid tics present an earlier onset age, are more likely to be male and have a family history of OCD, and experience symmetry symptoms.

III.B.4.b. Symptom-based approach. A study conducted by Leckman et al. in 1997 found four factors of OCD symptoms: obsessions and checking, symmetry and ordering, cleanliness and washing, and hoarding, being their results congruent with some earlier reports.

Mataix-Cols et al. (2005) conducted a recent review of factor-analytic studies related to symptom-based approaches. They stated that symptom dimensions derived from these studies are not mutually exclusive as the focus of their model is the symptoms or behaviours, not groups of patients. They found evidence for at least four symptom dimensions, which are contamination and cleaning, hoarding, symmetry and order, and obsessions and checking. Distinct patterns of co-morbidity, genetic transmission, neural substrates and treatment response were found among them (Fig. 5).

III.B.5. Child and adolescent considerations

Obsessions related to fear of harm and separation, compulsions without obsessions, and rituals involving family members are common in younger patients. Some authors claim that childhood

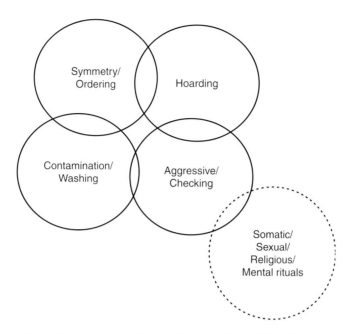

Fig. 5. Schematic representation of symptom clustering in Obsessive-Compulsive Disorder. Adapted from Mataix-Cols et al. (2006).

OCD frequently presents with obsessions based on magical ideation that do not necessarily correspond well with overt symptoms (McKay et al., 2004). A clinical study conducted by Rettew et al. (1992) supported that OCD is more variable in children than in adults. Paediatric OCD is more difficult to identify. Patients commonly lack the insight related to the nature of their obsessions and they have undeveloped verbal expression (Geller, 2006).

III.B.6. Cultural aspects
It may be that the phenomenology of OCD is relatively independent of cultural variations. The unique exception to this rule appears to be the content of the obsessions in which cultural factors may play a significant role. A recent study conducted in Brazil showed that a predominance of aggressive and religious obsessions was found only in Brazilian and Middle Eastern samples, respectively (Fontenelle et al., 2004).

III.C. Clinical course

III.C.1. Age of onset
Age-at-onset data have shown a bimodal distribution of age of onset in OCD, with one peak in preadolescent childhood and another in young adulthood. Childhood onset seems to be associated with a markedly increased risk for familial transmission of OCD, tic disorders and ADHD (Geller, 2006).

Many authors have described a slow onset of symptoms, taking years for phenomenological issues to become clear. However, rapid onset has been reported in relation with stress events.

A study comparing participants with late-onset OCD and early-onset OCD found that the early-onset group had higher rates of lifetime panic disorder, eating disorders and obsessive-compulsive personality disorder than late-onset OCD. There were also differences in the types of symptoms first noticed as well as on rates of current obsessions and compulsions (Pinto et al., 2006).

III.C.2. Course of the disorder

OCD has a typical gradual onset and a continuous course regardless of age at onset though it may come on suddenly in women after childbirth. Frequently, there is a substantial gap between its onset and the initiation of treatment. It frequently coexists with other psychiatric symptoms and leads to serious social and occupational impairment (Pinto et al., 2006).

However, good prognosis is associated with good social and occupational adjustment and an episodic nature of symptoms; childhood onset, bizarre compulsions and the presence of co-morbid psychiatric disorders are related to a chronic and severe course of the disorder (Nutt and Ballenger, 2005).

III.D. Epidemiology and social impact

III.D.1. Prevalence

III.D.1.a. General population. Earlier prevalence of OCD was estimated at around 0.05% (Nutt and Ballenger, 2005). However, in the last two decades, studies have suggested worldwide prevalence of OCD in around 2% of the general population, or even greater (Sasson et al., 1997). Robins et al. (1984) estimated a prevalence of 2.5% and several subsequent studies in the USA and other countries have supported this finding (Hollander, 1993; Angst et al., 2004).

Many studies have found slight gender differences in OCD prevalence rates, with a mild preponderance among women (Angst et al., 2004). However, some others report equal gender representation or a very slight female preponderance (Geller, 2006).

III.D.1.b. Children. The prevalence of OCD in childhood is similar to that for adults but has a different gender representation to adults, being clearly male predominant (Zohar et al., 1992; Masi et al., 2005). It shows high rates of associations with tic, mood and anxiety disorders, similar to the patterns in adults, but also association with disruptive behaviour disorders (ADHD and oppositional defiant disorder) and other specific and pervasive developmental disorders (Geller, 2006).

III.D.1.c. Elderly. OCD is one of the most frequently occurring psychiatric disorders in this age group with reports of atypical manifestations (Calamari et al., 1994).

III.D.2. Social impact considerations

Despite effective pharmacotherapy, OCD has a major effect on psychosocial functioning and quality of life. Social impairment includes low self-steem, lowered career aspirations and having fewer successful relationships, impact on family members and interference with their work functioning.

III.E. Conclusion

OCD is a multi-dimensional and aetiologically heterogeneous condition. It is currently proposed that it should be removed from the anxiety disorders category in the DSM-V and clustered with other putative obsessive-compulsive spectrum disorders. While classifying OCD into mutually exclusive subcategories would be a step back, a dimensional perspective could be to some extent a step forward, as mono-symptomatic patients are rare (Watson, 2005).

Whichever the new model is, it should provide clinicians and researchers with a more complete picture to use specific pharmacological treatments and behavioural interventions.

IV. Panic disorder

IV.A. Introduction

It was in the 18th and 19th centuries that panic symptoms were first described with attacks of 'overwhelming anxiety with dyspnoea (shortness of breath)', vertigo, sweating, palpitations and avoidance that reached a disabling level. Freud observed that agoraphobic patients presented a common state of panic and fear of repetition of this panic state when they believed they could not escape the situation. Kraepelin also contributed to the conceptualization of the diagnosis describing spontaneous panic attacks with fears of dying, somatic symptoms and classic agoraphobia.

Klein (1981) was the first to describe a pharmacological dissociation between panic anxiety and more generalized anxiety; imipramine, a tricyclic antidepressant that acts to block the reuptake of NE and 5HT, was discovered to be effective in panic. This discovery led to a reconceptualization of panic anxiety with three clusters of symptoms: spontaneous panic attacks, anticipatory anxiety and agoraphobic avoidance. PD was officially recognized in DSM-III, creating two diagnostic categories: (a) panic disorder and (b) agoraphobia with panic.

IV.B. Clinical features

IV.B.1. The phenomenology of panic disorder
The essential symptom in PD is the panic attack, which must be spontaneous. However, in DSM-IV, the additional symptom of 1-month anticipatory anxiety following a panic attack is required for the diagnosis. Agoraphobic avoidance can be an additional condition in PD in both ICD-10 and DSM-IV, but agoraphobia is considered a separate disorder when PD criteria are not fulfilled.

IV.B.1.a. The phenomenon of a panic attack
Description. A panic attack is defined as an abruptly developed feeling of intense anxiety or fear present for a discrete period of time, which has its peak in 2–10 min and involves different cognitive and physical symptoms (DSM-IV). At least four of the following symptoms are required, which are either cognitive or somatic symptoms in both DSM-IV and ICD-10 classifications:

Choking feelings, discomfort, fear of losing control, depersonalization, fear of going crazy, fear of dying, derealization, accelerated heart rate, palpitations, pounding heart, flushes, light headed, feeling unsteady or faint, numbness, tingling, chills, sweating, chest pain, nausea, trembling or shaking, shortness of breath or abdominal distress, or hot flushes.

Nature. Panic attacks can occur as a unique symptom in a wide range of mental disorders, especially in anxiety disorders, being very frequent in PTSD and SAnD. Within phobic conditions, panic attacks appear in specific feared situations, although they can paradoxically also occur in situations perceived as safe (Clark, 1986). In SAnD, they occur in association with public speaking, in OCD related to obsessional thoughts or a failure to carry out a compulsive act, and in PTSD, they are related to a violent assault or another traumatic incident. They may also include other psychiatric conditions like schizophrenia and depression. The nature of panic attacks can vary, but in PD some attacks must be spontaneous (Clark, 1986).

Frequency. The frequency of the attacks varies considerably from several attacks daily to weekly or monthly. ICD-10 considers a sub-classification based on this item: *moderate PD*, when at least four panic attacks are present in a 4-week period and *severe PD*, when at least four panic attacks are present per week in a 4-week period.

Cognitions of panic. There are two major viewpoints with regard to cognitions in PD. While one model suggests that the cognitive process is the source of panic (Clark's cognitive model), the other assumes that cognitive symptoms develop as a response to an unexplained physiological state (Klein's model).

Klein's physiological model: "beyond fear". The relative specificity of respiratory symptoms during spontaneous panic attacks and the evidence that patients with PD are especially sensitive to carbon dioxide (CO_2) inhalation led Klein to hypothesize that PD is a disturbance in a suffocation alarm system in which a physiological misinterpretation of suffocative produces respiratory distress, hyperventilation and panic (Klein, 1984).

This theoretical approach stated that fear and cognitive symptoms of anxiety are thus not central to the core concept of human PD, at least at the onset of the disorder, suggesting that such activations occur only later in the clinical evolution of PD when subjects have started developing anticipatory worry and anxiety. Building on this approach, Klein suggests that animal models of human PD should be designed to better reflect the distinction between unconditioned, sudden spells of physical anxiety, and the conditioned components associated to repeated occurrence of intense, sudden and originally unconditioned physical symptoms of internal impending alarm.

On this basis, it has been argued that it is incorrect to constrain investigation of the specific neural systems underlying PD to the fear and anxiety systems, suggesting that clinical observations of therapeutic and panicogenic substances are still needed (Klein, 1999). Specific responses to panicogenic agents observable in animal models can thus be taken as endophenotypes for the study of human PD.

Clark's cognitive model. Clark's model is based on the belief that a catastrophic misunderstanding of certain sensations is central to PD, and these derive from an alteration in their perception by the patient, which exaggerates the extent of the danger. It suggests that perceived threat leads to an apprehensive state accompanied by increased perception of body sensations. When interpreted in a catastrophic way, apprehension increases, and again body sensations increase, producing a vicious circle that becomes the panic attack (Clark, 1986). Several internal bodily sensations can be misinterpreted, mainly sensations involved in normal anxiety responses (palpitations, breathlessness, dizziness, etc.). However, this theory has been criticized, as it does not accommodate the variation in type and intensity of symptoms experienced during the attacks and does not explain why panic commonly occurs in states such as during sleep and relaxation.

Somatic symptoms. Somatic symptoms can lead to the misdiagnosis of several medical conditions, especially cardiologic and neurological diagnoses. Some researchers have been interested in the high cost of misdiagnosing non-cardiac chest pain, as it is important to recognize panic attacks and to distinguish them from cardiac disease, so avoiding the use of healthcare resources (Katon, 1990; Fleet et al., 2000; Potokar and Nutt, 2000). In a similar fashion, symptoms of choking and nausea relate to GI medicine; sweating to endocrinology; dizziness, trembling and paraesthesias are related to neurology; and flushes to the menopause clinic.

IV.B.1.b. Anticipatory anxiety. Some individuals who experience panic attacks do not have anxiety symptoms at other times. However, other patients develop anticipatory anxiety, which are considered essential in the DSM-IV criteria:

1. persistent concern about having another attack,
2. worry about the implications or consequences of the attacks or
3. significant behavioural changes related to the attacks.

IV.B.1.c. Agoraphobia–avoidance. The literal meaning of the term agoraphobia is 'fear of the market place', but the essential symptom is the anxiety in places or situations from where there is

1. difficulty in escaping or embarrassment in the event of panic or
2. difficulty in asking for help in the event of panic.

Because anticipated fear as well as internal stimuli may trigger the emergence of unpleasant bodily sensations, individuals start to restrict their activities to environments they see as safe, avoiding situations where attacks have occurred previously or not. Being alone outside home or being home alone, being in a crowd of people, travelling (especially by bus, train or aeroplane) and being on a bridge or on an elevator can be the most common. In the unlikely event of being faced with these situations, they are endured with marked distress or anxiety about having symptoms, and commonly require the presence of a companion.

IV.B.2. Specific subtypes of the disorder
Two symptom clusters, respiratory and cognitive, have been identified. The cognitive cluster focuses on the feelings of fear and danger (Clark, 1986).

The respiratory cluster is defined by the presence of respiratory symptoms, especially hyperventilation, shortness of breath, choking and smothering sensations. It relates either to the hyperventilation theory of panic by Ley (1985) or to the suffocation alarm theory of panic by Klein (1993).

Briggs et al. reported some data related to this issue evaluating 1,168 patients as part of the data of the Cross-National Collaborative Panic Study. They made a phenomenological description of two groups characterized by the presence or absence of prominent respiratory symptoms. The respiratory subgroup experienced more choking, smothering sensations, chest pain, numbness, tingling and fear of dying, and suffered more spontaneous panic attacks. The group without prominent respiratory symptoms experienced more palpitations, dizziness, flushes, trembling, sweating, and fear of going crazy or losing control, nausea and depersonalization, and suffered more situational panic attacks. A better response to imipramine was found in the respiratory subgroup, whereas the group without prominent respiratory symptoms responded better to alprazolam (Briggs et al., 1993).

The respiratory group has also been proposed to have more nocturnal panic attacks and have later panic onset, longer illness duration, higher cigarette consumption and increased agoraphobia (Nardi et al., 2004).

IV.B.2.a. Nocturnal panic. Many patients report nocturnal panic attacks in addition to daytime panic; however, they are rarely the only panic attacks the person experiences. Nocturnal panic leads to sudden awakening with a discrete period of intense fear or discomfort accompanied by marked physiological activation. It occurs in non-REM sleep, mostly in stages 2 and 3, between 30 and 225 min after sleep onset, and only occasionally happens more than once per night. The return to sleep is difficult because individuals become fearful to sleep in case they experience another attack. Avoidance of sleep may increase nocturnal panic because of sleep deprivation. A clinical presentation featuring multiple nocturnal panic attacks has also been well documented in PTSD (Craske and Tsao, 2005).

IV.B.2.b. Limited symptom attacks. Limited symptom attacks are simply panic attacks that do not meet DSM-IV or ICD-10 criteria for full panic attacks since there are less than 4 of the 13 recognized panic symptoms.

IV.B.3. Child and adolescent considerations

IV.B.3.a. Phenomenology. While some authors suggest that PD can emerge in childhood, others claim that antecedent childhood distress is found with excessive fearfulness and separation anxiety, but cannot be considered true panic disorder (Moreau and Weissman, 1992; Biederman et al., 1997; Diler et al., 2004).

The diagnosis of PD in children is difficult. First, their cognitive ability may be limited such that their awareness and ability to label symptoms may be less advanced than in adults. Moreover, it is also difficult to establish the boundary between phobia and panic symptoms in this subgroup.

Frequent symptoms in children are palpitations, trembling/shaking, nausea, abdominal distress, chills, hot flushes, sweating and dizziness. Some studies reported a major prevalence of dizziness, faintness and nausea in females compared to males.

IV.B.3.b. Separation anxiety and panic. Klein proposed that separation anxiety and disruptions in personal relationships in childhood are antecedents to adult PD and agoraphobia. While there is some evidence for this separation anxiety hypothesis (Battaglia et al., 1995; Pine et al., 1998), other retrospective familial aggregation studies have found that patterns of anxiety disorders do not support a specific association between childhood and adulthood disorders (Lipsitz et al., 1994; Aschenbrand et al., 2003).

IV.B.4. Medical associations

PD has shown high association rates with several medical conditions as asthma (Hasler et al., 2005a, b), the irritable bowel syndrome (Garakani et al., 2003), hypertension (Davies et al., 1999) and true cardiac illness (Katon, 1990).

IV.C. Clinical course

IV.C.1. Age of onset

The peak incidence of PD has been reported between 15 and 19 years of age, with nearly 20% of adults with PD reporting their first panic attack before age 10, even some reports at age 4; it is rare for PD to begin after the age of 40. Organic causes (e.g. thyroid and other endocrine disorders) and contributing medical problems should be carefully considered in later-onset presentations. It has been suggested that those who present later in life have less positive family history and disability and fewer symptoms (Raj et al., 1993).

IV.C.2. Clinical course of the disorder

Some studies suggest that it is an oversimplification to regard PD as a chronic condition. This is demonstrated in the comparison of lifetime, 12- and 1-month prevalence rates from the two large US epidemiological studies conducted over the last 15 years. Results suggest that there may be a subgroup of PD patients whose condition tends to be more chronic and follows a course progressing from situational to unexpected panic attacks,

phobic avoidance and full-blown agoraphobia. Many of the patients of this group remain without receiving clinical treatment. The available evidence for shorter follow-up periods (up to 6 years) suggests that full remission might occur in approximately 33% of patients who have undergone clinical treatment. At the other end of the spectrum of those patients who have received specialized psychiatric care, 20% follows an unremitting and severe chronic course.

Taken together, results suggest that the frequency and intensity of panic attacks at baseline have no predictive importance. Instead, a longer duration of the disorder and the presence of agoraphobia at baseline seem to be connected with a less favourable course and outcome.

The first panic attack is usually mediated by environmental stress factors; this then conditions inter-panic anxiety, increasing autonomic distress and sensitization, which lead to anticipatory anxiety and avoidance (see Fig. 6) (Klein, 1981).

It is thought that after the first spontaneous panic attack, there is a 33% risk of developing PD and a 20% risk of developing agoraphobia. A recent study conducted by Kessler et al. (2006) replicated this course model.

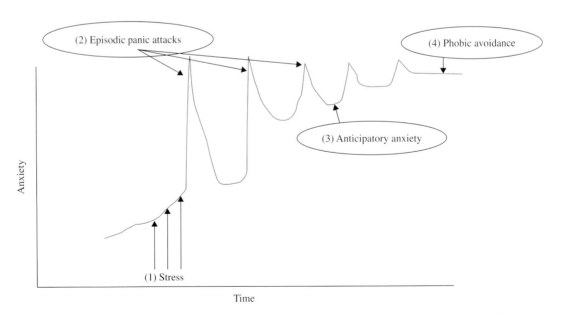

Fig. 6. Schematic representation of development of panic disorder, adapted from Klein (1981).

IV.D. Epidemiology and social impact

IV.D.1. Prevalence

IV.D.1.a. General population. Epidemiological studies have advanced the understanding of PD (Bland et al., 1988; Wittchen et al., 1992; Sheikh et al., 2002). Results from the NCS reported by Grant et al. (2006) estimated 12-month and lifetime prevalence rates in PD without agoraphobia up to 1.6 and 4.0%, exceeding those found in individuals with PD and agoraphobia, which were 0.6 and 1.1%, respectively. Rates of 12-month and lifetime agoraphobia without panic were extremely low, 0.05 and 0.17% (Grant et al., 2006). Kessler et al., 2006 replicated these data, estimating 4.7% for lifetime prevalence and 2.8% for 12-month prevalence. They also estimated lifetime and 12-month prevalence of panic attacks, which appeared to be 28.3 and 11.2%, respectively.

The differences between these studies could be attributable to the use of the more precise version of the CIDI DSM-IV than the CIDI DSM-III-R, supporting a past underestimation (Kessler et al., 2006). Some of these results suggest that PD with agoraphobia may be a more severe variant of PD and that agoraphobia should be a distinct clinical entity as defined in the DSM-IV.

However, certain issues related to panic epidemiology are still poorly understood, the main one being the fact that many people have isolated panic attacks that do not meet criteria for PD. Because of the impairment they cause, they have led to the view that panic attacks are fairly non-specific risk markers for psychopathology (Kessler et al., 2006).

IV.D.1.b. Children. Despite being considered less common in youth, the prevalence rates of PD in the community samples ranges between 0.5–5 and 0.2–10% in paediatric psychiatric clinics, notwithstanding the use of different criteria (Lewinsohn et al., 1993; Reed and Wittchen, 1998; Essau et al., 1999a, b).

Hayward et al. (2000) conducted a prospective study from a sample ($N = 2,365$) assessed over a 4-year period to identify risk factors for onset of panic attacks in adolescents to evaluate the risk factors such as negative affectivity, female sex, anxiety sensitivity and childhood separation anxiety disorder. Anxiety sensitivity appeared to be a specific factor that increased the risk for four-symptom panic attacks in adolescents, while negative affectivity appeared to be a non-specific risk factor for panic attacks and major depression.

IV.D.2. Social impact considerations

On an average, patients with PD use primary care three more times than the general population, also use emergency departments and inpatient and outpatient facilities (Fleet et al., 2000).

They often have financial problems, increased work absenteeism and lower productivity, and are more likely to be unemployed. They also have high levels of family and social dysfunction. A relatively higher risk of suicide has also been reported (Mendlowicz and Stein, 2000; Sareen et al., 2005).

IV.E. Conclusion

PD is a common disabling disorder. It has evolved from its early unitary conceptualization to a more heterogeneous syndrome associated with subtypes of phenomenological patterns and different medical conditions. Therefore, the difficulty in recognition and treatment of this disorder is increased by its complexity. Further research and approaches to the underlying neurobiology and phenomenology will surely improve the development of specific treatments.

V. Generalized anxiety disorder

V.A. Introduction

In spite of the fact that GAD is one of the most common anxiety disorders, it remains under-diagnosed and under-treated in clinical practice (Kessler et al., 1994). The concept of generalized anxiety disorder emerged from an overarching anxiety disorder diagnosis described by Freud as 'anxiety neurosis'. This syndromical description included four principal clinical features: general irritability, chronic apprehension/anxious expectation, anxiety attacks and secondary phobic avoidance and later appeared in DSM-I and -II.

However, once it became clear that there were several different anxiety disorders related to this construct, GAD was recognized as being a separate disorder from panic disorder and phobic conditions in DSM-III in which it appeared as a residual category or diagnosis of exclusion used for anxiety presentations that lacked the discrete attacks or situational fear and avoidance typical of these other disorders (Noyes et al., 1987). Diagnostic criteria were refined in DSM-III-R moving away from the notion of a residual category to provide more specific diagnostic criteria, with notably the addition of a requirement of a six month duration, while in DSM-IV core symptom of 'excessive or unrealistic worry' was outlined, underlining a complete departure from the residual category approach of DSM-III.

V.B. Clinical features

Despite the fact that diagnostic criteria for generalized anxiety disorder have undergone many revisions there is ample evidence to underpin its existence as a distinct disorder encompassing generalized and persistent anxiety and associated somatic symptoms (Watson, 2005).

V.B.1. The phenomenology of GAD
V.B.1.a. The phenomenon of worry. The existence of worry is essential in the diagnosis of GAD in current classifications.

The description of worry. The existence of worry is the main symptom in GAD. The approach to the term 'worry' has changed over the years. In DSM-III-R, it was redefined as 'apprehensive expectation'. In DSM-IV, the emphasis of 'lack of control' was the main feature of worry. The content or the degree to which the worry was unreasonable was not important anymore (Brown et al., 1994). ICD-10 does not specify the nature of worry, but added prominent tension and feelings of apprehension to its description.

Cognitions of worry. Studies suggest that specific worries may be more predominant in GAD, observing two different groups of worries: immediate problems and remote events. Dugas et al. (1998a,

b) found out that this second group may be a more specific distinctive feature of GAD. Recent data also supported that GAD patients report higher levels of intolerance to uncertainty and a more negative problem orientation (Dugas et al., 2005). Routine life situations such as job or career, misfortune to or health of family members, finances or minor matters related to home or time management, safety of children, interpersonal conflicts or the issue of acceptance by others are the most common. Patients usually have insight and realize that the extent of worry is out of proportion of the actual likelihood of the most feared outcomes.

V.B.1.b. Somatic symptoms. Somatic symptoms are essential criteria in current GAD classifications. In the early stages, they were included in three major clusters: (1) motor tension, (2) autonomic hyperactivity and (3) vigilance and scanning. However, new subcategories of symptoms emerged in current more recent research studies (Dugas et al., 2005).

DSM-IV considerations. Some authors suggested the removal of the autonomic hyperactivity symptoms concluding they were rare in GAD (Marten et al., 1993), and DSM-IV criteria excluded these. The remaining symptoms related to motor tension and vigilance are listed below:

- restlessness or feeling keyed up or on edge,
- being easily fatigued (probably secondary to increased muscle tension),
- difficulty in concentrating or mind going blank,
- irritability,
- muscle tension,
- sleep disturbance (difficulty in falling or staying asleep, or restless unsatisfying sleep).

This classification requires three of the somatic symptoms above. In the case of childhood GAD diagnosis, only one item is required.

ICD-10 considerations. ICD-10 gave more prominence to somatic symptoms (Tyrer and Baldwin, 2006). At least one symptom of autonomic arousal was essential for the diagnosis, together with three other symptoms that are subcategorized as follows, four of them being needed overall.

Autonomic arousal symptoms: palpitations or pounding heart or accelerated heart rate, sweating, trembling, shaking or dry mouth (one needed for the diagnosis).

Symptoms involving chest pain: difficulty in breathing, feeling of choking, chest pain or discomfort and nausea or abdominal distress.

Symptoms involving mental state: feeling dizzy, unsteady, faint or light headed, derealization or depersonalization, fear of losing control, going crazy or fear of dying.

General symptoms: hot flushes or cold chills, numbness or tingling sensations, muscle tension, restlessness and inability to relax, feeling keyed up on edge or mentally tense and a sensation of a lump in the throat or difficulty in swallowing.

Non-specific symptoms: exaggerated response to minor surprises; being startled, difficulty in concentrating or mind going blank, irritability, difficulty in getting to sleep because of worry or anxiety.

V.B.2. Child and adolescent considerations

In general, child and adolescent populations, sub-clinical anxiety symptoms are common and stable, especially in boys, and cause impairments in school achievement (Masi et al., 1999, 2004).

Some clinical studies report that children are highly symptomatic, presenting with feelings of tension, apprehension, reassurance, irritability, high sensitivity, negative self-image and physical complaints. The need for reassurance is more frequent in children than in adolescents. Physical complaints form a percentage of symptoms. Children tend to be very fearful of novelty and have a higher natural tendency to separation anxiety and to school missing and refusal (Wagner, 2001).

Their worries relate to school performance and can extend to social situations and natural issues (pollution, contamination, earthquakes, storms, etc.).

V.C. Clinical course

V.C.1. Age of onset

Many individuals report feeling anxious for their entire lives and over half of the patients report onset of anxiety in childhood or adolescence. Onset is typically suggested in the late teenage years, late 20s or early 30s, most of the times before the 40s (Wittchen et al., 1994).

Some data report a mean age of onset of 8.8 years, although a recent study conducted in the USA has estimated a much later mean onset age of 32.7 years (Grant et al., 2005). Other epidemiological surveys suggest a bimodal distribution, with peaks of both early onset and late onset (Blazer, 1991; Last et al., 1992). While the early onset has been described to be associated with problems of adjustment and childhood domestic disturbances, late onset bears relation to stressful life events (Blazer et al., 1987; Hoehn-Saric et al., 1993).

V.C.2. Course of the disorder

GAD has a chronic course, often persisting for a decade or longer. A prospective naturalistic study ($N = 711$ adults) conducted in the USA estimated that the likelihood of remission was 0.15 after 1 year and 0.25 after 2 years. The probability of becoming asymptomatic from all psychiatric symptoms was only 0.08 (Yonkers et al., 1996), and another study highlighted the lower likelihood of recovery from GAD compared with major depression (Baldwin et al., 2005). In contrast to this, Grant et al. (2005) estimated that the average duration of GAD episode was 11.1 months and that the average number of episodes was 3.4; differences between studies may be accounted for by different criteria (e.g. age at onset first symptoms versus full syndrome). Moderate-to-severe social disability is present in nearly 33% of the GAD patients, increasing to 59% in case of co-morbidity with major depression (Nutt et al., 2002).

V.D. Epidemiology and social impact

V.D.1. Prevalence

V.D.1.a. General population. The high prevalence of concurrent psychiatric disorders is the main problem in GAD. After DSM-III, several community-based surveys estimated a prevalence rate for GAD of 0.5–6.4%, being the lifetime prevalence 4–6.6%, with a 12-month prevalence between 1.6 and 2.5% (Baldwin et al., 2005). Higher prevalence rates were found if ICD-10 criteria were used, probably as a result of a broader definition of worrying and the requirement of less somatic symptoms in ICD-10.

In the first study conducted to estimate the prevalence rates of DSM-III disorders at a national scale, the national survey of psychotherapeutic drug use stated GAD to be the most prevalent disorder, 6.4% (Uhlenhuth et al., 1983). Faravelli et al. (1989) evaluated the prevalence of DSM-III-R GAD, estimating 2 and 3.9% in current and lifetime GAD, respectively. Wacker et al., 1992 compared DSM-III-R and ICD-10 GAD prevalence rates, stating that ICD-10 prevalence was four times higher than in DSM-III-R.

The NCS conducted in the USA was one of the largest epidemiological surveys (Kessler et al., 1994). The current prevalence rates for GAD were 1.6%, 3.1% for 12-month GAD and 5.1% for lifetime GAD. When ICD-10 classification was used, prevalence increased again to 8.9%.

A recent study conducted in the USA by Grant et al., 2005 using DSM-IV criteria estimated 12-month and lifetime prevalence of 2.1 and 4.1%, respectively. They found that GAD is more prevalent in African Americans and that Asian, Hispanic and Black have a reduced risk. These rates were slightly slower than the ones found in NCS Replication, probably because substance-induced GAD was not excluded (Kessler et al., 2005).

GAD is more common in women (2:1) and is also significantly greater in widowed, separated, divorced and those in urban areas and lower socioeconomic groups (Grant et al., 2005). It is more prevalent in clinical settings, particularly in primary care (Shear and Schulberg 1994).

V.D.1.b. Children.
GAD rates are similar in children despite a lack of epidemiological data using DSM-IV criteria. Findings from the NCS have estimated prevalence of 1.6 and 5.1% for current and lifetime, respectively (Wittchen and Hoyer, 2001). No differences in gender ratio or a predominance of girls are reported, together with an over-representation of the middle-upper class.

V.D.1.c. Elderly.
In the elderly, prevalence rates range from 0.7 to 7.3%, and GAD appears to account for the majority of anxiety disorders experienced in this age group (Flint, 1994; Beekman et al., 1998).

V.D.2. Social impact considerations
GAD was once considered a mild disorder, increasing in importance with the presence of co-morbidity. However, this is no longer the case. Individuals with GAD are heavy users of primary care and specialty healthcare resources, as they are often not aware of the anxiety-related nature of their symptoms. There is an excess in hospitalization and an increased suicide risk (Sareen et al., 2005). Data from the HARP study highlighted that 50% of the sample reported substantial day-life interference due to GAD symptoms (Shear et al., 1994; Wittchen et al., 1994).

Different surveys suggest there is on an average 45 lost days of work every year in GAD, increasing up to 57 lost days when a concomitant co-morbid disorder is present (Greenberg et al., 1999; Souetre et al., 1994) and a substantial loss in work productivity. GAD disability is comparable with the one produced by major depression (Grant et al., 2005).

V.E. Conclusion

There is an ongoing debate over how best to place GAD in anxiety disorders and even whether it is a distinct syndrome. General evidence indicates it may share phenotypical and genotypic similarities to unipolar mood disorders and it should be considered a distinct syndrome, more closely linked to depression rather than to other anxiety disorders.

There is an evidence both for and against this belief with several authors suggesting that in the forthcoming DSM-V, GAD should be placed with major depression, dysthymia and post-traumatic stress disorder in a category of distress disorders (Watson, 2005). However, evidence from studies of brain mechanisms, especially of circuits and sleep architecture, suggests that GAD is clearly different from major depression though may be more similar to minor depression (Nutt et al., 2002).

VI. Post-traumatic stress disorder

VI.A. Introduction

PTSD is a chronic and disabling disorder that has only recently been clearly defined despite the fact that trauma has been considered aetiological in anxiety symptoms since the twentieth century by many authors, and Shay in 1999 suggested that elements of this disorder could be identified in Homer's *Iliad*. Daly also argued that PTSD symptoms, including flashbacks, could be identified in the accounts of veterans of the American Civil War, based on the observations of Jacob Mendez Da Costa. The relatively high prevalence of this disorder among veterans of the Vietnam War was a major reason to expand its research.

Despite this history, PTSD was not officially considered a discrete disorder until DSM-III and ICD-10. Since then, considerable research effort has been conducted towards its characteristics and treatment and related and common co-morbid disorders (Andreasen, 2004; Nemeroff et al., 2006). DSM-IV and ICD-10 added a subjective component of the experience of the trauma, suggesting that the interpretation of the events affected the probability of developing PTSD, a change that has largely been supported (e.g. Ehlers et al., 1998). It is required that the person experiencing the event has to respond with intense fear, helplessness or horror. However, other emotions can be present, like being numb or in a daze during the event or even amnesia for the event, which may attenuate emotional intensity (Brewin et al., 2000a, b; Creamer et al., 2005).

VI.B. Clinical features

VI.B.1. Considerations about the traumatic event
Many individuals will develop an acute brief response to stress after a traumatic event, and they will not develop any long-lasting pathologic sequelae, whereas a smaller proportion will experience persistent PTSD, either alone or in combination with major depression, or just depression (Kindt and Engelhard, 2005; Vieweg et al., 2006). According to DSM-III, PTSD criteria required

being exposed to a stressor that was relevant because of its rare prevalence, and this stressor was such so as to evoke symptoms of distress in most people. Subsequently, many authors suggested that traumatic events are not as rare as supposed (Kessler et al., 1995), and this led DSM-IV to redefine the trauma not in relation with its prevalence but of its nature, describing the need to involve actual or threatened death or serious injury, or a threat to the physical integrity to self or others.

Several studies have claimed that the type of trauma is a predictor of PTSD; a higher risk being associated with assault violence, in particular being raped. Other events may also be highly associated with PTSD, such as the loss or the death of a loved one (Kessler et al., 1995).

VI.B.2. The phenomenology of PTSD
PTSD has always been considered as being conformed by three phenomenological distinct symptom clusters or sub-syndromes: re-experiencing/flashbacks, emotional numbing and other symptoms (e.g. hyperarousal, avoidance, survival guilt).

There are some slight differences in current classification criteria. While DSM-IV divides the phenomenology of PTSD in three: the re-experience phenomena, the avoidance/numbing response and the persistent symptoms of increased arousal, ICD-10 also includes the inability to recall some important aspects of the period exposure.

VI.B.2.a. The re-experience phenomenon
Criteria considerations. Repeated recurrence and concomitant distress are required in making the diagnosis of re-experiencing one or more of the following: recollections of the event including images, thoughts or perceptions; dreams of the event, including flashes, illusions, hallucinations or dissociative flashback episodes; acting or feeling as if the traumatic event were recurring, an intense psychological distress and physiological reactivity on exposure to internal or external cues that resemble the event.

Phenomenological considerations. Little is known about the phenomenology of re-experiencing.

Many studies have concluded that the most dramatic form of re-experiencing is the flashback. Nevertheless, theoretical approaches conclude that re-experiencing is related with the way trauma memories are encoded, organized in memory and retrieved (Ehlers et al., 2004).

Quality of memories. Intrusive memories are described as intrusive thoughts. However, research supports that intrusive memories are better considered as brief sensory fragments of the traumatic event, since it was found that visual sensations were the most common ones, followed by taste, smells, sounds and bodily sensations. Recent considerations claim that evaluative thoughts about the trauma and rumination should also be considered (Murray et al., 2002).

Re-experiencing phenomena are often felt as actually occurring; e.g. awareness that the content is related to the past is missing. Second, there may be a lack of context; original emotions and sensations are re-experienced despite acquiring new information that contradicts them. Some case reports have shown individuals with two contradictive intrusive memories, for example, that they were a victim and at the same time enjoyed aspects of the trauma (Ehlers et al., 2004).

Content of memories. It appears that the most common contents are related to either the onset of the trauma or the moments of largest emotional impact. Ehlers et al. (2004) suggested that because of temporal association with the event, these memories acquired the status of warning signals. Newspaper or TV reports of similar events can provoke intrusions. These are called trigger stimuli and can lead to re-experiencing associated with visual, physical or others senses, and as individuals tend not to be aware of them, so they appear to come unexpectedly. Recent approaches to re-experiencing have revealed that trauma memories may only occur in certain retrieval routes and memory processes or systems, for example, smells are very evocative whereas images may be less so.

VI.B.2.b. The avoidance and emotional numbing response.
These are a form of avoidance phenomena and are viewed as brain efforts to avoid thoughts, feelings, activities and situations that lead to recollections of the trauma. Numbing can lead to a very severe disruption of life as in agoraphobia or avoidance behaviour and may also contribute to the presence of secondary depression. DSM-IV specifically requires at least three of the following criteria: (1) efforts to avoid thoughts, feelings or conversations associated with the trauma; (2) efforts to avoid activities, places or people, that might lead to recollections of trauma; (3) inability to recall an important aspect of the trauma; (4) a diminished interest in related activities; (5) a feeling of detachment or estrangement from others; (6) restricted range of affect or (7) a sense of a foreshortened future.

An over-development of avoidance activities that appear to reduce the experience of trauma-related dysphoria is commonly present in PTSD. Examples of such responses are dissociation, substance abuse and tension reduction activities (Briere and Spinazzola, 2005).

Dissociation. In an attempt to reduce the emotional responses associated with triggered traumatic memories, dissociative responses may be present (Chu et al., 1999). Examples of them are depersonalization, derealization, fugue states and dissociative identity disorder.

Substance abuse. Epidemiological and clinical literature supports the frequent co-occurrence of substance use disorders and PTSD. Individuals with complex and chronic trauma histories may be more likely to use substance abuse as emotional avoidance. While some groups claim that substances are taken to anaesthetize negative affect associated with traumatic experiences or subsequent trauma memories, other clinical data suggest that they induce transient and predictable pleasurable bodily sensations or emotions, minimizing affective numbness in some trauma survivors.

Tension reduction. Tension reduction behaviours include compulsive sexual behaviour, binging and purging, self-mutilation and being suicidal. They are thought to work by providing temporary distraction or by inducing distress-incompatible affective states.

Increased arousal symptoms. These include sleep disturbance (nightmares replicating traumatic events) or difficulty initiating and maintaining sleep, hypervigilance, exaggerated startle response, irritability, angry outbursts and poor concentration. These often lead to major problems for partners and immediate family.

VI.B.3. Subtypes of the disorder

Acute PTSD is diagnosed if the duration of the symptoms is less than 3 months. Chronic PTSD is used when the symptoms last 3 month or longer, and delayed PTSD when at least 6 months have passed between the traumatic event and the onset of the symptoms.

VI.B.3.a. The acute stress disorder. This subcategory was added as a separate disorder in DSM-IV edition and describes post-traumatic stress symptoms with prominent dissociative symptoms occurring in the immediate period after a traumatic event.

Initial prospective studies found that acute stress disorder or response predicts extremely well the later emergence of PTSD. However, recent data suggest that acute stress disorder, as currently formulated, may be indistinct from PTSD without a duration criterion (Brewin et al., 2003).

VI.B.4. Child and adolescent considerations

After a frightening event, children are likely to become distressed. Slight phenomenological differences are seen in this group. Flashbacks are relatively rare in children, where repetitive and intrusive thoughts occur, especially when children are quiet. Sleep disturbances are also very frequent in the first weeks, with nightmares, fears of the dark and bad dreams and waking up at night. Separation difficulties are very frequent, even without wanting parents to be off their sight (Hawkins and Radcliffe, 2006).

Mood changes are also visible as many children become irritable. Cognitive changes are also reported by children, especially concentration and memory.

VI.C. Clinical course of the disorder

Some epidemiological studies have focused on the natural course of PTSD. About one-third remit, one-third stay somewhat impaired and one-third make minimal recovery (Perkonigg et al., 2005).

Previous vulnerability to depressive or anxiety disorders increases the likelihood that PTSD will develop, and a higher number of avoidant symptoms predict a chronic course. Also, patients become much more vulnerable to developing another episode of PTSD following another trauma.

VI.D. Epidemiology and social impact

VI.D.1. Prevalence

VI.D.1.a. General population. The experience of a traumatic event is surprisingly common in the general population, with estimated prevalence ranging from 51% in women to 61% in men (Kessler et al., 1995). The vast majority of individuals who experience trauma will recover, not developing PTSD.

The NCS conducted in the USA by Kessler and his colleagues (1995) estimated lifetime prevalence rates in DSM-III-R in the community to be 7.8% and 12-month prevalence 3.9%. Creamer et al. (2001) conducted a study estimating a 12-month DSM-IV prevalence of 1.33% and 12-month PTSD prevalence rates of 1.3%. Other studies have found lower lifetime prevalence rates (Davidson et al., 1991).

However, it is not rare that a higher lifetime PTSD prevalence of around 30% is reported in particular samples, as in Vietnam veterans or female victims of rape. A recent meta-analysis conducted by Brewin et al. (2000a, b) concluded that when different populations (soldiers and civilians) are exposed to traumatic events, the risk of PTSD is enhanced reliably, but to a relatively small extent by some factors, the most relevant being female gender, intellectual disadvantage, prior psychiatric history and various types of previous adversity, which increase risk, and greater social and educational attainments, which reduce risk, as well as by somewhat larger effects attributable to factors occurring during or after the trauma, especially social support.

VI.D.1.b. Children. After early observations that children did not develop PTSD subsequent studies have reported that among children surviving traumatic experiences the incidence of subsequent PTSD may be around 25%.

In specific childhood studies, 52% were found to have PTSD after the first weeks and 34% still met criteria after 5 years (Yule, 1992). Findings similar to estimated prevalence in adults have been reported among children; in many studies, finding of a higher risk of PTSD among girls than boys is consistent with this pattern.

VI.D.2. Social impact considerations

The social consequences of PTSD samples bear comparison with other seriously impairing mental disorders. Risk of suicide attempts is particularly high among people with PTSD. Different studies have reported direct consequences in PTSD and physical health, reporting increased physical symptoms and negative health behaviours. Direct consequences include increased doctors' visits, emergency rooms, psychiatric hospitalization and outpatient services (Tyndel, 1999). Social impairment also includes missing work, a decrease in productivity and even job loss in many cases. Social relationships are also affected often reflecting the greatest impairment with estrangement and detachment and frequently the avoidance of sexual intimacy. Moreover, individuals also report inability to care for children, marital problems resulting in divorce and family problems.

VI.E. Conclusion

PTSD is a common and impairing condition. There are several kinds of traumatic events and related factors that can increase the likelihood to develop it and, therefore, should be taken into account. It is also important to note that only a minority of people with PTSD obtain treatment and that to some extent, early and aggressive outreach to treat people with PTSD could help reduce the enormous societal costs of this disorder.

Current reconsideration of anxiety disorders state that PTSD could be re-conceptualized as a fear disorder, a distress disorder or a mix of both. Moreover, considerations regarding symptom subgroups need further research to resolve many outstanding issues (Watson, 2005).

VII. Conclusions

In this chapter, we have given a brief introduction to the various forms of anxiety disorders, focusing on their diagnostic criteria, prevalence and phenomenology. The treatments of these disorders are discussed in the chapter by Baldwin and Garner. Though these treatments are often effective, many patients do not respond or respond only partially, so there is a real need for new approaches.

A major challenge in neuroscience is to develop animal paradigms that more accurately model these human disorders so that the brain mechanisms can be more readily understood and new treatments developed. This is difficult especially for disorders such as GAD, where subjective worry is such a key element, but should be easier for disorders such as PTSD, which result from the experience of trauma, and for PD and SAnD, both of which seem to occur in rats and primates.

Abbreviations

GAD	generalized anxiety disorder
OCD	obsessive-compulsive disorder
PD	panic disorder
PTSD	post-traumatic stress disorder
SAnD	social anxiety disorder

References

Alfano, C.A., Beidel, D.C. and Turner, S.M. (2006) Cognitive correlates of social phobia among children and adolescents. J. Abnorm. Child Psychol., 34: 189–201.

Amies, P.L., Gelder, M.G. and Shaw, P.M. (1983) Social phobia: a comparative clinical study. Br. J. Psychiatry, 142: 174–179.

Andreasen, N.C. (2004) Acute and delayed posttraumatic stress disorders: a history and some issues. Am. J. Psychiatry, 161: 1321–1323.

Angst, J., Gamma, A., Endrass, J., Goodwin, R., Ajdacic, V., Eich, D. and Rossler, W. (2004) Obsessive-compulsive severity spectrum in the community: prevalence, comorbidity, and course. Eur. Arch. Psychiatry Clin. Neurosci., 254: 156–164.

Aschenbrand, S.G., Kendall, P.C., Webb, A., Safford, S.M. and Flannery-Schroeder, E. (2003) Is childhood separation anxiety disorder a predictor of adult panic disorder and agoraphobia? A seven-year longitudinal study. J. Am. Acad. Child Adolesc. Psychiatry, 42: 1478–1485.

Baldwin, D.S., Anderson, I.M., Nutt, D.J., Bandelow, B., Bond, A., Davidson, J.R., den Boer, J.A., Fineberg, N.A., Knapp, M., Scott, J. and Wittchen, H.U. (2005) Evidence-based guidelines for the pharmacological treatment of anxiety disorders: recommendations from the British Association for Psychopharmacology. J. Psychopharmacol., 19: 567–596.

Bartz, J.A. and Hollander, E. (2006) Is obsessive-compulsive disorder an anxiety disorder? Prog. Neuropsychopharmacol. Biol. Psychiatry, 30: 338–352.

Battaglia, M., Bertella, S., Politi, E., Bernardeschi, L., Perna, G., Gabriele, A. and Bellodi, L. (1995) Age at onset of panic disorder: influence of familial liability to the disease and of childhood separation anxiety disorder. Am. J. Psychiatry, 152: 1362–1364.

Beekman, A.T., Bremmer, M.A., Deeg, D.J., van Balkom, A.J., Smit, J.H., de Beurs, E., van Dyck, R. and van Tilburg, W. (1998) Anxiety disorders in later life: a report from the Longitudinal Aging Study Amsterdam. Int. J. Geriatr. Psychiatry, 13: 717–726.

Beidel, D.C., Turner, S.M. and Morris, T.L. (1999) Psychopathology of childhood social phobia. J. Am. Acad. Child Adolesc. Psychiatry, 38: 643–650.

Biederman, J., Faraone, S.V., Marrs, A., Moore, P., Garcia, J., Ablon, S., Mick, E., Gershon, J. and Kearns, M.E. (1997) Panic disorder and agoraphobia in consecutively referred children and adolescents. J. Am. Acad. Child Adolesc. Psychiatry, 36: 214–223.

Bland, R.C., Orn, H. and Newman, S.C. (1988) Lifetime prevalence of psychiatric disorders in Edmonton. Acta Psychiatr. Scand. Suppl., 338: 24–32.

Blazer, D., Hughes, D. and George, L.K. (1987) Stressful life events and the onset of a generalized anxiety syndrome. Am. J. Psychiatry, 144: 1178–1183.

Blazer, D.G. (1991) Generalized anxiety disorder. In: Robins, L.N. and Regier, D.A. (Eds.), Psychiatric Disorders in America: The Epidemiologic Catchment Area Study. The Free Press, New York, pp. 180–203.

Bogels, S.M. and Mansell, W. (2004) Attention processes in the maintenance and treatment of social phobia: hypervigilance, avoidance and self-focused attention. Clin. Psychol. Rev., 24: 827–856.

Brewin, C.R., Andrews, B. and Rose, S. (2000a) Fear, helplessness, and horror in posttraumatic stress disorder: investigating DSM-IV criterion A2 in victims of violent crime. J. Trauma. Stress, 13: 499–509.

Brewin, C.R., Andrews, B. and Rose, S. (2003) Diagnostic overlap between acute stress disorder and PTSD in victims of violent crime. Am. J. Psychiatry, 160: 783–785.

Brewin, C.R., Andrews, B. and Valentine, J.D. (2000b) Meta-analysis of risk factors for posttraumatic stress disorder in trauma-exposed adults. J. Consult. Clin. Psychol., 68: 748–766.

Briere, J. and Spinazzola, J. (2005) Phenomenology and psychological assessment of complex posttraumatic states. J. Trauma. Stress, 18: 401–412.

Briggs, A.C., Stretch, D.D. and Brandon, S. (1993) Subtyping of panic disorder by symptom profile. Br. J. Psychiatry, 163: 201–209.

Brown, T.A., Barlow, D.H. and Liebowitz, M.R. (1994) The empirical basis of generalized anxiety disorder. Am. J. Psychiatry, 151: 1272–1280.

Cairney, J., McCabe, L., Veldhuizen, S., Corna, L.M., Streiner, D. and Herrmann, N. (2007) Epidemiology of social phobia in later life. Am. J. Geriatr. Psychiatry, 15: 224–233.

Calamari, J.E., Faber, S.D., Hitsman, B.L. and Poppe, C.J. (1994) Treatment of obsessive-compulsive disorder in the elderly: a review and case example. J. Behav. Ther. Exp. Psychiatry, 25: 95–104.

Chavira, D.A. and Stein, M.B. (2000) Recent developments in child and adolescent social phobia. Curr. Psychiatry Rep., 2: 347–352.

Chu, J.A., Frey, L.M., Ganzel, B.L. and Matthews, J.A. (1999) Memories of childhood abuse: dissociation, amnesia, and corroboration. Am. J. Psychiatry, 156: 749–755.

Clark, D.M. (1986) A cognitive approach to panic. Behav. Res. Ther., 24: 461–470.

Clark, D.M. and Wells, A. (1995) A cognitive model of social anxiety disorder. In: Heimberg, R.G. Liebowitz, M.R. Hoper, D.A. and Schneier, F.R. (Eds.), Social Anxiety Disorder: Diagnosis, Assessment and Treatment. The Guilford Press, New York, pp. 69–93.

Craske, M.G. and Tsao, J.C. (2005) Assessment and treatment of nocturnal panic attacks. Sleep Med. Rev., 9: 173–184.

Creamer, M., Burgess, P. and McFarlane, A.C. (2001) Post-traumatic stress disorder: findings from the Australian National Survey of Mental Health and Well-being. Psychol. Med., 31: 1237–1247.

Creamer, M., McFarlane, A.C. and Burgess, P. (2005) Psychopathology following trauma: the role of subjective experience. J. Affect. Disord., 86: 175–182.

Daly, R.J. (1983) Samuel Pepys and post-traumatic stress disorder. Br. J. Psychiatry, 143: 64–68.

Davidson, J.R., Hughes, D., Blazer, D.G. and George, L.K. (1991) Post-traumatic stress disorder in the community: an epidemiological study. Psychol. Med., 21: 713–721.

Davies, S.J., Ghahramani, P., Jackson, P.R., Noble, T.W., Hardy, P.G., Hippisley-Cox, J., Yeo, W.W. and Ramsay, L.E. (1999) Association of panic disorder and panic attacks with hypertension. Am. J. Med., 107: 310–316.

Diler, R.S., Birmaher, B., Brent, D.A., Axelson, D.A., Firinciogullari, S., Chiapetta, L. and Bridge, J. (2004) Phenomenology of panic disorder in youth. Depress. Anxiety, 20: 39–43.

Dugas, M.J., Freeston, M.H., Ladouceur, R., Rheaume, J., Provencher, M. and Boisvert, J.M. (1998a) Worry themes in primary GAD, secondary GAD, and other anxiety disorders. J. Anxiety Disord., 12: 253–261.

Dugas, M.J., Gagnon, F., Ladouceur, R. and Freeston, M.H. (1998b) Generalized anxiety disorder: a preliminary test of a conceptual model. Behav. Res. Ther., 36: 215–226.

Dugas, M.J., Marchand, A. and Ladouceur, R. (2005) Further validation of a cognitive-behavioral model of generalized anxiety disorder: diagnostic and symptom specificity. J. Anxiety Disord., 19: 329–343.

Ehlers, A., Hackmann, A. and Michael, T. (2004) Intrusive re-experiencing in post-traumatic stress disorder: phenomenology, theory, and therapy. Memory, 12: 403–415.

Ehlers, A., Mayou, R.A. and Bryant, B. (1998) Psychological predictors of chronic posttraumatic stress disorder after motor vehicle accidents. J. Abnorm. Psychol., 107: 508–519.

Essau, C.A., Conradt, J. and Petermann, F. (1999a) Frequency and comorbidity of social phobia and social fears in adolescents. Behav. Res. Ther., 37: 831–843.

Essau, C.A., Conradt, J. and Petermann, F. (1999b) Frequency of panic attacks and panic disorder in adolescents. Depress. Anxiety, 9: 19–26.

Faravelli, C., Guerrini Degl'Innocenti, B. and Giardinelli, L. (1989) Epidemiology of anxiety disorders in Florence. Acta Psychiatr. Scand., 79: 308–312.

Faravelli, C., Zucchi, T., Viviani, B., Salmoria, R., Perone, A., Paionni, A., Scarpato, A., Vigliaturo, D., Rosi, S., D'Adamo, D., Bartolozzi, D., Cecchi, C. and Abrardi, L. (2000) Epidemiology of social phobia: a clinical approach. Eur. Psychiatry, 15: 17–24.

Fehm, L., Pelissolo, A., Furmark, T. and Wittchen, H.U. (2005) Size and burden of social phobia in Europe. Eur. Neuropsychopharmacol., 15: 453–462.

Fleet, R., Lavoie, K. and Beitman, B.D. (2000) Is panic disorder associated with coronary artery disease? A critical review of the literature. J. Psychosom. Res., 48: 347–356.

Flint, A.J. (1994) Epidemiology and comorbidity of anxiety disorders in the elderly. Am. J. Psychiatry, 151: 640–649.

Foa, E.B., Kozak, M.J., Goodman, W.K., Hollander, E., Jenike, M.A. and Rasmussen, S.A. (1995) DSM-IV field trial: obsessive-compulsive disorder. Am. J. Psychiatry, 152: 90–96.

Fontenelle, L.F., Mendlowicz, M.V., Marques, C. and Versiani, M. (2004) Trans-cultural aspects of obsessive-compulsive disorder: a description of a Brazilian sample and a systematic review of international clinical studies. J. Psychiatr. Res., 38: 403–411.

Garakani, A., Win, T., Virk, S., Gupta, S., Kaplan, D. and Masand, P.S. (2003) Comorbidity of irritable bowel syndrome in psychiatric patients: a review. Am. J. Ther., 10: 61–67.

Geller, D.A. (2006) Obsessive-compulsive and spectrum disorders in children and adolescents. Psychiatr. Clin. North Am., 29: 353–370.

Grant, B.F., Hasin, D.S., Stinson, F.S., Dawson, D.A., Goldstein, R.B., Smith, S., Huang, B. and Saha, T.D. (2006) The epidemiology of DSM-IV panic disorder and agoraphobia in the United States: results from the National Epidemiologic Survey on Alcohol and Related Conditions. J. Clin. Psychiatry, 67: 363–374.

Grant, B.F., Hasin, D.S., Stinson, F.S., Dawson, D.A., June Ruan, W., Goldstein, R.B., Smith, S.M., Saha, T.D. and Huang, B. (2005) Prevalence, correlates, co-morbidity, and comparative disability of DSM-IV generalized anxiety disorder in the USA: results from the National Epidemiologic Survey on Alcohol and Related Conditions. Psychol. Med., 35: 1747–1759.

Greenberg, P.E., Sisitsky, T., Kessler, R.C., Finkelstein, S.N., Berndt, E.R., Davidson, J.R., Ballenger, J.C. and Fyer, A.J. (1999) The economic burden of anxiety disorders in the 1990s. J. Clin. Psychiatry, 60: 427–435.

Hasler, G., Gergen, P.J., Kleinbaum, D.G., Ajdacic, V., Gamma, A., Eich, D., Rossler, W. and Angst, J. (2005a) Asthma and panic in young adults: a 20-year prospective community study. Am. J. Respir. Crit. Care Med., 171: 1224–1230.

Hasler, G., LaSalle-Ricci, V.H., Ronquillo, J.G., Crawley, S.A., Cochran, L.W., Kazuba, D., Greenberg, B.D. and Murphy, D.L. (2005b) Obsessive-compulsive disorder symptom dimensions show specific relationships to psychiatric comorbidity. Psychiatry Res., 135: 121–132.

Hawkins, S.S. and Radcliffe, J. (2006) Current measures of PTSD for children and adolescents. J. Pediatr. Psychol., 31: 420–430.

Hayward, C., Killen, J.D., Kraemer, H.C. and Taylor, C.B. (2000) Predictors of panic attacks in adolescents. J. Am. Acad. Child Adolesc. Psychiatry, 39: 207–214.

Hemmings, S.M., Kinnear, C.J., Lochner, C., Niehaus, D.J., Knowles, J.A., Moolman-Smook, J.C., Corfield, V.A. and Stein, D.J. (2004) Early- versus late-onset obsessive-compulsive disorder: investigating genetic and clinical correlates. Psychiatry Res., 128: 175–182.

Heyman, I., Mataix-Cols, D. and Fineberg, N.A. (2006) Obsessive-compulsive disorder. Br. Med. J., 333: 424–429.

Hirsch, C.R. and Clark, D.M. (2004) Information-processing bias in social phobia. Clin. Psychol. Rev., 24: 799–825.

Hoehn-Saric, R., Hazlett, R.L. and McLeod, D.R. (1993) Generalized anxiety disorder with early and late onset of anxiety symptoms. Compr. Psychiatry, 34: 291–298.

Hollander, E. (1993) Obsessive-compulsive spectrum disorders: an overview. Psychiatr. Ann., 23: 355–358.

Holt, C.S., Heimberg, R.G. and Hope, D.A. (1992) Avoidant personality disorder and the generalized subtype of social phobia. J. Abnorm. Psychol., 101: 318–325.

Kagan, J., Reznick, J.S. and Snidman, N. (1988) Biological bases of childhood shyness. Science, 240: 167–171.

Katon, W.J. (1990) Chest pain, cardiac disease, and panic disorder. J. Clin. Psychiatry, 51(Suppl): 27–30. (discussion 50-23).

Kessler, R.C., Berglund, P., Demler, O., Jin, R., Merikangas, K.R. and Walters, E.E. (2005) Lifetime prevalence and age-of-onset distributions of DSM-IV disorders in the National Comorbidity Survey Replication. Arch. Gen. Psychiatry, 62: 593–602.

Kessler, R.C., Chiu, W.T., Jin, R., Ruscio, A.M., Shear, K. and Walters, E.E. (2006) The epidemiology of panic attacks, panic disorder, and agoraphobia in the National Comorbidity Survey Replication. Arch. Gen. Psychiatry, 63: 415–424.

Kessler, R.C., McGonagle, K.A., Zhao, S., Nelson, C.B., Hughes, M., Eshleman, S., Wittchen, H.U. and Kendler, K.S. (1994) Lifetime and 12-month prevalence of DSM-III-R psychiatric disorders in the United States. Results from the National Comorbidity Survey. Arch. Gen. Psychiatry, 51: 8–19.

Kessler, R.C., Sonnega, A., Bromet, E., Hughes, M. and Nelson, C.B. (1995) Posttraumatic stress disorder in the National Comorbidity Survey. Arch. Gen. Psychiatry, 52: 1048–1060.

Kindt, M. and Engelhard, I.M. (2005) Trauma processing and the development of posttraumatic stress disorder. J. Behav. Ther. Exp. Psychiatry, 36: 69–76.

Klein, D.F. (1981) Anxiety reconceptualized. In: Klein, D.F. and Rabkin, J.G. (Eds.), Anxiety: New Research and Changing Concepts. Raven Press, New York, pp. 235–263.

Klein, D.F. (1984) Lactate provocation of panic attacks: I. Clinical and behavioural findings. Arch. Gen. Psychiatry, 41: 764–770.

Klein, D.F. (1993) False suffocation alarms, spontaneous panics, and related conditions. An integrative hypothesis. Arch. Gen. Psychiatry., 50: 306–317.

Klein, D.F. (1999) Panic disorder. Lancet, 353: 326–327.

La Greca, A.M. and Lopez, N. (1998) Social anxiety among adolescents: linkages with peer relations and friendships. J. Abnorm. Child Psychol., 26: 83–94.

Last, C.G., Perrin, S., Hersen, M. and Kazdin, A.E. (1992) DSM-III-R anxiety disorders in children: sociodemographic and clinical characteristics. J. Am. Acad. Child Adolesc. Psychiatry, 31: 1070–1076.

Leckman, J.F., Grice, D.E., Boardman, J., Zhang, H., Vitale, A., Bondi, C., Alsobrook, J., Peterson, B.S., Cohen, D.J., Rasmussen, S.A., Goodman, W.K., McDougle, C.J. and Pauls, D.L. (1997) Symptoms of obsessive-compulsive disorder. Am. J. Psychiatry, 154: 911–917.

Lensi, P., Cassano, G.B., Correddu, G., Ravagli, S., Kunovac, J.L. and Akiskal, H.S. (1996) Obsessive-compulsive disorder. Familial-developmental history, symptomatology, comorbidity and course with special reference to gender-related differences. Br. J. Psychiatry, 169: 101–107.

Lepine, J.P. and Lellouch, J. (1995) Classification and epidemiology of social phobia. Eur. Arch. Psychiatry Clin. Neurosci., 244: 290–296.

Lewinsohn, P.M., Hops, H., Roberts, R.E., Seeley, J.R. and Andrews, J.A. (1993) Adolescent psychopathology: I. Prevalence and incidence of depression and other DSM-III-R disorders in high school students. J. Abnorm. Psychol., 102: 133–144.

Ley, R. (1985) Agoraphobia, the panic attack and the hyperventilation syndrome. Behav. Res. Ther., 23: 79–81.

Lipsitz, J.D., Martin, L.Y., Mannuzza, S., Chapman, T.F., Liebowitz, M.R., Klein, D.F. and Fyer, A.J. (1994) Childhood separation anxiety disorder in patients with adult anxiety disorders. Am. J. Psychiatry, 151: 927–929.

Marten, P.A., Brown, T.A., Barlow, D.H., Borkovec, T.D., Shear, M.K. and Lydiard, R.B. (1993) Evaluation of the ratings comprising the associated symptom criterion of DSM-III-R generalized anxiety disorder. J. Nerv. Ment. Dis., 181: 676–682.

Masi, G., Millepiedi, S., Mucci, M., Bertini, N., Milantoni, L. and Arcangeli, F. (2005) A naturalistic study of referred children and adolescents with obsessive-compulsive disorder. J. Am. Acad. Child Adolesc. Psychiatry, 44: 673–681.

Masi, G., Millepiedi, S., Mucci, M., Poli, P., Bertini, N. and Milantoni, L. (2004) Generalized anxiety disorder in referred children and adolescents. J. Am. Acad. Child Adolesc. Psychiatry, 43: 752–760.

Masi, G., Mucci, M., Favilla, L., Romano, R. and Poli, P. (1999) Symptomatology and comorbidity of generalized anxiety disorder in children and adolescents. Compr. Psychiatry, 40: 210–215.

Mataix-Cols, D. (2006) Deconstructing obsessive-compulsive disorder: a multidimensional perspective. Curr. Opin. Psychiatry, 19: 84–89.

Mataix-Cols, D., Rosario-Campos, M.C. and Leckman, J.F. (2005) A multidimensional model of obsessive-compulsive disorder. Am. J. Psychiatry, 162: 228–238.

McKay, D., Abramowitz, J.S., Calamari, J.E., Kyrios, M., Radomsky, A., Sookman, D., Taylor, S. and Wilhelm, S. (2004) A critical evaluation of obsessive-compulsive disorder subtypes: symptoms versus mechanisms. Clin. Psychol. Rev., 24: 283–313.

Mendlowicz, M.V. and Stein, M.B. (2000) Quality of life in individuals with anxiety disorders. Am. J. Psychiatry, 157: 669–682.

Miguel, E.C., Leckman, J.F., Rauch, S., do Rosario-Campos, M.C., Hounie, A.G., Mercadante, M.T., Chacon, P. and Pauls, D.L. (2005) Obsessive-compulsive disorder phenotypes: implications for genetic studies. Mol. Psychiatry, 10: 258–275.

Mogg, K. and Bradley, B.P. (1998) A cognitive-motivational analysis of anxiety. Behav. Res. Ther., 36: 809–848.

Moreau, D. and Weissman, M.M. (1992) Panic disorder in children and adolescents: a review. Am. J. Psychiatry, 149: 1306–1314.

Murray, J., Ehlers, A. and Mayou, R.A. (2002) Dissociation and post-traumatic stress disorder: two prospective studies of road traffic accident survivors. Br. J. Psychiatry., 180: 363–368.

Nardi, A.E., Lopes, F.L., Valenca, A.M., Nascimento, I., Mezzasalma, M.A. and Zin, W.A. (2004) Psychopathological description of hyperventilation-induced panic attacks: a comparison with spontaneous panic attacks. Psychopathology, 37: 29–35.

Neal, J.A. and Edelmann, R.J. (2003) The etiology of social phobia: toward a developmental profile. Clin. Psychol. Rev., 23: 761–786.

Nemeroff, C.B., Bremner, J.D., Foa, E.B., Mayberg, H.S., North, C.S. and Stein, M.B. (2006) Posttraumatic stress disorder: a state-of-the-science review. J. Psychiatr. Res., 40: 1–21.

Noyes, R., Jr. Clarkson, C., Crowe, R.R., Yates, W.R. and McChesney, C.M. (1987) A family study of generalized anxiety disorder. Am. J. Psychiatry, 144: 1019–1024.

Nutt, D. and Malizia, A. (2006) Anxiety and OCD – the chicken or the egg? J. Psychopharmacol., 20: 729–731.

Nutt, D.J. and Ballenger, J. (2005) Anxiety Disorders, Blackwell Publishing, Oxford.

Nutt, D.J., Ballenger, J.C., Sheehan, D. and Wittchen, H.U. (2002) Generalized anxiety disorder: comorbidity, comparative biology and treatment. Int. J. Neuropsychopharmacol., 5: 315–325.

Pelissolo, A., Andre, C., Moutard-Martin, F., Wittchen, H.U. and Lepine, J.P. (2000) Social phobia in the community: relationship between diagnostic threshold and prevalence. Eur. Psychiatry, 15: 25–28.

Perkonigg, A., Pfister, H., Stein, M.B., Hofler, M., Lieb, R., Maercker, A. and Wittchen, H.U. (2005) Longitudinal course of posttraumatic stress disorder and posttraumatic stress disorder symptoms in a community sample of adolescents and young adults. Am. J. Psychiatry, 162: 1320–1327.

Pine, D.S., Cohen, P., Gurley, D., Brook, J. and Ma, Y. (1998) The risk for early-adulthood anxiety and depressive disorders in adolescents with anxiety and depressive disorders. Arch. Gen. Psychiatry, 55: 56–64.

Pinto, A., Mancebo, M.C., Eisen, J.L., Pagano, M.E. and Rasmussen, S.A. (2006) The Brown Longitudinal Obsessive Compulsive Study: clinical features and symptoms of the sample at intake. J. Clin. Psychiatry, 67: 703–711.

Potokar, J.P. and Nutt, D.J. (2000) Chest pain: panic attack or heart attack? Int. J. Clin. Pract., 54: 110–114.

Raj, B.A., Corvea, M.H. and Dagon, E.M. (1993) The clinical characteristics of panic disorder in the elderly: a retrospective study. J. Clin. Psychiatry, 54: 150–155.

Rao, P.A., Beidel, D.C., Turner, S.M., Ammerman, R.T., Crosby, L.E. and Sallee, F.R. (2007) Social anxiety disorder in childhood and adolescence: descriptive psychopathology. Behav. Res. Ther., 45: 1181–1191.

Rapee, R.M. and Heimberg, R.G. (1997) A cognitive-behavioral model of anxiety in social phobia. Behav. Res. Ther., 35: 741–756.

Rapee, R.M. and Lim, L. (1992) Discrepancy between self- and observer ratings of performance in social phobics. J. Abnorm. Psychol., 101: 728–731.

Reed, V. and Wittchen, H.U. (1998) DSM-IV panic attacks and panic disorder in a community sample of adolescents and young adults: how specific are panic attacks? J. Psychiatr. Res., 32: 335–345.

Rettew, D.C., Swedo, S.E., Leonard, H.L., Lenane, M.C. and Rapoport, J.L. (1992) Obsessions and compulsions across time in 79 children and adolescents with obsessive-compulsive disorder. J. Am. Acad. Child Adolesc. Psychiatry, 31: 1050–1056.

Robins, L.N., Helzer, J.E., Weissman, M.M., Orvaschel, H., Gruenberg, E., Burke, J.D. Jr. and Regier, D.A. (1984) Lifetime prevalence of specific psychiatric disorders in three sites. Arch. Gen. Psychiatry, 41: 949–958.

Sareen, J., Cox, B.J., Afifi, T.O., de Graaf, R., Asmundson, G.J., ten Have, M. and Stein, M.B. (2005) Anxiety disorders and risk for suicidal ideation and suicide attempts: a population-based longitudinal study of adults. Arch. Gen. Psychiatry, 62: 1249–1257.

Sasson, Y., Zohar, J., Chopra, M., Lustig, M., Iancu, I. and Hendler, T. (1997) Epidemiology of obsessive-compulsive disorder: a world view. J. Clin. Psychiatry, 58(Suppl. 12): 7–10.

Schlenker, B.R. and Leary, M.R. (1982) Social anxiety and self-presentation: a conceptualization and model. Psychol. Bull., 92: 641–669.

Schneier, F.R., Heckelman, L.R., Garfinkel, R., Campeas, R., Fallon, B.A., Gitow, A., Street, L., Del Bene, D. and Liebowitz, M.R. (1994) Functional impairment in social phobia. J. Clin. Psychiatry, 55: 322–331.

Schwartz, C.E., Snidman, N. and Kagan, J. (1999) Adolescent social anxiety as an outcome of inhibited temperament in childhood. J. Am. Acad. Child Adolesc. Psychiatry, 38: 1008–1015.

Shear, M.K. and Schulberg, H.C. (1995) Anxiety disorders in primary care. Bull. Menninger. Clin., 1995; 59 (2 Suppl A): A73–85.

Shay, J. (1999) Mental disorder after two wars: sauce for the goose, but none for the gander. [Review of: Dean ET. Shook over hell: post-traumatic stress, Vietnam, and the Civil War. Harvard University Press, 1997]. Rev. Am. Hist., 27: 149–155.

Sheikh, J.I., Leskin, G.A. and Klein, D.F. (2002) Gender differences in panic disorder: findings from the National Comorbidity Survey. Am. J. Psychiatry, 159: 55–58.

Souetre, E., Lozet, H., Cimarosti, I., Martin, P., Chignon, J.M., Ades, J., Tignol, J. and Darcourt, G. (1994) Cost of anxiety disorders: impact of comorbidity. J. Psychosom. Res., 38(Suppl. 1): 151–160.

Stein, M.B. (1996) How shy is too shy? Lancet, 347: 1131–1132.

Stein, M.B. and Chavira, D.A. (1998) Subtypes of social phobia and comorbidity with depression and other anxiety disorders. J. Affect. Disord., 50(Suppl. 1): S11–S16.

Stein, M.B., Walker, J.R. and Forde, D.R. (1996) Public-speaking fears in a community sample. Prevalence, impact on functioning, and diagnostic classification. Arch. Gen. Psychiatry, 53: 169–174.

Suzuki, K., Takei, N., Kawai, M., Minabe, Y. and Mori, N. (2003) Is taijin kyofusho a culture-bound syndrome? Am. J. Psychiatry, 160: 1358.

Turner, S.M., Beidel, D.C. and Townsley, R.M. (1992) Social phobia: a comparison of specific and generalized subtypes and avoidant personality disorder. J. Abnorm. Psychol., 101: 326–331.

Tyndel, M. (1999) Posttraumatic stress disorder and outcomes for functioning and quality of life. Am. J. Psychiatry, 156: 804–805.

Tynes, L.L., White, K. and Steketee, G.S. (1990) Toward a new nosology of obsessive compulsive disorder. Compr. Psychiatry, 31: 465–480.

Tyrer, P. and Baldwin, D. (2006) Generalised anxiety disorder. Lancet, 368: 2156–2166.

Uhlenhuth, E.H., Balter, M.B., Mellinger, G.D., Cisin, I.H. and Clinthorne, J. (1983) Symptom checklist syndromes in the general population. Correlations with psychotherapeutic drug use. Arch. Gen. Psychiatry, 40: 1167–1173.

Velting, O.N. and Albano, A.M. (2001) Current trends in the understanding and treatment of social phobia in youth. J. Child Psychol. Psychiatry, 42: 127–140.

Vieweg, W.V., Julius, D.A., Fernandez, A., Beatty-Brooks, M., Hettema, J.M. and Pandurangi, A.K. (2006) Posttraumatic stress disorder: clinical features, pathophysiology, and treatment. Am. J. Med., 119: 383–390.

Vriends, N., Becker, E.S., Meyer, A., Michael, T. and Margraf, J. (2007) Subtypes of social phobia: are they of any use? J. Anxiety Disord., 21: 59–75.

Wagner, K.D. (2001) Generalized anxiety disorder in children and adolescents. Psychiatr. Clin. North Am., 24: 139–153.

Wacker, H.R., Müllejans, R., Klein, K.H. and Battegay, R. (1992) Identification of cases of anxiety disorders and affective disorders in the community according to ICD-10 and DSM-III-R by using the Composite International Diagnostic Interview (CIDI). Int. J. Methods Psychiatr. Res., 2: 91–100.

Watson, D. (2005) Rethinking the mood and anxiety disorders: a quantitative hierarchical model for DSM-V. J. Abnorm. Psychol., 114: 522–536.

Wittchen, H.U., Essau, C.A., von Zerssen, D., Krieg, J.C. and Zaudig, M. (1992) Lifetime and six-month prevalence of mental disorders in the Munich Follow-Up Study. Eur. Arch. Psychiatry Clin. Neurosci., 241: 247–258.

Wittchen, H.U. and Fehm, L. (2003) Epidemiology and natural course of social fears and social phobia. Acta Psychiatr. Scand., 108(Suppl. 417): 4–18.

Wittchen, H.U. and Hoyer, J. (2001) Generalized anxiety disorder: nature and course. J. Clin. Psychiatry, 62(Suppl. 11): 15–19. (discussion 20-11).

Wittchen, H.U., Zhao, S., Kessler, R.C. and Eaton, W.W. (1994) DSM-III-R generalized anxiety disorder in the National Comorbidity Survey. Arch. Gen. Psychiatry, 51: 355–364.

Wood, S.R. and Tolin, D.F. (2002) The relationship between disgust sensitivity and avoidant behavior: studies of clinical and nonclinical samples. J. Anxiety Disord., 16: 543–559.

Wu, K.D., Clark, L.A. and Watson, D. (2006) Relations between obsessive-compulsive disorder and personality: beyond axis I–axis II comorbidity. J. Anxiety Disord., 20: 695–717.

Yonkers, K.A., Dyck, I.R. and Keller, M.B. (2001) An eight-year longitudinal comparison of clinical course and characteristics of social phobia among men and women. Psychiatr. Serv., 52: 637–643.

Yonkers, K.A., Warshaw, M.G., Massion, A.O. and Keller, M.B. (1996) Phenomenology and course of generalised anxiety disorder. Br. J. Psychiatry, 168: 308–313.

Yule, W. (1992) Post-traumatic stress disorder in child survivors of shipping disasters: the sinking of the 'Jupiter'. Psychother. Psychosom., 57: 200–205.

Zohar, A.H., Ratzoni, G., Pauls, D.L., Apter, A., Bleich, A., Kron, S., Rappaport, M., Weizman, A. and Cohen, D.J. (1992) An epidemiological study of obsessive-compulsive disorder and related disorders in Israeli adolescents. J. Am. Acad. Child Adolesc. Psychiatry, 31: 1057–1061.

CHAPTER 5.2

How effective are current drug treatments for anxiety disorders, and how could they be improved?

David S. Baldwin[1,2,]* and Matthew Garner[1,3]

[1]*Clinical Neuroscience Division, School of Medicine, University of Southampton, Southampton, UK*
[2]*Mood and Anxiety Disorders Service, Hampshire Partnership Trust, Southampton, Southampton, UK*
[3]*School of Psychology, University of Southampton, Southampton, UK*

Abstract: Although there are many psychotropic drugs and psychotherapies available for the treatment of patients with anxiety disorders, overall clinical outcomes and the standard of care for most patients with these common, persistent and impairing illnesses are usually far from optimal. The disorders typically follow a chronic or recurring course in which full symptomatic remission is uncommon; they are associated with the temporal accumulation of comorbid disorders and with an increased suicide risk; and treatment responsiveness may diminish over time. This chapter examines the efficacy of current pharmacological treatments in the three main anxiety disorders – generalised anxiety disorder (GAD), panic disorder and social anxiety disorder (social phobia) – and summarises how clinical outcomes might be improved by a number of alternative approaches, including the enhanced use of existing treatments, modifications to existing psychotropic drugs and the development of new targets for anxiolytic pharmacotherapy. It also describes how advances in genetics and neuroscience might lead towards more individualised drug treatments, whilst recognising that theoretical treatment advances can only improve outcomes if used rationally, in collaboration with the patient.

Keywords: psychopharmacology; pharmacotherapy; treatment efficacy; treatment response; generalised anxiety disorder; social anxiety disorder (social phobia); panic disorder; cognitive-behavioural therapy; combination treatment

I. Which pharmacological treatments are efficacious in anxiety disorders?

Systematic reviews and randomised placebo-controlled trials indicate that some selective serotonin reuptake inhibitors (SSRIs), the serotonin-noradrenaline reuptake inhibitors (SNRIs) venlafaxine and duloxetine, some benzodiazepines (alprazolam and diazepam), the tricyclic antidepressant (TCA) imipramine, the 5-HT$_{1A}$ partial agonist buspirone, the novel anticonvulsant pregabalin, the antipsychotic trifluoperazine and the antihistamine hydroxyzine are all efficacious in the acute treatment of patients with generalised anxiety disorder (GAD) (Baldwin and Polkinghorn, 2005; Mitte et al., 2005; Baldwin and Ajel, 2007). In long-term treatment, double-blind studies show that continuing with SSRI or SNRI treatment is associated with an increase in overall response rates, and placebo-controlled relapse-prevention studies in patients who have responded to acute SSRI treatment reveal a significant advantage for staying on active medication

*Corresponding author. E-mail: dsb1@soton.ac.uk

DOI: 10.1016/S1569-7339(07)00018-5

compared to switching to placebo, for up to 12 months (Baldwin et al., 2005). Placebo-controlled augmentation studies demonstrate that atypical antipsychotics (risperidone, olanzapine) may prove helpful, after non-response to first-line pharmacological treatment (Tyrer and Baldwin, 2006).

The situation is broadly similar in panic disorder, where randomised double-blind placebo-controlled trials indicate that all SSRIs, venlafaxine, the selective noradrenaline reuptake inhibitor (NRI) reboxetine, the TCAs clomipramine and imipramine and some benzodiazepines (alprazolam, clonazepam, diazepam and lorazepam) are efficacious in acute treatment. Buspirone is not efficacious in acute treatment in panic disorder, but most SSRIs and imipramine are efficacious in relapse prevention. Augmentation studies after initial non-response indicate that the effects of cognitive-behaviour therapy (CBT) can be enhanced by the SSRI paroxetine and the efficacy of fluoxetine by the beta-blocker and 5-HT autoreceptor antagonist pindolol (Baldwin et al., 2005).

In social anxiety disorder, there is evidence of acute treatment efficacy for SSRIs, venlafaxine, the monoamine oxidase inhibitors (MAOI) phenelzine and moclobemide, the benzodiazepines bromazepam and clonazepam, the anticonvulsants gabapentin and pregabalin and the antipsychotic olanzapine. Neither imipramine nor buspirone is efficacious in acute treatment (Blanco et al., 2003), but placebo-controlled studies demonstrate that clonazepam and some SSRIs can prevent relapse. Unlike the situation in panic disorder, pindolol does not appear efficacious as an augmentation agent after poor response to paroxetine.

II. What is the mechanism of action in anxiety disorders?

Investigations of altered serotonergic or noradrenergic function in the pathophysiology of anxiety disorders have produced rather inconsistent findings – whether this is in GAD, panic disorder or social phobia. However, the 'broad-spectrum' efficacy of SSRIs, SNRIs and benzodiazepines in anxiety disorders has naturally focused attention

on the possible role of enhanced serotonergic and noradrenergic neurotransmission, and altered function of the GABA-benzodiazepine receptor chloride ionophore complex, in the successful response to pharmacological treatment.

Two morphologically distinct major serotonergic systems have been implicated in the neurobiology of anxiety disorders. The two distinct systems originate from the dorsal and medial raphe nuclei and both innervate many regions of the brain, including the frontal cortex, cingulate gyrus and amygdala, but they have differing afferent and efferent projections and actions and dysfunction in different brain regions may relate to different forms of anxiety disorder. Projections from the medial raphe nuclei may be of primary importance in modulating fear and anticipatory anxiety, whereas the projections from the dorsal raphe nuclei may mediate the cognitive aspects of anxiety disorders (Grove et al., 1997). SSRIs enhance the availability of serotonin by blocking the presynaptic 5-HT transporter protein, but this effect is offset at first by the activity of presynaptic inhibitory 5-HT_{1A} receptors on raphe cell bodies which act to reduce 5-HT availability, and this may explain the initial increase in 'nervousness' that can be seen at the start of SSRI treatment. After two weeks of treatment, these receptors become desensitised and serotonin availability is increased.

The importance of enhanced serotonergic neurotransmission in the treatment response in patients with anxiety disorders is seen from findings of randomised controlled tryptophan depletion studies (Bell et al., 2001). In these, patients successfully treated with an SSRI experience a significantly greater return of psychological symptoms when subject to tryptophan depletion after exposure to stressful situations – such as reading autobiographical scripts for embarrassing situations in patients with social phobia (Argyropoulos et al., 2004) or administration of flumazenil in patients with panic disorder (Bell et al., 2002).

Noradrenergic neurones have their origin in the locus coeruleus and branch extensively throughout the forebrain: release of noradrenaline activates α_1 (postsynaptic) receptors involved in arousal; α_2 receptors linked to arousal, regulation of blood pressure and growth hormone release (postsynaptic) or in the inhibition of further noradrenaline release (presynaptic autoreceptors); and β receptors, whose central function is uncertain.

The different anxiety disorders may be characterised by differing perturbations of the adrenergic system: for example, administration of presynaptic α_2 receptor antagonists (yohimbine, idazoxan) increases anxiety in healthy volunteers (Goldberg et al., 1983; Krystal et al., 1992) and panic attack frequency in panic disorder patients (Charney et al., 1984), but is not anxiogenic in patients with obsessive-compulsive disorder (OCD) (Rasmussen et al., 1987) or GAD (Charney et al., 1989). Reflecting these findings, the centrally acting α_2 receptor partial agonist clonidine is anxiolytic in patients with panic disorder (Coplan et al., 1992), but ineffective in diminishing obsessive-compulsive symptoms (Hewlett et al., 1992). Investigations of postsynaptic α_2 receptor function demonstrate a blunting of the growth hormone response to clonidine challenge in panic disorder and GAD, with inconsistent results in social phobia and OCD.

Unlike the many studies of the effects of acute tryptophan depletion in patients who have responded successfully to SSRI treatment of anxiety disorders, there have been few investigations of catecholamine depletion in patients responding to noradrenergic compounds. Depletion of noradrenaline and adrenaline by α-methyl-p-tyrosine elicits depressive symptoms in patients who have responded to noradrenergic antidepressant treatment (Delgado et al., 1993), but not in drug-free patients with OCD (Longhurst et al., 1999). As in investigations of the effects of tryptophan depletion, the psychological effects of acute decreases in catecholamine availability may be more pronounced if biochemical challenges are accompanied by neuroendocrine or psychological challenge tests.

Benzodiazepines enhance the effects of the inhibitory neurotransmitter γ-aminobutyric acid (GABA) by acting as agonists at high-affinity sites on the $GABA_A$ receptor that allosterically modulates the GABA–chloride ionophore complex. Antagonists at this site, such as flumazenil, have minimal effect when administered alone, but reverse the actions of benzodiazepines and of

anxiogenic inverse agonists such as the B-carboline FG7142 (Jackson and Nutt, 1992). Patients with anxiety disorders may differ from healthy subjects in having an altered 'set-point' at benzodiazepine binding sites – for example, flumazenil administration precipitates panic attacks in patients but not controls (Nutt et al., 1990) and binding of radio-labelled flumazenil is reduced, particularly in orbitofrontal cortex and insula (Malizia et al., 1998).

Benzodiazepines are potent anxiolytic, anticonvulsant and myorelaxant drugs, but can be associated with troublesome sedation, memory problems, tolerance and discontinuation symptoms. The alpha-1 subunit of the $GABA_A$ receptor appears responsible for the sedative, amnestic and anticonvulsant properties of benzodiazepines, whereas the alpha-2 subunit appears involved in the anxiolytic effects. $GABA_A$ receptor subtype agonists or modulators may therefore be expected to exert anxiolytic effects with a reduced risk of unwanted sedation (Korpi and Sinkkonen, 2006).

Novel approaches to enhancing the effects of GABA include increasing its synthesis (topiramate, valproate); inhibiting its breakdown (vigabatrin); inhibiting its reuptake (tiagabine); through direct agonism at the benzodiazepine site (pagoclone) and use of GABA analogues (gabapentin and pregabalin). Tiagabine inhibits GABA reuptake into presynpatic and glial cells, in vivo microdialysis studies indicating reuptake inhibition is time-limited and dose-dependent (Ipponi et al., 1999). Furthermore, as the effects of tiagabine are most marked when synaptic release of GABA has occurred, it works in a more 'physiological' manner, which may reduce the potential for the development of tolerance. Early findings suggested tiagabine was efficacious in reducing core GAD symptoms such as anxious mood and tension (Pollack et al., 2005), but subsequent large randomised controlled trials have produced disappointing results.

The mechanism of action of pregabalin (the s-enantiomer of 3-isobutylgaba) differs to that of all other known anxiolytic drugs. Although a structural analogue of GABA it has no clinically significant effects at either $GABA_A$ or $GABA_B$ receptors, and is not converted into either GABA or a GABA agonist; furthermore, it does not act as an antagonist at glutamate receptors and has no effects on 5-HT reuptake (Kavoussi, 2006). It binds in a state-dependent manner to the alpha-2-delta subunit of P/Q-type voltage-gated calcium channels of 'over-excited' presynaptic neurones (Dooley et al., 2002; Fink et al., 2002), changing the channel conformation and reducing release of excitatory neurotransmitters, such as glutamate, aspartate and substance P. The consequent reduced stimulation of postsynaptic neurones is thought to be responsible for its anxiolytic, anticonvulsant and analgesic effects (Stahl, 2004). This proposed mechanism of action is supported by findings of pre-clinical studies in animal models demonstrating that binding to alpha-2-delta receptors is needed for pregabalin to exert anxiolytic-like effects.

III. Do randomised controlled trials reveal consistent differences in efficacy?

OCD, in which anxiety symptoms are common, appears to show a singular specificity of the acute treatment response, to compounds that primarily inhibit 5-HT reuptake, namely the SSRIs and clomipramine (Fineberg and Gale, 2005), whereas primarily noradrenaline reuptake inhibitors have little or no efficacy. The situation is quite different in the treatment of patients with the anxiety disorders GAD, panic disorder and social phobia, where a wide range of psychotropic drugs with varying pharmacological properties are efficacious, and where few comparative studies have revealed significant differences in treatment response between compounds.

In GAD, acute treatment studies have shown that escitalopram (20 mg/day) was marginally more efficacious than paroxetine (20 mg/day) (Baldwin et al., 2006), and that venlafaxine (75–225 mg/day) was superior to fluoxetine (20–60 mg/day) on some outcome measures in patients with comorbid GAD and major depression (Silverstone and Salinas, 2001); in addition, rather inconsistent evidence shows that psychological symptoms of anxiety in GAD may respond better to antidepressant drugs than to benzodiazepines (Baldwin and Polkinghorn, 2005). In randomised controlled

treatment studies in panic disorder, escitalopram appeared marginally superior to citalopram (Stahl et al., 2003) and the SSRIs paroxetine and fluvoxamine appeared more effective than the NRIs reboxetine or maprotiline, respectively (Den Boer and Westenberg, 1988; Bertani et al., 2004). In social phobia, escitalopram (20 mg/day) appeared more efficacious than paroxetine (20 mg/day) (Lader et al., 2004), whereas venlafaxine (75–225 mg/day) and paroxetine (20–50 mg/day) had similar efficacy in two placebo-controlled studies (Allgulander et al., 2004; Liebowitz et al., 2005). Therefore the only consistent observations of potential superior efficacy for a particular medication in anxiety disorders are for escitalopram over the SSRI paroxetine, reflecting similar findings in major depression (Kennedy et al., 2006): whether this stems from the actions of escitalopram at the allosteric site for the 5-HT transporter protein (Chen et al., 2005; Sánchez, 2006) is uncertain and requires further investigation.

IV. Why don't randomised controlled trials reveal more differences between treatments?

The inability of randomised controlled trials to reveal consistent clinically relevant differences between pharmacological treatments might simply reflect the limited impact that current approaches have in correcting the underlying pathophysiology in anxiety disorders. Novel treatments could result in improved efficacy and tolerability, but the design of phase II and III studies also needs to be refined, in order to be able to demonstrate potential advances convincingly. The lack of reliable, readily available diagnostic markers means anxiety disorders are essentially syndromes, probably arising from variable causes: as diagnosis is reliant on the reporting of symptoms, many of which are non-specific, studies unavoidably include undifferentiated patient subgroups. Furthermore, study sponsors are usually concerned to demonstrate differences between broad groups of patients treated either with active medication or with placebo, rather than the identification of subgroups of patients that might respond particularly well to treatment as this could limit the licensed indications for the drug, or restrict it to an uneconomic niche. Patients participating in treatment studies are often characterised rather poorly, with limited efforts to identify subgroups according to particular symptom clusters, or personality traits, dimensions and disorders: and yet these factors are important in predicting overall outcome (e.g. Mennin and Heimberg, 2000; Slaap and den Boer, 2001). As in randomised controlled trials in major depression, the exclusion of more severely ill patients from treatment studies means that the severity of symptoms at baseline may be insufficient to reveal reliable differences from placebo or between active compounds. In addition, the outcome measures that are commonly employed in trials can be inappropriate (such as measuring panic attack frequency rather than illness severity, in panic disorder); and traditional psychopathological rating scales may contain many non-specific and insensitive items (such as occurs in the Hamilton Anxiety Scale, in studies GAD), leading to reliance on large multi-centre studies with higher placebo response rates (Stein et al., 2006).

V. Could clinical outcomes be improved with better use of current treatments?

Patients included within randomised controlled trials in anxiety disorders are required by regulators to have low levels of coexisting depressive symptoms or comorbid disorders, are in generally good physical health, have limited use of concomitant medication and have anxiety symptoms that are neither too mild to be able to reveal efficacy nor too severe to comprise their participation in a treatment study. Even in these good prognosis patients who are subject to frequent assessments in a supportive environment, the effects of treatment can be disappointing. For example, average overall response rates in randomised controlled trials of SNRIs in the acute treatment of patients with GAD are approximately 60% with active medication compared with around 40% with placebo; in social phobia, average overall response rates in acute treatment studies are approximately 55% with an SSRI and 35% with placebo.

Clinical outcomes might be improved by the better use of existing treatment approaches, such as prescribing in accordance with evidence-based guidelines; the combination of multiple drug treatments; and the combination of anxiolytic agents with structured psychotherapies. As an example, randomised controlled trials of guideline-based treatment of depressed patients in primary care show that outcomes can be improved, with greater symptom reduction, improved social function and greater cost-effectiveness: interventions that improve outcomes typically also include 'case management' and some involvement of specialist mental health services (Von Korff and Goldberg, 2001).

Only few randomised controlled trials of the effects of implementing treatment guidelines for anxiety disorders within routine clinical practice have been performed, and have produced inconsistent results. A comparison of treatment guidelines, CBT and self-help techniques in patients with either GAD or panic disorder found no differences in outcomes at 12 weeks or after 9 months (Van Boeijen et al., 2005); and comparison of local broad guidelines with computerised patient-specific treatment recommendations in primary care patients with mild anxiety and depressive symptoms found no difference in outcomes at 6 months (Thomas et al., 2004). By contrast, case management (comprising preference assessment, psycho-education, monitoring and physician feedback) improved response rates compared to 'treatment as usual' (Rollman et al., 2005) in patients with either panic disorder or GAD; as did CBT combined with algorithm-based pharmacotherapy in patients with panic disorder (Roy-Byrne et al., 2005).

Randomised controlled trials of the first-line combination treatment of SSRIs with benzodiazepines in panic disorder suggest that the addition of benzodiazepines may produce an earlier reduction in symptom severity than is seen with SSRI treatment, given alone; but this combination is not associated with additional benefit at the end of the acute treatment period (Woods et al., 1992; Goddard et al., 2001; Pollack et al., 2003).

Combination approaches can also be used to minimise the adverse events of psychotropic medication: for example, in patients undergoing SSRI treatment, the prescription of modafinil to relieve fatigue and sleepiness (Fava et al., 2005); or the addition of buproprion or mirtazapine to reduce sexual dysfunction (Baldwin and Mayers, 2003), or the use of trazodone to minimise insomnia (Dording et al., 2002). The findings of placebo-controlled augmentation studies in patients with anxiety disorders who have responded poorly to initial treatment with a single compound have been summarised above.

VI. Can psychological therapies enhance the efficacy of pharmacological treatments?

Cognitive-behavioural therapy (CBT), the most extensively researched form of psychological treatment (Dobson, 2001), is effective in many anxiety disorders (Butler et al., 2006). Based on Beck's early cognitive model it assumes that biases in information processing which favour threat information increase perceptions of threat and danger, and thereby maintain anxiety disorders (Beck et al., 1985; Williams et al., 1997; Mogg and Bradley, 1998). Anxiety is thought to be characterised by the cognitive system functioning in a mode of preparedness for dealing with danger, including a basic 'threat' mode that includes a bias to evaluate external cues as being threatening, increased attentional vigilance and enhanced psychobiological and behavioural responsiveness to facilitate avoidance or escape from presumed danger (Ohman and Mineka, 2001). Neurobiological theories suggest that an interconnected neural system, involving subcortical and cortical structures such as the amygdala, thalamus and frontal cortex, underpins the activation of this anxious cognitive mode (LeDoux 1996; Davidson and Irwin, 1999). Consistent with these predictions, anxious individuals show dysfunctional biases in perception and attention when processing emotional material, including emotional facial expressions, words or pictures (Mathews and MacLeod, 2005; Garner et al., 2006). CBT aims to relieve anxiety symptoms by correcting

cognitive biases using integrated cognitive restructuring and behavioural exposure techniques. Recent advances in information-processing theories of pathological anxiety (Bouton et al., 2001; Clark and McManus, 2002) and in the experimental methods used to delineate disorder-specific cognitive biases have refined cognitive-behavioural treatments for the anxiety disorders. The efficacy of psychological and pharmacological approaches is broadly similar in the acute treatment of anxiety disorders (Gould et al., 1997; Baldwin et al., 2005) although there is some evidence that relapse rates are lower after an initial response to CBT-based therapies than after response to drug treatment (Gould et al., 1995; Simpson et al., 2004).

Neither pharmacotherapy nor CBT help all patients and even those who do improve are often troubled by residual symptoms. This has sparked interest in combining treatment approaches in order to improve clinical outcomes (Black, 2006). Medication might enhance the efficacy of CBT through reduction of heightened anxiety and arousal, thereby enabling patients to tolerate longer exposure to feared situations. Moderate intensity anxiety during exposure is thought to enhance processing of the corrective information embedded in the exposure situation and thereby ameliorate negative cognitions and reduce pathological fear (Foa et al., 2002). A review of combination treatments for anxiety disorders found that post-treatment and follow-up effect size and percentage responder data from randomised controlled trials did not demonstrate a consistent advantage or disadvantage for combined treatment over CBT alone, in OCD, social phobia or generalised anxiety disorder (Foa et al., 2002).

In GAD, it is uncertain whether combining pharmacological and psychological treatments is associated with greater overall efficacy than is seen with either treatment, when given alone (Durham and Turvey, 1987; Power et al., 1990; Lader and Bond, 1998). Similar uncertainty is seen in panic disorder (Van Balkom et al., 1997; Barlow et al., 2000), although combination treatment with exposure was superior to imipramine when given alone (Mavissakalian et al., 1983); combination treatment with paroxetine was superior to psychological treatment alone, in studies of bibliotherapy

(Dannon et al., 2002), 'very brief' CBT (Stein et al., 2000) and basic CBT (Oehrberg et al., 1995); buspirone treatment may enhance the short-term efficacy of CBT (Cottraux et al., 1995); and combination treatment seemed to offer initial advantages over CBT alone, but higher relapse rates after treatment was stopped (Marks et al., 1993; Barlow et al., 2000). In social phobia, combination treatment does not appear superior to psychological or pharmacological treatment, when given alone (Blomhoff et al., 2001; Clark et al., 2003; Davidson et al., 2004). Given the absence of consistent evidence for enhanced efficacy with combined psychological and pharmacological treatments, recent evidence-based guidelines for the treatment of patients with anxiety disorders recommend that combining CBT with drug treatment should only be considered after a non-response to drug treatment in patients with GAD, panic disorder, social phobia or post-traumatic stress disorder (PTSD): in OCD combination treatment is recommended, when efficacy needs to be maximised (Baldwin et al., 2005).

VII. Could clinical outcomes be improved, with new targets for anxiolytic drugs?

Advances in clinical neuroscience and awareness of the limited efficacy and adverse effects of current treatments for anxiety disorders have together encouraged the identification of many new targets for the development of potential new anxiolytic drugs. As described in detail in previous chapters, many putative anxiolytics are being evaluated, some in phase III studies; others have failed to sustain the promise of early findings and are no longer in development.

As reviewed above, although SSRIs have proven efficacy across the range of anxiety disorders, many patients do not respond and adverse effects such as sexual dysfunction reduce their acceptability in clinical practice (Baldwin, 2004). Buspirone has efficacy in GAD but it and other 5-HT$_{1A}$ partial agonist drugs with a similar mechanism of action are subject to extensive first-pass hepatic metabolism, and alternative methods of delivery such as a skin patch have the potential to increase bioavailability, and possibly efficacy. Combining 5-HT reuptake inhibition with 5-HT$_2$ antagonist properties may result in greater efficacy in relieving anxiety symptoms and reduced liability for treatment-emergent sleep disturbance or sexual dysfunction. In theory, combining an SSRI action with 5-HT1$_A$ and 5-HT1$_B$ autoreceptor antagonist properties may increase the availability of 5-HT within the synaptic cleft and thereby advance the onset of action of SSRIs. The 5-HT$_{2C}$ antagonist deramciclane was found efficacious in a preliminary double-blind placebo-controlled study in patients with GAD (Naukkarinen et al., 2005), but subsequent studies failed to replicate this finding. Similarly, the potential efficacy of 5-HT$_3$ antagonists (Costall and Naylor, 1993; Harmer et al., 2006b) has not been confirmed consistently within large randomised placebo-controlled studies (Lecrubier et al., 1993).

The melatonin agonist agomelatine (which also has 5-HT$_{2C}$ antagonist properties) has anxiolytic properties in animal models (Millan et al., 2005) and been found superior to placebo in randomised controlled trials in patients with major depression, with good relief of anxiety symptoms (Loo et al., 2002, 2003), few discontinuation symptoms and little sexual dysfunction (Montgomery et al., 2004; Montgomery, 2006): it is likely to become available for clinical use soon. Selective non-peptide antagonists for tachykinin receptors have been available for many years, but drug development has largely focused on the substance-P-preferring receptor known as neurokinin-1 (NK1). Originally developed as potential analgesics, NK1 receptor antagonists had properties in animal models suggesting possible antidepressant and anxiolytic effects (Stout et al., 2001), and a randomised controlled trial with the substance P antagonist MK 869 found significantly greater relief of anxiety symptoms than paroxetine, in patients with major depression (Kramer et al., 1998). Although subsequent studies with this compound could not confirm its efficacy, clinical investigations with other compounds with similar properties suggest that this approach may still offer some promise (Kramer, et al., 2004) and compounds with mixed substance P antagonist and 5-HT re-uptake blocking properties are in development.

Three classes of metabotropic G-protein-coupled glutamate receptors ($mGlu_{1-8}$) regulate glutamate release and modify postsynaptic excitability. In Group I, an $mGlu_1$ receptor agonist (*trans*-ACPD) enhances the startle response in rodents (Grauer and Marquis, 1999); and an $mGlu_5$ receptor antagonist (MPEP) has been found to exert anxiolytic-like effects (Ballard et al., 2005). In Group II, LY354740, an agonist at $mGlu_2$ receptors, limits glutamate release through a presynaptic mechanism and has an anxiolytic profile in animal models, where its effects are reversed by flumazenil; it prevents CO_2-induced anxiety in panic patients, and reduced anxiety symptoms in patients with GAD (Swanson et al., 2005). There are few ligands for Group III mGlu receptors, although the $mGlu_6$ receptor agonist MSOP has shown anxiolytic-like effects.

As described in previous chapters, many neurotransmitters exert direct or indirect effects on the $GABA_A$ receptor, including neurosteroids, corticotrophin-releasing factor (CRF), arginine vasopressin (AVP), neuropeptide-Y (NPY), cholecystokinin (CCK), substance P, neurotensin, glutamate, somatostatin, norepinephrine, dopamine, acetylcholine, serotonin and *N*-methyl-D-aspartate. Other potential targets for anxiolytic drugs include receptors for CCK, NPY, adenosine and AVP.

Although CCK-4 antagonists block the anxiogenic effects of CCK, efficacy of CCK-4 antagonists has not been demonstrated in placebo-controlled studies in patients with anxiety disorders. NPY may downregulate norepinephrine neurotransmission and can exert anxiolytic-like effects that are reversed by the alpha-2 antagonist idazoxan. Ligands at differing receptors exert differing effects: anxiolysis appears to be mediated by NPY_1 and NPY_5 receptors, whereas sedation may be mediated through the NPY_5 receptor only: anxiolytic effects are seen with NPY_1 agonists and NPY_2 antagonists. Caffeine is a non-specific antagonist at adenosine A_1 and A_{2A} receptors, and exerts anxiogenic effects: caffeine-induced wakefulness and presumably anxiogenesis is mediated through the A_{2A} receptor, as caffeine induces wakefulness in wild and A_1-knockout

mice but has no effects in A_{2A}-knockout mice (Huang et al., 2005). Polymorphisms for the A_{2A} receptor have been reported in patients with panic disorder (Hamilton et al., 2004). AVP is produced in the hypothalamus and is involved in regulation of corticotrophin secretion by the pituitary gland; AVP-containing neurones project to the limbic system, and vasopressin receptors (V_{1a} and V_{2a}) are located in the septum and hippocampus. An antagonist at vasopressin V_{1b} receptors (SSR149415) is effective in rodent models of anxiety and depression, these effects probably occurring through receptors in limbic structures (Griebel, 2002).

An alternative approach to antidepressant drug development has been to target the CRF receptor, and this approach may also yield potential anxiolytics. Two CRF subtypes are known to exist, differing in their localisation and receptor pharmacology: the CRF1 receptor is abundant within cerebral cortex, cerebellum and pituitary, whereas CRF2 receptors are found mainly in the septum, ventromedial hypothalamus and dorsal raphe nucleus (Chalmers et al., 1996). A number of selective CRF1 receptor antagonists have been developed, with some evidence of potential efficacy for the treatment of depression and anxiety disorders (Zobel et al., 2000; Nemeroff, 2002).

VIII. Could clinical outcomes be improved through using genetic approaches?

Certain demographic or clinical factors have been found predictive of treatment response or non-response in patients with anxiety disorders, but many individuals with factors that are predictive of a good response will still respond only poorly. Concerted efforts are therefore being made to establish whether a given patient is likely to respond particularly well to a given treatment, on the basis of their genetic profile. For example, genotyping for cytochrome P450 enzymes might be useful in deciding which SSRI to use, and at what dosage, as slow metabolisers would be predisposed to the development of higher concentrations and a greater burden of adverse effects. However, many other factors affect the pharmacokinetic properties of psychotropic drugs, including age, diet, smoking, concomitant treatment and physical ill-health and it is probably premature to incorporate P450 genotyping within routine clinical practice (Perlis, 2007).

Variations in the human genome account for the genetic component of susceptibility to disease and response to drug treatment. Much of the variation in the genome is due to single nucleotide polymorphisms (SNPs) where two alternate bases occur at one position (Taillon-Miller et al., 1998). Pharmacogenomic approaches use high-density SNP maps to correlate a patient's genetic profile with their likely response to a certain drug. For example, in patients with depressive disorders, particular genotypes could be found to predict the likelihood of an earlier onset of action and greater overall efficacy with a particular psychotropic drug, whereas other genotypes might be associated with better tolerability of treatment (Wong and Licinio, 2004). The goal of pharmacogenomic research is therefore to match an individual patient phenotype with an individual drug treatment, targeted against proteins containing functionally relevant SNPs (Roses, 2002): in this 'individualised medicine', tissue samples from patients could be removed and used to generate a multiplicity of treatments that would vary between individuals.

A less complex and for the moment more feasible approach would be to base the selection of a particular drug treatment upon the presence of an identified clinical biomarker that has been shown to be predictive of response: in 'personalised' or 'stratified' medicine, a patient is found to be similar to a cohort that has exhibited a particular treatment response (Trusheim et al., 2007). This approach is already used in other areas of medicine, such as identification of a genetic variant of the enzyme UDP-glucuronosyltransferase 1A1 that predisposes a patient to severe toxicity reactions with the oncology drug irinotecan (Paoluzzi et al., 2004). In the area of mental health, patients with particular polymorphisms for 5-HT$_{2C}$ receptors are predisposed to weight gain and drug-induced dyskinesias associated with atypical antipsychotic drug treatment (Reynolds et al., 2005), and 'bedside' testing for these polymorphisms may not be many years away.

IX. The insights offered by studies of pharmacological modulation of emotion processing

The similar overall efficacy of pharmacological, psychological and combination treatments raises questions regarding potential common mechanisms that might be involved in the treatment response. Recent years have seen much research involving pharmacological modulation of the dysfunctional cognitive processes proposed to maintain mood and anxiety disorders, and using advanced imaging techniques to probe the functional neuroanatomy of pharmacological and psychological treatments for anxiety disorders.

Various methods have been used to examine the effect of 5-HT on emotion processing, including the depletion of tryptophan (a 5-HT precursor) to decrease 5-HT function. Tryptophan depletion slows response times for happy but not sad targets in an affective go/no-go task (Murphy et al., 2002), decreases the ability to discriminate between large and small rewards in emotional decision-making (Rogers et al., 2003), impairs the identification of fearful facial expressions in healthy women (Harmer et al., 2003c), reduces the identification of happy faces and elevates eye-blink startle responses in recovered depressed patients (Hayward et al., 2005), increases the interference effect of threat words on a modified Stroop task in healthy volunteers and recovered depressed patients (Hayward et al., 2005), and increases the interference effect of social threat words on a modified Stroop task in recovered depressed patients taking medication (Munafo et al., 2006).

An alternative approach has been to assess the effect of increasing 5-HT function, either by tryptophan supplementation or through the administration of an SSRI. Tryptophan supplementation has been shown to increase the identification of happy faces in healthy female volunteers (Attenburrow et al., 2003; Murphy et al., 2006), and to decrease baseline startle responsivity and possibly decrease attentional bias for negative words for women, as suggested by error rates on a visual probe task (Murphy et al., 2006). These findings suggest that increasing 5-HT function in women may elicit a cognitive bias favouring positive information. These findings converge with the observations that a single dose of the SSRI citalopram increased the identification of happy faces in healthy controls (Harmer et al., 2003a), that administration of citalopram for 1 week decreased amygdala responses to masked threat faces (Harmer et al., 2006a) and that treatment with an SSRI (citalopram or paroxetine) for 4 weeks significantly reduced a measure of interpretative bias, namely the tendency to interpret ambiguous homophones negatively, in patients with GAD (Mogg et al., 2004).

With regard to the effect of NA on emotion processing, administration of the beta-adrenoceptor blocker propranolol has been shown to reduce the identification of sad facial expressions (Harmer et al., 2001), to impair the ability to discriminate between the magnitude of aversive outcomes in emotional decision-making (Rogers et al., 2004) and to reduce memory for emotional information (Chamberlain et al., 2006). Furthermore, acute potentiation of NA using a single dose of the NRI reboxetine is associated with a positive bias in the perception of happy facial expressions in healthy individuals (Harmer et al., 2003b), and with enhanced emotional memory for positive information (Chamberlain et al., 2006). In a comparison of the effects of citalopram with those of reboxetine on several emotion-processing tasks, in which each drug was administered for 7 days, both the SSRI and NRI reduced the identification of negative facial expressions (fear and anger) and increased the recall of positive, relative to negative, information (Harmer et al., 2004), which suggests that 5-HT and NA both play a role in modulating processing biases for emotional information.

Taken together, these studies indicate that manipulation of 5-HT and NA affects processing of emotional information, for example with increased 5-HT function being associated with an enhanced positive processing bias. Methodological differences between studies, such as the duration of pharmacological manipulation, possible dose effects and varying emotion-processing tasks undoubtedly complicate the comparison of findings across investigations, but these observations provide an intriguing insight into the mechanisms by which efficacious pharmacological treatments might improve psychological symptoms of anxiety, such as anxious apprehension and excessive worrying.

X. Do neuroimaging studies explain the neuroanatomy of the treatment response?

The number of studies that have used neuroimaging techniques to explicitly evaluate neural correlates of psychological and pharmacological treatment has steadily increased (Roffman et al., 2005). For example, successful behavioural therapy for OCD has been found associated with a decrease in metabolism in the caudate nucleus, consistent with the presumed pathophysiology of the disorder (Saxena et al., 1998). Moreover, both fluoxetine and psychotherapy for OCD appear to uncouple dysfunctional cortico-striatothalamic circuitry (Baxter et al., 1992; Schwartz et al., 1996). Significant deactivation within the anterior and superior cingulate cortex, the left hippocampus and the right thalamus has been observed in a mixed group of patients with anxiety disorders (OCD, PTSD, social phobia) following SSRI treatment, with greater deactivation within the precentral, right inferior, middle frontal and left prefrontal regions in treatment responders than in non-responders (Carey et al., 2004).

Studies in patients with phobic disorders reveal a reduction in limbic or paralimbic activity following treatment, consistent with the hypothesised pathophysiology (Charney, 2003). For example, in a controlled comparison of cerebral blood flow (CBF) in patients with social phobia before and after pharmacological or group CBT treatment, there was significantly greater attenuation of the rCBF response to a public-speaking challenge, bilaterally in the amygdala, hippocampus and the periamygdaloid, rhinal and parahippocampal cortices in patients than in control subjects, and in treatment responders than in non-responders (Furmark et al., 2002). Furthermore, after successful group CBT, patients with spider phobia showed significantly less activation in the parahippocampal gyrus and right dorsolateral prefrontal cortex (PFC) and increased activation in the right ventral PFC (Paquette et al., 2003). These findings arc consistent with the observed relationship between right ventral PFC activity and downregulation of negative effect and limbic outflow, when subjects were asked to de-emphasise affective responses to threat stimuli; this in turn suggesting the dorsal PFC plays a role in upregulating negative affect and limbic outflow under threat conditions, with treatment shifting activity to the ventral PFC and consequently dampening the fear reaction (Ochsner et al., 2004). Pharmacological and psychological treatments for anxiety disorders are therefore associated with attenuation of brain-imaging abnormalities in regions linked to the pathophysiology of anxiety, and with activation in regions related to positive reappraisal of anxiogenic stimuli (Roffman et al., 2005).

Functional neuroimaging techniques show promise as a clinical tool in the prediction of treatment response in patients with mood and anxiety disorders. Initial reports suggested that patterns of pre-treatment prefrontal and anterior cingulate brain activity could predict treatment outcome in depressed patients (Little et al., 1996; Mayberg et al., 1997; Brody et al., 1999). Pre-treatment orbitofrontal activity predicts outcome with drug treatment (Saxena et al., 1998; Rauch et al., 2002) or CBT (Brody et al. 1998) in patients with OCD (Karleyton et al., 2006). In anxious children and adolescents, significant negative associations are seen between left amygdala activation and measures of improvement with either CBT or SSRI treatment (McClure et al., 2007). In social phobia, the degree of amygdala-limbic attenuation following CBT and pharmacological treatment is linked to overall improvement at 1 year (Furmark et al., 2002); and higher anterior, lateral temporal cortical perfusion at baseline to the response to SSRI treatment (van der Linden et al., 2000). These findings emphasise the importance of limbic regions (amygdala and hippocampus) in mediating anxiety, and deepen our understanding of the mechanisms that might underlie the response to treatment in anxiety disorders. Extending our knowledge of the shared and unshared neurobiological mechanisms that are affected by pharmacological and psychological treatments, and their role in emotion processing, could together lead to innovative approaches that might combine the key therapeutic elements of current pharmacological and psychological treatments.

References

Allgulander, C., Mangano, R., Zhang, J., Dahl, A.A., Lepola, U., Sjodin, I. and Emilien, G. (2004) Efficacy of venlafaxine ER in patients with social anxiety disorder: a double-blind, placebo-controlled, parallel-group comparison with paroxetine. Hum. Psychopharmacol., 19: 387–396.

Argyropoulos, S.V., Hood, S.D., Adrover, M., Bell, C.J., Rich, A.S., Nash, J.R., Rich, N.C., Witchel, H.J. and Nutt, D.J. (2004) Tryptophan depletion reverses the therapeutic effect of selective serotonin reuptake inhibitors in social anxiety disorder. Biol. Psychiatry, 56: 503–509.

Attenburrow, M.J., Williams, C., Odontiadis, J., Reed, A., Powell, J., Cowen, P.J. and Harmer, C.J. (2003) Acute administration of nutritionally sourced tryptophan increases fear recognition. Psychopharmacology, 169: 104–107.

Baldwin, D.S. (2004) Sexual dysfunction associated with antidepressant drugs. Exp. Opin. Drug Safe., 3: 457–470.

Baldwin, D.S. and Ajel, K. (2007) The role of pregabalin in the treatment of generalized anxiety disorder. Neuropsychiatr. Dis. Treat., 3: 185–191.

Baldwin, D.S., Anderson, I.M., Nutt, D.J., Bandelow, B., Bond, A., Davidson, J.R., den Boer, J.A., Fineberg, N.A., Knapp, M., Scott, J. and Wittchen, H.-U. (2005) Evidence-based guidelines for the pharmacological treatment of anxiety disorders: recommendations from the British Association for Psychopharmacology. J. Psychopharmacol., 19: 567–596.

Baldwin, D.S., Huusom, A.K.T. and Maehlum, E. (2006) Escitalopram and paroxetine in the treatment of generalised anxiety disorder. Randomised, double-blind, placebo-controlled, double-blind study. Br. J. Psychiatry, 189: 264–272.

Baldwin, D.S. and Mayers, A.G. (2003) Sexual side effects of antidepressant and antipsychotic drugs. Adv. Psychiatr. Treat., 9: 202–210.

Baldwin, D.S. and Polkinghorn, C. (2005) Evidence-based pharmacotherapy of generalized anxiety disorder. Int. J. Neuropsychopharmacol., 8: 293–302.

Ballard, T.M., Wolley, M.L., Prinssen, E., Huwyler, J., Porter, R. and Spooren, W. (2005) The effect of the mGlu5 receptor antagonist MPEP in rodent tests of anxiety and cognition: a comparison. Psychopharmacology, 179: 218–229.

Barlow, D.H., Gorman, J.M., Shear, M.K. and Woods, S.W. (2000) Cognitive-behavioral therapy, imipramine, or their combination for panic disorder: a randomized controlled trial. JAMA, 283: 2529–2536.

406

Baxter, L.R., Schwartz, J.M., Bergman, K.S., Szuba, M.P., Guze, B.H., Mazziotta, J.C., Alazraki, A., Selin, C.E., Ferng, H.K., Munford, P. and Phelps, M.E. (1992) Caudate glucose metabolic rate changes with both drug and behavior therapy for obsessive-compulsive disorder. Arch. Gen. Psychiatry, 49: 681–689.

Beck, A.T., Emery, G. and Greenberg, R. (1985) Anxiety Disorders and Phobias: A Cognitive Perspective. Basic, New York.

Bell, C., Forshall, S., Adrover, M., Nash, J., Hood, S., Argyropoulosm, S., Rich, A. and Nutt, D.J. (2002) Does 5-HT restrain panic? A tryptophan depletion study in panic disorder patients recovered on paroxetine. J. Psychopharmacol., 16: 5–14.

Bell, C.J., Abrams, J.K. and Nutt, D.J. (2001) Tryptophan depletion and its implications for psychiatry. Br. J. Psychiatry, 178: 399–405.

Bertani, A., Perna, G., Migliarese, G., Di Pasquale, D., Cucchi, M., Caldirola, D. and Bellodi, L. (2004) Comparison of the treatment with paroxetine and reboxetine in panic disorder: a randomized, single-blind study. Pharmacopsychiatry, 37: 206–210.

Black, D.W. (2006) Efficacy of combined pharmacotherapy and psychotherapy versus monotherapy in the treatment of anxiety disorders. CNS Spectrosc., 11(Suppl.): 29–33.

Blanco, C., Raza, M.S., Schneier, F. and Liebowitz, M.R. (2003) The evidence-based pharmacotherapy of social anxiety disorder. Int. J. Neuropsychopharmacol., 6: 427–442.

Blomhoff, S., Haug, T.T., Hellstrom, K., Holme, I., Humble, M., Madsbu, H.P. and Wold, J.E. (2001) Randomised controlled general practice trial of sertraline, exposure therapy and combined treatment in generalised social phobia. Br. J. Psychiatry, 179: 23–30.

Bouton, M.E., Mineka, S. and Barlow, D.H. (2001) A modern learning theory perspective on the etiology of panic disorder. Psychol. Rev., 108: 4–32.

Brody, A.L., Saxena, S., Schwartz, J.M., Stoessel, P.W., Maidment, K., Phelps, M.E. and Baxter, L.R. (1998) FDG-PET predictors of response to behavioral therapy and pharmacotherapy in obsessive compulsive disorder. Psychiatr. Res., 84: 1–6.

Brody, A.L., Saxena, S., Silverman, D.H., Alborzian, S., Fairbanks, L.A., Phelps., M.E., Huang, S.C., Wu, H.M., Maidment, K. and Baxter, L.R. Jr. (1999) Brain metabolic changes in major depressive disorder from pre- to post-treatment with paroxetine. Psychiatr. Res., 91: 127–139.

Butler, A.C., Chapman, J.E., Forman, E.M. and Beck, A.T. (2006) The empirical status of cognitive-behavioural therapy: a review of meta-analyses. Clin. Psychol. Rev., 26: 17–31.

Carey, P.D., Warwick, J., Niehaus, D.J., van der Linden, G., van Heerden, B.B., Harvey, B.H., Seedat, S. and Stein, D.J. (2004) Single photon emission computed tomography (SPECT) of anxiety disorders before and after treatment with citalopram. BMC Psychiatry, 14: 4–30.

Chalmers, D., Lovenberg, T., Grigoriadis, D., Behan, D.P. and De Souza, E.B. (1996) Corticotropin-releasing factor receptors: from molecular biology to drug design. Trends Pharmacol. Sci., 17: 166–172.

Charney, D.S. (2003) Neuroanatomical circuits modulating fear and anxiety behaviors. Acta Psychiatr. Scand. Suppl., 417: 38–50.

Charney, D.S., Heninger, G.R. and Breier, A. (1984) Noradrenergic function and panic anxiety effects of yohimbine in healthy subjects and patients with agoraphobia and panic disorder. Arch. Gen. Psychiatry, 41: 751–763.

Charney, D.S., Woods, S.W. and Heninger, G.R. (1989) Noradrenergic function in generalized anxiety disorder: effects of yohimbine in healthy subjects and patients with generalized anxiety disorder. Psychiatry Res., 27: 173–182.

Chamberlain, S.R., Muller, U., Blackwell, A.D., Robbins, T.W. and Sahakian, B.J. (2006) Noradrenergic modulation of working memory and emotional memory in humans. Psychopharmacology, 188: 397–407.

Chen, F., Larsen, M.B. and Sánchez, C. (2005) The S-enantiomer of R, S-citalopram increases inhibitor binding to the human serotonin transporter by an allosteric mechanism: comparison with other serotonin transporter inhibitors. Eur. Neuropsychopharmacol., 15: 193–198.

Clark, D.M., Ehlers, A., McManus, F., Hackmann, A., Fennell, M., Campbell, H., Flower, T., Davenport, C. and Louis, B. (2003) Cognitive therapy versus fluoxetine in generalized social phobia: a randomized placebo-controlled trial. J. Consult. Clin. Psychol., 71: 1058–1067.

Clark, D.M. and McManus, F. (2002) Information processing in social phobia. Biol. Psychiatry, 51: 92–100.

Coplan, J.D., Liebowitz, M.R., Gorman, J.M., Fyer, A.J., Dillon, D.J., Campeas, R.B., Davies, S.O., Martinez, J. and Klein, D.F. (1992) Noradrenergic function in panic disorder. Effects of intravenous clonidine pretreatment on lactate induced panic. Biol. Psychiatry, 31: 135–146.

Costall, B. and Naylor, R.J. (1993) Anxiolytic potential of 5-HT3 antagonists. Pharmacol. Toxicol., 70: 157–162.

Cottraux, J., Note, I.D., Cungi, C., Legeron, P., Heim, F., Chneiweiss, L., Bernard, G. and Bouvard, M. (1995) A controlled study of cognitive behaviour therapy with buspirone or placebo in panic disorder with agoraphobia. Br. J. Psychiatry, 167: 635–641.

Dannon, P.N., Iancu, I. and Grunhaus, L. (2002) Psychoeducation in panic disorder patients: effect of a self-information booklet in a randomized, masked-rater study. Depress. Anxiety, 16: 71–76.

Davidson, J.R.T., Foa, E.B., Huppert, J., Keefe, F.J., Franklin, M.E., Compton, J.S., Zhao, N., Connor, K.M., Lynch, T.R. and Gadde, K.M. (2004) Fluoxetine, comprehensive cognitive behavioral therapy (CCBT) and placebo in generalized social anxiety disorder. Arch. Gen. Psychiatry, 61: 1005–1013.

Davidson, R.J. and Irwin, W. (1999) The functional neuroanatomy of emotion and affective style. Trends Cogn. Sci., 3: 11–21.

Delgado, P.L., Miller, H.L., Solomon, R.M., Licinio, J., Heninger, G.R., Gelenberg, A.J. and Charney, D.S. (1993) Monoamines and the mechanism of antidepressant action: effects of catecholamine depletion on mood of patients treated with antidepressants. Psychopharmacol. Bull., 29: 389–396.

Den Boer, J.A. and Westenberg, H.G. (1988) Effect of a serotonin and noradrenaline uptake inhibitor in panic disorder; a double-blind comparative study with fluvoxamine and maprotiline. Int. Clin. Psychopharmacol., 3: 59–74.

Dobson, K.S., (2001) Handbook of Cognitive-Behavioral Therapies. 2nd edn. Guilford Press, New York.

Dooley, D.J., Donovan, C.M., Meder, W.P. and Whetzel, S.Z. (2002) Preferential action of gabapentin and pregabalin at P/Q-type voltage-sensitive calcium channels: inhibition of K^+-evoked [3H]-norepinephrine release from rat neocortical slices. Synapse, 45: 171–190.

Dording, C.M., Mischoulon, D., Petersen, T.J., Kornbluh, R., Gordon, J., Nierenberg, A.A., Rosenbaum, J.E. and Fava, M. (2002) The pharmacologic management of SSRI-induced side effects: a survey of psychiatrists. Ann. Clin. Psychiatr., 14: 143–147.

Durham, R.C. and Turvey, A.A. (1987) Cognitive therapy versus behaviour therapy in the treatment of chronic generalised anxiety. Behav. Res. Ther., 25: 229–234.

Fava, M., Thase, M.E. and DeBattista, C. (2005) A multicenter, placebo-controlled study of modafinil augmentation in partial responders to selective serotonin reuptake inhibitors with persistent fatigue and sleepiness. J. Clin. Psychiatr., 66: 85–93.

Fineberg, N.A. and Gale, T.M. (2005) Evidence-based pharmacotherapy of obsessive-compulsive disorder. Int. J. Neuropsychopharmacol., 8: 107–129.

Fink, K., Dooley, D.J., Meder, W.P., Suman-Chauhan, N., Duffy, S., Clusmann, H. and Gothert, M. (2002) Inhibition of neuronal Ca(2+) influx by gabapentin and pregabalin in the human neocortex. Neuropharmacology, 42: 229–236.

Foa, E.B., Franklin, M.E. and Moser, J. (2002) Context in the clinic: how well do cognitive-behavioural therapies and medications work in combination? Biol. Psychiatry, 52: 987–997.

Furmark, T., Tillfors, M., Marteinsdottir, I., Fischer, H., Pissiota, A., Langstrom, B. and Fredrikson, M. (2002) Common changes in cerebral blood flow in patients with social phobia treated with citalopram or cognitive-behavioral therapy. Arch. Gen. Psychiatry, 59: 425–433.

Garner, M., Mogg, K. and Bradley, B.P. (2006) Orienting and maintenance of gaze to facial expressions in social anxiety. J. Abnorm. Psychol., 115: 760–770.

Goddard, A.W., Brouette, T., Almai, A., Jetty, P., Woods, S.W. and Charney, D. (2001) Early coadministration of clonazepam with sertraline for panic disorder. Arch. Gen. Psychiatry, 58: 681–686.

Goldberg, M.R., Hollister, A.S. and Robertson, D. (1983) Influence of yohimbine on blood pressure, autonomic reflexes and plasma catecholamines in humans. Hypertension, 5: 772–778.

Gould, R.A., Otto, M.W. and Pollack, M.H. (1995) A meta-analysis of treatment outcome for panic disorder. Clin. Psychol. Rev., 15: 819–844.

Gould, R.A., Otto, M.W. and Pollack, M.H. (1997) Cognitive behavioural and pharmacological treatment of generalised anxiety disorder: a preliminary meta-analysis. Behav. Ther., 28: 285–305.

Grauer, S.M. and Marquis, K.L. (1999) Intracerebral administration of metabotropic glutamate receptor agonists disrupts prepulse inhibition of acoustic startle in Sprague–Dawley rats. Psychopharmacology, 141: 405–412.

Griebel, G. (2002) Anxiolytic- and antidepressant-like effects of the non-peptide vasopressin V_{1b} receptor antagonist, SSR149415, suggest an innovative approach for the treatment of stress-related disorders. Proc. Natl. Acad. Sci. USA, 99: 6370–6375.

Grove, G., Coplan, J.D. and Hollander, E. (1997) The neuroanatomy of 5-IIT dysregulation and panic disorder. J. Neuropsychiatr. Clin. Neurosci., 9: 198–207.

Hamilton, S.P., Slager, S.L., De Leon, A.B., Heiman, G.A., Klein, D.F., Hodge, S.E., Weissman, M.M., Fyer, A.J. and Knowles, J.A. (2004) Evidence for genetic linkage between a polymorphism in the adenosine 2A receptor and panic disorder. Neuropsychopharmacology, 29: 558–565.

Harmer, C.J., Bhagwagar, Z., Perrett, D.I., Vollm, B.A., Cowen, P.J. and Goodwin, G.M. (2003a) Acute SSRI administration affects the processing of social cues in healthy volunteers. Neuropsychopharmacology, 28: 148–152.

Harmer, C.J., Perrett, D.I., Cowen, P.J. and Goodwin, G.M. (2001) Administration of the beta-adrenoceptor blocker propranolol impairs the processing of facial expressions of sadness. Psychopharmacology, 154: 383–389.

Harmer, C.J., Hill, S.A., Taylor, M.J., Cowen, P.J. and Goodwin, G.M. (2003b) Toward a neuropsychological theory of antidepressant drug action: increase in positive emotional bias after potentiation

408

of norepinephrine activity. Am. J. Psychiatry, 160: 990–992.

Harmer, C.J., Mackay, C.E., Reid, C.B., Cowen, P.J. and Goodwin, G.M. (2006a) Antidepressant drug treatment modifies the neural processing of nonconscious threat cues. Biol. Psychiatry, 59: 816–820.

Harmer, C.J., Reid, C.B., Ray, M.K., Goodwin, G.M. and Cowen, P.J. (2006b) 5HT(3) antagonism abolishes the emotion potentiated startle effect in humans. Psychopharmacology, 186: 18–24.

Harmer, C.J., Rogers, R.D., Tunbridge, E., Cowen, P.J. and Goodwin, G.M. (2003c) Tryptophan depletion decreases the recognition of fear in female volunteers. Psychopharmacology, 167: 411–417.

Harmer, C.J., Shelley, N.C., Cowen, P.J. and Goodwin, G.M. (2004) Increased positive versus negative affective perception and memory in healthy volunteers following selective serotonin and norepinephrine reuptake inhibition. Am. J. Psychiatry, 161: 1256–1263.

Hayward, G., Goodwin, G.M., Cowen, P.J. and Harmer, C.J. (2005) Low-dose tryptophan depletion in recovered depressed patients induces changes in cognitive processing without depressive symptoms. Biol. Psychiatry, 57: 517–524.

Hewlett, W.A., Vongradov, S. and Agras, W.S. (1992) Clomipramine, clonazepam and clonidine treatment of obsessive-compulsive disorder. J. Clin. Psychopharmacol., 12: 420–430.

Huang, Z.L., Qu, W.M., Eguchi, N., Chen, J.F., Schwarzschild, M.A., Fredholm, B.B., Urade, Y. and Hayaishi, O. (2005) Adenosine A2A, but not A1, receptors mediate the arousal effect of caffeine. Nat. Neurosci., 8: 858–859.

Ipponi, A., Lamberti, C., Medica, A., Bartolini, A. and Malmberg-Aiello, P. (1999) Tiagabine antinociception in rodents depends on GABA(B) receptor activation: parallel antinociception testing and medial thalamus GABA microdialysis. Eur. J. Pharmacol., 368: 205–211.

Jackson, H.C. and Nutt, D.J. (1992) Effects of benzodiazepine receptor inverse agonists on locomotor activity and exploration in mice. Eur. J. Pharmacol., 221: 199–204.

Karleyton, C.E., Dougherty, D.D., Pollack, M.H. and Rauch, S.L. (2006) Using neuroimaging to predict treatment response in mood and anxiety disorders. Ann. Clin. Psychiatry, 18: 33–42.

Kavoussi, R. (2006) Pregabalin: from molecule to medicine. Eur. Neuropsychopharmacol., 16(Suppl.): S128–S133.

Kennedy, S.H., Andersen, H.F. and Lam, R.W. (2006) Efficacy of escitalopram in the treatment of major depressive disorder compared with conventional selective serotonin reuptake inhibitors and venlafaxine XR: a meta-analysis. Rev. Psychiatr. Neurosci., 31: 122–131.

Korpi, E.R. and Sinkkonen, S.T. (2006) GABA-A receptor subtypes as targets for neuropsychiatric drug development. Pharmacol. Ther., 109: 12–32.

Kramer, M., Cutler, N. and Feighner, J., et al. (1998) Distinct mechanism for antidepressant activity by blockade of central substance P receptors. Science, 281: 1640–1645.

Kramer, M.S., Winokur, A., Kelsey, J., Preskorn, S.H., Rothschild, A.J., Snavely, D., Ghosh, K., Ball, W.A., Reines, S.A., Munjack, D., Apter, J.T., Cunningham, L., Kling, M., Bari, M., Getson, A. and Lee, Y. (2004) Demonstration of the efficacy and safety of a novel substance P (NK1) receptor antagonist in major depression. Neuropsychopharmacology, 29: 385–392.

Krystal, J.H., McDougle, C.J., Woods, S.W., Price, L.H., Heninger, G.R. and Charney, D.S. (1992) Dose-response relationship for oral idazoxan effects in healthy human subjects: comparison with oral yohimbine. Psychopharmacology, 108: 313–319.

Lader, M., Stender, K., Burger, V. and Nil, R. (2004) Efficacy and tolerability of escitalopram in 12- and 24-week treatment of social anxiety disorder: randomised, double-blind, placebo-controlled, fixed-dose study. Depress. Anxiety, 19: 241–248.

Lader, M.H. and Bond, A.J. (1998) Interaction of pharmacological and psychological treatments of anxiety. Br. J. Psychiatry, 173(Suppl.): 42–48.

Lecrubier, Y., Puech, A.J., Azcona, A., Bailey, P.E. and Lataste, X. (1993) A randomized double-blind placebo-controlled study of tropisetron in the treatment of outpatients with generalized anxiety disorder. Psychopharmacology, 112: 129–133.

LeDoux, J.E. (1996) The Emotional Brain. Simon & Schuster, New York.

Liebowitz, M.R., Gelenberg, A.J. and Munjack, D. (2005) Venlafaxine extended release vs. placebo and paroxetine in social anxiety disorder. Arch. Gen. Psychiatry, 62: 190–198.

Little, J.T., Ketter, T.A., Kimbrell, T.A., Danielson, A., Benson, B., Willis, M.W. and Post, R.M. (1996) Venlafaxine or bupropion responders but not non-responders show baseline prefrontal and paralimbic hypometabolism compared with controls. Psychopharm. Bull., 32: 629–635.

Longhurst, J.G., Carpenter, L.L., Epperson, C.N., Price, L.H. and McDougle, C.J. (1999) Effects of catecholamine depletion with AMPT (alpha-methyl-para-tyrosine) in obsessive-compulsive disorder. Biol. Psychiatry, 46: 573–576.

Loo, H., Dalery, J., Macher, J.P. and Payen, A. (2003) Pilot study comparing in blind the therapeutic effect of two doses of agomelatine, melatonin-agonist and selective 5HT2C receptor antagonist, in the treatment of major depressive disorders. Encephale, 29: 165–171.

Loo, H., Hale, A. and D'haenen, H. (2002) Determination of the dose of agomelatine, a melatonergic agonist and selective 5-HT(2C) antagonist, in the treatment of major depressive disorder: a placebo-controlled dose range study. Int. Clin. Psychopharmacol., 17: 239–247.

Malizia, A.L., Cunningham, V.J., Bell, C.J., Liddle, P.F., Jones, T. and Nutt, D.J. (1998) Decreased brain GABA-A -benzodiazepine receptor binding in panic disorder: preliminary results from a quantitative PET study. Arch. Gen. Psychiatry, 55: 715–720.

Marks, I.M., Swinson, R.P., Basaglu, M., Kuch, K., Norshirvani, H., O'Sullivan, G., Lelliott, P.T., Kirby, M., McNamee, G. and Sengun, S. (1993) Alprazolam and exposure alone and combined in panic disorder with agoraphobia: a controlled study in London and Toronto. Br. J. Psychiatry, 162: 776–787.

Mathews, A. and MacLeod, C. (2005) Cognitive vulnerability to emotional disorders. Ann. Rev. Clin. Psychol., 1: 167–195.

Mavissakalian, M., Michelson, L. and Dealy, R.S. (1983) Pharmacological treatment of agoraphobia: imipramine versus imipramine with programmed practice. Br. J. Psychiatry, 143: 348–355.

Mayberg, H.S., Brannan, S.K., Mahurin, R.K., Jerabek, P.A., Brickman, J.S., Tekell, J.L., Silva, J.A., McGinnis, S., Glass, T.G., Martin, C.C. and Fox, P.T. (1997) Cingulate function in depression: a potential predictor of treatment response. Neuroreport, 8: 1057–1061.

McClure, E.B., Adler, A., Monk, C.S., Cameron, J., Smith, S., Nelson, E.E., Leibenluft, E., Ernst, M. and Pine, D.S. (2007) fMRI predictors of treatment outcome in pediatric anxiety disorders. Psychopharmacology, 191: 97–105.

Mennin, D.S. and Heimberg, R.G. (2000) The impact of comorbid mood and personality disorders in the cognitive-behavioral treatment of panic disorder. Clin. Psychol. Rev., 20: 339–357.

Millan, M.J., Brocco, M., Gobert, A. and Dekeyne, A. (2005) Anxiolytic properties of agomelatine, an antidepressant with melatoninergic and serotonergic properties: role of 5-HT2C receptor blockade. Psychopharmacology, 77: 448–458.

Mitte, K., Noack, P., Steil, R. and Hautzinger, M. (2005) A meta-analytic review of the efficacy of drug treatment in generalized anxiety disorder. J. Clin. Psychopharmacol., 25: 141–150.

Mogg, K., Baldwin, D.S., Brodrick, P. and Bradley, B.P. (2004) Effect of short-term SSRI treatment on cognitive bias in generalised anxiety disorder. Psychopharmacology, 176: 466–470.

Mogg, K. and Bradley, B. (1998) A cognitive-motivational analysis of anxiety. Behav. Res. Ther., 36: 809–848.

Montgomery, S.A. (2006) Major depressive disorders: clinical efficacy and tolerability of agomelatine, a new melatonergic agonist. Eur. Neuropsychopharmacol., 16(Suppl.): S633–S638.

Montgomery, S.A., Kennedy, S.H., Burrows, G.D., Lejoyeux, M., Hindmarch, I. (2004) Absence of discontinuation symptoms with agomelatine and occurrence of discontinuation symptoms with paroxetine: a randomized, double-blind, placebo-controlled discontinuation study. Int. Clin. Psychopharmacol., 19: 271–280.

Munafo, M.R., Hayward, G. and Harmer, C. (2006) Selective processing of social threat cues following acute tryptophan depletion. J. Psychopharmacol., 20: 33–39.

Murphy, F.C., Smith, K.A., Cowen, P.J., Robbins, T.W. and Sahakian, B.J. (2002) The effects of tryptophan depletion on cognitive and affective processing in healthy volunteers. Psychopharmacology, 163: 42–53.

Murphy, S.E., Longhitano, C., Ayres, R.E., Cowen, P.J. and Harmer, C.J. (2006) Tryptophan supplementation induces a positive bias in the processing of emotional material in healthy female volunteers. Psychopharmacology, 181: 121–130.

Naukkarinen, H., Raassina, R., Penttinen, J., Ahokas, A., Jokinen, R., Koponen, H., Lepola, U., Kanerva, H., Lehtonen, L., Pohjalainen, T., Partanen, A., Maki-Ikola, O. and Rouru, J., Deramciclane Dose-Finding Study Group. (2005) Deramciclane in the treatment of generalized anxiety disorder: a placebo-controlled, double-blind, dose-finding study. Eur. Neuropsychopharmacol., 15: 617–623.

Nemeroff, C. (2002) New directions in the development of antidepressants: the interface of neurobiology and psychiatry. Hum. Psychopharmacol. Clin. Exp., 17: S13–S16.

Nutt, D.J., Glue, P., Lawson, C. and Wilson, S. (1990) Evidence for altered benzodiazepine receptor sensitivity in panic disorder: effects of the benzodiazepine receptor antagonist flumazenil. Arch. Gen. Psychiatry, 47: 917–925.

Ochsner, K.N., Ray, R.D., Cooper, J.C., Robertson, E.R., Chopra, S., Gabrieli, J.D. and Gross, J.J. (2004) For better or worse: neural systems supporting the cognitive down- and up-regulation of negative emotion. Neuroimage, 23: 483–499.

Oehrberg, S., Christiansen, P.E., Behnke, K., Borup, A.L., Severin, B., Soegaard, J., Calberg, H., Judge, R., Ohrstrom, J.K. and Manniche, P.M. (1995) Paroxetine in the treatment of panic disorder. A randomised, double-blind, placebo-controlled study. Br. J. Psychiatry, 167: 374–379.

Ohman, A. and Mineka, S. (2001) Fears, phobias, and preparedness: toward an evolved module of fear and fear learning. Psychol. Rev., 108: 483–522.

Paoluzzi, L., Singh, A.S., Price, D.K., Danesi, R., Mathijssen, R.H., Verweij, J., Figg, W.D. and Sparreboom, A. (2004) Influence of genetic variants in UGT1A1 and UGT1A9 on the in vivo glucuronidation of SN 38. J. Clin. Pharmacol., 44: 854–860.

Paquette, V., Levesque, J., Mensour, B., Leroux, J.M., Beaudoin, G., Bourgouin, P. and Beauregard, M.

(2003) "Change the mind and you change the brain": effects of cognitive-behavioral therapy on the neural correlates of spider phobia. Neuroimage, 18: 401–409.

Perlis, R.H. (2007) Cytochrome P450 genotyping and antidepressants. Br. Med. J., 334: 759.

Pollack, M.H., Roy-Byrne, P.P., Van Ameringen, M., Snyder, H., Brown, C., Ondrasik, J. and Rickels, K. (2005) The selective GABA reuptake inhibitor tiagabine for the treatment of generalized anxiety disorder: results of a placebo-controlled study. J. Clin. Psychiatry, 66: 1401–1408.

Pollack, M.H., Simon, N.M., Worthington, J.J., Doyle, A.L., Peters, P., Toshkov, F. and Otto, M.W. (2003) Combined paroxetine and clonazepam treatment strategies compared to paroxetine monotherapy for panic disorder. J. Psychopharmacol., 17: 276–282.

Power, K.G., Simpson, M.B., Swanson, V. and Wallace, L.A. (1990) A controlled comparison of cognitive-behaviour therapy, diazepam, and placebo in the management of generalized anxiety disorder. J. Anxiety Disord., 4: 267–292.

Rasmussen, S.A., Goodman, W.K., Woods, S.W., Heninger, G.R. and Charney, D.S. (1987) Effects of yohimbine in obsessive-compulsive disorder. Psychopharmacology, 93: 308–313.

Reynolds, G.P., Templeman, L.A. and Zhang, Z.J. (2005) The role of 5-HT2C receptor polymorphisms in the pharmacogenetics of antipsychotic drug treatment. Prog. Neuropsychopharmacol. Biol. Psychiatry, 29: 1021–1028.

Rogers, R.D., Lancaster, M., Wakeley, J. and Bhagwagar, Z. (2004) Effects of beta-adrenoceptor blockade on components of human decision-making. Psychopharmacology, 172: 157–164.

Rogers, R.D., Tunbridge, E.M., Bhagwagar, Z., Drevets, W.C., Sahakian, B.J. and Carter, C.S. (2003) Tryptophan depletion alters the decision-making of healthy volunteers through altered processing of reward cues. Neuropsychopharmacology, 28: 153–162.

Roffman, J.L., Marci, C.D., Glick, D.M., Dougherty, D.D. and Rauch, S.L. (2005) Neuroimaging and the functional neuroanatomy of psychotherapy. Psychol. Med., 35: 1385–1398.

Rauch, S.L., Shin, L.M., Dougherty, D.D., Alpert, N.M., Fischman, A.J. and Jenike, M.A. (2002) Predictors of fluvoxamine response in contamination-related obsessive compulsive disorder: a PET symptom provocation study. Neuropsychopharmacology, 27: 782–791.

Rollman, B.L., Belnap, B.H., Mazumdar, S., Houck, P.R., Zhu, F., Gardner, W., Reynolds, C.F., III Schulberg, H.C. and Shear, M.K. (2005) A randomized trial to improve the quality of treatment for panic and generalized anxiety disorders in primary care. Arch. Gen. Psychiatry, 62: 1332–1341.

Roses, A. (2002) Genome-based pharmacogenetics and the pharmaceutical industry. Nat. Drug Discov., 1: 541–549.

Roy-Byrne, P.P., Craske, M.G., Stein, M.B., Sullivan, G., Bystritsky, A., Katon, W., Golinelli, D. and Sherbourne, C.D. (2005) A randomized effectiveness trial of cognitive-behavioral therapy and medication for primary care panic disorder. Arch. Gen. Psychiatry, 62: 290–298.

Sánchez, C. (2006) The pharmacology of citalopram enantiomers: the antagonism by R-citalopram on the effect of S-citalopram. Basic Clin. Pharmacol. Toxicol., 99: 91–95.

Saxena, S., Brody, A.L., Schwartz, J.M. and Baxter, L.R. (1998) Neuroimaging and frontal-subcortical circuitry in obsessive-compulsive disorder. Br. J. Psychiatry, 35: 26–37.

Schwartz, J.M., Stoessel, P.W., Baxter, L.R., Martin, K.M. and Phelps, M.E. (1996) Systematic changes in cerebral glucose metabolic rate after successful behavior modification treatment of obsessive-compulsive disorder. Arch. Gen. Psychiatry, 53: 109–113.

Silverstone, P.H. and Salinas, E. (2001) Efficacy of venlafaxine extended release in patients with major depressive disorder and comorbid generalized anxiety disorder. J. Clin. Psychiatry, 62: 523–539.

Simpson, H.B., Liebowitz, M.R., Foa, E.B., Kozak, M.J., Schmidt, A.B., Rowan, V., Petkova, E., Kjernisted, K., Huppert, J.D., Franklin, M.E., Davies, S.O. and Campeas, R. (2004) Post-treatment effects of exposure therapy and clomipramine in obsessive-compulsive disorder. Depress. Anxiety, 19: 225–233.

Slaap, B.R. and den Boer, J.A. (2001) The prediction of nonresponse to pharmacotherapy in panic disorder: a review. Depress. Anxiety, 14: 112–121.

Stahl, S.M. (2004) Anticonvulsants as anxiolytics: Part 2. Pregabalin and gabapentin as alpha(2)delta ligands at voltage-gated calcium channels. J. Clin. Psychiatry, 65: 460–461.

Stahl, S.M., Gergel, I. and Li, D. (2003) Escitalopram in the treatment of panic disorder: a randomized, double-blind, placebo-controlled trial. J. Clin. Psychiatry, 64: 1322–1327.

Stein, D.J., Baldwin, D.S., Dolberg, O.T., Despiegel, N. and Bandelow, B. (2006) Which factors predict placebo response in anxiety disorders and major depression? An analysis of placebo-controlled studies of escitalopram. J. Clin. Psychiatry, 67: 1741–1746.

Stein, M.B., Ron Norton, G., Walker, J.R., Chartier, M.J. and Graham, R. (2000) Do selective serotonin reuptake inhibitors enhance the efficacy of very brief cognitive behavioral therapy for panic disorder? A pilot study. Psychiatry Res., 94: 191–200.

Stout, S., Owens, M. and Nemeroff, C. (2001) Neurokinin (1) receptor antagonists as potential antidepressants. Ann. Rev. Pharmacol. Toxicol., 41: 877–906.

Swanson, C.J., Bures, K., Johnson, M.P., Linden, A-M., Monn, J.A. and Schoepp, D.D. (2005) Metabotropic glutamate receptors as novel targets for anxiety and stress disorders. Nat. Rev. Drug Discov., 4: 131–144.

Taillon-Miller, P., Gu, Z., Li, Q., Hillier, L. and Kwok, P.Y. (1998) Overlapping genomic sequences: a treasure-trove of single-nucleotide polymorphisms. Genome Res., 8: 748–754.

Thomas, H.V., Lewis, G., Watson, M., Bell, T., Lyons, I., Lloyd, K., Weich, S. and Sharp, D. (2004) Computerised patient-specific guidelines for management of common mental disorders in primary care: a randomised controlled trial. Br. J. Gen. Pract., 54: 832–837.

Trusheim, M.R., Berndt, E.R. and Douglas, F.L. (2007) Stratified medicine: strategic and economic implications of combining drugs and clinical biomarkers. Nat. Rev. Drug Discov., 6: 287–293.

Tyrer, P.J. and Baldwin, D.S. (2006) Generalised anxiety disorder. Lancet, 368: 2156–2166.

van Balkom, A.J., Bakker, A., Spinhoven, P., Blaauw, B.M., Smeenk, S. and Ruesink, B. (1997) A meta-analysis of the treatment of panic disorder with or without agoraphobia: a comparison of psychopharmacological, cognitive-behavioral, and combination treatments. J. Nerv. Ment. Dis., 185: 510–516.

van Boeijen, C.A., van Oppen, P., van Balkom, A.J., Visser, S., Kempe, P.T., Blankenstein, N. and van Dyck, R. (2005) Treatment of anxiety disorders in primary care practice: a randomised controlled trial. Br. J. Gen. Pract., 55: 763–769.

Van der Linden, G., van Heerden, B., Warwick, J., Wessels, C., van Kradenburg, J., Zungu-Dirwayi, N. and Stein, D.J. (2000) Functional brain imaging and pharmacotherapy in social phobia: single photon emission computed tomography before and after treatment with the selective serotonin reuptake inhibitor citalopram. Prog. Neuropsychopharmacol. Biol. Psychiatry, 24: 419–438.

Von Korff, M. and Goldberg, D. (2001) Improving outcomes in depression. Br. Med. J., 323: 948–949.

Williams, J.M.G., Watts, F.N., MacLeod, C. and Mathews, A. (1997) Cognitive Psychology and Emotional Disorders. Wiley, Chichester.

Woods, S.W., Nagy, L.M., Koleszar, A.S., Krystal, J.H., Heninger, G.R. and Charney, D.S. (1992) Controlled trial of alprazolam supplementation during imipramine treatment of panic disorder. J. Clin. Psychopharmacol., 12: 32–38.

Wong, M.L. and Licinio, J. (2004) From monoamines to genomic targets: a paradigm shift for drug discovery in depression. Nat. Rev. Drug Discov., 3: 136–151.

Zobel, A., Nickel, T., Kunzel, H., Ackl, N., Sonntag, A., Ising, M. and Holsboer, F. (2000) Effects of the high-affinity corticotropin-releasing hormone receptor 1 antagonist R121919 in major depression: the first 20 patients treated. J. Psychiatr. Res., 34: 171–181.

Experimental models: panic and fear

Gabriel Esquivel*, Koen Schruers and Eric Griez

Experimental & Clinical Psychiatry Section, Department of Psychiatry & Neuropsychology, Faculty of Health, Medicine and Life Sciences, Maastricht University, Maastricht, The Netherlands

Abstract: The main paradigm of experimental psychiatry is the carefully controlled time-limited production of a pathological picture in volunteering subjects under safe laboratory conditions. Most often, such a procedure relies on either the manipulation of a physiological parameter or administration of a pharmacological agent in order to unveil underlying vulnerabilities believed to be directly related to the pathogenesis of the disorder. Because they intentionally put the organism under strain, such procedures have been referred to as "challenges". The interest of an experimental model mimicking a clinical condition lies in its validity. Insights in the underlying pathophysiology will progress to the extent that a particular challenge can be linked to a syndrome in particular individuals, who are also prone to the development of the same syndrome in real-life environment. In other words, experimental models are supposed to act as biological markers of clinical disorders. Human models of panic and fear are scrutinized under different aspects for their validation. These aspects include safety, convergence, discrimination, reliability, and clinical validity. However, these aspects of validation can become blurred without a clear agreement on what is called anxiety, fear, or panic, and their correspondence with spontaneous panic attack and situational panic attacks. In this scope, animal models that have mapped fear and anxiety in two different defense systems may contribute to clarify this issue. Ultimately, the identification of a reliable biomarker can pave the way for studies into the genetic determinants of susceptibility to fear and panic and new therapeutic approaches.

Keywords: panic; fear; experimental models; lactate; carbon dioxide; voluntary hyperventilation; doxapram; cholecystokinin

I. Introduction

The experimental method is a procedure designed to falsify a prediction that was constructed by means of inferences from observed phenomena in nature (Verburg et al., 2001). This procedure, which involves the manipulation of models of such phenomena in a laboratory, aids in the construction of knowledge that would be otherwise very difficult to access by other means. In this way, human and animal models of psychopathology complement each other in the sense that the former have a clear face validity, whereas in animals, these models can delineate the neurochemical and neuroanatomical underpinnings of the mental workings in a much more powerful way. Designing experimental models of fear and panic in humans is an exercise of making inferences that claim a correspondence between human linguistic labels of brain processes (LeDoux, 1996) and the observable defensive behavior of other mammals. Nevertheless, the need for human models of even one human anxiety disorder – panic – to be constantly reshaped by the

*Corresponding author.
E-mail: gabriel.esquivel@pn.unimaas.nl

R.J. Blanchard, D.C. Blanchard, G. Griebel and D. Nutt (Eds.)
Handbook of Anxiety and Fear, Vol. 17
ISBN 978-0-444-53065-3

413

DOI: 10.1016/S1569-7339(07)00019-7

overwhelming advances in the neurobiological understanding of defensive behavior in animals (and vice versa) cannot be understated (Gorman et al., 2000). In a broad sense, the ultimate goal of experimental models of panic, anxiety and fear is to achieve valid clinical diagnosis, currently based on epidemiological data (e.g. DSM-IV) and the development of means to effectively treat patients with anxiety disorders. Because these models intentionally put the organism under strain, such procedures have been referred to as "challenges". In fact, the principle of these challenges resembles some procedures used in clinical medicine, for instance the glucose tolerance test, or an effort ECG. In both cases the diagnostic procedure seeks to evidence an underlying vulnerability that may not be obvious during routine examination.

One straightforward approach to the human models of panic and fear is to look at their construct validity. In other words, investigate whether the observed pattern in a model corresponds to that of the real-life psychopathological process. In the case of panic for example, some authors have proposed the basic operational criteria required for a model validation (Guttmacher et al., 1983): safety, convergence, discrimination, reliability, and clinical validity:

1. *Safety*. When dealing with models that can elicit defensive responses, safety is an essential component of any procedure performed in human subjects. The symptoms provoked by an experimental maneuver should be temporary, short lived, readily reversible, and hold no foreseeable health risks.
2. *Convergence*. With regard to convergence, the experiences produced by the model should mimic naturally occurring cognitive and neurovegetative symptoms of fear and panic. Additionally, experiences should be idiosyncratic to each individual subject.
3. *Discrimination*. A feature that has received particular attention is discrimination (specificity) or the capability of the model to identify those with the affected condition from those without it. Although it might seem that absolute specificity is desirable, arguably, a relative specificity may actually better reflect

the psychopathological processes involved in panic disorder (PD). This notion stems from research that regards defensive behaviors as a neurobiological evolutionary derived function of the brain present in all mammals (McNaughton and Corr, 2004) as well as studies that suggest that vulnerability for PD, for instance, may obey homeostatic processes that follow a continuous distribution with those affected individuals in one extreme (Battaglia and Perna, 1995; Bellodi et al., 1998; Swain et al., 2003).

4. *Reliability* or re-test reliability refers to the reproducibility of the effects of the model after consecutive trials.
5. *Clinical validation*. Clinical validation relates to one of the most powerful and useful elements of construct validity. For example, medication that is effective for PD and reduces the effects of a panic-inducing experimental manipulation, can be linked to a large amount of pharmacological studies performed in animal models (Blanchard et al., 2003). Clinical validation should also include effective non-pharmacological interventions (i.e. cognitive-behavioral therapy) that effectively reduce the symptoms produced by a model.

It is clear that an agreement on what we call anxiety, fear, or panic is essential when describing experimental models for them. Unfortunately, a uniform definition does not exist to date. Hence, an important limitation in the validation of models for anxiety disorders is the controversy concerning the meaning of the concept of panic (or fear). Some suggest that it is an intense form of general anxiety, as opposed to those stressing that it is an evolutionary more primitive emotion, activated by physiological disturbances that warn the organism of impending danger (Andreatini et al., 2001). Allegations in favor of the idea of panic as an intense form of general anxiety (i.e. the idea that anxiety, fear, and panic are on a continuum) stem from the fact that anti-panic medication, such as anti-depressants and benzodiazepines, can also provide relief for phobias and generalized anxiety. Models that support this view have linked situational panic and laboratory-induced panic attacks, with neuroendocrine and physiological responses that activate defensive networks that are probably integrated in the amygdala (Charney, 2003), and provide a framework that may also explain phobic avoidance and agoraphobia (Gorman, 2003). On a different view, others have put forward that the phenomenon of spontaneous panic is clearly distinct from that of situational panic and other anxiety symptoms related to PD. They base their claim on animal research that has arranged defensive behavior in a two-dimensional hierarchically organized brain system (McNaughton and Corr, 2004). This concept integrates concepts of defensive distance and defensive direction (Blanchard et al., 2003). Defensive approach (i.e. anxiety) is favored when the distance from the source of danger allows the possibility for elaborate and complex behaviors, whereas defensive avoidance (i.e., fear and panic) will be predominant when it is necessary to deal with nose-to-nose danger (Graeff, 2004). In this view, (generalized) anxiety is: (i) linked to responses that deal with the conflicts of approach to potential danger (distant or imagined), (ii) suppressed by anxiolytic drugs, (iii) integrated in the amygdala and other forebrain structures, and (iv) activates the HPA axis. Fear (and spontaneous panic as its most primitive and intense form), on the contrary, is: (i) related to behavior adequate to escape imminent danger (i.e. suffocation), (ii) reduced by SSRIs, and (iii) organized in more primitive structures that do not activate the HPA system (Graeff, 2004; Graeff et al., 2005). Some support in favor of this notion is provided by studies showing that when spontaneous panic is distinguished from situational panic and anticipatory anxiety, the crucial role of respiratory symptoms (Briggs et al., 1993; Uhlenhuth et al., 2000) and lack of HPA axis activation (Graeff et al., 2005) becomes evident. Other studies have also shown that symptoms of human pathological fear are not related to HPA axis activation (Potts et al., 1991; Uhde et al., 1994; Martel et al., 1999).

This chapter will attempt to describe the most prominent and current experimental maneuvers that claim to model human panic. After a general description of the conception, the technique, and the possible mechanisms, the studies that validate the model according to the described basic criteria will follow. Finally, without trying to solve the anxiety–panic debate, studies that can potentially address this issue will be considered and incorporated throughout the description of each model.

II. Sodium lactate and other hyperosmotic infusion techniques

II.A. Background

Lactate, the dissociated cationic form of lactic acid in biological fluids, is a ubiquitous substance, constantly produced as result of mammalian anaerobic metabolism. Lactate has been historically demonized as a wastage product responsible for pain and exhaustion during exercise (Leverve and Mustafa, 2002). Nevertheless, it is actually actively recycled during physical exertion and may play an important role in energetic homeostasis in both physiological and extreme conditions. Moreover, lactate may be the most important source of energy for neurons where it is glycolytically converted by astrocytes from glucose (Tsacopoulos and Magistretti, 1996).

Lactate occurs in two stereoisometric forms, L-lactate and D-lactate, where the L-lactate is an abundant intermediate of mammalian metabolism, and D-lactate is usually of bacterial origin. Human metabolism of D-lactate is known to occur, but is only in a very small proportion of that of L-lactate (Kondoh et al., 1992).

The standardized use of lactate infusions as a panicogenic maneuver was established by Pitts and McClure (1967) initially to provoke anxiety in patients with anxiety neurosis (then, the term panic was not extensively used). Their idea stemmed from the previous work of Cohen and White (1951) in patients with neurocirculatory asthenia (a diagnostic entity that overlaps with PD) that showed abnormally high levels of blood lactate and a low oxygen uptake in response to physical exercise. The lactate infusion can probably still be regarded as the most extensively used panicogenic maneuver. The use of bicarbonate and hypertonic infusions, despite providing with interesting findings, is scarce.

II.B. Features and technique

As a model of panic provocation, sodium lactate (typically racemic) is intravenously administered in a 0.5 mol/L concentration dose of 10 mL/kg over 20 min. Pure D- or L-lactate infusions in panic patients have been performed. However, the results of these studies are not clear (Gorman et al., 1990a; Klein, 1993). A larger concentration of 1.0 mol/L has been used in a small sample of PD patients, nevertheless with inconclusive results (Ehlers et al., 1986; Klein and Ross, 1986). Sodium bicarbonate and hypertonic saline have been administered in a similar fashion as a 2.5 mL/kg of 8.4% and 10 mL/kg of 3%, respectively, with a point-to-panic usually reached after about 10 min (Liebowitz et al., 1985; Gorman et al., 1989; Peskind et al., 1998).

Lactate infusions produce various physiological changes in all subjects such as paradoxical hyperventilation, an increase in heart rate and in blood pressure (Liebowitz et al., 1985; Peskind et al., 1998). Because of the effects of lactate on cell metabolism there is a parallel increase of bicarbonate with blood lactate levels. In other words, the metabolism of lactate in the tricarboxylic-acid cycle leads to the cytosol consumption of a proton ion and therefore the generation of a bicarbonate ion (Zhou, 2005). Sodium bicarbonate infusions in PD patients also produce paradoxical hyperventilation (Gorman et al., 1989). More recent research on the effects of a sodium bicarbonate infusion on brain intracellular pH (Nakashima et al., 1996) shows that the maneuver produces a significant shift towards acidity that is likely to explain the hyperventilation seen with lactate and bicarbonate panic provocation challenges. Interestingly, a panicogenic hypertonic saline infusion does not provoke hyperventilation (Peskind et al., 1998). Increased heart rate and blood pressure is not surprising when the amount of hyperosmotic fluids administered that initially stimulate vasopressin and the locus ceruleus are considered: i.e. an infusion with lactate, bicarbonate, or hypertonic saline (King and Baertschi, 1992; Ganong, 1997). Other studies from the Bristol group suggest that lactate produces shifts in CNS brain electrolytes and glucose may provoke changes in noradrenergic and GABA tone in relevant brain structures (George et al., 1990, 1995). Additionally, some of the physiological changes during a lactate infusion can be attributed to a reduction in parasympathetic activity (George et al., 1989).

The idea that panic attacks are linked with HPA-axis activation still remains controversial (Graeff et al., 2005). Extensive work concludes that lactate-induced panic is not linked to HPA-axis activation (Hollander et al., 1989; Coplan et al., 1998) and at least one study suggests that neither is hypertonic saline-induced panic (Peskind et al., 1998). It has been speculated that the rise in atrial natriuretic peptide during a lactate infusion may blunt the cortisol response (Kellner et al., 1995). However, in another study pre-medication with atrial natriuretic peptide did not affect the characteristic HPA activation of the putative panicogen CCK (Wiedemann et al., 2001).

II.C. Underlying mechanisms

The mechanism behind lactate-induced panic remains obscure. Early studies have proposed and discarded the implication of peripheral and central adrenergic surge, ionized calcium, or metabolic alkalosis (Liebowitz et al., 1986b).

Because a noradrenergic disturbance has been postulated as an underlying mechanism in panic (Charney and Heninger, 1986), lactate infusions have been performed after premedication with the β-adrenergic blocker propranolol (Gorman et al., 1983) and the α-adrenergic agonist clonidine (Coplan et al., 1992). Propranolol did not have any effect on lactate panic-provocation, whereas clonidine had a partial panic-reducing effect. Clonidine, however, has shown to have a therapeutic effect (Valenca et al., 2004) and is associated with a release of atrial natriuretic peptide (Mukaddam-Daher et al., 1997; Strohle et al., 2001).

The fact that most of the racemic lactate (L-lactate) used in infusions is metabolized to pyruvate, with a consecutive increase in bicarbonate, has lead to the idea that the infusion could ultimately result in an increase in partial-pressure of CO_2 (pCO_2) by back-titration (i.e. HCO_3^- and $H^+ \rightarrow CO_2$ and H_2O). This metabolic hypothesis, that unified the mechanisms behind lactate and CO_2-induced panic, was tested in a protocol using bicarbonate (Gorman et al., 1989). Results from this study, however, suggest at best a contribution of lactate "metabolism" to CO_2 in lactate's panicogenic effect. The fact that D-Lactate has shown to also be panicogenic (Gorman et al., 1990a), thought not to have any metabolism to pyruvate, would exclude the possible contribution of CO_2. However, the large increases of bicarbonate seen in this trial cannot rule this out. A spectroscopy study indicating brain intracellular acidification after an infusion with bicarbonate (Nakashima et al., 1996) also lends some empirical support to the metabolic hypothesis of lactate-induced panic.

In the 1980s, Carr and Sheehan (1984) proposed a model where a lactate infusion and its metabolism to pyruvate would reduce NAD^+ to NADH and H^+ with a consecutive drop in neuronal pH, depending on its permeability through the blood–brain barrier. Although lactate probably does not cross the blood–brain barrier, work performed with proton-NMR spectroscopy to measure the brain lactate response during a racemic lactate infusion shows a larger diffuse brain lactate increase in PD patients (Dager et al., 1999). Additionally, acute and disproportionate brain lactate elevations are seen in PD after voluntary hyperventilation (VH) as measured with ^{1}H-NMR techniques (Dager et al., 1995). It is plausible that this metabolic scenario can lead to brain intracellular acidification (van Rijen et al., 1989; Maddock, 2001), potentially stimulating H^+/CO_2 chemoreceptors in the same fashion as CO_2 inhalations.

As mentioned, a lactate infusion (and hypertonic saline) constitutes a high volume hyperosmotic fluid load that provokes an increase in blood pressure, heart rate, and hemodilution. This brings about the possible role of the so-called osmosensitive circumventricular organs (Ganong, 1997). These areas, with fenestrated capillaries at many sites that have direct link to the hypothalamus and other structures involved in panic, are candidate sites for the action of hyperosmotic challenges (Shekhar and Keim, 1997). In an animal model with a disruption of GABA-mediated inhibition in the dorsal medial hypothalamus, the panic-like effect of lactate was mediated by angiotensin II (Shekhar et al., 2006). Shifts in neuroactive steroids that modulate GABA activity seem to be associated with lactate-induced panic in PD patients (Strohle et al., 2003) and are in line with a possible role of the circumventricular organs. It is attractive to speculate that the dorsal medial hypothalamus is involved in lactate-induced panic since it is considered a key anatomical structure in animal models of panic attacks and defensive behavior, together with the periaqueductal gray (PAG) and the amygdala (Canteras, 2002; Schenberg et al., 2001).

II.D. Validity

In those patients that respond to a lactate infusion there is a considerable symptom convergence with their reported natural spontaneous panic attacks (Liebowitz et al., 1984; Dillon et al., 1987; Goetz et al., 1994), except maybe for tingling which appears to be a specific hypocalcemic effect of the infusion. When a lactate infusion is compared to bicarbonate and hypertonic saline, the lactate-specific tingling seems to be absent only in the former (Gorman et al., 1989). However, a fundamental absence of the same degree of dyspnea is absent in the latter (Peskind et al., 1998). Some studies place emphasis on the lack of specificity for dyspnea in panic attacks (Vickers and McNally, 2005). However, this issue is clarified when a distinction is made between spontaneous panics and anticipation/situational anxiety attacks (Briggs et al., 1993) which are considered to have phenomenological overlap but a distinct neurobiology (Andreatini et al., 2001; Uhlenhuth et al., 2006).

A large body of evidence developed by the group from Columbia University (Gorman et al.,

1990b) has shown that PD patients are more vulnerable to a lactate infusion than healthy subjects, patients with depression, generalized anxiety disorder (GAD), obsessive compulsive disorder, social phobia (SP), or bulimia (Liebowitz et al., 1984). Moreover, lactate seems to be more specific to a history of panic attacks than the clinical diagnosis of PD (Cowley et al., 1986; Buller et al., 1989). The specificity of lactate in PD, however, is not without controversy as patients with GAD (Cowley et al., 1988) and premenstrual dysphoric disorder (Facchinetti et al., 1992) have a larger reaction than healthy controls, but smaller when compared to PD patients. Also, lactate infusions may provoke flashbacks in patients with post-traumatic stress disorder (PTSD) (Jensen et al., 1997). Panic rates for a classic racemic sodium lactate infusion vary, but a sample from two large studies report panic attacks in over 65% of PD patients and 0% of healthy controls (Liebowitz et al., 1984; Gorman et al., 1989).

A well-designed study to evaluate the reliability of lactate and isoproterenol-induced panic attacks, reveals that these maneuvers do not display any sensitizing or desensitizing effect on PD patients after three consecutive trials (Yeragani et al., 1988a). Many pharmacological substances and interventions that are therapeutic in PD have been used to block the effects of a lactate infusion. High potency benzodiazepines (e.g. Alprazolam) can cancel the panicogenic effects of lactate (Liebowitz et al., 1986a; Cowley et al., 1991) as opposed to diazepam which has shown to have no effect (Liebowitz et al., 1995). Anti-depressants such as tricyclics (Yeragani et al., 1988b) and SSRIs (Dager et al., 1997) when given for several weeks have also shown to reduce the effects of lactate on measures of panic.

III. Carbon dioxide

III.A. Background

Carbon dioxide, as lactate an end-product of carbohydrate metabolism, is constantly produced in the cell yet it rarely accumulates as it is readily processed by the bicarbonate system and transported from tissues to the lungs where it is finally excreted (Ganong, 1997).

Although the experimental panicogenic properties of CO_2 have been described since 1951 (Cohen and White, 1951), it was not until the 1980s when Van den Hout and Griez (1984) at Maastricht University applied inhalations with 35% CO_2, that were considered "anxiolytic" at the time, and found that PD patients experienced brief periods of intense cognitive and physical symptoms that resemble spontaneous panic attacks. About the same time, Gorman et al. (1984) at the University of Columbia in New York used a continuous inhalation of 5% CO_2 during VH as way of controlling hypocapnia, and unexpectedly found that using CO_2 was more panicogenic than the hyperventilation. Carbon dioxide challenges are currently one of the most extensively used models for panic.

III.B. Features and technique

The two main methods of delivering CO_2 as an experimental panicogen are: (i) a single- or a double-breath 35% inhalation through a mask (Van den Hout and Griez, 1984; Fyer et al., 1987) and (ii) the continuous 5–7% inhalation in a canopy for 15–20 min (Gorman et al., 1994). A single-breath 35% CO_2/65% O_2 mixture inhalation of at least 80% of the subject's vital capacity and subsequent breath holding for 4 s, is widely used (Perna et al., 1994a). Variations of the 35% CO_2 model include a double-breath hold with the mixture for 4–8 s (Nardi et al., 2006), a continuous inhalation for 30 s (Papp et al., 1993), and five repeated vital-capacity inhalations (Schmidt et al., 1997) which apparently increases sensitivity with a decrease in specificity. The 35% challenge elicits its panicogenic effects in a matter of seconds (Griez et al., 1987a), whereas the inhalation of 5–7% does the same after several minutes (Gorman et al., 1994). Other forms of administration include the Read re-breathing method with 7% CO_2 (Zandbergen et al., 1991), a continuous positive air pressure with 5.5% (Sanderson et al., 1989), and a 20-s inhalation of 20% CO_2 (Prenoveau et al., 2006). Simple breath-holding with room-air has been currently used as a method to endogenously increase body CO_2 levels where subjects are usually instructed to stop breathing following a normal exhalation and hold their breath for as long as possible (Nardi et al., 2003).

Because of the biological importance of its elimination, CO_2 elicits a powerful ventilatory stimulation mediated by peripheral and central CO_2/H^+ chemoreceptors. In the presence of carbonic anhydrase, CO_2 interacts with water to form carbonic acid, which is highly unstable and rapidly dissociates into H^+ and bicarbonate. The accumulation of H^+ without a compensatory increase of HCO_3^- would lead to a decrease in pH. The single inhalation of 35% CO_2 produces a rapid intravascular increase of pCO_2 and a decrease of pH that lasts about 10 s and is immediately followed by a 2-min hyperventilation-driven alkalosis (Griez et al., 1987a). Notoriously, CO_2 may also provoke a dramatic increase in cerebral blood flow (CBF) that is contingent on the perivascular levels of CO_2/H^+ (Pandit et al., 2003). Studies that have assessed the relationship between CBF and anxiety/panic during CO_2 provocation are not clear-cut. The 5% challenge has shown that higher subjective anxiety in a mixed GAD-healthy subject group is related to a lesser increase in CBF (Mathew and Wilson, 1988; Mathew et al., 1997a) as measured with the xenon-133 inhalation technique. On the other hand, more recent work with transcranial Doppler and the 35% CO_2 probe in PD patients shows that they display a larger increase in basilar artery blood flow velocity than healthy controls after the challenge.

Neuroendocrinological studies in CO_2-induced panic have revealed that the challenge can elicit a small HPA activation in healthy volunteers and PD patients (van Duinen et al., 2005, 2006). This activation however is not related to any subjective measures of panic nor does it discriminate panic patients from healthy controls. On the other hand, the Bristol group has found substantial cortisol and ACTH activations after a challenge with 35% CO_2 in healthy volunteers (Argyropoulos et al., 2002; Kaye et al., 2004). Remarkably, the latter study shows a moderate positive correlation between peak anxiety and plasma cortisol change.

III.C. Underlying mechanisms

The relatively recent discovery of acid-sensing ion channels involved in fear conditioning (Wemmie et al., 2003, 2004) and the pH chemosensitivity of midbrain 5-HT neurons (Severson et al., 2003; Richerson, 2004) makes it mechanistically tentative to view the response to the CO_2 inhalation as an affective expression related to brain acidosis.

In an effort to determine if central acidification was relevant to the subjective response to CO_2-induced symptoms in PD, two groups of researchers tested the subjective effects of 1 g of intravenous acetazolamide (Mathew et al., 1989; Gorman et al., 1993). Results from these studies are consistent with the fact that the maneuver does not provoke panic, and moreover, one group reported a reduction in the levels of anxiety with the medication (Gorman et al., 1993). It is remarkable that acetazolamide has shown to increase levels of CO_2 and decrease pH in the extracellular compartments of the brain, yet without an effect on cerebral intercellular pH (Bickler et al., 1988; Vorstrup et al., 1989). This finding may explain the drug's lack of an acute effect on ventilation (Mathew et al., 1989; Gorman et al., 1993) as minute ventilation in human healthy volunteers has an inverse relationship with brain intracellular pH (Jensen et al., 1988). One study specifically designed to determine if the response to CO_2 is dose-dependent, has shown that the panic reaction to a CO_2 challenge is related to the amount of CO_2 administered (Griez et al., 2007). In general, in studies that use a double inhalation versus a single inhalation or a continuous inhalation of 7 versus 5%, the larger dose of CO_2 is invariably related to a higher panic rate in PD patients (Nardi et al., 2006; Rassovsky and Kushner 2003).

Recently, Bailey et al. (2003) have put forward a hypothesis where CO_2-induced panic initiates in the brainstem chemosensory noradrenergic neurons including the locus ceruleus with a subsequent involvement of the central nucleus of the amygdala and the hypothalamus.

Neuroimaging studies have revealed that CO_2 inhalations and CO_2-induced breathlessness are related to activations in several brain structures that are thought to be implicated in affective responses including the midbrain, hypothalamus, hippocampus, cingulate gyrus, and cerebellum (Corfield et al., 1995; Liotti et al., 2001). Interestingly, activation of the cerebellum during CO_2-elicited breathlessness has been hypothesized to have a role beyond the traditional implication in motor activity to include primal emotions that would serve ecological purposes (i.e. escaping suffocation) (Parsons et al., 2001).

III.D. Validity

A diversity of studies confirms that the symptoms elicited by CO_2 inhalations are similar in quality, duration, and severity to panic attacks that occur naturally (Griez et al., 1987b; Perna et al., 1994a). The study by Perna et al. (1994a) additionally concludes that the risk of having a panic attack is significantly more reliably predicted by reactivity to CO_2 than by meeting diagnostic criteria for PD. In healthy volunteers, a positive response to a 20% CO_2 challenge predicted the future onset of spontaneous panic attacks in a 2-year prospective follow-up study (Schmidt et al., 2007). Taken together, these data are consistent with a psychological model of PD where a spontaneous panic attack is a core psychopathological element that, when present in individuals with an anxious cognitive style, can precipitate the dysfunctional set of behaviors and cognitions (Bouton et al., 2001) characteristic of PD.

A single 35% CO_2 inhalation after three consecutive challenges at a weekly interval has displayed good reliability (Perna et al., 1994a; Verburg et al., 1998), although there appears to be some desensitization after a prolonged series of challenges (van den Hout et al., 1987).

Carbon dioxide can elicit panic in 20–90% of patients with PD and 0–38% of healthy controls, depending on the gas concentration, method of delivery, and operational definition of a panic attack (Papp et al., 1997; Rassovsky and Kushner, 2003). The CO_2 challenge specifically elicits a panic reaction in PD patients as opposed to healthy subjects (Griez et al., 1987b). Similar results are obtained when PD patients are compared to patients with obsessive-compulsive disorder (OCD) (Griez et al., 1990) and subjects with other anxiety and mood disorders (Griez, 2001). Recent research suggest that a continuous inhalation of 7.5% CO_2 may be used as a model for GAD, based on the differential modification of its effects by lorazepam and paroxetine in healthy volunteers (Bailey et al., 2007). Nevertheless, patients with GAD have a smaller panic and anxiety response to 5 and 35% CO_2 compared with PD patients (Holt and Andrews, 1989; Verburg et al., 1995; Perna et al., 1999). Additionally, GAD patients show an anxiety response similar to that of healthy controls using the 5% CO_2 inhalation (Mathew and Wilson, 1988; Mathew et al., 1997). The Bristol group has shown, in separate studies, that healthy volunteers and GAD patients display increased anxiousness to the continuous inhalation of 7.5% CO_2 (Bailey et al., 2005; Seddon et al., in press).

Several studies confirm that effective anti-panic medications, such as MAOIs (Perna et al., 1994b), SSRIs (Pols et al., 1996b), and high-potency benzodiazepines (Pols et al., 1996a), are capable of significantly reducing the reaction to a CO_2 challenge in PD patients. Moreover, some of these medications have shown to be capable of blocking a CO_2 challenge after only a week of treatment and before a full therapeutic response was obtained (Perna et al., 1997).

IV. Cholecystokinin

IV.A. Background

In the early seventies, a small peptide with gastrin-like immunoreactivity was discovered in the mammalian brain (Vanderhaeghen et al., 1975). Despite a quite heterogeneous distribution, this substance, which was identified as the sulphated C-terminal octapeptide of the gut hormone CCK, proved to be the most abundant neuropeptide in the human brain. The octapeptide CCK-8S and, more important, corresponding receptors, were found mainly in the cortex, caudate nucleus, putamen, and hippocampus. Additionally, somewhat lower levels were found in the septum PAG and other limbic structures. It was later discovered that the tetrapeptide CCK-4, consisting of the very first CCK-8S amino acids, was able to activate brain receptors (CCK-B receptors). In the late eighties, an investigator noticed a brief, but strong feeling of anxiety after self-administration of CCK. This led to an open label trial in a group of 10 healthy volunteers, confirming that intravenous injections of CCK, in various dosages between 20 and 100 μg, had definite anxiogenic properties (de Montigny, 1989). In the mid nineties, investigators began to use pentagastrin, an easily available agonist of CCK receptors, as an alternative to CCK-4 for the experimental study of panic (Abelson and Nesse, 1994). Pentagastrin, a synthetic analogue of gastrin, was developed for the diagnostic evaluation of gastric acid secretory function. It is a 5-amino acid peptide, which with its four amino acids C-terminal sequence is identical to CCK-4.

IV.B. Features and technique

CCK-4 and pentagastrin are administered as a bolus intravenous infusion. CCK-4 is usually administered in a 1–3 mL saline solution with dosages of 25 μg in PD patients and 50 μg in healthy volunteers. Pentagastrin is generally administered in a less than 1 mL of saline solution with dosages from 0.5 to 0.6 μg per kg in both PD and healthy volunteers. The maneuver elicits its characteristic behavioral effects about 20 s after the infusion with a mean duration of about 20 min (Bradwejn et al., 1990).

CCK-B receptor agonist administration is accompanied by noticeable cardiorespiratory alterations. Well-controlled studies have shown a robust increase of heart rate, blood pressure, and minute ventilation only a few minutes after administration (Abelson and Nesse, 1994; Bradwejn et al., 1998; Koszycki et al., 1998). Research into the relationship between objective cardiorespiratory measures and subjective panic measures have shown that these are rather asynchronous. Although one study did find a relationship between diastolic blood pressure and a positive panic response to CCK-4, these findings have not been replicated in recent, carefully designed studies (Eser et al., 2007). Pentagastrin and CCK-4 also elicit a considerable activation of the HPA axis. Abelson et al. (1994) analyzed ACTH, cortisol, and growth hormone responses to the pentagastrin challenge. Pentagastrin produced a consistent and potent activation of the HPA axis, although interpretation of the authors was that HPA activation was not related to the anxiogenic response. Furthermore, a recent randomized, placebo-controlled study in 85 healthy volunteers using CCK-4 found no relationship between HPA activation and measures of panic response (Eser et al., 2007).

IV.C. Underlying mechanisms

Several neurotransmitter systems have been postulated to mediate the effects of CCK-4 and pentagastrin. The actions of CCK-B receptor agonists elicited panic symptoms can be almost entirely blocked by the CCK-B receptor antagonist L-365,260 in both healthy volunteers (Lines et al., 1995) and PD patients (Bradwejn et al., 1994b). CI-988, another CCK-B receptor antagonist, also showed to reduce the effects of CCK when administered to healthy volunteers (Bradwejn et al., 1995). However, its effects were modest which is probably due to a poor systemic availability. These finding altogether suggest a mediation of CCK-B receptors in the panicogenic effects of CCK-4 and pentagastrin in humans. This, in turn, has lead researchers to hypothesize that CCK receptors might play a major role in the underlying mechanisms of spontaneous panic attacks and PD. Unfortunately, well-controlled studies using CCK antagonists have failed to show any therapeutic effects in PD patients (Kramer et al., 1995; Pande et al., 1999). While some research suggests that the serotonergic, the noradrenergic, and the benzodiazepine receptor systems may modulate the panicogenic effects of CCK, their mediation is generally not supported (Bradwejn et al., 1994a; McCann et al., 1997a; Khan et al., 2004; Maron et al., 2004; Toru et al., 2006).

Based on findings from animal research, it is attractive to speculate that HPA-axis activation plays an important role in the panicogenic effects induced by CCK-B agonists (Strohle et al., 2000). As mentioned previously, CCK-4 and pentagastrin elicit a clear HPA-axis activation that is rather asynchronous with the provoked panic arousal (Graeff et al., 2005). In this scope, a recent study has shown that premedication with a mineralocorticoid antagonist before a CCK challenge in healthy men increased baseline cortisol. However, no effect was found on baseline ACTH, or either CCK-stimulated cortisol or ACTH (Otte et al., 2007). In a similar protocol, premedication with the synthetic progestational hormone megestrol blunted the HPA-axis activation typically seen with a CCK (Raedler et al., 2006). Thus, despite the modifications produced by the mineralocorticoid antagonist and megestrol on ACTH and cortisol activation, no effects were seen on the panicogenic effects of a CCK challenge. On a different perspective, some studies have explored the relationship between the CCK challenge and the activity of neuroactive steroids that can allosterically modulate neurotransmitter receptors. In this scope, changes in the plasma concentrations of progesterone metabolites, which are thought to parallel those in the brain, have been found to correlate with the CCK-elicited panic symptoms in PD patients (Strohle et al., 2003). As suggested in that report, the observed changes in neuroactive steroids can be linked to a central modulation of GABA-A receptor activity that would lead to a decrease in central GABA-ergic tone.

Neuroanatomical studies in both animal and human have yielded compelling results. Research has shown that the dorsal PAG CCK-2 (CCK-B) receptors modulate anxious behavior displayed by rodents in an elevated plus-maze model (Netto and Guimaraes, 2004) and freezing and escape behavior evoked by electrical stimulation (Bertoglio et al., 2007). The former study also showed that the administration of CCK-B agonists in the dorsal PAG induced Fos expression in other brain regions related to defensive behavior such as the raphe nuclei, medial amygdala, medial hypothalamus, and paraventricular hypothalamus. As mentioned earlier, the PAG, together with the medial hypothalamus and the amygdala, are key anatomical structures in animal models of panic attacks and defensive behavior (Schenberg et al., 2001; Canteras, 2002). A positron emission tomography (PET) study in healthy male volunteers was conducted to determine the changes in regional CBF in two time points after a CCK challenge (Javanmard et al., 1999). This study revealed an early involvement of the hypothalamus and a later asymmetrical activation of the claustrum-insular that positively correlated with increments in the measurements of panic. A more recent study, using functional magnetic resonance imaging recordings in healthy volunteers exposed to 50 µg of CCK-4, has found a blood oxygen level-dependent (BOLD) activation in the insular cortices, temporal poles, cingulate gyrus, thalamic region, and cerebellar vermis. These BOLD activations were more extensive and significant in those with a strong panic reaction to the challenge. Although the latter study does not report on any activation of the hypothalamus, as set forward by Javanmard et al., (1999), it is appealing to speculate an initial activation of the hypothalamus because of its interconnections with circumventricular organs including the area postrema, subfornical organ, and organum vasculosus lamina terminalis (Shekhar and Keim, 1997). Intravenous infusions with CCK-B agonists may exert their effect by leaking through circumventricular organs, such as the area postrema (Olson et al., 1993).

IV.D. Validity

The technique of using CCK-B agonists as a safe method has been well established with hundreds of subjects. The symptoms induced by CCK-B agonists in PD patients seem to resemble their spontaneous panic attacks (Bradwejn et al., 1990; Abelson and Nesse, 1994). At least one study attests the reproducibility of panic symptoms using an infusion with CCK-B receptor agonist in PD patients (Bradwejn et al., 1992b).

In randomized placebo-controlled studies the effects of CCK-B agonists appear to be dose dependent, with higher dosages increasing the number of subjects reporting panic sensations (Bradwejn et al., 1992a, 1991; van Megen et al., 1994). However, at a given dosage, there is a significant difference in sensitivity to CCK between normal controls and patients with PD, the latter group appearing definitively more vulnerable to the pharmacological effect of CCK agonists. A series of well-controlled studies have compared the CCK vulnerability in other anxiety disorders. A pentagastrin challenge in a small sample of OCD patients suggests that these are more prone to respond with a panic attack than healthy controls (de Leeuw et al., 1996). Additionally, OCD symptomatology was not affected. One study compared the responses of patients with PD, patients with SP, and healthy volunteers to pentagastrin (McCann et al., 1997b). Both groups of PD and social phobics panicked in the pentagastrin condition. And although patients with PD had a slightly higher rate of formally defined panic attacks, 64 versus 47%, the difference was not significant. The rate of panic in the healthy control group was 11%. This, together with a similar study (van Vliet et al., 1997), strongly suggests that patients with SP and PD have a similarly high sensitivity to CCK agonists. Nevertheless, Katzman et al. (2004) and coworkers did not replicate these findings when they compared the vulnerability of OCD patients, SP patients, and healthy volunteers to 20 μg of CCK-4. In this study, the small sample size may have precluded the finding of a significant difference between the 50% panic attack rates in social phobics and OCD and the 8.3% panic attack rate in healthy volunteers. One study addressed the issue of CCK sensitivity in GAD (Brawman-Mintzer et al., 1997). A limited sample of seven patients and seven age-matched healthy controls received a bolus infusion with 0.6 μg per kg of pentagastrin on one occasion, and saline placebo on another occasion, according to a single blind design. Results from this study suggest that GAD patients are highly vulnerable to a pentagastrin challenge. Overall, although the studies are relatively sparse and the samples quite small, most investigations reviewed above in other anxiety disorders with CCK analogues indicate that the high CCK sensitivity observed in PD may extend across the other main anxiety disorders.

Several investigations have shown that antipanic interventions can also reduce the effects of a challenge with CCK-B agonists. For instance, PD patients that respond to imipramine (Bradwejn and Koszycki, 1994), fluvoxamine (van Megen et al., 1997), and citalopram (Shlik et al., 1997) show a smaller reaction to CCK agonists. Benzodiazepines such as lorazepam and alprazolam have also shown to attenuate the effects produced by CCK-4 administration in healthy volunteers (de Montigny, 1989; Zwanzger et al., 2003a). The GABA neurotransmission enhancing drugs tiagabine and vigabatrin given for 1 week also reduce the vulnerability of healthy volunteers to 50 μg of CCK-4 (Zwanzger et al., 2001, 2003b), although these drugs have yet to show therapeutic usefulness in PD patients (Mula et al., 2007). Interestingly, an acute exercise session of 30 min can protect healthy volunteers from CCK-induced panic attacks when compared with 30 min of rest (Strohle et al., 2005). This is consistent with the therapeutic effects of an aerobic exercise program in PD patients (Broocks et al., 1998).

V. Voluntary hyperventilation

V.A. Background

It was found that a hyperventilation-driven reduction in pCO_2 is associated with vulnerability to sodium lactate induced panic attacks (Gorman et al., 1988). Moreover, there's an overlap in panic symptoms and the symptoms produced by acute respiratory alkalosis. Based on these findings, a VH model for panic was developed (Lum, 1987). Although hyperventilation is now largely disregarded as a cause of panic, the practical and non-invasive features of VH yielded a compelling and large amount of research (Maddock, 2001).

V.B. Features and technique

Many different methods of VH have been used across laboratories. However, most techniques of VH involve visual or auditory stimuli to indicate the frequency of 30 breathing cycles per minute for 4–15 min (Gorman et al., 1994; Papp et al., 1997; Nardi et al., 2001b) or visual feed-back for the subject to breathe as necessary to keep an end-tidal pCO_2 lower than 20 mmHg for 8 min (Maddock and Mateo-Bermudez, 1990; Maddock and Carter, 1991). Notably, one laboratory used a long tube attached to a mask to increase dead space and maintain baseline levels of pCO_2 as control isocapnic hyperventilation (Zandbergen et al., 1990).

Most techniques used in VH will usually produce drop in pCO_2 below 20 mmHg in less than 2 min (Wilhelm et al., 2001; Friedman et al., 2006). After hyperventilation, pCO_2 levels will recover slowly probably due to the typical accumulation of systemic and brain lactate during VH (Posse et al., 1997) that is probably mediated by the effects of respiratory alkalosis on carbohydrate metabolism (Siesjo, 1982; Maddock and Mateo-Bermudez, 1990). In contrast to an inhalation with CO_2, VH and the subsequent drop in pCO_2 induces a reduction in cerebral blood velocity (van Rijen et al., 1989). To our knowledge there is no systematic study on the relationship between the panicogenic effects of VH and HPA axis activation. Nevertheless, one report suggests that VH may lead to a mild increase in cortisol and plasma catecholamines after 10 min (Laderach and Straub, 2001) probably related to respiratory work and skeletal muscle contraction.

V.C. Underlying mechanisms

Hyperventilation has once been regarded not only as an experimental maneuver to induce panic but also the cause of naturalistic panic attacks (Lum, 1987; Ley, 1992). This idea of a causative role emphasizes on the sequelae of hyperventilation in the production of mild physical symptoms that in a cognitive vicious circle will render the development of full-blown panic. However, against this theory lies the fact that VH is a relatively weak and inconsistent method to induce panic (Zandbergen et al., 1990; Gorman et al., 1994). Studies that monitor pCO_2 levels of subjects during the recovery phase of VH show that panic-responsive PD patients have larger decreases and a longer recovery (Maddock and Carter, 1991; Wilhelm et al., 2001). This has lead to the suggestion that VH may produce a more downward adjustment in the CO_2

sensitivity of PD patients who then become more vulnerable to the rising than the absolute levels of CO_2 (Wilhelm et al., 2001).

Another proposed mechanism links VH with panic provocation induced by lactate. Acute and disproportionate brain lactate elevations are seen in PD after VH as measured with ^{1}H-NMR spectroscopy techniques (Dager et al., 1995). The proposed mechanisms behind this exaggerated lactate response to alkalotic challenges (including sodium lactate infusions) involve: hypoxia due to vasoconstriction, a disturbance in intracellular pH regulation, and enhanced glycolysis due to adrenergic activation (Maddock, 2001). In this regard, PD patients have shown a more pronounced reduction basilar artery flow during VH than healthy controls (Gibbs 1992; Ball and Shekhar, 1997).

V.D. Validity

The voluntary nature of hyperventilation techniques makes this maneuver very safe. The usual side effects such as dizziness and paresthesia are within the characteristic symptoms of a panic attack, but are usually present in all subjects that undergo VH, regardless of the subject's condition or challenge outcome. According to studies using a large sample of VH-sensitive PD patients, the frequencies of DSM-IV panic attack symptoms provoked by the maneuver were similar to those reported during the patients spontaneous panic attacks (Nardi et al., 2004). In a Dutch sample of 48 patients with PD, only 21% of subjects panicked during VH, but recognized the induced panic symptoms to be similar to their spontaneous panic attacks (Spinhoven et al., 1992). In conflict with this, previous reports are consistent in that VH produces an increase in somatic symptoms but no change in subjective measures of panic (Maddock and Carter, 1991; Griez et al., 1988).

A Brazilian group lead by Nardi et al. (2001a, b, 2002) published a series of studies that provide evidence towards a considerable discriminative power of VH when the panic response rates in PD patients are compared to those with major depression, OCD, and SP. Combining a number of their studies, Nardi et al. (2000, 2001a, b, 2002) have shown that 44 up till 64% of the subjects respond with a panic attack using VH as a challenge technique. Although other laboratories (Maddock et al., 1991; Wilhelm et al., 2001) report similar rates with fewer patients, other groups have found VH to have a very low sensitivity when compared to the rates of CO_2 induced panic in the same group of patients (Zandbergen et al., 1990; Papp et al., 1997). Conclusions from these latter studies are that VH is, at best, a weak panicogen when compared to CO_2. Overall, the symptom convergence and panic rates of VH in PD across laboratories are difficult to interpret because of differences in subject selection, procedures used for hyperventilation and operational criteria used to assess the occurrence of a panic attack. With regard to reliability, one study that compared the type and severity of VH-elicited symptoms reported by 14 PD patients and 14 healthy control subjects on two occasions, 1 week apart, revealed test–retest consistency (Lindsay et al., 1991). To our knowledge, no data support a clinical validation for VH as an experimental model for panic attacks as there are no systematic studies that test the VH challenge after the use of an anti-panic maneuver or treatment.

VI. Doxapram

VI.A. Background

Doxapram is a CNS stimulant (analeptic) commonly used in the management of respiratory failure. The capability of intravenous doxapram to induce hyperventilation and a consecutive drop in pCO_2 inspired its use as a model for panic (Lee et al., 1993).

VI.B. Features and technique

In panic provocation protocols, doxapram hydrochloride is administered as a 0.5 mg/kg dose in 10 mL of saline over 15 s (Gutman et al., 2005). As a respiratory stimulant, doxapram produces an increase in ventilation and a drop in pCO_2 of about 5% in healthy subjects and up till 20% in PD patients (Lee et al., 1993). Whether the

HPA-axis is activated after doxapram administration is not clear (Gutman et al., 2005; Abelson et al., 2006). In any case, the activation is unspecific and unrelated to the panic response (Gutman et al., 2005; Abelson et al., 2006).

VI.C. Underlying mechanisms

One proposed explanation states that doxapam (as well as most other panicogenic substances) produces physiological arousal, which in susceptible individuals leads to misinterpretation of bodily sensations, ultimately with stimulation of the amygdala and production of panic (Gutman et al., 2005). Some research provides elements to link doxapram to the same mechanisms involved in CO_2-induced panic. Doxapram could exert its effect by the inhibition of TASK-1 and TASK-3 (Cotton et al., 2006), which are pH-sensitive potassium channels expressed in brainstem serotonergic neurons (Washburn et al., 2002). By inhibition of these channels, doxapram may increase the excitability of brainstem CO_2-sensitive neurons that potentially warn the organism of detrimental effects of asphyxia.

VI.D. Validity

Doxapram can be regarded as safe when used at the conventional panicogenic dosages. However, its use should be restricted in subjects with risk of seizures or pharmacotherapy with MAOIs. The validity of doxapram as a model for panic is limited due to the lack of studies. In any case, doxapram seems to be a potent panicogen with panic rates ranging from 80 to 100% in PD patients and 0 to 20% in healthy control subjects (Lee et al., 1993; Gutman et al., 2005; Kent et al., 2005).

VII. Other experimental models of panic

VII.A. Flumazenil

Flumazenil is a benzodiazepine receptor antagonist used in research and in clinical practice for the management of benzodiazepine overdose. As an intravenous dose of 2 mg flumazenil is generally devoid of any significant symptomatic effect but may produce panic attack in PD patients (Nutt et al., 1990). This finding put forward the interesting hypothesis that PD patients may have an abnormal benzodiazepine receptor set point. A study performed by the Bristol group suggests that flumazenil has a robust panicogenic effect that can be blocked with standard anti-panic treatment with SSRIs (Bell et al., 2002). Although two studies have not replicated the previously described findings in PD patients (Strohle et al., 1999, 1998), methodological differences may account for these results (Potokar et al., 1999). The use of this model in panic has been very limited and further validation studies are timely.

VII.B. Caffeine

Caffeine is an adenosine receptor antagonist with widespread use as a stimulant. Although caffeine has been extensively used as a model for panic (Bourin et al., 1998) its rather unspecific effects are probably better related to generalized anxiety than to panic (Bruce et al., 1992). Additionally, to our knowledge no clinical validation studies have been performed and in the last decade the amount of research using caffeine as a model of panic has been scarce. However, recent studies suggest that PD patients that panic after caffeine administration are associated with having respiratory sub-type panic attacks and are more sensitive to CO_2 (Masdrakis et al., 2007; Nardi et al., 2007).

VII.C. Adrenergic challenges: yohimbine, isoprotenerol and epinephrine

In general, very little work has been done with noradrenergic challenges as models for panic in the last decade. Yohimbine is a $\alpha2$-antagonist that is thought to produce panic symptoms by increasing activity in the locus ceruleus (Bourin et al., 1998). Yohimbine has shown to provoke panic attacks in PD patients at a higher rate compared with healthy subjects (Charney et al., 1984). Additionally, patients with GAD or OCD are not panic sensitive to the $\alpha2$-antagonist challenge

(Rasmussen et al., 1987; Charney et al., 1989). On the other hand, two factors make yohimbine a questionable model for panic: (i) yohimbine elicits flashbacks and panic attacks in patients with PTSD (Southwick et al., 1997) and (ii) standard anti-panic treatment with imipramine does not reduce the effects of the challenge in patients with PD (Charney and Heninger, 1985).

Isoprotenerol is a peripherally active β-agonist that potentially induces panic attacks that are phenomenologically similar to those produced by a sodium lactate infusion and placebo dextrose infusions in PD patients (Balon et al., 1988). A challenge with isoprotenerol produces panic attacks in a greater proportion of PD patients as opposed to healthy volunteers (Pohl et al., 1988), which can be reduced by standard anti-panic treatment with imipramine (Pohl et al., 1990). Other studies that validate isoprotenerol as a model of panic are scant. In the case of epinephrine, very few studies address the validity of this model (Veltman et al., 1996).

VII.D. Serotonergic panicogens: d-Fenfluramine and mCPP

Fenfluramine, an acute 5-HT enhancer, has been describe to provoke more intense panic and anxiety in patients with PD than patients with major depressive disorder and healthy volunteers (Targum and Marshall, 1989). Nevertheless, these findings have been questioned as to whether they better account for anticipatory anxiety or generalized anxiety (Hollander et al., 1990). In fact, fenfluramine premedication has shown to increase anxiety and reduce the panicogenic effects of CO_2 in patients with PD (Mortimore and Anderson, 2000). These latter findings are explained in the context of a theory that attributes a dual role for 5-HT in anxiety (Deakin and Graeff, 1991).

*Meta*chlorophenylpiperazine (m-CPP) is mainly a 5-HT receptor agonist, however it also antagonizes 5-HT3 and $\alpha1$-adrenergic receptors (Kahn and Wetzler, 1991). results (as a model for panic) are not clear: (i) its panic effect depends on the route of administration, (ii) the challenge can exacerbate OCD symptoms in patients with this disorder (Erzegovesi et al., 2001) and anger and anxiety in GAD patients (Germine et al., 1992), (iii) findings are difficult to interpret as other 5-HT enhancers such as L-5 hydroxytyptophan not only does not provoke panic but reduces the effects of a 35% CO_2 challenge in patients with PD and healthy volunteers (Schruers et al., 2002).

VIII. General conclusions

The use of experimental models has aided our understanding of panic and fear. Together with animal studies, these models can help delineate the neurochemical and neuroanatomical underpinnings of defensive behavior. In any case, even a cautious interpretation of the modest evidence supports the assumption that pathological anxiety does not rely on one single mechanism.

This complexity is manifest when comparing the most well-studied panicogens (i.e. lactate, CO_2, and CCK) in the degree to which they meet the criteria for an ideal experimental model. Apparently, the vulnerability triggered by the different models of panic does not completely overlap, even though they may produce similar symptoms. For instance subjects with GAD or OCD are not affected by a CO_2 challenge or a lactate infusion in the same way as PD patients. In contrast, the studies published so far strongly suggest that CCK is as panicogenic in GAD and in OCD as it is in PD. This differential sensitivity, if confirmed, may pave the way for further pharmacologic dissection of defensive behavior.

Other experimental models are still in need of further validation. VH has been recently fairly validated, however the blockablity of the maneuver has not been systematically tested with standard anti-panic interventions. Moreover, the evidence so far suggests it is a weak panicogen when compared to CO_2. Doxapram is a promising agent that may meet criteria for an ideal experimental model provided additional validation.

Much work is still to be done. Experimental models of panic and fear can eventually be useful paradigms for proof-of-concept studies. Since the traditional ways of measuring the panic response to the different models depend on the conceptual cortico-linguistic abilities of the subjects being tested, there is a need to search for objective physiological measurements (e.g. cardiovascular, neuroendocrine, etc) that can predict a challenge response. This may be relevant in the search for biomarkers that are more objective and scientifically useful for studies into the genetic and neuroanatomical determinants of panic and fear susceptibility. This altogether may be relevant for better understanding of etiological mechanisms and accordingly, call for a revised nosology. Experimental challenges may finally prove useful in suggesting effective treatments for discrete anxiety disorders.

Abbreviations

BOLD	Blood oxygen level-dependent
CBF	Cerebral blood flow
GAD	Generalized anxiety disorder
NTS	Nucleus tractus solitarius
OCD	Obsessive-compulsive disorder
PAG	Periaqueductal gray
pCO_2	Partial-pressure of CO_2
PD	Panic disorder
PTSD	Post-traumatic stress disorder
VH	Voluntary hyperventilation

References

Abelson, J.L., Khan, S., Liberzon, I. and Young, E.A. (2006) HPA axis activity in patients with panic disorder: review and synthesis of four studies. Depress. Anxiety, 24: 66–76.

Abelson, J.L. and Nesse, R.M. (1994) Pentagastrin infusions in patients with panic disorder. I. Symptoms and cardiovascular responses. Biol. Psychiatry, 36: 73–83.

Abelson, J.L., Nesse, R.M. and Vinik, A.I. (1994) Pentagastrin infusions in patients with panic disorder. II. Neuroendocrinology. Biol. Psychiatry, 36: 84–96.

Andreatini, R., Blanchard, C., Blanchard, R., Brandao, M.L., Carobrez, A.P. and Griebel, G. (2001) The brain decade in debate: II. Panic or anxiety? From animal models to a neurobiological basis. Braz. J. Med. Biol. Res., 34: 145–154.

Argyropoulos, S.V., Bailey, J.E., Hood, S.D., Kendrick, A.H., Rich, A.S. and Laszlo, G. (2002) Inhalation of 35% CO(2) results in activation of the HPA axis in healthy volunteers. Psychoneuroendocrinology, 27: 715–729.

Bailey, J.E., Argyropoulos, S.V., Kendrick, A.H. and Nutt, D.J. (2005) Behavioral and cardiovascular effects of 7.5% CO_2 in human volunteers. Depress. Anxiety, 21: 18–25.

Bailey, J.E., Argyropoulos, S.V., Lightman, S.L. and Nutt, D.J. (2003) Does the brain noradrenaline network mediate the effects of the CO_2 challenge? J. Psychopharmacol., 17: 252–259.

Bailey, J.E., Kendrick, A., Diaper, A., Potokar, J.P. and Nutt, D.J. (2007) A validation of the 7.5% CO_2 model of GAD using paroxetine and lorazepam in healthy volunteers. J. Psychopharmacol., 21: 42–49.

Ball, S. and Shekhar, A. (1997) Basilar artery response to hyperventilation in panic disorder. Am. J. Psychiatry, 154: 1603–1604.

Balon, R., Yeragani, V.K. and Pohl, R. (1988) Phenomenological comparison of dextrose, lactate, and isoproterenol associated panic attacks. Psychiatry Res., 26: 43–50.

Battaglia, M. and Perna, G. (1995) The 35% CO_2 challenge in panic disorder: optimization by receiver operating characteristic (ROC) analysis. J. Psychiatr. Res., 29: 111–119.

Bell, C., Forshall, S., Adrover, M., Nash, J., Hood, S. and Argyropoulos, S. (2002) Does 5-HT restrain panic? A tryptophan depletion study in panic disorder patients recovered on paroxetine. J. Psychopharmacol., 16: 5–14.

Bellodi, L., Perna, G., Caldirola, D., Arancio, C., Bertani, A. and Di Bella, D. (1998) CO_2-induced panic attacks: a twin study. Am. J. Psychiatry, 155: 1184–1188.

Bertoglio, L.J., de Bortoli, V.C. and Zangrossi, H. Jr. (2007) Cholecystokinin-2 receptors modulate freezing and escape behaviors evoked by the electrical stimulation of the rat dorsolateral periaqueductal gray. Brain Res., 1156: 133–138.

Bickler, P.E., Litt, L., Banville, D.L. and Severinghaus, J.W. (1988) Effects of acetazolamide on cerebral acid–base balance. J. Appl. Physiol., 65: 422–427.

Blanchard, D.C., Griebel, G. and Blanchard, R.J. (2003) The mouse defense test battery: pharmacological and behavioral assays for anxiety and panic. Eur. J. Pharmacol., 463: 97–116.

Bourin, M., Baker, G.B. and Bradwejn, J. (1998) Neurobiology of panic disorder. J. Psychosom. Res., 44: 163–180.

Bouton, M.E., Mineka, S. and Barlow, D.H. (2001) A modern learning theory perspective on the etiology of panic disorder. Psychol. Rev., 108: 4–32.

Bradwejn, J. and Koszycki, D. (1994) Imipramine antagonism of the panicogenic effects of cholecysto-kinin tetrapeptide in panic disorder patients. Am. J. Psychiatry, 151: 261–263.

Bradwejn, J., Koszycki, D., Annable, L., Couetoux du Tertre, A., Reines, S. and Karkanias, C. (1992a) A dose-ranging study of the behavioral and cardiovascular effects of CCK-tetrapeptide in panic disorder. Biol. Psychiatry, 32: 903–912.

Bradwejn, J., Koszycki, D. and Bourin, M. (1991) Dose ranging study of the effects of cholecystokinin in healthy volunteers. J. Psychiatry Neurosci., 16: 91–95.

Bradwejn, J., Koszycki, D., Couetoux du Tertre, A., Paradis, M. and Bourin, M. (1994a) Effects of flumazenil on cholecystokinin-tetrapeptide-induced panic symptoms in healthy volunteers. Psychopharmacol. (Berl.), 114: 257–261.

Bradwejn, J., Koszycki, D., Couetoux du Tertre, A., van Megen, H., den Boer, J. and Westenberg, H. (1994b) The panicogenic effects of cholecystokinin-tetrapeptide are antagonized by L-365,260, a central cholecystokinin receptor antagonist, in patients with panic disorder. Arch. Gen. Psychiatry, 51: 486–493.

Bradwejn, J., Koszycki, D. and Meterissian, G. (1990) Cholecystokinin-tetrapeptide induces panic attacks in patients with panic disorder. Can. j. Psychiatry, 35: 83–85.

Bradwejn, J., Koszycki, D., Paradis, M., Reece, P., Hinton, J. and Sedman, A. (1995) Effect of CI-988 on cholecystokinin tetrapeptide-induced panic symptoms in healthy volunteers. Biol. Psychiatry, 38: 742–746.

Bradwejn, J., Koszycki, D., Payeur, R., Bourin, M. and Borthwick, H. (1992b) Replication of action of cholecystokinin tetrapeptide in panic disorder: clinical and behavioral findings. Am. J. Psychiatry, 149: 962–964.

Bradwejn, J., LeGrand, J.M., Koszycki, D., Bates, J.H. and Bourin, M. (1998) Effects of cholecystokinin tetrapeptide on respiratory function in healthy volunteers. Am. J. Psychiatry, 155: 280–282.

Brawman-Mintzer, O., Lydiard, R.B., Bradwejn, J., Villarreal, G., Knapp, R. and Emmanuel, N. (1997) Effects of the cholecystokinin agonist pentagastrin in patients with generalized anxiety disorder. Am. J. Psychiatry, 154: 700–702.

Briggs, A.C., Stretch, D.D. and Brandon, S. (1993) Subtyping of panic disorder by symptom profile. Br. J. Psychiatry, 163: 201–209.

Broocks, A., Bandelow, B., Pekrun, G., George, A., Meyer, T. and Bartmann, U. (1998) Comparison of aerobic exercise, clomipramine, and placebo in the treatment of panic disorder. Am. J. Psychiatry, 155: 603–609.

Bruce, M., Scott, N., Shine, P. and Lader, M. (1992) Anxiogenic effects of caffeine in patients with anxiety disorders. Arch. Gen. Psychiatry, 49: 867–869.

Buller, R., von Bardeleben, U., Maier, W. and Benkert, O. (1989) Specificity of lactate response in panic disorder, panic with concurrent depression and major depression. J. Affect. Disord., 16: 109–113.

Canteras, N.S. (2002) The medial hypothalamic defensive system: hodological organization and functional implications. Pharmacol. Biochem. Behav., 71: 481–491.

Carr, D.B. and Sheehan, D.V. (1984) Panic anxiety: a new biological model. J. Clin. Psychiatry, 45: 323–330.

Charney, D.S. (2003) Neuroanatomical circuits modulating fear and anxiety behaviors. Acta Psychiatr. Scand. Suppl., 108: 38–50.

Charney, D.S. and Heninger, G.R. (1985) Noradrenergic function and the mechanism of action of antianxiety treatment. II. The effect of long-term imipramine treatment. Arch. Gen. Psychiatry, 42: 473–481.

Charney, D.S. and Heninger, G.R. (1986) Abnormal regulation of noradrenergic function in panic disorders. Effects of clonidine in healthy subjects and patients with agoraphobia and panic disorder. Arch. Gen. Psychiatry, 43: 1042–1054.

Charney, D.S., Heninger, G.R. and Breier, A. (1984) Noradrenergic function in panic anxiety. Effects of yohimbine in healthy subjects and patients with agoraphobia and panic disorder. Arch. Gen. Psychiatry, 41: 751–763.

Charney, D.S., Woods, S.W. and Heninger, G.R. (1989) Noradrenergic function in generalized anxiety disorder: effects of yohimbine in healthy subjects and patients with generalized anxiety disorder. Psychiatry Res., 27: 173–182.

Cohen, M.E. and White, P.D. (1951) Life situations, emotions, and neurocirculatory asthenia (anxiety neurosis, neurasthenia, effort syndrome). Psychosom. Med., 13: 335–357.

Coplan, J.D., Goetz, R., Klein, D.F., Papp, L.A., Fyer, A.J. and Liebowitz, M.R. (1998) Plasma cortisol concentrations preceding lactate-induced panic. Psychological, biochemical, and physiological correlates. Arch. Gen. Psychiatry, 55: 130–136.

Coplan, J.D., Liebowitz, M.R., Gorman, J.M., Fyer, A.J., Dillon, D.J. and Campeas, R.B. (1992) Noradrenergic function in panic disorder. Effects of intravenous clonidine pretreatment on lactate induced panic. Biol. Psychiatry, 31: 135–146.

Corfield, D.R., Fink, G.R., Ramsay, S.C., Murphy, K., Harty, H.R. and Watson, J.D. (1995) Evidence for limbic system activation during CO_2-stimulated breathing in man. J. Physiol., 488: 77–84.

Cotton, J.F., Keshavaprasad, B., Laster, M.J., Eger, E.I. 2nd and Yost, C.S. (2006) The ventilatory stimulant doxapram inhibits TASK tandem pore (K2P) potassium channel function but does not affect minimum alveolar anesthetic concentration. Anesth. Analg., 102: 779–785.

Cowley, D.S., Dager, S.R. and Dunner, D.L. (1986) Lactate-induced panic in primary affective disorder. Am. J. Psychiatry, 143: 646–648.

Cowley, D.S., Dager, S.R., McClellan, J., Roy-Byrne, P.P. and Dunner, D.L. (1988) Response to lactate infusion in generalized anxiety disorder. Biol. Psychiatry, 24: 409–414.

Cowley, D.S., Dager, S.R., Roy-Byrne, P.P., Avery, D.H. and Dunner, D.L. (1991) Lactate vulnerability after alprazolam versus placebo treatment of panic disorder. Biol. Psychiatry, 30: 49–56.

Dager, S.R., Friedman, S.D., Heide, A., Layton, M.E., Richards, T. and Artru, A. (1999) Two-dimensional proton echo-planar spectroscopic imaging of brain metabolic changes during lactate-induced panic. Arch. Gen. Psychiatry, 56: 70–77.

Dager, S.R., Richards, T., Strauss, W. and Artru, A. (1997) Single-voxel ^{1}H-MRS investigation of brain metabolic changes during lactate-induced panic. Psychiatry Res., 76: 89–99.

Dager, S.R., Strauss, W.L., Marro, K.I., Richards, T.L., Metzger, G.D. and Artru, A.A. (1995) Proton magnetic resonance spectroscopy investigation of hyperventilation in subjects with panic disorder and comparison subjects. Am. J. Psychiatry, 152: 666–672.

Deakin, J.F.W. and Graeff, F.G. (1991) 5-HT and mechanisms of defence. J. Psychopharmacol., 5: 305–315.

de Leeuw, A.S., Den Boer, J.A., Slaap, B.R. and Westenberg, H.G. (1996) Pentagastrin has panic-inducing properties in obsessive compulsive disorder. Psychopharmacol. (Berl.), 126: 339–344.

de Montigny, C. (1989) Cholecystokinin tetrapeptide induces panic-like attacks in healthy volunteers. Preliminary findings. Arch. Gen. Psychiatry, 46: 511–517.

Dillon, D.J., Gorman, J.M., Liebowitz, M.R., Fyer, A.J. and Klein, D.F. (1987) Measurement of lactate-induced panic and anxiety. Psychiatry Res., 20: 97–105.

Ehlers, A., Margraf, J., Roth, W.T., Taylor, C.B., Maddock, R.J. and Sheikh, J. (1986) Lactate infusions and panic attacks: do patients and controls respond differently? Psychiatry Res., 17: 295–308.

Erzegovesi, S., Martucci, L., Henin, M. and Bellodi, L. (2001) Low versus standard dose mCPP challenge in obsessive-compulsive patients. Neuropsychopharmacology, 24: 31–36.

Eser, D., Schule, C., Baghai, T., Floesser, A., Krebs-Brown, A. and Enunwa, M. (2007) Evaluation of the CCK-4 model as a challenge paradigm in a population of healthy volunteers within a proof-of-concept study. Psychopharmacol. (Berl.), 192: 479–487.

Facchinetti, F., Romano, G., Fava, M. and Genazzani, A.R. (1992) Lactate infusion induces panic attacks in patients with premenstrual syndrome. Psychosom. Med., 54: 288–296.

Friedman, S.D., Mathis, C.M., Hayes, C., Renshaw, P. and Dager, S.R. (2006) Brain pH response to hyperventilation in panic disorder: preliminary evidence for altered acid–base regulation. Am. J. Psychiatry, 163: 710–715.

Fyer, M.R., Uy, J., Martinez, J., Goetz, R., Klein, D.F. and Fyer, A. (1987) CO_2 challenge of patients with panic disorder. Am. J. Psychiatry, 144: 1080–1082.

Ganong, W. (1997) Review of Medical Physiology, 18 ed.. Appleton and Lange, Stamford, CT.

George, D.T., Glue, P., Bacher, J.D., Waxman, R.P. and Nutt, D.J. (1990) Lactate-induced electrolyte changes in the cerebrospinal fluid of rabbits. Biol. Psychiatry, 27: 104–108.

George, D.T., Lindquist, T., Nutt, D.J., Ragan, P.W., Alim, T. and McFarlane, V. (1995) Effect of chloride or glucose on the incidence of lactate-induced panic attacks. Am J. Psychiatry, 152: 692–697.

George, D.T., Nutt, D.J., Walker, W.V., Porges, S.W., Adinoff, B. and Linnoila, M. (1989) Lactate and hyperventilation substantially attenuate vagal tone in normal volunteers. A possible mechanism of panic provocation? Arch. Gen. Psychiatry, 46: 153–156.

Germine, M., Goddard, A.W., Woods, S.W., Charney, D.S. and Heninger, G.R. (1992) Anger and anxiety responses to m-chlorophenylpiperazine in generalized anxiety disorder. Biol. Psychiatry, 32: 457–461.

Gibbs, D.M. (1992) Hyperventilation-induced cerebral ischemia in panic disorder and effect of nimodipine. Am. J. Psychiatry, 149: 1589–1591.

Goetz, R.R., Klein, D.F. and Gorman, J.M. (1994) Consistencies between recalled panic and lactate-induced panic. Anxiety, 1: 31–36.

Gorman, J.M. (2003) Does the brain noradrenaline network mediate the effects of the CO_2 challenge?. J. Psychopharmacol., 17: 265–268.

Gorman, J.M., Askanazi, J., Liebowitz, M.R., Fyer, A.J., Stein, J. and Kinney, J.M. (1984) Response to hyperventilation in a group of patients with panic disorder. Am. J. Psychiatry, 141: 857–861.

Gorman, J.M., Battista, D., Goetz, R.R., Dillon, D.J., Liebowitz, M.R. and Fyer, A.J. (1989) A comparison of sodium bicarbonate and sodium lactate infusion in the induction of panic attacks. Arch. Gen. Psychiatry, 46: 145–150.

Gorman, J.M., Goetz, R.R., Dillon, D., Liebowitz, M.R., Fyer, A.J. and Davies, S. (1990a) Sodium D-lactate infusion of panic disorder patients. Neuropsychopharmacology, 3: 181–189.

Gorman, J.M., Goetz, R.R., Uy, J., Ross, D., Martinez, J. and Fyer, A.J. (1988) Hyperventilation occurs during lactate-induced panic. Journal of Anxiety Disorders, 2: 193–202.

Gorman, J.M., Kent, J.M., Sullivan, G.M. and Coplan, J.D. (2000) Neuroanatomical hypothesis of panic disorder, revised. Am. J. Psychiatry, 157: 493–505.

Gorman, J.M., Levy, G.F., Liebowitz, M.R., McGrath, P., Appleby, I.L. and Dillon, D.J. (1983) Effect of acute beta-adrenergic blockade on lactate-induced panic. Arch. Gen. Psychiatry, 40: 1079–1082.

Gorman, J.M., Papp, L. and Donald, F.K. (1990b) Biological models of panic disorder. In: Noyes, R. Roth, M. and Burrows, G.D. (Eds.), Handbook of AnxietyVol. 3Elsevier, New York, NY.

Gorman, J.M., Papp, L.A., Coplan, J., Martinez, J., Liebowitz, M.R. and Klein, D.F. (1993) The effect of acetazolamide on ventilation in panic disorder patients. Am. J. Psychiatry, 150: 1480–1484.

Gorman, J.M., Papp, L.A., Coplan, J.D., Martinez, J.M., Lennon, S. and Goetz, R.R. (1994) Anxiogenic effects of CO_2 and hyperventilation in patients with panic disorder. Am. J. Psychiatry, 151: 547–553.

Graeff, F.G. (2004) Serotonin, the periaqueductal gray and panic. Neurosci. Biobehav. Rev., 28: 239–259.

Graeff, F.G., Garcia-Leal, C., Del-Ben, C.M. and Guimaraes, F.S. (2005) Does the panic attack activate the hypothalamic–pituitary–adrenal axis? An. Acad. Bras. Cienc., 77: 477–491.

Griez, E., de Loof, C., Pols, H., Zandbergen, J. and Lousberg, H. (1990) Specific sensitivity of patients with panic attacks to carbon dioxide inhalation. Psychiatry Res., 31: 193–199.

Griez, E., van den Hout, M.A. and Verstappen, F. (1987a) Body fluids after CO_2 inhalation: insight into panic mechanisms?. Eur. Arch. Psychiatry Neurol. Sci., 236: 369–371.

Griez, E., Zandbergen, J., Lousberg, H. and van den Hout, M. (1988) Effects of low pulmonary CO_2 on panic anxiety. Compr. Psychiatry, 29: 490–497.

Griez, E.J., Colasanti, A., van Diest, R., Salamon, E. and Schruers, K. (2007) Carbon dioxide inhalation induces dose-dependent and age-related negative affectivity. PLoS ONE, 2: e987.

Griez, E.J., Lousberg, H., van den Hout, M.A. and van der Molen, G.M. (1987b) CO_2 vulnerability in panic disorder. Psychiatry Res., 20: 87–95.

Griez, E.J.L. (2001) Anxiety disorders: an introduction to clinical management and research. Wiley, New York, NY.

Gutman, D.A., Coplan, J., Papp, L., Martinez, J. and Gorman, J. (2005) Doxapram-induced panic attacks and cortisol elevation. Psychiatry Res., 133: 253–261.

Guttmacher, L.B., Murphy, D.L. and Insel, T.R. (1983) Pharmacologic models of anxiety. Compr. Psychiatry, 24: 312–326.

Hollander, E., Liebowitz, M.R., DeCaria, C. and Klein, D.F. (1990) Fenfluramine, cortisol, and anxiety. Psychiatry Res., 31: 211–213.

Hollander, E., Liebowitz, M.R., Gorman, J.M., Cohen, B., Fyer, A. and Klein, D.F. (1989) Cortisol and sodium lactate-induced panic. Arch. Gen. Psychiatry, 46: 135–140.

Holt, P.E. and Andrews, G. (1989) Provocation of panic: three elements of the panic reaction in four anxiety disorders. Behav. Res. Ther., 27: 253–261.

Javanmard, M., Shlik, J., Kennedy, S.H., Vaccarino, F.J., Houle, S. and Bradwejn, J. (1999) Neuroanatomic correlates of CCK-4-induced panic attacks in healthy humans: a comparison of two time points. Biol. Psychiatry, 45: 872–882.

Jensen, C.F., Keller, T.W., Peskind, E.R., McFall, M.E., Veith, R.C. and Martin, D. (1997) Behavioral and neuroendocrine responses to sodium lactate infusion in subjects with posttraumatic stress disorder. Am. J. Psychiatry, 154: 266–268.

Jensen, K.E., Thomsen, C. and Henriksen, O. (1988) In vivo measurement of intracellular pH in human brain during different tensions of carbon dioxide in arterial blood. A ^{31}P-NMR study. Acta Physiol. Scand., 134: 295–298.

Kahn, R.S. and Wetzler, S. (1991) *m*-Chlorophenylpiperazine as a probe of serotonin function. Biol. Psychiatry, 30: 1139–1166.

Katzman, M.A., Koszycki, D. and Bradwejn, J. (2004) Effects of CCK-tetrapeptide in patients with social phobia and obsessive-compulsive disorder. Depress. Anxiety, 20: 51–58.

Kaye, J., Buchanan, F., Kendrick, A., Johnson, P., Lowry, C. and Bailey, J. (2004) Acute carbon dioxide exposure in healthy adults: evaluation of a novel means of investigating the stress response. J. Neuroendocrinol., 16: 256–264.

Kellner, M., Herzog, L., Yassouridis, A., Holsboer, F. and Wiedemann, K. (1995) Possible role of atrial natriuretic hormone in pituitary–adrenocortical unresponsiveness in lactate-induced panic. Am. J. Psychiatry, 152: 1365–1367.

Kent, J.M., Coplan, J.D., Mawlawi, O., Martinez, J.M., Browne, S.T. and Slifstein, M. (2005) Prediction of panic response to a respiratory stimulant by reduced orbitofrontal cerebral blood flow in panic disorder. Am. J. Psychiatry, 162: 1379–1381.

Khan, S., Liberzon, I. and Abelson, J.L. (2004) Effects of propranolol on symptom and endocrine responses to pentagastrin. Psychoneuroendocrinology, 29: 1163–1171.

King, M.S. and Baertschi, A.J. (1992) Ventral pontine catecholaminergic pathway mediates the vasopressin response to splanchnic osmostimulation in conscious rats. Brain Res., 580: 81–91.

Klein, D.F. (1993) False suffocation alarms, spontaneous panics, and related conditions. An integrative hypothesis. Arch. Gen. Psychiatry, 50: 306–317.

Klein, D.F. and Ross, D.C. (1986) Response of panic patients and normal controls to lactate infusions. Psychiatry Res., 19: 163–167.

Kondoh, Y., Kawase, M. and Ohmori, S. (1992) D-lactate concentrations in blood, urine and sweat before and after exercise. Eur. J. Appl. Physiol. Occup. Physiol., 65: 88–93.

Koszycki, D., Zacharko, R.M., Le Melledo, J.M. and Bradwejn, J. (1998) Behavioral, cardiovascular, and neuroendocrine profiles following CCK-4 challenge in healthy volunteers: a comparison of panickers and nonpanickers. Depress. Anxiety, 8: 1–7.

Kramer, M.S., Cutler, N.R., Ballenger, J.C., Patterson, W.M., Mendels, J. and Chenault, A. (1995) A placebo-controlled trial of L-365,260, a CCKB antagonist, in panic disorder. Biol. Psychiatry, 37: 462–466.

Laderach, H. and Straub, W. (2001) Effects of voluntary hyperventilation on glucose, free fatty acids and several glucostatic hormones. Swiss Med. Wkly., 131: 19–22.

LeDoux, J.E. (1996) The emotional brain: the mysterious underpinnings of emotional life. Simon & Schuster, New York, NY.

Lee, Y.J., Curtis, G.C., Weg, J.G., Abelson, J.L., Modell, J.G. and Campbell, K.M. (1993) Panic attacks induced by doxapram. Biol. Psychiatry, 33: 295–297.

Leverve, X.M. and Mustafa, I. (2002) Lactate: a key metabolite in the intercellular metabolic interplay. Crit. Care, 6: 284–285.

Ley, R. (1992) The many faces of Pan: psychological and physiological differences among three types of panic attacks. Behav. Res. Ther., 30: 347–357.

Liebowitz, M.R., Coplan, J.D., Martinez, J., Fyer, A.J., Dillon, D.J. and Campeas, R.B. (1995) Effects of intravenous diazepam pretreatment on lactate-induced panic. Psychiatry Res., 58: 127–138.

Liebowitz, M.R., Fyer, A.J., Gorman, J.M., Campeas, R., Levin, A. and Davies, S.R. (1986a) Alprazolam in the treatment of panic disorders. J. Clin. Psychopharmacol., 6: 13–20.

Liebowitz, M.R., Fyer, A.J., Gorman, J.M., Dillon, D., Appleby, I.L. and Levy, G. (1984) Lactate provocation of panic attacks. I. Clinical and behavioral findings. Arch. Gen. Psychiatry, 41: 764–770.

Liebowitz, M.R., Gorman, J.M., Fyer, A., Dillon, D., Levitt, M. and Klein, D.F. (1986b) Possible mechanisms for lactate's induction of panic. Am. J. Psychiatry, 143: 495–502.

Liebowitz, M.R., Gorman, J.M., Fyer, A.J., Levitt, M., Dillon, D. and Levy, G. (1985) Lactate provocation of panic attacks. II. Biochemical and physiological findings. Arch. Gen. Psychiatry, 42: 709–719.

Lindsay, S., Saqi, S. and Bass, C. (1991) The test–retest reliability of the hyperventilation provocation test. J. Psychosom. Res., 35: 155–162.

Lines, C., Challenor, J. and Traub, M. (1995) Cholecystokinin and anxiety in normal volunteers: an investigation of the anxiogenic properties of pentagastrin and reversal by the cholecystokinin receptor subtype B antagonist L-365,260. Br. J. Clin. Pharm., 39: 235–242.

Liotti, M., Brannan, S., Egan, G., Shade, R., Madden, L. and Abplanalp, B. (2001) Brain responses associated with consciousness of breathlessness (air hunger). Proc. Natl. Acad. Sci. USA, 98: 2035–2040.

Lum, L.C. (1987) Hyperventilation syndromes in medicine and psychiatry: a review. J. R. Soc. Med., 80: 229–231.

Maddock, R.J. (2001) The lactic acid response to alkalosis in panic disorder: an integrative review. J. Neuropsychiatry Clin. Neurosci., 13: 22–34.

Maddock, R.J. and Carter, C.S. (1991) Hyperventilation-induced panic attacks in panic disorder with agoraphobia. Biol. Psychiatry, 29: 843–854.

Maddock, R.J., Carter, C.S. and Gietzen, D.W. (1991) Elevated serum lactate associated with panic attacks induced by hyperventilation. Psychiatry Res., 38: 301–311.

Maddock, R.J. and Mateo-Bermudez, J. (1990) Elevated serum lactate following hyperventilation during glucose infusion in panic disorder. Biol. Psychiatry, 27: 411–418.

Maron, E., Toru, I., Vasar, V. and Shlik, J. (2004) The effect of 5-hydroxytryptophan on cholecystokinin-4-induced panic attacks in healthy volunteers. J. Psychopharmacol., 18: 194–199.

Martel, F.L., Hayward, C., Lyons, D.M., Sanborn, K., Varady, S. and Schatzberg, A.F. (1999) Salivary cortisol levels in socially phobic adolescent girls. Depress. Anxiety, 10: 25–27.

Masdrakis, V.G., Papakostas, Y.G., Vaidakis, N., Papageorgiou, C. and Pehlivanidis, A. (2007) Caffeine challenge in patients with panic disorder: baseline differences between those who panic and those who do not. *Depress. Anxiety* [Epub ahead of print].

Mathew, R.J. and Wilson, W.H. (1988) Cerebral blood flow changes induced by CO_2 in anxiety. Psychiatry Res., 23: 285–294.

Mathew, R.J., Wilson, W.H., Humphreys, D., Lowe, J.V. and Wiethe, K.E. (1997) Cerebral vasodilation and vasoconstriction associated with acute anxiety. Biol. Psychiatry, 41: 782–795.

Mathew, R.J., Wilson, W.H. and Tant, S. (1989) Responses to hypercarbia induced by acetazolamide in panic disorder patients. Am. J. Psychiatry, 146: 996–1000.

McCann, U.D., Morgan, C.M., Geraci, M., Slate, S.O., Murphy, D.L. and Post, R.M. (1997a) Effects of the 5-HT3 antagonist, ondansetron, on the behavioral and physiological effects of pentagastrin in patients with panic disorder and social phobia. Neuropsychopharmacology, 17: 360–369.

McCann, U.D., Slate, S.O., Geraci, M., Roscow-Terrill, D. and Uhde, T.W. (1997b) A comparison of the effects of intravenous pentagastrin on patients with social phobia, panic disorder and healthy controls. Neuropsychopharmacology, 16: 229–237.

McNaughton, N. and Corr, P.J. (2004) A two-dimensional neuropsychology of defense: fear/anxiety and defensive distance. Neurosci. Biobehav. Rev., 28: 285–305.

Mortimore, C. and Anderson, I.M. (2000) d-Fenfluramine in panic disorder: a dual role for 5-hydroxytryptamine. Psychopharmacol. (Berl.), 149: 251–258.

Mukaddam-Daher, S., Lambert, C. and Gutkowska, J. (1997) Clonidine and ST-91 may activate imidazoline binding sites in the heart to release atrial natriuretic peptide. Hypertension, 30: 83–87.

Mula, M., Pini, S. and Cassano, G.B. (2007) The role of anticonvulsant drugs in anxiety disorders: a critical review of the evidence. J. Clin. Psychopharmacol., 27: 263–272.

Nakashima, K., Yamashita, T., Kashiwagi, S., Nakayama, N., Kitahara, T. and Ito, H. (1996) The effect of sodium bicarbonate on CBF and intracellular pH in man: stable Xe-CT and 31P-MRS. Acta Neurol. Scand. Suppl., 166: 96–98.

Nardi, A.E., Lopes, F.L., Valenca, A.M., Nascimento, I., Mezzasalma, M.A. and Zin, W.A. (2004) Psychopathological description of hyperventilation-induced panic attacks: a comparison with spontaneous panic attacks. Psychopathology, 37: 29–35.

Nardi, A.E., Nascimento, I., Valenca, A.M., Lopes, F.L., Mezzasalma, M.A. and Zin, W.A. (2003) Panic disorder in a breath-holding challenge test: a simple tool for a better diagnosis. Arq. Neuropsiquiatr., 61: 718–722.

Nardi, A.E., Valenca, A.M., Lopes, F.L., de-Melo-Neto, V.L., Freire, R.C. and Veras, A.B. (2007) Caffeine and 35% carbon dioxide challenge tests in panic disorder. Hum. Psychopharmacol., 22: 231–240.

Nardi, A.E., Valenca, A.M., Lopes, F.L., Nascimento, I., Veras, A.B. and Freire, R.C. (2006) Psychopathological profile of 35% CO_2 challenge test-induced panic attacks: a comparison with spontaneous panic attacks. Compr. Psychiatry, 47: 209–214.

Nardi, A.E., Valenca, A.M., Nascimento, I., Mezzasalma, M.A. and Zin, W.A. (2001a) Hyperventilation in panic disorder and social phobia. Psychopathology, 34: 123–127.

Nardi, A.E., Valenca, A.M., Nascimento, I. and Zin, W.A. (2001b) Hyperventilation challenge test in panic disorder and depression with panic attacks. Psychiatry Res., 105: 57–65.

Nardi, A.E., Valenca, A.M., Nascimento, I. and Zin, W.A. (2002) Panic disorder and obsessive compulsive disorder in a hyperventilation challenge test. J. Affect. Disord., 68: 335–340.

Netto, C.F. and Guimaraes, F.S. (2004) Anxiogenic effect of cholecystokinin in the dorsal periaqueductal gray. Neuropsychopharmacology, 29: 101–107.

Nutt, D.J., Glue, P., Lawson, C. and Wilson, S. (1990) Flumazenil provocation of panic attacks. Evidence for altered benzodiazepine receptor sensitivity in panic disorder. Arch. Gen. Psychiatry, 47: 917–925.

Olson, B.R., Freilino, M., Hoffman, G.E., Stricker, E.M., Sved, A.F. and Verbalis, J.G. (1993) c-Fos expression in rat brain and brainstem nuclei in response to treatments that alter food intake and gastric motility. Molec. Cell. Neurosci., 4: 93–106.

Otte, C., Moritz, S., Yassouridis, A., Koop, M., Madrischewski, A.M. and Wiedemann, K. (2007) Blockade of the mineralocorticoid receptor in healthy men: effects on experimentally induced panic symptoms, stress hormones, and cognition. Neuropsychopharmacology, 32: 232–238.

Pande, A.C., Greiner, M., Adams, J.B., Lydiard, R.B. and Pierce, M.W. (1999) Placebo-controlled trial of the CCK-B antagonist, CI-988, in panic disorder. Biol. Psychiatry, 46: 860–862.

Pandit, J.J., Mohan, R.M., Paterson, N.D. and Poulin, M.J. (2003) Cerebral blood flow sensitivity to CO_2 measured with steady-state and Read's rebreathing methods. Respir. Physiol. Neurobiol., 137: 1–10.

Papp, L.A., Klein, D.F., Martinez, J., Schneier, F., Cole, R. and Liebowitz, M.R. (1993) Diagnostic and substance specificity of carbon-dioxide-induced panic. Am. J. Psychiatry, 150: 250–257.

Papp, L.A., Martinez, J.M., Klein, D.F., Coplan, J.D., Norman, R.G. and Cole, R. (1997) Respiratory psychophysiology of panic disorder: three respiratory challenges in 98 subjects. Am. J. Psychiatry, 154: 1557–1565.

Parsons, L.M., Egan, G., Liotti, M., Brannan, S., Denton, D. and Shade, R. (2001) Neuroimaging evidence implicating cerebellum in the experience of hypercapnia and hunger for air. Proc. Natl. Acad. Sci. USA, 98: 2041–2046.

Perna, G., Battaglia, M., Garberi, A., Arancio, C., Bertani, A. and Bellodi, L. (1994a) Carbon dioxide/oxygen challenge test in panic disorder. Psychiatry Res., 52: 159–171.

Perna, G., Bertani, A., Gabriele, A., Politi, E. and Bellodi, L. (1997) Modification of 35% carbon dioxide hypersensitivity across one week of treatment with clomipramine and fluvoxamine: a double-blind, randomized, placebo-controlled study. J. Clin. Psychopharmacol., 17: 173–178.

Perna, G., Bussi, R., Allevi, L. and Bellodi, L. (1999) Sensitivity to 35% carbon dioxide in patients with generalized anxiety disorder. J. Clin. Psychiatry, 60: 379–384.

Perna, G., Cocchi, S., Bertani, A., Arancio, C. and Bellodi, L. (1994b) Pharmacologic effect of toloxatone on reactivity to the 35% carbon dioxide challenge: a single-blind, random, placebo-controlled study. J. Clin. Psychopharmacol., 14: 414–418.

Peskind, E.R., Jensen, C.F., Pascualy, M., Tsuang, D., Cowley, D. and Martin, D.C. (1998) Sodium lactate and hypertonic sodium chloride induce equivalent panic incidence, panic symptoms, and hypernatremia in panic disorder. Biol. Psychiatry, 44: 1007–1016.

Pitts, F.N. Jr. and McClure, J.N. Jr. (1967) Lactate metabolism in anxiety neurosis. N. Engl. J. Med., 277: 1329–1336.

Pohl, R., Yeragani, V.K. and Balon, R. (1990) Effects of isoproterenol in panic disorder patients after antidepressant treatment. Biol. Psychiatry, 28: 203–214.

Pohl, R., Yeragani, V.K., Balon, R., Rainey, J.M., Lycaki, H. and Ortiz, A. (1988) Isoproterenol-induced panic attacks. Biol. Psychiatry, 24: 891–902.

Pols, H., Verburg, K., Hauzer, R., Meijer, J. and Griez, E. (1996a) Alprazolam premedication and 35% carbon dioxide vulnerability in panic patients. Biol. Psychiatry, 40: 913–917.

Pols, H.J., Hauzer, R.C., Meijer, J.A., Verburg, K. and Griez, E.J. (1996b) Fluvoxamine attenuates panic induced by 35% CO_2 challenge. J. Clin. Psychiatry, 57: 539–542.

Posse, S., Dager, S.R., Richards, T.L., Yuan, C., Ogg, R. and Artru, A.A. (1997) In vivo measurement of regional brain metabolic response to hyperventilation using magnetic resonance: proton echo planar spectroscopic imaging (PEPSI). Magn. Reson. Med., 37: 858–865.

Potokar, J., Lawson, C., Wilson, S. and Nutt, D. (1999) Behavioral, neuroendocrine, and cardiovascular response to flumazenil: no evidence for an altered benzodiazepine receptor sensitivity in panic disorder. Biol. Psychiatry, 46: 1709–1711.

Potts, N.L., Davidson, J.R., Krishnan, K.R., Doraiswamy, P.M. and Ritchie, J.C. (1991) Levels of urinary free cortisol in social phobia. J. Clin. Psychiatry Suppl., 52: 41–42.

Prenoveau, J.M., Forsyth, J.P., Kelly, M.M. and Barrios, V. (2006) Repeated exposure to 20% CO_2 challenge and risk for developing panic attacks: a controlled 6- and 12-month follow-up in a nonclinical sample. J. Anxiety Disord., 20: 1158–1167.

Raedler, T.J., Jahn, H., Goedeken, B., Gescher, D.M., Kellner, M. and Wiedemann, K. (2006) Megestrol attenuates the hormonal response to CCK-4-induced panic attacks. Depress. Anxiety, 23: 139–144.

Rasmussen, S.A., Goodman, W.K., Woods, S.W., Heninger, G.R. and Charney, D.S. (1987) Effects of yohimbine in obsessive compulsive disorder. Psychopharmacol. (Berl.), 93: 308–313.

Rassovsky, Y. and Kushner, M.G. (2003) Carbon dioxide in the study of panic disorder: issues of definition, methodology, and outcome. J. Anxiety Disord., 17: 1–32.

Richerson, G.B. (2004) Serotonergic neurons as carbon dioxide sensors that maintain pH homeostasis. Nat. Rev. Neurosci., 5: 449–461.

Sanderson, W.C., Rapee, R.M. and Barlow, D.H. (1989) The influence of an illusion of control on panic attacks induced via inhalation of 5.5% carbon dioxide-enriched air. Arch. Gen. Psychiatry, 46: 157–162.

Schenberg, L.C., Bittencourt, A.S., Sudre, E.C. and Vargas, L.C. (2001) Modeling panic attacks. Neurosci. Biobehav. Rev., 25: 647–659.

Schmidt, N.B., Maner, J.K. and Zvolensky, M.J. (2007) Reactivity to challenge with carbon dioxide as a prospective predictor of panic attacks. Psychiatry Res., 151: 173–176.

Schmidt, N.B., Trakowski, J.H. and Staab, J.P. (1997) Extinction of panicogenic effects of a 35% CO_2

challenge in patients with panic disorder. J. Abnorm. Psychol., 106: 630–638.

Schruers, K., van Diest, R., Overbeek, T. and Griez, E. (2002) Acute L-5-hydroxytryptophan administration inhibits carbon dioxide-induced panic in panic disorder patients. Psychiatry Res., 113: 237–243.

Seddon, K., Potokar, J., Rich, A., Bailey, J., Morris, K. and Nutt, D.J. (in press) The effects of a 7.5% CO_2 challenge in patients with generalised anxiety disorder. *J. Psychopharmacol.* (in press).

Severson, C.A., Wang, W., Pieribone, V.A., Dohle, C.I. and Richerson, G.B. (2003) Midbrain serotonergic neurons are central pH chemoreceptors. Nat. Neurosci., 6: 1139–1140.

Shekhar, A., Johnson, P.L., Sajdyk, T.J., Fitz, S.D., Keim, S.R. and Kelley, P.E. (2006) Angiotensin-II is a putative neurotransmitter in lactate-induced panic-like responses in rats with disruption of GABAergic inhibition in the dorsomedial hypothalamus. J. Neurosci., 26: 9205–9215.

Shekhar, A. and Keim, S.R. (1997) The circumventricular organs form a potential neural pathway for lactate sensitivity: implications for panic disorder. J. Neurosci., 17: 9726–9735.

Shlik, J., Aluoja, A., Vasar, V., Vasar, E., Podar, T. and Bradwejn, J. (1997) Effects of citalopram treatment on behavioural, cardiovascular and neuroendocrine response to cholecystokinin tetrapeptide challenge in patients with panic disorder. J. Psychiatry Neurosci., 22: 332–340.

Siesjo, B.K. (1982) Lactic acidosis in the brain: occurrence, triggering mechanisms and pathophysiological importance. Ciba. Found. Symp., 87: 77–100.

Southwick, S.M., Krystal, J.H., Bremner, J.D., Morgan, C.A., 3rd Nicolaou, A.L. and Nagy, L.M. (1997) Noradrenergic and serotonergic function in posttraumatic stress disorder. Arch. Gen. Psychiatry, 54: 749–758.

Spinhoven, P., Onstein, E.J., Sterk, P.J. and Le Haen-Versteijnen, D. (1992) The hyperventilation provocation test in panic disorder. Behav. Res. Ther., 30: 453–461.

Strohle, A., Feller, C., Onken, M., Godemann, F., Heinz, A. and Dimeo, F. (2005) The acute antipanic activity of aerobic exercise. Am. J. Psychiatry, 162: 2376–2378.

Strohle, A., Holsboer, F. and Rupprecht, R. (2000) Increased ACTH concentrations associated with cholecystokinin tetrapeptide-induced panic attacks in patients with panic disorder. Neuropsychopharmacology, 22: 251–256.

Strohle, A., Kellner, M., Holsboer, F. and Wiedemann, K. (1999) Behavioral, neuroendocrine, and cardiovascular response to flumazenil: no evidence for an altered benzodiazepine receptor sensitivity in panic disorder. Biol. Psychiatry, 45: 321–326.

Strohle, A., Kellner, M., Holsboer, F. and Wiedemann, K. (2001) Anxiolytic activity of atrial natriuretic peptide in patients with panic disorder. Am. J. Psychiatry, 158: 1514–1516.

Strohle, A., Kellner, M., Yassouridis, A., Holsboer, F. and Wiedemann, K. (1998) Effect of flumazenil in lactate-sensitive patients with panic disorder. Am. J. Psychiatry, 155: 610–612.

Strohle, A., Romeo, E., di Michele, F., Pasini, A., Hermann, B. and Gajewsky, G. (2003) Induced panic attacks shift gamma-aminobutyric acid type A receptor modulatory neuroactive steroid composition in patients with panic disorder: preliminary results. Arch. Gen. Psychiatry, 60: 161–168.

Swain, J., Koszycki, D., Shlik, J. and Bradwejn, J. (2003) Pharmacological challenge agents in anxiety. In: Nutt, D.J. and Ballenger, J.C. (Eds.), Anxiety disorders. Blackwell Science, Malden, MA, pp. xi, 542.

Targum, S.D. and Marshall, L.E. (1989) Fenfluramine provocation of anxiety in patients with panic disorder. Psychiatry Res., 28: 295–306.

Toru, I., Shlik, J., Maron, E., Vasar, V. and Nutt, D.J. (2006) Tryptophan depletion does not modify response to CCK-4 challenge in patients with panic disorder after treatment with citalopram. Psychopharmacol. (Berl.), 186: 107–112.

Tsacopoulos, M. and Magistretti, P.J. (1996) Metabolic coupling between glia and neurons. J. Neurosci., 16: 877–885.

Uhde, T.W., Tancer, M.E., Gelernter, C.S. and Vittone, B.J. (1994) Normal urinary free cortisol and postdexamethasone cortisol in social phobia: comparison to normal volunteers. J. Affect. Disord., 30: 155–161.

Uhlenhuth, E.H., Leon, A.C. and Matuzas, W. (2006) Psychopathology of panic attacks in panic disorder. J. Affect. Disord., 92: 55–62.

Uhlenhuth, E.H., Matuzas, W., Warner, T.D., Paine, S., Lydiard, R.B. and Pollack, M.H. (2000) Do antidepressants selectively suppress spontaneous (unexpected) panic attacks? A replication. J. Clin. Psychopharmacol., 20: 622–627.

Valenca, A.M., Nardi, A.E., Mezzasalma, M.A., Nascimento, I., Lopes, F.L. and Zin, W.A. (2004) Clonidine in respiratory panic disorder subtype. Arq. Neuropsiquiatr., 62: 396–398.

Van den Hout, M.A. and Griez, E. (1984) Panic symptoms after inhalation of carbon dioxide. Br. J. Psychiatry, 144: 503–507.

van den Hout, M.A., van der Molen, G.M., Griez, E., Lousberg, H. and Nansen, A. (1987) Reduction of CO_2-induced anxiety in patients with panic attacks after repeated CO_2 exposure. Am. J. Psychiatry, 144: 788–791.

Vanderhaeghen, J.J., Signeau, J.C. and Gepts, W. (1975) New peptide in the vertebrate CNS reacting with antigastrin antibodies. Nature, 257: 604–605.

van Duinen, M.A., Schruers, K.R., Maes, M. and Griez, E.J. (2005) CO_2 challenge results in hypothalamic–pituitary–adrenal activation in healthy volunteers. J. Psychopharmacol., 19: 243–247.

van Duinen, M.A., Schruers, K.R., Maes, M. and Griez, E.J. (2006) CO_2 challenge induced HPA axis activation in panic. Int. J. Neuropsychopharmacol., 1: 1–8.

van Megen, H.J., Westenberg, H.G., den Boer, J.A., Haigh, J.R. and Traub, M. (1994) Pentagastrin induced panic attacks: enhanced sensitivity in panic disorder patients. Psychopharmacol. (Berl.), 114: 449–455.

van Megen, H.J., Westenberg, H.G., den Boer, J.A., Slaap, B. and Scheepmakers, A. (1997) Effect of the selective serotonin reuptake inhibitor fluvoxamine on CCK-4 induced panic attacks. Psychopharmacol. (Berl.), 129: 357–364.

van Rijen, P.C., Luyten, P.R., van der Sprenkel, J.W., Kraaier, V., van Huffelen, A.C. and Tulleken, C.A. (1989) ^{1}H and ^{31}P NMR measurement of cerebral lactate, high-energy phosphate levels, and pH in humans during voluntary hyperventilation: associated EEG, capnographic, and Doppler findings. Magn. Reson. Med., 10: 182–193.

van Vliet, I.M., Westenberg, H.G., Slaap, B.R., den Boer, J.A. and Ho Pian, K.L. (1997) Anxiogenic effects of pentagastrin in patients with social phobia and healthy controls. Biol. Psychiatry, 42: 76–78.

Veltman, D.J., van Zijderveld, G.A. and van Dyck, R. (1996) Epinephrine infusions in panic disorder: a double-blind placebo-controlled study. J. Affect. Disord., 39: 133–140.

Verburg, K., Griez, E., Meijer, J. and Pols, H. (1995) Discrimination between panic disorder and generalized anxiety disorder by 35% carbon dioxide challenge. Am. J. Psychiatry, 152: 1081–1083.

Verburg, K., Perna, G. and Griez, E. (2001) A case study of the 35% CO_2 challenge. In: Griez, E.J.L. (Ed.), Anxiety disorders: an introduction to clinical management and research. Wiley, Chichester, NY, pp. xxii, 380.

Verburg, K., Pols, H., de Leeuw, M. and Griez, E. (1998) Reliability of the 35% carbon dioxide panic provocation challenge. Psychiatry Res., 78: 207–214.

Vickers, K. and McNally, R.J. (2005) Respiratory symptoms and panic in the National Comorbidity Survey: a test of Klein's suffocation false alarm theory. Behav. Res. Ther., 43: 1011–1018.

Vorstrup, S., Jensen, K.E., Thomsen, C., Henriksen, O., Lassen, N.A. and Paulson, O.B. (1989) Neuronal pH regulation: constant normal intracellular pH is maintained in brain during low extracellular pH induced by acetazolamide–^{31}P NMR study. J. Cereb. Blood Flow Metab., 9: 417–421.

Washburn, C.P., Sirois, J.E., Talley, E.M., Guyenet, P.G. and Bayliss, D.A. (2002) Serotonergic raphe neurons express TASK channel transcripts and a TASK-like pH- and halothane-sensitive K^+ conductance. J. Neurosci., 22: 1256–1265.

Wemmie, J.A., Askwith, C.C., Lamani, E., Cassell, M.D., Freeman, J.H. Jr. and Welsh, M.J. (2003) Acid-sensing ion channel 1 is localized in brain regions with high synaptic density and contributes to fear conditioning. J. Neurosci., 23: 5496–5502.

Wemmie, J.A., Coryell, M.W., Askwith, C.C., Lamani, E., Leonard, A.S. and Sigmund, C.D. (2004) Overexpression of acid-sensing ion channel 1a in transgenic mice increases acquired fear-related behavior. Proc. Natl. Acad. Sci. USA, 101: 3621–3626.

Wiedemann, K., Jahn, H., Yassouridis, A. and Kellner, M. (2001) Anxiolyticlike effects of atrial natriuretic peptide on cholecystokinin tetrapeptide-induced panic attacks: preliminary findings. Arch. Gen. Psychiatry, 58: 371–377.

Wilhelm, F.H., Gerlach, A.L. and Roth, W.T. (2001) Slow recovery from voluntary hyperventilation in panic disorder. Psychosom. Med., 63: 638–649.

Yeragani, V.K., Balon, R., Rainey, J.M., Ortiz, A., Berchou, R. and Lycaki, H. (1988a) Effects of laboratory-induced panic-anxiety on subsequent provocative infusions. Psychiatry Res., 23: 161–166.

Yeragani, V.K., Pohl, R., Balon, R., Rainey, J.M., Berchou, R. and Ortiz, A. (1988b) Sodium lactate infusions after treatment with tricyclic antidepressants: behavioral and physiological findings. Biol. Psychiatry, 24: 767–774.

Zandbergen, J., Lousberg, H.H., Pols, H., de Loof, C. and Griez, E.J. (1990) Hypercarbia versus hypocarbia in panic disorder. J. Affect. Disord., 18: 75–81.

Zandbergen, J., Pols, H., de Loof, C. and Griez, E.J. (1991) Ventilatory response to CO_2 in panic disorder. Psychiatry Res., 39: 13–19.

Zhou, F.Q. (2005) Pyruvate in the correction of intracellular acidosis: a metabolic basis as a novel superior buffer. Am. J. Nephrol., 25: 55–63.

Zwanzger, P., Baghai, T.C., Schuele, C., Strohle, A., Padberg, F. and Kathmann, N. (2001) Vigabatrin decreases cholecystokinin-tetrapeptide (CCK-4) induced panic in healthy volunteers. Neuropsychopharmacology, 25: 699–703.

Zwanzger, P., Eser, D., Aicher, S., Schule, C., Baghai, T.C. and Padberg, F. (2003a) Effects of alprazolam on cholecystokinin-tetrapeptide-induced panic and hypothalamic–pituitary–adrenal-axis activity: a placebo-controlled study. Neuropsychopharmacology, 28: 979–984.

Zwanzger, P., Eser, D., Padberg, F., Baghai, T.C., Schule, C. and Rotzer, F. (2003b) Effects of tiagabine on cholecystokinin-tetrapeptide (CCK-4)-induced anxiety in healthy volunteers. Depress. Anxiety, 18: 140–143.

CHAPTER 5.4

Principles and findings from human imaging of anxiety disorders

Andrea L. Malizia[1,2,*] and David Nutt[2]

[1]*Academic Unit of Psychiatry, University of Bristol, Bristol, UK*
[2]*Psychopharmacology Unit, University of Bristol, Bristol, UK*

Abstract: Investigating the human brain is difficult and until the advent of imaging techniques there were virtually no studies in the anxiety disorders. However, in the last 20 years the development of new techniques especially PET and SPET and MRI have allowed scientific exploration of the circuits and molecular mechanisms that may help us understand the nature of anxiety and the mode of action of anxiolytic treatments. These advances have already helped confirm the discrete nature of the distinct anxiety disorders as well as emphasising important overlaps in circuitry and to a less-studied extent the neurochemistry in these conditions. As such techniques offer huge potential to explore a much wider range of neurotransmitters, transporters and enzymes we can expect the field to develop enormously in the next few decades so the underlying principles behind the techniques is also described.

Keywords: PET; SPET; MRI; fMRI; brain circuits; receptors; transporters

I. Introduction

Anxiety disorders are common and result in a large burden to society and considerable individual disability. Up to 40% of individuals will experience an anxiety disorder in their lifetime and up to 5% will have recurrent or chronic anxiety disorders with relatively poor response to current treatment strategies. These disorders cause a great deal of personal distress, result in reduced life expectancy and, in the UK alone, have an estimated cost of approximately $7 billion per year.

The development of new, more effective treatments for these disorders depends on an understanding of their biological substrates. Unlike depressive disorders and schizophrenia, it is thought that anxiety and anxiety disorders are easier to

model in experimental animals and that such models can be robust in predicting therapeutic efficacy – indeed this volume is predicated on such a view! This is because anxiety allows an individual to prepare for, or respond to, changes in the environment and, as such, it is assumed to be present in experimental animals when a number of specific behaviours are observed. Thus, there is a large body of preclinical literature that describes pharmacological changes and their association with anxiety behaviours. In particular, molecular biology and behavioural sciences have advanced greatly in the last decade and provide a framework to understand brain function and dysfunction at a cellular, chemical and anatomical level. Examples related to anxiety include evidence of increased anxiety in $5HT_{1A}$ knockout mice (Sibille et al., 2000) and in γ_2 $GABA_A$-benzodiazepine receptor knockouts (Crestani et al., 1999), the need for α_2/α_3 $GABA_A$-benzodiazepine receptor expression for anxiolysis (Morris et al., 2006), data on specific neurochemical

*Corresponding author.
E-mail: andrea.l.malizia@bristol.ac.uk

R.J. Blanchard, D.C. Blanchard, G. Griebel and D. Nutt (Eds.)
Handbook of Anxiety and Fear, Vol. 17
ISBN 978-0-444-53065-3

437

DOI: 10.1016/S1569-7339(07)00020-3

effects on fear-potentiated startle (Walker and Davis, 2002) and on unconditioned fear responses (Adamec, 2001).

Nevertheless, human anxiety disorders have been difficult to model satisfactorily as it is not known whether they exist in experimental animals and the predictive validity of animal data have not been as robust as it had been hoped. One of the main issues is that this emotion is expressed inappropriately, spontaneously and idiosyncratically in people with anxiety disorders. In addition it can be manifest in many different guises where it forms part of a number of clinically very different syndromes such as panic disorder, obsessive-compulsive disorder (OCD), social anxiety disorder and post-traumatic stress disorder (PTSD) that have little in common with many of the preclinical models, which tend to focus on fearful responding in animals.

Despite a great deal of research, an adequate account of the molecular mechanisms that underlie these human disorders is still lacking and the principal challenge facing the investigators has been the lack of reciprocal mapping of preclinical and clinical knowledge. There are three fundamental problems in mapping preclinical findings onto human anxiety disorders. The first is that although there is evidence for evolutionary conservation of brain structure relationships across species, the human brain comprises extremely developed frontal lobes and language-related structures unmatched in extent or complexity in any other species. The second is that there is still no good knowledge of the mechanisms that are involved in the inappropriate trigger of pathological anxiety in anxiety and other psychiatric disorders. The third is the difficulty in designing preclinical and clinical experimental paradigms that are isomorphic; this being made more complex by the fact that there is a paucity of instruments that allow the investigation of neurochemical anatomy in man in vivo when symptoms are expressed. The new techniques of brain imaging are beginning to allow the necessary investigations of both circuits and receptors/enzymes in humans and the rest of this chapter gives an overview of this with implications for new drug discovery.

II. Choice of imaging modality

Imaging can be performed in a number of modalities ranging from the radioactive such as PET, SPET, CT through the various forms of MRI. The bulk of this chapter will review the topic of molecular imaging – the use of PET and SPET tracers to investigate receptors and enzyme alterations in anxiety – but first it is necessary to briefly review the issue of how best to investigate the brain circuits of anxiety and fear using many of these techniques have been used to explore the brain circuits involved in human fear and anxiety.

PET can be used to study brain circuitry by measuring changes in brain metabolism either directly using the glucose analogue flurodeoxyglucose (FDG) or in relation to changes in blood flow using radiolabelled water (^{15}O-water). SPET uses a blood-flow-sensitive tracer HMPAO to estimate regional variations in blood flow following stimulation. MRI offers the ability to measure brain volumes (volumetric MRI) and most especially to measure changes in brain metabolism due to anxiety stimuli using the BOLD response (functional or fMRI) which changes due to the coupling between blood flow and brain metabolism. Other newer MRI techniques, such as arterial spin labelling (ASL) may soon add to this dataset and have the advantage of providing fully quantitative rather than relative measures.

Each technique has its advantages and limitations. These are summarised for the three main techniques in Table 1. fMRI has good time resolution but is non-quantitative, FDG gives great regional specificity and resolution but only a single datum per scan with little opportunity for repetition. This is because PET and SPET suffer the limitations of radioactive exposure so repetition of scans is not easy. However, the greater tolerability of PET and SPET scanners for anxiety disorder patients makes them more viable techniques for the study of patient groups.

In this regard SPET has the added potential for administration of the tracer outside the scanner – one can induce an anxiety state, for example by exposure to a feared situation and then give the tracer before returning the subject to the hospital for scanning.

Table 1. Biological information obtainable with molecular imaging techniques

	PET	SPET
Physiology		
Blood volume	✓	
Gross atrophy	✓	✓
Mild neuronal loss	✓	✓
Perfusion	✓	✓
Regional rate of metabolism	✓	✓
Transport into brain	✓	✓
Pharmacology		
B available (receptor concentration available for binding)	✓	✓
Brain concentration of pharmaceuticals	✓	✓
Brain volume of distribution	✓	✓
Enzyme concentration	✓	
Intracellular signaling	✓	
Microglial activation	✓	✓
Neurotransmitter release (indirect)	✓	✓
Receptor binding potential	✓	✓
Transporter/reuptake site density	✓	✓

Whatever technique is used there is a general consensus that anxiety provocation produces increases in activation (increase in metabolism and/or blood flow) in brain regions known for many years to be involved in emotion – the limbic circuit and connected cortical areas (see earlier chapters). In particular the amygdala in humans seems generally activated by fearful inputs both visual and auditory. Many of these changes seem to be manipulated by drugs that reduce anxiety especially the benzodiazepines and antidepressants. They are also affected by genotypes – for example the 5HT transporter polymorphisms ss (short) and ll (long) forms can markedly alter the amygdala response to fearful faces (Hariri et al., 2002). Other gene variants that alter monoamine function, for example MAO and COMT variants also have similar effects.

The investigation of human brain networks related to anxiety experience and anxiety disorders is a big topic with many published papers in the past two decades, so we will not be trying to cover all these as recent reviews can be consulted (e.g. Bremner, 2004; Talbot, 2004; Miller et al., 2005; Deckersbach et al., 2006). The goal of much of this work is to use imaging studies to provide an important new concept – the endophenotype – and to use this then as the basis for new investigations into brain mechanisms, genetic factors and hopefully new drug discovery.

One approach to the question of brain circuitry in anxiety is provoked by Fig. 1 in the chapter by Nutt, Garcia de Miguel and Davies which provides a theoretical perspective of how we can reconcile the similarities and differences between the different disorders. It suggests that there will be a common pathway for the shared elements of each disorder, such as the physiological arousal, the escape and avoidance behaviour and elements of the learning. However, there will also be unique brain specifiers – probably distinct regions or sub-regions – that will be involved in the production of the unique symptoms of each of the disorders.

Based on this model, it is possible to integrate much of the current imaging findings relating to the brain circuitry involved in anxiety into an anatomical schema. In brief the evidence so far suggests that in OCD (for which there is the best and most consistent evidence) the circuitry involved is a loop from orbitofrontal cortex into the caudate nucleus; this system is overactive in the ill state and tends to normalise on treatment with either drugs or psychotherapy (Baxter et al., 1992). In panic the anatomical lesion is thought to be in the amygdala with perhaps some failure of orbitofrontal descending control, whereas in PTSD there is consistent evidence of a medial prefrontal cortex functional abnormality that is also mirrored by molecular imaging studies of the benzodiazepine receptor (see below). The situation in SAnD and generalised anxiety disorder (GAD) is less certain as there have been fewer studies, but in both cases a high prefrontal abnormality is postulated, with in the case of SAnD some possible involvement of accessory motor areas that are also involved in related disorders such as stuttering (Nutt et al., 1998).

Why should the brain show regional variations in function that are associated with – and possibly casual of – anxiety disorders? Perhaps the best explanation is that there may be regional differences in regulatory systems especially receptors that control activity in these brain regions, which is where molecular imaging approaches are necessary.

II.A. Pharmaco-MRI (pMRI)

One interesting new concept that has developed from the imaging endophenotype approach is to study the actions of drugs on such anxiety-related activations (Paulus et al., 2005) of brain function and the potential this might have for discovering or testing new drugs. For example, some have suggested that using an fMRI change in response to fear could give us a better measure of anxiolytic drug effects than subjective responses or especially clinical trials. If this were true then this could markedly accelerate drug discovery as it would allow a much faster screening of drugs in normal volunteers rather than doing patient studies. How likely is this? Currently we can only say that there is insufficient data to allow a decision either way. There has not been a systematic approach to the issue using a range of both active anxiolytic drugs and negative controls (e.g. anticholinergic drugs) in the same paradigm and similar sets of normal volunteers. Moreover, there are few studies that have examined whether patients with anxiety disorders show similar patterns of activation as normal volunteers – so the face validity of these tasks is still not proven. Indeed there are suggestions that patients may show a rather different pattern of response to fear provocation than volunteers, perhaps in an attempt to compensate for their ongoing distress. Moreover we have even less data in patients that have recovered from an anxiety disorder, where recovery is associated with 'normalisation' substituting this overactive amygdala response with abnormal brain responses, so the predictive validity of imaging parameters in terms of treatment outcome is not yet clear. PMRI provides an alternative way of describing brain function whereby drugs rather than psychological tasks are used as probes.

A good example of the pMRI sort of approach is the work of the Manchester group, Anderson and Deakin who have for example pioneered studies of the 5HT agonist drug mCPP and the indirect agonist SSRI citalopram. They have shown that the anxiety produced by mCPP relates to activation in temporal cortical regions, whereas the endocrine effects (prolactin release) correlates with hypothalamic activity (Anderson et al., 2002; McKie et al.,

2005). This value of such an approach to pharmacology is obvious and we can expect more studies in this field in future years.

III. Molecular imaging

Human in vivo molecular brain imaging is one of the few tools capable of bridging the clinical–preclinical chasm. These techniques have evolved since the late 1980s and can be used to map functional neurochemistry and pharmacology of the human brain with macro-anatomical (about 1 cm) resolution thus providing the necessary instruments for a more detailed examination of the human central nervous system. The remainder of this chapter discusses the principles of human molecular imaging and its application in anxiety disorders research.

III.A. Methods and reflections

Molecular imaging uses the techniques of PET and SPET, nuclear medicine techniques that can provide brain in vivo imaging information on a number of different tissue, cellular and molecular events. These are summarised in Table 2.

In this chapter, the discussion will be limited to pharmacological measures and in particular to receptor and transporter density. The spatial resolution of the techniques is of the order of 2–20 mm and the temporal resolution is of the order of minutes, neither of which are compatible with understanding the detailed course of cellular events. However, their great advantage is molecular specificity and sensitivity whereby picomolar concentrations of specific chemical structures of interest can be identified; this results in detection, for instance, of changes in receptor concentration even in areas that are poorly defined anatomically, such as the raphe nuclei.

III.A.1. Scientific principles of emission tomography
Emission tomography relies on scanners detecting photons emitted by the body. In order to achieve this, radioactively labelled molecules are injected.

Table 2. Three approaches for measuring brain circuitry/activation studies in anxiety-strengths and limitations

fMRI	Fast t resolution 2–5 s High statistical power High spatial resolution	Relative measure only Very stressful
PET, ^{15}O-water	Moderate t resolution = 90 s Good stat power in 6–12 scans Good spatial resolution	Inter-arterial line for absolute quantification
SPET, 99mTc-HMPAO	Can be given outside scanner = real-world situations Well tolerated	One (possibly 2) scans per session, poor power and lower spatial resolution

The half-life of the radioactive nuclei is about 2 min for ^{15}O, about 20 min for ^{11}C, about 120 min for ^{18}F, about 6 h for ^{99}Tc and about 13 h for ^{123}I, these being the most commonly used nuclei, the first three for PET and the last two for SPET. Note that with SPET tracers the incorporation of a radioactive nucleus will usually involve modifications of the structure of biologically active molecules, thus altering their pharmacological properties. The photons (singles for SPET, pairs for PET) are detected by scintillating crystals connected to photomultiplier tubes (amplifiers) and electronic devices. In SPET, detectors have to be heavily collimated in order to achieve some spatial selectivity that allows reconstruction of the lines of response (the volume from which the event was generated). In PET the radioactive nuclei decay releasing a positron (a positively charged electron); the positron travels for about 1 mm in tissue and is then annihilated on collision with an electron giving off two photons at almost 180° to each other. The line of response, establishing where the event has occurred, is determined without physical collimators by detecting coincident events, i.e. events that have caused two opposite detectors to scintillate within 6–12 ns. This is known as 'electronic collimation'.

Usually, all the events over a period of time are binned together and tomographically reconstructed using filtered backprojection and a number of other filters. More recently PET data can be acquired in 'list' mode that is where each event is tagged with its own time of occurrence. This allows for later rebinning of the data – a process that can increase the versatility of the dataset but that is computationally more intense. Another

development is the possibility of using iterative techniques (Mesina et al., 2003) to reconstruct the images – these are again more computationally expensive and not currently implemented in commercially available scanners but should improve data quality and statistics (Lubberink et al., 2004).

A number of corrections need to be applied to the acquired data. These are detailed below for PET data and include exclusion of random events, attenuation correction, scatter correction and partial volume correction. The situation is somewhat simpler for SPET; however, in SPET some corrections cannot be measured thus resulting in the technique not being fully quantitative.

Random photons, counted by crystals, are routinely and automatically eliminated by modern PET scanners. Attenuation is the process whereby some events are lost because the tissue absorbs photons; it can be corrected by measuring this attenuation prior to the scan. In the past this was always done with a low activity 511 keV emitter and with the patient in situ. However, the advent of PET/CT machines has resulted in the attenuation being measured with CT. This has two associated potential problems: increased exposure to radiation which, if unchecked could be significant for healthy volunteers, and the fact that the attenuation map has to be transformed with the aid of lookup tables as the X-ray energy is about one-third of the PET photons. Advantages are speed of acquisition and congruence of positioning in the chest and abdomen although the latter are not relevant to brain studies. Scatter is the process whereby photons are deflected resulting in false signal detections from inexistent lines of response.

Early corrections for these were either calculated (rather rudimentarily thus introducing bias) or measured (within a different energy window thus at the expense of some extra noise). Most current algorithms are calculated from sophisticated statistical simulations of the data. These seem to be rather robust especially when applied to brain scans. However, they may introduce biases that affect quantification. These should be understood and could be a particular problem when larger people are scanned whereby the body scatter is considerable. Partial volume effect describes the process whereby radioactive counts are erroneously attributed to a particular voxel because of the influence of neighbouring voxels. These can be rectified using MRI and statistical models (e.g. Aston et al., 2002).

III.A.2. Obtaining and modelling data

The data obtained is in the format of number of radioactive counts per unit volume. The unit volume is usually referred to as a 'voxel'. The information in any voxel comprises the total radionucleide counts in blood (plasma free and bound and intracellular) and in the tissue of interest (free, specifically and non-specifically bound) (Fig. 1).

Most often, the interest is in deriving parameters that describe binding or any other *physiological or pharmacological* process of interest and therefore a model has to be applied. In order to identify the signal, reference data are needed and these usually are either plasma (most usefully arterial) and/or an area of low or no binding in the brain.

One of the initial decisions in analysing the data is whether a model-lead or data-lead approach is preferable. These decisions will usually be based on the exploratory modelling studies that define the response characteristics of a particular ligand in the brain. The advantage of model-based analyses is that the parameter estimates correspond to a biological conceptual framework. The advantage of data-lead models is that they can be less noisy and more robust, however, interpretation of the pharmacological meaning of the results needs to be more cautious. Where there is numerical convergence averaging across models may be most robust

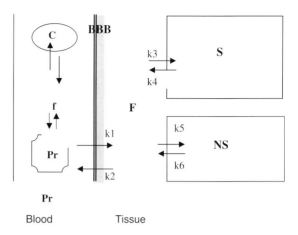

Fig. 1. Signal constituents for each brain voxel and rate constants relating 'compartments'. BBB, blood–brain barrier; C, cells; Pr, proteins; F, free radioligand in tissue; S, specifically bound radioligand in tissue; NS, non-specifically bound radioligand in tissue; f, unbound radioligand in blood. K1/k2 represents the equilibrium from plasma to brain. k3/k4 represents the specific binding equilibrium whereby $k3 = k_{on} \cdot B_{max}$ and k4 is k_{off}. k5/k6 represents the equilibrium with non-specific binding in the brain.

(Turkheimer et al., 2003). These issues are discussed in detail elsewhere (Lammertsma and Hume, 1996; Gunn et al., 1997, 2001, 2002; Slifstein and Laruelle, 2001; Laruelle et al., 2002). Inappropriate model selection or inappropriate choice of reference area/input function can lead to non-sensical data such as negative binding in areas of low (but not null) receptor density, profound influence of perfusion on binding parameters (Asselin et al., 2007) or fundamentally erroneous parameter estimates (Olsson and Farde, 2005).

Radiotracer properties and image robustness are related (Laruelle et al., 2003) and modelling can only work if some basic radioligand properties are met. These are summarised in Table 3.

In addition, experimental designs are also very important in determining pharmacological parameters. While full equilibrium experiments are preferred in order to achieve robust analysis, measures have also been robust in situations where a pulse of tracer is used for parameter estimation (Ito et al., 1998) or where only one of the ligands has been kept at equilibrium while the other

Table 3. Essential radioligand characteristic for successful quantification of brain pharmacological processes

- Ligand enters the brain and is not extruded by e.g. p-glycoproteins
- Tracer kinetics assumptions are not violated so that ligand occupies at most 1% of available specific sites
- Ratio of signal of interest to non-specific signal is at least 2:1 and preferably of the order of over 5:1
- Labelled metabolites in plasma are well understood and accounted for
- There are no labelled metabolites in tissue
- There are no competing 'cold' metabolites in tissue
- Physiology and pharmacology is well understood, e.g. does receptor internalise, is there a significant efflux?

(usually the radiolabel) is given as a pulse (Laruelle et al., 2002).

In conclusion, molecular imaging has the potential to deliver data that is important to understand receptor, transporter, enzyme and transmitter changes that are associated with anxiety disorders. However, a review of the existing literature reveals that the studies that have been carried out thus far are relatively few when compared with the amount of information present in the preclinical literature.

This is due to a number of factors:

- There is a paucity of good in vivo radioligands. This is explained by the methodological points made above. In order to penetrate the brain, ligands have to be lipophyllic, however this characteristic increases non-specific binding to an extent that most radiolabelled molecules produce too small a specific binding signal for its identifiability as part of the total signal recovered. The problem is made harder by the fact that not all molecules can be radiolabelled with ease and by the relative paucity of molecules available for specific targets. This situation can be improved by pharmaceutical industry if a concerted effort is made to discover potential in vivo radiotracers in the early, chemistry-dominated phases of molecule discovery and development. Such efforts are ongoing in the US where NIH/NIMH may act as 'honest broker' to coordinate efforts between industrial and academic partners.

- The discussion on methods points to the fact that some of these studies are methodologically difficult until the properties of the radioligand have been adequately assessed and modelled. This can take some years and currently there are only a few centres worldwide that are able to do so reliably.
- In vivo imaging is expensive. This is not entirely the case when the full costs are compared with many other experimental techniques, especially if the potential benefits are taken into account. However, the upfront technological costs are often enough to discourage more serious investment in this area.
- Biological variability and in some cases poor understanding of the methodological issues have resulted in apparently contrasting results being published; this has resulted in a degree of scepticism about the robustness of the techniques. This is a problem that appears in all biology and pertains equally to preclinical as to clinical studies. Some findings are easily replicated, while others are subject to sources of variation that is often only understood when greater knowledge is acquired.

IV. Molecular imaging in anxiety disorders

Most of the findings in anxiety disorders relate to existing GABAergic and serotonergic ligands (for GABA$_A$, 5HT1$_A$, 5HT2 receptors and 5HTT) and these will be dealt with separately. Data relating to the dopamine transporter (DAT) and NK1 receptors will also be discussed. It is of interest that there has been little exploration of the role of D1 and D2 receptors and of striatal dopamine release in the anxiety disorders despite the wide availability of these techniques. The only exception is of SAnD, where both decreased D2 receptors (Schneier et al., 2000) and DAT number (Tiihonen et al., 1997a, b) have been reported though not replicated.

IV.A. Why focus on GABA$_A$-benzodiazepine receptor imaging?

The GABA$_A$-benzodiazepine receptors are ionophores that modulate chloride flux into the neurons. GABA and other molecules, such as barbiturates, directly increase the frequency and length of opening of the channel. Antagonists at these receptors decrease the tonic effects of GABA and therefore reduce cellular hyperpolarisation leading to seizures and anxiety. Molecules that act at benzodiazepine sites on the pentamer, however, have a modulatory rather than direct function, thus increasing GABA effectiveness (agonists) or reducing it (inverse agonists). Antagonists at benzodiazepine sites, such as flumazenil, are on the whole silent, implying that if endogenous benzodiazepine-like molecules exist, their function is not tonic. The exact function of the various molecules that bind to this receptor is dependent on the receptor subtype; there are well over 100,000 theoretical combinations of the five protein subunits that make up the complex but it is likely that no more than 100 subtypes exist and that there are less than 20 commonly expressed.

There are a number of observations that link the $GABA_A$-benzodiazepine receptors and anxiety modulation in man (for review see Nutt and Malizia, 2001):

- Benzodiazepines are effective anxiolytics
- Benzodiazepine site inverse agonists are anxiogenic (Dorow et al., 1983; Drugan et al., 1985)
- GABAergic antagonists are anxiogenic (Rodin and Calhoun, 1970; File and Lister, 1984)
- GABAergic agonists are anxiolytic (Hoehn-Saric, 1983; Corbett et al., 1991)
- $GABA_A$ receptor numbers can change with environmental manipulation, such as chronic stress, that result in an increase in anxiety expression (Rago et al., 1988; Inoue et al., 1985; Weizman et al., 1989, 1990; Primus and Gallager, 1992). These changes may be mediated by corticosteroids (Weizman et al., 1990) and, indeed, exogenous corticosteroid administration mimics chronic stress and decreases benzodiazepine binding in specific brain structures (Orchinik et al., 2001)
- Developmental behavioural manipulations that result in life-long stress hyper-reactivity, such as repeated short-term maternal separation, result in decreased benzodiazepine binding in brain structures essential for anxiety experience (Kaufman et al., 2000)
- $GABA_A$ receptor subunit expression changes with hormonal changes associated with increased anxiety in man, such as a sudden drop in progesterone levels (Gulinello et al., 2001)
- $GABA_A$ receptor composition can change with chronic administration of neurosteroids (Yu et al., 1996) and their concentration is thought to be altered in some anxiety disorders (Strohle et al., 2002)
- Genetic manipulations can produce animals who have reduced expression of particular subunits (e.g. α_2, α_3 or γ_2) and increased anxiety or decreased sensitivity to anxiolysis (e.g. Crestani et al., 1999; Morris et al., 2006)

In addition, there appear to be differences in $GABA_A$-benzodiazepine receptor function in different anxiety disorders. For instance, the initial separation of generalised anxiety and panic disorder was made on the basis of observations that suggested that patients with panic disorder were less clinically responsive to benzodiazepine agonists. Subsequent experimentation suggested that the clinical observation was mirrored by the pharmacodynamic effects whereby panic disorder patients are less sensitive to benzodiazepines on a number of psychophysiological measures, such as saccadic eye movements to target and suppression of plasma noradrenaline appearance rate with orthostatic challenge (Roy-Byrne et al., 1989, 1990). These findings could be explained by the abnormal presence of a benzodiazepine site inverse agonist. However, Nutt et al. (1990) discovered that flumazenil, a benzodiazepine site antagonist, which has neutral or anxiolytic effects in control subjects, provokes panic attacks in patients with panic disorder. This disproved the putative benzodiazepine receptor inverse agonist theory that postulated that panic attacks and reduced sensitivity to full agonists were due to a phasic increase or presence of an endogenous anxiogenic inverse agonist. There are two possible explanations for the panicogenic effects of an antagonist, such as flumazenil in patients with panic disorder: the first is that subunit changes at the $GABA_A$-benzodiazepine receptor result in changed receptor function so that fluma-zenil behaves like an inverse agonist; the second is that flumazenil blocks a putative endogenous agonist which is present in a compensatory func-tion and which is however insufficient to prevent the emergence of panic attacks. Some recent evidence on the concentration of neurosteroid agents in panic disorder supports the latter (Strohle et al., 2002).

IV.B. GABA_A-benzodiazepine binding in anxiety disorders

Two ligands have been extensively used to measure benzodiazepine receptor density in man: [^{11}C]flu-mazenil (for PET) and [^{123}I]Iomazenil (for SPET). Full quantification can only be achieved with PET but rigorous methodology can be applied to SPET in order to achieve a robust estimate of receptor density (Tokunaga et al., 1997). The main metho-dological problem associated with Iomazenil is that tissue equilibrium (in terms of mapping receptor binding) is only achieved two or more hours after injection and therefore early scans are dominated by perfusion effects (Onishi et al., 1996): thus if subjects are scanned too early, the resulting maps will represent a mixture of binding and blood flow at the time of injection – these cannot be separated unless appropriate input function and time activity curves are generated. However, provided that methodology is sound, binding data can be obtained using these techniques allowing compar-ison of receptor expression between groups.

IV.B.1. Panic disorder

Decreased binding to flumazenil has been demon-strated in a fully quantitative study of benzodiaze-pine naïve subjects. Malizia et al. (1998) employed [^{11}C]flumazenil PET and found a 20% global decrease in binding in benzodiazepine naïve, drug-free patients with panic disorder who had no comorbid conditions and did not abuse alcohol (Fig. 2). These global changes were highly sig-nificant (p < 0.0005 by extent criteria in statistical parametric mapping (SPM)) and were maximal in orbitofrontal, anterior insula and anterior

temporal cortex areas thought to be pivotal for human anxiety.

A recent PET study also using [^{11}C]flumazenil PET (Cameron et al., 2007) demonstrated decreased benzodiazepine binding in the insula but no global changes when comparing 11 patients with panic disorder with 21 healthy controls. Another PET study (Abadie et al., 1999) compared patients with a number of anxiety disorders and healthy volunteers using [^{11}C]flumazenil PET. Variance in the reference area was very large and there were no significant differences in binding between healthy volunteers and controls. However, results for the 10 subjects (5 patients and 5 volunteers) who had arterial sampling show that flumazenil volume of distribution is lower in anxiety patients in all the areas sampled (Table 4).

The differences in the studies' results could all be accounted for by the different methods employed but the most robust interpretation is that reduced binding is present at least in some of the brain areas germane to anxiety modulation in panic disorder.

Using Iomazenil SPET, Schlegel et al. (1994) was the first to report decreased benzodiazepine recep-tor binding in panic disorder comparing, at 90–110 min post-injection, 10 patients with panic disorder with 10 patients with epilepsy on carba-mazepine. The decreases were significant in the occipital and frontal lobes and maximal in the tem-poral lobes. Kaschka et al. (1995) studied nine medicated patients with panic disorder *and* comor-bid depression with a matched group of medicated patients with dysthymia using Iomazenil SPET (2 h). Decreases in binding were seen in the inferior temporal lobes both medially and laterally and in the inferior frontal lobes. These changes were already detectable at 10 min post-injection reflect-ing changes dominated by delivery effects. All participants were on antidepressants. Tokunaga et al. (1997) published an elegant technical study, having followed a very rigorous scanning metho-dology. This study demonstrated reduced benzo-diazepine binding in anxiety patients but is limited by the uncertainty associated with the fact that a standard psychiatric classification was not used.

In contrast to these studies, increases in Ioma-zenil binding were shown by Kuikka et al. (1995) who studied 17 unmedicated patients with panic

446

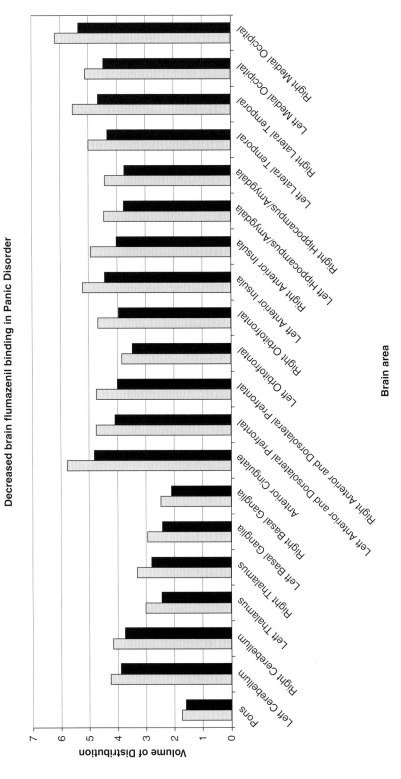

Fig. 2. Histogram showing brain area decreases in flumazenil binding in panic disorder patients compared with healthy volunteers. Lighter bars: flumazenil volume of distribution in healthy volunteers; black bars: flumazenil volume of distribution in panic disorder patients. For discussion see Malizia et al. (1998).

Table 4. Comparison of [^{11}C]flumazenil volumes of distribution values in the Malizia et al. (1998) panic disorder study and in the Abadie et al. (1999) anxiety disorders study

	Medial frontal	Right lateral frontal	Left lateral frontal	Anterior cingulate	Posterior occipital	Right lateral occipital	Left lateral occipital	Right lateral temporal	Left lateral temporal	Cerebellum
Abadie patients	4.8	4.1	4.3	5.1	5.3	4.1	4.6	4.2	4.1	2.9
Abadie controls	5.6	4.7	4.6	5.8	6.0	4.5	4.6	5.1	4.8	3.6
Malizia patients	4.2	4.0	4.1	4.8	4.9	4.5	4.7	4.7	4.3	3.8
Malizia controls	5.0	4.7	4.8	5.8	5.5	5.1	5.4	5.6	5.0	4.2

Data extracted from published tables.

disorder and 17 healthy age- and sex-matched controls using two different SPET cameras (at 90 min post-injection). The increase in signal was bilateral in the temporal cortex and in the right middle/inferior lateral frontal gyrus. Brandt et al. (1998) also reported that patients with panic disorder had a significant increase of benzodiazepine receptor binding in the right supraorbital cortex and a trend to an increased uptake in the right temporal cortex. Both these studies are difficult to interpret, as the data are likely to be influenced by ligand delivery. In the most recent SPET study, Bremner et al. (2000a, b) showed a relative decrease in measures of benzodiazepine receptor binding in left hippocampus and precuneus in panic disorder patients relative to controls. The group further observed that panic disorder patients who had a panic attack compared with patients who did not have a panic attack at the time of the scan also had a decrease in benzodiazepine receptor binding in prefrontal cortex. They also reported an increase in benzodiazepine binding in the right caudate, in the occipital lobes, in the middle temporal and in the middle frontal cortex. Although patients were drug free at the time of the scan none of them were benzodiazepine naïve. In summary, most SPET studies demonstrate decreases in benzodiazepine binding in panic disorder. All but the last one have significant methodological problems (inappropriate control groups, relative quantitation only, presence of medication, unclear diagnostic systems and most important too short an interval between injection and scanning to separate delivery effects from binding) which result in considerable difficulty in interpreting the data.

Decreased benzodiazepine receptor binding is consistent with the idea that panic disorder is due to a deficiency in brain inhibition that leads to, or allows, paroxysmal elevations in anxiety during panic attacks. The peak decreases in benzodiazepine binding are in anatomical areas (e.g. orbitofrontal cortex and insula) thought to be involved in the experience of anxiety in man and could represent a primary pathology. The reduction in binding not only explains some of the known features of benzodiazepine receptor function in panic disorder but is also congruent with animal data reviewed above showing that chronic stress decreases benzodiazepine binding (Inoue et al., 1985; Weizman et al., 1989, 1990) and that animals with genetically decreased flumazenil binding experience more anxiety (Crestani et al., 1999). It is thus possible that this finding could be the result of experiencing repeated panic attacks or the consequence of one or more of the aetiological factors, such as genetic predisposition or life events. These data does not exclude changes in other neurochemical systems thought to be involved in anxiety, particularly serotonin. Preclinical data suggests a cross-link between serotonin and $GABA_A$ receptor expression in that $5HT1_A$ knockout mice, who are more anxious, have decreased benzodiazepine binding and decreased α_1 and α_2 subunit mRNA expression in the amygdala (Sibille et al., 2000). This is further discussed below.

IV.B.2. Post-traumatic stress disorder

Exposure to chronic stress decreases benzodiaze-pine binding, this decrease being maximal in the frontal cortex in some animal experiments (Weizmann et al., 1989). The Yale group (Bremner et al., 2000a) investigated Vietnam veterans with PTSD using Iomazenil SPET and found that there was a significant decrease in the volume of distribution of benzodiazepine GABA$_A$ receptors in the frontal cortex of these patients in an area which corresponds to Brodmann area 9 (ventro-medial prefrontal cortex). This finding may be of particular significance as this area is involved in extinction of conditioned responses, (Milad et al., 2005) thus malfunction of local inhibitory circuits could be either a consequence or a predispositon to developing inappropriate responses to trauma.

IV.B.3. Generalised anxiety disorder

Benzodiazepine binding was also investigated in GAD using ^{123}I NNC 13-8241 SPET in Finland where Tiihonen et al. (1997a) compared 10 patients with 10 age- and sex-matched healthy volunteers finding decreased benzodiazepine GABA$_A$ binding in the left temporal pole. In addition they found a difference in fractal dimen-sions of the binding parameters, which the authors interpreted as a decrease in variation of cortical receptor density akin to the decrease variability of some heart rate parameters seen in cardiovascular disease. While intriguing, this interpretation is premature as the significance of changes in fractal parameters for binding have not been mapped to cellular or histological differences.

IV.C. Why image the serotonin system

The serotonergic system projecting from medial and dorsal raphe is widely associated with anxiety and the data is too numerous to summarise in this chapter.

In man there are a number of lines of evidence:

- Serotonin reuptake inhibitors (SSRIs) and 5HT1$_A$ agonists (e.g. buspirone) are effective in treating anxiety disorders although, unlike medicines that work on GABAA, their thera-peutic effects are delayed (Sheehan and Shee-han, 2007).
- Serotonergic modulation by medicines can produce short-term increases in anxiety in anxiety disorders, in healthy volunteers and in experimental animals (Bruce Lydiard et al., 1996; Browning et al., 2007; Burghardt et al., 2007).
- Serotonergic action is especially important in OCD where dopaminergic blockade can also be therapeutic. Interestingly, strategies to augment serotonergic action do not help people with treatment-resistant OCD unlike people with depressive disorders (Dell'Osso et al., 2007).
- Polymorphisms at the 5HT transporter influ-ence neuroticism and fearfulness and vulner-ability to life events (Caspi et al., 2003; Canli and Lesch, 2007). Further they have effects on 5HT1$_A$ receptors (David et al., 2005) whose expression regulates anxiety behaviours in mice.

IV.D. Findings at the 5HT receptors and transporters in human anxiety disorders

IV.D.1. Panic disorder

In man, Nash et al. (2004) using [^{11}C]WAY100635 (a highly selective antagonist tracer) demonstrated that 5HT1$_A$ binding was decreased throughout the brain in untreated patients with panic disorder when compared with healthy volunteers. The decreased binding was maximal and significant in the raphe and in areas germane to anxiety, such as medial temporal and orbitofrontal cortices and amygdala. However, comparison with treated panic disorder patients on SSRIs showed that while the decrease in raphe binding was of the same magnitude as in untreated patients (and similar to patients with depression), there were no differences in cortical binding between SSRI-treated panic disorder patients and healthy controls. [^{11}C] WAY100635 PET binding is not affected by in vivo changes in intrasynaptic serotonin and has been previously demonstrated not to change with SSRI treatment in depression (Sargent et al., 2000a, b) therefore the results in panic disorder patients can be interpreted as actual changes in binding rather than an effect of changes in synaptic serotonin on the PET measurement; therefore, if replicated, these data would speak to cortical $5HT1_A$ binding being a state marker of panic disorder. A comparable study published by Neumeister et al. (2004) using a modified ^{18}F-containing tracer ligand and studying patients with comorbid panic disorder and major depressive disorder as well as patients with pure panic disorder also showed a decrease of $5HT1_A$ binding in anterior and posterior cingulate and raphe compared with healthy controls. Other areas were not reported on because of the interference of fluorine incorporation in bone interferes with the brain imaging in regions such as temporal lobe proximal to the skull.

The general decrease in $5HT1_A$ and benzodiazepine binding could be the result of widespread neuronal loss, however MRI studies have demonstrated that decreases in grey matter in panic disorder are mainly found in the temporal cortex (Dantendorfer et al., 1996; Vythilingam et al., 2000); further, global decreases, where present, are of the order of 5–7%, this being less than the observed receptor changes; finally the $5HT1_A$ and benzodiazepine decreases have a different distribution pattern thus eschewing anatomical congruence and therefore speaking against the notion of changes secondary to generalised atrophy. In addition, the finding that $5HT1_A$ density in anterior cingulate and neocortex is inversely related to trait anxiety in healthy volunteers (Tauscher et al., 2001) aids interpretation as it implies that reduced postsynaptic expression may be important in the expression of anxiety behaviours.

One beta-CIT SPET study (Maron et al., 2004a, b) has investigated the integrity of presynaptic serotonergic anatomy by studying eight patients with current PD, eight patients with PD in remission and eight healthy control subjects. The patients with current PD showed a significant decrease in 5-HTT binding in the midbrain, in the temporal lobes and in the thalamus in comparison to the controls and 5-HTT binding was negatively correlated with the severity of panic symptoms. Patients in remission had lower density only in the thalamus.

IV.D.2. Obsessive-compulsive disorder

In OCD many studies report decreases in serotonin transporter in the raphe (Stengler-Wenzke et al., 2004; Hesse et al., 2005; Hasselbalch et al., 2007) although one group found increased availability (Pogarell et al., 2003) and one no significant changes (Simpson et al., 2003). In treatment studies, SSRI administration produces decreases in radioligand transporter binding that are of the same order of magnitude as in depression. The discrepancies are likely to reflect methodology and patient selection and these will only be resolved as more studies are carried out resulting in larger numbers. The interpretation of decreases in 5HTT would be consistent with specific decreases in presynaptic neuronal density or arborisation. This is consistent with a finding of increased postsynaptic 5HT2 binding in the caudate nuclei (region where 5HT2 binding can be measured with altanserin) in untreated OCD (Adams et al., 2005) that could reflect either an increase in (upregulation) B_{max} (app) or a decrease in serotonergic output. (B_{max} apparent is used as a shorthand in PET studies to emphasise that changes in receptor availability may not actually represent a change in the number of receptors but may be a result of changes in endogenous ligand, since the difference between the two is not identifiable. So, for example an increase in intrasynaptic ligand can manifest itself, for some systems and tracers, as a decrease in apparent B_{max} as fewer receptors are available for binding by the exogenous radiotracer due to decreases in serotonergic tone or by an upregulation secondary to decrease serotonergic function). The same authors found that the increase was reversed by treatment with SSRIs thus speaking to the increase being a state marker.

Decreases in transporter density in the raphe have also been found in Tourette's syndrome that shares some clinical characteristics with OCD (Muller-Vahl et al., 2005). Consistent with decreases in 5HTT density, many, but not all, studies have found compensatory increases in dopamine transporter density (Kim et al., 2003; van der Wee et al., 2004; Hesse et al., 2005) confirming that there is a reciprocal relationship between dopamine and serotonin function in

OCD. This is further supported by the finding that successful treatment with the SSRI fluvoxamine increases D2 availability, probably as a function of decreased dopaminergic function (Moresco et al., 2007).

IV.D.3. Other anxiety disorders

[^{11}C]WAY100635 has been used to measure 5HT1$_A$ density in social anxiety disorder where decreases were maximal and significant in the amygdala (Lanzenberger et al., 2007) and in PTSD where no differences with healthy controls were found (Bonne et al., 2005). The social anxiety disorder findings are consistent with other imaging findings that suggest a hyper-reactivity of the amygdalae in this condition. Maron et al. (2004b) investigated the density of the serotonin transporter in GAD finding no difference in density with healthy volunteers.

IV.E. Other findings of interest

Two intriguing findings have emerged that will merit further exploration – a decrease in mu receptor density in limbic areas with trauma exposure accompanied by differential binding in areas germane to anxiety between people who developed PTSD and people who did not (Liberzon et al., 2007) and the finding of decreased NK1 binding in the amygdala during specific phobic anxiety (Michelgard et al., 2007). Both, probably, speak to the novel ability to detect changes in transmitter release that accompany the experience of anxiety or the state of having an anxiety disorder. In our opinion, PET's ability to detect changes in endogenous neurotransmitter release is a robust development which merits further validation and research effort as it provides a unique window on the neurochemical pathology of anxiety disorders.

Another area of interest in relation to drug discovery is the development of new tracers that can be used to perform dose-occupation studies to ensure that optimal doses of drugs – both new and old – are used. The findings that NK1 antagonists were ineffective in depression (see chapter by Baldwin) were considerably strengthened by the prior dose-finding PET studies that allowed doses

that lead to >80% receptor occupation to be determined before the clinical trials started. Such trials can also help determine if a potential therapy even gets into the brain, so can prevent expensive trials that have little or no chance of success.

IV.F. Molecular imaging – conclusion

The paradigms here described are applicable to all areas of human anxiety disorders. So far, most molecular studies in anxiety disorders have been focused on the GABA$_A$ receptor and on 5HT1$_A$ receptors and the serotonin transporter. Many studies are difficult to interpret as the methodology has needed ongoing refinements; however, some of these initial findings provide a unique opportunity to link animal and human research.

The findings of decreased benzodiazepine and 5HT1$_A$ binding in panic disorder are intriguing and provide the first set of 'hard' data that links the preclinical pharmacology of stress with human receptor binding changes in vivo. This is invaluable as it allows completion of data-driven research cycle and allows us to re-focus preclinical research in areas where changes in human neurochemistry are observed. The main shortcoming of this process is the dearth of radioligand that are satisfactory for in vivo imaging. Thus, advances in this area will depend upon the discovery of new tracers with adequate characteristics for in vivo imaging.

Altogether, the last 10 years have seen a consolidation of molecular imaging techniques. These are now mature in many areas and are likely to provide fundamental contributions in our understanding of human anxiety disorders.

References

Abadie, P., Boulenger, J.P., Benali, K., Barre, L., Zarifian, E. and Baron, J.C. (1999) Relationships between trait and state anxiety and the central benzodiazepine receptor: a PET study. Eur. J. Neurosci., 11: 1470–1478.

Adamec, R. (2001) Does long term potentiation in periacqueductal gray (PAG) mediate lasting changes in rodent anxiety-like behavior (ALB) produced by predator stress? – effects of low frequency stimulation (LFS) of PAG on place preference and changes in ALB produced by predator stress. Behav. Brain Res., 120: 111–135.

Adams, K.H., Hansen, E.S., Pinborg, L.H., Hasselbalch, S.G., Svarer, C., Holm, S., Bolwig, T.G. and Knudsen, G.M. (2005) Patients with obsessive-compulsive disorder have increased 5-HT2A receptor binding in the caudate nuclei. Int. J. Neuropsychopharmacol., 8: 391–401.

Anderson, I.M., Clark, L., Elliott, R., Kulkarni, B. and Deakin, J.F.W. (2002) 5HT2C receptor activation by m-chlorophenylpiperazine detected in humans with fMRI. Neuroreport, 13: 1547–1551.

Asselin, M.C., Montgomery, A.J., Grasby, P.M. and Hume, S.P. (2007) Quantification of PET studies with the very high-affinity dopamine D2/D3 receptor ligand [^{11}C]FLB 457: re-evaluation of the validity of using a cerebellar reference region. J. Cereb. Blood Flow Metab., 27: 378–392.

Aston, J.A., Cunningham, V.J., Asselin, M.C., Hammers, A., Evans, A.C. and Gunn, R.N. (2002) Positron emission tomography partial volume correction: estimation and algorithms. J. Cereb. Blood Flow Metab., 22: 1019–1034.

Baxter, L.R., Jr. Schwartz, J.M., Bergman, K.S., Szuba, M.P., Guze, B.H., Mazziotta, J.C., Alazraki, A., Selin, C.E., Ferng, H.K. and Munford, P. (1992) Caudate glucose metabolic rate changes with both drug and behavior therapy for obsessive-compulsive disorder. Arch. Gen. Psychiatry, 49: 681–689.

Bonne, O., Bain, E., Neumeister, A., Nugent, A.C., Vythilingam, M., Carson, R.E., Luckenbaugh, D.A., Eckelman, W., Herscovitch, P., Drevets, W.C. and Charney, D.S. (2005) No change in serotonin type 1A receptor binding in patients with posttraumatic stress disorder. Am. J. Psychiatry., 162: 383–385.

Brandt, C.A., Meller, J., Keweloh, L., Hoschel, K., Staedt, J., Munz, D. and Stoppe, G. (1998) Increased benzodiazepine receptor density in the prefrontal cortex in patients with panic disorder. J. Neural Transm., 105: 1325–1333.

Bremner, J.D. (2004) Brain imaging in anxiety disorders. Expert Rev. Neurother., 4: 275–284.

Bremner, J.D., Innis, R.B., Southwick, S.M., Staib, L., Zoghbi, S. and Charney, D.S. (2000a) Decreased benzodiazepine receptor binding in prefrontal cortex in combat-related posttraumatic stress disorder. Am. J. Psychiatry, 157: 1120–1126.

Bremner, J.D., Innis, R.B., White, T., Fujita, M., Silbersweig, D., Goddard, A.W., Staib, L., Stern, E., Cappiello, A., Woods, S., Baldwin, R. and Charney, D.S. (2000b) SPET [I-123]iomazenil measurement of the benzodiazepine receptor in panic disorder. Biol. Psychiatry, 47: 96–106.

Browning, M., Reid, C., Cowen, P.J., Goodwin, G.M. and Harmer, C. (2007) A single dose of citalopram increases fear recognition in healthy subjects. J. Psychopharmacol., 1: 64–73.

Burghardt, N.S., Bush, D.E., McEwen, B.S. and Ledoux, J.E. (2007) Acute selective serotonin reuptake inhibitors increase conditioned fear expression: blockade with a 5-HT(2C) receptor antagonist. *Biol. Psychiatry*, (in press).

Cameron, O.G., Huang, G.C., Nichols, T., Koeppe, R.A., Minoshima, S., Rose, D. and Frey, K.A. (2007) Reduced gamma-aminobutyric acid(A)-benzodiazepine binding sites in insular cortex of individuals with panic disorder. Arch. Gen. Psychiatry, 64: 793–800.

Canli, T. and Lesch, K.P. (2007) Long story short: the serotonin transporter in emotion regulation and social cognition. Nat. Neurosci., 10: 1103–1109.

Caspi, A., Sugden, K., Moffitt, T.E., Taylor, A., Craig, I.W., Harrington, H., McClay, J., Mill, J., Martin, J., Braithwaite, A. and Poulton, R. (2003) Influence of life stress on depression: moderation by a polymorphism in the *5-HTT* gene. Science, 301: 386–389.

Corbett, R., Fielding, S., Cornfeldt, M. and Dunn, R.W. (1991) GABAmimetic agents display anxiolytic like effects in the social interaction and elevated plus maze procedures. Psychopharmacology (Berl.), 104: 312–316.

Crestani, F., Lorez, M., Baer, K. and Mohler, H. (1999) Decreased GABAA-receptor clustering results in enhanced anxiety and a bias for threat cues. Nat. Neurosci., 2: 833–839.

Dantendorfer, K., Prayer, D., Kramer, J., Amering, M., Baischer, W., Berger, P., Schoder, M., Steinberger, K., Windhaber, J., Imhof, H. and Katschnig, H. (1996) High frequency of EEG and MRI brain abnormalities in panic disorder. Psychiatry Res., 68: 41–53.

David, S.P., Murthy, N.V., Rabiner, E.A., Munafo, M.R., Johnstone, E.C., Jacob, R., Walton, R.T. and Grasby, P.M. (2005) A functional genetic variation of the serotonin (5-HT) transporter affects 5-HT1A receptor binding in humans. J. Neurosci., 25: 2586–2590.

Deckersbach, T., Dougherty, D.D. and Rauch, S.L. (2006) Functional imaging of mood and anxiety disorders. J. Neuroimaging, 16: 1–10.

Dell'Osso, B., Altamura, A.C., Mundo, E., Marazziti, D. and Hollander, E. (2007) Diagnosis and treatment of obsessive-compulsive disorder and related disorders. Int. J. Clin. Pract., 1: 98–104.

Dorow, R., Horowski, R., Paschelke, G. and Amin, M. (1983) Severe anxiety induced by FG 7142, a beta carboline ligand for benzodiazepine receptors. Lancet, 2: 98–99.

Drugan, R.C., Maier, S.F., Skolnick, P., Paul, S.M. and Crawley, J.N. (1985) An anxiogenic benzodiazepine receptor ligand induces learned helplessness. Eur. J. Pharmacol., 113: 453–457.

File, S.E. and Lister, R.G. (1984) Do the reductions in social interaction produced by picrotoxin and

452

pentylenetetrazole indicate anxiogenic actions? Neuropharmacology, 23: 793–796.

Gulinello, M., Gong, Q.H., Li, X. and Smith, S.S. (2001) Short-term exposure to a neuroactive steroid increases alpha4 GABA(A) receptor subunit levels in ssociation with increased anxiety in the female rat. Brain Res., 910: 55–66.

Gunn, R.N., Gunn, S.R. and Cunningham, V.J. (2001) Positron emission tomography compartmental models. J. Cereb. Blood Flow Metab., 21: 635–652.

Gunn, R.N., Gunn, S.R., Turkheimer, F.E., Aston, J.A. and Cunningham, V.J. (2002) Positron emission tomography compartmental models: a basis pursuit strategy for kinetic modeling. J. Cereb. Blood Flow Metab., 22: 1425–1439.

Gunn, R.N., Lammertsma, A.A., Hume, S.P. and Cunningham, V.J. (1997) Parametric imaging of ligand-receptor binding in PET using a simplified reference region model. Neuroimage, 6: 279–287.

Hariri, A.R., Mattay, V.S., Tessitore, A., Kolachana, B., Fera, F., Goldman, D., Egan, M.F. and Weinberger, D.R. (2002) Serotonin transporter genetic variation and the response of the human amygdala. Science, 297: 400–403.

Hasselbalch, S.G., Hansen, E.S., Jakobsen, T.B., Pinborg, L.H., Lonborg, J.H. and Bolwig, T.G. (2007) Reduced midbrain-pons serotonin transporter binding in patients with obsessive-compulsive disorder. Acta. Psychiatr. Scand., 115: 388–394.

Hesse, S., Muller, U., Lincke, T., Barthel, H., Villmann, T., Angermeyer, M.C. and Sabri, O. Stengler-Wenzke K. (2005) Serotonin and dopamine transporter imaging in patients with obsessive-compulsive disorder. Psychiatry. Res., 140: 63–72. Epub 2005 Oct 6.

Hoehn-Saric, R. (1983) Effects of THIP on chronic anxiety. Psychopharmacology (Berl.), 80: 338–341.

Inoue, O., Akimoto, Y., Hashimoto, K. and Yamasaki, T. (1985) Alterations in biodistribution of [3H]Ro 15 1788 in mice by acute stress: possible changes in in vivo binding availability of brain benzodiazepine receptor. Int. J. Nucl. Med. Biol., 12: 369–374.

Ito, H., Hietala, J., Blomqvist, G., Halldin, C. and Farde, L. (1998) Comparison of the transient equilibrium and continuous infusion method for quantitative PET analysis of [^{11}C]raclopride binding. J. Cereb. Blood Flow Metab., 18: 941–950.

Kaschka, W., Feistel, H. and Ebert, D. (1995) Reduced benzodiazepine receptor binding in panic disorders measured by iomazenil SPET. J. Psychiatr. Res., 29: 427–433.

Kaufman, J., Plotsky, P.M., Nemeroff, C.B. and Charney, D.S. (2000) Effects of early adverse experiences on brain structure and function: clinical implications. Biol. Psychiatry, 48: 778–790.

Kim, C.H., Koo, M.S., Cheon, K.A., Ryu, Y.H., Lee, J.D. and Lee, H.S. (2003) Dopamine transporter density of basal ganglia assessed with [123I] IPI SPET in obsessive-compulsive disorder. Eur. J. Nucl. Med. Mol. Imaging, 30: 1637–1643.

Kuikka, J.T., Pitkanen, A., Lepola, U., Partanen, K., Vainio, P., Bergstrom, K.A., Wieler, H.J., Kaiser, K.P., Mittelbach, L. and Koponen, H. (1995) Abnormal regional benzodiazepine receptor uptake in the prefrontal cortex in patients with panic disorder. Nucl. Med. Commun., 16: 273–280.

Lammertsma, A.A. and Hume, S.P. (1996) Simplified reference tissue model for PET receptor studies. Neuroimage, 4: 153–158.

Lanzenberger, R.R., Mitterhauser, M., Spindelegger, C., Wadsak, W., Klein, N., Mien, L.K., Holik, A., Attarbaschi, T., Mossaheb, N., Sacher, J., Geiss-Granadia, T., Kletter, K., Kasper, S. and Tauscher, J. (2007) Reduced serotonin-1A receptor binding in social anxiety disorder. Biol. Psychiatry., 61: 1081–1089.

Laruelle, M., Slifstein, M. and Huang, Y. (2002) Positron emission tomography: imaging and quantification of neurotransporter availability. Methods, 27: 287–299.

Laruelle, M., Slifstein, M. and Huang, Y. (2003) Relationships between radiotracer properties and image quality in molecular imaging of the brain with positron emission tomography. Mol. Imaging Biol., 5: 363–375.

Liberzon, I., Taylor, S.F., Phan, K.L., Britton, J.C., Fig, L.M., Bueller, J.A., Koeppe, R.A. and Zubieta, J.K. (2007) Altered central micro-opioid receptor binding after psychological trauma. Biol. Psychiatry, 61: 1030–1038.

Lubberink, M., Boellaard, R., van der Weerdt, A.P., Visser, F.C. and Lammertsma, A.A. (2004) Quantitative comparison of analytic and iterative reconstruction methods in 2- and 3-dimensional dynamic cardiac 18F-FDG PET. J. Nucl. Med., 45: 2008–2015.

Lydiard, R.B., Brawman-Mintzer, O. and Ballenger, J.C. (1996) Recent developments in the psychopharmacology of anxiety disorders. J. Consult. Clin. Psychol., 64: 660–668.

McKie, S., Del-Ben, C., Elliott, R., Williams, S., Delvai, N., Anderson, I. and Deakin, J.F.W. (2005) Neuronal effects of acte citalopram detected by pharmacoMRI. Psychopharmacology, 180: 680–686.

Malizia, A.L., Cunningham, V.J., Bell, C.J., Liddle, P.F., Jones, T. and Nutt, D.J. (1998) Decreased brain GABA(A)-benzodiazepine receptor binding in panic disorder: preliminary results from a quantitative PET study. Arch. Gen. Psychiatry, 55: 715–720.

Maron, E., Kuikka, J.T., Shlik, J., Vasar, V., Vanninen, E. and Tiihonen, J. (2004a) Reduced brain serotonin transporter binding in patients with panic disorder. Psychiatry Res., 132: 173–181.

Maron, E., Kuikka, J.T., Ulst, K., Tiihonen, J., Vasar, V. and Shlik, J. (2004b) SPET imaging of serotonin transporter binding in patients with generalized anxiety disorder. Eur. Arch. Psychiatry Clin. Neurosci., 254: 392–396.

Mesina, C.T., Boellaard, R., van den Heuvel, O.A., Veltman, D.J., Jongbloed, G., van der Vaart, A.W. and Lammertsma, A.A. (2003) Effects of attenuation correction and reconstruction method on PET activation studies. Neuroimage, 20: 898–908.

Michelgard, A., Appel, L., Pissiota, A., Frans, O., Langstrom, B., Bergstrom, M. and Fredrikson, M. (2007) Symptom provocation in specific phobia affects the substance P neurokinin-1 receptor system. Biol. Psychiatry, 61: 1002–1006.

Miller, L.A., Taber, K.H., Gabbard, G.O. and Hurley, R.A. (2005) Neural underpinnings of fear and its modulation: implications for anxiety disorders. J. Neuropsychiatry Clin. Neurosci., 17: 1–6.

Milad, M.R., Quinn, B.T., Pitman, R.K., Orr, S.P., Fischl, B. and Rauch, S.L. (2005) Thickness of ventromedial prefrontal cortex in humans is correlated with extinction memory. Proc. Natl. Acad. Sci. USA, 102: 10706–10711.

Moresco, R.M., Pietra, L., Henin, M., Panzacchi, A., Locatelli, M., Bonaldi, L., Carpinelli, A., Gobbo, C., Bellodi, L., Perani, D. and Fazio, F. (2007) Fluvoxamine treatment and D2 receptors: a pet study on OCD drug-naive patients. Neuropsychopharmacology, 32: 197–205.

Morris, H.V., Dawson, G.R., Reynolds, D.S., Atack, J.R. and Stephens, D.N. (2006) Both alpha2 and alpha3 GABAA receptor subtypes mediate the anxiolytic properties of benzodiazepine site ligands in the conditioned emotional response paradigm. Eur. J. Neurosci., 9: 2495–2504.

Muller-Vahl, K.R., Meyer, G.J., Knapp, W.H., Emrich, H.M., Gielow, P., Brucke, T. and Berding, G. (2005) Serotonin transporter binding in tourette syndrome. Neurosci. Lett., 9; 385: 120–125.

Nash, J.R., Sargent, P.A. and Rabiner, E.A. (2004) Altered 5HT1A binding in panic disorder demonstrated by positron emission tomography. Eur. Neuropsychopharmacol., 14: S322–S323.

Neumeister, A., Bain, E., Nugent, A.C., Carson, R.E., Bonne, O., Luckenbaugh, D.A., Eckelman, W., Herscovitch, P., Charney, D.S. and Drevets, W.C. (2004) Reduced serotonin type 1A receptor binding in panic disorder. J. Neurosci., 24: 589–591.

Nutt, D.J., Bell, C.J. and Malizia, A.L. (1998) Brain mechanisms of social anxiety disorder. J. Clin. Psychiatry, 59: 4–11.

Nutt, D.J., Glue, P., Lawson, C. and Wilson, S. (1990) Flumazenil provocation of panic attacks. Arch. Gen. Psychiatry, 47: 917–925.

Nutt, D.J. and Malizia, A.L. (2001) New insights into the role of the GABA(A)-benzodiazepine receptor in psychiatric disorder. Br. J. Psychiatry, 179: 390–396.

Olsson, H. and Farde, L. (2005) Half-life of receptor occupancy – a meaningless concept. Int. J. Neuropsychopharmacol., 8: 141–142.

Onishi, Y., Yonekura, Y., Tanaka, F., Nishizawa, S., Ozakawa, H., Ishizu, K., Fujita, T., Konishi, J. and Mukai, T. (1996) Delayed image of iodine-123 iomazenil as a relative map of benzodiazepine receptor binding: the optimal scan time. Eur. J. Nucl. Med., 23: 1491–1497.

Orchinik, M., Carroll, S.S., Li, Y.H., McEwen, B.S. and Weiland, N.G. (2001) Heterogeneity of hippocampal GABA(A) receptors: regulation by corticosterone. J. Neurosci., 21: 330–339.

Paulus, M.P., Feinstein, J.S., Castillo, G., Simmons, A.N. and Stein, M.B. (2005) Dose-dependent decrease of activation in bilateral amygdala and insula by lorazepam during emotion processing. Arch. Gen. Psychiatry, 62: 282–288.

Pogarell, O., Hamann, C., Popperl, G., Juckel, G., Chouker, M., Zaudig, M., Riedel, M., Simpson, H.B., Lombardo, I., Slifstein, M., Huang, H.Y., Hwang, D.R., Abi-Dargham, A., Liebowitz, M.R. and Laruelle, M. (2003) Serotonin transporters in obsessive-compulsive disorder: a positron emission tomography study with [(11)C]McN 5652. Biol. Psychiatry, 54: 1414–1421.

Pogarell, O., Poepperl, G., Mulert, C., Hamann, C., Sadowsky, N., Riedel, M., Moeller, H.J., Hegerl, U. and Tatsch, K. (2005) SERT and DAT availabilities under citalopram treatment in obsessive-compulsive disorder (OCD). Eur. Neuropsychopharmacol., 15: 521–524.

Primus, R.J. and Gallager, D.W. (1992) GABAA receptor subunit mRNA levels are differentially influenced by chronic FG 7142 and diazepam exposure. Eur. J. Pharmacol., 226: 21–28.

Rago, L., Kiivet, R.A., Harro, J. and Pold, M. (1988) Behavioral differences in an elevated plus maze: correlation between anxiety and decreased number of GABA and benzodiazepine receptors in mouse cerebral cortex. Naunyn Schmiedebergs Arch. Pharmacol., 337: 675–678.

Rodin, E.A. and Calhoun, H.D. (1970) Metrazol tolerance in a "normal" volunteer population. A ten year follow up report. J. Nerv. Ment. Dis., 150: 438–443.

Roy-Byrne, P.P., Cowley, D.S., Greenblatt, D.J., Shader, R.I. and Hommer, D. (1990) Reduced benzodiazepine sensitivity in panic disorder. Arch. Gen. Psychiatry, 47: 259–272.

Roy-Byrne, P.P., Lewis, N., Villacres, E., Diem, H., Greenblatt, D.J., Shader, R.I. and Veith, R. (1989) Preliminary evidence of benzodiazepine subsensitivity in panic disorder. Arch. Gen. Psychiatry, 46: 165–169.

Sargent, P.A., Kjaer, K.H., Bench, C.J., Rabiner, E.A., Messa, C., Meyer, J., Gunn, R.N., Grasby, P.M. and Cowen, P.J. (2000a) Brain serotonin1A receptor binding measured by positron emission tomography with [^{11}C]WAY-100635: effects of depression and antidepressant treatment. Arch. Gen. Psychiatry, 57: 174–180.

Sargent, P.A., Nash, J., Hood, S., Rabiner, E., Messa, C., Cowen, P., Nutt, D.J. and Grasby, P. (2000b) 5HT1A receptor binding in panic disorder: comaprison with depressive disorder and healthy volunteers using PET and [^{11}C] WAY 100635. Neuroimage, 11: s189.

Schneier, F.R., Liebowitz, M.R., Abi-Dargham, A., Zea-Ponce, Y., Lin, S.H. and Laruelle, M. (2000) Low dopamine D(2) receptor binding potential in social phobia. Am. J. Psychiatry, 157: 457–459.

Schlegel, S., Steinert, H., Bockisch, A., Hahn, K., Schloesser, R. and Benkert, O. (1994) Decreased benzodiazepine receptor binding in panic disorder measured by Iomazenil SPET. A preliminary report. Eur. Arch. Psychiatry Clin. Neurosci., 244: 49–51.

Sheehan, D.V. and Sheehan, K.H. (2007) Current approaches to the pharmacologic treatment of anxiety disorders. Psychopharmacol. Bull., 40: 98–109.

Sibille, E., Pavlides, C., Benke, D. and Toth, M. (2000) Genetic inactivation of the serotonin(1A) receptor in mice results in downregulation of major GABA(A) receptor alpha subunits, reduction of GABA(A) receptor binding, and benzodiazepine-resistant anxiety. J. Neurosci., 20: 2758–2765.

Simpson, H.B., Lombardo, I., Slifstein, M., Huang, H.Y., Hwang, D.R., Abi-Dargham, A, Liebowitz, M.R. and Laruelle, M. (2003) Serotonin transporters in obsessive-compulsive disorder: a positron emission tomography study with [(11)C]McN 5652. Biol. Psychiatry., 54: 1414–1421.

Slifstein, M. and Laruelle, M. (2001) Models and methods for derivation of *in vivo* neuroreceptor parameters with PET and SPECT reversible radio tracers. Nucl. Med. Biol., 28: 595–608.

Stengler-Wenzke, K., Muller, U., Angermeyer, M.C., Sabri, O. and Hesse, S. (2004) Reduced serotonin transporter-availability in obsessive-compulsive disorder (OCD). Eur. Arch. Psychiatry. Clin. Neurosci., 254: 252–255.

Stengler-Wenzke, K., Muller, U., Barthel, H., Angermeyer, M.C., Sabri, O. and Hesse, S. (2006) Serotonin transporter imaging with [123I]beta-CIT SPECT before and after one year of citalopram treatment of obsessive-compulsive disorder. Neuropsychobiology., 53: 40–45.

Strohle, A., Romeo, E., di Michele, F., Pasini, A., Yassouridis, A., Holsboer, F. and Rupprecht, R. (2002) GABA(A) receptor-modulating neuroactive steroid composition in patients with panic disorder before and during paroxetine treatment. Am. J. Psychiatry, 59: 145–147.

Talbot, P.S. (2004) The molecular neuroimaging of anxiety disorders. Curr. Psychiatry Rep., 6: 274–279.

Tauscher, J., Bagby, R.M., Javanmard, M., Christensen, B.K., Kasper, S. and Kapur, S. (2001) Inverse relationship between serotonin 5-HT(1A) receptor binding and anxiety: a [(11)C]WAY-100635 PET investigation in healthy volunteers. Am. J. Psychiatry, 158: 1326–1328.

Tiihonen, J., Kuikka, J., Bergstrom, K., Lepola, U., Koponen, H. and Leinonen, E. (1997a) Dopamine reuptake site densities in patients with social phobia. Am. J. Psychiatry, 154: 239–242.

Tiihonen, J., Kuikka, J., Rasanen, P., Lepola, U., Koponen, H., Liuska, A., Lehmusvaara, A., Vainio, P., Kononen, M., Bergstrom, K., Yu, M., Kinnunen, I., Akerman, K. and Karhu, J. (1997b) Cerebral benzodiazepine receptor binding and distribution in generalized anxiety disorder: a fractal analysis. Mol. Psychiatry, 2: 463–471.

Tokunaga, M., Ida, I., Higuchi, T. and Mikuni, M. (1997) Alterations of benzodiazepine receptor binding potential in anxiety and somatoform disorders measured by ^{123}I-iomazenil SPET. Radiat. Med., 15: 163–169.

Turkheimer, F.E., Hinz, R. and Cunningham, V.J. (2003) On the undecidability among kinetic models: from model selection to model averaging. J. Cereb. Blood Flow Metab., 23: 490–498.

van der Wee, N.J., Stevens, H., Hardeman, J.A., Mandl, R.C., Denys, D.A., van Megen, H.J., Kahn, R.S. and Westenberg, H.M. (2004) Enhanced dopamine transporter density in psychotropic-naive patients with obsessive-compulsive disorder shown by [123I]{beta}-CIT SPET. Am. J. Psychiatry, 161: 2201–2206.

Vythilingam, M., Anderson, E.R., Goddard, A., Woods, S.W., Staib, L.H., Charney, D.S. and Bremner, J.D. (2000) Temporal lobe volume in panic disorder – a quantitative magnetic resonance imaging study. Psychiatry Res., 99: 75–82.

Walker, D.L. and Davis, M. (2002) The role of amygdala glutamate receptors in fear learning, fear-potentiated startle, and extinction. Pharmacol. Biochem. Behav., 71: 379–392.

Weizman, A., Weizman, R., Kook, K.A., Vocci, F., Deutsch, S.I. and Paul, S.M. (1990) Adrenalectomy prevents the stress induced decrease in in vivo [3H]Ro15 1788 binding to GABAA benzodiazepine receptors in the mouse. Brain Res., 519: 347–350.

Weizman, R., Weizman, A., Kook, K.A., Vocci, F., Deutsch, S.I. and Paul, S.M. (1989) Repeated swim stress alters brain benzodiazepine receptors measured in vivo. J. Pharmacol. Exp. Ther., 249: 701–707.

Yu, R., Follesa, P. and Ticku, M.K. (1996) Downregulation of the GABA receptor subunits mRNA levels in mammalian cultured cortical neurons following chronic neurosteroid treatment. Brain Res. Mol. Brain Res., 41: 163–168.

CHAPTER 5.5

Stress hormones and anxiety disorders

Elizabeth A. Young[1,*], James L. Abelson[2] and Israel Liberzon[2]

[1]Molecular and Behavioral Neurosciences Institute, University of Michigan, Ann Arbor, MI, USA
[2]Department of Psychiatry, University of Michigan, Ann Arbor, MI, USA

Abstract: Conceptually stress and anxiety are tightly linked and animal studies find activation of the hypothalamic–pituitary–adrenal (HPA) axis in anxiogenic situations. However, disruption of the HPA axis in anxiety disorders is less robust than studies with major depression. In contrast, activation of the central noradrenergic system is a robust finding in anxiety disorders. Neuroanatomical and neurophysiological studies suggest that activation of these two stress systems are linked in other species. This chapter reviews the HPA axis and sympathetic nervous system (SNS) and their function in anxiety disorders particularly panic disorder and post-traumatic stress disorder (PTSD). The picture of activation of the central noradrenergic systems without clear evidence of HPA axis pathology in anxiety disorders has led some to conclude that anxiety patients may be hypoactive in regards to the HPA axis. While this may be true, an alternative is that the prolonged activation of the HPA axis as observed in major depression is beyond what is expected under "chronic stress," and thus the problem may be in our comparison group and expecting the HPA axis in anxiety disorders to look like that in depression. Studies of individuals under chronic stress do not by and large demonstrate an over-active HPA axis leading us to conclude that patients with anxiety disorders have a fundamentally normal HPA axis that is capable of responding and is regulated properly by inhibitory circuits of the brain.

Keywords: hypothalamic–pituitary–adrenal axis; cortisol; noradrenergic systems; clonidine; growth hormone; post-traumatic stress disorder

I. Introduction: stress, fear and anxiety

The following chapter reviews the laboratory and clinical findings of interaction between stress exposure, fear and anxiety, with particular emphasis on the possible role of stress in generation of anxiety symptoms and anxiety disorders. Careful examination of the interrelationships between of stress, anxiety and fear reveals an often confusing picture due to both the degree of conceptual overlap and the liberal use of these definitions in the literature. To minimize potential confusion, we will be using these concepts in the following

manner: stress represents an interaction between a particular type of environmental stimuli (stressors) and a number of specific stress response systems (namely hypothalamic–pituitary–adrenal (HPA) axis and/or catecholamines). Anxiety and fear, on the other hand, constitute a set of behavioral, cognitive and physiologic responses to threatening situations or uncertainty. While fear often constitutes a normal response to a well-defined threat, anxiety is often dissociated from the external stimulus, and is not necessarily associated with a particular physiological response. From these definitions one can appreciate the potential for conceptual overlap and confusion, stemming from two sources: (a) anxiety and fear can be a part of the stress response, and (b) anxiety and fear in turn

*Corresponding author. E-mail: eayoung@umich.edu

R.J. Blanchard, D.C. Blanchard, G. Griebel and D. Nutt (Eds.)
Handbook of Anxiety and Fear, Vol. 17
ISBN 978-0-444-53065-3

455

DOI: 10.1016/S1569-7339(07)00021-5

can constitute a component of a potential stressor. For example, fear or anxiety are used as a stressor, in humans in the Trier Social Stress Test and basic scientist often take advantage of certain anxiety tests like the open field or the elevated plus-maze, to measure the HPA axis response as well as fear behavior. In this chapter we will focus however on the long-lasting effects of stress on anxiety symptoms and behaviors, usually examining the relationships between stress exposure and symptoms of anxiety that are dissociated in time.

An additional important distinction is between "normal" or adaptive fear and anxiety and the pathological conditions. While the character of behavioral, cognitive and autonomic responses might not differ between the normal and the "pathological conditions," such as anxiety disorders, the context in which they occur, their intensity and the degree of their effects on overall behavior, defines the extent of the pathology. This phenomenological overlap leads at times to erroneous assumptions of identical neurophysiology underlying both normal and pathological anxiety. For example, animal models of "normal" fear demonstrated a central role of the amygdaloid complex in expression of fear and anxiety (see below). Interestingly, when researchers modeled abnormal fear, or pathological anxiety additional or "extra-amygdaloid" neuroanatomical regions have been often implicated as well as central gray or lateral hypothalamus. These regions exchange projections with the amygdaloid complex and it is possible that abnormal input or abnormal modulation of amygdaloid activity, originating from these regions, are involved in abnormal or pathological fear. However, it is also possible that abnormal function of these regions independent of the amygdaloid complex activity is involved in generation of pathological anxiety. A better understanding of pathological anxiety and valid animal models are needed in order to empirically test competing hypotheses.

The existing overlap between depression and pathological anxiety further complicates the picture and contributes to overlapping definitions. The role of stress in generation of depression has been described extensively (Brown and Harris, 1978; Brown et al., 1994; Frank et al., 1994), and often prominent anxiety symptoms are found in depressed patients. However, depression without anxiety symptoms can be also associated with stress, while abnormal anxiety can occur without obvious link to stress exposure – as exemplified by specific phobias. These observations suggest that more than a single mechanism might be involved both in generation of pathological anxiety and in the effects of stress on fear and mood regulation. A particularly interesting example of stress/anxiety interaction is the field of post-traumatic stress. Post-traumatic stress disorder (PTSD) is per definition a stress disorder (induced by trauma) and the clinical picture includes multiple manifestations of pathological anxiety (among other symptoms). Furthermore, laboratory findings in PTSD also suggest changes in hormonal systems involved in the stress response. Traditionally, stress studies have been primarily focused on the investigation of particular neuroendocrine axes, while studies of fear and anxiety focused on cognitive and psychophysiologic responses in humans and on behavioral responses in animals. A combination of these diverse modalities and both clinical and basic science approaches have contributed to substantial growth of knowledge in these fields lately, and even more integrative research will be needed in the future to further elucidate complex interaction between these systems.

II. Anxiety disorders and stressful events: is there a connection? – The role of life events

Since the early idea of stress and the description of the general adaptational syndrome by Selye, the association of psychiatric disorders with stress has persisted. The first effort to measure life events, and to relate them to onset, severity, and/or course of illness was by Holmes and Rahe (1967). There has been a substantial amount of research on the effects of social factors, "stress," and, specifically, life events on the occurrence of depression (Brown and Harris, 1978; Finlay-Jones, 1981; O'Connell and Mayo, 1988; Brown and Harris, 1989; Paykel, 1994). The preponderance of the data supports a role for life events in the occurrence of depression. There has been less research on the role of life events in people with anxiety disorders, although some research supports a role in anxiety disorders other than PTSD. Finlay-Jones and Brown (1981) reported that life events associated with danger were associated with anxiety symptomatology, while those associated with loss were associated with depression; subsequent research has provided some support for this finding (Miller and Ingham, 1983; Torgersen, 1985: Deadman et al., 1989), although not all studies agree (Eaton and Ritter, 1988). This group (Brown et al., 1993; Brown and Harris, 1993) has proposed a model, based on their data, in which childhood abuse and neglect lead to increased risk for both depression and anxiety, while recent stressful life events lead to depression.

Other investigators have also addressed this question in anxiety. Raskin et al. (1982) found that, in comparison to patients with generalized anxiety disorder, panic disorder patients reported more "grossly disturbed childhood environment." Faravelli (1985) reported that panic disorder patients showed a large increase in significant life events in the month before panic onset. Roy-Byrne and Uhde (1988) found that the occurrence of either loss or separation in panic disorder patients raised the likelihood of the subsequent occurrence of a depressive episode in these panic disorder patients, but did not influence the severity of the pre-existing panic disorder.

III. Stress response systems: stress and neuroendocrine regulation

Stress activates secretion of a number of hormones, but the main "stress" hormone system is the HPA axis. Stress-sensitive systems in multiple areas of the brain are activated by stress and integrated at the hypothalamus resulting in a hormonal cascade leading to cortisol secretion by the adrenal. Neurons in the paraventricular nucleus (PVN) of the hypothalamus synthesize corticotropin-releasing factor (CRF), the lead hormone in this cascade, which is secreted into the hypophyseal portal system via the median eminence (Swanson et al., 1983). In man, CRF is believed to be the primary secretagogue driving pituitary corticotropes to release ACTH. The majority of stressors that activate CRF secretion in humans are physiological/hormonal, such as exercise, insulin-induced hypoglycemia and infection, while evidence that psychological stressors activate CRF secretion in humans is inconsistent between individuals (Hellhammer and Wade, 1993). One exception is novelty, which many studies suggest activate the HPA axis in humans (Mason, 1968). A recent meta-analysis of 208 studies of psychosocial stress and cortisol release suggested that motivated performance in the context of uncontrollable challenges with social evaluative threat may also provide a potent activator of the HPA axis in humans (Dickerson and Kemeny, 2004).

CRF release stimulates the secretion of ACTH from pituitary corticotropes, which, in turn, stimulates the secretion of cortisol from the adrenal cortex in a feed forward cascade. Glucocorticoid secretion is tightly controlled and limited by negative feedback effects of glucocorticoids at both pituitary and brain sites. The ability of glucocorticoids to inhibit their own release has formed the basis for challenge studies such as the dexamethasone suppression test. Negative feedback of glucocorticoids on CRF and ACTH secretion can occur very rapidly, within 5–10 min, and provides real-time inhibition to limit the stress response and prevent over-secretion of glucocorticoids (Keller-Wood and Dallman, 1985). In addition to stress as an activator of CRF/ACTH/cortisol secretion, intrinsic rhythmic elements in the suprachiasmatic nucleus (SCN) drive secretion from the HPA axis in a circadian pattern. In man, the circadian rhythm in ACTH and cortisol secretion is entrained to the wake/sleep cycle (Krieger, 1979). The ACTH secretion is pulsatile in nature with the trough of secretion occurring in the evening and early night and the peak of secretion occurring just before awakening. Active secretion continues through the morning and early afternoon.

IV. Links between HPA and noradrenergic function in animal studies

In addition to stimulating the HPA axis, stressors activate both central and peripheral noradrenergic systems. These two systems may be linked via

CRF. Basic science studies on the biology of stress have suggested a central role for CRF in the coordination and integration of the stress response throughout the brain (Dunn and Berridge, 1990; Butler and Nemeroff, 1990). While the role of CRF from the PVN of the hypothalamus as the releasing factor for ACTH is well established (Dunn and Berridge, 1990), a wealth of information from studies in rodents suggests that CRF outside the PVN appears to mediate the general stress response, including the behavioral responses of decreased sleep, anorexia, inhibition of sexual receptivity, decreased locomotion, increased startle reflex and decreased exploratory behavior in novel environments (Dunn and Berridge, 1990; Butler and Nemeroff, 1990). Additionally, a number of behavioral effects of stress have been demonstrated to be reversed by central administration of alpha-helical CRF (9–41), a CRF antagonist (Koob et al., 1993). Following the initial isolation and sequencing of CRF by Vale and colleagues (129), Brown et al. (1982) demonstrated that injection of CRF activated the sympathetic nervous system (SNS) (130). While it was long known that stress activated the locus coeruleus (LC), studies demonstrating direct effects of CRF on LC neurons have been critical for understanding the role of CRF in mediating arousal (Valentino, 1989). Subsequent studies (Aston Jones et al., 1991) have demonstrated that the main afferent fibers to the LC contain CRF. Recent studies have demonstrated that interactions between the LC and the amygdala, a critical part of the anxiety/fear circuit, utilize CRF (Bouret et al., 2003). The amygdala also communicates directly and indirectly, via the bed nucleus of the stria terminalis, with the PVN (Sved et al., 2002). Central administration of CRF activates the amygdala in primates (Sved et al., 2002). Stimulation of the amygdala activates the HPA axis in animals and humans (Rubin et al., 1966; Van de Kar and Blair, 1999). In humans, the degree of left amygdala activation strongly correlates with stress-induced cortisol secretion (Drevets et al., 2002). Recent studies have also demonstrated CRF co-localized with serotonin in the dorsal raphe and the existence of CRF-containing axons from the dorsal raphe nucleus to the central nucleus of the amygdala (Commons et al., 2003).

These anatomical data illuminate pathways through which the LC can produce arousal/anxiety behavior following CRF administration. Noradrenergic stimulation also results in secretion of CRF into the hypophyseal portal blood (Plotsky et al., 1989), providing the link between LC and PVN. Studies in conscious rodents find that stimulation of the LC always results in HPA activation, as well as activation of SNS. Consequently, LC noradrenergic outflow can result in activation of the HPA axis (Plotsky, 1987). Finally, studies examining the effects of the HPA axis on LC have demonstrated that cortisol may inhibit LC activity; tyrosine hydroxylase mRNA levels in LC increase following adrenalectomy and SNS activation decreases following increases in circulating plasma glucocorticoid levels (Mc Ewen, 1995).

Taken together these studies demonstrate multiple interactions between limbic circuits involved in anxiety, including both the HPA axis and the SNS. A model of the interactions between these systems in normal individuals is shown in panel A of Fig. 1. Our previous studies support a correlation between tonic LC activity and HPA axis response to a stressor in normal and purely anxious subjects (Young et al., 2005). However, this relationship was disrupted in subjects with depression. One can conceptualize two different but related CRF systems, the PVN/HPA axis system and the limbic/LC system (see Fig. 1), with amygdala involvement with both systems. Fuller understanding of the interactions between these two systems in humans might help in efforts to better "dissect" the role of the HPA axis in depression and anxiety, and in efforts to understand the well-known clinical overlap between anxiety and depression. In depression, there is clear evidence of excessive HPA axis activation, consistent with CRF hyper-secretion from the PVN, and accounting for abnormal results in metyrapone and perhaps also in DST studies (panel B). Secondary, or concomitant, activation of the extra-PVN, amygdala/LC system has been proposed as an explanation of some of the behavioral symptoms present in depression (Butler and Nemeroff, 1990). Consistent with this, the changes in amygdala activation observed in depression are tonic rather than reactive to emotionally salient stimuli (Drevets, 2003) as seen

A

HPA Axis Interconnection with Autonomic Nervous System and
Other Critical Limbic Areas

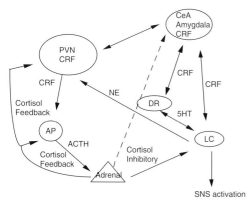

PVN=paraventricular Nucleus; AP=Anterior Pituitary; DR=dorsal raphe
LC= locus Coeruleus; SNS- sympathetic Nervous System
Cortisol Feedback inhibitory (solid line) and stimulatory (dotted line)

B

HPA Axis Interconnection with Autonomic Nervous System and
Other Critical Limbic Areas : Depression Model

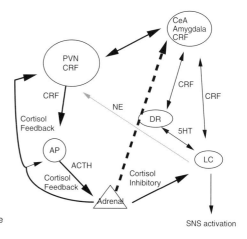

C

HPA Axis Interconnection with Autonomic Nervous System and
Other Critical Limbic Areas ; Anxiety Disorders

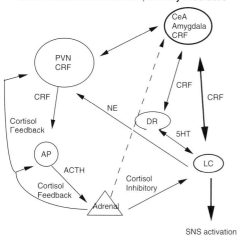

D

HPA Axis Interconnection with Autonomic Nervous System and
Other Critical Limbic Areas : Comorbid State

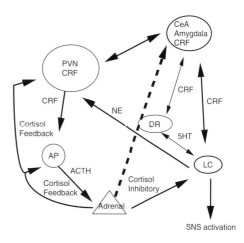

Fig. 1. Cortisol inhibitory feedback is solid line and stimulatory effect is dotted line. Thicker lines indicate greater activation of the pathway/feedback and thinner lines indicate lesser activation.

in anxiety disorders. Hormonal input from the PVN/HPA system can drive amygdala and may account for the increased tonic activation seen in major depression.

Animal studies suggest that central CRF administration is also an excellent model of anxiety symptoms (Butler and Nemeroff, 1990), and other evidence suggests that these symptoms involve

activity in limbic/LC circuits (Sullivan et al., 1999). Central CRF administration can intensify anxiety symptoms in anxiogenic situations and these behavioral effects are blocked by benzodiazepines and alcohol (Britton et al., 1985). These animal studies suggest a common substrate for some mood and anxiety disorder symptoms, and raise the possibility that comorbidity between depression and anxiety may be related to interconnections between these two related systems. Differences between the two types of disorders could relate to the origin of excessive activity within these circuits, whether it is from the PVN/HPA component (panel B) or the limbic/LC component (panel C), or the relative amount of activity in each one.

Genetic studies suggest a common neurobiological/genetic substrate for mood and anxiety disorders upon which stressful life experiences, which activate these central CRF systems, are superimposed (Brown and Harris, 1978; Finlay-Jones, 1981; Faravelli, 1985; O'Connell & Mayo, 1988; Checkley, 1992; Brown et al., 1994; Frank et al., 1994; Paykel, 1994). The emerging model would predict that HPA axis activation and central noradrenergic activation should be linked in most circumstances, as seen in animal models, but pathological states in mood or anxiety states could disrupt these linkages. Evidence from examining anxiety states, including reactions to exposure to phobic objects and to precipitated panic attacks, suggest that these clearly psychologically stressful events are not necessarily accompanied by activation of the HPA axis, despite profound changes in heart rate and blood pressure, physiological measures that are dependent upon activation of the SNS, and possibly upon catecholamine secretion (Nesse et al., 1985; Cameron et al., 1987). Activation of limbic/LC circuits does not apparently always lead to HPA activation. In our own work a psychosocial stress model that usually triggers an HPA response did not produce excessive activation in pure depressed or pure anxiety patients, but subjects with both types of disorders did show excessive ACTH release, without clear evidence of excessive cardiovascular responses (Young et al., 2004a, b, 2005). So the systems have some degree of functional autonomy, despite their clear interconnections. We hypothesize that the increased cortisol secretion seen in major depression is able to dampen the LC system to prevent over activation of the noradrenergic systems. When depression and anxiety occur together, particularly when anxiety is primary, cortisol is no longer able to dampen the LC and both "sides" of the system are activated, amplifying the HPA responses seen to stress. This is consistent with the findings that central noradrenergic input from LC can increase CRH secretion under stress. Our epidemiological data from subjects with both depression and PTSD also suggest increased urinary and salivary cortisol in the comorbid group, while subjects with a history of depression only show smaller increases (Young and Breslau, 2004a, b; Young et al., 2004a, b). This is also consistent with the model, suggesting that increased LC activity of anxiety may "amplify" quiescent period activity in the HPA axis. Accumulating data clearly suggest an important influence of comorbid anxiety on HPA axis regulation in depression.

In addition to feed forward, activational elements, glucocorticoids also have inhibitory feedback connections to the PVN, higher centers (particularly the hippocampus) and the LC (Mc Ewen, 1995). However, glucocorticoids are simultaneously stimulatory on the amygdalar CRF system, providing a mechanism by which stress and increased glucocorticoid secretion observed in major depression may drive the limbic/anxiety circuits and ultimately contribute additional PVN CRF "drive." This could play a role in leading to insensitivity to glucocorticoid feedback (Makino et al., 1994). Our studies examining response to a social stressor, the TSST (Young et al., 2004a, b), and growth hormone response to clonidine (Cameron et al., 2004) found a correlation between overall hormonal responses (AUC) to these two challenges in normal subjects, suggesting basal noradrenergic tone is a contributor to HPA axis stress reactivity in normal subjects (Young et al., 2005). A similar relationship was found in individuals with an anxiety disorder without depression, but was lost in those with major depression (Young et al., 2005). Ongoing study of how the HPA axis and the LC-noradrenergic systems interact with each other, in patients with various mood and anxiety disorders, and patients with mood-anxiety comorbidity, should help us better understand both normal and psychopathological functioning in these systems.

IV.A. The HPA axis in panic disorder and other anxiety disorders

The HPA axis has been examined in a number of anxiety disorders, with panic disorder and PTSD being the most extensively studied. Despite the profound psychological changes and intense distress induced by either spontaneous or laboratory-induced panic attack, there is little evidence that panic attacks per se are accompanied by cortisol secretion (Cameron et al., 1987; Abelson and Cameron, 1994; Abelson et al., 1996). There is evidence that cortisol levels are higher at the time of a real-life panic attack than they are 24 h later (Bandelow et al., 2000a), but these data cannot determine whether the cortisol elevation was a consequence of panic or perhaps a response to an environmental factor that triggered panic.

Feedback inhibition also appears relatively normal in panic – the overall incidence of cortisol non-suppression with dexamethasone challenge is 17% in panic disorder (13 studies), while the incidence for major depression is 50% (Abelson and Cameron, 1994). When non-suppression is seen it is more associated with depressive or agoraphobic symptoms, or long-term disability, than panic per se (Coryell and Noyes, 1988; Coryell et al., 1989; Westberg et al., 1991), suggesting that factors other than the anxiety disorder itself may be at play.

Studies of HPA basal activity or central drive in panic have produced mixed results. Abelson et al. (1996) studied 20 panic disorder patients and 12 normal controls with q15 min blood sampling for 24 h. Panic patients demonstrated an increase in 24 h mean cortisol levels at the trend level of significance, which was most pronounced in the 2 AM to 6 AM time block, during the time of circadian activation. The increase in cortisol secretion was seen almost entirely in the 6 patients who sought treatment, rather than the remaining 14 patients who responded to an advertisement for subjects with panic disorder. These two groups of patients did not differ in severity as rated by number of panic attacks/week nor did they differ on Ham-A anxiety ratings, but they did differ on level of functional impairment. HPA activity was associated with sleep disruption in this study, and panic patients may have slept less well than controls. These data thus suggest that the abnormalities seen may not be linked to panic pathophysiology itself, but to other factors that shape functional impairment or non-specific reactivity to the study context. Bandelow et al. (1997, 2000a)

also reported nocturnal elevations of cortisol in panic, but also observed that nocturnal awakenings could account for this finding (Bandelow et al., 1997). Urine sampling for 24 h cortisol secretion has shown normal levels in uncomplicated panic (Kathol et al., 1988; Uhde et al., 1988). When elevations have been noted using this methodology, they were linked to depression or agoraphobia, and not panic (Kathol et al., 1988; Lopez et al., 1990). Elevated "baseline" levels of cortisol have also been seen prior to challenge studies (Roy-Byrne et al., 1986a, b), but pre-challenge, baseline levels have been normal with more prolonged accommodation periods (Holsboer et al., 1987; Curtis et al., 1997), again suggesting other factors at work, perhaps hyper-reactivity to experimental context in panic patients. One anomaly in this emerging pattern is a study by Goldstein et al. (1987), which showed elevated cortisol across the afternoon in panic patients, though excessive reactivity to some aspect of the sampling paradigm cannot be ruled out entirely even in this study.

Studies with CRF challenge in panic disorder patients have demonstrated a decreased integrated ACTH response in comparison to controls in some studies (Roy-Byrne et al., 1986; Holsboer et al., 1987), but a normal response in others (Rapaport et al., 1989; Brambilla et al., 1992; Abelson et al., 1994a, b; Curtis et al., 1997). Similar to CRF challenge studies in depressed patients, "baseline" plasma cortisol was increased in patients with panic disorder who demonstrated blunted CRF responses in some of these studies (Roy-Byrne et al., 1986), so the blunted ACTH response may be attributable to an initial hyper-reactivity to context, leading to feedback restraint of CRH-stimulated ACTH. However, one study with a long accommodation period and normal pre-CRH cortisol did show blunted ACTH responses (Von Bardeleben and Holsboer, 1988). Furthermore, a study of central HPA drive using a combined dexamethasone-CRH paradigm also found an abnormal cortisol response in panic patients (Schreiber et al., 1996). However, the presence of confounding gender effects (Schreiber) and incomplete characterization of the patients studied (Von Bardeleben) make full interpretation of these findings difficult.

Hyper-reactivity of the HPA axis in panic has been seen in three other studies using pharmacological paradigms, involving yohimbine (Gurguis et al., 1997), fenfluramine (Targum and Marshall, 1989) and pentagastrin (Abelson et al., 1994a, b). In the pentagastrin study, however, the data suggested that the HPA abnormality in panic patients involved increased reactivity upon first visit to the laboratory setting and not a hypersensitivity to the pharmacological agent itself. The designs used in the yohimbine and fenfluramine studies cannot rule out this explanation in those paradigms as well. In a recent review (Abelson et al., 2007) of all of our own studies of HPA axis activity in panic patients, we concluded that the bulk of the data on HPA function in panic supports the hypothesis that the abnormalities reported in this system in these patients may well be due to acute hyper-reactivity to specific environmental stimuli, such as novelty cues. Studies specifically designed to test this hypothesis are needed.

IV.B. The HPA axis in PTSD

In general, the effects of repeated stress are of sensitization of the HPA axis to stressors, leading to a greater hormonal stress response over time, and increase in baseline cortisol (Young and Akil, 1985; Dallman, 1993). Thus, it was expected that PTSD patients would show HPA axis abnormalities similar to that seen in depressed patients or chronically stressed animals. However, that has clearly not been the case. An initial report by Mason et al. (1986) found that urinary free cortisol (UFC) excretion was lower in the PTSD than major depression patients, but that UFC excretion was similar between PTSD and paranoid schizophrenic patients. All patients were on psychotropic medications. After this initial report, Halbreich et al. (1988) noted that in patients with major depression, endogenous subtype, those who also met criteria for PTSD demonstrated significantly lower baseline and post-dexamethasone plasma cortisol than depressed patients without PTSD. Furthermore, none of the PTSD patients were dexamethasone non-suppressors. Both alcohol abuse and chronic pain were present in this PTSD

sample. Pittman and Orr (1990) found increased UFC excretion in outpatient PTSD veterans compared to combat controls without PTSD. In contrast Yehuda et al. (1991) reported decreased UFC excretion in PTSD veterans compared to normal controls. A clear difference between these two studies is the use of normal controls versus combat controls. No study of veterans has compared UFC excretion in PTSD patients, combat controls and normal controls not exposed to combat. The one study on response to CRF challenge in veterans with PTSD showed normal to increased plasma cortisol at the time of the CRH challenge (Smith et al., 1989). More recent studies have examined response to low-dose dexamethasone in PTSD veterans, veterans exposed to combat without PTSD and normal controls and found enhanced feedback to dexamethasone in veterans who met criteria for PTSD. The presence of comorbid major depression did not alter the picture. Combat exposed control veterans demonstrated normal supression compared to non-combat normal subjects (Yehuda et al., 1995a). The above study suggest that the abnormalities seen in PTSD are not a consequence of exposure to trauma per se, but either a reflection of the underlying disorder of PTSD or a pre-existing condition that may pre-dispose to PTSD. Although Yehuda has linked the "enhanced suppression" of cortisol to low-dose dexamethasone in PTSD veterans to increased numbers of glucocorticoid receptors in lymphocytes, increased numbers of glucocorticoid receptors were also seen in combat-exposed veterans without PTSD. Furthermore, lower plasma cortisol would produce decreased occupancy of glucocorticoid receptors and thus increased numbers of glucocorticoid receptors would be seen in receptor-binding assays. The most significant issue of the above studies remains the nature of the sample, veterans who are all males who also demonstrate substantial comorbid Axis I and Axis II disorders, particularly substance abuse, and may be very different endocrinologically and psychiatrically than women exposed to trauma.

In order to address some of the concerns about the ability to extrapolate from male veterans with significant past substance abuse to civilian populations including women, Yehuda et al.

(1995b) has examined UFC excretion in holocaust survivors. In this case three groups of subjects have been studied, Holocaust subjects with PTSD, Holocaust subjects without PTSD and age-matched normal subjects without exposure to the Holocaust. Again, these studies have shown reduced UFC excretion in subjects with PTSD compared to normal subjects and subjects exposed to trauma without PTSD. While these studies are promising with regards to replicating the work with veterans and extending it to individuals of both genders and reducing the problems with comorbid substance abuse, there are still problems with this population. The elderly nature of the population, the extremely long time since exposure to the trauma, the young age of the subjects at the time of trauma (often children and adolescents) which may result in different adaptations than would be observed in an adult, and the problems in classifying individuals who met criteria for PTSD in the past but who are now well, complicate interpretation of these data.

A number of other investigators have sought to address this problem by using non-veteran subjects recruited from clinics and the community. The majority of these studies have examined women with childhood sexual abuse. While some studies have demonstrated increased UFC (Lemieux and Coe, 1995), others have demonstrated similar plasma cortisol (Rasmusson et al., 2001) and still others have found lower cortisol and enhanced suppression to dexamethasone (Stein et al., 1997). The issue of comorbid depression in the PTSD population has not been well addressed, with most studies including comorbid individuals and few analyzing the data by the absence or presence of comorbid depression. The exception are the studies (Heim et al., 2000, 2001) focusing upon childhood abuse and MDD which examined multiple HPA axis challenges in the same subjects. These studies found an effect of early abuse (with comorbid PTSD in 11/13 subjects) and MDD on stress reactivity, with both an increased ACTH and cortisol response to the stressor compared to either controls or depressed patients without childhood abuse. In these same subjects, they found a blunted response to CRH challenge in MDD patients with or without childhood abuse, but an increased

response to CRH in abused without MDD. The abused subjects also showed a blunted cortisol response to ACTH 1–24. Thus, childhood abuse produced "enhanced pituitary response with counter-regulatory adrenal adaptations," a change compatible with low or normal basal cortisol. Furthermore, they found lower cortisol and enhanced feedback to low-dose dexamethasone in the same subjects (Newport et al., 2004). The latter study was also analyzed by the presence or absence of PTSD as the primary diagnosis and came to the same conclusion of enhanced feedback.

Epidemiological based samples in adults have focused upon natural disasters and have generally examined exposure with high and low PTSD symptoms (Davidson and Baum, 1986; Fukuda et al., 2000; Anisman et al., 2001), but without diagnostic information. The exception was the study of Maes et al. (1998) which looked at PTSD subjects recruited from community disasters and demonstrated increased UFC in PTSD. In general, community based studies suggest that exposure to disaster increases plasma (Fukuda et al., 2000) and saliva cortisol (Anisman et al., 2001) and UFC (Davidson and Baum, 1986). Studies examining motor vehicle accident survivors (Hawk et al., 2000) found no difference in cortisol between those with and without PTSD 6 months later. Studies of male and female adults with exposure to mixed traumas have found either no effect of PTSD on basal cortisol (Kellner et al., 2002, 2003; Young and Breslau, 2004a, b; Young et al., 2004a, b) or elevated basal cortisol (Lindley et al., 2004). The studies of adult trauma survivors generally include individuals with childhood exposure also, so determining differential effects of timing of trauma is not possible from existing studies. Our own analysis of recent trauma exposure in two community samples (Young and Breslau, 2004a; Young et al., 2004a, b) found increased cortisol in those with past year exposure to trauma, but no effect of greater than 1 year past trauma exposure and no effect of childhood abuse on basal saliva cortisol or UFC. To add further complexity, the majority of studies of trauma and PTSD included subjects with comorbid depression. In most studies, the majority of subjects had both PTSD and major depression. The PTSD studies generally report comorbid depression in their subjects; but studies of depression often fail to measure and report trauma histories. As a result, documented depression confounds much of the PTSD HPA axis literature and undocumented trauma and abuse may confound some of the depression HPA axis literature.

In addition to the issue of exposure to trauma, the persistence of the neuroendocrine changes following recovery from PTSD is unclear. In an early study Yehuda et al. (1995c) reported that holocaust survivors with past but not current PTSD demonstrated normal UFC, while later studies of offspring of holocaust survivors (Yehuda et al., 2002) suggested that changes in cortisol may persist beyond the duration of the symptoms, and thus may be a marker of underlying vulnerability to PTSD. The large analysis by Boscarino (1996) of cortisol data from several thousand combat veterans showed a very small effect of PTSD on basal cortisol, but a very clear effect of combat exposure with increasing levels of severity of combat exposure associated with increasingly lower cortisol.

Our recent studies of cortisol in PTSD from two epidemiological samples (Young and Breslau, 2004a, b; Young et al., 2004b) demonstrate normal UFC and saliva cortisol in the first representative community-based, biological study of individuals with "pure" and comorbid PTSD. However, both studies demonstrate a clear effect of lifetime comorbid major depression on cortisol. The comorbid MDD and PTSD group demonstrated higher urinary and salivary cortisol in the evening, compared to PTSD alone or MDD alone. In the Breslau study (Young and Breslau, 2004a) 2/3 of the subjects had adult trauma exposure only, while in the Women's Employment Study (Young et al., 2004a, b) cohort 50% of trauma-exposed individuals were exposed as adults only. These data suggest that PTSD secondary to adult trauma exposures combined with depression seems to be associated with increased activity in circadian activational elements of the HPA axis, evident during the usual nadir of the system's circadian rhythm. These epidemiological data suggest the hypothesis that increased HPA axis activation will be observed in the late afternoon/evening in patients who have both MDD and an adult onset anxiety disorder.

Studies examining the response to low-dose dexamethasone in PTSD veterans, combat exposed veterans without PTSD and normal controls found enhanced feedback to dexamethasone in veterans who met criteria for PTSD, whether or not comorbid MDD was present; combat exposed controls demonstrated normal suppression compared to non-combat normal subjects (Yehuda, 2002). Similar enhanced suppression to dexamethasone has been found by Yehuda (2002) in Holocaust survivors with PTSD and their offspring. This enhanced suppression to dexamethasone has been found in studies looking at either plasma or saliva cortisol (Yehuda, 2002). In Yehuda's (2002) studies, as well as the report by Stein et al. (1997) the enhanced suppression is also paired with low baseline cortisol. Lindley et al. (2004) examined a treatment seeking non-veteran PTSD population and found elevated basal cortisol and normal suppression to dexamethsone in subjects with PTSD. Kellner et al. (2002, 2003) examined response to low-dose dexamethasone in anxiety disorders and found a normal response in both PTSD and patients with panic disorders. Newport et al. (2004) examined dexamethasone suppression to low-dose dexamethasone in women with childhood abuse and depression and found enhanced suppression. They also analyzed their data with PTSD as the primary diagnosis and again found enhanced suppression to low-dose dexamethasone with childhood abuse. Few other groups have utilized the low-dose dexamethasone suppression test, to determine whether this is a replicable finding across PTSD samples and whether it is present in other anxiety disorders.

Activational challenges have generally used CRF challenge. An initial CRF challenge study in combat-related PTSD showed normal to increased plasma cortisol at time of challenge (Smith et al., 1989) and a decreased ACTH response in subjects with high baseline cortisol. A study by Rasmusson et al. (2001) examined women with history of childhood abuse who met criteria for PTSD. Women with PTSD showed enhanced cortisol response to CRF and to exogenous ACTH infusion, as well as a trend toward higher 24h UFC. Interestingly, all the women with PTSD had either past or current major depression, so comorbidity was the rule. In the study by Heim et al. (2001) examining response to CRF in women with major depression, with and without childhood abuse 14 of 15 childhood abuse MDD patients also met criteria for PTSD. This group, with comorbid MDD and PTSD, demonstrated a blunted ACTH response to CRF challenge, similar to that observed in MDD alone without PTSD. The abused groups also demonstrated lower baseline and stimulated cortisol in response to CRF challenge as well as following ACTH infusion. These same groups of women showed a significantly greater HPA response to the TSST, despite smaller responses to CRF (Heim et al., 2000). These studies certainly suggest that the picture is complicated in PTSD with comorbid depression; the findings of some studies look like depression while others look quite different, e.g., showing a smaller response to ACTH infusion when MDD patients show an augmented response. Age of trauma exposure may be one reason for contradictory data. Finally, one study by Yehuda (2002) of combat veterans with PTSD demonstrated greater rebound ACTH secretion compared to controls following administration of metyrapone in the morning, indicating that increased CRF drive is present in the morning and normally restrained by cortisol feedback. The other two studies examining metyrapone challenge in PTSD found a normal ACTH response to afternoon or overnight metyrapone as well as a normal response to cortisol infusion in PTSD subjects and panic disorder subjects (Kanter et al., 2001; Kellner et al., 2004a, b). These data lead us to hypothesize a normal response to metyrapone in patients with MDD+ PTSD with early trauma, or MDD with early onset SAD. In summary, these data suggest that there may be no simple relationship between diagnostic categories and specific HPA axis abnormalities. Timing of trauma or onset of anxiety disorder may differentially affect the HPA axis profile.

V. The SNS in anxiety disorders

Growth hormone response to clonidine has been widely used as a marker of central noradrenergic activity in psychiatric disorders. Clonidine is a selective alpha2-adrenergic receptor partial agonist which reduces central noradrenergic outflow by activation of presynaptic receptors at noradrenergic re-uptake sites. It releases GH through direct agonistic activity at postsynaptic sites. Blunted GH responses to clonidine are thought to reflect subsensitivity (downregulation) of these postsynaptic alpha2-adrenergic receptors (Siever et al., 1982). Downregulation presumably occurs in response to chronic, excessive noradrenergic outflow from the LC, which is thought to play a role in anxiety states (Uhde et al., 1992). Blunted GH response to clonidine is probably the best replicated biological abnormality thus far reported in patients with panic disorder (Charney and Heninger, 1986; Uhde et al., 1986; Nutt, 1989; Lee et al., 1990; Abelson et al., 1992; Schittecatte et al., 1992). This strongly suggests a noradrenergic dysregulation in these patients. However, the finding of blunted GH responses to GHRH, and possibly to other challenges, in panic has raised the possibility of a more generalized dysregulation of the hypothalamic–pituitary–somatrophic (HPS) axis in this disorder, which may not reflect a specific noradrenergic defect (Uhde et al., 1992). On the other hand, normal GH responses to apomorphine (Pichot et al., 1995), exercise and pyridostigmine and normal 24 h growth hormone secretion (Abelson and Curtis, 1996) are consistent with a specific GH-clonidine abnormality in panic. These findings, and basic science evidence (Devesa et al., 1991) continue to support the assumption that the GH response to clonidine provides a probe of the central, noradrenergic system and that the blunted response seen in panic patients reflects a specific noradrenergic abnormality. Our own data examining patients with social phobia, major depression or comorbid social phobia and major depression found blunted GH response to clonidine in those with an anxiety diagnosis but not in pure depression (Cameron et al., 2004). We found no relationship between anxiety symptoms and GH response but those who met criteria for anxiety diagnosis, with or without comorbid depression, demonstrated the abnormalities. We conclude that anxiety disorders themselves, and not just symptoms and not just panic disorder, may be associated with adrenergic dysregulation.

In addition to the blunted GH response to clonidine, there is other evidence of both central and peripheral noradrenergic abnormalities in these disorders. Catecholamine and MHPG levels appear to be either normal or mildly elevated in panic patients. However, there is no evidence that panic attacks are accompanied by peripheral secretion of catecholamines. Challenges with other pharmacological agents in addition to clonidine, primarily yohimbine, have been used, but non-specific anxiogenic effects have made results of pharmacological challenges difficult to interpret. This problem is also true for the beta-adrenergic agonist isoproterenol (as well as for a number of non-adrenergic challenge agents such as caffeine and carbon dioxide). However, a recent report of a challenge involving a sinble breath of 35% carbon dioxide has demonstrated activation of the HPA axis in normal subjects (Argyropoulos et al., 2002). Such a brief challenge would be useful in examining response to a physiological stressor in anxiety disorders. Results of adrenergic receptor binding on blood cells have been inconsistent, although in some groups, decreased platelet alpha2-adrenergic receptor binding has been consistently observed (Cameron et al., 1984, 1990). In addition, most data suggest decreases in beta-adrenergic receptor function of lymphocytes. Studies with depression and comorbid panic disorder demonstrated that unlike panic disorder patients, patients with major depression without panic disorder demonstrated an increase in platelet alpha2-adrenergic binding, while patients with comorbid depression plus panic disorder demonstrated a decrease in platelet alpha2-adrenergic binding that was even greater than the pure panic disorder patients, suggesting that the effects of noradrenergic hyperactivity predominate in the comorbid state (Grunhaus et al., 1990). Generalized anxiety disorder and PTSD appear similar to panic disorder, although less well studied, while another anxiety disorder (obsessive-compulsive disorder) does not show evidence of noradrenergic hyperactivity (Hollander et al., 1991). In general, measures under truly basal conditions are typically normal, but panic patients may be more reactive to provocative stimuli than are normal subjects. This is true not only for anxiogenic stimuli but also for physiologic stimuli

such as change in posture. There is evidence from some studies of differences between panic patients and control subjects in the hemodynamic and catecholamine responses to standing, suggesting an abnormality in systemic autonomic reactivity as reflected in control of vascular tone (Cameron et al., 1984).

V.A. Peripheral SNS function in PTSD

While increased adrenergic activation would appear to underlie the pathophysiology of several anxiety disorders, alterations in peripheral catecholamine systems has been difficult to demonstrate for any anxiety disorder, (Abelson and Cameron, 1994). The situation is similar in PTSD. Electrophysiological studies examining baseline heart rate, blood pressure and galvanic skin response have demonstrated no consistent alterations in veterans with PTSD. In contrast, challenge studies have demonstrated exaggerated autonomic reactivity in response to various combat-related stimuli but not in response to non-trauma-related stimuli. Pitman et al.'s (1987) studies have used "scripts" of the trauma situation, lending support for the idea that the memories of the trauma can activate these physiological parameters. These studies provide indirect evidence of a hyperactive SNS in PTSD patients, but suggest the abnormality may be present episodically, dependent upon environmental cues, specifically cues associated with the trauma (Pitman et al., 1987; Hamner et al., 1994; Murburg et al., 1994). Given that these autonomic measures are regulated in opposing directions by SNS and parasympathetic nervous system input, and that increase in a parameter can result from an increase in adrenegic tone or a decrease in vagal tone, more direct measures of SNS activity are necessary. SNS activity can be evaluated by measurement of plasma epinepherine (Epi) and norepinepherine (NE) or quantitation of urinary excretion. Three published studies have examined 24h urinary catecholamines in PTSD veterans, with conflicting results. The study by Kosten et al. (1987) and Yehuda et al. (1992) demonstrated an increase in urinary Epi and NE, in comparison to other psychiatric disorder controls (Kosten et al., 1987) or normal controls (Yehuda et al., 1992), while Pittman and Orr (1990) found no difference in PTSD veterans compared to combat controls. Our studies on a community-based sample examined the effects of PTSD and trauma exposure on 24 h urinary Epi and NE. We found that individuals with PTSD demonstrated significantly increased Epi, NE and dopamine excretion compared to either trauma exposed or non-exposed groups (Young and Breslau, 2004a, b).

Again the issue of the nature of the control group is critical, and it may be that exposure to trauma itself alters urinary Epi and NE. This possibility is supported by the studies of Davidson and Baum (1986), demonstrating increases in urinary NE in a civilian population exposed to the Three Mile Island explosion compared to individuals 80 miles away, as well as the studies of Rahe et al. (1990) demonstrating increased urinary catecholamine excretion in the American hostages shortly after they were freed from Iran. In our study of 24 h urine catecholamine secretion in the Detroit Area Study, the trauma-exposed group showed significantly lower urinary dopamine and Epi than the non-exposed group. We interpreted this as indicating that the unexposed group is a mixture of those both susceptible and not susceptible to PTSD. Those individuals with higher catecholamines pre-trauma exposure are at risk for PTSD and develop PTSD when exposed, so those who are exposed and do not develop PTSD show lower catecholamines compared to the mixed population of unexposed subjects. However, we cannot exclude that trauma has direct effects on long-term catecholamine levels. Overall the data suggest that exposure to trauma, per se, does not have any long-lasting effects on urinary catecholamines but that PTSD individuals show increased catecholamine secretion (Young and Breslau, 2004a).

In contrast to the data from urinary studies, plasma studies have found no elevation in baseline plasma catecholamines in PTSD patients compared to normal controls (McFall et al. 1990; Blanchard et al., 1991; Southwick et al., 1993; Hamner et al., 1994; Murburg et al., 1994), but increased catecholamine response to trauma-related stimuli were reported by Murburg et al. (1994). Interestingly, the PTSD patients in the Murburg study did not

have an exaggerated plasma catecholamine response to a stressful, but trauma-unrelated stimulus. These findings again suggest that the increases in catecholamines secretion may be occurring sporadically throughout the 24 h, perhaps in response to specific trauma-related cues. Supporting this possibility, Yehuda et al. (1992) found that urinary NE secretion correlated with the severity of intrusive symptoms. In summary, there are discrepancies between conclusions from urinary measures and plasma measures that could result from episodic activation of catecholamine secretion, which are captured by urinary measures but missed by plasma measures.

VI. Summary and conclusions

Anxiety disorders involve over-activation of certain areas of the brain (like amygdala) and underactivation of other areas (like anterior cingulate and dorsolateral prefrontal cortex) which have been shown to be critical circuits involved in HPA axis regulation in animal and human studies. Basic science studies provide ample evidence for the involvement of CRF in both activation of the HPA axis and in the generation of anxiety symptoms. Many of the regions involved in activation of fear and anxiety circuits utilize CRF as a neurotransmitter. Despite the involvement of these brain regions in the pathology of anxiety that should lead to over-activity to the HPA axis in anxiety disorders, this has not been found in most studies of anxiety disorders. The overall evidence suggests an over-reactivity to some contextual cues, like novelty, in panic disorder. Response to social stressors in social anxiety disorders has by and large been shown to be normal (Levin et al., 1993; Martel et al., 1999; Gerra et al., 2000; Young et al., 2004a, b). PTSD subjects do not appear to show elevated cortisol and in some cases they are found to show low cortisol. Thus, there is clear consistency in finding overall normal HPA axis functioning in anxiety disorders. In contrast, measures of SNS activation and evaluation of central noradrenergic tone using clonidine as a challenge have shown excessive activation of these systems in anxiety disorders. Our own studies suggest the importance of anxiety diagnosis as opposed to just symptoms in producing the latter findings. Interestingly, we found a clear relationship between tonic noradrenergic tone and ACTH response to a stressor in normal subjects, which persisted in anxiety subjects. This confusing picture of activation of the central noradrenergic systems without clear evidence of HPA axis pathology in anxiety disorders has led some to conclude that anxiety patients may be hypoactive in regards to the HPA axis. While this may be true, an alternative is that the prolonged activation of the HPA axis as observed in major depression is beyond what is expected under "chronic stress," and thus the problem may be in our comparison group and expecting the HPA axis in anxiety disorders to look like that in depression. Studies of individuals under chronic stress do not by and large demonstrate an over-active HPA axis (Ranjit et al., 2005), so patients with anxiety disorders may have a fundamentally normal HPA axis that is capable of responding and is regulated properly by inhibitory circuits of the brain, while major depression is clearly abnormal in this regard. The developmental context in which anxiety disorders occur may exert important modulation on HPA axis development and maturation, leading toward "homeostasis" in this system and by and large normal functioning despite excessive sensitivity to these anxiety cues. Among the various animals models of anxiety, the over-expression of glucocorticoid receptors is particularly intriguing, since this produces no overt pathology in the HPA axis except perhaps enhanced suppression to glucocorticoids (a pattern found in PTSD and following early life stress in humans and animals) but animals shows greater sensitivity to anxiogenic situations. Thus, while the HPA axis is "normal" in anxiety disorders, there may still be involvement of individual elements of this system, e.g., glucocorticoid receptors or CRFbp in producing both anxiety symptoms and normal regulation of the HPA axis.

References

Abelson, J.L. and Cameron, O.G. (1994) Adrenergic dysfunction in anxiety disorders. In: Cameron, O.G. (Ed.), Adrenergic Dysfunction and Psychobiology. AP Press, Washington, DC.

Abelson, J.L. and Curtis, G.C. (1996) Hypothalamic-pituitary-adrenal axis activity in panic disorder: 24-hour secretion of corticotropin and cortisol. Arch. Gen. Psychiatry, 53: 323–331.

Abelson, J.L., Glitz, D., Cameron, O.G., Lee, M.A., Bronzo, M. and Curtis, G.C. (1992) Endocrine, cardiovascular, and behavioral responses to clonidine in patients with panic disorder. Biol. Psychiatry, 32: 18–25.

Abelson, J.L., Khan, S., Liberzon, I. and Young, E.A. (2007) HPA axis activity in patients with panic disorder: review and synthesis of four studies. Depress. Anxiety, 24: 66–76.

Abelson, J.L., Nesse, R.M. and Vinik, A. (1994a) Pentagastrin infusions in panic disorder II. Neuroendocrinol. Biol. Psychiatry, 36: 73–78.

Abelson, J.L., Nesse, R.M. and Vinik, A. (1994b) Pentagastrin infusions in patients with panic disorder II. Neuroendocrinol.Biol. Psychiatry, 36: 84–96.

Abelson, J.L., Weg, J.G., Nesse, R.M. and Curtis, G.C. (1996) Neuroendocrine responses to laboratory panic: cognitive intervention in the doxapram model. Psychoneuroendocrinology, 21: 375–390.

Anisman, H., Griffiths, J., Matheson, K., Ravindran, A.V. and Merali, Z. (2001) Posttraumatic stress symptoms and salivary cortisol levels. Am. J. Psychiatry, 158: 1509–1511.

Argyropoulos, S.V., Bailey, J.E., Hood, S.D., Kendrick, A.H., Rich, A.S., Laszlo, G., Nash, J.R., Lightman, S.L. and Nutt, D.J. (2002) Inhalation of 35% CO_2 results in activation of the HPA axis in healthy volunteers. Psychoneuroendocrinology, 27: 715–729.

Aston Jones, G., Shipley, M.T. and Chouvet, G. (1991) Afferent regulation of locus coeruleus neurons: anatomy, physiology and pharmacology. Prog. Brain Res., 88: 47–75.

Bandelow, B., Sengos, G., Wedekind, D., Huether, G., Pilz, J., Broocks, A., Hajak, G. and Ruther, E. (1997) Urinary excretion of cortisol, norepinephrine, testosterone, and melatonin in panic disorder. Pharmacopsychiatry, 30: 113–117.

Bandelow, B., Wedekind, D., Pauls, J., Broocks, A., Hajak, G. and Ruther, E. (2000a) Salivary cortisol in panic attacks. Am. J. Psychiatry, 157: 454–456.

Bandelow, B., Wedekind, D., Sandvoss, V., Broocks, A., Hajak, G., Pauls, J., Peter, H. and Ruther, E. (2000b) Diurnal variation of cortisol in panic disorder. Psychiatry Res., 95: 245–250.

Blanchard, E.B., Kolb, L.C. and Prins, A. (1991) Changes in plasma norepinepherine in combat related stimuli among Vietnam veterans with PTSD. J. Nerv. Mental Dis., 179: 371–373.

Boscarino, J.A. (1996) Posttraumatic stress disorder, exposure to combat, and lower plasma cortisol among Vietnam veterans: findings and clinical implications. J. Consult. Clin. Psychol., 64: 191–201.

Bouret, S., Duvel, A., Onat, S. and Sara, S. (2003) Phasic activation of locus ceruleus neurons by central nucleus of the amygdala. J. Neurosci., 23: 3491–3497.

Brambilla, F., Bellodi, L., Perna, G., Battaglia, M., Sciuto, G., Diaferia, G., Petraglia, F., Panerai, A. and Sacerdote, P. (1992) Psychoimmunoendocrine aspects of panic disorder. Neuropsychobiology, 26: 12–22.

Britton, K.T., Morgan, J., Rivier, J., Vale, W. and Koob, G.F. (1985) Chlordiazepoxide attenuates response suppression induced by corticotropin-releasing factor in the conflict test. Psychopharmacology (Berl.), 86: 170–174.

Brown, G.W. and Harris, T. (1978) Social Origins of Depression: A Study of Psychiatric Disorder in Women. The Free Press, New York.

Brown, G.W. and Harris, T.O. (1989) Depression. In: Brown, G.W. and Harris, T.O. (Eds.), Life Events and Illness. The Guilford Press, New York, pp. 49–93.

Brown, G.W. and Harris, T.O. (1993) Aetiology of anxiety and depressive disorders in an inner-city population. 1. Early adversity. Psychol. Med., 23: 143–154.

Brown, G.W., Harris, T.O. and Eales, M.J. (1993) Aetiology of anxiety and depressive disorders in an inner-city population. 2. Comorbidity and adversity. Psychol. Med., 23: 155–165.

Brown, G.W., Harris, T.O. and Hepworth, C. (1994) Life events and endogenous depression. A puzzle reexamined. Arch. Gen. Psychiatry, 51: 525–534.

Brown, M.R., Fisher, L.A., Spiess, J., Rivier, C., Rivier, J. and Vale, W. (1982) Corticotropin releasing factor: actions on sympathetic nervous system and metabolism. Endocrinology, 111: 928–931.

Butler, P.D. and Nemeroff, C.B. (1990) Corticotropin releasing factor as a possible cause of comorbidity in anxiety and depressive disorders. In: Maser, J.D. and Cloninger, C.R. (Eds.), Comorbidity of Mood and Anxiety Disorders. American Psychiatric Press, Washington, DC.

Cameron, O.G., Abelson, J. and Young, E.A. (2004) Anxious and depressive disorders and their comorbidity: effect on central nervous system noradrenergic function. Biol. Psychiatry, 56: 875–883.

Cameron, O.G., Lee, M.A., Curtis, G.C. and McCann, D.S. (1987) Endocrine and physiological changes during "spontaneous" panic attacks. Psychoneuroendocrinology, 12: 321–331.

Cameron, O.G., Smith, C.B., Hollingsworth, P.J., Nesse, R.M. and Curtis, G.C. (1984) Platelet alpha2-adrenergic receptor binding and plasma catecholamines. Arch. Gen. Psychiatry, 41: 1144–1148.

Cameron, O.G., Smith, C.B., Lee, M.A., Hollingsworth, P.J., Hill, E.M. and Curtis, G.C. (1990) Adrenergic status in anxiety disorders: platelet alpha2-adrenergic receptor binding, blood pressure, and plasma catecholamines in panic and generalized anxiety disorder patients and normal subjects. Biol. Psychiatry, 28: 3–20.

Checkley, S. (1992) Neuroendocrine mechanisms and the precipitation of depression by life events. British. J. Psychiatry, 160: 7–17.

Charney, D.S. and Heninger, G.R. (1986) Abnormal regulation of noradrenergic function in panic disorder. Arch. Gen. Psychiatry, 43: 1042–1054.

Commons, K.G., Connalle, K.R. and Valentino, R.J. (2003) A neurochemically distinct dorsal raphe-limbic circuit with a potential role in affective disorders. Neuropsychopharmacology, 28: 206–215.

Coryell, W. and Noyes, R. (1988) HPA axis disturbance and treatment outcome in panic disorder. Biol. Psychiatry, 24: 762–766.

Coryell, W., Noyes, R. and Schlechte, J. (1989) The significance of HPA axis disturbance in panic disorder. Biol. Psychiatry, 25: 989–1002.

Curtis, G.C., Abelson, J.L. and Gold, P.W. (1997) Adrenocorticotropic hormone and cortisol responses to corticotropin-releasing hormone: changes in panic disorder and effects of alprazolam treatment. Biol. Psychiatry, 41: 76–85.

Dallman, M.F. (1993) Stress update: adaptation of the hypothalamaic-pituitary-adrenal axis to chronic stress. Trends Endocrinol. Metab., 4: 62–69.

Davidson, L.M. and Baum, A. (1986) Chronic stress and posttraumatic disorders. J. Consult. Clin. Psychol., 54: 303–308.

Deadman, J.M., Dewey, M.J., Owens, R.G., Leinster, S.J. and Slade, P.D. (1989) Danger and loss in breast cancer. Psychol. Med., 19: 677–681.

Devesa, J., Diaz, M.J., Tresguerres, J.A.F., Arce, V. and Lima, L. (1991) Evidence that alpha2-adrenergic pathways play a major role in growth hormone (GH) neuroregulation: alpha2-adrenergic agonism counteracts the inhibitory effect of muscarinic cholinergic receptor blockade on the GH response to GH-releasing hormone, while alpha2-adrenergic blockade diminishes the potentiating effect of increased cholinergic tone on such stimulation in normal men. J. Clin. Endocrinol. Metab., 73: 252–256.

Dickerson, S.S. and Kemeny, M.E. (2004) Acute stressors and cortisol responses: a theoretical integration and synthesis of laboratory research. Psychol. Bull., 130: 355–391.

Drevets, W. (2003) Neuroimaging abnormalities in the amygdala in mood disorders. Ann. N. Y. Acad. Sci., 985: 420–444.

Drevets, W.C., Price, J.L., Bardgett, M.E., Reich, T., Todd, R.D. and Raichle, M.E. (2002) Glucose metabolism in the amygdala in depression: relationship to diagnostic subtype and plasma cortisol levels. Pharmacol. Biochem. Behav., 71: 431–447.

Dunn, A.J. and Berridge, C.W. (1990) Physiological and behavioral responses to corticotropin-releasing factor administration: is CRF a mediator of anxiety or stress response. Brain Res. Rev., 15: 71–100.

Eaton, W.W. and Ritter, C. (1988) Distinguishing anxiety and depression with field survey data. Psychol. Med., 18: 155–166.

Faravelli, C. (1985) Life events preceding the onset of anxiety disorder. J. Affective Disord., 9: 103–105.

Finlay-Jones, R. (1981) Showing that life events are a cause of depression – a review. Aust. N.Z.J. Psychiatry, 15: 229–238.

Finlay-Jones, R. and Brown, G.W. (1981) Types of stressful life event and the onset of anxiety and depressive disorders. Psychol. Med., 11: 803–815.

Frank, E., Anderson, B., Reynolds, C.F., Ritenour, A. and Kupfer, D.J. (1994) Life events and the research diagnostic criteria endogenous subtype. A confirmation of the distinction using the Bedford College methods. Arch. Gen. Psychiatry, 51: 519–524.

Fukuda, S., Morimota, K., Kanae, M. and Maruyama, S. (2000) Effect of the Hanshin-Awaji earthquake on posttraumatic stress, lifestyle changes, and cortisol levels of victims. Arch. Environ. Health, 55: 121–125.

Gerra, G., Zaimovic, A., Zambelli, U., Timpano, M., Reali, N. and Bernasconi, S. (2000) Neuroendocrine responses to psychological stress in adolescents with anxiety disorder. Neuropsychobiology, 42: 82–92.

Goldstein, S., Halbreich, U., Asnis, G., Endicott, J. and Alvir, J. (1987) The hypothalamic-pituitary-adrenal system in panic disorder. Am. J. Psychiatry, 144: 1320–1323.

Grunhaus, L.J., Cameron, O.G., Pande, A.C., Haskett, R.F., Hollingsworth, P.J. and Smith, C.B. (1990) Comorbidity of panic disorder and major depressive disorder: effects on platelet alpha2-adrenergic receptors. Acta. Psychiatr. Scand., 81: 216–219.

Gurguis, G.N., Vitton, B.J. and Uhde, T.W. (1997) Behavioral, sympathetic and adrenocortical responses to yohimbine in panic disorder patients and normal controls. Psychiatry Res., 71: 27–39.

Halbreich, U., Olympia, J., Glogowski, J., Carson, S., Axelrod, S. and Yeh, C.M. (1988) The importance of past psychological trauma and pathophysiological process as determinants of current biologic abnormalities. Arch. Gen. Psychiatry, 45: 293–294.

Hamner, M.B., Diamond, B.I. and Hitri, A. (1994) Plasma norepinephrine and MHPG responses to exercise stress in PTSD. In: Murburg, M.M. (Ed.), Cathecolamine Function in Posttraumic Stress Disorder: Emerging Concepts. American Psychiatric Press, Washington, DC, pp. 221–232.

Hawk, L.W., Dougall, A.L., Ursano, R.J. and Baum, A. (2000) Urinary catecholamines and cortisol in recent-onset posttraumatic stress disorder after motor vehicle accidents. Psychosom. Med., 62: 423–434.

Heim, C., Newport, D.J., Bonsall, R., Miller, A.H. and Nemeroff, C.B. (2001) Altered pituitary-adrenal axis responses to provocative challenge tests in adult survivors of childhood abuse. Am. J. Psychiatry, 158: 575–581.

Heim, C., Newport, D.J., Heit, S., Graham, Y.P., Wilcox, M., Bonsall, R., Miller, A.H. and Nemeroff, C.B. (2000) Pituitary-adrenal and autonomic responses to stress in women after sexual and physical abuse in childhood. JAMA, 284: 592–597.

Hellhammer, D.H. and Wade, S. (1993) Endocrine correlates of stress vunerability. Psychother. Psychosomat., 60: 8–17.

Hollander, E., DeCaria, C., Nitescu, A., Cooper, T., Stover, B., Gully, R., Klein, D.F. and Liebowitz, M.R. (1991) Noradrenergic function in obsessive-compulsive disorder: behavioral and neuroendocrine responses to clonidine and comparison to healthy controls. Psychiatry Res., 37: 161–177.

Holmes, T.H. and Rahe, R.H. (1967) The social readjustment rating scale. J. Psychosom. Res., 11: 213–218.

Holsboer, F., von Bardeleben, U., Buller, R., Heuser, I. and Steiger, A. (1987) Stimulation response to corticotropin-releasing hormone (CRH) in patients with depression, alcoholism and panic disorder. Horm. Metab. Res., 16: 80–88.

Kanter, E.D., Wilkinson, C.W., Radant, A.D., Petrie, E.C., Dobie, D.J., McFall, M.E., Peskind, E.R. and Raskind, M.A. (2001) Glucocorticoid feedback sensitivity and adrenocortical responsiveness in posttraumatic stress disorder. Biol. Psychiatry, 50: 238–245.

Kathol, R.G., Anton, R., Noyes, R., Lopez, A.L. and Reich, J.H. (1988) Relationship of urinary free cortisol levels in patients with panic disorder to symptoms of depression and agoraphobia. Psychiatry Res., 24: 211–221.

Keller-Wood, M.E. and Dallman, M.F. (1985) Corticosteroid inhibition of ACTH secretion. Endocr. Rev., 5: 1–24.

Kellner, M., Baker, D.G., Yassouridis, A., Bettinger, S., Otte, C., Naber, D. and Wiedemann, K. (2002) Mineralocorticoid receptor function in patients with posttraumatic stress disorder. Am. J. Psychiatry, 159: 1938–1940.

Kellner, M., Otte, C., Yassouridis, A., Schick, M., Jahn, H. and Wiedemann, K. (2004a) Overnight metyrapone and combined dexamethasone/metyrapone tests in post-traumatic stress disorder: preliminary findings. Eur. Neuropsychopharmacol., 14: 337–339.

Kellner, M., Schick, M., Yassouridis, A., Struttmann, T., Wiedemann, K. and Alm, B. (2004b) Metyrapone tests in patients with panic disorder. Biol. Psychiatry, 56: 898–900.

Kellner, M., Yassouridis, A., Hubner, R., Baker, D.G. and Wiedemann, K. (2003) Endocrine and cardiovascular responses to corticotropin-releasing hormone in patients with posttraumatic stress disorder: a role for atrial natriuretic peptide? Neuropsychobiology, 47: 102–108.

Koob, G.F., Heinrichs, S.C., Pich, E.M., Menzaghi, F., Baldwin, H., Miczek, K. and Britton, K.T. (1993) The role of corticotropin-releasing factor in behavioral responses to stress. Ciba Found. Symp., 172: 277–289.

Kosten, T.R., Mason, J.W. and Giller, E.L. (1987) Sustained urinary norepinephine and epinephrine elevation in post-traumatic stress disorder. Psychoneuroendocrinology, 12: 13–20.

Krieger, D. (1979) Rhythms in CRH, ACTH and corticosteroids. Endocrine Rev., 1: 1–23.

Lee, M.A., Cameron, O.G., Gurguis, G.N.M., Glitz, D., Smith, C.B., Hariharan, M., Abelson, J.L. and Curtis, G.C. (1990) Alpha 2-adrenoreceptor status in obsessive-compulsive disorder. Biol. Psychiatry, 27: 1083–1093.

Lemieux, A.M. and Coe, C.L. (1995) Abuse-related posttraumatic stress disorder: evidence for chronic neuroendocrine activation in women. Psychosom. Med., 57: 105–115.

Levin, A.P., Saoud, J.B., Strauman, T., Gorman, J.M., Fyer, A.J. and Crawford, R. (1993) Responses of generalized and discrete social phobics during public speaking. J. Anxiety Disord., 7: 207–221.

Lindley, S.E., Carlson, E.B. and Benoit, M. (2004) Basal and dexamethasone suppressed salivary cortisol concentrations in a community sample of patients with posttraumatic stress disorder. Biol. Psychiatry, 55: 940–945.

Lopez, A.L., Kathol, R.G. and Noyes, R. (1990) Reduction in urinary free cortisol during benzodiazepine treatment of panic disorder. Psychoneuroendocrinology, 15: 23–28.

Maes, M., Lin, A., Bonaccorso, S., van Hunsel, F., Van Gastel, A., Delmeire, L., Biondi, M., Bosmans, E., Kenis, G. and Scharpe, S. (1998) Increased 24-hour urinary cortisol excretion in patients with posttraumatic stress disorder and patients with major depression, but not in patients with fibromyalgia. Acta Psychiatr. Scand., 98: 328–335.

Makino, S., Gold, P.W. and Schulkin, J. (1994) Corticosterone effects on corticotropin-releasing hormone mRNA in the central nucleus of the amygdala and the parvocellular region of the paraventricular nucleus of the hypothalamus. Brain Res., 640: 105–112.

Martel, F.L., Hayward, C., Lyons, D.M., Sanborn, K., Varady, S. and Schatzberg, A.F. (1999) Salivary cortisol levels in socially phobic adolescent girls. Depress. Anxiety, 10: 25–27.

Mason, J.W. (1968) A review of psychoendocrine research on the pituitary adrenal cortical system. Psychosom. Med., 30: 576–607.

Mason, J.W., Giller, E.L., Kosten, T.R., Ostroff, R.B. and Podd, L. (1986) Urinary free-cortisol levels in posttraumatic stress disorder patients. J. Nerv. Ment. Dis., 174: 145–149.

Mc Ewen, B.S. (1995) Adrenal steroid action on brain: dissecting the fine line between protection and damage. In: Friedman, M.J. Charney, D.S. and Deutch, A.Y. (Eds.), Neurobiological and Clinical Consequences of Stress: From Normal Adaptation to PTSD. Lippincott-Raven, Philadelphia, PA.

McFall, M., Murburg, M. and Ko, G. (1990) Autonomic response to stress in Vietnam combat veterans with post-traumatic stress disorder. Biol. Psychiatry, 27: 1165–1175.

Miller, P. and Ingham, J.G. (1983) Dimensions of experience. Psychol. Med., 13: 417–429.

Murburg, M.M., McFall, M.E. and Veith, R.C. (1994) Basal sympathoadrenal function in patients with PTSD and depression. In: Murburg, M.M. (Ed.), Catecholamine Function in Posttraumatic Stress Disorder: Emerging Concepts. American Psychiatric Press, Inc., Washington, DC, pp. 175–188.

Nesse, R.M., Curtis, G.C., Thyer, B.A., McCann, D.S., Huber-Smith, M.J. and Knopf, R.F. (1985) Endocrine and cardiovasular responses during phobic anxiety. Psychosom. Med., 47: 320–332.

Newport, D.J., Heim, C., Bonsall, R., Miller, A.H. and Nemeroff, C.B. (2004) Pituitary-adrenal responses to standard and low-dose dexamethasone suppression tests in adult survivors of child abuse. Biol. Psychiatry, 55: 10–20.

Nutt, D.J. (1989) Altered central alpha2-adrenoreceptor sensitivity in panic disorder. Arch. Gen. Psychiatry, 46: 165–169.

O'Connell, R.A. and Mayo, J.A. (1988) The role of social factors in affective disorders: a review. Hosp. Community Psychiatry, 39: 842.

Paykel, E.S. (1994) Life events, social support and depression. Acta Psychiatr. Scand., 377: 50–58.

Pichot, W., Hansenne, M., Gonzalez-Mareno, A. and Ansseau, M. (1995) Growth hormone response to aopmorphine in panic disorder: comparison with major depression and normal controls. Eur. Arch. Psychiatry Neurosci., 245: 306–308.

Pittman, R.G. and Orr, S.P. (1990) Twenty-four hour urinary cortisol and catecholamine excretion in combat-related posttraumatic stress disorder. Biol. Psychiatry, 27: 245–247.

Pitman, R.K., Orr, S.P., Forgue, D.F., deJong, J.B. and Claiborn, J.M. (1987) Psychophysiologic assessment of posttraumatic stress disorder imagery in Vietnam combat veterans. Arch. Gen. Psychiatry, 44: 970–975.

Plotsky, P.M. (1987) Facilitation of immunoreactive corticotropin-releasing factor secretion into the hypophyseal-portal circulation after activation of catechoaminergic pathways or central norepinepherine injection. Endocrinology, 121: 924–930.

Plotsky, P.M., Cunningham, E.T. and Widmaier, E.P. (1989) Catecholaminergic modulation of corticotropin-releasing factor and adrenocorticotropin secretion. Endocr. Rev., 10: 437–458.

Rahe, R.H., Karson, S. and Howard, N.S. (1990) Psychological and physiological assessment on American hostages freed from captivity in Iran. Psychosom. Med., 52: 1–16.

Ranjit, N., Young, E.A. and Kaplan, G.A. (2005) Material hardship alters the diurnal rhythms of salivary cortisol. Int. J. Epidemiol., 34: 1138–1143.

Rapaport, M.H., Risch, S.C., Golshan, S. and Gillin, J.C. (1989) Neuroendocrine effects of ovine corticotropin-releasing hormone in panic disorder patients. Biol. Psychiatry, 26: 344–348.

Raskin, M., Peeke, H.V., Dickman, W. and Pinsker, H. (1982) Anxiety and generalized anxiety disorders. Developmental antecedents and precipitants. Arch. Gen. Psychiatry, 39: 687–689.

Rasmusson, A.M., Lipschitz, D.S., Wang, S., Hu, S., Vojvoda, D., Bremner, J.D., Southwick, S.M. and Charney, D.S. (2001) Increased pituitary and adrenal reactivity in premenopausal women with posttraumatic stress disorder. Biol. Psychiatry, 50: 965–977.

Roy-Byrne, P.P. and Uhde, T.W. (1988) Exogenous factors in panic disorder: Clinical research implications. J. Clin. Psychiatry, 49: 56–61.

Roy-Byrne, P., Uhde, T.W., Post, R.M., Galucci, W., Chrosous, G.P. and Gold, P.W. (1986a) The corticotropin-releasing-hormone stimulation test in patients with panic disorder. Am. J. Psychiatry, 148: 896–899.

Roy-Byrne, P.P., Uhde, T.W., Post, R.M., Gallucci, W., Chrousos, G.P. and Gold, P.W. (1986b) The corticotropin-releasing hormone stimulation test in patients with panic disorder. Am. J. Psychiatry, 143: 896–899.

Rubin, R.T., Mandell, A.J. and Crandall, P.H. (1966) Corticosteroid responses to limbic stimulation in man: localization of stimulus sites. Science, 153: 767–768.

Schittecatte, M., Ansseau, M., Charles, G., Machowski, R., Papart, P., Pichot, W. and Wilmotte, J. (1992) Growth hormone response to clonidine in male patients with panic disorder untreated by antidepressants. Psychol. Med., 22: 1059–1062.

Schreiber, W., Lauer, C.J., Krumrey, K., Holsboer, F. and Krieg, J.C. (1996) Dysregulation of the hypothalamic-pituitary-adrenocortical system in panic disorder. Neuropsychopharmacology, 15: 7–15.

Siever, L.J., Uhde, T.W., Silberman, E.K., Jimerson, D.C., Aloi, J.A., Post, R.M. and Murphy, D.L. (1982) Growth hormone response to clonidine as a probe of noradrenergic receptor responsiveness in affective disorder patients and controls. Psychiatry Res., 6: 171–183.

Smith, M.A., Davidson, J., Ritchie, J.C., Kudler, H., Lipper, S., Chappell, P. and Nemeroff, C.B. (1989) The corticotropin-releasing hormone test in patients with posttraumatic stress disorder. Biol. Psychiatry, 26: 349–355.

Southwick, S.M., Krystal, J.H., Morgan, C.A., Johnson, D., Nagy, L.M., Nicolaou, A., Heninger, G.R. and Charney, D.S. (1993) Abnormal noradrenergic function in posttraumatic stress disorder. Arch. Gen. Psychiatry, 50: 266–274.

Stein, M.B., Yehuda, R., Koverola, C. and Hanna, C. (1997) Enhanced dexamethasone suppression of plasma cortisol in adult women traumatized by childhood sexual abuse. Biol. Psychiatry, 42: 680–686.

Sullivan, G.M., Coplan, J.D., Kent, J.M. and Gorman, J.M. (1999) The noradrenergic system in pathological anxiety: a focus on panic with relevance to generalized anxiety and phobias. Biol. Psychiatry, 46: 1205–1218.

Sved, A.F., Cano, G., Passerin, A.M. and Rabin, B.S. (2002) The locus coeruleus, Barrington's nucleus, and neural circuits of stress. Physiol. Behav., 77: 737–742.

Swanson, L.W., Sawchenko, P.E., Rivier, J. and Vale, W.W. (1983) Organization of ovine corticotropin-releasing factor immunoreactive cells and fibers in the rat brain. An immunohistochemical study. Neuroendocrinology, 36: 165–186.

Targum, S.D. and Marshall, L.E. (1989) Fenfluramine provocation of anxiety in patients with panic disorder. Psychiatry Res., 28: 295–306.

Torgersen, S. (1985) Developmental differentiation of anxiety and affective neuroses. Acta Psychiatr. Scand., 71: 304–310.

Uhde, T., Joffe, R.T., Jimerson, D.C. and Post, R.M. (1988) Normal urinary free cortisol and plasma MHPG in panic disorder: clinical and theoretical implications. Biol. Psychiatry, 23: 575–585.

Uhde, T.W., Vittone, B.J., Siever, L.J., Kaye, W.H. and Post, R.M. (1986) Blunted growth hormone response to clonidine in panic disorder patients. Biol. Psychiatry, 21: 1081–1085.

Uhde, T.W., Tancer, M.E., Rubinow, D.R., Roscow, D.B., Boulenger, J.P., Vittone, B., Gurguis, G., Geraci, M., Black, B. and Post, R.M. (1992) Evidence for hypothalamic-growth hormone dysfunction in panic disorder: profile of growth hormone (GH) responses to clonidine, yohimbine, caffeine, glucose, GRF and TRH in panic disorder patients versus healthy volunteers. Neuropsychopharmacology, 6: 101–118.

Valentino, R.J. (1989) Corticotropin-releasing factor: putative neurotransmitter in the noradrenergic nucleus locus coeruleus. Psychopharmacol. Bull., 25: 306–311.

Van de Kar, L.D. and Blair, M.L. (1999) Forebrain pathways mediating stress-induced hormone secretion. Front. Neuroendocrinol., 20: 1–48.

Von Bardeleben, U. and Holsboer, F. (1988) Human corticotropin releasing hormone: clinical studies in patients with affective disorders, alcoholism, panic disorder and in normal controls. Prog. Neuropsychopharmacol. Biol. Psychiatry, 12: S165–S187.

Westberg, P., Modigh, K., Lisjo, P. and Eriksson, E. (1991) Higher postdexamethasone serum cortisol levels in agoraphobic than in nonagoraphobic panic disorder patients. Biol. Psychiatry, 30: 247–256.

Yehuda, R. (2002) Current status of cortisol findings in post-traumatic stress disorder. Psychiatr. Clin. North Am., 25: 341–368.

Yehuda, R., Boisoneau, D., Lowy, M.T. and Giller, E.L. Jr. (1995a) Dose-response changes in plasma cortisol and lymphocyte glucocorticoid receptors following dexamethasone administration in combat veterans with and without posttraumatic stress disorder. Arch. Gen. Psychiatry, 52: 583–593.

Yehuda, R., Giller, E.L., Southwick, S.M., Lowy, M.T. and Mason, J.W. (1991) Hypothalamic-pituitary-adrenal dysfunction in posttraumatic stress disorder. Biol. Psychiatry, 30: 1031–1048.

Yehuda, R., Halligan, S.L., Grossman, R., Golier, J.A. and Wong, C. (2002) The cortisol and glucocorticoid receptor response to low dose dexamethasone administration in aging combat veterans and holocaust survivors with and without posttraumatic stress disorder. Biol. Psychiatry, 52: 393–403.

Yehuda, R., Kahana, B., Binder-Brynes, K., Southwick, S.M., Mason, J.W. and Giller, E.L. (1995b) Low urinary cortisol excretion in Holocaust survivors with posttraumatic stress disorder. Am. J. Psychiatry, 152: 982–986.

Yehuda, R., Kahana, B., Schmeidler, J., Southwick, S.M., Wilson, S. and Giller, E.L. (1995c) Impact of cumulative lifetime trauma and recent stress on current posttraumatic stress disorder symptoms in holocaust survivors. Am. J. Psychiatry, 152: 1815–1818.

Yehuda, R., Southwick, S., Giller, E.L., Ma, X. and Mason, J.W. (1992) Urinary catecholamine excretion and severity of PTSD symptoms in Vietnam combat veterans. J. Nerv. Ment. Dis., 180: 321–325.

Young, E.A., Abelson, J.L. and Cameron, O.G. (2004a) Effect of comorbid anxiety disorders on the HPA axis response to a social stressor in major depression. Biol. Psychiatry, 56: 113–120.

Young, E.A., Abelson, J.L. and Cameron, O.G. (2005) Interaction of brain noradrenergic system and the hypothalamic-pituitary-adrenal (HPA) axis in man. Psychoneuroendocrinology, 30: 807–814.

Young, E.A. and Akil, H. (1985) CRF stimulation of ACTH/β endorphin release: effect of acute and chronic stress. Endocrinology, 117: 23–30.

Young, E.A. and Breslau, N. (2004a) Cortisol and catecholamines in posttraumatic stress disorder: a community study. Arch. Gen. Psychiatry, 61: 394–401.

Young, E.A. and Breslau, N. (2004b) Saliva cortisol in a community sample with posttraumatic stress disorder. Biol. Psychiatry, 56: 205–209.

Young, E.A., Tolman, R., Witkowski, K. and Kaplan, G. (2004b) Salivary cortisol and PTSD in a low income community sample of women. Biol. Psychiatry, 55: 621–626.

The genetics of human anxiety disorders

Eduard Maron[1,*], John M. Hettema[2] and Jakov Shlik[3]

[1]*Department of Psychiatry, University of Tartu, Tartu, Estonia; and Research Department of Mental Health,
The North Estonian Regional Hospital, Psychiatry Clinic, Tallinn, Estonia*
[2]*Virginia Institute for Psychiatric and Behavioral Genetics, Department of Psychiatry, Virginia Commonwealth
University, Richmond, VA, USA*
[3]*Department of Psychiatry, University of Ottawa, Royal Ottawa Health Care Group, Ottawa, Ont., Canada*

Abstract: The anxiety disorders (ADs) are recognized as the most prevalent group of psychiatric diseases affecting up to about 25% of general population in lifetime. After demonstrating the heritable nature of anxiety traits, the genetic research has taken an important place in the investigation of the ethiopathogenesis of ADs. Despite the increasing efforts to determine vulnerability genes for ADs, current knowledge on genetic substrates of anxiety is still in early stage. In this chapter we review the data accumulated from epidemiological and molecular genetic studies conducted in ADs in order to better understand the role of genetic factors in the origins of pathological anxiety. We also address the novel approaches, including functional genetics, potentially advancing the investigations in this field.

Keywords: anxiety disorder; genetic; polymorphism; family; twin; association; linkage study; pharmacogenetic

I. Introduction

The evolutionary necessity and apparent heritability of anxiety traits have stimulated a growing interest in the genetic substrate and transmission of anxiety disorders (ADs). Research on the genetics of ADs has spanned from familial aggregation and twin studies to linkage and association studies aiming to identify genes and their variants affecting the disease susceptibility. In this chapter, we present the available human data on the genetic factors that contribute to the risk of specific ADs and highlight the trends and perspectives in this rapidly expanding area.

II. Genetic epidemiology

In this section, we review the available data on genetic epidemiology of ADs. The "chain of evidence" for genetic investigations of a medical condition begins with family studies, which compare rates of illness in relatives of those who have the condition (case probands) with rates in relatives of healthy controls. Higher rates in the former group of relatives suggest familial aggregation, i.e., there is an association of illness in probands with illness in their relatives. This association may be parameterized by the odds ratio (OR), calculated from 2×2 contingency tables constructed from these rates of affected versus unaffected relatives of cases versus control probands. The next step relies on either adoption studies (which are not available for ADs) or twin studies to differentiate genetic from non-genetic sources of familial aggregation. Twin studies compare resemblance for a condition between members of a twin pair, using the fact that identical (monozygotic, MZ) twins share 100% of their genes while non-identical (dizygotic, DZ) twins share only 50% of their genes on average. One commonly used measure of twin resemblance

*Corresponding author.
E-mail: Eduard.Maron@kliinikum.ee

R.J. Blanchard, D.C. Blanchard, G. Griebel and D. Nutt (Eds.)
Handbook of Anxiety and Fear, Vol. 17
ISBN 978-0-444-53065-3

475

DOI: 10.1016/S1569-7339(07)00022-7

is the probandwise concordance, i.e., the proportion of co-twins of affected index twins who are also affected. With larger twin samples, one may also estimate the proportion of individual differences for the condition due to the effects of genetic factors (heritability). For conditions with substantial heritability, gene finding (linkage or association) studies are possible to identify which genes contribute to risk.

One of us (JMH) published a meta-analysis to summarize findings across family and twin studies of ADs (Hettema et al., 2001a), the results of which will be referred to herein. We restricted our selection of studies to include only those that: (1) used operationalized diagnostic criteria, (2) systematically ascertained, and (3) directly interviewed the majority of subjects, (4) performed the diagnostic assessment of relatives blind to proband affection status, and (5) for the family studies, included a control group. This allowed us to (1) evaluate consistency across studies, and (2) combine data from multiple primary studies to provide more reliable, precise, and less-biased aggregate estimates of familial risk and heritability.

Given their high rates of comorbidity, we will also examine the data, where available, relating to shared genetic risk across anxiety and related disorders. This type of data has broad implications for the design of molecular genetic investigations of these conditions.

II.A. Family studies

II.A.1. Panic disorder

Five family studies of panic disorder (PD) met the inclusion criteria for the meta-analysis as described above. Some, but not all of these, included agoraphobia (AG) or other psychiatric disorders in their assessment. In the first, Noyes et al. examined rates of DSM-III psychiatric illness in 241 relatives of 40 PD patient probands, 40 patients with AG, and 113 relatives of 20 non-anxious controls (Noyes, et al., 1986). They found higher rates of PD in relatives of PD probands (17.3%) and AG probands (8.3%) compared to relatives of controls (4.2%). However, AG rates were only elevated in

relatives of AG probands (11.6%), leading the authors to conclude that PD with AG is a more severe variant of PD. They also reported no significantly greater risk for primary affective disorders among the relatives of agoraphobic or PD patients, suggesting independent familial aggregation for affective versus ADs. The OR (and 95% confidence interval, CI) for PD alone in this study was 4.8 (1.6–13.8).

In the second study, Mendlewicz et al. compared morbidity risk of DSM-III PD and several other ADs in the first-degree relatives (N_R) of four age- and sex-matched proband groups ($N_P = 25$ each) from a German clinical sample: those with PD ($N_R = 122$), generalized anxiety disorder (GAD) ($N_R = 102$), major depression (MD) ($N_R = 137$), and healthy controls ($N_R = 130$) (Mendlewicz et al., 1993). They found significantly higher morbidity risk for PD in relatives of PD probands (13.2%) compared to the other three groups (3.3, 1.9, and 0.9%, respectively – no significant differences), giving an OR for PD versus controls of 15.6 (95% CI 2.0–121).

The third PD family study examined rates of psychiatric illness in 174 relatives of 40 DSM-III-R PD patients without a history of psychotic disorders, MD, or alcoholism compared with families of 80 unscreened controls recruited from the general population (Maier et al., 1993). They reported an age-corrected PD morbidity risk of 7.9 versus 2.3% in relatives of PD probands compared to control probands, respectively, giving an OR of 3.6 (95% CI 1.3–10.2). They also found a trend-level elevation in risk of MD and alcoholism in the relatives of the PD probands compared to control relatives, not accounted for by comorbidity in these "pure" PD probands.

The Weissman et al. study included 193 probands from four mutually exclusive DSM-III-R diagnostic groups: PD without MD, PD plus MD, early-onset MD without PD, and healthy controls, in an attempt to control for the effects of proband comorbidity on estimates of familial co-aggregation (Weissman et al., 1993). They reported specific and independent transmission of PD and MD, with an OR for PD of 6.7 (95% CI 2.1–21.7).

In the fifth study, Fyer et al. similarly compared rates of PD and social phobia (SP) in relatives of four DSM-III-R proband groups (without additional lifetime AD comorbidity): (1) PD, (2) SP, (3) PD plus SP, and (4) never ill controls (Fyer et al., 1996). They found higher rates of PD in relatives of PD probands (10%) than relatives of controls (3.0%), with OR = 3.4 (95% CI 1.4–8.1). Rates of PD in the relatives of pure SP probands (2%) were comparable to those from control probands. The pattern for the combined PD plus SP group was similar to that of the pure PD group. However, although not statistically significant due to sample size, rates of SP were elevated in relatives of the pure PD proband group (9%) compared to control relatives (6%).

All five studies possessed OR greater than 1, supporting the familial aggregation of PD. In addition, the findings of a secondary analysis of the Weissman et al. data suggest higher familial risk associated with early-onset PD in the proband (Goldstein et al., 1997). The results of our meta-analysis showed a highly significant association between PD in the proband and PD in first-degree relatives (Mantel–Haenszel statistic 47.8, df = 1, $p < 0.0001$). The summary OR across the five studies was 5.0 (95% CI: 3.0–8.2), strongly supporting a familial component in liability to PD. The unadjusted aggregate risk across the studies based on 1,356 total first-degree relatives of PD probands was 10.0%, compared to 2.1% in 1,187 control relatives. Most of these studies support the hypothesis of that PD aggregates in families separately from MD and other ADs.

II.A.2. Generalized anxiety disorder

There is only one published family study of GAD that met all of the inclusion criteria from our meta-analysis. That study by Mendlewicz et al., cited in the previous section on PD, compared morbidity risks in the first-degree relatives of four age- and sex-matched proband groups ($N_P = 25$ each): PD, GAD, MD, and healthy controls (Mendlewicz et al., 1993). The age-corrected morbidity risk for GAD was higher in relatives of GAD probands (8.9 ± 1.2%) compared with relatives of PD (4.0 ± 0.8%), MD (4.9 ± 0.9%), and control probands (1.9 ± 0.5%), although these differences did not reach statistical significance as

a group. Comparing only the GAD and control proband groups, the OR for GAD is 5.0 (95% CI: 1.0–24.3).

In the meta-analysis, we included one additional study for comparison, that of Noyes et al., which met all criteria except blind assessment (Noyes, et al., 1987). This analysis extended their family study of PD cited above by comparing the relatives of four proband groups [GAD ($N_P = 20$, $N_R = 123$); PD ($N_P = 40$, $N_R = 241$); AG ($N_P = 40$, $N_R = 256$); controls ($N_P = 20$, $N_R = 113$)]. The rates of GAD were higher in the relatives of GAD compared to the other three proband groups, with a significant GAD–control proband difference (19.5 vs. 3.5%, $\chi^2 = 14.37$, df = 1, $p < 0.001$). The OR in GAD versus control probands is 6.6 (95% CI: 2.2–19.7).

Both studies support the familial aggregation of GAD, and together they show a significant association between GAD in the proband and in their first-degree relatives (Mantel–Haenszel statistic = 19.1, df = 1, $p < 0.0001$), with a Mantel–Haenszel summary OR of 6.08 (95% CI: 2.5–14.9). They each exhibit trend level familial coaggregation of GAD with other disorders, although proband comorbidity is a potential confound.

A recent report examined DSM-III GAD in a community-based sample including 160 case probands, 764 controls, and 2,386 first-degree relatives, as opposed to the samples described above that utilized clinically derived probands (Newman and Bland, 2006). That study, which also attempted to control for potential confounding by comorbid MD and other ADs diagnoses, reported more modest rates of familial aggregation for GAD (OR ranging from ~1.5 to 3 depending upon the types of relatives analyzed).

II.A.3. Phobias

Given the relatively few genetic studies of the phobias, specific phobias (P), SP, generalized SP (GSP), and AG will be grouped together in this section. The family study of Noyes et al., summarized in the section on PD above (Noyes, et al., 1986), separately analyzed rates of illness in relatives of AG versus PD probands. They found higher rates of AG in relatives of probands with AG compared to control relatives (11.6 vs. 4.2%, OR = 3.0).

Fyer and colleagues performed a series of analyses examining simple, social, and AGs and their relationship with each other and PD (Fyer et al., 1996, 1995). The sample sizes varied somewhat by analysis but are represented as follows: simple phobia ($N_P = 15$, $N_R = 79$), SP ($N_P = 39$, $N_R = 178$), PD $\pm$ AG ($N_P = 58$, $N_R = 236$), controls ($N_P = 77$, $N_R = 380$). They reported higher rates of P in relatives of P probands compared with control relatives (31 vs. 9%), higher rates of SP in relatives of SP probands compared with control relatives (16 vs. 5%), and higher rates of AG in relatives of AG probands (10 vs. 3%). They also found relative specificity in the familial aggregation of these disorders, although there was a trend for higher rates of P in the relatives of SP probands. A re-analysis of their SP data found that probands with only the generalized subtype transmitted higher rates of SP to relatives (16%), with the rates in relatives of discrete subtype probands equal to those in control probands (6%) (Mannuzza et al., 1995).

A study by Stein et al. extended these findings by assessing the rates of separate SP subtypes in relatives of 23 GSP probands and 24 comparison probands without SP (Stein et al., 1998a, b). They found that only the generalized type aggregated in the families of these patients, with other forms equally common in the two groups of relatives. That study also found increased rates of PD, post-traumatic stress disorder (PTSD), and MD in the relatives of GSP probands, though these differences did not achieve statistical significance due to the size of the sample. Also, this study did not control for rates of comorbidity in the probands.

All studies support the familial aggregation of phobias. The results of our meta-analysis across these studies found a highly significant association between phobia in the proband and in first-degree relatives (Mantel–Haenszel statistic 52.3, $df = 1$, $p < 0.0001$). The summary OR was 4.07 (95% CI: 2.7–6.1), supporting a familial risk for phobic disorders similar to that for PD and GAD.

II.A.4. Obsessive-compulsive disorder
There were four family studies of obsessive-compulsive disorder (OCD) that met our inclusion

criteria and one that met all except blind assessment. That last one, by McKeon et al., found similarly low rates of OCD in relatives of OCD and control probands (0.7%) with non-specific elevations in "mental illness" in the relatives of cases probands (McKeon and Murray, 1987). A small study by Black et al. likewise found little difference in rates of full OCD between 120 relatives of 32 OCD probands and 129 relatives of 33 OCD probands (2.6 vs. 2.2%, OR = 1.1), although sub-clinical OCD symptomatology was more frequent in relatives of OCD probands (Black et al., 1992). They did find higher rates of ADs in relatives of OCD probands, however. These two studies, by themselves, provide little support for familiarity of OCD.

Three subsequent family studies found evidence for familial aggregation of OCD. Preliminary results of a family study by Fyer and colleagues supported familial aggregation of OCD (OR = 3.9, 95% CI = 0.49–31.9) and were included in the meta-analysis. These results were extended in a recent publication from that study, examining a total of 263 relatives of 72 OCD probands and 154 relatives of 32 control probands, finding significant familial aggregation of OCD (Fyer et al., 2005). In addition, they found a trend for familial co-aggregation for GAD. That group also published a replication study examining familial aggregation in another set of 57 OCD and 41 control probands (Lipsitz et al., 2005). In that study, they reported statistically significant aggregation only when examining the broader phenotype of OCD or OC symptoms, with an overall hazard ratio of about 5. There also they found significant evidence for familial co-aggregation of OCD with GAD, and also SP, with trends for depressive disorders as well. Pauls et al. compared 466 relatives of 100 OCD clinical probands with 113 relatives of 33 control probands, finding significantly higher rates of OCD in the former group (10.3 vs. 1.9%) with OR = 5.9 (95% CI 1.4–24.8) (Pauls et al., 1995). Similarly, a study by Nestadt et al. found 11.7% of the 326 relatives of 80 OCD probands with OCD compared with only 2.7% of the 297 relatives of 73 control probands surveyed (OR = 4.8, 95% CI = 2.2–10.3) (Nestadt et al., 2000). In a follow-up analysis of this sample, they reported that GAD, PD, AG, separation AD, and MD were more frequent in relatives of OCD probands, but only GAD and AG remained significant after controlling for comorbid OCD in the relatives, leading the authors to conclude that these two ADs may share a common familial etiology with OCD (Nestadt et al., 2001). Both this study and a follow-up analysis of the Pauls et al. study (Grados et al., 2001) reported higher rates of tics in relatives of OCD versus control probands, supporting the hypothesis of familial co-aggregation of these two types of disorders, or that tic disorders may be an alternate expression of the OCD phenotype.

Separately, these studies provide mixed support for familial aggregation of OCD. Taken together, however, there is a highly significant association between OCD in the proband and OCD in first-degree relatives (Mantel–Haenszel statistic 25.1, $df = 1$, $p < 0.0001$). The Mantel–Haenszel summary OR across the five studies was estimated at 4.0 (95% CI: 2.2–7.1), supporting the familial aggregation of OCD. The unadjusted aggregate risk based on 1,209 total first-degree relatives of OCD probands equaled 8.2 versus 2.0% in 746 control relatives. Several other family studies not meeting our inclusion criteria generally support these findings (Brown, 1942; Rudin, 1953; Kringlen, 1965; Lo, 1967; Rosenberg, 1967; Insel et al., 1983; Rasmussen and Tsuang, 1986; Lenane et al., 1990; Riddle et al., 1990; Bellodi et al., 1992; Nicolini et al., 1993; Sciuto et al., 1995; Thomsen, 1995).

Some interesting corollary findings were reported by these studies. The Pauls et al. study performed a secondary analysis that examined whether age of onset was related to risk among relatives. They found an approximately twofold higher risk of OCD among relatives of probands with early (<18 years) age of onset than among relatives of probands with later onset. This was confirmed by similar findings in the Nestadt et al. study but not in the Fyer et al. study. Thus, younger age of onset may increase familial risk for OCD. This appears to be supported by two family studies of childhood-onset OCD, where ODs for OCD in pediatric proband versus control relatives were even higher than those seen in the adult proband studies above (Hanna et al., 2005; do Rosario-Campos et al., 2005).

II.A.5. Post-traumatic stress disorder

The study of the genetics of PTSD is complicated by the requirement of a specific environmental exposure in its diagnostic criteria. The classification of a subject as not carrying an increased risk for PTSD (i.e., "healthy") is predicated on the condition that they are unaffected only *after* experiencing a significant trauma. Nonetheless, a handful of published family studies exist, mostly examining general psychopathology in the relatives of PTSD probands to identify correlated familial risk factors. Early family history studies generally found an increase in familial anxiety in patients with PTSD. While a family interview study of chronic PTSD following rape in 127 female proband and their 639 first-degree relatives reported a trend in this direction, the main finding of that study was an increase in MD in the relatives of PTSD probands with comorbid MD (Davidson et al., 1998). In a family study of substance abuse and ADs in 263 probands and 1,206 adult first-degree relatives, an association between affective disorders and vulnerability to PTSD was reported in female relatives, with a parallel association between drug abuse and PTSD in male relatives but no specific elevation in PTSD risk in the relatives of probands with PTSD (Dierker and Merikangas, 2001). In an urban sample of 1,007 young adults, Breslau et al. examined the risk factors for exposure to trauma and for development of PTSD given that exposure occurred, finding that neuroticism and familial anxiety, among other factors, increased the risk for PTSD given the experience of a traumatic event (Breslau et al., 1991). Thus, a family history of either anxiety or depressive disorders or both may increase an individual's risk for developing PTSD after experiencing a significant trauma.

II.B. Twin studies

II.B.1. Panic disorder

A number of studies of PD using twins have been published. In a study of approximately 300 same-sex Norwegian adult twin pairs in which 85 twins had DSM-III-diagnosed ADs, Torgersen found a twofold increase in frequency of ADs in the co-twins of MZ compared with DZ twins (Torgersen, 1983). For PD or AG with panic attacks specifically, the probandwise concordance was 31% in MZ versus 0% in DZ twins. In another Norwegian sample of 81 adult twins with DSM-III-R ADs, Skre et al. reported MZ:DZ concordance ratios of more than 2:1 (41.7 vs. 16.7%) (Skre et al., 1993). Perna et al. examined panic attacks and PD in a small population-based sample of Italian twins ($N = 120$), finding four of seven MZ pairs versus zero of six DZ pairs concordant for PD (Perna et al., 1997). The finding of larger MZ than DZ concordance rates in these smaller twin studies suggests that the etiologic basis for PD is at least, in part, genetic.

The two largest sources of twin data for PD are the population-based Virginia Adult Twin Study of Psychiatric and Substance Use Disorders (VATSPSUD), and the Vietnam Era Twin (VET) Registry. The former consists of approximately 6,000 twins from male and female same-sex and opposite sex pairs, while the latter is of comparable size but contains only male twins who served during the Vietnam War. The size of these samples permits the use of structural equation modeling (Neale and Cardon, 1992) to assess the relative contributions of genetics, common family (shared) environment, and individual specific (non-shared) environment to the liability of PD. However, even in these samples, diagnostic criteria were broadened to overcome power limitations introduced by the relatively low prevalence of PD (2–3%) in the general population.

The VATSPSUD examined panic syndromes in two studies of same-sex female (Kendler et al., 1993b) and same-sex male and female and opposite-sex pairs (Kendler et al., 2001a), respectively, while the VET study analyzed the relationship between panic and generalized anxiety syndromes (Scherrer et al., 2000). Both samples are consistent with each other in attributing 30–40% of the variance in liability of PD to genetic risk factors, with the remainder deriving from individual specific environment. They did not find a significant role for common family environment

in the etiology of PD, suggesting that the basis for its familial aggregation is genetic in origin. In addition, the VATSPSUD found no evidence that genetic risk factors differ between men and women.

II.B.2. Generalized anxiety disorder

The Norwegian study of 81 adult twins with DSM-III-R ADs cited above reported a trend-level elevated probandwise concordance in MZ versus DZ twin pairs (3/5 and 1/7, respectively) (Skre et al., 1993). Both the VATSPSUD and the VET Registry used broadened GAD-like syndromes (1-month duration and less restrictive diagnostic criteria) to obtain sufficient power for modeling. The VATSPSUD examined GAD syndromes in two separate studies: the first in same-sex female twin pairs (Kendler et al., 1992a) and the second in same-sex male and female and opposite-sex pairs (Hettema et al., 2001b); the VET study for PD and GAD in males is that cited above (Scherrer et al., 2000). Although the best-fitting model varied somewhat across syndromic definitions and interview waves of the VATSPSUD (the latter likely due to poor reliability of GAD), the overall picture suggests that GAD may have only modest heritability (15–30%). The VET Registry study reported a slightly higher heritability of 38%. An overall heritability estimate of 31.6% (95%CI: 24–39%) was obtained when data from both samples were combined in a meta-analytic fashion.

II.B.3. Phobias

The only adult twin studies of phobias that meet our inclusion criteria are from the VATSPSUD. However, those analyses suggest that irrational fears and phobias represent differing levels of severity on the same underlying dimension of liability. Therefore, we will describe twin studies of phobic fears together with those of clinically defined phobias in this section. In his early studies of Norwegian twins, Torgersen found that genetic factors played a role in several categories of common phobic fears (Torgersen, 1979), but this could not be established unambiguously for phobia diagnoses (Torgersen, 1983). A more recent study using a small Norwegian sample of 23 MZ and

38 DZ pairs reported moderate heritability estimates of 0.47 for social and animal fears, 0.30 for agoraphobic fears, and 0 for situational fears (Skre et al., 2000). Cary and Gottesman examined 49 twin pairs from the Maudsley Twin Registry made up of twins hospitalized for obsessional neurosis, obsessional personality, or phobic neurosis (Carey and Gottesman, 1981). They reported concordance rates of 13% for MZ and 8% for DZ twin pairs who had a treatment episode involving phobias and 88% for MZ and 38% for DZ pairs with "phobic symptoms or features", i.e., symptoms with or without associated impairment. Rose and colleagues performed genetic analyses on fear survey symptoms in 151 same-sex twin pairs and their families from an Indiana sample, finding higher MZ than DZ twin correlations for all fear types and heritability estimates ranging from 0.24 for fear of deep water to 0.78 for fear of death of a loved one (Rose et al., 1981). Heritability estimates of 0.3–0.5 were reported for a variety of fears examined in a small sample of child and adolescent twins, extending the applicability of the findings from the adult studies (Stevenson et al., 1992). A recent report examining anxiety symptoms and disorders in 6-year-old twins from the UK Twins Early Development Study (TEDS) sample reported heritability of 80% for phobic symptoms and 60% for specific phobia diagnoses (Bolton et al., 2006). Overall, these studies support a significant genetic component for fear symptoms.

The only large, adult twin sample that has comprehensively examined the genetics of phobias in adults is the VATSPSUD. Kendler et al. reported best-fit models suggesting that genetics is responsible for twin resemblance in females for AG, SP, and animal phobias, with no significant role for shared environmental factors (Kendler et al., 1992c). However, in this analysis for situational phobias, and for blood/needle/hospital/illness (BNHI) phobias reported Neale et al. (1994b), the best-fit models suggested that common family environment was the driver for twin resemblance. Given that even large twin samples such as this one often lack sufficient power to completely differentiate between these two competing sources of variance, this may not represent a true difference (Neale et al., 1994a). In fact, a follow-up analysis that included measurement reliability from two assessments 8 years apart found that twin resemblance was due solely to genetic factors for all but animal phobias, and that when fears and phobias were combined using a multiple threshold model, genetics alone accounted for twin resemblance in all of the phobic categories (Kendler et al., 1999). In these analyses, the reliability-corrected heritability estimates ranged from 0.46 for situational phobia to 0.67 for AG. For the male–male twins in the VATSPSUD sample, the analyses also supported a modest role for genetic factors in the etiology of all phobic subtypes, with the remainder of the variance explained by non-shared environmental factors (Kendler et al., 2001b). Finally, analyses combining fear/phobia data from same- and opposite-sex twin pairs suggest that some phobic subtypes may have sex-specific genetic risk factors, although statistical power limitations make these findings tentative until replicated in other samples (Kendler et al., 2002).

Although only one large, adult twin sample exists that has made a comprehensive study of the phobias, it supports the familial aggregation seen in the family studies. In addition, it predicts that genetics is largely responsible for this aggregation, explaining from 1/3 to 2/3 of individual differences for fears and phobias. Some of these findings are supported by studies in three other, large population-based twin registries. A study of blood fears and fainting in 659 complete twin pairs from the Australian Twin Registry estimates that about 2/3 of the variance of these two phenotypes is explained by genetics and the remaining by non-shared environmental risk factors (Page and Martin, 1998). An analysis in 3,372 pairs of male twins from the VET Registry reported an OR = 5.7 that the cotwin has AG with panic attacks if their twin brother also has it (Tsuang et al., 2004). A trivariate model examining SP, MD, and alcohol dependence in 1,344 subjects from the Missouri Adolescent Female Twin Study reported that genetics accounted for 28% of the variance in risk for SP, with the remainder due to non-shared environment (Nelson et al., 2000).

II.B.4. Obsessive-compulsive disorder

Due to the complex assessment requirements and relatively low prevalence rates of diagnostically defined OCD, many twin studies have only examined broadened phenotypes consisting of OC symptoms or features, which we will include in this section. Rasmussen and Tsuang (1986) reviewed early literature reports of twins with OCD. Most of these were case studies lacking data for DZ twins, but an overall MZ concordance rate of 63% was reported. The study by Carey and Gottesman mentioned in the phobia section above reported twin concordance rates for different levels of obsessive and compulsive symptoms or features in 15 MZ and 15 DZ pairs (Carey and Gottesman, 1981). The MZ and DZ concordance rates for OC symptoms or features were 87 and 47%, respectively, but only 33 and 7% for episodes requiring treatment. Clifford et al. (1984) analyzed OC traits and symptoms assessed by the Leyton Obsessional Inventory in 419 complete pairs from a London-based volunteer twin registry. They reported heritability estimates of 44% for OC traits and 47% for symptoms, with the remainder of the variance for these measures explained by non-shared environment. Self-report obsessive and compulsive symptoms from the Padua Inventory were examined in 527 female twin pairs from the VATSPSUD (Jonnal et al., 2000). Factor analysis identified two major factors accounting for 62% of the variance that appeared to roughly correspond to obsessions and compulsions, with heritabilities of 33 and 26%, respectively.

Two recent studies examined OC syndromes in large, population-based pediatric twin samples. Bolton et al. analyzed a sub-threshold OCD syndrome requiring a positive response to the OC screening and persistence questions of the Anxiety Disorders Interview Schedule for Children and Parents (ADIS-C/P) but not distress, resistance, or impairment in 854 6-year-old twin pairs from the UK TEDS sample (Bolton et al., 2007). They found that 47% of the etiologic influence was from familial sources but could not sufficiently distinguish between genetic and family environment as drivers for this. They also reported strong familial co-aggregation between this OCD syndrome and both tics and other ADs as a group.

In the largest twin study to date, Hudziak and colleagues used an 8-item OC scale contained in the Child Behavior Checklist (CBCL) in their study combining over 8,500 twin pairs aged 7, 10, or 12 from the Netherlands Twin Registry (NTR) with about 1,500 pairs from the Missouri Twin Study (Hudziak et al., 2004). They estimated an overall heritability of about 55%, with the remainder of the variance accounted for primarily by unique (non-shared) environmental factors. For a recent review that examines the broader OCD phenotype, see van Grootheest et al. (2005).

II.B.5. Post-traumatic stress disorder

Two published twin studies of PTSD currently exist. The first, from the VET Registry, analyzed 15 self-report symptoms of PTSD from the re-experiencing, avoidance, and hyperarousal clusters in 4,042 complete male twin pairs (True et al., 1993). The MZ twin correlations were higher than the DZ correlations for all of the symptoms, and heritabilities in the range 30–35% were estimated for most of the individual symptoms after controlling for the effects of trauma exposure, with non-shared environment explaining the rest of the variance in liability to PTSD. Although the majority of the traumatic events were likely combat-related, similar results obtained for a smaller sub-sample of 1,694 pairs who did not serve in Southeast Asia, suggesting that these findings may generalize to civilian populations.

A second, smaller twin study extended these findings to female subjects and PTSD resulting from civilian traumas (Stein et al., 2002). The sample consisted of 291 female–female, 75 male–male, and 40 opposite-sex complete twin pairs ascertained from the general population in the Vancouver area of Canada. For pairs in which both twins were exposed to trauma, MZ pairs were more highly correlated than DZ pairs for all of the PTSD symptom clusters, and modeling results produced heritability estimates in a similar range as those from the VET Registry study.

II.B.6. Comorbidity

While most, but not all, family studies of the ADs reported relative specificity in their familial aggregation, this is not the case with twin studies. As discussed earlier, Torgersen reported a 2:1 MZ:DZ concordance ratio for all AD, but found no MZ pairs in which twins had the same disorder, most likely due to the limited sample size (Torgersen, 1983). Similarly, Skre et al. reported higher rates of any AD in co-twins of MZ probands with AD than DZ, both of which were higher than rates in co-twins of comparison mood or substance use disorder probands (Skre et al., 1993). A study of 446 adult twin pairs with anxiety or depressive disorders from the Australian Twin Registry found no MZ:DZ concordance ratios that differed significantly from unity in various disorder grouping schemes, although a trend existed for GAD and for other ADs without GAD for greater MZ than DZ concordance (Andrews et al., 1990). The small sizes of these earlier twin studies limited their ability to adequately examine models of comorbidity for the ADs.

Studies in the VATSPSUD sample have found genetic and environmental factors are, to a greater or lesser extent, shared across most of the ADs and MD. The twin studies cited earlier in the phobia section reported multivariate modeling that tested whether there was a common factor of "phobia proneness" that increased liability across classes of phobic fears and whether it was genetic, environmental, or both in origin. For both the male (Kendler et al., 2001b) and female (Kendler et al., 1992c) subjects the findings were similar: the best-fitting models contained both common and disorder-specific genetic and environmental influences on all of the phobia subtypes examined, with the proportion of genetic variance explained by common genes varying somewhat by disorder and gender. Bivariate analyses between both 12-month (Kendler, 1996) and lifetime (Kendler et al., 1992b) MD and GAD in female twins from the VATSPSUD, as well as lifetime MD and GAD in same-sex male and female and opposite sex twins from the Swedish Twin Registry (Roy et al., 1995) produced identical findings: MD and GAD share the majority of their genetic risk in common but only a modest proportion of environmental risk factors. On the other hand, analyses examining the relationship between MD and various phobia subtypes in female twins found estimated genetic correlations of only about 35% between MD and AG, animal, or SPs, with no genetic correlation between MD and situational phobia (Kendler et al., 1993a).

Several studies from the VATSPSUD tested broader models of comorbidity between the ADs, or between the ADs, MD, and other psychiatric syndromes. One such analysis examined the relationships between PD, GAD, AG, social, animal, and situational phobias in over 5,000 same-sex male and female twin pairs (Hettema et al., 2005). In the best-fitting model, the genetic influences on anxiety susceptibility for both sexes were best explained by two additive genetic factors common across the disorders, with only significant specific (non-shared) genetic risk for AG. The first factor loaded most strongly on GAD, PD, and AG, while the second loaded primarily on the two specific phobias. SP was intermediate, in that it was influenced by both common genetic factors. This is generally consistent with an even broader analysis that still attempted to identify the risk structure of a wide range of psychiatric and substance use syndromes. That study found that genetic risk could be broadly defined as internalizing (primarily affecting MD, GAD, and phobias) and externalizing (primarily affecting alcohol dependence, illicit drug dependence, adult antisocial behavior, and conduct disorder) (Kendler et al., 2003). The internalizing genetic factor was further broken down into one of "anxiety-misery" loading primarily on MD and GAD, and "fear", loading primarily on animal and situational phobias, with PD intermediate.

Analyses from other large twin datasets support the hypothesis of a shared genetic diathesis between the AD or between AD and MD. The VET Registry found significant genetic correlations between GAD and PD (Scherrer et al., 2000), and between these syndromes and PTSD (Chantarujikapong et al., 2001), with some role for panic- and PTSD-specific genetic influences. The adolescent twin study by Nelson et al. found significant sharing of the genetic vulnerability between SP and MD, and modest sharing between SP and alcohol dependence (Nelson et al., 2000).

II.C. Summary

Overall, genetic epidemiological studies support a moderate level of familial aggregation (OR ~4–6) for the ADs. The source of this familial risk is predominantly genetic in origin, with heritability of about 30–50%, depending upon the disorder and sample analyzed. Although some of the family studies are at odds with these findings, twin studies suggest a role for common genetic factors that may non-specifically increase risk across these conditions. This appears to be supported by some of the molecular genetic studies that are finding association of several candidate genes to more than one AD phenotype (see following sections).

Thus, one possible initial strategy for identifying susceptibility genes for the ADs would be to group together subjects with various ADs as cases in linkage or association studies in order to find those genes that increase risk across disorders. Once these are identified, one may then search for residual susceptibility genes that differentially affect risk for specific conditions. Several linkage studies for ADs have begun to use this approach (Boomsma et al., 2000; Kirk et al., 2000; Thorgeirsson et al., 2003; Kaabi et al., 2006), finding that using broader phenotypic definitions (implying, among other things, more potential case subjects) increases power to detect linkage signals. One of us (JMH) has adopted this strategy for genetic association by selecting twin pairs scoring at the extremes of a latent genetic risk factor that underlies susceptibility to neuroticism, MD, GAD, PD, AG, and SP, from the VATSP-SUD (Hettema et al., 2006b). Subjects from these pairs at high and low genetic risk are entered as cases and controls, respectively, in candidate gene association analyses (Hettema et al., 2006a).

III. Molecular genetics

The research on the heritability of ADs has further employed linkage and association analyses aimed to clarify the molecular basis of the genetic epidemiological findings. Linkage studies provide an approximate chromosomal location of the gene or genes associated with a familial transmission of AD phenotypes. These studies use the logarithm of the odds (LOD) to estimate the likelihood of two gene loci to be inherited together. More recent efforts focus on candidate gene studies, where the current knowledge of the pathophysiology of anxiety and the mode of action of drugs and challenge agents, along with the findings in other psychiatric disorders, are used to make judicious choice of the specific genes for testing. This approach aims to link the illness to common variations in DNA sequence, such as sequence repeats or single nucleotide polymorphisms (SNP) and patterns of their proximate occurrence (haplotypes). These studies commonly employ an association paradigm with case–control design and/or family-based analyses. In this section we review the extant literature on molecular genetics of the ADs addressing the promises and caveats of these studies often characterized by negative, inconsistent, or unreplicated results. For a simplified overview, the key findings from the published genetic association studies are summarized in Tables 1–3.

III.A. Panic disorder

Several multi-family, genome-wide linkage analyses of PD, including some studies on a broader panic-related phenotype have been published. A first-pass genome scan was conducted by the Columbia University group in 23 families from two different generations having at least three affected relatives with PD with or without AG (Knowles et al., 1998). Using both parametric and non-parametric linkage analyses they revealed six markers with LOD scores between 1.0 and 2.0 on chromosomes 1p, 20p, (dominant model) and 7p, 17p, 20q, X/Y (recessive model), falling substantially short of the threshold LOD score of 3.3 required for definite linkage to a complex trait like PD. In their later linkage analysis performed in 60 multiplex pedigrees of broad syndromes, including PD, bladder problems, severe headaches, mitral valve prolapse, and thyroid conditions, the significant linkage on chromosomes 13q, and possibly, 22 under a dominant genetic model was found (Hamilton et al., 2003). The linkage with

Table 1. Association studies in panic disorder

Investigated genes	Number of investigated polymorphisms	Number of studies	Main findings
5-HT related genes			
5-HTT	5	7	Association with LL genotype and L allele of 5-HTTLPR in Estonian sample (158 cases/215 controls; $p = 0.01$–0.02) [Maron et al., 2005a]
MAO-A	2	5	Association with longer alleles of VNTR polymorphism in different female samples ($p = 0.001$–0.02), but not males [Deckert et al., 1999, Maron et al., 2005a]
TPH1	3	5	No associations
TPH2	5	2	Association with rs1386494 SNP only in females with pure phenotype (58 cases/212 controls; $p = 0.01$–0.02) [Maron et al., 2007]
5-HTR1A	3	4	Association between the −1019C–G polymorphism and some phenotypes ($p = 0.03$–0.05) [Rothe et al., 2004a, Maron et al., 2005b]
5-HTR1Dß	10	3	No association
5-HTR2A	4	4	Association between 102T–C polymorphism and only pure phenotype in both Japanese ($n = 63$; $p = 0.016$) and Estonian ($n = 42$; $p = 0.01$) samples [Inada et al., 2003, Maron et al., 2005b]
5-HTR2C	4	4	Association between Cys23Ser polymorphism and comorbid phenotype in Estonian sample ($p = 0.03$) [Maron et al., 2005b]
5-HTR3A	2	1	No association [Maron et al., 2005b]
CCK-related genes			
CCK	4	6	Association with SNP 1270C–G in Estonian sample (127 cases/146 controls; $p = 0.03$), supported by haplotype analysis ($p = 0.04$) [Maron et al., 2005b]
CCKR1	8	4	Associations with both -81A/G and −128G/T polymorphisms, supported by haplotype analyses in Japanese sample (109 patients/400 controls; $p < 0.0001$) [Miyasaka et al., 2004].
CCKR2	7	7	Association with promoter CT repeat polymorphism in both Canadian ($n = 99$) and German ($n = 111$) samples ($p = 0.002$–0.004) [Kennedy et al., 1999, Hosing et al., 2004]. Suggestive association with −215C–A SNP in Estonian sample ($n = 127$; $p = 0.05$) [Maron et al., 2005b]
DA-related genes			
DRD1	7	1	Association with −94G–A polymorphism only in pure phenotype ($n = 42$; $p = 0.02$), supported by haplotype analysis ($p = 0.03$) [Maron et al., 2005b]
DRD2	12	1	No association
DRD3	3	1	No association
DRD4	8	2	Association with −1217del-G SNP in Estonian sample ($n = 127$; $p = 0.03$) [Maron et al., 2005b]
DRD5	1	1	No association
DAT	1	1	No association
TH	2	1	No association
COMT	9	6	Association with Val158Met polymorphism in different samples (most $p < 0.01$) [Hamilton et al., 2002; Woo et al., 2002; Domschke et al., 2004; Rothe et al., 2006]

Table 1 (*continued*)

Investigated genes	Number of investigated polymorphisms	Number of studies	Main findings
Adenosine-related genes			
A1AR	1	1	No association [Deckert et al. (1998)]
A2aAR	5	4	Association with both the 1083T allele ($p = 0.01$) and 1083T/T genotype ($p = 0.024$) in German sample ($n = 89$) [Deckert et al., 1998]. Linkage for 1083C/T (LOD score 2.98) in 70 multiplex pedigrees [Hamilton et al., 2004]
Opioid-related genes			
OPRM1	4	1	No association [Maron et al., 2005b]
OPRD1	2	1	No association
OPRK1	7	1	No association
POMC	6	1	No association
PENK	2	1	No association
Other genes			
ACE	1	2	Non-replicated association with I/D polymorphism in male (24 cases vs. 192 controls; $p = 0.005$), but not female (48 cases/243 controls) patients [Olsson et al., 2004]
AGT	1	1	No association [Olsson et al., 2004]
ATr1	1	1	No association [Olsson et al., 2004]
ApoE	1	1	No association [Martinez-Barrondo et al., 2006]
BDNF	2	2	No association [Lam et al., 2004, Shimizu et al., 2005]
CHRNA4	3	1	No association [Steinlein et al., 1997]
CREM	8	2	Association with shorter P2 promoter eight repeat trinucleotide allele in German sample ($n = 88$; $p = 0.001$–0.02), but not in Italian ($n = 76$) or Spanish ($n = 62$) [Domschke et al., 2003]
CRHR2	1	1	No association [Tharmalingam et al., 2006]
ELN	3	1	No association [Philibert et al., 2003]
ESR1	3	1	No association [Sand et al., 2002]
GABA(B)R1	3	1	No association [Sand et al., 2000]
GLO1	1	1	Association with Ala111Glu polymorphism in Italian patients without AG (61 cases/288 controls; $p < 0.025$), but not in total sample ($n = 162$) or with AG [Politi et al., 2006]
HW	2	1	Associations with G2457A polymorphism in Japanese males ($n = 21$, $p = 0.011$–0.026), but not in females ($n = 20$) [Nakamura et al., 1999]
NET	9	2	Associations with both G/C (rs2397771) and T/C (rs2242446) polymorphisms ($p = 0.004$–0.02), supported by haplotype analysis ($p = 0.03$) in German sample without AG (83 cases/115 controls), but not in total sample ($n = 115$) or with AG [Lee et al., 2005b]
NTRK3	4	1	Association with allele 2 of the SNP in the 5′UTR-region in Spain sample (59 cases/86 controls; $p = 0.02$) [Armengol et al., 2002]
NPY	1	1	No association [Lindberg et al., 2006]
PBR	1	1	Association with 485 G > A polymorphism in Japanese sample (91 cases/178 controls; $p = 0.014$–0.021) [Nakamura et al., 2006]
Progesterone receptor	2	1	Association with G331A polymorphism in Caucasian females (48 cases vs. 253 controls; $p = 0.0009$; OR = 3.5), but not in males (24 cases/197 controls; $p = 0.1$) [Ho et al., 2004]
Rgs2	4	1	Association with four SNPs in German sample (173 cases/173 controls; $p = 0.02$–0.05), supported by haplotype analysis [Leygraf et al., 2006]

Table 2. Association studies in obsessive-compulsive disorder

Investigated genes	Number of investigated polymorphisms	Number of studies	Main findings
5-HT related genes			
5-HTT	3	13	Inconsistent or controversial results among studies. Supported association between 5-HTTLPR and early-onset phenotype in pooled analysis ($p = 0.005–0.02$) [Dickel et al., 2007]. Significant excess of allele 12 of VNTR polymorphism in Spanish patients (97 cases/406 controls; $p = 0.008$, OR = 3.6) [Baca-Garcia et al., 2007]
MAO-A	2	3	The gender different associations with both EcoRV and Fnu4HI polymorphisms in comorbid phenotype [Camarena et al., 1998, 2001a, Karayiorgou et al., 1999]
TPH2	3	2	Preferential transmission of haplotype G–C of SNP rs4565946 to patients in 71 trios ($p = 0.035$) [Mossner et al., 2006b]
5-HTR1Dβ	1	8	Non-replicated association with G861C polymorphism
5-HTR2A	3	8	Association with −1438G/A polymorphism in two from five independent samples ($p < 0.05$) [Walitza et al., 2002, Enoch et al., 2001]. Association with C516T polymorphism (79 cases/202 controls; $p = 0.00007–0.0002$) [Meira-Lima et al., 2004]
5-HTR2C	1	1	No association [Cavallini et al., 1998]
DA-related genes			
DRD2	1	2	Association with TaqI A polymorphism only in male patients (51 cases/67 controls $p = 0.02–0.049$) [Denys et al., 2006a]
DRD3	1	2	No association [Catalano et al. (1994)]
DRD4	2	7	Association with 48bp VNTR polymorphism in both family- and population-based studies in the different samples ($p = 0.0001–0.03$) [Millet et al., 2003, Cruz et al., 1997, Hemmings et al., 2004, Camarena et al., 2007]
DAT	1	3	No association [Billett et al., 1998, Hemmings et al., 2003]
COMT	2	12	Insufficient evidence to support an association [Azzam and Mathews, 2003]
Glutamate-related genes			
GRIK2	3	1	No association [Delorme et al., 2004]
GRIK3	1	1	No association [Delorme et al., 2004]
GRIN2B	3	1	Association with 5072T/G polymorphism in 130 families ($p = 0.014$); supported by haplotype analysis ($p = 0.002$) [Arnold et al., 2004]
SLC1A1	9	2	Association with various SNPs particularly in male probands, supported by haplotype analysis [Dickel et al., 2006, Arnold et al., 2006]
Other genes			
ApoE	1	1	No association [Nicolini et al. (2001)]
BDNF	4	5	Non-replicated preferential transmission of the Val66 variant [Hall et al., 2003, Mossner et al., 2005]
ERE 6	1	1	No association [Kinnear et al., 2001]
GABA(B)R1	5	1	A trend of over-transmission of −7265A allele to 159 affected probands in the TDT analysis ($p = 0.071$) [Zai et al., 2005]
MOG	4	1	Significantly biased transmission of allele 2 at a tetranucleotide TAAA repeat polymorphism in 160 nuclear families ($p = 0.02$); positive haplotypic association ($p = 0.01$) [Zai et al., 2004]
NET	1	1	No association [Miguita et al., 2006]
OPRM1	2	1	No association [Urraca et al., 2004]
SGCE	1	1	No association [de Carvalho et al., 2004]
TNF-α	1	1	No association [Zai et al., 2006]

Table 3. Association studies in generalized anxiety disorder (GAD), social phobia (SP), and post-traumatic stress disorder (PTSD)

Investigated genes	Number of investigated polymorphisms	Number of studies	Main findings
5-HTT	1	3	Association with S allele of 5-HTTLPR in Korean patients with PTSD (100 cases/197 controls; $p = 0.044$, OR $= 1.65$) [Lee et al., 2005a]. No association in GAD or phobias [Stein et al., 1998a, b, Samochowiec et al., 2004]
5-HTR2A	1	1	No linkage in SP [[Stein et al., 1998a, b]
MAO-A	2	2	Association with T941G SNP in patients with GAD (50 cases/276 controls; $p = 0.009$, OR $= 2.1$) [Tadic et al., 2003]. Association with longer alleles of VNTR polymorphism in females with GAD (48 cases/148 controls; $p = 0.01$) [Samochowiec et al., 2004]
DRD2	1	3	No linkage in SP [Kennedy et al., 2001]. No consistent association in PTSD [Gelernter et al., 1999]
DRD3	1	1	No linkage in SP [Kennedy et al., 2001]
DRD4	1	1	No linkage in SP [Kennedy et al., 2001]
DAT	1	2	No linkage in SP [Kennedy et al., 2001]. Association with the SLC6A3 9 repeat allele ($p = 0.012$, OR $= 1.72$) and nine repeat homozygous genotype ($p = 0.047$) in Jewish PTSD sample (102 case/104 controls) [Segman et al., 2002]
COMT	1	3	No association in GAD or phobias [Ohara et al., 1998, Samochowiec et al., 2004], however increased risk of phobic anxiety was observed for COMT Val/Val genotype (OR $= 1.99$, 95% CI $= 1.17$–3.40) [McGrath et al., 2004]
BDNF	3	1	No association in PTSD [Zhang et al., 2006]

chromosome 7p15 with maximum LOD score of 2.23 was also reported in 23 multiplex families by research group from the University of Iowa (Crowe et al., 2001). A re-analysis of this data using a Bayesian approach obtained an 80% probability of linkage to marker D16S749 in that region (Logue et al., 2003). The other study performed by the University of Yale group in a set of 20 pedigrees detected two regions on chromosome 1 and 11, respectively, with suggestive linkage to PD (Gelernter et al., 2001). The results of linkage analyses in a set of 25 families from the Icelandic population with at least one member affected with PD were reported by Thorgeirsson et al. (2003). The highest LOD score in this study was 4.18 obtained for a region on chromosome 9q31, corresponding to a genome wide significance level of $p < 0.05$. In addition, LOD scores between 1 and 2 were also observed on chromosomes 3, 4, 15, 18, and X. Notably, the region on the chromosome 9 is near the one with

a LOD score of 2.0 from the second Columbia study. However, the results of the Icelandic study on this region were not replicated by study of Wang et al. (2006) in an isolated population of the Faroe Islands, probably due to small sample size.

Recently Kaabi et al. (2006) used a new multi-phenotype approach to ADs (PD, SP, and P) in a subset of the families from the prior Yale study. They have found a strong evidence of linkage with genome-wide significance at $p < 0.05$ for a region on chromosome 4q31-q34, at marker D4S413, in a set of 19 extended American pedigrees (219 subjects) ascertained through the probands with PD. Notably, this chromosome region includes the site of a neuropeptide Y receptor gene (NPY1R) and NPY has been implicated in the etiology of PD (Boulenger et al., 1996). Suggestive linkage was also demonstrated in several other regions on four chromosomes (4q21.21-22.3, 5q14.2-14.3, 8p23.1, and 14q22.3-23.3). Finally, a genome scan using parametric two-point, multipoint, and non-parametric analyses was performed recently in 120 multiplex PD pedigrees consisting of 1,591 individuals (Fyer et al., 2006) reported recently. Evidence for linkage reached genome-wide significance in one region on chromosome 15q (near GABA-A receptor subunit genes) and was suggestive at loci on 2p, 2q, and 9p. The support at one locus on 2q increased to genome-wide significance and an additional region of suggestive linkage on 12q was identified when analyses for sex-specific theta's were performed. These data provide evidence for chromosomal regions on 15q and 2q that may be important in genetic susceptibility to PD.

III.A.1. Serotonin related genes

An effort to determine anxiety vulnerability genes in the serotonin (5-HT) system has been driven by the established efficacy of 5-HT reuptake blockers and other 5-HT-acting drugs in the treatment of ADs. Despite being favored candidate genes in association studies, there are only few reports implicating their involvement in susceptibility to ADs and particularly to PD.

III.A.1.a. Serotonin transporter gene. 5-HT transporter (5-HT), the key protein regulating 5-HT neurotransmission, contains a functional polymorphism in the 5′ regulatory promoter region (5-HTTLPR), involving two alleles, corresponding to a 44-bp insertion (long or L-allele) or deletion (short or S-allele). This polymorphism became the main candidate in genetic studies after Lesch et al. (1996) reported a decreased 5-HTT transcriptional activity and diminished 5-HT uptake of S-variant in comparison to LL genotype and on a positive association of S-allele with anxiety traits in humans. Nevertheless, a number of case–control association studies in different ethnic populations argue against the major role of 5-HTTLPR in PD (Deckert et al., 1997; Ishiguro et al., 1997; Matsushita et al., 1997; Kim et al. 2006). As well, neither linkage nor association between this polymorphism and PD were observed in a family-based study; however, a more frequent occurrence of 5-HTTLPR LL genotype was detected in female PD probands (Hamilton et al., 1999). Our group have

recently observed a significant difference in the distribution of 5-HTTLPR genotypes and allele frequencies between Estonian PD patients ($n = 158$) and controls ($n = 215$), with the LL genotype and L allele variant being more frequent in the patients (Maron et al., 2005a). Pertinently, we have also found that healthy females with the LL genotype were more sensitive to cholecystokinin (CCK) tetrapeptide induced panic attacks than those carrying the S allele (Maron et al., 2004). Also Schmidt et al. (2000) have reported that subjects homozygous for the L-variant were at a greater risk for behavioral hyper-reactivity to 35% CO_2 challenge than those with S-allele genotypes. On the contrary, in the patients with PD, CO_2 reactivity was not influenced by 5-HTTLPR genetic variants (Perna et al., 2004). A number of other known 5-HTT polymorphisms were not found to be associated with PD clinical phenotypes (Maron et al., 2005b).

III.A.1.b. Monoamine oxidase A gene. Monoamine oxidase (MAO) existing in two isoforms (MAO-A and MAO-B) catalyzes the oxidative deamination of a number of biogenic amines, including 5-HT. Previously, the transcriptionally more active longer alleles and genotypes of a functional polymorphism of the *MAO-A* gene, uVNTR, demonstrated a significant association with PD in female but not male patients (Deckert et al., 1999). We found a similar gender-dependent association with longer allele genotypes in female PD patients with AG (Maron et al., 2005a). Samochowiec et al. (2004) observed a significant association with longer alleles in females with panic attack phenotypes. Again, this association was absent in males. These studies suggest an impact of MAO-A promoter region polymorphism on vulnerability to PD in females; however, a family-based study with a separate analysis for females did not support these findings (Hamilton et al., 2000b). Another polymorphism of the MAO-A, Fnu4H1, was not associated with PD (Tadic et al., 2003).

III.A.1.c. Tryptophan hydroxylase gene. Tryptophan hydroxylase (TPH) catalyzes the first and rate-limiting step in the biosynthesis of 5-HT converting L-tryptophan to 5-hydroxytryptophan. Numerous studies have looked for a connection between *TPH* gene polymorphisms and PD. However no associations with PD were found for various variants of tryptophan hydroxylase isoform 1 (*TPH1*) gene (Han et al., 1999; Fehr et al., 2001; Maron et al., 2005b; Kim et al., 2006). The newly identified isoform 2 of *TPH* gene (*TPH2*), which is preferentially expressed in neuronal tissue may be a more promising candidate gene having functional polymorphisms involved in the regulation of brain 5-HT synthesis (Zhang et al., 2004). Despite this, a recent association study by Mossner et al. (2006a) did not find an association between PD ($n = 134$) and two common SNPs, rs4570625 and rs4565946, located in the putative transcriptional control region and in intron 2 of TPH2, respectively. Also in our recent study there were no significant associations with *TPH2* gene SNPs rs1386494 and rs1386483 in 213 (163 females and 50 males) patients with PD when compared to 303 (212 females and 91 males) matched healthy control subjects (Maron et al., 2007). However, an association with rs1386494 SNP was observed in this study in a subgroup of females with pure PD phenotype ($n = 52$), indicating possible gender-specific effect of *TPH2* gene variants in PD.

III.A.1.d. Serotonin receptor genes. A common −1018C–G (−1019C–G) functional polymorphism in the promoter region of the human 5-HT receptor (*5-HTR*) *1A* gene has been well described (Wu and Comings, 1999; Lemonde et al., 2003). Lemonde et al. (2003) postulated that the −1019 G allele results in impaired repression of the *5-HTR1A* gene, leading to elevated levels of 5-HTR1A autoreceptor and inhibition of basal raphe neuronal activity. So far, the relationship between this polymorphism and 5-HTR1A binding in the prefrontal cortex was not confirmed (Huang et al., 2004), suggesting that 5-HTR1A responsiveness in the adult brain is not robustly influenced by variants of this gene (Lesch and Gutknecht, 2004). A recent study by Rothe et al. (2004a) showed an association between the −1019C–G polymorphism and PD with AG ($n = 101$), but no association in the total sample of German PD patients ($n = 133$). Our study

demonstrated a suggestive association of this SNP with PD phenotype in a sample consisting of 123 Estonian patients (Maron et al., 2005b). However, Rothe et al. (2004a) showed a significant association with the G allele, whereas our results indicated an association with the C allele. Association of 5-HTR1A −1019C–G with the presence of panic attacks was also observed in other psychiatric disorders, including MD, bipolar disorder, and schizophrenia; however, this association was not present in the patients with a concurrent diagnosis of PD, probably due to the lower diagnostic reliability in the last group (Huang et al., 2004). Other data have shown lack of associations between PD phenotypes and several other 5-HTR1A polymorphisms (Inada et al., 2003; Maron et al., 2005b).

The *5-HTR1Dβ* gene 861G–C polymorphism did not demonstrate any significant association in patients with PD (Fehr et al., 2000a; Maron et al., 2005a). Furthermore, no associations were found between PD phenotypes and a large number of SNPs in this gene, excluding the major role of the *5-HTR1Dβ* gene in PD (Maron et al., 2005b).

Inada et al. (2003) have detected a significant association with 5-HTR2A silent 102T–C polymorphism in Japanese PD patients with pure phenotype ($n = 63$) and in particular with AG ($n = 33$). Our study also indicated a significant association with the 5-HTR2A 102T–C polymorphism in Estonian patients with pure ($n = 42$), but not in comorbid PD (Maron et al., 2005b). Both studies showed a higher frequency of 102C allele among patients, suggesting its role in the predisposition to PD. On the contrary, the effect of the 5-HTR2A 102T–C polymorphism in PD was not supported in a study of Rothe et al. (2004b). Neither transmission disequilibrium nor allelic or genotypic differences were detected between 102T–C polymorphism and PD in this study consisting of German ($n = 86$) and Canadian ($n = 94$) patients and matched controls. Also, Fehr et al. (2001) did not find significant association with the 102T–C polymorphism of the *5-HTR2A* gene in their smaller German sample of PD patients without AG ($n = 35$). Possibly, the ethnic and phenotype variance may explain these discrepant findings. In our study, no associations were observed between PD phenotypes and several other known polymorphisms in this gene (Maron et al., 2005b).

The results of two studies argued against a major role for the 5-HTR2C Cys23Ser polymorphism in PD (Fehr et al., 2000b; Inada et al., 2003). In our study, this polymorphism was significantly associated with PD in a sample of patients that allowed for comorbidity with mood disorders (Maron et al., 2005b). Previously, a role for Cys23Ser polymorphism was suggested in MD and bipolar disorder (Lerer et al., 2001). Thus, this polymorphism may have non-specific links to comorbid phenotypes of PD, but its specific impact on the predisposition to PD remains unclear. Two novel adjacent dinucleotide polymorphisms in the 5-HTR2C gene promoter region, (12–18)G–T and (4–5)C–T, were not associated with PD phenotype (Deckert et al., 2000). Nevertheless, a significant excess of genotypes containing long haplotypes of these polymorphisms was observed in this study among PD females in their German ($n = 87$), but not in their Italian sample ($n = 124$). This study demonstrated that, similar to other X-chromosomal gene markers, such as MAO-A VNTR, the 5-HTR2C gene promoter length polymorphisms may have gender-dependent effects on the genetic vulnerability to PD.

III.A.2. Cholecystokinin-related genes

Strong evidence suggests that CCK system plays an important role in the neurobiology of panic attacks (Bradwejn, 1993; Shlik et al., 1997). Two types of CCK receptors, CCK1R and CCK2R, have been described and implicated in regulation of anxiety. A CT repeat polymorphism of the CCK2R has been associated with PD in two case–control studies (Kennedy et al., 1999; Hosing et al., 2004), but not in a family-based study (Hamilton et al., 2001). In the SNP-array study by our group (Maron et al., 2005b), no significant associations were found between various CCK-related polymorphisms and pure PD phenotype, although CCK2R polymorphism –215C–A showed an association in the PD group that included comorbid mood disorders. Also we detected an association of CCK1R 246G–A polymorphism with the

phenotype of comorbid, but not pure PD. Among the CCK gene polymorphisms, the SNP 1270C–G showed an association particularly in the PD group comorbid with MD. In addition, the haplotype analysis demonstrated that CCK gene haplotype – 45T/1270G was associated with the phenotype of PD with affective comorbidity. A study by Hattori et al. (2001) showed a lack of association with PD for –45C–T (–36C–T) and –196G–A (–188A–G) polymorphisms of CCK gene. Thus, the role of CCK gene variants in predisposition to PD, initially suggested by the study of Wang et al. (1998), remains inconclusive. The functional role of CCK receptor genetic variants in PD warrants further studies.

III.A.3. Dopamine-related genes

Our results showed that dopamine (DA) type 1 receptor (DRD1) polymorphism –94G–A was significantly associated with the pure PD phenotype, the DRD1 allele –94A being less frequent in the patients with pure PD (Maron et al., 2005b). The haplotype analysis in this study supported an association between a lower risk for pure PD phenotype and DRD1 CAA haplotype formed by –800T–C –94G–A –48G–A SNPs and carrying a –94G–A individual effect. We have also found that the –1217del-G polymorphism of the DRD4 gene was associated with PD in the group allowing for comorbid affective disorders. A number of other DA polymorphisms were not associated with PD (Maron et al., 2005b). Previously, no association was detected between the DRD4 or DA transporter (DAT) gene polymorphisms and PD in multiplex families (Hamilton et al., 2000a).

III.A.3.a. Catechol-O-methyltransferase gene. A functional variant Val158Met (472G/A-Val/Met) in the coding sequence of the catechol-O-methyltransferase (COMT) gene, has attracted a number of studies in PD. A significant linkage for this along with some other polymorphisms was demonstrated by the Columbia group in their family-based sample of 70 PD pedigrees and 83 parent–offspring triads (Hamilton et al., 2002). The association with this COMT polymorphism was recently examined in 115 patients with PD and

age- and sex-matched controls by Domschke et al. (2004). In this study, a significant excess of the high-activity valine allele was detected in patients ($p = 0.04$) and particularly in females ($p = 0.01$), but not in males ($p = 1.0$). In contrast, Woo et al. (2002) described a significant association ($p = 0.005$) of the low-activity allele in 51 PD patients of Korean origin. An additional study with a larger number of participants did not replicate this result, but showed a borderline significant association with the low-activity Met/Met genotype in another Korean sample of 178 PD patients (Woo et al., 2004). Ohara et al. (1998) investigated a sample of patients with ADs ($n = 108$) including a small number of PD patients ($n = 29$) and found no association, likely due to very low power. More recently, Rothe et al. (2006) have found a significant association between the valine allele of the Val158Met COMT polymorphism and PD in two independent samples, one of nuclear families and another of case–controls. The fact that positive results have been observed not only in the studies with case–control design, but also in the family samples indicates that these findings were not confounded by population stratification.

III.A.3.b. Adenosine receptor gene. The observations of an anxiogenic effect of caffeine administration have implicated adenosine and particularly adenosine A2a receptor (A2aAR) in PD (Boulenger et al., 1984; Charney et al., 1985). Deckert et al. (1998) first showed that a silent coding polymorphism (1976T > C, formerly 1083T > C) in exon 2 of the *A2aAR* gene was associated with PD in a German sample. This polymorphism and particularly 1976T/T genotype was also associated with higher anxiety response to caffeine administration in healthy subjects (Alsene et al., 2003). The association with the A2 receptor gene was partially replicated in a recent study by Hamilton et al. (2004) which provided an evidence for linkage between the A2aAR locus and PD in a Caucasian sample of Western European background. However, this association was not found in a Japanese (Yamada et al., 2001) or Chinese population (Lam et al., 2005). The fact that a positive association between this polymorphism

and PD was found in Western but not in Asian population indicates that the relationship may be ethnicity-specific.

III.A.4. Other genes
A large number of other genes from various neuronal systems have been recently investigated. Overall, these studies demonstrated that most of new gene candidates are not likely to have a major role in the susceptibility to PD (Table 1). The preliminary findings with certain variants of cAMP responsive element modulator (CREM), peripheral benzodiazepine receptor, progesterone receptor, and regulator of G-protein signaling two genes need to be followed-up in larger independent studies.

III.B. Generalized anxiety disorder

GAD remains the less investigated AD in regards to its molecular genetics probably due to some disagreement among clinicians on its diagnostic validity and a low prevalence of pure GAD phenotype. Recently Tadic et al. (2003) reported a positive association between MAO-A T941G SNP and GAD, but not PD. Specifically, over-representation of the 941T allele was detected in small sample of patients suffering from GAD ($n = 50$, 34 females and 16 males) when compared to 276 healthy volunteers ($p < 0.01$).

III.C. Phobias

The Yale group has reported evidence of linkage in phobias for different chromosome markers using a previously described set of pedigrees ascertained through probands with PD. Significant linkage (LOD scores > 3.0) on chromosome 14 and a suggestive linkage (LOD > 2.0) on chromosome 8 were reported in the first scan among 129 subjects from 14 families with two or more members affected by simple phobia (Gelernter et al., 2003). Their second genome-wide linkage scan conducted in 163 subjects (at least 56 was affected) from 17 pedigrees found a suggestive linkage of a region on chromosome 16 to SP

(Gelernter et al., 2004). The few molecular studies failed to find linkage of 5-HT or DA candidate genes to SP (Stein et al., 1998a, b; Kennedy et al., 2001); however an increased risk for phobic anxiety in a female control sample was associated with COMT Val158Met polymorphism (McGrath et al., 2004).

III.D. Obsessive-compulsive disorder

Several potential regions (4q, 5q, and 17q) with significant linkage to OC symptoms were identified in the previous genome-wide scan performed in the cohort of 77 sib pairs who were concordant for Tourette syndrome (Zhang et al., 2002). Tic disorders are frequently comorbid with OCD and appear to share a portion of their neurobiology and genetic predisposition. Additionally, Hanna et al. (2002) found a suggestive evidence for linkage on 9p (LOD ~2.0) and two other regions on 6p and 19q with LOD scores between 1 and 2. In this study among seven probands with early-onset OCD three also had a history of Tourette syndrome and two of the 25 relatives with OCD had a tic history. The findings on 9p were replicated in a follow-up linkage study targeting this region conducted by the Johns Hopkins group in 50 OCD families with no probands with Tourette syndrome (Willour et al., 2004). Recently, Shugart et al. (2006) presented the first large-scale model-free linkage analysis of both extended and nuclear families using both "broad" (definite and probable diagnoses) and "narrow" (definite only) definitions of OCD. Genome-scan analyses were performed in 219 families collected in the OCD Collaborative Genetics Study. The probands with a history of Tourette syndrome were excluded. The findings showed suggestive linkage signals by multipoint analysis on chromosomes 3q27-28 ($p = 0.0003$), 6q ($p = 0.003$), 7p ($p = 0.001$), 1q ($p = 0.003$), and 15q ($p = 0.006$). Using the "broad" OCD definition, they observed the strongest evidence for linkage on chromosome 3q27-28. Interestingly, that one of the markers in this region with the highest LOD score, D3S1262, is 2.5 Mb downstream from *5-HT3R* gene. This indicates the relevance of *5-HT3R* gene

polymorphisms to further genetic association studies in OCD.

III.D.1. Serotonin-related genes

III.D.1.a. Serotonin transporter gene. The *5-HTT* gene (SLC6A4) polymorphisms have been tested in OCD in a number of case–control and family-based studies with no consistent results. McDougle et al. (1998) were first to provide a preliminary support for association and linkage disequilibrium between the long allele of 5-HTTLPR and OCD. This association was confirmed in another population-based analysis in 75 OCD Caucasian patients and 397 ethnically matched individuals (Bengel et al., 1999). However, other studies (Billett et al., 1997; Kinnear et al., 2000; Camarena et al., 2001b) have failed to find a significant association with 5-HTTLPR. Lack of association between 5-HTTLPR and OCD was also observed in both case–control and family association samples from another study (Chabane et al., 2004). In contrast to these earlier findings, a recent study of Hasler et al. (2006) demonstrated that the frequencies of the S allele and SS genotype of 5-HTTLPR were associated with certain symptom clusters of OCD. An association with S-allele was also found in female OCD patients in another recent case–control study (Denys et al., 2006b). Dickel et al. (2007) recently concluded that a pooled analysis of five replication studies of the 5-HTTLPR in early-onset OCD supports association. Furthermore, a rare functional variant, I425V, in *5-HTT* gene was associated with OCD by way of a higher occurrence of the V425 variant in the patients (Ozaki et al., 2003; Delorme et al., 2005). The potential role of SLC6A4 V425 in the susceptibility to OCD is obscured by its low frequency and the fact that it was detected in a few controls.

III.D.1.b. Monoamine oxidase A gene. Two polymorphisms in *MAO-A* gene, namely *Fnu4HI* and *EcoRV*, were associated with OCD in a gender-dependent manner (Camarena et al., 1998; Karayiorgou et al., 1999). When Camarena et al. (2001a) re-examined the EcoRV polymorphism in 124 Mexican patients with OCD compared to

122 controls, they found that the low activity-related allele of this polymorphism was significantly more frequent in OCD females, confirming gender differences of *MAO-A* gene in susceptibility for OCD.

III.D.1.c. Tryptophan hydroxylase gene. Mossner et al. (2006b) have studied two common SNPs of TPH2, rs4570625 and rs4565946, in a family-based sample of OCD patients with an early onset of disease comprising 71 complete independent trios. The results showed a significant preferential transmission of a haplotype G–C and a trend towards preferential transmission of the C allele of SNP rs4565946 in the patients. The genotype relative-risk estimate for the homozygous C allele carriers of SNP rs4565946 was 2.58 (95% CI 0.98–6.82). Although replication in larger samples is warranted, this preliminary evidence links *TPH2* gene polymorphisms to the pathogenesis of early-onset OCD.

III.D.1.d. Serotonin receptor genes. The role of at least two 5-HTR genes, *5-HTR1Dβ* and *5-HTR2A*, in the predisposition to OCD has been examined by several groups. Linkage disequilibrium between the G861C variant of *5-HTR1Dβ* gene and OCD reported in one study (Mundo et al., 2000, 2002) was not confirmed by other case–control and family-based association analyses (Di Bella et al., 2002a; Hemmings et al., 2003; Camarena et al., 2004; Denys et al., 2006b). However, a quantitative trait analysis, performed by Camarena et al. (2004) showed higher YBOCS obsessions scores in the patients with a preferential transmission of the G861 variant compared to the C861 allele carriers, suggesting possible role of this allele in the severity of OCD symptoms. Findings on the association of OCD with *5-HTR2A* gene polymorphisms have also been inconsistent. The reported evidence of a link between the A-allele of –1438G/A polymorphism in *5-HTR2A* gene and OCD (Enoch et al., 2001; Walitza et al., 2002) was not confirmed in later studies (Tot et al., 2003; Denys et al., 2006b; Dickel et al., 2007). However, an over-representation of G-allele and GG genotype in Caucasian patients from the Netherlands with a positive family history and early onset of OCD in the study of Denys et al. (2006b) suggests a difference in the risk effect of this polymorphism that may depend either on ethnicity or phenotype specifics. Another *5HTR2A* gene polymorphism, T102C, was not associated with OCD in 79 OCD patients compared to 202 control subjects. However, this study found significant associations for the C516T *5HTR2A* gene polymorphism showing differences in genotypic distribution ($p = 0.0002$) and allelic frequencies ($p = 0.00007$) (Meira-Lima et al., 2004).

III.D.2. Dopamine-related genes
Various DA-related genes have been tested for their implication in OCD. Significant decrease (uncorrected for multiple testing) of the 2–4 genotype of a polymorphic 48 base-pair repeat polymorphism of DRD4 was observed in 118 OCD patients compared to 118 control subjects (Billett et al., 1998). However, a subsequent case–control study in Ashkenazi and non-Ashkenazi Jews did not replicate this finding (Frisch et al., 2000). In additional, no significant genotypic or allelic associations with OCD were detected in a case–control association study in Afrikaner population looking at selected polymorphic variants in DA system (Hemmings et al., 2003). However, their later study demonstrated a significant association with the allele distribution of DRD4 VNTR polymorphism in the South African Caucasian sample with an early-onset OCD (Hemmings et al., 2004). Previously, a higher frequency of the allele 7 was reported in OCD patients with comorbid vocal or motor tics when compared to those without tics or to 12 healthy controls matched for age and gender (Cruz et al., 1997), but this allelic difference was not confirmed in two other studies (Millet et al., 2003; Camarena et al., 2007). To further explore the potential role of *DRD4* gene variants in OCD, Millet et al. (2003) examined the transmission of the 48 bp *DRD4* gene polymorphism in nuclear families of 55 OCD probands and also compared the distribution between OCD patients and controls in a French Caucasian population. A significantly lower frequency of the allele 2 was observed in the OCD, but no association was detected in the

subgroup of patients with comorbid tics. Finally, a significant association with the 48-bp polymorphism and particularly a lower frequency of allele 4R was recently demonstrated in a sample of 210 OCD patients when compared to 202 healthy controls. However, this association was not confirmed by their further family-based association analysis in a sub-sample of 86 OCD families (Camarena et al., 2007).

III.D.2.a. *Catechol-O-methyltransferase gene.*

The *COMT* gene polymorphism in OCD has been investigated by several groups using both case–control and family-based association tests with contrasting results (Schindler et al., 2000; Alsobrook et al., 2002; Erdal et al., 2003; Meira-Lima et al., 2004). A recent systematic review and meta-analysis of the both published and unpublished data (Azzam and Mathews, 2003) revealed insufficient evidence to support an association between the COMT and OCD.

III.D.3. *Other genes*

A number of various candidate genes for OCD have recently attracted attention (Table 2). Among the most studied are the genes from glutamate system, brain-derived neurotrophic factor, GABA and μ(mu)-opioid receptors. Overall, these studies have demonstrated only suggestive or not yet replicated associations with the OCD phenotype. Furthermore, the gender difference in particular for glutamatergic polymorhisms was proposed to play a role in the genetic susceptibility to OCD.

III.E. *Post-traumatic stress disorder*

To date there are no published linkage studies in PTSD. Similarly to other ADs the findings from association studies are too preliminary to support the involvement of any specific genetic loci in the development of PTSD. The strongest evidence for an association with PTSD was demonstrated for *DAT* gene (SLC6A3) polymorphism by Segman et al. (2002). They compared a group of 102 patients with chronic PTSD with 104 trauma survivors who did not develop PTSD. Their results point to a significant association between the SLC6A3 nine repeat allele and nine repeat homozygous genotype and susceptibility to a chronic PTSD. Another recent study has linked severe re-experiencing symptoms and impaired memory in the patients with PTSD to the apolipoprotein E 2 allele genotype, but the interpretation of these data was limited by a small sample size in this study (Freeman et al., 2005).

IV. Functional genetics

IV.A. *Pharmacogenetics*

Pharmacogenetic studies have multiplied in the past decade giving a promise to find the genetic predictors of treatment response and tolerability informative for clinical practice (Pickar and Rubinow, 2001). The 5-HTTLPR polymorphism has been the most investigated object in the studies of treatment response to antidepressants, particularly selective 5-HT re-uptake inhibitors (SSRIs) (Serretti et al., 2005). However, there are only sparse published reports available on pharmacogenetic studies in ADs. For example, Perna et al. (2005) have shown that the high-expressive L variant of 5-HTTLPR was associated with a better response to 12-weeks treatment with an SSRI paroxetine in female ($n = 51$), but not male ($n = 39$) patients with PD. In this study the presence of the long allelic variant was associated with a better response in the symptom domain of panic attacks but not in anticipatory anxiety or phobic avoidance. However, a study in the Korean population (Kim et al., 2006) showed lack of association between 5-HTTLPR as well as TPH A218C polymorphisms with the outcomes of a 10-week treatment with paroxetine in 143 PD patients. On the other hand, treatment response to paroxetine was related to a COMT polymorphism in Korean PD patients (Woo et al., 2004). Recently, Stein et al. (2006) have demonstrated that in the patients with SP ($n = 32$), the allelic variation in 5HTTLPR may predict response to SSRIs. Earlier studies in OCD patients ($n < 100$) showed that the response to SSRIs treatment was unrelated to this polymorphism (Billett et al., 1997; Di Bella et al., 2002b). Taken together, the search for genetic factors influencing drug response or drug tolerability in the ADs is in early stage and more studies applying novel methodologies in larger samples are warranted.

IV.B. Brain imaging genetics

Use of brain imaging to study the gene effects on emotional processing is a novel strategy to study the genetic basis of anxiety regulation. Dubbed as ''imaging genomics'' (Hariri and Weinberger, 2003) this approach links the gene markers to discrete brain circuits during specific forms of information processing (e.g., visual, auditory, cognitive, emotional). Most of the studies so far have been focusing on the link between the ''usual suspect'', 5-HTTLPR polymorphism, and the brain correlates of emotional reactivity. In a pioneering study, Hariri et al. (2002) detected a higher activation in the right amygdala in response to fearful and angry faces in healthy volunteers carrying S allele genotypes of the 5-HTTLPR. Subsequently, the hyper-reactivity of the amygdala to emotionally salient stimuli in S allele carriers has been reported in different separate cohorts of healthy subjects (Bertolino et al., 2005; Canli et al., 2005b; Heinz et al., 2005; Brown and Hariri, 2006; Heinz et al., 2007) as well as in the patients with PD (Domschke et al., 2007) and SP (Furmark et al., 2004). In addition, Hariri et al. (2005) have replicated their original finding in a large, independent cohort of volunteers ($N = 92$) demonstrating that the effect of S allele on the amygdala activation was independent from allele load or sex. Thus, in line with the groundbreaking study of Lesch et al. (1996) showing that healthy S allele carriers displayed higher levels of trait anxiety, the neuroimaging studies extend this link to the amygdala-mediated anxiety regulation.

Another study has demonstrated a significantly lower activation in several brain regions, including the right ventromedial, orbitofrontal, and the anterior cingulate cortex, in PD patients homozygous for the G high-risk allele of the 5-HTR1A −1019C/G polymorphism during processing of anxiety-related emotional face stimuli (Domschke et al., 2006). This study found that both, the 5-HTR1A 1019C/G and the 5-HTTLPR polymorphisms may increase the risk of PD by contributing to an altered emotional processing. In addition, a variance in the reactivity of the amygdala has been linked to the genetic variants of *TPH2* gene (Brown et al., 2005, Canli et al., 2005a). Taken together, the initial findings suggest a major potential of imaging genomics to broaden the understanding of the interplay between the genetic and neurobiological bases of anxiety regulation.

V. Summary and further directions

The genetic research on ADs has grown tremendously in the last decade. The genetic association studies suggest some role of genetic variability in the risk for ADs, but most of the positive findings are difficult to replicate. Notably, the associations between the studied genetic polymorphisms and psychopathology are not specific to ADs. For many of them the relationships have also been found in schizophrenia (Shifman et al., 2002), MD (Massat et al., 2005), rapid cycling in bipolar illness (Kirov et al., 1998), and anxiety-related personality traits (Lesch et al., 1996; Stein et al., 2005). This may indicate that the involvement of genetic variants confer a ''general susceptibility'' predisposing to several syndromes rather than a ''specific susceptibility'' to a particular AD. The limited success of genetic studies in ADs as well as in other psychiatric disorders has raised questions concerning the definition of genetically relevant phenotypes and the number and the nature of the underlying genes. Failure to replicate, and thus to confirm, previously identified susceptibility loci could result from a number of reasons, including the potential for population admixture, the clinical heterogeneity of ADs, small sample sizes (and subsequent lack of power), publication bias, epistasis, or failure to account for multiple testing (Hemmings and Stein, 2006). Reducing phenotypic heterogeneity may considerably increase the power of genetic studies (Hasler et al., 2004). Furthermore, it has been suggested that different classes of gene action have to be taken into account; some genes may influence susceptibility only, others may influence clinical features as quantitative traits only (i.e., pure modifier genes), and others may have a mixed effect (Fanous and Kendler, 2005). Supporting this view, the reviewed findings, particularly in PD, demonstrate that genetic influence may be differently related to PD phenotypes (with or without AG; pure or comorbid) and may be gender-dependent.

To date, the molecular genetic studies of ADs have been primarily restricted to relatively small data sets derived from ethnically heterogeneous populations, with genotyping of a single SNP or limited numbers of SNPs. Recent advances in genomic information, novel statistical genetic methods, and genotyping technologies provide the means for far more comprehensive and powerful studies. Recently, the International Hap Map Consortium completed genotyping of over 3.8 million SNPs in three major populations, and the results of studying patterns of linkage disequilibrium indicate that characterization of 300,000–500,000 tag SNPs is sufficient to provide good genomic coverage for linkage-disequilibrium-based association studies in many populations. Lately, Gunderson et al. (2006) described the development of a whole-genome genotyping (WGG) assay that enables unconstrained SNP selection and effectively unlimited multiplexing from a single sample preparation. The real promise of microarrays in detecting the genetic basis of ADs may lay in large studies, in which thousands of variants in hundreds of candidate genes are genotyped, or millions of variants chosen without an a priori hypothesis used to scan the genome for associations with multiple phenotypes or treatment outcomes. However, there is a controversy as to whether the genome-wide studies designed to detect millions of genotypes with microarrays will lead to new genetic discoveries more than a more focused, hypothesis-driven approach (Murphy, 2006). It has been proposed that no knowledge of the biology of the drug or potential marker SNPs is required, as long as there are a sufficient number of markers across the entire genome (Taillon-Miller et al., 2004; Hirschhorn and Daly, 2005). To obtain sufficient power to detect a genetic effect, it is thought that millions of SNPs must be genotyped in a "hypothesis-free" genome-wide association study (Carlson et al., 2004). The success of these studies may depend on whether most psychiatric diseases and pharmacogenetic effects are due to rare variants or more common variants (Pritchard and Cox, 2002; Lohmueller et al., 2003), which is currently unknown. At present, the most promising way forward could be to use the WGG as a first step for generating candidate loci and then, based on the most plausible hypothesis, to perform a detailed gene (or pathway)-based association analysis.

The second way to find new potential risk genes of ADs in addition to the WGG method is the analysis of the gene expression, using again the whole genome approach. Gene expression profiling can be studied during the course of ADs and their treatment, thereby providing clues to molecular pathogenesis. Although the gene expression levels in the brain are probably different from the periphery, blood cells are easily available for studying and could be a more realistic target than the brain itself, at least presently. To this point, the application of microarray gene expression in human lymphocytes has shown some promise for psychiatry (Gladkevich et al., 2004). Moreover, gene expression signatures in the blood cells were found to be predictive of outcome and correlated with the essential neuropsychiatric dimensions of PTSD (Segman et al., 2005) and may differentiate PD patients from healthy subjects (Philibert et al., 2007). These technologies may be particularly applicable to the pharmacogenetic and treatment efficacy studies of ADs. Lastly, with a heritability estimate not exceeding 30–50%, the role of gene–environment interaction in the development and outcomes of ADs deserves more scientific attention.

Abbreviations

ACE	angiotensin converting enzyme
AGT	angiotensinogen
ATr1	angiotensin receptor type 1
ApoE	apolipoprotein E
A1AR	adenosine receptor A1
A2aAR	adenosine receptor A2a
BDNF	brain-derived neurotrophic factor

CCK	cholecystokinin
CCKR	cholecystokinin receptor
CHRNA4	neuronal nicotinic acetylcholine receptor alpha 4 subunit
COMT	catechol O-methyltransferase
CREM	cAMP responsive element modulator
CRHR2	corticotrophin-releasing hormone receptor 2
DA	dopamine
DAT	dopamine transporter
DRD	dopamine receptor
ELN	elastin gene
ERE 6	estrogen response element in the promoter area of COMT
ESR1	estrogen receptor 1
GABA(B)R1	gamma-amino-butyric acid type B receptor 1
GLO1	glyoxalase I
GRIK	glutamate receptor
GRIN2B	glutamate receptor, ionotropic, N-methyl-D-aspartate 2B
hW	-human homolog of the *Drosophila* white gene
MAO-A	monoamine oxidase A
MOG	myelin oligodendrocyte glycoprotein
NET	norepinephrine transporter
NPY	neuropeptide Y
NTRK3	high-affinity receptor for neurotrophin 3
OPRD1	δ-opioid receptor
OPRK1	κ-opioid receptor
OPRM1	μ-opioid receptor
PBR	peripheral benzodiazepine receptor
PENK	proenkephalin
POMC	proopiomelanocortin
Rgs2	regulator of G-protein signaling 2
SGCE	ε-sarcoglycan
SLC1A1	glutamate transporter gene solute carrier family 1
SLC6A3	dopamine transporter gene
SLC6A4	serotonin transporter gene
TH	tyrosine hydroxylase
TNF-α	tumor necrosis factor-alpha
TPH	tryptophan hydroxylase
5-HT	serotonin
5-HTR	serotonin receptor
5-HTT	serotonin transporter

References

Alsene, K., Deckert, J., Sand, P. and de, W.H. (2003) Association between A2a receptor gene polymorphisms and caffeine-induced anxiety. Neuropsychopharmacology, 28: 1694–1702.

Alsobrook, J.P., Zohar, A.H., Leboyer, M., Chabane, N., Ebstein, R.P. and Pauls, D.L. (2002) Association between the COMT locus and obsessive-compulsive disorder in females but not males. Am. J. Med. Genet., 114: 116–120.

Andrews, G., Stewart, G., Allen, R. and Henderson, A.S. (1990) The genetics of six neurotic disorders: a twin study. J. Affect. Disord., 19: 23–29.

Armengol, L., Gratacos, M., Pujana, M.A., Ribases, M., Martin-Santos, R. and Estivill, X. (2002) 5′ UTR-region SNP in the *NTRK3* gene is associated with panic disorder. Mol. Psychiatry, 7: 928–930.

Arnold, P.D., Rosenberg, D.R., Mundo, E., Tharmalingam, S., Kennedy, J.L. and Richter, M.A. (2004) Association of a glutamate (NMDA) subunit receptor gene (GRIN2B) with obsessive-compulsive disorder: a preliminary study. Psychopharmacology, 174: 530–538.

Arnold, P.D., Sicard, T., Burroughs, E., Richter, M.A. and Kennedy, J.L. (2006) Glutamate transporter gene *SLC1A1* associated with obsessive-compulsive disorder. Arch. Gen. Psychiatry, 63: 769–776.

Azzam, A. and Mathews, C.A. (2003) Meta-analysis of the association between the catecholamine-O-methyltransferase gene and obsessive-compulsive disorder. Am. J. Med. Genet. B Neuropsychiatr. Genet., 123: 64–69.

Baca-Garcia, E., Vaquero-Lorenzo, C., az-Hernandez, M., Rodriguez-Salgado, B., Dolengevich-Segal, H., rrojo-Romero, M., Botillo-Martin, C., Ceverino, A., Piqueras, J.F., Perez-Rodriguez, M.M. and Saiz-Ruiz, J. (2007) Association between obsessive-compulsive disorder and a variable number of tandem repeats polymorphism in intron 2 of the serotonin transporter gene. Prog. Neuropsychopharmacol. Biol. Psychiatry, 31: 416–420.

Bellodi, L., Sciuto, G., Diaferia, G., Ronchi, P. and Smeraldi, E. (1992) Psychiatric disorders in the families of patients with obsessive-compulsive disorder. Psychiatry Res., 42: 111–120.

Bengel, D., Greenberg, B.D., Cora-Locatelli, G., Altemus, M., Heils, A., Li, Q. and Murphy, D.L. (1999) Association of the serotonin transporter promoter regulatory region polymorphism and obsessive-compulsive disorder. Mol. Psychiatry, 4: 463–466.

Bertolino, A., Arciero, G., Rubino, V., Latorre, V., De, C.M., Mazzola, V., Blasi, G., Caforio, G., Hariri, A., Kolachana, B., Nardini, M., Weinberger, D.R. and Scarabino, T. (2005) Variation of human amygdala response during threatening stimuli as a function of 5'HTTLPR genotype and personality style. Biol. Psychiatry, 57: 1517–1525.

Billett, E.A., Richter, M.A., King, N., Heils, A., Lesch, K.P. and Kennedy, J.L. (1997) Obsessive compulsive disorder, response to serotonin reuptake inhibitors and the serotonin transporter gene. Mol. Psychiatry, 2: 403–406.

Billett, E.A., Richter, M.A., Sam, F., Swinson, R.P., Dai, X.Y., King, N., Badri, F., Sasaki, T., Buchanan, J.A. and Kennedy, J.L. (1998) Investigation of dopamine system genes in obsessive-compulsive disorder. Psychiatr. Genet., 8: 163–169.

Black, D.W., Noyes, R., Jr. Goldstein, R.B. and Blum, N. (1992) A family study of obsessive-compulsive disorder. Arch. Gen. Psychiatry, 49: 362–368.

Bolton, D., Eley, T.C., O'connor, T.G., Perrin, S., Rabe-Hesketh, S., Rijsdijk, F. and Smith, P. (2006) Prevalence and genetic and environmental influences on anxiety disorders in 6-year-old twins. Psychol. Med., 36: 335–344.

Bolton, D., Rijsdijk, F., O'connor, T.G., Perrin, S. and Eley, T.C. (2007) Obsessive-compulsive disorder, tics and anxiety in 6-year-old twins. Psychol. Med., 37: 39–48.

Boomsma, D.I., Beem, A.L., van den, B.M., Dolan, C.V., Koopmans, J.R., Vink, J.M., De Geus, E.J. and Slagboom, P.E. (2000) Netherlands twin family study of anxious depression (NETSAD). Twin Res., 3: 323–334.

Boulenger, J.P., Jerabek, I., Jolicoeur, F.B., Lavallee, Y.J., Leduc, R. and Cadieux, A. (1996) Elevated plasma levels of neuropeptide Y in patients with panic disorder. Am. J. Psychiatry, 153: 114–116.

Boulenger, J.P., Marangos, P.J., Patel, J., Uhde, T.W. and Post, R.M. (1984) Central adenosine receptors: possible involvement in the chronic effects of caffeine. Psychopharmacol. Bull., 20: 431–435.

Bradwejn, J. (1993) Neurobiological investigations into the role of cholecystokinin in panic disorder. J. Psychiatry Neurosci., 18: 178–188.

Breslau, N., Davis, G.C., Andreski, P. and Peterson, E. (1991) Traumatic events and posttraumatic stress disorder in an urban population of young adults. Arch. Gen. Psychiatry, 48: 216–222.

Brown, F.W. (1942) Heredity in the psychoneuroses. Proc. R. Soc. Med., 35: 785–790.

Brown, S.M. and Hariri, A.R. (2006) Neuroimaging studies of serotonin gene polymorphisms: exploring the interplay of genes, brain, and behavior. Cogn. Affect. Behav. Neurosci., 6: 44–52.

Brown, S.M., Peet, E., Manuck, S.B., Williamson, D.E., Dahl, R.E., Ferrell, R.E. and Hariri, A.R. (2005) A regulatory variant of the human tryptophan hydroxylase-2 gene biases amygdala reactivity. Mol. Psychiatry, 10: 884–888. 805.

Camarena, B., Aguilar, A., Loyzaga, C. and Nicolini, H. (2004) A family-based association study of the 5-HT-1Dbeta receptor gene in obsessive-compulsive disorder. Int. J. Neuropsychopharmacol., 7: 49–53.

Camarena, B., Cruz, C., de, l.F. Jr. and Nicolini, H. (1998) A higher frequency of a low activity-related allele of the MAO-A gene in females with obsessive-compulsive disorder. Psychiatr. Genet., 8: 255–257.

Camarena, B., Loyzaga, C., Aguilar, A., Weissbecker, K. and Nicolini, H. (2007) Association study between the dopamine receptor D(4) gene and obsessive-compulsive disorder. Eur. Neuropsychopharmacol, 17: 406–409.

Camarena, B., Rinetti, G., Cruz, C., Gomez, A., de, L.F. Jr. and Nicolini, H. (2001a) Additional evidence that genetic variation of MAO-A gene supports a gender subtype in obsessive-compulsive disorder. Am. J. Med. Genet., 105: 279–282.

Camarena, B., Rinetti, G., Cruz, C., Hernandez, S., de, l.F. Jr. and Nicolini, H. (2001b) Association study of the serotonin transporter gene polymorphism in obsessive-compulsive disorder. Int. J. Neuropsychopharmacol., 4: 269–272.

Canli, T., Congdon, E., Gutknecht, L., Constable, R.T. and Lesch, K.P. (2005a) Amygdala responsiveness is modulated by tryptophan hydroxylase-2 gene variation. J. Neural Transm., 112: 1479–1485.

Canli, T., Omura, K., Haas, B.W., Fallgatter, A., Constable, R.T. and Lesch, K.P. (2005b) Beyond affect: a role for genetic variation of the serotonin transporter in neural activation during a cognitive attention task. Proc. Natl. Acad. Sci. USA, 102: 12224–12229.

Carey, G. and Gottesman, I.I. (1981) Twin and family studies of anxiety, phobic, and obsessive disorders. In: Klein, D.F. and Rabkin Anxiety, J. (Eds.), New research and changing concepts. Raven Press, New York, NY, pp. 117–136.

Carlson, C.S., Eberle, M.A., Rieder, M.J., Yi, Q., Kruglyak, L. and Nickerson, D.A. (2004) Selecting a maximally informative set of single-nucleotide polymorphisms for association analyses using linkage disequilibrium. Am. J. Hum. Genet., 74: 106–120.

Catalano, M., Sciuto, G., Di Bella, D., Novelli, E., Nobile, M. and Bellodi, L. (1994) Lack of association between obsessive-compulsive disorder and the dopamine D3 receptor gene: some preliminary considerations. Am. J. Med. Genet., 54: 253–255.

Cavallini, M.C., Di Bella, D., Pasquale, L., Henin, M. and Bellodi, L. (1998) 5HT2C CYS23/SER23 polymorphism is not associated with obsessive-compulsive disorder. Psychiatry Res., 77: 97–104.

Chabane, N., Millet, B., Delorme, R., Lichtermann, D., Mathieu, F., Laplanche, J.L., Roy, I., Mouren, M.C.,

Hankard, M., Maier, W., Launay, J.M. and Leboyer, M. (2004) Lack of evidence for association between serotonin transporter gene (*5-HTTLPR*) and obsessive-compulsive disorder by case control and family association study in humans. Neurosci. Lett., 363: 154–156.

Chantarujikapong, S.I., Scherrer, J.F., Xian, H., Eisen, S.A., Lyons, M.J., Goldberg, J., Tsuang, M. and True, W.R. (2001) A twin study of generalized anxiety disorder symptoms, panic disorder symptoms and post-traumatic stress disorder in men. Psychiatry Res., 103: 133–145.

Charney, D.S., Heninger, G.R. and Jatlow, P.I. (1985) Increased anxiogenic effects of caffeine in panic disorders. Arch. Gen. Psychiatry, 42: 233–243.

Clifford, C.A., Murray, R.M. and Fulker, D.W. (1984) Genetic and environmental influences on obsessional traits and symptoms. Psychol. Med., 14: 791–800.

Crowe, R.R., Goedken, R., Samuelson, S., Wilson, R., Nelson, J. and Noyes, R. Jr. (2001) Genomewide survey of panic disorder. Am. J. Med. Genet., 105: 105–109.

Cruz, C., Camarena, B., King, N., Paez, F., Sidenberg, D., de, l.F. Jr. and Nicolini, H. (1997) Increased prevalence of the seven-repeat variant of the dopamine D4 receptor gene in patients with obsessive-compulsive disorder with tics. Neurosci. Lett., 231: 1–4.

Davidson, J.R., Tupler, L.A., Wilson, W.H. and Connor, K.M. (1998) A family study of chronic post-traumatic stress disorder following rape trauma. J. Psychiatr. Res., 32: 301–309.

de Carvalho, A.P., Fazzari, M., Jankovic, J. and Ozelius, L.J. (2004) Examination of the SGCE gene in Tourette syndrome patients with obsessive-compulsive disorder. Mov. Disord., 19: 1237–1238.

Deckert, J., Catalano, M., Heils, A., Di Bella, D., Friess, F., Politi, E., Franke, P., Nothen, M.M., Maier, W., Bellodi, L. and Lesch, K.P. (1997) Functional promoter polymorphism of the human serotonin transporter: lack of association with panic disorder. Psychiatr. Genet., 7: 45–47.

Deckert, J., Catalano, M., Syagailo, Y.V., Bosi, M., Okladnova, O., Di Bella, D., Nothen, M.M., Maffei, P., Franke, P., Fritze, J., Maier, W., Propping, P., Beckmann, H., Bellodi, L. and Lesch, K.P. (1999) Excess of high activity monoamine oxidase A gene promoter alleles in female patients with panic disorder. Hum. Mol. Genet., 8: 621–624.

Deckert, J., Meyer, J., Catalano, M., Bosi, M., Sand, P., DiBella, D., Ortega, G., Stober, G., Franke, P., Nothen, M.M., Fritze, J., Maier, W., Beckmann, H., Propping, P., Bellodi, L. and Lesch, K.P. (2000) Novel 5′-regulatory region polymorphisms of the 5-HT2C receptor gene: association study with panic disorder. Int. J. Neuropsychopharmacol., 3: 321–325.

Deckert, J., Nothen, M.M., Franke, P., Delmo, C., Fritze, J., Knapp, M., Maier, W., Beckmann, H. and Propping, P. (1998) Systematic mutation screening and association study of the A1 and A2a adenosine receptor genes in panic disorder suggest a contribution of the *A2a* gene to the development of disease. Mol. Psychiatry, 3: 81–85.

Delorme, R., Betancur, C., Wagner, M., Krebs, M.O., Gorwood, P., Pearl, P., Nygren, G., Durand, C.M., Buhtz, F., Pickering, P., Melke, J., Ruhrmann, S., Anckarsater, H., Chabane, N., Kipman, A., Reck, C., Millet, B., Roy, I., Mouren-Simeoni, M.C., Maier, W., Rastam, M., Gillberg, C., Leboyer, M. and Bourgeron, T. (2005) Support for the association between the rare functional variant I425 V of the serotonin transporter gene and susceptibility to obsessive compulsive disorder. Mol. Psychiatry, 10: 1059–1061.

Delorme, R., Krebs, M.O., Chabane, N., Roy, I., Millet, B., Mouren-Simeoni, M.C., Maier, W., Bourgeron, T. and Leboyer, M. (2004) Frequency and transmission of glutamate receptors GRIK2 and GRIK3 polymorphisms in patients with obsessive compulsive disorder. Neuroreport, 15: 699–702.

Denys, D., Van, N.F., Deforce, D. and Westenberg, H. (2006a) Association between the dopamine D2 receptor TaqI A2 allele and low activity COMT allele with obsessive-compulsive disorder in males. Eur. Neuropsychopharmacol., 16: 446–450.

Denys, D., Van, N.F., Deforce, D. and Westenberg, H.G. (2006b) Association between serotonergic candidate genes and specific phenotypes of obsessive compulsive disorder. J. Affect. Disord., 91: 39–44.

Di Bella, D., Cavallini, M.C. and Bellodi, L. (2002a) No association between obsessive-compulsive disorder and the *5-HT(1Dbeta)* receptor gene. Am. J. Psychiatry, 159: 1783–1785.

Di Bella, D., Erzegovesi, S., Cavallini, M.C. and Bellodi, L. (2002b) Obsessive-compulsive disorder, 5-HTTLPR polymorphism and treatment response. Pharmacogenomics J., 2: 176–181.

Dickel, D.E., Veenstra-VanderWeele, J., Bivens, N.C., Wu, X., Fischer, D.J., Van Etten-Lee, M., Himle, J.A., Leventhal, B.L., Cook, E.H. Jr. and Hanna, G.L. (2007) Association studies of serotonin system candidate genes in early-onset obsessive-compulsive disorder. Biol. Psychiatry, 61: 322–329.

Dickel, D.E., Veenstra-VanderWeele, J., Cox, N.J., Wu, X., Fischer, D.J., Van Etten-Lee, M., Himle, J.A., Leventhal, B.L., Cook, E.H. Jr. and Hanna, G.L. (2006) Association testing of the positional and functional candidate gene *SLC1A1/EAAC1* in early-onset obsessive-compulsive disorder. Arch. Gen. Psychiatry, 63: 778–785.

Dierker, L.C. and Merikangas, K.R. (2001) Familial psychiatric illness and posttraumatic stress disorder: findings from a family study of substance abuse and anxiety disorders. J. Clin. Psychiatry, 62: 715–720.

Domschke, K., Braun, M., Ohrmann, P., Suslow, T., Kugel, H., Bauer, J., Hohoff, C., Kersting, A., Engelien, A., Arolt, V., Heindel, W. and Deckert, J. (2006) Association of the functional −1019C/G 5-HT1A polymorphism with prefrontal cortex and amygdala activation measured with 3 T fMRI in panic disorder. Int. J. Neuropsychopharmacol., 9: 349–355.

Domschke, K., Freitag, C.M., Kuhlenbaumer, G., Schirmacher, A., Sand, P., Nyhuis, P., Jacob, C., Fritze, J., Franke, P., Rietschel, M., Garritsen, H.S., Fimmers, R., Nothen, M.M., Lesch, K.P., Stogbauer, F. and Deckert, J. (2004) Association of the functional V158M catechol-O-methyl-transferase polymorphism with panic disorder in women. Int. J. Neuropsychopharmacol., 7: 183–188.

Domschke, K., Kuhlenbaumer, G., Schirmacher, A., Lorenzi, C., Armengol, L., DiBella, D., Gratacos, M., Garritsen, H.S., Nothen, M.M., Franke, P., Sand, P., Fritze, J., Perez, G., Maier, W., Sibrowski, W., Estivill, X., Bellodi, L., Ringelstein, E.B., Arolt, V., Martin-Santos, R., Catalano, M., Stogbauer, F. and Deckert, J. (2003) Human nuclear transcription factor gene *CREM*: genomic organization, mutation screening, and association analysis in panic disorder. Am. J. Med. Genet. B Neuropsychiatr. Genet., 117: 70–78.

do Rosario-Campos, M.C., Leckman, J.F., Curi, M., Quatrano, S., Katsovitch, L., Miguel, E.C. and Pauls, D.L. (2005) A family study of early-onset obsessive-compulsive disorder. Am. J. Med. Genet. B Neuropsychiatr. Genet., 136: 92–97.

Enoch, M.A., Greenberg, B.D., Murphy, D.L. and Goldman, D. (2001) Sexually dimorphic relationship of a 5-HT2A promoter polymorphism with obsessive-compulsive disorder. Biol. Psychiatry, 49: 385–388.

Erdal, M.E., Tot, S., Yazici, K., Yazici, A., Herken, H., Erdem, P., Derici, E. and Camdeviren, H. (2003) Lack of association of catechol-O-methyltransferase gene polymorphism in obsessive-compulsive disorder. Depress. Anxiety, 18: 41–45.

Fanous, A.H. and Kendler, K.S. (2005) Genetic heterogeneity, modifier genes, and quantitative phenotypes in psychiatric illness: searching for a framework. Mol. Psychiatry, 10: 6–13.

Fehr, C., Grintschuk, N., Szegedi, A., Anghelescu, I., Klawe, C., Singer, P., Hiemke, C. and Dahmen, N. (2000a) The HTR1B 861G>C receptor polymorphism among patients suffering from alcoholism, major depression, anxiety disorders and narcolepsy. Psychiatry Res., 97: 1–10.

Fehr, C., Schleicher, A., Szegedi, A., Anghelescu, I., Klawe, C., Hiemke, C. and Dahmen, N. (2001) Serotonergic polymorphisms in patients suffering from alcoholism, anxiety disorders and narcolepsy. Prog. Neuropsychopharmacol. Biol. Psychiatry, 25: 965–982.

Fehr, C., Szegedi, A., Anghelescu, I., Klawe, C., Hiemke, C. and Dahmen, N. (2000b) Sex differences in allelic frequencies of the 5-HT2C Cys23Ser polymorphism in psychiatric patients and healthy volunteers: findings from an association study. Psychiatr. Genet., 10: 59–65.

Freeman, T., Roca, V., Guggenheim, F., Kimbrell, T. and Griffin, W.S. (2005) Neuropsychiatric associations of apolipoprotein E alleles in subjects with combat-related posttraumatic stress disorder. J. Neuropsychiatry Clin. Neurosci., 17: 541–543.

Frisch, A., Michaelovsky, E., Rockah, R., Amir, I., Hermesh, H., Laor, N., Fuchs, C., Zohar, J., Lerer, B., Buniak, S.F., Landa, S., Poyurovsky, M., Shapira, B. and Weizman, R. (2000) Association between obsessive-compulsive disorder and polymorphisms of genes encoding components of the serotonergic and dopaminergic pathways. Eur. Neuropsychopharmacol., 10: 205–209.

Furmark, T., Tillfors, M., Garpenstrand, H., Marteinsdottir, I., Langstrom, B., Oreland, L. and Fredrikson, M. (2004) Serotonin transporter polymorphism related to amygdala excitability and symptom severity in patients with social phobia. Neurosci. Lett., 362: 189–192.

Fyer, A.J., Hamilton, S.P., Durner, M., Haghighi, F., Heiman, G.A., Costa, R., Evgrafov, O., Adams, P., de Leon, A.B., Taveras, N., Klein, D.F., Hodge, S.E., Weissman, M.M. and Knowles, J.A. (2006) A third-pass genome scan in panic disorder: evidence for multiple susceptibility loci. Biol. Psychiatry, 60: 388–401.

Fyer, A.J., Lipsitz, J.D., Mannuzza, S., Aronowitz, B. and Chapman, T.F. (2005) A direct interview family study of obsessive-compulsive disorder. I. Psychol. Med., 35: 1611–1621.

Fyer, A.J., Mannuzza, S., Chapman, T.F., Lipsitz, J., Martin, L.Y. and Klein, D.F. (1996) Panic disorder and social phobia: effects of comorbidity on familial transmission. Anxiety, 2: 173–178.

Fyer, A.J., Mannuzza, S., Chapman, T.F., Martin, L.Y. and Klein, D.F. (1995) Specificity in familial aggregation of phobic disorders. Arch. Gen. Psychiatry, 52: 564–573.

Gelernter, J., Bonvicini, K., Page, G., Woods, S.W., Goddard, A.W., Kruger, S., Pauls, D.L. and Goodson, S. (2001) Linkage genome scan for loci predisposing to panic disorder or agoraphobia. Am. J. Med. Genet., 105: 548–557.

Gelernter, J., Page, G.P., Bonvicini, K., Woods, S.W., Pauls, D.L. and Kruger, S. (2003) A chromosome 14 risk locus for simple phobia: results from a genome-wide linkage scan. Mol. Psychiatry, 8: 71–82.

Gelernter, J., Page, G.P., Stein, M.B. and Woods, S.W. (2004) Genome-wide linkage scan for loci predisposing to social phobia: evidence for a chromosome 16 risk locus. Am. J. Psychiatry, 161: 59–66.

Gelernter, J., Southwick, S., Goodson, S., Morgan, A., Nagy, L. and Charney, D.S. (1999) No association between D2 dopamine receptor (DRD2) "A" system alleles, or DRD2 haplotypes, and posttraumatic stress disorder. Biol. Psychiatry, 45: 620–625.

Gladkevich, A., Kauffman, H.F. and Korf, J. (2004) Lymphocytes as a neural probe: potential for studying psychiatric disorders. Prog. Neuropsychopharmacol. Biol. Psychiatry, 28: 559–576.

Goldstein, R.B., Wickramaratne, P.J., Horwath, E. and Weissman, M.M. (1997) Familial aggregation and phenomenology of 'early'-onset (at or before age 20 years) panic disorder. Arch. Gen. Psychiatry, 54: 271–278.

Grados, M.A., Riddle, M.A., Samuels, J.F., Liang, K.Y., Hoehn-Saric, R., Bienvenu, O.J., Walkup, J.T., Song, D. and Nestadt, G. (2001) The familial phenotype of obsessive-compulsive disorder in relation to tic disorders: the Hopkins OCD family study. Biol. Psychiatry, 50: 559–565.

Gunderson, K.L., Steemers, F.J., Ren, H., Ng, P., Zhou, L., Tsan, C., Chang, W., Bullis, D., Musmacker, J., King, C., Lebruska, L.L., Barker, D., Oliphant, A., Kuhn, K.M. and Shen, R. (2006) Whole-genome genotyping. Methods Enzymol., 410: 359–376.

Hall, D., Dhilla, A., Charalambous, A., Gogos, J.A. and Karayiorgou, M. (2003) Sequence variants of the brain-derived neurotrophic factor (*BDNF*) gene are strongly associated with obsessive-compulsive disorder. Am. J. Hum. Genet., 73: 370–376.

Hamilton, S.P., Fyer, A.J., Durner, M., Heiman, G.A., Baisre de, L.A., Hodge, S.E., Knowles, J.A. and Weissman, M.M. (2003) Further genetic evidence for a panic disorder syndrome mapping to chromosome 13q. Proc. Natl. Acad. Sci. USA, 100: 2550–2555.

Hamilton, S.P., Haghighi, F., Heiman, G.A., Klein, D.F., Hodge, S.E., Fyer, A.J., Weissman, M.M. and Knowles, J.A. (2000a) Investigation of dopamine receptor (DRD4) and dopamine transporter (DAT) polymorphisms for genetic linkage or association to panic disorder. Am. J. Med. Genet., 96: 324–330.

Hamilton, S.P., Heiman, G.A., Haghighi, F., Mick, S., Klein, D.F., Hodge, S.E., Weissman, M.M., Fyer, A.J. and Knowles, J.A. (1999) Lack of genetic linkage or association between a functional serotonin transporter polymorphism and panic disorder. Psychiatr. Genet., 9: 1–6.

Hamilton, S.P., Slager, S.L., Heiman, G.A., Haghighi, F., Klein, D.F., Hodge, S.E., Weissman, M.M., Fyer, A.J. and Knowles, J.A. (2000b) No genetic linkage or association between a functional promoter polymorphism in the monoamine oxidase-A gene and panic disorder. Mol. Psychiatry, 5: 465–466.

Hamilton, S.P., Slager, S.L., De Leon, A.B., Heiman, G.A., Klein, D.F., Hodge, S.E., Weissman, M.M., Fyer, A.J. and Knowles, J.A. (2004) Evidence for genetic linkage between a polymorphism in the adenosine 2A receptor and panic disorder. Neuropsychopharmacology, 29: 558–565.

Hamilton, S.P., Slager, S.L., Heiman, G.A., Deng, Z., Haghighi, F., Klein, D.F., Hodge, S.E., Weissman, M.M., Fyer, A.J. and Knowles, J.A. (2002) Evidence for a susceptibility locus for panic disorder near the catechol-O-methyltransferase gene on chromosome 22. Biol. Psychiatry, 51: 591–601.

Hamilton, S.P., Slager, S.L., Helleby, L., Heiman, G.A., Klein, D.F., Hodge, S.E., Weissman, M.M., Fyer, A.J. and Knowles, J.A. (2001) No association or linkage between polymorphisms in the genes encoding cholecystokinin and the cholecystokinin B receptor and panic disorder. Mol. Psychiatry, 6: 59–65.

Han, L., Nielsen, D.A., Rosenthal, N.E., Jefferson, K., Kaye, W., Murphy, D., Altemus, M., Humphries, J., Cassano, G., Rotondo, A., Virkkunen, M., Linnoila, M. and Goldman, D. (1999) No coding variant of the tryptophan hydroxylase gene detected in seasonal affective disorder, obsessive-compulsive disorder, anorexia nervosa, and alcoholism. Biol. Psychiatry, 45: 615–619.

Hanna, G.L., Himle, J.A., Curtis, G.C. and Gillespie, B.W. (2005) A family study of obsessive-compulsive disorder with pediatric probands. Am. J. Med. Genet. B Neuropsychiatr. Genet., 134: 13–19.

Hanna, G.L., Veenstra-VanderWeele, J., Cox, N.J., Boehnke, M., Himle, J.A., Curtis, G.C., Leventhal, B.L. and Cook, E.H. Jr. (2002) Genome-wide linkage analysis of families with obsessive-compulsive disorder ascertained through pediatric probands. Am. J. Med. Genet., 114: 541–552.

Hariri, A.R., Drabant, E.M., Munoz, K.E., Kolachana, B.S., Mattay, V.S., Egan, M.F. and Weinberger, D.R. (2005) A susceptibility gene for affective disorders and the response of the human amygdala. Arch. Gen. Psychiatry, 62: 146–152.

Hariri, A.R., Mattay, V.S., Tessitore, A., Kolachana, B., Fera, F., Goldman, D., Egan, M.F. and Weinberger, D.R. (2002) Serotonin transporter genetic variation and the response of the human amygdala. Science, 297: 400–403.

Hariri, A.R. and Weinberger, D.R. (2003) Functional neuroimaging of genetic variation in serotonergic neurotransmission. Genes Brain Behav., 2: 341–349.

Hasler, G., Drevets, W.C., Manji, H.K. and Charney, D.S. (2004) Discovering endophenotypes for major depression. Neuropsychopharmacology, 29: 1765–1781.

Hasler, G., Kazuba, D. and Murphy, D.L. (2006) Factor analysis of obsessive-compulsive disorder YBOCS-SC symptoms and association with 5-HTTLPR SERT polymorphism. Am. J. Med. Genet. B Neuropsychiatr. Genet., 141: 403–408.

Hattori, E., Yamada, K., Toyota, T., Yoshitsugu, K., Toru, M., Shibuya, H. and Yoshikawa, T. (2001) Association studies of the CT repeat polymorphism in the 5′ upstream region of the cholecystokinin B receptor gene with panic disorder and schizophrenia in Japanese subjects. Am. J. Med. Genet., 105: 779–782.

Heinz, A., Braus, D.F., Smolka, M.N., Wrase, J., Puls, I., Hermann, D., Klein, S., Grusser, S.M., Flor, H., Schumann, G., Mann, K. and Buchel, C. (2005) Amygdala-prefrontal coupling depends on a genetic variation of the serotonin transporter. Nat. Neurosci., 8: 20–21.

Heinz, A., Smolka, M.N., Braus, D.F., Wrase, J., Beck, A., Flor, H., Mann, K., Schumann, G., Buchel, C., Hariri, A.R. and Weinberger, D.R. (2007) Serotonin transporter genotype (5-HTTLPR): effects of neutral and undefined conditions on amygdala activation. Biol. Psychiatry, 61: 1011–1014.

Hemmings, S.M., Kinnear, C.J., Lochner, C., Niehaus, D.J., Knowles, J.A., Moolman-Smook, J.C., Corfield, V.A. and Stein, D.J. (2004) Early- versus late-onset obsessive-compulsive disorder: investigating genetic and clinical correlates. Psychiatry Res., 128: 175–182.

Hemmings, S.M., Kinnear, C.J., Niehaus, D.J., Moolman-Smook, J.C., Lochner, C., Knowles, J.A., Corfield, V.A. and Stein, D.J. (2003) Investigating the role of dopaminergic and serotonergic candidate genes in obsessive-compulsive disorder. Eur. Neuropsychopharmacol., 13: 93–98.

Hemmings, S.M. and Stein, D.J. (2006) The current status of association studies in obsessive-compulsive disorder. Psychiatr. Clin. North Am., 29: 411–444.

Hettema, J.M., An, S.S., Neale, M.C., Bukszar, J., van den Oord, E.J., Kendler, K.S. and Chen, X. (2006a) Association between glutamic acid decarboxylase genes and anxiety disorders, major depression, and neuroticism. Mol. Psychiatry, 11: 752–762.

Hettema, J.M., Neale, M.C. and Kendler, K.S. (2001a) A review and meta-analysis of the genetic epidemiology of anxiety disorders. Am. J. Psychiatry, 158: 1568–1578.

Hettema, J.M., Neale, M.C., Myers, J.M., Prescott, C.A. and Kendler, K.S. (2006b) A population-based twin study of the relationship between neuroticism and internalizing disorders. Am. J. Psychiatry, 163: 857–864.

Hettema, J.M., Prescott, C.A. and Kendler, K.S. (2001b) A population-based twin study of generalized anxiety disorder in men and women. J. Nerv. Ment. Dis., 189: 413–420.

Hettema, J.M., Prescott, C.A., Myers, J.M., Neale, M.C. and Kendler, K.S. (2005) The structure of genetic and environmental risk factors for anxiety disorders in men and women. Arch. Gen. Psychiatry, 62: 182–189.

Hirschhorn, J.N. and Daly, M.J. (2005) Genome-wide association studies for common diseases and complex traits. Nat. Rev. Genet., 6: 95–108.

Ho, H.P., Westberg, L., Annerbrink, K., Olsson, M., Melke, J., Nilsson, S., Baghaei, F., Rosmond, R., Holm, C., Bjorntorp, P., Andersch, S., Allgulander, C. and Eriksson, E. (2004) Association between a functional polymorphism in the progesterone receptor gene and panic disorder in women. Psychoneuroendocrinology, 29: 1138–1141.

Hosing, V.G., Schirmacher, A., Kuhlenbaumer, G., Freitag, C., Sand, P., Schlesiger, C., Jacob, C., Fritze, J., Franke, P., Rietschel, M., Garritsen, H., Nothen, M.M., Fimmers, R., Stogbauer, F. and Deckert, J. (2004) Cholecystokinin- and cholecystokinin-B-receptor gene polymorphisms in panic disorder. J. Neural Transm. Suppl., 68: 147–156.

Huang, Y.Y., Battistuzzi, C., Oquendo, M.A., Harkavy-Friedman, J., Greenhill, L., Zalsman, G., Brodsky, B., Arango, V., Brent, D.A. and Mann, J.J. (2004) Human 5-HT1A receptor C(−1019)G polymorphism and psychopathology. Int. J. Neuropsychopharmacol., 7: 441–451.

Hudziak, J.J., van Beijsterveldt, C.E., Althoff, R.R., Stanger, C., Rettew, D.C., Nelson, E.C., Todd, R.D., Bartels, M. and Boomsma, D.I. (2004) Genetic and environmental contributions to the Child Behavior Checklist Obsessive-Compulsive Scale: a cross-cultural twin study. Arch. Gen. Psychiatry, 61: 608–616.

Inada, Y., Yoneda, H., Koh, J., Sakai, J., Himei, A., Kinoshita, Y., Akabame, K., Hiraoka, Y. and Sakai, T. (2003) Positive association between panic disorder and polymorphism of the serotonin 2A receptor gene. Psychiatry Res., 118: 25–31.

Insel, T.R., Hoover, C. and Murphy, D.L. (1983) Parents of patients with obsessive-compulsive disorder. Psychol. Med., 13: 807–811.

Ishiguro, H., Arinami, T., Yamada, K., Otsuka, Y., Toru, M. and Shibuya, H. (1997) An association study between a transcriptional polymorphism in the serotonin transporter gene and panic disorder in a Japanese population. Psychiatry Clin. Neurosci., 51: 333–335.

Jonnal, A.H., Gardner, C.O., Prescott, C.A. and Kendler, K.S. (2000) Obsessive and compulsive symptoms in a general population sample of female twins. Am. J. Med. Genet., 96: 791–796.

Kaabi, B., Gelernter, J., Woods, S.W., Goddard, A., Page, G.P. and Elston, R.C. (2006) Genome scan for loci predisposing to anxiety disorders using a novel multivariate approach: strong evidence for a chromosome 4 risk locus. Am. J. Hum. Genet., 78: 543–553.

Karayiorgou, M., Sobin, C., Blundell, M.L., Galke, B.L., Malinova, L., Goldberg, P., Ott, J. and Gogos, J.A. (1999) Family-based association studies support a sexually dimorphic effect of COMT and MAOA on genetic susceptibility to obsessive-compulsive disorder. Biol. Psychiatry, 45: 1178–1189.

Kendler, K.S. (1996) Major depression and generalised anxiety disorder, (partly) different environments – revisited. Br. J. Psychiatry, 168: 68–75.

Kendler, K.S., Gardner, C.O. and Prescott, C.A. (2001a) Panic syndromes in a population-based sample of male and female twins. Psychol. Med., 31: 989–1000.

Kendler, K.S., Jacobson, K.C., Myers, J. and Prescott, C.A. (2002) Sex differences in genetic and environmental risk factors for irrational fears and phobias. Psychol. Med., 32: 209–217.

Kendler, K.S., Karkowski, L.M. and Prescott, C.A. (1999) Fears and phobias: reliability and heritability. Psychol. Med., 29: 539–553.

Kendler, K.S., Myers, J., Prescott, C.A. and Neale, M.C. (2001b) The genetic epidemiology of irrational fears and phobias in men. Arch. Gen. Psychiatry, 58: 257–265.

Kendler, K.S., Neale, M.C., Kessler, R.C., Heath, A.C. and Eaves, L.J. (1992a) Generalized anxiety disorder in women. A population-based twin study. Arch. Gen. Psychiatry, 49: 267–272.

Kendler, K.S., Neale, M.C., Kessler, R.C., Heath, A.C. and Eaves, L.J. (1992b) Major depression and generalized anxiety disorder. Same genes, (partly) different environments? Arch. Gen. Psychiatry, 49: 716–722.

Kendler, K.S., Neale, M.C., Kessler, R.C., Heath, A.C. and Eaves, L.J. (1992c) The genetic epidemiology of phobias in women. The interrelationship of agoraphobia, social phobia, situational phobia, and simple phobia. Arch. Gen. Psychiatry, 49: 273–281.

Kendler, K.S., Neale, M.C., Kessler, R.C., Heath, A.C. and Eaves, L.J. (1993a) Major depression and phobias: the genetic and environmental sources of comorbidity. Psychol. Med., 23: 361–371.

Kendler, K.S., Neale, M.C., Kessler, R.C., Heath, A.C. and Eaves, L.J. (1993b) Panic disorder in women: a population-based twin study. Psychol. Med., 23: 397–406.

Kendler, K.S., Prescott, C.A., Myers, J. and Neale, M.C. (2003) The structure of genetic and environmental risk factors for common psychiatric and substance use disorders in men and women. Arch. Gen. Psychiatry, 60: 929–937.

Kennedy, J.L., Bradwejn, J., Koszycki, D., King, N., Crowe, R., Vincent, J. and Fourie, O. (1999) Investigation of cholecystokinin system genes in panic disorder. Mol. Psychiatry, 4: 284–285.

Kennedy, J.L., Neves-Pereira, M., King, N., Lizak, M.V., Basile, V.S., Chartier, M.J. and Stein, M.B. (2001) Dopamine system genes not linked to social phobia. Psychiatr. Genet., 11: 213–217.

Kim, W., Choi, Y.H., Yoon, K.S., Cho, D.Y., Pae, C.U. and Woo, J.M. (2006) Tryptophan hydroxylase and serotonin transporter gene polymorphism does not affect the diagnosis, clinical features and treatment outcome of panic disorder in the Korean population. Prog. Neuropsychopharmacol. Biol. Psychiatry, 30: 1413–1418.

Kinnear, C., Niehaus, D.J., Seedat, S., Moolman-Smook, J.C., Corfield, V.A., Malherbe, G., Potgieter, A., Lombard, C. and Stein, D.J. (2001) Obsessive-compulsive disorder and a novel polymorphism adjacent to the oestrogen response element (ERE 6) upstream from the COMT gene. Psychiatr. Genet., 11: 85–87.

Kinnear, C.J., Niehaus, D.J., Moolman-Smook, J.C., du Toit, P.L., van, K.J., Weyers, J.B., Potgieter, A., Marais, V., Emsley, R.A., Knowles, J.A., Corfield, V.A., Brink, P.A. and Stein, D.J. (2000) Obsessive-compulsive disorder and the promoter region polymorphism (5-HTTLPR) in the serotonin transporter gene (SLC6A4): a negative association study in the Afrikaner population. Int. J. Neuropsychopharmacol., 3: 327–331.

Kirk, K.M., Birley, A.J., Statham, D.J., Haddon, B., Lake, R.I., Andrews, J.G. and Martin, N.G. (2000) Anxiety and depression in twin and sib pairs extremely discordant and concordant for neuroticism: prodromus to a linkage study. Twin Res., 3: 299–309.

Kirov, G., Murphy, K.C., Arranz, M.J., Jones, I., McCandles, F., Kunugi, H., Murray, R.M., McGuffin, P., Collier, D.A., Owen, M.J. and Craddock, N. (1998) Low activity allele of catechol-O-methyltransferase gene associated with rapid cycling bipolar disorder. Mol. Psychiatry, 3: 342–345.

Knowles, J.A., Fyer, A.J., Vieland, V.J., Weissman, M.M., Hodge, S.E., Heiman, G.A., Haghighi, F., de Jesus, G.M., Rassnick, H., Preud'homme-Rivelli, X., Austin, T., Cunjak, J., Mick, S., Fine, L.D., Woodley, K.A., Das, K., Maier, W., Adams, P.B., Freimer, N.B., Klein, D.F. and Gilliam, T.C. (1998) Results of a genome-wide genetic screen for panic disorder. Am. J. Med. Genet., 81: 139–147.

Kringlen, E. (1965) Obsessional neurotics: a long-term follow-up. Br. J. Psychiatry, 111: 700–722.

Lam, P., Cheng, C.Y., Hong, C.J. and Tsai, S.J. (2004) Association study of a brain-derived neurotrophic factor (Val66Met) genetic polymorphism and panic disorder. Neuropsychobiology, 49: 178–181.

Lam, P., Hong, C.J. and Tsai, S.J. (2005) Association study of A2a adenosine receptor genetic polymorphism in panic disorder. Neurosci. Lett., 378: 98–101.

Lee, H.J., Lee, M.S., Kang, R.H., Kim, H., Kim, S.D., Kee, B.S., Kim, Y.H., Kim, Y.K., Kim, J.B., Yeon, B.K., Oh, K.S., Oh, B.H., Yoon, J.S., Lee, C., Jung, H.Y., Chee, I.S. and Paik, I.H. (2005a) Influence of the serotonin transporter promoter gene polymorphism on susceptibility to posttraumatic stress disorder. Depress. Anxiety, 21: 135–139.

Lee, Y.J., Hohoff, C., Domschke, K., Sand, P., Kuhlenbaumer, G., Schirmacher, A., Freitag, C.M., Meyer, J., Stober, G., Franke, P., Nothen, M.M., Fritze, J., Fimmers, R., Garritsen, H.S., Stogbauer, F. and Deckert, J. (2005b) Norepinephrine transporter (NET) promoter and 5′-UTR polymorphisms:

association analysis in panic disorder. Neurosci. Lett., 377: 40–43.

Lemonde, S., Turecki, G., Bakish, D., Du, L., Hrdina, P.D., Bown, C.D., Sequeira, A., Kushwaha, N., Morris, S.J., Basak, A., Ou, X.M. and Albert, P.R. (2003) Impaired repression at a 5-hydroxytryptamine 1A receptor gene polymorphism associated with major depression and suicide. J. Neurosci., 23: 8788–8799.

Lenane, M.C., Swedo, S.E., Leonard, H., Pauls, D.L., Sceery, W. and Rapoport, J.L. (1990) Psychiatric disorders in first degree relatives of children and adolescents with obsessive compulsive disorder. J. Am. Acad. Child Adolesc. Psychiatry, 29: 407–412.

Lerer, B., Macciardi, F., Segman, R.H., Adolfsson, R., Blackwood, D., Blairy, S., Del, F.J., Dikeos, D.G., Kaneva, R., Lilli, R., Massat, I., Milanova, V., Muir, W., Noethen, M., Oruc, L., Petrova, T., Papadimitriou, G.N., Rietschel, M., Serretti, A., Souery, D., Van, G.S., Van, B.C. and Mendlewicz, J. (2001) Variability of 5-HT2C receptor cys23ser polymorphism among European populations and vulnerability to affective disorder. Mol. Psychiatry, 6: 579–585.

Lesch, K.P., Bengel, D., Heils, A., Sabol, S.Z., Greenberg, B.D., Petri, S., Benjamin, J., Muller, C.R., Hamer, D.H. and Murphy, D.L. (1996) Association of anxiety-related traits with a polymorphism in the serotonin transporter gene regulatory region. Science, 274: 1527–1531.

Lesch, K.P. and Gutknecht, L. (2004) Focus on The 5-HT1A receptor: emerging role of a gene regulatory variant in psychopathology and pharmacogenetics. Int. J. Neuropsychopharmacol., 7: 381–385.

Leygraf, A., Hohoff, C., Freitag, C., Willis-Owen, S.A., Krakowitzky, P., Fritze, J., Franke, P., Bandelow, B., Fimmers, R., Flint, J. and Deckert, J. (2006) *Rgs 2* gene polymorphisms as modulators of anxiety in humans? J. Neural Transm., 113: 1921–1925.

Lindberg, C., Koefoed, P., Hansen, E.S., Bolwig, T.G., Rehfeld, J.F., Mellerup, E., Jorgensen, O.S., Kessing, L.V., Werge, T., Haugbol, S., Wang, A.G. and Woldbye, D.P. (2006) No association between the −399 C > T polymorphism of the neuropeptide Y gene and schizophrenia, unipolar depression or panic disorder in a Danish population. Acta Psychiatr. Scand., 113: 54–58.

Lipsitz, J.D., Mannuzza, S., Chapman, T.F., Foa, E.B., Franklin, M.E., Goodwin, R.D. and Fyer, A.J. (2005) A direct interview family study of obsessive-compulsive disorder. II. Contribution of proband informant information. Psychol. Med., 35: 1623–1631.

Lo, W.H. (1967) A follow-up study of obsessional neurotics in Hong Kong Chinese. Br. J. Psychiatry, 113: 823–832.

Logue, M.W., Vieland, V.J., Goedken, R.J. and Crowe, R.R. (2003) Bayesian analysis of a previously published genome screen for panic disorder reveals new and compelling evidence for linkage to chromosome 7. Am. J. Med. Genet. B Neuropsychiatr. Genet., 121: 95–99.

Lohmueller, K.E., Pearce, C.L., Pike, M., Lander, E.S. and Hirschhorn, J.N. (2003) Meta-analysis of genetic association studies supports a contribution of common variants to susceptibility to common disease. Nat. Genet., 33: 177–182.

Maier, W., Lichtermann, D., Minges, J., Oehrlein, A. and Franke, P. (1993) A controlled family study in panic disorder. J. Psychiatr. Res., 27: 79–87.

Mannuzza, S., Schneier, F.R., Chapman, T.F., Liebowitz, M.R., Klein, D.F. and Fyer, A.J. (1995) Generalized social phobia: reliability and validity. Arch. Gen. Psychiatry, 52: 230–237.

Maron, E., Lang, A., Tasa, G., Liivlaid, L., Toru, I., Must, A., Vasar, V. and Shlik, J. (2005a) Associations between serotonin-related gene polymorphisms and panic disorder. Int. J. Neuropsychopharmacol., 8: 261–266.

Maron, E., Nikopensius, T., Koks, S., Altmae, S., Heinaste, E., Vabrit, K., Tammekivi, V., Hallast, P., Koido, K., Kurg, A., Metspalu, A., Vasar, E., Vasar, V. and Shlik, J. (2005b) Association study of 90 candidate gene polymorphisms in panic disorder. Psychiatr. Genet., 15: 17–24.

Maron, E., Tasa, G., Toru, I., Lang, A., Vasar, V. and Shlik, J. (2004) Association between serotonin-related genetic polymorphisms and CCK-4-induced panic attacks with or without 5-hydroxytryptophan pretreatment in healthy volunteers. World J. Biol. Psychiatry, 5: 149–154.

Maron, E., Toru, I., Must, A., Tasa, G., Toover, E., Vasar, V., Lang, A. and Shlik, J. (2007) Association study of tryptophan hydroxylase 2 gene polymorphisms in panic disorder. Neurosci. Lett., 411: 180–184.

Martinez-Barrondo, S., Saiz, P.A., Morales, B., Garcia-Portilla, M.P., Coto, E., Alvarez, V., Bascaran, M.T., Bousono, M. and Bobes, J. (2006) Negative evidences in association between apolipoprotein E polymorphism and panic disorder. Eur. Psychiatry, 21: 59–61.

Massat, I., Souery, D., Del-Favero, J., Nothen, M., Blackwood, D., Muir, W., Kaneva, R., Serretti, A., Lorenzi, C., Rietschel, M., Milanova, V., Papadimitriou, G.N., Dikeos, D., Van, B.C. and Mendlewicz, J. (2005) Association between COMT (Val158Met) functional polymorphism and early onset in patients with major depressive disorder in a European multi-center genetic association study. Mol. Psychiatry, 10: 598–605.

McDougle, C.J., Epperson, C.N., Price, L.H. and Gelernter, J. (1998) Evidence for linkage disequilibrium between serotonin transporter protein gene (*SLC6A4*) and obsessive compulsive disorder. Mol. Psychiatry, 3: 270–273.

McGrath, M., Kawachi, I., Ascherio, A., Colditz, G.A., Hunter, D.J. and De, V.I. (2004) Association between catechol-O-methyltransferase and phobic anxiety. Am. J. Psychiatry, 161: 1703–1705.

McKeon, P. and Murray, R. (1987) Familial aspects of obsessive-compulsive neurosis. Br. J. Psychiatry, 151: 528–534.

Meira-Lima, I., Shavitt, R.G., Miguita, K., Ikenaga, E., Miguel, E.C. and Vallada, H. (2004) Association analysis of the catechol-o-methyltransferase (*COMT*), serotonin transporter (*5-HTT*) and serotonin 2A receptor (*5HT2A*) gene polymorphisms with obsessive-compulsive disorder. Genes Brain Behav., 3: 75–79.

Mendlewicz, J., Papadimitriou, G.N. and Wilmotte, J. (1993) Family study of panic disorder: comparison with generalized anxiety disorder, major depression and normal subjects. Psychiatr. Genet., 3: 73–78.

Miguita, K., Cordeiro, Q., Shavitt, R.G., Miguel, E.C. and Vallada, H. (2006) Association study between the 1287 A/G exonic polymorphism of the norepinephrine transporter (*NET*) gene and obsessive-compulsive disorder in a Brazilian sample. Rev. Bras. Psiquiatr., 28: 158–159.

Millet, B., Chabane, N., Delorme, R., Leboyer, M., Leroy, S., Poirier, M.F., Bourdel, M.C., Mouren-Simeoni, M.C., Rouillon, F., Loo, H. and Krebs, M.O. (2003) Association between the dopamine receptor D4 (*DRD4*) gene and obsessive-compulsive disorder. Am. J. Med. Genet. B Neuropsychiatr. Genet., 116: 55–59.

Miyasaka, K., Yoshida, Y., Matsushita, S., Higuchi, S., Shirakawa, O., Shimokata, H. and Funakoshi, A. (2004) Association of cholecystokinin-A receptor gene polymorphisms and panic disorder in Japanese. Am. J. Med. Genet. B Neuropsychiatr. Genet., 127: 78–80.

Mossner, R., Freitag, C.M., Gutknecht, L., Reif, A., Tauber, R., Franke, P., Fritze, J., Wagner, G., Peikert, G., Wenda, B., Sand, P., Rietschel, M., Garritsen, H., Jacob, C., Lesch, K.P. and Deckert, J. (2006a) The novel brain-specific tryptophan hydroxylase-2 gene in panic disorder. J. Psychopharmacol., 20: 547–552.

Mossner, R., Walitza, S., Geller, F., Scherag, A., Gutknecht, L., Jacob, C., Bogusch, L., Remschmidt, H., Simons, M., Herpertz-Dahlmann, B., Fleischhaker, C., Schulz, E., Warnke, A., Hinney, A., Wewetzer, C. and Lesch, K.P. (2006b) Transmission disequilibrium of polymorphic variants in the tryptophan hydroxylase-2 gene in children and adolescents with obsessive-compulsive disorder. Int. J. Neuropsychopharmacol., 9: 437–442.

Mossner, R., Walitza, S., Lesch, K.P., Geller, F., Barth, N., Remschmidt, H., Hahn, F., Herpertz-Dahlmann, B., Fleischhaker, C., Schulz, E., Warnke, A., Hinney, A. and Wewetzer, C. (2005) Brain-derived neurotrophic factor V66M polymorphism in childhood-onset obsessive-compulsive disorder. Int. J. Neuropsychopharmacol., 8: 133–136.

Mundo, E., Richter, M.A., Sam, F., Macciardi, F. and Kennedy, J.L. (2000) Is the 5-HT(1Dbeta) receptor gene implicated in the pathogenesis of obsessive-compulsive disorder? Am. J. Psychiatry, 157: 1160–1161.

Mundo, E., Richter, M.A., Zai, G., Sam, F., McBride, J., Macciardi, F. and Kennedy, J.L. (2002) 5HT1Dbeta receptor gene implicated in the pathogenesis of obsessive-compulsive disorder: further evidence from a family-based association study. Mol. Psychiatry, 7: 805–809.

Murphy, G.M. Jr. (2006) Application of microarray technology in psychotropic drug trials. J. Psychopharmacol., 20: 72–78.

Nakamura, K., Yamada, K., Iwayama, Y., Toyota, T., Furukawa, A., Takimoto, T., Terayama, H., Iwahashi, K., Takei, N., Minabe, Y., Sekine, Y., Suzuki, K., Iwata, Y., Pillai, A., Nakamoto, Y., Ikeda, K., Yoshii, M., Fukunishi, I., Yoshikawa, T. and Mori, N. (2006) Evidence that variation in the peripheral benzodiazepine receptor (*PBR*) gene influences susceptibility to panic disorder. Am. J. Med. Genet. B Neuropsychiatr. Genet., 141: 222–226.

Nakamura, M., Ueno, S., Sano, A. and Tanabe, H. (1999) Polymorphisms of the human homologue of the *Drosophila* white gene areassociated with mood and panic disorders. Mol. Psychiatry, 4: 155–162.

Neale, M.C. and Cardon, L.R. (1992) Methodology for Genetic Studies of Twins and Families. Kluwer Academic Publishers B.V. Dordrecht, Dordrecht, The Netherlands.

Neale, M.C., Eaves, L.J. and Kendler, K.S. (1994a) The power of the classical twin study to resolve variation in threshold traits. Behav. Genet., 24: 239–258.

Neale, M.C., Walters, E.E., Eaves, L.J., Kessler, R.C., Heath, A.C. and Kendler, K.S. (1994b) Genetics of blood-injury fears and phobias: a population-based twin study. Am. J. Med. Genet., 54: 326–334.

Nelson, E.C., Grant, J.D., Bucholz, K.K., Glowinski, A., Madden, P.A.F., Reich, W. and Heath, A.C. (2000) Social phobia in a population-based female adolescent twin sample: co-morbidity and associated suicide-related symptoms. Psychol. Med., 30: 797–804.

Nestadt, G., Samuels, J., Riddle, M., Bienvenu, O.J., III Liang, K.Y., LaBuda, M., Walkup, J., Grados, M. and Hoehn-Saric, R. (2000) A family study of obsessive-compulsive disorder. Arch. Gen. Psychiatry, 57: 358–363.

Nestadt, G., Samuels, J., Riddle, M.A., Liang, K.Y., Bienvenu, O.J., Hoehn-Saric, R., Grados, M. and Cullen, B. (2001) The relationship between obsessive-compulsive disorder and anxiety and affective disorders: results from the Johns Hopkins OCD Family Study. Psychol. Med., 31: 481–487.

Newman, S.C. and Bland, R.C. (2006) A population-based family study of DSM-III generalized anxiety disorder. Psychol. Med., 36: 1275–1281.

Nicolini, H., Urraca, N., Camarena, B., Gomez, A., Martinez, H., Rinetti, G., Campillo, C., Castelli, P., Apiquian, R., Fresan, A., Garcia-Anaya, M. and Cruz, C. (2001) Lack of association of apolipoprotein E polymorphism in obsessive-compulsive disorder. CNS. Spectr., 6: 978–979. 992.

Nicolini, H., Weissbecker, K., Mejia, J.M. and Sanchez, D.C. (1993) Family study of obsessive-compulsive disorder in a Mexican population. Arch. Med. Res., 24: 193–198.

Noyes, R., Jr. Clarkson, C., Crowe, R.R., Yates, W.R. and McChesney, C.M. (1987) A family study of generalized anxiety disorder. Am. J. Psychiatry, 144: 1019–1024.

Noyes, R., Jr. Crowe, R.R., Harris, E.L., Hamra, B.J., McChesney, C.M. and Chaudhry, D.R. (1986) Relationship between panic disorder and agoraphobia. A family study. Arch. Gen. Psychiatry, 43: 227–232.

Ohara, K., Nagai, M., Suzuki, Y., Ochiai, M. and Ohara, K. (1998) No association between anxiety disorders and catechol-O-methyltransferase polymorphism. Psychiatry Res., 80: 145–148.

Olsson, M., Annerbrink, K., Westberg, L., Melke, J., Baghaei, F., Rosmond, R., Holm, G., Andersch, S., Allgulander, C. and Eriksson, E. (2004) Angiotensin-related genes in patients with panic disorder. Am. J. Med. Genet. B Neuropsychiatr. Genet., 127: 81–84.

Ozaki, N., Goldman, D., Kaye, W.H., Plotnicov, K., Greenberg, B.D., Lappalainen, J., Rudnick, G. and Murphy, D.L. (2003) Serotonin transporter missense mutation associated with a complex neuropsychiatric phenotype. Mol. Psychiatry, 8: 933–936.

Page, A.C. and Martin, N.G. (1998) Testing a genetic structure of blood-injury-injection fears. Am. J. Med. Genet., 81: 377–384.

Pauls, D.L., Alsobrook, J.P., Goodman, W., Rasmussen, S. and Leckman, J.F. (1995) A family study of obsessive-compulsive disorder. Am. J. Psychiatry, 152: 76–84.

Perna, G., Caldirola, D., Arancio, C. and Bellodi, L. (1997) Panic attacks: a twin study. Psychiatry Res., 66: 69–71.

Perna, G., Di Bella, D., Favaron, E., Cucchi, M., Liperi, L. and Bellodi, L. (2004) Lack of relationship between CO_2 reactivity and serotonin transporter gene regulatory region polymorphism in panic disorder. Am. J. Med. Genet. B Neuropsychiatr. Genet., 129: 41–43.

Perna, G., Favaron, E., Di Bella, D., Bussi, R. and Bellodi, L. (2005) Antipanic efficacy of paroxetine and polymorphism within the promoter of the serotonin transporter gene. Neuropsychopharmacology, 30: 2230–2235.

Philibert, R.A., Crowe, R., Ryu, G.Y., Yoon, J.G., Secrest, D., Sandhu, H. and Madan, A. (2007) Transcriptional profiling of lymphoblast lines from subjects with panic disorder. Am. J Med. Genet. B Neuropsychiatr. Genet., 144: 674–682.

Philibert, R.A., Nelson, J.J., Bedell, B., Goedken, R., Sandhu, H.K., Noyes, R. Jr. and Crowe, R.R. (2003) Role of elastin polymorphisms in panic disorder. Am. J. Med. Genet. B Neuropsychiatr. Genet., 117: 7–10.

Pickar, D. and Rubinow, K. (2001) Pharmacogenomics of psychiatric disorders. Trends Pharmacol. Sci., 22: 75–83.

Politi, P., Minoretti, P., Falcone, C., Martinelli, V. and Emanuele, E. (2006) Association analysis of the functional Ala111Glu polymorphism of the glyoxalase I gene in panic disorder. Neurosci. Lett., 396: 163–166.

Pritchard, J.K. and Cox, N.J. (2002) The allelic architecture of human disease genes: common disease – common variant…or not? Hum. Mol. Genet., 11: 2417–2423.

Rasmussen, S.A. and Tsuang, M.T. (1986) Clinical characteristics and family history in DSM-III obsessive-compulsive disorder. Am. J. Psychiatry, 143: 317–322.

Riddle, M.A., Scahill, L., King, R., Hardin, M.T., Towbin, K.E., Ort, S.I., Leckman, J.F. and Cohen, D.J. (1990) Obsessive compulsive disorder in children and adolescents: phenomenology and family history. J. Am. Acad. Child Adolesc. Psychiatry, 29: 766–772.

Rose, R.J., Miller, J.Z., Pogue-Geile, M.F. and Cardwell, G.F. (1981) Twin-family studies of common fears and phobias. In: Gedda, L. Parisi, P. and Nance, W.E. (Eds.), Twin Research 3: Intelligence, Personality, and Development. Alan R. Liss, Inc., New York, NY, pp. 169–174.

Rosenberg, C.M. (1967) Familial aspects of obsessional neurosis. Br. J. Psychiatry, 113: 405–413.

Rothe, C., Gutknecht, L., Freitag, C., Tauber, R, Mossner, R., Franke, P., Fritze, J., Wagner, G., Peikert, G., Wenda, B., Sand, P., Jacob, C., Rietschel, M., Nothen, M.M., Garritsen, H., Fimmers, R., Deckert, J. and Lesch, K.P. (2004a) Association of a functional 1019C > G 5-HT1A receptor gene polymorphism with panic disorder with agoraphobia. Int. J. Neuropsychopharmacol., 7: 189–192.

Rothe, C., Koszycki, D., Bradwejn, J., King, N., De, L.V., Shaikh, S., Franke, P., Garritsen, H., Fritze, J., Deckert, J. and Kennedy, J.L. (2004b) Association study of serotonin-2A receptor gene polymorphism and panic disorder in patients from Canada and Germany. Neurosci. Lett., 363: 276–279.

Rothe, C., Koszycki, D., Bradwejn, J., King, N., Deluca, V., Tharmalingam, S., Macciardi, F., Deckert, J. and Kennedy, J.L. (2006) Association of the Val158Met catechol O-methyltransferase genetic polymorphism with panic disorder. Neuropsychopharmacology, 31: 2237–2242.

Roy, M.A., Neale, M.C., Pedersen, N.L., Mathe, A.A. and Kendler, K.S. (1995) A twin study of generalized anxiety disorder and major depression. Psychol. Med., 25: 1037–1049.

Rudin, E. (1953) Ein beitrag zur frage der zwangskrankheit insbesondere ihrer hereditaren beziehungen. Arch. Psychiatr. Nervenkrankheit, 191: 14–54.

Samochowiec, J., Hajduk, A., Samochowiec, A., Horodnicki, J., Stepien, G., Grzywacz, A. and Kucharska-Mazur, J. (2004) Association studies of MAO-A, COMT, and 5-HTT genes polymorphisms in patients with anxiety disorders of the phobic spectrum. Psychiatry Res., 128: 21–26.

Sand, P.G., Godau, C., Riederer, P., Peters, C., Franke, P., Nothen, M.M., Stober, G., Fritze, J., Maier, W., Propping, P., Lesch, K.P., Riess, O., Sander, T., Beckmann, H. and Deckert, J. (2000) Exonic variants of the GABA(B) receptor gene and panic disorder. Psychiatr. Genet., 10: 191–194.

Sand, P.G., Schlurmann, K., Luckhaus, C., Gotz, M., Stober, G., Lesch, K.P., Riederer, P., Franke, P., Maier, W., Nothen, M.M., Propping, P., Fritze, J. and Deckert, J. (2002) Estrogen receptor 1 gene (ESR1) variants in panic disorder. Am. J. Med. Genet., 114: 426–428.

Scherrer, J.F., True, W.R., Xian, H., Lyons, M.J., Eisen, S.A., Goldberg, J., Lin, N. and Tsuang, M.T. (2000) Evidence for genetic influences common and specific to symptoms of generalized anxiety and panic. J. Affect. Disord., 57: 25–35.

Schindler, K.M., Richter, M.A., Kennedy, J.L., Pato, M.T. and Pato, C.N. (2000) Association between homozygosity at the COMT gene locus and obsessive compulsive disorder. Am. J. Med. Genet., 96: 721–724.

Schmidt, N.B., Storey, J., Greenberg, B.D., Santiago, H.T., Li, Q. and Murphy, D.L. (2000) Evaluating gene × psychological risk factor effects in the pathogenesis of anxiety: a new model approach. J. Abnorm. Psychol., 109: 308–320.

Sciuto, G., Pasquale, L. and Bellodi, L. (1995) Obsessive compulsive disorder and mood disorders: a family study. Am. J. Med. Genet., 60: 475–479.

Segman, R.H., Cooper-Kazaz, R., Macciardi, F., Goltser, T., Halfon, Y., Dobroborski, T. and Shalev, A.Y. (2002) Association between the dopamine transporter gene and posttraumatic stress disorder. Mol. Psychiatry, 7: 903–907.

Segman, R.H., Shefi, N., Goltser-Dubner, T., Friedman, N., Kaminski, N. and Shalev, A.Y. (2005) Peripheral blood mononuclear cell gene expression profiles identify emergent post-traumatic stress disorder among trauma survivors. Mol. Psychiatry, 10: 500–513. 425.

Serretti, A., Benedetti, F., Zanardi, R. and Smeraldi, E. (2005) The influence of serotonin transporter promoter polymorphism (SERTPR) and other polymorphisms of the serotonin pathway on the efficacy of antidepressant treatments. Prog. Neuropsychopharmacol. Biol. Psychiatry, 29: 1074–1084.

Shifman, S., Bronstein, M., Sternfeld, M., Pisante-Shalom, A., Lev-Lehman, E., Weizman, A., Reznik, I., Spivak, B., Grisaru, N., Karp, L., Schiffer, R., Kotler, M., Strous, R.D., Swartz-Vanetik, M., Knobler, H.Y., Shinar, E., Beckmann, J.S., Yakir, B., Risch, N., Zak, N.B. and Darvasi, A. (2002) A highly significant association between a COMT haplotype and schizophrenia. Am. J. Hum. Genet., 71: 1296–1302.

Shimizu, E., Hashimoto, K., Koizumi, H., Kobayashi, K., Itoh, K., Mitsumori, M., Ohgake, S., Okamura, N., Koike, K., Matsuzawa, D., Zhang, L., Kumakiri, C., Nakazato, M., Komatsu, N. and Iyo, M. (2005) No association of the brain-derived neurotrophic factor (BDNF) gene polymorphisms with panic disorder. Prog. Neuropsychopharmacol. Biol. Psychiatry, 29: 708–712.

Shlik, J., Vasar, V., Aluoja, A., Kingisepp, P.H., Jagomagi, K., Vasar, E., Rago, L. and Bradwejn, J. (1997) The effect of cholecystokinin tetrapeptide on respiratory resistance in healthy volunteers. Biol. Psychiatry, 42: 206–212.

Shugart, Y.Y., Samuels, J., Willour, V.L., Grados, M.A., Greenberg, B.D., Knowles, J.A., McCracken, J.T., Rauch, S.L., Murphy, D.L., Wang, Y., Pinto, A., Fyer, A.J., Piacentini, J., Pauls, D.L., Cullen, B., Page, J., Rasmussen, S.A., Bienvenu, O.J., Hoehn-Saric, R., Valle, D., Liang, K.Y., Riddle, M.A. and Nestadt, G. (2006) Genomewide linkage scan for obsessive-compulsive disorder: evidence for susceptibility loci on chromosomes 3q, 7p, 1q, 15q, and 6q. Mol. Psychiatry, 11: 763–770.

Skre, I., Onstad, S., Torgersen, S., Lygren, S. and Kringlen, E. (1993) A twin study of DSM-III-R anxiety disorders. Acta Psychiatr. Scand., 88: 85–92.

Skre, I., Onstad, S., Torgersen, S., Philos, D.R., Lygren, S. and Kringlen, E. (2000) The heritability of common phobic fear: a twin study of a clinical sample. J. Anxiety Disord., 14: 549–562.

Stein, B., Chartier, J., Kozak, M.V., King, N. and Kennedy, J.L. (1998a) Genetic linkage to the serotonin transporter protein and 5HT2A receptor genes excluded in generalized social phobia. Psychiatry Res., 81: 283–291.

Stein, M.B., Chartier, M.J., Hazen, A.L., Kozak, M.V., Tancer, M.E., Lander, S., Furer, P., Chubaty, D. and Walker, J.R. (1998b) A direct-interview family study of generalized social phobia. Am. J. Psychiatry, 155: 90–97.

Stein, M.B., Fallin, M.D., Schork, N.J. and Gelernter, J. (2005) COMT polymorphisms and anxiety-related personality traits. Neuropsychopharmacology, 30: 2092–2102.

Stein, M.B., Jang, K.L., Taylor, S., Vernon, P.A. and Livesley, W.J. (2002) Genetic and environmental influences on trauma exposure and posttraumatic stress disorder symptoms: a twin study. Am. J. Psychiatry, 159: 1675–1681.

Stein, M.B., Seedat, S. and Gelernter, J. (2006) Serotonin transporter gene promoter polymorphism predicts SSRI response in generalized social anxiety disorder. Psychopharmacology, 187: 68–72.

Steinlein, O.K., Deckert, J., Nothen, M.M., Franke, P., Maier, W., Beckmann, H. and Propping, P. (1997) Neuronal nicotinic acetylcholine receptor alpha 4 subunit (CHRNA4) and panic disorder: an association study. Am. J. Med. Genet., 74: 199–201.

Stevenson, J., Batten, N. and Cherner, M. (1992) Fears and fearfulness in children and adolescents: a genetic analysis of twin data. J. Child Psychol. Psychiatry, 33: 977–985.

Tadic, A., Rujescu, D., Szegedi, A., Giegling, I., Singer, P., Moller, H.J. and Dahmen, N. (2003) Association of a *MAOA* gene variant with generalized anxiety disorder, but not with panic disorder or major depression. Am. J. Med. Genet. B Neuropsychiatr. Genet., 117: 1–6.

Taillon-Miller, P., Saccone, S.F., Saccone, N.L., Duan, S., Kloss, E.F., Lovins, E.G., Donaldson, R., Phong, A., Ha, C., Flagstad, L., Miller, S., Drendel, A., Lind, D., Miller, R.D., Rice, J.P. and Kwok, P.Y. (2004) Linkage disequilibrium maps constructed with common SNPs are useful for first-pass disease association screens. Genomics, 84: 899–912.

Tharmalingam, S., King, N., De, L.V., Rothe, C., Koszycki, D., Bradwejn, J., Macciardi, F. and Kennedy, J.L. (2006) Lack of association between the corticotrophin-releasing hormone receptor 2 gene and panic disorder. Psychiatr. Genet., 16: 93–97.

Thomsen, P.H. (1995) Obsessive-compulsive disorder in children and adolescents: a study of parental psychopathology and precipitating events in 20 consecutive Danish cases. Psychopathology, 28: 161–167.

Thorgeirsson, T.E., Oskarsson, H., Desnica, N., Kostic, J.P., Stefansson, J.G., Kolbeinsson, H., Lindal, E., Gagunashvili, N., Frigge, M.L., Kong, A., Stefansson, K. and Gulcher, J.R. (2003) Anxiety with panic disorder linked to chromosome 9q in Iceland. Am. J. Hum. Genet., 72: 1221–1230.

Torgersen, S. (1979) The nature and origin of common phobic fears. Br. J. Psychiatry, 134: 343–351.

Torgersen, S. (1983) Genetic factors in anxiety disorders. Arch. Gen. Psychiatry, 40: 1085–1089.

Tot, S., Erdal, M.E., Yazici, K., Yazici, A.E. and Metin, O. (2003) T102C and −1438 G/A polymorphisms of the 5-HT2A receptor gene in Turkish patients with obsessive-compulsive disorder. Eur. Psychiatry, 18: 249–254.

True, W.R., Rice, J., Eisen, S.A., Heath, A.C., Goldberg, J., Lyons, M.J. and Nowak, J. (1993) A twin study of genetic and environmental contributions to liability for posttraumatic stress symptoms. Arch. Gen. Psychiatry, 50: 257–264.

Tsuang, M., Domschke, K., Jerskey, B.A. and Lyons, M.J. (2004) Agoraphobic behavior and panic attack: a study of male twins. J. Anxiety Disord., 18: 799–807.

Urraca, N., Camarena, B., Gomez-Caudillo, L., Esmer, M.C. and Nicolini, H. (2004) Mu opioid receptor gene as a candidate for the study of obsessive compulsive disorder with and without tics. Am. J. Med. Genet. B Neuropsychiatr. Genet., 127: 94–96.

van Grootheest, D.S., Cath, D.C., Beekman, A.T. and Boomsma, D.I. (2005) Twin studies on obsessive-compulsive disorder: a review. Twin Res. Hum. Genet., 8: 450–458.

Walitza, S., Wewetzer, C., Warnke, A., Gerlach, M., Geller, F., Gerber, G., Gorg, T., Herpertz-Dahlmann, B., Schulz, E., Remschmidt, H., Hebebrand, J. and Hinney, A. (2002) 5-HT2A promoter polymorphism −1438G/A in children and adolescents with obsessive-compulsive disorders. Mol. Psychiatry, 7: 1054–1057.

Wang, A.G., Dahl, H.A., Vang, M., Als, T.D., Ewald, H., Kruse, T.A. and Mors, O. (2006) Genetics of panic disorder on the Faroe Islands: a replication study of chromosome 9 and panic disorder. Psychiatr. Genet., 16: 99–104.

Wang, Z., Valdes, J., Noyes, R., Zoega, T. and Crowe, R.R. (1998) Possible association of a cholecystokinin promoter polymorphism (CCK-36CT) with panic disorder. Am. J. Med. Genet., 81: 228–234.

Weissman, M.M., Wickramaratne, P., Adams, P.B., Lish, J.D., Horwath, E., Charney, D., Woods, S.W., Leeman, E. and Frosch, E. (1993) The relationship between panic disorder and major depression. A new family study. Arch. Gen. Psychiatry, 50: 767–780.

Willour, V.L., Yao, S.Y., Samuels, J., Grados, M., Cullen, B., Bienvenu, O.J., III Wang, Y., Liang, K.Y., Valle, D., Hoehn-Saric, R., Riddle, M. and Nestadt, G. (2004) Replication study supports evidence for linkage to 9p24 in obsessive-compulsive disorder. Am. J. Hum. Genet., 75: 508–513.

Woo, J.M., Yoon, K.S., Choi, Y.H., Oh, K.S., Lee, Y.S. and Yu, B.H. (2004) The association between panic disorder and the L/L genotype of catechol-O-methyltransferase. J. Psychiatr. Res., 38: 365–370.

Woo, J.M., Yoon, K.S. and Yu, B.H. (2002) Catechol O-methyltransferase genetic polymorphism in panic disorder. Am. J. Psychiatry, 159: 1785–1787.

Wu, S. and Comings, D.E. (1999) A common C-1018G polymorphism in the human 5-HT1A receptor gene. Psychiatr. Genet., 9: 105–106.

Yamada, K., Hattori, E., Shimizu, M., Sugaya, A., Shibuya, H. and Yoshikawa, T. (2001) Association studies of the cholecystokinin B receptor and A2a adenosine receptor genes in panic disorder. J. Neural Transm., 108: 837–848.

Zai, G., Arnold, P., Burroughs, E., Barr, C.L., Richter, M.A. and Kennedy, J.L. (2005) Evidence for the gamma-amino-butyric acid type B receptor 1 (*GABBR1*) gene as a susceptibility factor in obsessive-compulsive disorder. Am. J. Med. Genet. B Neuropsychiatr. Genet., 134: 25–29.

Zai, G., Arnold, P.D., Burroughs, E., Richter, M.A. and Kennedy, J.L. (2006) Tumor necrosis factor-alpha gene is not associated with obsessive-compulsive disorder. Psychiatr. Genet., 16: 43–45.

Zai, G., Bezchlibnyk, Y.B., Richter, M.A., Arnold, P., Burroughs, E., Barr, C.L. and Kennedy, J.L. (2004) Myelin oligodendrocyte glycoprotein (*MOG*) gene is associated with obsessive-compulsive disorder. Am. J. Med. Genet. B Neuropsychiatr. Genet., 129: 64–68.

Zhang, H., Leckman, J.F., Pauls, D.L., Tsai, C.P., Kidd, K.K. and Campos, M.R. (2002) Genomewide scan of hoarding in sib pairs in which both sibs have Gilles de la Tourette syndrome. Am. J. Hum. Genet., 70: 896–904.

Zhang, H., Ozbay, F., Lappalainen, J., Kranzler, H.R., van Dyck, C.H., Charney, D.S., Price, L.H., Southwick, S., Yang, B.Z., Rasmussen, A. and Gelernter, J. (2006) Brain derived neurotrophic factor (*BDNF*) gene variants and Alzheimer's disease, affective disorders, posttraumatic stress disorder, schizophrenia, and substance dependence. Am. J. Med. Genet. B Neuropsychiatr. Genet., 141: 387–393.

Zhang, X., Beaulieu, J.M., Sotnikova, T.D., Gainetdinov, R.R. and Caron, M.G. (2004) Tryptophan hydroxylase-2 controls brain serotonin synthesis. Science, 305: 217.

Subject Index